TEXAS CIVIL PROCEDURE: PRETRIAL LITIGATION

2010–2011 Edition

TEXAS CIVIL PROCEDURE: PRETRIAL LITIGATION
2010–2011 Edition

William V. Dorsaneo III
Chief Justice John and Lena Hickman Distinguished Faculty Fellow
and Professor of Law
Southern Methodist University Dedman School of Law

Elizabeth Thornburg
Professor of Law
Southern Methodist University Dedman School of Law

Elaine Grafton Carlson
Stanley J. Krist Distinguished Professor of Law
South Texas College of Law

David Crump
John B. Neibel Professor of Law & Director of CLE
University of Houston Law Center

Library of Congress Card Number:

ISBN: 978-1-4224-7768-7

Library of Congress Cataloging-in-Publication Data

Texas civil procedure : pretrial litigation / William V. Dorsaneo III ... [et al.]. -- 2010-2011 ed.
p. cm.
Includes index.
ISBN 978-1-4224-7768-7 (soft cover)
I. Dorsaneo, William V.
KFT1737.D67 2010
347.764'072--dc22

2010022140

This publication is designed to provide accurate and authoritative information in regard to the subject matter covered. It is sold with the understanding that the publisher is not engaged in rendering legal, accounting, or other professional services. If legal advice or other expert assistance is required, the services of a competent professional should be sought.

Editorial Offices
21 Chanlon Rd., New Providence, NJ 07974 (908) 464-6800
Mission St., San Francisco, CA 94105-1831 (415) 908-3200
lexisnexis.com

W BENDER

(2010–Pub.709)

PREFACE

Texas civil procedure is a constantly moving target, with both court decisions and legislative changes keeping both students and practitioners on the alert. This new edition of Texas Civil Procedure: Pretrial Litigation incorporates important developments since the last edition went to press in the spring of 2009. Most notably, this new edition:

- incorporates important changes in probate court jurisdiction;
- contains important new Texas Supreme Court decisions on default judgments, service of process, and the strict compliance standard;
- enhances the chapter on parties with new cases on interpleader and class actions;
- includes the Texas Supreme Court decision regarding the forum non conveniens statute;
- adds new developments in the discovery area, including e-discovery, HIPAA, "snap back" of privileged documents, and spoliation sanctions; and
- inserts a new Texas Supreme Court case on summary judgment evidence.

In addition, to help students review the material and prepare for the Texas bar examination, the Appendices have been updated to include questions from the 2009 and 2010 bar exams.

We hope you enjoy the new material.

William V. Dorsaneo III
Elizabeth Thornburg
Elaine Grafton Carlson
David Crump

April 2010

Introduction

This book is the first in a two-part series that will teach you how lawsuits are handled in the Texas courts, from the earliest client contact through a final appeal to the Texas Supreme Court. You have already studied one procedural system — the federal one — in your first year Civil Procedure course. As you learn about the Texas system, you will see both similarities and differences in rules and in attitudes. This book will introduce you to the pre-trial phases of litigation, from pre-filing activities through attempts at alternative dispute resolution. The Texas Trial and Appellate Procedure book will cover merits-related procedural issues such as trial settings, motions for continuance, jury selection, trial procedures, jury instructions, non-jury trials, appealable orders, and post-trial motions. It will also deal with all aspects of appeals and original proceedings in the appellate courts in Texas, including standards of review, appellate deadlines, handling appeals, and review in the Texas Supreme Court.

It is not possible to learn all the details of Texas procedure in a single course. But this book hopes to introduce you to the most important concepts at a level of sophistication that will put you in good stead as you begin to litigate in Texas courts. In addition to cases,[1] statutes, and rules, the book uses Notes to provide supplementary information as well as discussion questions designed to probe your understanding of the material and the policy issues underlying the technical rules. Many sections of the book also contain Practice Exercises so that you can test your ability to apply the rules. Finally, a number of chapters are followed by an appendix containing actual Texas bar examination questions, which should be helpful both in learning about practice and in preparing you for the Texas Procedure & Evidence portion of the bar exam.

We hope you will find this book to be helpful and enlightening.

William V. Dorsaneo III
Elizabeth Thornburg
Elaine Grafton Carlson
David Crump

April 2010

---

[1] Case footnotes are numbered as in the original and are otherwise omitted. Citations have sometimes been removed from within cases without ellipses in the interest of readability.

TABLE OF PRACTICE EXERCISES

Table of Contents

Table of Contents

Chapter 1

THE PRE-LITIGATION PHASE OF A CIVIL DISPUTE

Scope

This chapter examines the early phases of a civil dispute from the perspective of the attorney taking on a new case, focusing on the period before litigation is filed. After an overview of the litigation process, the chapter covers the initiation of the attorney-client relationship, including negotiating and preparing fee contracts, case evaluation, and the ethical considerations that are related to the initiation of the relationship. It then discusses matters to which the attorney must attend at the very outset of the dispute, particularly compliance with statutory pre-filing requirements and the statute of limitations.

§ 1.01 OVERVIEW OF THE PRE-TRIAL PROCESS

There are numerous steps required to initiate a lawsuit and steer it through the dispute resolution process. As we study each individual component of litigation, it is easy to lose track of how it fits into the larger picture. This section therefore provides an overview of the activities generally involved in a fully-litigated civil case.

The story generally begins with the client, and the lawyer's decision about whether to represent the client in this case. This requires the attorney to be aware of his or her ethical duties to the client, and to negotiate and draft a fair contract of employment. In deciding whether to file a lawsuit, the attorney must begin by researching both law and facts, making sure that there is a good faith basis to bring suit on the client's behalf. This may require interviewing witnesses, looking at documents, and consulting experts. It can also require some time in the law library, checking on the elements of the client's cause of action, any preliminary procedural requirements, and the applicable statutes of limitations. Occasionally the lawyer will need to invoke special procedures such as attachment, garnishment, sequestration, or temporary restraining orders in order to make sure that relief will be available should the plaintiff prevail.

Once it is clear that a suit will be filed, the lawyer must determine which courts have *subject matter jurisdiction* — the power to hear cases of this type. This will be based on the amount in controversy and on the nature of the case. Often in Texas more than one court will have *concurrent jurisdiction* and the decision about where to file will be strategic as well as technical. The lawyer must also check to see that all prospective defendants have enough contacts with Texas so that they are subject to *personal jurisdiction* in the Texas courts. While you studied personal jurisdiction cases in federal procedure, you will add to that knowledge by studying Texas long-arm statutes as well as Texas cases interpreting the requirements of due process of law. A third consideration in determining where to file a case is *venue*.

Texas has its own system that determines which counties in Texas are proper — generally this will include at least the defendant's residence (or, for an entity, principal office) and the county in which a substantial part of the acts or omissions giving rise to the claim occurred. But you will see that in the Texas system there are also numerous exceptions to the general rule, and some situations in which venue is mandatory rather than permissive. Again, the rules may make several counties proper and the lawyer will need to make strategic decisions about the best place to file.

For lawyers representing plaintiffs, the next step is to draft, file, and serve the initial pleading, which in Texas is called a *petition*. The primary function of the petition is to provide the defendant a "short statement of the cause of action sufficient to give fair notice of the claim involved" and the relief requested. Unlike in the federal system, the concept of a "cause of action" remains central in Texas, and pleadings are traditionally more factually detailed than those in federal court. Service of the petition is governed by rules specifying who can serve and be served, and they vary depending on whether the defendant is inside or outside of Texas.

Defendants can file various non-merits defenses, some of which must be filed before others or they are waived. Personal jurisdiction is challenged through a *special appearance*, and venue with a *motion to transfer venue*. Subject matter jurisdiction is challenged through a *plea to the jurisdiction*, and there is a "catchall" *plea in abatement* to raise fundamental defects such as the prior pendency of another action or the non-joinder of a person needed for just adjudication. A Texas device called the *special exception* fills the role of two federal pleadings: the motion for more definite statement and the motion to dismiss for failure to state a claim. When it comes to the merits of the case, Texas allows a *general denial* of all of the plaintiff's claims, regardless of whether the defendant has a factual basis for the denial. There are certain kinds of denials, however, that must be made specifically or under oath. A defendant may also raise *affirmative defenses*, independent grounds for defeating plaintiff's recovery, or *inferential rebuttal defenses*, factual allegations that indirectly negate some element of the plaintiff's cause of action.

Joinder of claims and parties is quite similar to what you learned in federal procedure. There is again free joinder of claims when the suit involves only a single plaintiff and single defendant. Once multiple parties are joined, however, the rules require that the joined claims arise out of the same transaction, occurrence, or series of transactions or occurrences and share common questions of law or fact. It is likely, because of differences in the state and federal rules, that joinder in Texas courts is more restrictive than in federal court. In Texas as in federal practice there are counterclaims, cross-claims, and third party claims, intervention, interpleader, and joinder of parties needed for just adjudication. There are also class actions, although recent rule changes and decisions may make certain kinds of class actions more difficult to maintain in Texas than elsewhere.

The joinder rules generally permit but do not require the addition of various claims. Nevertheless, rules of preclusion may mean that a claim that was not brought was lost forever. They may also mean that certain litigated fact findings will bind the parties, even in a future lawsuit. For that reason, litigators must also be mindful of the rules of *issue preclusion (res judicata)* and *claim preclusion (collateral estoppel)*.

Discovery plays an important part in the pre-trial process in Texas, and the concepts are quite similar to those in federal court, but there are important differences as well. Discovery is proper as to information that is relevant but not privileged. As in federal court, the relevance concept is somewhat fluid and incorporates a balancing of materiality and burden as well as concerns about privacy. Rules regarding *electronic discovery* are somewhat different in this regard than their federal counterparts. The discovery devices parallel those you know (*interrogatories, requests for production, depositions, physical and mental examinations, and requests for admission*), but the Texas system of disclosures requires a *Request for Disclosure*; it is not automatic. Texas also has "discovery levels" — presumptive limits on the use of certain discovery devices depending on the amount in controversy and complexity of the lawsuit. There are also *sanctions* for misconduct during discovery.

In some cases, after an adequate time for discovery, it will appear that there is no need for a jury trial because one of the parties is entitled to *summary judgment* — there is no genuine issue of material fact. Texas has a two-track system for summary judgment motions. The "traditional" motion requires the movant to prove his or her right to recover as a matter of law. Even for defendants moving on the ground that the plaintiff will not prove her case, the traditional motion is more like the pre-*Celotex* federal practice, and defendant must disprove some element of the plaintiff's claim. However, Texas has more recently adopted a "no-evidence" summary judgment motion. Defendants filing this type of motion make an argument more like the one you learned about in federal procedure. Texas also has an extensive body of law about what kinds of materials are proper summary judgment evidence, and about the time at which a party needs to object to the inadequacies of an opponent's evidence or risk waiving the objection.

In Texas as in the federal courts, many more cases *settle* or are otherwise disposed of before trial. This can be the result of direct negotiation between the parties, or the product of some kind of *alternative dispute resolution* mechanism. The latter are increasingly used across numerous types of cases and, indeed, are sometimes required by the courts before the parties will be allowed a trial setting.

In terms of attitude, the Texas courts are in a period of transition. In some ways they retain their older literal approach to rules and procedures. Such attitudes can create traps for the unwary lawyer — failure to do exactly the right thing at exactly the right moment may waive a client's rights forever. In other ways, Texas courts have adopted the more discretionary approach characteristic of the federal courts, giving judges discretion to forgive legal lapses in the interests of disposing of cases on the merits. While one can hope for discretion and beg forgiveness under this scheme, a careful lawyer will try to know the rules and meet their requirements, rather than scrambling to avoid the consequences of error.

§ 1.02 INITIATING THE ATTORNEY-CLIENT RELATIONSHIP

[A] Fees and Fee Contracts

Suppose that you have met with a prospective client and want to take the case. What kind of agreement should you negotiate with the client, and how should it be documented? Getting it right is very important both to the lawyer and to the client, and attention to the matter at the outset can help avoid serious difficulties later in the relationship.

[1] Propriety of Fee

Lawyers are prohibited from entering into an arrangement for, charging, or collecting illegal or unconscionable fees. State Bar Rules, Art. 10 § 9, Rule 1.04(a); *Hoover Slovacek LLP v. Walton*, 206 S.W.3d 557 (Tex. 2006) (termination fee provision, requiring immediate payment of contingent interest, violated public policy and was unconscionable). In this regard, a fee is "unconscionable" if a competent lawyer could not form a reasonable belief that the fee is reasonable. State Bar Rules, Art. 10 § 9, Rule 1.04(a).

Among the factors that may be taken into account in determining the reasonableness of a fee are the following:

1. The time and labor required.
2. The novelty and difficulty of questions involved.
3. The skill needed to perform the legal service properly.
4. The likelihood, if apparent to the client, that the acceptance of the particular employment will preclude other employment by the lawyer.
5. The customary fee in the locality for similar legal services.
6. The amount involved in the matter and the results obtained by the lawyer.
7. The time limitations imposed by the client or by circumstances.
8. The nature and length of the professional relationship between the lawyer and the client.
9. The ability, experience, and reputation of the lawyer or lawyers performing the services.
10. Whether the fee is fixed or contingent.

State Bar Rules, Art. 10 § 9, Rule 1.04(b).

Although Disciplinary Rule 1.04(b) lists factors that may be considered in determining the reasonableness of a fee, these factors do not exclude other reasonable factors, including evidence regarding the attorney's billing practices. When a lawyer has not regularly represented the client, the basis or rate of the fee must be communicated to the client, preferably in writing. This should be done before or shortly after the representation commences. State Bar Rules, Art. 10 § 9, Rule 1.04(c).

[2] Client's Consent to Split Fee

Effective March 1, 2005, lawyers who are not members of the same firm may not divide a fee or enter into an arrangement to divide a fee unless they comply with certain requirements State Bar Rules, Art. 10 § 9, Rule 1.04(f). A fee division is permitted only if:

1. The division is in proportion to the professional services performed by each lawyer; or
2. The division is made between lawyers who assume joint responsibility for the representation.

The client must consent in writing to the terms of the arrangement before the time of the association or referral proposed, including: (1) the identity of all lawyers or lawyers who will participate in the fee-sharing arrangement; (2) whether fees will be divided based on the proportion of services performed, or by lawyers agreeing to assume joint responsibility for the representation; and (3) the share of the fee that each lawyer or law firm will receive or, if the division is based on the proportion of services performed, the basis on which the division will be made. The aggregate fees must not violate Rule 1.04(a) as to unconscionability. *See* State Bar Rules, Art. 10 § 9, Rule 1.04(f)(3).

Every agreement that allows a lawyer or law firm to associate other counsel in the representation of a person, or to refer the person to other counsel for representation, and that results in an association with, or referral to, a different law firm or lawyer in a different firm, must be confirmed by an arrangement conforming to Rule 1.04(f). Consent by a client or prospective client without knowledge of the information set out in Rule 1.04(f)(2) does not constitute confirmation. An attorney may not collect or seek to collect fees or expenses in connection with an agreement that is not confirmed in this way, except for:

1. The reasonable value of legal services provided to that person; and
2. The reasonable and necessary expenses actually incurred on behalf of that person.

[3] Contingent Fee Contracts

Generally, a lawyer's fee may be contingent on the outcome of the matter for which the service is rendered. Contingent fee agreements must be in writing and must state the method by which the fee is to be determined. If different percentages are to be paid to the lawyer in the event of settlement, trial, or appeal, those percentages must be stated in the contract. The agreement must state the expenses, litigation or otherwise, that will be deducted from the recovery, and whether the expense deduction is taken before or after the contingent fee is calculated. When a contingent fee matter is concluded, the lawyer must provide the client with a written statement that describes the outcome of the matter, and, in the case of a recovery, shows the remittance to the client and the method of determining that amount.

The burden is on the lawyer to inform the client of the basis or rate of the fee at the outset of the matter, including whether the contingent fee will be calculated on non-cash benefits as well as monetary damages. In a case in which a damage award was offset by a counterclaim, the Texas Supreme Court determined that the attorney was entitled only to a percentage of the amount actually received by the clients after the offset was deducted, rather than a percentage of the full amount of the award without considering the counterclaim. *Levine v. Bayne, Snell & Krause, Ltd.*, 40 S.W.3d 92, 95–96 (Tex. 2001).

A contingent fee contract is voidable by the client if it results from conduct that violates Texas laws or state bar rules regarding barratry, the improper institution of litigation, or improper solicitation of employment by attorneys or other persons.

[4] Informing Client of Fee

An attorney should not hesitate to discuss fees with the client on the first visit. If the amount to be charged the client is not based on an agreement that specifies the fee, but rather is based on an understanding that the attorney is entitled to a reasonable fee for services, collection will be facilitated if the statement sent to the client contains details of the services rendered. An itemization of the fee may also be helpful in some instances. The attorney should keep detailed records indicating precisely what he or she has done (particularly with regard to telephone calls and office conferences that are often overlooked) so that the statement for services can be specific and detailed and the amount of the bill can be readily justified should any question arise.

The attorney should bill the client promptly, because the longer the delay after the completion of the services, the greater the likelihood that the client will have forgotten the services actually rendered. If prolonged litigation is not being handled on a contingent fee basis, the attorney ordinarily will want to bill the client at regular monthly intervals rather than waiting until completion of the litigation.

How should an attorney balance the need to protect the client's interest and his or her own interest in being compensated for the work done? Are there any limits on contractual provisions regarding payment if the attorney is discharged without cause? Consider these issues, particularly with regard to the court's discussion of a clause regarding the effect of termination, in the case that follows.

HOOVER SLOVACEK LLP v. WALTON

206 S.W.3d 557 (Tex. 2006)

JEFFERSON, C.J.

In this case, we must determine whether an attorney hired on a contingent-fee basis may include in the fee agreement a provision stating that, in the event the attorney is discharged before completing the representation, the client must immediately pay a fee equal to the present value of the attorney's interest in the client's claim. We conclude that this termination fee provision is contrary to public policy and unenforceable. We affirm the court of appeals' judgment in part, reverse in part, and remand to the court of appeals for further proceedings.

I. Background

In June 1995, John B. Walton, Jr. hired attorney Steve Parrott of Hoover Slovacek LLP (Hoover) to recover unpaid royalties from several oil and gas companies operating on his 32,500 acre ranch in Winkler County. The engagement letter granted Hoover a 30% contingent fee for all claims on which collection was achieved through one trial. Most significantly, the letter included the following provision:

> You may terminate the Firm's legal representation at any time . . . . Upon termination by You, You agree to immediately pay the Firm the then present value of the Contingent Fee described [herein], plus all Costs then owed to the Firm, plus subsequent legal fees [incurred to transfer the representation to another firm and withdraw from litigation].

Shortly after signing the contract, Walton and Parrott agreed to hire Kevin Jackson as local counsel and reduced Hoover's contingent fee to 28.66%. Parrott negotiated settlements exceeding $200,000 with Texaco and El Paso Natural Gas, and Walton paid Hoover its contingent fee. Parrott then turned to Walton's claims against Bass Enterprises Production Company (Bass), and hired accountant Everett Holseth to perform an audit and compile evidence establishing the claims' value.[1] Meanwhile, Walton authorized Parrott to settle his claims against Bass for $8.5 million.

In January 1997, Parrott made an initial settlement demand of $58.5 million. Bass's attorney testified that Parrott was unable to support this number with any legal theories, expert reports, or calculations, and that the demand was so "enormous" he basically "quit listening." The following month, however, Bass offered $6 million not only to settle Walton's claims, but also to purchase the surface estates of eight sections of the Winkler County ranch, acquire numerous easements, and secure Walton's royalty interests under the leases. Walton refused to sell, but authorized Parrott to accept $6 million to settle only Walton's claims for unpaid royalties. Walton also wrote Parrott and expressed discontent that Parrott did not consult him before making the $58.5 million demand. According to Walton, Parrott responded by pressuring him to sell part of the ranch and his royalties for $6 million. In March 1997, Walton discharged Parrott, complaining that Parrott was doing little to prosecute his claims against Bass and had damaged his credibility by making an unauthorized and "absurd" $58.5 million demand.

Walton then retained Andrews & Kurth LLP, which, in November 1998, settled Walton's claims against Bass for $900,000. By that time, Hoover had sent Walton a bill for $1.7 million (28.66% of $6 million), contending that Bass's $6 million offer,

---

[1] Holseth never completed the audit, but testified that he estimated the value of Walton's claims at $2 million to $4 million.

and Walton's subsequent authorization to settle for that amount, established the present value of Walton's claims at the time of discharge. Walton paid Andrews & Kurth approximately $283,000 in hourly fees and costs, but refused to pay Hoover.

When Hoover sought to intervene in the settlement proceedings between Walton and Bass, the trial court severed Hoover's claim, and the parties tried the case before a jury. Richard Bianchi, a former state district judge in Harris County, testified as Hoover's expert witness. Bianchi opined that a 28.66% contingent fee was, "if anything, lower than normal, but certainly reasonable under these circumstances," and that "it would only be unconscionable to ignore the agreement of the parties." He also testified that charging more than Walton ultimately recovered from Bass "doesn't change the deal they made. That's just a bad business deal." In contrast, Walton's local counsel, Kevin Jackson, testified that he had never heard of attorneys charging a percentage based on the present value of a claim at the time of discharge rather than the client's actual recovery, and that the $1.7 million fee was unconscionable.

The jury failed to find that Walton discharged Hoover for good cause or that Hoover's fee was unconscionable. The trial court entered judgment on the verdict, which awarded Hoover $900,000. The court of appeals reversed and rendered a take-nothing judgment for Walton, concluding that Hoover's fee agreement was unconscionable as a matter of law. We granted Hoover's petition for review. Because our reasoning differs from the court of appeals' in some respects, we affirm its judgment in part, reverse in part, and remand this case to the court of appeals.

II. Discussion

When interpreting and enforcing attorney-client fee agreements, it is "not enough to simply say that a contract is a contract. There are ethical considerations overlaying the contractual relationship." *Lopez v. Munoz, Hockema & Reed, L.L.P.*, 22 S.W.3d 857, 868 (Tex. 2000) (Gonzales, J., concurring and dissenting).

> In Texas, we hold attorneys to the highest standards of ethical conduct in their dealings with their clients. The duty is highest when the attorney contracts with his or her client or otherwise takes a position adverse to his or her client's interests. As Justice Cardozo observed, "[a fiduciary] is held to something stricter than the morals of the marketplace. Not honesty alone, but the punctilio of an honor the most sensitive, is then the standard of behavior." Accordingly, a lawyer must conduct his or her business with inveterate honesty and loyalty, always keeping the client's best interest in mind.

Id. at 866–67 (alteration in original) (citations omitted). The attorney's special responsibility to maintain the highest standards of conduct and fair dealing establishes a professional benchmark that informs much of our analysis in this case.

Although contingent fee contracts are increasingly used by businesses and other sophisticated parties, their primary purpose is to allow plaintiffs who cannot afford an attorney to obtain legal services by compensating the attorney from the proceeds of any recovery. *Arthur Andersen & Co. v. Perry Equip. Corp.*, 945 S.W.2d 812, 818 (Tex. 1997). The contingent fee offers "the potential of a greater fee than might be earned under an hourly billing method" in order to compensate the attorney for the risk that he or she will receive "no fee whatsoever if the case is lost." *Id.* In exchange, the client is largely protected from incurring a net financial loss in connection with the representation. This risk-sharing feature creates an incentive for lawyers to work diligently and obtain the best results possible. A closely related benefit is the contingent fee's tendency to reduce frivolous litigation by discouraging attorneys from presenting claims that have negative value or otherwise lack merit.

In Texas, if an attorney hired on a contingent-fee basis is discharged without cause before the representation is completed, the attorney may seek compensation in quantum meruit or in a suit to enforce the contract by collecting the fee from any damages the client subsequently recovers. *Mandell & Wright v. Thomas*, 441 S.W.2d 841, 847 (Tex. 1969). Both remedies are subject to the prohibition against charging or collecting an unconscionable fee. Tex. Disciplinary R. Prof'l Conduct 1.04(a), *reprinted in* TEX. GOV'T CODE, tit. 2, subtit. G, app. A (Tex. State Bar R. art. X, § 9).[2] Whether a particular fee amount or contingency percentage charged by the attorney is unconscionable under all relevant circumstances of the representation is an issue for the factfinder. On the other hand, whether a contract, including a fee agreement between attorney and client, is contrary to public policy and unconscionable at the time it is formed is a question of law.

Hoover's termination fee provision purported to contract around the *Mandell* remedies in three ways. First, it made no distinction between discharges occurring with or without cause. Second, it assessed the attorney's fee as a percentage of the present value of the client's claim at the time of discharge, discarding the quantum meruit and contingent fee measurements. Finally, it required Walton to pay Hoover the percentage fee immediately at the time of discharge.

In allowing the discharged lawyer to collect the contingent fee from any damages the client recovers, *Mandell* complies with the principle that a contingent-fee lawyer "is entitled to receive the specified fee only when and to the extent the client receives payment." RESTATEMENT (THIRD) OF THE LAW GOVERNING LAWYERS § 35(2) (2000). Hoover's termination fee, however, sought immediate payment of the firm's contingent interest without regard for when and whether Walton eventually prevailed. Public policy strongly favors a client's freedom to employ a lawyer of his choosing and, except in some instances where counsel is appointed, to discharge the lawyer during the representation for any reason or no reason at all. *See Martin v. Camp*, 114 N.E. 46, 48 (N.Y. 1916) (describing this policy as a "firmly established rule which springs from the personal and confidential nature" of the attorney-client relationship); *see also* TEX. DISCIPLINARY R. PROF'L CONDUCT 1.15 cmt. 4 ("A client has the power to discharge a lawyer at any time, with or without cause . . . ."). Nonetheless, we recognize the valid competing interests of an attorney who, like any other professional, expects timely compensation for work performed and results obtained. Thus, attorneys are entitled to protection from clients who would abuse the contingent fee arrangement and avoid duties owed under contract. Striving to respect both interests, *Mandell* provides remedies to the contingent-fee

---

[2] Although the Disciplinary Rules do not define standards of civil liability for attorneys, they are persuasive authority outside the context of disciplinary proceedings, and we have applied Rule 1.04 as a rule of decision in disputes concerning attorney's fees.

lawyer who is fired without cause. Hoover's termination fee provision, however, in requiring immediate payment of the firm's contingent interest, exceeded *Mandell* and forced the client to liquidate 28.66% of his claim as a penalty for discharging the lawyer. Because this feature imposes an undue burden on the client's ability to change counsel, Hoover's termination fee provision violates public policy and is unconscionable as a matter of law.

Notwithstanding its immediate-payment requirement, several additional considerations lead us to conclude that Hoover's termination fee provision is unenforceable. In *Levine v. Bayne, Snell & Krause, Ltd.*, we refused to construe a contingent fee contract as entitling the attorney to compensation exceeding the client's actual recovery. 40 S.W.3d 92, 95 (Tex. 2001). In that case, the clients purchased a home containing foundation defects, and stopped making mortgage payments when the defects were discovered. They agreed to pay their lawyer one-third of "any amount received by settlement or recovery." A jury awarded the clients $243,644 in damages, but offset the award against the balance due on their mortgage, resulting in a net recovery of $81,793. The lawyer sued to collect $155,866, a fee equaling one-third of the gross recovery plus pre- and post-judgment interest and expenses. In refusing to interpret "any amount received" as permitting collection of a contingent fee exceeding the client's net recovery, we emphasized that the lawyer is entitled to receive the contingent fee "only when and *to the extent the client receives payment*." A reasonable client does not expect that a lawyer engaged on a contingent-fee basis will charge a fee equaling or, as in this case, exceeding 100% of the recovery.[3] In *Levine*, we noted that "[l]awyers almost always possess the more sophisticated understanding of fee arrangements. It is therefore appropriate to place the balance of the burden of fair dealing and the allotment of risk in the hands of the lawyer in regard to fee arrangements with clients." We believe Hoover's termination fee provision is unreasonably susceptible to overreaching, exploiting the attorney's superior information, and damaging the trust that is vital to the attorney-client relationship.

The Disciplinary Rules provide that a contingent fee is permitted only where, quite sensibly, the fee is "contingent on the outcome of the matter for which the service is rendered." TEX. DISCIPLINARY R. PROF'L CONDUCT 1.04(d). Hoover's termination fee, if not impliedly prohibited by Rule 1.04(d), is directly forbidden by Rule 1.08(h), which states that "[a] lawyer shall not acquire a proprietary interest in the cause of action or subject matter of litigation the lawyer is conducting for the client, except that the lawyer may . . . contract in a civil case with a client for a contingent fee that is permissible under Rule 1.04." *Id.* 1.08(h)(2). Thus, even if Hoover's termination fee provision is viewed as transforming a traditional contingent fee into a fixed fee, it nonetheless impermissibly grants the lawyer a proprietary interest in the client's claim by entitling him to a percentage of the

---

[3] Hourly fee agreements and cases in which the prevailing party recovers attorney's fees from an opposing party do not implicate the concerns presented here. Thus, pursuant to statute or a contract between the parties, it is not uncommon for courts to approve fee-shifting awards that exceed the damages recovered by the client. *See, e.g.*, *Hruska v. First State Bank of Deanville*, 747 S.W.2d 783, 785 (Tex. 1988) (upholding $12,570 fee where the client recovered $2,920); *Sibley v. RMA Partners, L.P.*, 138 S.W.3d 455, 458–59 (Tex. App. — Beaumont 2004, no pet.) (upholding $82,748 fee where the client stood to recover approximately $43,000).

claim's value without regard to the ultimate results obtained.

Examining the risk-sharing attributes of the parties' contract reveals that Hoover's termination fee provision weighs too heavily in favor of the attorney at the client's expense. Specifically, it shifted to Walton the risks that accompany both hourly fee and contingent fee agreements while withholding their corresponding benefits. In obligating Walton to pay a 28.66% contingent fee for any recovery obtained by Parrott, the fee caused Walton to bear the risk that Parrott would easily settle his claims without earning the fee. But Walton also bore the risk inherent in an hourly fee agreement because, if he discharged Hoover, he was obligated to pay a 28.66% fee regardless of whether he eventually prevailed. This "heads lawyer wins, tails client loses" provision altered *Mandell* almost entirely to the client's detriment. Indeed, the only scenario in which Hoover's termination fee provision would benefit Walton is if he expected the value of his claim to significantly increase after discharging Hoover. In that case, Walton could limit Hoover's fee to 28.66% of a relatively low value, and avoid paying 28.66% of a much larger recovery eventually obtained with new counsel. Thus, it is conceivable that a client viewing the events in hindsight could find that the arrangement worked out to his benefit. At the time of contracting, however, the client has no reason to desire such a provision because the winning scenario is not only unlikely, but also entirely arbitrary in relation to its timing and occurrence. Moreover, to the extent the client believes the value of his claim will increase as a result of employing new counsel, a rational client would forego the representation altogether rather than agree to the provision. In sum, the benefits of Hoover's termination fee provision are enjoyed almost exclusively by the attorney.

Hoover's termination fee provision is also antagonistic to many policies supporting the use of contingent fees in civil cases. Most troubling is its creation of an incentive for the lawyer to be discharged soon after he or she can establish the present value of the client's claim with sufficient certainty. Whereas the contingent fee encourages efficiency and diligent efforts to obtain the best results possible, Hoover's termination fee provision encourages the lawyer to escape the contingency as soon as practicable, and take on other cases, thereby avoiding the demands and consequences of trials and appeals. Moreover, the provision encourages litigation of a subset of claims that would not be pursued under traditional contingent fee agreements.

Finally, Hoover's termination fee provision creates problems relating to valuation and administration, but not in the manner articulated by the court of appeals. The court of appeals viewed the parties' contract as empowering Parrott alone to determine the value of Walton's claims at the time of discharge, concluding that "[a]n agreement that leaves the damages to be paid upon termination by one party wholly within the unfettered discretion of the other party is so one-sided as to be substantively unconscionable." We disagree, because nothing in their fee agreement indicates that Parrott retained such discretion. On the contrary, the contract is silent with respect to valuation. Nevertheless, its silence in that respect exposes an additional defect — the contract fails to explain how the present value of the claims will be measured. It does not describe how the nature and severity of the client's injuries will be characterized, nor does it state whether any other factors, such as venue, availability and quality of witnesses, the defendant's wealth and the strength of its counsel, and the reprehensibility of the defendant's conduct will apply to the calculation. Lawyers have a duty, at the outset of the representation, to "inform a client of the basis or rate of the fee" and "the contract's implications for the client." *Levine*, 40 S.W.3d at 96 (citing RESTATEMENT (THIRD) OF THE LAW GOVERNING LAWYERS §§ 38(1), 18. We have stated that "to impose the obligation of clarifying attorney-client contracts upon the attorney 'is entirely reasonable, both because of [the attorney's] greater knowledge and experience with respect to fee arrangements and because of the trust [the] client has placed in [the attorney].' " *Levine*, 40 S.W.3d at 95 (quoting *Cardenas v. Ramsey County*, 322 N.W.2d 191, 194 (Minn. 1982)) (alterations in original). For these reasons, the "failure of the lawyer to give at the outset a clear and accurate explanation of how a fee was to be calculated" weighs in favor of a conclusion that the fee may be unconscionable. TEX. DISCIPLINARY R. PROF'L CONDUCT 1.04 cmt. 8. And while experts can calculate the present value of a claim at the time of discharge, this extra time, expense, and uncertainty can be avoided under hourly billing and the traditional contingent fee, even in cases in which a discharged attorney seeks compensation from a disgruntled client.

Our conclusion that Hoover's termination fee provision is unconscionable does not render the parties' entire fee agreement unenforceable. *See* RESTATEMENT (SECOND) OF CONTRACTS § 208 (1981) ("If a contract or term thereof is unconscionable at the time the contract is made a court may refuse to enforce the contract, or may enforce the remainder of the contract without the unconscionable term, or may so limit the application of any unconscionable term as to avoid any unconscionable result."); *Williams v. Williams*, 569 S.W.2d 867, 871 (Tex. 1978) (explaining that an illegal provision generally may be severed if it does not constitute the essential purpose of the agreement). Walton paid Hoover its contingent fee for settlements that Parrott negotiated with Texaco and El Paso Natural Gas, and Walton does not contend that this portion of the agreement is unconscionable. On the contrary, in his brief to the court of appeals, Walton argued in the alternative that Hoover was limited to recovering 28.66% of the $900,000 settlement reached in the Bass litigation and requested rendition of judgment in that amount. Severing the termination fee provision, the remainder of the fee agreement is enforceable. Thus, if Hoover were discharged without cause, it would be entitled to either its contingent fee or compensation in quantum meruit. *Mandell*, 441 S.W.2d at 847.

The court of appeals rendered a take-nothing judgment against Hoover, holding the entire fee agreement unenforceable and denying a recovery in quantum meruit because Hoover failed to present evidence of the reasonable value of its services. We agree that Hoover no longer has a claim for quantum meruit, but we disagree with the take-nothing judgment. In the trial court, Hoover sought to enforce the contract's termination fee provision. Our holding, however, severs the termination fee provision, leaving a contingent fee contract subject to *Mandell*. The jury (1) found that Walton did not comply with the contract and (2) failed to find that Walton had good cause to discharge Hoover. Under *Mandell*, therefore, Hoover was entitled to its contingent fee: 28.66% of $900,000, or $257,940. In the trial court, and again in his appellate brief, Walton argued that Hoover was entitled to only this amount, and Hoover requested this relief in the alternative in its brief to this Court.

In the court of appeals, however, Walton challenged the factual and legal sufficiency of the evidence supporting the jury's finding on the good-cause issue. Because the court of appeals reversed and rendered judgment, it did not reach Walton's sufficiency points. Accordingly, we remand the case to that court for consideration of those issues.

III. Conclusion

Hoover's termination fee provision penalized Walton for changing counsel, granted Hoover an impermissible proprietary interest in Walton's claims, shifted the risks of the representation almost entirely to Walton's detriment, and subverted several policies underlying the use of contingent fees. We hold that this provision is unconscionable as a matter of law, and therefore, unenforceable. We affirm that part of the court of appeals' judgment reversing the trial court's judgment, but reverse its take-nothing judgment, and remand this case to the court of appeals for further proceedings. Tex. R. App. P. 60.2(a), (d).

[The dissenting opinion of Justices Hecht, Medina and Willett is omitted.]

NOTES AND QUESTIONS

(1) *Fiduciary Duties and Ethical Considerations.* In *Hoover Slovacek,* the Court begins its analysis by explaining that because an attorney-client relationship is a fiduciary relationship, ethical considerations require the lawyer to keep the client's best interest in mind. Does this mean that the lawyer must subordinate his or her own interests to the interests of the client even before any attorney-client relationship is established? *See* Disciplinary R. Prof'l Conduct 1.04, cmt. 4 ("The determination of a proper fee requires consideration of the interests of both client and lawyer. The determination of reasonableness requires consideration of all relevant circumstances . . . ."). What does the Court conclude about the propriety of the contingent fee contract made between the Hoover Slovack firm and Walton? To what extent was the contract enforceable?

(2) *Limits on Contingent Fee Contracts.* Contingent fee contracts are well-recognized in civil cases, with the exception of family law cases in which such fees are "rarely justified." *See* Disciplinary R. Prof'l Conduct 1.04, cmt. 9. Based on *Hoover Slovacek*, contingent fee contracts are improper if they contain termination provisions requiring immediate payment of a firm's contingent interest because "this feature, imposes an undue burden on the client's ability to change counsel." Similarly, a contingent fee must not be crafted in such a way that the fee contract entitles the attorney to compensation, exceeding the client's actual recovery. *See* Disciplinary R. Prof'l Conduct 1.04(d) (fee is "contingent on the outcome of the matter for which the service is rendered."). *See also* Disciplinary R. Prof'l Conduct 1.08(h) (a "lawyer shall not acquire a proprietary interest in the cause of action or subject matter of litigation . . . , except that the lawyer . . . may contract in a civil case with a client for a contingent fee that is permissible under Rule 1.04."). Perhaps more fundamentally, in *Hoover Slovacek*, the Court explains that lawyers have the obligation to "inform a client of the basis or rate of a fee" and "the contract's implications for the client." *See* Disciplinary R. Prof'l Conduct 1.04, cmt. 5 ("When there is doubt about whether a particular fee arrangement is consistent

with the client's best interest, the lawyer should discuss with the client alternative bases for the fee and explain their implications.").

(3) *Attorney's Remedies.* Under the principle established in *Mandell & Wright v. Thomas*, 441 S.W.2d 841, 847 (Tex. 1969), if an attorney hired on a contingent-fee basis is discharged without cause before the representation is completed, he or she may enforce the contingent fee contract by collecting the fee from any damages the client subsequently recovers or may seek compensation in quantum meruit. In contrast, it is unclear whether an attorney who was discharged for good cause is allowed to recover the reasonable value of services rendered up to the time of discharge. *See Rocha v. Ahmad*, 676 S.W.2d 149 (Tex. App. — San Antonio 1984, writ dism'd); *Howell v. Kelly*, 534 S.W.2d 737, 739 (Tex. Civ. App. — Houston (1st Dist.) 1976, no writ) (summarizing conflicting cases). Finally, attorneys who breach fiduciary duties to their clients may be required to forfeit all or part of the fee, even if the breach caused the client no actual damages. *Burrow v. Arce*, 997 S.W.2d 229, 237–40 (Tex. 1999) (aggregate settlement in violation of Disciplinary Rule 1.08(f) is violation warranting fee forfeiture).

After reading *Hoover Slovacek*, you may be wondering what fee agreements generally look like. Consider the following form, adapted from section 3.100 of WILLIAM V. DORSANEO III, TEXAS LITIGATION GUIDE.

CONTINGENT FEE CONTRACT

[*Name of client*], of [*address*], referred to as the Client, and [*name of attorney or law firm or professional corporation*], of [*address*], referred to as the Attorney, agree as follows:

1. Purpose of Representation

The Client retains and employs the Attorney to: [*state purpose of contractual relationship, e.g.*, sue for and recover all damages and compensation to which the Client may be entitled as well as to compromise and settle all claims arising out of the ____________ (*specify, e.g.*, automobile accident) that occurred on or about ____________ (*date*), at ____________ (*location of occurrence*) or represent the Client in contesting the will of ____________ (*name*), deceased, dated ____________]. To secure the performance of Client's obligations, as set forth below, the Client hereby transfers and assigns to the Attorney an undivided interest in the Client's claim, this interest being equivalent to the amount or percentage that the Client, by this agreement, promises to pay for the services of the Attorney.

2. Attorney's Fees

In consideration of services rendered and to be rendered by the Attorney, the Client agrees to pay to the Attorney [*specify percentage, e.g.*, 40] percent of all money and property collected [*optional*: and all economic benefits obtained] whether from the proceeds of any suit and judgment or from a settlement after trial. However, if the claim and cause of action is such that the fee allowed to an attorney is set by law, the amount payable to the Attorney shall be limited to the maximum so allowed by law. In the event the case is settled before trial, the Client agrees to pay [*specify percentage, e.g.*, 33 1/3] percent of the recovery as attorney's fees.

3. Approval Necessary for Settlement

No settlement of any nature will be made for any of the claims of the Client without the complete approval of the Client.

4. Deduction of Expenses

The costs of court and all reasonable expenses advanced or incurred by the Attorney in the handling of this claim will be deducted by the Attorney from the Client's share of any recovery that is obtained. The Client will remain liable for all expenses in the event that a recovery is not obtained or in the event that the recovery obtained is less than the expenses incurred.

All medical expenses and charges of any nature will be paid by the Client. In the event of a recovery, the Client agrees that the Attorney may pay any unpaid bills from the Client's share of the recovery, but the Attorney is not bound to pay any of these expenses or charges.

5. Calculation and Explanation of Contingency

The percentage paid to the attorney will be calculated [before *or* after] expenses and costs are deducted from the amount of the recovery. At the conclusion of the matter, the Attorney will provide the Client with a statement clearly detailing the determination of the fee and any remittance to Client.

6. Cooperation of Client

The Client will keep the Attorney advised of the Client's whereabouts at all times, will appear on reasonable notice at any and all depositions and court appearances, and will comply with all reasonable requests of the Attorney in connection with the preparation and presentation of the claim.

7. Permission to Withdraw

In case the Attorney determines after conducting a preliminary investigation that the Client's claim should not be pursued further, the Client agrees that the Attorney may withdraw from the representation of the Client by sending written notice of the Attorney's intention to withdraw to the Client at the Client's last known address. In such event, the Client will not be obligated to pay any fees to the Attorney, but the Attorney will be entitled to reimbursement of any expenses, charges, or costs that the Attorney may have advanced or incurred during the course of the representation.

8. Texas Law to Apply

This agreement will be construed in accordance with the laws of the State of Texas, and all obligations of the parties are performable in ____________ County, Texas.

9. Parties Bound

This agreement is binding on and inures to the benefit of the parties and their respective heirs, executors, administrators, legal representatives, successors, and assigns.

10. Legal Construction

In case any one or more of the provisions contained in this agreement is held to be invalid, illegal, or unenforceable in any respect, such invalidity, illegality, or unenforceability will not affect any other provision, and this agreement will be construed as if such invalid, illegal, or unenforceable provision did not exist.

11. Prior Agreements Superseded

This agreement constitutes the only agreement of the parties and supersedes any prior understandings or written or oral agreements between the parties respecting the subject matter.

12. Notice to Client

The State Bar of Texas requires that we provide the following information [Gov. C. § 81.079]:

The State Bar of Texas investigates and prosecutes professional misconduct committed by Texas attorneys. Although not every complaint against or dispute with a lawyer involves professional misconduct, the State Bar Office of General Counsel will provide you with information about how to file a complaint. For more information, call toll-free 1-800-932-1900.

[*Signatures*]

NOTES AND QUESTIONS

(1) *The Client's Obligations.* How much of the contract between lawyer and client should be concerned with obligations of the client in addition to paying the fee? For example, does the client have an obligation to keep in touch with the lawyer if the client changes his or her address (a frequent and serious problem)? What does the lawyer do if the client is "too nervous" to have a deposition taken by the opponent and refuses to appear (a not unheard-of problem)? Finally, what does the lawyer do if, in a contingent fee case in which the lawyer has invested considerable time and money, the client insists on perjury or requests an unethical course of conduct for the lawyer? Can these matters be covered in a written

document, and is it worthwhile to do so?

Note that the form contract from the *Texas Litigation Guide*, excerpted above, has a section covering "Cooperation of Client." There are varying schools of thought as to whether it is best to set forth a general duty to cooperate or whether it is better to specify by listing a number of duties the client is to perform, together with an explicit statement that the attorney may withdraw and collect the earned portion of the fee on breach.

(2) *Discuss Fees Sooner Rather Than Later.* An attorney should not hesitate to discuss fees with the client on the first visit. You may be surprised to learn that there is virtual unanimity among writers on this conclusion. The reason is apparently that clients themselves wish to have the matter clarified. Of course, the problem with discussing fees at the first visit is that the attorney generally does not yet know how much effort it will take to solve the client's problem. Accordingly, the setting of fees is an art, and a very important one for the lawyer to learn. What disadvantageous consequences can occur if a lawyer overestimates the time and effort required and quotes a fee arrangement that is too high? What disadvantages flow from setting a fee that is too low?

(3) *Adversarial Client Relationships.* Does it appear from these materials that the lawyer may sometimes have an adversarial relationship with his or her own client? If that thought seems disturbing, consider the matter this way. A stranger to the lawyer has just contacted the lawyer and has asked him or her to spend time and money to pursue a claim, the merits of which the lawyer has heard only from the prospective client, a stranger. The lawyer has no accurate way to judge whether the stranger is telling the truth. The action the stranger is requesting is that the lawyer initiate a suit, an act which, by itself, will cause harm and expense to another party, the defendant. The lawyer also does not know whether the stranger will pay for the lawyer's efforts, will fulfill his or her own obligations, or will look for opportunities to accuse the lawyer of wrongdoing. It is not that the lawyer assumes the worst about these matters, it is simply that the lawyer does not know. Is this picture overdrawn?

(4) *Enforcing the Fee Contract.* What should be done about the situation in which the lawyer does considerable work and spends money on a case only to find that the client has previously hired another lawyer? What of the lawyer who is "fired" by the client after spending considerable effort and money? Does the device of assigning an interest in the litigation provide adequate protection? How else can a lawyer protect himself or herself? Note that the situation of the client who hires two separate lawyers without telling either about the other is not unknown. The problem can be an acute one for personal injury lawyers who advance money for expenses.

(5) *Withdrawal of Counsel.* One of the problems (from the lawyer's standpoint) about the attorney-client relationship is that it can, at times, be a difficult one to terminate. If one is attorney of record in a litigation matter, termination is not accomplished merely by the attorney's unilateral decision, nor is it accomplished even by the agreement of the client. A motion to withdraw should be filed with the court, accompanied by a proposed form of order, indicating whether the withdrawal is with the client's consent and, if not, the reasons. Although such a

motion will ordinarily be granted, the court is not required to grant it (except in exceptional circumstances such as those posing a conflict of interest). In particular, a tardy motion may be denied if it would result in delay. A lawyer may be required to spend valuable time and money when previous time and money have been uncompensated (or worse, be forced to represent the views of a client with whom the attorney has serious personality or ethical differences).

[B] Avoiding Conflicts of Interest

As you have seen in the materials above, the attorney owes special duties to the client. In addition to being sure that the fee agreement is reasonable and clearly communicated, the lawyer must avoid certain actions and relationships which would cause the lawyer's personal interests to conflict with the interests of the client.

[1] General Rule

The Disciplinary Rules address conflict of interest in general and in particular types of situations. The basic rule on the subject is also the simplest: a lawyer is prohibited from representing opposing parties to the same litigation. Parties are opposing for purposes of this rule if a judgment favorable to one of the parties will directly impact unfavorably on the other party.

Loyalty to a client also prevents representation in situations that involve conflicting interests but not the same litigation. In general, a lawyer must not represent a person if the representation would involve a substantially related matter in which that person's interests are materially and directly adverse to the interests of another client of the lawyer or the lawyer's firm. This ban on representation also extends to situations in which representation of the person reasonably appears to be or become adversely limited by the lawyer' or law firm's responsibilities to another client or to a third person, or by the lawyer's or law firm's own interests.

Despite the general prohibition, however, a lawyer may represent a client in either of the two situations described in the preceding paragraphs if both of the following are true: (1) the lawyer reasonably believes that the representation of each client will not be materially affected; and (2) each affected or potentially affected client consents to the representation after full disclosure of the existence, nature, implications, and possible adverse consequences of the common representation and the advantages involved, if any. When a disinterested lawyer would conclude that the client should not agree to the representation under the circumstances, the lawyer involved should not ask for the client's agreement or provide representation on the basis of the client's consent. Moreover, it may be impossible to make the full disclosure necessary to obtain informed consent if, for example, one client refuses to consent to the disclosure of confidential information necessary to permit the other client to make an informed decision. If a lawyer would be prohibited by Rule 1.06 from representing one or more persons, no other lawyer who is a member of or associated with that lawyer's firm may represent those persons either.

[2] Prohibited Transactions

[a] Business Transactions

A lawyer may not enter into a business transaction with a client unless:

1. The transaction and terms on which the lawyer acquires an interest are fair and reasonable to the client and have been fully disclosed in a manner that the client can reasonably understand.
2. The client is given a reasonable opportunity to seek the advice of independent counsel in the transaction.
3. The client consents to the transaction in writing.

The term "business transaction" as used in this rule does not include standard commercial transactions between the lawyer and the client for products or services that the client generally markets to others.

[b] Gifts

An attorney is not prohibited from receiving reasonable gifts from a client, such as a simple gift to commemorate a holiday or express appreciation. However, a lawyer is forbidden to prepare an instrument that gives any substantial gift from a client, including a testamentary gift, to the lawyer or to the lawyer's parent, child, sibling, or spouse, unless the client is related to the donee. If the effectuation of a substantial gift requires preparing a legal instrument such as a will or conveyance, the client should have the detached advice that another lawyer can provide.

[c] Literary Rights

Conflicts of interest may arise if a lawyer acquires literary or media rights that relate to a representation. Measures suitable in the representation of the client may detract from the publication value of an account of the representation. Therefore, until the conclusion of all aspects of the matter giving rise to the lawyer's employment, a lawyer is precluded from making or negotiating an agreement with a client, prospective client, or former client that gives the lawyer literary or media rights to a portrayal or account based substantially on information relating to the representation.

Rule 1.08 does not prevent a lawyer who represents a client in a transaction concerning literary property from agreeing that the lawyer's fee shall consist of a share in ownership in the property, subject to the rules governing fees contained in Rule 1.04 and the limitations of Rule 1.08(h) concerning the acquisition of a proprietary interest in the subject matter of litigation.

[d] Acquisition of Proprietary Interest

A lawyer is prohibited from acquiring a proprietary interest in the cause of action or subject matter of the litigation that the lawyer is conducting for a client, except that the lawyer may (1) acquire a lien granted by law to secure the lawyer's fee or expenses, and (2) contract in a civil case with a client for a contingent fee that meets the requirements set forth in Rule 1.04.

[e] Payment for Legal Services

A lawyer is generally not permitted to provide financial assistance to a client in connection with pending or contemplated litigation or administrative proceedings. However there are two exceptions to this general rule. First, a lawyer may advance or guarantee court costs, expenses of litigation or administrative proceedings, and reasonably necessary medical and living expenses. Furthermore, the repayment of these amounts may be made contingent on the matter's outcome. Second, a lawyer who represents indigent clients may pay court costs and litigation expenses on their behalf.

The Disciplinary Rules also place restrictions on a lawyer's right to be paid by a third party for representing a client. A lawyer is not allowed to accept compensation from a third party unless (1) the client consents, (2) the arrangement does not interfere with the lawyer's independent professional judgment or with the attorney-client relationship, and (3) information relating to the client's representation is protected in compliance with the rules of confidentiality.

[f] Aggregate Settlement

A lawyer who represents two or more clients is forbidden to participate in making an aggregate settlement of the claims of or against the clients unless each client has consented to the settlement after a consultation that included disclosure of the existence and nature of all involved claims or pleas involved and disclosure of the nature and extent of the participation of each person in the settlement.

[g] Limitation of Liability

Lawyers are not permitted to make agreements prospectively limiting their malpractice liability unless the agreement is permitted by law and the client is independently represented in making the agreement. In addition, it is prohibited for a lawyer to settle a claim for malpractice liability with an unrepresented client or former client without first advising that person in writing that independent representation is appropriate in connection with the settlement.

[3] Former Client

A lawyer's duty to a client to avoid conflicts of interest does not cease to exist when a particular matter is resolved or a representation ends. Conflicts between duties to former and current clients have generated considerable controversy in many cases, often resulting in disqualification motions. Without prior consent, a lawyer who personally represented a client in a matter may not afterwards represent another person in a matter adverse to the former client in any of the following circumstances:

1. If the subsequent representation is in the same or a substantially related matter.

2. If the matter is one in which the other person questions the validity of the lawyer's services or work product for the former client.

3. If the representation in reasonable probability will involve a violation of the rule relating to the preservation of confidential information.

In general, when lawyers are or have become members of or associated with a firm, all of them are prohibited from knowingly representing a client if any one of them practicing alone would be prohibited from doing so by the rule stated above. This prohibition does not apply to the extent that representation is authorized by the rule relating to successive government and private employment.

When the association of a lawyer with a firm has terminated, the lawyers who were formerly associated with that lawyer are forbidden from knowingly representing a client if the lawyer whose association has terminated would be prohibited from representing that client, either because it would be representation in a matter adverse to a former client in the same or a substantially related matter or because the representation in reasonable probability will involve a violation of the rule relating to the preservation of confidential information.

The Texas Supreme Court has noted the distinction that Rule 1.09 makes between current and prior firms. *See In re Mitcham*, 133 S.W.3d 274, 276 (Tex. 2004). Rule 1.09 prohibits a lawyer from representing a current client against a former client in a matter that (1) questions the validity of the earlier representation, (2) involves a reasonable probability that confidences will be violated, or (3) is substantially related to the earlier representation. Other members of a disqualified lawyer's prior firm are disqualified only in the first two instances: (1) matters attacking the prior work, (2) and matters risking disclosure of confidences.

Rule 1.09(a)(2) prohibits representing a client in a dispute with a former client if the matters are "substantially related." For purposes of this provision, a "substantial" relationship exists if the facts of the previous representation are so related to the facts in the present litigation that a genuine threat exists that confidences revealed by the former client could be divulged to a present client. A "substantial relationship" primarily involves situations in which a lawyer could have acquired confidential information concerning a prior client that could be used either to that prior client's disadvantage or for the advantage of the lawyer's current client or some other person. Whether information was actually received from a former client is immaterial to the existence of a substantial relationship.

In this context, "confidential information" includes not only privileged information but "all information relating to a client or furnished by the client . . . acquired by the lawyer during the course of or by reason of the representation."

§ 1.03 CASE EVALUATION, ACCEPTANCE, AND SETTLEMENT

The vast majority of cases (probably in excess of 90 percent of cases filed) are settled without trial. Another very substantial proportion of litigation is settled without suit being filed. Consequently, ascertaining the "settlement value" of a case is integral to proper case evaluation. It is important to realize that this process is not a low form of intellectual endeavor, and it is not done without effort and work.

These materials cover the techniques involved in evaluating a case and negotiating for fair settlement value.

D. Reneker,
GEARY, STAHL, AND SPENCER LITIGATION SECTION ORIENTATION*

Settlements. The majority of the litigation matters the firm handles are concluded by means of compromise settlements that are negotiated by the lawyers with the consent of the clients. Accordingly, the prospects of settlement should be borne in mind throughout each stage of the litigation process.

The client makes the final decision as to whether a case is to be settled, and on what basis. For this reason, it is never appropriate for us to commit to a settlement without the client's express authorization. The client's decision, however, as to whether and on what terms to settle should not be made on the basis of his layman's view of the case; to the contrary, it should be made only after we have given the client the benefit of our recommendations.

In order for us to make appropriate recommendations about settlement, we must make an analysis of the case for the purpose of determining its "settlement value." The "settlement value" of a case is the amount a reasonable plaintiff would accept or a reasonable defendant would pay to avoid the risks inherent in a trial, given a full understanding of all significant factors in the case.

The significant factors to be analyzed in determining the reasonable settlement value of a case are (1) liability, (2) damages, and (3) ability to pay. The manner in which these factors relate to each other is best described by the use of several examples of situations that may arise within a general factual framework. Assume a personal injury case involving a two-car automobile collision. One of the cars was driven by our client, the plaintiff, who is a wealthy businessman, age 45, with a demonstrated ability to earn over $100,000 per year. The other car was driven by the defendant, a retired schoolteacher, age 75, who has no non-exempt assets and whose income consists of a pension and social security benefits.

EXAMPLE NO. 1

Liability: Undisputed evidence shows that defendant ran a red light.

---

* Reprinted by permission of Geary, Stahl & Spencer.

Damages: Plaintiff suffered severe brain damage, can no longer work and requires constant medical care.

Ability to Pay: Defendant carries liability insurance that provides coverage up to $1,000,000.

Settlement Value: Very high.

EXAMPLE NO. 2

Liability: Evidence conflicts as to which party ran a red light.

Damages: Plaintiff suffered severe brain damage, can no longer work and requires constant medical care.

Ability to Pay: Defendant carries liability insurance that provides coverage up to $1,000,000.

Settlement Value: Moderate; discount due to reduced liability factor.

EXAMPLE NO. 3

Liability: Undisputed evidence shows that defendant ran a red light.

Damages: Plaintiff suffered cuts and bruises and no lost time from work and required minimal medical care.

Ability to Pay: Defendant carries liability insurance that provides coverage up to $1,000,000.

Settlement Value: Nominal; discount due to reduced damages.

EXAMPLE NO. 4

Liability: Undisputed evidence shows that defendant ran a red light.

Damages: Plaintiff suffered severe brain damage, can no longer work and requires constant medical care.

Ability to Pay: Defendant uninsured.

Settlement Value: Nominal; discount due to lack of ability to pay.

We normally make our recommendations with a view toward the reasonable settlement value of a case. This is not to say, however, that the client is bound to accept our recommendations. As you will learn, however, the client will be more likely to accept our recommendations if he has been conditioned to do so from the outset and has been given reason to have confidence in our ability to give sound advice.

Settlements are normally reached through the process of negotiation, which involves offers and counter-offers. No attempt will be made here to review all the tactics that may be involved in negotiating with another lawyer. Several broad principles, however, are generally applicable. First of all, the opposing lawyer is not likely to want to "talk settlement" until he is generally familiar with the strengths and weakness of his case. Secondly, it is usually incumbent on the claimant to make the first offer. Thirdly, an offer once made, to which no response is given, should be withdrawn within a reasonable time; or, conversely, a time frame within which the offer must be accepted or rejected may be established when the offer is made. Finally, once an offer is made, a counter-offer is appropriate; accordingly, we should not "bargain with ourselves" by making a lower offer, if the first offer is rejected and no counter-offer is made.

Once a settlement is orally agreed to between the lawyers and the parties, it must be fully documented in writing as soon as practicable. Settlement documents may consist, in some cases, of no more than a release from one party to the other. Ordinarily, however, they are much more involved because many settlements contain terms that require actions other than the payment of money. The nature and extent of the settlement documents will depend on the nature of the case. The objective, of course, is to resolve all disputes between the parties, leaving no "loose ends," and to fully and fairly set forth the terms that have been agreed on, so that there can be absolutely no question about what is intended, what constitutes performance, what constitutes default and what rights and remedies are available to the parties upon performance or default, as the case may be.

§ 1.04 PRE-LITIGATION FACT-GATHERING: INVESTIGATION AND INTERVIEWING

THE CLIENT INTERVIEW

Good interviewing requires proper preparation, proper questioning, and proper interview structure. It requires the ability to break communications barriers. It requires the ability to detect and deal with intended or unintended falsehood.

Structure: Beginning the Interview. If the interviewee is a client, it is generally useful to begin the interview by finding out what the client wants.

The point appears obvious and most lawyers observe it intuitively to some degree, but proper interviewing means encouraging the client to express, and express completely, what he or she wants, before moving on. "I want a divorce" may mean just that, or it may mean the opposite. "I've been sued and I don't know what to do" may lead to the conclusion that the client wants a little more time to pay and is fearful that this supplier will tell others of the default.

The best beginning may be to ask the client, "How may I serve you?" or some similarly broad question. It is equally important, though, to realize that the initial response may be incomplete. Probing may be in order. "How do you feel about that?" or "Tell me what consequences you see that this might have for you personally?" might be the kind of follow-up that would be appropriate.

Before discussing the structure of the remainder of the interview, it may be useful here to distinguish between "hard" and "soft" information, because the structure sometimes depends on that distinction.

"Hard" and "Soft" Information. Evidence that is clear, definite, and unlikely to be successfully disputed may be called "hard" information. Other information is "soft." In a contract dispute, for instance, an order form sent by one party and

stamped with the other party's indication that it was received is relatively hard information. The recollection of one of the parties as to the contents of a telephone call, on the other hand, is relatively soft information.

Generally speaking, it is best to assemble hard points of data first to the extent they are available and then fill in the gaps with soft information. That is to say, the best approach may be to collect all pieces of paper related to the dispute, put them in chronological order and then attempt to reconstruct the remainder of the story with the aid of the chronology thus established.

Several further points about this principle need explanation. First, it is important to realize that "hard" and "soft" are relative terms. A document may turn out to be false, misleading, or ambiguous. A telephone conversation may become a hard data point if it is the subject of identical and positive recollection by both parties. One must, therefore, be willing to consider even the "hard" structure as changeable. Second, "soft" information may be just as valuable as "hard." The most important issues in the case may be, and frequently are, controlled more by soft than by hard evidence; this is because soft evidence is susceptible to differing versions. The versions naturally take the shape of the disputants' interests and become the battleground of the case. Third, although every case has some hard information, there are great differences in the degree to which hard information controls the interview process.

If the case is one in which hard information is voluminous, the collection of that hard information ordinarily must precede an in-depth reconstruction of the event. It may be possible to have the client collect the hard data in advance. If not, sequential interviews will likely be necessary. It may be advisable in any event to obtain an overview before looking for hard information.

Structure: The Interview as a Whole. The structure of the interview thus depends somewhat on whether the available hard data have been assimilated. After the problem identification stage at the beginning of the interview, it may be advisable to pause to collect further hard information or it may not, depending on the situation. If the interview is continued, the remainder of the interview may be concerned with three categories of activity: "Getting out the story," formulating theories or proposed courses of action, and testing the theories.

First, getting the story: This aspect of the interview is usually best conducted in a chronological manner. There are essentially two problems with a chronological approach: finding an appropriate starting point, and proceeding, step-by-step, without getting sidetracked or missing an important item. These are more formidable problems than they appear. For example, if the lawyer asks, "When did this all begin?" and the response is, "In 1969, when I met my partner," does the lawyer develop the story chronologically by asking for a complete statement of the relationship between the client and the partner, or does the lawyer do better to say, "And what was the next important event?"

Second, formulating courses of action: It is important to be tentative at this stage. In the litigation context, this step generally consists of formulating theories about the situation.

Third, testing the theories: If the lawyer has tentatively identified a defense of self-defense to an assault suit, or a fraud claim against the partner, the lawyer should not conclude the interview without comparing the elements of that legal theory against the facts the client can furnish. In other words, the lawyer should test the theory.

To recapitulate: A well-structured client interview would begin with a complete examination of the client's own conception of his or her desires. "What can I do to help you?" "Have you told me everything about this that bothers you?" The next step would be a chronological development of the story. "Suppose we go back to the beginning and you tell me what happened." "Is that really where it started?" This development may require careful direction to keep from getting sidetracked. Next, there should be formulation of integrating theories in a tentative way and the testing of these theories against the client's perceptions.

Questioning Techniques. There are many different kinds of questions. One of the most fundamental distinctions is that between leading and non-leading questions. "You were frightened, right?" is more leading than "Tell me how you felt." The leading question is susceptible to a greater danger of producing misleading information, but it is sometimes necessary for direction of the interview or to test a hypothesis.

Sometimes, "questioning" may be done by utterances that do not seem to involve questions at all. Reflecting the client's statements back to him or her, or what is called "active listening" (consisting of reactions indicating absorption of the client's statements) may be considered questioning techniques in that they prompt the client to provide further information. "Let me see whether I understand what you're saying . . . " or simply "I see, uh-huh," are examples of these techniques. At the opposite end of the spectrum, urging a position or rejecting one ("Oh, no, I certainly wouldn't say that") are techniques akin to questioning. The different approaches might be thought of as falling along a continuum from least leading or suggestive to most leading with silence (or active listening) at the lower end of the spectrum, non-leading questioning or reflection in the middle, and urging or rejection at the higher end.

The Funnel Sequence.

It follows from this discussion of question types that some should be used in some situations, others in other situations. It is inadvisable to begin a client interview pertaining to a complex event by asking the client a highly leading question. Likewise, once the client has exhausted the narrative possibilities, it is not appropriate to say, "Uh-huh, I see" and leave the matter at that. The sequence that is usually best is the opposite of this example: a sequence from less-leading to more-leading questions. To be more descriptive, a proper sequence often resembles a funnel, in that it starts with broad questions and proceeds to narrower ones. Writers in the area describe the sequence as "funnelling" or "T-funnelling" (the latter signifying that one questions broadly, across the bar of the "T," before zeroing in on particulars). An upside-down metaphor to similar effect is the pyramid, which has a broad base and builds to a narrow point.

The technique is easier to describe than it is to apply. The trickiest part is to know when and how to switch from broad to narrow questions. Switching too early may well cause important details to be missed. Switching too late can cause a half-hour interview to consume an afternoon, and it can mean failure to get to necessary subjects. The most common problem, however, is missed details because the lawyer does not know of them and the client does not see their relevance. "Why didn't you tell me that?" "Because you didn't ask," is the result that a switch too early from broad to narrow questions may produce.

As in the beginning of the interview, it is important in the funnel sequence to "squeeze" the client (here the metaphor being that of a sponge), albeit gently. The message should be, "Have you told me everything?" Example:

> Tell me what happened.
>
> I went in the bar and he hit me.
>
> Can you tell me a little more about how it happened?
>
> Well, I was walking to my table, and he come up to me and says, "What did you say?" and I says, "I didn't say anything."

Notice that the interviewer has resisted the temptation, after the first question and answer, to proceed to narrower questions, because the "squeezing" process has only begun. The squeeze produces more, but still incomplete, information. What should be the next question? An interviewer might ask: "Do you suppose he might have mistaken you for someone else?," but that would not be the sort of question the funnel sequence would dictate. "What led up to his saying that?" or better yet, "Can you tell me more about what happened?" would be more in line with the funnel sequence. The dangers of the leading question at this stage are twofold: it detracts from the client's free-form narrative, which may uncover useful information to which it is unlikely the lawyer will direct a specific question, and furthermore, it may suggest to the client a direction the interviewer wants the client to take with all subsequent responses.

After the client has been thoroughly squeezed, the interviewer is ready to explore aspects the lawyer has seen but the client has not. For instance, the setting. What was the bar like? The questioning should begin at that level of generality, not with "How many people were there in the bar?" or "Was it dark?" The question, "What was the bar like?" is intermediate in the funnel sequence. It is important, eventually, to ask about the number of people and the lighting after the client's narrative potential has been exhausted by broader questions and careful squeezing.

Preparation; Interviewing Forms. Interview forms or checklists are useful, but there is a wide variety of views about their proper place. Some lawyers use long and detailed checklists. Some use forms to be filled out by clients. Others use neither or use checklists only as a vague guide.

The degree to which interview forms can be useful depends on several factors, including the kind of information to be gathered, the frequency with which the attorney gathers this kind of information, the nature of the clientele and the personality of the individual client. For gathering personal data on the client, forms are quite useful. Thus, in obtaining the client's name, address, telephone, employment location, next of kin, and the like, forms are a means of ensuring complete, accurate, and efficient data collection. For certain information in certain types of cases — property and income information in a divorce case, the factors necessary for a commercial collection suit, the damage and liability factors in an automobile collision case — forms may likewise be extremely useful.

Should the client be asked to fill out a form, or should the attorney question from it? The answer depends on the complexity of the questions and the nature of the client. If the form is longer than one or two pages, the sheer intimidation factor, surprisingly, may dictate against its use. Many clients, even intelligent ones, will be incapable of filling in a form of any complexity without assistance — and clients who are intelligent enough are sometimes offended. A few lawyers are successful in sending interview forms in the mail in advance of the interview. Doing so requires great sensitivity and willingness to consider that the client may appear without the form filled in (or may be offended or intimidated by it), but pays great dividends if done successfully.

The obtaining of information or documents by the client in advance is another important problem. In general, it is better to tell the client to be inclusive in bringing documents. Don't say, "Bring me that life insurance policy." Instead, say: "Go through your house from top to bottom and bring me everything that has the word insurance on it or has anything to do with insurance." Deciding that a homeowner's policy, or a liability policy, or some other kind of insurance policy does not cover the event is a task to be done by the lawyer, not the client.

In the office, the lawyer may interview the client in free-flow fashion and then have the client fill in a form or write a narrative. Another alternative may be to have a legal assistant conduct a more in-depth interview or assist the client to fill in a form. Forms and free-flow interviewing should be viewed as complementing each other. It is important to keep in mind that a form cannot substitute for a free-flow interview. It is equally important, but less obvious, to recognize that a free-flow interview is sometimes not a substitute for a systematic form.

Interviewing structure requires some problem-identification at the beginning. It also requires the building of some rapport. These factors may explain the difficulty of mailed interview forms. They also, in all probability, dictate that the free-flow interview should be placed before the use of a form (unless the form is used in a limited fashion to gather such information as name and address).

Reluctance.

In some instances, obtaining information from a client may be difficult not because the interviewer uses the wrong questioning sequence, but because the interviewee has a reluctance to express something important. There are several kinds of blocking factors that may be at work.

To see what they might be, we will consider a simple example. Assume that the client (the husband) is being interviewed in connection with potential divorce proceedings. He is on the brink of insolvency because of a parasitic illness. He does not particularly wish to discuss either the insolvency or the illness. The reasons may include:

(1) *Fear that disclosure may hurt his legal position.* He may feel that admitting these facts will hurt his legal position. (Actually, the opposite may be true if, for example, he is concerned about property division or holding child support to a reasonable amount; or it may be that the facts would indeed hurt him but would best be known by his lawyer, such as if, for example, a custody dispute is possible.) In either event, the client does not perceive the need for disclosure as a lawyer would.

(2) *Social embarrassment.* It is not easy for anyone except a clinician to discuss a parasitic disease, and then only if it is someone else's. Many people do not feel it is the kind of thing one brings up in polite conversation. Even if the client sees the purpose of the interview, he may unconsciously refrain from disclosure.

(3) *Self-esteem.* The client may have higher self-esteem if he refuses to recognize these facts.

(4) *Desire to talk about other subjects.* In a divorce situation, a client often wishes to catalogue completely his complaint about the other spouse and may do so to the exclusion of subjects he sees as less important.

(5) *Differences in status.* Sometimes communication is inhibited because the client perceives himself as of a different social class from the lawyer. Personal matters may be difficult to discuss with one of another social class.

(6) *Failure to recognize relevance.* Clients often think of information as categorized into "legal" and "non-legal" or they may simply fail to see the relevance of the issue. Indeed, unless one has either a curious mind or awareness of legal issues, it may be hard to see how a disease or insolvency relates to divorce. If the lawyer asks, after the proceeding, "Why didn't you tell me that?" a client who failed to see its relevance will reply, "Because you didn't ask me."

(7) *Concern for confidentiality.* The client may fear that the lawyer will disclose the matter carelessly. (Such a fear is not totally unfounded.)

These factors may operate singly or in tandem. The most insidious thing about them is that they do not operate in the open and they operate to mask subjects about which the lawyer may not know to ask in the first place. Thus there are two kinds of problems that may affect each other: (1) the lawyer does not broach the subject; and (2) even if the lawyer does, the client resists providing the information.

Dealing With Reluctance. There are many means of dealing with these problems, including:

(1) *Expression of Understanding.* "In a divorce, there are usually things we have to talk about that are embarrassing. I understand that. You're probably feeling embarrassed just talking to a complete stranger about the whole thing, right?" The same technique can be used in response to the revelation of a traumatic event: "I can imagine how upset you must have been when she asked you for money and you didn't have any."

(2) *Praise.* "These are hard things to talk about and you're doing pretty well at telling me about them."

(3) *Assurance Against Certain Harms.* Explicit expression of, and explanation of, the attorney-client privilege, together with a statement of a determination to follow it, is sometimes useful, as is an expression of loyalty. In some instances, the statement "Sometimes people think they may be hurt by information they give me. I'm not going to hurt you" is useful.

(4) *Statement of Expectation.* "I know that if you try, you can remember at least something about it, and whatever you remember will help." Acting as though the interviewer expects the client to make disclosure often produces the disclosure.

(5) *Explanation of Law or Analogy.* Explaining the legal elements of a claim or defense is a way of preventing the "failure-to-recognize-relevance" blocking factor from operating. "We don't recover anything unless we prove the defendant was 'negligent.' 'Negligent' means the defendant was 'careless.' Any information you have that might possibly show that would be useful." The technique is subject to the criticism that it may produce falsehood. However, it often operates to extract truthful information that would otherwise have remained buried. A related idea is to give an example: "In the so-and-so case, we were able to find out that the defendant had done such-and-such. That's the sort of thing that would be useful to find out here."

(6) *Helpfulness to Legal Position.* With respect to the "legal position" blocking factor, sometimes the best antidote is to convince the client that disclosure not only will not hurt the case, but it will help the case. "I can't defend you until I know everything you know." "Even the most seemingly irrelevant detail might help." Explaining forthrightly that even harmful information should be disclosed so that it can be dealt with in the adversary context, together with an example or analogy illustrating this principle, is useful.

(7) *Appeal to Pride.* Sometimes an appeal to higher values helps. This is particularly true of disinterested witnesses ("You don't want to see a horribly injured man unable to pay his medical bills, do you?"), but sometimes it is useful as to the client as well. "You owe it to every physician who is wrongly sued, as you are, to search your memory carefully."

The careful development of rapport and respect, of course, is the best way around some blocking factors. For some of them patience and persistence are also the best curatives.

Falsehood. Clients fabricate more than beginning lawyers usually expect they will. In a way, falsehood is human. Some falsehood is necessary to normal living, as an incident of common courtesy. Other falsehood is necessary to defend the ego. The experienced lawyer, although not completely accepting falsehood, learns to expect it and tends to judge it slightly less harshly than the beginning lawyer.

The easiest and most effective method of detecting fabrication is also the most obvious. A story that is unreasonable, inconsistent with human nature, filled with physical improbabilities, or inconsistent with social custom to a marked degree should be recognized as a red flag. "So you say that, although you usually don't do it, on this occasion, you looked to the left side, then looked to the right side, then turned back and looked to the other side again, and the first time you saw this car was when it hit you?" "You say you were never angry when you spanked little Johnny?"

The obviousness of the technique, however, does not mean that it is easy to employ. In the first place, litigators are usually dealing with extraordinary situations; those are the kinds of situations that create litigation. Recognizing the unusual that is also unreasonable is harder than it sounds. Second, the recognition that the interviewee is one's client and is lying is difficult. Third, a trusting relationship between lawyer and client is a good thing, and disbelief interferes with that relationship. Fourth, the most effective technique for dealing with the falsehood may not be to confront it directly (indeed, in the short run, it may be to ignore it), and it is easier to ignore it if one fails to recognize it in the first place. Finally, a great deal of popular wisdom ("A lawyer's got to believe his client") tells the lawyer to suspend disbelief. Hence, while the statement, "You say you were never angry when you spanked little Johnny?" may bring broad smiles from parents who know otherwise, when it is put forth sincerely by a credible client who has paid a fee, it tends not to raise a red flag.

There are other means of detecting deception. One is recognizing reluctance. Reluctance to talk about the subject may indicate falsehood (it may also indicate blocking factors, of course; falsehood is not always indicated). A story that shifts and contains internal inconsistencies is another. Yet another method is to ask the client what hostile persons will say about him or her, under the ostensible guise of obtaining information for the case. "Of course, the driver of the car doesn't necessarily always tell the story the same way. Even if he's not going to tell the truth, we want to know what he's going to say. You might know or have some idea. Do you think he's going to say you looked both ways?"

The methods of dealing with fabrication are also varied. One is to ignore the matter at first, waiting until rapport has been built before confronting it. As an alternative to direct confrontation, the lawyer may ask the client to explain an inconsistent version given by a third person; in this situation, the third party, not the lawyer, does the confronting, so that the relationship is not damaged. Another means of indirect confrontation is to explore areas of reluctance by probing questions. Understand that case relation or similar "blockbreakers" should accompany the use of these techniques. Non-verbal communication, such as a cold stare or a start of surprise can sometimes be effective. Sometimes the best approach is direct confrontation, which can be done by an expression of the reasons for disbelief in a polite manner, or can be done by the conclusory statement, "Look, you're lying your head off to me and I can't represent you in that situation." Which technique to use depends on the magnitude of the falsehood, the motivation for its use, and the attorney's concern for the trusting relationship that is needed.

Conclusion. The techniques of interviewing are simple to describe, intuitively obvious to many, but hard to employ in practice. A good interview is one that is properly structured, uses different questioning types in funnelling sequence where appropriate, recognizes inhibitions and deals with them, and recognizes and deals with falsehood. The use of forms can often enhance interviewing if it does not take over the interviewing process.

§ 1.05 WHEN TO FILE THE LAWSUIT: COMPLIANCE WITH PRELIMINARY PROCEDURAL REQUIREMENTS IMPOSED BY STATUTE

A wide variety of claims require plaintiffs to fulfill prefiling or prelitigation requirements as a prerequisite to suit and, in some cases, as a prerequisite to liability. For example, most Texas municipalities have enacted charter provisions stating that the city will not be liable for any damages unless proper and timely notice is given prior to the filing of any suit against the city. *See City of Houston v. Torres*, 621 S.W.2d 588, 590 (Tex. 1981). The Tort Claims Act expressly recognizes and adopts these charter or comparable local ordinance provisions for tort claims filed against municipalities. *See* C.P.R.C. § 101.101(b). Similarly, a claimant asserting liability against any governmental unit under the Tort Claims Act must give the governmental unit notice of the claim against it not later than six months after the incident giving rise to the claim occurred. The notice must reasonably describe the damage or injury claimed, the time and place of the incident and the incident itself. C.P.R.C. § 101.101(a). Failure to give the notice bars the tort claim, unless the governmental unit has actual notice. *See Reese v. State Dep't of Highways & Pub. Transp.*, 831 S.W.2d 529, 530 (Tex. App. — Tyler 1992, pet. denied).

Both state and federal statutes governing particular types of employment litigation also require claimants to satisfy presuit requirements by filing a charge of discrimination with the EEOC within 300 days of the allegedly unlawful practice. 42 U.S.C. §§ 2000e-5(e)(1), 12117(a). At the conclusion of the administrative process, the EEOC will issue a right to sue notice to the plaintiff, who must file suit within 90 days of receipt of the notice. 42 U.S.C. § 2000e-5(f)(1). Both Title VII of the Civil Rights Act of 1964 and the Americans with Disabilities Act of 1990 require the exhaustion of Title VII's administrative remedies as a jurisdictional prerequisite to suit. Similarly the Texas Commission on Human Rights Act also requires a claimant to exhaust comparable administrative remedies before the Texas Workforce Commission to prosecute a private right of action. In addition, before bringing suit against a state or local governmental body under the Texas Whistleblower Act, an employee must at least invoke the employer's grievance procedure within 90 days after the alleged violation occurred. If a final decision is not rendered within 60 days after the procedures are initiated, the employee may either exhaust the procedures or bring suit. Gov. C. § 554.006(d).

A number of other statutes contain even more elaborate pre-filing or prelitigation requirements. These requirements are designed to facilitate the resolution of particular kinds of disputes and to screen particular types of claims out of the litigation process because they are unmeritorious. For example, in most actions brought under the Deceptive Trade Practices Act (DTPA), a consumer must give written notice at least 60 days prior to filing a suit for damages under the DTPA to a prospective defendant in reasonable detail of the consumer's specific complaint and the amount of damages, both for economic loss and mental anguish, and expenses, including attorney's fees, if any, reasonably incurred by the consumer in asserting the claim against the defendant. Bus. & Com. C. § 17.505(a).

The only exceptions to the requirement that the consumer give 60 days' written notice prior to filing suit are if (1) the need to file suit prior to the expiration of the statute of limitations renders the notice impracticable, or (2) the consumer's claim is asserted by a counterclaim. Bus. & Com. C. § 17.505(b). Actual or oral notice is not an acceptable substitute for the written notice required by the statute. *The Moving Co. v. Whitten*, 717 S.W.2d 117, 123 (Tex. App. — Houston [14th Dist.] 1986, writ ref'd n.r.e.), *disapproved on other grounds by Hines v. Hash*, 843 S.W.2d 464, 469–470 (Tex. 1992).

During the 60-day period between the time the notice is given and the suit is filed, the person given the notice may make a written request to inspect, in a reasonable manner and at a reasonable time and place, the goods that are the subject of the action or claim. Bus. & Com. C. § 17.505(a); *see* Bus. & Com. C. § 17.50(b).

A person against whom a suit is pending who does not receive the required written notice may file a plea in abatement not later than the 30th day after the filing of the original answer. The plea is not available if notice was excused by the need to avoid the running of the statute of limitation, or if the consumer's claim was asserted as a counterclaim. Bus. & Com. C. § 17.505(c).

The court must abate the suit if, after a hearing, it finds proper notice was not provided. A suit is automatically abated without the order of the court beginning on the 11th day after the date a plea in abatement is filed if the plea is verified and alleges that the person against whom the suit is pending did not receive the required written notice and if that affidavit is not controverted by an affidavit filed by the consumer before the 11th day after the date on which the plea in abatement is filed. Bus. & Com. C. § 17.505(d). An automatic abatement continues until the 60th day after the date that proper written notice is served. Bus. & Com. C. § 17.505(e).

A party may file a motion to compel mediation of a DTPA claim. This motion must be filed within 90 days of the service of a pleading in which DTPA relief is sought. Bus. & Com. C. § 17.5051(a). Within 30 days of the filing, the court must sign an order setting the time and place of the mediation. If the parties do not agree on a mediator, the court must appoint the mediator. Mediation must be held within 30 days after the date the order is signed, unless the parties agree otherwise or the court determines that additional time, not to exceed an additional 30 days is warranted. Bus. & Com. C. § 17.5051(b)–(d). Except as agreed by all parties who have appeared in the action, each party who has appeared must participate in the mediation and share the mediation fee. Bus. & Com. C. § 17.5051(e). Nevertheless, a party may not compel mediation if the amount of economic damages claimed is less than $15,000, unless the party seeking to compel mediation agrees to pay the costs of the mediation. Bus. & Com. C. § 17.5051(f).

DTPA defendants may limit their exposure to liability by making a statutorily-sanctioned "offer of settlement." A person who receives proper notice of a DTPA claim may tender an "offer of settlement" at any time during the period beginning on the date the notice is received and ending on the 60th day after that date. Bus. & Com. C. § 17.5052(a). If mediation is not compelled, the person may tender an "offer of settlement" at any time during the period beginning on the date an original answer is filed and ending on the 90th day after that date. If a mediation is compelled, a person against whom a DTPA claim is pending may tender an "offer of settlement" during the period beginning on the day after the date that the mediation ends and ending on the 20th day after that date. Bus. & Com. C. § 17.5052(b), (c).

An "offer of settlement" must include an offer to pay the following amounts of money, separately stated, Bus. & Com. C. § 17.5052(d):

- An amount of money or other consideration, reduced to its cash value, as settlement of the consumer's claim for damages.
- An amount of money to compensate the consumer for the consumer's reasonable and necessary attorneys' fees incurred as of the date of the offer. *See Cain v. Pruett*, 938 S.W.2d 152, 157 (Tex. App. — Dallas 1996, no writ) (settlement offer that did not include agreement to reimburse plaintiffs for reasonable attorney's fees did not limit recovery of damages or fees, although it did affect calculation of prejudgment interest.

Unless both required parts of an offer of settlement are accepted by the consumer not later than the 30th day after the date the offer is made, the offer is rejected. Bus. & Com. C. § 17.5052(e). A proper settlement offer that has been rejected by the consumer may be filed with the court, accompanied by an affidavit certifying the offer's rejection. If the court finds that the amount tendered in the settlement offer for damages is the same as, substantially the same as, or more than the damages found by the trier of fact, the consumer may not recover as damages any amount in excess of the lesser of (1) the amount of damages tendered in the settlement offer, or (2) the amount of damages found by the trier of fact. Bus. & Com. C. § 17.5052(f), (g). If the court makes the foregoing finding, it must determine reasonable and necessary attorney's fees to compensate the consumer for attorney's fees incurred before the date and time of the rejected settlement offer to compensate the consumer for attorney's fees. If the offer of attorney's fees is the same as, substantially the same as, or more than the amount of reasonable and necessary attorney's fees incurred by the consumer as of the date of the offer, the consumer may not recover attorney's fees greater than the amount of fees tendered in the settlement offer. Bus. & Com. C. § 17.5052(h). In contrast, if the court finds that the offering party could not perform the offer at the time the offer was made or that the offering party substantially misrepresented the cash value of the offer, the foregoing limitations on recovery do not apply. Bus. & Com. C. § 17.5052(j); *see* Bus. & Com. C. § 17.506.

An "offer of settlement" is not an admission of engaging in an unlawful act, practice, or liability under the DTPA. An offer or a rejection of an offer may not be used in evidence at trial except in connection with the DTPA settlement procedure as described above. Bus. & Com. C. § 17.5052(k).

The DTPA's "offer of settlement" provisions, which are designed to avoid liability for attorney's fees, are in addition to the cost-shifting provisions contained in Chapter 42 of the Civil Practice and Remedies Code and in Civil Procedure Rule 167, both of which apply to actions filed on or after January 1, 2004.

A settlement offer that does not comply with DTPA standards may still affect the calculation of prejudgment interest, even though it will not limit the award of damages or attorney's fees. Under the Finance Code, prejudgment interest may be eliminated during the period that the settlement offer may be accepted, if the offer is for more than the ultimate judgment. *Cain v. Pruett*, 938 S.W.2d 152, 157–58 (Tex. App. — Dallas 1996, no writ); *see* FIN. C. § 304.105.

Very similar presuit notice, mediation and settlement provisions are applicable to private causes of action brought under Chapter 541 of the Insurance Code.

Perhaps the most elaborate prelitigation and prefiling requirements are applicable to health care liability claims. Chapter 74 of the Civil Practice and Remedies Code requires that any person asserting a health care liability claim must give written notice of the claim by certified mail, return receipt requested, to each physician and health care provider against whom the claim is being made, at least 60 days before the filing of a suit in any Texas court based on the claim. C.P.R.C. § 74.051(a); *see De Checa v. Diagnostic Center Hosp., Inc.*, 852 S.W.2d 935, 938–39 (Tex. 1993) (separate notice required for each person sued). The notice should identify the claimant, describe the essential facts of the claim and state the purpose of the notice, including any settlement demand. C.P.R.C. § 74.051(c). Presumably, the purpose of the notice is to encourage the defendant or defendants to conduct an investigation and evaluation of the claim to facilitate settlement. The notice must be accompanied by an authorization form for the release of protected health information. C.P.R.C. §§ 74.051(a), 74.052(a).

If the claimant fails to give the required notice to each defendant, any defendants who do not receive the notice may obtain a 60-day abatement of the action on request. *See De Checa v. Diagnostic Center Hosp., Inc.*, 852 S.W.2d 935, 938–39 (Tex. 1993). In addition, failure to provide the authorization for release of health information along with the notice of claim causes all further proceedings against the physician or other health care provider receiving the notice to be abated until 60 days following receipt by the physician or health care provider of the authorization. C.P.R.C. § 74.052(a).

If the pre-suit notice is given, the statute of limitations is tolled "to and including a period of 75 days following the giving of the notice" for all parties and potential parties, C.P.R.C. § 75.01(c). This means that the running of limitations is suspended for 75 days. *See Phillips v. Sharpstown General Hosp.*, 664 S.W.2d 162, 165 (Tex. App. — Houston [1st Dist.] 1983, no writ).

In addition, a claimant who has filed a petition asserting a health care liability claim must serve on each party or the party's attorney one or more expert reports, with a curriculum vitae of each expert listed in the report for each physician or health care provider against whom a liability claim is asserted, not later than the 120th day after the petition is filed. Each defendant physician or health care provider whose conduct is implicated in a report must file and serve any objection to the sufficiency of the report not later than the 21st day after the date it was served, failing which all objections are waived. C.P.R.C. § 74.351.

The "expert report" must provide a fair summary of the expert's opinions as of the date of the report regarding applicable standards of care, the manner in which the care rendered by the physician or health care provider failed to meet the standards, and the causal relationship between that failure and the injury, harm or damages claimed. C.P.R.C. § 74.351(r)(6). Subject to the provision for one 30-day extension to cure a deficient report (*see* C.P.R.C. § 74.351(c)), unless the date for serving the report is extended by written agreement of the affected parties (C.P.R.C. § 74.351(a)), if the plaintiff does not file a sufficient report within the 120-day limit, on motion of the affected physician or health care provider, the court must dismiss the case with prejudice and award the movant reasonable attorney's fees and costs of court. C.P.R.C. § 74.351(b).

Until a claimant has served the required report and curriculum vitae, all discovery in a suit based on a health care liability claim is stayed except for the acquisition by the claimant of information, including medical and hospital records, related to the patient's health care through written discovery, depositions on written questions and discovery from nonparties under Civil Procedure Rule 205. C.P.R.C. § 74.351(g).

§ 1.06 WHEN TO FILE THE LAWSUIT: STATUTES OF LIMITATIONS AND STATUTES OF REPOSE

The failure to observe time deadlines, including the statutes of limitation, is a great source of actionable attorney malpractice in the trial area. Trial attorneys typically have from 100 to 300 ongoing matters at any one time. New information is obtained daily and must be assimilated. Each matter involves not just one deadline, but rather a series of deadlines. In cases in which suit has not yet been filed, the attorney may be engaged in settlement negotiations, cogitation on theories of suit, investigation, or the like. Missing a deadline under these conditions is not something that happens only to the slovenly. It happens even to skilled, conscientious lawyers. In addition to careful calendaring practices, knowledge of relevant statutes of limitations is invaluable in avoiding the loss of a client's rights through the lawyer's default.

Chapter 16 of the Civil Practice and Remedies Code contains a number of provisions that create either statutes of limitation (that run from the accrual of the cause of action) or statutes of repose (that create absolute time limits on the right to sue certain kinds of defendants, even if the particular plaintiff's claim has not yet arisen).

§ 16.002. *One-Year Limitations Period.*

(a) A person must bring suit for malicious prosecution, libel, slander, or breach of promise of marriage not later than one year after the day the cause of action accrues . . . .

§ 16.003. *Two-Year Limitations Period.*

(a) Except as provided by Sections 16.010 and 16.0045, a person must bring suit for trespass for injury to the estate or to the property of another, conversion of personal property, taking or detaining the personal property of another, personal injury, forcible entry and detainer, and forcible detainer not later than two years after the day the cause of action accrues.

(b) A person must bring suit not later than two years after the day the cause of action accrues in an action for injury resulting in death. Thc cause of action accrues on the death of the injured person.

§ 16.004. *Four-Year Limitations Period.*

(a) A person must bring suit on the following actions not later than four years after the day the cause of action accrues:

(1) specific performance of a contract for the conveyance of real property;

(2) penalty or damages on the penal clause of a bond to convey real property;

(3) debt;

(4) fraud; or

(5) breach of fiduciary duty.

(b) A person must bring suit on the bond of an executor, administrator, or guardian not later than four years after the day of the death, resignation, removal, or discharge of the executor, administrator, or guardian.

(c) A person must bring suit against his partner for a settlement of partnership accounts, and must bring an action on an open or stated account, or on a mutual and current account concerning the trade of merchandise between merchants or their agents or factors, not later than four years after the day that the cause of action accrues. For purposes of this subsection, the cause of action accrues on the day that the dealings in which the parties were interested together cease.

§ 16.0045. *Five-Year Limitations Period.*

(a) A person must bring suit for personal injury not later than five years after the day the cause of action accrues if the injury arises as a result of conduct that violates:

(1) Section 22.011, Penal Code (sexual assault);

(2) Section 22.021, Penal Code (aggravated sexual assault);

(3) Section 21.02, Penal Code (continuous sexual abuse of young child or children);

(b) In an action for injury resulting in death arising as a result of conduct described by Subsection (a), the cause of action accrues on the death of the injured person.

(c) The limitations period under this section is tolled for a suit on the filing of a petition by any person in an appropriate court alleging that the identity of the defendant in the suit is unknown and designating the unknown defendant as "John or Jane Doe." The person filing the petition shall proceed with due diligence to discover the identity of the defendant and amend the petition by substituting the real name of the defendant for "John or Jane Doe" not later than the 30th day after the date that the defendant is identified to the plaintiff. The limitations period begins running again on the date that the petition is amended.

§ 16.008. *Architects, Engineers, Interior Designers, and Landscape Architects Furnishing Design, Planning, or Inspection of Construction of Improvements.*

(a) A person must bring suit for damages for a claim listed in Subsection (b) against a registered or licensed architect, engineer, interior designer, or landscape architect in this state, who designs, plans, or inspects the construction of an improvement to real property or equipment attached to real property, not later than 10 years after the substantial completion of the improvement or the beginning of operation of the equipment in an action arising out of a defective or unsafe condition of the real property, the improvement, or the equipment.

(b) This section applies to suit for:

(1) injury, damage, or loss to real or personal property;

(2) personal injury;

(3) wrongful death;

(4) contribution; or

(5) indemnity.

(c) If the claimant presents a written claim for damages, contribution, or indemnity to the architect, engineer, interior designer, or landscape architect within the 10-year limitations period, the period is extended for two years from the day the claim is presented.

§ 16.009. *Persons Furnishing Construction or Repair of Improvements*

(a) A claimant must bring suit for damages for a claim listed in Subsection (b) against a person who constructs or repairs an improvement to real property not later than 10 years after the substantial completion of the improvement in an action arising out of a defective or unsafe condition of the real property or a deficiency in the construction or repair of the improvement.

(b) This section applies to suit for:

(1) injury, damage, or loss to real or personal property;

(2) personal injury;

(3) wrongful death;

(4) contribution; or

(5) indemnity.

(c) If the claimant presents a written claim for damages, contribution, or indemnity to the person performing or furnishing the construction or repair work during the 10-year limitations period, the period is extended for two years from the date the claim is presented.

(d) If the damage, injury, or death occurs during the 10th year of the limitations period, the claimant may bring suit not later than two years after the day the cause of action accrues.

(e) This section does not bar an action:

(1) on a written warranty, guaranty, or other contract that expressly provides for a longer effective period;

(2) against a person in actual possession or control of the real property at the time that the damage, injury, or death occurs; or

(3) based on wilful misconduct or fraudulent concealment in connection with the performance of the construction or repair.

(f) This section does not extend or affect a period prescribed for bringing an action under any other law of this state.

§ 16.010. *Misappropriation of Trade Secrets.*

(a) A person must bring suit for misappropriation of trade secrets not later than three years after the misappropriation is discovered or by the exercise of reasonable diligence should have been discovered.

(b) A misappropriation of trade secrets that continues over time is a single cause of action and the limitations period described by Subsection (a) begins running without regard to whether the misappropriation is a single or continuing act.

§ 16.012. *Products Liability.*

(a) In this section:

(1) "Claimant," "seller," and "manufacturer" have the meanings assigned by Section 82.001.

(2) "Products liability action" means any action against a manufacturer or seller for recovery of damages or other relief for harm allegedly caused by a defective product, whether the action is based in strict tort liability, strict products liability, negligence, misrepresentation, breach of express or implied warranty, or any other theory or combination of theories, and whether the relief sought is recovery of damages or any other legal or equitable relief, including a suit for:

(A) injury or damage to or loss of real or personal property;

(B) personal injury;

(C) wrongful death;

(D) economic loss; or

(E) declaratory, injunctive, or other equitable relief.

(b) Except as provided by Subsections (c), (d), and (d-1), a claimant must commence a products liability action against a manufacturer or seller of a product before the end of 15 years after the date of the sale of the product by the defendant.

(c) If a manufacturer or seller expressly warrants in writing that the product has a useful safe life of longer than 15 years, a claimant must commence a products liability action against that manufacturer or seller of the product before the end of the number of years warranted after the date of the sale of the product by that seller.

(d) This section does not apply to a products liability action seeking damages for personal injury or wrongful death in which the claimant alleges:

(1) the claimant was exposed to the product that is the subject of the action before the end of 15 years after the date the product was first sold;

(2) the claimant's exposure to the product caused the claimant's disease that is the basis of the action; and

(3) the symptoms of the claimant's disease did not, before the end of 15 years after the date of the first sale of the product by the defendant, manifest themselves to a degree and for a duration that would put a reasonable person on notice that the person suffered some injury.

(d-1) This section does not reduce a limitations period for a cause of action described by Subsection (d) that accrues before the end of the limitations period under this section.

(e) This section does not extend the limitations period within which a products liability action involving the product may be commenced under any other law.

(f) This section applies only to the sale and not to the lease of a product . . . .

§ 16.051. *Residual Limitations Period.* Every action for which there is no express limitations period, except an action for the recovery of real property, must be brought not later than four years after the day the cause of action accrues.

In addition to chapter 16 of the Civil Practice and Remedies Code, other Texas laws contain their own statute of limitations provision. Here are some of the most common examples.

Bus. & Comm. C. § 2.725. *Statute of Limitations in Contracts for Sale*

(a) An action for breach of any contract for sale must be commenced within four years after the cause of action has accrued. By the original agreement the parties may reduce the period of limitation to not less than one year but may not extend it.

(b) A cause of action accrues when the breach occurs, regardless of the aggrieved party's lack of knowledge of the breach. A breach of warranty occurs when tender of delivery is made, except that where a warranty explicitly extends to future performance of the goods and discovery of the breach must await the time of such performance the cause of action accrues when the breach is or should have been discovered.

(c) Where an action commenced within the time limited by Subsection (a) is so terminated as to leave available a remedy by another action for the same breach such other action may be commenced after the expiration of the time limited and within six months after the termination of the first action unless the termination resulted from voluntary discontinuance or from dismissal for failure or neglect to prosecute.

(d) This section does not alter the law on tolling of the statute of limitations nor does it apply to causes of action which have accrued before this title becomes effective.

Bus. & Comm. C. § 17.565. *Limitation in Deceptive Trade Practices Cases*

All actions brought under this subchapter must be commenced within two years after the date on which the false, misleading, or deceptive act or practice occurred or within two years after the consumer discovered or in the exercise of reasonable diligence should have discovered the occurrence of the false, misleading, or deceptive act or practice. The period of limitation provided in this section may be extended for a period of 180 days if the plaintiff proves that failure timely to commence the action was caused by the defendant's knowingly engaging in conduct solely calculated to induce the plaintiff to refrain from or postpone the commencement of the action.

Ins. C. § 541.162. *Limitations Period for Claims Against Insurers for Unfair Competition or Unfair Practices*

(a) A person must bring an action under this chapter before the second anniversary of the following:

(1) the date the unfair method of competition or unfair or deceptive act or practice occurred; or

(2) the date the person discovered or, by the exercise of reasonable diligence, should have discovered that the unfair method of competition or unfair or deceptive act or practice occurred.

(b) The limitations period provided by Subsection (a) may be extended for 180 days if the person bringing the action proves that the person's failure to bring the action within that period was caused by the defendant's engaging in conduct solely calculated to induce the person to refrain from or postpone bringing the action.

The Civil Practice and Remedies Code also contains provisions that limit or otherwise affect the operation of the limitation statutes.

§ 16.001. *Effect of Disability.*

(a) For the purposes of this subchapter, a person is under a legal disability if the person is:

(1) younger than 18 years of age, regardless of whether the person is married;

(2) imprisoned; or

(3) of unsound mind.

(b) If a person entitled to bring a personal action is under a legal disability when the cause of action accrues, the time of the disability is not included in a limitations period.

(c) A person may not tack one legal disability to another to extend a limitations period.

(d) A disability that arises after a limitations period starts does not suspend the running of the period.

§ 16.063. *Temporary Absence From State.* The absence from this state of a person against whom a cause of action may be maintained suspends the running of the applicable statute of limitations for the period of the person's absence.

[Note, however, that the Texas Supreme Court has held that if a nonresident is amenable to service of process under the long-arm statute and has contacts with the state that are sufficient to support personal jurisdiction, this statute does not toll the statute of limitations. *Kerlin v. Sauceda*, 263 S.W.3d 920, 927 (2008).]

§ 16.062. *Effect of Death.*

(a) The death of a person against whom or in whose favor there may be a cause of action suspends the running of an applicable statute of limitations for 12 months after the death.

(b) If an executor or administrator of a decedent's estate qualifies before the expiration of the period provided by this section, the statute of limitations begins to run at the time of the qualification.

§ 16.065. *Acknowledgment of Claim.* An acknowledgment of the justness of a claim that appears to be barred by limitations is not admissible in evidence to defeat the law of limitations if made after the time that the claim is due unless the acknowledgment is in writing and is signed by the party to be charged.

§ 16.068. *Amended and Supplemental Pleading.* If a filed pleading relates to a cause of action, cross action, counterclaim, or defense that is not subject to a plea of limitation when the pleading is filed, a subsequent amendment or supplement to the pleading that changes the facts or grounds of liability or defense is not subject to a plea of limitation unless the amendment or supplement is wholly based on a new, distinct, or different transaction or occurrence.

§ 16.069. *Counterclaim or Cross Claim.*

(a) If a counterclaim or cross claim arises out of the same transaction or occurrence that is the basis of an action, a party to the action may file the counterclaim or cross claim even though as a separate action it would be barred by limitation on the date the party's answer is required.

(b) The counterclaim or cross claim must be filed not later than the 30th day after the date on which the party's answer is required.

§ 16.070. *Contractual Limitations Period.*

(a) Except as provided by Subsection (b), a person may not enter a stipulation, contract, or agreement that purports to limit the time in which to bring suit on the stipulation, contract, or agreement to a period shorter than two years. A stipulation, contract, or agreement that establishes a limitations period that is shorter than two years is void in this state.

(b) This section does not apply to a stipulation, contract, or agreement relating to the sale or purchase of a business entity if a party to the stipulation, contract, or agreement pays or receives or is obligated to pay or entitled to receive consideration under the stipulation, contract, or agreement having an aggregate value of not less than $500,000.

Knowing the number of years allowed is only part of the problem of calculating the deadline for filing suit. It can also be tricky to determine the time at which the statute of limitations starts to run. Sometimes limitations will begin to run whether or not the plaintiff knows of her injury; other times it will not begin to run until the injury is or should be discovered. Consider the court's application of the discovery rule in the following case.

S.V. v. R.V.

933 S.W.2d 1 (Tex. 1996)

Hecht, J.

R. intervened in her parents' divorce proceeding, alleging that her father, S., was negligent by sexually abusing her until she was seventeen years old. (Given the sensitive nature of these allegations, we refer to the parties only by initials to avoid the use of proper names.) Because R. did not sue her father within two years of her eighteenth birthday as required by the applicable statutes of limitations, her action is barred as a matter of law unless the discovery rule permits her to sue within two years of when she knew or reasonably should have known of the alleged abuse. R. contends that the discovery rule should apply in this case because she repressed all memory of her father's abuse until about a month after she turned twenty, some three months before she intervened in the divorce action. The district court directed a verdict against R. on the grounds that the discovery rule does not apply in this case, and that R. adduced no evidence of abuse. A divided court of appeals reversed and remanded for a new trial. We reverse the judgment of the court of appeals and affirm the judgment of the district court on limitations grounds.

I

Before we review the evidence in this case it is important to have clearly in mind the issue that is crucial in determining whether to apply the discovery rule. To pose that issue we begin with an analysis of our discovery rule jurisprudence.

We have long recognized the salutary purpose of statutes of limitations. In

Gautier v. Franklin, 1 Tex. 732, 739 (1847), we wrote that statutes of limitations

> are justly held "as statutes of repose to quiet titles, to suppress frauds, and to supply the deficiencies of proof arising from the ambiguity, obscurity and antiquity of transactions. They proceed upon the presumption that claims are extinguished, or ought to be held extinguished whenever they are not litigated in the proper forum at the prescribed period. They take away all solid ground of complaint, because they rest on the negligence or laches of the party himself; they quicken diligence by making it in some measure equivalent to right." [*Joseph P. Story, Conflicts of Law* 482.]

More recently, we explained:

> Limitations statutes afford plaintiffs what the legislature deems a reasonable time to present their claims and protect defendants and the courts from having to deal with cases in which the search for truth may be seriously impaired by the loss of evidence, whether by death or disappearance of witnesses, fading memories, disappearance of documents or otherwise. The purpose of a statute of limitations is to establish a point of repose and to terminate stale claims.

Murray v. San Jacinto Agency, Inc., 800 S.W.2d 826, 828 (Tex. 1990).

The enactment of statutes of limitations is, of course, the prerogative of the Legislature. At the time this case was filed and tried, the applicable statute was the one governing personal injury actions generally, which provided: "A person must bring suit for . . . personal injury . . . not later than two years after the day the cause of action accrues." The code contains two other provisions relevant to this case. One is: "If a person entitled to bring a personal action is under a legal disability when the cause of action accrues, the time of the disability is not included in the limitations period." Tex. Civ. Prac. & Rem. Code § 16.001(b). The other is: "For the purposes of this subchapter, a person is under a legal disability if the person is: (1) younger than 18 years of age . . . ." *Id.* § 16.001(a). Thus, a person has until his or her twentieth birthday to bring suit for personal injury from sexual assault if — and here we come to the root of the problem in the case before us — the cause of action "accrued" while the person was a minor.

In 1995, the Legislature enacted a special five-year statute of limitations for sexual abuse cases: "A person must bring suit for personal injury not later than five years after the day the cause of action accrues if the injury arises as a result of conduct that violates: (1) Section 22.011, Penal Code (sexual assault); or (2) Section 22.021, Penal Code (aggravated sexual assault)." Tex. Civ. Prac. & Rem. Code § 16.0045(a). This new statute was not enacted until long after the present case was filed and tried and therefore does not govern. We mention it here to point out that under both the new statute and its predecessor, the prescribed period begins to run on the day the cause of action "accrues."

Many other statutes peg the beginning of the limitations period on the date the cause of action "accrues." Occasionally the date of accrual is defined. *E.g.*, Tex. Civ. Prac. & Rem. Code § 16.003(b) (a wrongful death cause of action "accrues on the death of the injured person"). More often, however, the definition of accrual is not prescribed by statute and thus has been left to the courts. As a rule, we have held that a cause of action accrues when a wrongful act causes some legal injury, even if the fact of injury is not discovered until later, and even if all resulting damages have not yet occurred. *Trinity River Auth. v. URS Consultants, Inc.*, 889 S.W.2d 259, 262 (Tex. 1994); *Quinn v. Press*, 140 S.W.2d 438, 440 (1940). We have not applied this rule without exception, however, and have sometimes held that an action does not accrue until the plaintiff knew or in the exercise of reasonable diligence should have known of the wrongful act and resulting injury. *Trinity River Auth.*, 889 S.W.2d at 262 (deferring accrual and thus delaying the commencement of the limitations period is distinct from suspending or tolling the running of limitations once the period has begun).

We first referred to this exception as the "discovery rule" in *Gaddis v. Smith*, 417 S.W.2d 577, 578 (Tex. 1967). We have sometimes used the phrase to refer generally to all instances in which accrual is deferred, including fraud and fraudulent concealment. At other times we have distinguished between fraudulent concealment and the discovery rule. Strictly speaking, the cases in which we have deferred accrual of causes of action for limitations purposes fall into two categories: those involving fraud and fraudulent concealment, and all others. The deferral of accrual in the latter cases is properly referred to as the discovery rule. We observe the distinction between the two categories because each is characterized by different substantive and procedural rules.

We have considered the applicability of the deferred accrual exception to the legal injury rule in an assortment of settings.

The justifications we have offered for deferring accrual have been diverse, somewhat inconsistent, and often overly broad. Fraud, we have said, in and of itself prevents running of the statute of limitations, as does fraudulent concealment. We have applied the discovery rule because of a special relationship between the plaintiff and defendant. *E.g.*, *Willis*, 760 S.W.2d at 645–46 (attorney and client); *Slay*, 187 S.W.2d at 388–93 (trustee and beneficiary). Even apart from such a relationship, we have indicated that the discovery rule applies when it is otherwise difficult for the injured party to learn of the wrongful act. *Gaddis*, 417 S.W.2d at 580 (leaving surgical sponge in plaintiff's body). We have characterized barring claims before plaintiffs knew they had them "shocking results." *Id.* at 581. On the other hand, we have observed:

> Statutes of limitations are not directed to the merits of any individual case, they are a result of legislative assessment of the merits of cases in general. The fact that a meritorious claim might thereby be rendered nonassertible is an unfortunate, occasional by-product of the operation of limitations. All statutes of limitations provide some time period during which the cause of action is assertible. However, preclusion of a legal remedy alone is not enough to justify a judicial exception to the statute. The primary purpose of limitations, to prevent litigation of stale or fraudulent claims, must be kept in mind.

Robinson, 550 S.W.2d at 20. A principal factor in deciding whether to apply the discovery rule has been to what extent the claim was objectively verifiable. *E.g.*, *Gaddis*, 417 S.W.2d at 581 (leaving a surgical sponge in a body "is a peculiar type of case which is not particularly susceptible to fraudulent prosecution"); *Robinson*,

550 S.W.2d at 21 ("Unlike *Gaddis v. Smith* there exists in the present case [alleging misdiagnosis of herniated intervertebral disc] no physical evidence which in-and-of-itself establishes the negligence of some person."); *Kelly*, 532 S.W.2d at 949 (credit defamation clear from written report).

While the language in the opinions in these cases varies, a general principle unites them. *Computer Associates International, Inc. v. Altai, Inc.*, 918 S.W.2d 453 (Tex. 1996). Accrual of a cause of action is deferred in two types of cases. In one type, those involving allegations of fraud or fraudulent concealment, accrual is deferred because a person cannot be permitted to avoid liability for his actions by deceitfully concealing wrongdoing until limitations has run. The other type, in which the discovery rule applies, comprises those cases in which "the nature of the injury incurred is inherently undiscoverable and the evidence of injury is objectively verifiable." *Id.* at 456. These two elements of inherent undiscoverability and objective verifiability balance the conflicting policies in statutes of limitations: the benefits of precluding stale or spurious claims versus the risks of precluding meritorious claims that happen to fall outside an arbitrarily set period. Restated, the general principle is this: accrual of a cause of action is deferred in cases of fraud or in which the wrongdoing is fraudulently concealed, and in discovery rule cases in which the alleged wrongful act and resulting injury were inherently undiscoverable at the time they occurred but may be objectively verified. This principle, while not expressed in every deferred accrual case, is derived from them and best defines when the exception to the legal injury rule has been and should be applied.

We have considered the "inherently undiscoverable" element of the discovery rule in several cases. The common thread in these cases is that when the wrong and injury were unknown to the plaintiff because of their very nature and not because of any fault of the plaintiff, accrual of the cause of action was delayed.

To be "inherently undiscoverable," an injury need not be absolutely impossible to discover, else suit would never be filed and the question whether to apply the discovery rule would never arise. Nor does "inherently undiscoverable" mean merely that a particular plaintiff did not discover his injury within the prescribed period of limitations; discovery of a particular injury is dependent not solely on the nature of the injury but on the circumstances in which it occurred and plaintiff's diligence as well. An injury is inherently undiscoverable if it is by nature unlikely to be discovered within the prescribed limitations period despite due diligence. *Computer Associates*, 918 S.W.2d at 456.

We have also considered the "objectively verifiable" element of the rule in a number of cases. In *Gaddis*, a patient claimed that her doctors were negligent in leaving a sponge inside her body after surgery. The presence of the sponge in her body — the injury — and the explanation for how it got there — the wrongful act — were beyond dispute. The facts upon which liability was asserted were demonstrated by direct, physical evidence. In contrast, *Robinson* involved a claim by a patient against his doctors for misdiagnosis of his back condition. We summarized the issue this way:

> Plaintiff, to prove his cause of action, faces the burden of proving both a mistake in professional judgment and that such mistake was negligent. Expert testimony would be required. Physical evidence generally is not

> available when the primary issue relevant to liability concerns correctness of past judgment. Unlike *Gaddis v. Smith* there exists in the present case no physical evidence which in-and-of-itself establishes the negligence of some person. What physical evidence was to the cause of action alleged in *Gaddis v. Smith*, expert testimony is to the cause of action in the present case. Even the fact of injury is a matter of expert testimony.

550 S.W.2d at 21. Expert testimony, we concluded, did not supply the objective verification of wrong and injury necessary for application of the discovery rule.

We have adhered to the requirement of objective verification fairly consistently in our discovery rule cases, although we have not always emphasized the requirement because the alleged injury was indisputable.

In the present case plaintiff R. claims that her father sexually abused her and that she unconsciously repressed all memory of it for years. If the legal injury rule were applied, R.'s claims against S. would each have accrued on the date the alleged incident of abuse occurred. In applying the statute of limitations, however, the years of her minority are not included. In effect, then, under the legal injury rule, R. is in the same position as if her claims all accrued on her eighteenth birthday and limitations began to run on that date, expiring about four months before she filed suit. R.'s claims are therefore barred unless she is entitled to an exception to the legal injury rule. R. does not allege fraud or fraudulent concealment . . . . For the discovery rule to apply, R.'s claim must have been inherently undiscoverable within the limitations period and objectively verifiable.

We have twice held a fiduciary's misconduct to be inherently undiscoverable. *Willis*, 760 S.W.2d at 645 (attorney); *Slay*, 187 S.W.2d at 394 (trustee). The reason underlying both decisions is that a person to whom a fiduciary duty is owed is either unable to inquire into the fiduciary's actions or unaware of the need to do so. While a person to whom a fiduciary duty is owed is relieved of the responsibility of diligent inquiry into the fiduciary' conduct, so long as that relationship exists, when the fact of misconduct becomes apparent it can no longer be ignored, regardless of the nature of the relationship. Because parents generally stand in the role of fiduciaries toward their minor children, R. was not obliged to watch for misconduct by her father as long as she was a minor. Again, however, R. does not claim to have been misled.

Nevertheless, given the special relationship between parent and child, and the evidence reviewed in detail below that some traumas are by nature impossible to recall for a time, we assume without deciding that plaintiff can satisfy the inherent undiscoverability element for application of the discovery rule. We therefore focus on the second element of objective verifiability. The question is whether there can be enough objective verification of wrong and injury in childhood sexual abuse cases to warrant application of the discovery rule. To answer this question, we look first at the facts of this case and then at the general nature of such cases.

II

[The court reviews the family's history, R.'s delayed recall of repressed memories of repeated sexual abuse by S., R.'s experiences in counseling, and psychological testing of both R. and S.]

III

R. sued S. for negligence "[d]uring the years 1973 through 1988, inclusively," in engaging or attempting to engage in sexual acts or contacts with her, and exposing himself to her while he was nude and aroused. She alleged that S.'s negligence was a breach of her right to privacy and caused her damages not in excess of $10 million . . . . As we have already explained, R.'s claims were subject to the two-year statute of limitations which did not begin to run until R.'s eighteenth birthday, October 15, 1988. R. has not complained of any occurrence after her eighteenth birthday. R.'s claims were thus barred by limitations after October 15, 1990, more than four months before she filed suit. She pleaded, however, that she was entitled to the benefit of the discovery rule.

Trial commenced to a jury. At the close of plaintiff's case, S. moved for directed verdict on two grounds: that the discovery rule did not apply and R.'s action was therefore barred by limitations as a matter of law; and that R. had failed to offer any evidence of sexual abuse. The district court granted S.'s motion without explanation and rendered judgment accordingly. The court of appeals, by a divided vote, reversed the judgment of the district court and remanded the case for further proceedings.

. . . .

The only physical evidence to support R.'s allegations consists of her symptoms and to a lesser extent her behavioral traits, as described by her and the experts who testified on her behalf. In every instance this evidence was inconclusive. The experts testified that R.'s symptoms could have been caused by other things than sexual abuse by her father. While R. fit a behavioral profile for someone who has been sexually abused, the experts acknowledged that that did not mean she had actually been abused. Tests on S. were also inconclusive. While he had many of the characteristics of a sex abuser, he did not match a characteristic profile, and even if he had, it would not prove that he abused R. Thus, there is no physical or other evidence in this case to satisfy the element of objective verifiability for application of the discovery rule.

The kinds of evidence that would suffice would be a confession by the abuser; a criminal conviction; contemporaneous records or written statements of the abuser such as diaries or letters; medical records of the person abused showing contemporaneous physical injury resulting from the abuse; photographs or recordings of the abuse; an objective eyewitness's account; and the like. Such evidence would provide sufficient objective verification of abuse, even if it occurred years before suit was brought, to warrant application of the discovery rule.

Although we indicated in *Robinson* that expert testimony would not alone provide the objective verification of a claim necessary to invoke the discovery rule, we have not held that such testimony can never suffice, at least in connection with other evidence, such as the symptoms of a survivor of abuse. We have held only that the bar of limitations cannot be lowered for no other reason than a swearing match between parties over facts and between experts over opinions. It is quite possible that recognized expert opinion on a particular subject would be so near consensus that, in conjunction with objective evidence not based entirely on the plaintiff's assertions, it could provide the kind of verification required. That is not true in this case, but we must explain why.

IV

. . . In sum, the literature on repression and recovered memory syndrome establishes that fundamental theoretical and practical issues remain to be resolved. These issues include the extent to which experimental psychological theories of amnesia apply to psychotherapy, the effect of repression on memory, the effect of screening devices in recall, the effect of suggestibility, the difference between forensic and therapeutic truth, and the extent to which memory restoration techniques lead to credible memories or confabulations. Opinions in this area simply cannot meet the "objective verifiability" element for extending the discovery rule . . . .

The Texas Legislature entered this area just last year, enacting a special statute of limitations for civil actions for sexual abuse which extends the period for filing suit from two years to five years. However, the new limitations period, like the old one, begins on the day the cause of action accrues. The Legislature did not define accrual for purposes of the new statute, although it certainly could have done so, just as it could have chosen a different starting date altogether. It could also have prescribed application of the discovery rule as it has done in other statutes. *E.g.*, Tex. Bus. & Com. Code § 17.565 ("All actions brought under [the Deceptive Trade Practices-Consumer Protection Act] must be commenced within two years after the date on which the false, misleading, or deceptive act or practice occurred or within two years after the consumer discovered or in the exercise of reasonable diligence should have discovered the occurrence of the false, misleading, or deceptive act or practice."). It did not do so, just as it has not done so in criminal sexual abuse cases. Tex. Code Crim. Proc. arts. 12.01(2)(D) & 12.03 (criminal action must be brought within ten years from the date of the commission of the offense). We must assume that the Legislature did not intend for sexual abuse cases to be treated differently from any other case in applying the discovery rule. The Legislature is in the best position to determine and accommodate the complex and conflicting policies involved in determining an appropriate limitations period, and it has done so.

. . . .

VII

Accordingly, we conclude that the discovery rule does not apply in this case . . . .

We do not, of course, impose any additional requirements on proof of a childhood sexual abuse case brought within the applicable limitations period. The objective verifiability requirement of the discovery rule does not apply in proving the case on the merits.

. . . .

The judgment of the court of appeals is reversed and the judgment of the district court is affirmed.

[The concurring opinion of Justices Gonzalez and Cornyn are omitted.]

OWEN, J, dissenting.

. . . The linchpin of the Court's decision today is its conclusion that repressed memory does not warrant the application of the discovery rule unless the sexual abuse is "objectively verifiable." In so holding, the Court ignores the fact that physical evidence may have been available at the time of the molestation but repression of memory and thus the unavailability of such evidence is often the direct consequence of the abuser's reprehensible acts. Allowing the statute of limitations to preclude R.V.'s cause of action would violate the principle "deeply rooted in our jurisprudence" that "no man may take advantage of his own wrong." *Glus v. Brooklyn E. Dist. Terminal*, 359 U.S. 231, 232 (1959) (holding that the plaintiff's claims were not time-barred where the defendant misrepresented the number of years in which the plaintiff had to sue). Because of the age of the victims and their psychological vulnerability, many years may pass before they are able to recall the event. In many cases, recollections do not occur until the victims are able to distance themselves from the physical presence and the emotional influence of the abuser.

It is disturbing that the Court requires "physical or other evidence" in this case in addition to the vivid (albeit recalled) memories of R.V. She testified directly and extensively about abuse at the hands of her father. Yet, the Court also requires:

> a confession by the abuser; a criminal conviction; contemporaneous records or written statements of the abuser such as diaries or letters; medical records of the person abused showing contemporaneous physical injury resulting from the abuse; photographs or recordings of the abuse; an objective eyewitness's account; and the like.

This is reminiscent of the days when the crime of rape went unpunished unless corroborating evidence, above and beyond the victim's testimony, was available. *See* SPOHN & HORNEY, RAPE LAW REFORM: A GRASSROOTS REVOLUTION & ITS IMPACT 24–25 (1992) (discussing the origins of the common-law requirement that the testimony of a rape victim, unlike that of other crime victims, be corroborated, including fears of the "danger of false charges by vindictive or mentally disturbed women" and fear of "memory falsification"). The Court's opinion perpetuates the attitudes reflected in that era. Today in Texas, no corroboration is required to convict a criminal defendant of the rape of a minor. Similarly, no corroboration should be required of a victim of childhood sexual abuse who seeks to invoke the discovery rule in a civil suit . . . .

NOTES AND QUESTIONS

(1) *Legal Injury Rule*. The legal injury rule provides that a cause of action accrues when all facts come into existence that authorize a claimant to seek a judicial remedy, even if all damages have not yet occurred or become apparent. Accrual does not depend on when the plaintiff learns of the injury (except in those

cases in which the discovery rule applies). *Murphy v. Campbell*, 964 S.W.2d 265, 270 (Tex. 1997). Thus, when the defendant's act is a legal injury in itself, the cause of action accrues at the time of the act. For example, because a defendant's tortious act is considered a legal injury in itself, under the legal injury rule the cause of action accrues on the date of the wrongful act, notwithstanding that damages may not be ascertainable at that time. It is not always easy to determine when the complainant has suffered a legal injury. *Atkins v. Crosland*, 417 S.W.2d 150, 153 (Tex. 1967) (latest possible date from which statute could begin to run in accounting malpractice case based on faulty tax advice was date plaintiff received notice of deficiency from IRS). Similarly a cause of action for breach of contract generally accrues when the contract is breached, and the limitation period commences at the time of the breach. *See Hurbrough v. Cain*, 571 S.W.2d 216, 221 (Tex. Civ. App. — Tyler 1978, no writ).

(2) *The Discovery Rule*. The discovery rule may make the legal injury rule irrelevant. As Justice Hecht's opinion in *S.V. v. R.V.* makes plain, the common law discovery rule is only applicable in a limited range of cases. The discovery rule applies in defamation cases, actions against fiduciaries, including legal and accounting malpractice actions [see notes (3) and (4) below] and may be applicable to negligent misrepresentation claims. The discovery rule also applies to cases in which an injured party was exposed to a latent disease and remained asymptomatic for an extended time, beyond the statute of limitations. The Court has also held that the question of whether the discovery rule applies is based on a "categorical approach" in which the court examines the general type of injury alleged rather than the injury in the specific case. *Apex Towing Co. v. Tolin*, 41 S.W.3d 118, 122 (Tex. 2001); *Via Net v. TIG Ins. Co.*, 211 S.W.3d 310, 315 (Tex. 2006) ("the focus is on whether a type of injury rather than a particular injury was discoverable").

The Texas Supreme Court has explained that "the discovery rule operates to defer accrual of a cause of action until a plaintiff discovers or, through the exercise of reasonable care and diligence, should discover the 'nature of his injury.' . . . Thus, when the discovery rule applies, accrual is tolled until a claimant discovers or in the exercise of reasonable diligence should have discovered the injury and that it was likely caused by the wrongful act of another. But once these requirements are satisfied, limitations commences, even if the plaintiff does not know the identity of the wrongdoer." *Childs v. Haussecker*, 974 S.W.2d 31, 36–45 (Tex. 1998) (latent occupational diseases silicosis and asbestosis); *cf. Howard v. Fiesta Texas Show Park, Inc.*, 980 S.W.2d 716, 720–22 (Tex. App. — San Antonio 1998, pet. denied) (plaintiff's injury arose from single event and was not inherently undiscoverable notwithstanding fact that injured party did not immediately know extent of injuries).

In the context of asbestos-related latent diseases, the Texas Supreme Court has held that neither the single action rule nor the statute of limitations bars a plaintiff who settled an asbestosis suit with one defendant from bringing suit against different defendants later for asbestos-related cancer. *Pustejovsky v. Rapid-American Corp.*, 35 S.W.3d 643 (Tex. 2000). The new cause of action for the malignant asbestos-related condition begins "when a plaintiff's symptoms manifest themselves to a degree or for a duration that would put a reasonable person on notice that he or she suffers from some injury and he or she knows, or with reasonable diligence should know, that the malignant asbestos-related condition is likely work-related."

(3) *Accounting Malpractice.* Professional liability in areas such as accounting or law may require application of the discovery rule, which delays the accrual of a cause of action until the earliest date when the plaintiff should be aware of a legal injury through the exercise of reasonable diligence. In *Murphy v. Campbell*, 964 S.W.2d 265 (Tex. 1997), the Court held that a person suffers legal injury from faulty professional advice when the advice is taken, but also found that the discovery rule may apply, given the difficulty a layperson would typically have in recognizing the faulty advice. Thus, a cause of action based on accounting malpractice rendered to the *Murphy* plaintiffs accrued when they received a deficiency notice from the Internal Revenue Service, which was when they first should have known of their injury.

(4) *Legal Malpractice.* The discovery rule applies to cases of legal malpractice. *Willis v. Maverick*, 760 S.W.2d 642, 645 (Tex. 1988). In addition, a special tolling doctrine applies in legal malpractice cases such that the limitations period is suspended until all appeals are exhausted in the underlying action if it is alleged that legal malpractice occurred in the prosecution or defense of that suit. *Hughes v. Mahaney & Higgins*, 821 S.W.2d 154, 157 (Tex. 1991). In *Apex Towing Co. v. Tolin*, 41 S.W.3d 118 (Tex. 2001), the Texas Supreme Court held that continued representation by the allegedly malpracticing attorney is not required to toll the statute of limitation in a legal malpractice case based on the attorney's alleged malpractice in the prosecution or defense of a claim that results in litigation. In *Apex*, the Court reiterated the tolling rule announced in *Hughes* as follows: "When an attorney commits malpractice in the prosecution or defense of a claim that results in litigation, the statute of limitation on a malpractice claim against that attorney is tolled until all appeals on the underlying claim are exhausted or the litigation is otherwise finally concluded." In *Underkofler v. Vanasek*, 53 S.W.3d 343 (Tex. 2001), the Court applied its holding in *Apex* to the plaintiff's malpractice claim, but held that the *Hughes* tolling rule does not apply to claims under the Deceptive Trade Practices Act.

(5) *Medical Malpractice.* A special limitations statute applies in medical malpractice cases:

> C.P.R.C. § 74.251 *Statute of Limitations on Health Care Liability Claims*
>
> (a) Notwithstanding any other law and subject to Subsection (b), no health care liability claim may be commenced unless the action is filed within two years from the occurrence of the breach or tort or from the date the medical or health care treatment that is the subject of the claim or the hospitalization for which the claim is made is completed; provided that, minors under the age of 12 years shall have until their 14th birthday in which to file, or have filed on their behalf, the claim. Except as herein provided this section applies to all persons regardless of minority or other legal disability.

> (b) A claimant must bring a health care liability claim not later than 10 years after the date of the act or omission that gives rise to the claim. This subsection is intended as a statute of repose so that all claims must be brought within 10 years or they are time barred.

Under Section 74.251(a), suit must be brought within two years of the date of the occurrence of the breach or tort, or within two years from the date the medical or health care that is the subject of the claim is completed. The Texas Supreme Court has explained that "the Legislature's intent in passing the predecessor to this statute was to abolish the discovery rule in cases governed by the Medical Liability Act." *Morrison v. Chan*, 699 S.W.2d 205, 208 (Tex. 1985). A wrongful death plaintiff suing on a medical negligence theory does not have two full years from the time of death in which to sue, but rather must sue within the time allowed by Section 74.251. In addition, the Texas Supreme Court has interpreted the statutory language to mean that "[w]hen the precise date of the specific breach or tort is ascertainable from the facts of the case . . . , [the statute] requires the limitations period to run from the date of the breach or tort" rather than from the date the patient's health care treatment was completed. *Kimball v. Brothers*, 741 S.W.2d 370, 372 (Tex. 1987).

The statutory phrase "[n]otwithstanding any other law" purports to eliminate a number of tolling provisions that normally apply to extend the period in which suit may be filed. For example, limitations on medical malpractice claims are not tolled while the defendant is absent from the state. C.P.R.C. § 16.063. The tolling provision that applies while the plaintiff is of unsound mind is also inapplicable to medical malpractice claims (C.P.R.C. § 16.001), as is the statute tolling limitations for one year or until the qualification of a personal representative of the decedent's estate for causes of action in favor of a decedent. C.P.R.C. § 16.062; *see also Bala v. Maxwell*, 909 S.W.2d 889, 892–893 (Tex. 1995) (medical malpractice limitation scheme rather than wrongful death limitation scheme applies).

The same facts that would delay the running of limitations under the discovery rule, or that would toll the running of limitations under a tolling statute, may operate to allow a plaintiff more time to sue under certain circumstances. The Texas Constitution contains a section known as the "open courts" provision (Article 1, Section 13), which provides that "[a]ll courts shall be open, and every person for an injury done him, in his lands, goods, person or reputation, shall have remedy by due course of law." This provision has been held to preclude the legislature from making a remedy contingent on an impossible condition, such as requiring suit to be brought when the nature of the injury could not have been discovered before limitations ran. *Diaz v. Westphal*, 941 S.W.2d 96, 99 (Tex. 1997). Because the "open courts" provision is different from the "discovery rule," and because its protection is constitutional, "open courts" protection is not abrogated by Section 74.251. Therefore, a claimant who could not reasonably have discovered his or her injury within the relevant two-year period has a "reasonable time" after the time the injury could reasonably have been discovered to bring suit. *Nelson v. Krusen*, 678 S.W.2d 918, 923 (Tex. 1984). The plaintiff does, however, have to exercise reasonable diligence to discover her injuries and file suit to avoid the bar of limitations. *Yancy v. United Surgical Partners Int'l, Inc.*, 236 S.W.3d 778, 784–85 (Tex. 2007). This "reasonable time" begins to run once the plaintiff becomes aware of both the injury and the facts giving rise to the cause of action, even if the plaintiff does not yet know the precise extent of the consequences of the alleged malpractice. *Hooten v. Fleckenstein*, 836 S.W.2d 300, 301–302 (Tex. App. — Tyler 1992, writ dism'd w.o.j.) (relevant date was when patient learned that doctor failed to diagnose fractured elbow, not when patient learned of loss of mobility).

A person who is incompetent is not able to discover his or her injury or the facts giving rise to a cause of action. Thus, a medical malpractice suit filed by a plaintiff who has been continuously incompetent from the time of the alleged malpractice until suit is filed is not barred by limitations. *Felan v. Ramos*, 857 S.W.2d 113, 117–18 (Tex. App. — Corpus Christi 1993, writ denied). This protection comes from the open courts provision rather than from the tolling statute. Similarly, the open courts provision makes Section 74.251 unconstitutional as it applies to minors because it effectively abrogates their right to bring well-established common law causes of action. *Weiner v. Wasson*, 900 S.W.2d 316, 321 (Tex. 1995). Thus, a person who suffers medical malpractice while under the age of 18 has until his or her 20th birthday to file suit on that claim.

The open courts provision, however, applies only to common law causes of action. *Rose v. Doctors Hosp.*, 801 S.W.2d 841, 843 (Tex. 1990). Thus, the protection provided by the open courts provision does not apply to wrongful death and survival actions based on medical malpractice, because wrongful death and survival actions are purely statutory. The tolling provision for minors does not apply to a wrongful death action brought by an adult based on the death of a child. Nor does the open courts provision apply to a minor's wrongful death action based on allegedly negligent treatment of a parent. If the decedent did not file a timely claim for medical malpractice, and that claim would have been barred by the medical malpractice statute of limitation at the time of death, no wrongful death action accrues. On the other hand, if the decedent dies after a malpractice action was timely filed, the petition may be amended to assert a wrongful death cause of action arising out of the same transaction or occurrence. The wrongful death action will relate back to the time the malpractice suit was filed.

(6) *Fraudulent Concealment*. As the court mentions in *S.V.*, a separate doctrine, called fraudulent concealment, suspends the limitations period if a defendant makes fraudulent representations or conceals facts that would reveal the existence of a cause of action, until the time the defendant's wrongful conduct is discovered or should have been discovered in the exercise of reasonable diligence. *See American Petrofina, Inc. v. Allen*, 887 S.W.2d 829, 830 (Tex. 1994). The elements of fraudulent concealment include the following: (1) the existence of the underlying cause of action; (2) the defendant's knowledge of the cause of action; (3) the defendant's use of deception to conceal the cause of action; and (4) the plaintiff's reasonable reliance on the deception to his or her detriment. *Mitchell Energy Corp. v. Bartlett*, 958 S.W.2d 430, 439 (Tex. App. — Fort Worth 1997, pet. denied).

Chapter 2

EMERGENCY AND INTERIM RELIEF (SPECIAL REMEDIES)

SCOPE

Emergency judicial intervention involves procedural problems that must be considered in the context of the need to obtain interim relief before final adjudication. As a general principle, interim relief is used to preserve the status quo pending a determination of the primary proceeding. Although coverage of extraordinary creditors' remedies is provided in more specialized courses devoted to them, this chapter provides overview coverage of the most important special remedies.

§ 2.01 TEMPORARY RESTRAINING ORDERS AND INJUNCTIONS

Read TEX. R. CIV. P. 680–689, 692.

J. Weber, *So You Need a Temporary Restraining Order?*, 41 TEX. B.J. 728 (1978).*

Imagine this situation:

You are sitting at your desk at 2:00 P.M. on Friday. The telephone rings. One of your better clients, Sam Successful, is frantic! Sam has recently purchased a beautiful 50-acre tract of woodlands on which he and his wife plan to build a summer home. Today Sam received word from an adjoining landowner that Landeater Lumber Company has cut his fence, and begun cutting the timber on his homesite. Landeater has a timber deed by which it claims the right to cut the timber. Landeater refused to cease operations and hopes to have the land cleared before the weekend is over. Sam wants you to stop Landeater immediately, before the entire tract is ruined. You need a temporary restraining order!

The facts always differ, but two things are always the same: there is a crisis, and both you and your client are in a hurry. This note will not deal with the substantive issue of whether Sam is entitled to a TRO (temporary restraining order). Instead, it presents the practical aspects of: (a) preparing the proper pleadings; (b) "greasing the skids"; and (c) effectively pursuing the TRO through so as to fully accomplish your purpose: to halt the cutting of trees pending a determination of the parties' rights.

The process of obtaining a TRO is complex. There are many details, legal and practical, all of which *must* be taken into account if you are to reach your objective.

 (References to federal practice have been omitted).

I. What Papers Do We Need?

These are the items the lawyer must have ready when he or she applies for his temporary restraining order:

A. The petition.

B. The temporary restraining order itself.

C. The restraining order bond.

D. The filing fee.

These items will be discussed in detail but remember — by now *it is 2:30* on Friday afternoon. You must make the practical arrangements to see that the necessary people are available to issue and serve the writ. This is "greasing the skids."

II. Greasing the Skids

You cannot issue and serve the temporary restraining order yourself. You will need the cooperation of the district judge, the district clerk, and the county sheriff. Each of these persons has a role to play and each must be available.

A. *Call the District Clerk:* A personal call to the clerk's office and a conversation with the deputy who will be handling the application for the TRO is a must. Give the clerk an estimate of when the papers will be prepared and the application filed. In counties with multiple judges, one judge may be designated the injunction judge. The clerk can give you this information. Rule 685, T.R.C.P., provides for presentment of the application for TRO to the judge *prior* to filing the petition with the district clerk. Therefore, especially on weekends and after hours, a hearing can be arranged with the judge prior to filing the pleadings with the clerk. Since the clerk does not issue the citation and writ until after the order has been signed and the bond posted, this procedure will require the clerk to make only one special trip to the courthouse. The clerk can file the application when you meet him or her at his or her office for preparation of the citations and writ.

B. *Contact the Judge:* You should immediately contact the injunction judge to determine his or her availability. Has he or she left for the weekend? Where can he or she be reached? Can another judge hear the matter? If it is necessary to present the application to the court at home, arrangements should be made in advance. The judge may want you to advise Landeater or his lawyer to be present. Furthermore, an advance call to the judge emphasizes the urgency of the proceeding. During this conference you may apprise the court of the circumstances of the case, thus minimizing the actual time required to present the matter to the court. Also, the judge might be asked the amount of the bond he or she is inclined to set so you can have it prepared in advance.

C. *Contact the Sheriff:* The TRO is worthless to the lawyer unless he or she can get it served on Landeater and its employees. The lawyer must confer with the sheriff . . . to schedule service of the restraining order after it is issued. If after hours, do not ask the sheriff or marshall to meet you at the courthouse at the same time you have arranged to meet the clerk. The filing of the petition, issuance of citation and preparation of copies of the order to be served may take some time, especially if there are many persons to be served, . . . and the sheriff may not be needed for an hour or so.

III. Preparing the Papers

A. *The Bond.* The bond is the last instrument you will need, but the first you need to prepare. [T]he rules require posting of a bond in almost all cases before issuance of a restraining order. Tex. R. Civ. P. 684.

If you intend to post a corporate surety bond, you should contact the bonding or insurance agent immediately. By now *it is 3:30 P.M.* and the bond must be prepared quickly, before the bonding company closes. The clerk will probably honor your own personal or firm check for the bond, but it [is] preferable that if your client intends to post cash, he should make arrangements to have the cash available or to have the district clerk approve his personal check.

B. *Prepare the Facts.* Who and where are the parties? Sam must supply you with basic information concerning Landeater Lumber Company, including some address where the sheriff or marshal can find its management, in order to serve the TRO.

Get a good factual summary of the events giving rise to your case. Hard, specific facts are needed for the application for temporary restraining order, to show that Sam owns the property in question, that Landeater has actually begun cutting timber without permission, and that, unless Landeater is restrained, Sam will suffer irreparable harm for which there is no adequate remedy at law. *Remember* you or your client must swear to the factual allegations . . . and, under the Texas Rules, an affidavit based only on information and belief is not sufficient. Tex. R. Civ. P. 682.

C. *The Petition* . . . . The petition or complaint will contain five parts, many of which are common to any original petition:

(1) *The names of the parties* and places where the defendant can be served with citation;

(2) *The factual allegations* giving rise to your right to relief, i.e., that Sam owns the land and that Landeater is cutting the timber without right or authority. Sam must further allege and show that irreparable harm will result if the temporary restraining order is not granted, to-wit: that the land upon which he is hoping to build his summer home is being ruined by the cutting of the timber, that his remedy at law of money damages is not adequate to protect him, and that Landeater is unable to respond in money damages anyway. These allegations must be of specific facts — pleading legal conclusions is not sufficient.

(3) *The prayer* should ask for not only a temporary restraining order but also that Landeater be cited to appear and show cause why the restraining order should not be converted into a temporary injunction. The prayer should further request a permanent injunction upon final hearing on the merits.

(4) *The affidavit:* [The] rules require verified pleading. Although Rule 14, T.R.C.P., allows the applicant's attorney to make the affidavit, it is not sufficient that the affidavit be upon information and belief. Further, an

affidavit made by the applicant's attorney must state his authority to do so.

(5) *Certificate of Counsel:* Texas Rule 680 provides that no temporary restraining order shall be granted without notice unless it clearly appears from specific facts shown by affidavit or the complaint that immediate and irreparable harm will result before notice can be served. The allegations made in your state court petition should satisfy this requirement.

D. *Temporary Restraining Order.* The requirements of the order itself are set out in Rules 680 and 683, T.R.C.P. The order should track the petition in:

(1) defining the injury in specific factual terms;

(2) stating specifically why the injury is irreparable; mere conclusory statements will not suffice;

(3) stating why the order was granted without notice;

(4) providing for the posting of a bond as a prerequisite to the clerk's issuing writs of injunction.(*Note:* the amount of the bond can be left blank to be filled in by the judge when the order is signed.)

(5) *specifically* setting out the act or acts being enjoined.

(6) specifically stating that the order is binding on the parties, their officers, agents, servants, employees, attorneys, and those persons in active concert with them who receive actual notice of the order by personal service or otherwise (TEX. R. CIV. P. 683);

(7) setting a date, within [fourteen] days, for a hearing on application for temporary injunction.

IV. Hearing, Filing and Followup

A. *The Hearing.* Now that the skids are greased and the pleadings prepared, you are ready for the hearing. The judge may have instructed you to advise Landeater. He or she may not have. At any rate, you should appear wherever you have arranged to meet the judge with your client, Sam Successful. Sam should be prepared to testify to the matters set out in your pleadings. If the judge grants your TRO, he will (a) fill in the amount of the bond; (b) set a date, within [fourteen] days for hearing the application for temporary injunction; and (c) sign the order.

B. *Don't Forget the Filing Fee.* Check cost schedules to determine the amount of the filing fee. In state court, you should give consideration to the number of citations to be served and include in the filing fee an amount sufficient for service of enough citations to serve Landeater and its employees out on the land.

C. *Copies of Pleadings.*

(1) Copies of Petition: The lawyer will need sufficient copies of his or her original petition or complaint to serve one on each named defendant.

(2) Certified Copies of TRO: You will need sufficient certified copies of the TRO for service upon all defendants. Further, if you contemplate serving Landeater's unnamed employees out in the woods (John Doe citations) you

will need additional certified copies of the TRO for service on these agents and employees.

D. *Get the TRO Served.* The sheriff should be given any assistance necessary to find the defendants and have them served. Furthermore, the lawyer should usually go to the site of the activity. Many times problems may come up at this stage which might thwart the restraining effort if the lawyer is not there to respond immediately.

In the rare instance where a party may defy the restraining order, the lawyer's presence is even more necessary. He or she can prepare, on the spot, the affidavit which will support a citation for contempt. The affidavit will set out what the offending defendant or person has done and is continuing to do in disregard of the court's order after service of same upon him. The lawyer can obtain the officer's signature on the affidavit and present it to the court with an order requiring that the contemptuous person be brought into Court to show cause why he should not be held in contempt.

E. *Prepare for the Temporary Injunction Hearing.* Finally, the lawyer must prepare for the hearing on temporary injunction to be held at the date and time set out in the TRO.

V. Congratulations!

By noon Saturday all is peaceful. Landeater has withdrawn from Sam's land. Sam lost a few trees, but serious damage has been averted. If you have obtained the TRO, had it served, and stopped the cutting smoothly and without a hitch, you have done an outstanding job of legal planning and organization. Sam should be pleased and impressed with a job well done.

NOTE

A temporary restraining order may only be extended once, *for a like period,* absent an agreement to the contrary. Tex. R. Civ. P. 686. The extension order must be made in writing. An oral extension of a temporary restraining order is ineffective and will not support an order of contempt absent notice to the contemnor of the written extension before the alleged contemptuous conduct occurs. *Ex parte Lesikar,* 899 S.W.2d 654 (Tex. 1995). The time limits on TROs must be taken seriously. The Texas Supreme Court has ruled that mandamus relief is available to remedy a temporary restraining order that violates the Rule 680 time limits. *In re TNRCC,* 85 S.W.3d 201 (Tex. 2002).

A judge granting an injunction before a full evidentiary hearing risks creating serious harm by either granting an injunction when she should not, or by denying an injunction that should be granted. For that reason, the rules require an explanation of the reasons for the judge's ruling. The following case considers that requirement.

CHARTER MEDICAL CORP. v. MILLER

547 S.W.2d 77 (Tex. Civ. App. — Dallas 1977, no writ)

ROBERTSON, J.

This appeal is from a temporary injunction, enjoining appellants, Charter Medical Corporation, Mesquite Memorial Hospital, Inc., and Howard Mulcay, and all others acting in concert with them, from attempting to enforce the provisions of the amended bylaws of Mesquite Memorial Hospital or in any manner attempting to interfere with or limit the appellees' rights to practice podiatry in the hospital as they existed prior to the adoption of the amendment. The order granting the temporary injunction set forth the reasons for its issuance as follows:

> . . . Plaintiffs have established by full and satisfactory proof all elements required for such injunction, including their probable right to recovery and irreparable damage herein and injury by virtue of the Defendants' conduct; . . . .

We hold that the recital in this order does not comply with the requirement of TEX. R. CIV. P. 683 that every order granting an injunction shall set forth specific reasons for its issuance. Accordingly, we dissolve the temporary injunction.

In *State v. Cook United, Inc.*, 464 S.W.2d 105, 106 (Tex. 1971), the supreme court stated that a trial court need not explain its reasons for believing an applicant has shown a probable right of recovery on the merits, but must give the reasons why injury will be suffered if the temporary injunction is not ordered. *See Transport Co. of Texas v. Robertson Transports*, 261 S.W.2d 549 (1953). The specific reasons are to be stated in lieu of mere conclusory statements. When a temporary injunction order is issued which does not conform to the requirements of the rule, it necessarily constitutes an abuse of the trial court's discretion and requires reversal. *Crouch v. Crouch*, 164 S.W.2d 35, 38 (Tex. Civ. App. — Waco 1942, no writ). The recital of "irreparable damage herein and injury by virtue of the Defendants' conduct" lacks the specificity required by Rule 683 and by the above decisions. Accordingly, we hold that the trial court abused its discretion.

In view of this holding it would be inappropriate for us to decide the points raised concerning appellees' probable right to permanent injunctive relief, and thus to render, in effect, an advisory opinion. A hearing on an application for temporary injunction does not serve the same purpose as a trial on the merits, nor should an appeal from a preliminary order be used to obtain an advance ruling thereon. Neither should it delay a trial on the merits.

Finally, this appeal, like many other temporary injunction appeals, appears to be entirely unnecessary. Presumably, the trial judge, after granting the temporary injunction, would have given the case a preferred setting for an early trial on the merits on request of either party so that the substantial questions involved in this litigation could be decided finally and expeditiously, as directed by the supreme court in *Texas Foundries, Inc. v. International Moulders & Foundry Workers, Union*, 248 S.W.2d 460, 464 (1952). We see no reason why the case could not have been prosecuted to final judgment in less time than that required by this interlocutory appeal, which decides nothing except whether the status quo should be preserved pending trial on the merits. The most expeditious way of obviating the hardship of an unfavorable preliminary order is to try the case and thus secure a hearing in which both facts and law may be fully developed, and then both trial and appellate courts can render judgment finally disposing of the controversy. *Southwest Weather Research, Inc. v. Jones*, 327 S.W.2d 417, 422 (1959).

Accordingly, we reverse the judgment of the trial court and dissolve the temporary injunction order.

§ 2.02 INTERIM RELIEF FOR SECURED CREDITORS AND OTHER CLAIMANTS

[A] Sequestration

Sequestration is a purely ancillary statutory procedure. The purpose of the procedure is to take specified property, in which the claimant asserts a preexisting property interest, out of the possession of a party to a suit and place it in the custody of the court pending final judgment on the issue of who is entitled to the property. *Harding v. Jesse Dennett, Inc.*, 17 S.W.2d 862, 864 (Tex. Civ. App. — San Antonio 1929, writ ref'd). The procedure is designed to preserve the property until a final determination on this issue has been made. *See Radcliff Fin. Corp. v. Industrial State Bank of Houston*, 289 S.W.2d 645, 649 (Tex. Civ. App. — Beaumont 1956, no writ). Sequestration is available only when provided for by statute, and strict compliance with the statute and applicable rules of procedure is required. *See American Mortgage Corp. v. Samuell*, 108 S.W.2d 193, 196 (1937); *Hunt v. Merchandise Mart, Inc.*, 391 S.W.2d 141, 144–45 (Tex. Civ. App. — Dallas 1965, writ ref'd n.r.e.).

CIVIL PRACTICE AND REMEDIES CODE CHAPTER 62

AVAILABILITY OF A REMEDY

§ 62.001. *Grounds.* A writ of sequestration is available to a plaintiff in a suit if:

(1) the suit is for title or possession of personal property or fixtures or for foreclosure or enforcement of a mortgage, lien, or security interest on personal property or fixtures and a reasonable conclusion may be drawn that there is immediate danger that the defendant or the party in possession of the property will conceal, dispose of, ill-treat, waste, or destroy the property or remove it from the county during the suit;

(2) the suit is for title or possession of real property or for foreclosure or enforcement of a mortgage or lien on real property and a reasonable conclusion may be drawn that there is immediate danger that the defendant or the party in possession of the property will use his possession to injure or ill-treat the property or waste or convert to his own use the timber, rents, fruits, or revenue of the property;

(3) the suit is for the title or possession of property from which the plaintiff has been ejected by force or violence; or

(4) the suit is to try the title to real property, to remove a cloud from the title of real property, to foreclose a lien on real property, or to partition real property and the plaintiff makes an oath that one or more of the defendants is a nonresident of this state.

§ 62.002. *Pending Suit Required.* A writ of sequestration may be issued at the initiation of a suit or at any time before final judgment.

§ 62.003. *Available for Claim Not Due.* A writ of sequestration may be issued for personal property under a mortgage or a lien even though the right of action on the mortgage or lien has not accrued. The proceedings relating to the writ shall be as in other cases, except that final judgment may not be rendered against the defendant until the right of action has accrued.

ISSUANCE

§ 62.021. *Who May Issue.* A district or county court judge or a justice of the peace may issue writs of sequestration returnable to his court.

§ 62.022. *Application.* The application for a writ of sequestration must be made under oath and must set forth:

(1) the specific facts stating the nature of the plaintiff's claim;

(2) the amount in controversy, if any; and

(3) the facts justifying issuance of the writ.

§ 62.023. *Required Statement of Rights.*

(a) A writ of sequestration must prominently display the following statement on the face of the writ:

> YOU HAVE A RIGHT TO REGAIN POSSESSION OF THE PROPERTY BY FILING A REPLEVY BOND. YOU HAVE A RIGHT TO SEEK TO REGAIN POSSESSION OF THE PROPERTY BY FILING WITH THE COURT A MOTION TO DISSOLVE THIS WRIT.

(b) The statement must be printed in 10-point type and in a manner intended to advise a reasonably attentive person of its contents.

DISSOLUTION AND REPLEVY

§ 62.041. *Motion for Dissolution; Stay.*

(a) The defendant may seek dissolution of an issued writ of sequestration by filing a written motion with the court.

(b) The right to seek dissolution is cumulative of the right of replevy.

(c) The filing of a motion to dissolve stays proceedings under the writ until the issue is determined.

§ 62.042. *Hearing on Motion.* Unless the parties agree to an extension, the court shall conduct a hearing on the motion and determine the issue not later than the 10th day after the motion is filed.

§ 62.043. *Dissolution.*

(a) Following the hearing, the writ must be dissolved unless the party who secured its issuance proves the specific facts alleged and the grounds relied on for issuance.

(b) If the writ is dissolved, the action proceeds as if the writ had not been issued.

§ 62.044. *Compulsory Counterclaim for Wrongful Sequestration.*

(a) If a writ is dissolved, any action for damages for wrongful sequestration must be brought as a compulsory counterclaim.

(b) In addition to damages, the party who sought dissolution of the writ may recover reasonable attorney's fees incurred in dissolution of the writ.

§ 62.045. *Wrongful Sequestration of Consumer Goods.*

(a) If a writ that sought to sequester consumer goods is dissolved, the defendant or party in possession of the goods is entitled to reasonable attorney's fees and damages equal to the greater of:

(1) $100;

(2) the finance charge contracted for; or

(3) actual damages.

(b) Damages may not be awarded for the failure of the plaintiff to prove by a preponderance of the evidence the specific facts alleged if the failure is the result of a bona fide error. For a bona fide error to be available as a defense, the plaintiff must prove the use of reasonable procedures to avoid the error.

(c) In this section, "consumer goods" has the meaning assigned by the Business & Commerce Code.

§ 62.046. *Liability for Fruit of Replevied Property.*

(a) In a suit for enforcement of a mortgage or lien on property, a defendant who replevies the property is not required to account for the fruits, hire, revenue, or rent of the property.

(b) This section does not apply to a plaintiff who replevies the property.

RULES OF CIVIL PROCEDURE

Read Tex. R. Civ. P. 696–716.

Issuance of the Writ of Sequestration. The application for the issuance of the writ must be made under oath and must set forth specific facts stating the nature of the plaintiff's claim, the amount in controversy, the statutory grounds relied on, and specific facts relied on by the plaintiff to justify findings of fact that support the statutory ground or grounds relied on. Tex. R. Civ. P. 696. Under Civil Procedure

Rule 696, the application must comply with all statutory requirements and must be supported by affidavits. The supporting affidavits may be based on information and belief only if the grounds for such belief are specifically stated. The application for the writ must also include a sufficient description of the property to be sequestered to identify it and to distinguish it from similar property. The application must state the value of each article of property and the county in which it is located. TEX. R. CIV. P. 696.

The clerk may issue the writ only on a written order following a hearing, which may be ex parte. The court's written order granting the application must contain specific findings of fact to support the statutory grounds which support the application and the writ. Property to be sequestered must be described in the court order with sufficient certainty to distinguish it from other similar property; in addition to this identification, the order must state the value of each item to be sequestered and the county in which it is located. TEX. R. CIV. P. 696. Before the writ of sequestration can issue, the plaintiff must file a sufficient bond with the court. TEX. R. CIV. P. 698. The court must specify the amount of bond required of the plaintiff in the court order granting the writ. The bond must, in the opinion of the court, be sufficient to "adequately compensate defendant in the event plaintiff fails to prosecute his suit to effect and pay all damages and costs as shall be adjudged against him for wrongfully suing out the writ." TEX. R. CIV. P. 696. Either party may challenge the amount of the bond or the sufficiency of the sureties. TEX. R. CIV. P. 698. The court must also indicate in its order the amount of bond required of the defendant to replevy. TEX. R. CIV. P. 696. Civil Procedure Rule 696 establishes the amount of the bond at the value of the property sequestered or the amount of the plaintiff's claim plus interest if allowed by law on the claim, whichever is less, plus court costs.

Contents of the Writ and Service on the Defendant. Civil Procedure Rule 700a requires that the copy of the writ served on the defendant prominently display in 10-point type, in a manner calculated to advise a reasonably attentive person, the following message:

> YOU HAVE A RIGHT TO REGAIN POSSESSION OF THE PROPERTY BY FILING A REPLEVY BOND. YOU HAVE A RIGHT TO SEEK TO REGAIN POSSESSION OF THE PROPERTY BY FILING WITH THE COURT A MOTION TO DISSOLVE THIS WRIT.

TEX. R. CIV. P. 700a. This language, and the rights of dissolution and modification granted under Civil Procedure Rule 712a, help protect the Texas sequestration procedure from constitutional attack.

The writ of sequestration must be directed to a sheriff or any constable within the State of Texas and must command him or her to take possession of the property, subject to the right of replevy and further order of the court. TEX. R. CIV. P. 699. The defendant must be served with a copy of the writ, the application of the plaintiff, accompanying affidavits, and orders of the court. Service may be made in any manner prescribed for service of citation or as provided in Civil Procedure Rule 21a. Service must occur as soon as practicable following the levy of the writ. TEX. R. CIV. P. 700a. On the face of the writ, before the required 10-point language quoted above, the writ must state:

To — —, Defendant:

> You are hereby notified that certain properties alleged to be claimed by you have been sequestered. If you claim any right in such property, you are advised: [The quoted language above in 10-point type must be placed here]. TEX. R. CIV. P. 700a.

Dissolution or Modification of the Writ of Sequestration. Under Civil Procedure Rule 712a, the defendant may, for any extrinsic or intrinsic ground or cause, seek by sworn written motion to vacate, dissolve, or modify the writ and the order directing the issuance of the writ. The motion to dissolve, modify, or vacate must admit or deny each finding in the court order authorizing the issuance of the writ. If, however, the moving party is unable to admit or deny a finding contained in the order, that party must state the reasons for the inability to admit or deny it. The motion must then be heard promptly, after reasonable notice to the plaintiff (which may be less than three days) and the issue shall be determined not later than 10 days after the motion is filed. TEX. R. CIV. P. 712a.

Once a Rule 712a motion has been filed, all other proceedings under the writ are stayed except for orders relating to the care and preservation of the property. This stay remains in effect until a hearing is had on the motion and the issue is decided. TEX. R. CIV. P. 712a.

Generally, the writ of sequestration is to be dissolved if the plaintiff fails to prove the grounds relied on for issuance of the writ. The movant, however, has the burden of proving, if he or she so contends, that the reasonable value of the property sequestered exceeds the amount necessary to secure the sum total of the debt, interest for one year, and probable costs. TEX. R. CIV. P. 712a.

In ruling on a motion, the court may make its determination on the basis of uncontroverted affidavits that set forth facts that would be admissible in evidence. If the affidavits are controverted, the court must make its determination on the basis of evidence submitted by the parties in the normal manner. In addition to dissolving the writ, the rules give the court great latitude in modifying its previous order on the writ if dissolution is not appropriate. If the court determines that the order or the writ should not be vacated or dissolved, but only modified, it may make further orders with respect to a replevy bond filed by the defendant that are consistent with the modification. TEX. R. CIV. P. 712a.

Replevy. The defendant may replevy the property at any time before judgment. TEX. R. CIV. P. 701. "If the movant has given a replevy bond, an order to vacate or dissolve the writ shall vacate the replevy bond and discharge the sureties." TEX. R. CIV. P. 712a. Replevin requires that the defendant give bond with sufficient sureties; the surety or sureties must be approved by the officer who levied the writ and must be payable to the plaintiff. The amount of the bond is the amount fixed by the original court order; that is, an amount equivalent to the value of the property or the amount of the plaintiff's claim and one year's interest, whichever is the lesser amount, and the probable costs of court. TEX. R. CIV. P. 701. *See* TEX. R. CIV. P. 702, 703 (condition of bond for personal property and real estate).

If the bond is objectionable to either party, that party, on motion and notice to the opposing party, has the right to a prompt judicial review of the amount of the bond required, denial of bond, sufficiency of sureties, or to the estimated value of the property in question. Judicial review of these issues is to be made by the court that authorized the issuance of the writ on the basis of evidence submitted, or uncontroverted affidavits setting forth facts that would be admissible. TEX. R. CIV. P. 701.

If the defendant fails to replevy the property within 10 days after levy of the writ and the service of notice, the plaintiff may replevy by giving bond payable to the defendant in an amount not less than the amount fixed by the court's order, with sufficient sureties to be approved by the levying officer. TEX. R. CIV. P. 708. Under Rule 708, if the property to be replevied is personalty, the bond must provide that the plaintiff will either preserve the property in the same condition as when it is replevied, together with the value of the fruits or revenue thereof, to abide the decision of the court, or that the plaintiff will pay the value thereof, or the difference between its value at the time of replevy and the time of judgment. If the property is realty, the bond must provide that the plaintiff will not injure the property and will pay the value of the rents if required to do so. On proper notice by either party, the complaining party can obtain judicial review of the plaintiff's replevy, just as in the case of defendant's replevy.

For further discussion and forms, see WILLIAM V. DORSANEO III, TEXAS LITIGATION GUIDE, Ch. 40, *Sequestration* (2006). *See also* Luke Soules, *Attachment, Sequestration, and Garnishment: The 1977 Rules*, 32 SW. L.J. 753 (1978).

[B] Notice of Lis Pendens

Another method of preserving the subject matter of the litigation pending final resolution is the notice of lis pendens. The procedure is controlled by the following sections of the Property Code:

§ 12.007. *Lis Pendens.*

(a) After the plaintiff's statement in an eminent domain proceeding is filed or during the pendency of an action involving title to real property, the establishment of an interest in real property, or the enforcement of an encumbrance against real property, a party to the action who is seeking affirmative relief may file for record with the county clerk of each county where a part of the property is located a notice that the action is pending.

(b) The party filing a lis pendens or the party's agent or attorney shall sign the lis pendens, which must state:

(1) the style and number, if any, of the proceeding;

(2) the court in which the proceeding is pending;

(3) the names of the parties;

(4) the kind of proceeding; and

(5) a description of the property affected.

(c) The county clerk shall record the notice in a lis pendens record. The clerk shall index the record in a direct and reverse index under the name of each party to the proceeding.

§ 13.004. *Effect of Recording Lis Pendens.*

(a) A recorded lis pendens is notice to the world of its contents. The notice is effective from the time it is filed for record, regardless of whether service has been made on the parties to the proceeding.

(b) A transfer or encumbrance of real property involved in a proceeding by a party to the proceeding to a third party who has paid a valuable consideration and who does not have actual or constructive notice of the proceeding is effective, even though the judgment is against the party transferring or encumbering the property, unless a notice of the pendency of the proceeding has been recorded under that party's name in each county in which the property is located.

The following excerpt from *King v. Tubb*, 551 S.W.2d 436, 443–444 (Tex. Civ. App. — Corpus Christi 1977, no writ), sets out the purpose and the effect of the notice of lis pendens:

> The ultimate effect of lis pendens is to prevent either party to certain litigation from alienating the property that is in dispute. It is a well settled rule of law in this State that a purchaser of land pendente lite stands in no better attitude than his vendor. The very purpose of the statutory *lis pendens* notice is to put those interested in the land on inquiry as to the status of the land. Therefore, it is apparent that the filing of the *lis pendens* notice by Tubb and Allison rendered King's title to the land defective and justified Middlebrook's failure to consummate the sale, resulting in his claim for the return of his $20,000.00 earnest money . . . . Since the trial court was correct in holding that the *lis pendens* rendered the contract unperformable, it is unnecessary for us to consider the propriety of the trial court's findings that the property description in the contract was too vague and indefinite and was incapable of being located on the ground.

For a discussion of the relationship of the lis pendens statutes to receivership, see *First S. Properties, Inc. v. Vallone*, 533 S.W.2d 339, 342–43 (Tex. 1976) (holding property in receivership in custodia legis; "We hold that compliance with Articles 6640 and 6642 is not required to prevent lands in receivership from being acquired under attempted sales by third parties . . . " without court approval).

[C] Self-Help Repossession by Secured Party

Section 9.609 of the Texas Business and Commerce Code provides, "Unless otherwise agreed a secured party has on default the right to take possession of the collateral. In taking possession a secured party may proceed without judicial process if this can be done without breach of the peace or may proceed by action. If the security agreement so provides the secured party may require the debtor to assemble the collateral and make it available to the secured party at a place to be designated by the secured party which is reasonably convenient to both parties. Without removal a secured party may render equipment unusable, and may dispose of collateral on the debtor's premises under [Business and Commerce Code] Section 9.[609]." Bus. & Com. C. § 9.609. The scope of this statute depends on a number of definitions of terms set out elsewhere in the code (*see* Bus. & Com. C. §§ 1.201 (action; party), 9.102 (collateral; debtor; secured party; security agreement), 9.109 (equipment)) and on the definition of two terms (default, breach of the peace), which the code does not define.

§ 2.03 INTERIM RELIEF FOR THE GENERAL (UNSECURED) CREDITOR

[A] Attachment

The purpose of attachment is to impound and fix a lien on the nonexempt property of a debtor before judgment. Property of a debtor that is exempt from attachment, execution, or other seizure for the satisfaction of liabilities is set forth in Property Code Sections 41.001–41.004. The remedy is structured primarily to prevent a debtor from making himself or herself judgment proof during the pendency of litigation. *Midway Nat'l Bank of Grand Prairie v. West Tex. Wholesale Co.*, 447 S.W.2d 709, 710–11 (Tex. Civ. App. — Fort Worth 1969), *writ ref'd n.r.e. per curiam*, 453 S.W.2d 460 (Tex. 1970). Attachment is in the nature of execution before judgment. When the writ of attachment is levied on the nonexempt property of the debtor, the creditor obtains a lien on the property. In other words, the general (unsecured) creditor becomes a judicial lien creditor from the date of levy. The type of suit that will normally support the issuance of the writ is a suit for a debt, which is defined as an obligation to pay a liquidated sum on an express or implied contract. C.P.R.C. § 61.001. *El Paso Nat'l Bank v. Fuchs*, 34 S.W. 206, 207 (Tex. 1896).

CIVIL PRACTICE AND REMEDIES CODE CHAPTER 61

AVAILABILITY OF REMEDY

§ 61.001. *General Grounds.* A writ of original attachment is available to a plaintiff in a suit if:

(1) the defendant is justly indebted to the plaintiff;

(2) the attachment is not sought for the purpose of injuring or harassing the defendant;

(3) the plaintiff will probably lose his debt unless the writ of attachment is issued; and

(4) specific grounds for the writ exist under Section 61.002.

§ 61.002. *Specific Grounds.* Attachment is available if:

(1) the defendant is not a resident of this state or is a foreign corporation or is acting as such;

(2) the defendant is about to move from this state permanently and has refused to pay or secure the debt due the plaintiff;

(3) the defendant is in hiding so that ordinary process of law cannot be served on him;

(4) the defendant has hidden or is about to hide his property for the purpose of defrauding his creditors;

(5) the defendant is about to remove his property from this state without leaving an amount sufficient to pay his debts;

(6) the defendant is about to remove all or part of his property from the county in which the suit is brought with the intent to defraud his creditors;

(7) the defendant has disposed of or is about to dispose of all or part of his property with the intent to defraud his creditors;

(8) the defendant is about to convert all or part of his property into money for the purpose of placing it beyond the reach of his creditors; or

(9) the defendant owes the plaintiff for property obtained by the defendant under false pretenses.

ISSUANCE

§ 61.021. *Who May Issue.* The judge or clerk of a district or county court or a justice of the peace may issue a writ of original attachment returnable to his court.

To obtain a writ of attachment, the plaintiff must make an affidavit and execute a bond. The affidavit must state three things (C.P.R.C. § 61.022):

(1) general grounds for issuance under C.P.R.C. §§ 61.001(1), (2), and (3);

(2) the amount of the demand; and

(3) specific grounds for issuance under C.P.R.C. § 61.002.

The writ of attachment may also be issued in suits based on tort or unliquidated demands if personal service on the defendant cannot be obtained within Texas. C.P.R.C. § 61.005. A writ of attachment may be issued either at the initiation of the suit or during its pendency but may not be issued before suit has been initiated (C.P.R.C. § 61.003) and it may be issued even though the plaintiff's debt or demand is not due. C.P.R.C. § 61.004. However, a final judgment may not be rendered against the defendant until the debt or demand becomes due.

The rules of civil procedure supplement the statutes concerning the remedy of attachment.

Read Tex. R. Civ. P. 592–609.

Issuance of the Writ of Attachment. Civil Procedure Rule 592 establishes specific procedures governing the plaintiff's application for, and the court's issuance of, a writ of attachment. Rule 592 was designed to meet the constitutional demands of due process. The specificity requirements are similar to the requirements for the application for the writ of sequestration described above.

Civil Procedure Rule 592a requires that the plaintiff file an attachment bond before the writ will be issued and provides for judicial review, if requested by either party, of the amount of the bond or the sufficiency of the sureties. The bond required of the plaintiff is designed to compensate the defendant adequately in the event the plaintiff fails to prosecute the suit to effect and to compensate the defendant sufficiently for all damages and costs that may be adjudged against the plaintiff for wrongfully suing out the writ of attachment. Tex. R. Civ. P. 592. If the attachment is wrongful, there are remedies available to the defendant. If none of the grounds stated in the plaintiff's affidavit for the issuance of the writ is true, then the attachment is wrongful. This is true notwithstanding the plaintiff's good faith. The party whose property was wrongfully attached must prove interference with his or her property rights to be entitled to more than nominal damages. When, however, the attachment creditor has acted maliciously and without probable cause, exemplary damages may be available. The attachment bond requirement is almost identical to the bond required by the rules for sequestration.

Contents of the Writ and Service on the Defendant. The writ of attachment must be directed to a sheriff or any constable within the state. The instructions to the sheriff or constable direct the officer to attach property "of a reasonable value in approximately the amount fixed by the court." Tex. R. Civ. P. 593. The levy of the writ fixes a lien on personalty. A lien on real estate is affixed by an "office levy." This procedure involves endorsement of the writ with a description of the realty and recordation of the writ and the return in the county in which the realty is located. The writ of attachment must inform the defendant of the right to replevy and regain possession by filing a motion to dissolve the writ. *See* Tex. R. Civ. P. 598a.

Dissolution or Modification of the Writ of Attachment. Civil Procedure Rule 608 governs dissolution and modification of the writ of attachment. Rule 608 provides for a prompt hearing at which the burden of persuasion is on the attaching creditors.

Replevy. Civil Procedure Rule 599 provides that the defendant may replevy on the filing of the required bond. The amount of the bond required of the defendant is the amount of the plaintiff's claim, one year's accrued interest if allowed by law, and the estimated costs of court. At the election of the defendant, however, the bond may be set at the value of the property the defendant seeks to replevy. Either party is entitled to judicial review of the amount of the bond, denial of bond, sufficiency of the sureties, and the estimated value of the property attached. Tex. R. Civ. P. 599. Rule 599 further provides that the defendant may move to have property of equal value substituted for the property attached.

[B] Prejudgment Garnishment

Prejudgment garnishment is also provided for by statute and is available (1) when an original attachment has issued; or (2) when suit is brought for a debt owed and an affidavit is made by the plaintiff to the effect that the debt is just, due and unpaid and that the defendant does not possess property in Texas subject to execution sufficient to satisfy the debt and the plaintiff is not seeking to injure or harass the defendant or the garnishee with the garnishment. C.P.R.C. § 63.001. The debt must be liquidated. *See Cleveland v. San Antonio Bldg. & Loan Ass'n*, 223 S.W.2d 226, 228 (Tex. 1949).

The effect of the service of the writ is set forth in the Civil Practice and Remedies Code:

§ 63.003. *Effect of Service.*

(a) After service of a writ of garnishment, the garnishee may not deliver any effects or pay any debt to the defendant. If the garnishee is a corporation or joint-stock company, the garnishee may not permit or recognize a sale or transfer of shares or an interest alleged to be owned by the defendant.

(b) A payment, delivery, sale, or transfer made in violation of Subsection (a) is void as to the amount of the debt, effects, shares, or interest necessary to satisfy the plaintiff's demand.

Only personalty (tangible or intangible) can be "seized" by the service of the writ. Moreover, certain property is exempt from garnishment. *See* C.P.R.C. § 63.004. Tex. Const. Art. 16, § 28 provides, "No current wages for personal service shall ever be subject to garnishment, except for the enforcement of court-ordered (1) child support payments; or (2) spousal maintenance." The Texas Family Code provides statutory authority for withholding income for these purposes. *See* Tex. Fam. Code §§ 8.101, 158.001.

The rules of civil procedure also must be consulted on the subject of prejudgment garnishment.

Read Tex. R. Civ. P. 657–679.

Issuance of the Writ of Garnishment. The requirements of an application for and issuance of the writ of garnishment are essentially the same as for the writ of attachment. A prejudgment garnishment bond is required. *See* Tex. R. Civ. P. 658a. The bond must be sufficient to cover any potential damages for wrongful garnishment. Tex. R. Civ. P. 658. The remedies for wrongful garnishment remain. Garnishment is wrongful if the prescribed allegations set forth in the garnishor's affidavit are untrue. As in attachment, good faith is no defense. Although good faith is not a defense, the garnishee cannot recover exemplary damages unless he or she can prove that the garnishment was obtained maliciously and without probable cause. Third parties whose property interests are wrongfully garnished as belonging to the garnishment debtor may also maintain an action against the erring creditor.

After the writ of garnishment is served on the garnishee, the garnishee must answer as in other civil actions. If the garnishee's uncontroverted answer reflects that he or she is indebted to the defendant or has possession of property of the defendant, after due notice to the defendant, the court in which the garnishment is pending may, on hearing, reduce the required amount of the bond to double the sum of the garnishee's indebtedness to the defendant, plus the value of the property in his or her possession that belongs to the defendant. TEX. R. CIV. P. 658a.

Garnishment involves a separate ancillary lawsuit between the garnishor and the garnishee (the third party). The garnishment action cannot be concluded with a judgment against the garnishee until the primary action for the debt between the plaintiff (garnishor) and the defendant (debtor) ends. The court dockets the case in the name of the plaintiff as plaintiff and of the garnishee as defendant. TEX. R. CIV. P. 659. The court must immediately issue a writ of garnishment if the application and the bond requirements are fulfilled. TEX. R. CIV. P. 659, 661. Under Civil Procedure Rule 659, the writ should command the garnishee to appear and answer under oath what, if anything, is owed to the defendant-debtor, and what the debt was to the defendant-debtor at the time the writ was served. The garnishee must also reveal what property of the defendant-debtor is in his or her possession presently, and what property was possessed when the writ was served. Finally, the garnishee must reveal any other persons known who are indebted to the defendant-debtor, or have property belonging to that person, in their possession. TEX. R. CIV. P. 659.

Contents of the Writ and Service on the Defendant. After the court orders issuance of the writ, which may be in the form prescribed by Civil Procedure Rule 661, the defendant-debtor is required to be served with a copy of the writ, the application, accompanying affidavits, and orders of the court as soon as practicable following the service of the writ on the garnishee. TEX. R. CIV. P. 663a. As in the case of attachment, the writ must inform the defendant of the right to replevy and to regain possession by filing a motion to dissolve the writ. TEX. R. CIV. P. 663a.

Dissolution or Modification of the Writ. Civil Procedure Rule 664a controls dissolution or modification of the writ and the order directing its issuance. It is similar to counterpart rules concerning dissolution or modification of the writs of sequestration and attachment.

Replevy. The defendant-debtor may replevy at any time before judgment if the garnished property has not been previously claimed or sold. TEX. R. CIV. P. 664. The defendant-debtor may replevy the property, any part thereof, or the proceeds from the sale of the property if it has been sold under a court order. The procedure necessary to entitle the defendant-debtor to replevy in garnishment is the same as in attachment. Also, as in attachment, the defendant-debtor may move to have property substituted for the garnished property. TEX. R. CIV. P. 664.

Garnishment After Judgment Distinguished. Garnishment after judgment is also available. Post-judgment garnishment is a procedure available to a judgment-creditor to satisfy a money judgment from the judgment-debtor's nonexempt personal property in the possession of a third person. Post-judgment garnishment is only available when the plaintiff has a valid, subsisting judgment and the judgment-debtor does not have property in his or her possession within the state subject to execution to satisfy the judgment. C.P.R.C. § 63.001(3). This statute governing post-judgment garnishment has been found constitutional notwithstanding that post-judgment garnishment does not require that a writ of execution be issued, or issued and returned unsatisfied. No bond is required for post-judgment garnishment.

Garnishment and Financial Institutions. In 2005, the Texas legislature passed a statute limiting the liability of financial institutions when they fail to respond to the writ of garnishment, resulting in a default judgment. The default judgment is only as to the issue of liability, not the amount of damages. This statute supersedes the effect of Civil Procedure Rule 667 and requires proof to support a declaratory judgment against the garnishor. *Regions Bank v. Centerpoint Apartments*, 290 S.W.3d 510, 514 (Tex. App. — Amarillo 2009, no pet.). Here is the statute:

Texas Finance Code § 276.002. Garnishment of Financial Institution Account

(a) Notwithstanding the Texas Rules of Civil Procedure, if a financial institution fails to timely file an answer to a writ of garnishment issued before or after a judgment is rendered in the case, a court may enter a default judgment against the financial institution solely as to the existence of liability and not as to the amount of damages.

(b) A financial institution against which a default judgment is entered under Subsection (a) is not deemed to have in the financial institution's possession or to have knowledge of sufficient debts, assets, or personal effects of the debtor to satisfy the debtor's obligations to the garnishor.

(c) After a default judgment is entered against a financial institution as to the existence of liability as provided by Subsection (a), the garnishor has the burden to establish the amount of actual damages proximately caused to the garnishor by the financial institution's default.

(d) The court may award to the garnishor:

(1) damages in the amount determined under Subsection (c); and

(2) for good cause shown, reasonable attorney's fees incurred by the garnishor in establishing damages under Subsection (c).

(e) Notwithstanding Section 22.004, Government Code, the supreme court may not amend or adopt rules in conflict with this section.

PRACTICE EXERCISE #1

Decide what prelitigation special remedy or other action, if any, would be appropriate in each of the following situations. Take into account both legal and practical considerations (that is, try to decide on the most expeditious and inexpensive method, but one that is legally justified under the circumstances).

1. Big-Hearted Ben, a car dealer, sold a new Hellcat Spyder automobile to Dan Deadbeat. Dan has stopped making payments to Ben. He keeps the car parked on the street at night; Ben, of course, has no key to it. The contract of sale provides Ben with a lien and with all remedies allowed under the Uniform Commercial Code. What can Ben do? REPO / WRIT OF SEQUESTRATION? W/O Breach of Peace

2. Assume the same situation as in (1), but with the additional fact that Dan keeps the car in his locked garage at night, is a light sleeper, can see the garage door from

his bedroom window, and has a loaded shotgun nearby. In addition, Dan has announced to Ben his intention to drive the car to California to get it where Ben cannot get to it and to "take a sledgehammer to it" if Ben does. What can Ben do now?

3. Don Debtor has defaulted on an unsecured promissory note to Carl Creditor. He has told Carl that he intends to remove all his non-exempt property to California, and has, to Carl's knowledge, already begun doing so.

4. Diane Debtor owes $10,000 to Carol Creditor and Carol has learned that Diane has $100,000 in one bank account and $200,000 in another. Both accounts have maintained that balance for the past year. Diane disputes the debt and has refused to pay for that reason.

5. Assume the same situation as (4), except that Diane's accounts total only $15,000, her cash requirements for her business are about $20,000 per month, her balance has been steadily diminishing, and Diane has stated to Carol that she owes the debt but "can't pay it because I need the money for other things."

§ 2.04 WRONGFUL USE OF SPECIAL REMEDIES

[A] Due Process Problems

When a court authorizes the seizure of a person's property based on summary procedures, it creates the potential for a violation of the Due Process Clause of the U.S. Constitution. In the following case, the debtor claimed that he did not receive adequate notice and hearing before his car was seized. How much protection does the Due Process Clause provide?

MONROE v. GENERAL MOTORS ACCEPTANCE CORP.

573 S.W.2d 591 (Tex. Civ. App. — Waco 1978, no writ)

McDonald, C.J.

This is an appeal by defendant from judgment against him for the unpaid balance of a retail installment contract, secured by a 1976 Chevrolet, and foreclosure of security interest of plaintiff in such automobile.

On October 26, 1977 plaintiff GMAC, sued defendant Monroe on a retail installment contract executed by defendant in the credit purchase of a 1976 Chevrolet automobile; alleging plaintiff is owner of such contract; that defendant is in arrears in his payments; that plaintiff has declared the entire principal balance due as provided in the contract; and sought judgment for the balance of principal and interest due, attorney's fees, and foreclosure of security interest in the automobile.

On the same date plaintiff filed the affidavit of its manager A.B. Rich for writ of sequestration of the automobile, and on such date the Judge of the 74th District Court issued writ of sequestration commanding the Sheriff to take possession of the automobile and keep same subject to further order of the court. On October 29,

1977 the Sheriff took possession of the automobile pursuant to the writ of sequestration.

On October 31, 1977 defendant filed Motion to Dissolve the Writ of Sequestration, and the trial court after hearing, on November 4, 1977 overruled same.

Trial on the merits was to a jury which found:

(1) Plaintiff GMAC requested defendant Monroe to surrender possession of the 1976 Chevrolet.

(2) The unpaid balance of the installment contract was $4,597.34.

(3) It was necessary for GMAC to secure an attorney.

(4) GMAC declared the entire principal balance of the installment contract due.

(5) GMAC did not waive its right to accelerate maturity.

(6) A.B. Rich made the sequestration affidavit at a time when he had reasonable knowledge to fear defendant would conceal, dispose of, ill treat, waste, destroy, or remove the 1976 Chevrolet from the jurisdiction of the court.

It was stipulated a reasonable attorney's fee would be $1000.

The trial court rendered judgment on the verdict for plaintiff for $5,597.34 (unpaid balance of the installment contract plus $1000 attorney's fee); and for foreclosure of security interest in the automobile.

Defendant appeals on 11 points which we summarize as 4 main contentions.

(1) The trial court erred in issuing the writ of sequestration because plaintiff's affidavit was insufficient as a matter of law in not setting forth:

a) specific facts as to the amount in controversy;

b) specific facts justifying issuance of the writ;

c) sufficient facts from which a reasonable conclusion may be drawn that defendant would conceal, dispose, ill treat, waste, destroy or remove the property during pendency of suit.

(2) The trial court erred in overruling defendant's motion to dissolve the writ because:

a) there was no evidence of any grounds and specific facts relied on by plaintiff for issuance of the writ as required by statute;

b) the evidence was insufficient to prove the grounds and specific facts relied on for issuance of the writ.

(3) The trial court erred in not assessing attorney's fees and damages against plaintiff.

(4) The Sequestration Statute [Article 6840] is unconstitutional in that it fails to provide for notice and opportunity for a hearing at a meaningful time

and in a meaningful manner before depriving a defendant of his property, thereby depriving the defendant of procedural due process.

. . . .

Contention 1 asserts plaintiff's affidavit insufficient as a matter of law.

Section 2 Article 6840 requires the affidavit to state the nature of plaintiff's claim, the amount in controversy, and the facts justifying the issuance.

Plaintiff's affidavit for writ of sequestration filed herein states "Plaintiff sues for the title and possession of the hereinafter described property and for foreclosure of a security interest therein [describing the 1976 Chevrolet] of the value of $6,987.96; the said property is now in the possession of the defendant . . . and the plaintiff fears that there is immediate danger that the defendant in possession thereof will conceal, dispose of, ill treat, waste or destroy such property, or remove the same out of the jurisdiction of this court during the pendency of this suit."

We think the affidavit is in substantial and sufficient compliance with the statute to authorize the judge to issue the writ.

Contention 2 asserts the trial court erred in overruling defendant's motion to dissolve the writ because there was no evidence or insufficient evidence of any grounds or specific facts to sustain issuance of the writ.

At the hearing on the motion to dissolve it was undisputed that defendant owed a debt (the installment contract), secured by a lien (security interest) on the automobile, and that defendant was delinquent 3 monthly payments of $166.38 each; that defendant had been in default before; that plaintiff's agents had contacted defendant by telephone and personally urged him to pay up; that he said "he didn't have the money and there was no way we could get the car at his place of business or at his home." Defendant at other times agreed to pay up his delinquent payments by times certain, but failed to do so. An automobile is a rapid depreciation chattel, and in the hands of defendant who did not make his payments but was continuing to use the vehicle, we think the trial court authorized to overrule the motion to dissolve the writ, and that the evidence is ample to sustain such order.

Contention 3 asserts the trial court erred in not assessing damages and attorney's fees against the plaintiff. Attorney's fees and damages against the plaintiff are authorized only if the writ is dissolved.

Contention 4 asserts the sequestration statute is unconstitutional in that it does not provide for notice and hearing at a meaningful time and in a meaningful manner before depriving defendant of his property.

Defendant relies on *Fuentes v. Shevin*, 407 U.S. 67 (1972), which held statutes in Florida and Pennsylvania invalid which permitted a creditor to obtain a prejudgment writ of replevin through summary process of ex parte application upon posting a bond. The court held that procedural due process requires an opportunity for a hearing before the State authorizes its agents to seize property from the party in possession.

The same court in *Mitchell v. W. T. Grant Co.*, 416 U.S. 600 (1974), held a Louisiana sequestration statute valid, which like the Texas statute provides that the debtor may immediately seek dissolution of the writ, which must be ordered unless the creditor proves grounds for issuance. The court held "it comports with due process to permit the initial seizure on sworn ex parte documents, followed by the early opportunity to put the creditor to his proof."

And the court recognizes the distinction between *Fuentes* and *Mitchell* in the 1975 case of *North Georgia Finishing, Inc. v. Di-Chem, Inc.*, 419 U.S. 601.

All defendant's points and contentions have been considered and are overruled.

[B] The Tort of Wrongful Attachment, Garnishment, and Sequestration

Sometimes the manner in which property is seized can form the basis for a tort claim against the party who took control of the property. The next cases consider the elements of such a tort claim.

CHANDLER v. CASHWAY BUILDING MATERIALS, INC.

584 S.W.2d 950 (Tex. Civ. App. — El Paso 1979, no writ)

Osborn, J.

This is an appeal from a summary judgment entered against a party seeking to recover damages in a suit for wrongful garnishment. We reverse and remand.

In June, 1977, Cashway Building Materials, Inc., sued Richard L. Chandler dba Skyline Hardware in Cause No. 39938-1 in County Court at Law No. 1 in El Paso to recover a debt of $1,276.24. In September, a default judgment was entered for $1,583.75, which amount included the amount of the debt, interest in the amount of $57.51 and attorney fees of $250.00. Execution was issued in November, 1977, for $1,833.75 (recited as being $1,583.75 and $250.00). Another execution was issued in March, 1978, for $1,583.75. The record does not reflect the return on those writs.

In March, 1978, Cashway filed in Cause No. 41705-1 in the County Court at Law No. 1 an Application for Writ of Garnishment after Judgment. El Paso National Bank was named garnishee and the writ was served on it on March 20, 1978. It answered on March 23, 1978, that the account of Skyline showed a balance of $5,945.35. On hearing Chandler's "Motion to Dismiss Garnishment," the Court authorized the Bank to release to Chandler any and all amounts over the sum of $1,150.00 which was required to be paid into the registry of the Court and the sum of $275.00 as attorney fees which were awarded to the garnishee.

Subsequently, the attorneys approved an "Agreed Judgment" styled Cashway Building Materials, Inc., Plaintiff, v. Richard L. Chandler d/b/a Skyline Hardware, Defendant, in No. 39938-1, in the County Court at Law No. 1, El Paso County, Texas. That judgment then recites:

> "On this day the 24th day of April, 1978, came on to be heard the above styled cause and the parties appeared by and through their attorneys of record and announced to the Court that they had compromised and settled all of the issues of fact and of law in dispute.

On the 4th day of April, 1978, the Court issued an order modifying the writ of garnishment in the case styled CASHWAY BUILDING MATERIALS, INC., Garnishor v. EL PASO NATIONAL BANK, Garnishee No. 41705-1 ordering the Garnishee to pay into the registry of the Court the sum of $1,150.00 to be taken from the garnished funds. The parties now wish to settle cause No. 39938-1 in the following manner:

1. The sum of $1,000.00 is to be paid from the funds in the registry of the Court to the Plaintiff CASHWAY BUILDING MATERIALS, INC. as an all inclusive settlement.

2. The remaining $150.00 is awarded to the Defendant RICHARD L. CHANDLER d/b/a SKYLINE HARDWARE.

A jury having been waived, the Court proceeded to hear the evidence and argument of counsel supporting such settlement agreement and is of the opinion and finds that such settlement agreement should be and is hereby, approved and made a part of this judgment.

It is accordingly ORDERED, ADJUDGED, AND DECREED that Plaintiff recover from the Defendant the sum of $1,000.00 in accordance with the settlement agreement and that the Defendant be awarded the remaining $150.00. All other relief prayed for is denied."

The trial judge struck through the cause number as typed on the judgment and with a pen changed the cause number to 41705-1. Thus, we have a judgment reciting "came on to be heard the above styled cause" in which Chandler is named as defendant, being entered in another cause in which he is not defendant and in which the El Paso National Bank is garnishee. That judgment recites that "The parties now wish to settle cause No. 39938-1 . . . " but makes no mention of settling No. 41705-1 in which the judgment was actually entered. Of course, the original judgment in No. 39938-1 became final many months earlier and no new judgment could be entered in that case. Thus, the trial judge entered the judgment in the only pending case between these parties. It appears the parties should have prepared a release of judgment to be filed in No. 39938-1 and an agreed judgment in No. 41705-1 reciting a desire or intention to settle that case. They, of course, did neither.

In May, 1978, Chandler filed this suit against Cashway seeking damages for wrongful garnishment. Cashway answered and filed a motion for summary judgment on the grounds that (1) there was no final judgment, but merely an agreed judgment in the garnishment case, (2) the suit was barred under the doctrine of res judicata, and (3) the claim is barred under the doctrine of estoppel by judgment. Chandler also filed a motion for summary judgment. The trial Court entered judgment as follows:

"IT IS THEREFORE ORDERED, ADJUDGED AND DECREED as follows:

1. The Motion for Summary Judgment filed by Plaintiff CHANDLER is in all things denied;

2. The Amended Motion for Summary Judgment filed by Defendant CASHWAY in in all things granted;

3. Plaintiff CASHWAY be dismissed and costs of suit be taxed against Plaintiff CHANDLER."

We don't know if the Court intended to say "Plaintiff Chandler" or "Defendant Cashway" at the beginning of paragraph 3 of the judgment. The judgment never recites that the Plaintiff take nothing from the Defendant as it should . . . .

The Appellant presents twelve points of error and in the sixth point urges that the trial Court erred in granting summary judgment when the proof did not establish, as a matter of law, that there was no genuine issue of fact as to one or more of the essential elements of Appellant's claim. We first consider the contention by the Appellee that there was no wrongful garnishment because there was no final judgment but only an agreed judgment entered in the garnishment case. Whether a garnishment is wrongful depends upon whether the steps taken by the parties seeking the writ comply with the statute authorizing such relief, and not the type of judgment entered. Article 4076, Tex. Rev. Civ. Stat. Ann., authorizes the issuance of a writ of garnishment:

> "Where the plaintiff has a valid, subsisting judgment and makes affidavit that the defendant has not, within his knowledge, property in his possession within this State, subject to execution, sufficient to satisfy such judgment."

The garnishment is wrongful if the facts set forth in the affidavit prescribed by Art. 4076, Tex. Rev. Civ. Stat. Ann. (1966), are untrue. *Peerless Oil & Gas Co. v. Teas*, 138 S.W.2d 637 (Tex. Civ. App. — San Antonio 1940), *aff'd* 158 S.W.2d 758 (Tex. 1942). In this case, Cashway obtained a judgment against Chandler for $1,583.75 but the Application for Writ of Garnishment, which was sworn to as being true and correct, asserted it was based upon a judgment for $1,833.75, "that said judgment is valid and existing," and that after payment of $500.00 the balance of $1,333.75 remains unsatisfied and that defendant has not, within the knowledge of plaintiff, property in his possession within this state, subject to execution, sufficient to satisfy said judgment. The affidavit incorrectly stated the amount of the judgment and the amount due after the payment.

In Plaintiff's Original Petition, it is alleged that Cashway's attorney was advised by the deputy sheriff, who had attempted to complete a writ of execution, as to the location and value of sufficient nonexempt property to satisfy the judgment. If that be true, the affidavit was incorrect in that regard. In order to be entitled to a summary judgment, the burden was on Cashway to conclusively rebut as a matter of law this allegation. *Zale Corporation v. Rosenbaum*, 520 S.W.2d 889 (Tex. 1975). There is no such proof in this case. In addition, Cashway in its motion for summary judgment assumed all of the facts of the plaintiff's original petition to be true. Thus, the Appellee's first contention fails to support the granting of the motion for summary judgment.

. . . .

Certainly, the suit for wrongful garnishment was not a compulsory counter-claim under Rule 97(a), Tex. R. Civ. P., because that claim did not arise out of the transaction or occurrence that is the subject matter of the opposing party's claim, in this case a debt for goods sold . . . .

It should be noted that a 1971 amendment to Rule 97(a) provides:

> ". . . that a judgment based upon a settlement or compromise of a claim of one party to the transaction or occurrence prior to a disposition on the merits shall not operate as a bar to the continuation or assertion of the claims of any other party to the transaction or occurrence unless the latter has consented in writing that said judgment shall operate as a bar."

We believe that amendment was to provide for the problem arising from such cases as *Akers v. Simpson*, 445 S.W.2d 957 (Tex. 1969). *See* McElhaney, *Texas Civil Procedure*, 24 Sw. L.J. 179 at 184 (1970). But it appears that even if this claim for wrongful garnishment did arise out of the opposing party's claim, the compulsory counterclaim rule would not be applicable under the 1971 amendment of the Rule as set forth above. Clearly, the agreed judgment which was based upon a settlement of Cashway's claim does not reflect that Chandler has consented in writing that the judgment shall bar his claim.

In *Hardeman & Son v. Morgan*, 48 Tex. 103 (1877), the court recognized the right of a defendant in an attachment suit to file a cross-action for wrongful attachment but concluded that he is not compelled to seek redress in this way. The court said: "He may undoubtedly, if he prefers it, bring his separate suit in the court having jurisdiction of such a demand, without regard to the tribunal in which the plaintiff's action may be pending." In this connection, we note that Chandler's suit for wrongful garnishment which seeks 1.5 million dollars in damages was not within the jurisdiction of the County Court at Law where the garnishment proceedings had been filed by Cashway. *See* 2 McDonald, Texas Civil Practice sec. 7.49-(III)(a) (1970).

. . . .

We sustain the Appellant's Point of Error Number Six, and reverse and remand the case to the trial Court.

BARFIELD v. BROGDON

560 S.W.2d 787 (Tex. Civ. App. — Amarillo 1978, writ ref'd n.r.e.)

Robinson, C.J.

The trial court entered judgment for defendant on a jury verdict on his cross-claim for actual and exemplary damages for wrongful sequestration. Affirmed subject to a remittitur.

Plaintiff, Robert E. Barfield, an attorney, took his lawn mower to Profitt's Lawn Mower Service owned by defendant, J. Darrell Brogdon, for a tune-up. Barfield testified that the price of the tune-up was agreed to be $14.00. Brogdon testified that (1) the agreed price was $14.50 plus the cost of parts; (2) he wrote "14.50 plus parts" on the repair order in the presence of Mr. Barfield; and (3) a large poster inside the shop showed that the standard tune-up charge was $14.50 plus parts. Barfield returned to pick up his lawn mower after the tune-up had been completed.

Barfield refused to pay the $24.32 charges ($14.50 plus $9.82 for parts), and Brogdon refused to relinquish possession of the lawn mower. The following day Barfield filed suit by a sworn petition, alleging that he was the owner and entitled to possession of the lawn mower, seeking return of the lawn mower and $500.00 attorney's fees. Barfield later amended his petition to allege that Brogdon withheld the lawn mower for the purpose of defrauding Barfield and extorting money from him and asked for an additional $3,000.00 as exemplary damages. No affidavit for sequestration meeting the statutory requirements for issuance of sequestration as set out in Rule 696, Tex. R. Civ. P. and Art. 6840, Tex. Rev. Civ. Stat. was filed.

Rule 696 provides:

> Rule 696. Applicant's Affidavit
>
> No sequestration shall issue in any cause until the party applying therefore shall file an affidavit in writing stating:
>
> (a) That he is the owner of the property sued for, or some interest therein specifying such interest, and is entitled to the possession thereof; or,
>
> (b) If the suit be to foreclose a mortgage or enforce a lien upon the property, the fact of the existence of such mortgage or lien, and that the same is just and unsatisfied, and the amount of the same still unsatisfied, and the date when due.
>
> (c) The property to be sequestered shall be described with such certainty that it may be identified and distinguished from property of a like kind, giving the value of each article of the property and the county in which the same is situated.
>
> (d) It shall set forth one or more of the causes named in Art. 6840 of the Revised Civil Statutes of Texas, 1925, entitling him to the writ. The writ shall not be quashed because two or more grounds are stated conjunctively or disjunctively.

The relevant part of Art. 6840 at that time provided:

> Judges and clerks of the district and county courts, and justices of the peace shall, at the commencement or during the progress of any civil suit, before final judgment, have power to issue writs of sequestration, returnable to their respective courts, in the following cases:
>
> . . . .
>
> 2. When a person sues for the title or possession of any personal property of any description, and makes oath that he fears the defendant or person in possession thereof will injure, ill-treat, waste or destroy such property, or remove the same out of the limits of the county during the pendency of the suit.

Despite Barfield's failure to comply with the statute, a writ of sequestration was issued and served. Barfield obtained possession of the lawn mower by filing a replevy bond. He has since worn out and discarded the mower. Brogdon answered and cross-claimed for actual and exemplary damages alleging that Barfield acted "willfully, intentionally, unlawfully and maliciously" in causing the writ of sequestration to be issued when he knew or should have known that he was not entitled to it.

Trial was held and the jury answered the corresponding numbered special issues as follows:

(1) Brogdon did not agree to repair the lawn mower for $14;

(2) The reasonable value of parts and labor to repair the lawn mower was $24.32;

(3) $74.32 would compensate Brogdon for his damages as a result of the wrongful issuance and execution of the writ of sequestration;

(4) Barfield knew or should have known that he had no right to possession of the lawn mower;

(5) Barfield knew or should have known that he violated the statutory sequestration procedures in causing the writ to be issued and executed;

(6) Barfield knew or should have known of the unconstitutionality of the sequestration statute.

An exemplary damage issue was submitted conditioned on an affirmative answer to Issue 4, 5, or 6. The jury found:

(7) Brogdon is entitled to $3,000 as exemplary damages for the wrongful sequestration of the lawn mower.

The trial court entered judgment for Brogdon for $3,074.32 based on the verdict of the jury. Barfield appeals.

On appeal Barfield contends that jury findings on which the exemplary damage issue was conditioned, i.e., that he knew or should have known that he did not have a right to sequester the property, are insufficient to support a judgment for exemplary damages.

It is well settled that to justify the recovery of exemplary damages, the issuance of a writ of sequestration must not only be wrongful, but procured without probable cause and maliciously. In the case of *Hamlett v. Coates*, 182 S.W. 1144, 1148 (Tex. Civ. App. — Dallas 1915, writ ref'd), the court discussed the requirement for malice as follows:

> Malice is where the facts and circumstances show not only that the grounds upon which the writ of sequestration issued were untrue and that there was no probable cause for believing them to be true, but evidences bad motives or such reckless disregard of the rights of the party against whom it is sued out as satisfies the mind that the unlawful act was willfully and purposely done to the injury of such party.

. . . .

We conclude that Issues 4, 5, and 6 were each defective or improper submissions of a controlling issue necessary for an award of exemplary damages. [The court then concludes that Barfield did not properly object to the charge and therefore waived his right to complain that they incorrectly stated the law.]

. . . .

Plaintiff next contends that as a matter of law Brogdon sustained no actual damages because plaintiff had posted adequate sequestration and replevy bonds. We overrule the contention. The filing of a sequestration bond does not preclude actual damages. On the contrary it guarantees the payment of damages and costs in case it is decided that the sequestration was wrongfully issued. Rule 698. *See Kelso v. Hanson*, 388 S.W.2d 396, 399 (Tex. 1965). The undisputed evidence establishes that Brogdon suffered actual damage in that he lost possession of the lawn mower which he was entitled to hold as security for the repair bill. There is no point of error that the jury finding of actual damages is excessive. There was no objection to the charge challenging the elements of damage which the jury was instructed that it could consider in connection with Special Issue No. 3.

. . . .

After considering the evidence in the light most favorable to the verdict and judgment and in the light of the authorities already cited we overruled plaintiff's contention that there was no evidence that plaintiff acted with malice, ill will, or reckless disregard for the rights of others in causing the writ of sequestration to be issued.

As above stated, certain of appellant plaintiff's points of error are not properly before us. We have considered and overrule each point of error before us except for the point of error presenting his contention that the jury finding of $3,000.00 exemplary damages is excessive. After consideration of the record as a whole, we are of the opinion that the verdict and judgment is excessive in the amount of $2,000.00.

If appellee files a remittitur of $2,000.00 within 15 days, the judgment will be reformed and affirmed. Otherwise, the judgment will be reversed and the cause remanded to the trial court for a new trial. Rule 440, Tex. R. Civ. P.

[The concurring and dissenting opinion of Justice Reynolds is omitted.]

NOTES AND QUESTIONS

(1) *Client Counseling.* Assume that, in the context of a bitter dispute, your client is considering sequestration of goods sold a consumer-debtor. How would you counsel this client? What cautionary advice would you offer? Try to create an informal, mental "checklist" of pre-sequestration considerations.

(2) In view of Barfield's ownership of the lawn mower, why did he not have the right to its possession? What does this have to do with the outcome of the case? If Barfield had peaceably and privately obtained possession, would Brogdon have had the right to sequestration himself?

(3) Cashway's application was defective. In what respect? What does this fact have to do with the outcome?

(4) Of what relevance is the applicant's good faith?

Chapter 3

THE SUBJECT MATTER JURISDICTION OF THE TEXAS TRIAL COURTS

SCOPE

This chapter covers the subject matter jurisdiction of Texas courts in civil cases. It begins with an overview of the Texas court system, and then focuses on trial level courts. Texas allocates jurisdiction among the various courts in a combination of constitutional and statutory provisions that focus primarily on the subject matter of the case and the amount in controversy. The courts' jurisdiction may be exclusive or concurrent; there are large areas in which jurisdiction overlaps. The chapter also discusses two particularly tricky issues involving overlapping jurisdiction: land title and probate matters. It ends with a brief discussion of justiciability and an examination of a statute that may help a party who has mistakenly filed a case in a court that lacks jurisdiction.

§ 3.01 AN OVERVIEW OF THE TEXAS COURT SYSTEM

[A] The Texas Appellate Courts

The Texas Supreme Court reviews questions of law, and has discretion regarding which cases to hear on appeal. It may deny review if it believes that the court of appeals' error, if any, is not sufficiently important to the jurisprudence of the state. Gov. Code § 22.001(a)(6). In a few situations, the Texas Supreme Court has discretion to hear an appeal directly from a trial court order. The courts of appeal consider both factual and legal issues, and must rule on timely appeals from cases in which county or district courts have or assume original jurisdiction when the judgment or the amount in controversy exceeds $250. The Texas Appellate Procedure book covers matters of appellate court jurisdiction in detail.

[B] A Simplified Description of the Texas Trial Courts

Texas has four primary types of trial courts: 1) district courts; 2) county courts; 3) justice courts; and 4) statutory county courts (also called legislative county courts or county courts at law). The first three are established by the Texas Constitution, although the legislature has the power to vary the constitutional pattern. The Texas legislature created the statutory county courts, often on a county-by-county basis. The table below shows the most common jurisdictional range for each type of court, but in practice it can vary substantially. We will consider the jurisdiction of each type of court in detail in the sections that follow.

As the table shows, the amount in controversy is the main factor that determines a court's subject matter jurisdiction. However, jurisdiction over certain categories of cases is given to specific courts regardless of the amount in controversy. Also notice the large areas in which the jurisdiction of two or more courts overlap. When this is the case, the plaintiff may choose to file suit in any of the jurisdictionally proper courts.

SUBJECT MATTER JURISDICTION OF THE TEXAS TRIAL COURTS SUMMARY OF COMMON PROVISIONS

Court	General AIC Range	Jurisdiction Granted	Jurisdiction Denied
Justice Courts	.01-10,000.00 (excluding interest)	Forcible entry and detainer (FED); deed restrictions	suit in behalf of the state to recover a penalty etc; divorce; slander or defamation; title to land; enforcement of a lien on land. No injunctions
Small Claims Courts (same judge as Justice Courts)	.01-10,000.00	recovery of money	suits by assignees of a claim; persons primarily engaged in the business of loaning money at interest; and collection agencies
Constitutional County Courts	200.01-10,000 (excluding interest)	appeals from justice courts over $250; often probate (uncontested); all writs	slander or defamation; enforcement of a lien on land; escheat; divorce; forfeiture of a corporate charter; trial of the right to property valued at $500 or more and levied on under a writ of execution, sequestration, or attachment; suit for the recovery of land
County Courts at Law	200.01-100,000 (excluding interest eo nomine, statutory or punitive damages and penalties, and attorney's fees)	all jurisdiction of constitutional county courts; appeal from justice courts; workers' comp. appeals; probate; eminent domain; family law	slander or defamation; enforcement of a lien on land; escheat; divorce; forfeiture of a corporate charter; trial of the right to property valued at $500 or more and levied on under a writ of execution, sequestration, or attachment; suit for the recovery of land
District Courts	500.01(?) and up (excluding interest)	residual; see exclusions from other courts	

§ 3.02 CONSTITUTIONAL AND STATUTORY PROVISIONS: AN OVERVIEW

The Texas Constitution gives the legislature great power to create and change the jurisdiction of the Texas courts. Article 5, section 1 provides that "[t]he judicial power of this State of Texas shall be vested in one Supreme Court, in one Court of Criminal Appeals, in Courts of Appeals, in District Courts, in County Courts, in Commissioners Courts,* in Courts of Justices of the Peace, and in such other courts as may be provided by law." It goes on to give the legislature permission to "establish such other courts as it may deem necessary and prescribe the jurisdiction and organization thereof, and may conform the jurisdiction of the district and other inferior courts thereto." This broad grant of power eliminates the need to seek a state constitutional amendment every time court jurisdiction changes. However, it means that it is imperative to check the statutes governing particular counties when deciding issues of subject matter jurisdiction. To add to the confusion, the Constitution defines the jurisdiction of the district courts, which are the state's primary courts of general jurisdiction, by process of elimination:

> District Court jurisdiction consists of exclusive, appellate, and original jurisdiction of all actions, proceedings, and remedies, except in cases where exclusive, appellate, or original jurisdiction may be conferred by this Constitution or other law on some other court, tribunal, or administrative body. District Court judges shall have the power to issue writs necessary to enforce their jurisdiction.

It was undoubtedly a mistake to include a comma after the second "exclusive." Read literally, the district courts would only have jurisdiction when no other court has jurisdiction. Read without the comma, on the other hand, district courts have jurisdiction whenever no other court or body has exclusive jurisdiction.

Because the jurisdiction of the district courts is defined by elimination, we will look at each type of trial court, beginning with the lower courts and working up to the district courts.

[A] Justice Courts

Read the following provisions describing the powers of the Justice Courts:

Texas Constitution Article 5 § 19

Justice of the peace courts shall have . . . exclusive jurisdiction in civil matters where the amount in controversy is two hundred dollars or less, and such other jurisdiction as may be provided by law.

Government Code § 27.031

(a) In addition to the jurisdiction and powers provided by the constitution and other law, the justice court has original jurisdiction of:

---

* Commissioners Courts are not really courts but rather county legislative branches.

(1) civil matters in which exclusive jurisdiction is not in the district or county court and in which the amount in controversy is not more than $10,000, exclusive of interest;

(2) cases of forcible entry and detainer; and

(3) foreclosure of mortgages and enforcement of liens on personal property in cases in which the amount in controversy is otherwise within the justice court's jurisdiction.

(b) A justice court does not have jurisdiction of:

(1) a suit in behalf of the state to recover a penalty, forfeiture, or escheat;

(2) a suit for divorce;

(3) a suit to recover damages for slander or defamation of character;

(4) a suit for trial of title to land; or

(5) a suit for the enforcement of a lien on land.

Government Code § 27.032

A justice of the peace may issue writs of attachment, garnishment, and sequestration within the justice's jurisdiction in the same manner as judges and clerks of the district and county courts.

---

[1] Justice Court Jurisdiction and Powers

As you can see from the above provisions, unless another court has been granted jurisdiction over the subject matter of a case, justice courts have exclusive original jurisdiction over civil cases when the amount in controversy is $200 or less. Tex. Const. art. 5, § 19. The justice courts share concurrent original jurisdiction with the county courts in civil cases in which the amount in controversy exceeds $200 but does not exceed $10,000, exclusive of interest, and with district courts in civil cases in which the amount in controversy exceeds $500 but does not exceed $10,000, exclusive of interest. *See* Tex. Const. art. 5, §§ 8, 16, 19; Gov. C. §§ 26.042(a), 27.031(a)(1). The 2007 amendments to statutes governing the justice courts also provides that "[a] corporation need not be represented by an attorney in justice court," thus, for example, allowing landlords to be represented by leasing agents, and creditors to be represented by non-lawyers in collection matters for amounts under $10,000. Gov. C. § 27.031(c) (effective in cases filed on or after September 1, 2007).

Justice courts have original jurisdiction over forcible entry and detainer cases (i.e., a special kind of speedy action designed to evict tenants, in which the issue is the right of possession but in which title is not in issue). *See* Gov. C. § 27.031(a)(2), (b)(4). The justice courts' jurisdiction over forcible entry and detainer actions exists regardless of the value of the land and occasionally a large commercial lease involving millions of dollars becomes the basis of a detainer action in a justice court. A claim for unpaid rent or other damages is not part of the claim for possession, therefore the rent or damages sought must be within the jurisdiction of the court.

Even for matters within their jurisdiction, the powers of the Justices of the Peace are somewhat limited. They can foreclose liens, but only liens on *personal* property. Similarly, the justice courts may issue writs of attachment, garnishment, and sequestration in cases otherwise within their jurisdiction (Gov. C. § 27.032) but have no authority to issue writs of mandamus or injunction.

Justice courts also have the power to hear "suits relating to enforcement of a deed restriction of a residential subdivision that does not concern a structural change to a dwelling." The justice courts' jurisdiction is concurrent with the district court, and exists "regardless of amount in controversy." In 1999, the legislature amended the statute, adding a new provision that states: "Nothing in this section authorizes a justice of the peace to grant a writ of injunction." Gov. C. § 27.034(j). Because justice courts do not generally have the power to issue writs of injunction, the result is that the justice courts can hear these deed restriction cases but cannot grant injunctive relief. How, then, will they serve the purpose of providing a speedy and inexpensive method for enforcing deed restrictions?

The Government Code also contains provisions providing that the justice courts do *not* have jurisdiction over certain matters. Justice courts are expressly denied jurisdiction of suits on behalf of the state to recover penalties, forfeitures and escheats; suits for divorce; suits to recover damages for slander or defamation of character; suits for the trial of title of land; and suits for the enforcement of liens on land. Gov. C. § 27.031(b). This rule effectively grants jurisdiction to the district court in these matters.

[2] Small Claims Courts

Another unusual feature of the justice courts is that the same judges also preside over small claims courts. Gov. C. §§ 28.001–28.002. The small claims court has concurrent jurisdiction with the justice court in actions by any person for the recovery of money in which the amount involved, exclusive of costs, does not exceed $10,000. Gov. C. § 28.003. A plaintiff must therefore choose whether to file the plaintiff's case as a small claims case or a justice court case. While there are some procedural differences between the two courts, their operation is very similar. Justice Hecht described the origin and nature of the small claims courts in a recent Texas Supreme Court opinion:

> The Small Claims Court Act was enacted in 1953 and has since been recodified and amended . . . . The purpose of the Act, according to the Legislature, was to address "the fact that many citizens of the State of Texas are now in effect denied justice because of the present expense and delay of litigation when their claims involve small sums of money," but it is doubtful whether the Act did much to facilitate the adjudication of small claims already being handled by the same justices of the peace in the justice courts. The Act prescribed procedures that are less extensive than the rules applicable in justice courts but not appreciably simpler in actual practice. For example, the Act permits an action to be commenced by filing a simple, sworn statement, but does not permit oral pleadings, which are

standard in justice court. Discovery is permitted in justice court, and while it was not expressly permitted at first in small claims courts, it is now. Perhaps the most significant difference between the two courts was the Act's admonition, inapplicable in justice court, that:

"In every case before the Small Claims Court, it shall be the duty of the judge to develop all of the facts in the particular case. In the exercise of this duty, the judge may propound any question of any witness or party to the suit or upon his own motion may summon any party to appear as witness in the suit as, in the discretion of the judge, appears necessary to effect a correct judgment and speedily dispose of such case . . . ."

This is in contrast to cases holding that, although a trial judge may examine a witness during a bench trial, a trial judge should not examine witnesses who are testifying before a jury. A jury trial may be demanded in either court.

Sultan v. Mathew, 178 S.W.3d 747, 753, 755 (Tex. 2005) (Hecht, J., dissenting).

There are further limits on small claims court jurisdiction. It can only hear actions for the recovery of money. Suits by the assignees of a claim, by persons primarily engaged in the business of loaning money at interest, and by collection agencies are excluded. In addition, the justice of the peace while acting as the judge of the small claims court cannot issue writs of attachment or sequestration. For a very helpful discussion choosing between justice and small claims courts, see the website for the Collin County Justices of the Peace, www.co.collin.tx.us/justices_peace/civil.jsp#1 (Civil and Small Claims).

[B] Constitutional County Courts

Read the following provisions concerning the power of the constitutional county courts:

Gov. C. § 26.042. *Civil Jurisdiction*

(a) A county court has concurrent jurisdiction with the justice courts in civil cases in which the matter in controversy exceeds $200 in value but does not exceed $10,000, exclusive of interest . . .

(d) A county court has concurrent jurisdiction with the district court in civil cases in which the matter in controversy exceeds $500 but does not exceed $10,000, exclusive of interest.

(e) A county court has appellate jurisdiction in civil cases over which the justice courts have original jurisdiction in cases in which the judgment appealed from or the amount in controversy exceeds $250, exclusive of costs.

Gov. C. § 26.043. *Civil Matters in Which County Court is Without Jurisdiction*

A county court does not have jurisdiction in:

(1) a suit to recover damages for slander or defamation of character;

(2) a suit for the enforcement of a lien on land;

(3) a suit in behalf of the state for escheat;

(4) a suit for divorce;

(5) a suit for the forfeiture of a corporate charter;

(6) a suit for the trial of the right to property valued at $500 or more and levied on under a writ of execution, sequestration, or attachment;

(7) an eminent domain case; or

(8) a suit for the recovery of land.

Gov. C. § 26.051. *Writ Power*

A county judge, in either term time or vacation, may grant writs of mandamus, injunction, sequestration, attachment, garnishment, certiorari, and supersedeas and all other writs necessary to the enforcement of the court's jurisdiction.

C.P.R.C. § 51.001. *Appeal From Justice Court to County or District Court*

(a) In a case tried in justice court in which the judgment or amount in controversy exceeds $250, exclusive of costs, or in which the appeal is expressly provided by law, a party to a final judgment may appeal to the county court.

(b) In a county in which the civil jurisdiction of the county court has been transferred to the district court, a party to a final judgment in a case covered by this section may appeal to the district court.

Certain counties have varied the jurisdiction of their county courts by statute. For example:

Gov. C. § 26.104. *Aransas County*

The County Court of Aransas County has no probate, juvenile, civil, or criminal jurisdiction.

Gov. C. § 26.111. *Bastrop County*

(a) If the county judge is licensed to practice law in this state, the County Court of Bastrop County has jurisdiction concurrent with the County Court at Law of Bastrop County over all causes and proceedings, civil and criminal, juvenile and probate, original and appellate, over which by the constitution and general laws of this state county courts have jurisdiction.

(b) If the county judge is not licensed to practice law in this state, the County Court of Bastrop County has concurrent jurisdiction with the county court at law only in probate proceedings, administrations of estates, guardianship proceedings, mental illness proceedings, and juvenile jurisdiction as provided by Section 26.042(b).

Constitutional county courts (to be distinguished from statutory county courts) occupy the next rung on the trial court ladder. The Texas Constitution provides that "[t]he County Court has jurisdiction as provided by law." TEX. CONST. art. 5, § 16. This constitutional provision has been implemented by statutes contained in the Government Code. These courts usually have jurisdiction in cases in which the amount in controversy is $200.01 through $10,000. Unless a cause is specifically assigned to another court because of its subject matter, a constitutional county court has concurrent jurisdiction:

1. with the justice courts in civil cases in which the amount in controversy exceeds $200 but does not exceed $10,000, exclusive of interest, and
2. with the district court in civil cases in which the amount in controversy exceeds $500 but does not exceed $10,000, exclusive of interest.

See GOV. C. §§ 26.042(a), (d), 27.031(a)(1). A county court has civil appellate jurisdiction over cases arising in the justice courts or small claims court when the judgment rendered exceeds $250, exclusive of costs. Review is by a trial de novo. *See* TEX. CONST. art. 5, § 16; C.P.R.C. § 51.001; GOV. C. § 28.052.

Constitutional county courts have limited probate jurisdiction in many counties, but ordinarily these courts do not have authority to resolve contested probate matters. Probate jurisdiction is summarized in [E][2], *below*.

A constitutional county court may issue writs of injunction, mandamus, certiorari, and all other writs necessary to enforce its jurisdiction. *See* TEX. CONST. art. 5, § 16; GOV. C. §§ 26.044, 26.051; C.P.R.C. §§ 61.021, 62.021, 63.002, 65.021.

The statutes governing the constitutional county courts also contain a list of cases over which those courts do *not* have jurisdiction. Constitutional county courts have no jurisdiction in (1) a suit to recover damages for slander or defamation of character; (2) a suit for the enforcement of a lien on land; (3) a suit in behalf of the state for escheat; (4) a suit for divorce; (5) a suit for the forfeiture of a corporate charter; (6) a suit for the trial of the right to property valued at $500 or more and levied on under a writ of execution, sequestration, or attachment; (7) an eminent domain case; or (8) a suit for the recovery of land. GOV. C. § 26.043. Once again, this withholding of jurisdiction from the county court becomes a grant of jurisdiction to the district courts.

The legislature, on a county-by-county basis, has also added to or subtracted from the jurisdiction of the courts in particular counties. See, for example, the provisions regarding Aransas and Bastrop County printed above. To get a better feel for the variations throughout the state, browse sections 26.101 through 26.354 to find the provisions for other counties.

[C] Statutory Courts

The above discussion deals primarily with the constitutional jurisdictional scheme. The following subsections pertain to statutory county courts (which are sometimes referred to as "county courts at law" or "legislative county courts"), statutory probate courts, and family district courts created by the Texas legislature pursuant to its constitutional authorization. *See* TEX. CONST. art. 5, § 1, as well as statutory alteration of the constitutional jurisdictional pattern.

[1] Statutory Courts Exercising District Court Jurisdiction

The Texas Supreme Court has held that the legislature may not restrict the jurisdiction of a district court. *Lord v. Clayton*, 352 S.W.2d 718, 721–22 (1961). On the other hand, the constitutional power to establish "other courts" permits the creation of statutory district courts with limited jurisdiction. *See Cook v. Nelius*, 498 S.W.2d 455 (Tex. Civ. App. — Houston [1st Dist.] 1973, no writ). The legislature can also change a "statutory" court into a constitutional district court by increasing its jurisdiction to constitutional proportions. For example, the legislature has established family district courts that have primary responsibility for family law matters such as divorce, annulment, child conservatorship and support and with jurisdiction "concurrent with that of other district courts in the county in which it is located." Gov. C. § 24.601(a). At one time, these courts were called "domestic relations" and "juvenile" courts and had more rigidly defined jurisdiction. Now, as family district courts, they can exercise jurisdiction over all matters within the competence of district courts without impediment, although they will still deal primarily with family law matters.

[2] Statutory County Courts

Read the following Government Code provisions concerning the powers of statutory county courts:

Subchapter A

§ 25.0001. *Application of Subchapter*

(a) This subchapter applies to each statutory county court in this state. If a provision of this subchapter conflicts with a specific provision for a particular court or county, the specific provision controls.

(b) A statement in Subchapter C . . . that a general provision of this subchapter does not apply to a specific statutory court or the statutory courts of a specific county does not affect the application of other laws on the same subject that may affect the court or courts.

§ 25.0003. *Jurisdiction*

(a) A statutory county court has jurisdiction over all causes and proceedings, civil and criminal, original and appellate, prescribed by law for county courts . . . .

(c) In addition to other jurisdiction provided by law, a statutory county court exercising civil jurisdiction concurrent with the constitutional jurisdiction of the county court has concurrent jurisdiction with the district court in:

> (1) civil cases in which the matter in controversy exceeds $500 but does not exceed $100,000, excluding interest, statutory or punitive damages and penalties, and attorney's fees and costs, as alleged on the face of the petition; and

(2) appeals of final rulings and decisions of the Texas Workers' Compensation Commission, regardless of the amount in controversy.

(d) Except as provided by Subsection (e), a statutory county court has, concurrent with the county court, the probate jurisdiction provided by general law for county courts.

(e) In a county that has a statutory probate court, a statutory probate court is the only county court created by statute with probate jurisdiction.

§ 25.0004. *Powers and Duties*

(a) A statutory county court or its judge may issue writs of injunction, mandamus, sequestration, attachment, garnishment, certiorari, supersedeas, and all writs necessary for the enforcement of the jurisdiction of the court. It may issue writs of habeas corpus in cases where the offense charged is within the jurisdiction of the court or any court of inferior jurisdiction in the county.

(b) A statutory county court or its judge may punish for contempt as prescribed by general law.

(c) The judge of a statutory county court has all other powers, duties, immunities, and privileges provided by law for county court judges.

Subchapter C

§ 25.2222. *Tarrant County Court at Law Provisions*

(a) A county court at law in Tarrant County has jurisdiction over all civil matters and causes, original and appellate, prescribed by law for county courts. The County Court at Law No. 1 of Tarrant County also has jurisdiction over all criminal matters and causes, original and appellate, prescribed by law for county courts. The County Courts at Law Nos. 2 and 3 of Tarrant County do not have criminal jurisdiction.

(b) A county court at law has concurrent jurisdiction with the district court in:

(1) civil cases in which the matter in controversy exceeds $500 and does not exceed $100,000, excluding mandatory damages and penalties, attorney's fees, interest, and costs;

(2) nonjury family law cases and proceedings;

(3) final rulings and decisions of the Texas Workers' Compensation Commission, regardless of the amount in controversy;

(4) eminent domain proceedings, both statutory and inverse, regardless of the amount in controversy;

(5) suits to decide the issue of title to real or personal property;

(6) suits to recover damages for slander or defamation of character;

(7) suits for the enforcement of a lien on real property;

(8) suits for the forfeiture of a corporate charter;

(9) suits for the trial of the right to property valued at $200 or more that has been levied on under a writ of execution, sequestration, or attachment; and

(10) suits for the recovery of real property.

(b) A county court at law has concurrent jurisdiction with the district court in nonjury family law cases and proceedings.

§ 25.0592. *Dallas County Court at Law Provisions*

(a) In addition to the jurisdiction provided by Section 25.0003 and other law, a county court at law in Dallas County has concurrent jurisdiction with the district court in civil cases regardless of the amount in controversy . . . .

§ 25.1032. *Harris County Civil Court at Law Provisions*

(a) A county civil court at law in Harris County has jurisdiction over all civil matters and causes, original and appellate, prescribed by law for county courts, but does not have the jurisdiction of a probate court. A county civil court at law has jurisdiction in appeals of civil cases from justice courts in Harris County. . . .

(c) A county civil court at law has exclusive jurisdiction in Harris County of eminent domain proceedings, both statutory and inverse, regardless of the amount in controversy. In addition to other jurisdiction provided by law, a county civil court at law has jurisdiction to:

(1) decide the issue of title to real or personal property;

(2) hear a suit to recover damages for slander or defamation of character;

(3) hear a suit for the enforcement of a lien on real property;

(4) hear a suit for the forfeiture of a corporate charter;

(5) hear a suit for the trial of the right to property valued at $200 or more that has been levied on under a writ of execution, sequestration, or attachment; and

(6) hear a suit for the recovery of real property.

Because the Texas legislature is empowered by the Texas Constitution to "establish such other courts as it may deem necessary," to prescribe the jurisdiction of such statutory courts, and because the legislature "may conform the jurisdiction of the district and other inferior courts thereto" (Tex. Const., art. 5, § 1), the jurisdiction of statutory county courts can be confusing. The basic jurisdictional provision is contained in Government Code section 25.0003. Section 25.0003(a) of the Government Code is an important general provision that provides simply that statutory county courts have jurisdiction over all causes and proceedings prescribed by law for county courts. Gov. C. § 25.0003(a). Accordingly, $200.01 is the minimum amount in controversy for statutory county courts, unless a specific statute provides otherwise. Gov. C. §§ 25.0003(a), 26.042(a). (In *USAA v. Brite*, 215 S.W.3d 400 (Tex.

2007), the court in dictum referred to $500 as the county court at law's "statutory minimum," but the comment is made only in passing and the jurisdictional minimum was not at issue in *Brite*.) Similarly, because section 25.0003(a) embraces the jurisdiction prescribed by law for county courts, statutory county courts have the same subject matter exclusions as county courts, unless a specific statute provides otherwise. *See* Gov. C. § 26.043. Notice, however, that the amount in controversy is calculated differently for the statutory county courts than for the other Texas trial courts — the calculation excludes "interest, statutory or punitive damages and penalties, and attorney's fees and costs." Gov. C. § 25.003(c)(1).

The maximum jurisdiction for statutory county courts, unless changed by a specific statute, is $100,000. This is also subject to statutory variation. Some counties, for example, give the statutory county courts the same jurisdiction as the district courts. *See* Gov. C. § 25.0592. Others change the method for calculating amount in controversy. *See* Gov. C. § 25.2222.

The jurisdiction of statutory county courts is governed by both general provisions contained in Subchapter A of Chapter 25 of the Government Code and by specific provisions relating to particular statutory county courts on a county-by-county basis set forth in Subchapter C of Chapter 25. If a general provision conflicts with a specific provision for a particular court or county, the specific provision controls. Gov. C. § 25.0001(a). In order to determine the exact contours of a particular statutory county court's jurisdiction, the particular statute should first be consulted to determine what it provides about a statutory county court's jurisdictional role in the county in which it operates. *See* Gov. C. § 25.0032 et seq. For those counties for which detailed provisions have been enacted, the specific statutory provisions will contain most of the pertinent information. For other counties, very little information is contained in the specific provisions and, consequently, the general provisions must be consulted to determine a statutory county court's jurisdictional role.

[D] District Courts

Read the following provisions concerning the power of the district courts:

Texas Constitution, Article 5, § 8. *Jurisdiction of District Court*

District Court jurisdiction consists of exclusive, appellate, and original jurisdiction of all actions, proceedings, and remedies, except in cases where exclusive, appellate, or original jurisdiction may be conferred by this Constitution or other law on some other court, tribunal, or administrative body. District Court judges shall have the power to issue writs necessary to enforce their jurisdiction.

Government Code § 24.007. *Jurisdiction*

The district court has the jurisdiction provided by Article V, Section 8, of the Texas Constitution.

Government Code § 24.008. *Other Jurisdiction*

The district court may hear and determine any cause that is cognizable by courts of law or equity and may grant any relief that could be granted by either courts of law or equity.

Government Code § 24.011. *Writ Power*

A judge of a district court may, either in termtime or vacation, grant writs of mandamus, injunction, sequestration, attachment, garnishment, certiorari, and supersedeas and all other writs necessary to the enforcement of the court's jurisdiction.

The district courts are the primary Texas trial courts, and are constitutional courts of general jurisdiction. Article 5, section 8 of the Texas Constitution states broadly that district courts have jurisdiction over all proceedings except those reserved exclusively to other courts.

The lower limit on amount in controversy jurisdiction of the district courts is unclear at this time. For years, the minimum was set at $500. Did that minimum survive the re-codification of subject matter jurisdiction? The most sensible hypothesis is that the court's lower limit is now $500.01. *See Gulf, C. & S. F. Ry. Co. v. Rainbolt*, 4 S.W. 356 (1887) (resolving conflict in former constitutional provisions and setting lower limit at $500). The Texas Supreme Court has hinted, but has not held, that under the current statutes the district court has no minimum. *Farmers Texas County Mut. Ins. Co. v. Griffin*, 955 S.W.2d 81, 83–84 (Tex. 1997); *Peek v. Equipment Serv. Co. of San Antonio*, 779 S.W.2d 802, 803 n.4 (Tex. 1989). The intermediate appellate courts in the state have split on this issue. For example, the Tyler Court of Appeals has held that the $500 minimum survives. *Chapa v. Spivey*, 999 S.W.2d 833, 835 (Tex. App. — Tyler 1999 no pet.) (per curiam) (holding that the 1985 changes were non-substantive). The Texarkana and Beaumont courts, however, believe that the district court minimum is now $200.01. *Arteaga v. Jackson*, 994 S.W.2d 342, 342 (Tex. App. — Texarkana 1999, pet. denied) (minimum comes from Tex. Const. art. 5 § 19 giving justice courts exclusive jurisdiction when amount in controversy is $200 or less); *Acreman v. Sharp*, 282 S.W.3d 251 (Tex. App. — Beaumont, no pet.) (noting unresolved issue and surveying cases).

The confusion likely stems from the way in which the legislature structured the jurisdictional statutes: the jurisdiction of the district court is defined by reference to the jurisdiction of the other courts. It is therefore important that the statute defining the jurisdiction of the county courts provides that *those* courts have concurrent jurisdiction with the district courts when the matter in controversy "exceeds $500." Gov. C. §§ 25.0003(c)(1), 26.042(d). Because the jurisdiction of the county court itself begins at $200.01, the only purpose of this reference to $500 can be to confirm that the district courts' jurisdiction begins at $500. The minimum was not eliminated from the statutes; it was moved due to the legislature's odd choice to draft the statute defining the jurisdiction of the state's main general jurisdiction trial courts in a way that requires constant cross-referencing of other statutes.

Whatever the minimum, there is no maximum jurisdictional limit.

Another line of cases has begun to suggest that because they are courts of general jurisdiction, the district courts are *presumed* to have jurisdiction, at least as compared to a tribunal with more limited power. In *Dubai Petroleum Co. v. Kazi*, 12 S.W.3d 71, 75 (Tex. 2000), the Texas Supreme Court rejected an argument that Texas courts lacked jurisdiction of the wrongful death claim of a foreign national because his homeland lacked "equal treaty rights" with the United States. In dictum, the court noted that because district courts are courts of general jurisdiction, "all claims are presumed to fall within the jurisdiction of the district court unless the Legislature or Congress has provided that they must be heard elsewhere." Next, the court repeated the "presumed jurisdiction" idea in *In re Entergy Corp.*, 142 S.W.3d 316, 322 (Tex. 2004), rejecting an argument that an agency had exclusive jurisdiction over the dispute. The court commented that "district courts are courts of general jurisdiction and generally have subject matter jurisdiction absent a showing to the contrary." *See also Tomball Hosp. Auth. v. Harris County*, 178 S.W.3d 244, 250–53 (Tex. App. — Houston [14th Dist.] 2005, pet. granted.) (jurisdictional challenge to district court based on statute giving jurisdiction to county court).

Certain types of cases can be heard *only* in the district courts. As provided in the Texas Constitution, district courts have original jurisdiction over all types of claims over which justice and constitutional county courts do not have jurisdiction, regardless of the amount in controversy. This concept is called "residual jurisdiction." In other words, *the district court's jurisdiction is ascertainable by the process of elimination.* Therefore, the types of cases denied to the justice and county courts are within the jurisdiction of the district courts. *See* Gov. C. §§ 26.043, 27.031(b). Cases that are not considered to have an amount in controversy and that are not assigned by subject matter to another court are within the district courts' residual jurisdiction.

[E] Shared Jurisdiction, Filing, and Transfer

When jurisdiction is shared between courts of the same or different levels, a number of questions arise. For example, in a county containing multiple district courts, where should an action appropriate for district court adjudication be filed? Can the case be transferred from one district court to the other? What happens when the provisions creating constitutional and/or statutory county courts for a given county result in shared jurisdiction between county courts or between the county courts and a district court, as may occur in the areas of probate and eminent domain? Where should the action be filed? When can the action be transferred? The following subsections discuss the provisions that pertain to the division of adjudicative responsibilities among courts of overlapping jurisdiction.

[1] Adjudicative Responsibility and Transfer: District Courts and Statutory Courts

Exchange of Benches by District Courts.

When a county contains two district courts having civil jurisdiction, responsibilities for adjudication are not located exclusively in one court or the other. Article 5, section 11 of the Texas Constitution and Civil Procedure Rule 330 provide that district court judges may, in their discretion, exchange benches or districts, and may transfer cases or proceedings from one court to another. Civil Procedure Rule 330 provides further that any district judge may in his or her own courtroom try and determine any case or proceeding pending in another court without having the case transferred, or may sit in any other district court and hear and determine any case pending there. The rule applies strictly to district courts. *See G.C.D. v. State*, 577 S.W.2d 302, 303–04 (Tex. Civ. App. — Beaumont 1978, no writ) (Keith, J., concurring).

Court Administration Act; Transfer and Shared Adjudicative Responsibility

The Court Administration Act requires counties to create comprehensive plans for judicial administration. The state is divided into nine administrative judicial regions (Gov. C. § 74.042), and the governor (with the advice and consent of the Texas Senate) appoints a judge to be the presiding judge of each region. Gov. C. § 74.005(a). Each county has a local administrative judge (Gov. C. § 74.091), whose duties include the assignment, docketing, transfer, and hearing of cases. Gov. C. § 74.092(1). The Act authorizes the district and statutory county court judges in each county to adopt local rules to provide for the "assignment, docketing, transfer, and hearing of all cases, subject to jurisdictional limitations of the district courts and statutory county courts." Gov. C. § 74.093(b)(1). A rule "relating to the transfer of cases and proceedings shall not allow the transfer of cases from one court to another unless the cases are within the jurisdiction of the court to which it is transferred." Gov. C. § 74.093(d).

Even without transfer, however, section 74.094(a) of the Court Administration Act provides that district and statutory county court judges may hear and determine a matter pending in any district or statutory court in the county and may sign a judgment or order regardless of whether the case has been transferred. Gov. C. § 74.094(a). As a result of the repeal of a provision limiting a statutory county court judge's ability to act for a district judge in a case in which the statutory county court lacked jurisdiction, section 74.094(a) "allow[s] a statutory county court judge to hear, determine, and sign a judgment in a matter pending in district court outside his court's jurisdiction" without transferring the case. *Camacho v. Samaniego*, 831 S.W.2d 804, 811 (Tex. 1992); *see also Texas Animal Health Comm'n v. Garza*, 980 S.W.2d 776, 777 (Tex. App. — San Antonio 1998, no pet.) (county judge could hear matter outside his court's jurisdiction as long as case was not transferred).

Section 74 also contains transfer provisions that govern other Texas trial courts. Statutory county court judges may transfer a case to the district court docket, as long as the district judge consents and the case is within the district court's jurisdiction. Gov. C. § 74.121(b). In addition, judges of constitutional county courts, statutory county courts, justice courts, and small claims courts in a county may transfer cases to and from the dockets of their respective courts, as long as the judge of the court to which it is transferred consents and the case is within the jurisdiction of the court to which it is transferred. Gov. C. § 74.121(a).

A complete understanding of the system requires a consideration of the Rules of Judicial Administration, adopted by the Texas Supreme Court. Rule 3 creates a "council of presiding judges," which is composed of the Chief Justice of the Texas Supreme Court and the nine presiding judges of the administrative regions. This council's task is to oversee dockets and case loads and to promote such uniformity in local rules as is practicable and consistent with local conditions. TEX. R. JUD. ADMIN. 3.

Rule 4 creates a "council of judges" within each administrative region, which is composed of the presiding judge and all qualified district and statutory county court judges for the region, including retired and former judges. This council's main goals include monitoring case loads and the promulgation of regional rules. TEX. R. JUD. ADMIN. 4.

Multidistrict Litigation

Effective September 1, 2003, notwithstanding any other law to the contrary, the judicial panel on multidistrict litigation, designated by the Texas Supreme Court, may transfer civil actions involving one or more common questions of fact pending in the same or different constitutional courts, county courts at law, probate courts, or district courts to any district court for consolidated or coordinated pretrial proceedings, including summary judgment or other dispositive motions, but not for trial on the merits. Gov. C. §§ 74.161, 74.162(a). Such a transfer may be made if the judicial panel determines that the transfer will (1) be for the convenience of the parties and witnesses, and (2) promote the just and efficient conduct of the actions. Gov. C. § 74.162(b). Administrative Rule 13 governs the transfer of cases under this provision. For a discusion of the MDL statute and rules, see Lonny Hoffman, *The Trilogy of 2003: Venue, Forum Non Conveniens and Multidistrict Litigation*, THE ADVOCATE 74 (Fall 2003); Stephen G. Tipps, *MDL Comes to Texas*, 46 S. TEX. L. REV. 829 (2005).

For advice on strategic use of MDL procedures, see Lynne Liberato & Laurie Ratliff, *Not Just for Toxic Tort Cases*, 71 TEX. BAR J. 98 (2008).

Consolidating Related Lawsuits

When related lawsuits are pending in the same county, there are likely to be local rules governing whether and where they should be consolidated. The Cameron County rules discussed above are an example of such rules. Dallas County's Local Rule 1.06 provides that "Whenever any pending case is so related to another case previously filed in or disposed of by another Court of Dallas County having subject matter jurisdiction that a transfer of the later case to such other Court would facilitate orderly and efficient disposition of the litigation, the Judge of the Court in which the earlier case is or was pending may, upon notice to all affected parties and Courts and hearing, transfer the later case to such Court." It is therefore extremely important to check the local rules for the county in which cases will be filed to determine the treatment of related cases.

What happens, however, when related cases are not pending in the same county? Such cases will be governed by the Multidistrict Rules. The panel on Multidistrict Litigation will decide whether cases should be consolidated, and what court should hear the consolidated matter.

Assignment of Judges

Think about the power involved in choosing a particular court to hear consolidated cases, particularly in mass tort cases such as the one above. Could such power be exercised in a way that might affect the parties' comparative procedural advantages or disadvantages?

Panel on Multidistrict Litigation

The panel on Multidistrict Litigation, which has five members, is appointed by the Chief Justice of the Supreme Court of Texas "from time to time." It has issued orders in a number of high-profile cases, including silicosis cases such as the ones discussed above, asbestos claims, Vioxx claims, Ford/Firestone claims, and cases arising out of a bus fire involving Hurricane Rita evacuees. The panel's orders (including dissents) are published at www.supreme.courts.state.tx.us/MDL_Orders/current.asp., under the name *Multidistrict Litigation Orders.*

[2] Adjudicative Responsibility and Transfer in Cases Involving Eminent Domain and Probate

The statutory county courts are an integral part of the jurisdictional scheme in cases involving eminent domain and probate. Notice the way in which some matters are transferred between county, statutory county, and district court, and sometimes transferred back again. As is so often the case in Texas, the implementation of the scheme will vary by county.

Eminent Domain

District courts have jurisdiction concurrent with the county courts at law in eminent domain cases. The constitutional county courts do not have jurisdiction over such cases. *See* Gov. C. § 26.043(7). Since not all statutory county courts have eminent domain jurisdiction, the statutes pertaining to the relevant county must be consulted. The relevant sections of the Property Code provide:

> § 21.001. *Concurrent Jurisdiction*
>
> District courts and county courts at law have concurrent jurisdiction in eminent domain cases. A county court has no jurisdiction in eminent domain cases.
>
> § 21.002. *Transfer of Case*
>
> If an eminent domain case is pending in a county court at law and the court determines that the case involves an issue of title or any other matter that cannot be fully adjudicated in that court, the judge shall transfer the case to a district court.
>
> § 21.013. *Venue; Fees and Processing for Suit Filed in District Court*

(b) Except where otherwise provided by law, a party initiating a condemnation proceeding in a county in which there is one or more county courts at law with jurisdiction may file the petition with any clerk authorized to handle filings for that court or courts.

(c) A party initiating a condemnation proceeding in a county in which there is not a county court at law must file the condemnation petition with the district clerk.

Probate

A number of different courts share probate jurisdiction, and the distribution of authority varies among counties. The courts involved include constitutional county courts and district courts. Statutory county courts are often given probate jurisdiction. In addition, a few counties have "statutory probate courts," a special kind of court created by the legislature. Statutory probate courts have very broad powers over probate-related matters. Do not confuse "statutory probate courts" with "statutory courts" that have been given probate jurisdiction; they are not the same thing.

1. Counties having no statutory court with probate jurisdiction and no statutory probate court

In counties without a statutory probate court, county court at law, or other statutory court exercising probate jurisdiction, probate cases are filed in the county court. If probate matters are contested, the county judge may (and on motion of a party, must) either request the assignment of a statutory probate judge to hear the contested part of the proceeding or transfer the contested matters to the district court. In such transferred contested matters, the district court has the general jurisdiction of a probate court, concurrently with the county court. Prob. C. §§ 4C & 4D.

2. Counties with a statutory court with probate jurisdiction but no statutory probate court

In counties that do have a county court of law or other statutory court exercising the jurisdiction of a probate court, probate cases are filed and heard in those courts and in the constitutional county court, rather than in the district court, unless otherwise provided by the legislature. The judge of a constitutional county court may not determine contested matters, but may (and on motion of a party, must) transfer the proceeding to the statutory probate court, county court at law, or other statutory court exercising probate jurisdiction. The transferee court then hears the proceeding as if it were originally filed in that court. Prob. C. §§ 4C & 4E..

3. Counties with a statutory probate court

In counties that have a "statutory probate court," all probate matters are filed and determined in those courts. Prob. C. § 4C. Statutory probate courts have extremely broad powers with regard to matters related to estates. Probate jurisdiction as it relates to these courts has become quite complex, and is discussed further in § 3.04[B].

[F] Summary

As a result of legislative action, many counties have unique provisions governing their courts. The reason may be the county's special needs, its population, the particular mix of cases, or simply the county's political situation. As a result, the jurisdiction of Texas trial courts resembles an asymmetrical quilt: confusing, overlapping, and not always consistent or rationally based. The Texas Supreme Court has voiced concern over the difficulties created "for the bench, the bar, and the public by the organization of Texas' several trial courts" (*Continental Coffee Prods. v. Cazarez*, 937 S.W.2d 444, 449 (Tex. 1996)), acknowledging that "confusion and inefficiency are endemic to a judicial structure with different courts of distinct but overlapping jurisdiction." *Camacho v. Samaniego*, 831 S.W.2d 804, 811 (Tex. 1992). One Justice has characterized the situation as a "jurisdictional scheme that has gone from elaborate . . . to Byzantine." *Sultan v. Mathew*, 178 S.W.3d 747, 753 (Tex. 2005) (Hecht, J., dissenting). Numerous committees have been established to make recommendations regarding the structure of the Texas trial courts, but the system remains largely unreformed. In 2007, the Texas legislature came close to adopting a bill that would have eliminated small claims courts as separate "courts," changed the statutory county courts with jurisdiction over $100,000 into district courts, and made other changes with regard to transfer of cases. However, this bill was sidelined at the last minute through a point of order. Many of these proposals, which are sponsored by Texans for Lawsuit Reform, may return in the next session of the legislature.

PRACTICE EXERCISE #2

(1) *Determining Jurisdiction.* For each of the following claims, identify what court or courts would have jurisdiction. Assume that the counties involved have not varied the general legislative scheme. If there is more than one court, specify each. Give the basis for your answer, and if there is another court that at first glance seems to have jurisdiction but for some special reason does not, explain why.

How to Approach Jurisdiction Questions

One method for analyzing these problems is to consider the jurisdiction of each type of court in turn. First, see if the justice court has jurisdiction under Government Code § 27.031. Be sure to look at both the amount in controversy and any subject matter specifically granted to or denied the justice courts. In addition, consider whether the court has the power to issue the type of order that the plaintiff requests. Do the same for each county level court under chapters 25 and 26 of the Government Code. Then consider the jurisdiction of the district courts. If neither the justice courts nor the county level courts have jurisdiction, then the district court has residual jurisdiction under Article 5, section 8 of the Texas Constitution. Even if one or more of the other courts does have jurisdiction, unless that jurisdiction is exclusive, the district court will have concurrent jurisdiction under Article 5, section 8, unless some statute or statutes provide otherwise. You should therefore see if the district court has jurisdiction based on the amount in controversy, and check to see if some other statute grants or denies district court jurisdiction of the subject matter of the problem case.

(a) Suit for $495.00 for defamation.

(b) Suit for forcible entry and detainer on the ground the defendant has failed to pay rent amounting to $6,000.00.

(c) Suit for divorce, in which the community estate is alleged to be worth $495.00.

(d) Suit for an oil and gas pipeline easement in which the owner has refused an offer of $10,000.00. (Hint: What type of power do utilities have to secure land necessary to their endeavors that ordinary citizens do not have?)

(e) Suit by a policyholder against a fire insurance company for $4,000 fire damage to a building.

(f) Suit to foreclose a lien on a parcel of real property.

(g) Suit in trespass to try title and to oust defendant's tenant from the land in question, claiming that plaintiff and not defendant has title to the property. (Note: trespass to try title is a special procedural vehicle used to determine title to real property.)

(h) Probate of a will in a case involving no contested issues.

(2) *Good Neighbors Are Hard to Find.* One of the authors of this book once had an acquaintance who filed suit to enjoin his neighbor from allowing his dog to bark (a true story!). What court or courts would have jurisdiction over such an action, assuming one were inclined to bring it? Why?

(3) *Strategic Considerations.* What sort of strategic considerations would govern the choice of court in each of the following situations?

(a) Suit to collect $750 on a promissory note.

(b) Same as (a), except that the action is based on the federal Truth in Lending Act (for which there is a special statute conferring federal jurisdiction without regard to amount in controversy, but not exclusive jurisdiction).

§ 3.03 AMOUNT IN CONTROVERSY

The amount in controversy determines which court(s) are proper in cases not otherwise assigned to a particular court based on their subject matter. This section discusses the various rules for computing this amount.

[A] General Rule

The amount in controversy is determined by an examination of the good-faith allegations of the plaintiff's petition. *See Texas Dept. of Parks & Wildlife v. Miranda*, 133 S.W.3d 217, 224 n.4 (Tex. 2004) (plaintiff's allegations in petition of amount in controversy control for jurisdictional purposes unless party challenging jurisdiction pleads and proves that plaintiff's allegations of amount in controversy were made fraudulently for purpose of obtaining jurisdiction). The petition should contain allegations indicating a claim for an amount that is within the jurisdiction of the court, as well as allegations that would sustain a recovery of that amount. If the petition shows that part of the damages, such as a claim for attorney's fees, is not allowed by law, that part of the claim is disregarded for jurisdictional purposes.

[B] Increase Above Court's Maximum

As a general rule, when jurisdiction is acquired lawfully and properly, no subsequent fact or event will defeat that jurisdiction, absent bad faith or fraud. Thus, a plaintiff who seeks additional damages due to the passage of time may file amended pleadings increasing the amount in controversy above the jurisdictional limits of the court, and judgment may be rendered accordingly. *Continental Coffee Products v. Cazarez*, 937 S.W.2d 444, 449 (Tex. 1996) (plaintiff testified that increase in damage claim was because "it is getting worser all the time"). However, the trial court may not render judgment in excess of its jurisdictional limit when the damages do *not* accrue as a result of the mere passage of time. *See Picon Transp., Inc. v. Pomerantz*, 814 S.W.2d 489, 490–91 (Tex. App. — Dallas 1991, writ denied) (jury verdict on unliquidated claim was reduced to bring award within court's jurisdiction and judgment was modified accordingly).

Claims for damages that will accrue in the future make it especially difficult to draw the line between damages that accrue due to passage of time (in which the court retains jurisdiction), and a claim, made from the outset, for the present value of future losses. The Texas Supreme Court confronted that issue in the following case. As you read it, consider whether the result turns on: 1) the plaintiff's defective initial pleading of jurisdiction; 2) on the difference between post-filing damages and post-trial damages; or 3) both. Would the case come out differently if Mr. Brite had only included in his petition a claim for "lost wages"? What if he had pleaded that his damages were "within the jurisdictional limits of the court"?

UNITED SERVICES AUTOMOBILE ASSOCIATION v. BRITE

215 S.W.3d 400 (Tex. 2007)

MEDINA, J.

County courts at law are courts of limited jurisdiction and many, including the county court at law in this case, lack jurisdiction over a "matter in controversy" that exceeds $100,000. *See* TEX. GOV'T CODE § 25.0003(c)(1); *see also id.* § 25.0172 (Bexar County Court at Law Provisions). The question here is whether the value of this case at filing (commonly referred to as the amount in controversy) exceeded the court's $100,000 jurisdictional limit. To answer that question, we must decide whether the amount in controversy includes the total amount of the damages the plaintiff seeks to recover, or whether it excludes damages that are uncertain in duration or amount. Because we hold that the "matter in controversy" includes all of the damages the plaintiff seeks to recover at the time suit is filed, we conclude that the case's value here at the time of filing exceeded $100,000 and that the county court at law therefore lacked jurisdiction over this matter. Accordingly, we reverse the judgment of the court of appeals and dismiss the case for want of jurisdiction.

James Steven Brite was employed by United Services Automobile Association (USAA) from 1977 to 2001. In 2001, USAA undertook a reduction in force and terminated Brite's employment. Brite subsequently filed an age-discrimination lawsuit against USAA, alleging that he was selected for a layoff because of his age.

Brite filed his suit in the Bexar County Court at Law No. 7, which has jurisdiction . . . in "civil cases in which the matter in controversy . . . does not exceed $100,000, excluding interest, statutory or punitive damages and penalties, and attorney's fees and costs, as alleged on the face of the petition." In his original petition, Brite pleaded that his damages exceeded the statutory minimum . . . , but he did not plead that his damages were below the $100,000 maximum limits. Although he did not specify amounts, his pleadings did seek the recovery of back pay, front pay, punitive damages, and attorney's fees. Brite's pleading did not use the terms "back pay" and "front pay" but rather described his damages as "compensation due Plaintiff that accrued at the time of filing this Petition" (back pay) and "the present value of unaccrued wage payments" (front pay). [Brite's petition asked for: "damages in a sum exceeding the minimum jurisdictional limits of the [county court]," including (i) "wage payments, vacation pay, bonuses and all other compensation due Plaintiff that accrued at the time of the filing of [the] Petition" and (ii) "a further sum representing the *present value* of unaccrued wage payments, vacation pay, bonuses and all other compensation due Plaintiff for the period following the date of judgment, calculated as of the date of judgment for the losses that Plaintiff has to sustain in the future." *U.S. Auto. Ass'n v. Brite*, 161 S.W.3d 566, 571 (Tex. App. — San Antonio 2005) (reversed by this case) (emphasis added). — Eds.]

Subsequently, Brite amended his petition to state that he sought damages of $1.6 million. He did not specify how much of that amount consisted of punitive damages or attorney's fees, but in a later discovery response, Brite admitted that "his lost wages and benefits in the future, until age 65, total approximately $1,000,000.00."

USAA filed a plea to the jurisdiction, asserting that the county court at law lacked jurisdiction because Brite sought damages greater than $100,000. The trial court denied the plea, and, after a jury trial, the court ultimately awarded Brite $188,406 for back pay, $350,000 for front pay, $300,000 in punitive damages, $129,387 in attorney's fees, and prejudgment interest. The court of appeals, with one justice dissenting, affirmed the trial court's judgment.

USAA argues here that the court of appeals erred in affirming the trial court's judgment because the amount in controversy at the time Brite filed suit exceeded

$100,000, thus depriving the county court at law of jurisdiction over the matter. We agree.

Texas Rule of Civil Procedure 47(b) requires that an original pleading "contain . . . the statement that damages sought are within the jurisdictional limits of the court." Moreover, we have said that "[t]he general rule is that the allegations of the plaintiff's petition must state facts which affirmatively show the jurisdiction of the court in which the action is brought." *Richardson v. First Nat'l Life Ins. Co.*, 419 S.W.2d 836, 839 (Tex. 1967). Brite's petition did not comply with these authorities because it failed to assert that the matter in controversy was  within the monetary limitations of the county court at law's jurisdiction. His petition was therefore defective. He could have remedied this defect, however, by proving jurisdiction in the trial court, as his original petition did not "affirmatively demonstrate an absence of jurisdiction." *See Peek v. Equip. Serv. Co.*, 779 S.W.2d 802, 804 (Tex. 1989) ("Even if the jurisdictional amount is never established by pleading, in fact, a plaintiff may recover if jurisdiction is proved at trial.").

Brite asserts that he established jurisdiction by proof at trial that, at the time he filed his petition, his back-pay damages totaled less than $100,000. USAA, on the other hand, argues that Brite's request for front-pay damages must also be included in calculating the amount in controversy. Because Brite's alleged front-pay damages alone exceeded $100,000 at the time he filed suit, including these damages would mean that the county court at law did not have jurisdiction over the case.

We have previously held that the amount in controversy is determined by the amount the plaintiff seeks to recover. *Tune v. Tex. Dep't of Pub. Safety*, 23 S.W.3d 358, 361 (Tex. 2000) ("It has long been the law that the phrase 'amount in controversy,' in the jurisdictional context, means 'the sum of money or *the value of the thing* originally sued for . . . .' " quoting *Gulf, C. & S. F. Ry. Co. v. Cunnigan*, 67 S.W. 888, 890 (Tex. 1902) (emphasis in original)). Brite argues, however, that we should abandon this rule in favor of another that takes into consideration the probability that plaintiff will succeed. Thus, he submits that the amount in controversy should not be calculated by the damages originally sued for, but instead by the amount of damages that, more likely than not, the plaintiff would recover. Under his proposed rule, Brite asserts that front pay should not be included in the amount in controversy because it was unlikely that he would recover those damages at the time he filed suit. Although Brite sued for front pay, asserting that he would "[i]n all reasonable probability" sustain those damages, he now submits that he was unlikely to prevail on this claim because the front-pay remedy is disfavored by the courts.

The court of appeals accepted this argument, holding that because of the "speculative nature of the front-pay damages," the trial court did not err in excluding those damages from its calculation of the amount in controversy. A dissenting justice disagreed, noting that "[f]or purposes of determining the 'amount in controversy,' the question is not what a plaintiff will recover or is likely to recover; it is what the plaintiff seeks to recover." *Id.* at 586 (Duncan, J. dissenting). We agree with the dissenting justice.

The jurisdictional statute for county courts at law values the matter in controversy on the amount of damages "alleged" by the plaintiff, not on the amount the plaintiff is likely to recover. . . . Because the statute bases jurisdiction on the damages "alleged on the face of the petition" and makes no exclusion based on the plaintiff's likelihood of recovery, it does not allow front-pay damages to be excluded from the amount in controversy. We therefore hold that front-pay damages must be included when determining the amount in controversy.

The amount in controversy in this case exceeded $100,000 at the time Brite filed suit, and thus the county court at law lacked jurisdiction over this matter. Accordingly, we reverse the court of appeals' judgment and, without reference to the merits, dismiss the case for want of jurisdiction.

NOTES AND QUESTIONS

(1) *Unmatured Claims.* As the Court notes, when a court originally acquires jurisdiction, changes that arise merely from the passage of time do not divest the court of jurisdiction. These "passage of time" increases generally accrue as unmatured claims mature. Thus, note payments that were not yet due at the time the suit was filed, but which became due by the time of trial, will justify a judgment in excess of the court's jurisdictional maximum. *Flynt v. Garcia*, 587 S.W.2d 109 (Tex. 1979). The Texas Supreme Court has explained that this result is preferable to the inefficiency of requiring multiple lawsuits to recover claims as they accrue.

Carrying this concept a bit farther, the Dallas Court of Appeals has held that this theory supports jurisdiction over awards of claims that do not accrue until after judgment. In *Standard Fire Ins. Co. v. Stigger*, 635 S.W.2d 667 (Tex. App. — Dallas 1982, no writ), a workers' compensation claimant was allowed a judgment that exceeded the court's jurisdictional maximum, including disability payments to accrue after trial. The court held that "where no question of bad faith or fraud in invoking the trial court's jurisdiction is presented, the court is empowered to grant complete relief on the claims its jurisdiction was invoked to adjudicate, even if such relief requires a judgment in excess of the court's jurisdictional limits. Accordingly, we hold that the trial court had jurisdiction to determine all the issues in this case, including unmatured benefit installments." *Id.* at 670. In *Stigger*, the injured worker had prayed for benefits in an unspecified amount within the jurisdictional limits of the court. Had he requested post-trial benefits from the beginning, would they have been included in the amount in controversy (and thus exceeded the statutory county court's jurisdiction)? The Dallas Court of Appeals' decision in this case was also influenced by the mechanical nature of workers' compensation payments, once liability is determined, and by the fact that Stigger was asserting a counterclaim in a forum chosen by the insurer. Nonetheless, *Stigger* may go farther than *Brite* would allow and therefore be incorrect.

"Front pay," the remedy sought by Brite, is an equitable remedy sometimes awarded in employment discrimination cases to make the plaintiff whole when reinstatement is not feasible. Keep in mind that in *Brite* the Court interpreted the plaintiff's original petition as requesting that lost future income be reduced to *present value*, thus claiming the entire amount of lost wages from the beginning, rather than as it accrued, and thus exceeding the jurisdictional maximum from the outset. Understood in this way, jurisdiction is *never* proper and the problem is not an increase due to the passage of time. Is Brite's claim for front pay different from Stigger's future disability benefits? Is it different from the claim in *Cazarez* that the plaintiff's pain and suffering was increasing as time passed?

(2) *Pleading Jurisdiction.* Part of Brite's problem is that his lawyer did not properly plead jurisdiction. What did he leave out? Would the jurisdictional problem have gone away had Plaintiff's Original Petition sought "damages within the jurisdictional limits of the court" (the language of Rule 47(b) since 1990) instead of "damages in excess of the jurisdictional minimum of the court" (the language often used to invoke district court jurisdiction, where there is no maximum)? If so, is it efficient to undo the work of the trial and appellate courts in order to require the proper verbal formula?

(3) *Disproving Jurisdiction.* Brite's problem may have gone beyond a pleading deficiency. Even when a plaintiff properly pleads jurisdiction, a defendant can defeat that claim by pleading and proving that the plaintiff's allegations of the amount in controversy were made fraudulently for the purpose of obtaining jurisdiction. USAA also raised this argument in the trial court. It presented affidavits seeking to establish that Brite's existing damages alone (including punitive damages and attorney's fees) exceeded $100,000 at the time his lawsuit was filed, as well as that the value of his front pay claims far exceeded $100,000. The San Antonio Court of Appeals concluded that due to factual disputes, USAA failed to prove that Brite's claim to jurisdiction was a sham (although the dissenting justice disagreed).

(4) *Strategy.* Brite's lawyer filed his case in the county court at law when he could have filed it in district court. USAA removed the case to federal court, and Brite dropped the claims that provided federal jurisdiction in order to get back into state court. Faced with an immediate plea to the jurisdiction, Brite continued to fight to remain in the county court at law. In response to a special exception, Brite amended his petition to claim damages of approximately $1.6 million, and the trial judge repeatedly warned Brite that his recovery might be limited to $100,000. Although Brite's lawyer may not have realized it, had his case been dismissed for lack of jurisdiction, Brite could have refiled in the district court where there was no jurisdictional problem. C.P.R.C. § 16.064. *See* § 3.06, *infra.* Why do you suppose Brite was so determined to try his case in the county court at law? Brite was 52 years old when he was laid off by USAA in 2001, after working for them for 24 years. What will happen to Brite's case now?

[C] Non-Monetary Relief

What court has jurisdiction if the claim is not for the recovery of money damages? For example, what of an action to recover possession of personalty? The fair market value of the personalty controls. What of a foreclosure on personalty? The amount in controversy is either the value of the property sought to be foreclosed on or the amount of the underlying debt, whichever is larger. *Walker Mercantile Co. v. J. R. Raney Co.*, 154 S.W. 317, 318 (Tex. Civ. App. — Austin 1913, no writ). Claims for injunctive relief or mandamus, too, may involve an amount in controversy. *See, e.g., City of Lubbock v. Green*, 312 S.W.2d 279, 283–84 (Tex. Civ. App. — Amarillo 1958, no writ) (suit to enjoin foreclosure upon property of the value of $400 could be brought in county court). Remember, however, that it is possible for a suit to involve no amount in controversy, and in that event jurisdiction is in the district court. *Super X Drugs, Inc. v. State*, 505 S.W.2d 333, 336 (Tex. Civ. App. — Houston [1st Dist.] 1974, no writ) (residual jurisdiction).

[D] Included and Excluded Elements of Recovery

Unless otherwise provided by statute, exemplary damages, attorney's fees, penalties, and like recoveries *are* counted as part of the amount in controversy, provided the claim for them is not invalid on its face. *Bybee v. Fireman's Fund Ins. Co.*, 331 S.W.2d 910, 913–14 (Tex. 1960). This rule governs most justice courts, constitutional county courts, and district courts. However, *statutory* county courts exercising civil jurisdiction must *not* include "interest, statutory or punitive damages and penalties, and attorney's fees and costs, as alleged on the face of the petition" in the amount in controversy calculation. Gov. C. § 25.0003(c). [Remember that in certain counties, the particular statute provides a different list of inclusions and exclusions. *See, e.g.*, Gov. C. § 25.2222 (Tarrant County)]. More specifically:

1. *Interest.* The definition of a trial court's monetary jurisdiction is invariably cast in terms that *exclude* interest from the calculation of the amount in controversy. Gov. C. §§ 25.0003(c), 26.042(a), 27.031(a). The definition is deceptive, for only interest *eo nomine* (interest "by name," also called "interest as interest"), is excluded.

a. Interest *eo nomine* includes conventional interest expressly provided for in a written contract or promissory note, regardless of whether or not it has accrued at the time of suit, and most types of interest allowed by specific statutory provisions. An example of the latter is Finance Code § 302.002, which provides that when no specified rate of interest is agreed on by the parties, interest at the rate of 6 percent per year is allowed on the principal amount of the credit extended, beginning on the 30th day after the date on which the amount is due and payable.

b. Interest as "damages" *is* included when calculating the amount in controversy. Interest as damages is a concept that was created when courts wanted to make plaintiffs whole (including their loss for the time value of money), but when no contract or statute provided for the award of "interest" For example, the Texas Supreme Court allowed an award of interest as "damages" in a suit on a contract that did not provide a measure of damages, and therefore could not accrue interest under the predecessor to Finance Code § 302.002. *Perry Roofing v. Olcott*, 744 S.W.2d 929, 930 (Tex. 1988). *But see Great Am. Ins. Co. v. North Austin Mun. Util. Dist. No. 1*, 950 S.W.2d 371 (Tex. 1997) (interest as damages, rather than statutory interest, only recoverable when the contract fails to fix a measure by which the amount of damages can be ascertained with reasonable certainty). The best current example of interest as damages comes in conversion cases, in which loss of use damages can be measured by interest on the value of the converted item.

c. The most common type of interest as "damages" used to be equitable pre-judgment interest awarded in personal injury and wrongful death cases. *Cavnar v. Quality Control Parking, Inc.*, 696 S.W.2d 549 (1985). Thus common law prejudgment interest is also considered interest as damages. Now, however, the system under *Cavnar* has been replaced by statute, and those statutes govern prejudgment interest in wrongful death, personal injury, and property damage cases. *See* Fin. C. § 304.101 et seq. It is not clear whether this statutory interest — like its common law predecessor — will be considered interest as damages or interest *eo nomine* for jurisdictional purposes. It is a substitute for a type of "interest as damages" that did count toward the amount in controversy, but it is now a form of statutory interest, which is generally "interest as interest" that does not count toward the amount in controversy. At least one court of appeals has classified statutory prejudgment interest as interest *eo nomine* that is not taken into account in determining the jurisdiction of the court. *Weidner v. Sanchez*, 14 S.W.3d 353, 362 (Tex. App. — Houston [14th Dist.] 2000, no pet.).

2. *Attorney's Fees*. The definition of a trial court's monetary jurisdiction may exclude attorney's fees from the calculation of the amount in controversy. *See, e.g.*, Gov. C. § 25.0003(c) (governing statutory county courts). However, if they are recoverable in the case, attorney's fees are normally part of the amount in controversy, regardless of whether or not the right to the fees is fixed in a contract or arises by statute. The fact that the attorney's fees may be taxed as costs does not change the result.

3. *Punitive Damages*. If punitive damages are recoverable under the applicable law, then they will be included when computing the amount in controversy for the justice courts, constitutional county courts, and district courts. They are excluded, however, for computations of amount in controversy for statutory county courts. *See* Gov. C. § 25.0003(c).

4. *Passage of Time*. As you have seen in *Brite*, the rule about the tie between jurisdictional limits and increasing demands for damages is easy to state, but not always so easy to apply. If the increase is due solely to the passage of time, the court does not lose jurisdiction. If not, the court does not have jurisdiction to render a judgment in excess of its limits. But when is the difference due to the passage of time? *Flynt v. Garcia*, 587 S.W.2d 109 (Tex. 1979), is a straightforward example. Flynt brought an action against Garcia to recover a debt. By trial amendment, Flynt increased her demand beyond the trial court's jurisdictional amount to include an obligation which did not mature prior to trial. The Texas Supreme Court concluded that judgment for the entire amount was proper, because her additional damages accrued naturally as more time passed and additional payments became due. *Continental Coffee Products v. Cazarez*, 937 S.W.2d 444, 449 (Tex. 1996), represents a closer call. Cazarez sued claiming retaliatory discharge in statutory county court, originally seeking actual damages of $100,000. Seven months later, she raised her damages claim to $250,000, and the trial court awarded her $150,000 in actual damages. In considering defendant's challenge to the court's jurisdiction, the trial court found that increased damages had accrued because of passage of time, based on the plaintiff's testimony that "it is getting worser every day."

5. *Costs.* Statutes defining the amount in controversy for specific courts do not always exclude costs, even when they exclude interest. Some courts count them and require a reduction from the statutory maximum. Some do not. This is another area in which lawyers should carefully consider the Government Code provisions governing the court in which the lawsuit is pending.

[E] Multiple Parties

When one plaintiff asserts multiple claims against only one defendant, the separate claims are added together to determine the amount in controversy. Be careful to distinguish between multiple claims [add them together] and the assertion of a single claim through alternative theories [do not add them together]. In the latter case, jurisdiction is determined by looking to the theory that would yield the largest award. If there are multiple plaintiffs, each making a good-faith claim against one defendant, the claims will be aggregated for purposes of determining the jurisdictional amount. Gov. C. § 24.009. Although the aggregation statute is codified only in Government Code chapter 24 (governing district courts), the same approach is probably applicable to each of the other types of trial courts. *But see Dubai Petroleum Co. v. Kazi*, 12 S.W.3d 71, 75 n.4 (Tex. 2000) (24.009 "may be irrelevant to district courts, where there may no longer be a jurisdictional minimum . . . ").

Claims against multiple defendants are *not* aggregated. When one plaintiff asserts separate, independent, and distinct, though joinable, claims against multiple defendants, the claim against each defendant is judged on its own, and independently must meet the jurisdictional limit of the court.

It is somewhat unsettled as to whether the claim of an intervening plaintiff should be aggregated with the claims of the "persons [who] originally join in one suit" in a way that would exceed the maximum and oust the court of jurisdiction. According to section 82.07 of the *Texas Litigation Guide*, "Intervention should not deprive a court of jurisdiction over a case. The statutory rule is that if two or more persons originally and properly join in one suit, the suit for jurisdictional purposes will be treated as if one party was suing for the aggregate amount of all their claims added together, exclusive of interest and costs. *See* Gov. C. § 24.009. An intervenor's claims, however, need not be aggregated since an intervenor is, by definition, not a person originally joining in the suit. Thus, an intervenor ought not to be able to destroy jurisdiction of the original claim by increasing the amount in controversy."

[F] Ancillary Claims

Counterclaims, cross-claims, and third party claims are normally judged on their own merits in determining whether they present an amount in controversy that is within the court's jurisdiction. Under some circumstances, however, there may be a kind of ancillary jurisdiction over these claims. If the amount sought *exceeds* the court's monetary limit, the added claims belong in another court and should be dismissed. But when the amount sought in the added claim is *below* the court's jurisdictional minimum, the court will normally exercise ancillary jurisdiction to avoid a multiplicity of suits if the court has jurisdiction over the plaintiff's claims and the counterclaim grows out of the same subject matter as the original suit.

In courts with a maximum jurisdictional limit, multiple counterclaims are not aggregated to defeat jurisdiction for multiple defendants each of whose counterclaims are properly joined. The aggregation statute, Government Code § 24.009, requires aggregation only with respect to co-plaintiffs who originally join together to assert related claims against a common defendant, and was intended to allow such claims to be aggregated to reach the jurisdictional minimum. *Smith v. Clary Corp.*, 917 S.W.2d 796, 798–99 (Tex. 1996).

PRACTICE EXERCISE #3

Explain what would be the proper computation of the amount in controversy in each of the following situations, assuming that all courts have the standard amounts in controversy. Also note which court(s) would have jurisdiction of the case.

(1) A suit to enjoin the foreclosure of a lien on a chattel alleged to be worth $750, when the lien secures an indebtedness of $300.

(2) A suit by two plaintiffs against a single defendant, each claiming $3,000.

(3) A suit by a single plaintiff against two defendants, allegedly each owing the plaintiff $75,000.

(4) A class action by a group of plaintiffs, including 6 named plaintiffs each of whom claims approximately $100, with the class including more than 2,000 persons (whose claims are also about $100 apiece).

(5) A suit on a note for $4000 plus $1500 interest, which has accrued in accordance with the interest provisions of the note, plus $900 attorney's fees, which are expressly payable under the terms of the note, filed in the district court. What about the same claim filed in the statutory county court?

(6) A suit to enjoin the operation of a bar based on noise levels and the behavior of the bar's patrons.

(7) A claim for $5,000 in personal injuries allegedly caused by a defective product, in which the plaintiff has two claims against the defendant, one for negligence and one for a design defect.

(8) A suit in the district court claiming $5,000 for conversion of a car by an auto body shop, with a $175 counterclaim for work done but not paid for.

(9) A suit in the constitutional county court for an unpaid medical bill in the amount of $1200, with a counterclaim for medical malpractice in the amount of $500,000.

(10) A suit in the county court at law by two plaintiffs against two defendants, with each plaintiff seeking $40,000 against each defendant for breach of a contract, with counterclaims by each defendant against Plaintiff #1, one in the amount of $60,000 and the other in the amount of $50,000.

[G] Defective Pleading of Amount in Controversy

What happens if the plaintiff never pleads an amount in controversy or that the amount is within the jurisdictional limits of the court? Does it matter whether the defendant raises the issue, or does the court lack jurisdiction from the beginning? Does it depend on whether the case could be too small for the court's bottom limit or too big for its top limit? At what point would a plaintiff finally fail to demonstrate that the trial court has jurisdiction? Consider the following cases.

PEEK v. EQUIPMENT SERVICE CO.
779 S.W.2d 802 (Tex. 1989)

PHILLIPS, C. J.

These cases present the question of whether a plaintiff seeking damages under the wrongful death and survival statutes invokes the jurisdiction of a district court by filing a petition which fails to allege either a specific amount of damages or that the damages sustained exceed the court's minimum jurisdictional limits. The district court held that its jurisdiction was not invoked by such a pleading. Because plaintiffs did not file a pleading properly alleging damages until after the applicable statute of limitations had run, the district court dismissed the suit. The court of appeals, in two unpublished opinions, affirmed. We reverse the judgments of the court of appeals and remand this consolidated cause to the trial court because the original pleading, although defective, was sufficient to invoke the court's jurisdiction and prevent the running of limitations.

. . . .

[Plaintiffs' initial petition did not specify an amount in damages, or allege that the damages sought exceeded the jurisdictional minimum of the district court.] The Peeks amended their petition on December 16, 1986, but made no changes in their defective allegations of damages. In a second amended pleading, filed January 14, 1987, the Peeks sought $3,750,000 actual damages and $5,000,000 exemplary damages against the defendants, jointly and severally. This pleading, however, came more than two years after Clyde's death. All defendants except Oshman's Sporting Goods, Inc. filed motions to dismiss, alleging that the Peeks had failed to invoke the jurisdiction of the district court prior to the running of the two-year statute of limitations. TEX. CIV. PRAC. & REM. CODE ANN. 16.003(b). The trial court granted these motions at various times, and severance orders were signed so that these judgments became final.

The Peeks timely appealed to the court of appeals, which affirmed the judgments of the trial court in two opinions. From both judgments of the court of appeals, the Peeks applied to this court for writ of error. After granting both writs, we consolidated the two causes for oral argument and decision.

The parties here have assumed the minimum monetary jurisdictional limit of the district court to be $500.00. Although recent constitutional and legislative changes call this assumption into question,[1] we will also assume, for purposes of our decision, that the jurisdiction of the district court does not extend to controversies involving sums of less than $500.00.

In this case, all parties agree that the trial court's jurisdiction was invoked not later than the filing of the Peeks' second amended petition. The respondents, however, argue that the Peeks did not invoke jurisdiction by the first two pleadings, and hence did not obtain jurisdiction until after limitations had run. The Peeks, on the other hand, asserted that their original petition did invoke the trial court's jurisdiction, although the petition did not expressly allege that the amount sought was within the court's jurisdiction. In fact, the Peeks argue that the nature of the loss sustained and the claims asserted made it absolutely apparent that plaintiffs sought damages far in excess of five hundred dollars.

. . . .

In the instant case, however, the Peeks' original and first amended petitions did not affirmatively demonstrate an absence of jurisdiction. Under these circumstances, a liberal construction of the pleadings is appropriate. As we wrote in *Pecos & Northern Texas Railway Co. v. Rayzor*, 172 S.W. 1103, 1105 (Tex. 1915): "In any doubtful case all intendments of the plaintiff's pleading will be in favor of the jurisdiction." Unless it is clear from the pleadings that the court lacks jurisdiction of the amount in controversy, it should retain the case. *Dwyer v. Bassett & Bassett*, 63 Tex. 274, 276 (1885). As one court recently said: "[W]e must presume in favor of the jurisdiction unless lack of jurisdiction affirmatively appears on the face of the petition." *Smith v. Texas Improvement Co.*, 570 S.W.2d 90, 92 (Tex. Civ. App. — Dallas 1978, no writ).

The failure of a plaintiff to state a jurisdictional amount in controversy in its petition, without more, thus will not deprive the trial court of jurisdiction. *See* W. Dorsaneo, 1 Texas Litigation Guide 11.02(4)(a) (1989); Newton, *Conflict of Laws*, 33 Sw. L.J. 425, 431–32 (1979). Even if the jurisdictional amount is never established by pleading, in fact, a plaintiff may recover if jurisdiction is proved at trial. Dorsaneo, *supra*, § 2.01(4)(b); 2 R. McDonald, Texas Civil Practice in District and County Courts § 6.09.1 (rev. 1982). This result is consistent with our holdings in cases when a plaintiff has failed to plead facts which state a cause of action. Unless the petition affirmatively demonstrates that no cause of action exists or that plaintiff's recovery is barred, we require the trial court to give the plaintiff an opportunity to amend before granting a motion to dismiss or a motion for summary judgment. *Texas Dept. of Corrections v. Herring*, 513 S.W.2d 6, 10 (Tex. 1974). And unless defendant objects, the plaintiff may proceed to trial, however

[1] The minimum monetary limit was formerly found in article V, section 8 of the Texas Constitution and article 1906 of the Texas Revised Civil Statutes. Both limited the jurisdiction of the district court to controversies involving at least $500.00. In 1985, however, this provision of the constitution was amended to delete any reference to the minimum monetary jurisdiction of the district court. Also in 1985, article 1906 was repealed and recodified with the enactment of the Government Code. In the recodification of article 1906, the legislature deleted the specific description of the district court jurisdiction, including the minimum monetary limit of $500.00. Tex. Gov. Code Ann. § 24.007. One commentator has suggested that a $500.00 minimum remains a limitation of the jurisdiction of the district courts despite its removal from the constitution and statute. *See* W. Dorsaneo, 1 Texas Litigation Guide § 2.01[3][b][ii] (1989). We do not decide this question because it is not necessary to our decision in this matter.

defective its allegations. So it is here. In the absence of special exceptions or other motion, defendant waives the right to complain of such a defect if plaintiff establishes the trial court's jurisdiction before resting its case. *See Olivares v. Service Trust Co.*, 385 S.W.2d 687 (Tex. Civ. App. — Eastland 1964, no writ).

In summary, we hold that the omission of any allegation regarding the amount in controversy from plaintiff's petition did not deprive the court of jurisdiction, but was instead a defect in pleading subject to special exception and amendment. Although defective, the original petition filed in this cause was sufficient to invoke the jurisdiction of the district court. The court of appeals therefore erred in affirming the judgments of dismissal, as the Peeks amended their petition and cured the defect prior to the rendition of the judgments which dismissed their claims. Accordingly, the judgments of the court of appeals are reversed and the causes remanded to the trial court for further proceedings.

Pet AMENDED
Remand new trial

NOTES AND QUESTIONS

(1) *Pleading Defects.* The court holds that the Peeks' failure to plead an amount in controversy was "a defect in pleading subject to special exception and amendment." We will consider the issue of waiver of pleading defects in greater detail in Chapter Six, Pleadings. In *Brite*, the defendant filed a plea to the jurisdiction rather than a special exception and, as in *Peek*, the plaintiff did not amend his petition to correctly allege subject matter jurisdiction.

(2) *Can All Pleading Defects Be Cured?* The Texas Supreme Court states that Brite could have cured his pleading defect by his proof at trial, citing *Peek*. If, based on the types of damages Brite alleged, he could have recovered more than $100,000 from the outset of the case, how could he have cured the pleading defect at trial? Does this mean that had Brite only proved the right to recover $100,000, the court would have had jurisdiction from the beginning?

(3) *Failure to Plead vs. Failure to Prove.* In *Peek*, the court finds that although the Peeks failed to properly plead jurisdiction, they nevertheless established jurisdiction through evidence offered at trial. The result would change with different trial evidence. Suppose a plaintiff never pleads an amount in controversy, and does not allege that the amount is within the jurisdictional limits of the court.

• *Damages proved too small.* At trial in the county court at law, the evidence offered conclusively proves that the amount in controversy is less than $200. In such a situation, the plaintiff has not "establishe[d] the trial court's jurisdiction before resting its case."

• *Damages proved too large.* At trial in the county court, the evidence conclusively proves that the amount in controversy has since filing been more than $500,000. In such a situation, the plaintiff has also failed to establish the trial court's jurisdiction before resting its case.

§ 3.04 COMPETING JURISDICTIONAL GRANTS: PARTICULAR CONTROVERSIES

[A] The District Court Land-Title Grant Collides With the Justice Court: Forcible Entry and Detainer

Read Tex. R. Civ. P. 738, 739, 746, 748, 749.

Justice courts have exclusive jurisdiction over actions for forcible entry and detainer, a special procedure designed to provide quick resolution of issues of right to possession of property. Justice courts do not, however, have the power to decide questions of title to land. Attempts to evict a tenant in cases in which title is also in issue therefore present jurisdictional difficulties. As you read the following case, think about what is actually at stake. Why would a litigant prefer to treat its claim through the FED procedure or through the district court? What is the difference between the cases in which the courts find and reject justice court jurisdiction?

DASS, INC. v. BENJIE SMITH D/B/A/ OAK CLIFF METALS

206 S.W.3d 197 (Tex. App. — Dallas 2006, no pet.)

LANG-MIERS, J.

This is an accelerated interlocutory appeal in which Dass, Inc. complains of the trial court's order granting a temporary injunction enjoining it from evicting Falcon Transit, Inc. from real property located at 523 Pontiac Avenue in Dallas. Dass argues the trial court lacked jurisdiction to grant the injunction, Benjie Smith lacked standing to seek an injunction, and the trial court abused its discretion by granting the injunction. We affirm.

BACKGROUND

Falcon Transit, a corporation owned by Benjie Smith, leased property located at 523 Pontiac Avenue in Dallas from Dass, a corporation owned by Steve McFalls, for thirty months beginning February 1, 1999 and expiring on or about August 1, 2001, for the operation of a scrap metal business called Oak Cliff Metals. The lease terms provided that when the lease expired, Falcon Transit would become a month-to-month tenant.

By letter dated October 26, 2005, Dass notified Falcon Transit it was terminating its lease and that Falcon Transit should vacate the property by December 1, 2005. On January 24, 2006, Smith filed this lawsuit seeking, among other things, a temporary injunction to prevent Dass from evicting Falcon Transit. Smith alleged that when the lease term expired in 2001, he purchased the property located at 523 Pontiac from McFalls and has the right to possession and title to the property.

At the temporary injunction hearing, Smith testified McFalls approached him when the lease expired in 2001 about buying the property and the equipment Smith had leased from Texas Industrial Recycling, a company also owned by McFalls.

Smith agreed to purchase the property and the equipment. Smith introduced into evidence a document entitled "Pending Sale of Land," which was purportedly signed on August 31, 2001 by Smith and McFalls and purported to sell the property to Smith individually. Smith also introduced into evidence a canceled check dated August 2, 2001, from Smith to McFalls in the amount of $175,000, which Smith said was a down payment on the purchase price of the land and equipment. Smith testified the amount of the monthly payments due under the sale agreement was $1450 (down from $2000 per month under the lease). Smith introduced into evidence canceled checks from Oak Cliff Metals to Dass for $1450 or multiples thereof, which he testified fully paid, if not overpaid, the amount due under the sale agreement.

McFalls also testified at the hearing. He said he did not sign the "pending sale of land" agreement and that his signature was forged. He said Dass did not sell the property to Smith. He explained that Smith asked if he could purchase the equipment and if he could reduce his monthly lease payment for the property from $2000 to $1450. McFalls agreed to sell him the equipment for $200,000 and testified the check for $175,000 was in partial payment of that purchase. He also agreed temporarily to accept a reduced lease payment of $1450.

After hearing the evidence, the trial court granted the temporary injunction. The order states:

> Defendants Steve McFalls, Texas Industrial Recycling Company and Dass, Inc. intend to evict and/or remove Benjie Smith and/or Falcon Transit, Inc. from the real property located at 523 Pontiac Avenue, Dallas, Texas before the Court can render judgment in this cause; that if Defendants carry out that intention, Benjie Smith will suffer loss or disruption of his business; and that unless Defendants are deterred from carrying out that intention, Plaintiff Benjie Smith will be without any adequate remedy at law, the loss or disruption of Plaintiff's business will be an irreparable harm, and Plaintiff and/or Falcon Transit, Inc. will be deprived of the use and enjoyment of the real property at 523 Pontiac Avenue, Dallas, Texas.

DISCUSSION

Jurisdiction

In its first issue, Dass argues the trial court lacked jurisdiction to issue a temporary injunction because exclusive jurisdiction in forcible detainer actions lies with the justice court. It argues the justice court is deprived of jurisdiction only if the right to immediate possession necessarily requires resolution of a title dispute, citing our opinion in *Rice v. Pinney*, 51 S.W.3d 705 (Tex. App. — Dallas 2001, no pet.), and that Smith offered no evidence to show he has any right to immediate possession of 523 Pontiac. Smith argues there is a dispute about who has the right to title to the property and, as a result, jurisdiction properly lies in the district court. We agree.

The justice court has original jurisdiction of cases of forcible entry and detainer.

Tex. Gov't Code Ann. § 27.031(a)(2); Tex. Prop. Code Ann. § 24.004; *Rice*, 51 S.W.3d at 708. The only issue to be decided in a forcible detainer action is which party has the right to immediate possession of the property. *See Rice*, 51 S.W.3d at 709. A forcible detainer action is dependent on proof of a landlord-tenant relationship. *Rice*, 51 S.W.3d at 712; *Haith v. Drake*, 596 S.W.2d 194, 196 (Tex. Civ. App. — Houston [1st Dist.] 1980, writ ref'd n.r.e.). Unless there is a landlord-tenant relationship, the justice court cannot determine the issue of immediate possession without also necessarily determining the owner of the property. *Rice*, 51 S.W.3d at 712–13. When the right to immediate possession necessarily requires resolution of a title dispute, the justice court has no jurisdiction to enter a judgment and may be enjoined from doing so. *See* Tex. Gov't Code Ann. § 27.031(b)(4); *Rice*, 51 S.W.3d at 709; *Haith*, 596 S.W.2d at 196.

Dass argues that because the "pending sale of land" document is silent about the right to possess the property, the only document to support the right to possession is the commercial lease between Dass and Falcon Transit. Dass further argues that because the lease shows that only Dass has an immediate right to possession of the property, Dass should be allowed to file its forcible detainer action in justice court while Smith maintains a parallel proceeding in district court to resolve the title dispute. We disagree.

In *Rice*, we concluded a landlord-tenant relationship existed and that the landlord could pursue a forcible detainer action in justice court while the tenant pursued a title dispute in district court. *See generally Rice*, 51 S.W.3d at 705–13; *see also Haith*, 596 S.W.2d at 197 (sales contract stated that landlord-tenant relationship formed when contract breached). But here, unlike in *Rice* and *Haith*, we have evidence the landlord-tenant relationship between Dass and Falcon Transit ended and a buyer-seller relationship between Dass and Smith began in 2001. Consequently, *Rice* and *Haith* are distinguishable from the facts of this case and do not control our decision.

Smith testified that when the lease expired in August 2001, McFalls agreed to sell the property and Smith agreed to buy it. Smith offered evidence that he made payments in consideration of that agreement. According to Smith, the relationship that existed with appellant after August 2001 was one of seller-buyer, not landlord-tenant. On the other hand, McFalls testified he did not agree to sell the property to Smith and claimed the signature on the sale agreement was forged. According to McFalls, there was no seller-buyer relationship but only a landlord-tenant relationship.

We conclude the determination of the right to immediate possession of the property necessarily requires a resolution of the title dispute and jurisdiction properly lies with the district court. *See Rice*, 51 S.W.3d at 712–13; *see also Guyer v. Rose*, 601 S.W.2d 205, 206 (Tex. Civ. App. — Dallas 1980, writ ref'd n.r.e.); *American Spiritualist Ass'n v. Ravkind*, 313 S.W.2d 121, 124 (Tex. Civ. App. — Dallas 1958, writ ref'd n.r.e.). We overrule appellant's first issue . . . .

We affirm the trial court's order.

NOTES AND QUESTIONS

(1) *What is a Title Dispute?* The *Dass* case applies the correct rule for determining FED jurisdiction: if the right to possession cannot be determined without deciding an issue or issues of title, the justice court lacks jurisdiction to determine the possession issue. The attempt to separate questions of title from questions of possession leads to a set of cases that make intricate (and not always sensible) distinctions. For example, *Dass* distinguishes an earlier Dallas Court of appeals case, *Rice v. Pinney*, 51 S.W.3d 705 (Tex. App. — Dallas 2001, no pet.). The dispute about possession in *Rice* followed a foreclosure that the Rices claimed was improper. The court relied on language in the Rice's deed of trust providing that foreclosure created a tenancy: "If any of the property is sold under this Deed of Trust, Grantor shall immediately surrender possession to the purchaser. If Grantor fails to do so, Grantor shall become a tenant at sufferance of the purchaser, subject to an action for forcible detainer." The court of appeals in *Rice* interpreted this clause as agreement to become a tenant at sufferance in the event of foreclosure, whether or not the foreclosure was proper. Under this debatable interpretation, immediate possession went to Pinney because the Rices became tenants at sufferance. The court of appeals held that the justice court had jurisdiction to decide this possession issue.

The question of whether the foreclosure was proper, which itself depended on whether the Rices defaulted, was left for determination in the district court. This later district court action between the Rices and Pinney, which was a title suit, would be the place to resolve the default and foreclosure issues. Presumably, if the Rices prevailed in that action, Pinney would be ordered to surrender possession to the Rices. Does any of this make sense? Is it efficient to require the Rices to move out, only to move back in again if they prevail in the district court? If the court of appeals' interpretation of the language in the deed of trust was not correct, then the result in *Rice* should have been the same as in *Dass*: right to possession turns on an issue of title, and so the justice court lacks jurisdiction to determine possession.

(2) *Incidental Determinations of Title.* Another line of Texas cases deals with title questions that are merely "incidental" to other, more substantial issues within the jurisdiction of a county or justice court. For example, in *Johnson v. Fellowship Baptist Church*, 627 S.W.2d 203 (Tex. App. — Corpus Christi 1981, no writ), justice and county courts ordered a writ of restitution in a forcible detainer action against a tenant, Johnson. Johnson sought an injunction from the district court on issuance of the writ. She argued that the justice and county courts, in deciding whether restitution should be made to Fellowship Baptist Church or Mayfair Park Baptist Church, both of whom could assert title to the property, had impermissibly determined a title issue. The Court of Civil Appeals affirmed the district court's denial of injunctive relief. The court stated, "In the case before us, there was never a claim of title by Mrs. Johnson. The only dispute involving title arose between Fellowship Baptist Church and Mayfair Park Baptist Church. It was not beyond the authority of the county court to determine title on this collateral matter." *Johnson v. Fellowship Baptist Church*, 627 S.W.2d 203, 204 (Tex. App. — Corpus Christi 1981, no writ).

(3) *Equitable Title and Equitable Rights.* Under Texas law, a purchaser under a contract for the conveyance of land acquires equitable title once the purchaser has performed its contractual obligations. *Johnson v. Wood*, 157 S.W.2d 146 (Tex. 1941); *Trans-World Bonded Whses. & Storage v. Garza*, 570 S.W.2d 2, 5 (Tex. Civ. App. — San Antonio 1978, writ ref'd n.r.e.). In *Haith v. Drake*, 596 S.W.2d 194, 197 (Tex. Civ. App. — Houston [1st Dist.] 1980, no writ), cited by *Dass*, the court of appeals distinguished between "equitable title" and an "equitable right" to possession. Because the defendant in the justice court was held to have no "equitable title," the justice court had jurisdiction to determine the question of possession. "Until he has fully performed his obligations under the contract [for deed] Dr. Drake possesses only equitable rights, not equitable title." Disputes about equitable title, however, may not be brought in the justice courts.

(4) *Concurrent Jurisdiction of Disputes About Possession.* A forcible detainer action is *not* an exclusive remedy and does not preclude concurrent actions for trespass, damage, waste, rent or profits. Prop. C. § 24.008. Forcible detainer actions and trespass to try title actions or other actions for possession brought in district court are cumulative remedies. District courts have concurrent jurisdiction with justice courts in trying possession rights to land. *McCloud v. Knapp*, 507 S.W.2d 644 (Tex. Civ. App. — Dallas, 1974, no writ). It is also proper for the district courts to hear title disputes at the same time justice courts are using FED procedures to determine the immediate right to possession.

(5) *Appeals to County Court.* A final judgment of a county court in a forcible entry and detainer suit may not be appealed on the issue of possession unless the premises in question are being used for residential purposes only. Prop. C. § 24.007. The same statute provides that a county court judgment may not be stayed unless the appellant files a supersedeas bond in the amount set by the county court, within 10 days of the signing of the judgment.

[B] Problems With Probate Jurisdiction

[1] Statutory Probate Courts

[a] Generally

As noted above, probate jurisdiction varies dramatically depending on the statutes for a particular county. In counties that have "statutory probate courts," additional complications arise. What are statutory probate courts? They are defined as follows in section 3(ii) of the Probate Code: " 'Statutory probate court' means a statutory court designated as a statutory probate court under Chapter 25, Government Code. A county court at law exercising probate jurisdiction is not a statutory probate court under this Code unless the court is designated a statutory probate court under Chapter 25, Government Code." Chapter 25 of the Government Code, in sections dealing with particular counties, designates counties that have statutory probate courts. As of 2010, eleven counties have statutory probate courts. They are: Bexar, Brazoria, Collin, Dallas, Denton, El Paso, Galveston, Harris, Hidalgo, Tarrant, and Travis Counties.

Statutory probate courts have broader powers than county courts at law exercising probate jurisdiction. In addition, Section 5B of the Probate Code provides that "[a] judge of a statutory probate court, on the motion of a party to the action or on the motion of a person interested in an estate, may transfer to the judge's court from a district, county, or statutory court a cause of action related to a probate proceeding pending in the statutory probate court or a cause of action in which a personal representative of an estate pending in the statutory probate court is a party and may consolidate the transferred cause of action with the other proceedings in the statutory probate court relating to that estate." This power to transfer is also known as "pull down" authority.

[b] Wrongful Death and Survival Claims

The cases in this section show the Texas Supreme Court's attempts to define "appertaining to" and "incident to" an estate, and to establish the limits of the pull down power. This is particularly problematic in the context of wrongful death and survival claims involving the decedent. Before reading these statutes and cases, it is important to understand the nature of wrongful death and survival claims and the identity of the persons who can bring them.

Two separate and distinct actions may be brought when wrongfully inflicted injuries result in death. One is based on the Wrongful Death Act. C.P.R.C. §§ 71.001 et seq. That act provides a statutory cause of action on behalf of the surviving spouse, children, and parents of the decedent, which is intended to compensate them for the losses they suffer as a result of the wrongful death. Each of them may bring the action for the benefit of all. If none of the statutory beneficiaries "have begun an action within three calendar months after the death of the injured individual, his executor or administrator shall bring and prosecute the action unless requested not to by all those individuals." C.P.R.C. § 71.004. Because the statutory beneficiaries generally choose to bring the claim themselves, most wrongful death actions, then, will not be brought by the administrator of the decedent's estate.

The other action that may be brought because of tortious injuries that result in death is a common-law action for damages sustained by the decedent. C.P.R.C. § 71.021(a). If the injured party dies, the action survives to and in favor of the decedent's estate, heirs, and legal representative. C.P.R.C. § 71.021(b). While there are circumstances in which the survival claim may be brought by the heirs, most survival claims brought on behalf of a decedent will be brought by the representative of the estate. *Austin Nursing Ctr., Inc. v. Lovato*, 171 S.W.3d 845, 848 (Tex. 2005).

The survival statute also provides that claims *against* the decedent survive against the decedent's estate. Suit may be instituted and prosecuted as if the decedent were alive. C.P.R.C. § 71.021(b), (c). A claim against the decedent, then, will normally be brought against the representative of the estate. Keep these probate provisions in mind when reading Probate Code sections 4B(a)(1)-(3); 4B(c)(2); 4H(1) & (4); 5(e); and 5B.

Read the following provisions. Be sure to distinguish between the provisions that govern only "statutory probate courts" and those that govern other courts exercising probate jurisdiction.

[c] Probate Code

§ 4A. *General Probate Court Jurisdiction; Appeals*

(a) All probate proceedings must be filed and heard in a court exercising original probate jurisdiction. The court exercising original probate jurisdiction also has jurisdiction of all matters related to the probate proceeding as specified in Section 4B of this code for that type of court.

(b) A probate court may exercise pendent and ancillary jurisdiction as necessary to promote judicial efficiency and economy.

(c) A final order issued by a probate court is appealable to the court of appeals.

§ 4B. *Matters Related to Probate Proceeding*

(a) For purposes of this code, in a county in which there is no statutory probate court or county court at law exercising original probate jurisdiction, a matter related to a probate proceeding includes:

(1) an action against a personal representative or former personal representative arising out of the representative's performance of the duties of a personal representative;

(2) an action against a surety of a personal representative or former personal representative;

(3) a claim brought by a personal representative on behalf of an estate;

(4) an action brought against a personal representative in the representative's capacity as personal representative;

(5) an action for trial of title to real property that is estate property, including the enforcement of a lien against the property; and

(6) an action for trial of the right of property that is estate property.

§ 4C. *Original Jurisdiction for Probate Proceedings*

(a) In a county in which there is no statutory probate court or county court at law exercising original probate jurisdiction, the county court has original jurisdiction of probate proceedings.

(b) In a county in which there is no statutory probate court, but in which there is a county court at law exercising original probate jurisdiction, the county court at law exercising original probate jurisdiction and the county court have concurrent original jurisdiction of probate proceedings, unless otherwise provided by law. The judge of a county court may hear probate proceedings while sitting for the judge of any other county court.

(c) In a county in which there is a statutory probate court, the statutory probate court has original jurisdiction of probate proceedings.

§ 4D. *Jurisdiction of Contested Probate Proceeding in County with no Statutory Probate Court or Statutory County Court*

(a) In a county in which there is no statutory probate court or county court at law exercising original probate jurisdiction, when a matter in a probate proceeding is contested, the judge of the county court may, on the judge's own motion, or shall, on the motion of any party to the proceeding, according to the motion:

(1) request the assignment of a statutory probate court judge to hear the contested matter, as provided by Section 25.0022, Government Code; or

(2) transfer the contested matter to the district court, which may then hear the contested matter as if originally filed in the district court.

(b) If a party to a probate proceeding files a motion for the assignment of a statutory probate court judge to hear a contested matter in the proceeding before the judge of the county court transfers the contested matter to a district court under this section, the county judge shall grant the motion for the assignment of a statutory probate court judge and may not transfer the matter to the district court unless the party withdraws the motion.

(c) A party to a probate proceeding may file a motion for the assignment of a statutory probate court judge under this section before a matter in the proceeding becomes contested, and the motion is given effect as a motion for assignment of a statutory probate court judge under Subsection (a) of this section if the matter later becomes contested.

(d) Notwithstanding any other law, a transfer of a contested matter in a probate proceeding to a district court under any authority other than the authority provided by this section:

(1) is disregarded for purposes of this section; and

(2) does not defeat the right of a party to the proceeding to have the matter assigned to a statutory probate court judge in accordance with this section.

(e) A statutory probate court judge assigned to a contested matter under this section has the jurisdiction and authority granted to a statutory probate court by this code. On resolution of a contested matter for which a statutory probate court judge is assigned under this section, including any appeal of the matter, the statutory probate court judge shall return the matter to the county court for further proceedings not inconsistent with the orders of the statutory probate court or court of appeals, as applicable.

(f) A district court to which a contested matter is transferred under this section has the jurisdiction and authority granted to a statutory probate court by this code. On resolution of a contested matter transferred to the district court under this section, including any appeal of the matter, the district court shall return the matter to the county court for further proceedings not inconsistent with the orders of the district court or court of appeals, as applicable.

(g) The county court shall continue to exercise jurisdiction over the management of the estate, other than a contested matter, until final disposition of the contested matter is made in accordance with this section. After a contested matter is transferred to a district court, any matter related to the probate proceeding may be brought in the district court. The district court in which a matter related to the probate proceeding is filed may, on its own motion or on the motion of any party, find that the matter is not a contested matter and transfer the matter to the county court with jurisdiction of the management of the estate.

(h) If a contested matter in a probate proceeding is transferred to a district court under this section, the district court has jurisdiction of any contested matter in the proceeding that is subsequently filed, and the county court shall transfer those contested matters to the district court. If a statutory probate court judge is assigned under this section to hear a contested matter in a probate proceeding, the statutory probate court judge shall be assigned to hear any contested matter in the proceeding that is subsequently filed.

(i) The clerk of a district court to which a contested matter in a probate proceeding is transferred under this section may perform in relation to the contested matter any function a county clerk may perform with respect to that type of matter.

§ 4E. *Jurisdiction of Contested Probate Proceeding in County with no Statutory Probate Court*

(a) In a county in which there is no statutory probate court, but in which there is a county court at law exercising original probate jurisdiction, when a matter in a probate proceeding is contested, the judge of the county court may, on the judge's own motion, or shall, on the motion of any party to the proceeding, transfer the contested matter to the county court at law. In addition, the judge of the county court, on the judge's own motion or on the motion of a party to the proceeding, may transfer the entire proceeding to the county court at law.

(b) A county court at law to which a proceeding is transferred under this section may hear the proceeding as if originally filed in that court. If only a contested matter in the proceeding is transferred, on the resolution of the matter, the matter shall be returned to the county court for further proceedings not inconsistent with the orders of the county court at law.

§ 4F. *Exclusive Jurisdiction of Probate Proceeding in County with Statutory Probate Court*

(a) In a county in which there is a statutory probate court, the statutory probate court has exclusive jurisdiction of all probate proceedings, regardless of whether contested or uncontested. A cause of action related to the probate proceeding must be brought in a statutory probate court unless the jurisdiction of the statutory probate court is concurrent with the jurisdiction of a district court as provided by Section 4H of this code or with the jurisdiction of any other court.

(b) This section shall be construed in conjunction and in harmony with Section 145 of this code and all other sections of this code relating to independent executors, but may not be construed to expand the court's control over an independent executor.

§ 4H. *Concurrent Jurisdiction with District Court*

A statutory probate court has concurrent jurisdiction with the district court in:

(1) a personal injury, survival, or wrongful death action by or against a person in the person's capacity as a personal representative;

(2) an action by or against a trustee;

(3) an action involving an inter vivos trust, testamentary trust, or charitable trust;

(4) an action involving a personal representative of an estate in which each other party aligned with the personal representative is not an interested person in that estate;

(5) an action against an agent or former agent under a power of attorney arising out of the agent's performance of the duties of an agent; and

(6) an action to determine the validity of a power of attorney or to determine an agent's rights, powers, or duties under a power of attorney.

§ 5. *Jurisdiction with Respect to Probate Proceedings*

(e) A statutory probate court has concurrent jurisdiction with the district court in all personal injury, survival, or wrongful death actions by or against a person in the person's capacity as a personal representative, in all actions by or against a trustee, in all actions involving an inter vivos trust, testamentary trust, or charitable trust, and in all actions involving a personal representative of an estate in which each other party aligned with the personal representative is not an interested person in that estate. For purposes of this section, "charitable trust" includes a charitable trust as defined by Section 123.001, Property Code.

§ 5B. *Transfer of Proceeding*

(a) A judge of a statutory probate court, on the motion of a party to the action or on the motion of a person interested in an estate, may transfer to the judge's court from a district, county, or statutory court a cause of action related to a probate proceeding pending in the statutory probate court or a cause of action in which a personal representative of an estate pending in the statutory probate court is a party and may consolidate the transferred cause of action with the other proceedings in the statutory probate court relating to that estate.

(b) Notwithstanding any other provision of this chapter, the proper venue for an action by or against a personal representative for personal injury, death, or property damages is determined under Section 15.007, Civil Practice and Remedies Code.

PRACTICE EXERCISE #4
READING THE STATUTE

In order to be sure you have understood the operation of these jurisdictional provisions, answer the following questions:

(1) In a county in which there is no statutory court with probate jurisdiction, what happens to a contested matter? After the contest is decided, what happens to the remainder of the case?

(2) In a county in which there is a constitutional county court and a statutory court exercising probate jurisdiction (but no statutory probate court), what happens to a contested matter?

(3) In counties in which probate jurisdiction is shared by the constitutional and statutory county courts, what kind of matters are "related to a probate proceeding"?

(4) In counties with a statutory probate court, what kind of matters are "related to a probate proceeding"?

(5) In situations in which both the statutory probate court and the district court have jurisdiction over a claim, where should the suit be filed?

[2] Defining "Related to a Probate Proceeding"

Controlling Issue Test

For a very long time, the Probate Code defined the jurisdiction of courts handling probate matters to include issues "incident to an estate" or "appertaining to an estate." Former section 5(d) of the Probate Code provided that "all courts exercising original probate jurisdiction shall have the power to hear all matters incident to an estate." The Texas legislature is in the process of re-writing the Probate Code — a project scheduled to be completed and codified in 2014 — and as part of that project the legislature in 2009 rewrote the jurisdictional sections of the Probate Code. In the new versions, the language "incident to an estate" has been changed to "related to a probate proceeding." The parts of the Probate Code that relate to guardianship retain the old "incident to" and "appertaining to" language. *See, e.g.*, Prob. C. §§ 606-607.

The phrase "incident to an estate" has given rise to extensive litigation, especially when controversies not traditionally part of the administration of a decedent's estate were filed in probate courts. The Texas Supreme Court defined the term in *Seay v. Hall*, 677 S.W.2d 19 (Tex. 1984), in the context of wrongful death and survival claims brought on behalf of the decedent and his family in the statutory probate court in Dallas County. After reviewing the legislative history, which emphasized the desire to limit probate jurisdiction, the Court held that the "incident to" and "appertaining to" language included only matters "in which the *controlling issue* was the settlement, partition, or distribution of an estate." Therefore, it did not include wrongful death or survival claims.

The Texas Supreme Court reaffirmed the "controlling issue" test from *Seay* as the correct measure of whether a claim is appertaining to or incident to an estate in 2002. *In re SWEPI*, 85 S.W.3d 800 (Tex. 2002), was an extremely complex dispute involving oil and gas royalties. The Denton County statutory probate court tried to obtain jurisdiction over a royalty dispute on the basis that it might have a collateral estoppel effect on other claims belonging to the decedent's estate. The Court thought this went too far, and held that the possibility of an indirect effect on the decedent's estate was not sufficient to satisfy the "controlling issue" test.

A Different Definition for Statutory Probate Courts

Section 4B of the Probate Code now provides broader jurisdiction for statutory probate courts than for other courts exercising probate jurisdiction, and section 4H provides that certain types of statutory probate court jurisdiction are concurrent with that of the district court.

Somewhat ironically, therefore, the basic definition of incident to/appertaining to/related to an estate no longer governs the jurisdiction of statutory probate courts in wrongful death and survival matters. The Texas legislature has gradually increased the jurisdiction of statutory probate courts. Under the current version of the statute, the statutory probate court has concurrent jurisdiction with the district court "in all personal injury, survival, or wrongful death actions by or against a person in the person's capacity as a personal representative." Prob. C. §§ 4H(1); 5(e). *See also* § 4B(c)(2) ("any cause of action in which a personal representative of an estate pending in the statutory probate court is a party in the representative's capacity as personal representative"). As you read in section [B][1][b] above, this will mean that survival claims, which are generally brought by (or against) the representative of the estate, fall within the jurisdiction of the statutory probate court. In addition, Probate Code section 4A gives probate courts "pendent and ancillary jurisdiction as necessary to promote judicial efficiency and economy." This power would allow a statutory probate court to exercise jurisdiction over wrongful death and personal injury claims that involve the same basic factual disputes as the survival claims.

When a cause of action is "related to the probate proceeding," it usually *must* be brought in the statutory probate court, even if under other circumstances additional courts would have jurisdiction over that type of claim. In other words, the statutory probate court has exclusive jurisdiction over those claims. However, for claims listed in Probate Code section 4H — including the personal injury, survival, and wrongful death claims just discussed — the probate court has concurrent jurisdiction with the other courts, and they need not be filed in the statutory probate court. *See* Prob. C. § 4F(a).

Guardianships and "Incident to Estates"

Section 608 of the Texas Probate Code authorizes a statutory probate court to transfer to itself a matter appertaining or incident to a guardianship estate. The Texas Supreme Court was faced with the question of whether a statutory probate court has the authority to transfer to itself from district court a divorce action when one spouse is a ward of the probate court. *In re Graham*, 971 S.W.2d 56 (Tex. 1998). In *Graham*, Gitta and Richard Milton married in July 1991 and had one child. In April 1995, Mr. Milton attempted suicide, after which he became incapacitated and resided in an Austin nursing home. Following Mr. Milton's attempted suicide, the probate court appointed Mrs. Milton guardian of her husband's person and estate. Later, Mrs. Milton filed for divorce in a Travis County district court; she resigned as guardian the next day. The probate court then transferred the divorce proceeding to itself under Probate Code section 608.

The Texas Supreme Court upheld the statutory probate court's assumption of jurisdiction over the divorce proceeding:

> We must next determine whether the divorce proceeding itself is appertaining to or incident to the guardianship estate. Courts have determined that a variety of matters are appertaining or incident to an estate. *See Lucik v. Taylor*, 596 S.W.2d 514, 516 (Tex. 1980) (holding that suits "incident to an estate" include determining whether property was part of marital estate); *Potter v. Potter*, 545 S.W.2d 43, 44 (Tex. Civ. App. — Houston [1st Dist.] 1976, writ ref'd n.r.e.) (concluding that probate court has jurisdiction to determine whether shares of stock were part of community estate or separate property) . . . . To determine whether this is such a proceeding, we review Mrs. Milton's pleadings. In her original divorce petition, she requested (1) a disproportionate share of the parties' estate, (2) reimbursement to the community estate for funds used to benefit Mr. Milton's separate estate, (3) reimbursement to her separate estate for funds used to benefit Mr. Milton's separate estate, and (4) reimbursement to her separate estate for funds used to benefit the community estate. Mrs. Milton also sought temporary orders (1) awarding her exclusive control of all community property, (2) enjoining Mr. Milton's guardian from entering, operating, or exercising control over the community property, (3) ordering the guardianship estate to pay child support, and (4) ordering Mr. Milton's separate estate to pay interim attorney's fees. Thus, the outcome of this divorce proceeding, which involves child support but not child custody or visitation, necessarily appertains to Mr. Milton's estate because it directly impacts the assimilation, distribution, and settlement of his estate.

[3] Pull-Down Jurisdiction vs. Venue

Statutory probate courts have the power to transfer to themselves lawsuits pending elsewhere that are incident to the estate. This can include cases that are pending in other courts in other counties. Those other cases would be governed by specific venue provisions — laws specifying which counties can hear which cases. What if the statutory probate court is not in a county where venue over the matter would be proper? Read the following case, and consider whether the statutory probate court's pull-down jurisdiction can overcome a problem of improper venue.

GONZALEZ v. RELIANT ENERGY, INC.

159 S.W.3d 615 (Tex. 2005)

Owen, J.

Two interlocutory appeals in the same underlying case present the issue of whether section 15.007 of the Texas Civil Practice and Remedies Code places venue limitations on a statutory probate court's discretionary authority, pursuant to section 5B of the Texas Probate Code, to transfer to itself a wrongful death, personal injury, or property damage case in which a personal representative of an estate pending in that court is a party. The court of appeals held that under section 15.007, a statutory probate court cannot effectuate such a transfer unless venue in the county in which the probate court is located would be proper under section 15.002 of the Civil Practice and Remedies Code. We affirm.

I

Guadalupe Gonzalez, Jr., lived with his wife Jannete and their children in Hidalgo County. Guadalupe Gonzalez was killed in an accident while working at a Reliant Energy power plant in Fort Bend County, near Houston. Jannete Gonzalez initiated an estate administration proceeding in statutory probate court in Hidalgo County and was appointed dependent administrator of her husband's estate. While the administration of the estate was pending, Gonzalez filed a wrongful death and survival action against Reliant in the Hidalgo County statutory probate court. Reliant moved to transfer venue of the wrongful death and survival case to a district court in Harris County, where its principal place of business is located. The probate court denied the motion.

Meanwhile, Gonzalez filed an identical wrongful death and survival action in a Harris County district court and ten days later filed a motion in the Hidalgo County probate court asking that court to transfer the Harris County suit to Hidalgo County and consolidate the two actions, citing former section 5B of the Texas Probate Code. The version of section 5B that was in effect prior to the 2003 amendments applies to this suit, and it provided:

> A judge of a statutory probate court, on the motion of a party to the action or on the motion of a person interested in an estate, may transfer to his court from a district, county, or statutory court a cause of action appertaining to or incident to an estate pending in the statutory probate court or a cause of action in which a personal representative of an estate pending in the statutory probate court is a party and may consolidate the transferred cause of action with the other proceedings in the statutory probate court relating to that estate.

Back in Harris County, Reliant answered in the Harris County suit and . . . argued that section 15.007 of the Civil Practice and Remedies Code rendered venue of that suit improper in Hidalgo County and that the Harris County court had dominant jurisdiction over Gonzalez's wrongful death and survival claims even though they were first filed and remained pending in Hidalgo County. Section 15.007 provides:

> Notwithstanding Sections 15.004, 15.005, and 15.031, to the extent that venue under this chapter for a suit by or against an executor, administrator, or guardian as such, for personal injury, death, or property damage conflicts with venue provisions under the Texas Probate Code, this chapter controls.

[Ultimately the Hidalgo County Probate Court granted Gonzalez' motion to transfer her suit out of the Harris County district court and into the Hidalgo County statutory probate court. After considerable procedural wrangling in the respective trial courts, the central questions concerning the relationship of Probate Code § 5B to C.P.R.C. § 15.007 were presented to the First Court of Appeals sitting *en banc*.]

The court of appeals concluded that section 5A of the Probate Code gives the Hidalgo County statutory probate court concurrent jurisdiction with the Harris County district court over the wrongful death and survival suit at hand, but held that section 5A does not "dispense with the requirement that proper venue must lie for a statutory probate court to exercise its concurrent jurisdiction."

Similarly, the court of appeals held that section 5B of the Probate Code, which gives a statutory probate court discretionary authority to transfer to itself a cause of action in which a personal representative of an estate pending in that court is a party, does not dispense with the requirement that venue of the wrongful death and survival action must be proper in the probate court. The court rejected Gonzalez's argument that the Hidalgo County probate court had dominant jurisdiction over the case, holding "it is axiomatic that a court cannot have 'dominant jurisdiction' if it does not have proper venue."

Finally, the court of appeals concluded that venue was improper in Hidalgo County due to section 15.007 of the Civil Practice and Remedies Code, which states that "to the extent venue under this chapter for a suit by or against an executor, administrator, or guardian as such, for personal injury, death, or property damage conflicts with venue provisions under the Texas Probate Code, this chapter controls." . . .

II

It is undisputed that Gonzalez's estate administration proceeding was properly brought in the Hidalgo County statutory probate court. That court has jurisdiction over the proceeding pursuant to section 5 of the Texas Probate Code, and venue is proper under section 6 of the Probate Code, which governs venue for the probate of wills and administration of estates. Gonzalez's husband was domiciled in Hidalgo County at the time of his death.

It is also undisputed that the Hidalgo County statutory probate court has jurisdiction over Gonzalez's wrongful death and survival action. Former section 5A(c)(1), which governs this suit, provided that "[a] statutory probate court has concurrent jurisdiction with the district court in all actions: (1) by or against a person in the person's capacity as a personal representative." This Court held in *Palmer v. Coble Wall Trust Co.* that this provision, added in 1985 and then contained in section 5A(b), gave probate courts jurisdiction over wrongful death and survival actions. However, this provision does not confer venue. Venue in wrongful death and survival actions is governed by section 15.002 of the Civil Practice and Remedies Code, which provides:

§ 15.002. Venue: General Rule

(a) Except as otherwise provided by this subchapter or Subchapter B or C, all lawsuits shall be brought:

(1) in the county in which all or a substantial part of the events or omissions giving rise to the claim occurred;

(2) in the county of defendant's residence at the time the cause of action accrued if defendant is a natural person;

(3) in the county of the defendant's principal office in this state, if the defendant is not a natural person; or

(4) if Subdivisions (1), (2), and (3) do not apply, in the county in which the plaintiff resided at the time of the accrual of the cause of action.

The accident that caused the death of Gonzalez's husband occurred in Fort Bend County, and Reliant's principal place of business is in Harris County. Accordingly, venue in Hidalgo County was not proper unless some provision of the Probate Code overrides section 15.002 with respect to wrongful death and survival actions. Gonzalez contends that even if she could not have filed and maintained her wrongful death and survival claims in Hidalgo County over Reliant's objection that venue was improper, the 1999 version of section 5B of the Probate Code, which governs this case, gave the probate court unfettered authority to transfer wrongful death and personal injury claims to itself. Accordingly, Gonzalez contends that the Hidalgo County probate court had the power to transfer her Harris County suit to Hidalgo County even though venue in Hidalgo County would otherwise be improper. Neither the wording nor the history of section 5B of the Probate Code or section 15.007 of the Civil Practice and Remedies Code supports this position.

. . . [T]he question is whether section 5B of the Probate Code authorized the Hidalgo County statutory probate court's transfer of the wrongful death case to itself from the Harris County district court despite section 15.007 and the fact that venue of the suit is not otherwise proper in Hidalgo County. We hold that section 15.007 of the Civil Practice and Remedies Code prohibits such a transfer when there is a timely objection.

Section 15.007 clearly curbs a party's ability to initially bring a lawsuit involving personal injury, death, or property damage in a statutory probate court when venue of the suit is not proper under Chapter 15 in the county in which the probate court is located, even if the probate court has jurisdiction to hear the suit. Section 15.007 also limits the probate court's discretion to transfer those kinds of cases to itself if venue is improper under Chapter 15.

Gonzalez's main argument — that section 5B is not a venue provision and that section 15.007 is therefore inapplicable because it governs only when there is a conflict between Chapter 15 and the venue provisions of the Probate Code — is unpersuasive. Section 5B permits a transfer. The transfer of a case pertains to venue, not jurisdiction. While section 5A grants concurrent jurisdiction in probate and district courts, section 15.007 makes clear that the transfer authority granted in section 5B is limited by the venue constraints set forth in Chapter 15 for wrongful death, personal injury, and property damage claims. Hidalgo County is not a county of proper venue for the wrongful death suit under section 15.002, as it is not a "county in which all or a substantial part of the events or omissions giving rise to the claim occurred" or the "county of the defendant's principal office in this state." The venue provisions in Chapter 15 govern regardless of whether the issue is the propriety of bringing the suit in the Hidalgo County probate court in the first instance or the probate court's authority to transfer the case. The fact that suit was first brought in another county does not make venue any more proper in Hidalgo County.

The Legislature chose between competing policy considerations in enacting section 5B of the Probate Code and section 15.007 of the Civil Practice and Remedies Code. On the one hand, the Legislature has "persistently expanded" the statutory probate courts' jurisdiction over the years. On the other hand, the venue statutes were revised in 1995 — the same year section 15.007 was added — in an effort to reduce forum shopping. Section 15.007 thus evidences a policy choice by the Legislature in favor of ensuring that suits involving death, personal injury, and property damage are filed in accordance with Chapter 15's venue statutes.

Because Hidalgo County was not a county of proper venue for the wrongful death suit, the Hidalgo County statutory probate court erred in granting Gonzalez's section 5B motion to transfer. In doing so, the probate court "actively interfered with the jurisdiction" of the Harris County court.

III

With regard to the parties' arguments as to which court had "dominant jurisdiction" over the wrongful death suit, we agree with the court of appeals that unless venue would be proper in both Harris and Hidalgo counties, the concept of "dominant jurisdiction" is inapplicable to this case. The court in which suit is first filed generally acquires dominant jurisdiction to the exclusion of other courts if venue is proper in the county in which suit was first filed. "As long as the forum is a proper one, it is the plaintiff's privilege to choose the forum."

For the foregoing reasons, we affirm the court of appeals' judgment.

NOTES

(1) *Probate Court Venue*. We will consider venue in detail in Chapter 5. For purposes of thinking about *Gonzalez*, however, it helps to know where probate matters are normally filed. Venue for the probate of wills and the administration of decedents' estates is in the following counties, in descending order:

1. The county where the deceased resided, if he or she had a domicile or fixed place of residence in Texas.
2. If the deceased had no domicile or fixed place of residence in Texas, but died in Texas, either the county where his or her principal property was at the time of death or the county where death occurred.
3. If the deceased had no domicile or fixed place of residence in Texas, and died outside of Texas, any county in Texas where his or her nearest of kin resides.
4. If the deceased had no kindred in Texas, the county where his or her principal estate was situated at the time of death.
5. If the only purpose of administration is the receipt of funds or money due to a deceased person or a deceased person's estate from any governmental source or agency, the county where the applicant resides, provided that if someone other than the mother, father, spouse, or adult child of the deceased is the applicant, citation must be served personally on any living

> parents, spouse, and adult children whose addresses are known to the applicant.

See Prob. C. § 6. The drafters of the Probate Code intended that its venue provisions not be jurisdictional. Thus, those provisions may be waived, and probate proceedings in counties other than those specified in the statutes are not void. *See* Prob. C. § 6, interpretative commentary.

The venue provisions of section 6 of the Probate Code apply only to proceedings to probate wills and to grant letters testamentary or of administration. Texas Litigation Guide § 393.02. Other related proceedings, such as suits to construe wills, are governed by the general venue statutes in the Civil Practice and Remedies Code. For negligence-based claims against the estate, including personal injury, wrongful death and survival claims, section 15.031 provides:

> If the suit is against an executor, administrator, or guardian, as such, to establish a money demand against the estate which he represents, the suit may be brought in the county in which the estate is administered, or if the suit is against an executor, administrator, or guardian growing out of a negligent act or omission of the person whose estate the executor, administrator, or guardian represents, the suit may be brought in the county in which the negligent act or omission of the person whose estate the executor, administrator, or guardian represents occurred.

(2) *Distinguishing Between Jurisdiction and Venue.* The court in *In re Graham*, 971 S.W.2d 56 (Tex. 1998), affirmed the power of the statutory probate court to acquire "pull down" jurisdiction over the ward's divorce case. In that case, both the district court and the statutory probate court were located in Travis County. In *Gonzalez*, however, the court held that the statutory probate court's pull-down power is limited by the normal venue rules in chapter 15 of the Civil Practice and Remedies Code. Although the statutory probate courts have *jurisdiction* over these cases, they may not hear them either by transfer or if initially filed in the statutory probate court unless *venue* is otherwise proper.

PRACTICE EXERCISE #5

(1) Sadie Smith died, at age 75, at her home in Eastland County, Texas. In Eastland County, general probate jurisdiction is exercised by the constitutional county court. There is no statutory county court or statutory probate court. The 91st Judicial District Court also has jurisdiction in Eastland County. Where should Sadie's will be filed for probate?

(2) Sadie's will leaves her entire estate to her final caregiver, Buck Benson. Sadie's two surviving children want to challenge the will, alleging that Buck exerted undue influence over Sadie. Who should hear and decide the will contest? What happens when the contested portion has been resolved?

(3) Zeke Jones died. He was domiciled in Cameron County. In Cameron County, both the constitutional county court and the statutory county courts exercise probate jurisdiction. Zeke's will disinherits his son Hickory. Hickory believes that

this will is a forgery, and that his father actually split his estate equally between him and his brother Hunk. Both Hickory and Hunk live in Cameron County. Hickory wants to contest the will. Who should hear and decide the will contest?

(4) Zeke died in a car wreck in Cameron County after spending two days in intensive care. The police investigation indicates that Elmira (also a Cameron County resident), the driver of the other car, survived the accident, and was intoxicated and at fault in the accident. The executor of Zeke's estate wants to bring survival claims on behalf of Zeke's estate against Elmira. Should the executor file those claims in the probate action or somewhere else?

(5) Emily lived in Denton County. When she was driving her motorcycle in Bee County, Emily was in an accident in which she was killed and Dorothy, the driver of the other vehicle, a resident of Bee County, was injured. Dorothy has sued Emily's estate (by suing the executor) in district court in Bee County. Emily's estate is being probated in the statutory probate court in Denton County. The executor, who resides in Denton County, has asked the Denton judge to transfer the Bee County suit to himself. Can the statutory probate judge do that?

(6) Henry, the executor of Emily's estate as well as her surviving spouse, thinks that the accident was Dorothy's fault. He has sued Dorothy for negligently causing Emily's death, bringing both wrongful death (for himself personally) and survival (on behalf of Emily's estate) claims against Dorothy in the statutory probate court of Denton County. Can the Denton court properly hear Henry's claims?

§ 3.05 JUSTICIABILITY, STANDING, AND RELATED DOCTRINES

There must be a justiciable controversy between the parties that will actually be determined by the court before a court has jurisdiction to proceed. A judicial decision reached in the absence of a "case or controversy" is an advisory opinion, which is barred by the separation of powers provision of the Texas Constitution. *See* Tex. Const. art. 2, § 1; *see also Brooks v. Northglen Ass'n*, 141 S.W.3d 158, 163–64 (Tex. 2004). When there is no case or controversy, there is no subject matter jurisdiction.

Petitions requesting declaratory judgments are often given special scrutiny. Texas has a declaratory judgment statute (C.P.R.C. § 37.003), but the courts look with some care to the effect the declaration will have. *See Farmers Texas County Mutual Ins. v. Griffin*, 955 S.W.2d 81 (Tex. 1997) (parties may secure a declaratory judgment on the insurer's duty to indemnify before the underlying tort suit proceeds to judgment). *Northglen*, for example, was an action between a homeowners' association and property owners. Two of the subdivisions (the association represented six subdivisions) were not represented by any property owners, and the Texas Supreme Court held that the trial court did not have jurisdiction to issue a declaratory judgment with respect to those two subdivisions; any opinions as to those two would be purely advisory.

The terms "justiciable controversy" and "advisory opinion" refer to two prerequisites for a declaratory judgment action: (1) there must be a real controversy between the parties; and (2) the controversy must be one that will actually be determined by the judicial declaration sought. C.P.R.C. § 37.008.

The Texas Supreme Court is also permitted to answer questions of law certified to it by any federal appellate court if that court is presented with determinative questions of Texas law on which there is no controlling Texas Supreme Court precedent. *See* Tex. R. App. P. 58.

The mootness doctrine is similar to the justiciable controversy doctrine. If a case or controversy existed at one time, but by the time of suit the requested relief would not redress the alleged wrong, Texas courts (like other courts throughout the nation) will consider the matter "moot" and dismiss it. In *Ben Robinson Co. v. Texas Workers' Comp. Comm'n*, 934 S.W.2d 149, 152 (Tex. App. — Austin 1996, writ denied), the plaintiff-company challenged the Commission's designation of the company as an "extra hazardous employer." The Commission alleged the complaint was moot, because the designation had been lifted before the trial court's judgment was rendered. The court disagreed; the requested relief would effectively purge the designation from state records and reverse the detrimental consequences to the company due to the designation (such as higher insurance premiums), whereas the mere lifting of the designation did not bring such relief. Because removal of the designation did not "leave the Company in the position it was in before being labeled extra-hazardous," the controversy was not moot.

The court went further and suggested that even if the case were moot, it would fall within the "capable of repetition yet evading review" exception to the mootness doctrine. Under this exception, the court will review a moot controversy so as to assure that the plaintiff has judicial review that would otherwise not be available to the plaintiff due to the circumstances of the controversy. In the case of an extra hazardous designation, an employer is required to take certain actions to immediately remedy the allegedly hazardous workplace conditions. Given severe penalties for noncompliance, the result is that in most cases the designation lasts for less than 10 months. If mootness were applied in such a situation to dismiss a plaintiff's claim, the plaintiff would never be able to obtain review of an allegedly erroneous designation. The court concluded, "Because the short duration of an employer's extra-hazardous status renders it nearly impossible for an employer to obtain judicial review while that status remains pending, we would hold that this case falls within the 'capable of repetition yet evading review' exception to the mootness doctrine." *Ben Robinson Co. v. Texas Workers' Comp. Com'n*, 934 S.W.2d 149, 153 (Tex. App. — Austin 1996, writ denied).

Another exception to the mootness doctrine is the "collateral consequences" exception. This exception prevents dismissal when prejudicial events have occurred whose effects will continue to stigmatize helpless or hated individuals long after the moot judgment ceases to operate because such effects will not be resolved by the dismissal of the case as moot. *See General Land Office v. Oxy U.S.A., Inc.*, 789 S.W.2d 569, 571 (Tex. 1990).

Conversely, if the suit is not ripe (i.e., if a matter essential to the claim has not yet occurred or may never occur), the courts will find that there is no justiciable controversy. A court's abstention on grounds of ripeness is also based on the prohibition against issuing advisory opinions. To rule on a case in which the claim depends on the occurrence of future events that may or may not occur "would be the essence of an advisory opinion, advising what the law would be on a hypothetical set of facts." *See Save Our Springs Alliance v. City of Austin*, 149 S.W.3d 674 (Tex. App. — Austin 2004, no pet.) (dismissing because when city changed challenged ordinance, claim challenging former rule was moot and claim challenging new rule was not ripe); *Patterson v. Planned Parenthood*, 971 S.W.2d 439, 444 (Tex. 1998) (holding not ripe for review a suit for declaratory judgment to declare a legislative appropriations rider unconstitutional because the state had not yet implemented the rider and was considering a plan under which plaintiff's funding would not be affected anyway).

The concept of "standing" is also essential to subject matter jurisdiction. *See Texas Ass'n of Business v. Air Control Bd.*, 852 S.W.2d 440, 443–44 (Tex. 1993) (discussion of constitutional bases of "standing" requirement). Standing requirements may also be imposed by statute. *See Bowles v. Wade*, 913 S.W.2d 644, 647 (Tex. App. — Dallas 1995, pet. denied). Otherwise, under the general rule of standing, a person has standing to sue only when the person is personally aggrieved as a result of the invasion of the person's "justiciable interest." Borrowing from federal jurisprudence, many Texas cases hold that whether a plaintiff is personally aggrieved depends on whether the plaintiff has factually suffered the right kind of "particularized" or "concrete" injury. *Polaris Industries v. McDonald*, 119 S.W.3d 331, 338 (Tex. App. — Tyler 2003, no pet.); *cf. Housing Auth. v. State ex rel Velasquez*, 539 S.W.2d 911, 914–15 (Tex. Civ. App. — Corpus Christi 1976, writ ref'd n.r.e.) (citing *Association of Data Processing Serv. Orgs., Inc. v. Camp*, 397 U.S. 150 (1970). A different line of Texas cases equates standing with the existence of a *legally* cognizable claim. *Nobles v. Marcus*, 533 S.W.2d 923, 927 (Tex. 1976) ("Only the person whose primary legal right has been breached may seek redress for an injury."); *Donman v. Citgo Pipeline Co.*, 123 S.W.3d 728, 732 (Tex. App. — Texarkana 2003, no pet.) ("Without a breach of a legal right belonging to the plaintiff, . . . no standing.").

The Texas Supreme Court recently addressed the requirement that a plaintiff must have an injury that is "concrete" and "actual or imminent" in order to have standing. In *DaimlerChrysler Corp. v. Inman*, 2008 Tex. LEXIS 91 (Tex. Feb. 1, 2008), a five-Justice majority dismissed the claims of three plaintiffs suing DaimlerChrysler over alleged defects in seat belt buckles. All three plaintiffs claimed that the "Gen-3" buckles released too easily, creating a danger of injury. However, two of the plaintiffs had not experienced inadvertent buckle release, and the third was not sure whether or not he had. The Court found the possibility of injury too remote to provide standing, and thus ordered the case dismissed for lack of subject matter jurisdiction. In explaining the relevant law, the Court noted:

> For standing, a plaintiff must be personally aggrieved; his alleged injury must be concrete and particularized, actual or imminent, not hypothetical. A plaintiff does not lack standing simply because he cannot prevail on the merits of his claim; he lacks standing because his claim of injury is too slight for a court to afford redress.

2008 Tex. LEXIS at *13 (footnotes omitted). Denying the dissent's charge that they had conflated a decision on the merits and a standing inquiry, the majority held that

"We do not rule out the possibility that somewhere there may be owners or lessees of vehicles with Gen-3 seatbelt buckles that can allege concrete injury. Our focus is on [the three plaintiffs in this case], and they have not shown that they can." *Id.* at *19–20.

Certain areas of the law have specific "standing" requirements. For example, for an antitrust plaintiff to have standing, the plaintiff's injury must correspond "to an injury of the same type to the relevant market." *Roberts v. Whitfill*, 191 S.W.3d 348 (Tex. App. — Waco 2006, no pet.). Thus a business that did not show that a preferential pricing system harmed the market lacked antitrust standing, and the court lacked subject matter jurisdiction over the antitrust claim.

Associations may have standing to raise issues on behalf of their members if its members would otherwise have standing to sue in their own right, if the interests the association seeks to protect are germane to its purpose, and if neither the claim asserted nor the relief requested requires participation of association members. *Texas Ass'n of Business v. Texas Air Control Bd.*, 852 S.W.2d 440, 443 (Tex. 1993) ("standing is implicit in the concept of subject matter jurisdiction").

The "political question" doctrine and the doctrine of "primary jurisdiction" are also concepts followed in Texas. A political question is one that is entrusted to the judgment of a governmental branch other than the judiciary. If a person disagreed with an appointment made by the governor of the state, for example, the person probably could not bring suit against the governor to rescind it (at least if the governor had acted within his or her legitimate political authority).

The doctrine of "primary jurisdiction" is related. It deals with disputes that the law has entrusted to administrative agencies or other tribunals other than the courts for the formulation of the initial decision. The Texas Supreme Court addressed primary jurisdiction issues in a series of three cases. The first case, *Cash America Internat'l, Inc. v. Bennett*, 35 S.W.3d 12, 14–16 (Tex. 2000), dealt with a pledgor's cause of action against a pawn shop for conversion and negligence and the pawn shop's attempt to take the matter before the Consumer Credit Commissioner via primary jurisdiction. The next two cases, *Subaru of America, Inc. v. David McDavid Nissan, Inc.*, 84 S.W.3d 212 (Tex. 2002), and *Butnaru v. Ford Motor Co.*, 84 S.W.3d 198 (Tex. 2002), were both breach of contract cases concerning the power of the Motor Vehicle Board to hear these claims. The court decided that the doctrine of primary jurisdiction is prudential in nature, meaning that it does not affect a court's subject-matter jurisdiction. The court also determined that when faced with agency primary jurisdiction, a court should abate the litigation.

The First Amendment to the federal Constitution also creates a limit on subject matter jurisdiction. Civil courts are not to intrude "into the church's governance of 'religious' or 'ecclesiastical' matters, such as theological controversy, church discipline, ecclesiastical government, or the conformity of members to standards of morality." Matters involving civil, contract, or property rights stemming from a church controversy can be considered, so long as they can be decided by applying neutral principles of law. Applying these principles, the Fort Worth Court of Appeals held that a case involving a controversy among church members should have been dismissed. *Dean v. Alford*, 994 S.W.2d 392, 395–96 (Tex. App. — Fort Worth 1999, no pet.) (controversy regarding whether pastor should be retained was ecclesiastical dispute; court may not intervene despite fact that independent status of congregation left church members without adequate remedy).

§ 3.06 CONSEQUENCES OF LACK OF JURISDICTION OVER THE SUBJECT MATTER AND RELATED PROBLEMS

The rule in Texas is that a court lacking jurisdiction over the subject matter of an action has jurisdiction to do nothing but dismiss. However, given the ambiguity of some jurisdictional grants, it is to be expected that some cases will be filed in the wrong court even when an attorney is well informed and careful. It may take months or years to determine the jurisdictional issue; the statute of limitations may run in the meantime. What should happen in such a situation? The following materials deal with that question.

C.P.R.C. § 16.064. *Effect of Lack of Jurisdiction*

(a) The period between the date of filing an action in a trial court and the date of a second filing of the same action in a different court suspends the running of the applicable statute of limitations for the period if:

(1) because of lack of jurisdiction in the trial court where the action was first filed, the action is dismissed or the judgment is set aside or annulled in a direct proceeding; and

(2) not later than the 60th day after the date the dismissal or other disposition becomes final, the action is commenced in a court of proper jurisdiction.

(b) This section does not apply if the adverse party has shown in abatement that the first filing was made with intentional disregard of proper jurisdiction.

Section 16.064 is meant to help litigants who, in good faith, file their lawsuits in the wrong courts. One issue in the following case is what types of dismissals fall under the statute. Also, in a complex case, the timing requirements can be quite tricky. When does the 60-day deadline start to run in the following case? It may help to make yourself a timeline including the date the cause of action accrued, and the dates on which claims were filed and dismissed.

VALE v. RYAN

809 S.W.2d 324 (Tex. App. — Austin 1991, no writ)

Jones, J.

Margaret Portz Vale sued Vernon McKenzie, Lanny Ryan, and others for false arrest, false imprisonment, and malicious prosecution. The trial court rendered a take-nothing summary judgment on the ground that the limitations period for Vale's cause of action had expired before she filed suit. Vale appeals, asserting that the trial court erred in granting summary judgment because sixty days had not passed between the dismissal of her identical federal action and the filing of this suit in state court. The issues in this appeal are whether: (1) a federal court's refusal to exercise jurisdiction over pendent state claims constitutes a dismissal for lack of jurisdiction under the Texas "saving statute," Tex. Civ. Prac. & Rem. Code Ann. § 16.064 (1986); and (2) the dismissal here was final for purposes of the same statute on the date of the federal district court's dismissal order. We will reverse the summary judgment and remand the cause.

The facts are undisputed. McKenzie, a Temple police sergeant, had participated in a drug "sting" operation. Apparently as the result of a name error, McKenzie incorrectly testified to a Bell County grand jury that Vale was a known drug offender and had received delivery of controlled substances. After hearing only McKenzie's testimony, the grand jury indicted Vale. She was arrested and jailed on November 17, 1982. The following day McKenzie's misidentification was discovered, and Vale was released.

On June 28, 1984, Vale brought suit in federal court against various defendants, including McKenzie, alleging violations of federal civil rights statutes. Vale also alleged, under the doctrine of federal courts' "pendent jurisdiction," state-law causes of action arising from the same facts. McKenzie was not initially a defendant in the federal suit; Vale filed a motion for leave to add him on November 20, 1984. On August 15, 1985, the federal district court granted McKenzie's motion to dismiss her action as to him on the basis of limitations. However, the court refused to sever Vale's cause against McKenzie from those against the other defendants, effectively preventing the summary judgment in McKenzie's favor from becoming final and appealable. As a result, Vale did not obtain appellate review of the dismissal until 1989, when the United States Court of Appeals for the Fifth Circuit held that the district court should have preserved her pendent state claims for prosecution in state court. *Vale v. Adams*, 885 F.2d 869 (5th Cir. 1989). The Fifth Circuit modified the district court's judgment to reflect that, as to McKenzie, the dismissal was "without prejudice." On April 16, 1990, the United States Supreme Court denied certiorari.

While the federal cause was still wending its way through the federal appellate system, Vale began to seek relief in state court. On October 18, 1985, following the federal district court dismissal but before its disposition on appeal, Vale filed the present state-court suit, asserting the same state claim she had previously alleged as pendent to her federal action. On August 21, 1986, the state district court granted McKenzie's motion for partial summary judgment on the ground that limitations had run on Vale's state claim. The parties agreed to continue the matter without a final judgment until the Fifth Circuit's disposition of the federal appeal.

Despite the Fifth Circuit's holding that Vale's pendent state claim should have been dismissed as a matter of judicial discretion, and without prejudice to its being refiled in state court, the state court refused to reconsider its earlier summary-judgment ruling. On February 23, 1990, the state district court severed the summary judgment in McKenzie's favor from the remainder of the state suit, allowing it to become final. Vale appeals from this judgment.

McKenzie obtained his summary judgment in state court by asserting the defense of limitations, arguing that Vale had filed her suit more than two years after the events giving rise to her cause of action. [One claim was based on the fact that the amendment adding McKenzie to the federal suit was filed three days after the statute of limitations ran. Based on a different tolling provision dealing with the defendant's absence from the state, the court held that McKenzie had not proved this limitations defense as a matter of law. McKenzie next claimed that the state court suit was filed too late because section 16.064 did not apply to toll the statute of limitations when the earlier case was dismissed on prudential rather than jurisdictional grounds.]

Vale asserts that the trial court incorrectly interpreted a portion of the saving statute, section 16.064, and erroneously concluded that her limitations period had expired before she filed suit. Section 16.064 and its predecessor statute . . . were designed to protect litigants from the running of limitations in certain circumstances. Section 16.064 provides:

> The period between the date of filing an action in a trial court and the date of a second filing of the same action in a different court suspends the running of the applicable statute of limitations for the period if:
>
> (1) because of *lack of jurisdiction* in the trial court where the action was first filed, the action is dismissed or the judgment is set aside or annulled in a direct proceeding; and
>
> (2) not later than the 60th day after the date the dismissal or other disposition *becomes final*, the action is commenced in a court of proper jurisdiction.

(Emphasis added.) These tolling provisions are remedial in nature and are to be liberally construed. *Republic Nat'l Bank v. Rogers*, 575 S.W.2d 643, 647 (Tex. Civ. App. — Waco 1978, writ ref'd n.r.e.).

First, McKenzie asserts that section 16.064 does not apply because the federal court dismissed appellant's state claims "as a matter of judicial discretion," rather than for "lack of jurisdiction" as required by the statute. This distinction, he argues, removes Vale's state claims from the umbrella of the saving statute's protection. We disagree. Ct says NO, it applies

When state and federal claims arise from a common nucleus of operative facts, a federal court may hear and determine the state claims as well as the federal ones by exercising its pendent jurisdiction. *United Mine Workers v. Gibbs*, 383 U.S. 715 (1966). However, the federal court's power to hear a pendent state claim does not create for the plaintiff a right to federal-court disposition of such state-law claims. The federal court, in its discretion, may decline to hear pendent state claims based on "considerations of judicial economy, convenience and fairness to litigants." *Id.* at 726. The first question, then, is whether such a dismissal constitutes a dismissal for "lack of jurisdiction" within the meaning of section 16.064.

One commentator has observed that the saving statute "applies whether the dismissed action was filed in the state or the federal court, and whether the dismissal is one for want of jurisdiction of the subject matter or one based upon the *impropriety of exercising jurisdiction in a particular action*." 4 McDonald, Texas Civil Practice § 17.20, at 123 (rev. ed. 1984) (emphasis added); *see also* Annotation,

Statute Permitting New Action after Failure of Original Action Commenced within Period of Limitation, as Applicable in Cases Where Original Action Failed for Lack of Jurisdiction, 6 A.L.R.3d 1043 (1966).

This Court has previously held the tolling provision to apply in cases like the present one. In *Burford v. Sun Oil Co.*, 186 S.W.2d 306 (Tex. Civ. App. — Austin 1945, writ ref'd w.o.m.), this Court considered whether the predecessor to section 16.064 applied to toll limitations in circumstances almost identical to those in the present cause. In concluding that the saving statute applied, this Court stated in *Burford* that

> the governing factor in determining whether [the saving statute] applies, is the same in any event — appellees were denied the right to litigate their suit as to state law issues in the federal court because the state courts afforded the appropriate remedy. The effect of the order as one of dismissal for want of jurisdiction cannot be obviated by means of nomenclature. And this is true in the instant case regardless of the distinction in a proper case between want of jurisdiction and refusal to exercise it.

186 S.W.2d at 318. We believe, as did the court in *Burford*, that a litigant who chooses the federal forum in good faith should not suffer a penalty merely for having made that selection. *Id.* at 309. We conclude that, for purposes of the applicability of section 16.064, a federal court's refusal to exercise jurisdiction over a pendent state claim is tantamount to a dismissal for lack of jurisdiction.

McKenzie also contends that Vale did not file her state court action within sixty days of the federal district court's dismissal. Therefore, he argues, she cannot avail herself of the saving statute because she has not satisfied the second requirement of section 16.064. We disagree.

Until September 6, 1989, when the Fifth Circuit ruled that the federal district court's dismissal of the pendent state claims should have been discretionary rather than on the merits, Vale did not have a cause to which the saving statute could apply. Therefore, the earliest date from which the sixty-day period could begin to run was September 6, 1989. Vale filed her cause in state district court on October 18, 1985, well before the date of the Fifth Circuit's opinion. Therefore, she has met the saving statute's second requirement.[4]

We conclude that the saving statute applied to toll limitations during the pendency of Vale's federal suit. Consequently, we sustain her first point of error. Because of our disposition of Vale's first point, it is unnecessary for us to address her remaining points. That portion of the cause relating to appellee Lanny Ryan is severed, and the judgment is affirmed as to him. We reverse the summary judgment in McKenzie's favor and remand that portion of the cause to the trial court for further proceedings.

---

[4] We do not address the question of when a disposition becomes final for purposes of section 16.064 where, for example, a district-court dismissal for lack of jurisdiction is later *affirmed* on appeal.

NOTES AND QUESTIONS

(1) *Additional Applications of the Statute.* As you can see from *Vale*, the statute applies to jurisdictional dismissals from the federal courts as well as from a Texas state court. It also applies to dismissals based on lack of personal jurisdiction from the courts of another state. *Long Island Trust Co. v. Dicker*, 659 F.2d 641, 647 (5th Cir. 1981) (New York state court dismissed and case refiled in federal district court in Texas). In addition, the Fifth Circuit has held that a dismissal because of forum non conveniens comes within the statute. *See Hotvedt v. Schlumberger Ltd. (N.V.)*, 914 F.2d 79, 81 (5th Cir. 1990).

(2) *The Court's Footnote 4.* The court does not decide a different but related issue with respect to tolling. In *Vale v. Ryan*, the federal court of appeals reversed the trial court's dismissal with prejudice (based on limitations) and turned it into a discretionary dismissal of a pendent state claim. Consider a situation in which the district court dismisses a case for want of jurisdiction, and the court of appeals affirms the dismissal on appeal. When do you think the deadline to refile should begin to run in that situation? Why is that a different issue? Given the uncertainty, when should careful counsel re-file in the correct court?

(3) *Another Tolling Provision.* The federal supplemental jurisdiction statute also contains a tolling provision of its own. "The period of limitations for any [pendent state claim] and for any other claim in the same action that is voluntarily dismissed at the same time as or after the dismissal [of the pendent state claim] shall be tolled while the claim is pending and for a period of 30 days after it is dismissed unless State law provides for a longer tolling period." 28 U.S.C. § 1367(d). Would this statute have helped the plaintiff in *Vale v. Ryan*? Since the Texas court interpreted 16.064 to apply to discretionary dismissals, the plaintiff didn't need the help of the federal savings provision. The Texas statute provides for 60 rather than 30 days to refile and is thus more generous than the federal provision. Lawyers should nevertheless be aware of section 1367, in case the Texas Supreme Court disagrees with *Vale* at some point, and also for occasions in which they might be practicing in a state other than Texas.

Chapter 4

JURISDICTION OF PERSONS AND PROPERTY

SCOPE

A state may compel a person to appear in a court in its jurisdiction only if the defendant or his conduct has sufficient contact with the state. This chapter examines the courts' jurisdiction over people and property, including in personam jurisdiction and in rem jurisdiction, long-arm statutes that provide for jurisdiction over people outside Texas, service of process generally, and challenges to jurisdiction.

§ 4.01 GENERAL PRINCIPLES GOVERNING JURISDICTION

You learned about federal constitutional limits on a court's jurisdiction over defendants in your first year Civil Procedure class. As you will remember, they apply to limit the jurisdictional reach of both state and federal courts. State courts must interpret and apply these doctrines to cases brought in their court systems. Accordingly, this chapter begins with a brief review of the due process limitations on personal jurisdiction as developed in cases decided by the U.S. Supreme Court.

[A] Territoriality

When a court exercises jurisdiction over the parties to a dispute, it is exercising power over them. Traditionally, this power was based on the sovereign's authority over the people and property within his realm. The government, through its courts, could exercise jurisdiction only over what was "present" in the territory of the state. *See Pennoyer v. Neff*, 95 U.S. 714 (1878). This system worked adequately in a society in which people largely stayed in their home towns and property took mostly physical form. But two features of modern America put increasing strain on the territorial theory behind the system. First, technological innovations — first the car, then the telephone, and now the internet — made interactions between residents of different states more and more common. Second, the domination of commerce by large corporations gave them the ability to contract or commit torts across great distances without any physical presence in jurisdictions that might want to hold them accountable for harm to their citizens. All of this culminated in a changed method of jurisdictional analysis based more on concepts of fairness than of territoriality.

[B] The "Minimum Contacts" Doctrine

The landmark case of *International Shoe v. Washington*, 326 U.S. 310, 316 (1945), enunciated the current test for personal jurisdiction: defendants must have "certain minimum contacts [with the forum state] such that the maintenance of the suit does not offend traditional notions of fair play and substantial justice." Later cases refined this analysis to focus on the *defendant's* deliberate contacts with the forum. "It is essential in each case that there be some act by which the defendant purposely avails itself of the privilege of conducting activities within the forum state." *Hanson v. Denckla*, 357 U.S. 235, 253 (1958). As time went on, the Supreme Court decided cases that provide examples that help to flesh out the meaning of these relatively cryptic quotations. They also treated the *International Shoe* test as having two parts: 1) the sufficiency of the defendant's purposeful contacts with the forum; and 2) the fairness of asserting jurisdiction over the defendant, taking into consideration the comparative burdens on the parties and the interests of the forum state and other states in adjudicating the dispute. These two parts of the test can interact with each other. For example, even in a case in which the defendant has sufficient contacts with the forum, the defendant has the opportunity to demonstrate that it would nevertheless be unfair to subject it to jurisdiction.

[C] Specific vs. General Jurisdiction

In most cases, the plaintiff's claim against the defendant arises out of or is related to the defendant's forum contacts. Such cases are referred to as involving "specific personal jurisdiction," and the minimum contacts test described above is applied.

In some cases, however, the plaintiff's claim is not related to the defendant's contacts with the forum. This is referred to as "general jurisdiction." If the defendant's forum contacts are substantial, the Constitution still allows jurisdiction over the defendant; those contacts must be substantial, continuous, and systematic before they can justify jurisdiction over an unrelated claim. In the earliest such case, *Perkins v. Benguet Consolidated Mining Co.*, 342 U.S. 437 (1952), the Court upheld jurisdiction over a company that was temporarily headquartered in the forum state. However, in a Texas case, *Helicopteros Nacionales de Colombia, S.A. v. Hall*, 466 U.S. 408 (1984), the Court rejected a series of multi-million dollar purchases of helicopters, parts, and training as a sufficient basis for general jurisdiction.

In many cases, especially those involving large national corporations, the defendant has both contacts that give rise to the cause of action and contacts that do not. The courts will therefore analyze both whether the forum state may constitutionally assert jurisdiction over the defendant under a specific jurisdiction theory and under a general jurisdiction theory, and in doing so should be careful about which contacts "count." Commentators have also suggested that the specific jurisdiction/general jurisdiction dichotomy is a false one, and that courts should instead use a more nuanced analysis that considers both the extent of defendant's forum contacts and the degree of relatedness between those contacts and the plaintiff's cause of action. *See, e.g.*, KEVIN M. CLERMONT, PRINCIPLES OF CIVIL PROCEDURE 224–25 (2005).

[D] Other Bases of Jurisdiction

[1] Consent

Defendants may also consent to jurisdiction in several ways. First, consent may arise from a contract signed before suit is brought, as when the contract contains a choice of forum clause or appoints an in-state agent for service of process. For the federal courts, the Supreme Court has enforced such agreements despite due process challenges. *See National Equipment Rental, Ltd. v. Szukhent*, 375 U.S. 311 (1964); *Carnival Cruise Lines v. Shute*, 499 U.S. 585 (1991). Corporations may also explicitly consent to jurisdiction when registering to do business in a state. In addition, defendants may consent to jurisdiction after suit is filed by appearing in the case without making a timely objection to personal jurisdiction.

[2] In Rem and Quasi in Rem Jurisdiction

The types of jurisdiction discussed above are all jurisdiction over the defendant's person, or *in personam* jurisdiction. Personal jurisdiction can result in a judgment imposing a personal obligation on the defendant in favor of the plaintiff. But this is not the only way in which a forum state can get the power to adjudicate a dispute. *In rem* jurisdiction involves an action against a thing. Jurisdiction in rem can result in a judgment affecting the interests of all persons in a particular thing — but no personal liability results. Examples of proceedings in rem include probate jurisdiction, actions to register title to land, and forfeiture actions. Jurisdiction over a person's *status* can also be thought of as a type of in rem jurisdiction, and the court can make a determination about that status. For example, in a divorce case the state where one spouse is domiciled can grant a divorce without having jurisdiction over the other spouse — and declare the status of marriage terminated — but cannot order support payments as part of this status determination.

Stretching the concept a little further, there is also *quasi in rem* jurisdiction. This kind of jurisdiction can result in a judgment affecting only the interests of *particular* persons in the thing. Although the action is brought against the defendants (rather than the thing itself), only their interests in the thing are at stake. There are two types of quasi in rem jurisdiction: 1) the plaintiff seeks to establish an interest in the thing, an interest that pre-dated the lawsuit; 2) the plaintiff seeks to apply the defendant's property to satisfy a claim against the defendant that is *not* related to the property. In *Shaffer v. Heitner*, 433 U.S. 186, 204 (1977), the Supreme Court held that the second type of traditional quasi in rem case is inconsistent with "the standards set forth in *International Shoe* and its progeny." Due process requires an examination of the relationship "among the defendant, the forum, and the litigation" and not just the presence of property in the forum. The court noted that all claims of personal jurisdiction would be held to the *International Shoe* standards of minimum contacts and fair play and substantial justice.

[3] Transient Jurisdiction

The *Shaffer* approach made people doubt the continuing viability of another traditional basis of jurisdiction: transient jurisdiction based on in-state service on the defendant. Under the old common law principles, being served with process within a jurisdiction was a sufficient basis for the exercise of personal jurisdiction because at the time of service, the defendant was "present" there. Would it satisfy a due process fairness test? In *Burnham v. Superior Court*, 495 U.S. 604 (1990), the Supreme Court unanimously (but for very different reasons) upheld the use of transient jurisdiction to give California the power to adjudicate child support issues affecting an ex-husband who lived in New Jersey because he was served with process in California. Justice Scalia used his "original intent" analysis to approve of transient jurisdiction, along with all traditional bases of jurisdiction; Justice White refused to say that all traditional bases were acceptable but found transient jurisdiction so deeply rooted as to need no case-specific analysis; Justice Brennan applied a due process analysis to the facts of the case but found that presence in the state was sufficient to support jurisdiction in most cases. Justice Stevens also upheld jurisdiction, noting briefly that "the historical evidence and consensus identified by Justice Scalia, the considerations of fairness identified by Justice Brennan, and the common sense displayed by Justice White, all combine to demonstrate that this is, indeed, a very easy case."

In addition to being bound by the Due Process Clause of the federal Constitution, states may create limits for themselves, because they are not required to extend their jurisdiction all the way to the constitutionally permissible limits. State courts must be authorized by state legislatures to exercise jurisdiction over out-of-state defendants; this authorization comes in the form of long-arm statutes. The next section of the chapter turns to Texas statutes and cases. What limits, if any, has Texas put on its courts' ability to adjudicate the alleged harms done by non-Texan defendants? We begin by examining the general long-arm statute.

§ 4.02 PERSONAL JURISDICTION IN TEXAS

[A] The General Long-Arm Statute

The current version of the general long-arm statute is located in chapter 17 of the Civil Practice and Remedies Code. It is one source of authority under state law outlining what kind of contacts are necessary for jurisdiction, and it also provides information about *how* nonresidents are served with process. As you read the statute, see if you can make a chart showing who gets served in what manner.

§ 17.041. *Definition.* In this subchapter, "nonresident" includes:

(1) an individual who is not a resident of this state; and

(2) a foreign corporation, joint-stock company, association, or partnership.

§ 17.042. *Acts Constituting Business in This State.* In addition to other acts that may constitute doing business, a nonresident does business in this state if the nonresident:

(1) contracts by mail or otherwise with a Texas resident and either party is to perform the contract in whole or in part in this state;

(2) commits a tort in whole or in part in this state; or

(3) recruits Texas residents, directly or through an intermediary located in this state, for employment inside or outside this state.

§ 17.043. *Service on Person in Charge of Business.* In an action arising from a nonresident's business in this state, process may be served on the person in charge, at the time of service, of any business in which the nonresident is engaged in this state if the nonresident is not required by statute to designate or maintain a resident agent for service of process.

§ 17.044. *Substituted Service on Secretary of State.*

(a) The secretary of state is an agent for service of process or complaint on a nonresident who:

(1) is required by statute to designate or maintain a resident agent or engages in business in this state, but has not designated or maintained a resident agent for service of process;

(2) has one or more resident agents for service of process, but two unsuccessful attempts have been made on different business days to serve each agent; or

(3) is not required to designate an agent for service in this state, but becomes a nonresident after a cause of action arises in this state but before the cause is matured by suit in a court of competent jurisdiction.

(b) The secretary of state is an agent for service of process on a nonresident who engages in business in this state, but does not maintain a regular place of business in this state or a designated agent for service of process, in any proceeding that arises out of the business done in this state and to which the nonresident is a party.

(c) After the death of a nonresident for whom the secretary of state is an agent for service of process under this section, the secretary of state is an agent for service of process on a nonresident administrator, executor, or personal representative of the nonresident. If an administrator, executor, or personal representative for the estate of the deceased nonresident is not appointed, the secretary of state is an agent for service of process on an heir, as determined by the law of the foreign jurisdiction, of the deceased nonresident.

(d) If a nonresident for whom the secretary of state is an agent for service of process under this section is judged incompetent by a court of competent jurisdiction, the secretary of state is an agent for service of process on a guardian or personal representative of the nonresident.

§ 17.045. *Notice to Nonresident.*

(a) If the secretary of state is served with duplicate copies of process for a nonresident, he shall require a statement of the name and address of the nonresident's home or home office and shall immediately mail a copy of the process to the nonresident.

(b) If the secretary of state is served with process under Section 17.044(a)(3), he shall immediately mail a copy of the process to the nonresident (if an individual), to the person in charge of the nonresident's business, or to a corporate officer (if the nonresident is a corporation).

(c) If the person in charge of a nonresident's business is served with process under Section 17.043, a copy of the process and notice of the service must be immediately mailed to the nonresident or the nonresident's principal place of business.

(d) The process or notice must be sent by registered mail or by certified mail, return receipt requested.

(e) If the secretary of state is served with duplicate copies of process as an agent for a person who is a nonresident administrator, executor, heir, guardian, or personal representative of a nonresident, the secretary shall require a statement of the person's name and address and shall immediately mail a copy of the process to the person.

NOTES AND QUESTIONS

(1) *Interpreting the Statute.* There are a number of ways in which the language of the long-arm statute could be read to differ from the jurisdiction permitted by the Constitution. For example, there is language in sections 17.043 and 17.044(b) that seems to rule out the exercise of general jurisdiction over a defendant "engaged in business" in Texas ("in an action arising from a nonresident's business in this state"; "any proceeding that arises out of the business done in this state and to which the nonresident is a party"). On the other hand, section 17.044(a)(1) extends long-arm jurisdiction over a nonresident that "engages in business in this state" without regard to whether the plaintiff's claim arises from the business. But for the reach of the statute to match principles of general jurisdiction, the words "engages in business" in 17.044(a)(1) must mean more extensive activities than the amount of business needed for specific jurisdiction provided for in sections 17.043 and 17.044(b). As you will see in the cases that follow, the Texas Supreme Court has consistently held that the long-arm statute goes to the limits of due process despite the statutory language and without following normal methods of statutory construction, which pay considerably more attention to the statutory language to ascertain legislative intent. *See* § 4.02[B], *infra.*

(2) *Why Worry About Long-Arm Statutes?* Since the Texas Supreme Court disregards the language of the long-arm statute when considering the jurisdictional limits of Texas courts, why should Texas lawyers worry about the statute? One reason is the statute's function in mandating the method for service of process. Knowing what statutory provision authorizes jurisdiction is crucial for knowing what methods of service are proper — and Texas courts *are* exceedingly demanding about service of process in default judgment cases. *See* § 4.04[B][6], *infra.* Another reason is that there are actually a number of long-arm statutes in

Texas, and each has its own theoretical justifications and limitations. *See, e.g.*, § 4.03, *infra* (discussing personal jurisdiction limits in family law cases); C.P.R.C. § 17.061 (non-resident motorist statute); INS. C. § 804.103 (jurisdiction over out-of-state insurers).

Long-arm statutes can also act as an expression of a state's intention to exercise its power over certain types of defendants in certain situations, and these expressions can influence courts' decisions about jurisdiction. For example, in *Kulko v. Superior Court*, 436 U.S. 84 (1978), there is a suggestion that long-arm provisions could be more persuasive if they enumerate the specific fact situation in which jurisdiction may be obtained. "California has not attempted to assert any particularized interest in trying such cases in its courts by, e.g., enacting a special jurisdictional statute." *Id.* at 98.

(3) *"Doing Business" Concept.* The decision that the statute goes as far as due process will permit stems in part from the "doing business" language in the statute. Notice that while there are specific examples given of conduct that will constitute doing business, the list is not exhaustive ("[i]n addition to other acts that may constitute doing business . . . "). The phrase itself comes from old personal jurisdiction cases and indicated that a defendant was sufficiently "present" in the jurisdiction to be sued there. *See Philadelphia & Reading Railway Co. v. McKibbin*, 243 U.S. 264, 265 (1917) ("A foreign corporation is amenable to process to enforce a personal liability, in the absence of consent, only if it is *doing business* within the State in such manner and to such extent as to warrant the inference that it is *present* there.") (emphasis added). This is another indication that the reach of the general long-arm statute was intended to equal the limits of due process.

(4) *Serving the Person in Charge.* In some cases, the nonresident may actually have a presence in Texas complete with a "person in charge." If so, section 17.043 requires service on this person if the nonresident is not required to designate or maintain a resident agent for service of process. Failure to make the proper allegations and serve the proper person could result in the loss of a default judgment. This issue will be discussed later in the chapter. *See McKanna v. Edgar*, discussed in section 4.04[B][6].

(5) *Serving the Secretary of State.* Section 17.044 describes the situations in which the secretary of state becomes a non-resident's agent for service. This can happen if: 1) the corporation was required to designate an agent but did not do so [17.044(a)(1)]; 2) the corporation has a resident agent but two separate attempts to serve the agent have been unsuccessful [17.044(a)(2)]; 3) the defendant becomes a nonresident after the cause of action accrues but before the suit is filed [17.044(a)(3)]; and 4) if the nonresident "engages in business" in Texas but does not maintain a regular place of business or a designated agent here [17.044(b)]. Note, therefore, that service on the secretary of state is not proper if the defendant maintains a regular place of business in Texas or a designated agent is available. When the secretary of state is the proper agent for service of process, service on the secretary *is* service on the defendant. The secretary is required to mail a copy of the process to the nonresident, both by the long-arm statute and by the Texas Business Organizations Code.

(6) *Serving the Resident Agent for Service of Process.* Most types of business organizations formed under and governed as to internal affairs by the laws of jurisdictions other than Texas must designate and maintain registered offices and agents in Texas for service of process — if the organizations do enough intrastate business in Texas. Section 9.001 of the Texas Business Organizations Code provides that virtually all limited-liability entities [foreign corporations; foreign limited partnerships; foreign limited liability companies; foreign business trusts; foreign real estate investment trusts; foreign cooperatives; foreign public or private limited companies; other foreign entities which if formed in Texas would require a certificate of formation; and any foreign entity that affords limited liability for any member or owner under the law of the jurisdiction of its formation] must register to transact business in Texas and maintain the organization's registration while transacting business in Texas. TBOC § 9.001. In contrast, foreign general partnerships and foreign unincorporated nonprofit associations are not required to register to transact business in Texas. *See* TBOC § 9.002(c)–(d) and Revisor's Notes ("The primary foreign entity not required to register is a foreign general partnership."). Chapter 5 of the Texas Business Organizations Code requires "foreign filing entities," defined as foreign entities "other than foreign limited liability partnerships," that are required to register under Chapter 9 [TBOC § 1.002(31)], to "designate and continuously maintain" a registered agent and registered office for service of process in Texas. Bus. Orgs. C. § 5.201. While the phrase "transacting business" is not defined affirmatively, section 9.251 contains a long list of activities that do *not* constitute "transacting business." They include engaging in litigation, carrying on internal affairs, maintaining a bank account, maintaining an office to deal with the entity's securities, selling through an independent contractor, creating or acquiring a security interest, conducting an isolated transaction, exercising various mineral interests, and the like.

For either a foreign or domestic entity that did not designate or maintain a registered agent as required by the TBOC, or whose agent cannot reasonably be found, the secretary of state becomes its agent for service of process:

Bus. Orgs. C. § 5.251. *Failure to Designate Registered Agent*

The secretary of state is an agent of an entity for purposes of service of process, notice, or demand on the entity if:

(1) the entity is a filing entity or a foreign filing entity and:

(A) the entity fails to appoint or does not maintain a registered agent in this state; or

(B) the registered agent of the entity cannot with reasonable diligence be found at the registered office of the entity; or

(2) the entity is a foreign filing entity and:

(A) the entity's registration to do business under this code is revoked; or

(B) the entity transacts business in this state without being registered as required by Chapter 9.

These provisions dovetail fairly well with C.P.R.C. § 17.044 (discussed in the previous note) although one could wish that the Texas legislature would use more informative terminology instead of alternating between "doing business," and "engaging in business" in the general long-arm statue and using the term "transacting business" in the TBOC. The "transacting business" language comes from a different line of cases involving the Privileges and Immunities Clause of the U.S. Constitution and the state's power to require nonresident corporations to register. What do each of these terms mean? Which ones are synonymous and which one is not?

(7) *Serving Agent Not Enough to Provide Jurisdiction.* Probably because the foregoing statutes and their predecessors do not state that a nonresident that "transacts business" in Texas consents to Texas jurisdiction, some intermediate appellate courts have ruled that the appointment of a registered agent is not necessarily sufficient for jurisdiction. For example, in *Juarez v. UPS de Mexico S.A. de C.V.*, 933 S.W.2d 281 (Tex. App. — Corpus Christi 1996, no writ), the court declined to exercise personal jurisdiction in a personal injury suit between Mexican citizens and a Mexican corporation, arising out of an accident that took place wholly in Mexico. The defendant corporation had regular contacts in Texas (though the contacts were unrelated to the accident) and had appointed an agent for service of process in Texas. Nonetheless, the court of appeals held that an appointed agent for service was, of itself, insufficient to indicate consent to general jurisdiction, but rather was only one factor to be considered in the overall jurisdictional analysis. Furthermore, considering the defendant's minimal contacts, the court ruled that the exercise of jurisdiction would offend traditional notions of fair play and substantial justice, emphasizing the lack of connection to Texas, the burden on the defendants of defending in Texas, and Mexico's interest in providing a forum and a remedy for disputes between its citizens. For cases holding that registration to do business and the appointment of an agent for service of process *does* constitute a sufficient basis for jurisdiction, see *Goldman v. Pre-Fab Transit Co.*, 520 S.W.2d 597, 598 (Tex. Civ. App. — Houston [14th Dist.] 1975, no writ); *Acacia Pipeline Corp. v. Champlin Exploration, Inc.*, 769 S.W.2d 719 (Tex. App. — Houston [1st Dist.] 1989, no writ). The Fifth Circuit, purporting to apply Texas law, has held that registration to do business does not constitute consent, but it failed to cite *Goldman* or *Acacia*. *See Wenche Siemer v. Learjet Acquisition Corp.*, 966 F.2d 179, 180 (5th Cir. 1992).

Early U.S. Supreme Court cases distinguish between defendants who have actually appointed a registered agent (and thereby actually consented to jurisdiction) and defendants whose consent to be served through the secretary of state is merely implied (as to whom only specific jurisdiction is proper). *ComparePennsylvania Fire Ins. Co. v. Gold Issue Mining & Milling Co.*, 243 U.S. 93, 94–96 (1917) (agent appointed and jurisdiction upheld), *withSimon v. Southern Ry.*, 236 U.S. 115, 128–32 (1915) (implied consent means suit must relate to defendant's forum activities).

(8) *Other Provisions Regarding Who to Serve.* Subchapter B of chapter 17 of the Civil Practice and Remedies Code contains miscellaneous statutory provisions concerning service on noncorporate business agents (C.P.R.C. § 17.021), partnerships (C.P.R.C. § 17.022), joint-stock associations (C.P.R.C. § 17.023), and political subdivisions (C.P.R.C. § 17.024). Unfortunately, the Civil Practice and Remedies

Code is only a partial recodification of the statutes concerning service and personal jurisdiction. Other codes dealing with specific subjects often contain additional provisions that supplement or effectively supersede the general jurisdictional provisions. *See, e.g.*, FAM. C. §§ 6.305, 102.011.

(9) *Rule 108: An Alternative to the Long-Arm Statute.* The Texas Rules of Civil Procedure also contain a provision allowing service on nonresidents. Read Rule 108. It allows service on nonresidents in the same manner as on residents, and then states: "A defendant served with such notice shall be required to appear and answer in the same manner and time and under the same penalties as if he had been personally served with citation within this State to the full extent that he may be required to appear and answer under the Constitution of the United States in an action either in rem or in personam." This, then, is another source of authority over nonresidents going to the limits of due process. While it was argued that only the legislature (and not the court, the body that adopts procedure rules) has the authority to create a long-arm provision, the Texas Supreme Court has recognized Rule 108 as "a valid procedural alternative to service under the long-arm statute" and rejected the "contention that Rule 108 impermissibly abridges substantive rights." *Paramount Pipe & Supply Co. v. Muhr*, 749 S.W.2d 491, 495 (Tex. 1988). When would it be easier to use Rule 108 than the general long-arm statute in order to serve the defendant?

PRACTICE EXERCISE #6

(1) McMamouth Corporation is a Delaware corporation with its principal place of business in California. It also does a significant amount of business within Texas, and has registered to do business in Texas and appointed Ronald Donald as its registered agent for service of process. Polly Petal contracted with McMamouth to provide live floral arrangements to all of its Dallas area stores. Polly did so, but McMamouth refuses to pay. Polly wants to sue McMamouth for breach of contract. How should she serve it with process under the general long-arm statute?

(2) Runaway Bride Emily Johnson has filed suit against the International Star for libel. Shortly after Emily returned home to face the music, the Star published an article claiming that Emily had been arrested for possession of crack cocaine when she was a student at the University of Texas. The Star is a Nevada corporation with its principal place of business in Florida. It registered to do business in Texas, where it sells thousands of papers weekly. The Star appointed Ewan Calder as its registered agent for service of process. The process server hired by Emily's attorney has tried to serve Calder four times without success — he never seems to be available. How can Emily get service on the Star?

(3) Acme Corporation is headquartered in New Mexico, where it manufactures explosive devices. It sells those devices in New Mexico, Arizona, and occasionally in Texas. Acme has a small office in Lubbock where its Texas sales representative keeps a warehouse full of merchandise and has his office. It has not registered to do business in Texas or appointed an agent for service of process, nor did the law require it to do so. One of the devices malfunctioned and injured Texas resident Wiley Coyote. Coyote wants to sue Acme in a Texas court. Who should be served

with process under the general long arm statute?

(4) Walker was a resident of Texas. While living here, he defrauded the widow Tucker out of her life savings. Before she could file suit and serve him with process, Walker moved to California. Does the general long arm statute provide a method of service of process for a situation such as this?

(5) XYZ Corporation is a Delaware corporation with its principal place of business in Illinois. XYZ operates a nationwide network of "Spuds-A-Plenty" restaurants, which sell only french fries and super-sized cola drinks. There are quite a few restaurants in Texas, and XYZ has appointed Wesley "Booger" King as its registered agent for service of process. Wendy Fillay slipped and fell in the Spuds-A-Plenty in Waco. She wants to sue XYZ, and thinks that it may be hard to locate King to serve him with process. May she serve XYZ by serving the secretary of state?

(6) Jenna Tree lives in Austin. After a catalogue came to her home, she ordered a crystal decanter from a mail order company in Indiana, Pot U.S. Inc. (POTUS). When it arrived it was broken in a million small pieces, but POTUS refuses to refund her purchase price. She knows the name and address of the president of POTUS. Jenna would like to avoid dealing with the secretary of state. Is there another way to serve POTUS with process?

[B] Texas Courts Apply the Statute and Constitution: Specific Jurisdiction

Based on these long arm provisions and the due process cases, the Texas courts have put their own spin on the requirements for minimum contacts and fairness. In the first case, the Justices of the Texas Supreme Court explain the doctrine as they understand it, and apply it in the context of an international defendant. This is the case in which the Texas courts began to articulate a personal jurisdiction analysis in a way that parallels the U.S. Supreme Court. Do they find sufficient contacts? Do they find that exercising jurisdiction over the defendant would be fair?

GUARDIAN ROYAL EXCHANGE v. ENGLISH CHINA CLAYS

815 S.W.2d 223 (Tex. 1991)

HIGHTOWER, J.

The issue before this court is whether it is consistent with the requirements of due process of law under the United States Constitution for Texas courts to assert in personam jurisdiction over Guardian Royal Exchange Assurance, Ltd. ("Guardian Royal"), an English insurance company. Southern Clay products, Inc. ("Southern Clay"), Gonzales Clay Corporation ("Gonzales Clay"), English China Clays Overseas Investments Ltd. ("Overseas Investments") and English China Clays, P.L.C. ("English China") sued Guardian Royal in Gonzales County, Texas. The trial court granted Guardian Royal's special appearance and dismissed the cause. The court of appeals reversed the judgment of the trial court and remanded the cause for trial. We reverse the judgment of the court of appeals and affirm the judgment of the trial court.

Guardian Royal is an English insurance company with its office and principal place of business in England. English China is an English company with American subsidiaries including Southern Clay and Gonzales Clay, which are Texas corporations. In 1980–81, Guardian Royal issued an insurance policy including several endorsements[2] to English China providing coverage for third party liability occurring anywhere in the world English China and its subsidiary companies did business. These transactions occurred in England between an English insurer and an English insured. All acts concerning the negotiation, implementation and performance of the policy and endorsement (including the payment of premiums) occurred in England between Guardian Royal and English China.

Guardian Royal asserts that the coverage was extended to the American subsidiaries on the understanding that they would obtain underlying liability insurance from American insurers. Although the endorsement to the policy listed Southern Clay and Gonzales Clay as located in the "U.S.A.," there was no indication that these subsidiaries were located in Texas. Furthermore, Guardian Royal did not know whether English China or its American subsidiaries did business in Texas or sent products to Texas. Subsequently Southern Clay acquired liability coverage from United States Fire Insurance Company ("U.S. Fire") and others.

In 1982, an employee of Southern Clay was killed in an on-the-job accident in Gonzales County, Texas. The deceased's family filed wrongful death lawsuits against the English China entities and others in federal and state courts in Texas. The English China entities settled the lawsuits and U.S. Fire contributed approximately $600,000 to the settlement. Asserting that the policy covered English China and its subsidiaries only for liability in excess of the coverage provided by American insurers, Guardian Royal declined to participate in or contribute to the settlement of the lawsuits. The English China entities asserted that Guardian Royal should "reimburse" U.S. Fire[3] for its settlement contribution on their behalf because Guardian Royal was the "primary insurer." After Guardian Royal refused to "reimburse" U.S. Fire, the English China entities sued Guardian Royal. Guardian Royal filed a special appearance pursuant to Rule 120a of the Texas Rules of Civil Procedure asserting that it did not have such minimum contacts with Texas as would allow the court to exercise personal jurisdiction without offending traditional notions of fair play and substantial justice. The trial court granted the special appearance and dismissed the cause. The court of appeals reversed the judgment of the trial court and remanded the cause for trial.

Guardian Royal argues that it is inconsistent with federal constitutional requirements of due process for Texas courts to assert *in personam* jurisdiction over Guardian Royal in this cause. We agree.

---

[2] The endorsements substantially altered the terms of the original policy. Among other things, the endorsements (1) extended coverage to English China's subsidiaries including Southern Clay and Gonzales Clay, (2) extended the definition of "Insured" to include any associated or subsidiary company of English China anywhere in the world, and (3) deleted the policy's geographical limits.

[3] As a result of the settlement, U.S. Fire has been subrogated to the rights of the English China entities in this cause. Therefore, U.S. Fire is the real party in interest.

The Texas long-arm statute authorizes the exercise of jurisdiction over nonresidents "doing business" in Texas, Tex. Civ. Prac. & Rem. Code Ann. section 17.042 (Vernon 1986). Although it lists particular acts which constitute "doing business," the statute also provides that the nonresident's "other acts" may satisfy the "doing business" requirement. *Id. See Schlobohm v. Schapiro*, 784 S.W.2d at 357; *U-Anchor Advertising, Inc. v. Burt*, 553 S.W.2d 760, 762 (Tex. 1977). As a result, we consider only whether it is consistent with federal constitutional requirements of due process for Texas courts to assert in personam jurisdiction over Guardian Royal. *See Helicopteros Nacionales de Colombia v. Hall*, 466 U.S. 408, 413–14 (1984).

Federal constitutional requirements of due process limit the power of the state to assert personal jurisdiction over a nonresident defendant such as Guardian Royal . . . . The United States Supreme Court divides the due process requirements into two parts: (1) whether the nonresident defendant has purposely established "minimum contacts" with the forum state; and (2) if so, whether the exercise of jurisdiction comports with "fair play and substantial justice." *Burger King Corp. v. Rudzewicz*, 471 U.S. 462, 475–76 (1985). *See Helicopteros*, 466 U.S. at 414.

I.

Under the minimum contacts analysis, we must determine whether the nonresident defendant has purposefully availed itself of the privilege of conducting activities within the forum state, thus invoking the benefits and protection of its laws. *Burger King*, 471 U.S. at 474–75. This "purposeful availment" requirement ensures that a nonresident defendant will not be haled into a jurisdiction based solely upon "random," "fortuitous" or "attenuated" contacts or the "unilateral activity of another party or a third person." *Burger King*, 471 U.S. at 475; *Helicopteros*, 466 U.S. at 417; *World-Wide Volkswagen Corp. v. Woodson*, 444 U.S. 286, 298.

The exercise of personal jurisdiction is proper when the contacts proximately result from actions of the nonresident defendant which create a substantial connection with the forum state, *Burger King*, 471 U.S. at 474–75. The substantial connection between the nonresident defendant and the forum state necessary for a finding of minimum contacts must come about by action or conduct of the nonresident defendant purposefully directed toward the forum state. *Burger King*, 471 U.S. at 472–76. However, "the constitutional touchstone remains whether the [nonresident] defendant purposefully established 'minimum contacts' in the forum State." *Burger King*, 471 U.S. at 474.

Foreseeability is also an important consideration in deciding whether the nonresident defendant has purposely established "minimum contacts" with the forum state. However, "foreseeability" is not necessarily determinative when considering whether the nonresident defendant purposefully established "minimum contacts" with the forum state. Although not an independent component of the minimum contacts analysis, the concept of "foreseeability" is implicit in the requirement that there be a "substantial connection" between the nonresident defendant and Texas arising from action or conduct of the nonresident defendant purposefully directed toward Texas. *World-Wide Volkswagen*, 444 U.S. at 297; *Burger King*, 471 U.S. at 474. "Foreseeability" is especially pertinent when the nonresident defendant is an insurance company . . . . Thus, when the nonresident defendant is an insurance company, the following factors, when appropriate, should be considered when determining whether the nonresident defendant has purposely established "minimum contacts" with the forum state: (a) the insurer's awareness that it was responsible to cover losses arising from a substantial subject of insurance regularly present in the forum state; and (b) the nature of the particular insurance contract and its coverage.

The United States Supreme Court has refined the minimum contacts analysis into specific and general jurisdiction. When specific jurisdiction is asserted, the cause of action must arise out of or relate to the nonresident defendant's contact with the forum state in order to satisfy the minimum contacts requirement. *Helicopteros*, 466 U.S. at 414 n.8. *See World-Wide Volkswagen*, 444 U.S. at 293–94. However, the contact must have resulted from the nonresident defendant's purposeful conduct and not the unilateral activity of the plaintiff or others. *See Helicopteros*, 466 U.S. at 417; *World-Wide Volkswagen*, 444 U.S. at 298. Furthermore, the nonresident defendant's activities must have been "purposefully directed" to the forum and the litigation must result from alleged injuries that "arise out of or relate to" those activities. *Burger King*, 471 U.S. at 472; *Zac Smith & Co.*, 734 S.W.2d at 663. When specific jurisdiction is asserted, the minimum contacts analysis focuses on the relationship among the defendant, the forum and the litigation. *Helicopteros*, 466 U.S. at 414; *Schlobohm*, 784 S.W.2d at 357.

General jurisdiction may be asserted when the cause of action does not arise from or relate to the nonresident defendant's purposeful conduct within the forum state but there are continuous and systematic contacts between the nonresident defendant and the forum state. *Helicopteros*, 466 U.S. at 414–16; *Schlobohm*, 784 S.W.2d at 357. When general jurisdiction is asserted, the minimum contacts analysis is more demanding and requires a showing of substantial activities in the forum state. *Schlobohm*, 784 S.W.2d at 357.

II.

Once it has been determined that the nonresident defendant purposefully established minimum contacts with the forum state, the contacts are evaluated in light of other factors to determine whether the assertion of personal jurisdiction comports with fair play and substantial justice. *Asahi Metal Indus. Co. v. Superior Court*, 480 U.S. 102 (1987); *Burger King*, 471 U.S. at 476. These factors include (1) "the burden on the defendant," (2) "the interests of the forum state in adjudicating the dispute," (3) "the plaintiff's interest in obtaining convenient and effective relief,"[4] (4) "the interstate judicial system's interest in obtaining the most efficient resolution of controversies,' ' and (5) "the shared interest of the several States in furthering fundamental substantive social policies." *World-Wide Volkswagen*, 444

[4] This factor was fully described in *World-Wide Volkswagen* as "the plaintiff's interest in obtaining convenient and effective relief . . . at least when that interest is not adequately protected by the plaintiff's power to choose the forum . . . ." 444 U.S. at 292 (citations omitted).

U.S. at 292; *Burger King*, 471 U.S. at 477; *Asahi*, 480 U.S. at 113. "These considerations sometimes serve to establish the reasonableness of jurisdiction upon a lesser showing of minimum contacts than would otherwise be required." *Burger King*, 471 U.S. at 477. However, regardless of these factors, it must be established that the nonresident defendant purposely established minimum contacts with the forum state. Even if the nonresident defendant has purposely established minimum contacts with the forum state, the exercise of jurisdiction may not be fair and reasonable under the facts in a particular case. *Burger King*, 471 U.S. at 477–78.

When the defendant is a resident of another nation, the court must also consider the procedural and substantive policies of other nations whose interests are affected by the assertion of jurisdiction by a state court:

> *World-Wide Volkswagen* also admonished courts to take into consideration the interests of the "several States," in addition to the forum State, in the efficient judicial resolution of the dispute and the advancement of substantive policies. In the present case, this advice calls for a court to consider the procedural and substantive policies of other nations whose interests are affected by the assertion of jurisdiction by the California court. The procedural and substantive interests of other nations in a state court's assertion of jurisdiction over an alien defendant will differ from case to case. In every case, however, those interests, as well as the Federal Government's interest in its foreign relations policies, will be best served by a careful inquiry into the reasonableness of the assertion of jurisdiction in the particular case, and an unwillingness to find the serious burdens on an alien defendant outweighed by minimal interests on the part of the plaintiff or the forum State. "Great care and reserve should be exercised when extending our notions of personal jurisdiction into the international field." *United States v. First National City Bank*, 379 U.S. 378, 404 (1965) (Harlan, J., dissenting).

Asahi, 480 U.S. at 115. "The unique burdens placed upon one who must defend oneself in a foreign legal system should have significant weight in assessing the reasonableness of stretching the long arm of personal jurisdiction over national borders." *Asahi*, 480 U.S. at 114. Thus, when an "international dispute" is involved, the following factors, when appropriate, should also be considered: (a) the unique burdens placed upon the defendant who must defend itself in a foreign legal system; and (b) the procedural and substantive policies of other nations whose interests are affected as well as the federal government's interest in its foreign relations policies.

The state's regulatory interests are also an important consideration in deciding whether the exercise of jurisdiction is reasonable. Other courts have recognized that the states have a legitimate concern in areas in which the state possesses a manifest regulatory interest such as insurance, securities and hazardous and toxic waste. *See Shaffer v. Heitner*, 433 U.S. 186, 222–26 (1977) (Brennan, J., concurring in part and dissenting in part).[5] Traditionally, regulation of the "business of

[5] A "State's valid substantive interests are important considerations in assessing whether it constitutionally may claim jurisdiction over a given cause of action." *Shaffer*, 433 U.S. at 233 (Brennan,

insurance" has bee n delegated to the states by the federal government. *See* McCarran-Ferguson Act, 15 U.S.C. § 1012 (1976); Reyes, *Insurance Company Liquidation in Texas — "The Basics"*, 51 TEX. B.J. 957 (1988).

The State of Texas has a special interest in regulating certain areas such as insurance, and the Texas courts have implicitly recognized the role of that interest for purposes of determining personal jurisdiction . . . . We find that a state's regulatory interest in a certain area or activity such as insurance is an important consideration in deciding whether the exercise of jurisdiction is reasonable and that a state's regulatory interest may establish the reasonableness of jurisdiction upon a lesser showing of minimum contacts than would otherwise be required. However, a state's regulatory interest alone is not in and of itself sufficient to provide a basis for jurisdiction . . . .

IV.

Today, we . . . clarify the jurisdictional formula to ensure compliance with federal constitutional requirements of due process. First, the nonresident defendant must have purposefully established "minimum contacts" with Texas.[6] There must be substantial connection between the nonresident defendant and Texas arising from action or conduct of the nonresident defendant purposefully directed toward Texas. When specific jurisdiction is asserted, the cause of action must arise out of or relate to the nonresident defendant's contacts with Texas. When general jurisdiction is alleged, there must be continuous and systematic contacts between the nonresident defendant and Texas. General jurisdiction requires a showing of substantial activities by the nonresident defendant in Texas.

Second, the assertion of personal jurisdiction must comport with fair play and substantial justice. In this inquiry, it is incumbent upon the defendant to present "a compelling case that the presence of some consideration would render jurisdiction unreasonable." *Burger King*, 471 U.S. at 477; *see also Zac Smith & Co.*, 734 S.W.2d at 664.[7]

. . . Only in rare cases, however, will the exercise of jurisdiction not comport with fair play and substantial justice when the nonresident defendant has purposefully

---

J., concurring in part and dissenting in part). "State courts have legitimately read their jurisdiction expansively when a cause of action centers in an area in which the forum State possesses a manifest regulatory interest." 433 U.S. at 223 (Brennan, J., concurring in part and dissenting in part). *See, e.g.*, *McGee v. International Life Ins. Co.*, 355 U.S. 220 (1957) (insurance regulation: "It cannot be denied that California has a manifest interest in providing effective means of redress for its residents when their insurers refuse to pay claims."); *O'Neil v. Picillo*, 682 F. Supp. 706, 714 n.1 (D.R.I. 1988) (heavily regulated activities-hazardous/toxic substances); *Wichita Federal Savings & Loan Ass'n v. Landmark Group, Inc.*, 674 F. Supp. 321, 326 (D. Kan. 1987) (securities regulation: "It is also relevant to this inquiry that the defendants are engaging in a highly regulated activity, making it more foreseeable that they might have to litigate in a distant forum.").

[6] In analyzing minimum contacts, it is not the number, but rather the quality and nature of the nonresident defendant's contacts with the forum state that is important. *Texas Commerce Bank v. Interpol '80 Ltd.*, 703 S.W.2d 765, 772 (Tex. App. — Corpus Christi 1985, no writ).

[7] We have previously held that the nonresident defendant must negate all bases of personal jurisdiction. *Zac Smith & Co.*, 734 S.W.2d at 664; *Siskind v. Villa Foundation for Education, Inc.*, 642 S.W.2d at 438.

established minimum contacts with the forum state. *See Burger King*, 471 U.S. at 477–78; *see also Schlobohm*, 784 S.W.2d at 358 ("it has become less likely that the exercise of jurisdiction will fail a fair play analysis."). The stringent standard to be applied is set forth in *Burger King*:

> [W]here a defendant who purposefully has directed his activities at forum residents seeks to defeat jurisdiction, he must present a compelling case that the presence of some other considerations would render jurisdiction unreasonable. Most such considerations usually may be accommodated through means short of finding jurisdiction unconstitutional. For example, the potential clash of the forum's laws with the *fundamental substantive social policies* of another State may be accommodated through application of the forum's choice-of-law rules. Similarly, a defendant claiming substantial inconvenience may seek a change of venue.

471 U.S. at 477 (emphasis added) (footnotes omitted); *see also Zac Smith & Co.*, 734 S.W.2d at 664 (quoting same language). Nor is distance alone ordinarily sufficient to defeat jurisdiction: "modern transportation and communication have made it much less burdensome for a party sued to defend himself in a State where he engages in economic activity." *McGee*, 355 U.S. at 223.

V.

. . . .

We must first determine whether Guardian Royal purposefully established "minimum contacts" with Texas; in other words, whether there was a "substantial connection" between Guardian Royal and Texas arising from action or conduct of Guardian Royal purposefully directed toward Texas. The policy and endorsements provided coverage for third party liability occurring anywhere in the world English China did business. Among other things, the policy stated that "[t]he words 'The Insured' wherever they appear shall apply to each party described in the Schedule as if a separate insurance policy had been issued to each . . . ." The endorsements to the policy (1) extended coverage to English China's subsidiaries including Southern Clay and Gonzales Clay, (2) extended the definition of "Insured" to include any associated and subsidiary company of English China anywhere in the world, and (3) deleted the policy's geographical limits. Furthermore, under these facts and circumstances, it is apparent that the nature of the insurance contract between Guardian Royal and English China and its coverage are sufficient to establish that Guardian Royal purposefully established "minimum contacts" with Texas. As the insurer of English China and its approximately 120 subsidiary companies located in many countries in the world including the United States and the issuer of an insurance policy providing coverage for third party liability occurring anywhere in the world English China and its subsidiary companies did business, Guardian Royal could reasonably anticipate the significant risk (if not the probability) that a subsidiary would become involved in disputes and litigation in many countries in the world including any state in the United States. In addition, Guardian Royal could reasonably anticipate the significant risk concerning the litigation brought in one of many countries including any state in the United States. Furthermore, the policy language that "the words 'The Insured,' wherever they appear, shall apply to each [subsidiary] . . . as if a separate insurance [policy] had been issued to each [subsidiary]" acknowledges the formation of a significant relationship between Guardian Royal and each subsidiary including Southern Clay. Under these facts and circumstances, we find that Guardian Royal purposefully established "minimum contacts" with Texas.

VI.

Second, we must determine whether the assertion of personal jurisdiction comports with fair play and substantial justice . . . .

Requiring Guardian Royal, an English insurer unaffiliated with American companies, to submit its dispute with its English insured to a foreign nation's judicial system is burdensome. All acts concerning the negotiation, implementation and performance of the policy and endorsements (including the payment of premiums) occurred in England. Frequently the interests of the forum state and the plaintiff will justify the severe burden placed upon the nonresident defendant. *See Asahi*, 480 U.S. at 114. In this case, however, the interests of Texas in adjudicating the dispute and the English China entities in obtaining convenient and effective relief are minimal. Like California, Texas "has a manifest interest in providing effective means of redress for its residents when their insurers refuse to pay claims. These residents would be at a severe disadvantage if they were forced to follow the insurance company to a distant State in order to hold it legally accountable." *McGee*, 355 U.S. at 223. However, this is a dispute between two insurers — Guardian Royal and U.S. Fire as subrogee to the rights of the English China entities. Among other things, U.S. Fire is seeking "reimbursement" for its contribution to the settlement of the wrongful death lawsuits against the English China entities. The family of the deceased employee of Southern Clay has been compensated and th e English China entities, the insureds, were defended and indemnified. Thus, in reality, U.S. Fire is the real party in interest and neither the family of the deceased employee nor the English China entities have an interest in the outcome of this lawsuit. In addition, since Guardian Royal and U.S. Fire are neither Texas consumers nor insureds, Texas' interest in adjudicating the dispute (including its special interest in regulating insurance) is considerably diminished. While Texas "has a manifest interest in providing effective means of redress for its residents when their insurers refuse to pay claims," Texas does not have a compelling interest in providing a forum for resolution of disputes between these insurers. Under these facts and circumstances, we find that the assertion of personal jurisdiction over Guardian Royal is unreasonable and does not comport with fair play and substantial justice. Accordingly, we hold that it is inconsistent with federal constitutional requirements of due process for Texas courts to assert in personam jurisdiction over Guardian Royal in this case.

For the reasons explained herein, we reverse the judgment of the court of appeals and affirm the judgment of the trial court.

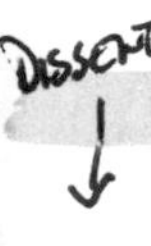

[Justice Mauzy dissented, arguing that it was reasonably foreseeable that Guardian Royal would be haled into court in Texas. He reasoned that "Guardian Royal's willingness to being haled into court in a foreign state was an express, and very marketable, feature of its policy. The company's contacts with the state of

Texas cannot be viewed as 'random' or 'fortuitous.' Since Guardian Royal purposefully availed itself of the privilege of conducting business with English China and its Texas subsidiaries, it now has the burden of presenting 'a compelling case that the presence of some other considerations would render jurisdiction unreasonable.' *Burger King Corp. v. Rudzewicz*, 471 U.S. 462, 477 (1985). There is no such compelling case here . . . . The fact that United States Fire Insurance Company subrogated to the interest of the insured should not be relevant. A subrogee 'stands in the shoes' of his subrogor . . . . The result here should be no different than if Gonzales Clay and Southern Clay brought this lawsuit directly . . . ."]

A "stream of commerce" kind of case is one in which a manufacturer of a product delivers it into the normal channels of commercial activity, and the product makes it way to the forum state. The U.S. Supreme Court has split on the issue of the requirements for purposeful minimum contacts in this context. In *Asahi Metal Industry Co. v. Superior Court*, 480 U.S. 102 (1987), Justice O'Connor (writing for four Justices) stated that "a defendant's awareness that the stream of commerce may or will sweep the product into the forum state does not convert the mere act of placing the product into the stream into an act purposefully directed at the form state." Instead, some evidence of "plus factors" showing that the defendant was "seeking to serve" the forum market is necessary. Justice Brennan (also writing for four Justices) argued that actual knowledge that defendant's products ended up in the forum was sufficient. Justice Stevens also expressed his reservations with the O'Connor approach. He first observed that the discussion of minimum contacts was unnecessary to the Court's resolution of the case, and then remarked that, even assuming the O'Connor test should have been applied, Asahi's regular course of dealing that resulted in deliveries of over 100,000 units annually over a period of several years would constitute "purposeful availment" even though the item delivered to the forum state was a standard product marketed throughout the world.

The Texas Supreme Court has adopted the O'Connor approach. In *CSR Ltd. v. Link*, 925 S.W.2d 591 (Tex. 1996), the Court ruled that an Australian company was not subject to personal jurisdiction, even though it sold its raw asbestos fiber to Johns-Manville knowing that Johns-Manville had a plant in Texas, when the company did not advertise in Texas, did not provide advice to Texas buyers, and did not create, control, or employ the distribution system that brought the asbestos into Texas. Under these circumstances, and because Johns-Manville plants were also located in four other states (Louisiana, New Jersey, Illinois and California), the Court held that there was no purposeful act directed toward Texas that would subject the defendant to jurisdiction.

The next case continues the Texas Supreme Court's development of its minimum contacts analysis, extending the "stream of commerce" reasoning to a case that arises out of the defendant's sale and delivery of a product to a Texas customer. Does it create a new "isolated occurrence" test? Should the court have distinguished between a defendant who sells products through a distributor directly to the forum and a defendant whose products reach the forum more indirectly and without its control through the "stream of commerce"?

CMMC v. SALINAS

929 S.W.2d 435 (Tex. 1996)

HECHT, J.

The sole question in this case is whether the Fourteenth Amendment permits a state court to take personal jurisdiction over a foreign manufacturer merely because it knew its allegedly defective product would be shipped to that state. We answer no, and thus reverse the judgment of the court of appeals and affirm the judgment of the trial court.

Hill Country Cellars, a small winery located in Cedar Park, Texas, ordered a winepress from KLR Machines, Incorporated, an independent distributor of equipment used in the wine and juice industries. KLR, in turn, ordered the winepress for Hill Country Cellars from CMMC, a French manufacturer, instructing CMMC to wire the press for electrical use in the United States. KLR quoted the price to Hill Country Cellars in deutch [sic] marks, although it would accept payment in U.S. dollars at the current exchange rate. KLR instructed CMMC to arrange with A. Germaine, a freight forwarder paid by KLR, to transport the press from the CMMC's factory in Chalonnes, France, to the ship on which it would travel to the United States, and to arrange for the press to be shipped FOB the port of Houston. CMMC complied and thus knew that the destination of the press was Texas. Hill Country Cellars took title to the winepress [from KLR] in Houston and paid for transportation to its winery. Shortly after it began to use the press, Hill Country Cellars made a warranty claim to KLR. KLR satisfied the claim by having an electrical motor rewound for proper use in the United States, for which it paid $529.57. KLR in turn presented the claim to CMMC, which agreed to credit KLR.

CMMC, a French corporation owned since 1986 by a German manufacturer, sells wine production equipment primarily in Europe. It does not directly market or advertise its equipment in the United States, other than by providing promotional materials to KLR. A buyer may acquire products from CMMC directly or through KLR. CMMC and KLR have no contractual arrangement and share no employees. KLR advertises CMMC products, but CMMC does not specifically authorize or approve the ads. CMMC has sold equipment in the United States, including a direct sale to another winery in Texas. CMMC has never had a place of business, distributor, or representative in Texas, or any other contacts with Texas. Hill Country Cellars never had any direct contact with CMMC.

KLR, a New York corporation with offices in Sebastopol, California, and Bath, New York, has never had offices or employees in Texas. In the ten years preceding this case it made only three or four equipment sales in Texas. It has never had any other contacts with Texas. KLR sells the equipment of numerous manufacturers, only one of which is CMMC. KLR directs its marketing efforts primarily toward California but also advertises in nationally circulated wine industry magazines. KLR advertisements have never pictured the particular press Hill Country Cellars purchased, although it was a KLR ad that led to the sale to Hill Country Cellars.

Ambrocio Salinas, a Hill Country Cellars employee, injured his arm while cleaning the press and filed this lawsuit for damages against CMMC, asserting strict product liability and negligence claims. The district court sustained CMMC's special appearance and dismissed the case for want of personal jurisdiction. The court of appeals reversed and remanded, holding that a Texas court's assertion of personal jurisdiction over CMMC could be based solely on CMMC's knowledge that the winepress would be shipped to Texas, and that this assertion would not offend traditional notions of fair play and substantial justice.

We have so frequently and so recently reiterated the constitutional standards for determining personal jurisdiction that we need not restate them yet again here . . . . Suffice it to say that the rule in these cases is that a state court can take personal jurisdiction over a defendant only if it has some minimum, purposeful contacts with the state, and the exercise of jurisdiction will not offend traditional notions of fair play and substantial justice.

CMMC's only contacts with Texas are that it made isolated sales of equipment to customers here, and that it knew the machine it sold KLR was being shipped here. Salinas argues, and the court of appeals agreed, that CMMC's release of its winepress into the stream of commerce with knowledge of the intended destination is sufficient to subject it to personal jurisdiction under our decisions in *Keen v. Ashot Ashkelon, Ltd.*, 748 S.W.2d 91 (Tex. 1988), and *Kawasaki Steel Corp. v. Middleton*, 699 S.W.2d 199 (Tex. 1985) (per curiam), which follow the rule of *World-Wide Volkswagen Corp. v. Woodson*, 444 U.S. at 286 and *Asahi Metal Industry v. Superior Court*, 480 U.S. at 102.

[The Court here summarizes the "stream of commerce" cases and O'Connor/Brennan split in the *Asahi* case.]

For now, we need not take sides in the *Asahi* debate over the stream-of-commerce doctrine because of the difference in the factual circumstances of that case and the one now before us. Asahi's products were regularly sold in California, although not by Asahi. CMMC's wine-producing equipment did not regularly find its way to Texas. Neither CMMC nor KLR made any effort to market CMMC's equipment in Texas, other than by advertisements in magazines with national circulation. Hill Country Cellars' purchase was an isolated event. KLR did not contact Hill Country Cellars; Hill Country Cellars contacted KLR. Hill Country Cellars never had any contacts at all with CMMC. CMMC's mere knowledge that its winepress was to be sold and used in Texas and its wiring the machine for use in the United States were not sufficient to subject CMMC to the jurisdiction of Texas courts. This evidence simply does not show that CMMC designed products for use in Texas, or that it made any effort to market them here, or that it took any other action to purposely avail itself of this market. Even Justice Brennan's view of the stream-of-commerce doctrine would not allow jurisdiction absent a "regular and anticipated flow of products from manufacture to distribution to retail sale." *Id.* There is no flow of products from CMMC to Texas; there is scarcely a dribble.

The court of appeals cited two Fifth Circuit cases recognizing that even one act by a defendant can support jurisdiction. *Ruston Gas Turbines, Inc. v. Donaldson Co.*, 9 F.3d 415, 419 (5th Cir. 1993); *Irving v. Owens-Corning Fiberglas Corp.*, 864 F.2d 383, 385 (5th Cir. 1989). Still, that act must be purposefully directed at the forum state so that the defendant could foresee being haled into court there. *See,*

e.g., *Burger King*, 471 U.S. at 475; *World-Wide Volkswagen*, 444 U.S. at 297–298; *Ruston*, 9 F.3d at 419; *Irving*, 864 F.2d at 385–386. Single or even occasional acts are not sufficient to support jurisdiction if, as here, " 'their nature and quality and the circumstances of their commission' create only an 'attenuated' affiliation with the forum." *Burger King*, 471 U.S. at 475, n.18 (citing *International Shoe*, 326 U.S. at 318).

This Court has followed the United States Supreme Court's stream-of-commerce rule, as of course we must. In *Kawasaki*, we held that a foreign steel manufacturer that confirmed orders for millions of dollars of steel annually to be shipped to Texas consumers had sufficient contacts to be subject to suit here. 699 S.W.2d at 201. The result would have been the same under either of the views expressed in *Asahi*. We cited *Kawasaki* and *Asahi* in *Keen*, stating: "A defendant's delivering of its product into the stream of commerce with the expectation that the product will enter the forum state will ordinarily satisfy the due process requirement of minimum contacts so as to afford that state personal jurisdiction over the defendant." *Keen*, 748 S.W.2d at 93. We did not by this one sentence extend the reach of Texas jurisdiction beyond that allowed by *World-Wide Volkswagen*, or even beyond that which Justice Brennan would have allowed in *Asahi*. Indeed, we could not have done so even if we had wanted to, bound as we are in this area by the decisions of the United States Supreme Court. To the contrary, we cited Justice O'Connor's plurality opinion twice and did not mention Justice Brennan's concurring opinion. If anything, *Keen* suggests that we would follow Justice O'Connor's formulation of the stream-of-commerce rule in Texas.

It is neither unfair nor unjust to require Salinas to litigate his disputes with CMMC at CMMC's place of business when neither he nor his employer ever had any contact whatever with CMMC in Texas. A manufacturer cannot fairly be expected to litigate in every part of the world where its products may end up; its contacts with the forum must be more purposeful, even in Justice Brennan's view, before it can constitutionally be subjected to personal jurisdiction. As we recently stated, echoing *Burger King Corp. v. Rudzewicz*, "[a] defendant should not be subject to the jurisdiction of a foreign court based upon 'random,' 'fortuitous,' or 'attenuated' contacts." *CSR*, 925 S.W.2d at 594 (quoting *Burger King*, 471 U.S. at 475). "Minimum contacts are particularly important when the defendant is from a different country because of the unique and onerous burden placed on a party called upon to defend a suit in a foreign legal system." *Id.* at 595. Here, those contacts are missing.

Accordingly, the judgment of the court of appeals is reversed and the judgment of the district court dismissing CMMC is affirmed.

The Texas Supreme Court's next case went even further, treating a direct sale to a Texas consumer as the equivalent of the consumer's fortuitous Oklahoma car wreck in *World-Wide Volkswagen*. Consider the following case.

MICHIANA EASY LIVIN' COUNTRY, INC. v. HOLTEN

168 S.W.3d 777 (Tex. 2005)

Justice Brister delivered the opinion of the Court, in which Chief Justice Jefferson, Justice Hecht, Justice Owen, and Justice Green joined. Justice Medina filed a dissenting opinion, in which Justice O'Neill joined. Justice Wainwright and Justice Johnson did not participate in the decision.

James Holten decided to buy a $64,000 Coachmen recreational vehicle sight unseen. Eschewing every RV dealer in Texas, he sought a lower price from Michiana Easy Livin' Country, Inc., an outlet store that only did business in Indiana. Holten called Michiana in Indiana, sent payment to Indiana, paid for delivery from Indiana, and agreed to resolve every dispute in Indiana. But when a dispute actually arose, he filed suit in Texas.

The trial court and court of appeals denied Michiana's special appearance . . . . Finding Michiana does not have minimum contacts with Texas, we reverse . . . .

II

A. Background

As its name invertedly suggests, Michiana is located in Indiana a few miles from the Michigan border. It is a separate legal entity from the manufacturer or any other dealers of Coachmen RVs. It has neither employees nor property in Texas, and is not authorized to do business here. It does not advertise in Texas or on the Internet, and thus did not solicit business from Holten or anyone else in Texas.

The sale at issue here was initiated entirely by Holten. Seeking a cheaper price than he could get from any of Coachmen's many dealers in Texas, Holten called the Coachmen factory. He was informed that Coachmen did not sell directly from the factory, but that a lower price could be obtained from Michiana, a "factory outlet." Holten obtained Michiana's number from the factory and placed the call that initiated the transaction here.

The RV was constructed and equipped outside Texas. It was paid for outside Texas. It was shipped to Texas at Holten's request and entirely at his expense.

The question presented is whether suit can be brought in Texas based on a nonresident's alleged misrepresentations in a telephone call with a Texas resident. The courts of appeals are split on this question of specific jurisdiction — some holding it would violate constitutional standards, and others (including the lower court here) that it would not.

B. Purposeful Availment

For half a century, the touchstone of jurisdictional due process has been "purposeful availment." Since *Hanson v. Denckla*, "it is essential in each case that there be some act by which the *defendant purposefully avails* itself of the privilege of conducting activities within the forum State, thus invoking the benefits and protections of its laws."

Three aspects of this requirement are relevant here. First, it is only the defendant's contacts with the forum that count: purposeful availment "ensures that a defendant will not be haled into a jurisdiction solely as a result of . . . the 'unilateral activity of another party or a third person.' " *Burger King Corp. v. Rudzewicz*, 471 U.S. 462, 475 (1985).

Second, the acts relied on must be "purposeful" rather than fortuitous. Sellers wh o "reach out beyond one state and create continuing relationships and obligations with citizens of another state" are subject to the jurisdiction of the latter in suits based on their activities. By contrast, a defendant will not be haled into a jurisdiction solely based on contacts that are "random, isolated, or fortuitous."

Third, a defendant must seek some benefit, advantage, or profit by "availing" itself of the jurisdiction. Jurisdiction is premised on notions of implied consent — that by invoking the benefits and protections of a forum's laws, a nonresident consents to suit there. By contrast, a nonresident may purposefully avoid a particular jurisdiction by structuring its transactions so as neither to profit from the forum's laws nor be subject to its jurisdiction.

C. Stream of Commerce

In the context of product sales, a nonresident need not have offices or employees in a forum state in order to meet the purposeful availment test. In *International Shoe Co. v. Washington*, a nonresident corporation had neither offices nor inventory in the state of Washington, but did have a dozen resident salesmen on commission who exhibited samples, solicited orders, and transmitted them to other states for shipment to resident consumers. The operation of a sales and distribution network rendered the nonresident subject to the state's jurisdiction.

Thus, a nonresident that directs marketing efforts to Texas in the hope of soliciting sales is subject to suit here in disputes arising from that business. Advertising in telephone directories in Texas cities, operating an office for sales information and support, and certain activities over the Internet all meet this standard.

It is less clear whether a nonresident "purposefully avails" itself of a forum when it benefits from a major market without doing any of the marketing. Almost twenty years ago, four justices of the United States Supreme Court held that a nonresident's mere awareness that thousands of its products were ultimately being sold in the forum state established purposeful availment; four others held that "additional conduct" was required (e.g., designing the product for or advertising it in the forum State); the ninth held that, assuming "additional conduct" was required, regular sales resulting in thousands of products reaching the forum state over many years would suffice "in most circumstances."

Since that time, we have noted that our cases appear to follow the "additional conduct" standard. Thus, for example, we have held that shipping hundreds of tons of raw asbestos to Houston was insufficient to establish jurisdiction absent evidence that a nonresident participated in the decision to send it there.

Whichever of these standards is ultimately correct, Michiana's conduct meets none of them. Michiana did not place large numbers of RVs in a "stream of commerce" flowing to Texas; as we have noted before, stream-of-commerce jurisdiction requires a stream, not a dribble. Nor is there any evidence of any "additional conduct" — Michiana did not design, advertise, or distribute RVs in Texas. Exercising jurisdiction here would go far beyond anything we have approved in other commercial cases.

D. Single Sales

The court of appeals relied on several cases by intermediate courts in Texas holding that a single contact with the state is sufficient to establish jurisdiction. But the United States Supreme Court has emphatically answered the question whether a single contract with a Texas resident can automatically establish jurisdiction — "the answer clearly is that it cannot."

Both the United States Supreme Court and this Court have found no purposeful availment in cases involving isolated sales solicited by consumers who proposed to use the product in a state where the defendant did no business. In *World-Wide Volkswagen Corp. v. Woodson*, the Supreme Court held that dealers who sold a car in New York could not be sued in Oklahoma just because the buyers were involved in a collision there:

> We find in the record before us a total absence of those affiliating circumstances that are a necessary predicate to any exercise of state-court jurisdiction. Petitioners carry on no activity whatsoever in Oklahoma. They close no sales and perform no services there. They avail themselves of none of the privileges and benefits of Oklahoma law. They solicit no business there either through salespersons or through advertising reasonably calculated to reach the State. Nor does the record show that they regularly sell cars at wholesale or retail to Oklahoma customers or residents or that they indirectly, through others, serve or seek to serve the Oklahoma market. In short, respondents seek to base jurisdiction on one, isolated occurrence and whatever inferences can be drawn therefrom: the fortuitous circumstance that a single Audi automobile, sold in New York to New York residents, happened to suffer an accident while passing through Oklahoma.

World-Wide Volkswagen Corp. v. Woodson, 444 U.S. at 295.

The facts here are not the same as those in *Woodson*, but do not differ in any material respect. Michiana *knew* Holten would take his RV to Texas, while it was merely *foreseeable* to the defendant in *Woodson* that its buyer would drive his Audi to Oklahoma. But in either case the choice was entirely that of the purchaser; the seller had no say in the matter. Under Holten's theory, Michiana could be sued in any state or country from which he chose to place his call and take delivery. But as the Supreme Court stated, "unilateral activity . . . cannot satisfy the requirement of contact with the forum State."

This Court addressed the same question in 1996 in *CMMC v. Salinas*. In that case, a French manufacturer had made no effort to market its winepress equipment in Texas, had made only one other sale in Texas, and did not initiate the sale at issue to a Texas buyer. We held that the Due Process Clause prohibited specific jurisdiction of a tort suit in Texas based on injuries resulting from alleged defects. As Michiana's contacts here are certainly no more and arguably somewhat less than those in *CMMC*, the result must be the same, as the Due Process Clause has not changed in the interim.

It is true that in some circumstances a single *contract* may meet the purposeful-availment standard, but not when it involves a single *contact* taking place outside the forum state. A long-term franchise agreement may establish minimum contacts because, though it stems from a single contract, it involves many contacts over a long period of time. Similarly, a life-insurance policy may stem from a single contract, but necessarily involves a series of contacts until death does the parties part. *McGee v. International Life Ins. Co.*, 355 U.S. 220, 223 (1957).

Certainly a nonresident corporation ought to be subject to suit in any jurisdiction where it "enjoys the benefits and protection of the laws of that state." Here, it is hard to imagine what possible benefits and protection Michiana enjoyed from Texas law. Holten paid for the RV in advance, and could not have planned on taking it to Indiana regularly for service. Everything Michiana wanted out of the contract it had in hand. Indeed, it is hard to imagine how Michiana would have conducted its activities any differently if Texas had no law at all.

Clearly, Michiana anticipated some profit from this single sale, at least until the litigation started. But "financial benefits accruing to the defendant from a collateral relation to the forum State will not support jurisdiction if they do not stem from a constitutionally cognizable contact with that State." *Woodson*, 444 U.S. at 299. We find none here.

III

The court of appeals affirmed on the basis of two contacts between Michiana and Texas: (1) misrepresentations Michiana allegedly made in response to a phone call from Holten, and (2) Michiana's arrangements with a shipper to deliver the RV to Holten for use in Texas. Neither is sufficient.

A. Shipping to Texas

The second ground is easily disposable. Delivery in Texas was at Holten's sole request and sole expense. If a seller of chattels is subject to suit wherever a customer requests delivery, then the chattel has become its agent for service of process — a conclusion the United States Supreme Court has expressly rejected.

We too rejected this argument in *CMMC*, in which we stated: "The sole question in this case is whether the Fourteenth Amendment permits a state court to take personal jurisdiction over a foreign manufacturer merely because it knew its allegedly defective product would be shipped to that state. *We answer no*, and thus reverse . . . ." 929 S.W.2d at 436. Accordingly, we must do the same here.

B. Committing a Tort "in" Texas

The court of appeals relied most heavily on the first ground — Holten's allegation that Michiana committed a tort in Texas.

Allegations that a tort was committed in Texas satisfy the Texas Long-Arm Statute, but not necessarily the U.S. Constitution; the broad language of the former extends only as far as the latter will permit. Thus, for example, the plaintiffs in both *Woodson* and *CMMC* alleged torts, and the defendants surely foresaw that defective products could harm local buyers — but in neither case was that enough to establish jurisdiction.

The court below joined many of its sister courts in stating the following as a rule of jurisdiction: "If a tortfeasor knows that the brunt of the injury will be felt by a particular resident in the forum state, he must reasonably anticipate being haled into court there to answer for his actions." But neither this Court nor the United States Supreme Court has ever said so.

To the contrary, twenty years ago the United States Supreme Court wrote: "Although it has been argued that foreseeability of causing injury in another State should be sufficient to establish such contacts there when policy considerations so require, the Court has consistently held that this kind of foreseeability is not a 'sufficient benchmark' for exercising personal jurisdiction." *Burger King Corp. v. Rudzewicz*, 471 U.S. at 474. This Court too has expressly rejected jurisdiction "based solely upon the effects or consequences of an alleged conspiracy" in the forum state. *National Indus. Sand Ass'n v. Gibson*, 897 S.W.2d 769, 773 (Tex. 1995). Instead, it is "the defendant's conduct and connection with the forum" that are critical. *Burger King*, 471 U.S. at 474 (quoting *Woodson*, 444 U.S. at 297).

It is true that on one occasion the United States Supreme Court found specific jurisdiction based on alleged wrongdoing intentionally directed at a forum resident. In *Calder v. Jones*, 465 U.S. 783, 785 n.2 (1984), a reporter and editor collaborated on an allegedly defamatory article, but they did so knowing the article was for their employer, the *National Enquirer*, which sold more than 600,000 copies in the forum state every week. Whether or not a jury found the article defamatory, there was no question the defendant's article constituted a substantial "presence" in the state.

Texas courts that base jurisdiction on torts committed during the receipt of an out-of-state phone call apparently assume that *Calder* would have come out the same way if the defamation had occurred in a single unsolicited phone call a nonresident answered from a single private individual in the forum state. But if "the defendant's conduct and connection with the forum" must play a critical role, the two cases cannot be the same.

A companion case decided by the same Court on the same day as *Calder* shows that the important factor was the extent of the defendant's activities, not merely the residence of the victim. In *Keeton v. Hustler Magazine, Inc.*, 465 U.S. 770, 772 (1984), the victim of another allegedly defamatory article sued not in the state where she lived, but in a different state with a longer statute of limitations. Noting that the defendant had sold more than 10,000 copies of its magazine every month in the forum state, the Supreme Court held that "it must reasonably anticipate being haled into court there."

Our dissenting colleagues cite no other authority that a single conversation with a private citizen constitutes purposeful availment of any jurisdiction in which that citizen happens to live. While torts were alleged in some of the cases cited in the dissent, the defendant's conduct in each case was much more extensive and was aimed at getting extensive business in or from the forum state. Exercising jurisdiction here would go far beyond anything we have approved in other tort cases.

C. The Consequences

Several problems arise if jurisdiction turns not on a defendant's contacts, but on where it "directed a tort." First, it shifts a court's focus from the "relationship among the *defendant*, the forum, and the litigation" to the relationship among the "*plaintiff*, the forum . . . and the litigation." The place where a plaintiff relies on fraud may determine the choice of law, but choice-of-law analysis considers all parties, local courts, legal policies, interested states, and the interstate and international systems. By contrast, minimum-contacts analysis focuses solely on the actions and reasonable expectations of the defendant.

Second, directed-a-tort jurisdiction confuses the roles of judge and jury by equating the jurisdictional inquiry with the underlying merits. If purposeful availment depends on whether a tort was directed toward Texas, then a nonresident may defeat jurisdiction by proving there was no tort. Personal jurisdiction is a question of law for the court, even if it requires resolving questions of fact. But what if a judge and jury could disagree? May a trial judge effectively grant summary judgment in a local jurisdiction by deciding contested liability facts in favor of the defendant? And if a jury absolves a defendant of tort liability, is the judgment void because the court never had jurisdiction of the defendant in the first place?

Business contacts are generally a matter of physical fact, while tort liability (especially in misrepresentation cases) turns on what the parties thought, said, or intended. Far better that judges should limit their jurisdictional decisions to the former rather than involving themselves in trying the latter.

Third, in cases dealing with commerce, a plaintiff often has the option to sue in either contract or tort. Here, for example, Holten alleged tort, contract, and statutory claims, as Texas law often allows a plaintiff to do. If directing a tort at Texas is enough, then personal jurisdiction arises when plaintiffs allege a tort, but not when they allege breach of contract. Thus, the purposeful availment depends on the form of claim selected by the *plaintiff*.

Fourth, changes in technology have made reliance on phone calls obsolete as proof of purposeful availment. While the ubiquity of "caller ID" may allow nonresidents to know a caller's telephone number, that number no longer necessarily indicates anything about the caller's location. If jurisdiction can be based on phone conversations "directed at" a forum, how does a defendant avail itself of any jurisdiction when it can never know where the other party has forwarded calls or traveled with a mobile phone?

In their dissenting opinion, our colleagues remind us seven times that Michiana did not deny Holten's fraud allegations. Of course, Michiana did deny his allegations in its answer, but rightly focused its jurisdictional affidavits on lack of *contacts* rather than lack of *culpability*. Jurisdiction cannot turn on whether a defendant denies wrongdoing — as virtually all will. Nor can it turn on whether a plaintiff merely alleges wrongdoing — again as virtually all will. If committing a tort establishes jurisdiction, our colleagues will have to decide who is correct — and then the Texas jurisdictional rule will be: guilty nonresidents can be sued here, innocent ones cannot. The dissenting opinion shows little doubt on that score; but if we address jurisdictional questions in this spirit, nonresidents will avoid not just our courts but our state and all its residents as well.

For the reasons stated above, we disapprove of those opinions holding that (1) specific jurisdiction is necessarily established by allegations or evidence that a nonresident committed a tort in a telephone call from a Texas number, or that (2) specific jurisdiction turns on whether a defendant's contacts were tortious rather than the contacts themselves.

. . . .

Michiana's only contact with Texas was Holten's decision to place his order from there, we reverse the court of appeals' judgment and render judgment dismissing the claims against Michiana for want of jurisdiction.

Justice Medina, joined by Justice O'Neill, dissenting.

[Justices Medina and O'Neill dissented, distinguishing *CMMC* and arguing that a direct sale of a product by the defendant to Texas could serve as the basis for personal jurisdiction. "Here, there is evidence that any misrepresentation was knowingly aimed at Texas because Michiana, with the knowledge that Holten was a Texas resident who expected the motor home to be delivered to Texas, made representations to him regarding the custom motor home."]

NOTES AND QUESTIONS

(1) *Advertising and "Seeking to Serve" the Texas Market.* Justice O'Connor's opinion in *Asahi* listed "advertising in the forum state" as one indicator that a defendant had purposely done business in the forum. In *CMMC*, the Texas Supreme Court seems to reject advertising in "magazines with national circulation" as evidence that the defendant has purposefully done business with Texas, despite the fact that such magazines solicit business from Texas residents, among others. At least in the context of general jurisdiction cases, intermediate appellate courts have made this same distinction between national and local publications, holding that national advertising does not constitute a purposeful contact with Texas. *See Stowers v. Roberts*, 2001 Tex. App. LEXIS 8397 at *16 (Tex. App. — Austin Dec. 20, 2001, no pet.) ("advertising in national media, as contrasted with state or local publications directed specifically at Texas residents, is not evidence of systematic and continuous activities purposefully directed at Texas to establish general jurisdiction"); *Michel v. Rocket Eng'g Corp.*, 45 S.W.3d 658, 673 (Tex. App. — Fort Worth 2001, no pet.); *Clark v. Noyes*, 871 S.W.2d 508, 519 (Tex. App. — Dallas 1994, no pet.) (publishing scholarly articles in national journals not purposeful availment).

(2) *The Supreme Court Finds Sufficient Contacts for Specific Jurisdiction.* In *Moki Mac River Expeditions v. Drugg*, 221 S.W.3d 569, 577–578 (Tex. 2007), the Court discussed the defendant's contacts with Texas:

> Unlike in *Michiana*, the evidence in this case indicates that Moki Mac does intend to serve the Texas market. Moki Mac knowingly sells rafting trips to Texas residents and purposefully directs marketing efforts to Texas with the intent to solicit business from this state. In addition to sending the brochures and release to the Druggs, the evidence shows that Moki Mac regularly advertised in Texas. It has placed advertisements in a variety of nationally circulated publications that have Texas subscribers. Moki Mac also hired public relations firms to target media groups and tour operators, some of whom were located in Texas. In 1996, Moki Mac promoted its trips within Texas by taking out an advertisement in the Austin Chronicle. We have said that a nonresident defendant's advertising in local media "in and of itself, is a sufficiently purposeful act that is done in Texas." *Siskind v. Villa Found. for Educ., Inc.*, 642 S.W.2d 434, 436 (Tex. 1982).
>
> Moki Mac's efforts to solicit business in Texas, however, go further. It solicited Texas residents through mass and targeted direct-marketing email campaigns. Moki Mac compiled a mailing list by collecting contact information from interested parties either by phone, email, or through the company's website. In addition, Moki Mac obtained a list of potential customers from a commercial source. Both its own mailing list and the commercial mailing list included Texas residents. The company would automatically send brochures and trip information to people who had previously expressed interest in a trip, even in years when that person had not expressed interest. As part of those promotions, Moki Mac offered "a free float" as an incentive to customers who coordinated a group of ten or more. Moki Mac provided this compensation to at least two Texas residents. Moki Mac occasionally provided musicians to accompany float trips free of charge. On one particular trip, Moki Mac permitted a string quartet from Fort Worth to accompany a Texas group on its float trip, free of charge to the musicians. Moki Mac also paid a fee to a travel agency located in Houston, resulting in multiple trips involving Texas residents.
>
> In addition, Moki Mac established channels of regular communication with its customers in Texas. It was Moki Mac's practice to utilize particular customers, who would become de facto group leaders, to plan, organize, and promote its trips. Annie Seals was one such contact. By communicating with all of its customers through correspondence with a single group leader, Moki Mac streamlined its reservations process. The company kept these communication channels open; it was Moki Mac's practice to automatically send information regarding new trips, schedules, and prices to those on its mailing list who had been a customer or who had simply expressed interest in a trip within a three-year period. . . . Moki Mac's contacts with Texas did not result, as did the defendant's in *Michiana*, from the mere fortuity that the Druggs happened to reside here. Rather, the contacts it had with Texas resulted from additional conduct through which it aimed to get extensive business in or from this state.

The Court, however, found that the Druggs' cause of action did not arise out of these contacts sufficiently to invoke specific jurisdiction, and remanded for a determination of whether Moki Mac's contacts would support general jurisdiction. This portion of the case is discussed in the next section.

Similarly, in *Retamco Operating, Inc. v. Republic Drilling Co.*, No. 07–0599, 2009 Tex. LEXIS 38 (Tex. Feb. 27, 2009), the Texas Supreme Court found that a California company that knowingly took an assignment of Texas oil and gas interests "reached out and created a continuing relationship in Texas." Under the assignment, it is liable for obligations and expenses related to the interests. This ownership also allows Republic to 'enjoy . . . the benefits and protection of [Texas laws].' *Michiana*, 168 S.W.3d at 787 (citing *Int'l Shoe*, 326 U.S. at 319). Unlike personal property, Republic's real property will always be in Texas, which leaves no doubt of the continuing relationship that this ownership creates." Thus Texas courts had jurisdiction over Republic in a case alleging that the assignment constituted a fraudulent transfer.

(3) *Use of "Stream of Commerce" Precedent.* In both *CMMC* and *Michiana*, the Texas Supreme Court relies on the U.S. Supreme Court's "stream of commerce" cases. In those cases, the defendant's product reached the forum state indirectly. In *World-Wide Volkswagen*, it was the New York consumer who brought the car sold by the defendant to Oklahoma while in the process of moving to Arizona, all without the defendant's knowledge. In that case, the manufacturer of the car and the national importer *were* subject to jurisdiction in Oklahoma. In *Asahi*, the defendant was a manufacturer of component parts whose valves ended up in tires that ended up in motorcycles that ended up in California. The defendant knew about (and profited from) but did not control the valves' destinations. On that record, five Supreme Court Justices would have found sufficient contacts with the forum, although eight Justices agreed that under the facts of that case, an assertion of jurisdiction would be unfair. How does CMMC's sale differ from these cases? How does Michiana's sale differ?

(4) *Reading* Calder v. Jones *Narrowly*. The majority opinion relies on footnote 2 in *Calder v. Jones* to support its contention that it was the volume of National Enquirer sales in California that was the basis for jurisdiction in that case. But that footnote ("A geographic analysis of the total paid circulation for the September 18, 1979, issue of the Enquirer showed total sales, national and international, of 5,292,200. Sales in California were 604,431. The State with the next highest total was New York, with 316,911") was used by the U.S. Supreme Court to explain why there was jurisdiction over the publication itself (which did not even challenge personal jurisdiction), not why there was jurisdiction over the editor and reporter who "directed" their intentional torts at California. Nevertheless, intermediate appellate courts have already begun to follow the Supreme Court's narrowing of *Calder*. *See, e.g.*, *Niehaus v. Cedar Bridge, Inc.*, 208 S.W.3d 575, 584 (Tex. App. — Austin, 2006, no pet.) (citing *Michiana* as holding that "the important factor [in *Calder*] was the extent of the defendant's activities, not merely the residence of the victim."); *Lewis v. Indian Springs Land Corp.*, 175 S.W.3d 906, 914 (Tex. App. — Dallas 2005, no pet.) (noting that "the decision in *Michiana* confirmed the rule that jurisdiction must turn on defendant's contacts, not where it 'directed a tort.' "). *See also Credit Commer. de France, S.A. v. Morales*, 195 S.W.3d 209, 223 (Tex. App. —

San Antonio 2006, pet. denied) (referring disparagingly to "direct-a-tort" jurisdiction). In fact, the Fourteenth Court of Appeals has indicated its belief that *Michiana* eliminates the effects test. *See Johns Hopkins University v. Nath*, 238 S.W.3d 492 (Tex. App. — Houston [14th] 2007, pet. denied) (commenting that the *Michiana* court construed *Calder's* finding of specific jurisdiction as turning on the defendants' "substantial 'presence' " in the forum state based on the fact that the allegedly defamatory article on which the defendants collaborated was for their employer, the National Enquirer, which sold more than 600,000 copies in the forum state every week).

(5) *Holten's Contract Claims.* As the majority opinion points out, plaintiffs often have claims based on both contract and tort theories all arising out of the same transaction. In *Michiana*, for example, the plaintiff claimed factually that at the time he purchased the motor home, Michiana represented to him that the motor home would (1) be constructed of solid wood fastened with screws, (2) not contain nails or staples, (3) contain a bathtub and shower, (4) contain a double-pedal foot-flush toilet, and (5) be serviceable by any authorized Ford dealer. Holten also alleged that these representations turned out to be false. Based on these factual allegations, Holten included claims for breach of warranty, breach of contract, and breach of the Deceptive Trade Practices Act.

What about Holten's contract and DTPA claims? Does the court consider the contract line of cases (such as *McGee* and *Burger King*) in deciding whether Michiana's entering into a contract with a resident of Texas can subject it to personal jurisdiction? The majority in *Burger King* holds that purposeful availment analysis in contract cases requires "a 'highly realistic' approach that recognizes that a 'contract' is ordinarily but an intermediate step serving to tie up prior business negotiations with future consequences which themselves are the real object of the business transaction. It is these factors — prior negotiations and contemplated future consequences, along with the terms of the contract and the parties' actual course of dealing — that must be evaluated in determining whether the defendant purposefully established minimum contacts within the forum." Note that although Holten's claims of fraud all arose out of a single telephone conversation, the course of dealings between the parties included multiple conversations as well as a written contract. What would be the likely result of such an analysis?

(6) *Tort v. Contract Claims.* Justice Brister argues that "intentionally causing effects in the forum" is too broad a grant of jurisdiction, because it would make jurisdiction easier to obtain for tort claims than for contract claims. "If directing a tort at Texas is enough, then personal jurisdiction arises when plaintiffs allege a tort, but not when they allege breach of contract. Thus, the *defendant's* purposeful availment depends on the form of claim selected by the *plaintiff*." What is wrong with treating different claims differently if the conduct giving rise to the claims differs and the effects also differ?

(7) *Playing with Precedent.* In the area of personal jurisdiction, the outcome of cases is extremely fact-dependent. In addition, the U.S. Supreme Court's cases are not particularly consistent. They also tend to contain long discussions of due process jurisprudence. Perhaps because of this, courts writing opinions in personal jurisdiction cases have a tendency to lift quotes that support the point they want to

make, without regard to whether the cited case in fact reaches a result consistent with the excerpted language. For example, the majority opinion in *Michiana* quotes *Burger King* for the following proposition:

> Although it has been argued that foreseeability of causing injury in another State should be sufficient to establish such contacts there when policy considerations so require, the Court has consistently held that this kind of foreseeability is not a 'sufficient benchmark' for exercising personal jurisdiction.

Burger King Corp. v. Rudzewicz, 471 U.S. at 474. But *Burger King*, as you recall from your first year Civil Procedure class, was a case in which the Supreme Court upheld Florida's jurisdiction over an individual Michigan resident who had a Michigan Burger King franchise supervised by a Michigan district office. It did so on the basis of telephone conversations with Florida headquarters, a one-time purchase of equipment from Florida, and the terms of a franchise contract (that would have involved a 20 year relationship but that ended almost before it began) that contained a Florida choice of law clause and from which the Michigan defendant had negotiated the removal of a Florida choice of forum clause. That defendant, the Court held, should have foreseen being sued in Florida. Suppose the *Michiana* court had chosen instead this quote from *Burger King*, which is in the same section of the case as the one above:

> Moreover, where individuals "purposefully derive benefit" from their interstate activities, . . . it may well be unfair to allow them to escape having to account in other States for consequences that arise proximately from such activities; the Due Process Clause may not readily be wielded as a territorial shield to avoid interstate obligations that have been voluntarily assumed . . . . Jurisdiction is proper . . . where the contacts proximately result from actions by the defendant himself that create a "substantial connection" with the forum State . . . . So long as it creates a "substantial connection" with the forum, even a single act can support jurisdiction.

Id. at 474, 476. Would it support the result in *Michiana*? Because selected quotations can be used to justify almost any position in personal jurisdiction cases, be sure to focus on the ways in which those courts applied (or didn't) the propositions contained in their general discussions of jurisdiction.

While some cases have read *Michiana* broadly, others have distinguished it and found sufficient purposeful contacts with Texas. For example, the court in *Glencoe Capital Partners II, L.P. v. Gernsbacher*, 269 S.W.3d 157 (Tex. App. — Fort Worth 2008, no pet.), found jurisdiction based on a series of conference call-board meetings with known Texas residents. "The circumstances of this case are markedly different from the single, unsolicited, unilateral phone call in *Michiana*. . . . [T]his case involves many telephonic board meetings at regular intervals over a span of years. . . . Even if [the defendants] did not know that [the plaintiffs] participated in the meetings from Texas, that ignorance alone is not enough to negate specific jurisdiction because it was foreseeable that their activity directed toward Texas

residents would subject them to Texas jurisdiction." Read the following case which, like *Michiana*, involves a Texas resident contacting a non-Texas seller and purchasing an expensive single item. In light of *Michiana* and this case, consider how to draw the line between products that are delivered in Texas and outside of Texas, and whether the technicalities of passage of title should make the difference between the presence and absence of personal jurisdiction.

GJP, INC. v. GHOSH

251 S.W.3d 854 (Tex. App. — Austin 2008, no pet.)

PEMBERTON, J.

This appeal concerns a dispute arising from the purchase of a used 1967 Jaguar sports car by appellee, Avijit Ghosh, from appellants GJP Inc. and Richard D. Herting. Complaining that he had been misled regarding the Jaguar's condition, Ghosh filed suit against appellants and two other defendants, alleging violations of the Texas Deceptive Trade Practices Act, among other claims. His claims were tried to a jury. Based on the jury's favorable findings on Ghosh's DTPA claims, the trial court rendered judgment against all defendants, jointly and severally, for $11,500 in actual damages and $112,500 in attorney's fees; $20,000 in additional damages against appellants, jointly and severally, based on findings of knowing conduct; plus another $3,000 in damages against GJP. Appellants bring twenty-seven points of error challenging, among other things, the trial court's personal jurisdiction over them. . . . For the reasons explained herein, we will affirm the judgment.

BACKGROUND

According to the evidence presented at trial, GJP is a South Dakota-based company principally engaged, at relevant times, in the plastering business. At pertinent times, GJP was owned by Gerald Johnson, a South Dakota resident. Johnson testified that the company, in addition to its primary business focus, also held title to approximately a dozen Jaguar automobiles. Johnson explained that acquiring and restoring Jaguars was a hobby of his and that he found it "convenient" to place the cars' title in his company. Richard Herting, a longtime friend of Johnson and fellow South Dakota resident, was an authorized agent of GJP who handled various business dealings of the company. He also shared Johnson's interest and work with his Jaguar collection. Appellants concede that, at all relevant times, Herting was acting within his authority as an agent of GJP.

Among the Jaguars in the collection was a red 1967 E-type Jaguar convertible. When purchased by GJP in 1999, this vehicle had been partially disassembled and was missing bumpers, door handles, most of the interior, and parts of the engine. Johnson and Herting reassembled it and, among other work, repainted it red, installed an interior and top, cleaned out and "redid" the gas tank, got "most of the wiring to work," and installed new wheels and tires. Johnson explained that he later chose to resell the 1967 E-type because he was restoring a 1968 E-type and "just didn't need two of them"; he added that he had lost interest in the 1967 vehicle once the "puzzle" of repairs had been completed. GJP had not previously sold one of its Jaguars, and Johnson denied that he had purchased the car with the intent to resell it. At trial, Ghosh questioned this explanation, suggesting that appellants had chosen to sell the car because they were aware of problems with it.

Herting advertised the red Jaguar on three websites around the world where, he testified, such vehicles were sold or traded — eBay, based in California; Jag-Lovers, based in Bergen, Norway; and Classic Jaguar, an Austin-based company that specialized in restorations of E-type vehicles. Herting explained that he chose Classic Jaguar because it was well-known and well-respected among Jaguar enthusiasts worldwide; there was also evidence that Herting and GJP had previously purchased parts from Classic Jaguar for use in their restorations, including the red Jaguar. Classic Jaguar is owned by Dan Mooney. Herting emailed information regarding the car to Mooney, who crafted, and Herting approved, an advertisement that Mooney placed on a portion of the Classic Jaguar website dedicated to similar "for sale" postings. The ad displayed two photographs of the red E-type and stated, "Believed low mileage (30,000) matching number car," "Strong mechanicals," and "New floors, sills, paint, interior (less seats), windshield, wiring, brakes, suspension, tyres and wheels." It listed an asking price of $38,000 and directed inquires to Herting's South Dakota telephone number, also providing Herting's email address.

In the meantime, Ghosh, a Houston resident, had been searching websites with an interest in purchasing a used E-type Jaguar. . . . Ghosh found the Classic Jaguar website, and inquired with Classic and Mooney about a blue Jaguar featured in one of the site's "for sale" ads. During a discussion about the blue car and the difficulty of finding reasonably priced E-types in general, Ghosh claims that Mooney mentioned, "Well, actually, there's an excellent car on our website right now," and referred him to appellants' ad for the red Jaguar.

Ghosh testified that Mooney vouched for Herting's experience and capability as a Jaguar restorer and his work on the red Jaguar in particular, indicating that Herting had used parts purchased from Classic Jaguar. Relying on Mooney's remarks about Herting and the car, Ghosh called Herting at his South Dakota phone number. The parties gave differing accounts of ensuing events. Ghosh testified that he called Herting four to five times before the Jaguar came to Texas. Herting testified that he received several calls from Ghosh, among a "few dozen" he received inquiring about the car. Ghosh claimed that during their first call, Herting made various representations echoing the statements in the website ad, explained the work he had done to the car, and stated that the car drove well and was in fine running order, that it was "rust-free," and that he had been storing the car in a heated garage. Ghosh claimed that he was impressed by Herting's apparently extensive knowledge of Jaguars and the fact that he had maintained and worked on so many other Jaguars in the GJP collection. Ghosh gained further confidence in Herting, he testified, because Herting made apparently forthcoming acknowledgments that the hood "didn't fit exactly right," the seats had not been replaced, and the right rear quarter of the car was not original. After their first phone conversation, Herting emailed Ghosh approximately twenty photographs of the red Jaguar. Ghosh added that, at some point, he inquired about having the Jaguar inspected in South Dakota, but Herting had dissuaded him by claiming that Ghosh would be unable to find an impartial opinion because all of the potential inspectors knew him. Herting, by contrast, explained that while any potential

South Dakota inspectors would know him because he and Johnson had essentially the only Jaguar collection in the state, he had suggested that Ghosh have the car inspected in a neighboring state.

Ghosh called Herting and offered him a price of $35,000, $3,000 below the asking price. Herting testified that Ghosh offered that price in exchange for taking the car "as-is" and without inspection. Both Herting and Johnson testified that it was not unusual in the marketplace for buyers to purchase used Jaguars without inspection, and that they had previously done so. Ghosh denies that he offered to purchase the car "as-is." He admits that he elected not to have the car inspected, blaming Herting and Mooney for inducing him into such a high level of confidence in the red Jaguar that he believed none was warranted.

In response to Ghosh's offer, Herting indicated that he needed to consult with his partner and asked Ghosh to call him back later. When Ghosh called, Herting accepted the offer on behalf of GJP. The parties agreed that they would meet at Classic Jaguar in Austin to conclude the transaction. It is undisputed that this location was chosen because Herting had previously planned a trip to Austin with an empty trailer to pick up a race car GJP had purchased from Classic Jaguar. Johnson and Herting added that these terms were part of the parties' deal: they claimed that Ghosh agreed to forego an inspection if Herting would deliver the car to Texas at no charge. . . .

Ghosh arranged with Mooney, in advance of his meeting with Herting, to have work done on the red Jaguar, including a hood realignment and installation of seat belts. He also made plans to drive the car over the weekend (the agreed-upon meeting date was a Friday) before returning the car to Classic on the following Monday to have the work performed. But Ghosh, at trial, dismissed as "complete nonsense" the notion that he had agreed to purchase the Jaguar while it was still in South Dakota. Instead, he characterized the parties' "deal" as being limited only to the price Ghosh would pay *if* he decided to purchase the car upon seeing it in Austin. According to Ghosh, "the car was being brought down to Texas for me to look at and any deal that was going to be conducted was going to be conducted here."

With what he testified was his understanding that he had a firm sale, Herting loaded the red Jaguar on the empty trailer and, accompanied by his wife, drove to Austin. On the appointed date, Ghosh arrived from Houston with a $35,000 cashier's check dated the preceding day. He testified that he had already planned to spend the weekend driving the car in the Hill Country with his girlfriend, who had accompanied him to Austin. Ghosh entered Classic Jaguar, where he met Herting and Mooney in person, and walked outside to where the red Jaguar was parked. Herting briefly pointed out various features of the work he had done to the car. Ghosh testified that he noticed a paint chip on the trunk and that the trunk did not appear flush with the rest of the car when closed. Herting assured him that the effect was likely attributable to new rubber seals that would eventually compress. Ghosh testified that he did not regard either of these problems as sufficiently serious to deter him from purchasing the car, and that the car looked to him as it had been represented. Ghosh and Herting then went inside the dealership.

According to Mooney's testimony, he allowed Herting and Ghosh to use an empty office in which to meet. Ghosh gave his cashier's check to Herting, and Herting handed over the car's South Dakota title, repair and parts receipts, and keys. When they emerged from the office after ten or fifteen minutes, Ghosh exclaimed, "Dan, I own my first E Type" and then asked Mooney to "look at a couple of things on the car" for him. Specifically, Ghosh asked whether the trunk lid needed to be adjusted and whether the floors were new. Although Mooney glanced at some of these exterior features, he testified that his 30-second look at the car was by no means an inspection, which, he explained, requires two to three hours to complete. . . .

Approximately eight to ten miles into his Hill Country excursion, Ghosh encountered what he perceived to be several problems with the car, including an overheating engine and leaking fluids. He ultimately had the car towed back to Classic Jaguar. Ghosh requested Classic Jaguar to inspect the car. The eventual inspection revealed, among other problems, cracks and other structural weaknesses in the engine frames — which, Johnson admitted at trial, created a danger to the driver — a blown head gasket, missing bolts, oil and water leaks, and corrosion.

Ghosh eventually filed suit in the trial court against GJP, Herting, Mooney, and Classic Jaguar. Appellants entered special appearances to contest personal jurisdiction, which the trial court denied. . . .

DISCUSSION

[The court first held that the defendants' failure to take an interlocutory appeal from the denial of their special appearances did not waive their right to raise the issue on appeal. It also concluded that it would make its decision based on all of the evidence in the record, not just the record from the special appearance motion and hearing.]

. . . .

It is undisputed that both Herting and GJP are South Dakota residents, that neither maintains a place of business in Texas or has employees, servants, or agents within the state, and that neither is required to maintain nor maintains a registered agent for service in Texas. The evidence is also not disputed that the only business Herting or GJP had previously transacted in Texas was purchasing parts by mail from Classic Jaguar and purchasing a race car on eBay that Classic had advertised for sale on that site. . . .

Appellants equate the underlying facts to those of the Texas Supreme Court's seminal decision in *Michiana Easy Livin' Country, Inc. v. Holten*. 168 S.W.3d 777. In *Michiana*, the court addressed "whether suit can be brought in Texas based on a nonresident's alleged misrepresentations in a telephone call with a Texas resident." *Id.* at 784. [The court here summarizes the facts and holding of *Michiana* before applying it to the facts of this case.]

Appellants urge that *Michiana* compels us to hold they did not purposefully avail themselves to the privilege of doing business in Texas so as to invoke the benefits and protections of its laws. Ghosh, like Holten, sued appellants based on misrepresentations allegedly made from out of state during one or more telephone calls. Each of these phone calls, Herting testified without dispute, was initiated by Ghosh. The mere allegation or proof that Ghosh relied on these out-of-state representations in Texas cannot support jurisdiction, appellants contend, nor are these phone calls proof of purposeful availment. Appellants add that there is no evidence they purposefully solicited Ghosh's business in a manner that could give rise to specific jurisdiction. To the contrary, they emphasize Ghosh's admissions that he had learned about Herting and the Jaguar from Mooney (a third party) and called Herting in reliance on Mooney's vouching for both the car and Herting's work. *See Michiana*, 168 S.W.3d at 785 (only defendant's acts count in determining whether it purposefully availed itself to the forum). Consequently, appellants maintain, the only Texas connection between the phone conversations and the parties' ultimate "deal" was that Ghosh happened to live in Texas.

Unlike Michiana, appellants did advertise on the Internet. Nonetheless, they point out that under the "Texas law on Internet activities" recognized in *Michiana*, a mere "passive" website advertisement — one that does not permit interactivity — does not constitute purposeful availment to the viewer's forum. Appellants emphasize that Herting's ad consisted only of photographs and statements, listed an asking price of $38,000, and directed inquires to Herting's South Dakota telephone number and email address, but did not enable a viewer to interact online with Herting. The fact that the owner of the website was Austin-based Classic Jaguar, appellants further assert, does not distinguish their passive website advertisement from one posted anywhere else in the world. Appellants stress that Herting posted similar ads on two other websites around the world that were calculated to reach Jaguar enthusiasts worldwide — Jag-Lovers, based in Bergen, Norway and eBay, located in California. The Classic Jaguar website was included among these, Herting testified without dispute, not because of its geographic location but because it, like the other two sites, was well-known and well-respected within the global community of Jaguar enthusiasts. . . .

As for Herting's conduct in Texas, appellants dismiss it as akin to Michiana's shipping the RV to Holten in Texas. *See Michiana*, 168 S.W.3d at 788 ("If a seller of chattels is subject to suit wherever a customer requests delivery, then the chattel has become its agent for service of process — a conclusion the United States Supreme Court has expressly rejected.") (citing *World-Wide Volkswagen*, 444 U.S. at 296); *see also CMMC*, 929 S.W.2d at 437–40 (finding no personal jurisdiction over manufacturer that knew a machine it sold a Texas buyer was being shipped here F.O.B. Houston). In appellants' view, they executed a sale contract with Ghosh before the Jaguar ever left South Dakota and were merely performing under that agreement while in Texas. *Michiana*, 168 S.W.3d at 787 (mere existence of a contract with a forum resident does not constitute purposeful availment). The fact that performance took place in Texas as opposed to South Dakota or somewhere else, appellants add, stems from the fortuities that (1) Herting had already made plans to travel to Classic Jaguar with a trailer to pick up the race car appellants had purchased; and (2) that location also happened to be convenient to Ghosh, who lived in Houston and desired to have Classic work on the car. Appellants add that Herting's trip to Texas did not seek or obtain benefits or protections from Texas law, but merely provided a courtesy to Ghosh that saved him the costs and inconvenience of having to make separate shipping and payment arrangements to gain possession of the car.

Although attributing somewhat greater jurisdictional significance to appellants' advertisement on the Classic Jaguar website and his telephone conversations with Herting, Ghosh acknowledges that personal jurisdiction ultimately hinges on the implications of Herting's acts while physically present in Texas. He urges that Herting availed himself of the benefits and protections of Texas law by traveling to Texas and selling him the Jaguar here. As noted, Ghosh disputes appellants' view of the "deal" they struck by telephone as "complete nonsense," claiming that he had agreed only to a *price* of $35,000 *if* he decided to purchase the car after seeing it in Austin and that "any deal that was going to be conducted was going to be conducted here." In the alternative, Ghosh argues that if the parties had executed a sale contract by phone, appellants purposefully availed themselves to Texas by agreeing to deliver the car and accept payment here.

Assuming without deciding that the "deal" the parties struck by telephone constituted a contract for sale, as appellants contend, we nonetheless conclude that Herting's acts in Texas constituted purposeful availment of the privilege of conducting activities in Texas so as to invoke the benefits and protections of Texas law. To understand why, we first consider the nature of the duties that Herting would have assumed under this sale contract. Both Texas and South Dakota have adopted the Uniform Commercial Code, and the applicable provisions of each state's version are materially identical. It is undisputed that Herting agreed to deliver the Jaguar to Ghosh in Austin. Upon tender of delivery in Austin, title would pass to Ghosh. *See* Tex. Bus. & Com. Code Ann. §§ 2.401(b), 2.503; S.D. Codified Laws §§ 57A-2–401(2), 57A-2–503 (2004). Tender of delivery was a condition to Ghosh's duty to accept the Jaguar and, unless otherwise agreed, to pay for it. *See* Tex. Bus. & Com. Code Ann. § 2.507(a) (1994); S.D. Codified Laws § 57A-2–507(1) (2004). Conversely, unless otherwise agreed, Ghosh's tender of payment was a condition to Herting's duty to tender and complete delivery. *See* Tex. Bus. & Com. Code Ann. § 2.511(a) (1994); S.D. Codified Laws § 57A-2–511(1) (2004). Here, it is undisputed that Herting had agreed to accept payment from Ghosh upon his delivery of the Jaguar in Austin.

The obligation to tender delivery required Herting to place at Ghosh's disposal a Jaguar conforming to their sale agreement. *See* Tex. Bus. & Com. Code Ann. §§ 2.201, 2.313 (1994), § 2.503(a); S.D. Codified Laws §§ 57A-2–201, 57A-2–313, 57A-2–503(1) (2004). Ghosh had the right to reject the Jaguar if it did not conform to the sale contract. *See* Tex. Bus. & Com. Code Ann. §§ 2.508(a), 2.510(a), 2.601, 2.602 (1994); S.D. Codified Laws §§ 57A-2–508(1), 57A-2–510(1), 57A-2–601, 57A-2–602 (2004). The U.C.C. also entitled Ghosh to inspect the car before payment or acceptance. *See* Tex. Bus. & Com. Code Ann. § 2.513 (1994); S.D. Codified Laws § 57A-2–513 (2004). Ghosh accepted the Jaguar and paid Herting. *See* Tex. Bus. & Com. Code Ann. § 2.606 (1994); S.D. Codified Laws § 57A-2–606 (2004).

We consider whether Herting's agreement to undertake these acts in Texas and his subsequent performance constitutes purposeful availment under the principles identified in *Michiana* and *CMMC*. The mere fact that Herting executed a sale contract with Ghosh would not suffice. Nor would it appear, especially under

CMMC, that Herting's tender of delivery in Texas and transfer of title here is alone sufficient to support personal jurisdiction.

For the same reasons, the fact that Herting personally delivered the Jaguar would not necessarily distinguish these facts from those of *CMMC*, as the third-party shipper there was acting as the French company's agent when delivering the winepress equipment and transferring title in Texas. More generally, territorial presence can be a key factor tending to enhance a potential defendant's affiliation with a state and demonstrating the purposefulness of the contact, but *Michiana* makes clear that the bare fact of physical presence in a state does not necessarily equal purposeful availment. . .

On the other hand, there are factual distinctions between the actions Herting agreed to perform here and those of the sellers in *Michiana* and *CMMC*. In neither of those cases did the seller pay for delivery: In *Michiana*, the supreme court emphasized that Holten paid for delivery himself, whereas in *CMMC*, shipment was paid for by the French company's independent distributor through whom the Texas company had placed its order. Herting, by contrast, delivered the Jaguar to Texas at his sole expense. Additionally, the parties agreed that payment would be made upon delivery of the Jaguar in Austin. In *Michiana*, in regard to whether the company had availed itself to the benefits and protections of Texas law, the Texas Supreme Court emphasized that "Holten paid for the RV in advance, and . . . [e]verything Michiana wanted out of the contract it had in hand." *Michiana*, 168 S.W.3d at 787.

In sum, assuming appellants' characterization of the "deal" struck by phone as a contract for sale of the Jaguar, the contract provided that the entire sale was to be performed in Texas. *See* Tex. Bus. & Com. Code Ann. § 2.106(a) (a "sale" consists in the passing of title from the seller to the buyer for a price); S.D. Codified Laws § 57A-2–106(1) (2004) (same). In this way, the transaction was directed to Texas to a degree that those in *Michiana* and *CMMC* were not.

We cannot agree with appellants that Herting's physical presence in Texas when closing the sale is "fortuitous" rather than "purposeful" in the sense the United States and Texas supreme courts have employed those concepts. Although his previously-planned trip to pick up the race car from Classic Jaguar may have fortuitously created a good *opportunity* to perform the sale in Texas, Herting nonetheless acted purposefully in opting to do so. In contrast [to] Michiana, who had no say over where the RV would end up, there is legally and factually sufficient evidence to support the trial court's implied findings that Herting had discretion and control over whether he would close the sale in Texas. As the Texas Supreme Court observed in *Michiana*, the purposeful-availment concept is based on implied consent — a nonresident may structure its transactions so as either to invoke the benefits and protections of Texas laws, thus impliedly consenting to suit there, or to "purposefully avoid [Texas] by structuring its transactions so as neither to profit from the forum's laws nor be subject to its jurisdiction." *Michiana*, 168 S.W.3d at 785. Herting's actions are much closer to the former than the latter.

We also cannot agree with appellants' contention that Herting's actions, even if purposeful, did not constitute availment to the benefits and protections of Texas law. Herting realized a significant benefit from his actions in Texas: he closed the

sale and left with a $35,000 check. He enjoyed the benefits and protections of Texas law in the process. These facts stand in contrast to *Michiana*, where "[e]verything Michiana wanted out of the contract it had in hand" before the RV ever left Indiana. *See Michiana*, 168 S.W.3d at 787. Nor did Herting evidence any intent to avoid the application of Texas law to his actions in our capitol city. *Cf. id.* at 792-93 (discussing forum-selection clauses as proof of intent not to avail oneself to a forum).

We hold that Herting purposefully availed himself of the benefits and protections of Texas law when closing the sale of the red Jaguar in Texas. [The court then finds that defendants' liability arises from its contacts with Texas.]

PRACTICE EXERCISE #7A

(1) *Affecting Texas Residents.* Robin, a resident of Texas, traveled to Hot Springs, Arkansas on vacation. While there, he was shopping for souvenirs and was assaulted by Guy, the store owner (who overheard Robin making fun of some of the items on sale). The store has never advertised outside of Arkansas. Back home in Texas, Robin filed suit against Guy based on the Arkansas assault. Can a Texas court constitutionally assert jurisdiction over Robin's claim against Guy?

(2) *Other Contacts with Texas.* Guy has made a special appearance, claiming that he cannot be sued in Texas. Robin has learned that on five occasions in the past Guy's store has sold archery sets and shipped them to Texas residents who had called the store and ordered them. Will this improve Robin's chances of getting jurisdiction over Guy in his case?

(3) *Seeking to Serve the Market.* Will is a Texas musician, and he placed a telephone order for a set of 10 CDs of folk music oldies from Sherwood Music. Sherwood advertises both in national magazines and in local music stores throughout the United States, including Texas. It sells about 50,000 CDs a year (10% of its total sales) to Texas customers. When the CDs arrive, Will learns that they are scratched and won't play without skipping badly. He wants to sue Sherwood for a refund (sadly, he paid cash for his order). Can Texas constitutionally assert jurisdiction over Sherwood in Will's case?

(4) *Single Sales and Advertising.* Sherwood also sells large tree houses for families to buy for their children to play in. These are very posh tree houses, and sell for about $15,000 apiece. In response to an ad in a national magazine called *Elite Parents*, Marian called Sherwood and ordered a tree house for her home in San Antonio. Sherwood custom-designed it for the San Antonio location, including southwest-style furniture, burnt orange decor, and an air conditioner. Sherwood had the tree house delivered to Marian in Texas, shipping it FOB Essex, California. All was fine for a while, but then one day when little John was playing in the tree house, the floor collapsed and he fell to the ground, breaking his leg. It turns out the floor was unsound. This is the only tree house that Sherwood has ever sold in Texas. Marian wants to sue Sherwood for negligence and breach of warranty, and she wants to sue them in Texas — would that be constitutional? What if Sherwood had also advertised in the sister publication, *Elite Texas Parents*?

The next section also examines the due process limits on personal jurisdiction, but it deals with cases in which the plaintiff's cause of action is not related to the defendant's contacts with the forum. In these cases, a different test for the quantity and quality of defendant's contacts with the forum state applies, and a significantly greater degree of contacts are required. Drawing the line between general and specific jurisdiction turns on the degree of relatedness between cause of action and contacts. The Texas Supreme Court has recently addressed this issue as well.

[C] Texas Courts Apply the Statute and Constitution: General Jurisdiction

[1] Distinguishing Specific and General Jurisdiction: The Substantial Connection Test

When the plaintiff's cause of action arises out of or is related to the defendant's contacts with Texas, the plaintiff only needs to show that the defendant has sufficient "minimum contacts" with Texas, as discussed above. Sometimes the relationship between contacts and the plaintiff's injury is very direct. When the relationship is more tangential, however, it can be difficult to decide whether the connection is strong enough to allow the exercise of jurisdiction based on the less demanding specific jurisdiction test. The next case discusses this issue in detail. Consider whether the test the Texas Supreme Court articulates is preferable to the ones it purports to reject.

MOKI MAC RIVER EXPEDITIONS v. DRUGG

221 S.W.3d 569 (Tex. 2007)

O'NEILL, J.

A Texas court may assert specific jurisdiction over an out-of-state defendant if the defendant's contact with this state is purposeful and the injury arises from or relates to those contacts. In this wrongful-death case against a Utah-based river-rafting outfitter, the defendant contends the plaintiff's death on a Grand Canyon hiking trail did not arise from or relate to its in-state commercial activities so as to establish specific jurisdiction over it in Texas. We agree. Accordingly, we reverse and remand the case to the court of appeals to determine whether general jurisdiction exists.

I. Background

Charles and Betsy Drugg's thirteen-year-old son, Andy, died on a June 2001, river-rafting trip in Arizona with Moki Mac River Expeditions, a Utah-based river-rafting outfitter. Moki Mac did not directly solicit the Druggs to participate in the trip. Instead, the Druggs learned about Moki Mac's excursions from a fellow Texas resident, Annie Seals, who had contacted the company regarding a rafting trip in the Grand Canyon. There was no space available for her at that time, but Seals's contact information was placed on Moki Mac's computerized mailing list so that she would automatically receive a brochure for the 2001 season when it became available. Moki Mac subsequently sent two brochures to Seals in Texas detailing pricing and schedules for upcoming excursions. Seals informed Moki Mac of the interest of several others in Texas with whom she shared the literature, including Andy and members of his family.

Betsy Drugg reviewed the brochures and information from Moki Mac's website. After corresponding with Moki Mac representatives from her home in Texas, Betsy ultimately decided to send Andy on the rafting trip. Andy's grandmother sent Moki Mac an application and payment for herself and Andy. As was its practice, Moki Mac sent a letter confirming payment to the Druggs' home in Texas along with an acknowledgment-of-risk and release form, which the company requires participants to sign as a prerequisite to attendance. Both Andy and his mother signed the form and returned it to Moki Mac.

The Druggs allege that on the second day of Andy's fourteen-day trip, Moki Mac guides led the group up an incline on a trail that narrowed around and was obstructed by a large boulder. The guides were positioned at the head and rear of the group, but no guide was present near the boulder. As Andy attempted to negotiate the boulder-blocked path, requiring him to lean back while attempting to cross a very narrow ledge, he fell backwards approximately fifty-five feet and was fatally injured.

The Druggs filed suit in Texas for wrongful death due to Moki Mac's negligence and for intentional and negligent misrepresentation.[1] The trial court denied Moki Mac's special appearance and the court of appeals affirmed on the basis of specific jurisdiction, holding that the Druggs' misrepresentation claim arose from, and related to, Moki Mac's purposeful contacts with Texas. Because the court of appeals found specific jurisdiction, it did not consider whether general jurisdiction was proper. We granted Moki Mac's petition for review to consider the extent to which a claim must "arise from or relate to" forum contacts in order to confer specific jurisdiction over a nonresident defendant. . . .

* * *

IV. Jurisdictional Analysis

The Druggs assert that Moki Mac established sufficient minimum contacts with Texas by making material misrepresentations to them here, upon which they relied, regarding the nature of the services that would be provided on its trips. The wrongful death of their son, the Druggs argue, arose from or related to the fact that Moki Mac's services did not meet the standards it represented in Texas. Moki Mac's principal argument is that there is an insufficient nexus between any alleged misrepresentations that it made in Texas and Andy's wrongful death in Arizona to

[1] The Druggs also claimed Moki Mac breached its agreement to provide the safety measures represented in its materials. Because the Druggs did not argue their breach-of-contract claim in the court of appeals and do not do so in their briefs to this Court, we only address the Druggs' wrongful-death claim.

satisfy jurisdictional due process. According to Moki Mac, Andy's death might have arisen out of or related to alleged negligence that occurred in Arizona, but it had no meaningful connection to Moki Mac's alleged misrepresentations in Texas.

For a Texas forum to properly exercise specific jurisdiction in this case, (1) Moki Mac must have made minimum contacts with Texas by purposefully availing itself of the privilege of conducting activities here, and (2) Moki Mac's liability must have arisen from or related to those contacts. *American Type Culture Collection, Inc.*, 83 S.W.3d at 806. Before deciding whether Moki Mac's liability arose from or related to its forum contacts, we must first examine the nature of those contacts and whether Moki Mac purposefully availed itself of the privilege of conducting business here. *See Michiana*, 168 S.W.3d at 784–85.

. . . .

B. Relatedness Requirement

The "arise from or relate to" requirement lies at the heart of specific jurisdiction by defining the required nexus between the nonresident defendant, the litigation, and the forum. To support specific jurisdiction, the Supreme Court has given relatively little guidance as to how closely related a cause of action must be to the defendant's forum activities. In assessing the relationship between a nonresident's contacts and the litigation, most courts have focused on causation, but they have differed over the proper causative threshold. *See Nowak v. Tak How Invs., Ltd.*, 94 F.3d 708, 714 (1st Cir. 1996) (discussing various causative approaches). Some courts have pursued an expansive but-for causative approach, others have adopted a restrictive relatedness view requiring forum contacts to be relevant to a necessary element of proof, and some have applied a sliding-scale analysis that attempts to strike a balance between the two. *See* Mark M. Maloney, *Specific Jurisdiction and the "Arise From or Relate to" Requirement . . . What Does it Mean?*, 50 WASH. & LEE L. REV. 1265, 1276, 1299 (1993). Each approach has proponents and detractors, for the reasons we examine below.

1. "But-For" Relatedness

. . . .

Courts that support the but-for approach have said that a cause of action arises from or relates to a defendant's forum contacts when, but for those contacts, the cause of action would never have arisen. . . . Rather than considering only isolated contacts that relate to a specific element of proof or the proximate cause of injury, the but-for analysis considers jurisdictional contacts that occur over the "entire course of events" of the relationship between the defendant, the forum, and the litigation. . . .

Few courts beyond the Ninth Circuit have adopted the but-for approach to relatedness. Specifically, both the Fifth and Sixth Circuits have signaled a movement away from such a broad test. We agree with those courts and commentators who view the but-for test as too broad and judicially unmoored to satisfy due-process concerns.

2. Substantive Relevance/Proximate Cause

Far more structured than the but-for approach is the restrictive view of relatedness known as "substantive relevance." As the name implies, this test requires forum-related contacts to be substantively relevant, or even necessary, to proof of the claim. *See Tecre Co. v. Buttonpro, Inc.*, 387 F. Supp. 2d 927, 933 (E.D. Wis. 2005). One iteration of this standard is known as the "proximate cause" test, reasoning that a contact that is the proximate or legal cause of an injury is substantively relevant to a cause of action that arises from it. The First, Second, and Eighth Circuits appear to have followed this approach. . . .

Proximate cause requires the defendant's conduct to be both the cause in fact and the foreseeable cause of injury. *See Doe v. Boys Clubs of Greater Dallas, Inc.*, 907 S.W.2d 472, 477 (Tex. 1995). Under this more stringent relatedness standard, the purposeful contact that is a proximate cause of injury is an essential liability element and is thus substantively relevant to a plaintiff's claim of harm.

Although Moki Mac urges us to follow the substantive-relevance approach, we have generally eschewed pinning jurisdictional analysis on the type of claim alleged. *See, e.g.*, *Michiana*, 168 S.W.3d at 791–92. In *Michiana*, we warned against the dangers of the plaintiff's pleadings driving the analysis, stating that such an approach "shifts a court's focus from the relationship among the *defendant*, the forum, and the litigation to the relationship among the plaintiff, the forum . . . and litigation." *Id.* at 790 (emphasis in original) (internal citations omitted). We reject a categorical approach that runs the danger of posing too narrow an inquiry. Although ostensibly imbued with a bright-line benefit, in practice it would require a court to delve into the merits to determine whether a jurisdictional fact is actually a legal cause of the injury. *See* Maloney, *supra* at 1290. Moreover, ease of application should not overshadow the principal constitutional due-process inquiry, which is whether the defendant has "certain minimum contacts with [the forum state] such that the maintenance of the suit does not offend 'traditional notions of fair play and substantial justice.'" *International Shoe*, 326 U.S. at 316. We note, too, that the substantive-relevance/proximate-cause standard is more stringent than the Supreme Court has, at least thus far, required. *Helicopteros*, 466 U.S. at 415 n.10.

3. "Sliding Scale" Relationship

Attempting to moderate the seemingly categorical effects of the but-for and substantive-relevance tests, some commentators have espoused, and a few courts have adopted, a "sliding scale" approach that examines the relationship between forum contacts and the litigation along a continuum. Under this view, as the extent of forum contacts goes up, the degree of relatedness to the litigation necessary to establish specific jurisdiction goes down, and *vice versa*. . . .

Although the sliding scale jurisdictional analysis studiously avoids the extremes that the other two relatedness tests present, it too presents a number of problems. Most significantly, deciding jurisdiction based on a sliding continuum blurs the distinction between general and specific jurisdiction that our judicial system has firmly embraced and that provides an established structure for courts to analyze questions of *in personam* jurisdiction. . . . Removing the jurisdictional analysis from these judicial underpinnings allows general and specific jurisdiction "to melt together in the middle . . . severely weaken[ing] the defendant's ability to anticipate the jurisdictional consequences of its conduct." Linda Sandstrom Simard, *Meeting Expectations: Two Profiles for Specific Jurisdiction*, 38 IND. L. REV. 343, 366 (2005). In sum, "this tradeoff does not fulfill the underlying goals of either general or specific jurisdiction" and "may raise far more difficult questions than it resolves." *Id.* at 366–67. For these reasons, we decline to adopt the sliding-scale approach to relatedness.

4. Substantial Connection to Operative Facts

As we have said, the but-for relatedness test is too broad and conceptually unlimited in scope, the substantive-relevance/proximate-cause test poses too narrow an inquiry, and the sliding-scale analysis conflates the fundamental distinction between general and specific jurisdiction that is firmly embedded in our jurisprudence. In light of these concerns, some courts have applied alternative approaches, requiring that a cause of action "lie in the wake of the [defendant's] commercial activities" in the forum, *Deluxe Ice Cream Co. v. R.C.H. Tool Corp.*, 726 F.2d 1209, 1215–16 (7th Cir. 1984), or that the forum contacts be "critical steps in the chain of events that led to the [injury]," *In re Oil Spill by Amoco Cadiz*, 699 F.2d 909, 915–16 (7th Cir. 1983). The Sixth Circuit has generally applied a test that falls somewhere between "proximate cause" and "but-for," requiring a "substantial connection" between the defendant's contacts and the plaintiff's claim to warrant the exercise of specific jurisdiction. *See Wedge Group, Inc.*, 882 F.2d at 1091 (6th Cir. 1989); *Southern Mach. Co. v. Mohasco Indus., Inc.*, 401 F.2d 374, 384 n.27 (6th Cir. 1968). In *Wedge Group, Inc.*, the court explained that the specific jurisdiction's relatedness element "does not require that the cause of action formally 'arise from' defendant's contacts with the forum [but instead requires] that the cause of action, of whatever type, *have a substantial connection with* the defendant's in-state activities." *Wedge Group Inc.*, 882 F.2d at 1091 (emphasis in original) (quoting *Southern Mach. Co.*, 401 F.2d at 384 n.27).

The Supreme Court has yet to explicate the degree of relatedness necessary to support specific jurisdiction over a nonresident defendant. However, in *Rush v. Savchuk*, the Court did consider the relation between forum contacts and the litigation in a case filed in Minnesota for personal injuries arising from an Indiana automobile accident. 444 U.S. 320, 324 (1980). The plaintiff claimed jurisdiction was proper in Minnesota because the defendant's insurance company did business there, and the insurer's obligation to defend and indemnify its insured in the accident litigation was inevitably the focus that would determine the victim's rights and obligations. *Id.* at 327–28. Holding that the insurance company's contacts could not be imputed to the defendant for the purpose of establishing jurisdiction, the Court concluded there were not "significant contacts between the litigation and the forum" because "the insurance policy is not the subject matter of the case . . . nor is it related to the operative facts of the negligence action." *Id.* at 329. The Court concluded that the insurance contract pertained only to the conduct and "not the substance [] of the litigation," and therefore the forum's jurisdiction was not affected. *Id.*

Our limited jurisprudence similarly suggests a middle ground, more flexible than substantive relevance but more structured than but-for relatedness, in assessing the strength of the necessary connection between the defendant, the forum, and the litigation. *See Guardian Royal*, 815 S.W.2d at 229–33. In *Guardian Royal*, we spoke in terms of a "substantial connection" between the nonresident defendant and Texas arising from purposeful action or conduct directed here. *Id.* at 226 (citing *Burger King*, 471 U.S. at 475 n.18) (stating "[s]o long as it creates a 'substantial connection' with the forum, even a single act can support jurisdiction"); *See also Shell Compania Argentina de Petroleo, S.A. v. Reef Exploration, Inc.*, 84 S.W.3d 830, 837 (Tex. App. — Houston [1st Dist.] 2002, pet. denied) (stating contacts "must have a 'substantial connection' that results in the alleged injuries") (citing *Guardian Royal*, 815 S.W.2d at 226). Considering our own jurisprudence and the Supreme Court's analysis in *Rush*, we believe that for a nonresident defendant's forum contacts to support an exercise of specific jurisdiction, there must be a substantial connection between those contacts and the operative facts of the litigation.

C. Relatedness of Moki Mac's Contacts

Betsy Drugg alleges she was induced to send Andy on the rafting trip by Moki Mac's direct solicitation, which included statements made in Moki Mac's brochures and in the release it sent to the Druggs. Specifically, Andy's mother claims she made the decision to send Andy on the trip based on Moki Mac's assurances that "[y]ou don't need 'mountain man' camping skills to participate in one of our trips," children age twelve or above are suited to participate, and "Moki Mac has taken reasonable steps to provide you with appropriate equipment and/or skilled guides." But for these promises, the Druggs claim, they would not have sent Andy on the rafting trip and he would not have fallen on the hiking trail.

Certainly on a river rafting trip safety is a paramount concern, and we accept as true the Druggs' claim that Andy might not have gone on the trip were it not for Moki Mac's representations about safety. However, the operative facts of the Druggs' suit concern principally the guides' conduct of the hiking expedition and whether they exercised reasonable care in supervising Andy. The events on the trail and the guides' supervision of the hike will be the focus of the trial, will consume most if not all of the litigation's attention, and the overwhelming majority of the evidence will be directed to that question. Only after thoroughly considering the manner in which the hike was conducted will the jury be able to assess the Druggs' misrepresentation claim. In sum, "the [alleged misrepresentation] is not the subject matter of the case . . . nor is it related to the operative facts of the negligence action." *Rush*, 444 U.S. at 329. Whatever connection there may be between Moki Mac's promotional materials sent to Texas and the operative facts that led to Andy's death, we do not believe it is sufficiently direct to meet due-process concerns. Analogous cases from other courts support our view.

Federal district courts in Texas have generally held that a nonresident's in-state advertising is insufficiently related to a negligence claim based on personal injury that occurs out of state to support an exercise of specific jurisdiction. In *Kervin v. Red River Ski Area, Inc.*, for example, the plaintiff fell while descending a flight of wooden steps leading to her ski lodge in New Mexico. 711 F. Supp. at 1385. The

Kervins sued the ski resort in Texas alleging negligence in failing to maintain safe premises. *Id.* The plaintiffs asserted *in personam* jurisdiction based on the resort's contacts with Texas, which included television and print advertising and mailing brochures to potential customers. *Id.* at 1386. The court determined that "[*i*] *n personam* jurisprudence has taken a restrictive view of the relationship between causes of action and contacts, seemingly to require virtually a direct link between [the] claim and [the] contacts." *Id.* at 1389. Although the court ultimately determined that general jurisdiction was proper, it held that specific jurisdiction was not because there was no substantial connection between the resort's advertising in Texas and its negligent maintenance of the stairwell in New Mexico. *Id.*

In *Gorman v. Grand Casino of Louisiana, Inc.-Coushatta*, the plaintiff, a Texas resident, sued a Louisiana casino in Texas claiming that its employee intentionally served her a drink containing Benzodiazepine (one of the "date-rape" drugs) and then made advances to her. 1 F. Supp. 2d at 658. The court held that there was an insufficient link between Gorman's sexual-harassment claim and the casino's marketing scheme in Texas to support the exercise of specific jurisdiction, concluding "[b]illboard advertisements of slot machine payouts . . . ha[ve] nothing to do with the conduct of that casino's employees." *Id.*; *see also Luna*, 851 F. Supp. at 832–33 (holding claim involving plaintiff's death in a plane crash over Panama arose not from her ticket purchase in Texas but from alleged negligence in Panama).

Courts in other jurisdictions have similarly addressed the issue, concluding that claims arising out of personal injury that occurs outside the forum do not arise from or relate to a defendant's forum advertising. In *Oberlies v. Searchmont Resort, Inc.*, a Michigan resident visited a Canadian ski resort after seeing the resort's advertisement in a Michigan newspaper. 633 N.W.2d 408, 411 (Mich. App. 2001). Claiming she was injured when resort employees negligently loaded her onto a ski lift, the plaintiff filed suit in Michigan. *Id.* The court concluded that the resort's advertising activities in the forum were insufficient to support *in personam* jurisdiction, and that it would violate due process to hale the Canadian resort into a Michigan court:

> [n]otwithstanding defendant's purposeful availment of Michigan business opportunities through its advertising, we are compelled to find that the presence of other factors render the exercise of jurisdiction unreasonable. Simply put, the connection between plaintiff's cause of action [negligence] and defendant's Michigan advertising is so attenuated that it is unreasonable to exercise jurisdiction over defendant. . . .

Id. at 416.

Somewhat analogous to advertising cases are those that concern efforts to recruit forum residents. Most courts have held that merely mailing letters and exchanging phone calls in recruitment efforts is insufficient to support specific jurisdiction over nonresidents for claims that arise outside the forum, although some courts have exercised jurisdiction when the defendant physically recruited in the forum. For example, in *Cassell v. Loyola University*, a Florida student who was a resident of Tennessee was recruited to play basketball for a New Orleans university. 294 F. Supp. 622, 622–23 (E.D. Tenn. 1968). When the university subsequently refused to grant Cassell a scholarship, he sued for breach of contract in Tennessee. *Id.* at 623. The only connections with the forum were that it was the student's domicile, it was where his father had signed the recruitment contract, and agents of the university had communicated there by mail and telephone. *Id.* The court held that the "asserted cause of action does not arise out of business transacted in Tennessee" and thus there was an insufficient connection between the forum and the litigation to justify personal jurisdiction. *Id.* at 624. (In doing so, the court distinguished college athletic recruiting from ordinary commercial activities.)

In *Kelly v. Syria Shell Petroleum Development B.V.*, two Texas oil well workers who had contracted their services to Syrian oil companies were killed while performing work in Syria. 213 F.3d at 855. Their families sued for wrongful death in Texas, but the Fifth Circuit held there was no specific jurisdiction over their claims. *Id.* at 844. The court noted that, even assuming the Syrian company possessed minimum contacts with Texas, including signing a contract for the well workers' services, "specific jurisdiction does *not* exist . . . because Appellants' claims do *not* arise out of those contacts. Instead, they arise out of alleged tortious acts committed . . . in Syria." *Id.* at 855 (emphasis in original).

The Druggs cite our decision in *Siskind* [*v. Villa Found. for Educ., Inc.*, 642 S.W.2d 434 (Tex. 1982)] to support their claim that Moki Mac's solicitations in Texas and Andy's death on the Arizona hiking trail are sufficiently related to support specific jurisdiction. *Siskind*, 642 S.W.2d at 437. But the operative facts in Siskind that supported liability and related to the defendant's forum contacts differ significantly from those presented here. The school solicited students in Texas through national magazines and local telephone books and the contract between Siskind and the school specifically provided that, if Siskind's son left during the school year, his tuition would be reimbursed. *Id.* at 435–36. When his son was expelled, the school refused to refund Siskind's tuition. *Id.* Siskind sued the school in Texas for the promised refund. *Id.* Under these circumstances, we held there was "a connection between Siskind's claim for breach of contract and Villa's contacts with Texas." *Id.* at 437. Here, however, Moki Mac's statements in its brochures and release do not bear the same direct link to Andy's injury as did Siskind's claim to recover money lost under the contract. Moki Mac's promotional representations, while theoretically related to Andy's injury on the hiking trail in the sense that but for them he might not have been there, are not sufficiently related to the operative facts underlying Andy's injury for which the Druggs seek recovery in wrongful death to sustain the exercise of specific jurisdiction.

This case more closely resembles the situation presented in *Brocail v. Anderson*, 132 S.W.3d 552 (Tex. App. — Houston [14th Dist.] 2004, pet. denied). In that case, Brocail, a former Detroit Tigers baseball player, underwent treatment by a team physician in Michigan. *Id.* at 555. Of his own volition, Brocail moved to his home in Texas during his rehabilitation, and at Brocail's request, his doctor, Anderson, prescribed follow-up treatments that were administered by a healthcare group in Houston. *Id.* at 555–56. Brocail sued Anderson in Texas for medical negligence and fraud related to his physical therapy, and alleged Texas had specific jurisdiction because Anderson had faxed prescriptions to Texas and communicated with the Texas healthcare group regarding Brocail's progress. *Id.* at 558. Brocail also asserted jurisdiction was proper because Anderson had made misrepresentations in Texas by failing to fully disclose the true extent of Brocail's injuries in his forum contacts. *Id.* at 563. The court of appeals held that Brocail's claims did not arise from or relate to any Texas contacts because "Brocail is complaining about a physical injury based on a course of treatment. Any tort occurred in the exercise of medical judgment in prescribing a course of physical therapy in Michigan, not from the communication of that prescription [to Texas]." *Id.* Similarly, the injuries for which the Druggs seek recovery are based on Andy's death on the hiking trail in Arizona, and the relationship between the operative facts of the litigation and Moki Mac's promotional activities in Texas are simply too attenuated to satisfy specific jurisdiction's due-process concerns.

V. Conclusion

We reverse the court of appeals' judgment and remand the case to that court to consider the Druggs' assertion that Moki Mac is subject to general jurisdiction in Texas.

NOTES AND QUESTIONS

(1) *Purposeful Availment Revisited.* The majority's opinion in *Moki Mac* also revisits the analysis of the level of deliberate contacts needed to satisfy due process in specific jurisdiction cases. Although it concludes that Moki Mak has ample contacts for specific jurisdiction, it also finds that this case does not belong in the specific jurisdiction category. On remand, the Court of Appeals must determine whether Moki Mac has enough contacts with Texas for general jurisdiction to be appropriate. A finding of general jurisdiction would provide proper personal jurisdiction over Moki Mac for *any* claim against it, even claims that have nothing whatsoever to do with its Texas activities. For example, jurisdiction would be proper over a claim by a resident of Maine arising out of an injury in Colorado on a trip solicited in New York. On remand, the Dallas Court of Appeals found that Moki Mac's contacts with Texas were not sufficient to support general jurisdiction. *Moki Mac River Expeditions v. Drugg*, 270 S.W.3d 799 (Tex. App. — Dallas 2008, no pet.).

(2) *Relatedness Tests.* The opinion discusses several possible methods for categorizing personal jurisdiction cases as specific or general, and rejects the argument that case law actually demonstrates a kind of sliding scale in which there is an inverse relationship between the quantity of contacts and the degree of relatedness (more related/fewer contacts required; less related/more contacts required). Of the "but for" test and the "substantive relevance" tests, which would be the easiest to satisfy? Which would be the hardest? How is the Texas court's "substantial connection" test different from the "substantive relevance" test? From the "but for" test?

[2] Substantial, Continuous, and Systematic Contacts

In an early case involving general jurisdiction, the Texas Supreme Court upheld jurisdiction based on relatively few contacts with Texas. *See Schlobohm v. Schapiro*, 784 S.W.2d 355 (Tex. 1990) (finding general jurisdiction over Pennsylvania father who invested in and ultimately owned all stock in his son's Texas business). As you read the following case, try to articulate the court's test for when contacts are sufficient to justify general jurisdiction. What advice would you give a client in this area?

PHC-MINDEN v. KIMBERLY-CLARK CORP.

235 S.W.3d 163 (Tex. 2007)

JEFFERSON, C.J.

The United States Constitution prohibits a court from exercising jurisdiction over a party that lacks minimum contacts with the forum. Personal jurisdiction has been described as either specific — that is, based on contacts arising from the dispute at issue — or general, predicated on a party's "continuous and systematic" contacts with the forum. Minimum-contacts analysis is easily muddled, however, as courts frequently import contacts relevant to one type of jurisdiction when deciding the other. Additionally, courts sometimes impute contacts of related entities to each other, when mere relatedness is an insufficient basis on which to confer jurisdiction. Today, we must determine whether a Louisiana hospital, either independently or through its parent corporation, has continuous and systematic contacts with Texas. We conclude that it does not.

I

Factual and Procedural Background

While traveling through Louisiana on December 10, 2000, Texas resident Jajah Eddington sought medical care at MHC-Minden Hospital ("Minden Hospital"), a 159-bed acute care hospital located in Minden, Louisiana. Medical personnel treated Eddington's flu-like symptoms in the emergency room and advised her to consult her primary care physician if her condition did not improve. Four days later, Eddington was admitted to Good Shepherd Medical Center in Longview, Texas, where she ultimately was diagnosed with toxic shock syndrome. That infection led to her death on December 28, 2000.

DeWayne Eddington, individually and as next friend of Devvyn Eddington, and as representative of Jajah Eddington's estate, sued Kimberly-Clark Corporation asserting product liability, breach of warranty, and negligence claims. He alleged that Eddington's use of Kotex tampons led to the infection that caused her death. On February 28, 2003, Kimberly-Clark filed a third-party petition against PHC-Minden, L.P. ("Minden"), which owns Minden Hospital, asserting that Minden's negligence proximately caused Eddington's death. Minden is a nonresident of Texas and a wholly owned subsidiary of Province Health Care ("Province"). Kimberly-Clark pleaded that Province, whose headquarters is in Tennessee, did business in Texas and that its forum-related acts should be imputed to Minden because: (1) Province owns Minden; (2) Province and Minden share officers, directors, and "common departments or business"; (3) Province and Minden do not differentiate their operations and have failed to erect "formal barriers" between themselves; and (4) Province's officers and directors control Minden's policies. Minden filed a special appearance and, subject thereto, a general denial. The parties conducted extensive discovery relating to the jurisdictional issue. After a hearing, the trial court concluded it had general jurisdiction over Minden and denied the special appearance.

The court of appeals affirmed, reasoning that (1) Minden itself had "continuous and systematic contacts with Texas"; and (2) Minden and Province operated as a single business enterprise, and Minden, through Province, did business in Texas. We granted Minden's petition for review to decide whether Texas courts have general jurisdiction over Minden.

II

General Jurisdiction

The Texas long-arm statute governs Texas courts' exercise of jurisdiction over nonresident defendants. *See* TEX. CIV. PRAC. & REM. CODE §§ 17.041–.045. That statute permits Texas courts to exercise jurisdiction over a nonresident defendant that "does business" in Texas, and the statute identifies some activities that constitute "doing business." *Id.* § 17.042. The list, however, is not exclusive. We have held that section 17.042's language extends Texas courts' personal jurisdiction "as far as the federal constitutional requirements of due process will permit." *U-Anchor Adver., Inc. v. Burt*, 553 S.W.2d 760, 762 (Tex. 1977). Thus, we rely on precedent from the United States Supreme Court and other federal courts, as well as our own decisions, in determining whether a nonresident defendant has negated all bases of jurisdiction. Personal jurisdiction over nonresident defendants is constitutional when: (1) the defendant has established minimum contacts with the forum state, and (2) the exercise of jurisdiction comports with traditional notions of fair play and substantial justice. *Int'l Shoe Co. v. Washington*, 326 U.S. 310, 316 (1945).

In *Helicopteros Nacionales de Colombia, S.A. v. Hall*, the Supreme Court adopted the terms "specific" and "general" to describe the differing types of personal jurisdiction. *Helicopteros*, 466 U.S. 408, 414 (1984) (citing Arthur T. von Mehren & Donald T. Trautman, *Jurisdiction to Adjudicate: A Suggested Analysis*, 79 HARV. L. REV. 1121, 1144–64 (1966)). The Court defined specific jurisdiction as "arising out of or related to the defendant's contacts with the forum." By contrast, the Court referred to general jurisdiction as "personal jurisdiction over a defendant in a suit not arising out of or related to the defendant's contacts with the forum."

In *Helicopteros*, the Court concluded that Texas courts did not have general jurisdiction over a Colombian company, Helicol. One of Helicol's helicopters had been involved in a crash in Peru, and the survivors and representatives of the decedents sued Helicol in state district court in Harris County, Texas. Helicol filed a special appearance and moved to dismiss the case, but the trial court denied the motion. The court of appeals, however, agreed with Helicol that in personam jurisdiction over Helicol was lacking. Our Court reversed. *Hall v. Helicopteros Nacionales de Colombia, S.A.*, 638 S.W.2d 870 (Tex. 1982).

The Supreme Court granted certiorari, and it summarized the pertinent jurisdictional facts:

> It is undisputed that Helicol does not have a place of business in Texas and never has been licensed to do business in the State. Basically, Helicol's contacts with Texas consisted of sending its chief executive officer to Houston for a contract-negotiation session; accepting into its New York bank account checks drawn on a Houston bank; purchasing helicopters, equipment, and training services from Bell Helicopter for substantial sums; and sending personnel to Bell's facilities in Fort Worth for training.

Helicopteros, 466 U.S. at 416. The Court concluded that the CEO's trip to Houston could not be described as a "continuous or systematic" contact. *Id.* Similarly, it held that Helicol's acceptance of checks drawn on a Houston bank was of "negligible significance." *Id.* at 416. The Court held, relying on a 1923 unanimous opinion written by Justice Brandeis, that "purchases and related trips, standing alone, are not a sufficient basis for a State's assertion of jurisdiction." *Id.* at 417 (citing *Rosenberg Bros. & Co. v. Curtis Brown Co.*, 260 U.S. 516 (1923)).

The point at which jurisdictional contacts reach a tipping point, however, has eluded precise formulation. Beyond stating that mere purchases and related travel are not enough, the Supreme Court has given little guidance on the appropriate inquiry for general jurisdiction, although its *Helicopteros* conclusion that general jurisdiction was improper suggests that the requisite level of contacts is fairly substantial. 16 James Wm. Moore et al., Moore's Federal Practice § 108.41[3] (3d ed. 2007); 4 Charles Alan Wright & Arthur R. Miller, Federal Practice & Procedure § 1067.5 (2007) (noting that the Court's rejection of each contact and its failure to aggregate contacts "suggests very strongly that the threshold contacts required for a constitutional assertion of general jurisdiction over a nonresident defendant are very substantial, indeed"). *Perkins v. Benguet Consolidated Mining Co.*, the only case in which that court has upheld a finding of general jurisdiction, offers an insight into the nature of the contacts required. *Perkins*, 342 U.S. 437 (1952). In assessing whether the nonresident defendant's Ohio contacts were sufficient to warrant a finding of general jurisdiction, the Court noted that the company's president, who was also the general manager and principal shareholder, maintained an Ohio office in which he "did many things on behalf of the company." He maintained company files in Ohio, carried on correspondence from there, drew and distributed salary checks from his Ohio office, used two Ohio bank accounts for company funds and had an Ohio bank act as transfer agent for the company's stock, held directors' meetings in Ohio, supervised policies dealing with the rehabilitation of the corporation's properties in the Philippines there, and dispatched funds from Ohio bank accounts to cover purchases of machinery for such rehabilitation. The Court concluded that the company "carried on in Ohio a continuous and systematic supervision of the necessarily limited wartime activities of the company," and even though "no mining properties in Ohio were owned or operated by the company, many of its wartime activities were directed from Ohio and were being given the personal attention of its president in that State at the time he was served with summons." The Court held that "under the circumstances above recited, it would not violate federal due process for Ohio either to take or decline jurisdiction of the corporation in this proceeding."

A general jurisdiction inquiry, therefore, is very different from a specific jurisdiction inquiry and involves a "more demanding minimum contacts analysis," *CSR Ltd. v. Link*, 925 S.W.2d 591, 595 (Tex. 1996), with a "substantially higher" threshold, 4 WRIGHT & MILLER, FEDERAL PRACTICE & PROCEDURE § 1067.5. Usually, "the defendant must be engaged in longstanding business in the forum state, such as marketing or shipping products, or performing services or maintaining one or more offices there; activities that are less extensive than that will not qualify for general in personam jurisdiction." 4 WRIGHT & MILLER, FEDERAL PRACTICE & PROCEDURE § 1067.5; *see also Hall*, 638 S.W.2d at 882 (Pope, J., dissenting) (noting that "substantial and continuous activity" required for general jurisdiction suggests that defendant "must establish some close substantial connection with the state approaching the relationship between the state and its own residents"); 16 MOORE'S FEDERAL PRACTICE § 108.41[3] (stating that general jurisdiction "typically requires the defendant to have an office in the forum state"); Lea Brilmayer, *A General Look at General Jurisdiction*, 66 TEX. L. REV. 723, 742 (1988) (proposing that "the basic inquiry must be whether the defendant's level of activity rises to the level of activity of an insider, so that relegating the defendant to the political processes is fair"); Charles W. "Rocky" Rhodes, *Clarifying General Jurisdiction*, 34 SETON HALL L. REV. 807, 811 (2004) (suggesting that a proper general jurisdiction query should evaluate whether the defendant engaged in activities in the forum state similar in frequency and nature to the activities of local businesses); Mary Twitchell, *The Myth of General Jurisdiction*, 101 HARV. L. REV. 610, 635 (1988) (noting that "traditional indicia" of general jurisdiction are "a home base, an agent for the service of process, a local office, or the pursuance of business from a tangible locale within the state").

General jurisdiction has been described as "dispute-blind," an exercise of the court's jurisdiction made without regard to the nature of the claim presented. It involves a court's ability to exercise jurisdiction over a nonresident defendant based on any claim, including claims unrelated to the defendant's contacts with the state. Some commentators suggest that courts assessing general jurisdiction employ an analytical device to determine whether the jurisdiction is, in fact, dispute-blind. They propose that the court construct a hypothetical claim without any forum connection "to insure that any related forum activities of the defendant are not improperly infiltrating the dispute-blind query." For example:

> [A]re the corporate defendant's actual activities in California so pervasive and extensive that it should be amenable to the adjudicatory jurisdiction of California for a hypothetical employment discrimination claim filed by a New York citizen employed at corporate headquarters in New York? Or, with respect to a foreign corporation, do the corporation's actual California contacts support jurisdiction even for a hypothetical cause of action arising from its sale of a product in Germany that injured a German citizen?

Such an inquiry properly frames the issue, as general jurisdiction is based solely on the defendant's "continuous and systematic" contacts with the forum.

A

Minden's Contacts

With this in mind, we turn to an analysis of Minden's Texas contacts, as the court of appeals concluded that Minden had "continuous and systematic contacts with Texas" sufficient to support general jurisdiction. We first determine the appropriate time period for assessing contacts for purposes of general jurisdiction, an issue on which our courts of appeals are in conflict. Some examine the defendant's forum-related activities up to the time of the occurrence that prompted the suit. Others focus on contacts up to the time of filing suit. Another — the court of appeals in this case — noted the conflict and assessed contacts under both timetables.

We conclude that the relevant period ends at the time suit is filed. As noted above, general jurisdiction is dispute-blind; accordingly, and in contrast to specific jurisdiction, the incident made the basis of the suit should not be the focus in assessing continuous and systematic contacts — contacts on which jurisdiction over any claim may be based. *See* Charles W. "Rocky" Rhodes, *The Predictability Principle in Personal Jurisdiction Doctrine: A Case Study of the Effects of a "Generally" Too Broad, But "Specifically" Too Narrow Approach to Minimum Contacts*, 57 Baylor L. Rev. 135, 238 (2005) (noting that "analyzing the contacts at the time of accrual is not appropriate under the proper explanation of general jurisdiction as dispute-blind general adjudicative authority"); *see also* 4 Wright & Miller, Federal Practice & Procedure § 1067.5 (noting that "a court should consider all of a defendant's contacts with the forum state prior to the filing of the lawsuit"). We also agree that "a mere one-time snapshot of the defendant's in-state activities" may not be sufficient, and contacts should be assessed over a reasonable number of years, up to the date suit is filed. This includes contacts at the time the cause of action arose, and it comports with the Supreme Court's guidance on the issue, as well as our prior caselaw. *See Helicopteros*, 466 U.S. at 409–11 (evaluating contacts over the seven-year period before suit was filed); *American Type Culture Collection, Inc. v. Coleman*, 83 S.W.3d 801, 807–08 (Tex. 2002) (assessing contacts over the twenty-year period preceding suit).

We now turn to Minden's contacts up to the time of suit. A general jurisdiction inquiry can be tedious, as it "demands . . . that all contacts be carefully investigated, compiled, sorted, and analyzed for proof of a pattern of continuing and systematic activity." *Schlobohm v. Schapiro*, 784 S.W.2d 355, 359 (Tex. 1990). In conducting this dispute-blind inquiry, Jajah's Eddington's status as a Texas resident, her treatment in Minden Hospital's emergency room, and her family's choice not to sue Minden are irrelevant. Instead, we focus solely on Minden's contacts with Texas. Minden is a nonresident limited partnership that owns a hospital licensed by the state of Louisiana. Minden's only facility is in Minden, Louisiana, and ninety percent of its patients reside within a twenty-five mile radius of Minden Hospital. Minden does not advertise in Texas. It owns no Texas property and has no Texas office or bank accounts, nor does it maintain a registered agent for service of process here. The court of appeals relied on three categories of contacts in determining that Minden's Texas contacts were continuous and systematic: (1) Minden employees' attendance at seminars in Texas; (2) Minden's purchases from vendors with Texas addresses; and (3) three contracts with Texas entities. We examine each in turn.

1. Texas Trips

The evidence showed that, since 1999, Minden employees attended two Province-sponsored meetings in Dallas. These isolated trips fall short of the "continuous and systematic contact" the Supreme Court requires. In *Helicopteros*, the Supreme Court rejected the notion that multiple trips to Fort Worth supported general jurisdiction, noting that the trips did not "in any way enhance[] the company's contacts with Texas." We agree with that analysis.

2. Payments to Texas Vendors

Since October 1, 1999, Minden paid $1,508,467.20 to 136 entities with Texas addresses. The largest payment, $515,650.15, was to Alcon Laboratories in Dallas, Texas, and the second largest, $209,997.36, to Centerpoint Energy in Houston, Texas. Most of the remaining payments are for less than $10,000.00 each. In *Helicopteros*, the Supreme Court held that "mere purchases, even if occurring at regular intervals, are not enough to warrant a State's assertion of in personam jurisdiction over a nonresident corporation in a cause of action not related to those purchase transactions." And we have recognized that "purchases from Texas vendors will not alone support the exercise of general jurisdiction." *American Type Culture Collection*, 83 S.W.3d at 808. We conclude that the payments to Texas vendors do not support general jurisdiction over Minden in Texas.

3. Contracts with Texas Entities

The court of appeals also identified three contracts with a Texas connection: (1) a September 23, 2003 contract with Cox Business Services, a Tyler, Texas-based company, for internet service (at a charge of $59.95 per month) and a cable modem; (2) a July 2002 contract with Lone Star Research, located in The Woodlands, Texas, pursuant to which Lone Star Research would conduct a one-time marketing survey of 200 adult residents in Minden Hospital's service area; and (3) an April 2001 professional services agreement with Horizon Radiology, P.A., a Texas company, whereby Horizon would provide specialty coverage (via teleradiology equipment) to Minden Hospital, in exchange for $1600 per month.

We agree with the court of appeals that the 2003 Cox contract, entered into after suit was filed, is irrelevant to the jurisdictional inquiry here. The 2002 Lone Star contract pursuant to which a Texas company conducted a marketing study of residents in Minden Hospital's service area — presumably Louisiana, as ninety percent of the hospital's patients live within twenty-five miles of the hospital — does not establish a continuous and systematic Texas contact. Lone Star agreed to conduct 200 telephone interviews and analyze the data within a week of the survey's completion, in exchange for $5,200. This type of sporadic Texas contact is not substantial enough for general jurisdiction.

Of the three contracts, the Horizon agreement has the most substantial connection to Texas. The agreement, signed in 2001 and renewed twice thereafter, required that Louisiana-licensed physicians (located in Texas) provide teleradiology services, for which Minden supplied the necessary equipment, in exchange for $1600 per month. Even this agreement, however, does not support general jurisdiction. Hiring a contractor to perform such limited services in the forum state does not equate to "continuous and systematic contacts."

Even when amassed, Minden's Texas contacts simply are not "continuous and systematic general business contacts" sufficient to support general jurisdiction, particularly when compared to the substantial, regular business activities conducted by the nonresident defendant in *Perkins*. Instead, the facts here are more like those described in *Helicopteros:* the nonresident defendant had limited contacts with Texas but none sufficient to support general jurisdiction. Accordingly, the court of appeals erred in holding otherwise.

B

Jurisdictional Veil-Piercing

As its second basis for general jurisdiction, the court of appeals imputed Province's Texas contacts to Minden, concluding the two entities operated as a single business enterprise and that Minden, through Province, did business in Texas. In 1925, the Supreme Court of the United States considered whether a North Carolina court had jurisdiction over a nonresident parent corporation whose subsidiary did business in North Carolina. *Cannon Mfg. Co. v. Cudahy Packing Co.*, 267 U.S. 333, 335 (1925). In affirming the district court's dismissal for lack of jurisdiction, the Court held:

> Through ownership of the entire capital stock and otherwise, the defendant dominates [its subsidiary], immediately and completely; and exerts its control both commercially and financially in substantially the same way, and mainly through the same individuals, as it does over those selling branches or departments of its business not separately incorporated which are established to market the [defendant's] products in other states. The existence of the [subsidiary] as a distinct corporate entity is, however, in all respects observed. Its books are kept separate. All transactions between the two corporations are represented by appropriate entries in their respective books in the same way as if the two were wholly independent corporations.

Id. The Court concluded that "the corporate separation, though perhaps merely formal, was real. It was not pure fiction." *Id.* at 337.

The Court has never disavowed *Cannon*, despite an opportunity to do so. Instead, it essentially echoed the *Cannon* rule in *Keeton v. Hustler Magazine, Inc.*, 465 U.S. 770, 781 n.13 (1984). In that case, then-Justice Rehnquist, writing for the Court, noted that "jurisdiction over a parent corporation [does not] automatically establish jurisdiction over a wholly owned subsidiary. . . . Each defendant's contacts with the forum State must be assessed individually." *Keeton*, 465 U.S. at 781 n.13.

The Fifth Circuit Court of Appeals followed *Cannon* in *Hargrave v. Fibreboard Corp.*:

> *Cannon* . . . stands for the proposition that so long as a parent and subsidiary maintain separate and distinct corporate entities, the presence of one in a forum state may not be attributed to the other. Cases in this circuit appear to have followed the *Cannon* rule in applying the Texas long-arm statute, although sometimes without explicit citation. We have noted often that 100% stock ownership and commonality of officers and directors are not alone sufficient to establish an alter ego relationship between two corporations. Generally, our cases demand proof of control by the parent over the internal business operations and affairs of the subsidiary in order to fuse the two for jurisdictional purposes. The degree of control exercised by the parent must be greater than that normally associated with common ownership and directorship. All the relevant facts and circumstances surrounding the operations of the parent and subsidiary must be examined to determine whether two separate and distinct corporate entities exist.

Hargrave, 710 F.2d 1154, 1160 (5th Cir. 1983). The court held that the two corporations at issue "maintained a degree of corporate separation that was more than superficial" and "[t]he policy making authority held and exercised by [the parent] was no more than that appropriate for a sole shareholder of a corporation" and not enough to warrant the extraterritorial exercise of jurisdiction over that shareholder. The court concluded: "The Lone Star of Texas may shine brightly throughout the world, but its long arm is not judicially all encompassing."

We recently followed *Hargrave* (and, by implication, *Cannon*) in explaining when the contacts of a related corporate entity may be considered for purposes of determining general jurisdiction. *BMC Software Belg., N.V. v. Marchand*, 83 S.W.3d 789, 795–96 (Tex. 2002). We held that "[p]ersonal jurisdiction may exist over a nonresident defendant if the relationship between the foreign corporation and its parent corporation that does business in Texas is one that would allow the court to impute the parent corporation's 'doing business' to the subsidiary." *Id.* at 798. The rationale for exercising jurisdiction is that "the parent corporation exerts such domination and control over its subsidiary 'that they do not in reality constitute separate and distinct corporate entities but are one and the same corporation for purposes of jurisdiction.' " *Id.* (quoting *Hargrave*). We required that the party seeking to ascribe one corporation's actions to another by disregarding their distinct corporate entities prove this allegation, because Texas law presumes that two separate corporations are distinct entities. We concluded that there was no evidence to support the trial court's finding of general jurisdiction over a Belgian subsidiary based on allegations it was the alter ego of its American parent.

1. Single Business Enterprise

Here, the court of appeals held that Province and Minden operated as a single business enterprise — a theory we have never endorsed — and, therefore, Province's Texas contacts could be imputed to Minden. In doing so, the court of appeals examined eight factors as they related to Minden and Province: (1) common employees, (2) common offices, (3) centralized accounting, (4) payment of wages by one corporation to another corporation's employees, (5) common business name, (6) services rendered by the employees of one corporation on behalf of another corporation, (7) undocumented transfers of funds between corporations, and (8) unclear allocation of profits and losses between corporations. The court's analysis failed to recognize, however, that veil-piercing for purposes of liability ("substantive veil-piercing") is distinct from imputing one entity's contacts to another for jurisdictional purposes ("jurisdictional veil-piercing").

Courts have acknowledged that jurisdictional veil-piercing and substantive veil-piercing involve different elements of proof. *See, e.g., Wells Fargo & Co. v. Wells Fargo Express Co.*, 556 F.2d 406, 425 (9th Cir. 1977) (noting that undercapitalization, "which is important to deciding whether to pierce the veil raised by a subsidiary corporation in order to hold the parent corporation liable for failure of the subsidiary to meet its debts, may not be relevant to a showing that the two corporations are in fact one so as to establish that the out-of-state corporation — be it parent or subsidiary — is present within the forum for jurisdictional purposes"; instead, "the operative question is whether the two corporations are in fact mere 'divisions' or 'branches' of a larger whole"); *Daimler-Benz Aktiengesellschaft v. Olson*, 21 S.W.3d 707, 721 n.5 (Tex. App. — Austin 2000, pet. dism'd w.o.j.) ("Although many of the factors relevant to [determining whether subsidiaries' contacts should be imputed to parent] may also be relevant in determining whether a parent corporation should be liable for the actions of its subsidiary, the determination whether two corporate entities are one and the same for jurisdictional purposes is distinct."); *see also* 2-32 William V. Dorsaneo, Texas Litigation Guide § 32.06 (2005). This makes sense in light of the fact that personal jurisdiction involves due process considerations that may not be overriden by statutes or the common law. *Cf.Michiana Easy Livin' Country, Inc. v. Holten*, 168 S.W.3d 777, 790–91 (Tex. 2005) (rejecting theory that where defendant "directed a tort" was relevant inquiry for specific jurisdiction, as such a rule improperly "equat[ed] the jurisdictional inquiry with the underlying merits"); *National Indus. Sand Ass'n v. Gibson*, 897 S.W.2d 769, 773 (Tex. 1995) (observing that "[c]onspiracy as an independent basis for jurisdiction has been criticized as distracting from the ultimate due process inquiry: whether the out-of-state defendant's contact with the forum was such that it should reasonably anticipate being haled into a court in the forum state" and declining to recognize personal jurisdiction based on conspiracy allegation); John A. Swain & Edwin E. Aguilar, *Piercing the Veil to Assert Personal Jurisdiction Over Corporate Affiliates: An Empirical Study of the Cannon Doctrine*, 84 B.U.L. Rev. 445, 453 (2004) (noting that "the principle of limited liability is statutory and does not speak to judicial jurisdiction").

For this reason, fraud — which is vital to piercing the corporate veil under section 21.223 of the Business Organizations Code — has no place in assessing contacts to determine jurisdiction. Similarly, some of the factors courts look to in determining whether an entity may be held liable as a "single business enterprise" are irrelevant to an analysis of jurisdictional contacts. For example, the court of appeals examined whether Province and Minden shared a common name and concluded that "[Minden's] partnership name and initials, PHC-Minden, L.P. can be construed as a reference to Province Healthcare Company." Whether two related entities share a common name, however, does not affect whether each has sufficient contacts with the forum for jurisdictional purposes.

2. Factors

Instead, we recently outlined the relevant factors for jurisdictional veil-piercing:

> To "fuse" the parent company and its subsidiary for jurisdictional purposes, the plaintiffs must prove the parent controls the internal business operations and affairs of the subsidiary. But the degree of control the parent exercises must be greater than that normally associated with common ownership and directorship; the evidence must show that the two entities cease to be separate so that the corporate fiction should be disregarded to prevent fraud or injustice.

BMC Software, 83 S.W.3d at 799. We also relied on our prior precedent, which held that "[a] subsidiary corporation will not be regarded as the alter ego of its parent merely because of stock ownership, a duplication of some or all of the directors or officers, or an exercise of the control that stock ownership gives to stockholders." *Gentry v. Credit Plan Corp. of Houston*, 528 S.W.2d 571, 573 (Tex. 1975). A leading treatise suggests that in determining whether a subsidiary corporation is subject to the jurisdiction of a forum state because its parent corporation is present or doing business there, courts should determine whether the subsidiary is "separate and distinct from its parent corporation for personal jurisdiction purposes," taking into account the amount of the subsidiary's stock owned by the parent corporation, the existence of separate headquarters, the observance of corporate formalities, and the degree of the parent's control over the general policy and administration of the subsidiary. 4A Wright & Miller, Federal Practice & Procedure § 1069.4.

Here, the court of appeals cited the following as evidence that Province and Minden were a single business enterprise:

> the record shows that Province and [Minden] have at least one common employee and that Province pays certain [Minden] employees, although the salaries are intercompany payables. The names of the two companies are similar, and Province employees provide various services to assist [Minden] in its operations. Province exercises control over [Minden]'s revenues and expenditures and oversees [Minden]'s operations, financial performance, and completion of strategic initiatives. Further, Province audits [Minden]'s financial goals to determine if [Minden] will be able to meet these goals. Considering the totality of this evidence, we conclude that Province and [Minden] have integrated their resources to achieve a common business purpose.

Upon closer examination, however, it is clear that Province does not exercise the sort of control over Minden that is required to fuse them for jurisdictional purposes. Much of the evidence cited points to parental involvement — involvement consistent with its investor status — not atypical control. *See* 16 Moore's Federal Practice § 108.42[3][b]. "Appropriate parental involvement includes monitoring the subsidiary's performance, supervision of the subsidiary's finance and capital budget decisions, and articulation of general policies." What is lacking here is the "plus" factor, "something beyond the subsidiary's mere presence within the bosom of the corporate family." *Dickson Marine, Inc. v. Panalpina, Inc.*, 179 F.3d 331, 338 (5th Cir. 1999). The two entities maintain separate headquarters, Minden in Louisiana and Province in Tennessee. Minden's Board of Governors approves Minden's budget and oversees day-to-day operations, and Minden alone establishes its policies and procedures for providing health care to patients. Province is not involved in Minden's physician recruitment, and the two entities share no directors. While Minden's chief executive officer, chief nursing officer, and chief financial officer receive their paychecks from Province, their salaries are intercompany payables; that is, the monies come from Minden's revenues. Similarly, while Province provides Minden's general liability insurance and a group health insurance policy for its employees, the policies are funded from Minden's revenues. There is no indication that Minden and Province have disregarded corporate formalities. The court of appeals cited evidence that two Minden employees received Province stock options, but we have said that "a parent company's offering a stock option plan to a subsidiary's employees is acceptable under IRS regulations and is not evidence of abnormal control over the subsidiary." *BMC Software*, 83 S.W.3d at 800. Put simply, we find no evidence of control other than that consistent with Province's investor status, and the court of appeals erred in imputing Province's Texas contacts to Minden.

III

Conclusion

Minden does not have continuous and systematic contacts with Texas, nor is there any basis for imputing Province's Texas contacts to Minden. We reverse the court of appeals' judgment and render judgment dismissing the claims against Minden for want of jurisdiction.

NOTES AND QUESTIONS

(1) *Time for Assessing Contacts.* The Court's opinion in *Minden* resolved a split among the intermediate appellate courts about the relevant end point in considering the defendant's contacts with Texas when the issue is general jurisdiction. Rejecting the analysis of lower courts who only considered contacts through the time of the occurrence giving rise to the lawsuit, the Court held that contacts through the filing of the lawsuit could be counted. As to the beginning point, the Court noted only that courts should look at a "reasonable period of time" rather than a snapshot, and cited cases going back seven (*Helicopteros*) and twenty (*ATCC*) years.

(2) *Theoretical Basis for General Jurisdiction.* In the article by Professor Rocky Rhodes, cited by the Court, he recommends a two-part test for general jurisdiction. "First, the court should conduct a qualitative analysis of the substantiality of the nature of the defendant's forum activities. Second, the court should perform a quantitative analysis of the continuity and regularity of such activities. With respect to both analyses, the court should appraise the defendant's

forum activities in light of the activities of a local business." Did the Texas Supreme Court's *Minden* opinion follow this methodology?

(3) *Interrelated Entities: The Issue.* Corporations and other business entities that have parent-subsidiary relationships, control over one another, joint venture agreements, or simply patterns of dealing present frequent, and knotty, due process issues. Courts have struggled to decide when the relationship is strong enough so that the contacts of one entity will be attributed to the other for purposes of analyzing the sufficiency of the defendant's purposeful contacts with the forum state. *Minden* is the Texas Supreme Court's most recent discussion of the problem of interrelated businesses.

(4) *Interrelated Entities: Substance Versus Procedure.* A related doctrine, which often goes by the sexy title "piercing the corporate veil," governs the liability of one entity for the acts of a related one. As the *Minden* court notes, the law with regard to substantive veil piercing is not identical to that for jurisdictional purposes. For articles tracing the development of the alter ego doctrine, see Lea Brilmayer & Kathleen Paisley, *Personal Jurisdiction and Substantive Legal Relations: Corporations, Conspiracies, and Agency*, 74 Cal. L. Rev. 1 (1986); Lonny Sheinkopf Hoffman, *The Case Against Vicarious Jurisdiction*, 152 U. Pa. L. Rev. 1023 (2004).

[D] Internet Contacts and Jurisdiction

During the early period of its evolution, the constitutional limit on personal jurisdiction dealt with contacts that were primarily physical: defendant personally traveled to the forum state, or shipped some physical good to the forum state. The doctrine adapted to the sorts of "virtual" contacts involved in modern business dealings, such as mail, telephone calls, and faxes. But what about activity that takes place wholly or partially in cyberspace? Does it have a physical location that can be used to find "minimum contacts"? Where does an internet sale take place? Where is an internet libel published? Does a web site that is available in the forum target forum residents? Both in the context of specific jurisdiction and of general jurisdiction, the courts have struggled to fit internet contacts into the constitutional calculus. Texas courts have decided only a few such cases. Consider the following case.

CHOICE AUTO BROKERS, INC. v. DAWSON

274 S.W.3d 172 (Tex. App. — Houston [1st Dist.] 2008, no pet.)

Nuchia, J.

CAB is a Florida corporation that sells automobiles using both its own website and the internet auction site, eBay. Dawson is a Texas resident, who purchased an automobile from CAB. Dawson found the automobile on CAB's website, which had a hyperlink to eBay to enable visitors to bid on vehicles through the online auction site. Because the website required that bidders who lacked a certain bidding history on eBay call before placing a bid, Dawson called CAB. He later purchased the car through eBay using the auction-ending function, "Buy It Now." Dawson's father took receipt of the car in Florida on Dawson's behalf. Due to mechanical problems, Dawson's father was unable to drive the car to Texas, and Dawson had it shipped to Texas.

Dawson sued for damages under the DTPA, alleging that CAB had not been truthful about the car's age and condition. Dawson argued that jurisdiction was proper because: (1) CAB had previously sold 43 vehicles to Texas residents over a three-year period; (2) CAB transported or arranged for the transportation of 19 of these to Texas; (3) CAB's website states in more than one place that a bid on a vehicle is a legally binding contract. In addition, CAB's website links directly to eBay, where customers can bid on the vehicles advertised on CAB's website.

CAB filed a special appearance, alleging that it does no business in Texas and was, therefore, not subject to personal jurisdiction in Texas. CAB stipulated that: (1) it maintained a website at the time of the sale; (2) visitors to its website could view pictures and specific details of vehicles it was offering for sale; (3) via the website, visitors could schedule a test drive of the vehicles; and (4) via the website, visitors could request additional information. CAB also provided printouts as exemplars of how the website looked at the time of the sale. In an affidavit attached to Defendant's Second Amended Special Appearance, Jean-Luc Ferrigno, the president of CAB, testified that: (1) CAB is a Florida corporation that does no business in the State of Texas; (2) CAB has no offices, employees, or facilities in Texas, nor does CAB own any property in Texas; (3) CAB does not engage in advertising that specifically targets Texas residents, as opposed to the residents of any other state; (4) CAB's advertising consists of paying a company that promotes vehicles for sale on behalf of numerous clients through internet listings that do not target the residents of any particular state; (5) unless otherwise requested by a client, the place of delivery is Florida; (6) CAB offers some of its products for sale through eBay and provides a link to eBay from its web page; (7) customers cannot purchase products from CAB through CAB's website; (8) customers can call CAB directly to negotiate a sale over the telephone; (9) the "Make an Offer" function on the CAB website sends an email to CAB; (10) in response to such an email, CAB calls the customer to discuss a potential sale; (11) CAB does not ship vehicles to Texas but will arrange for transportation outside of Florida through a third party; (12) a customer can request a test drive through the website, but the test drive must occur in Florida; and (13) CAB provides no warranties.

The trial court denied CAB's special appearance, and CAB timely appealed.

[The court first discussed the general principles of personal jurisdiction.]

Internet Use & Personal Jurisdiction

Internet usage is divided into three categories, using a sliding scale, for the purposes of establishing personal jurisdiction. *Reiff v. Roy*, 115 S.W.3d 700, 705 (Tex. App. — Dallas 2003, pet. denied). "At one end of the scale are websites clearly used for transacting business over the Internet, such as entering into contracts and knowing and repeated transmission of files of information, which may be sufficient to establish minimum contacts with a state." *Id.* "On the other end of the spectrum are 'passive' websites that are used only for advertising over the Internet and are not sufficient to establish minimum contacts even though they are accessible to residents of a particular state." *Id.* at 705–06. "In the middle are 'interactive' websites that allow the 'exchange' of information between a potential customer and a host computer." *Id.* at 706. Jurisdiction in cases involving interactive websites is determined by the degree of interaction. *Id.*

Discussion

CAB's website was more than a purely passive website. The website provided advertising and some interactivity, because customers were able to email CAB through the website to schedule a test drive or request additional information about the vehicle. But the website did not allow a customer to enter into a contract or purchase a vehicle directly; rather, it routed the customer to eBay, where CAB had no control over who would be the highest bidder. Because the degree of interactivity falls between the two extremes, we look beyond the internet activity to the degree of interaction between the parties.

As to specific jurisdiction, the record shows that Dawson initiated the conversations with CAB and received the vehicle in Florida. There is no evidence that CAB made misrepresentations to Dawson in Texas. In fact, the record shows that the car initially malfunctioned while outside of Texas as well. Nothing in the record suggests that CAB's potential liability arises from or is related to an activity conducted within the forum. Therefore, we conclude that specific jurisdiction does not exist. NO SPECIFIC JX

As to general jurisdiction, the record shows that CAB sold 43 vehicles to Texas purchasers, but the record does not quantify CAB's total sales. During the same time period CAB shipped, or arranged for shipping, nineteen of those vehicles to Texas. There is no indication in the record that CAB targeted Texas customers in any way. Nothing in the record shows that CAB maintained a physical presence in Texas, performed any business activities in Texas, or otherwise structures its business affairs to benefit from the Texas laws.

The Texas Supreme Court has held that an 18-year history of sales to Texas residents was insufficient to confer general jurisdiction, when Texas sales accounted for 3.5% of its total sales and title to the goods purchased passed outside of Texas. *American Type Culture Collection*, 83 S.W.3d 801, 807-09 (Tex. 2002). In *American Type Culture Collection*, the defendant also purchased supplies from over 33 Texas vendors over a five-year period and sent representatives to five scientific conferences in Texas over a seven-year period. But the defendant did not advertise in Texas or maintain a physical presence in Texas. It performed its business services outside of Texas and constructed its contracts to ensure it did not benefit from Texas laws. The supreme court concluded that these factors, taken together, did not establish a pattern of continuing and systematic activity sufficient to support the exercise of personal jurisdiction in Texas.

Likewise, we hold that CAB's activities do not establish a pattern of continuing and systematic activity sufficient to support the exercise of personal jurisdiction in Texas. We hold that the trial court erred in denying CAB's special appearance.

NO GEN JX

NOTES AND QUESTIONS

(1) *The Sliding Scale.* The court analyzes website-based contacts using a sliding scale that turns on the nature of the website. This approach was first used in *Zippo Manufacturing Co. v. Zippo Dot Com.* The *Zippo* test, and its use by Texas courts, is discussed in Charles W. "Rocky" Rhodes, *The Predictability Principle in Personal Jurisdiction Doctrine: A Case Study on the Effects of a "Generally" Too Broad, but "Specifically" Too Narrow Approach to Minimum Contacts,* 57 BAYLOR L. REV. 135, 198–201, 231–33 (2005).

(2) *General Jurisdiction and Websites.* The *Choice Auto Brokers* court, using the Supreme Court's test from *Moki Mac,* concludes that the internet advertising was not sufficiently related to the plaintiff's claim to fall within the category of specific jurisdiction. Further, general jurisdiction would require a finding of substantial, continuous and systematic activity in Texas. Although a few early Texas cases found that the "continuous and systematic" internet presence was sufficient for general jurisdiction, those cases are almost certainly incorrect. As this case holds, the fiction that a website is always present in the state is not sufficient to create the kind of contacts needed for general jurisdiciton. *See also Amquip Corp. v. Cloud,* 73 S.W.3d 380, 388 (Tex. App. — Houston [1st Dist.] 2002, no pet.).

(3) *Sales Solely Through E-Bay.* Most internet jurisdiction cases are based on the interactivity of the defendant's own website. But what about defendants who sell online with the help of eBay, or a similar web-based business? In *Karstetter v. Voss,* 184 S.W.3d 396, 405 (Tex. App. — Dallas 2006, no pet.), the court refused to enforce a Kansas judgment against a Dallas car dealer who had sold a truck, through eBay, to a Kansas resident. The court found that the Kansas court lacked personal jurisdiction:

> This case would fall into the middle category of the [*Zippo*] sliding scale used to evaluate internet usage for purposes of establishing jurisdiction since eBay would be characterized as an "interactive website." Appellees [sellers] had to register and list the truck on eBay before appellant could bid on it. However, appellees had no control over who would be the highest bidder. Therefore, we have to look beyond the internet activity to the degree of interaction between the parties. *See generally Shamsuddin v. Vitamin Research Products,* 346 F. Supp. 2d 804, 810 (D. Md. 2004) (many courts have held that selling goods through internet auction sites does not subject a defendant to the jurisdiction of the purchaser).
>
> The record shows that the interaction between the parties was minimal. The email correspondence between the parties relating to the single purchase was initiated by appellant [buyer]. There was no evidence that appellees traveled to Kansas or engaged in other transactions with appellant or other Kansas residents either through the eBay service or otherwise. Although appellees did seek some benefit, advantage or profit by selling the truck to a Kansas resident, their contact with Kansas was random, isolated, and fortuitous. The interaction between the parties did not rise to a level such that appellees should have reasonably foreseen that they would be haled into a Kansas court.

(4) *Other Types of Analysis.* As courts become more familiar with internet technology, and as the types of internet contacts become more varied, the *Zippo* test is not always used. It is also arguable that the eBay case above cites but does not actually use *Zippo* as the basis for its decision. For thoughtful discussions of alternative methods of approaching internet jurisdiction cases, see A. Benjamin Spencer, *Jurisdiction and the Internet: Returning to Traditional Principles to Analyze Network-Mediated Contacts*, 2006 U. ILL. L. REV. 71; Michael A. Geist, *Is There a There There? Toward Greater Certainty for Internet Jurisdiction*, 16 BERKELEY TECH. L.J. 1345 (2001).

PRACTICE EXERCISE #7B

(1) *General Jurisdiction over National Businesses.* McCartney's is a national chain of fast food restaurants catering to vegetarians. Its corporate headquarters are in Vermont. It has at least a dozen restaurants in each state, including Texas. Ronnie was eating at a McCartney's in Orlando, Florida, and was served a spinach salad that gave him food poisoning, which put him in the hospital for several days. Ronnie is back home in Texas now and wants to sue McCartney's in Texas rather than in Florida. Could the Texas courts get jurisdiction over McCartney's for Ronnie's case? McCartney's has a website that is available to anyone in Texas with an internet connection; will that suffice for personal jurisdiction in Texas?

(2) *General Jurisdiction Over Texas Businesses.* RealBigChemicals (RBC) is a Texas corporation with its principal place of business in Texas. It sells test tubes to high school chemistry labs all over the world. One of those test tubes exploded and injured Jessica, a chemistry teacher, when she was demonstrating an experiment in her classroom in Alaska. Jessica's pretty face was scarred by flying glass, and she wants to sue RBC. Jessica grew up in Texas and has gone home to live with her parents while she has plastic surgery to try to fix the damage, and so she'd like to sue RBC in Texas. Would that be constitutional?

(3) *Alter Ego Jurisdiction.* The Lochland Distillery is a British company, a celebrated maker of single-malt whisky. In addition to making whisky, it sells specially fired oak casks to people who want to experiment with home brews, although it sells only to consumers in Europe. (Lochland refers potential customers from the U.S. to its U.S. subsidiary). Lochland is the parent company of Lakeland Whiskeys, a Delaware corporation with its headquarters in Amarillo, Texas. The two companies have interlocking boards of directors, use the same accounting firm, share common letterhead, have connected websites, and the President of Lakeland is a Senior Vice President of Lochland. The two companies are privately owned, and consolidate their balance sheets for the purpose of soliciting investors. Lochland's management must approve all hires of Lakeland executives. Lakeland does, however, respect corporate formalities like board meetings and minutes, and it keeps its own books and has its own bank accounts and line of credit. Tommy and Jeff, who wanted to go into the whiskey business, ordered two dozen oak casks from Lakeland, and Lakeland shipped the casks to Austin as requested. Much to Tommy and Jeff's horror, the casks turned out to be so leaky that they were unsuitable for distilling. They want to sue Lakeland and Lochland in Texas. Lochland's only contact with Texas is its relationship to Lakeland. Can Tommy and Jeff successfully get jurisdiction over Lochland in Texas?

[E] Consent

Forum selection clauses are enforceable in Texas. In fact, enforcement of forum-selection clauses is mandatory unless the party opposing enforcement "clearly show[s] that enforcement would be unreasonable and unjust, or that the clause was invalid for such reasons as fraud or overreaching." *In re AIU Ins. Co.*, 148 S.W.3d 109, 112–14 (Tex. 2004); *see also In re Automated Collection Techs., Inc.*, 156 S.W.3d 557, 559 (Tex. 2004). The Texas Supreme Court has continued to affirm its support for forum selection clauses, noting that "[f]orum selection clauses are generally enforceable, and the party attempting to show that such a clause should not be enforced bears a heavy burden." *In re International Profit Associates*, 274 S.W.3d 672, 675 (Tex. 2009). Further, the party seeking to enforce a forum selection clause does not need to prove that it showed the clause to other contracting parties. *In re International Profit Associates*, 286 S.W.3d 921, 924 (Tex. 2009).

Courts considering contractual forum selection clauses must consider whether the clause provides an additional forum or an exclusive one. This was the issue before the court in *Southwest Intelecom, Inc. v. Hotel Networks Corp.*, 997 S.W.2d 322, 325 (Tex. App. — Austin 1999, pet. denied). In that case, Intelecom sued HNC, seeking money damages and declaratory relief based on allegations of fraud in the inducement, failure of consideration, and breach of contract. The contract between the parties contained the following clause: "The Parties stipulate to jurisdiction and venue in Ramsey County, Minnesota." Nevertheless, Intelecom brought suit in Texas. The trial court dismissed the case based on the choice of forum clause, but the Austin Court of Appeals reversed, upholding the Texas court's jurisdiction. The appellate court explained, "We believe that the jurisdiction clause . . . requires that the parties submit to jurisdiction in the courts of Ramsey County, Minnesota, in the event that a suit related to the agreement is brought there. We do not, however, interpret the clause to mandate that Minnesota courts have exclusive jurisdiction. The plain language of the jurisdiction clause neither prohibits litigation in jurisdictions other than Ramsey County, Minnesota, nor provides that Minnesota courts have exclusive jurisdiction over all claims arising out of the contract." The court contrasted the language in this case with that of other forum selection clauses that have been held to be binding, e.g., "The parties hereby agree that any legal action concerning this Agreement shall be brought in a court of competent jurisdiction in the State of Oregon." For an extensive discussion of the issues raised by forum selection clauses, see Paul Yetter & Richard Farrer, *The Evolution of Forum-Selection-Clause Enforcement in Texas*, 73 Tex. Bar J. 274 (April 2010).

§ 4.03 OTHER LONG-ARM STATUTES: THE FAMILY CODE

The long-arm provisions of the Texas Family Code are contained in sections 6.305 and 102.011. As you will see below, section 6.305 deals with the exercise of personal jurisdiction over a nonresident respondent in a suit to dissolve the matrimonial relationship whereas section 11.051 concerns suits affecting the parent-child relationship:

Fam. C. § 6.305. *Acquiring Jurisdiction Over Nonresident Respondent*

(a) If the petitioner is a resident or a domiciliary of this state at the time the suit for dissolution is filed, the court may exercise personal jurisdiction over the respondent, or the respondent's personal representative, although the respon dent is not a resident of this state if:

(1) this state is the last marital residence of the petitioner and the respondent and the suit is commenced within two years after the date on which marital residence ended; or

(2) there is any basis consistent with the constitutions of this state and the United States for the exercise of the personal jurisdiction.

(b) A court acquiring jurisdiction under this section also acquires jurisdiction over the respondent in a suit affecting the parent-child relationship.

FAM. C. § 102.011. *Acquiring Jurisdiction Over Nonresident*

(a) The court may exercise status or subject matter jurisdiction over the suit as provided by Chapter 152 [containing provisions of the Uniform Child Custody Jurisdiction Act].

(b) The court may also exercise personal jurisdiction over a person on whom service of citation is required or over the person's personal representative, although the person is not a resident or domiciliary of this state, if:

(1) the person is personally served with citation in this state;

(2) the person submits to the jurisdiction of this state by consent, by entering a general appearance, or by filing a responsive document having the effect of waiving any contest to personal jurisdiction;

(3) the child resides in this state as a result of the acts or directives of the person;

(4) the person resided with the child in this state;

(5) the person resided in this state and provided prenatal expenses or support for the child;

(6) the person engaged in sexual intercourse in this state and the child may have been conceived by that act of intercourse; or

(7) there is any basis consistent with the constitutions of this state and the United States for the exercise of the personal jurisdiction.

To interpret these provisions and understand their application, you must bring to bear your understanding of the Full Faith and Credit Clause and Due Process Clause. *See* William V. Dorsaneo III, *Due Process, Full Faith and Credit, and Family Law Litigation*, 36 SW. L.J. 1085 (1983). Because of considerations associated with full faith and credit and due process, the treatment of custody and termination has bedeviled the courts at all levels. Lower courts have struggled with custody cases more than virtually any other species of domestic relations litigation. One result of the confusion has been the passage of uniform state legislation such as the Uniform Child Custody Jurisdiction Enforcement Act. How does it affect the results of the following case?

IN RE FORLENZA

140 S.W.3d 373 (Tex. 2004)

O'NEILL, J.

After the trial court in this case made an initial child-custody determination, the children lived with their custodial parent in four different states over a five and one-half year period while the non-custodial parent remained in Texas. In this modification suit, we must decide whether significant connections with Texas exist or substantial evidence is available here such that the initial trial court retained exclusive continuing jurisdiction under section 152.202(a)(1) of the Texas Family Code. Based on the record presented, we hold that the trial court retained exclusive continuing jurisdiction over the modification proceedings and the court of appeals erred in concluding otherwise. Because the relator lacks an adequate remedy by appeal, we grant the petition for writ of mandamus and order the court of appeals to vacate its order directing the trial court to dismiss the case for lack of jurisdiction.

I

Ann Marie and Robert Joseph Forlenza were divorced in Collin County, Texas, on March 1, 1996. On July 23, 1997, the trial court signed an agreed modification order, modifying the original divorce decree, that granted Robert primary custody of their two children, now ten and fourteen years old, and the exclusive right to establish their primary physical residence. That same month, the children moved with Robert to Issaquah, Washington. Over the next five years, Robert moved with the children three more times — on August 30, 1998, they moved to Ohio, on February 19, 1999, they moved to Virginia, and on August 27, 2002, they moved to Colorado where they now reside.[1]

The current dispute arose in 2001 when Robert lost his job in Virginia and was offered a two-year contract job in Taipei, Taiwan. Claiming that she had experienced difficulty in exercising her possession rights, Ann filed this suit on September 10, 2001, seeking to modify the prior agreed possession order. She also requested a restraining order prohibiting Robert from relocating the children outside the United States, which the trial court granted. Robert filed a counter-motion to clarify and, alternatively, to modify prior orders. In his motion, Robert averred that the Collin County court had exclusive continuing jurisdiction over the suit as a result of prior proceedings. Shortly thereafter, on October 8, 2001, Robert filed a motion to dismiss alleging that the trial court did not have jurisdiction to issue an initial child-custody order, and alternatively requesting the trial court to decline jurisdiction in favor of Virginia, where the children then resided with their

---

[1] On August 6, 2002, Robert sent Ann notice that he was moving with the children back to Washington where he had a job offer. While visiting his family in Colorado en route to Washington, Robert decided to permanently move to Colorado.

father and his new wife. After a hearing on November 29, 2001, the court denied Robert's motion and the parties proceeded to prepare the case for trial, which was ultimately set for February 3, 2003.

During a pretrial conference seven days before the scheduled trial date, Robert filed a second motion to dismiss alleging that the court did not have exclusive continuing jurisdiction under Texas Family Code section 152.202(a) to modify its previous child-custody order. The trial court conducted another evidentiary hearing and denied the motion. The court of appeals, however, concluded that the trial court had abused its discretion and granted Robert's petition for writ of mandamus, ordering the trial court to vacate its prior order and dismiss the case.We granted Ann's petition to determine whether the trial court retained exclusive continuing jurisdiction under the Uniform Child Custody Jurisdiction Enforcement Act (UCCJEA).

II

Effective September 1, 1999, Texas adopted the UCCJEA, replacing the previous Uniform Child Custody Jurisdiction Act (UCCJA). The UCCJEA was designed, in large part, to clarify and to unify the standards for courts' continuing and modification jurisdiction in interstate child-custody matters. The Act that the UCCJEA replaced, the UCCJA, was drafted in 1968 as a model act designed to prevent repeated custody litigation. But even though all fifty states adopted the UCCJA, some did so with significant departure from the original text. As a result, states often interpreted the Act inconsistently and child-custody determinations made in one state were often not accorded full faith and credit in another.

To address some of these problems, in 1980 Congress enacted the Parental Kidnaping Prevention Act (PKPA), which requires states to accord full faith and credit to custody decrees issued by sister states that substantially comply with the PKPA. 28 U.S.C. § 1738A (2000). The PKPA authorizes exclusive continuing jurisdiction in the state that issued the original decree as long as one parent or child remains there and that state has exclusive continuing jurisdiction under its own law. *Id.* § 1738A(d). The UCCJA, though, which the states had adopted, does not clearly articulate when a decree-granting state retains exclusive continuing jurisdiction. As states adopted different interpretations of continuing jurisdiction and reached conflicting conclusions about the circumstances under which it endures, the law's uniformity diminished, often resulting in simultaneous proceedings and conflicting custody decrees. The UCCJEA was designed to eliminate inconsistent state interpretations of the UCCJA's jurisdictional aspects and to harmonize the UCCJA with the PKPA. *See Id.*

Article 2 of the UCCJEA specifically grants exclusive continuing jurisdiction over child-custody disputes to the state that made the initial custody determination and provides specific rules on how long this jurisdiction continues. *See* UNIF. CHILD CUSTODY JUR. & ENF. ACT § 202, 9 U.L.A. 673–74 (Supp. 2004). Rules that prevent another state from modifying a child-custody determination while exclusive continuing jurisdiction remains in the original-decree state complement these provisions.[3] Texas adopted Article 2 without substantial variation from the UCCJEA.

Robert's challenge involves the proper interpretation of section 152.202(a), which governs the duration of the decree-granting state's exclusive continuing jurisdiction. That section provides that a court of this state that has made an initial child-custody determination consistent with section 152.201 has exclusive continuing jurisdiction over the determination until

(1) a court of this state determines that *neither the child, nor the child and one parent,* nor the child and a person acting as a parent, *have a significant connection with this state and* that *substantial evidence is no longer available in this state* concerning the child's care, protection, training, and personal relationships; or

(2) a court of this state or a court of another state determines that the child, the child's parents, and any person acting as a parent do not presently reside in this state.

TEX. FAM. CODE § 152.202(a) (emphasis added). Robert does not challenge the prior child-custody order's compliance with section 152.201. And section 152.202(a)(2) does not apply because Ann continues to reside in Texas. Therefore, we must decide whether the trial court properly applied section 152.202(a)(1) in deciding that it had exclusive continuing jurisdiction over these modification proceedings. Statutory construction is a question of law that we review de novo. *McIntyre v. Ramirez*, 109 S.W.3d 741, 745 (Tex. 2003).

Robert's jurisdictional plea contends that Ann failed to establish that a significant connection with Texas exists and that substantial evidence is available here concerning the children's care, protection, training, and personal relationships. As a preliminary matter, Robert asserts that, in making this determination, the court may not consider any contacts that occurred or any evidence that was created after September 10, 2001. We agree that jurisdiction must be determined at the proceeding's commencement, which section 152.102(5) defines as the filing of the first pleading — in this instance, Ann's motion to modify the prior agreed possession order. *See* TEX. FAM. CODE § 152.102(5). However, we disagree with Robert's contention that it was Ann's burden in the first instance to establish that the children have a significant connection with Texas and that substantial evidence is available here. As a general matter, the pleader must allege facts that affirmatively demonstrate the court's jurisdiction to hear the case. *See Texas Ass'n of Bus. v. Texas Air Control Bd.*, 852 S.W.2d 440, 446 (Tex. 1993). Under the statute, a court acquires exclusive continuing jurisdiction by virtue of a prior child-custody determination. TEX. FAM. CODE § 152.202(a). By alleging that the court's prior orders conferred exclusive continuing jurisdiction, Ann satisfied

[3] Section 203 provides that "a court of this State may not modify a child-custody determination made by a court of another State unless a court of this State has jurisdiction to make an initial determination under Section 201(a)(1) or (2) and: (1) the court of the other State determines it no longer has exclusive, continuing jurisdiction under Section 202 or that a court of this State would be a more convenient forum under Section 207; or (2) a court of this State or a court of the other State determines that the child, the child's parents, and any person acting as a parent do not presently reside in the other state."

her initial statutory burden. The statute specifically provides that a court *retains* exclusive continuing jurisdiction *until* it determines that the significant-connection and substantial-evidence requirements are no longer met. *Id.* Robert may challenge whether the statutory elements are satisfied, or the court may consider them sua sponte, but Ann has satisfied her initial jurisdictional burden under the statute.

Robert contends that the children no longer have a significant connection with Texas because (1) the children visited here only five times in the four-year period preceding this action, and (2) Ann's residence in Texas is not sufficient, as the commentary to section 152.202 specifically notes that the presence of one parent remaining in the state is not determinative. *See* UNIF. CHILD CUSTODY JUR. & ENF. ACT § 152.202 cmt. 1, 9 U.L.A. 674. But Ann does not rely on her mere presence in Texas to establish a significant connection under the statute. Contrary to Robert's briefing, the record indicates that the children actually visited Texas six times in the relevant period. On four of these occasions the children lived with Ann for considerable periods, each lasting approximately one month during the summer. *See Fish v. Fish*, 596 S.E.2d 654, 656 (Ga. Ct. App. 2004) (pointing to extended custodial visitation in state to support court's finding of a significant connection); *Ruth v. Ruth*, 83 P.3d 1248, 1254 (Kan. Ct. App. 2004) (same). Moreover, we presume that the trial court accepted as true Ann's testimony that more visitation would have occurred in Texas but for Robert's actions and the fact that the children were not allowed to fly to Texas.

Other courts commonly consider visitation within the state as evidence of a significant connection. In addition, numerous relatives, including Ann's mother and sister and Robert's sister and sister-in-law, live in Texas and maintain a relationship with the children.

Moreover, the evidence in this case clearly indicates that Ann maintained a significant relationship with her children. *See* UNIF. CHILD CUSTODY JUR. & ENF. ACT § 202 cmt. 1, 2, 9 U.L.A. 674 ("If the relationship between the child and the person remaining in the State with exclusive, continuing jurisdiction becomes so attenuated that the court could no longer find significant connections and substantial evidence, jurisdiction would no longer exist . . . . The significant connection to the original decree State must relate to the child, the child and a parent, or the child and a person acting as a parent."); *see also* CONN. GEN. STAT. § 46b-115l (2003) (altering the language of the UCCJEA to clarify that significant connection refers to the relationship with the remaining parent); *Fish*, 596 S.E.2d at 656 ("Based on [father's] continuous residency, the significant relationship he maintains with his children, and the extended visitation in this State, it cannot be said that neither the children nor the parents in this case have a substantial connection with Georgia."); *Ruth*, 83 P.3d at 1254 (inquiring whether the father's relationship with his children was substantial); Kelly Gaines Stoner, *The Uniform Child Custody Jurisdiction & Enforcement Act (UCCJEA)*, 75 N.D. L. REV. 301, 316 (1999) ("If the relationship between the child and the person remaining in the state becomes so tenuous that the court could no longer find a significant connection to the state, jurisdiction would no longer exist."); *cf.In the Matter of M.B. II*, 756 N.Y.S.2d at 712–13 (rejecting assertion that incidental contacts with New York, such as a visit for a cousin's communion, constitute a significant connection with New York). To accommodate the children's schedule over the years, Ann repeatedly flew to Washington, Ohio, and Virginia to see them. Robert admits that Ann made at least fifteen such trips in the four-year period under review. Because the record establishes that the children visited Texas on a number of occasions and maintained a close relationship with their mother and other relatives residing in Texas, all important considerations under the UCCJEA, we hold that the children have a significant connection with Texas sufficient to support the trial court's exclusive continuing jurisdiction over the modification proceedings.

Robert nevertheless claims that the children's contacts with Texas do not rise to the level other Texas courts have required. Specifically, Robert cites *In the Interest of Bellamy*, 67 S.W.3d 482 (Tex. App. — Texarkana 2002, no pet.), and *In the Interest of C.C.B. & M.J.B.*, 2002 WL 31727247, at *4 (Tex. App. — El Paso 2002, no pet.) (not designated for publication). Those cases, however, do not focus exclusively on the number of times the child has had contact with the state, as Robert suggests. In *Bellamy*, the original child-custody determination was made in Texas, where the parents were divorced. 67 S.W.3d at 483. The father later sought to modify the custody order, at which time the child's home state was Louisiana. *Id.* Although the child lived in Louisiana with her mother, she attended school daily across the border in Texas, regularly visited her father and his family in Texas, and visited doctors and dentists in Texas. *Id.* at 485. Based on these facts, the trial court determined that section 152.202(a)(1)'s significant-connection element was satisfied. *Id.* But nowhere did the court suggest that this quantum of physical contact was necessary to meet the statutory standard, as Robert contends. Rather, the court emphasized the nature and quality of the child's relationship with the father and family members who resided in Texas. *Id.*

Robert also relies on *In the Interest of C.C.B. and M.J.B.*, in which the court stated that the contacts in *Bellamy* are "the types of significant contacts that might cause a Texas court to retain jurisdiction in Texas even when a child moves from the state." 2002 WL 31727247, at *4. To the extent this statement concerns the nature and quality of the child's contacts with the resident parent, it is consistent with *Bellamy* and the UCCJEA. But insofar as the statement might suggest that such a high level of physical presence in Texas is necessary to satisfy section 202(a)'s significant-connection standard, we disapprove it. *See also Fish*, 596 S.E.2d at 656; *Ruth*, 83 P.3d at 1254; *In re Dale McCormick*, 87 S.W.3d 746, 751 (Tex. App. — Amarillo 2002, no pet.); *Lord v. Lord*, 2001 Conn. Super. LEXIS 2646 (Conn. Super. Ct. Sept. 14, 2001) (not designated for publication).

Robert claims that no other court has exercised exclusive continuing jurisdiction over children who have resided out of state for more than five years. We disagree. In *Fish*, the Georgia Court of Appeals determined that the trial court had exclusive continuing jurisdiction pursuant to a prior divorce decree even though the mother and the children had lived in Florida for seven years. 596 S.E.2d 654. Similarly, in *Ruth*, the Kansas Court of Appeals determined that the trial court had jurisdiction pursuant to a prior divorce decree after the mother and children had lived in Missouri for approximately six years. 83 P.3d at 1254. And in *Heath v. Heath*, a Connecticut court exercised exclusive continuing jurisdiction even though the children had lived in California for eight years. 2000 Conn. Super. LEXIS 3054 (Conn. Super. Ct. Nov. 21, 2000) (not designated for publication). Moreover, contrary to Robert's argument, the UCCJEA does not premise the exclusive continuing jurisdiction determination on which state has the *most* significant connection with the child. *See In re Dale McCormick*, 87 S.W.3d at 750 (stating that "although evidence was admitted which establishes that [the child] has significant ties with the state of Kansas, that fact does not necessarily mean that there is no significant connection with Texas or that substantial evidence cannot be found here"). This relative type of inquiry is appropriate under section 152.207, which allows a court with exclusive continuing jurisdiction to decline it in favor of a more convenient forum, but it does not affect the initial section 152.202 jurisdictional analysis. *See* TEX. FAM. CODE § 152.207. Importantly, the only issue before us is whether the Texas court retained jurisdiction; the court could still decline to exercise that jurisdiction if another forum was more convenient. In this case, though, the children's almost continual change of residence supports the trial court's conclusion that the children had a significant connection with Texas based on their visits here and their personal relationships maintained in this state.

Finally, Robert argues that substantial evidence does not exist in Texas regarding the children's care, protection, training, and personal relationships, and section 152.202(a)(1) requires the trial court to find *both* a significant connection with Texas *and* that substantial evidence exists here before it can exercise exclusive continuing jurisdiction. For this proposition, Robert relies upon the court of appeals' statement in *Bellamy* that "Texas retains jurisdiction [under section 152.202(a)] . . . so long as there is still a significant connection with Texas and substantial evidence is still available in Texas." 67 S.W.3d at 484. Robert also cites the commentary to section 152.202, which notes that the original-decree state retains exclusive jurisdiction even if the child has acquired a new home state "so long as the general requisites of the 'substantial connection' jurisdiction provisions of Section 201 are met." UNIF. CHILD CUSTODY JUR. & ENF. ACT § 202 cmt. 1, 9 U.L.A. 674. Because section 201, which governs the initial custody determination, requires both a significant connection and substantial evidence, Robert concludes that section 202 must as well. We disagree.

Robert's strained construction of the statutory scheme ignores section 152.202(a)(1)'s plain language. That section specifically states that jurisdiction continues until the court determines that there is not a significant connection with Texas *and* that substantial evidence concerning the children's care, protection, training, and personal relationships is no longer available here. *See* TEX. FAM. CODE § 152.202(a)(1). Clearly, exclusive jurisdiction continues in the decree-granting state as long as a significant connection exists *or* substantial evidence is present.[4]

[4] We note that our interpretation comports with that of other jurisdictions. *See Fish v. Fish*, 596 S.E.2d 654, 656 (Ga. Ct. App. 2004) (stating that for exclusive continuing jurisdiction to be lost "two findings [no significant connection and no substantial evidence] must be made"); *Ruth v. Ruth*, 83 P.3d 1248, 1254 (Kan. Ct. App. 2004) (affirming trial court's exercise of jurisdiction after determining the children have a significant connection with Kansas); *Benson v. Benson*, 667 N.W.2d 582, 585 (N.D. 2003) ("Because [the father] still resides in the state, North Dakota retains exclusive, continuing jurisdiction until a court of this state determines [the child] no longer has a significant connection with the state and the state no longer has substantial evidence concerning [the child]."); *Lord v. Lord*, 2001 Conn. Super. LEXIS 2646 (Conn. Super. Ct. Sept. 14, 2001) (determining that exclusive continuing jurisdiction exists in Connecticut because the child's relationship with the resident parent is significant, even though the court found that substantial evidence is no longer available). *But see In re Marriage of David Medill*, 40

To the extent that *Bellamy* is inconsistent with our holding today, we disapprove it. Because we conclude that the trial court did not err in concluding that the children had a substantial connection with Texas on September 10, 2001, we need not address whether substantial evidence existed here as well.

III

For the foregoing reasons, we hold that the trial court had exclusive continuing jurisdiction over this modification proceeding and that mandamus relief is justified. *See Geary v. Peavy*, 878 S.W.2d 602, 603 (Tex. 1994); *see also* TEX. FAM. CODE § 152.107. Accordingly, we conditionally grant the writ of mandamus and direct the court of appeals to vacate its order directing the trial court to dismiss the case for lack of jurisdiction. The writ will issue only if the court of appeals does not comply.

NOTES AND QUESTIONS

(1) *Civil Status Determinations.* Courts have long held that jurisdiction over civil "status" requires a different analysis from other assertions of personal jurisdiction. Why should that be true? Consider the following excerpt from *Dosamantes v. Dosamantes*, 500 S.W.2d 233, 236 (Tex. Civ. App. — Texarkana 1973, writ dism'd):

> It is urged that the District Court of Titus County lacked jurisdiction to grant appellee a divorce, irrespective of whether or not appellant was properly served, because the jurisdiction of the Texas court could not extend beyond Texas' territorial borders to affect the rights or the status of a citizen of Mexico.
>
> Historically, it has been recognized that a state court in the United States has the jurisdiction to determine or alter the status of a marriage relationship when one of the parties thereto is a domiciliary of that state, even though the other party thereto is a nonresident or a citizen of another state . . . . The basis for this power is that domicile in itself creates a relationship to the state which is sufficient for the exercise of state power. It has been said that domicile implies a nexus between person and place of such permanence as to authorize the control of the legal status, relationships and responsibilities of the domiciliary. The state, as sovereign, has an important and legitimate interest in the marital status of persons domiciled within its borders and consequently, it may determine, regulate and alter that status. As held by the United States Supreme Court in the case of *Williams v. North Carolina*, 317 U.S. 287:
>
> Thus it is plain that each state by virtue of its command over its domiciliaries and its large interest in the institution of marriage can alter within its own borders the marriage status of the spouse domiciled there, even though the other spouse is absent.

P.3d 1087, 1093 (Or. Ct. App. 2002) (finding that the trial court would only have continuing exclusive jurisdiction if both requirements were satisfied).

> Divorce actions are not mere in personam actions, but are quasi in rem. *Williams v. North Carolina*, 317 U.S. 287. In such cases the court is not exercising personal jurisdiction over the nonresident, but is exercising jurisdiction over the subject matter — that is, the marital status of its citizen. Thus, in this case, Texas was not attempting to extend its laws so as to give them extraterritorial effect in Mexico. Rather, it was exercising jurisdiction over the legal status and relations of its own citizen. The fact that such action affects a citizen of another sovereign does not prevent the exercise of such power any more than the exercise of jurisdiction over a true "res" located within the borders of the acting sovereign would be prohibited simply because the adjudication affects the rights of nonresidents of whom the sovereign has no personal jurisdiction.

Most of the cases decided on this question involve divorces where one of the parties is a citizen of another state of the United States, but the rule applies with equal force when the nonresident is a resident of a foreign nation. *Risch v. Risch*, 395 S.W.2d 709 (Tex. Civ. App. — Houston 1965, dism'd).

Is this consistent with the requirement that all assertions of personal jurisdiction meet the requirements of due process? What about division of marital property located within the state? What of suits affecting (terminating) the parent-child relationship? See *May v. Anderson*, 345 U.S. 528 (1953), which sets forth the traditional rule that custody awards require in personam jurisdiction. *See also Spitzmiller v. Spitzmiller*, 429 S.W.2d 557 (Tex. Civ. App. — Houston [1st Dist.] 1968, writ ref'd n.r.e.), which is to the same effect. Before the adoption of the parent-child long-arm provision of the Texas Family Code, personal jurisdiction of the parents was not sufficient unless the child was either domiciled in Texas or physically present. *See Ex parte Birmingham*, 244 S.W.2d 977 (Tex. 1952). As stated by Professor Jack Sampson, "This disability is what the parent-child long-arm statute is designed to correct to the maximum extent possible." Jack Sampson, *Jurisdiction in Divorce and Conservatorship Suits*, 8 TEX. TECH L. REV. 159, 173 (1976).

(2) *Statutes Regulating Jurisdiction over Custody Disputes*. The Uniform Child Custody Jurisdiction Act (UCCJA) preceded the UCCJEA. Virtually all jurisdictions adopted some variant of the act, Texas doing so originally in 1983. Texas adopted a revised version, the Uniform Child Custody Jurisdiction and Enforcement Act (UCCJEA) in 1999, codified in Chapter 152 of the Family Code. The new law brings Texas law more in line with the provisions of the Parental Kidnapping Prevention Act (PKPA).

(3) *Initial Child Custody Determinations*. Family Code Section 152.201, defines the circumstances under which a Texas court has jurisdiction to make an "initial child custody determination." This happens when (1) Texas is the home state of the child on the date of the commencement of the proceeding, or was the home state of the child within six months before the commencement of the proceeding and the child is absent from Texas but a parent or person acting as a parent continues to live in Texas; or (2) a court of another state does not have jurisdiction, or a court of the home state of the child has declined to exercise jurisdiction on the ground that Texas is the more appropriate forum based on inconvenience or unjustifiable

conduct and (a) the child and the child's parents, or the child and at least one parent or a person acting as a parent, have a significant connection with Texas other than mere physical presence and (b) substantial evidence is available in Texas concerning the child's care, protection, training, and personal relationships. The term "home state" means "the state in which a child lived with a parent or person acting as a parent for at least six consecutive months immediately before the commencement of a child custody proceeding. In the case of a child less than six months of age, the term means the state in which the child lived from birth with a parent or person acting as a parent. A period of temporary absence of a parent or a person acting as a parent is part of the period." FAM. C. § 152.102(7).

Except in cases of temporary emergencies, a Texas court may not modify a child custody determination made by a court of another state unless a Texas court has jurisdiction to make an initial determination and (1) the court of the *other* state determines it no longer has exclusive continuing jurisdiction or that a Texas court would be a more convenient forum; or (2) a Texas court or a court of the other state determines that the child, the child's parents, and any person acting as parent do not presently reside in the other state. FAM. C. § 152.203.

As you read in *In re Forlenza*, when a Texas court has made an initial determination or modification permitted by the sections described above, it has exclusive continuing jurisdiction until (1) a Texas court determines that neither the child, nor the child and one parent, nor the child and a person acting as a parent, have significant connection with Texas and that substantial evidence is no longer available in this state concerning the child's care, protection, training, and personal relationships; or (2) a court determines that the child, the child's parents, and any person acting as a parent do not presently reside in Texas.

(4) *Relationship to Minimum Contacts Doctrine*. Section 152.106 provides that a child custody determination made by a Texas court that had jurisdiction "binds all persons who have been served in accordance with the laws of this state or notified in accordance with Section 152.108 [notice by service of process under laws of Texas or the place where served] or who have submitted to the jurisdiction of the court and who have been given an opportunity to be heard. As to those persons, the determination is conclusive as to all decided issues of law and fact except to the extent the determination is modified." This means a non-Texas parent who has received notice is bound by the court's decision, whether or not that person would otherwise be subject to the personal jurisdiction of the Texas courts under the minimum contacts doctrine. Note, however, that if a parent has brought a child to Texas under circumstances that constitute "unjustifiable conduct," the Texas court is directed to decline to exercise its jurisdiction. FAM. C. § 152.208.

(5) *Subject Matter Jurisdiction and the UCCJEA*. The problem of jurisdiction in custody disputes is complicated by the fact that the UCCJEA involves the issue of subject matter jurisdiction. In *In re J.S.*, 175 S.W.3d 526, 527 (Tex. App. — Texarkana 2005, no pet.), the court held that personal jurisdiction over the out-of-state spouse is not sufficient to allow a Texas court to make a custody decision without meeting the requirements of the UCCJEA:

> Joseph James, Jr., filed a petition affecting the parent-child relationship, alleging that he is the father of J.S. and that Taneska Stout is the child's

mother. In his original petition, Joseph alleged Taneska is a nonresident of Texas and could be served with process at Fortson, Georgia. Joseph further alleged J.S. was born December 25, 2003, and resided in Harris County, Georgia. Joseph requested that the court enter an order appointing him and Taneska as joint managing conservators. Taneska filed a response entitled Special Answer and Special Motion to Dismiss, in which she specifically denied that the Jefferson County, Texas, court had jurisdiction. She further alleged that the minor child had resided in the State of Georgia since birth and that Georgia was the home state of the child in accordance with the Uniform Child Custody Jurisdiction and Enforcement Act (UCCJEA). The trial court considered the motion for temporary orders February 7, 2005, and determined jurisdiction was not proper in the State of Texas and dismissed the case without prejudice March 7, 2005. Joseph appeals alleging Taneska had sufficient contacts with the State of Texas to allow the district court to exercise jurisdiction.

Joseph argues that Taneska previously attended school in Texas and that the child was conceived in Texas, thereby authorizing Texas courts to exercise jurisdiction. These allegations are relevant as to personal jurisdiction; however, this case is controlled by subject-matter jurisdiction. Subject-matter jurisdiction exists when the nature of the case falls within a general category of cases that the court is empowered, under applicable statutory and constitutional provisions, to adjudicate . . . . Subject-matter jurisdiction is essential to the authority of a court to decide a case . . . . Subject-matter jurisdiction over custody issues in Texas is governed by the UCCJEA. TEX. FAM. CODE ANN. §§ 152.001–152.317. That Act provides mandatory jurisdictional rules for an original child custody proceeding. Georgia has also adopted the UCCJEA. *See* GA. CODE ANN. § 19-9-61. A Texas court must have jurisdiction under the UCCJEA to make a child custody determination.

(6) *Enforcing Sister State Custody Orders.* The Parental Kidnaping Prevention Act of 1980 (PKPA) contains a section that requires that decrees rendered by sister states be enforced, generally without modification. The following summary of the federal act is taken from William V. Dorsaneo III, *Interstate Modification and Enforcement: A Pilgrim's Progress Through UCCJA, PKPA and Section 14.10*, State Bar of Texas, Marriage Dissolution Institute, Chapter B (1981).*

PARENTAL KIDNAPING PREVENTION ACT OF 1980

1. *Child Custody Determination.* This term is defined as follows: " 'Custody determination' means a judgment, decree, or other order of a court providing for the custody or visitation of a child, and includes permanent and temporary orders, and initial orders and modifications." 28 U.S.C. § 1738A(b)(3).

2. *When Enforcement Mandatory.* "The appropriate authorities of every State shall enforce according to its terms, and, shall not modify except as provided in subsection (f) of this section, any child custody determination made consistently with the provisions of this section by a court of another State." 28 U.S.C. § 1738A(a).

3. *When Modification Permissible.* Subsection (f) permits modification if: (a) the court of the State in which modification is sought has jurisdiction to make a child custody determination, and (b) the court of the State which made the decree no longer has jurisdiction, or it has declined to exercise it. 28 U.S.C. § 1738A(f).

4. *When Determination Made Consistently with PKPA Requirements.*

(a) The court must have jurisdiction under the law of the state in which it sits to make the child custody determination. If it does not, then the determination is not consistent with PKPA.

(b) In addition, one of the following conditions must be met before a state court's exercise of jurisdiction is consistent with PKPA.

(1) the state is the child's "home state" [" 'home state' means the State in which, immediately preceding the time involved, the child lived with his parents, a parent, or a person acting as a parent for at least six consecutive months . . . " 28 U.S.C. § 1738A(b)(4)]; or

(2) the state had been the "home state" within six months of the date suit was brought and one "contestant" [" 'contestant' means a person, including a parent, who claims a right to custody or visitation of a child" 28 U.S.C. § 1738A(b)(2)] "continues to live in such State"; or

(3) if and only if there is no "home state" and the second alternative also does not apply, *and* it is in the child's best interest that the state assume jurisdiction because the child and at least one contestant have a significant connection with the State and substantial evidence exists in the State; or

(4) the child is physically present in the State *and* has been abandoned *or* requires emergency treatment as a result of actual or threatened mistreatment or abuse; or

(5) none of the above are applicable *or* another state has declined to exercise jurisdiction on the ground that the State whose jurisdiction is in issue is the more appropriate forum *and* it is in the best interest of the child for it to exercise jurisdiction;

(6) "the court has continuing jurisdiction pursuant to subsection d of this section." 28 U.S.C. § 1738A(c)(2)(e). Subsection (d) provides: "The jurisdiction of a court of a State which has made a child custody determination consistently with the provisions of this section continues as long as the requirement of subsection (c)(1) ['such court has jurisdiction under the law of such State'] of this section continues to be

met and such State remains the residence of the child or of any contestant."

(7) *Concurrent Jurisdiction: Comity.* The PKPA also provides that: "A court of a State shall not exercise jurisdiction in any proceeding for a custody determination commenced during the pendency of a proceeding in a court of another State where such court of that other State is exercising jurisdiction consistently with the provisions of this section to make a custody determination." 28 U.S.C. § 1738A(g).

§ 4.04 SERVICE OF PROCESS

[A] Due Process Requirements

Service of process is the way in which the defendant gets notice of the claim against him and its allegations. The U.S. Supreme Court has held that due process requires "notice reasonably calculated, under the circumstances, to apprise interested parties of the pendency of the action and afford them the opportunity to present their objections." *Mullane v. Central Hanover Bank & Trust Co.*, 339 U.S. 306, 314 (1950). When a default judgment is entered against a defendant in the absence of constitutionally-adequate notice, the judgment may be collaterally attacked. In the following case, the U.S. Supreme Court considered the Texas procedure for setting aside a default judgment in light of due process notice requirements. Can there be due process when the defendant is never served at all?

PERALTA v. HEIGHTS MEDICAL CENTER, INC.

485 U.S. 80 (1988)

Peralta sought relief in Texas state court to set aside a default judgment entered against him two years earlier and to void a subsequent sale of his property to satisfy the judgment. He alleged that because the original service of process itself showed that it was defective and, in fact, he had never been personally served, the judgment was void under Texas law. The Texas courts denied relief on the ground that Peralta failed to show he would have had a meritorious defense, even if he had had notice. The Texas courts rejected Peralta's contention that the meritorious defense requirement violated his due process rights under the Fourteenth Amendment, finding the requirement "not onerous."

The U.S. Supreme Court unanimously reversed. The Court first noted that all parties agreed Peralta had never been personally served and had no notice of the judgment. "[U]nder our cases, a judgment entered without notice or service is constitutionally infirm. 'An elementary and fundamental requirement of due process in any proceeding which is to be accorded finality is notice reasonably calculated, under the circumstances, to apprise interested parties of the pendency of the action and afford them the opportunity to present their objections.' *Mullane v. Central Hanover Bank & Trust Co.*, 339 U.S. 306, 314 (1950). Failure to give notice violates the most rudimentary demands of due process of law." The Court rejected the argument that without a meritorious defense the same judgment would again be entered against Peralta, and therefore he suffered no harm from the judgment. "[T]his reasoning is untenable . . . . [H]ad he notice of the suit, [Peralta] might have impleaded the employee whose debt had been guaranteed, worked out a settlement, or paid the debt. He would also have preferred to sell his property himself in order to raise funds rather than to suffer it sold at a constable's auction."

NOTES AND QUESTIONS

(1) *Complete Absence of Service of Process.* A defendant who has not been served may file a bill of review proceeding, even if his appellate deadlines have otherwise passed. The bill of review plaintiff's burdens are also satisfied through proof of non-service. The Texas Supreme Court explained:

> We begin by considering what a bill of review plaintiff must prove when claiming lack of service of process. A bill of review is an equitable proceeding brought by a party seeking to set aside a prior judgment that is no longer subject to challenge by a motion for new trial or appeal. Bill of review plaintiffs must ordinarily plead and prove (1) a meritorious defense to the underlying cause of action, (2) which the plaintiffs were prevented from making by the fraud, accident or wrongful act of the opposing party or official mistake, (3) unmixed with any fault or negligence on their own part.
>
> Bill of review plaintiffs claiming non-service, however, are relieved of two elements ordinarily required to be proved in a bill of review proceeding. First, if a plaintiff was not served, constitutional due process relieves the plaintiff from the need to show a meritorious defense. *Peralta v. Heights Med. Ctr., Inc.*, 485 U.S. 80, 86–87 (1988) (holding that the meritorious defense requirement in a bill of review proceeding violates due process where the bill of review plaintiff has no notice of the proceeding in which the default judgment was rendered). Second, the plaintiff is relieved from showing that fraud, accident, wrongful act or official mistake prevented the plaintiff from presenting such a defense. Bill of review plaintiffs alleging they were not served, however, must still prove the third and final element required in a bill of review proceeding — that the judgment was rendered unmixed with any fault or negligence of their own . . . . [T]his third and final element is conclusively established if the plaintiff can prove that he or she was never served with process. An individual who is not served with process cannot be at fault or negligent in allowing a default judgment to be rendered. Proof of non-service, then, will conclusively establish the third and only element that bill of review plaintiffs are required to prove when they are asserting lack of service of process as their only defense.

Caldwell v. Barnes, 154 S.W.3d 93, 96–97 (Tex. 2004).

(2) *Ex Parte Proceedings and Due Process.* At times, the Texas legislature creates expedited processes designed to provide fast and inexpensive relief. In the late 1990s, concerned that members of the former "Republic of Texas" were filing frivolous liens against the property of persons they viewed as enemies, the legislature passed the following statute.

Government Code § 51.901. *Fraudulent Document or Instrument*

> (a) If a clerk . . . has a reasonable basis to believe in good faith that a document or instrument previously filed or recorded or offered or submitted for filing or for filing and recording is fraudulent the clerk shall . . .
>
> provide written notice of the filing, recording, or submission for filing or for filing and recording to the stated or last known address of the person named in the document or instrument as the obligor or debtor and to any person named as owning any interest in the real or personal property described in the document or instrument . . . .
>
> (c) For purposes of this section, a document or instrument is presumed to be fraudulent if: . . .
>
> (2) the document or instrument purports to create a lien or assert a claim against real or personal property or an interest in real or personal property and:
>
> (A) is not a document or instrument provided for by the constitution or laws of this state or of the United States; [or]
>
> (B) is not created by implied or express consent or agreement of the obligor . . . .

On receiving this notice, the property owner may file a sworn "Motion for Judicial Review of Documentation or Instrument Purporting to Create a Lien or Claim." This motion is not, apparently, served on anyone. Gov. C. § 51.903 ("The court's finding may be made solely on a review of the documentation or instrument attached to the motion and without hearing any testimonial evidence. The court's review may be made ex parte without delay or notice of any kind."). The district judge may make findings that the lien is not provided for by statute or that it has not been agreed to by the debtor, although in theory the judge's order "makes no finding as to any underlying claims of the parties involved, and expressly limits its finding of fact and conclusion of law to the review of a ministerial act."

Consider this story, reported on January 29, 2007, in the *Dallas Morning News*:

Michael Grabell
IN TAX FIGHT, A PAPER CHASE: ENTREPRENEUR FLOODS COURTS WITH LAWSUITS IN BATTLING INCOME LEVY
DALLAS MORNING NEWS (Jan. 2007)*

There are three things in life that are inevitable — death, taxes and people who fight their taxes. And ironically, they're using a state law meant to stop tax protesters from flooding the courts with legal filings to flood the courts with legal filings. The new tactic is part of a long history of anti-tax sentiment that goes back to the Boston Tea Party and begat a large but fragmented group of conspiracy theorists who believe that powerful bankers took over the government in the early 1900s and forced through an illegal income tax. More recently, a militant group of Republic of Texas members who want to secede from the U.S. fought taxes so aggressively that the Texas Legislature passed the law against so-called paper terrorism in 1997 after numerous false liens were filed against public officials. But even the Republic of Texas wants to distance itself from tax protesters using these tactics.

For Ben Richard Drum, the spicy-ketchup maker, the last several years have been a patriotic crusade against the Internal Revenue Service. He has been trying to prove the federal income tax is "just a big money scam." "I have come to believe the labor of a human being is not a revenue-taxing activity," he said. "Have you heard of the Declaration of Independence? It says that it's self-evident that we're endowed by our government with certain inalienable rights — life, liberty and the pursuit of happiness. How can you pursue happiness if you don't work?" Mr. Drum said he has dedicated four hours a day, five days a week for four years to the cause . . . .

Adding fuel to the fire was a Dallas County judge's ruling late last year that Mr. Drum was right. Mr. Drum and Preston Hollow dentist Wesley David Bowden filed motions under the paper terrorism law, arguing that the IRS was filing numerous false tax liens against them. Associate District Judge Sheryl Day McFarlin approved the motions in November and December, voiding five of Mr. Drum's liens and 10 against Dr. Bowden and his wife. The judge said the IRS had violated a Texas law by failing to file a copy of a court judgment with the county clerk's office. "All 10 said liens are declared to be unlawfully filed . . . and therefore are fraudulent, and therefore should be fully removed from the Dallas County record indexes," the Bowden order said. It was a rare judgment that tax experts say could have hampered the IRS' ability to go after delinquent taxpayers.

Suppose you are an attorney with the IRS in a case like this. You were not served with the taxpayer's motion and had no chance to appear to contest the argument about the tax liens. In fact, by the time you found out that your lien (acquired pursuant to federal law) had been declared invalid, the district judge had lost power over the case, and your deadline for a normal appeal had expired. Will *Peralta* and *Caldwell* help you?

[B] Texas' Statutory and Rule-Based Requirements

[1] The Strict Compliance Standard

In addition to the due process notice requirements, Texas has a series of quite specific rules governing service of process: who can serve, who can be served, what they should be served with, and what kind of documentation must be maintained to prove the service. Further, Texas courts require strict compliance with these rules, absent which a default judgment based on that service will be set aside. The next case is an example. Did the defendant there have actual knowledge of the suit? If so, why should the judgment be set aside?

Read TEX. *R.* CIV. *P. 106.*

WILSON v. DUNN
800 S.W.2d 833 (Tex. 1990)

HECHT, J.

The district court in this case authorized substitute service of suit papers upon defendant without an affidavit or other evidence justifying such service as required by Rule 106(b) of the Texas Rules of Civil Procedure. Defendant nevertheless received citation and plaintiff's petition, but did not answer, and the trial court rendered default judgment against him. The court of appeals reversed the default judgment because of the defect in service and remanded the case to the trial court for further proceedings. We affirm.

I

Jesse Wilson sued Michael Dunn for damages resulting from Dunn's negligent operation of a motor vehicle. Wilson alleged that Dunn could be served with citation at his apartment, where, in fact, Dunn was then residing and has resided at all times material to this case. Repeated, sustained efforts to serve Dunn there, however, both in person and by mail, proved unsuccessful.

After several months, Wilson's attorney filed a motion for substitute service under Rule 106(b). Rule 106(b) states:

> Upon motion *supported by affidavit* stating the location of the defendant's usual place of business or usual place of abode or other place where the defendant can probably be found and stating specifically the facts showing that service has been attempted under either (a)(1) or (a)(2) at the location named *in such affidavit* but has not been successful, the court may authorize service
>
> (1) by leaving a true copy of the citation, with a copy of the petition attached, with anyone over sixteen years of age at the location specified *in such affidavit*, or
>
> (2) in any other manner that the *affidavit* or other evidence before the court shows will be reasonably effective to give the defendant notice of the suit.

(Emphasis added.) Contrary to the explicit requirement of the rule, Wilson's motion was not verified or supported by affidavit or other evidence. Nonetheless, the judge of the 236th District Court to which the case was assigned granted the motion and ordered that citation be served upon Dunn either by attaching it to the door of his apartment or by delivering it to the apartment manager at Dunn's address. However, the judge instructed the clerk to attach a note to the docket sheet stating that no default judgment was to be taken. The return of citation authorized by the district court stated that it had been served by a deputy constable "by delivering to the within named Michael Donell [sic] Dunn by delivering to his agent for service,

Carol Berlinger, apartment manager" a copy of the citation and plaintiff's original petition. Dunn actually received the papers, as he later acknowledged in a sworn statement given to Wilson's attorney:

> . . . I received some suit papers from [Wilson's attorney]. These papers were placed in my apartment by the apartment manager where I live after the Constable served the papers on her. Within five days from the date that I received the suit papers, I hand delivered them to my insurance agent . . . .

Within a few weeks an adjuster for Dunn's insurer telephoned Wilson's attorney to discuss the case. Following up their conversation, the adjuster wrote Wilson's attorney requesting him to agree that, pending efforts to obtain Dunn's cooperation and to settle Wilson's claim, Dunn would not be required to file an answer in the case and no default judgment would be taken without ten days' notice. Wilson's attorney wrote at the bottom of the letter, "I agree to the above," signed it, and returned it to the adjuster. Shortly thereafter the adjuster retained an attorney to monitor the case. The attorney telephoned the clerk of the court on at least two occasions and was told that at the court's instruction a note had been attached to the file that no default judgment could be taken in the case. The attorney did not contact Dunn but the adjuster finally did, and obtained a statement from him. About the same time, however, the insurer transferred the case to another adjuster, and Wilson's attorney was not informed that Dunn had been contacted.

Concerned that the second anniversary of the accident was approaching, Wilson's attorney wrote Dunn a letter dated February 19, 1987, urging him to cooperate with his insurer and warning him of the possible consequences of failing to do so. Specifically, the letter stated, "we are going to ask the Court for the Default Judgment against you during the second week of March, 1987." Wilson's attorney sent a copy of the letter to the adjuster and the attorney retained by the adjuster. In response to the letter, the sometimes elusive Dunn contacted Wilson's attorney and arranged to meet with him. Dunn gave Wilson's attorney a sworn statement in which he indicated that he had not failed to communicate with his insurer.

Convinced that the adjuster had not been fully candid with him, Wilson's attorney went to the 236th District Court on February 27, 1987, to obtain a default judgment. Finding that the judge of that court was not available, Wilson's attorney requested the file from the clerk so that he could take it to another judge for hearing on his request for a default judgment. The clerk was reluctant to give Wilson's attorney the file because the judge had told her that default judgment was not to be taken in the case. She pointed out to Wilson's attorney the note the judge had instructed her to attach to the file, but he insisted on taking it, and she finally relented. On the way to a hearing before the judge of the 67th District Court, Wilson's attorney removed the note from the file and threw it away.

Wilson's original petition requested $144 damages for past medical expenses, and unspecified amounts for future medical expenses, lost wages, loss of earning capacity, and past and future physical pain and mental anguish. After hearing, the judge of the 67th District Court rendered default judgment for Wilson for $475,000. Later the same day Wilson's attorney told the judge who granted the default judgment that he had removed the prior judge's note from the file because Dunn had actual knowledge of the suit and default was therefore appropriate. The judge who granted the default judgment strongly reproved Wilson's attorney but did not set aside the judgment.

Neither Dunn nor his insurer learned of the default judgment until after it was signed. Dunn filed a motion for new trial, which was also presented to the judge of the 67th District Court. The motion did not complain of the defect in service. After hearing evidence, the trial court denied the motion. The trial court concluded that substitute service was appropriate, and that Dunn had received actual notice of the suit. The trial court also concluded that Dunn's failure to file an appearance was due to the conscious indifference of his insurer.

On appeal, Dunn argued that service was defective and could not support the default judgment. Dunn also argued that the trial court's conclusion that he was not entitled to a new trial was against the great weight of the evidence and manifestly unjust. The appeals court agreed with Dunn's defective service argument and did not address his other arguments. Thus, the only issue presented to us is the sufficiency of service.

II

For well over a century the rule has been firmly established in this state that a default judgment cannot withstand direct attack by a defendant who complains that he was not served in strict compliance with applicable requirements. *See, e.g.*, *Uvalde Country Club v. Martin Linen Supply Co.*, 690 S.W.2d 884, 886 (Tex. 1985) (per curiam); *McKanna v. Edgar*, 388 S.W.2d 927, 929 (Tex. 1965); *Sloan v. Batte*, 46 Tex. 215, 216 (1876); *see also* R. McDonald, Texas Civil Practice in District and County Courts § 17.23.2, at 134–144 (F. Elliott rev. 1984). This Court only recently reasserted:

> There are no presumptions in favor of valid issuance, service, and return of citation in the face of a [direct] attack on a default judgment . . . . Moreover, failure to affirmatively show strict compliance with the Rules of Civil Procedure renders the attempted service of process invalid and of no effect.

Uvalde, 690 S.W.2d at 885. *See Higginbotham v. General Life & Acc. Ins. Co.*, 796 S.W.2d 695, 697 (Tex. 1990).

In this case, Dunn was not strictly served in compliance with Rule 106(b) because substitute service was not properly authorized absent the affidavit explicitly required by the rule. The express requirement of an affidavit in support of a motion for substitute service was added effective in 1981. It appears, however, that prior to that change in the text of the rule the courts uniformly held that substitute service could be authorized only upon probative evidence of the impracticality of personal service. Since the 1981 change in Rule 106(b) the courts have consistently held that substitute service may not properly issue on a motion supported by an affidavit that is conclusory or otherwise insufficient. We agree and hold that substitute service is not authorized under Rule 106(b) without an affidavit which meets the requirements of the rule demonstrating the necessity for other than personal service.

Wilson acknowledges that service on Dunn was defective because of the failure to comply with Rule 106(b), but argues that the default judgment rendered against Dunn should nevertheless stand because Dunn actually received the suit papers and actually knew of the pendency of the suit. We disagree. Actual notice to a defendant, without proper service, is not sufficient to convey upon the court jurisdiction to render default judgment against him. *See Harrell v. Mexico Cattle Co.*, 11 S.W. 863, 865 (Tex. 1889). Rather, jurisdiction is dependent upon citation issued and served in a manner provided for by law. Absent service, waiver, or citation, mere knowledge of a pending suit does not place any duty on a defendant to act. Consequently, Dunn's knowledge that Wilson had sued him and his actual receipt of suit papers is not sufficient to invoke the district court's jurisdiction to render default judgment against him.

Wilson relies heavily upon section 3 of the Restatement (Second) of Judgments (1982), which states: "When actual notice of an action has been given, irregularity in the content of the notice or the manner in which it was given does not render the notice inadequate." Wilson fails to note, however, that this rule does not apply to default judgments. As comment d to section 3 explains:

> The objection to the regularity of notice also often arises in the context of an application for relief from a default judgment. Here again there is a rational basis for treating an irregularity in notice-giving as significant even though actual notice has been conferred. To do so is to apply a rule of parity among the parties concerning formal defects in procedure.
>
> A default judgment is awarded not because the court is entirely satisfied that the claim has substantive merit . . . but because the party in default was derelict in complying with the rules of procedure governing how he may make his defense. An applicant for relief from such dereliction must show that he acted with due diligence after having become aware of the default and that he has a good case on the merits . . . . Assuming he makes such a showing, the only ground supporting the judgment is that the defendant has failed to respond to the action in conformity with applicable procedure for doing so. If the defendant can then show that the person commencing the action was guilty of comparable nonconformity with procedural rules, under a principle of equality the derelictions offset each other and the merits of the controversy may be brought forward for consideration.

This authority contradicts, rather than supports, Wilson's position.

Wilson also contends that Dunn is foreclosed from complaining that service was defective because he has admitted receipt of the suit papers. We agree that Dunn could have waived his complaint of defective service by conceding the issue, but he has not done so. Dunn has admitted receipt, not service. Indeed, the issue presented is whether actual receipt can cure defective service in this context. The two cases upon which Wilson relies demonstrate this distinction. In both *First Nat'l Bank v. Peterson*, 709 S.W.2d 276, 280 (Tex. App. — Houston [14th Dist.] 1986, writ ref'd n.r.e.), and *Hurst v. A.R.A. Manufacturing Co.*, 555 S.W.2d 141, 142 (Tex. Civ. App. — Fort Worth 1977, writ ref'd n.r.e.), the defendant admitted not simply that process was received, but that it was "duly served." The distinction between actual receipt and proper service is precisely what gives rise to the issue we address here. We hold that a default judgment is improper against a defendant who has not been served in strict compliance with law, even if he has actual knowledge of the lawsuit. *See Higginbotham v. General Life & Acc. Ins. Co.*, 796 S.W.2d 695, 697 (Tex. 1990). Finally, Wilson argues that Dunn has failed to preserve any complaint of defective service by not raising the issue in his motion for new trial. Rule 324 imposes no such requirement for preservation of such error. Tex. R. Civ. P. 324. . . . We hold that Dunn's complaint was preserved for appeal.

III

Accordingly, we conclude that the default judgment against Dunn was improper. We therefore affirm the judgment of the court of appeals reversing the judgment of the district court and remanding the case to that court for further proceedings.

NOTES

(1) *Strict Compliance.* As *Wilson* indicates, Texas courts require strict compliance with the requirements for service, in the default judgment context. Actual receipt will not cure defective service, as it will in many other jurisdictions. *See also Primate Construction, Inc. v. Silver*, 884 S.W.2d 151, 153 (Tex. 1994) ("It is the responsibility of the one requesting service, not the process server, to see that service is properly accomplished . . . . This responsibility extends to seeing that service is properly reflected in the record.").

The Texas Supreme Court continued its strict compliance philosophy for default judgment cases in *Insurance Co. of the State of PA v. Lejeune*, 297 S.W.3d 254, 255 (Tex. 2009) (per curiam), in which the Court overturned a default judgment because the clerk's endorsement of the return of service did not include the *hour* of receipt, as required by Rules 16 and 105. "Here, although Lejeune served Insurance Co. by certified mail, the record shows that the return of citation lacks the required notation showing the hour of receipt of citation. Lejeune's default judgment, therefore, cannot stand."

(2) *Another Example of the Strict Compliance Standard.* When the defendant is an entity rather than a human, the return must reflect that service was on the entity by serving an appropriate person. In *Benefit Planners, L.L.P. v. Rencare, Ltd.*, 81 S.W.3d 855 (Tex. App. — San Antonio 2002, pet. denied), citation was issued to "Benefit Partners, L.L.P., Tom Cusick, Jr. (Registered Agent)." The return of citation stated that the citation was delivered to "Tom P. Cusick, Jr., Reg. Agent." Citing other Texas cases, the San Antonio court held that this return was defective because it did not reflect that *Benefit Planners* was served. "Even when a return establishes that the person served was an agent for service of process, the return is still defective if it does not establish that the corporation was served by reciting that the corporation was served by serving on or through the agent." *Id.* at 859.

(3) *Corporations as Registered Agents for Service.* Under Texas law, a corporation may designate another corporation as its registered agent for service of process. However, physical service still involves delivery to some individual. In

Reed Elsevier Inc. v. Carrollton-Farmers Branch ISD, 180 S.W.3d 903 (Tex. App. — Dallas 2005, pet. denied), the court addressed this situation. It held:

> The record must show whether the person served was in fact such an agent for the corporation acting as the registered agent . . . . In this case, the return does not indicate the capacity of "Danielle Smith" or why she was served with process. Her name is handwritten on the face of the citation without designation of her status with Lexis Document Services, Inc. The return merely recites service "by delivering to Danielle Smith," without explaining her authority to receive service. Neither the return nor any other portion of the record designates her authority to receive service on behalf of Reed Elsevier's registered agent. Without indication of her capacity to receive service on the face of the record, the granting of the default judgment was improper.

(4) *Variance Between Citation and Return.* Even a strict compliance approach will let some tiny variances slide. The Dallas Court of Appeals, in *Myan Management Group L.L.C. v. Adam Sparks Family Revocable Trust*, 292 S.W.3d 750, 752-53 (Tex. App. — Dallas 2009, no pet.), refused to set aside a default judgment of a claim brought against "Myan Management Group, L.L.C.," with citation omitting the periods from LLC, and the return reflecting citation on "Myan Management." The court noted that "service is invalid if the name on the return alters the identity of the defendant. . . . The name of the defendant is altered if it is changed to the extent that the court cannot determine if the name of the citation is the same person or entity identified on the return." The opinion then surveys prior cases. These changes were held to be alterations that invalidated default judgments: 1) Henry Bunting, Jr. changed to Henry Bunting; 2) Mr. Christ Lytle changed to Christopher Lytle; and 3) Brown-McKee, Inc. changed to Brown-McKee Const. Co. On the other hand, earlier cases held these changes not to be alterations: 1) removal of a middle initial; 2) omission of the corporate designation "Inc"; 3) the lack of an accent mark on a corporate name; and 4) substituting @ for "at." The court held that the change from Myan Management Group, LLC to Myan Management fell into the latter category.

[2] Techniques of Service

Issuance and Service of Citation

Read Tex. R. Civ. P. 99.

Section 17.027 of the Civil Practice and Remedies Code allows the plaintiff to prepare the appropriate citation for the defendant as long as the citation is prepared in the form prescribed in Tex. R. Civ. P. 99(b) and served in the manner prescribed by law. Although the clerk may charge for the issuance of a citation, the clerk may not charge for signing his/her name and affixing the seal to a citation that is prepared by the plaintiff or his/her attorney in accordance with Section 17.027.

Serving Persons in Texas — Basic Methods

Read Tex. R. Civ. P. 103, 106, 107.

THE METHOD OF SERVICE

Unless the citation otherwise directs, it may be served by either of two alternate methods:

a. *Personal Delivery*

Civil Procedure Rule 103 provides that citation may be served by any sheriff or constable, any person authorized by law or by written court order who is not less than 18 years of age, or by any person certified under order of the Texas Supreme Court. Rule 106(a) allows "any person authorized by Rule 103" to accomplish service by "delivering to the defendant in person." Sheriffs and constables are not restricted to their counties for purposes of service of process. In addition, "[t]he order authorizing a person to serve process may be made without written motion and no fee shall be imposed for issuance of such order." TEX. R. CIV. P. 103. The provision creating a category of persons "certified under order of the Supreme Court" is a new one and, since considerable money is at stake, has generated a certain amount of controversy. For a discussion of the process for certification and a complete list of certified process servers, see Texas Judiciary Online, Process Server Review Board, *at* www.supreme.courts.state.tx.us/psrb/psrbhome.asp.

b. *By Mail*

Service by mail is authorized "by any person authorized by Rule 103 by . . . mailing to the defendant by registered or certified mail, return receipt requested, a true copy of the citation with a copy of the petition attached thereto." TEX. R. CIV. P. 106(a)(2). No court order is necessary to authorize service by certified mail under Civil Procedure Rule 106(a)(2).

THE PERSON TO SERVE

When the defendant is an entity rather than a person, service is ordinarily accomplished by the delivery of citation to one of its authorized agents. Hence, the addressee to whom delivery is restricted under Civil Procedure Rule 106(a)(2) should be the defendant or an agent authorized to accept service of citation.

Various Texas statutes have provided for service upon resident defendants by serving some person other than the named defendant. A few are noted here:

1. *Domestic Corporations.* The president, vice-president, or registered agent for service are the appropriate service agents. BUS. ORGS. C. §§ 5.201, 5.255. If a domestic corporation fails to appoint a registered agent, the secretary of state serves as the registered agent.

2. *Partnerships.* Service should be made on a partner or local agent of the partnership in the county in which the local agent transacts business, in all suits or actions growing out of or connected with such business and brought in the county in which office, place of business or agency is located. C.P.R.C. §§ 17.021, 17.022 ("Citation served on one member of a partnership authorizes judgment against the partnership and the partner actually served"). Business Organization Code section 5.255 provides that "each partner of a domestic or foreign general partnership is an agent of that partnership" for the purpose of service of process. However, service on

one partner is not sufficient for a personal judgment against other partners who have not been served. C.P.R.C. § 31.003.

3. *Limited Liability Partnerships.* Each general partner of a domestic or foreign limited partnership is an agent of the limited partnership. Bus. Org. Code § 5.255. Limited partnerships also are required to have a registered agent for service and a registered office. Bus. Org. Code. § 5.201.

4. *Limited Liability Companies.* Service agents are the managers, if any, and the registered agents for service of process. Bus. Orgs. C. §§ 5.201, 5.255(3).

5. *Joint Stock Associations.* Service agents are the president, vice-president, secretary, cashier, assistant cashier, or treasurer of the association, or the local agent of the association in the county in which suit will be filed. C.P.R.C. § 17.023.

6. *Real Estate Investment Trusts.* Service agents are any resident trust manager or any officer of trust. Bus. Orgs. C. §§ 1.002(22), 5.255(4).

7. *Domestic Insurance Companies.* Service agents are the president, active vice president, secretary, and attorney in fact. Ins. C. § 804.101(b).

8. *Counties.* Service agent is the county judge. C.P.R.C. § 17.024(a).

9. *Municipalities.* Service agents are mayor, clerk, secretary, or treasurer. C.P.R.C. § 17.024(b).

10. *School Districts.* Service agents are the president of the school board or the superintendent. C.P.R.C. § 17.024(c).

11. *State of Texas.* The secretary of state is the service agent for the State of Texas. C.P.R.C. § 101.102(c).

Alternative Methods of Service

When "service has been attempted" under either Civil Procedure Rule 106(a)(1) or 106(a)(2) but has not been successful, the court, on motion, may authorize service in some other reasonably effective manner. *See* Tex. R. Civ. P. 106(b). Particular methods suggested by the rule are as follows:

1. Leaving a true copy of the citation, with a copy of the petition attached, with anyone over 16 years of age at the location of the defendant's usual place of business or usual place of abode or other place where the defendant can probably be found; or

2. Any other manner that is shown by affidavit or other evidence to be reasonably effective to give the defendant notice of the suit.

The party requesting alternate service must file a motion supported by an affidavit that sets forth the location of the defendant's usual place of business, abode, or other place and that states service was attempted either in person or by certified mail and that this attempt failed. The affidavit must specifically state factual propositions and not be conclusory. *Sgitcovich v. Sgitcovich*, 241 S.W.2d 142, 146 (Tex. 1951). Cases decided under an earlier version of the rule held that a trial court should not sign an order authorizing alternate service without hearing and considering evidence to the effect that it was impractical to obtain personal service. A record of the hearing should be made. *See Kirkegaard v. First City Nat'l Bank of Binghamton, N.Y.*, 486 S.W.2d 893, 894 (Tex. Civ. App. — Beaumont 1972, no writ). Affidavits will suffice. *Smith v. Texas Discount Co.*, 408 S.W.2d 804, 806 (Tex. Civ. App. — Austin 1966, no writ). Failure to make a record may result in the reversal of a default judgment. *Spencer v. Texas Factors, Inc.*, 366 S.W.2d 699, 700 (Tex. Civ. App. — Dallas 1963, writ ref'd n.r.e.). More recent practice allows proof to be made by affidavit. It would also be wise to include in the order for alternate service the method for a proper return of service, as strict compliance is required in this area as well.

Waiver of Process

Read Tex. R. Civ. P. 119.

1. Waiving Proper Delivery of Lawsuit Papers

Under the provisions of Civil Procedure Rule 119, a defendant may waive the issuance and service of citation by filing among the papers of the cause a verified written memorandum "signed by him, or by his duly authorized agent or attorney, *after* suit is brought."

In addition, section 30.001 of the Civil Practice and Remedies Code prohibits pre-suit waivers of service of process:

> In an instrument executed before suit is brought, a person may not accept service and waive process, enter an appearance in open court, or confess a judgment.

2. Waiving Objections to Amenability to Process

Do not confuse these provisions invalidating pre-suit waiver of proper service of process with statutory or contractual consent to *jurisdiction*, which may be permissible. Contractual consent to jurisdiction satisfies due process unless the consent is not valid because it is not voluntarily, knowingly or intelligently made. *See National Equip. Rental, Ltd. v. Szukhent*, 375 U.S. 311 (1964) (Michigan residents validly consented to substituted service on a named person in New York — someone they did not know personally — when they entered into a lease that named that person as their agent).

3. Pre-Filing Waivers in Cases Terminating Parental Rights

In cases arising under Texas Family Code provisions pertaining to termination of parental rights, pre-filing waivers are permissible. *Brown v. McLennan County Children's Protective Services*, 627 S.W.2d 390 (Tex. 1982), upheld the constitutionality of the Code's provisions authorizing a parent's waiver of citation prior to filing of suit for termination of parental rights where such waiver was voluntarily, intelligently, and knowingly made. *See* FAM. C. § 15.02. Why would the state choose to make it easier for a person to waive such a fundamental right?

Subsequent Pleadings

Read Tex. R. Civ. P. 124, 21a, 92.

1. Cross-Claims and Counterclaims

Is service of citation necessary for a counterclaim? How about for a cross-claim? *See* Tex. R. Civ. P. 124; *see also Galloway v. Moeser*, 82 S.W.2d 1067, 1069 (Tex. Civ. App. — Eastland 1935, no writ) (no citation needed for cross-claim when parties had all appeared).

2. Amended Pleadings

If the opposing party has not appeared, an amended petition must be served on him, but a majority of the Texas Supreme Court has held that the amended petition may be served under the less onerous requirements of Civil Procedure Rule 21a. In *In re E.A.*, 287 S.W.3d 1, 4 (Tex. 2009), the Court rejected the rule that service of a new citation is required to support a default judgment based on a more onerous amended petition. The majority reasoned:

> Rule 21a applies to all pleadings required to be served under Rule 21 other than the original petition and except as provided in the rules. Nothing in the rules requires a plaintiff to serve a nonanswering defendant with new citation for a more onerous amended petition. While a nonanswering defendant must be served with a more onerous amended petition in order for a default judgment to stand, we agree with the court of appeals that Rule 21a service satisfies that requirement.

The Court therefore overruled *Weaver v. Hartford Accident and Indemnity Co.*, 570 S.W.2d 367, 370 (Tex. 1978), to the extent that it is inconsistent with Rule 21a.

Justices Brister, Wainwright, and Willett disagreed. "There are good reasons," they wrote in concurrence, for the requirement of new service of citation. "A citation is an official notice from a court officer, is accompanied by the petition, and warns recipients that they must answer by a stated deadline or 'judgment by default may be rendered for the relief demanded in the petition.' A person served with citation can be under no misconceptions about the effect of ignoring that petition. By contrast, a petition received in the mail is not an official notice from a court but an adversary's list of complaints. . . . It states no deadlines, no actions necessary to avoid default, not even a hint that default might occur." *Id.* at 6-7.

[3] Service of Process and the Statute of Limitations

Sometimes failure to achieve prompt service on the defendant will cause a case to be dismissed based on the statute of limitations, even if the case was filed before the statute ran. To "bring suit" within the limitations period, the plaintiff must not only file suit within the applicable limitations period, but also must use diligence in having the defendant served with process. For example, in *Taylor v. Thompson*, 4 S.W.3d 63, 66 (Tex. App. — Houston [1st Dist.] 1999, pet. denied), the plaintiff filed her original negligence petition on August 30, 1996, in a case arising out of a car wreck on January 16, 1995. Two days before limitations ran in January of 1997, the plaintiff requested a private process server to obtain service on the defendants.

The district clerk's office issued citation a week after limitations ran and two defendants were served that same day. A third defendant was not served until almost a month after limitations ran. The court affirmed summary judgment in favor of all defendants based on limitations. The court explained, "Because [plaintiff] failed to serve citations on [defendants] within the period of limitations, she had the burden to prove that she used due diligence in procuring the subsequent issuance and service of citation upon the defendants . . . . An unexplained delay in effecting service constitutes a lack of due diligence." Because the plaintiff waited four months after filing, and until two days before limitations ran, to request a private firm to serve the defendants, the court found that she did not use due diligence. The record did not reflect any efforts to serve the defendants earlier. The court held that as a matter of law there was no valid excuse and no due diligence. It further found that the defendants did not waive the running of the statute of limitations when they filed a general appearance after statute of limitations had run without asserting the affirmative defense of limitations until a later amendment to the answer. The trial court's summary judgment was affirmed, even as to the defendants who were served with process very shortly after the expiration of the statute of limitations.

Diligent efforts at service, especially when coupled with the defendant's efforts to evade service, will sometimes be sufficient to avoid a summary judgment based on limitations. In *Proulx v. Wells*, 235 S.W.3d 213, 214 (Tex. 2007), the plaintiff's lawyers utilized two process servers and two investigators to try to locate the defendant, and 30 attempts were made to serve the defendant at five different addresses. The second investigator opined that the defendant was "moving from relative to relative and doing his best to avoid service from the courts and creditors." Although service was not finally accomplished (through substituted service on a relative) until eight months after the statute of limitations ran, the Texas Supreme Court reversed summary judgment for the defendant.

The Court also clarified the operation of burdens of proof in this area:

> Once a defendant has affirmatively pled the limitations defense and shown that service was effected after limitations expired, the burden shifts to the plaintiff "to explain the delay." Thus, it is the plaintiff's burden to present evidence regarding the efforts that were made to serve the defendant, and to explain every lapse in effort or period of delay. In some instances, the plaintiff's explanation may be legally improper to raise the diligence issue and the defendant will bear no burden at all. But if the plaintiff's explanation for the delay raises a material fact issue concerning the diligence of service efforts, the burden shifts back to the defendant to conclusively show why, as a matter of law, the explanation is insufficient. In assessing diligence, the relevant inquir y is whether the plaintiff acted as an ordinarily prudent person would have acted under the same or similar circumstances and was diligent up until the time the defendant was served. Generally, the question of the plaintiff's diligence in effecting service is one of fact, and is determined by examining the time it took to secure citation, service, or both, and the type of effort or lack of effort the plaintiff expended in procuring service.

Proulx, 235 S.W.3d at 216 (citations omitted).

[4] Proof of Service: The Return

Read Tex. R. Civ. P. 103, 105, 107, 109a, and 124.

[a] Personal Service

The person serving process must make a return of service that shows:

(1) The day and hour on which citation was received. Tex. R. Civ. P. 105.

(2) The day on which citation was served and the manner of service. Tex. R. Civ. P. 107. *See Brown-McKee, Inc. v. J.F. Bryan & Associates*, 522 S.W.2d 958, 959 (Tex. Civ. App. — Texarkana 1975, no writ).

[b] Certified or Registered Mail Service

If service is by registered or certified mail, the return must also contain the return receipt with the addressee's signature. Tex. R. Civ. P. 107, 109a.

[c] Returns for Alternative Service

If service is made pursuant to court order, strict compliance with the court order is required. *Broussard v. Davila*, 352 S.W.2d 753, 754 (Tex. Civ. App. — San Antonio 1961, no writ). When service is by a disinterested person or in some other manner reasonably effective to give defendant notice of the suit (Tex. R. Civ. P. 106(b)), proof of service must be made in the manner ordered by the court. Tex. R. Civ. P. 107.

As with other kinds of service, substituted service requires strict compliance with service and return rules. In *Bautista v. Bautista*, 9 S.W.3d 250, 251 (Tex. App. — San Antonio 1999, no pet.), the plaintiff's motion for substituted service of process was granted, and the trial court ordered the defendant served by serving any person over sixteen at a specified address. The return was executed and signed by a private process server, who completed the "Certificate of Delivery" at the bottom of the return, certifying that he delivered a copy of the "instrument" to Andres Salas Bautista, Sr. (the defendant's father). Unfortunately, the return was not verified. Because Civil Procedure Rule 107 requires a return of citation by a private process server to be verified before a notary public, and the order for substituted service did not change that requirement, the return was defective on its face and the record did not show strict compliance with the rules. The default judgment entered based on the defective return was reversed.

[d] Amending Flawed Returns

ReadTex. R. Civ. P. 107, 118.

If the process server's return is defective in some way, can it be fixed? If so, is there a deadline?

BAVARIAN AUTOHAUS, INC. v. HOLLAND

570 S.W.2d 110 (Tex. Civ. App. — Houston [1st Dist.] 1978, no writ)

PEDEN, J.

Bavarian Autohaus, Inc. and BMW of North America, Inc. (BMW) appeal . . . from a default judgment in favor of David Holland, who claimed unliquidated damages under the Deceptive Trade Practices and Consumer Protection Act (Tex. Bus. & Com. Code, Chapter 17) as a result of the defendants' alleged misrepresentations concerning the quality of their automobiles and their repair service. The trial court heard testimony on the plaintiff's damages and entered a judgment of $5,000 plus costs against the defendants jointly and severally. Bavarian Autohaus asserts error in the trial court's finding that citation was served on it, and both appellants contend that the plaintiff did not offer adequate proof of damages. The appellee has not responded. We reverse and remand . . . .

Bavarian Autohaus argues under its first eight points of error that the default judgment should be set aside because the record does not affirmatively show that citation was properly served upon it. Ordinarily, presumptions are made in support of due service when it is recited in the judgment but not when a direct attack is made upon a default judgment. *McKanna v. Edgar*, 388 S.W.2d 927, 929 (Tex. 1965). In that case, jurisdiction must affirmatively appear on the face of the record. *Flynt v. City of Kingsville*, 82 S.W.2d 934 (Tex. 1935).

The citation recites that it was to be issued to Bavarian Autohaus, Inc., a Texas corporation, by serving its agent, Charles Vann. The original sheriff's return states that it was delivered to "Clint Hughes-V. Pres."

The amended return states:

> "Received this writ on the *3* day of *FEB*, 1977, at 10:49 o'clock A.M., and executed the same in Harris County Texas, on the *9* day of *FEB*, 1977, at 2:50 o'clock P.M., by summoning the *BAVARIAN AUTOHAUS, INC.*, a corporation by delivering to *Clint Hughes*, in person *Vice President* of the said *Corporation* a true copy of this writ, together with accompanying certified copy plaintiff's original petition."

The amended return relates back and is regarded as filed when the original return was filed. *Lafleaur v. Switzer*, 109 S.W.2d 239, 241 (Tex. Civ. App. — Beaumont 1937, no writ); *Nash v. Boyd*, 225 S.W.2d 649 (Tex. Civ. App. — Dallas 1949, no writ); 2 McDONALD, TEXAS CIVIL PRACTICE 406, § 9.19 (1970).

Article 2.11 of the Texas Business Corporation Act makes the president, all vice presidents and the registered agent of a corporation agents for service of process. The original officer's return did not state that Bavarian Autohaus was served by serving "Clint Hughes-V. Pres." It did not recite, as it must, that process was delivered to the defendant, Bavarian Autohaus, through its named agent. *Brown-McKee, Inc. v. J.F. Bryan & Associates*, 522 S.W.2d 958, 959 (Tex. Civ. App. — Texarkana 1975, no writ); *Firman Leather Goods Corp. v. McDonald & Shaw*, 217 S.W.2d 137, 140 (Tex. Civ. App. — El Paso 1948, no writ).

This original return was fatally defective, but the appellee procured an amended return sometime prior to the day of the hearing. Rule 118, Texas Rules of Civil Procedure, provides:

> "At any time in its discretion and upon such notice and on such terms as it deems just, the court may allow any process or proof of service thereof to be amended, unless it clearly appears that material prejudice would result to the substantial rights of the party against whom the process issued."

When this case was before the trial judge for assessment of damages, he noted that the court file did not show service of citation on Bavarian Autohaus, whereupon the appellee produced the amended return described above from his file and related that his secretary had taken it to the constable's office for correction. Further discussion followed, outside the hearing of the court reporter.

It is obvious that the trial court allowed the amended return to be filed before entering judgment next day. Although the statement of facts does not show that the provisions of Rule 118 were specifically invoked in the trial court, it appears that they were complied with. Bavarian Autohaus has not asserted that it was misled by the earlier return on the citation. We cannot say the trial court erred in allowing the already-amended return to be filed or in not requiring that notice of the amendment be given to Bavarian Autohaus . . . .

[Although the court upheld the amendment of the return, it reversed and remanded for a new hearing on the issue of damages.]

[5] Citation by Publication

Read Tex. R. Civ. P. 109-117a, 244, 329.

[a] Generally

The pejorative term "constructive service" is frequently employed to describe citation by publication. It also has been accurately described as a "sham upon due process." Merlin O. Johnson, *Citation by Publication: A Sham Upon Due Process*, 36 TEX. B.J. 205 (Mar. 1973). Traditionally, it has been restricted to proceedings that are classifiable as in rem or quasi in rem. Modern due process notions reject the idea that a determination of the type of action as either in rem or in personam controls the availability of publication. On the other hand, the application of the traditional categories has led courts to conclude that publication is ordinarily not available *unless* the action is in rem, at least where non-domiciliaries are concerned. Some Texas cases indicate that it is not available in actions to obtain personal judgments against non-domiciliaries of Texas. *In the Interest of A.B.*, 207 S.W.3d 434, 439 (Tex. App. — Dallas 2006, no pet.); *Sgitcovich v. Sgitcovich*, 241 S.W.2d 142, 146 (Tex. 1959). *Compare* TEX. R. CIV. P. 117a. *See also Mullane v. Central Hanover Bank & Trust Co.*, 339 U.S. 306, 314 (1950).

[b] Specific Uses

Citation by publication is specifically authorized in the following circumstances:

(1) *Partition.* In an action to partition when some portion of the land described in the petition is owned by a person who is unknown to the plaintiff or whose residence is unknown to the plaintiff. Tex. R. Civ. P. 758.

(2) *Defunct Corporations.* In an action against unknown heirs or stockholders of a defunct corporation. Tex. R. Civ. P. 111; C.P.R.C. § 17.004.

(3) *Land.* In an action against unknown owners or claimants of interests in land. Tex. R. Civ. P. 112, 113; C.P.R.C. § 17.005.

(4) *Marriage Dissolution.* In an action for divorce or annulment of marriage in which the defendant cannot be notified by personal service or registered or certified mail. Fam. C. § 3.521.

(5) *Ad Valorem Taxes.* In suits for the collection of delinquent ad valorem taxes. Tex. R. Civ. P. 117a.

(6) *Whereabouts of Defendant Unknown.* When the defendant's residence is unknown and cannot be ascertained after reasonable diligence, or the defendant is a transient person whose whereabouts are unknown and cannot be ascertained, or the defendant is absent from or a nonresident of Texas and service under Tex. R. Civ. P. 108 has been attempted unsuccessfully. Tex. R. Civ. P. 109.

Whenever citation by publication is authorized, the court may, on motion, prescribe a different method of service if the court finds, and so recites in its order, that the method so prescribed would be as likely as publication to give the defendant actual notice. Tex. R. Civ. P. 109a. *See also* Tex. R. Civ. P. 329.

NOTES AND QUESTIONS

(1) *Constitutionally Adequate Notice.* In light of the standard articulated in *Peralta*, above, when will you use publication?

(2) *Publication and Default Judgments.* Read Tex. R. Civ. P. 244 and 329. Can there be a true default judgment when citation is by publication? How long does the nonresident have to reopen a default? This is another reason not to use service by citation when a better method is available.

[6] Special Requirements for Service on the Secretary of State Under the General Texas Long-Arm Statute

[a] Pleading Requirements

As you learned in § 4.02 above, the Texas long arm statute contains intricate requirements that govern which nonresidents should be served by what method. Service on the nonresident must also be consistent with the requirements of due process. Compliance with these requirements must be properly pleaded, or a default judgment will be vulnerable to challenge. What did the plaintiff's lawyer in the next case fail to plead? Why did that matter?

McKANNA v. EDGAR

388 S.W.2d 927 (Tex. 1965)

[Edgar sued McKanna in Travis County, Texas on a promissory note payable by its terms in Austin. Service was purportedly done through the secretary of state pursuant to the general Texas long-arm statute. A default judgment was rendered against McKanna, which the court of civil appeals affirmed. McKanna attacked the judgment on appeal on the ground that the record failed to show the conditions required by the general Texas long-arm statute. The Texas Supreme Court agreed and reversed.]

Section 3 of [the former general Texas long-arm statute], here to be construed, reads in part as follows:

> "Any . . . non-resident natural person that engages in business in this State . . . and does not maintain a place of regular business in this State or a designated agent upon whom service may be made . . . , the act or acts of engaging in such business . . . shall be deemed equivalent to an appointment . . . of the Secretary of State of Texas as agent upon whom service of process may be made . . . ."

Edgar alleged in his petition that Eileen Ann McKanna resided in Orange County, California, and that she executed and delivered to Edgar her note "payable to the order of plaintiff at 1210 Perry-Brooks Building, Austin, Texas . . . ." These allegations comply with the requirements of Section 3 of [the general Texas long-arm statute] that McKanna be a nonresident and, as stipulated, be doing business in this State. But there are no allegations that McKanna "does not maintain a place of regular business in this State or a designated agent upon whom service may be made." The nonexistence of those two conditions is shown to be a necessary prerequisite to the applicability of Section 3 because of the language used in Section 2. Section 2 provides:

> "When any . . . non-resident natural person . . . shall engage in business in this State . . . service may be made by serving a copy of the process with the person who . . . is in charge of any business in which the defendant or defendants are engaged . . . ."

If the defendant had a regular place of business or a designated agent in Texas, we doubt that it could be successfully contended that service of process could be made on the Secretary of State. We hold under the clear language of [the general Texas long-arm statute] that "the intent is to permit resort to Section 3 only if Section 2 is not available." Counts, *More on Rule 120a*, 28 Tex. B.J. 95, 137 (Feb. 1965). This holding is in accord with the established law of this State that it is imperative and essential that the record affirmatively show a strict compliance with the provided mode of service.

[The Court next rejected two arguments relied on by the court of civil appeals. First, although there is a presumption in favor of most judgments, that rule does not apply to default judgments or to jurisdictional allegations subjected to direct attack. Secondly, although the cases indicate that actual *proof* of certain kinds of jurisdictional facts need not be made on default, they must at least be *alleged*.]

The judgments of the courts below are reversed, and the cause remanded to the District Court for a trial on the merits.

Issues of pleading specificity also arise in challenges to default judgments. Because the defendant has the burden of *disproving* contacts, it seems logical to require notice of the contacts on which plaintiff relies. Should this sort of notice be required to appear in the petition, and if so, what degree of specificity should be required? In *Paramount Pipe & Supply Co. v. Muhr*, 749 S.W.2d 491 (Tex. 1988), the Texas Supreme Court upheld two default judgments after addressing the adequacy of the jurisdictional allegations:

> So long as the allegations confronting Muhr were sufficient to satisfy due process requirements, the trial court had jurisdiction to render judgment by default against him. The only question, then, is whether the jurisdictional allegations in the petitions were sufficient, under the Constitution of the United States, to require Muhr to answer. Tex. R. Civ. P. 108.
>
> The petitions in both cases alleged that the defendants, including Muhr, engaged in business in Texas and further that the causes of action arose from and were connected with "purposeful acts committed by Defendant Western International Petroleum Corporation, acting for itself and as agent for Defendant Ulrich Muhr." The petitions went on to allege, in substance, that Western International made and breached contracts in Texas as Muhr's agent and on his behalf. These allegations against Western International (which, by default, admittedly was acting for Muhr) are sufficient to satisfy the rule stated in *Siskind v. Villa Foundation for Education, Inc.*, 642 S.W.2d 434 (Tex. 1982), and we perceive no due process violation. We conclude that the trial court did have in personam jurisdiction and constitutionally rendered judgments by default on the allegations made against Muhr.

[b] Method of Service

*The Mechanics of Service on the Secretary of State.*Section 17.026 of the Civil Practice and Remedies Code provides that in an action in which citation may be served on the secretary of state, service may be made by certified mail, return receipt requested, by the clerk of the court in which the case is pending or by the party or the representative of the party. C.P.R.C. § 17.026. Two copies of process and the requisite fees must be sent to the secretary. For more information on how the secretary of state serves process, and what is normally included on the certificate, see www.sos.state.tx.us/statdoc/forms/2401.htm.

[c] Proof of Long-Arm Service: The Return

If a defendant is served through the secretary of state pursuant to the general Texas long-arm statute, the service is accomplished once the secretary has been served. The nonresident defendant's time to answer begins to run when the secretary is served, not when the defendant receives the certified mailing.

Accordingly, the return will show that it was served on the secretary, the date and hour, etc.

The general long-arm statute does not specify a particular method by which the return of citation must be made. Typically, when the secretary of state is served under the general long-arm statute, a return will be filed showing service on the secretary of state. Moreover, if service is effected under the provisions of the long-arm statute that permit service of citation in person, in Texas, on the person in charge of the defendant's business in Texas (C.P.R.C. § 17.043), there is no reason why the return may not be in the same form as is used for service on residents. *See* Tex. R. Civ. P. 107.

More importantly, the default judgment record must include proof of service in the form of a certificate from the secretary of state showing receipt of process on a particular date as agent for the nonresident defendant and the forwarding of the process to the nonresident defendant at a particular address by certified or register mail. *Whitney v. L&L Realty Corp.*, 500 S.W.2d 94, 95–96 (Tex. 1973). The Texas Supreme Court has also held that, absent fraud or mistake, a certificate from the secretary of state is "conclusive evidence" that the secretary of state was served with process and forwarded the papers as required by statute. *Capitol Brick, Inc. v. Fleming Mfg. Co.*, 722 S.W.2d 399, 401 (Tex. 1986).

Is the secretary of state's certificate sufficient even in a default judgment situation if the record does not contain the return showing service on the secretary of state? The next case discusses this point further.

CAMPUS INVESTMENTS, INC. v. CULLEVER

144 S.W.3d 464 (Tex. 2004)

Per Curiam

The evidence at the trial of this bill of review showed that a certificate of service from the Secretary of State was on file ten days before the underlying default judgment was granted, but citation and return were not. *See* Tex. R. Civ. P. 107. Relying on its opinion in *G.F.S. Ventures, Inc. v. Harris*, 934 S.W.2d 813 (Tex. App. — Houston [1st Dist.] 1996, no writ), the First Court of Appeals held this was sufficient. Petitioner points out that this opinion conflicts with the Sixth Court of Appeals' opinion to the contrary in *Onyx TV v. TV Strategy Group, LLC*, 990 S.W.2d 427 (Tex. App. — Texarkana 1999, no pet.). Finding the First Court's analysis correct, we approve the former, disapprove the latter, and affirm.

Anthony Sean Cullever and Kevin Michael Els brought suit alleging they suffered injuries during a robbery that took place at the adult book store where they allege they were employees of Campus Investments, Inc. After several unsuccessful attempts to serve the latter's registered agent, they requested service on the Secretary of State. Tex. Bus. Corp. Act art. 2.11, § B. The Secretary subsequently issued a certificate that he had received and forwarded a copy of the citation and Second Amended Original Petition to Campus by certified mail, which was returned marked "Attempted — Not Known."

Rule 107 prohibits a default judgment until citation and proof of service have been on file for ten days. TEX. R. CIV. P. 107. In *Whitney v. L & L Realty Corp.*, we reversed a default judgment because the record included proof of service on the Secretary of State, but not a certificate that the Secretary had forwarded process to the defendant. 500 S.W.2d 94, 95–96 (Tex. 1973). There was such a certificate in *Capitol Brick, Inc. v. Fleming Mfg. Co.*, so we held that "absent fraud or mistake, the Secretary of State's certificate is conclusive evidence that the Secretary of State, as agent of [the defendant], received service of process for [the defendant] and forwarded the service as required by the statute." 722 S.W.2d 399, 401 (Tex. 1986); *see also* TEX. BUS. CORP. ACT art. 9.05, § A (providing that certificates issued by the Secretary are prima facie evidence of facts recited therein).

The First Court of Appeals interpreted *Capitol Brick* to dispense with any requirement that the default judgment record include the citation and return. 141 S.W.3d 641; *G.F.S. Ventures*, 934 S.W.2d at 818. The Sixth Court of Appeals noted, however, that without the citation it will be impossible to tell whether the defendant was informed of the many details necessary to respond to the lawsuit. *Onyx TV*, 990 S.W.2d at 430–31; *see* TEX. R. CIV. P. 99 (requiring citation to contain 12 discrete items, including time when answer is due and warning regarding default).

We agree with the First Court. When substituted service on a statutory agent is allowed, the designee is not an agent for *serving* but for *receiving* process on the defendant's behalf. *See Capitol Brick*, 722 S.W.2d at 401; *World Distribs. v. Knox*, 968 S.W.2d 474, 479 (Tex. App. — El Paso 1998, no pet.). A certificate like the one here from the Secretary of State *conclusively* establishes that process was served. *Capitol Brick*, 722 S.W.2d at 401. As the purpose of Rule 107 is to establish whether there has been proper citation and service, the Secretary's certificate fulfills that purpose.

We recognize that service of a *defective* citation through substituted service on the Secretary of State could mislead a defendant and lead to an improper default judgment. In such cases, a defendant may bring a bill of review and establish those facts. *Caldwell v. Barnes*, 975 S.W.2d 535, 537, 539 (Tex. 1998) (holding affidavits filed in bill of review proceeding corroborating lack of service raised fact question for trial). But Campus was not misled here because — as it had failed to update addresses for its registered agent and registered office — it never received

anything the Secretary sent. Accordingly, Campus was negligent in failing to comply with its statutory duties. *See, e.g.*, TEX. BUS. CORP. ACT arts. 2.10–2.11, 8.09. We hold there is some evidence to support the trial court's denial of the bill of review. *Wembley Inv. Co. v. Herrera*, 11 S.W.3d 924, 927 (Tex. 1999) (per curiam) (holding that bill of review claimant must show prior judgment did not result from own fault or negligence).

Accordingly, without hearing oral argument, we grant the petition for review, and affirm the judgment of the court of appeals. TEX. R. APP. P. 59.1.

[7] An Alternate Way to Serve Nonresident Defendants — Rule 108

Read Tex. R. Civ. P. 108.

Rule 108 provides that service of process on a nonresident defendant or on any defendant who is absent from Texas may be made in the same manner as that provided for service of citation on residents under Rule 106. Rule 106 permits service of citation by delivery, in person, of a copy of the citation with a copy of the petition attached. Service by registered or certified mail may, if requested, be made by the clerk of the court. Civil Procedure Rule 108 provides further that nonresident "notice may be served by any disinterested person competent to make oath of the fact in the same manner as provided in Rule 106."

Since Rule 108 permits service of process on a nonresident defendant by any method authorized by Rule 106, service on nonresidents by mail is also proper. Rule 106 permits service of a copy of the citation and the petition on the defendant by registered or certified mail, return receipt requested. Rule 106 permits this type of service without prior court order. Rule 106 also provides that the citation may be served by a person authorized to serve citation by Rule 103. Rule 103 permits service by registered or certified mail by the clerk of the court in which the action is pending if such service is requested, as well as by sheriffs, constables, disinterested persons over 18 authorized by law or court order, and persons certified by order of the Supreme Court.

Rule 108's incorporation of the other rules for in-state service should also make alternative service available when unsuccessful attempts have been made to serve the defendant by the usual means.

PRACTICE EXERCISE #8

(1) Peter, from Dallas County, wants to sue Doug, also from Dallas County, for breach of contract. He has prepared a brilliant Petition and has a perfect citation. Who could serve Doug with process on Peter's behalf?

(2) Suppose that Peter's sixteen-year-old nephew, Fred, is really good at finding people. Can Peter get an order allowing Fred to serve the citation?

(3) Peter, a litigious fellow, also wants to sue Dallas County. The County also breached a contract with Peter. Who should he serve with process?

(4) Sally, from Texas, sued RobCo, from New York. Sally's petition has this to say about service of process: "RobCo may be served by serving the Secretary of State, who should forward process to RobCo's president, Rob Petrie, at his office address of 123 Main Street, New Rochelle, New York." Other than this, the other allegations of the petition concerned Sally's cause of action. Citation was properly served on the secretary of state, who properly forwarded the documents to Rob, who accepted the documents and signed the card. Sally filed the proper documents with the Texas trial court. Rob did not answer the petition, and a default judgment was entered against him. If this judgment is properly challenged by an appeal, will

Sally be able to hang on to the default judgment?

(5) Pam sues Daniel Toone. Daniel is served with process by the county sheriff. The return notes service on "Dan Boone." There is no question that the papers were handed to the correct person. Everything has been on file for the requisite number of days. Should Pam go ahead and get a default judgment based on the record as it stands? If not, what should she do?

(6) Paulette has sold some of her personally designed fashions to XYZ Company, a New Mexico boutique, but XYZ has failed to pay for them. Her attorneys served XYZ by serving the secretary of state (XYZ has no office in Texas and no registered agent for service of process). The secretary of state has forwarded process to XYZ, has provided Paulette's attorneys with a certificate attesting that process was forwarded to XYZ, and has attached the card showing that XYZ received the documents. Paulette's attorneys file this return with the court. XYZ has never responded to the suit. Assuming that at least ten days have passed since the filing of the secretary of state's certificate, is the case ready for a default judgment?

(7) Olivia sues Elliot for breach of contract, seeking damages of $1,000. Although properly served with process, Elliot fails to respond. Olivia's lawyer realizes that he has failed to request consequential damages, which were substantial: Olivia also lost profits of $25,000. Can Olivia go ahead and get a default judgment for $26,000 based on Elliot's default, or is there something else her lawyer needs to do first?

§ 4.05 CHALLENGES TO JURISDICTION BY NONRESIDENTS

Read Tex. R. Civ. P. 120a, 122.

[A] The Special Appearance

[1] History and Procedure

In 1846, in the earliest days of Texas statehood, the First Legislature enacted a procedural statute that recognized a plea to the jurisdiction. The First Legislature also enacted another statute that provided that "[n]o judgment shall in any case be rendered against any defendant unless upon service, or acceptance, or waiver of process, or upon an appearance by the defendant, as prescribed in this chapter, except where otherwise expressly provided by law." Under these provisions, Texas courts apparently did allow nonresidents to appear specially to challenge the exercise of in personam jurisdiction.

Probably as a result of the Civil War, the legal landscape was changed radically by the inclusion of "general appearance" provisions in the Revised Statutes of 1879. First, Article 1242 stated, "The filing of an answer constitutes an appearance of the defendant so as to dispense with the necessity for the issuance or service citation upon him." Second, Article 1243 provided that if service were quashed on motion, the defendant was deemed to have entered his appearance at the next term of court. Third, Article 1244 added that if the judgment was reversed on appeal for want of service or defects in service, the defendant was deemed to have entered his appearance to the term of the trial court where he filed the mandate.

In 1889, these statutory provisions were interpreted by the Texas Supreme Court to mean that every appearance, even one made specially by a nonresident to challenge the exercise of jurisdiction, constituted a general appearance. In *York v. State*, the State of Texas brought suit against York, a resident of Missouri, to recover on a lease contract. York was served in Missouri. York appeared in the Texas court and made what he thought was a "special appearance" for the purpose of contesting personal jurisdiction. The court overruled his plea. When the case came to trial, York appeared, waived his demand for a jury, and relied solely on his plea to the jurisdiction for his defense. Judgment was rendered against York. On appeal, the Supreme Court of Texas held that Articles 1242, 1243, and 1244 had abolished the special appearance. The Court further held that every defensive pleading was part of the answer, and by statute the answer was a general appearance that dispensed with the necessity of valid service on the defendant. Hence, as a result of York's appearance, the Texas trial court had jurisdiction and the judgment was affirmed.

Thereafter, York appealed his case to the Supreme Court of the United States, contending that the denial of a special appearance was a denial of due process under the Constitution's Fourteenth Amendment. Somewhat surprisingly, the Supreme Court affirmed the judgment holding that "the state has full power over remedies and procedures in its own courts, and can make any order it pleases in respect thereto provided that substance of right is secured without unreasonable burden to parties and litigants." *York v. State*, 137 U.S. 15 (1890). As Professor Thode has explained, in many quarters the Texas Supreme Court's decision was considered "the ultimate in jurisdictional provincialism until it was eliminated in 1962." *See* E. Wayne Thode, *In Personam Jurisdiction, Article 2031B, the Texas "Long-Arm" Jurisdiction Statute, and the Appearance to Challenge Jurisdiction in Texas and Elsewhere*, 42 TEX. L. REV. 279 (1964).

As *York* demonstrates, a nonresident defendant who appeared in a Texas judicial proceeding for the purpose of challenging the court's jurisdiction was deemed to have consented to its jurisdiction by making an appearance. Professor Thode has suggested that the defendant appeared in the majority of the cases and contested on the merits rather than suffer a default judgment. Under this analysis, Texas attorneys representing defendants were undoubtedly employed by non-residents to contest more cases on the merits than had been the experience of defendants' attorneys in other states.

In 1962, by amendment of the rules of procedure, nonresidents again became authorized to make special appearances under Civil Procedure Rule 120a. Until relatively recently, the requirements of 120a have been construed strictly against nonresidents.

It may help you to understand how a special appearance works if you see what the paperwork looks like. The following Special Appearance is taken from WILLIAM

V. Dorsaneo III, Texas Litigation Guide, § 60.100[2].*

SPECIAL APPEARANCE TO PRESENT MOTION OBJECTING TO JURISDICTION

TO THE HONORABLE COURT:

____________ [*Name*], defendant in this cause, makes this special appearance under the authority of Texas Rule of Civil Procedure 120a for the purpose of objecting to the jurisdiction of the Court over the person and property of the defendant, and as grounds shows the following:

I.

This special appearance is made to ____________ [the entire proceeding or the severable claim asserted by plaintiff wherein plaintiff seeks ____________ (*specify such severable claim*)].

II.

This special appearance is filed prior to a motion to transfer or any other plea, pleading, or motion.

III.

This Court does not have jurisdiction over the defendant for the reason that the party is not amenable to process issued by the courts of Texas. In this connection, defendant would further show that: ____________ [*negate all theories of jurisdiction, e.g.*,

1. Defendant is not a resident of Texas, and neither is required to maintain nor maintains a registered agent for service in Texas.

2. Defendant does not now engage and has not engaged in business in Texas nor committed any tort, in whole or in part, within the state.

3. Defendant does not maintain a place of business in Texas, and has no employees, servants, or agents within the state.]

IV.

The assumption of jurisdiction by the Court over this defendant would offend traditional notions of fair play and substantial justice, depriving the defendant of due process as guaranteed by the Constitution of the United States.

WHEREFORE, defendant requests that this motion be set for hearing on notice to ____________ [*name*], plaintiff, and upon such hearing, this motion be in all things sustained and ____________ [*the entire proceeding or specify severable claim*] be dismissed for want of jurisdiction.

Respectfully submitted,

[signature block]

VERIFICATION

STATE OF TEXAS

COUNTY OF ____________

BEFORE ME, the undersigned Notary Public, on this day personally appeared ____________ [*name*], who, being by me duly sworn on oath deposed and said that ____________ [he *or* she] is the ____________ [*insert appropriate party designation, e.g.*, defendant or duly authorized agent for ____________ (*name*)] in the above-entitled and numbered cause; that ____________ [he *or* she] has read the above SPECIAL APPEARANCE TO PRESENT MOTION OBJECTING TO JURISDICTION; and that every statement contained in the SPECIAL APPEARANCE is within ____________ [his *or* her] personal knowledge and is true and correct. ____________

[*signature of affiant*]

SUBSCRIBED AND SWORN TO BEFORE ME on the ____________ day of ____________, 200______, to certify which witness my hand and official seal.

[*Seal*] ____________ [*signature*]

____ [*typed name*]

Notary Public in and for the State of Texas

My commission expires ____________

[certificate of service]

NOTES AND QUESTIONS

(1) *Requirements of Motion.* Do you see how the above motion tracks the requirements of Rule 120a? Why does the motion contain a notary's certificate?

(2) *Amenability to Process.* From the time of its first reported judicial construction, Rule 120a has been interpreted to place the burden of showing a lack of amenability to process on the nonresident. This is contrary to the federal practice, under which the plaintiff bears the ultimate burden to show that the defendant is subject to the court's jurisdiction. *See* FED. R. CIV. P. 12(b)(2). Which approach is more sensible? Defective jurisdictional allegations in the petition, defective service of process, and defects in the citation must be challenged by a motion to quash, not a special appearance. *See Kawasaki Steel Corp. v. Middleton*, 699 S.W.2d 199, 203 (Tex. 1985).

(3) *The Nonresident's Burden.* In determining a special appearance motion, the relationship of the nonresident's "burden of proof to negate all bases of personal jurisdiction" to the plaintiff's jurisdictional allegations continues to trouble the bench and bar. Many courts require the defendants to negate only those bases for jurisdiction specifically pleaded by the plaintiff. *See, e.g.*, *Temperature Sys., Inc. v. Bill Pepper, Inc.*, 854 S.W.2d 669, 673–74 (Tex. App. — Dallas 1993, writ dism'd by agr.) (when there are no jurisdictional allegations in the plaintiff's petition, proof

that defendant is nonresident is sufficient to meet burden, but proof of nonresidency is not sufficient when plaintiff alleges jurisdictional facts). Given this confusion, as well as the possibility of a default judgment, the plaintiff should be sure to include in the petition allegations that would justify jurisdiction over the defendant. Other cases, however, find no basis for a specific pleading requirement to activate a defendant's necessity to disprove jurisdiction. *See, e.g., Huynh v. Nguyen*, 180 S.W.3d 608 (Tex. App. — Houston [14th Dist.] 2005, no pet.), which held that:

> There is no requirement that plaintiffs or other claimants plead in their petition the theories or bases of personal jurisdiction upon which they rely; rather, the only relevant pleading requirement flows from the need to plead allegations sufficient to bring nonresident defendants within the provisions of the long-arm statute. *See Am. Type Culture Collection*, 83 S.W.3d at 807 (stating plaintiffs bear the initial burden of pleading allegations sufficient to bring nonresident defendants within the provisions of the long-arm statute); *Siskind v. Villa Found. For Educ., Inc.*, 642 S.W.2d 434, 437–38 (Tex. 1982) (indicating that plaintiffs must allege an act by nonresident defendants in Texas in their petition to avoid a dismissal for lack of personal jurisdiction). This minimal pleading requirement is satisfied by an allegation that the nonresident defendants are doing business in Texas. *See Perna v. Hogan*, 162 S.W.3d 648, 652–53 (Tex. App. — Houston [14th Dist.] 2005, no pet.) (indicating that pleading requirement can be satisfied by alleging that defendant is doing business in Texas or that defendant has committed any act in Texas); *El Puerto De Liverpool, S.A. de C.V. v. Servi Mundo Llantero S.A. de C.V.*, 82 S.W.3d 622, 629 (Tex. App. — Corpus Christi 2002, pet. dism'd w.o.j.) (indicating that pleading requirement can be satisfied by alleging that defendant is doing business in Texas).

Although it was not a disputed issue in the case, the Texas Supreme Court recently described special appearance burdens: "The plaintiff bears the initial burden of pleading sufficient allegations to invoke jurisdiction under the Texas long-arm statute. . . . The nonresident defendant then assumes the burden of negating all bases of jurisdiction in those allegations." *Moki Mac River Expeditions v. Drugg*, 221 S.W.3d 569 (Tex. 2007).

(4) *Alter Ego Cases.* When the basis for assertion of jurisdiction over a defendant is its relationship to a related entity, the burden is on the *plaintiff* to prove that the parent controls the internal business operations and affairs of the subsidiary rather than on the defendant to prove that such control is absent. *BMC Software Belg., N.V. v. Marchand*, 83 S.W.3d 789, 799 (Tex. 2002).

(5) *The Hearing on the Special Appearance.* The court is directed to hold a hearing and rule on the special appearance before any other plea or pleading. The court can consider the pleadings, stipulations, affidavits, discovery products, and live testimony. Tex. R. Civ. P. 120a(3).

(6) *The Effect of Improper Removal.* The filing of a notice of removal to federal court before a special appearance does not waive the right to thereafter challenge personal jurisdiction before a Texas court on remand. *Antonio v. Marino*, 910 S.W.2d 624, 629 (Tex. App. — Houston [14th Dist.] 1995, no writ).

(7) *An End Run?* Can the plaintiff eliminate the personal jurisdiction problem by serving the defendant with process while he is in the state to testify at the special appearance hearing? No. In *Oates v. Blackburn*, 430 S.W.2d 400, 403 (Tex. Civ. App. — Houston [14th Dist.] 1968, no writ), the court of civil appeals held that the presence is privileged because otherwise Civil Procedure Rule 120a would be rendered ineffective. In fact, nonresident defendants are generally exempt from service of process while in the state to testify, even in unrelated judicial proceedings. *See Vega v. Davila*, 31 S.W.3d 376, 379 (Tex. App. — Corpus Christi 2000, no pet.).

[2] Strict Compliance Standard?

As noted above, the rule in Texas has been that anything other than a special appearance, perfect in form and timing, constitutes a general appearance — thus subjecting the defendant to the jurisdiction of Texas courts. This may no longer be true. Read the following case carefully and consider whether and how the Texas Supreme Court has loosened that standard.

DAWSON-AUSTIN v. AUSTIN

968 S.W.2d 319 (Tex. 1998)

HECHT, J.

The issues we address in this divorce action are whether the district court had in personam jurisdiction over the wife, and if not, whether the court nevertheless had jurisdiction to divide the marital estate. The court of appeals upheld personal jurisdiction. We disagree.

I

Since 1970, William Franklin Austin has been the president, chief executive officer, sole director, and sole stockholder of Starkey Laboratories, Inc., a Minnesota corporation in the business of manufacturing and distributing hearing aids. In 1977, Austin met Cynthia Lee Dawson at a seminar in Oregon, where she was living, and persuaded her to come to work for Starkey at its headquarters in Minnesota. Austin was 35 years old and divorced, and Dawson was 30 years old and separated from her husband. Dawson soon moved into Austin's Minnesota home and continued working for Starkey. On a business trip to China in 1980, Austin and Dawson recited marriage vows in a Beijing restaurant. Two years later they filed a marriage certificate in Minnesota. At some point Dawson assumed the surname, Dawson-Austin.

Dawson-Austin worked for Starkey until shortly after she and Austin separated in 1992. Over the years the business had grown. In 1980 Starkey was worth about $1.5 million with some $12 million in net revenues. By 1992 the company had become the second largest manufacturer of hearing aids in the world with sales totaling more than $200 million and a net worth of at least $40 million.

Throughout the marriage the couple's principal residence was in Minnesota, although they also owned homes elsewhere, including one they acquired in California in 1984. They never resided in Texas, and neither of them ever came to the state except on business, and then only a few times. When they separated in February 1992, Dawson-Austin was living in their California home, and she remained there. Austin moved to Texas on March 10. On April 10 Dawson-Austin filed for divorce in California but did not serve Austin until October 16. Austin filed for divorce in Texas on September 10, the first day he could do so under Texas law, Tex. Fam. Code § 6.301 (formerly Tex. Fam. Code § 3.21), and served Dawson-Austin four days later.

Dawson-Austin filed a special appearance and an amended special appearance, both of which the district court overruled. Dawson-Austin requested the court in dividing the couple's property to apply Minnesota law, under which she contends she would be entitled to a part of the increase in value of petitioner's Starkey stock attributable to the efforts of either spouse. The court refused and instead applied Texas law, holding that the stock was Austin's separate property subject only to any right of reimbursement of the community estate. The district court also struck Dawson-Austin's two expert witnesses retained to testify on the value of the community and its right of reimbursement, on the grounds that they were not timely identified in discovery. In a bench trial, Austin stipulated to Dawson-Austin's valuation of the community estate at $3,750,000. The court awarded Dawson-Austin 55.59% of the community — a little over $2 million.

Dawson-Austin appealed. The court of appeals in its initial opinion reversed the decree, holding that Minnesota law should have been applied in dividing the marital estate. On rehearing, however, a divided court of appeals affirmed the decree in all respects.

II

We first consider whether, as a matter of procedure, Dawson-Austin made a general appearance in the case.

Dawson-Austin filed *pro se* a single instrument including a special appearance, a motion to quash service of citation, a plea to the jurisdiction of the court, a plea in abatement, and subject to all of the above, an original answer. Only the answer was expressly made subject to the special appearance; the motion and pleas were not. The instrument contained a verification of the facts and allegations stated in each component of the instrument except the special appearance. Dawson-Austin contends that the failure to include the special appearance in the verification was a typographical error. The district court overruled Dawson-Austin's special appearance because it was not sworn as required by Rule 120a(1), Tex. R. Civ. P., and because a motion to quash service of citation, plea to the jurisdiction, and plea in abatement, all included in the same instrument with the special appearance, were not expressly made subject to the special appearance.

The day after the court's overruling of the special appearance, Dawson-Austin filed a motion for reconsideration and an amended special appearance. The court denied the amended special appearance "on the merits," in the court's words, and did not rule on the motion to reconsider.

The court of appeals held that Dawson-Austin's special appearance was properly overruled because it was unsworn. The court did not consider whether the other pleadings in the same instrument should have been expressly subjected to the special appearance. The court also held that Dawson-Austin waived her amended special appearance because, before it was filed, Dawson-Austin argued her motion to quash and did not object to the district court's consideration of it.

Austin argues that there are yet other reasons, in addition to those given by the lower courts, for concluding that Dawson-Austin made a general appearance in the proceeding. We address each of these arguments in turn.

A

As the lower courts both held, an unsworn special appearance does not comply with Rule 120a(1), Tex. R. Civ. P., and thus is ineffectual to challenge in personam jurisdiction. The lower courts also held, however, that the lack of verification can be cured by amendment. Austin argues that an unsworn special appearance cannot be cured and is itself a general appearance. Austin's argument is contrary to the express provision of Rule 120a(1) that a special appearance "may be amended to cure defects." By "cure," the rule means to restore the special appearance. The rule does not limit the kinds of defects that can be cured. The absence of a verification is such a defect, and an amendment that adds a verification cures the special appearance. Every court that has considered the issue agrees. *See Villalpando v. De La Garza*, 793 S.W.2d 274, 275–76 (Tex. App. — Corpus Christi 1990, no writ); *Carbonit Houston, Inc. v. Exchange Bank*, 628 S.W.2d 826, 828 (Tex. App. — Houston [14th Dist.] 1982, writ ref'd n.r.e.); *Stegall & Stegall v. Cohn*, 592 S.W.2d 427, 429 (Tex. App. — Fort Worth 1979, no writ); *Dennett v. First Continental Inv. Corp.*, 559 S.W.2d 384, 385–86 (Tex. App. — Dallas 1977, no writ).

Austin argues, alternatively, that even if an unsworn special appearance can be cured by amendment, the amendment must be filed before the special appearance is ruled on. This argument, too, finds no footing in Rule 120a(1). The rule simply does not require that an amendment be filed before a ruling on the special appearance, as long as the amendment is filed before there is a general appearance. *See Dennett*, 559 S.W.2d at 386 ("[T]he crucial focus is on the *allowance* of amendment, and the *timing* of the amendment is not determinative.") (emphasis in original).

Austin's arguments are not only contradicted by both the language and silence of Rule 120a, they misperceive what constitutes a general appearance. One court has explained:

> A party enters a general appearance whenever it invokes the judgment of the court on any question other than the court's jurisdiction; if a defendant's act recognizes that an action is properly pending or seeks affirmative action from the court, that is a general appearance.

Moore v. Elektro-Mobil Technik GMBH, 874 S.W.2d 324, 327 (Tex. App. — El Paso 1994, writ denied). Another court has stated the same proposition in the negative:

> [A]lthough an act of defendant may have some relation to the cause, it does not constitute a general appearance, if it in no way recognizes that the cause is properly pending or that the court has jurisdiction, and no affirmative action is sought from the court.

Investors Diversified Servs., Inc. v. Bruner, 366 S.W.2d 810, 815 (Tex. Civ. App. — Houston [1st Dist.] 1963, writ ref'd n.r.e.). These courts have accurately restated the principle underlying a general appearance. An unverified special appearance neither acknowledges the court's jurisdiction nor seeks affirmative action. While it cannot be used to disprove jurisdiction, it certainly does not concede it.

Thus, Dawson-Austin did not enter a general appearance by filing an unsworn special appearance or by amending it only after it was overruled.

B

Austin argues that Dawson-Austin made a general appearance by filing a motion to quash service, a plea to the jurisdiction, and a plea in abatement, all in the same instrument with the special appearance and all following the special appearance in the instrument, but none expressly made subject to the special appearance. The district court agreed with this argument; the court of appeals did not address it. The argument is contrary to Rule 120a, which states: "a motion to transfer venue and any other plea, pleading, or motion may be contained in the same instrument or filed subsequent thereto without waiver of such special appearance." The rule makes matters in the same instrument and subsequent matters subject to the special appearance without an express statement to that effect for each matter.

A few courts have referred to other matters being made subject to a special appearance but do not hold that "subject to" language is required to avoid waiver. [citations omitted]. Only two courts have addressed whether "subject to" language is required. In *Antonio v. Marino*, 910 S.W.2d 624, 629 (Tex. App. — Houston [14th Dist.] 1995, no writ), the court held that filing a stipulation without making it subject to the special appearance did not waive the special appearance. In *Portland Sav. & Loan Ass'n v. Bernstein*, 716 S.W.2d 532, 534–35 (Tex. App. — Corpus Christi 1985, writ ref'd n.r.e.), the court held that motions for sanctions and to disqualify counsel that were not filed subject to the special appearance did not "comply with Rule 120a" and therefore constituted a general appearance. *Portland* is contrary to the plain language of Rule 120a and to that extent is overruled.

Because Dawson-Austin's motion and pleas fully complied with Rule 120a, they did not constitute a general appearance.

C

The hearing on Dawson-Austin's special appearance, motion to quash service of process, plea to the jurisdiction, and plea in abatement was requested by Austin, not Dawson-Austin, because he wished the Texas court to proceed before the California court. As Austin's counsel told the district court, "we can't protect ourselves against the California lawsuit if we don't proceed today." Dawson-Austin did not ask the district court for a hearing on any of the matters she filed. On the contrary,

Dawson-Austin filed a motion for continuance the day of the hearing on the grounds that she had not been given the requisite notice for the hearing, her counsel had just been hired to make an appearance and he was in a jury trial at the time of the hearing, discovery was needed on the special appearance, and discovery was needed on the motion to quash. Dawson-Austin's counsel reurged the motion for continuance throughout the hearing, and also requested a postponement because of Austin's and Dawson-Austin's unavailability to testify. The district court denied the continuance.

Austin argues that Dawson-Austin's motion for continuance was not made subject to the special appearance and was therefore a general appearance. The district court appears to have rejected this argument, and the court of appeals did not address it. Austin's argument is incorrect for several reasons. First, as already discussed, Rule 120a expressly states that pleadings and motions may be "filed subsequent [to a special appearance] without waiver of such special appearance." Dawson-Austin's motion for continuance was filed subsequent to her special appearance and thus, by the plain language of the rule, was not a general appearance. Second, the motion for continuance did not request affirmative relief inconsistent with Dawson-Austin's assertion that the district court lacked jurisdiction, which, as we have noted, is the test for a general appearance. Rather, the motion asked the court to defer action on all matters. Third, the motion was particularly appropriate, given that Austin, not Dawson-Austin, set the matters for hearing. Dawson-Austin was obliged to request that hearing of her motion and pleas be deferred until after the special appearance. Rule 120a(2) states: "A ny motion to challenge the jurisdiction provided for herein shall be heard and determined before a motion to transfer venue or any other plea or pleading may be heard." She could not request a postponement of the special hearing without also requesting a postponement of her other matters on which Austin, not Dawson-Austin, had requested a hearing. Dawson-Austin was also entitled to seek a postponement of the special appearance hearing until she could complete discovery, as expressly permitted by Rule 120a, and she was entitled to ask for more time for discovery on her motion to quash, provided she did not attempt to take that discovery before the special appearance was decided.

Dawson-Austin was entitled to request more time to prepare for the special appearance hearing that Austin set. Her request to postpone consideration of her other matters was required if the special appearance hearing were to be delayed. Dawson-Austin's motion for continuance in no way constituted a general appearance.

D

[In this section, the Court concludes that Dawson-Austin properly entered a special appearance only with respect to the claim for division of the marital estate, because that claim is severable from the action for divorce. The district court had jurisdiction to grant the divorce even without jurisdiction over Dawson-Austin.]

E

Finally, Austin argues and the court of appeals held that Dawson-Austin, by asserting her motion to quash service of process at the conclusion of the hearing on her special appearance, made a general appearance before filing her amended special appearance the next day. The record does not support this argument.

Again, it must be recalled that Austin, not Dawson-Austin, requested the hearing on the motion to quash, along with the special appearance and Dawson-Austin's other matters, and insisted on going forward. Dawson-Austin did not raise any of the matters at the hearing; on the contrary, Dawson-Austin, as has been noted, repeatedly requested a postponement as to all of them. As soon as the district court overruled Dawson-Austin's special appearance, the following colloquy occurred:

> [Austin's Attorney]: Your Honor, if I may, I would like to proceed on their — They have a motion before the Court to quash the process in this case, and I —
>
> THE COURT: Let me ask you this. We don't get that a lot, but I thought that under the rules if you filed a Motion to Quash the service of process and the Court quashes the service of process, then that day becomes the day you're served, and then you have the Monday next after the expiration of twenty days for service from that day to file your Answer.
>
> [Austin's Attorney]: Process is moot at this point.
>
> THE COURT: But they have already filed their Answer.
>
> [Austin's Attorney]: Process is moot at this point because they filed an Answer. So actually we don't need to approach that question.
>
> THE COURT: Okay, I agree. Do you disagree with that?
>
> [Dawson-Austin's Attorney]: Yes, Your Honor, because there's no — the construction of pleadings is that you can have it all contained in the same pleadings.
>
> THE COURT: No, I'm not talking about that. I'm talking — I'm only talking about the Motion to Quash the Citation. If you have a bad citation and you come into court and get the citation quashed, then the day the Court quashes your citation is the day you're served.
>
> [Dawson-Austin's Attorney]: That's right.
>
> THE COURT: Right?
>
> [Dawson-Austin's Attorney]: So we —
>
> THE COURT: Then you have until the Monday next to file an Answer.
>
> [Dawson-Austin's Attorney]: Plus twenty.
>
> THE COURT: Am I with you? Or are you with me?
>
> [Dawson-Austin's Attorney]: Yes, Your Honor.
>
> THE COURT: But she's already filed.

> [Dawson-Austin's Attorney]: Well, Your Honor, if it's bad service — if it's a bad service, then — and that's the way the motion is presented to the Court that it's a bad service, and if you were to quash it today, then she would have twenty days plus a Monday to enter the Answer, because —
>
> THE COURT: I wouldn't be quashing her general denial. She's already filed a general denial.
>
> [Dawson-Austin's Attorney]: She hasn't waived, Your Honor, unless the Court is ruling that she waived it, that by presenting it in a pleading to the Court.
>
> THE COURT: Oh, that the general denial is subject to the ruling?
>
> [Dawson-Austin's Attorney]: Yes, Your Honor.
>
> THE COURT: Well, I don't think that waived it, but I think the fact that — I think that the intrinsic deficiencies in her Special Appearance waives it. I think she does become here at that point.
>
> [Austin's Attorney]: Your Honor, then that being the case, that was the only other motion we wanted to urge today.

As the record shows, Dawson-Austin's counsel did not raise or argue the motion to quash or any other matter. Austin's counsel raised the motion to quash, and the court ruled it moot without a word from Dawson-Austin's counsel. Only then did the court ask Dawson-Austin's counsel whether he agreed, and he essentially conceded. Nothing else transpired before the filing and hearing of Dawson-Austin's amended special appearance. Thus, the district court properly considered the special appearance on the merits.

III

A

However, the district court erred in overruling Dawson-Austin's amended special appearance. Section 6.305(a) of the Family Code provides:

> If the petitioner in a suit for dissolution of a marriage is a resident or a domiciliary of this state at the time the suit for dissolution is filed, the court may exercise personal jurisdiction over the respondent or over the respondent's personal representative although the respondent is not a resident of this state if:
>
> (1) this state is the last marital residence of the petitioner and the respondent and the suit is commenced within two years after the date on which marital residence ended; or
>
> (2) there is any basis consistent with the constitutions of this state and the United States for the exercise of the personal jurisdiction.

Tex. Fam. Code § 6.305(a) (formerly Tex. Fam. Code § 3.26(a)). Austin had been domiciled in Texas exactly six months to the day when he filed suit for divorce. *See id.* § 6.301 ("A suit for divorce may not be maintained in this state unless at the time the suit is filed either the petitioner or the respondent has been . . . a domiciliary of this state for the preceding six-month period . . . ") (formerly TEX. FAM. CODE § 3.21). Dawson- Austin, however, neither was nor ever had been a Texas resident. Thus the district court did not have in personam jurisdiction over Dawson-Austin unless it was under Section 6.305(a)(2).

The United States Constitution permits "a state court [to] take personal jurisdiction over a defendant only if it has some minimum, purposeful contacts with the state, and the exercise of jurisdiction will not offend traditional notions of fair play and substantial justice." *CMMC v. Salinas*, 929 S.W.2d 435, 437 (Tex. 1996) (citing cases); *International Shoe Co. v. Washington*, 326 U.S. 310 (1945). Dawson-Austin had no "minimum, purposeful contacts" with Texas. At the time Austin filed suit, Dawson-Austin resided in California, as Austin's petition itself alleged. She was served in California. At the hearing on her amended special appearance, she testified unequivocally and without contradiction from Austin that her only contact with the State of Texas had been to attend a business convention nine or ten years earlier. She had never lived in Texas, and Austin had not lived here before March 1992. There was no basis for the district court to exercise personal jurisdiction over Dawson-Austin, and Austin does not contend otherwise.

B

Even though the district court did not have in personam jurisdiction over Dawson-Austin, it is possible under the United States Constitution, and thus under Texas law, for the court to have had jurisdiction to divide the marital estate located in Texas. The property in Texas in which the parties claimed an interest was Austin's Dallas home and Texas bank accounts, which the parties agreed was community property, and the stock certificate evidencing Austin's shares in Starkey. As we have previously stated, Austin contends that his Starkey stock is separate property, while Dawson-Austin claims that she is entitled under Minnesota law to part of the increase in value of the stock attributable to her and Austin's efforts during marriage.

In *Pennoyer v. Neff*, 95 U.S. 714 (1878), the United States Supreme Court held that a state court could exercise jurisdiction over property within the state's borders and determine the rights and interests of non-residents. But in *Shaffer v. Heitner*, 433 U.S. 186 (1977), the Court abandoned this position and concluded instead that jurisdiction over property, like jurisdiction over persons, must be based on minimum, purposeful contacts and must not offend traditional notions of fair play and substantial justice.

> The fiction that an assertion of jurisdiction over property is anything but an assertion of jurisdiction over the owner of the property supports an ancient form without substantial modern justification. Its continued acceptance would serve only to allow state-court jurisdiction that is fundamentally unfair to the defendant.
>
> We therefore conclude that all assertions of state-court jurisdiction must be evaluated according to the standards set forth in *International Shoe* and

its progeny.

Id. at 212. *Shaffer* was a shareholder derivative suit against officers and directors of two Delaware corporations. A Delaware court sequestered defendants' stock in the corporations, even though neither defendants nor their stock were physically present in Delaware, basing its jurisdiction to do so on a Delaware statute that deemed Delaware the situs of ownership of all stock in Delaware corporations. The Supreme Court held that neither defendants nor their stock had sufficient contacts with Delaware to justify the state court's exercise of jurisdiction over them.

In the present case, the location in Texas of property that either is or is claimed to be part of the marital estate does not supply the minimum contacts required for the court to exercise jurisdiction over Dawson-Austin. Austin bought his Dallas home, opened his Texas bank accounts, and brought his Starkey stock certificate to Texas after he separated from Dawson-Austin. We do not believe that one spouse may leave the other, move to another state in which neither has ever lived, buy a home or open a bank account or store a stock certificate there, and by those unilateral actions, and nothing more, compel the other spouse to litigate their divorce in the new domicile consistent with due process. One spouse cannot, solely by actions in which the other spouse is not involved, create the contacts between a state and the other spouse necessary for jurisdiction over a divorce action. *See In the Interest of S.A.V.*, 837 S.W.2d 80, 83–84 (Tex. 1992) (holding that without personal jurisdiction over one parent, a court could still decide custody of a child living in the State, but could not determine support and visitation). Moreover, Dawson-Austin's claim to a part of the value of the Starkey stock is completely unrelated to the situs of the certificate; rather, it is based on the parties' efforts to increase the value of Starkey, most of which occurred in Minnesota. In no sense can it be said that Dawson-Austin ever "purposefully availed" herself of the privilege of owning property in this State. *See Burger King Corp. v. Rudzewicz*, 471 U.S. 462 (1985) (citing *Hanson v. Denckla*, 357 U.S. 235, 253 (1958)).

Thus, the district court lacked jurisdiction to adjudicate Dawson-Austin's claim to part of the value of the Starkey stock or to divide the marital estate . . . .

The district court had jurisdiction only to grant a divorce and not to determine the parties' property claims. Accordingly, the judgment of the court of appeals is reversed and the case is remanded to the district court for rendition of judgment divorcing Austin and Dawson-Austin and dismissing all other claims for relief for want of jurisdiction.

BAKER, J., dissenting, joined by JUSTICES ENOCH and ABBOTT.

I respectfully dissent. After determining that it had jurisdiction, the trial court dissolved the parties' marriage, characterized Austin's Starkey Corporation stock as his separate property, and distributed about fifty-five percent of the community estate to Dawson-Austin and about forty-five percent to Austin. The court of appeals affirmed the trial court's judgment. I would affirm the court of appeals.

. . . .

B. Analysis

Because Dawson-Austin's original special appearance was not sworn, it was defective. *See* Tex. R. Civ. P. 120a(1). While Rule 120a allows for amendment, any amendment to cure a defective special appearance must be accomplished *before* arguing other matters. *See* Tex. R. Civ. P. 120a(2). Dawson-Austin did not amend her special appearance until *after* she argued other matters, namely her motion to quash and about discovery related to that motion. By doing so, Dawson-Austin invoked the trial court's jurisdiction and generally appeared. *See* Tex. R. Civ. P. 120a(1) and (2); *see also Elektro-Mobil Technik GMBH*, 874 S.W.2d at 327; *Portland Sav. & Loan Ass'n*, 716 S.W.2d at 535.

Dawson-Austin argues that because she sought a continuance before the hearing on her original special appearance, she could present her other motions before amending her special appearance. I would reject this argument. I generally agree that a motion for continuance is not a general appearance. A continuance would allow a party to amend its special appearance under Rule 120a. A continuance request for that purpose in no way invokes the trial court's judgment about anything other than the court's jurisdiction. *See Elektro-Mobil Technik GMBH*, 874 S.W.2d at 327. However, that is not what occurred in this case. Dawson-Austin did not seek a continuance to cure her defective special appearance, but instead contended that she needed time to take depositions to support *her motion to quash*. Regardless, Dawson-Austin did not provide the court of appeals with any briefing about whether the trial court improperly denied her a continuance. She did not raise the issue in this Court.

Also, like the court of appeals, I reject Dawson-Austin's argument that she should be excused from arguing her motion to quash because Austin set the hearing. Dawson-Austin did not object to the trial court proceeding with her motion to quash or indicate to the trial court that she wanted to amend her special appearance before proceeding further. By arguing her motion to quash before amending her special appearance, Dawson-Austin committed a fatal procedural error and therefore generally appeared. *See Kawasaki Steel Corp.*, 699 S.W.2d at 201, 203. The Court should affirm the court of appeals . . . .

Today the Court permits less than strict compliance with Rule 120a. I believe that Dawson-Austin's efforts to specially appear were flawed. Therefore, she made a general appearance and the trial court properly exercised its jurisdiction. I would affirm the courts below. Because the Court holds otherwise, I dissent.

NOTES AND QUESTIONS

(1) *Cases Applying the* Dawson-Austin *General Appearance Standard.* Applying the *Dawson-Austin* general appearance standard and the express language of Rule 120a(1), the Texas Supreme Court has ruled that:

a) the mere inclusion of a challenge to the method of serving citation in the same instrument as a special appearance motion does not waive the jurisdictional challenge that the defendant is not amenable to process. *GFTA v. Varme*, 991 S.W.2d 785 (Tex. 1999).

b) the filing of a Rule 11 Agreement that extends a defendant's time to file a responsive pleading before filing a special appearance motion also does not violate Rule 120a's "due-order-of pleading" requirement and does not constitute a general appearance. *Exito Electronics Co., Ltd. v. Trejo*, 142 S.W.3d 302, 306 (Tex. 2004). Neither, as the Court explained in *Dawson-Austin*, does the filing of an unverified or a defectively verified special appearance motion concede jurisdiction. *Id.* at 307–08 ("Any defect in proof goes to the merits; it is simply not a waiver issue.").

c) Rule 120a(1)'s language concerning "the use of discovery processes" means that engaging in discovery and obtaining the trial court's rulings on discovery motions concerning discovery related to a special appearance "does not amount to a recognition that the action is properly pending or a request for affirmative relief inconsistent with the jurisdictional challenge." *Id.* at 306–07.

(2) *Due Order.* The concept of due order of pleadings has another non-obvious aspect. Due order pleas must be heard and *determined* in "due order," not merely filed in the right order. *See* Tex. R. Civ. P. 84. Based on Cynthia Dawson-Austin's experience, what procedures will you follow in making a special appearance?

(3) *Motions to Quash.* As the judge notes in the colloquy quoted in *Dawson-Austin*, the motion to quash, even if granted, is relatively pointless because a defendant who prevails on the motion is not entitled to be served correctly. Rather, the order quashing service acts as service on the defendant and merely extends the period to answer.

[B] Postjudgment Challenges by Nonresidents

Despite the clear suggestion in the last sentence of Civil Procedure Rule 120a(1) that a special appearance motion cannot be made after judgment, several cases have authorized post-judgment special appearance motions as long as they are filed in due order. *Koch Graphics, Inc. v. Avantech, Inc.*, 803 S.W.2d 432 (Tex. App. — Dallas 1991, no writ) (court can consider special appearance after default judgment). Counsel must be very careful, however, to take the action required to get a default judgment set aside without taking an action that constitutes a general appearance.

The Texas courts continue to struggle with the problem of post-default special appearances. In *Transportes Aereos De Coahuila, S.A. v. Falcon*, 5 S.W.3d 712, 717 (Tex. App. — San Antonio 1999, pet. denied), the court had to determine whether the defendant, TACSA, waived its special appearance when it filed an agreed motion for new trial to set aside a default judgment. The plaintiff, Falcon, brought separate but related lawsuits against TACSA. Following removal to federal court and remand to state court, TACSA inadvertently filed a special appearance in only one of the two cases. The plaintiffs moved for a default judgment in the case in which no responsive pleading had been served. However, TACSA did file a special appearance before the entry of default judgment. On realizing this, the parties filed an agreed motion for new trial, and the trial court entered an order setting aside the default judgment before ruling on the special appearance. The court of appeals rejected the claim that this waived TACSA's special appearance.

> We are not convinced that [drafting the agreed motion and order and submitting it to the trial court] is sufficient to waive TACSA's special appearance. The mere filing of a motion for new trial, without a request that it be set for hearing before the hearing on the special appearance, is not a request for affirmative relief inconsistent with the assertion that the district court lacks jurisdiction.

Id. In making this decision, the court distinguished the Texas Supreme Court's decision in *Liberty Enterprises, Inc. v. Moore Transp. Co., Inc.*, 690 S.W.2d 570, 571 (Tex. 1985), in which the defendant's agreeing to the court's order reinstating the cause of action and statement that it was "ready to try this case when it is properly set for trial" constituted a general appearance.

It is, however, imperative that the postjudgment special appearance motion be heard and determined before the nonresident's motion for new trial. In *Landry v. Daigrepont*, 35 S.W.3d 265, 267 (Tex. App. — Corpus Christi 2000, no pet.), the defendant's counsel argued a new trial motion and approved the court's order granting new trial before the court ruled on defendant's special appearance. The court therefore held that the defendant had waived its special appearance. Contrast this result with *Lang v. Capital Resource Investments I*, 102 S.W.3d 861, 864–65 (Tex. App. — Dallas 2003, no pet.), in which the special appearance motion was not waived because the defendant did not participate in the hearing and objected to the court's decision to proceed on the new trial motion before ruling on the special appearance.

Restricted appeals based on improper service, even if they succeed in setting aside a default judgment, also create a general appearance risk. In *Boyd v. Kobierowski*, 283 S.W.3d 19 (Tex. App. — San Antonio, no pet.), a Texas resident obtained a default judgment against Boyd, a California resident, in a suit over Boyd's sale of a California vehicle advertised on the internet. Boyd filed a restricted appeal, and the court reversed the default judgment based on defective personal service. After remand to the trial court, Boyd failed during a period of six months either to answer or to file a special appearance, and the Texas plaintiff once again took a default judgment against Boyd. In response, Boyd filed a special appearance and motion for new trial subject to the special appearance. Unfortunately for Boyd, this action came too late. Civil Procedure Rule 123 provides that when a judgment "is reversed on appeal . . . because of defective service of process, no new citation shall be issued or served, but the defendant shall be presumed to have entered his appearance." While the special appearance rule, Rule 120a, creates an opportunity for a nonresident defendant to except to the provision in Rule 123 that creates a general appearance, Boyd did not do so correctly.

The court explained that a nonresident defendant "may avoid a general appearance by properly employing the special appearance exception. For instance, a non-resident defendant may enter a special appearance after a judgment is reversed for defective or no service. However, failure to file a special appearance upon remand results in a general appearance." Nor did Boyd's special appearance filed after the second default judgment cure this defect. "[F]ailing to file a special appearance is not a defect that can be cured by amendment under Rule 120a." Boyd thus subjected himself to the jurisdiction of the Texas court.

Is the *Boyd* case correct? A defendant who files a timely motion to quash citation before making a special appearance enters a general appearance; do the rules provide a different result for a restricted appeal based on defective service of process? Should they?

PRACTICE EXERCISE #9

(1) You represent Computer Corporation (CC), a North Dakota corporation that has been sued in Texas by a competitor seeking damages for theft of trade secrets. You see a number of potential procedural defenses before you even get to the merits of the case. First of all, the citation was mistakenly served on a mail-room employee, and the return — which you checked at the courthouse — is defective. More significantly, you don't think CC has enough contacts with Texas to be sued there. You want to be sure not to default, though, so you're tempted to file an answer on the substantive merits of the claims and defenses while you research Texas cases on personal jurisdiction and object to that later. Would that be a good idea?

(2) On second thought, you don't really want to answer yet. But service was definitely done improperly. What about filing a motion to quash service while you review your law school notes on "minimum contacts"? Would that help?

(3) You have now dithered around so long that the plaintiff, Doll Computers, has taken a default judgment against CC. What should you do, and in what order should you do it, to try to get the default judgment set aside?

§ 4.06 THE DOCTRINE OF FORUM NON CONVENIENS

Under the U.S. Supreme Court's two-part analysis of due process, the parties' relative convenience and the interests of the forum state are part of the basic decision about personal jurisdiction. Nevertheless, there is also a separate doctrine called "forum non conveniens," which gives the court some discretion to dismiss — even if the court has jurisdiction — if the forum is relatively inconvenient and another forum exists that is significantly more convenient.

Probably the best known case discussing the doctrine is *Gulf Oil Corp. v. Gilbert*, 330 U.S. 501 (1947), a decision by the United States Supreme Court. Forum non conveniens is not a doctrine frequently resorted to in the federal courts today because 28 U.S.C. § 1404(a) gives the federal courts power to transfer cases among themselves for the convenience of the parties and witnesses or in the interest of justice. Still, the doctrine does appear occasionally, because the section 1404(a) transfer provision does not apply if the more convenient forum is the court of another nation. State courts, lacking a nationwide system that would allow transfers, invoke the doctrine of forum non conveniens more frequently. Texas courts have come to the doctrine more recently, as for a while it was held to be inapplicable to personal injury and death cases. *Dow Chemical v. Alfaro*, 786 S.W.2d 674 (Tex. 1990) (overruled by statute).

[A] The Common Law Doctrine

The party moving for forum non conveniens dismissal must make two showings: 1) there is an adequate alternate forum available; and 2) the balance of relevant private and public factors favors dismissal.

The private factors concern the relative benefits and burdens of litigation for the parties. They include: 1) relative ease of access to sources of proof; 2) availability of compulsory process to obtain the attendance of unwilling witnesses; 3) the cost of obtaining the attendance of willing witnesses; 4) the possibility of viewing the premises, where that is relevant; and 5) all other practical problems that would affect the efficiency of trial in the competing forums. Some of the "practical problems" noted by courts include the defendant's inability to implead a third-party defendant, the cost of obtaining or translating evidence, and the financial hardship that the plaintiff might incur if forced to try the case in the alternative forum.

The public factors include: 1) any administrative difficulties that arise from court congestion (including a comparison of the dockets of the competing forums); 2) the burden on the community of jury duty in a matter over which they have little interest; 3) the inability of people who are concerned about the controversy to get news of the litigation; 4) the "local interest in having localized controversies decided at home"; and 5) the preference for having a case tried in the jurisdiction whose law will apply (and for avoiding difficult choice of law issues).

Notice that this list of factors was devised in 1947, and technological developments since then may have decreased the inconvenience of distant litigation and increased the sharing of news and information across the miles. Nevertheless, the doctrine of forum non conveniens remains a powerful one, and has become a battleground in struggles between plaintiffs and defendants to obtain a favorable forum.

The common law version of forum non conveniens applies only when the balance of factors so strongly favors trying the case in another jurisdiction that, in the interest of justice, the case should be dismissed. The party seeking dismissal has the burden of proving that the balance of factors strongly favors trying the case in the other jurisdiction. The trial court should consider not only the advantages and disadvantages of the plaintiff's forum choice, but also the advantages and disadvantages of the alternative forum. Unless the balance is strongly in favor of defendant, the plaintiff's choice of forum should not be disturbed. *Gurvich v. Tyree*, 694 S.W.2d 39, 46 (Tex. App. — Tyler 1985, writ denied). Case law, however, gives less deference to the plaintiff's choice of forum when the plaintiff is not suing at home.

Texas cases applying the common law doctrine of forum non conveniens include *In re Smith Barney, Inc.*, 975 S.W.2d 593 (Tex. 1998); *Flaiz v. Moore*, 359 S.W.2d 872 (Tex. 1962); *Sarieddine v. Moussa*, 820 S.W.2d 837 (Tex. App. — Dallas 1991, writ denied); *Direct Color Services, Inc. v. Eastman Kodak Co.*, 929 S.W.2d 558 (Tex. App. — Tyler 1996, writ denied). On appeal, the trial court's decision is reviewed for abuse of discretion.

The Texas Supreme Court has addressed the question of when forum non conveniens motions may properly be raised:

> If the court is to decline jurisdiction, . . . the question must be raised at a time and in a manner that will give the parties an opportunity to present evidence regarding the circumstances that are relevant for a determination of whether jurisdiction should or should not be retained.

Flaiz, supra, at 875. One Texas appellate court has upheld the timeliness of a motion filed nine months after the case began. *Direct Color, supra.* The Texas forum non conveniens statute, on the other hand, provides a much earlier deadline [see section 4.06[B], *infra*], and it is possible that even when considering a common law motion, the court might be influenced by the policy determination reflected in the statutory deadline. The amount of case activity before filing may also matter: federal authorities have held that even if the defendant has moved in a timely fashion, if extensive discovery on the merits has taken place or if the court has expended significant resources on the case, considerations of judicial economy weigh in favor of retaining the action. *See Lony v. E.I. Du Pont de Nemours & Co.*, 935 F.2d 604, 607 (3d Cir. 1991); *Empresa Lineas Maritimas Argentinas v. Schichau-Unterweser, A.G.*, 955 F.2d 368, 372 (5th Cir. 1992) (upholding district court's determination that progress of litigation was not so significant as to merit retention of the action).

[B] The Statute

If the plaintiff's claim is for personal injuries or wrongful death, the application of the doctrine of forum non conveniens is governed by the Civil Practice and Remedies Code:

§ 71.051. *Forum Non Conveniens*

(a) [Repealed in 2003].

(b) If a court of this state, on written motion of a party, finds that in the interest of justice and for the convenience of the parties a claim or action to which this section applies would be more properly heard in a forum outside this state, the court shall decline to exercise jurisdiction under the doctrine of forum non conveniens and shall stay or dismiss the claim or action. In determining whether to grant a motion to stay or dismiss an action under the doctrine of forum non conveniens, the court shall consider whether:

(1) an alternate forum exists in which the claim or action may be tried;

(2) the alternate forum provides an adequate remedy;

(3) maintenance of the claim or action in the courts of this state would work a substantial injustice to the moving party;

(4) the alternate forum, as a result of the submission of the parties or otherwise, can exercise jurisdiction over all the defendants properly joined to the plaintiff's claim;

(5) the balance of the private interests of the parties and the public interest of the state predominate in favor of the claim or action being

brought in an alternate forum, which shall include consideration of the extent to which an injury or death resulted from acts or omissions that occurred in this state; and

(6) the stay or dismissal would not result in unreasonable duplication or proliferation of litigation.

(c) The court may set terms and conditions for staying or dismissing a claim or action under this section as the interests of justice may require, giving due regard to the rights of the parties to the claim or action. If a moving party violates a term or condition of a stay or dismissal, the court shall withdraw the order staying or dismissing the claim or action and proceed as if the order had never been issued. Notwithstanding any other law, the court shall have continuing jurisdiction for purposes of this subsection.

(d) A request for stay or dismissal under this section is timely if it is filed not later than 180 days after the time required for filing a motion to transfer venue of the claim or action. The court may rule on a motion filed under this section only after a hearing with notice to all parties not less than 21 days before the date specified for the hearing. The court shall afford all of the parties ample opportunity to obtain discovery of information relevant to the motion prior to a hearing on a motion under this section. The moving party shall have the responsibility to request and obtain a hearing on such motion at a reasonable time prior to commencement of the trial, and in no case shall the hearing be held less than 30 days prior to trial.

(e) The court may not stay or dismiss a plaintiff's claim under Subsection (b) if the plaintiff is a legal resident of this state. If an action involves both plaintiffs who are legal residents of this state and plaintiffs who are not, the court may not stay or dismiss the action under Subsection (b) if the plaintiffs who are legal residents of this state are properly joined in the action and the action arose out of a single occurrence. The court shall dismiss a claim under Subsection (b) if the court finds by a preponderance of the evidence that a party was joined solely for the purpose of obtaining or maintaining jurisdiction in this state and the party's claim would be more properly heard in a forum outside this state.

(f) A court that grants a motion to stay or dismiss an action under the doctrine of forum non conveniens shall set forth specific findings of fact and conclusions of law.

(g) Any time limit established by this section may be extended by the court at the request of any party for good cause shown.

(h) In this section:

(1) "Legal resident" means an individual who intends the specified political subdivision to be his permanent residence and who intends to return to the specified political subdivision despite temporary residence elsewhere or despite temporary absences, without regard to the individual's country of citizenship or national origin. The term does not include an individual who adopts a residence in the specified political subdivision in bad faith for purposes of avoiding the application of this section.

(2) "Plaintiff" means a party seeking recovery of damages for personal injury or wrongful death. In a cause of action in which a party seeks

recovery of damages for personal injury to or the wrongful death of another person, "plaintiff" includes both that other person and the party seeking such recove ry. The term does not include a counterclaimant, cross-claimant, or third-party plaintiff or a person who is assigned a cause of action for personal injury, or who accepts an appointment as a personal representative in a wrongful death action, in bad faith for purposes of affecting in any way the application of this section.

Texas's forum non conveniens statute is very similar to the common law doctrine, but section (b) contains a specific list of factors that the court "shall consider" in determining whether "in the interest of justice and for the convenience of the parties a claim or action . . . would be more properly heard in a forum outside this state." Do the items on the list have the same meaning as their common law counterparts? Who must provide evidence to support these factors, and what happens if they do not all point in the same direction? Consider the following case.

IN RE GENERAL ELECTRIC COMPANY

271 S.W.3d 681 (Tex. 2008)

JOHNSON, J.

ON PETITION FOR WRIT OF MANDAMUS

Although Austin Richards never lived or worked in Texas, he sued numerous defendants in Dallas County as a result of alleged exposure to asbestos at his jobsite in Maine. He alleged that he developed mesothelioma as a result of the exposure and that the defendants were liable to him because they produced or were involved in furnishing the asbestos. Several defendants moved for dismissal on the basis of forum non conveniens. The trial court denied the motions. At issue in this mandamus proceeding is whether the trial court abused its discretion by denying the defendants' motions to dismiss. We conclude that it did and conditionally grant mandamus relief.

I. Background

Aside from a period of military service, Austin Richards lived in Maine his entire life. He worked in Maine for over thirty years as a mason handling pipe-covering insulation. In December 2005, he was diagnosed with mesothelioma. Richards and his wife (collectively "Richards") filed suit in Dallas County against General Electric and over twenty other companies, three of are headquartered in Texas. Richards alleged that the defendants mined, processed, manufactured, sold, or distributed asbestos which caused or contributed to his disease. The case was transferred to the asbestos multi-district litigation court in Harris County. *See* TEX. R. JUD. ADMIN. 13.

Seven defendants moved for dismissal of Richards's suit based on forum non conveniens. *See* TEX. CIV. PRAC. & REM. CODE § 71.051. They argued that the suit had no connection to Texas and that Maine was an adequate alternative forum for the case. Richards responded that the trial court should deny the motions to dismiss because the defendants had not met their burden of proof regarding the section 71.051 factors. He especially emphasized that the defendants had not proved the existence of an adequate alternative forum in which the claim could be tried. Richards asserted that if his case were dismissed and he refiled in Maine, the case would be vulnerable to removal to federal court and if removed, it would be transferred to the federal Multi-District Litigation Court No. 875 (MDL 875) for pretrial proceedings. *See In re Asbestos Prods. Liab. Litig.*, 771 F. Supp. 415, 422-24 (J.P.M.L. 1991). Richards further argued that cases transferred to MDL 875 do not get tried and "virtually nothing happens to them at all." Richards urged that he was seriously ill from his disease and that if the Texas trial court declined to exercise jurisdiction, MDL 875 would not be adequate because he would not survive long enough to have his case tried. [In fact, Mr. Richards died before this opinion was written. — Eds.]

At the hearing on the motion to dismiss, the judge asked whether the defendants would agree that they would not attempt to remove the case to federal court if he granted the motion to dismiss. Several defendants, including General Electric, did not agree to waive their removal rights. The judge sent a letter to the parties indicating that he would deny the motion to dismiss and expressing concern that if he granted the motion and the case were refiled in Maine, it would be removed to federal court and transferred to MDL 875 where it would "sit . . . for several years." The judge wrote that his ruling on the motion might have been different if the defendants had waived their right of removal.

The defendants filed a motion to reconsider. They asserted that even if their motions to dismiss were granted and Richards refiled his case in Maine, removal to federal court was speculative, the criticisms of MDL 875 were unfounded as recent activity there refuted any argument that it did not provide an adequate remedy, and the court's ruling should not depend on the defendants' waiver of their removal rights. After another hearing, the trial court granted the motion to reconsider, set aside the letter in which he stated the grounds for his previous ruling, and denied the motion to dismiss without stating a reason.

Three defendants — General Electric, Warren Pumps, and Ingersoll-Rand (defendants) — seek mandamus relief directing the trial court to grant their motions to dismiss. They argue that on this record, the statutory forum non conveniens factors require dismissal.

II. Discussion

* * *

B. Forum Non Conveniens

1. General

The defendants claim that the trial court had no discretion but to apply the factors found in the forum non conveniens statute and dismiss Richards's claim because those factors weigh in favor of a forum other than Texas. Richards argues that even considering the statutory factors, the trial court had discretion to determine whether a forum non conveniens dismissal would serve the interest of justice, which in this case it would not. [The Court next quotes the language of section 71.051(b).]

Prior to 2003, section 71.051 provided that a case brought by a United States resident "may" be stayed or dismissed under the doctrine of forum non conveniens. In 2003, the Legislature amended the statute. Among other changes, the amended statute provided that a trial court "shall" dismiss a claim or action if the court found that in the interest of justice and for the convenience of the parties a claim or action would be more properly heard in a forum outside Texas. Before the 2005 amendments the statute also provided that when determining whether to dismiss an action based on forum non conveniens, a trial court "may" consider the factors specified in section 71.051(b). In 2005, the Legislature amended the statute to its current form. It now provides that when determining whether to dismiss an action based on forum non conveniens, a trial court "shall" consider the factors specified in section 71.051(b).

The defendants claim that the amended statute takes away much of a trial court's discretion in regard to forum non conveniens motions by requiring the court to weigh the statutory factors and decline to exercise jurisdiction if the factors weigh in favor of granting the motion. Richards claims, however, that the Legislature has always provided trial courts discretion to deny forum non conveniens motions, and the statute does not remove that discretion. Instead, the statute merely requires that dismissals serve the interests of justice--an inherently discretionary standard.

Use of the word "shall" in a statute imposes a duty. Tex. Gov't Code § 311.016(2). We agree with defendants that by using the word "shall" in regard to a trial court's consideration of the factors listed in section 71.051(b), the Legislature has essentially defined the terms "interest of justice" and "convenience of the parties" as they are used in section 71.051(b). Tex. Civ. Prac. & Rem. Code § 71.051(b). The Legislature also, by use of the word "shall," requires dismissal of the claim or action if the statutory factors weigh in favor of the claim or action being more properly heard in a forum outside Texas. *See In re Pirelli Tire*, 247 S.W.3d at 675 n.3 (noting that with the 2003 amendment, the Legislature now mandates dismissal if the trial court finds that the case would be more properly heard in another forum).

Richards asserts that the defendants, as movants, had the burden to prove that each factor weighed in favor of dismissal and urges that they failed to meet the burden. We disagree. Prior to 2003, the statute provided that a trial court could stay or dismiss a claim under the forum non conveniens statute "if the party seeking to stay or dismiss proves" the enumerated factors "by a preponderance of the evidence." However, the statute was amended to provide only that a trial court "shall consider" the factors. Tex. Civ. Prac. & Rem. Code § 71.051(b). The statute does not mandate that a movant prove each factor or that each factor must weigh in favor of dismissal to require a motion to be granted. . . . The statute does not contain language placing the burden of proof on a particular party in regard to the factors, as was the situation with the prior version. Nor does the statute require that a party prove each factor of section 71.051(b). The statute simply requires the trial court to consider the factors, and it must do so to the extent the factors apply. To the extent evidence is necessary to support the positions of the parties, the trial court must base its findings and decision on the weight of the evidence, and certainly is entitled to take into account the presence or absence of evidence as to some issue or position of a party.

With the foregoing in mind, we turn to the enumerated factors to determine whether the trial court abused its discretion in failing to grant the motions to dismiss.

2. Section 71.051(b)(1) and (2) — Adequate Alternate Forum

The first two factors in section 71.051(b) are: (1) whether an alternate forum exists where the claim may be tried, and (2) whether the alternate forum provides an adequate remedy. The defendants assert that Maine, where Richards lived and was allegedly exposed to asbestos, is such an alternate forum. Richards does not dispute that Maine state courts are an alternate forum or that those courts provide an adequate remedy. He urges in his brief that had defendants agreed not to remove the case to federal court, the Texas case would have been dismissed and the case would have been tried in Maine. But he contends the defendants have not proved the availability of an alternate forum where the claims may be *tried*. He takes that position because none of the defendants in this case maintain a principal place of business or are incorporated in Maine. Therefore, his case would be vulnerable to removal to federal court on diversity jurisdiction grounds. He claims that once removed to federal court, his case would almost certainly be transferred to MDL 875, and it is widely accepted that cases transferred to MDL 875 do not get tried. For support, he quotes from an opinion of the federal district court in Maine: "If these claims return to state court, they will proceed to resolution. If they remain in federal court, they will encounter significant delay upon their transfer [to MDL 875] where no asbestos trials or discovery takes place in deference to global settlement efforts." *In re Maine Asbestos Cases*, 44 F. Supp. 2d 368, 374 (D. Me. 1999). He also quotes from *Madden v. Able Supply Co.*, 205 F. Supp. 2d 695, 702 (S.D. Tex. 2002): "There are thousands of asbestos cases pending in [MDL 875] and, if history be any indicator, Plaintiff's claims . . . will not be heard for many years." Richards also points to data from the Judicial Panel on Multidistrict Litigation indicating that as of August 10, 2000, 32,892 cases were pending in MDL 875 and only 199 cases had been remanded in the preceeding year. He claimed in the trial court, and continues to claim in this Court, that because of the situation in MDL 875, dismissal would not work justice, but would work injustice. Richards argued that a transfer to MDL 875 would work an injustice because he would have no chance at a trial before his death and that because claims languish in MDL 875, it is not an alternate forum in which the claim may be tried as required by section 71.051(b)(1).

The defendants claim that because the state courts of Maine comprise an adequate alternate forum and remedy, Richards's arguments about MDL 875 are irrelevant. Section 71.051(b), they posit, does not allow the trial court to deny their motions based on speculation about what might happen procedurally in another venue, nor does it allow the trial court to speculate about whether the case would be refiled in Maine or some other alternate forum. Even though their position is that the status of MDL 875 is irrelevant, they also counter Richards's claims as to that court with more recent documents showing that progress is being made in regard to moving asbestos cases through the federal pretrial process.

Ordinarily, an alternate forum is shown if the defendant is "amenable to process" in the other jurisdiction. *Piper Aircraft Co. v. Reyno*, 454 U.S. 235, 254 n.22 (1981). There may be circumstances where an alternate forum is not adequate because the remedies it offers are so unsatisfactory that they really comprise no remedy at all. But, comparative analyses of procedures and substantive law in different forums should be given little weight in forum non conveniens analysis because such analyses pose significant practical problems. Comparison of the "rights, remedies, and procedures" available in each forum would require complex exercises in comparative law that the forum non conveniens doctrine is designed to help courts avoid. Therefore, a comparative analysis of the procedures, rights, and remedies available in Texas, Maine, and federal courts should only be given weight if Maine (and a potential transfer to MDL 875) would in substance provide no remedy at all.

The disadvantages Richards perceives in MDL 875 proceedings are ones of comparative speed to disposition of his case. His objection is based on comparative analysis of procedural processes and times to trial. That is the type of exercise that is disfavored when forum non conveniens motions are considered. Delay in disposition of a case might happen in any jurisdiction depending on docket congestion, statutes, and procedures mandating preferential settings for certain types of cases, fiscal conditions of the judiciary, and numerous other possible conditions and events. The many known and unknown matters affecting pretrial events and trial settings are necessarily speculative and are reasons comparative analyses have been termed "complex" and should be avoided in forum non conveniens consideration. *See Piper Aircraft Co.*, 454 U.S. at 251.

Furthermore, even if Richards's case is dismissed in Texas, filed in Maine, and transferred to MDL 875 for pretrial proceedings, Richards will not be deprived of all remedies for purposes of forum non conveniens analysis. *See In re Union Carbide Corp. Gas Plant Disaster at Bhopal, India*, 634 F. Supp. 842, 848-49 (S.D.N.Y. 1986), *aff'd*, 809 F.2d 195 (2d Cir. 1987) (rejecting plaintiffs' claims that a suit should not be dismissed on forum non conveniens grounds because the alternate forum had problems of delay and backlog, and lacked the wherewithal to deal effectively and expeditiously with the suit). Though Richards (and others) may be critical of the methods used and time taken to dispose of pretrial matters in the federal asbestos MDL scheme, the scheme is designed to resolve asbestos cases, not deprive injured parties of a remedy. The federal Constitution guarantees Richards the right to a jury trial and due process, and the Maine and federal courts are bound to afford those rights to Richards. U.S. Const. amend. VII, amend XIV, § 1. We believe, therefore, that Maine, and even MDL 875, come within the Legislature's intent that the alternate forum be one "in which the claim or action may be tried." Tex. Civ. Prac. & Rem. Code § 71.051(b).

We conclude that on balance, the factors set out in sections 71.051(b)(1) and (2) weigh strongly, if not conclusively, in favor of Richards's action being heard in a forum outside Texas.

3. Section 71.051(b)(3) — Substantial Injustice to Defendants by Litigating in Texas

The defendants point to private interest considerations in support of their assertion that litigating this case in Texas will work a substantial injustice to them. *See* TEX. CIV. PRAC. & REM. CODE § 71.051(b)(3). They also point to the increased costs of traveling to Maine to depose witnesses for trial in Texas. Richards argues that the defendants' claims in this regard are conclusory allegations which are insufficient to support dismissal. He also claims that regardless of the forum, expert witnesses in asbestos cases reside all over the country and attorneys must routinely travel to take depositions.

While some travel in this case will almost certainly occur regardless of the forum in which the case is ultimately litigated, that aspect does not override the fact that the evidence and witnesses relevant to the issue of Richards's asbestos exposure and his damages are outside the subpoena power of Texas courts. TEX. R. CIV. P. 176.3. At the hearing on the defendants' motions to dismiss, Richards agreed that if the trial court denied the motions but it later became clear to the defendants that trial in Texas would be impossible due to the unavailability of witnesses and evidence, Richards would not object to motions to dismiss on the basis of timeliness, even if they were filed shortly before trial. But requiring parties to litigate a case such as this in Texas until it becomes clear that it is "impossible" to defend the case due to unavailability of evidence and fact witnesses because they are beyond the reach of compulsory process is a waste of private and public resources. *See Gulf Oil Corp. v. Gilbert*, 330 U.S. 501, 511 (1947) ("Certainly to fix the place of trial at a point where litigants cannot compel personal attendance and may be forced to try their case on deposition, is to create a condition not satisfactory to court, jury or most litigants."). Further, while Richards argues that defendants have not identified any specific witness or evidence they are unable to obtain, such a showing is not necessary. *See Reyno*, 454 U.S. at 258 (noting that requiring detail and extensive investigation regarding witnesses beyond the reach of compulsory process would defeat the purpose of a forum non conveniens motion).

We conclude that the section 71.051(b)(3) factor — whether maintaining the action in Texas would work a substantial injustice to defendants--weighs strongly in favor of the claim being more properly heard in a forum outside Texas.

4. Section 71.051(b)(4) — Jurisdiction Over all Defendants

Richards claims the evidence did not show that all the defendants in this case are subject to the jurisdiction of Maine courts, or have consented to jurisdiction in Maine. *See* TEX. CIV. PRAC. & REM. CODE § 71.051(b)(4). The defendants that filed motions to dismiss stipulated to jurisdiction in Maine, agreed to submit to jurisdiction there, or admitted they were subject to jurisdiction under the Maine long-arm statute. Further, the defendants argue that under the Maine long-arm statute, courts in Maine will have jurisdiction over all defendants *properly* joined as parties.

Maine courts have jurisdiction over any person as to a cause of action arising from "[d]oing or causing a tortious act to be done, or causing the consequences of a tortious act to occur within this State." 14 ME. REV. STAT. § 704-A(2)(B). Richards claims that this statute only allows an assumption that all defendants are subject to jurisdiction in Maine and that dismissal of a case based on a mere assumption would itself be an abuse of discretion. But there is no dispute that the exposure and injuries alleged by Richards occurred in Maine. Richards has not identified any defendant over which Maine courts would not have jurisdiction under the Maine long-arm statute. And this Court has recognized that the possibility an alternate forum may not accept jurisdiction does not overcome other factors weighing in favor of dismissal, particularly when a court may condition its dismissal order on the acceptance of jurisdiction by the alternate forum. *In re Pirelli*, 247 S.W.3d at 677-78; *see* Tex. Civ. Prac. & Rem. Code § 71.051(c) (allowing a court to set terms and conditions for dismissal of a claim based on forum non conveniens). . . .

The Maine long-arm statute is plain and speaks for itself. This record presents no reason to do what typically is not done in forum non conveniens analyses — perform a comprehensive comparative consideration of Maine jurisprudence in regard to each party to Richards's suit. Requiring Texas trial courts and appellate courts to engage in such exercises would slow down and complicate forum non conveniens hearings and decisions to the point that they could become major detriments to disposition of cases. This record presents no reason, for purposes of forum non conveniens analysis, to consider Maine's long-arm statute further than its plain words. The section 71.051(b)(4) factor — whether the alternate forum can exercise jurisdiction over all defendants properly joined to the plaintiff's claim — weighs in favor of the claim being more properly heard in a forum outside Texas.

5. Section 71.051(b)(5) — Public and Private Interest

Richards contends the defendants did not demonstrate that the balance of public and private interests weigh in favor of a Maine forum. Generally, the public interest factors to be considered are administrative difficulties related to court congestion, burdening the people of a community with jury duty when they have no relation to the litigation, local interest in having localized controversies decided at home, and trying a case in the forum that is at home with the law that governs the case. The private interest considerations generally are considered to be the ease of access to proof, the availability and cost of compulsory process, the possibility of viewing the premises, if appropriate, and other practical problems that make trial easy, expeditious, and inexpensive.

As to the public interest factors, the parties do not disagree that Maine law will apply in this case. Maine undoubtedly has an interest in ensuring that its citizens are not exposed to hazardous materials in the workplace. Absent some overriding consideration, the citizens of Texas should not be burdened with jury duty in a complex asbestos exposure case that has no relationship to Texas. In this case, most evidence and fact witnesses are admittedly located in Maine. Richards's treating physicians, co-worker witnesses, and family members are there. The paper mill where Richards was allegedly exposed to asbestos is in Maine. Compulsory process is unavailable to require attendance at a Dallas County trial by witnesses approximately two thousand miles away. *See* Tex. R. Civ. P. 176.3. Richards says that he has already provided or will provide copies of his medical records to the defendants. But a promise to produce some or even most evidence does not cure the logistical problems created by lack of effective compulsory process for trial. Richards also asserts the defendants' claim that there is no compulsory process for witnesses who reside in Maine is an insufficient, "unsubstantiated, conclusory allegation" because the defendants have never identified a witness whose appearance they will be unable to obtain at a Texas trial. But detail regarding which witnesses would be called and what evidence would be unavailable is not necessary in a case such as this where the practical problems of trying a personal injury case hundreds of miles from the scene of the occurrence, the place where the lay witnesses reside, and where most other evidence is located is manifest. *See Reyno*, 454 U.S. at 258. Reasonable access to witnesses and evidence is a fundamental need in regard to any trial — asbestos or otherwise.

Richards also points to the recently decided case of *Sales v. Weyerhaeuser*, 177 P.3d 1122 (Wash. 2008), in which the Washington Supreme Court concluded that a trial court should have considered the effect of MDL 875 when analyzing the convenience of forums for forum non conveniens purposes. In *Sales*, Charles Sales filed suit in Washington against Weyerhaeuser, a Washington corporation that owned a lumber mill in Arkansas. Sales alleged he was exposed to asbestos in Arkansas and that the exposure caused him to develop mesothelioma. The trial court granted Weyerhaeuser's motion to dismiss on forum non conveniens grounds over Sales's arguments that if he refiled the suit in Arkansas it would be removed to federal court and transferred to MDL 875 which would impede the progress of his suit based on the inherent delays there. The Washington Supreme Court concluded that the trial court should have considered the effect of MDL 875 on the convenience of litigating in Arkansas. It did not conclude that MDL 875 proceedings would make Washington the more convenient setting, but rather, it concluded that the trial court should have considered whether MDL 875 proceedings would impact the speed, ease, and expense of the proceedings which would weigh in favor of litigation in Washington over Arkansas.

A trial court must take all relevant factors into consideration with regard to the public and private interest factors. However, in this case, even including the effect of a possible transfer to MDL 875 does not change the balance: the factors in section 71.051(b)(5) weigh in favor of Maine as an alternate forum for Richards's claim. First and foremost, and as previously noted, is the fact that both Maine and MDL 875 are subject to the federal Constitution and the rights it guarantees to Richards. Further, there is only a potential that the case will end up in MDL 875. There are a number of events that could occur that would prevent that from happening (such as if Richards decides to file suit in a state other than Maine). Additionally, if Richards refiles the case in Maine and it is transferred to MDL 875, there is still only the potential for delay. Richards presented statistics from 1999 and cases indicating that claims were left pending for many years and the MDL 875 judge, Judge Weiner, resolved cases through negotiation not trial. The defendants pointed out that Judge Wiener was no longer presiding over MDL 875. He was replaced by Judge Giles who had issued orders outlining changes to docket management and directed quarterly meetings of all counsel to address the processing and administration of claims.

Section 71.051(b)(5) requires a trial judge to balance the public and private interests to determine whether those factors predominate in favor of the claim being more properly heard in a forum outside Texas, and on balance, it is clear that the factors weigh in favor of Richards's action being heard in Maine.

6. Section 71.051(b)(6) — Unreasonable Duplication of Litigation

Richards asserts that the defendants failed to show dismissal would not result in unreasonable duplication of litigation. He claims dismissal would result in two lawsuits: the Texas case against the nonmoving defendants would remain pending while a new suit would be filed against the moving defendants in Maine. We disagree that had the trial court granted the defendants' motions to dismiss, this would have resulted in unreasonable duplication of litigation. Section 71.051(b) currently provides that if a court decides "a claim or action" would be more properly heard in another forum, the court shall stay or dismiss "the claim or action." The language is broad and does not require that a trial court dismiss only the claims or actions against moving defendants. *See* Tex. Civ. Prac. & Rem. Code § 71.051(b) (requiring dismissal of a claim or action on written motion of "a" party).

In all the motions to dismiss, the defendants requested dismissal of the entire case, not just the claims against themselves. For example, General Electric concluded its motion by stating "this case should be dismissed because it would be in the interest of justice and convenience to do so." It argued throughout the motion that the statutory factors weighed in favor of dismissal for all the defendants.

If Richards's action or part of the action is dismissed for forum non conveniens, the extent to which his litigation might be fragmented or duplicated lies in his hands, not those of the Texas court. If he were to refile suit in a jurisdiction other than Maine, then he might again be met with assertions by defendants that the action or a claim in the action is subject to a forum non conveniens challenge. But those contingencies depend on decisions by Richards to file suits in forums other than Maine and run the risk of multiple suits in multiple venues.

We disagree with Richards's position in regard to the section 71.051(b)(6) factor. The potential that a trial court might grant a motion to dismiss as to only part of an action and that some duplication of litigation could occur, depending on Richards's own litigation decisions, does not turn the trial court's decision to grant motions to dismiss such as the ones in this case into decisions causing unreasonable duplication of litigation. Under the circumstances, the section 71.051(b)(6) factor — that the stay or dismissal would not result in unreasonable duplication or proliferation of litigation — weighs in favor of the claim being more properly heard in a forum outside Texas.

III. Conclusion

When all section 71.051(b) factors in a case favor the conclusion that an action or claim would be more properly held in a forum outside Texas, as they do here, the statute requires the trial court to grant motions requesting that it decline to exercise its jurisdiction. The trial court's denial of the relators' motions to dismiss violated the forum non conveniens statute and was an abuse of its discretion. We conditionally grant the petition for writ of mandamus and direct the trial court to grant the relators' motions. The writ will issue only if the trial court fails to comply.

NOTES AND QUESTIONS

(1) Do you agree with the Court's assessment of the statutory factors in the preceding case? What standard is it using in resolving disputed facts, such as the adequacy of MDL 875, the availability of witnesses in Texas, and Maine's jurisdiction over all defendants? [To update the MDL statistics, as of March 31, 2010, there were 48,136 cases pending, although the pace of disposition had increased. For current information on the consolidated asbestos cases, see http://www.paed.uscourts.gov/mdl875.asp.]

(2) *Common Law vs. CPRC.* In what ways does the statutory regime differ from the common law doctrine?

(3) *Non-Texas Plaintiffs and the Statute of Limitations.* Chapter 71 also puts additional limits on non-resident plaintiffs seeking to recover damages for personal injuries or wrongful death. In an attempt to prevent forum-shopping to avoid limitations, non-resident plaintiffs are bound by the limitation period prescribed by the state of the plaintiff's residence. C.P.R.C. § 71.031. Residence is determined as of the time the plaintiff's cause of action accrues. *See Tullis v. Georgia-Pacific Corp.*, 45 S.W.3d 118, 128 (Tex. App. — Fort Worth 2000, no pet.).

APPENDIX — PERSONAL JURISDICTION AND THE TEXAS BAR EXAM

Texans frequently interact with people and entities from outside Texas. When those interactions end badly and the Texans want to sue at home, personal jurisdiction issues arise. These are frequently tested on the Texas bar exam. The following are questions from past exams, reprinted with the permission of the Texas Board of Law Examiners, which owns the copyright to these questions. You can see more questions, and the examiners' comments on the answers, by visiting the Board's website at www.ble.state.tx.us/past_exams/main_pastexams.htm.

In formulating your answers, keep in mind that on the bar exam you will have only five lines to answer each question.

February 2001

Paul Palmer, a resident of Bell County, has filed a negligence, breach of warranty, and product liability suit in state district court in Hill County, Texas. Palmer alleges that a curling iron, which he had bought for his daughter from Dad's Department Store ("Dad's"), was defective, overheated, and caused a fire in his home. Palmer, who is uninsured, seeks to recover the cost of repairing the damage to his home and for injuries to his minor daughter, and he alleges damages in excess of $50,000. Palmer sued two defendants: the retailer, Dad's, a sole proprietorship in Waco, Texas (McLennan County); and Kurlee, Inc., the manufacturer, a Vermont corporation with its headquarters in Vermont.

Kurlee does in fact make curling irons, but maintains that it sells them only to distributors in New England and that it shipped no curling irons to Texas or to any intermediaries that do business in Texas.

1. You are counsel for Palmer. Based on the facts provided, what must Palmer plead and prove in order to invoke Texas Long-Arm Jurisdiction over Kurlee, Inc.?

2. You are counsel to Kurlee, Inc. State (a) what pleading you should file to contest personal jurisdiction; (b) what you should say in that pleading; (c) whether the pleading must be verified; (d) whether Kurlee's participating in discovery waives Kurlee's contest of jurisdiction; (e) in what forms you may present evidence for consideration by the court in deciding jurisdiction.

July 2002

Pam, a resident of Bowie County, was injured in a three-car automobile collision while she was driving her car in Travis County. The other two drivers were Don, a resident of Oklahoma, and Jim, who is a resident of Potter County. Pam sues both of the other drivers in state district court in Texas.

1. Don decides to contest the lawsuit. He has been served with citation through the Texas Secretary of State. In order to preserve his objection to jurisdiction in a Texas court: (a) what motion must Don file; (b) in what form must it be presented; and (c) when should he file it?

2. Don sends written discovery requests to Pam with his objection to jurisdiction. Pam contends that, by participating in discovery under the Texas Rules of Civil Procedure, Don has subjected himself to the jurisdiction of the Texas court and has waived his objection to jurisdiction. Assuming that this argument is properly raised by Pam, how should the court rule? Explain fully.

February 2003

Pat, doing business as "Wonder Widgets," is a retailer of specialized high tech widgets. Her store is in Fort Worth, Tarrant County, Texas. These widgets only function if constantly maintained at a regulated temperature. They must be handled carefully at each stage of the commercial chain by the manufacturer, shippers, wholesalers, and retailers.

Pat has two wholesale suppliers, Don Ho Wholesale Supply, Inc. ("Don Ho"), and Jim Dandy Specialty Warehouse, Inc. ("Jim Dandy"). The wholesalers warrant that the widgets have been kept continuously at the approved temperature. Both operate under identical contracts with Pat to deliver widgets, per her orders, to her warehouse in Tarrant County. Don Ho is incorporated and located in Kansas. Jim Dandy is incorporated in Texas and its principal office is in Denton County.

Pat has experienced numerous complaints from her customers about the widgets not performing as they should, allegedly because the temperature at which they have been stored has deviated from the approved temperature. Pat has received numerous returns of widgets and suffered serious loss of business as a result. Pat wants to bring one suit against both Don Ho and Jim Dandy.

Assume that Pat files suit against Don Ho and Jim Dandy in a state district court in Texas. What basis does Pat have for maintaining personal jurisdiction over Don Ho in Texas? Explain fully.

July 2005

Laura has been a life-long resident of Harris County, Texas. She was injured on January 15, 2002, when she slipped and fell in a grocery store in Dallas County, Texas. The owner and operator of the store was Food, Inc., a Texas corporation with its principal office in Bexar County. Laura returned home after the incident, but she never fully recovered from her injuries. Laura sought legal advice from a lawyer who practices in Travis County, Texas. The lawyer recommended that Laura file a lawsuit.

Laura's lawyer filed the lawsuit on January 14, 2004. He did not request the issuance of process until June 15, 2004. Defendant was served with the petition and citation on October 30, 2004. What affirmative defense, if any, should Defendant assert in its answer to the suit? Explain fully.

February 2009

Paul, a resident of Nueces County, Texas, went to the local hardware store, Supplies, Inc., ("Supplies"), to purchase an electric saw. Supplies is a Texas corporation with its principal place of business in Nueces County, Texas. After purchasing the saw, Paul asked David, a salesman for Supplies, to demonstrate how the saw operated. When David turned on the saw, its blade came loose, resulting in serious injuries to Paul's arm. David is a resident of San Patricio County, Texas. In addition to working for Supplies, David is also a representative for the manufacturer of the saw, Tools, Inc., ("Tools"), a Delaware corporation. Tools regularly advertises and sells its products in Texas through hardware stores like Supplies. Paul sues David, Supplies, and Tools in a state district court in Nueces County, Texas. Paul's lawsuit seeks damages resulting from the injuries he sustained in the incident in question. All of the defendants are properly served with citation and a copy of the original petition.

1. Tools wants to object to the jurisdiction of the Nueces County district court on the ground that it is not amenable to process issued by a Texas court. What pleading, if any, must Tools file to present such objection and when must it file such pleading? Explain fully.

2. Assume that Tools properly presents its objection to the Court's jurisdiction over it. What may the Court consider in ruling on the objection? How should the Court rule on the objection? Explain fully.

Chapter 5

VENUE

SCOPE

This chapter discusses venue within the state of Texas: in which county or counties can a case properly be heard? It also covers the procedures used for challenging and securing appellate review of venue decisions. The Texas scheme is somewhat complex: it includes both general rules and exceptions, provisions that are mandatory and others that are permissive. On top of that it contains a provision for transfer of venue in the interest of justice as well as a transfer to avoid local prejudice. In the cases, decisions about proper venue are intertwined with decisions about venue procedure, and so you should review some of the earlier materials when considering procedure later in the chapter.

§ 5.01 THE BASIC VENUE SCHEME

Texas venue law has gone through numerous changes. In early days it was heavily influenced by Spanish law, which insisted on fixing venue at the defendant's domicile, and this remained the basic scheme for years. As time went by, however, more and more statutory exceptions were added based on the type of cause of action or on the identity of the defendant. In addition, decisions on venue were immediately appealable, leading to much expense and delay. The first major overhaul came in 1983, along with new procedural rules and the elimination of interlocutory appeals. In 1995, however, the legislature again made wholesale revisions, primarily intended to limit the venue choices available to plaintiffs in actions against business entities, and brought back interlocutory appellate review in a few controversial areas.

The current general rule creates two primary options for venue: 1) the defendant's residence (humans) or principal office (entities); and 2) the place where important events or omissions occurred.

Read the following sections of the Civil Practice and Remedies Code.

§ 15.002. *Venue: General Rule.*

(a) Except as otherwise provided by this subchapter [general rule] or Subchapter B [mandatory venue exceptions] or C [permissive venue exceptions], all lawsuits shall be brought:

(1) in the county in which all or a substantial part of the events or omissions giving rise to the claim occurred;

(2) in the county of defendant's residence at the time the cause of action accrued if defendant is a natural person;

(3) in the county of the defendant's principal office in this state, if the defendant is not a natural person; or

(4) if Subdivisions (1), (2), and (3) do not apply [i.e. there is no county in Texas in which venue is proper under the general rule or exceptions], in the county in which the plaintiff resided at the time of the accrual of the cause of action.

§ 15.001. *Definitions.*

(b) "Proper venue" means:

(1) the venue required by the mandatory provisions of Subchapter B or another statute prescribing mandatory venue; or

(2) if Subdivision (1) does not apply, the venue provided by this subchapter [the general rule] or Subchapter C [permissive venue provisions].

The next two sections will consider the meanings of the general rule provisions. Although some were decided under earlier versions of the venue statutes, their interpretations of identical language should still be reliable. Note that pre-1983 cases may refer to the process of challenging venue as a "plea of privilege."

[A] Defendant's Residence (Natural Persons)

When a dispute arises about a person's "residence" for venue purposes, the court must decide whether the person has sufficient ties to the county to say that he or she resides there. This is different from identifying a person's permanent home. The next case discusses these issues.

MIJARES v. PAEZ

534 S.W.2d 435 (Tex. Civ. App. — Amarillo 1976, no writ)

ROBINSON, J.

Plaintiff Maria Rosario Paez brought a paternity suit against Carlos Javier Mijares in Lubbock County. Defendant Mijares [sought to have the venue of the action transferred to El Paso County and contended] . . . that the trial court "erred in finding" that appellant resided in Lubbock County for venue purposes . . . . Affirmed.

Defendant was not a minor at any time pertinent to this suit. He testified that he enrolled in Texas Tech University in Lubbock County, Texas, in January, 1974, and was still enrolled there in the fall semester of 1975. During the spring and fall semesters of 1974 he resided in university housing. He returned to El Paso during the summer of 1974 and at Christmas. He was enrolled in Texas Tech University during both the spring and summer semesters of 1975, as well as during the fall semester of 1975 when the hearing was held.

The defendant registered to vote in Lubbock County, listing his dormitory address in Lubbock County as his home address. At the time of the hearing, he was maintaining an apartment in Lubbock where he took his meals. He was served with citation in Lubbock County.

The defendant testified that he intended to complete a bachelor's degree at Texas Tech, but that he was only in Lubbock County to go to school, that he did not like Lubbock, and that it would never be his home.

When the defendant registered to vote in Lubbock County, giving his dormitory address as his residence, he represented that Lubbock County was his "current permanent residence address." V.A.T.S. Election Code, Art. 5.13b, subd.1(8).

Furthermore, the defendant could be a resident of Lubbock County for venue purposes even if his domicile were elsewhere. Although a person may have only one domicile, he may establish more than one residence for venue purposes. Even a rented room may qualify and the intent to make a permanent home is not necessary to the establishment of a second residence away from the domicile. *Snyder v. Pitts*, 241 S.W.2d 136, 150 Tex. 407 (1951). In *Snyder*, the Supreme Court announced a three element test to determine whether a second residence away from a domicile has been established. The proof must show that (1) the defendant possesses a fixed place of abode, (2) occupied or intended to be occupied consistently over a substantial period of time, (3) which is permanent rather than temporary.

The court in *Ward v. Lavy*, 314 S.W.2d 381 (Tex. Civ. App. — Eastland 1958, no writ) applied the *Snyder* test to facts similar to those before us. It held that a student at Hardin-Simmons University located in Taylor County had established residence in Taylor County for venue purposes by virtue of his enrollment in that university with the intention of remaining one or two years together with his rental of an apartment there.

We conclude that the trial court did not err in finding that the defendant was a resident of Lubbock County for venue purposes.

The order of the trial court overruling defendant's plea of privilege and retaining venue in Lubbock County is affirmed.

NOTES AND QUESTIONS

(1) *Distinguishing "Residence" and "Domicile."* As the court notes in *Mijares*, the concept of residence for venue is not the same as that of domicile. At least under the traditional approach, a person may have only one domicile. The Texas Supreme Court, in the *Snyder* case cited above, explained that *domicile* is the place where a person resides and has voluntarily fixed his abode, with an intention to remain and make such place his permanent home, and to which, whenever he is absent, he has the intention of eventually returning. The court also said that "intent to make it a permanent home" is not required for a *residence*, although it did list "permanent rather than temporary" as part of the residence requirement. What's the difference?

(2) *Applying the Venue Residence Test.* What is a "substantial period of time"? Would six months qualify? The issue may involve intent as much as it does the duration of the time period. What does "permanent" mean in light of the result

reached in *Mijares*? In *Snyder*, the court found that defendant's residence was sufficiently permanent, holding:

> Defendant Snyder had been regularly and consistently commuting between his room in Dalhart and his home in Vernon for a period of fifteen months at the time the plea of privilege was filed and for two years at the time it was tried. The question of whether a stay is temporary or permanent is a question of intent to be proved by declarations and acts. Here the Defendant Snyder made excursions out from Dalhart and returned. It was headquarters for his business. Under the facts here there is no dispute that Defendant Snyder had not abandoned his plan for living part time in Dalhart. Defendant Snyder occupied consistently and with continuity a fixed place of abode in Dalhart in such a manner that the trial court could find that he had ceased to be a visitor and that the proof supplied this element of the definition of a residence.

241 S.W.2d at 141 (citations omitted).

(3) *The Relevant Moment in Time for "Residence."* The "general rule" (*see* C.P.R.C. § 15.002, above) and most exceptions focus on the residence of natural persons at the time the cause of action accrued rather than on residence at the time suit was filed.

(4) *Venue at Plaintiff's Residence.* Suit can be brought in the county in which the plaintiff resides at the time the cause of action accrued only if C.P.R.C. § 15.002(1)–(3) do not apply. C.P.R.C. § 15.002(4). As a result, venue is ordinarily not proper in the county of plaintiff's residence. In fact, only two mandatory exceptions (*see* C.P.R.C. §§ 15.017, 15.018) and two permissive exceptions (*see* C.P.R.C. §§ 15.032, 15.033) offer the plaintiff's residence (at the time when the cause of action accrued) as a venue choice.

(5) *No Valid Claim Against Resident Defendant.* When the claim that the plaintiff has asserted against the resident defendant is legally invalid, the fact of residence alone will not provide a basis for proper venue. *Garrett v. Patterson-UTI Drilling Co., L.P.*, 299 S.W.3d 911, 914 (Tex. App. — Eastland 2009, no pet.). In *Union Pacific RR Co. v. Cezar*, 293 S.W.3d 800 (Tex. App. — Beaumont 2009, no pet.), plaintiffs sued a number of defendants for injuries caused when a train hit a pickup truck at a crossing in Vinton, Louisiana. The case was filed in Jefferson County, Texas, and the plaintiffs alleged that venue was proper there because an individual defendant, Mann, resided in Jefferson County. Mann was a claims investigator who had investigated prior accidents at the same crossing where this accident occurred but who had not closed the crossing or posted warnings there. When the case went to trial, Mann was still a defendant, but the trial court granted a directed verdict in his favor. The court of appeals agreed with the directed verdict, holding that Mann owed no duty to the travelling public, including the plaintiffs, as a matter of law. Therefore, proper venue in Jefferson County could not be sustained based on Mann's residence there.

Notice the serious consequences that can attend this kind of problem. Although the plaintiffs had won a judgment against Union Pacific that was supported by some evidence, the case was reversed and remanded to the trial court with instructions to transfer the case to Harris County, where the railroad's principal office was located, for a new trial. (On appeal, venue is judged based on the whole record, and trial in a county of improper venue is never harmless error. *See* § 5.03, *infra*; CIV. PRAC. & REM. CODE § 15.064(b)).

[B] Defendant's Principal Office (Legal Persons)

C.P.R.C. § 15.001. *Definitions.* In this chapter:

(a) "Principal office" means a principal office of the corporation, unincorporated association, or partnership in this state in which the decision makers for the organization within this state conduct the daily affairs of the organization. The mere presence of an agency or representative does not establish a principal office.

For many companies, it may be easy to determine where a "principal office" lies. But what about companies that do business throughout Texas? What is the test for "principal office"? And can a company have more than one? Consider the following case.

IN RE MISSOURI PACIFIC RAILROAD CO.

998 S.W.2d 212 (Tex. 1999)

GONZALEZ, J.

These consolidated mandamus proceedings concern the mandatory venue statute for suits brought under the Federal Employers' Liability Act (FELA). In each case the key issue is whether the plaintiff in the underlying lawsuit sued the corporate defendant in a county where it maintains "a principal office," as defined in the venue statutes. We conclude that the plaintiffs in all of the suits failed to prove that the corporate defendant has a principal office in the county of suit, so we direct the trial courts in Jefferson County and Tarrant County to transfer the cases to a proper county.

I

These mandamus proceedings arise out of three FELA lawsuits filed in Jefferson County, and three filed in Tarrant County. Section 15.018(b) of the venue statutes gives three choices:

> (b) All suits brought under [FELA] shall be brought:
>
> (1) in the county in which all or a substantial part of the events or omissions giving rise to the claim occurred;
>
> (2) in the county where the defendant's principal office in this state is located; or
>
> (3) in the county where the plaintiff resided at the time the cause of action accrued.

Subparts (b)(1) and (b)(3) do not apply here because none of the plaintiffs reside in the county of suit and none claim the cause of action arose there. All the plaintiffs in the Jefferson County cases claim damages for an injury occurring outside of Texas. Freddie Burleigh, a Louisiana resident, sued his employer, Missouri Pacific Railroad Company (Mo-Pac), for injuries he suffered in Louisiana. Terriance Spiller and Juanita Spiller, residents of Harris County, sued Mo-Pac for injuries Terriance Spiller received in Louisiana. Tamara L. Weston resides in Dalhart, Hartley County. She sued Southern Pacific Transportation Company and Mo-Pac in Jefferson County for an injury she suffered near Obar, New Mexico.

Each plaintiff in the Tarrant County suits against Union Pacific Railroad alleged he suffered an injury in his home state outside Texas. Ronald E. Smirl, a resident of Oklahoma, sued for an injury suffered in Chickasha, Oklahoma. Bobby Ray Martin, a Louisiana resident, sued for an incident occurring in Shreveport, Louisiana. Willie B. Williams is a resident of Arkansas who alleges an injury in Gurdon, Arkansas.

The venue challenges proceeded much the same in all the cases. The plaintiff alleged that the railroad maintained a principal office in the county of suit. The railroad denied that it had a principal office in the county of suit or that venue was proper there, and moved to transfer venue to Harris County where the railroad had principal offices in Texas. In each case the trial court denied the motion and retained venue, resulting in these mandamus proceedings.

II

Section 15.0642 of the Texas Civil Practice and Remedies Code directs appellate courts to enforce the mandatory venue statutes by mandamus:

> A party may apply for a writ of mandamus with an appellate court to enforce the mandatory venue provisions of this chapter. An application for the writ of mandamus must be filed before the later of:
>
> (1) the 90th day before the date the trial starts; or
>
> (2) the 10th day after the date the party receives notice of the trial setting.

Section 15.0642 does not detail the scope of mandamus review of mandatory venue decisions. Traditionally, mandamus will not issue (1) unless the trial court has committed a clear abuse of discretion, (2) for which appeal is not an adequate remedy. We determined in a prior case that the usual mandamus standard of review, abuse of discretion, applies to a section 15.0642 mandamus. But we have not considered whether a party challenging a mandatory venue decision also must show that appeal is an inadequate remedy. The railroads argue that it is presumed that there is no adequate remedy for a failure to enforce a mandatory venue statute-, . . . [because] it would undermine the purpose of section 15.0642 if a relator were forced to show inadequate remedy by appeal. We agree.

We have repeatedly denied mandamus to review the merits of a venue decision because we considered it an incidental trial ruling correctable by appeal. Before 1983, venue rulings were immediately correctable by interlocutory appeal under the former plea of privilege practice. In 1983, the Legislature replaced interlocutory venue appeals with the rule that in an ordinary post-trial appeal, improper venue is not subject to harmless error analysis, virtually guaranteeing reversal[1] . . . .

We reiterated in early 1995 that "Texas law is quite clear that venue determinations are not reviewable by mandamus." But a few months later, the Legislature enacted section 15.0642 authorizing parties to seek mandamus "to enforce the mandatory venue provisions," along with a timetable for seeking mandamus. The Legislature left in place the "presumed harm" rule for challenging venue in an appeal after trial. Thus, section 15.0642 poses a conundrum: venue decisions are not reviewable by mandamus because they are correctable by appeal, but section 15.0642 authorizes mandamus review of mandatory venue decisions. Either the availability of mandamus relief under the statute is largely illusory, or we must dispense with the requirement of showing inadequate appellate remedy in mandatory venue cases.

Our goal in construing a statute is to carry out the Legislature's intent. The language of section 15.0642 seems to contemplate a review of the merits of the trial court's decision on mandatory venue. Yet if we still insist on a particularized showing of inadequate remedy by appeal, then a court could rarely, if ever, "enforce the mandatory venue provisions" by mandamus . . . . We do not lightly presume that the Legislature may have done a useless act. Rather, we presume the Legislature intended "a result feasible of execution." To effectuate the Legislature's intent, we conclude that adequacy of an appellate remedy is not a requisite of a mandatory venue mandamus under section 15.0642.

III

Thus, the focus of a mandamus proceeding under section 15.0642 is whether the trial court abused its discretion. The trial court has no discretion in determining the legal principles controlling its ruling or in applying the law to the facts. A trial court does not have the discretion to make an erroneous legal conclusion even in an unsettled area of law. Therefore, we review in these cases whether the trial courts failed to analyze or apply the law correctly when they refused to transfer the cases to the defendants' chosen venue.

The parties' pleading and proof limits a trial court's discretion to determine venue. A plaintiff's choice of venue stands unless challenged by proper motion to transfer venue. Once challenged, the plaintiff has the burden to present prima facie proof by affidavit or other appropriate evidence that venue is maintainable in the county of suit. The plaintiff's prima facie proof is not subject to rebuttal, cross-examination, impeachment, or disproof. However, if the plaintiff fails to discharge the burden, the right to choose a proper venue passes to the defendant, who must then prove that venue is proper in the defendant's chosen county. The controlling issue here is what the plaintiffs had to plead and prove to establish venue in "the

[1] On rare occasion we have issued mandamus to correct improper venue procedure but not to review the propriety of venue in the county of suit. *See, e.g.*, *In re Masonite*, 997 S.W.2d 194 (Tex. 1999); *HCA Health Serv., Inc. v. Salinas*, 838 S.W.2d 246, 248 (Tex. 1992); *Union Carbide Corp. v. Moye*, 798 S.W.2d 792, 793 (Tex. 1990); *Henderson v. O'Neill*, 797 S.W.2d 905, 905 (Tex. 1990).

county where the defendant's principal office in this state is located" under the FELA venue statute.

The railroads contend that a foreign corporation only has one principal office under the mandatory venue statutes for FELA actions. If the FELA venue statute is read in isolation, the provision for suit "in the county where the defendant's principal office in this state is located" would indicate a company's Texas headquarters. However, that view is complicated by the general definition of "principal office" in section 15.001:

In this chapter:

> (a) "Principal office" means a principal office of the corporation . . . in this state in which the decision makers for the organization within this state conduct the daily affairs of the organization. The mere presence of an agency or representative does not establish a principal office.

The plaintiffs respond that the phrase "*a* principal office" indicates that there can be more than one principal office. Further, the plaintiffs argue, the "daily affairs" of these defendants consist of operating trains, so that a principal office is wherever a railroad official makes decisions about operating trains.

We agree with the plaintiffs that a corporation can have more than one principal office. We are bound by the statutory definition of "principal office" as "a" principal office. Thus, when we apply the general definition of "principal office" to the FELA venue statute, we must assume a defendant company could have more than one principal office.

But we reject the plaintiffs' argument that the statute clearly defines a principal office as any place where a company official makes decisions about the company's business. Such a broad definition would include agencies and representatives, which the statute expressly rejects. Agencies and representatives, as we defined them under the former venue statutes, are officials who possess broad power and discretion to act for the corporation. Thus, "decision makers" who "conduct the daily affairs" are officials of a different order than agents or representatives. Moreover, even though "a principal office" suggests there can be more than one office, the term "principal" indicates some sort of primacy. It is unlikely that an office clearly subordinate to and controlled by another Texas office could be "a principal office." Finally, in context, "the daily affairs" of a company cannot mean relatively common, low-level managerial decisions.

Beyond these preliminary observations, the statute is not entirely clear in all its particulars. The language of the statute could support more than one reasonable interpretation and therefore is ambiguous. Because it is ambiguous, we may turn to extratextual sources such as the statute's legislative history.

IV

Sections 15.001 and 15.018 codify parts of Senate Bill 32, enacted by the 74th Legislature. The railroads contend that Senate Bill 32's legislative history supports its interpretation of the venue statutes. The plaintiffs argue to the contrary, that the bill's history supports their own interpretation. Both the House and Senate proposed changes to the venue statutes for corporations during the 74th regular session of the Legislature, House Bill 6 and Senate Bill 32. As the plaintiffs readily concede, and legislative history bears out, a major purpose of the 1995 amendments was to reduce or limit forum shopping. As initially proposed, Senate Bill 32 did not define "principal office." The Senate Committee on Economic Development added the definition of "a" principal office, but also provided that courts would determine a single county as the principal office in this state for any corporate defendant.

The definition of "a principal office" remained in Senate Bill 32, but the provision for a single principal office was not included in the version the Senate adopted on April 19, 1995. The House substituted House Bill 6 with Senate Bill 32 and amended section 15.001(a) to provide that the mere presence of an agency or representative does not establish a principal office. The House passed Senate Bill 32 as amended on May 4, 1995, and the Senate concurred four days later . . . .

We find nothing in the legislative history to dissuade us from our initial observations about the meaning of section 15.001. Rather, the legislative history supports our conclusion that: (1) a company may have more than one principal office, (2) the "decision makers" who conduct the "daily affairs" of the company are officials who run the company day to day, (3) a mere agent or representative is not a "decision maker" nor is a principal office one where only decisions typical of an agency or representative are made, and (4) a principal office is not an office clearly subordinate to and controlled by another Texas office.

The debates on the floor of the House and the Senate confirm that the Legislature did not intend to limit venue to only one county where the company maintains a corporate office if the facts do not warrant it. A company may control or direct its daily affairs in Texas through decision makers of substantially equal responsibility and authority in different offices in the state. In that case each office may be a principal office of the company.

Necessarily, courts must look at the corporation's structure to determine a company's principal office or offices. The titles of the company officials in a particular office are not as informative as a description of their responsibility and authority, relative to other company officials within the state. We recognize that our interpretation does not provide a precise test. But we believe the Legislature intended a flexible test to allow for the myriad forms that corporate structures can take.

V

. . . .

The plaintiffs' evidence focused largely on the extent of operations and equipment in Jefferson County, Texas. The evidence showed that the railroad's corporate headquarters were in Omaha, Nebraska, and many of the executive and administrative decisions were made there. The evidence did little to define the role of any of the decision makers in Jefferson County relative to the rest of the company in Texas. A party cannot prove a prima facie case that a county has a principal office without evidence of the corporate structure and the authority of the officers in the county of suit as compared with the remainder of the state. The only company officials in Jefferson County the plaintiffs' evidence identified were a manager of train operations, a manager of yard operations, and a "maintenance and way" foreman. There was testimony that the railroads' corporate headquarters delegated some policy-making to the local level. However, there is little evidence of the kinds of decisions the Jefferson County officials could make. More importantly, there is no evidence of how the Jefferson County officials' authority compared to others statewide, so that the court could make a meaningful determination whether Jefferson County is in any sense a "principal office."

VI

The Tarrant County plaintiffs put on more extensive evidence of Union Pacific's organization structure in Texas. Union Pacific is divided into four regions. The southern region includes most of Texas and parts of Louisiana. The southern region is further divided into six divisions. In answer to interrogatories, the railroad identified the "decision makers" who office in Harris County as a general solicitor, a vice president for transportation, a general manager, two general supervisors, a chief engineer, and two division superintendents. All but the division superintendents are considered executive officers of the company. The former general solicitor stated in a deposition that "the real policy decisions and real serious operational decisions are made by persons at the level of superintendent or above." The only official the plaintiffs claim is a "decision maker" in Tarrant County is a division superintendent for the Fort Worth service unit. He testified in his deposition that his duties included coordinating the movement of trains, staffing the crews within the area, and ensuring rules compliance and discipline. The division superintendent also said that the southern region is based in Houston, and his boss is the general manager in Harris County.

This evidence is sufficient to characterize a division superintendent as a decision maker under the statute. However, it fails to establish prima facie that the Tarrant County office is a principal office when compared to the responsibility and authority exercised by company officials elsewhere in Texas. The evidence shows that the division superintendent in Tarrant County is not an executive officer and has the least authority of any of the decision makers with any real discretion or authority. In contrast, there are six executive officers in Harris County. The two highest ranking officers in Texas, general solicitors, conduct the affairs of the railroad from offices in Harris County. They oversee legal affairs such as FELA litigation in Texas for the railroads. The general manager of transportation is responsible for the transportation plan for the southern region of the Company, which includes Texas and Louisiana. The general manager supervises the assistant general manager and the general superintendent. The general supervisor also supervises six division superintendents, two in Houston, three in other Texas offices, and one in Louisiana. The general superintendent performs the logistics for deciding train starts and yard starts. Finally, the chief engineer directs the activities of local maintenance-of-way and signal service units throughout the region.

VII

The plaintiffs failed to establish Jefferson County or Tarrant County as principal offices of the railroads. The burden shifted to the defendants to prove that Harris County is a proper venue. The venue facts bear out that Harris County is "a" principal office of the railroads, and therefore a proper venue under the mandatory FELA statute. The trial courts abused their discretion by not sustaining the motions to transfer. Accordingly, we conditionally issue writs of mandamus directing the trial courts to sustain the railroads' motions to transfer the cases to Harris County. The writs will not issue unless the trial courts fail to act in accordance with this opinion.

NOTES AND QUESTIONS

(1) *Mandamus Review.* In addition to discussing the meaning of "principal office," this case is noteworthy for its discussion of the availability of immediate review (through mandamus) of mandatory venue rulings. The Civil Practice and Remedies Code provides for mandamus review of venue rulings in order to "enforce" the mandatory venue provisions. In *Missouri Pacific Railroad*, the Court held that the legislature intended section 15.0642 to provide for immediate review of mandatory venue rulings. Therefore, despite the fact that the vehicle for review is "mandamus," these cases need not satisfy the normal requirement that there be no adequate remedy by appeal.

The Court has also allowed the use of mandamus to provide an immediate review of a venue ruling when the trial court has used an improper procedure. *See In re Masonite Corp.*, 997 S.W.2d 194 (Tex. 1999); *In re Team Rocket, L.P.*, 256 S.W.3d 257 (Tex. 2008).

(2) *How Much Authority is Required?* Under the 1995 version of the venue statutes, a corporation could often be sued in the county in which it had an "agent or representative." As under the current statute, disputes centered around the level of activity that a corporation needed to have in a county before it could be sued there. The Texas Supreme Court had held that "agency or representative" required the presence of an employee with broad discretionary powers. *Ruiz v. Conoco, Inc.*, 868 S.W.2d 752, 759 (Tex. 1993). The Court in *Missouri Pacific* says that a mere "agency or representative" is not enough to meet the requirements of a "principal office." When do broad discretionary powers (not enough for a principal office) shade into " 'decision makers' who conduct the 'daily affairs' of the company [and] run the company day to day" (sufficient for principal office)?

(3) *Single Texas Office. Missouri Pacific* dealt with a situation in which a corporation had multiple Texas offices, and the Court required evidence comparing the functions of the different offices. What if a corporation has its main office outside of Texas, but does have one Texas office. Is that office by definition a "principal office"? Does it have to have a decision maker with greater power than an "agency or representative"? If so, would authority over all of the Texas operations be sufficient, even if those operations are comparatively limited?

[C] County in Which All or a Substantial Part of the Events or Omissions Giving Rise to the Claim Occurred

In addition to residence and principal office, venue is proper under the general rule in any county where "all or a substantial part of the events or omissions giving rise to the claim occurred." The language is modeled after the federal venue statute, 28 U.S.C. § 1391. Under the federal statute, it is clear that there may be more than one district that meets the definition. Texas courts have begun to interpret this new language, trying to discern when events are sufficiently central to a claim to qualify as a "substantial part." Consider the following cases.

[1] Tort Claims

VELASCO v. TEXAS KENWORTH CO.

144 S.W.3d 632 (Tex. App. — Dallas 2004, pet. denied)

MORRIS, J.

In this wrongful death case, appellant Rutilio Ignacio Velasco, individually and as next friend to Jose Velasco, a minor, Erick Velasco, a minor, and Steven Velasco, a minor, and as Representative of the Estate of Gloria Oviedo Velasco, appeals the trial court's final judgment dismissing his claims with prejudice. On appeal, appellant . . . asserts his case was improperly transferred from Johnson County to Dallas County . . . . Because we conclude appellant's case was transferred to Dallas County in error, we vacate the Dallas County trial court's final summary judgment and remand the case to that court for transfer back to the trial court in Johnson County.

Appellant filed this lawsuit after his wife died in a multi-vehicle collision in Johnson County, Texas. In his petition, appellant alleged that a used Kenworth semi-tractor purchased by Johnson County from the Kenworth appellees shortly before the accident had faulty brakes and was a proximate cause of the collision. Appellant asserted claims for negligence, strict liability, breach of warranty, and misrepresentation. Kenworth filed an answer denying each allegation in appellant's petition and filed a motion to transfer the case from Johnson County to Dallas County [because Kenworth's principal place of business was in Dallas County] . . . . Appellant asserted venue was proper in Johnson County because it is the location where a substantial part of the events or omissions giving rise to his claims occurred . . . . The trial court . . . granted Kenworth's motion to transfer appellant's lawsuit to Dallas County. In Dallas, Kenworth filed a traditional and a no-evidence motion for summary judgment. The trial court granted summary judgment in Kenworth's favor and rendered a final judgment . . . . It is from this judgment that appellant appeals.

In his first point of error, appellant complains about the trial court's order transferring his lawsuit from Johnson County to Dallas County. Texas venue law is well-established. The plaintiff has the first choice to fix venue in a proper county. *See Wilson v. Texas Parks & Wildlife Dept.*, 886 S.W.2d 259, 261 (Tex. 1994). It is

reversible error to transfer venue from a proper venue even if the county of transfer would have been proper if originally chosen by the plaintiff. *See id.* at 262. To determine whether a trial court improperly transferred the case, we must consider the entire record, including any trial on the merits. *Ruiz v. Conoco, Inc.*, 868 S.W.2d 752, 758 (Tex. 1993). If there is any probative evidence that supports venue in the county of suit, the trial court must deny the transfer. *Bonham State Bank v. Beadle*, 907 S.W.2d 465, 471 (Tex. 1995). This is true even if the evidence preponderates to the contrary. *Id.*

In the case before us, appellant relies on section 15.002(a)(1) of the Texas Civil Practices and Remedies Code to establish venue in Johnson County. This section provides that venue is proper in the county where "all or a substantial part of the events or omissions giving rise to the claim occurred." Tex. Civ. Prac. & Rem. Code Ann. § 15.002(a)(1). This provision limits the number of counties where venue can be maintained to those with a substantial connection with the lawsuit. *Chiriboga v. State Farm Mut. Auto Ins. Co.*, 96 S.W.3d 673, 681 (Tex. App. — Austin 2003, no pet.). Appellant's factual basis for maintaining venue in Johnson County is that Johnson County is where the accident occurred, where appellant's wife died, where the bid for the semi-tractor was submitted and opened by Johnson County representatives, and where [defendant Mark] Sims talked to Johnson County representatives about the semi-tractor. Thus, appellant contends, Johnson County became the site for a substantial part of the facts giving rise to his claims. We agree.

Appellant's wrongful death claim arose when his wife died in the accident in Johnson County. *See Ray v. Farris*, 887 S.W.2d 164, 166 (Tex. App. — Texarkana 1994, *rev'd on other grounds*, 895 S.W.2d 351 (Tex. 1995)). Additionally, appellant's petition complains about the failure of Kenworth to inform or warn Johnson County about the dangerous condition of the semi-tractor, the breach of various warranties contained in the bid proposal, and misrepresentations made to Johnson County with respect to the character or quality of the semi-tractor. Appellant complains that these omissions or acts occurred at the time the bid was delivered to Johnson County representatives in Johnson County. Because a substantial number of the essential facts upon which appellant's claims are based occurred in Johnson County, we conclude venue was proper in Johnson County.

Conceding that there is no dispute that appellant's claim arose when the accident occurred in Johnson County, Kenworth argues that for purposes of a venue analysis under subsection (a)(1), we must focus solely on the defendant's action or inaction giving rise to appellant's claims. Specifically, Kenworth asserts that because appellant's petition alleges that it failed to properly repair, service, or inspect the brakes on the semi-tractor, Tarrant County is the proper venue under subsection (a)(1) because that is where these alleged acts or omissions occurred. Initially, we note that there is no indication that the present venue statute contemplates only one county can satisfy the requirements of subsection (a)(1). Indeed at least one appellate court has concluded more than one county may qualify as proper venue under subsection (a)(1) provided a "substantial part of the event or omissions" giving rise to the claim occurred there. *See Southern County Mut. Ins. Co. v. Ochoa*, 19 S.W.3d 452, 458 (Tex. App. — Corpus Christi 2000). Therefore, to succeed on its motion to transfer, Kenworth had to establish that no substantial part of the events giving rise to appellant's claims occurred in Johnson County, not merely that a substantial part of the events or omissions occurred in another county. Kenworth has failed to do so. Even assuming that Tarrant County qualified as a county where a substantial part of the events or omissions giving rise to appellant's cause of action occurred, there was probative evidence that Johnson County also satisfied subsection (a)(1)'s requirements. Accordingly, the trial court erred in transferring the case from Johnson County.

Although our research has revealed no Texas case directly on point, we find support for our conclusion in several federal cases. Because subsection (a)(1) appears to have been patterned after a federal venue statute, we may presume the legislature intended to adopt the construction placed on that wording by the federal courts and look to federal cases to guide our interpretation of the state statute. *See id.* at 457. The ninth circuit has reasoned that because the harm a plaintiff experienced occurred in Nevada, venue was proper there as the location where a substantial part of the events and omission giving rise to the claim occurred. *See Myers v. Bennett Law Offices*, 238 F.3d 1068, 1075 (9th Cir. 2001). In product liability cases against manufacturers, other courts have stated the accident or crash constituted a substantial part of the events giving rise to the claim such that venue is appropriate where the crash or accident occurred. *Cali v. East Coast Aviation Servs., Ltd.*, 178 F. Supp. 2d 276, 282 (E.D.N.Y. 2001) (venue proper where airplane crashed); *Roll v. Tracor, Inc.*, 26 F. Supp. 2d 482, 485 (W.D.N.Y. 1998) (venue proper where accident occurred); and *Dwyer v. General Motors Corp.*, 853 F. Supp. 690, 692 (S.D.N.Y. 1994). Contrary to Kenworth's position, federal courts have interpreted the subsection (a)(1)'s federal counterpart to allow venue in a district where acts or omissions closely related to the legal action occurred, even if none of those acts or omissions were the act or omission that allegedly caused the injury. *See e.g., Ciena Corp. v. Jarrard*, 203 F.3d 312, 315–16 (4th Cir. 2000).

Because the accident, appellant's wife's death, and other events of which appellant complains occurred in Johnson County, we conclude that Johnson County has a close connection to this lawsuit and that the requirements of subsection (a)(1) have been satisfied. We therefore sustain appellant's first point of error. Because our determination on the venue question is dispositive, we do not address appellant's remaining points of error. *See* Tex. R. App. P. 47.1.

We vacate the judgment of the trial court and remand this case to the trial court for transfer to the Johnson County trial court for further proceedings consistent with this opinion.

NOTE

Torts: Breach vs. Injury. In *Eddins v. Parker*, 63 S.W.3d 15 (Tex. App. — El Paso 2001, pet. denied), the plaintiff filed suit in Harris County, alleging that the defendant doctor negligently treated her in Grayson County, but that she suffered the consequences of that negligence in Harris County. The court held that since the doctor treated the patient in Grayson County, that was "the only county in which all or a substantial part of the events or omissions giving rise to the claim occurred."

[2] Contract Claims

KW CONSTRUCTION v. STEPHENS & SONS CONCRETE CONTRACTORS, INC.

165 S.W.3d 874 (Tex. App. — Texarkana 2005, pet. denied)

CARTER, J.

KW Construction appeals the judgment entered following a bench trial in which plaintiff, Stephens & Sons Concrete Contractors, Inc., recovered $12,500.00, plus pre- and post-judgment interest and $7,500.00 in attorney's fees in its suit for breach of an oral contract or, in the alternative, under a theory of quantum meruit. Stephens & Sons alleged there existed an oral contract between the parties in which the parties agreed that Stephens & Sons would repair and construct certain concrete structures under a general contract awarded to KW Construction by the Sabine River Authority (SRA) to construct an office complex in Rains County. After a payment dispute went unresolved, Stephens & Sons brought suit in Lamar County. KW Construction unsuccessfully moved the trial court to transfer the case to Rains County. On appeal, KW Construction complains of the trial court's refusal to transfer the case. KW Construction also contends there is legally and factually insufficient evidence to support both the conclusion that an oral contract was formed between the parties and the trial court's finding of $12,500.00 as the reasonable value of work performed. We will affirm.

I. FACTUAL AND PROCEDURAL HISTORY

KW Construction is a sole proprietorship owned by Kenneth Brown, with its primary place of business in Rains County. KW Construction was awarded the general contract for the SRA to build an office complex in Rains County. The original concrete subcontractor left the job before completion of the concrete work. The work that had been completed to that point was unacceptable because it was not level.

In 1999, Brown contacted Todd Stephens of Stephens & Sons Concrete Contractors, Inc. to discuss the task of repairing and completing the concrete work. Brothers Todd and Paul Stephens traveled from the company's office in Lamar County to meet with Brown and Steve Hunt and to assess the project at the job site in Rains County. After the site inspection, the men met at Brown's house in Rains County to further discuss the project.

Initially, Stephens and Brown agreed that Stephens & Sons would "cap" the defective slab, if the SRA approved the procedure, and complete the remaining concrete work. The "capping" process would have taken approximately two to three days to complete. According to Stephens' testimony, he and Brown agreed that the price associated with the "capping" process would not exceed $18,000.00, the amount representing the remainder of the amount KW Construction had budgeted for construction work on the SRA project. A few days later, Brown called Stephens at his office in Lamar County to inform him that the SRA had rejected the "capping" process as a repair. During this telephone conversation, the two agreed instead that Stephens & Sons would grind and level the existing 5,568 square feet of defective concrete slab, a more difficult and more expensive process than "capping." In addition, Stephens & Sons was to pour approximately 200 square feet of structural slab; pour 2,352 square feet of sidewalk, mechanical pad, and porch; and pour 916 linear feet of curb and gutter.

A dispute concerning payment arose and, eventually, Stephens & Sons left the job incomplete for nonpayment, having substantially completed the grinding and leveling of the defective concrete slab and having poured approximately 100 linear feet of curb and gutter, 215 square feet of porch, and 200 square feet of structural slab. The payment dispute continued and resulted in litigation. Stephens & Sons brought suit in Lamar County against KW Construction to recover funds owed to Stephens & Sons under an oral contract or, alternatively, under a theory of quantum meruit. KW Construction unsuccessfully moved the trial court to transfer the case to Rains County.

II. VENUE

A. Permissive Venue and Review of Ruling on Motion to Transfer Venue

First, we note that a substantial part of the events or omissions giving rise to a claim may occur in more than one county. *See Southern County Mut. Ins. Co. v. Ochoa*, 19 S.W.3d 452, 458 (Tex. App. — Corpus Christi 2000, no pet.). Plaintiffs are accorded the right to choose venue first as long as suit is initially filed in a county of proper venue. *Wilson v. Texas Parks & Wildlife Dep't*, 886 S.W.2d 259, 261 (Tex. 1994). When the county in which the plaintiff files suit is at least a permissive venue and when no mandatory provision applies, the plaintiff's venue choice cannot be disturbed. *See id.*; *Chiriboga v. State Farm Mut. Auto. Ins. Co.*, 96 S.W.3d 673, 677 (Tex. App. — Austin 2003, no pet.). If the parties' dispute involves two counties of permissive venue, transferring the case is improper. *Wilson*, 886 S.W.2d at 262.

[The court then discussed the proper procedure for asserting and challenging venue and for review of venue determinations on appeal.]

In this case, no mandatory venue provision applies. Therefore, venue here is governed by the general venue rule contained in Section 15.002(a) . . . .

The language pertinent to the venue issue before us is found in Section 15.002(a)(1), which provides that venue is proper in the county where "all or a substantial part of the events or omissions giving rise to the claim occurred." Tex. Civ. Prac. & Rem. Code Ann. § 15.002(a)(1). We must determine whether the record contains any probative evidence to support the trial court's implied ruling that "all or a substantial part of" the events giving rise to this suit occurred in Lamar County.

B. Venue Facts

KW Construction maintains its place of business in Rains County; Stephens & Sons maintains its place of business in Lamar County. The record is clear that Brown first contacted Stephens & Sons by placing a telephone call to Stephens in

Lamar County. After the initial telephone conversation, the Stephens brothers traveled to Rains County to assess the project. Brown then again called Stephens' office in Lamar County. The parties disagree as to whether they agreed to a price during this telephone conversation and, if so, on what price they agreed. But it is undisputed that, during this telephone call, the men came to an agreement as to the scope of the work to be done, since Brown informed Stephens that the SRA rejected the "capping" proposal. Instead, the two men agreed during this conversation that Stephens & Sons would grind and level the defective slab.

Subsequently, all the concrete work was performed in Rains County. By affidavit, Stephens stated it was agreed that payment was to be sent to Stephens & Sons in Lamar County. Brown sent to the Stephens & Sons office in Lamar County a check in the amount of $4,717.00 bearing the notation "paid in full." Stephens returned the check. The trial court concluded that the parties agreed that payment would be made in Lamar County.

C. Former Venue Provision: Accrual of a Cause of Action

Before 1995, the relevant venue provision did not contain a substantiality requirement and, instead, pointed to "the county in which all or part of the cause of action accrued." *See Krchnak v. Fulton*, 759 S.W.2d 524, 525 (Tex. App. — Amarillo 1988, writ denied). A "cause of action" consists of a plaintiff's primary right and the defendant's act or omission which violates that right. *Id.* at 526. A "cause of action" comprises every fact which is necessary for a plaintiff to prove in order to obtain judgment. *Id.* The accrual of a cause of action means the right to institute and maintain a suit, and whenever one person may sue another, a cause of action has accrued. *Id.* The court in *Krchnak* noted that, as early as 1854, the Texas Supreme Court held that, in a suit for breach of contract, the contract, its performance, and its breach were all essential parts of the cause of action. *Phillio v. Blythe*, 12 Tex. 124, 127–28 (1854); *Krchnak v. Fulton*, 759 S.W.2d 524 at 526.

To illustrate, we look to a case that, although decided under the "all or part" language of the pre-1995 venue provisions, is factually analogous to the case before us. In *Krchnak*, plaintiff Fulton and defendant Krchnak entered into an oral agreement that Fulton would board Krchnak's mare. The mare was to be boarded and services rendered in Lee County. The defendant was a resident of Austin County. After Krchnak's failure to pay for Fulton's services, Fulton brought suit in Lubbock County, alleging that the agreement was entered into in Lubbock County and that the agreement provided that payment was to be made in Lubbock County.

The essential elements, then, of Fulton's cause of action were that an agreement existed under which services were rendered by appellee for which payment was not made by appellant. The court went on to conclude that "[a] part of that underlying contract would be an agreement that payment would be made in Lubbock County." *Id.* Venue was proper in Lubbock County because Fulton's prima facie proof showed that the agreement to pay for his services was entered into in Lubbock County and that the contract provided for payment to be made in Lubbock County. Again, under the former general rule, the court held that the "cause of action accrued" in Lubbock County. *Id.*; *see also Whitworth v. Kuhn*, 734 S.W.2d 108, 111 (Tex. App. — Austin 1987, no writ) (cause of action for breach of lease accrued in county where rental payments to be made, although leased premises were in different county).

Both parties rely to an extent on the opinion in *Krchnak*. KW Construction distinguishes the rule in *Krchnak* to support its argument that the place to which KW Construction sent partial payment is not an element of Stephens & Sons' cause of action. Going further, KW Construction points out that no longer is any fact connected to the lawsuit sufficient to establish venue as it was under the venue scheme prior to the 1995 amendments. *See Chiriboga*, 96 S.W.3d at 681. Stephens & Sons relies on the rule in *Krchnak* for the proposition that, if payment under a contract is to be made in a certain county but a party fails to make payment, a cause of action for breach of contract accrues in the county in which payment was to be received. Stephens & Sons argue that, according to *Krchnak*, the telephone discussions in which Brown first contacted Stephens & Sons and in which the two came to an agreement regarding the scope of the work to be done and Brown's later failure to pay Stephens & Sons in accordance with the terms of the agreement constitute a substantial part of the events giving rise to the breach of contract claim.

From *Krchnak*, we know that a part of a cause of action accrues in the county in which the agreement was made and payment was to be made. Now we must measure those events in terms of Section 15.002's substantiality requirement. In other words, we must determine whether those events constitute a *substantial* part of the plaintiff's claim.

A more recent case, one decided under the amended venue provision, lends us guidance in this inquiry. *See Kay v. North Tex. Rod & Custom*, 109 S.W.3d 924, 926 (Tex. App. — Dallas 2003, no pet.). Kay sued North Texas Rod & Custom in Dallas County for breach of contract. North Texas Rod & Custom successfully moved the trial court to transfer the case to Kaufman County, the county in which North Texas Rod & Custom's place of business was located. The trial court concluded no fact supported Kay's choice of venue. After reviewing the record, the Dallas Court of Appeals agreed, concluding that no evidence in the record supported Kay's allegation that North Texas Rod & Custom solicited Kay's business by placing a telephone call to Kay's place of business in Dallas County. That being the case, the trial court's order transferring the case to Kaufman County was proper. The implied holding of *Kay* is that, had there been evidence to support Kay's allegation that North Texas Rod & Custom did contact him by placing a telephone call to Dallas County, such evidence would have been sufficient to support venue in Dallas County, even under the more rigorous standard in the post-1995 general venue scheme.[4]

---

[4] Additionally, the reasoning in *National Family Care Life Ins. Co. v. Fletcher*, 57 S.W.3d 662, 665 (Tex. App. — Beaumont 2001, pet. denied), supports the conclusion that the place of payment is a relevant consideration in reviewing venue issues involving suits for breaches of contract. In *Fletcher*, the court points out that the evidence demonstrated, *inter alia*, that "appellants issued and [the appellee] received some commission checks in [the county in which the appellee brought suit]" which, along with evidence of other connections to the county in which plaintiff brought suit, was sufficient to constitute probative value to support the finding that venue was proper in the plaintiff's choice of venue. *Id.* at 665–66.

D. Venue Proper in Lamar County

Applying reasoning similar to that in *Krchnak* to the converse factual situation as that presented in *Kay*, we hold that the record before us contains probative evidence to support the trial court's implied ruling that "all or a substantial part of" the events giving rise to this suit occurred in Lamar County. KW Construction first contacted Stephens & Sons in Lamar County in November 2000 to seek its services. Later, Brown again called Stephens in Lamar County to clarify the scope of work to be done. According to Stephens' testimony, during this conversation, the parties also agreed that the price would be determined on a "time and materials" basis. Further, Stephens stated by affidavit that payment was to be made by Brown to Stephens in Lamar County. The fact that Brown sent a later-rejected $4,717.00 check to Stephens in Lamar County as an attempted payment in full supports the conclusion that payment was to be made to Stephens & Sons in Lamar County.

The elements of a breach of contract claim are (1) existence of a valid contract, (2) performance or tendered performance by the plaintiff, (3) breach of the contract by the defendant, and (4) damages to the plaintiff resulting from the breach. *Id.* at 927. So, in terms of the venue provision and Stephens' claim for breach of contract, the evidence here connects at least two elements — the existence of a contract and the defendant's breach — to Lamar County. We conclude events or omissions pertaining to two elements of Stephens & Sons' breach of contract claim are sufficient to qualify as a "substantial part" of the plaintiff's claim and sufficiently connect the claim to Lamar County. We hold that these facts constitute probative evidence supporting venue in Lamar County. We, therefore, must not disturb the trial court's denial of Brown's motion to transfer venue . . . .

V. CONCLUSION

Having determined that the trial court properly denied KW Construction's motion to transfer venue and that the evidence was legally and factually sufficient to support the trial court's finding that the parties entered into an oral contract and the reasonable value of the work performed was $12,500.00, we overrule KW Construction's point of error. Accordingly, we affirm the trial court's judgment.

NOTE

Contract Formation. In *Old Am. Co. Mut. Fire Ins. Co. v. Renfro*, 90 S.W.3d 810 (Tex. App. — Fort Worth 2002, no pet.), the court held that the county where a contract was made is not a "county in which all or a substantial part of the events or omissions giving rise to the claim occurred" when all other events took place elsewhere. "Certainly there could not be a suit had the contract not been formed, and thus the acts constituting contract formation are among the events giving rise to the lawsuit. However, the suit was concerned with construing the contract in light of a discrete set of events. All of these events . . . took place in Wise County." Similarly, in *Levine v. Bayne, Snell & Krause, Ltd.*, 92 S.W.3d 1, 8 (Tex. App. — San Antonio 1999, pet. denied), the court held that the county where a contingency fee contract was reviewed, discussed, executed, and performed is the county in which a substantial part of the events giving rise to the claim occurred.

[D] Transfer Based on Convenience

The general venue statute also provides for a venue transfer based on convenience. Specifically, C.P.R.C. § 15.002(b) provides:

> (b) For the convenience of the parties and witnesses and in the interest of justice, a court may transfer an action from a county of proper venue under this subchapter or Subchapter C [the general rule or a permissive venue exception] to any other county of proper venue on motion of a defendant filed and served concurrently with or before the filing of the answer, where the court finds:
>
> (1) maintenance of the action in the county of suit would work an injustice to the movant considering the movant's economic and personal hardship;
>
> (2) the balance of interests of all the parties predominates in favor of the action being brought in the other county; and
>
> (3) the transfer of the action would not work an injustice to any other party.

Although facially similar to federal statutory provisions (28 U.S.C. § 1404(a)), a number of differences exist. Under the Texas version, only the defendant may seek a transfer urging a more convenient county. Further, while both statutes speak of transfer "for the convenience of the parties and witnesses and in the interest of justice," the Texas statute lists three additional factors (*see* (b)(1)–(3), above) to support a transfer.

The Texas statute also has two noteworthy procedural provisions: 1) the motion must be urged at the very outset of the case, "filed and served concurrently with or before the filing of the answer"; and 2) trial court decisions about venue convenience are completely unreviewable. Subdivision (c) provides that "[a] court's ruling or decision to grant or deny a transfer under Subsection (b) is not grounds for appeal or mandamus and is not reversible error."

The latter provision precludes appeal of orders that grant motions to transfer grounded on claims of improper venue and inconvenience. In one case, the defendant filed a motion to transfer, asserting both improper venue and inconvenience. The trial court granted the motion and transferred the case to Hidalgo County without specifying the grounds for the transfer. The plaintiff was dissatisfied with the outcome of the trial and appealed the judgment. The court of appeals reversed the judgment, refusing to follow the normal appellate presumption that affirmance is required if there is any basis for upholding the order challenged on appeal. The Texas Supreme Court reversed the court of appeals. The Court explained that "[b]ecause the transfer order here includes no reasoning, we cannot ascertain on which of the two grounds it was granted; one ground was convenience, and the evidence showed most of the witnesses and all of the events took place in Hidalgo County. As the Starr County judge certainly might have intended to grant it on convenience grounds, we cannot ignore the Legislature's ban on reviewing such orders by adopting a new presumption so we can review them anyway." *Garza v. Garcia*, 137 S.W.3d 36, 39 (Tex. 2004).

The "no appeal" provision probably means that little or no case law can develop interpreting and applying the statute. Nevertheless, the provision raises a number of interesting questions, including:

- Who bears the burden of proof on a motion to transfer based on convenience? Presumably, the defendant, as movant, bears the burden.
- What is appropriate proof that the "convenience of the parties and witnesses and the interest of justice" support a transfer, that the "balance of interests of all the parties predominates" in favor of a transfer, and the transfer "would not work an injustice to any other party"? Are the only relevant factors access to evidence and party convenience, or is the forum's interest (or lack thereof) in the controversy also relevant?
- What is the interplay between a motion to transfer based on convenience and a plea of forum non conveniens? If the more convenient forum is outside Texas, the latter doctrine should be urged.
- May a transferee court "reconsider" a motion to transfer based on convenience? Could the case be transferred a second time? In a number of federal cases, multiple motions to transfer have been granted giving rise to "the appearance of judicial ping-pong." David E. Steinberg, *The Motion to Transfer and the Interests of Justice*, 66 Notre Dame L. Rev. 443, 482 (1990). Do the time limits mandated in the Texas statute for raising venue complaints solve this problem?

§ 5.02 EXCEPTIONS TO THE GENERAL RULE

[A] Types of Exceptions

Texas statutes contain a number of "exceptions" to the general venue rules discussed above. Some of the exceptions overlap significantly with the general rules. Many are contained in Chapter 15 of the Civil Practice and Remedies Code, but many others lurk in other statutes. The C.P.R.C. exceptions are printed below. When reading them, keep in mind that there are a number of types of exceptions.

First, there are a number of exceptions based on the substantive nature of the plaintiff's cause of action. For example, some exceptions apply to contract actions [C.P.R.C. §§ 15.033, 15.035], some to tort actions [C.P.R.C. §§ 15.017, 15.033], some to actions involving real property [C.P.R.C. § 15.011], some to suits for specialized types of injunctive relief [C.P.R.C. §§ 15.012, 15.013], and some to claims against various departments of state government [C.P.R.C. § 15.014]. The 1995 amendments added mandatory exceptions for landlord-tenant litigation [C.P.R.C. § 15.0115], FELA and Jones Act cases [C.P.R.C. § 15.018], and inmate litigation [C.P.R.C. § 15.019].

Other exceptions depend on the type of defendant. For example, particular exceptions apply to counties [C.P.R.C. § 15.015], certain other political subdivisions [C.P.R.C. § 15.0151], insurance companies [C.P.R.C. § 15.032], manufacturers of consumer goods [C.P.R.C. § 15.033], and transient persons [C.P.R.C. § 15.039].

There are many venue provisions contained in other statutes. For example, Chapter 65 of the Civil Practice and Remedies Code contains a section concerning the venue of suits for injunctive relief. Under this provision, venue for injunction suits is mandatory in the county of the defendant's "domicile." *See* C.P.R.C. § 65.023. But the injunction venue statute applies only to suits in which the relief sought is purely or primarily injunctive. *See In re Continental Airlines*, 988 S.W.2d 733, 735–36 (Tex. 1998) (suit for declaratory relief coupled with request for temporary, but not permanent, injunction was not primarily injunctive and so not governed by mandatory venue provision for injunctions). In addition, the Texas Tort Claims Act (which governs tort claims against the government) provides that "[a] suit under this chapter shall be brought in the county in which the cause of action or a part of the cause of action arises." *See* C.P.R.C. § 101.102. Specific sections of the basic venue statute set forth in Chapter 15 of the Civil Practice and Remedies Code make it clear that when venue is dealt with in another statute, there is no conflict because the other statute takes precedence. *See* C.P.R.C. § 15.016 (other mandatory venue), 15.038 (other permissive venue). *But see In re Fort Bend County*, 278 S.W.3d 842 (Tex. App.—Houston [14th Dist.] 2009) (mandatory venue provision of section 15.015, suits against counties, controls over section 15.016, other mandatory venue, despite mandatory venue provisions of Texas Tort Claims Act found in section 101.102).

[B] Mandatory and Permissive Exceptions

When an exception provides that an action "shall be brought" in a particular county, the requirement is mandatory in the sense that it controls over permissive exceptions as well as the general rule. Subchapter B of Chapter 15 of the Civil Practice and Remedies Code contains mandatory exceptions. Subchapter C of Chapter 15, on the other hand, talks about where actions "may" be brought, and these exceptions are called "permissive." Permissive exceptions do not override the general rule. They provide alternative venue choices to plaintiffs.

Thus, a plaintiff may choose to rely on a mandatory exception, a permissive exception or an application of the general rule. Similarly, a defendant moving to transfer venue may ask that the case be moved to a county that is proper under a mandatory exception, a permissive exception or an application of the general rule.

If a mandatory provision applies, venue is not proper elsewhere, assuming that the defendant challenges the plaintiff's choice of venue by a proper motion to transfer venue based on the mandatory provision. If more than one mandatory provision applies so that an apparent conflict between two provisions of equal rank occurs, the "principal relief sought" is said to determine venue. This tie-breaker is easy to articulate but difficult to apply. *See Brown v. Gulf Television Co.*, 306 S.W.2d 706, 709 (1957); *cf. Gonzalez v. Texaco, Inc.*, 645 S.W.2d 324 (Tex. App. — Corpus Christi 1982, no writ) (considering conflict between land title and injunction mandatory venue provisions). In addition, when litigation includes a claim covered by a mandatory venue exception as well as others that would be merely permissive, all of the claims or causes of action arising from the "same transaction, occurrence, or series of transactions or occurrences" as the mandatory venue claim must be brought in the county required by the mandatory venue provision. C.P.R.C. § 15.004.

A defendant that bases a motion to transfer on a permissive exception or an application of the general rule must establish that the basis for the plaintiff's venue choice is inapplicable and that venue is proper in the defendant's chosen county.

Before considering certain of the venue provisions in detail, it is helpful to have a general overview of the structure of the statute. Read the following sections of the Civil Practice and Remedies Code.

SUBCHAPTER B. MANDATORY VENUE

§ 15.011. *Land.* Actions for recovery of real property or an estate or interest in real property, for partition of real property, to remove encumbrances from the title to real property, for recovery of damages to real property, or to quiet title to real property shall be brought in the county in which all or a part of the property is located.*

§ 15.0115. *Landlord-Tenant.*

(a) Except as provided by another statute prescribing mandatory venue, a suit between a landlord and a tenant arising under a lease shall be brought in the county in which all or a part of the real property is located.

(b) In this section, "lease" means any written or oral agreement between a landlord and a tenant that establishes or modifies the terms, conditions, or other provisions relating to the use and occupancy of the real property that is the subject of the agreement.

§ 15.012. *Injunction Against Suit.* Actions to stay proceedings in a suit shall be brought in the county in which the suit is pending.

§ 15.013. *Injunction Against Execution of Judgment.* Actions to restrain execution of a judgment based on invalidity of the judgment or of the writ shall be brought in the county in which the judgment was rendered.

§ 15.014. *Head of State Department.* An action for mandamus against the head of a department of the state government shall be brought in Travis County.

§ 15.015. *Counties.* An action against a county shall be brought in that county.

§ 15.0151. *Certain Political Subdivisions.*

---

* This statute has been strictly construed by the courts, and is triggered only if an action clearly falls within one of the enumerated types of causes of action. It will not apply merely because a lawsuit involves land in some manner. The Texas Supreme Court has recently signaled its intent to read the statute's language in a more straightforward way. *See In re Applied Chem. Magnesias Corp.*, 206 S.W.3d 114 (Tex. 2006) (looking to "essence" of dispute and finding that declaratory judgment action involving mining rights fell within section 15.011).

(a) Except as provided by a law not contained in this chapter, an action against a political subdivision that is located in a county with a population of 100,000 or less shall be brought in the county in which the political subdivision is located. If the political subdivision is located in more than one county and the population of each county is 100,000 or less, the action shall be brought in any county in which the political subdivision is located.

(b) In this section, "political subdivision" means a governmental entity in this state, other than a county, that is not a state agency. The term includes a municipality, school or junior college district, hospital district, or any other special purpose district or authority.

§ 15.016. *Other Mandatory Venue.* An action governed by any other statute prescribing mandatory venue shall be brought in the county required by that statute.

§ 15.017. *Libel, Slander, or Invasion of Privacy.* A suit for damages for libel, slander, or invasion of privacy shall be brought and can only be maintained in the county in which the plaintiff resided at the time of the accrual of the cause of action, or in the county in which the defendant resided at the time of filing suit, or in the county of the residence of defendants, or any of them, or the domicile of any corporate defendant, at the election of the plaintiff.

§ 15.018. *Federal Employers' Liability Act and Jones Act.*

(a) This section only applies to suits brought under the federal Employers' Liability Act (45 U.S.C. Section 51 et seq.) or the Jones Act (46 U.S.C. Section 688).

(b) All suits brought under the federal Employers' Liability Act or the Jones Act shall be brought:

(1) in the county in which all or a substantial part of the events or omissions giving rise to the claim occurred;

(2) in the county where the defendant's principal office in this state is located; or

(3) in the county where the plaintiff resided at the time the cause of action accrued.

§ 15.019. *Inmate Litigation.*

(a) Except as provided by Section 15.014, an action that accrued while the plaintiff was housed in a facility operated by or under contract with the Texas Department of Criminal Justice shall be brought in the county in which the facility is located.

(b) An action brought by two or more plaintiffs that accrued while the plaintiffs were housed in a facility operated by or under contract with the Texas Department of Criminal Justice shall be brought in a county in which a facility that housed one of the plaintiffs is located.

(c) This section does not apply to an action brought under the Family Code.

§ 15.020. *Major Transactions: Specification of Venue by Agreement.*

(a) In this section, "major transaction" means a transaction evidenced by a written agreement under which a person pays or receives, or is obligated to pay or entitled to receive, consideration with an aggregate stated value equal to or greater than $1 million. The term does not include a transaction entered into primarily for personal, family, or household purposes, or to settle a personal injury or wrongful death claim, without regard to the aggregate value.

(b) An action arising from a major transaction shall be brought in a county if the party against whom the action is brought has agreed in writing that a suit arising from the transaction may be brought in that county.

(c) Notwithstanding any other provision of this title, an action arising from a major transaction may not be brought in a county if:

(1) the party bringing the action has agreed in writing that an action arising from the transaction may not be brought in that county, and the action may be brought in another county of this state or in another jurisdiction; or

(2) the party bringing the action has agreed in writing that an action arising from the transaction must be brought in another county of this state or in another jurisdiction, and the action may be brought in that other county, under this section or otherwise, or in that other jurisdiction.

(d) This section does not apply to an action if:

(1) the agreement described by this section was unconscionable at the time that it was made;

(2) the agreement regarding venue is voidable under section 35.52, Business & Commerce Code; or

(3) venue is established under a statute of this state other than this title.

(e) This section does not affect venue and jurisdiction in an action arising from a transaction that is not a major transaction.*

SUBCHAPTER C. PERMISSIVE VENUE

§ 15.031. *Executor; Administrator; Guardian.* If the suit is against an executor, administrator, or guardian, as such, to establish a money demand against the estate which he represents, the suit may be brought in the county in which the estate is administered, or if the suit is against an executor, administrator, or guardian growing out of a negligent act or omission of the person whose estate the executor, administrator, or guardian represents, the suit may be brought in the county in which the negligent act or omission of the person whose estate the executor, administrator, or guardian represents occurred.

---

* Texas courts will consider the terms of a contract in order to determine whether it meets the $1 million requirement for major transactions. *See In re Texas Assoc. of School Boards, Inc.*, 169 S.W.3d 653 (Tex. 2005) (premiums paid, not insured value, is the relevant amount); *In re Royalco Oil & Gas Corp.*, 287 S.W.3d 398 (Tex. App. — Waco 2009, orig. proceeding) (value of lease agreement should be measured by its full term); *Spin Doctor Golf, Inc. v. Paymentech L.P.*, 296 S.W.3d 354 (Tex. App. — Dallas 2009, pet. denied) ($5 million in annual sales volume sufficient despite allegation of forgery).

§ 15.032. *Insurance.* Suit against fire, marine, or inland insurance companies may also be commenced in any county in which the insured property was situated. A suit on a policy may be brought against any life insurance company, or accident insurance company, or life and accident, or health and accident, or life, health, and accident insurance company in the county in which the company's principal office in this state is located or in the county in which the loss has occurred or in which the policyholder or beneficiary instituting the suit resided at the time the cause of action accrued.

§ 15.033. *Breach of Warranty by Manufacturer.* A suit for breach of warranty by a manufacturer of consumer goods may be brought in any county in which all or a substantial part of the events or omissions giving rise to the claim occurred, in the county in which the manufacturer has its principal office in this state, or in the county in which the plaintiff resided at the time the cause of action accrued.*

§ 15.035. *Contract in Writing.*

(a) Except as provided by Subsection (b), if a person has contracted in writing to perform an obligation in a particular county, expressly naming the county or a definite place in that county by that writing, suit on or by reason of the obligation may be brought against him either in that county or in the county in which the defendant has his domicile.

(b) In an action founded on a contractual obligation of the defendant to pay money arising out of or based on a consumer transaction for goods, services, loans, or extensions of credit intended primarily for personal, family, household, or agricultural use, suit by a creditor on or by reason of the obligation may be brought against the defendant either in the county in which the defendant in fact signed the contract or in the county in which the defendant resides when the action is commenced. No term or statement contained in an obligation described in this section shall constitute a waiver of these provisions.**

---

* Note that this section applies only to a defendant who is the manufacturer, not the retailer, and only if the product in question is a consumer good.

** Beware of contracts involving Texas cities that are located in more than one county. *See Southwest Inv. Co. v. Shipley*, 400 S.W.2d 304 (Tex. 1966) ("payable in Amarillo, Texas" was insufficient because Amarillo lies within two counties).

Several cases make it clear that the contractual provision providing for performance in a particular county must be at least one of the obligations sued on. The fact that one obligation under a contract is to be performed under the contractual terms at a specific place does not mean that another distinct contractual undertaking (obligation) is also to be performed there. *See Rorschach v. Pitts*, 248 S.W.2d 120 (Tex. 1952) (court would not imply that a provision that required a gas processing plant to take delivery of gas in Hutchinson County also required that the place of payment for the gas was in Hutchinson County).

Note that section 15.035(b) limits the application of section 15.035(a). If the action involves a breach of a contractual obligation to pay money arising out of most types of *consumer* transactions, suit may only be brought in either the county where the contract was signed or the county where the defendant resides when the action is commenced. *See* C.P.R.C. § 15.035(b). It is also worth noting that filing suit in any county other than the county in which the defendant resides at the time of the commencement of the action, or in which the defendant in fact signed the contract, may be a deceptive trade practice. *See* Bus. & Com. C. § 17.46(b)(22).

§ 15.038. *Other Permissive Venue.* An action governed by any other statute prescribing permissive venue may be brought in the county allowed by that statute.

§ 15.039. *Transient Person.* A transient person may be sued in any county in which he may be found.

Tex. Bus. & Com. C. § 17.56 *Actions for Deceptive Trade Practices.* An action brought under this subchapter may be brought:

(1) in any county in which venue is proper under Chapter 15, Civil Practice and Remedies Code; or

(2) in a county in which the defendant or an authorized agent of the defendant solicited the transaction made the subject of the action at bar.*

PRACTICE EXERCISE #10

(1) There is a car accident. Plaintiff Peter is a resident of Dallas County. Darwin, an individual, has always been a resident of Tarrant County. The accident took place in Denton County. Where may Peter file suit?

(2) Peter has decided that he would rather sue Darwin's employer, because Darwin was working when the accident occurred. The employer is a Texas corporation with its headquarters in Harris County and a permanent office (but not its main office) in Dallas County. The Dallas County office makes some decisions about operations in Dallas County but it is subordinate to the Harris County office. Now where may Peter file suit?

(3) Polly has been a lifelong resident of Harris County. She was injured on January 15, 2005, when she slipped and fell in a grocery store in Dallas County. The owner and operator of the store was Food, Inc., a Texas corporation with its principal place of business in Bexar County. Polly returned home after the incident, but she never fully recovered from her injuries. Polly sought legal advice from a lawyer who practices in Travis County. The lawyer has recommended that Polly file a lawsuit. In what county or counties may Polly properly file her suit?

(4) Fred, after extensive negotiations were conducted in Potter County, contracted with InkMe, a Georgia corporation with its principal place of business in Georgia, to acquire the first-ever InkMe franchise in Texas. InkMe provides emergency home deliveries to people whose printers run out of ink just as some crucial print job must be completed. The contract was signed in Dallas County (at Love Field), and Fred's franchise was to operate in Tarrant County. The contract called for Fred to make payments to InkMe by wire transfer to InkMe's bank account in Georgia. InkMe fails to deliver on its promises, and Fred wants to sue them in Texas. Assuming that personal jurisdiction is proper, in what counties can Fred properly file suit?

---

* The issue in these cases may be whether the defendant's agent solicited the transaction in the county of suit. *See Dairyland County Mutual Ins. Co. v. Harrison*, 578 S.W.2d 186, 191 (Tex. Civ. App. — Houston [14th Dist.] 1979, no writ) (telephone directory advertisement was sufficient proof of business solicitation in particular county); *Jim Walter Homes, Inc. v. Altreche*, 605 S.W.2d 733 (Tex. Civ. App. — Corpus Christi 1980, no writ) (telephone directory used to show solicitation must date from proper time period).

(5) Fran was visiting her daughter in Denton County. While there she had a medical emergency that required minor outpatient surgery. Dr. Drew performed the operation. Fran returned home to Travis County, and once there it became clear that something had gone terribly wrong, as she started bleeding profusely and had to be rushed to an Austin hospital. Now Fran wants to sue Dr. Drew for malpractice in Travis County. Would venue there be proper?

[C] Multiple Claims and Parties

First, a Word About Joinder

When it comes to venue rules and their application to cases involving multiple claims or multiple parties, the joinder rules apply. You therefore need a preview of these rules, so that you will be able to say when claims or parties are "properly joined."

The Texas joinder of claims rule (Tex. R. Civ. P. 51) was taken without modification from the 1937 version of its federal counterpart, Fed. R. Civ. P. 18(a). Under the Texas rule, in a case involving only one plaintiff and one defendant, there can be no misjoinder of claims, because the claims need not arise from the same transaction or occurrence or series of transaction or occurrences. *Cf.* Tex. R. Civ. P. 40.

For example, imagine that Paulette and David are involved in a traffic accident in which Paulette's car is damaged. Coincidentally, David owes Paulette $1,000 because he agreed to pay her to paint his house. Paulette may sue David both for negligence in the traffic accident and for the money owed on the painting contract in the same lawsuit, even though the claims are not related.

When there are multiple plaintiffs or multiple defendants (or both), Rule 40 also applies. Persons may join as plaintiffs or be joined as defendants when the claims by or against them arise out of the same transaction, occurrence, or series of transactions or occurrences, and when they share a question of law or fact common to all parties joined.

Courts use tests such as whether claims will include significant evidence overlap and whether the claims are "logically related" in determining whether they arise out of the "same transaction or occurrence."

[1] Multiple Claims

The traditional rule in Texas is that if venue is proper as to one of several claims made against the same defendant, other claims against that defendant that are properly joined can be litigated in the same venue. *Middlebrook v. David Bradley Mfg. Co.*, 26 S.W. 935 (1894). This rule is referred to as the *Middlebrook* doctrine, and it is intended to promote efficiency by avoiding a multiplicity of suits. It was, from its inception, a derivative venue provision created by the courts rather than the legislature. The *Middlebrook* doctrine, for a brief period, was reinforced by the venue statutes, but when the legislature amended the venue statutes in 1995, it did not explicitly include the *Middlebrook* provisions applicable to claims by one plaintiff against one defendant.[*] Although one might argue that the legislature thereby intended to eliminate the *Middlebrook* doctrine, a combination of legislative history and statutory construction makes this unlikely. *See* William D. Underwood, *Reconsidering Derivative-Venue in Cases Involving Multiple Parties and Multiple Claims*, 56 Baylor L. Rev. 579, 649–57 (2004).

As to any one defendant, then, if there is one good claim against that defendant that makes venue proper in the county of suit, venue is also proper as to other related and unrelated claims by the same plaintiff against that defendant.

In contrast, C.P.R.C. § 15.004 expressly provides that if one of the joined claims is subject to a mandatory venue exception, all of the claims arising from the same transaction or occurrence or series of transactions or occurrences must be brought in the county required by the mandatory venue provision. Presumably, mandatory venue controls over the *Middlebrook* doctrine so that a claim governed by a mandatory venue provision as well as other connected claims must be filed in the county of mandatory venue. Elaine A. Grafton Carlson, 2 McDonald & Carlson Texas Civil Practice § 6:57 (2d ed. 2006).

PRACTICE EXERCISE #11

(1) Assume that Doug, the sole proprietor of a small business and resident of Travis County, executed three contracts to provide services for the Procedure Corporation (PC), whose principal office is in Dallas County. Only one of the contracts provides that it is to be performed in Harris County, Texas. (The others do not specifically provide for a place of performance.) PC claims that Doug has failed to perform his obligations under the contracts, and wants to sue Doug on all three contracts in a single suit in Harris County. Is venue proper on all claims there? What if the *Middlebrook* doctrine is no longer a part of Texas venue law?

(2) Patty, a resident of Wise County, gets in a terrible argument with her boss and is fired from her job. Her employer is DataCorp, a Texas corporation with its principal office in Dallas County. Patty sues DataCorp in Tarrant County (she likes Fort Worth), alleging a breach of contract, defamation, and intentional infliction of emotional distress claims, all based on facts concerning the argument and her firing. DataCorp establishes mandatory venue in Wise County because of the defamation claim. What part of the case will be transferred to Wise County?

[*] *Compare* current § 15.005 *with* former § 15.061 ("When . . . two or more claims or causes of action are properly joined in one action and the court has venue of [a] claim against any one defendant, the court also has venue of all claims or actions against all defendants unless one or more of the claims or causes of action is governed by [a mandatory venue provision].")

[2] Multiple Defendants

When a lawsuit involves multiple defendants the statute is much clearer. There is also an anti-waiver provision. Read the following provisions from the Civil Practice and Remedies Code.

> § 15.005. *Multiple Defendants.* In a suit in which the plaintiff has established proper venue against a defendant, the court also has venue of all the defendants in all claims or actions arising out of the same transaction, occurrence, or series of transactions or occurrences.

> § 15.0641. *Venue Rights of Multiple Defendants.* In a suit in which two or more defendants are joined, any action or omission by one defendant in relation to venue, including a waiver of venue by one defendant, does not operate to impair or diminish the right of any other defendant to properly challenge venue.

As you can see, proper venue against one defendant can create proper venue as to all of the other defendants properly joined. Keep in mind, however, that the claim against the lynch-pin defendant must be a legitimate one.

PRACTICE EXERCISE #12

(1) Assume that an automobile collision occurs in Dallas County. Assume further that the injured claimant resides in Harris County, that the driver and owner of the pizza delivery car that collided with the claimant's vehicle resides in Travis County and that his employer is a Texas corporation with its principal office in Collin County. What venue choices are open to the claimant?

(2) Assume the same facts as in (1) above. Also assume that the claimant actually wants to bring suit in Harris County against all of the parties mentioned above and also wants to sue the manufacturer of his own car, a corporation with a principal office in Texas in Travis County (he asserts that the design of the vehicle added to his injuries in the collision). He will assert causes of action for negligence, strict liability, and breach of warranty. What effect does joinder of the manufacturer have?

(3) The Student Bar Association (SBA) had its annual retreat at Shrub's Watering Hole in Bexar County. The SBA is a Texas non-profit corporation with its principal office in Dallas County. Shrub's is a Texas corporation with its principal office in Travis County. Phillip, a resident of Collin County, was severely injured during the hayride in Bexar County when he fell off the hay wagon. Some say the truck pulling the wagon suddenly jerked, knocking Phillip off. The truck was manufactured by Acme Trucking Company, a Michigan corporation with its principal office in Detroit and its sole Texas office in Bell County. The Bell County office merely processes paperwork, and no employee there has any significant decision-making power. The driver of the wagon, David, is an officer of the SBA who resides in Ellis County. In what counties could Phillip properly file suit? He wants to include claims for negligent hiring, negligence, and breach of warranty.

(4) Pam, Dan, and Dora are involved in a three-way traffic accident in Kaufman County. Pam, who is from El Paso County, files a negligence claim there against

Dan and Dora, who are both residents of Grayson County. Dan files a motion to transfer venue, seeking transfer of the case to Grayson County. Dora, however, files an answer without challenging venue, thus waiving her right to complain about venue. Does C.P.R.C. § 15.005 make venue proper in El Paso County for both Dan and Dora?

[3] Multiple Plaintiffs; Intervention

The 1995 amendments created new limitations on the ability of multiple plaintiffs to base venue on the claims of others — essentially each plaintiff must now independently establish venue unless each plaintiff can make very difficult showings like an "essential need" to be in the county of suit. The statute was again amended in 2003 to provide more clearly for interlocutory appeals from decisions under this section. Read the following C.P.R.C. provision:

§ 15.003. *Multiple Plaintiffs and Intervening Plaintiffs.*

(a) In a suit in which there is more than one plaintiff, whether the plaintiffs are included by joinder, by intervention, because the lawsuit was begun by more than one plaintiff, or otherwise, each plaintiff must, independently of every other plaintiff, establish proper venue. If a plaintiff cannot independently establish proper venue, that plaintiff's part of the suit, including all of that plaintiff's claims and causes of action, must be transferred to a county of proper venue or dismissed, as is appropriate, unless that plaintiff, independently of every other plaintiff, establishes that:

(1) joinder of that plaintiff or intervention in the suit by that plaintiff is proper under the Texas Rules of Civil Procedure;

(2) maintaining venue as to that plaintiff in the county of suit does not unfairly prejudice another party to the suit;

(3) there is an essential need to have that plaintiff's claim tried in the county in which the suit is pending; and

(4) the county in which the suit is pending is a fair and convenient venue for that plaintiff and all persons against whom the suit is brought.

(b) An interlocutory appeal may be taken of a trial court's determination under Subsection (a) that:

(1) a plaintiff did or did not independently establish proper venue; or

(2) a plaintiff that did not independently establish proper venue did or did not establish the items prescribed by Subsections (a)(1)–(4).

(c) An interlocutory appeal permitted by Subsection (b) must be taken to the court of appeals district in which the trial court is located under the procedures established for interlocutory appeals. The appeal may be taken by a party that is affected by the trial court's determination under Subsection (a). The court of appeals shall:

(1) determine whether the trial court's order is proper based on an independent determination from the record and not under either an abuse

of discretion or substantial evidence standard; and

(2) render judgment not later than the 120th day after the date the appeal is perfected.

(d) An interlocutory appeal under Subsection (b) has the effect of staying the commencement of trial in the trial court pending resolution of the appeal.

You will not be surprised to learn that one of the most difficult issues faced by the courts in interpreting section 15.003 has been deciding when a would-be plaintiff has demonstrated "essential need" to join the litigation. The following case expresses the Texas Supreme Court's views on the issue. NOTE: Because this case raises issues of venue procedure, you may wish to read § 5.03, Litigating Venue Rights, before considering the *Surgitek* case.

SURGITEK, BRISTOL-MYERS CORP. v. ABEL
997 S.W.2d 598 (Tex. 1999)

ENOCH, J.

This case presents several issues concerning section 15.003 of the Texas Civil Practice and Remedies Code. Section 15.003 limits when a plaintiff may join an action in a venue that would otherwise be improper for that plaintiff. Here, 104 plaintiffs who could not independently establish venue in Bexar County attempted to join two plaintiffs in a Bexar County action against makers of silicone-gel breast implants. Concluding that the 104 plaintiffs were improperly joined, the trial court granted the defendants' motion to transfer venue of those plaintiffs' claims. A divided court of appeals reversed, with one justice concurring and one justice dissenting. We conclude that: . . . (2) a trial court may limit the scope of evidence on its section 15.003(a) joinder determination to pleadings and affidavits, but it has discretion to consider a broader range of evidence, including live testimony; (3) appellate courts should conduct a de novo review of the propriety of a trial court's section 15.003 joinder decision; and (4) the plaintiffs here did not establish an "essential need" to have their claims tried in Bexar County. Consequently, we reverse the court of appeals' judgment and reinstate the trial court's venue transfer order.

BACKGROUND

One-hundred-six plaintiffs sued Surgitek, Bristol-Myers Squibb Co., and Medical Engineering Corp. (Surgitek) for injuries they allegedly sustained from defective breast implants. Surgitek moved to transfer venue of 104 of these plaintiffs' claims, asserting that none could establish proper venue in Bexar County and that none could establish that they were entitled to join the Bexar County suit under section 15.003. [The court next quotes the statute.]

The trial court agreed with Surgitek that 104 plaintiffs did not establish that their joinder in the Bexar County suit was proper. The trial court transferred venue of 103 of these plaintiffs to Dallas County, Surgitek's principal place of business in Texas, and one plaintiff to Tarrant County, that plaintiff's residence. (While this action was pending in this Court, 45 plaintiffs, including the Tarrant County plaintiff, have, through settlement or nonsuit, ceased being parties to this appeal. Fifty-nine plaintiffs remain, and our opinion and judgment apply only to those parties.)

The plaintiffs appealed the trial court's order to the court of appeals, which, after determining that it had jurisdiction to hear the appeal, reversed and remanded . . . .

BURDEN OF PROOF

The parties disagree about which party has the burden of proof, and the nature of that burden, under section 15.003(a). The court of appeals concluded that the Legislature, in enacting section 15.003(a), did not intend to alter pre-existing statutory standards for venue hearings and proof. Thus, it stated that in a section 15.003(a) determination, a trial court is to look only to the pleadings and affidavits, and not to any other proof, such as live testimony. And it determined that the trial court should consider only whether the plaintiff presented prima facie proof that joinder under section 15.003(a) is appropriate; if so, the plaintiff has established her right to join. We disagree that a trial court is so limited in conducting a section 15.003(a) hearing and determination.

The fact that section 15.003(a) appears in the venue chapter of the Civil Practice and Remedies Code informs but does not control what type of hearing or standard of proof governs a section 15.003(a) joinder determination. Ultimately, we resolve the issue of what quantum-of-proof and nature-of-proof standards are established by section 15.003(a) not just by looking at where it was placed in the Civil Practice and Remedies Code, but also by considering legislative intent as reflected in its plain language.

Section 15.003(a) takes as its starting point a "person who is unable to establish proper venue." Thus, before the trial court even reaches the joinder elements, it first has to determine whether a plaintiff can independently establish proper venue. This determination, of course, is made using venue proof standards — if the plaintiff offers prima facie proof through pleadings and affidavits that venue is proper, the inquiry is over.

But when a plaintiff cannot establish proper venue, section 15.003(a) expressly places the burden on the plaintiff to "establish" four elements before she can join venue for the suit. The plaintiffs urge that we construe this requirement to mean only that they must offer the same quantum of prima facie proof required to establish venue. Surgitek argues that the plaintiffs must prove the four elements by a preponderance of the evidence, and that the trial court should conduct a full evidentiary hearing as it would in a normal joinder matter.

We conclude that the plain language of section 15.003(a) places the burden on the plaintiff in the first instance to offer prima facie proof of the four elements, but that it contemplates the admission, in some instances, of a broader range of evidence than would be admissible in a venue hearing. The Legislature used the same word — establish — in section 15.003(a) to describe both venue proof ("Any person who is unable to *establish* proper venue . . . ") and joinder proof (" . . . unless the person . . . *establishes* [the four elements.]"). Because a plaintiff need only offer prima facie proof to "establish" venue, it follows that, at least initially, a plaintiff must offer prima facie proof of each joinder element. And if the defendant offers no rebuttal evidence, the inquiry is over.

But Surgitek is correct that the four elements a plaintiff must establish under section 15.003(a) do not lend themselves readily to the prima facie standard applied in venue hearings. The usual types of prima facie proof in a venue determination — pleadings and affidavits establishing places of residence, principal offices, and even where the cause of action accrued — are usually objective enough that pleadings and affidavits can fairly be said to enable the trial court to correctly decide the issue. But the section 15.003(a) elements — joinder under the Texas Rules of Civil Procedure, unfair prejudice, essential need, and fairness and convenience — are relatively subjective and not as readily susceptible to proof by affidavit or pleading. Thus, the defendant must be afforded the opportunity to rebut the plaintiff's prima facie proof.

Accordingly, we conclude that the trial court has discretion to allow a broader range of proof in making a section 15.003(a) joinder determination than it would in a venue hearing. Specifically, a trial court may allow the parties to offer testimony, if the trial court believes it would be useful to its determination. Moreover, a trial court may order limited discovery on the joinder elements, affording the parties the opportunity to more fully develop evidence on the issues raised. To the extent that a defendant's joinder evidence rebuts the plaintiff's prima facie proof on any of the joinder elements, a trial court has discretion to consider all available evidence to resolve any disputes that the parties' proof creates. A trial court's decision to limit the scope of evidence is an abuse of discretion only if a party is materially prejudiced by its inability to offer further proof.

SCOPE AND STANDARD OF REVIEW

The court of appeals expressly limited its review in this case to the affidavits and pleadings. Its decision to do so logically followed from its conclusion that under section 15.003(a) a trial court could only consider affidavits and pleadings. But just as that determination was error, so too was the standard of review the court of appeals employed.

Section 15.003(c)(1) describes the proper standard for the court of appeals to apply:

> "The court of appeals shall . . . determine whether the joinder or intervention is proper based on an independent determination from the record, and not under either an abuse of discretion or substantial evidence standard."

Construing this language, as we must, by its plain meaning, we conclude that a court of appeals should conduct a de novo review of the entire record to determine whether a trial court's section 15.003(a) joinder determination was proper. The phrase "independent determination," coupled with the admonition not to conduct an abuse of discretion or a substantial evidence review, suggests that the court of appeals should make its own determination of the propriety of joinder under section 15.003(a), with no deference to the trial court's ruling. Thus, its review of the merits of the joinder determination should be de novo. And the phrase "from the record" indicates that the court of appeals is not constrained solely to review the pleadings and affidavits, but should consider the entire record, including any evidence presented at the hearing.

On the other hand, the court of appeals should employ an abuse of discretion standard to review a party's contention that it was improperly denied the opportunity to present further proof. While the plain language of section 15.003(c)(1) prevents a court of appeals from using an abuse of discretion standard when reviewing the propriety of a trial court's section 15.003(a) joinder determination, nothing in section 15.003(c)(1) precludes employment of that standard for reviewing the trial court's decision to limit the scope of evidence.

ANALYSIS

With the proper burden of proof and scope and standard of review in mind, we turn now to the record in this case.

The evidence plaintiffs offered to establish their right to join the Bexar County litigation consisted of affidavits from the two plaintiffs who could independently establish venue in Bexar County, pleadings Surgitek filed in the multi-district federal breast implant litigation, an affidavit from the plaintiffs' counsel, and Surgitek's witness designations. The plaintiffs offered Surgitek's MDL pleadings as evidence that in another proceeding Surgitek took the position that some common questions of fact and law exist across breast implant cases, thus showing that joinder was proper under Rule 40 of the Texas Rules of Civil Procedure. Plaintiffs' counsel's affidavit reiterated the commonality of fact questions, and further stated that Surgitek designated the same expert witnesses in each case. Finally, the plaintiffs offered Surgitek's witness list to demonstrate that these witnesses were located all over the country, thus showing that no matter where the cases are tried the witnesses will have to travel.

The court of appeals held that this evidence was sufficient to satisfy all four section 15.003(a) elements for joinder. We disagree.

Section 15.003(a)(3) requires the plaintiff to establish that "there is an essential need to have the person's claim tried in the county in which the suit is pending." The court of appeals held that the plaintiffs established their "essential need" to try their claims against Surgitek in Bexar County "by proving the need to pool resources against common experts and issues." But that is not enough. The trial court's order in this case kept all of the remaining plaintiffs together in a single action, thereby allowing them to pool resources. Thus, if the need to pool resources were dispositive, the plaintiffs could have no complaint.

We agree with Surgitek that the "essential need" element requires each plaintiff seeking joinder to demonstrate that there is an "essential need" for her claim to be tried in Bexar County. The plain language of section 15.003(a)(3) compels this result: "[the person seeking joinder must establish that] there is an essential need to have the person's claim tried *in the county in which the suit is pending.*" Citing a legal dictionary definition of "essential," Surgitek argues that an "essential need" is one that is "indispensably necessary." Another dictionary likewise defines "essential" as "necessary, such that one cannot do without it." We recognize that this burden is very high, but the language of the statute makes it so. Here, the plaintiffs did not establish that it was "indispensably necessary" to try their claims in Bexar County. Because we conclude that the plaintiffs failed to establish this joinder element, we need not consider whether they established the other three.

Accordingly, we reverse the court of appeals' judgment and reinstate the trial court's order transferring venue of the 59 remaining plaintiffs' claims to Dallas County.

NOTES AND QUESTIONS

(1) *The "Essential Need" Requirement.* Under the Texas Supreme Court's analysis, when would a plaintiff be able to show "essential need" to join a case in a particular county? Would it be enough to show that all plaintiffs are represented by the same lawyer, were treated by the same doctor, share the same medical expert witness, and live near the county of suit? That the case could go to trial quickly in the county of the plaintiff's choice but would be subject to a two- to three-year delay in the county requested by the defendants?

(2) *Applying* Surgitek *Standard.* The courts of appeals have generally held that plaintiffs cannot satisfy the "essential need" element. Consider these examples:

- In *Ramirez v. Collier, Shannon, Scott, PLLC*, an intervening plaintiff claimed to need "the use of a common investigator" with the original plaintiff, to need to "pool[] resources" with the original plaintiff, to litigate "common facts and issues" with the original plaintiff, and to work with the original plaintiff regarding "the location of witnesses across the country." The *Ramirez* court rejected this argument, holding that "the desire to pool resources against common defendants and experts is not enough to establish essential need." 123 S.W.3d 43, 53 (Tex. App. — Houston [1st Dist.] 2003, pet. denied).
- In *Smith v. Adair*, "essential need" was also not shown. The would-be plaintiff swore that "his lawyers [would] have to do twice the work and the division of labor would cause him to lose the full attention of his attorneys," "his expert witnesses would have to duplicate their efforts," his witnesses lived in the county of original suit, and "if this case [were] tried in two separate venues, the first to finish might cause collateral estoppel to apply." 96 S.W.3d 700, 707 (Tex. App. — Texarkana 2003, pet. denied).
- In *American Home Products v. Bernal*, the court rejected an attempt to show "essential need" through counsel's sworn testimony that, through joinder, plaintiffs could "achieve mutual support" and "derive a significant economic benefit," achieve significant efficiencies in discovery, and benefit economically from counsel's reviewing defendant's documents once rather than twenty times. 5 S.W.3d 344, 348 (Tex. App. — Corpus Christi 1999, no pet.)

- In *American Home Products v. Burroughs*, sworn testimony that "plaintiffs could not economically afford to try their cases without combining their resources to cover the cost of litigation" did not show "essential need." 998 S.W.2d 696, 700 (Tex. App. — Eastland 1999, no pet.)

In sum, courts have consistently held that "the mere fact that a related suit is already proceeding in a county" and related arguments are "insufficient to establish that it is indispensably necessary for the plaintiff seeking joinder or intervention to try his or her claims there." *See generally* James Holmes, *House Bill 4's Impact on Multi-Plaintiff Joinder and Intervention and on Forum Non Conveniens*, 46 S. Tex. L. Rev. 775, 785–06 (2005).

So far, the Corpus Christi Court of Appeals is the only one to have held in favor of a plaintiff seeking to show essential need. In *Teco-Westinghouse Motor Co. v. Gonzalez*, 54 S.W.3d 910 (Tex. App. — Corpus Christi 2001, no pet.), the court found "essential need" because the testimony of an essential witness was only available in the desired county. In another case, the court found that "essential need" can be shown if the party seeking to join as a plaintiff would be bound by the results of the pending case under the doctrine of collateral estoppel. *National Union Fire Ins. Co. v. Valero Energy Corp.*, 143 S.W.3d 859 (Tex. App. — Corpus Christi 2004, pet. denied).

(3) *Procedural Requirements.* In addition to its holding about the meaning of "essential need," *Surgitek* discusses the proper method of proving section 15.003 venue, the availability of interlocutory review of these decisions, and the standard of review that the court of appeals should apply. These are all somewhat different from the normal rules for venue, which are discussed in §§ 5.03[B] and [C].

PRACTICE EXERCISE #13

(1) Bill, who resides in Matagorda County, purchased a Ford F-150 pickup truck from Uptown Ford in Nueces County, Texas. Before the purchase, Bill had received numerous mail and telephone solicitations at his Matagorda County home from Ford, urging him to shop for trucks at Uptown. Bill believes that the truck is defective and unmerchantable in breach of implied warranties. He has claims for breach of warranty and for violation of the Texas Deceptive Trade Practices Act. What venue choices are available to Bill if he wants to sue Ford? (You may assume that Ford has no principal office in Texas.)

(2) Bill wants to file suit against Ford in Matagorda County. Bill's lawyer is aware of about a dozen other people who purchased similar trucks from Ford in North Texas. They also claim breach of warranty for the same defect as does Bill. These plaintiffs, however, do not reside in Matagorda County, nor did Ford solicit their business there. If they join as plaintiffs, what type of showing will be needed to keep the case in Matagorda County if Ford contests venue?

(3) Assume the same facts as in (2), above. Can other plaintiffs from other counties solve their venue problem by intervening *after* the original plaintiff's venue rights have been determined?

(4) Assume the same facts as in (2) above. This time also assume that all of the would-be plaintiffs are represented by the same lawyer. Also assume that they share the same expert witness, David Carr, and that Carr is a resident of Matagorda County. Carr is one of the country's leading experts on the particular kind of defect alleged, but is in poor health and it is difficult for him to travel far from home. Would this establish "essential need" to hear all of the plaintiffs' claims in Matagorda County?

[D] Counterclaims, Cross-Claims, and Third Party Actions

Another Note About Joinder

Plaintiffs aren't the only ones who can add claims to lawsuits. Defendants can do the same. Here are three types of claims filed primarily by defendants (although under certain circumstances plaintiffs may do so as well).

1. Counterclaims are claims seeking relief against an "opposing party." If they arise out of the same transaction or occurrence as the opposing party's claim, they are "compulsory" (in the sense of "use them or lose them.") If not, they are "permissive." Tex. R. Civ. P. 97(a) & (b).

2. Cross-claims are claims made against co-parties, as, for example, claims for contribution or indemnity made between co-defendants. Tex. R. Civ. P. 97(c).

3. Third Party Claims (also called "impleader") are claims brought by a defendant against a person "not a party to the action who is or may be liable" to the defendant or to the plaintiff for all or part of the plaintiff's claim against the defendant. Tex. R. Civ. P. 38.

The Civil Practice and Remedies Code addresses the way in which these claims are treated for venue purposes.

§ 15.062. *Counterclaims, Cross Claims, and Third-Party Claims.*

(a) Venue of the main action shall establish venue of a counterclaim, cross claim, or third-party claim properly joined under the Texas Rules of Civil Procedure or any applicable statute.

(b) If an original defendant properly joins a third-party defendant, venue shall be proper for a claim arising out of the same transaction, occurrence, or series of transactions or occurrences by the plaintiff against the third-party defendant if the claim arises out of the subject matter of the plaintiff's claim against the original defendant.

§ 5.03 LITIGATING VENUE RIGHTS

The plaintiff has the first choice to fix venue in a proper county, which is done by filing suit in the county of choice, and is ordinarily bound by this choice. But what if defendant claims that plaintiff has chosen a county in which venue is *not* proper? This section discusses the ways in which those issues are raised and litigated.

Read Tex. R. Civ. P. 86 through 89.

[A] Raising the Issue of Improper Venue

A defendant seeking a venue change should file a motion to transfer venue. Generally, a motion to transfer venue on the basis that venue is improper must be made at the earliest opportunity. Objections to improper venue are waived unless made by written motion filed before or concurrently with any other plea, pleading, or motion except a special appearance motion. Tex. R. Civ. P. 86(1). The primary basis for transfer (other than on grounds of inconvenience or inability to obtain a fair trial) is that venue is not proper in the county of suit and is proper in the county to which transfer is sought (or that venue is mandatory in a particular county despite the fact that venue would otherwise have been proper where the action was filed); no response is necessary except as required by Civil Procedure Rule 87(3)(a). A trial court has no discretion to transfer venue on its own motion, even to a county of proper venue. *See In re Masonite Corp.*, 997 S.W.2d 194, 198 (Tex. 1999).

[B] Venue "Hearings"

Before September 1, 1983, it was often necessary for the plaintiff to prove a cause of action as one of the venue facts. At the venue hearing, live testimony was required to establish the venue facts. Affidavits were not a permissible substitute. Do not, therefore, rely on pre-1983 cases on questions of the proper procedure to contest venue.

Each of these aspects of former venue practice was eliminated by the 1983 amendments. First, the amendments eliminated the former requirement that a plaintiff who based venue on a particular kind of cause of action had to call witnesses to prove that cause of action in order to demonstrate that venue was correct. Instead, the statute now provides, "In all venue hearings, no factual proof concerning the merits of the case shall be required to establish venue." *See* C.P.R.C. § 15.064(a); *see also* Tex. R. Civ. P. 87(2)(b). Second, to eliminate "minitrials" on venue issues altogether, the statute was amended to provide that "[t]he court shall determine venue on the basis of the pleadings and affidavits." C.P.R.C. § 15.064(a).

Under Rule 86, a defendant who wants to challenge venue files a timely motion to transfer venue. The motion should name the county to which the defendant seeks transfer. Tex. R. Civ. P. 86. If the defendant has specifically denied the venue facts that plaintiff pleaded, then the plaintiff must make "prima facie proof" that venue is correct by supplying affidavits swearing to the venue facts. If plaintiff does so, the facts are sufficiently established. Tex. R. Civ. P. 87.

But what happens when there are conflicting factual allegations? Rule 87 provides that a claimant's prima facie proof that venue is proper will prevent a venue transfer — the court will not look at a defending party's response unless the venue transfer motion is based on the grounds that an impartial trial cannot be held in the county of suit or "on an established ground of mandatory venue" as reflected in the movant's "prima facie proof." TEX. R. CIV. P. 87(3)(a)-(c). This procedure creates an incentive for a plaintiff to provide false affidavits in order to secure a desirable venue. Therefore, a matching disincentive exists by way of the treatment of the issue on appeal. As more fully explained in the next subsection, "[o]n appeal from the trial on the merits, if venue was improper, it shall in no event be harmless error and shall be reversible error" and "[i]n determining whether venue was or was not proper, the appellate court shall consider the entire record, including the trial on the merits." C.P.R.C. § 15.064(b). Thus, plaintiffs were provided ample statutory encouragement to avoid unfounded venue claims.

The way the system works may be more clear to you if you review the papers that would be filed in a typical venue dispute. Take a look at the following forms from William V. Dorsaneo III, *Texas Litigation Guide*, chapter 61 (Venue). First come the venue allegations in the Plaintiff's Original Petition.

___ [*paragraph number*]

Plaintiff's action against ______ [name] as defendant is properly maintainable in the county of suit for the following reasons:

[*Alternative One. When venue is based on county where events occurred*]

______ [*Allege facts indicating that all or substantial part of events giving rise to claim took place in county of suit, e.g.*, Negotiations that formed the basis of plaintiff's contract with defendant occurred on ______ (*date*), at ______ (*address of location of negotiations*) in ______ County.] Accordingly, venue is proper in ______ County, Texas.

[*Alternative Two. When venue is based on county of defendant's residence*]

Defendant ______ [*name*], a natural person, maintains a venue residence at ______ [*address of residence*], in ______ [*county of suit, e.g.*, Dallas] County. This residence is within the possession of defendant ______ [*name*], and ______ [______ (he *or* she) has occupied it consistently for a substantial period of time or ______ (he *or* she) intends to occupy it on a permanent basis consistently for a substantial period of time]. Accordingly, venue is proper in ______ County, Texas.

If the defendant believes that the venue chosen is improper, the defendant should file a motion to transfer venue. A motion to transfer venue based on improper venue and seeking transfer to a county where venue is permitted by statute must allege that venue is not proper in the county of suit under any application of the general venue rule, any mandatory venue exception, or any permissive venue exception properly raised by the plaintiff's pleadings. The defendant's motion must state the "legal and factual basis" for the transfer of the action. Consequently, the motion should state specifically why venue is not proper in the county of suit. Tex. R. Civ. P. 86(3).

Because all venue facts, when properly pleaded, are taken as true unless specifically denied by the adverse party, the motion must contain specific denials of the venue facts pleaded by the plaintiff in the petition that would support venue in the county of suit. Tex. R. Civ. P. 87(3)(a). This requires more than a statement that the defendant "specifically denies those venue facts pleaded in Plaintiff's Original Petition that purport to establish venue." *See Maranatha Temple, Inc. v. Enterprise Prods. Co.*, 833 S.W.2d 736, 740 (Tex. App. — Houston [1st Dist.] 1992, pet. denied).

The motion must also request that the action be transferred to another specified county of proper venue, setting out the legal and factual basis supporting venue in the county to which transfer is sought Tex. R. Civ. P. 86(3). Facts supporting venue in the county to which transfer is sought should be specific, as venue facts in a defendant's motion to transfer are also taken as true unless specifically denied. Tex. R. Civ. P. 87(3)(a). A defendant may plead that *if* a cause of action exists, all or part of it accrued in the county to which transfer is sought. Doing so does not constitute an admission that a cause of action in fact exists. Tex. R. Civ. P. 87(2)(b). The motion would look something like this [*Litigation Guide* § 61.110]:

I.

Defendant objects to venue in ______ [*name of county of suit, e.g.*, Dallas County], the county in which this action was instituted, on the ground that this county is not a proper county. No basis exists mandating or permitting venue in this county.

Defendant specially denies the venue facts pleaded in plaintiff's petition. More specifically, defendant is not a resident of ______ County, Texas. ______ [He *or* She] was not a resident of ______ County, Texas, when the alleged cause of action accrued. Defendant also specifically denies that all or a substantial part of the alleged events or omissions set out in the petition occurred in ______ County, Texas. ______ [*Continue with specific denials that alleged cause of action accrued in county of suit, e.g.*, The defendant did not sign the alleged contract in Dallas County, and none of the performance of the alleged contract was to take place in Dallas County].

II.

[*Optional. If petition alleges venue based on specified mandatory or permissive venue statute*]

In addition, venue is improper because the ______ [mandatory *or* permissive] grounds for venue alleged in plaintiff's petition do not apply in this case. ______ [*Continue with specific denials of legal and factual basis for venue, e.g.*, The mandatory venue statute for real property actions, Civil Practice and Remedies Code Section 15.011, does not govern plaintiff's cause of action. Plaintiff is not seeking to recover an interest or estate in real property, to remove encumbrances from the title to real property, to quiet title to real property, or to partition real property. Instead, the property in question is involved only incidentally and not directly].

III.

Defendant requests that this action be transferred to a district court of ______ [*name of county to which transfer is sought, e.g.*, Travis County, Texas], where proper venue lies in this cause.

IV.

Venue is proper in ______ County, Texas, in that ______ [*state legal and factual basis for transfer to county of proper venue, e.g.*, plaintiff's action is founded on an alleged contractual obligation of defendant to pay money arising out of a consumer transaction for goods primarily intended for personal, family, or household use. The alleged contract was signed in ______ County, Texas, on ______ (*date*), and the defendant resided in ______ County, Texas, when this suit was commenced or the defendant resided in ______ County, Texas, when this suit was commenced].

A plaintiff wanting venue to remain in the county in which the suit was originally filed may need to respond to the motion and demonstrate that venue is proper or that venue would be improper in the county requested by the motion to transfer. Properly pleaded venue facts in the defendant's motion to transfer must be taken as true unless specifically denied. TEX. R. CIV. P. 87(3)(a). Specific denial of the venue facts contained in the motion to transfer will compel the defendant to present prima facie proof of his or her venue allegations. TEX. R. CIV. P. 87(3)(a). Similarly, when the defendant's motion specifically denies venue facts contained in the petition, the plaintiff must make prima facie proof. Prima facie proof requires that venue facts be properly pleaded and that an affidavit and any relevant discovery products that set forth facts supporting the pleading be filed. TEX. R. CIV. P. 87(3)(a); *see also* TEX. R. CIV. P. 88 (discovery products may be considered by court in making venue determinations). Therefore, a plaintiff's response should be accompanied by affidavits and attached discovery products proving venue facts in the petition that were specifically denied in the motion to transfer venue. It is recommended that the response itself outline the venue facts that will be established by the affidavits and attachments.

A response will therefore look something like this [*Litigation Guide* § 61.120]:

I.

On ______ [*date*], plaintiff filed in this cause ______ [his *or* her] ______ [*designate current trial pleading, e.g.*, First Amended Original Petition], which is incorporated by reference as if fully copied and set forth at length. The allegations of that petition are true and correct.

II.

As alleged in that petition and as supported and established by the attached affidavits and attachments to this response, plaintiff's suit is ______ [*state nature of case, e.g.*, a suit for damages for libel against defendant in his individual capacity *or* a suit for damages for libel against a corporate defendant that has its principal place of business and is domiciled in Dallas County].

III.

______ [*Allege venue facts supported by prima facie proof established in affidavits and attachments, e.g.*, Defendant is a resident of ______ County, Texas *or* Defendant corporation's principal office is located in ______ County, Texas].

IV.

By reason of the above, venue of this suit as to ______ [*name*] is ______ [proper *or* mandatory] in ______ County, Texas, under the provisions of [*cite statutory authority, e.g.*, Section 15.017 of the Civil Practice and Remedies Code].

[If plaintiff also believes that venue would be incorrect in the county to which defendant seeks transfer, deny those venue facts.]

PRACTICE EXERCISE #14

(1) A car wreck between Paula and Darwin happens near the Dallas County/Tarrant County border. Darwin resides in Tarrant County. Paula sues Darwin in Collin County despite her Petition's allegations that the accident occurred in Dallas County and that Darwin resides in Tarrant County. Darwin files a timely motion to transfer venue to Tarrant County. Does Darwin need to include special denials in this motion? If Paula does not respond, how should the judge rule?

(2) Assume the same facts as in (1), but this time Paula files suit in Dallas County, alleging that the accident happened there. Darwin files a motion to transfer venue to Tarrant County, and his motion states that he resides in Tarrant County. He specifically denies that the accident happened in Dallas County. Paula responds by objecting to transfer, and she files an affidavit stating that the accident occurred in Dallas County. How should the judge rule?

(3) Pam and Dirk are co-owners of a house in Collin County (they used to live together there). Since they both moved out, they have used the house as rental property. Dirk wants to continue to do so, but Pam needs cash now and wants to sell the house. Dirk refuses to agree, and so Pam files an action for partition of the property. She files the action in Dallas County, where Dirk now resides. Dirk would rather litigate the case in Collin County. What should he do?

(4) Plaintiff Patsy has sued defendant Doug for breach of contract. She has filed the suit in Harris County, which is where both parties met and signed the contract. Her petition alleges that a substantial part of the events giving rise to her claim took place in Harris County. Defendant Doug prefers venue in Bexar County, where the contract was to be performed. (Doug lives in Bexar County, and promised in the

contract to provide cleaning services for Patsy's office in San Antonio. Patsy promised to pay Doug by mailing a check to Doug's San Antonio address.) You represent Doug. Using the forms on the preceding pages, draft Doug's Motion to Transfer Venue.

The following case illustrates proper (and improper) ways in which to litigate issues of venue, and serves as a warning about how easy it is for a litigant to waive his or her objection to venue. Not all courts take such a strict approach but some do, and so the prudent practitioner will take care to avoid waiving the client's venue rights. What should Carlile have done differently in the following case?

CARLILE v. RLS LEGAL SOLUTIONS, INC.

138 S.W.3d 403 (Tex. App. — Houston [14th Dist.] 2004, no pet.)

Guzman, J.

David C. Carlile appeals a judgment rendered in favor of RLS Legal Solutions, Inc. ("RLS"), on three grounds: (1) the trial court erred in denying his motion to transfer venue; (2) there was legally and factually insufficient evidence to support the jury's award of attorney's fees; and (3) the trial court erred in excluding evidence. We affirm.

I. FACTS AND PROCEDURAL HISTORY

Carlile is an attorney practicing law in Harrison County, Texas. The subject of this appeal stems from a toxic tort case styled *Frazier v. Ashland* ("*Frazier* litigation"), filed by Carlile in Harrison County on behalf of approximately 600 plaintiffs and involving over 170 defendants. In connection with that case, Carlile requested copies of various discovery documents from defense counsel Baker Botts pursuant to Texas Rule of Civil Procedure 203.3. Baker Botts, in turn, referred Carlile to RLS to obtain the copies because the *Frazier* defendants had contracted with RLS to act as a repository and document retrieval system on their behalf.

RLS furnished the requested copies to Carlile; however, a dispute arose over the charges billed. Consequently, RLS filed suit against Carlile in a Harris County court on a sworn account and asserting breach of contract and quantum meruit claims. Both Carlile and RLS filed a number of pretrial motions, including a motion to transfer venue filed by Carlile in January 2001. The trial court heard Carlile's venue motion on March 18, 2002. The following day, March 19, the case proceeded to trial. The jury rendered a verdict in favor of RLS awarding the amount due on the account, attorney's fees, and interest. On March 20, the court signed an order denying Carlile's venue motion and entered judgment in accordance with the jury's verdict. This appeal ensued.

II. VENUE

In his first issue, Carlile argues the trial court erred in denying his motion to transfer venue because RLS failed to properly plead and prove venue. According to Carlile, because RLS's original petition alleged venue was proper in Dallas County pursuant to section 15.011 of the Texas Civil Practice and Remedies Code [the mandatory real property provision], RLS failed to establish that venue was proper in Harris County. RLS contends Carlile waived his venue objections.

The trial court's order denying Carlile's venue motion does not indicate whether it was denied because the court deemed the venue objection waived or concluded venue was proper in Harris County. Thus, we address the waiver issue first . . . .

A party may also expressly waive venue rights by clear, overt acts evidencing an intent to waive, or impliedly, by taking some action inconsistent with an intent to pursue the venue motion. Generally, these actions invoke the judicial power of the courts. A movant may urge a preliminary motion without waiving venue objections, provided the motion does not involve a hearing on the merits.

In this case, RLS filed its original petition against Carlile in November 2000. Both RLS and Carlile assert Carlile originally filed his motion to transfer venue in January 2001; however that document is not contained in the record. Instead, the next document in the record relative to the venue issue is a motion for summary judgment filed by RLS on May 25, 2001. The trial court granted the summary judgment on June 26, 2001, and awarded RLS damages, attorney's fees, and judgment interest. Notice of the judgment was mailed on that same day. On July 25, 2001, Carlile filed a motion for new trial.

In the initial paragraph of his motion for new trial, Carlile noted that he had attempted to file a response, entitled "Defendant's Motion for Continuance, Motion to Set a Hearing to Transfer Venue, Special Exceptions and Objections to the Plaintiff's Offer of Proof as to Plaintiff's Motion for Summary Judgment, and Response to Motion for Summary Judgment" ("Response"), to RLS's summary judgment motion. However, Carlile stated the county clerk mistakenly refused to file his Response and instead, returned it. Following this paragraph, Carlile's motion requested the court vacate the order granting summary judgment, stating:

> The Court committed error in the application of the law and abused its discretion by granting [RLS's] motion without considering Defendant's response. Defendant would show that the Harris County Clerk exceeded her authority by refusing to file Defendant's response to [RLS's] motion for summary judgment . . . . Thus, the Court should have considered Defendant's response to [RLS's] motion for summary judgment . . . .

In the motion, Carlile argued further that his Response raised a fact issue on the existence of a contract, its terms, and attorney's fees; Carlile also challenged RLS's summary judgment evidence. Importantly, however, Carlile did not assert any arguments regarding venue. He did not reassert his venue objections or make the motion for new trial subject to his venue motion . . . .

At least one Texas appellate court has concluded that filing a motion for new trial can be an action inconsistent with an intent to continue to assert an objection to improper venue, (thus waiving the venue motion). . . . As described by the court, by filing a motion for new trial when the venue motion was pending, the defendant engaged in "an act seeking to invoke the authority of the court whose authority" he challenged . . . .

A venue motion is an appearance on the venue issue and, like a special appearance, must be filed prior to or concurrently with any other plea, pleading, or motion. *See* Tex. R. Civ. P. 86. Arguably then, because Carlile's motion for new trial was a pleading which addressed the merits of the summary judgment before Carlile pursued a ruling on his venue motion, the motion for new trial could be construed as an "affirmative action" by which he submitted to the jurisdiction of the trial court. By invoking the judicial power of the trial court in this manner, Carlile acted inconsistently with his objections to venue in Harris County. However, we need not look solely to Carlile's motion for new trial as an implied waiver of his venue motion. The record reflects additional actions which, when examined in conjunction with the motion for new trial, constitute waiver of the venue motion.

A party filing a venue motion has the burden to diligently request a setting on the motion and obtain a ruling prior to a trial on the merits. A delay in obtaining a hearing provides a basis for the trial court to deny a venue motion. Here, the record reflects the venue motion was not heard until March 18, 2002 and was not ruled upon until one day after trial. Assuming Carlile filed his original venue motion in January 2001, approximately fourteen months elapsed before Carlile obtained a hearing on the motion, indicating a lack of diligence in securing the hearing . . . .

Carlile asserts however that the record is "replete" with his attempts to challenge venue. First, Carlile points to his Response dated June 14, 2001, returned to him by the county clerk. As we noted, Carlile did present a request to the trial court for a hearing on his venue motion in those documents. When the clerk returned the documents to Carlile, in June 2001, the clerk also provided Carlile with forms reflecting submission docket procedures. However, the record indicates that Carlile's next attempt to obtain a hearing was on November 26, when he filed a "Motion for Continuance, Motion to Set a Hearing to Transfer of Venue, and Response to Motion for Summary Judgment," in response to another summary judgment motion filed by RLS on November 1. [A]lthough the record reflects Carlile requested a hearing, it does not reflect that he pursued the matter to conclusion, indicating he was perhaps less than diligent — particularly because Carlile was advised of the trial court's docketing procedures in June 2001, and already had suffered an adverse judgment in the case.

Regardless, in February 2002, RLS filed a no-evidence summary judgment motion. Carlile responded by filing a "Motion to Compel, Motion for Continuance, and Response to No Evidence Motion for Summary Judgment." In his motion, Carlile requested the court (1) compel RLS to respond to discovery, and (2) reset the hearing on RLS's summary judgment motion because RLS had not produced requested discovery. *See* Tex. R. Civ. P. 166a(g) (allowing a continuance for discovery to be had). Carlile's motion also addressed the merits of RLS's request for summary judgment. However, again, Carlile did not assert any arguments regarding venue, make the motion subject to his venue motion, nor request a continuance so the venue motion could be heard. By filing a motion for continuance, not conditioned upon his venue motion, Carlile invoked the jurisdiction of the trial court and acted inconsistently with an intent to insist upon his venue motion.

In sum, even assuming that none of Carlile's actions or lack of diligence alone sufficed to waive his venue motion, collectively these actions establish a waiver of the motion.

In response to Carlile's argument that we must reverse the trial court's judgment because RLS failed to establish venue was proper in Harris County, we note that because Carlile waived his venue motion, RLS was not required to produce proof of venue. We find Carlile waived his venue objections. Thus, the trial court did not abuse its discretion in denying his motion to transfer venue. Accordingly, we overrule Carlile's first issue.

[The court also affirmed the judgment below as to attorney's fees and found that Carlile failed to preserve error on his evidence point.]

NOTES AND QUESTIONS

(1) *Timing Considerations.* Civil Procedure Rule 86 provides that an objection to improper venue is waived if not made by written motion filed before or concurrently with any other plea, pleading or motion. *See also* C.P.R.C. § 15.063. A defendant may subpoena witnesses and use the various discovery devices without waiving the venue challenge. *See* Tex. R. Civ. P. 88.

(2) *Waiver by Pursuing Other Motions.* Counsel must be very careful before taking other actions that could be construed as being inconsistent with the venue challenge, as *Carlile* demonstrates. And *Carlile* has company. In *Nacol v. Williams*, 554 S.W.2d 286, 288 (Tex. Civ. App. — Eastland 1977, writ dism'd), the defendant was held to have waived the basic venue privilege existing under prior law by *presenting* a motion to require the plaintiff to post security for costs even though the motion was filed after the venue challenge! Consider the following excerpt:

> This case is distinguishable from *Talbert v. Miles*, 477 S.W.2d 710 (Tex. Civ. App. — Waco 1972, no writ) relied on by appellant in that in *Talbert* there was no evidence the motion to rule for costs was submitted to the court for determination or that any action of any nature was taken on the motion by anyone after it was filed. In the case at bar, when the appellant filed his motion with an order attached for the judge to sign, the court had a duty to act on the motion.

(3) *Waiver Through Delay.* The *Carlile* court also relied on the defendant's delay in securing a ruling on his venue motion. This, too, is consistent with other cases. As reflected in the following excerpt from *Whitworth v. Kuhn*, 734 S.W.2d 108, 111 (Tex. App. — Austin 1987, no writ), a movant must take the initiative to present a motion to transfer to the trial court:

> Texas R. Civ. P. 87(1) provides in part:
>
> The determination of a motion to transfer venue shall be made promptly by the court and such determination must be made in a reasonable time prior to commencement of the trial on the merits. The movant has the duty

to request a setting on the motion to transfer.

It is apparent that this language contemplates a speedy determination of a venue question. Indeed, we find it implicit in the language and purpose of this rule that a movant may not sit on his rights indefinitely without incurring waiver. *See* 3 W. Dorsaneo, Texas Litigation Guide § 61.05[4] (1987). Thus, while a trial court may rule on a venue motion without a hearing, the movant is under a duty to request a hearing to urge his motion within a reasonable time. Here, Whitworth waited more than a year after filing his motion to transfer venue before requesting a hearing on that motion. His complete lack of diligence is inconsistent with the purpose of Rule 87(1), and the trial court could have refused his motion on that basis.

(4) *The Scope of Waiver.* C.P.R.C. § 15.0641 resolves a split among Texas intermediate courts and clarifies that waiver by one defendant of its right to contest venue does not operate as a waiver to a co-defendant's right to timely challenge venue.

(5) *The Effect of a Nonsuit on Venue Determination.* Under pre-1983 venue practice, if a plaintiff took a nonsuit while the defendant's plea of privilege was pending, venue was fixed in the county to which transfer was sought. *See Tempelmeyer v. Blackburn*, 175 S.W.2d 222, 224 (Tex. 1943); *see also Ruiz v. Conoco, Inc.*, 868 S.W.2d 752, 756–57 (Tex. 1993). Under post-1983 practice, when a nonsuit is filed, the trial court and any reviewing court "must consider the state of the record at that point." *GeoChem Tech Corp. v. Verseckes*, 962 S.W.2d 541, 543 (Tex. 1998). Thus, if an objection to venue has been filed and the plaintiff then takes a nonsuit and has not specifically denied the venue facts alleged by the party seeking transfer, the venue facts are taken as true. Once the first court has ruled, however, venue is fixed. The Supreme Court addressed this issue in *In re Team Rocket, L.P.*, 256 S.W.3d 257 (Tex. 2008), which involved plaintiffs who mistakenly filed suit in Harris County. The defendants filed a motion to transfer to Williamson County, their principal office and residence, and the trial court granted the motion. The plaintiffs then took a nonsuit and immediately refiled the case in Fort Bend County, the place where the acts giving rise to the claim occurred. The defendants filed a motion to transfer the case to Williamson county based on the original trial court's transfer order, but the Fort Bend trial court refused to transfer the case. The Supreme Court granted mandamus relief, holding that "once a venue determination has been made, that determination is conclusive as to those parties and claims. . . . Once the Harris County trial court transferred the cause to the proper venue of Williamson County, venue was fixed permanently in Williamson County for these causes of action between these parties. That venue was also proper in Fort Bend County does not change the result." *Id.* at 260.

(6) *Venue Hearings.* Normally, the trial court is directed to make venue decisions based solely on pleadings and affidavits, and to look only to see whether the plaintiff made a prima facie case of its venue facts without resolving factual disputes. Re-read the *Surgitek* case in § 5.02[D][3] above. How does the evidentiary hearing described in that case differ from a normal venue hearing? Can you think of any other venue provisions for which the Texas Supreme Court might find an evidentiary hearing to be appropriate? *See, e.g.*, C.P.R.C. § 15.002(b) (transfers based on

convenience); TEX. R. CIV. P. 257–259 (transfers for impartial trial).

[C] Appellate Review of Venue Rulings

Because of the importance of a party's venue rights, as well as the elimination of evidentiary hearings on most venue disputes, the 68th Texas Legislature developed an unusual rule for the appeal of venue rulings. Section 15.064 of the Civil Practice and Remedies Code provides:

> (a) In all venue hearings, no factual proof concerning the merits of the case shall be required to establish venue. The court shall determine venue questions from the pleadings and affidavits. No interlocutory appeal shall lie from the determination.
>
> (b) On appeal from the trial on the merits, if venue was improper it shall in no event be harmless error and shall be reversible error. In determining whether venue was or was not proper, the appellate court shall consider the entire record, including the trial on the merits.

This standard causes considerable confusion, because: 1) it reverses the normal "harmless error" rule; and 2) it directs the court of appeals to make a decision on a different basis and on different facts than the trial court whose actions it is reviewing. The Texas Supreme Court discussed this dilemma, and its proper treatment, in the following cases.

[1] The Standard of Review on Appeal

RUIZ v. CONOCO, INC., 868 S.W.2d 752 (Tex. 1993). Javier Ruiz, a resident of Hidalgo County, suffered severe head injuries in Webb County while working for Cameron Iron Works, Inc. on a well owned by Conoco, Inc. Ruiz ultimately sued Conoco in Starr County through his wife who had been appointed his guardian. Ruiz claimed that venue was proper in Starr County under a former permissive venue exception that was repealed in 1995 under which: "Foreign corporations . . . not incorporated by the laws of this state, and doing business in this state, may be sued in any county in which . . . the company may have an agency or representative." Conoco sought to have the action transferred to Harris County. Despite the fact that it ruled as a matter of law that Conoco had no agency or representative in Starr County, the Texas Supreme Court interpreted Civil Practice and Remedies Code Section 15.064(b) by devising the following deferential standard of review:

> The procedure mandated by this statute is fundamentally flawed because it allows appellate review of venue on a basis different from that on which it was decided. In deciding a motion to transfer venue, the trial court is required by Rule 87, Tex. R. Civ. P., to take as true those facts of which prima facie proof is made by the party with the burden of such proof; yet in reviewing the trial court's decision, an appellate court must reverse (there cannot be harmless error) if other evidence in the record, even evidence adduced after venue was determined, destroys the prima facie proof on which the trial court relied. Prima facie proof is not subject to rebuttal, cross-examination, impeachment or even disproof. The evidence

as a whole may well show that prima facie proof was misleading or wrong. But while the wisdom of the statute may be challenged, there is no misunderstanding its plain language: an appellate court is obliged to conduct an independent review of the entire record to determine whether venue was proper in the ultimate county of suit.

This review should be conducted like any other review of a trial court's fact findings and legal rulings, except that the evidence need not be reviewed for factual sufficiency. If there is probative evidence to support the trial court's determination, even if the preponderance of the evidence is to the contrary, we believe the appellate court should defer to the trial court. A remand to reconsider the issue, which is the relief ordinarily afforded for factual insuffi ciency of the evidence, would only increase the expense and delay of litigation in order to resolve an issue which, though important, is unrelated to the merits. Moreover, it exacerbates the difficulties already present in the rule if the appellate court decides, based on all the evidence, that the case should be remanded for a redetermination of venue, based on prima facie proof. (Would a second trial be required?) The statute does not mandate factual sufficiency review, and we believe it is neither necessary nor wise.

Therefore, if there is any probative evidence in the entire record, including trial on the merits, that venue was proper in the county where judgment was rendered, the appellate court must uphold the trial court's determination. If there is no such evidence, the judgment must be reversed and the case remanded to the trial court. The error cannot be harmless, according to the statute. If there is any probative evidence that venue was proper in the county to which transfer was sought, the appellate court should instruct the trial court to transfer the case to that county. Only if there is no probative evidence that venue was proper either in the county of suit or in the county to which transfer was sought should the appellate court remand the case to the trial court to conduct further proceedings on the issue of venue. This is one instance in which remand cannot be avoided. Rule 87(3)(d), Tex. R. Civ. P., contemplates that additional proof may be ordered in connection with a motion to transfer if neither party makes the required showing at first. In the unusual instance where there is no probative evidence in the record that venue is proper anywhere, a remand is unavoidable.

The issue for us, then, is whether there is any probative evidence in the record to support the trial court's determination that venue was proper in Starr County. As in any other situation, we view the record in the light most favorable to the trial court's ruling. We do not defer, however, to the trial court's application of the law.

868 S.W.2d 752, 757–58 (Tex. 1993). The Court then applied these standards and concluded that there was no evidence in the whole record of the case that venue was proper in Starr County, as the defendant's managerial employee there had the authority only to order parts and services in an amount not to exceed $500. It therefore affirmed the court of appeals decision reversing and remanding the case

with instructions to transfer to Harris County.

[2] Reversible Error

The venue statutes' appellate review provisions create another quandary — what happens if the trial court transfers a case when it should not have done so, but it transfers the case to a county in which venue would have been proper from the outset? Is it still automatically reversible error?

WILSON v. TEXAS PARKS AND WILDLIFE DEPT.

886 S.W.2d 259 (Tex. 1994)

Hightower, J.

This cause requires that we determine whether a trial court commits reversible error by transferring a civil lawsuit filed in a Texas county that qualifies as a proper venue to another county that originally might have been considered a proper venue. Lydia Wilson, Curtis Wilson, Angela Wilson Kramm, and Lila Wilson (collectively "Plaintiffs") sued the Texas Parks and Wildlife Department ("Department") in district court in Travis County, alleging that the Department's negligence caused the drowning deaths of Wilford and Wilton Wilson. The Department filed a motion to transfer venue of Plaintiffs' action to Blanco County. The motion was granted and the case was transferred to Blanco County where, after a jury trial, a take-nothing judgment was rendered in favor of the Department. The court of appeals affirmed, holding that the transfer of a lawsuit from one county of proper venue to another county of proper venue is not reversible error. For the reasons explained herein, we reverse the judgment of the court of appeals, remand this cause to the trial court in Blanco County, and order that the cause be transferred to Travis County for a new trial.

I.

On the afternoon of May 16, 1987, the Wilson fishing party, including Wilford and Wilton Wilson, arrived at Pedernales Falls State Park ("the Park") to go fishing. The Park is located in Blanco County and is owned and operated by the Department. The fishing party walked and waded across one-hundred yards of river bed to get to their fishing spot. By 4:00 p.m., the party was fishing from atop a rock surrounded by water. At 8:00 p.m., the party was joined by two additional members of the Wilson family. Shortly thereafter, the party noticed rising water and attempted to retrace their steps across the river bed. Wilford and Wilton Wilson were unable to cross the river and drowned.

Plaintiffs sued the Department in Travis County, alleging that the Department's negligence caused the drowning deaths of Wilford and Wilton Wilson. Specifically, Plaintiffs alleged that the Department was negligent in the design, implementation, and maintenance of the Park's flood early warning system and in the training of Park personnel. The Department filed a motion to transfer venue of the suit to Blanco County, the site of the drownings. The motion was granted and the suit was transferred. Trial was to a jury who found that the Department was negligent, but failed to find that this negligence was a proximate cause of the deaths. Additionally, the jury found that Wilford and Wilton Wilson's negligent conduct was a proximate cause of their deaths. Finally, the jury found that the Wilson fishing party was not fishing within the park boundaries. Based on the jury's verdict, the trial court rendered a take-nothing judgment in favor of the Department. The court of appeals affirmed, holding that the transfer of a lawsuit from a county of proper venue to another county of proper venue is not reversible error.

II.

The Department contends that the transfer of a civil lawsuit from a county that qualifies as a proper venue to another county that might originally have been considered a proper venue is not reversible error as a matter of law. We disagree . . . .

Together, Rule 87-3(c) and section 15.063(1) require that a lawsuit pleaded and proved to be filed in a county of proper venue may not be transferred. Therefore, if the plaintiff chooses a county of proper venue, and this is supported by proof as required by Rule 87, no other county can be a proper venue in that case.[2] This rule gives effect to the plaintiff's right to select a proper venue.

The Department urges that reversible error exists only if the county of trial was one where permissive or mandatory venue never could have been sustained. Such a rule would eviscerate the plaintiff's right to select venue. The First Court of Appeals correctly understood the harsh effect of such a rule:

> [W]hen the plaintiff files suit in a permissible county, and the trial court wrongly transfers venue to another county, even a permissible one, the plaintiff has lost his right to choose where to bring his suit. He has neither waived his option by filing in an impermissible county nor had his suit transferred because the defendant has properly shown that it should be. Yet, he lost the right to bring suit in the permissible county of his choice. He has lost a right which he neither waived nor was rightfully divested of. The harmless error rule should not apply to such a circumstance.

Id.[3] Furthermore, the Department asks us to fashion a rule that runs contrary to the mandatory admonishment of Rule 87-3(c) and that renders section 15.063(1) meaningless. This we cannot do. Tex. Gov't Code Ann. 311.021(2) ("In enacting a statute, it is presumed that . . . the entire statute is intended to be effective.");

[2] This opinion only addresses transfer of venue pursuant to section 15.063(1) of the Texas Civil Practice and Remedies Code and expresses no opinion regarding transfer of venue pursuant to sections 15.063(2) and (3). We recognize that these sections may apply to make transfer of venue appropriate.

[3] The court in *Maranatha Temple, Inc.* recognized additional beneficial effects of the rule we announce today: "Parties who would otherwise be likely to knowingly assert faulty grounds for a transfer of venue will be less likely to do so if they face automatic reversal once it is determined on appeal that the transfer was erroneous . . . [and such a rule] . . . will guard against the forum shopping that occurs when a party intentionally asserts faulty, invalid grounds for a change of venue from one permissible county to another permissible county which he perceives is more favorable." 883 S.W.2d at 741.

Monsanto Co. v. Cornerstones Mun. Util. Dist., 865 S.W.2d 937, 939 (Tex. 1993) (stating that this court seeks the intent of the legislature as found in the plain and common meaning of the words and terms used).

Accordingly, we hold that if a plaintiff files suit in a county of proper venue, it is reversible error to transfer venue under section 15.063(1) even if the county of transfer would have been proper if originally chosen by the plaintiff. We now consider whether venue was proper in the county where suit was initially brought in this case.

III.

The standard of appellate review is governed by section 15.064(b) of the Texas Civil Practice and Remedies Code which provides:

> On appeal from the trial on the merits, if venue was improper it shall in no event be harmless error and shall be reversible error. In determining whether venue was or was not proper, the appellate court shall consider the entire record, including the trial on the merits.

Tex. Civ. Prac. & Rem. Code Ann. 15.064(b); *Ruiz v. Conoco, Inc.*, 868 S.W.2d 752, 757 (Tex. 1993). The "appellate court is obligated to conduct an independent review of the entire record to determine whether venue was proper in the ultimate county of suit." *Ruiz*, 868 S.W.2d at 758. Under the rule announced today, if Travis County, the venue chosen by Plaintiffs, was a county of proper venue, then Blanco County cannot be a county of proper venue as a matter of law.[4]

[The Court then concludes that the record contained some probative evidence that venue was proper in Travis County, noting that "Tom McGlathery, Regional Park Director for the Department, testified that the decision not to arm the Johnson City River Bridge sensor was made, in part, by Barry Bennett at the Department's headquarters in Travis County. Mr. McGlathery also testified that the individuals responsible for the content of the signs and map handouts detailing the Park's flood early warning system were employed at the Department's headquarters in Travis County. Wilbur Mengers, superintendent of the Park, testified that the signs and maps concerning the flood early warning system came from Travis County. Together, this testimony constitutes probative evidence that acts giving rise to the Plaintiffs' cause of action occurred in Travis County."]

Because we find that Travis County, the venue chosen by Plaintiffs, was a county of proper venue, we hold that Blanco County was an improper venue as a matter of law. The trial of this lawsuit in Blanco County constitutes reversible error. *See* Tex. Civ. Prac. & Rem. Code Ann. § 15.064(b).

For the reasons explained herein, we reverse the judgment of the court of appeals, remand this cause to the trial court in Blanco County, and order that the cause be transferred to Travis County for a new trial.

---

[4] The parties agree that Blanco County would have been a proper venue had the Plaintiffs originally filed suit there.

NOTES AND QUESTIONS

(1) *What is the "Entire Record"?* As *Ruiz* and *Wilson* note, the statute requires the court of appeals to review the "entire record, including trial on the merits" when deciding whether venue was proper. Venue was proper in the county where filed if there is "any probative evidence" in the entire record that supports venue. But do they really mean the "entire record," or do they just mean the trial record? In cases in which venue was challenged, the plaintiff's affidavit used to sustain venue will be part of the "entire record," and it would constitute some probative evidence. It appears that the Court disregards the "prima facie proof" from the venue hearing in doing "entire record" review, although it has not explicitly so held since it has so far found "probative evidence" in support of venue in the trial record.

(2) *Effect of Changes on Review.* Suppose that venue in a county is based on the residence of one of multiple defendants or one of multiple claims. What happens if the claim on which venue is based is eliminated by summary judgment? If the defendant files a timely motion to transfer venue, will the elimination of the in-county claim destroy the basis for venue? *See Pines of Westbury, Ltd. v. Paul Michael Constr., Inc.*, 993 S.W.2d 291, 294 (Tex. App. — Eastland 1999, pet. denied) (venue based on claim against defendant Hart; venue was correctly sustained at original venue hearing based on prima facie evidence presented about Hart at that time; claim against Hart eliminated on the merits by summary judgment; on appeal, court must review entire record and because of the summary judgment there is no probative evidence to support the claim and therefore no probative evidence to support the court's venue determination; reversed and remanded with directions to transfer the case as requested by defendants).

(3) *Reconsideration of Prior Ruling.* Assuming that the result in *Pines*, above, is correct, what should a trial court do about venue after dismissing the claim against the defendant whose presence justifies venue? Whole record review will show that venue was incorrect and venue errors will lead to reversal. The parties are not permitted to file a new motion to transfer. Can the defendant ask the court to rehear the original motion? One court of appeals has held that the language of Tex. R. Civ. P. 87(5) prohibits reconsideration and that mandamus is available to correct the "void" order. *Dorchester M.L.P. v. Anthony*, 734 S.W.2d 151, 152 (Tex. App. — Houston [1st Dist.] 1987, no writ):

> Relator's predecessor in interest, Dorchester Gas Producing Company, filed the underlying suit in December, 1983, seeking to recover money damages against Cabot Pipeline Corporation and other defendants for the alleged conversion of gas from producing wells located in the Panhandle Field in Gray and Carson Counties. On May 23, 1984, Judge Ken Harrison, then Presiding Judge of the 334th District Court, entered an order denying the defendants' motion to transfer venue. On February 27, 1987, the defendants filed a second motion to transfer venue, and on May 18, 1987, Judge Anthony, on her own motion, entered a purported order of transfer, stating that she had considered, *sua sponte*, the correctness of venue of the case and determined that proper venue was in Gray County. Judge

> Anthony's order also purported to vacate, sua sponte, "any previous orders relating to venue" in the case . . . .
>
> Here, the [original] court *sustained* venue in the county of suit and denied the defendants' motion to transfer. Under such a circumstance, the express provisions of Rule 87(5) mandate that "no further motions to transfer shall be considered . . . ." We accordingly hold that Judge Anthony's venue order dated May 18, 1987, is void in that it purports to reconsider and vacate Judge Harrison's prior order that sustained venue in Harris County. Because the order is void, mandamus is an appropriate action to compel that the order be vacated, that the transmitted papers be returned to the 334th Judicial District Court, and that Judge Anthony proceed to trial. *See Brown v. Brown*, 566 S.W.2d 378, 380 (Tex. Civ. App. — Corpus Christi 1978, no writ).

However, at the time *Anthony* was decided, the heading of Civil Rule 87(5) read "No Rehearing." Since then, the Rule's language has been changed to read "Motion for Rehearing," and the text of the rule itself never prohibited the court from reconsidering an earlier motion — just from considering a "further motion." Perhaps, then, a subsequent event that makes venue improper would allow the court to reconsider venue, as that would be more efficient than trying the case where "whole record" review will result in reversible error.

(4) *"Void" Transfer Orders*. In *City of La Grange v. McBee*, 923 S.W.2d 89, 90 (Tex. App. — Houston [1st Dist.] 1996, writ denied), the court held that a case transferred pursuant to a void order remains on the docket of the court from which the transfer is attempted, and the transferee court obtains no jurisdiction. Accordingly, any judgment entered by the transferee court under those circumstances is fundamental error and may be attacked for the first time on appeal.

§ 5.04 CONTRACTING FOR VENUE

Traditionally, forum selection clauses that prescribed venue in a particular Texas county in derogation of Texas venue statutes were considered to be against public policy. *See International Travelers' Assoc. v. Branum*, 212 S.W. 630, 632 (Tex. 1919); *see also Fidelity Union Life Ins. Co. v. Evans*, 477 S.W.2d 535, 537 (Tex. 1972). More recently, the Texas Supreme Court has ruled that forum selection clauses prescribing venue in another state should be enforced unless the party opposing the clause clearly shows that enforcement would be unreasonable and unjust, or that the clause was invalid for such reasons as fraud or overreaching. *See In re AIU Ins. Co.*, 148 S.W.3d 109, 111–15 (Tex. 2004) (trial court abused its discretion in failing to enforce clause selecting New York as forum). It is not clear whether this attitude will expand into venue agreements within the state of Texas. At least in the context of mandatory venue rules, one Texas court has reaffirmed traditional practice, holding that "a party's pre-suit agreement to set venue in a particular county that is contrary to a mandatory venue statute is void and unenforceable." *In re Great Lakes Dredge & Dock Co.*, 251 S.W.3d 68 (Tex. App. — Corpus Christi 2008, orig. proc.). The court specifically rejected the argument that the Supreme Court, having discarded the "ouster" doctrine on which the earlier forum selection cases were based, would reach the same conclusion in venue cases. *Id.* at 77-79.

Under the venue statute, however, forum selection clauses are enforceable if (and only if) they arise out of certain transactions that qualify as "major transactions." Generally, this refers to transactions involving an "aggregated stated value" of $1 million or more. C.P.R.C. § 15.020(e). [Re-read this section, which is located in § 5.02[B]]. Such agreements are binding unless unconscionable when made, and control over other provisions of Chapter 15. They do not, however, control over the venue provisions of statutes outside of Chapter 15 of the Civil Practice and Remedies Code.

Although, with the exception of "major transactions," the parties may not contract out of the basic venue scheme, a contract that provides for performance in a particular county of the obligation sought to be enforced may provide the basis for venue in the county of performance. In this sense, then, parties may indirectly choose venue. *See* C.P.R.C. § 15.035(a). This power is limited in most contract cases brought against consumers. In these cases, the contract is not enforceable unless it provides for venue "either in the county in which the defendant in fact signed the contract or in the county in which the defendant resides when the action is commenced."

Parties may also contract with respect to venue after suit is filed. The court must transfer an action to another county if the parties file a written consent to transfer to that county. C.P.R.C. § 15.063(3). Also, if a motion to transfer on the grounds of inability to obtain an impartial trial is granted, the parties may agree on the particular county to which venue will be transferred. Tex. R. Civ. P. 259(d)(2). A written agreement made in accordance with Civil Procedure Rule 11 entered into before a case is transferred and filed with the transferee court, operates as an express waiver of the venue issue on appeal. *Farris v. Ray*, 895 S.W.2d 351, 352 (Tex. 1995).

§ 5.05 CHANGE OF VENUE BECAUSE IMPARTIAL TRIAL CANNOT BE HAD

The rules on change of venue to secure an impartial trial predate the 1983 venue statutes, and were always a separate category from the basic venue rules. The current codification, however, creates uncertainty about the extent to which Rules 257–259 are governed by chapter 15 and Rules 86–87. One important question concerns whether the new stripped-down venue procedure, with its paper-based prima facie cases, applies to impartial trial issues, or whether a live evidentiary hearing is permissible. The other question concerns the timing requirements: must an impartial trial motion also be filed before answering?

Read Tex. R. Civ. P. 86(1), 87(2)(c)(5), 257, 258, 259.

NOTES AND QUESTIONS

(1) *Type of Hearing.* If a motion to transfer venue is based on the grounds that an impartial trial may not be had in the county where the action is pending, the matter is to be determined in accordance with Civil Procedure Rules 257 through 259. Given that the language of Rule 258 is taken (except for the last sentence)

verbatim from former Rule 258, prior case law is instructive for interpreting its meaning.

Assuming the movant complies with the requirements of Rule 257, i.e., submits an affidavit as well as those of three credible persons residing in the county of suit showing inability to obtain an impartial trial, transfer is mandatory unless the adverse party attacks the credibility of the movant by submitting the affidavit of a credible person. *See City of Abilene v. Downs*, 367 S.W.2d 153, 155–56 (Tex. 1963). When the credibility of the moving party, the means of knowledge of affiants, or truth of facts set out in the motion are attacked by the affidavit of a credible person, the motion will be tried by the judge.

It is not clear whether the trial court may, should, or must hear live testimony in connection with a motion to transfer venue due to an inability to obtain an impartial trial. The 1983 revisions of the venue statutes and companion procedural rules contained a number of provisions directed at eliminating the practice of essentially trying the merits of the case twice. *See* C.P.R.C. § 15.064(a); Tex. R. Civ. P. 87(3)(a). The first sentence of Section 15.064(a) provides: "In all venue hearings, no factual proof concerning the merits of the case shall be required to establish venue." However, when the sole issue is the availability of an impartial forum, the venue hearing is concerned with the existence of prejudice and favoritism, not the merits of the case. The rules for this type of venue hearing specify that a controverted motion shall be "tried" by the judge, but do not indicate whether such a trial will involve the testimony of live witnesses.

Cases interpreting this rule prior to the 1983 revisions of the venue statutes held that such a motion could not be resolved solely on the basis of affidavits and discovery products. After the 1983 revisions, however, section 15.064(a) states that venue questions shall be determined from the pleadings and affidavits. The Texas Supreme Court was faced with this discrepancy in a 1990 case and did not resolve the issue, instead addressing the other issue on appeal. *Union Carbide Corp. v. Moye*, 798 S.W.2d 792, 792 (Tex. 1990) (majority addressed issue of whether defendant was entitled to continuance). Two concurring opinions, however, suggested that defendants should have been allowed to present live testimony in the venue hearing. Justice Hecht took the position that the trial court should be allowed to hear oral testimony if it is necessary to resolve the issues, but should not be required to hear live testimony if the issues could be decided on the written evidence. Justice Raul Gonzalez went further, declaring that there should be a right to an oral hearing under Civil Procedure Rule 258. Allowing live testimony under at least some circumstances would also be consistent with the court's decision in *Surgitek*, in § 5.02[D][3] above, that recommended "a broader range of proof" in disputes over the fairness and convenience elements of section 15.003 joinder disputes.

(2) *Timing Considerations.* It is not clear whether a motion to transfer venue based on the inability to obtain an impartial trial must be filed and served concurrently with or before the filing of the answer. Section 15.063 of the Civil Practice and Remedies Code provides that a motion to transfer venue must be granted if filed and served concurrently with or before the answer, and lists inability to obtain an impartial trial as one of the three grounds for transfer.

Civil Procedure Rule 258 does not indicate a specific time for the filing of a motion to transfer venue on impartial trial grounds, but it does indicate that the motion should be "duly made." Cases interpreting the impartial trial venue rules prior to the 1983 revisions of the venue rules held that application based on impartial trial grounds could be made after the answer was filed. *City of Abilene v. Downs*, 367 S.W.2d 153, 155–56 (Tex. 1963); *Atchison, Topeka & Sante Fe Ry. Co. v. Holloway*, 479 S.W.2d 700, 706 (Tex. Civ. App. — Beaumont 1972, writ ref'd n.r.e.). The 1983 amendments to the venue rules left the rules bearing on this point virtually intact, which may mean that the Texas Supreme Court intended to leave the timing of the impartial trial venue motion unchanged.

It is difficult to reconcile the current text of section 15.063 with prior law, even though the imposition of a due order rule for impartial trial cases is not a good idea. The conditions giving rise to inability to obtain an impartial trial, e.g., publicity resulting in widespread community feeling about the case, may not arise until after the answer is filed. In his concurring opinion in *Union Carbide*, Justice Gonzalez stated that section 15.063 does not supplant the rules and decisions allowing for a motion based on prejudice that manifests itself after the answer has been filed. However, even if filing after the answer is allowed, it would be prudent for counsel to show why a delay is justified, or how the motion is nevertheless "duly" made. *See, e.g., Lone Star Steel Co. v. Scott*, 759 S.W.2d 144, 157–58 (Tex. App. — Texarkana 1988, pet. denied). In this regard, the last two sentences of Civil Procedure Rule 86(1) were certainly designed to suggest that due order rules should not apply to transfers on impartial trial grounds or consent-based transfers. *See* Tex. R. Civ. P. 86(1) ("A written consent of the parties to transfer the case to another county may be filed with the clerk of the court at any time. A motion to transfer venue because an impartial trial cannot be had in the county where the action is pending is governed by the provisions of Rule 257.").

(3) *To What County?* If the motion to transfer is sustained, the judge must transfer the case as specified in Civil Procedure Rule 259. In line with the language of section 15.063 of the Civil Practice and Remedies Code, Rule 259 states that the court must transfer the case to a county of proper venue if one is available. Under this rule, the court must first try to find an adjoining county of proper venue. If there is no proper adjoining county, transfer must be made to *any* county of proper venue. Only if there is no county of proper venue other than the county of suit may the court transfer the case to an adjoining county without regard to its being a proper one, but because an impartial trial can be had there. As before, if the motion to transfer is sustained, the parties may agree on a transferee county and the court must transfer the case to that county.

(4) *The Collision Between Appellate Rule 44 and C.P.R.C. § 15.064.* Appellate Rule 44, the harmless error rule, applies to all procedural errors including the violation of apparently mandatory rules such as Civil Procedure Rule 258. A judgment is not to be reversed for an error of law unless the error amounts to a denial of the appellant's rights that was reasonably calculated to cause the rendition of an improper judgment. *See Lone Star Steel Co. v. Scott*, 759 S.W.2d 144, 147 (Tex. App. — Texarkana 1988, writ denied) (holding that error in not transferring case was harmless). Does this holding conflict with the language in section 15.064(b) that "if venue was improper it shall in no event be harmless error

and shall be reversible error"? Does section 15.064 have anything to do with Rules 257–259?

§ 5.06 MULTIDISTRICT LITIGATION

In 2003, the Texas Legislature directed the Supreme Court to adopt rules to allow for the temporary transfer of related cases to one district court for consolidated or coordinated pretrial proceedings. The cases are to be remanded to their original courts after those pretrial proceedings are concluded. The Supreme Court responded by adopting Rule 13 of the Texas Rules of Judicial Administration. It applies to civil actions involving one or more common questions of fact that were filed in a constitutional county court, county court at law, probate court, or district court on or after September 1, 2003.

Read Tex. R. Jud. Admin. 13.

13.2 Definitions. — As used in this rule:

(a) MDL Panel means the judicial panel on multidistrict litigation designated pursuant to section 74.161 of the Texas Government Code, including any temporary members designated by the Chief Justice of the Supreme Court of Texas in his or her discretion when regular members are unable to sit for any reason.

(b) Chair means the chair of the MDL Panel, who is designated by the Chief Justice of the Supreme Court of Texas.

(c) MDL Panel Clerk means the Clerk of the Supreme Court of Texas.

(d) Trial court means the court in which a case is filed.

(e) Pretrial court means the district court to which related cases are transferred for consolidated or coordinated pretrial proceedings under this rule.

(f) Related means that cases involve one or more common questions of fact.

(g) Tag-along case means a case related to cases in an MDL transfer order but not itself the subject of an initial MDL motion or order.

13.3 Procedure for Requesting Transfer.

(a) Motion for transfer; who may file; contents. — A party in a case may move for transfer of the case and related cases to a pretrial court. The motion must be in writing and must:

(1) state the common question or questions of fact involved in the cases;

(2) contain a clear and concise explanation of the reasons that transfer would be for the convenience of the parties and witnesses and would promote the just and efficient conduct of the cases;

(3) state whether all parties in those cases for which transfer is sought agree to the motion; and

(4) contain an appendix that lists:

(A) the cause number, style, and trial court of the related cases for which transfer is sought; and

(B) all parties in those cases and the names, addresses, telephone numbers, fax numbers, and email addresses of all counsel.

(b) Request for transfer by judges. — A trial court or a presiding judge of an administrative judicial region may request a transfer of related cases to a pretrial court. The request must be in writing and must list the cases to be transferred.

(c) Transfer on the MDL Panel's own initiative. — The MDL Panel may, on its own initiative, issue an order to show cause why related cases should not be transferred to a pretrial court.

(d) Response; reply; who may file; when to file. — Any party in a related case may file:

(1) a response to a motion or request for transfer within twenty days after service of such motion or request;

(2) a response to an order to show cause issued under subparagraph (c) within the time provided in the order; and

(3) a reply to a response within ten days after service of such response.

. . . .

(*l*) Decision. — The MDL Panel may order transfer if three members concur in a written order finding that related cases involve one or more common questions of fact, and that transfer to a specified district court will be for the convenience of the parties and witnesses and will promote the just and efficient conduct of the related cases.

. . . .

(o) Retransfer. — On its own initiative, on a party's motion, or at the request of the pretrial court, the MDL Panel may order cases transferred from one pretrial court to another pretrial court when the pretrial judge has died, resigned, been replaced at an election, requested retransfer, recused, or been disqualified, or in other circumstances when retransfer will promote the just and efficient conduct of the cases.

13.4 Effect on the Trial Court of the Filing of a Motion for Transfer.

(a) No automatic stay. — The filing of a motion under this rule does not limit the jurisdiction of the trial court or suspend proceedings or orders in that court.

(b) Stay of proceedings. — The trial court or the MDL Panel may stay all or part of any trial court proceedings until a ruling by the MDL Panel.

13.5 Transfer to a Pretrial Court.

(a) Transfer effective upon notice. — A case is deemed transferred from the trial court to the pretrial court when a notice of transfer is filed with the trial court and the pretrial court . . . .

(b) No further action in trial court. — After notice of transfer is filed in the trial court, the trial court must take no further action in the case except for good cause stated in the order in which such action is taken and after conferring with the pretrial court. But service of any process already issued by the trial court may be completed and the return filed in the pretrial court.

. . . .

(e) Transfer of tag-along cases. — A tag-along case is deemed transferred to the pretrial court when a notice of transfer — in the form described in Rule 13.5(a) — is filed in both the trial court and the pretrial court. Within 30 days after service of the notice, a party to the case or to any of the related cases already transferred to the pretrial court may move the pretrial court to remand the case to the trial court on the ground that it is not a tag-along case. If the motion to remand is granted, the case must be returned to the trial court, and costs including attorney fees may be assessed by the pretrial court in its remand order. The order of the pretrial court may be appealed to the MDL Panel by a motion for rehearing filed with the MDL Panel Clerk.

13.6 Proceedings in Pretrial Court.

(a) Judges who may preside. — The MDL Panel may assign as judge of the pretrial court any active district judge, or any former or retired district or appellate judge who is approved by the Chief Justice of the Supreme Court of Texas. An assignment under this rule is not subject to objection under chapter 74 of the Government Code. The judge assigned as judge of the pretrial court has exclusive jurisdiction over each related case transferred pursuant to this rule unless a case is retransferred by the MDL Panel or is finally resolved or remanded to the trial court for trial.

(b) Authority of pretrial court. — The pretrial court has the authority to decide, in place of the trial court, all pretrial matters in all related cases transferred to the court. Those matters include, for example, jurisdiction, joinder, venue, discovery, trial preparation (such as motions to strike expert witnesses, preadmission of exhibits, and motions in limine), mediation, and disposition by means other than conventional trial on the merits (such as default judgment, summary judgment, and settlement). The pretrial court may set aside or modify any pretrial ruling made by the trial court before transfer over which the trial court's plenary power would not have expired had the case not been transferred.

(c) Case management. — The pretrial court should apply sound judicial management methods early, continuously, and actively, based on its knowledge of each individual case and the entire litigation, in order to set fair and firm time limits tailored to ensure the expeditious resolution of each case and the just and efficient conduct of the litigation as a whole. After a case is transferred, the pretrial court should, at the earliest practical date, conduct a hearing and enter a case management order. The pretrial court should consider at the hearing, and its order should address, all matters pertinent to the conduct of the litigation, including:

(1) settling the pleadings;

(2) determining whether severance, consolidation, or coordination with other actions is desirable and whether identification of separable triable

portions of the case is desirable;

(3) scheduling preliminary motions;

(4) scheduling discovery proceedings and setting appropriate limitations on discovery, including the establishment and timing of discovery procedures;

(5) issuing protective orders;

(6) scheduling alternative dispute resolution conferences;

(7) appointing organizing or liaison counsel;

(8) scheduling dispositive motions;

(9) providing for an exchange of documents, including adopting a uniform numbering system for documents, establishing a document depository, and determining whether electronic service of discovery materials and pleadings is warranted;

(10) determining if the use of technology, videoconferencing, or teleconferencing is appropriate;

(11) considering such other matters the court or the parties deem appropriate for the just and efficient resolution of the cases; and

(12) scheduling further conferences as necessary.

(d) Trial settings. — The pretrial court, in conjunction with the trial court, may set a transferred case for trial at such a time and on such a date as will promote the convenience of the parties and witnesses and the just and efficient disposition of all related proceedings. The pretrial court must confer, or order the parties to confer, with the trial court regarding potential trial settings or other matters regarding remand. The trial court must cooperate reasonably with the pretrial court, and the pretrial court must defer appropriately to the trial court's docket. The trial court must not continue or postpone a trial setting without the concurrence of the pretrial court.

13.7 Remand to Trial Court.

(a) No remand if final disposition by pretrial court. — A case in which the pretrial court has rendered a final and appealable judgment will not be remanded to the trial court.

(b) Remand. — The pretrial court may order remand of one or more cases, or separable triable portions of cases, when pretrial proceedings have been completed to such a degree that the purposes of the transfer have been fulfilled or no longer apply . . . .

13.8 Pretrial Court Orders Binding in the Trial Court After Remand.

(a) Generally. — The trial court should recognize that to alter a pretrial court order without a compelling justification would frustrate the purpose of consolidated and coordinated pretrial proceedings. The pretrial court should recognize that its rulings should not unwisely restrict a trial court from responding to circumstances that arise following remand.

(b) Concurrence of the pretrial court required to change its orders. — Without the written concurrence of the pretrial court, the trial court cannot, over objection, vacate, set aside, or modify pretrial court orders, including orders related to summary judgment, jurisdiction, venue, joinder, special exceptions, discovery, sanctions related to pretrial proceedings, privileges, the admissibility of expert testimony, and scheduling.

(c) Exceptions. — The trial court need not obtain the written concurrence of the pretrial court to vacate, set aside, or modify pretrial court orders regarding the admissibility of evidence at trial (other than expert evidence) when necessary because of changed circumstances, to correct an error of law, or to prevent manifest injustice. But the trial court must support its action with specific findings and conclusions in a written order or stated on the record.

(d) Unavailability of pretrial court. — If the pretrial court is unavailable to rule, for whatever reason, the concurrence of the MDL Panel Chair must be obtained.

13.9 Review.

(a) MDL Panel decision. — An order of the MDL Panel, including one granting or denying a motion for transfer, may be reviewed only by the Supreme Court in an original proceeding.

(b) Orders by the trial court and pretrial court. — An order or judgment of the trial court or pretrial court may be reviewed by the appellate court that regularly reviews orders of the court in which the case is pending at the time review is sought, irrespective of whether that court issued the order or judgment to be reviewed. A case involving such review may not be transferred for purposes of docket equalization among appellate courts.

(c) Review expedited. — An appellate court must expediate review of an order or judgment in a case pending in a pretrial court.

APPENDIX — VENUE AND THE TEXAS BAR EXAM

Venue is a key concept that affects every lawsuit filed in Texas, and venue issues are frequently tested on the Texas Bar Exam. The following are questions from past exams, reprinted with the permission of the Texas Board of Law Examiners, which owns the copyright to these questions. You can see more questions, and the examiners' comments on the answers, by visiting the Board's website at www.ble.state.tx.us/past_exams/main_pastexams.htm.

In considering the questions, keep in mind that on the bar exam your answer is always limited to five lines.

February 2001

Paul Palmer, a resident of Bell County, has filed a negligence, breach of warranty, and product liability suit in state district court in Hill County, Texas. Palmer alleges that a curling iron, which he had bought for his daughter from Dad's Department Store ("Dad's"), was defective, overheated, and caused a fire in his home. Palmer, who is uninsured, seeks to recover the cost of repairing the damage to his home and for injuries to his minor daughter, and he alleges damages in excess of $50,000. Palmer sued two defendants: the retailer, Dad's, a sole proprietorship in Waco, Texas (McLennan County); and Kurlee, Inc., the manufacturer, a Vermont corporation with its headquarters in Vermont.

You are counsel for Dad's and are in the process of drafting an answer. Dad's has just noticed that the suit was filed in Hill County, instead of McLennan County. Dad's does not do business in Hill County. Dad's would like to have the case moved to McLennan County, where it is well known.

1. State (a) what motion must be filed to move the case to a different county; (b) what must be said in the motion; (c) at what stage in the proceedings must the motion be filed; (d) in what form you must present evidence for consideration by the court in determining the motion; (e) what party will have the burden of proof.

Assume that Dad's did not seek to move the case to another county before filing the answer. Now you are Kurlee, Inc.'s counsel. Kurlee, Inc. also wants to try to have the case moved to another county.

2. Assuming Kurlee, Inc. is subject to jurisdiction in Texas and that it has not yet filed any papers with the trial court, state whether or not it is too late for Kurlee, Inc. to request that the case be moved to another county and why.

3. Assume that Kurlee, Inc. is subject to jurisdiction and is the only defendant in the case. Kurlee, Inc. wishes to move the case to another county. State which county Kurlee, Inc. has the best chance for moving the case to, and why.

February 2002

On August 24, 2001, Peter Payne visited the Big Box Store in Amarillo, Potter County, Texas with his friends to browse and see the latest television and sound equipment. Big Box Warehouse is a national chain of electronic appliance warehouse stores that offers a big inventory of the latest products. It stores the electronics in their original unopened boxes on racks and shelves ranging from 3 to 20 feet above the floor . . . . Peter is injured when a boxed television falls from a stack of 4 on the top shelf, 20 feet from the floor, and hits him. Peter is dazed but laughs it off and leaves the store with his friends. He does not report to the store the incident or any injury until 3 days later . . . . After his continued complaints of pain, his grandmother takes him to the doctor, who diagnoses muscle strain and bruises, and some possible nerve damage to his neck and back, the symptoms of which have mostly gone away after several weeks of treatment.

1. The accident took place while Peter was visiting his grandparents for the summer in Potter County, where he had lived with his parents until he was 12. His family had moved to McAllen, Texas, and at the time of the accident his residence was with his parents in McAllen (Hidalgo County). Peter's lawyer has his law office in McAllen and prefers to bring suit in a Texas state court in Hidalgo County. There are no Big Box Warehouse stores in Hidalgo County. Big Box Warehouse is incorporated in Idaho and owns stores in several larger Texas cities. Would venue be sustained in Hidalgo County over Big Box's timely motion to transfer? Explain fully.

2. Peter's suit is pending in Hidalgo County district court. Big Box wants to file a motion to transfer venue to Potter County. Big Box has filed its answer early, some 10 days before the answer was due, and now files its motion to transfer 7 days before its original answer was due. Does the motion to transfer timely raise the venue issue? Explain fully.

3. Big Box has also considered moving to transfer venue to Bexar County, the county with a Big Box store nearest to Hidalgo County. What grounds, if any, does Big Box have for alleging in a motion to transfer that venue is mandatory or permissive in Bexar County? Explain fully.

July 2003

Pam, a resident of Bowie County, was injured in a three-car automobile collision while she was driving her car in Travis County. The other two drivers were Don, a resident of Oklahoma, and Jim, who is a resident of Potter County.

1. Under the general venue rule, in what county or counties can Pam bring her suit in Texas district court against Don and Jim? Explain fully.

2. Pam files suit in Travis County. Jim answers by filing a general denial. Don files a motion objecting to venue, subject to his objection to personal jurisdiction. Pam responds that Don is already subject to venue in Travis County because Jim did not object to venue in Travis County and waived his potential venue objection, and thus established venue for all defendants. How should the court rule on Pam's argument that Jim's waiver precludes Don's venue objections? Explain fully.

3. Assume that Don files a motion to transfer venue and specially denies the venue facts pled by Pam. Further assume that Pam does not raise the waiver argument. What, if anything, must Pam file and when will it be due? Explain fully.

February 2003

Pat, doing business as "Wonder Widgets," is a retailer of specialized high tech widgets. Her store is in Fort Worth, Tarrant County, Texas. These widgets only function if constantly maintained at a regulated temperature. They must be handled carefully at each stage of the commercial chain by the manufacturer, shippers, wholesalers, and retailers.

Pat has two wholesale suppliers, Don Ho Wholesale Supply, Inc. ("Don Ho"), and Jim Dandy Specialty Warehouse, Inc. ("Jim Dandy"). The wholesalers warrant that the widgets have been kept continuously at the approved temperature. Both operate under identical contracts with Pat to deliver widgets, per her orders, to her warehouse in Tarrant County. Don Ho is incorporated and located in Kansas. Jim Dandy is incorporated in Texas and its principal office is in Denton County.

Pat has experienced numerous complaints from her customers about the widgets not performing as they should, allegedly because the temperature at which they have been stored has deviated from the approved temperature. Pat has received numerous returns of widgets and suffered serious loss of business as a result. Pat wants to bring one suit against both Don Ho and Jim Dandy.

1. Pat files suit against Don Ho and Jim Dandy in Tarrant County. Many of Pat's most important customers are major employers in Tarrant County. Their employees are outraged at the widget failures. Critical news coverage of the failure of widgets in several high technology businesses has been extensive in print and broadcast media in the county. Aside from mandatory or permissive venue issues, do defendants have any other basis for a change of venue and, if so, what is required to bring the argument before the court? Explain fully.

2. Pat has established venue against Jim Dandy because their contract specified venue in Tarrant County, Texas. However, there is no venue provision in the contract between Pat and Don Ho. Does Don Ho have any valid objections to venue? Explain fully.

July 2009

Extra Good Plumbing ("Extra") was a Texas sole proprietorship with a principal place of business in Nueces County, Texas. Bill resided in Kleberg County, Texas. Bill requested that Extra send an employee to his residence to check a possible gas leak. Extra dispatched an employee, Ray, to Bill's residence. Ray resides in Brooks County, Texas. Ray had been a plumber for one month. Ray discovered a gas valve leak inside Bill's residence. Ray told Bill he could try to replace the valve, but that he was not certified to replace any type of leaking gas valve. Bill told Ray he did not care about any certification and that he wanted Ray to replace the valve. Ray turned the gas off at Bill's gas meter. Ray installed a replacement valve manufactured by Plumber Parts, Inc. ("Parts"). Parts is not a Texas corporation, but it had over $2,000,000 in sales in Texas in the year of the valve replacement. In spite of a city ordinance to the contrary, Bill turned his gas back on at the gas meter without contacting the local gas utility. The next day, Bill's house exploded and he sustained serious personal injuries. Bill hired a lawyer to sue Ray and Extra for his personal injuries sustained in the explosion and fire.

1. What county or counties would be proper venue for such a lawsuit? Explain fully.

2. Bill sues Extra and Ray in Brooks County. Extra wants to contest venue in Brooks County and move the case to Nueces County. What pleading must Extra file to challenge venue in Brooks County? When must the pleading be filed? Explain fully.

Chapter 6

PLEADINGS

SCOPE

This chapter covers pleadings. It will discuss the historical background of pleadings and then consider basic pleading requirements, including the requirement to state a "cause of action," and the requirement to give "fair notice" of legal theories and factual elements. The chapter also considers the requirements for defendants' pleadings, as well as the methods for complaining about pleading defects in order to avoid waiving them and the consequences of failure to appear and answer. The chapter concludes with an examination of two types of cases with special pleading requirements: sworn accounts and trespass to try title.

§ 6.01 HISTORICAL BACKGROUND

In 1840, the Fourth Congress of the Republic of Texas implemented the constitutional directive, contained in the Constitution of 1836, to adopt the common law of England "with such modifications as our circumstances . . . may require." (Section 13, Article IV, 1 LAWS OF TEXAS 1074 (Gammel, 1898)). Section 1 of the act of February 6, 1840 provided:

> [T]he adoption of the common law shall not be construed to adopt the common law system of pleading, but the proceedings in all civil suits shall, as heretofore, be conducted by petition and answer; but neither petition nor answer shall be necessary in a cause to recover money before a justice of the peace.

2 H. Gammel, LAWS OF TEXAS 262–67 (1898).

As Professor McKnight has explained, "It is chiefly because the Spanish system of pleading was simple and direct that it was so well suited to the needs of frontier life. Unlike English common law pleading, no premium was placed on great formalities or the niceties of pleas that can be mastered only by the most exacting training. The Spanish system of pleading by simple petition and answer was ideally suited to frontier conditions — and the ignorance (or lack of training) of local judges. The willingness with which Anglo-Texas frontiersmen accepted this system was probably influenced by an impatience with the fine distinctions of common law pleading encountered in the United States, at least in matters involving any substantial amount of money or property." Joseph Webb McKnight, *The Spanish Influence on the Texas Law of Civil Procedure*, 38 TEX. L. REV. 24, 26 (1959).

The nature of the simplified system of pleading, or at least the attitude with which the pleading process was approached, is described in Hamilton v. Black, Dallam 586 (1844), in which the Texas Supreme Court said: "The object of our statutes on the subject of pleading, is to simplify as much as possible that branch of the proceedings in courts which by the ingenuity and learning of both common and civil law lawyers and judges, has become so refined in its subtleties as to substitute in many instances the shadow for the substance. Our statutes require, at the hands of the petitioner to a court of justice[,] only a statement of the names of the parties plaintiff and defendant, a full and fair exposition of his cause of action, and finally the relief which he seeks." This sensible attitude was gradually replaced by a mass of technicalities. *See* Thos. A. Franklin, *Simplicity in Procedure*, 4 TEX. L. REV. 83 (1925). Former Article 1997 of the Revised Civil Statutes of 1925, originally enacted in the late 1870s, required a pleader to allege the "facts constituting the cause of action or the defendant's grounds of defense."

A movement for procedural change that focused, in part, on a simplification of the pleading rules was made manifest in 1938 as a result of the adoption of the Federal Rules of Civil Procedure. The general federal pleading rule, Federal Civil Procedure Rule 8(a), requires "a short and plain statement of the claim showing that the pleader is entitled to relief." The value-laden terms "facts" and "cause of action" were not included because of the technical baggage that accompanied them. Although no definition was attempted in the federal rules of the meaning of the term "claim," the forms the federal drafters prepared as examples reflect a substantial departure from the detailed, long-form pleading required previously. *See* Charles Clark, *The Texas and the Federal Rules of Civil Procedure*, 20 TEX. L. REV. 4 (1941); Robert W. Stayton, *The Scope and Function of Pleading Under the New Federal and Texas Rules: A Comparison*, 20 TEX. L. REV. 16 (1941).

Effective May 15, 1939, the Supreme Court of Texas was vested with full rulemaking power in "practice and procedure" in civil actions. Shortly thereafter, the Court appointed a committee of lawyers, judges, and law professors to suggest a set of rules for the control of civil actions, including rules to govern the pleading process. Although the Texas rules concerning pleadings were patterned in part on the Federal Rules of Civil Procedure, the drafters made a conscious decision to avoid wholesale adoption of the federal short form of pleading on the theory that the federal form of pleading would be incompatible with Texas jury submission practice, which in turn required considerable factual specificity. Moreover, the general denial, which had been abolished between the years 1913 and 1915 in Texas, was retained because it had been in use for over a century. *See* Stayton, *supra* at 20–21 (1941). *See also* Robert W. Stayton, *The General Issue in Texas*, 9 TEX. L. REV. 1, 12–18 (1930).

Under the Texas Rules of Civil Procedure as originally promulgated in 1940 (effective September 1, 1941), the pleading rules eliminated the requirement that the pleader plead the "facts constituting the plaintiff's cause of action or the defendant's ground of defense." *See* former R.C.S. Art. 1997. This requirement to plead "facts" as distinguished from "evidence" or "legal conclusions" was replaced by a requirement that pleadings "consist of a statement in plain and concise language of the plaintiff's cause of action or the defendant's grounds of defense." *See* TEX. R. CIV. P. 45. Significantly, the concept of "fair notice" was added as the principal pleading requirement. *See* TEX. R. CIV. P. 45 ("That an allegation be evidentiary or be of legal conclusion shall not be grounds for objection when fair notice to the opponent is given by the allegations as a whole"). This odd mixture of old and new pleading concepts was accompanied by another major change. The "new rules" abolished the general demurrer as a procedural device and provided for the waiver of pleading defects, unless the defect is raised by an "exception in writing . . . brought to the attention of the judge in the trial court before the instruction or charge to the jury or, in a non-jury case, before the judgment is signed." *See* Tex. R. Civ. P. 90. Before the adoption of Civil Procedure Rule 90, pleading defects could be raised for the first time in a motion for new trial.

§ 6.02 AN OVERVIEW OF TEXAS PLEADINGS AND THEIR FUNCTIONS

To understand Texas pleading, a new terminology must be mastered. The following pleadings are in current use in Texas and the following descriptions give a basic understanding of their functions:

[A] Plaintiff's Pleadings

Plaintiff's Original Petition. In Texas, the plaintiff's pleading that commences the action is called an original petition (not a complaint). An original petition should contain certain formal elements, such as allegations of jurisdiction, venue, the pertinent discovery level and the names of the parties and their residences. It must also allege the cause or causes of action and include a prayer for relief.

Plaintiff's Supplemental Petition. For historical reasons, a plaintiff's reply to a defendant's answer is called a supplemental petition. It may include special exceptions and denials or avoidances of pleas included in the answer.

Amended Pleadings. A plaintiff may also amend existing pleadings to make additions, corrections or other changes. An amended pleading generally supersedes its predecessor in the pleading process. A supplemental pleading does not supersede an original petition.

[B] Defendant's Pleadings

The Special Appearance Motion. We have already considered special appearance practice in Chapter 4 on jurisdiction over the person, but you should be aware that a special appearance motion contesting a nonresident's amenability to process is a defendant's plea that, if filed, must be filed first.

Motion to Transfer Venue. The motion to transfer venue because the county where the action is pending is not a proper county or because the venue selected by the claimant is inconvenient is covered in Chapter 5 on venue. It is mentioned here so that it can be placed in its proper place in the pleading scheme. An objection to improper or inconvenient venue is waived if the motion to transfer is not filed prior to or concurrently with any other plea except a special appearance motion.

Motion to Quash Citation. A defendant may attack the propriety of the service by this plea. As you learned in Chapter 4, it is seldom used, however, because even when citation is quashed, the only effect is to delay the appearance day. A motion to quash is a general appearance and should not be filed by a nonresident who contests personal jurisdiction.

Plea in Abatement. The plea in abatement is the method of raising a fundamental defect in the mode of bringing the action, other than on personal jurisdiction, citation, or venue grounds. It is thus a "catchall" type of plea. Its most frequent use is to raise such matters as the prior pendency of another action or the nonjoinder of a person needed for just adjudication.

Plea to the Jurisdiction. As you learned in Chapter 3, a challenge to the court's exercise of jurisdiction of the subject matter of the action is made by a plea to the jurisdiction. Customarily, the pleading is sworn, although no rule of procedure requires it.

Special Exceptions. This plea attacks the sufficiency of the opponent's pleadings, raising defects of either form or substance. In other words, if the pleading is vague, contains improper matter or fails to state grounds on which relief can legally be granted, the special exception is a proper vehicle for raising these defects. The special exception fulfills the function that the motion to dismiss for failure to state a claim and the motion for more definite statement fulfill in federal court.

General Denial. Texas allows the defendant to deny the petition generally, putting the plaintiff to proof on most issues. The general denial is not subject to the requirement that pleadings be made only with a good faith belief in their factual and legal propriety.

Specific Denials and Denials Under Oath. A defendant may choose to deny given facts specifically even when a general denial is permitted. However, in some instances, a defendant is required to deny allegations specifically, and a general denial is ineffective to require the plaintiff to prove these allegations.

Affirmative Defenses. An affirmative defense is one that sets up an independent ground defeating plaintiff's recovery, i.e., one that does not operate by denying elements of the claim. Affirmative defenses must be alleged affirmatively, as well as proved, by the defendant. A general denial is ineffective to raise them.

§ 6.03 SAMPLE PLEADINGS

On the pages that follow is a plaintiff's negligence petition in traditional Texas format. As you will see, the factual allegations are quite detailed, and the allegations of negligence are tied to particularized factual theories. As you read the materials in section 6.04, consider whether this degree of specificity is required under current Texas practice, and what role the petition plays in the processing and determination of the dispute.

Original Petition

<table>
<tr>
<td>JASON PINKTON, and
MARCY PINKTON, Plaintiffs
vs.
ACE CONSTRUCTION,
TERRY ACE, and LARRY ACE,
jointly and severally</td>
<td>IN THE DISTRICT COURT OF
DALLAS COUNTY, TEXAS
192nd JUDICIAL DISTRICT</td>
</tr>
</table>

PLAINTIFFS' ORIGINAL PETITION

TO THE HONORABLE JUDGE OF SAID COURT:

NOW COME Marcy Pinkton and her husband, Jason Pinkton, hereinafter called Plaintiffs, complaining of Ace Construction, a partnership composed of Jerry Ace and Larry Ace, individually and doing business as Ace Construction, hereinafter called Defendants, and by way of Petition and for cause of action Plaintiffs would respectfully show the Court the following:

I.

Plaintiffs are resident citizens of Dallas County, Texas. The Defendant, Ace Construction, maintains an office and place of business in the City of Dallas, Dallas County, Texas, and may be served by serving its general partner, Jerry Ace, at 123 Main Street, Dallas, Dallas County, Texas. Defendant Larry Ace, individually and doing business as Ace Construction, resides in the County of Dallas, State of Texas, where he may be found for purpose of service of citation herein at his home address of 42 Spring Hill Road, Dallas, Texas. The Defendant, Jerry Ace, individually and doing business as Ace Construction, resides in the County of Dallas, State of Texas, where he may be served with process at 123 Main Street, Dallas, Dallas County, Texas.

II.

Your Plaintiffs would show that at all times material to this cause of action, Ace Construction was engaged in the business of erecting houses and other structures. In connection with its business operations it used, owned and maintained various motor vehicles, the basis of this suit. On the afternoon of January 31, 1949, Marcy Pinkton was riding as a passenger in a Mercury automobile which was being operated in a northerly direction along Swanee Street in the City of Dallas, Dallas County, Texas. Such Mercury automobile was being operated by Jason Pinkton, who was in all things conducting himself in a careful, lawful and prudent manner and who was exercising due care for his own safety and that of his passenger. At or about the hour of 1 o'clock P.M. on January 31, 1949, the vehicle in which Marcy Pinkton was riding as a passenger approached the intersection of Swanee Street and Maple Glen Road. At such intersection, traffic is controlled by signal lights. There was displayed a red traffic signal light and Jason Pinkton brought the Mercury automobile to a stop behind another car, which was also proceeding in a northerly direction along Swanee Street. When the light changed to green for northbound traffic on Swanee Street, the first automobile proceeded forward and Jason Pinkton started his car forward. After the Mercury automobile in which Marcy Pinkton was riding as a passenger had crossed Maple Glen Road, the vehicle proceeding ahead of it was brought to a stop for the purpose of making a left turn, which could not be made immediately because of the approach of southbound traffic. Jason Pinkton brought the Mercury automobile to a stop and then suddenly and without warning the pick-up truck of Jerry Ace crashed into the rear of the Mercury automobile. This pick-up truck was on such occasion being operated by Jerry Ace, who was then and there acting in the course and scope of his representation of Ace Construction, a partnership composed of the said Jerry Ace and Larry Ace. As a result thereof, Marcy Pinkton was caused to suffer serious bodily injuries, which will be described hereinafter with particularity.

III.

The collision of January 31, 1949, out of which this suit arises, resulted from the negligence of Jerry Ace, while acting as the representative of Ace Construction, a partnership composed of Jerry Ace and Larry Ace, in some one or more of the following particulars:

1. In failing to maintain a proper lookout.
2. In failing to make proper application of the brakes on the pick-up truck.
3. In failing to make timely application of the brakes on the pick-up truck.
4. In failing to bring the pick-up truck to a stop before it struck the rear of the Mercury automobile in which Marcy Pinkton was riding as a passenger.
5. In failing to maintain proper stopping distance behind the Mercury automobile.
6. In following the Mercury automobile more closely than was reasonable and prudent under the existing circumstances, having due regard for the condition of and traffic upon Swanee Street, in violation of law.
7. In failing to turn the pick-up truck to the right to avoid striking the rear of the Mercury automobile.
8. In operating the pick-up truck at a rate of speed in excess of that at which it would have been operated by a person of ordinary prudence in the exercise of ordinary care under the same or similar circumstances.
9. In failing to maintain proper control of the pick-up truck.

Each and all of the above and foregoing acts, both of omission and commission, were negligent and constituted negligence and were each and all a proximate cause of the collision made the basis of this suit, of the injuries suffered by Marcy Pinkton, and of the damages sustained by your Plaintiffs as a result thereof.

IV.

In the collision of January 31, 1949, which is made the basis of this suit, Marcy Pinkton was caused to be thrown about violently in the car in which she was riding as a passenger. She suffered a severe whiplash injury to her neck and cervical spine. Her shoulders and upper back were injured and damaged. She has been caused to experience frequent severe headaches and spells of dizziness. She suffered a severe traumatic nervous shock, which has produced great nervousness. It was necessary for her attending physician to apply traction to her neck and head and to use diathermy treatments. Her injuries and the effects thereof have caused Marcy Pinkton to suffer from great and excruciating physical pain and mental anguish and she will in all reasonable probability continue to suffer from such physical pain and mental anguish, as well as from great nervousness, for a long time in the future, if not for the balance of her natural life. On January 31, 1949, Marcy Pinkton was a woman of the age of twenty-eight years, who had a life expectancy of seventy-two years according to the Standard Ordinary Tables of Mortality. She was a housewife, who customarily maintained her home for her husband and family. She has been handicapped in the discharge of her household duties and has required the assistance of others. It is reasonably probable that she will continue to be handicapped in the discharge of her household duties in the future and that she will continue to require assistance from others. Her activities since January 31, 1949, have been and it is reasonably probable that her future activities will be engaged in under the handicaps of pain and suffering. Marcy Pinkton has required medical care and will in the future in reasonable probability require additional medical care. Plaintiffs have been required to pay and incur liability to pay and will in the future in reasonable probability be required to pay and incur liability to pay the charges which have been made and which will be made for the services rendered and to be rendered unto Marcy Pinkton. The charges which have been made and which will be made have represented and will represent the usual, reasonable and customary charges for like and similar services in the vicinity where they have been and will be made necessary in connection with the proper treatment of the injuries suffered by Marcy Pinkton in the collision of January 31, 1949, which is made the basis of this suit. By reason of all of the above and foregoing, your Plaintiffs have been caused to suffer damages within the jurisdictional limits of the court.

WHEREFORE, Premises Considered, the Defendant, Jerry Ace, individually and doing business as Ace Construction, having heretofore appeared and answered herein, Plaintiffs pray that the Defendants, Ace Construction, a partnership composed of Jerry Ace and Larry Ace, be served in terms of the law to appear and answer herein and that upon final trial of this cause, Plaintiffs have judgment against the Defendants, jointly and severally, for $50,000 damages; that they have pre- and post-judgment interest at the legal rate; that they recover their costs of Court in this behalf incurred, and that they have such other and further relief, general and special, at law and in equity, to which they may show themselves justly entitled and in duty bound will ever pray.

NOTES AND QUESTIONS

(1) *Analyze the Petition.* What is the purpose of the first numbered paragraph? What cause or causes of action have the plaintiffs alleged? What is the purpose of each paragraph before the final paragraph? What relief and what kinds of damages have they requested, and why?

In the materials that follow, we will see that a plaintiff's original petition should allege proper causes of action and give "fair notice" of the legal theories and factual elements comprising them. Consider whether the degree of detail contained in this petition is required to satisfy the fair notice requirement.

(2) *The Function of the Petition.* As we begin to consider various kinds of pleadings, it might be worthwhile to ask: What functions do the pleadings fulfill, or what functions are they supposed to accomplish? Before the advent of discovery, pleadings were designed to initiate the lawsuit, provide notice of the parties' claims and defenses, share relevant information about the case, and in some cases to dispose of the action completely. Under a modern system, in which discovery is available to provide information to the litigants, what functions should pleadings serve? What mechanisms exist for early disposition of unwarranted claims? Under what circumstances should the pleadings be a sufficient basis for a decision on the merits?

§ 6.04 PLAINTIFF'S PETITION

[A] General Considerations and Formal Elements

Read Tex. R. Civ. P. 22, 28, 45, 47, 48, 50, 58, 78, 79, 190.

The primary function of the petition is to provide the defendant or defendants "a short statement of the cause of action sufficient to give fair notice of the claim involved" and the relief requested. It is not grounds for objection that an allegation is "evidentiary" or is a "legal conclusion" when fair notice is given by the allegations of the petition as a whole. Specific rules of procedure supplement and clarify the method of giving fair notice. *See, e.g.*, Tex. R. Civ. P. 56. Civil Procedure Rule 47 requires that pleadings seeking unliquidated damages contain a statement that the damages sought are "within" the jurisdictional limits of the court, not that they exceed the court's minimum jurisdictional limits.

Although no specific rule requires it, the petition should contain allegations that demonstrate the basis for the court's subject matter jurisdiction, jurisdiction over the person or property of the defendant(s), and the propriety of the venue. The problem of pleading jurisdiction is exemplified by cases in Chapter 3 on subject matter jurisdiction, such as *Peek v. Equipment Service Co. of San Antonio*, 779 S.W.2d 802 (Tex. 1989). Jurisdictional allegations concerning nonresidents must also be drafted with care to avoid a motion to quash service of citation and to support a default judgment against a direct attack. *Kawasaki Steel Corp. v. Middleton*, 699 S.W.2d 199, 203 (Tex. 1985). Jurisdiction of a person who resides within Texas is usually shown by showing that fact and indicating where service can be effectuated.

The rules also contain some technical requirements for petition drafting. They must be correctly "indorsed" (named) to show their chronological position (e.g. "original petition"; "first amended original petition" etc.). Tex. R. Civ. P. 78. The petition must state the names of the parties and their residences. Tex. R. Civ. P. 79. The petition should set out its claims in numbered paragraphs, "each of which shall be limited as far as practicable to a statement of a single set of circumstances." Tex.

R. Civ. P. 50. Statements in a pleading can be adopted by reference either later in the same pleading or in later pleadings or motions. Tex. R. Civ. P. 58. The attorney of record must sign the pleading in his or her individual name, including the State Bar identification number, address, telephone number, and fax number. Tex. R. Civ. P. 57.

As a result of the 1999 amendments to the Texas Rules of Civil Procedure, a plaintiff must allege in the first numbered paragraph of the original petition whether discovery is intended to be conducted under Level 1, 2, or 3 of Civil Procedure Rule 190. Tex. R. Civ. P. 190.1. The choice of Level 1 discovery has a significant impact on the pleadings rules, because it binds the pleader to a maximum claim of no more than $50,000. No post-verdict amendment for a recovery of a greater amount of damages is allowed in these cases. Tex. R. Civ. P. 190, Comment 2 ("the rule in *Greenhalgh v. Service Lloyds Ins. Co.*, 787 S.W.2d 938 (Tex. 1990) does not apply").

[B] Pleading a "Cause of Action"

Read Tex. R. Civ. P. 45, 47.

The concept of cause of action is essential to a proper understanding of procedure. It is important in pleading because the Texas rules require a statement of a "cause of action." It is likewise important to an understanding of permissive and required joinder of claims and parties, res judicata (which prohibits the splitting of a cause of action), and jury submission (because the charge should contain all elements of the cause of action that are contested). Incidentally, understanding of the notion of a cause of action is important not only in Texas but in other procedural systems.

The concept of cause of action is embedded in its historical context. Hence, this section begins with attempts made to define it both recently and historically.

[1] Basic Pleading Requirements: Defining a "Cause of Action"

Consider the following excerpt from a treatise on common-law pleading, the original home to the concept of "cause of action":

> The declaration must state distinctly and with certainty every fact that is essential to the plaintiff's prima facie case. No essential allegation can be imported into the declaration by inference or intendment. The principal points necessary to be shown in the statement of a cause of action are:
>
> (a) the plaintiff's right;
>
> (b) the defendant's wrongful act violating that right;
>
> (c) the consequent damages.

Shipman, Handbook on Common-Law Pleading, 3d ed. (H.B. Ballantine, ed. 1923) at 196.

Texas cases trying to define a cause of action point alternately to the collection of facts and to the legal theory. The authorities have generally held that a cause of action at law consists of the existence of a right in the plaintiff and an invasion of that right by some act or omission on the part of the defendant, and, when necessary for recovery according to the substantive law, the consequent damages. Some of the cases have held that the *facts* alleged which establish the existence of the right and its violation *constitute the cause of action*. On the other hand, it has also been said that the cause of action does *not* consist of the allegations of *facts* but of the unlawful *violation of a right* which these facts show. In either case, traditional Texas law required the plaintiff to identify the legal theory or theories on which the plaintiff based its suit, and to allege in a relatively specific way the facts corresponding to each element of the legal theory.

In interpreting the 1941 Rules of Civil Procedure, the Amarillo Court of Civil Appeals, in *Christy v. Hamilton*, 384 S.W.2d 795, 796 (Tex. Civ. App. — Amarillo 1964, no writ), put the matter in the following terms:

> It is elementary that a plaintiff's petition shall contain a statement in plain and concise language of the plaintiff's cause of action and shall give fair notice of the claim involved. Rule 47, Texas Rules of Civil Procedure. It must also appear from the face of a petition that a primary legal right rests in the plaintiff, that there is a primary legal duty connected with this right resting on the defendant, and that there has been a breach of this duty by the defendant.

NOTES AND QUESTIONS

(1) *Sufficiency of Petition.* Consider the following two examples. Based on the discussion and examples above, would they satisfy basic pleading requirements? The first example (in (a), *below*) is taken from a suit brought by the owners of the surface estate against lessees under an oil and gas lease for alleged damages to the plaintiffs' land and cattle. The second example (in (b), *below*) is taken from the forms devised to aid in the interpretation of Fed. R. Civ. P. 8(a) ("short and plain statement of the claim showing that the pleader is entitled to relief").

> (a) That the defendants have heretofore during the last year, drilled several oil and gas wells upon the above tract of land, the surface of which belongs to these plaintiffs; and that during the process of drilling, operating and connecting the same to pipeline which crosses plaintiffs said land, the defendants, their agents, servants or employees have conducted such operations, drilling and connecting with the said pipeline across plaintiffs' said property that they have damaged these plaintiffs in the following manner.
>
> . . . .
>
> That the damages to these plaintiffs grassland over which defendants laid connecting lines from the pipeline to the wells, as well as the driving of the heavy machinery, trucks and numerous vehicles on and across said

> grassland to the reasonable damage of $50.00 per well of $200.00, plus the damage of $1.00 per rod for the damages due to the laying of 320 rods of pipeline across this land; that the oil and debris were allowed to pollute the plaintiffs [sic] fish pond on this property in the sum of $200.00.

Christy v. Hamilton, 384 S.W.2d 795 (Tex. Civ. App. — Amarillo 1964, no writ).

> (b) On ___ [date], at ___ [place], the defendant negligently drove a motor vehicle against the plaintiff. As a result, the plaintiff was physically injured, lost wages or income, suffered physical and mental pain, and incurred medical expenses of $___. Therefore, the plaintiff demands judgment against the defendant for $___, plus costs.

Appendix of Forms, Federal Rules of Civil Procedure Form 11. Form 11 is sufficient to satisfy the federal pleading rules. Would the *Christy* court uphold it if challenged?

(2) *Contrasting Christy and Federal Form 11.* What additional information is added by the word "negligently?" Would naming this cause of action have satisfied the court in *Christy*? Does use of the term provide "fair notice" in Form 11? Consider, for example, whether there is more than one way to drive "negligently"? Should it be necessary to identify the specific acts and omissions? Are the allegations in Form 11 sufficient to apprise the defendant of the evidence plaintiff will introduce at trial? Is that the function of pleadings? As you can see, the concept of fair notice requires attention both to the plaintiff's legal theory and to the extent of factual specificity that the court will require. The next two sections of the chapter discuss these issues.

[2] "Fair Notice" of the Substantive Legal Theory

The following cases consider whether the petitions in question sufficiently inform the defendant of the legal theory underlying the plaintiff's cause of action. Consider, when you read them, whether the problem is poor drafting or an attempt to plead a non-existent cause of action. Notice also the problems of waiver: assuming that the plaintiff's petition is defective, the defendant must — in the correct way and at the correct time — bring the defect to the trial court's attention, or the defect may not be raised on appeal.

CASTLEBERRY v. GOOLSBY BLDG. CORP.

617 S.W.2d 665 (Tex. 1981)

CAMPBELL, J.

This is a suit for actual and exemplary damages under Article 5525, the Texas Survival Statute. The trial court rendered summary judgment that Plaintiff Clarence E. Castleberry take nothing as to Defendant Goolsby Building Corporation. The Court of Civil Appeals affirmed the judgment of the trial court. 608 S.W.2d 763. We affirm the judgment of the Court of Civil Appeals.

Richard Ernest Castleberry was employed by Goolsby Building Corporation. On June 5, 1978, he was killed in an industrial accident while in the course of his employment. Clarence E. Castleberry, Individually as surviving natural parent and as Administrator of the Estate of Richard Ernest Castleberry, Deceased, (Administrator) sued the City of Corpus Christi and Goolsby Building Corporation. The Administrator alleged Richard's death was caused by certain "acts and/or omissions to act, which . . . constitute gross, wanton, and willful negligence," "grossly negligent acts," "negligent, or grossly negligent, acts and omissions" and "ordinary or gross negligence." Goolsby Building Corporation alleged in its motion for summary judgment that the Administrator failed to state a cause of action. The trial court rendered summary judgment that the Administrator take nothing against Goolsby Building Corporation.

The Administrator argues the Workers' Compensation Act does not bar a deceased's cause of action for intentional injuries which survive to the estate under Article 5525, the Texas Survival Statute. We agree . . . . The Workers' Compensation Act exempts employers from common law liability based on negligence or gross negligence, except in [wrongful] death cases for exemplary damages . . . . The Act does not exempt employers from common law liability for intentional injuries. We hold the Workers' Compensation Act does not bar a deceased's cause of action for intentional injuries which survive to the estate under Article 5525.

The Administrator further argues the pleadings are sufficient to allege an "intentional injury" to Richard Castleberry by Goolsby Building Corporation.

Under Rules 45 and 47, pleadings are sufficient if they give the opposing attorney fair notice of the claim involved. Tex. R. Civ. P. 45 and 47; *Stone v. Lawyers Title Ins. Corp.*, 554 S.W.2d 183 (Tex. 1977). The object and purpose of pleading is to give fair and adequate notice to the party being sued of the nature of the cause of action asserted against him so he may adequately prepare his defense. *McCamey v. Kinnear*, 484 S.W.2d 150 (Tex. Civ. App. — Beaumont 1972, writ ref'd n.r.e.). The Administrator's allegations are insufficient to give the opposing attorney fair notice that this cause of action was for an "intentional injury."

The Administrator contends an allegation of willful negligence or willful gross negligence is sufficient to allege an "intentional injury." An allegation of willful negligence or willful gross negligence is an allegation based upon negligence and is insufficient to allege an "intentional injury." An injury caused by willful negligence or willful gross negligence is not an intentional injury necessary to avoid the effect of the Workers' Compensation Act.

The judgments of the courts below are affirmed.

CITY OF HOUSTON v. CRABB

1995 Tex. App. LEXIS 1698 (Tex. App. — Houston [14th] 1995, no pet.)

Fowler, J.

This is an appeal from a judgment on a jury verdict awarding appellees damages for the City of Houston's demolishing a house owned by appellees Crabb and

Griffin. The jury found that the house was not a public nuisance on the day it was demolished, and awarded appellees the difference between the market value of the property before and after the demolition of the house, and the reasonable cost of repairs expended by McKenzie, a prospective buyer of the property. Because appellees stated a cause of action for compensation under the Texas Constitution's Takings Clause, the evidence presented supports the jury verdict, and the trial court properly determined the starting date for prejudgment interest, we affirm.

FACTS

Appellees Harrel Crabb and Saundra Griffin are co-owners of a piece of property located in Houston. In 1981, they sold the property for $30,000 to a man who operated a nursery business. There was a house on the property, which the man gutted for the use of his business, leaving the outer walls intact. In 1985, the nursery owner could not make his payments, so Crabb and Griffin had to foreclose. The nursery owner left some trash and old tires on the property, which Crabb and Griffin did not clean up, because they wanted to sell it again. As time passed, the property fell into disrepair. Although Crabb and Griffin kept the fence around the property locked, children would occasionally break in and play in the house.

In early 1987, Crabb received a notice from the City of a dangerous building hearing. Attached to the notice was a "Major Building Deficiencies Form," which contained a list of potential deficiencies for a structure that could make it dangerous. All of the possible defects were checked on the form, even though Crabb knew the house was not deficient in several of the listed areas. Crabb attended the hearing and told the inspector he intended to secure the building and sell the property. After the hearing, on April 30, 1987, Crabb received the Order of the Building Official (the Order), which contained checks by all the defects listed in the Major Building Deficiencies Form. The Order stated that the building was to be posted immediately as a dangerous building, and gave Crabb fifteen days, until May 15th, to notify the City of his intention to repair or demolish the building. If he did not repair or demolish the building by June 30, 1987, the City would demolish the building. Crabb sent the City a letter stating he was going to remove the trash, secure the building, and keep it boarded up, all of which he did. He did not inform the City that many of the alleged deficiencies were inaccurate — that had been done at the hearing, to no avail.

One year after the City sent the Order to Crabb, in April 1988, a city appraiser went to the property to complete a form entitled "Condemned Structure Appraisal." The appraiser recommended that the City not destroy the structure, and wrote on the form "DO NOT DESTROY, PROPERTY DOES NEED MAJOR RENOVATION." Unaware that the City still might be considering destroying the building, Crabb and Griffin signed an earnest money contract for the property in August, 1988, with George McKenzie, a roofer and building contractor. McKenzie was going to fix up the house with his own resources and pay them $30,000 for the property. McKenzie had a buyer lined up who was going to buy the property for $48,000 after he finished his work on the house.

McKenzie went to work on the house. He put on a new roof, put in all new walls, and purchased all new fixtures, including a whirlpool bathtub and new hot water heater to install in the house. He also completely relandscaped the yard. The neighbors thought the property was looking "real pretty." All together, McKenzie spent $13,000 of his own money fixing up the property.

Then, on December 22, 1988, without any warning, the City came in and bulldozed down the house, even though one of the demolition workers commented after they had torn down the house that he would have liked to live in the house, and that it "was a pretty little place." The demolition contractor took away all the fixtures and lumber from the demolished house. The demolition occurred almost two years after the City had sent out its Order notifying Crabb of its intent to demolish if he did not repair the building. No other notices were sent or posted on the property, nor was the demolition order filed with the deed records.

After the City destroyed the house, McKenzie refused to buy the property, which was then worth only $5000.

PRIOR POSTURE

Crabb, Griffin, and McKenzie sued the City of Houston and the demolition contractor, Foursome, Inc., under five legal theories: (1) "wrongful destruction of property," (2) negligence, (3) gross negligence, (4) conversion, and (5) due process violation. The City filed no special exceptions to the pleadings. It answered, claiming that (i) its conduct was an exercise of its governmental functions, and it was therefore immune; (ii) the plaintiffs consented to the demolition, and were estopped from suing for damages; and (iii) the plaintiffs were themselves negligent. The City also filed a counterclaim for the cost of the demolition. Foursome filed a cross claim against the City for indemnification.

The jury returned a verdict that the house was not a nuisance on the day the City demolished it, the difference in the market value of the property immediately before and after the demolition was $38,000, and the reasonable cost of repairs made by McKenzie was $13,000.

The trial court entered judgment that Crabb, Griffin, and McKenzie were to recover $38,000 plus prejudgment interest from the City of Houston. The court also entered take-nothing judgments on the plaintiffs' claims against Foursome, on Foursome's claim against the City, and on the City's counterclaim against the plaintiffs. . . .

JUDGMENT NOTWITHSTANDING THE VERDICT

In its first point of error, the City argues the trial court erred in failing to grant judgment notwithstanding the verdict. Generally, a complaint on appeal that the trial court erred in refusing to grant a judgment notwithstanding the verdict raises only a "no evidence" point for review. However, the City's discussion under its point of error does not comport with a "no evidence" claim. Instead, the City seems to be contending that appellees could not recover as a matter of law because they did not plead the elements required to support the jury's verdict. . . .

[T]he City argues that appellees may not recover under article 1, section 17 of the Texas Constitution, the "Takings Clause," because they did not plead a cause of action under article 1, section 17. Article 1, section 17 provides:

> No person's property shall be taken, damaged, or destroyed for or applied to the public use without adequate compensation being made, unless by the consent of such person . . . .

Tex. Const. art. 1, 17. Appellees' petition alleged liability on the City's part for "Wrongful Destruction of Property," claiming:

> At the time that Defendants demolished Plaintiffs' property, the property was not a public nuisance. Thus, there was no reason for Defendants to demolish it, and they became liable to Plaintiffs for their damages when they wrongfully destroyed the property.

Pleadings are to be liberally construed in favor of the pleader, particularly when the complaining party has not filed any special exceptions. *Boyles v. Kerr*, 855 S.W.2d 593, 601 (Tex. 1993). Rule 45 of the Texas Rules of Civil Procedure requires that pleadings give fair notice of the claim asserted. *Paramount Pipe & Supply Co. v. Muhr*, 749 S.W.2d 491, 494 (Tex. 1988). The purpose of the fair notice requirement is to provide the opposing party with enough information to enable him to prepare a defense. *Id.*; *Roark v. Allen*, 633 S.W.2d 804, 810 (Tex. 1982). A petition is sufficient if a cause of action may be reasonably inferred from what is specifically stated, even if an element of the cause of action is not specifically alleged. *Boyles*, 855 S.W.2d at 601; *Gulf, Colorado & Santa Fe Ry. v. Bliss*, 368 S.W.2d 594, 599 (Tex. 1963).

Here, although appellees did not specifically cite article 1, section 17 in their petition, it is evident that appellees were asking for damages based on the City's destruction of their property. Because the City did not file special exceptions asking for a clearer statement of the cause of action, we apply a liberal construction of appellees' pleadings and find that appellees stated a cause of action for compensation under article 1, section 17 for the destruction of their property.

[The court went on to hold that the burden was on the City to plead and prove that the property owners had consented to the taking, and that it had paid adequate compensation. The owners' failure to plead lack of consent and inadequate compensation was therefore proper. After rejecting the City's other points of error, the court affirmed the trial court's judgment.]

NOTES AND QUESTIONS

(1) *Fair Notice and Special Exceptions.* How should the City of Houston have objected to the defects in the plaintiffs' pleading? If an "objection" had been properly made, would it have been error not to sustain it? *See* Tex. R. Civ. P. 90, 91. What is necessary to give "fair notice" of the substantive legal theory relied on if a special exception is made? Should the pleading be upheld "even if some element of a cause of action has not been specifically alleged" when an objection is leveled at the pleading imperfection?

(2) *Fair Notice and Pleading Negligence Per Se. Castleberry* states that fair and adequate notice of the cause of action is required so that the defendant can adequately prepare a defense. *Murray v. O & A Express, Inc.*, 630 S.W.2d 633 (Tex. 1982), arising from the nighttime collision of an automobile with an improperly

parked truck, elaborates on this notion. The driver of the automobile and the estate of a passenger killed in the wreck filed suit for negligence and wrongful death against the truck driver and the company for which he worked. The pleadings asserted that the truck driver was negligent in parking the truck so that it protruded into the plaintiffs' lane of traffic, in failing to put out warning signals or devices, and "in other acts of negligence." At trial, however, plaintiffs' attorney did not pursue a theory of common law negligence, but instead relied on negligence per se. Negligence per se, advanced in the opening statement, maintained throughout the trial, and addressed in the jury charge, was predicated on the idea that the truck's protrusion and the lack of warning signals violated statutory provisions. From a judgment for the plaintiffs, the defendants appealed, alleging error in the *variance* between the pleadings and the jury charge, which stated that the truck driver's violation of the statute constituted negligence as a matter of law.

In its opinion in *Murray*, the Texas Supreme Court, after noting that pleadings are required to provide fair and adequate notice on which to prepare a defense, stated:

> The unexcused violation of a penal statute constitutes negligence as a matter of law [negligence per se] if such statute was designed to prevent injuries to a class of persons to which the injured party belongs . . . . When a defendant is alleged to be negligent as a matter of law because of the violation of a statute and a statutory violation is proven, the defendant's negligence is not at issue unless evidence of excuse is presented . . . . The defendant in such a suit must frame his defense in terms of the recognized excuses for violation of a statute. Since these excuses must be affirmatively raised by the evidence, it is important that the party alleged to be negligent as a matter of law be informed prior to trial that the opposing party relies upon the statutory violation. Thus, a party relying upon a statutory violation should plead this reliance on that basis. Further, the pleader should reasonably identify the statute relied upon.

630 S.W.2d at 636.

(3) *Fair Notice and Variance Between Pleading and Proof.* Notwithstanding the failure of the plaintiffs' pleadings to comply with these rules, the *Murray* court affirmed the trial court's judgment for plaintiffs because such failure was never raised at trial:

> O & A made no special exceptions to the pleadings of Murray even though those pleadings were general. Moreover, O & A did not object to the opening statement of Murray which made clear his reliance upon the statutes. Murray's evidence of statutory violations was likewise admitted without objection to the lack of pleadings. Finally, O & A never excepted to the lack of pleadings supporting the court's charge which instructed the jury that O & A and Young were negligent as a matter of law. Having failed to except to the lack of pleadings at any point during trial, O & A has waived any error in the pleadings of Murray.

630 S.W.2d at 636–37.

(4) *Waiving Variance Problems.* Some complaints about plaintiff's petition, then, are waived at the pleading stage. This includes errors that are clear from the face of the pleadings, such as vagueness. Complaints about variance between pleading and proof are not waived at the pleading stage (there is no variance yet to complain about), but can be waived at trial. In a non-jury trial, the variance is waived when defendant fails to object to the introduction of evidence that is clearly outside the pleadings. In a jury trial, waiver occurs when the defendant fails to object to submitting unpleaded issues to the jury. In either case, note that the plaintiff has the option of asking the court for a trial amendment to cure the variance problem. This issue of trial amendments is discussed in more detail in section 6.06.

WAIVER OF PLAINTIFF'S PLEADING DEFECTS

<table>
<tr><th>Pretrial Stage — Rule 90</th><th colspan="2">Trial Stage — Rules 66–67</th><th>Jury Instruction Stage — Rule 274–278</th></tr>
<tr><td>Problem:
1) vague pleading
2) omission of element of cause of action</td><td colspan="2">Problem: evidence offered that clearly relates solely to unpleaded issue</td><td>Problem: jury charge requested on unpleaded issue on which evidence was received without objection</td></tr>
<tr><td>If no special exception, opponent waives right to object to introduction of evidence due to vagueness or incompleteness of pleading. Does not waive opponent's need for proof of each element of claim or defense.</td><td>Bench Trial — If no objection to evidence based on lack of pleading, tried by consent. If evidence objected to, court may allow trial amendment unless opposing party shows prejudice</td><td>Jury Trial — No waiver from failing to object to evidence</td><td>If no objection to charge based on lack of pleading, unpleaded matter is tried by consent [but Rule 67 still requires written pleadings to support submission to jury. See note 5 below]. If charge objected to, court may allow trial amendment based on lack of surprise to opponent who heard evidencewithout objection.</td></tr>
<tr><td>If special exception overruled, opponent should also object to introduction of evidence at trial</td><td colspan="2">Party objecting to opponent's trial amendment must also request a continuance in order to preserve complaint</td><td></td></tr>
<tr><td colspan="4">But waiver is only by the "party seeking reversal on such account."</td></tr>
</table>

(4) *Surplusage?* A number of cases state the principle that a general allegation that is accompanied by specific allegations should be considered as "mere surplusage." *See, e.g., Weingartens, Inc. v. Price*, 461 S.W.2d 260 (Tex. Civ. App. — Houston [14th Dist.] 1970, writ ref'd n.r.e.). Does this rule of construction make sense? Taken

literally it means that a general allegation is limited by the specific and cannot provide "fair notice" of any other claims that might have been encompassed by the more general allegation. It also means that questions of whether the proof offered varies from the pleadings will be determined by the most specific allegations of the petition.

(5) *More on Preserving Error.* Even if a party properly asserts a special exception objecting to defects in pleading, if the special exception is overruled by the court, another step may be required before the pleading deficiency can be raised on appeal. One court of appeals has ruled that the aggrieved party must also object to testimony when it is offered in order to avoid trial of the unpleaded issue by consent. Nonetheless, based on the proviso at the end of Civil Procedure Rule 67, written pleadings are necessary to support a party's right to the submission of jury questions even when unpleaded issues are tried by consent. *See Elbaor v. Smith*, 845 S.W.2d 240, 243–44 (Tex. 1992); *Gibbins v. Berlin*, 162 S.W.3d 335, 340–42 (Tex. App. — Fort Worth 2005, no pet.); *Republic Bankers Life Ins. Co. v. McCool*, 441 S.W.2d 314, 317 (Tex. Civ. App. — Tyler 1969, no writ).

[3] "Fair Notice" of Factual Theories

WHITE v. JACKSON

358 S.W.2d 174 (Tex. Civ. App. — Waco 1962, writ ref'd n.r.e.)

TIREY, J.

This is an appeal by writ of error from a default judgment.

A statement is necessary. In May 1961, Willie Jackson filed his original petition in the District Court of Dallas County against Henry White, a resident of Dallas County, and caused citation to be issued and served on White, but he failed to answer. We quote the pertinent parts of the petition:

> "On or about the 7th day of June 1959, plaintiff sustained severe and extensive injuries and damages as a direct and proximate result of the negligence of defendant, all to the actual damage of plaintiff in an amount greatly in excess of One Thousand Dollars ($1000.00) and within the jurisdiction of the District Court.
>
> "Wherefore, premises considered, plaintiff prays that defendant be cited to appear and answer herein, and that upon final trial, plaintiff have judgment against defendant for all damages proved, costs of court, interest at the rate of 6% per annum from the date of the judgment until same is paid, and for such other and further relief as to which plaintiff may be justly entitled, whether at law or in equity."

On June 12, 1961, judgment was rendered against defendant in favor of plaintiff, and in the judgment we find this recital:

> "the matters of fact and things in controversy being submitted to the court in their due and regular order, and it appearing to the court upon

good and sufficient evidence that plaintiff is entitled to recover of and from Henry White, defendant, the sum of $20,510."

. . . .

The judgment is assailed on 5 Points. They are substantially to the effect that the Trial Court erred in entering judgment: (1 and 2) Based upon appellee's petition for the reason that the petition is not sufficient to support a default judgment, because it failed to allege any facts or circumstances from which it could be found that appellant breached any duty whatsoever which he might have owed appellee in connection with whatever act or omission of the appellant is claimed as negligence; and failed to allege any act or omission whatsoever of appellant which could constitute negligence; (3 and 4) That the Court erred in entering judgment for any amount of money for the reason that appellee's petition failed to allege any injury, fact or act from which any damages could have resulted to appellee; and that the Court erred in entering judgment in the sum of $20,510.00 in favor of appellee for the reason that his petition could in no event support a judgment substantially in excess of $1,000.00; (5) That the judgment of $20,510.00 is erroneous, because such petition did not give appellant notice as to the nature of appellee's claim and the relief sought as required by the Fourteenth Amendment of the Constitution of the United States, and as also required by Article 1, Sec. 19 of the Constitution of the State of Texas, Vernon's Ann. St.

. . . .

Going back to appellee's petition, we find that it fails to allege any act or omission on the part of appellant which constituted negligence; we find no allegation of fact indicating that appellant owed appellee any duty whatsoever in connection with whatever might be the basis of appellee's claim against him. No facts are alleged in the petition. The only word contained in appellee's petition which might be considered any clue as to the nature of appellee's claim is the word "negligence." But, there can be no negligence unless a duty is present, and here none is alleged. The term "negligence" is not used to characterize any specific act or omission made by appellant, and there is no way of ascertaining from the pleading that appellant may or might have owed appellee a duty of any kind whatsoever. So the word "negligence," standing alone, provides the only starting point for determination of whether or not appellee's petition was sufficient to support a default judgment . . . . In *Missouri Pacific Ry. Co. v. Hennessey*, 12 S.W. 608, we find this statement of the Rule:

"A mere abstract proposition that defendant was guilty of negligence which resulted in injury to the plaintiff would not be sufficient. The act done or omitted constituting negligence must be averred and proved. Hence it follows that an act done or omitted which is relied on to establish negligence must be alleged, or proof of it will not be allowed. Where, from the nature of the case, the plaintiff would not be expected to know the exact cause, or the precise negligent act which becomes the cause, of an injury, and where the facts are peculiarly within the knowledge of the defendant, he would not be required to allege the particular cause, but it would be sufficient to allege the fact in a general way, as that there was a defect of machinery of structure, or want of skill in operating on the part of defendant or its

> servants, or some such fact as would give the defendant notice of the character of proof that would be offered to support the plaintiff's case . . . . If an injury occurs under such circumstances that a negligent act on the part of defendant cannot be alleged or proved, and where no relation exists between the parties that demands immunity from injury, there can be no recovery."

The foregoing rule is very broad and comprehensive and our Supreme Court has not seen fit to change it. It seems to us that appellee alleged no more than a legal conclusion to the effect that appellant was liable to him as a result of negligence; that appellee's pleading is and was fatally defective; that in effect it contained nothing more than the unsupported statement that appellant is liable to appellee because of some unknown act or omission of negligence resulting in some unknown injury or damage to appellee; such allegations are obviously a conclusion on the part of appellee and do not furnish any information whatsoever from which such conclusion could be drawn. The allegation of negligence is a mere conclusion of the pleader, and such allegation is not admitted by either a general demurrer or by default, and such allegation in the petition could in no event support a judgment by default under Rules 45, 47 and 90, T.R.C.P.

Needless to say that appellee's pleading was wholly insufficient to permit appellant to identify anything or to estimate the scope of the dispute, which is well illustrated by a judgment for $20,510.00 against him, based upon a petition alleging damages only "in excess of $1,000.00." We think for the reasons stated that Points 1 and 2 must be sustained, and this will require that the cause be reversed and remanded.

Appellant's 3rd Point is substantially that the Court erred in entering judgment for any amount of money, for the reason that the petition failed to allege any injury, fact or act from which any damages could have resulted to appellee. We think it is obvious that this point must be sustained. For the rules prescribing the detail with which the damages must be alleged, *see* Vol. 2, McDonald, Texas Civ. Prac., Sec. 6.17, at p. 576. Going back to the appellee's petition in this cause, the defendant was not advised of the alleged damages and injuries to appellee, either to his person or to his property. We think that a pleading which wholly failed to state whether or not the alleged injuries or damages were personal or whether the damage was to property, is fatally defective and will certainly not support a judgment by default for any amount. The petition, as we have stated before, does not allege any act, circumstance or injury from which damages normally flow or can be remotely implied. Certainly none can be supplied by the court. It is the general rule of pleadings that fair notice is a guide for determining whether or not a petition contains sufficient allegations on which to base an award of damages in any amount. *See* Rules 45 and 47, T.R.C.P. *See also* 17 Tex. Jur. 2d, Damages, Sec. 192. The petition here does not allege any facts from which the court can supply any measure of damages whatsoever, and we think such failure requires the judgment to be reversed and remanded. *See Caswell v. J.S. McCall & Sons*, Tex. Civ. App., 163 S.W. 1001, n.w.h.

We have carefully considered Points 4 and 5, and we think each should be sustained. Since we are of the view that the cause must be reversed and remanded, it will unduly extend this opinion to make further comment on Points 4 and 5, and for that reason we do not do so. Accordingly, this cause is reversed and remanded.

McDonald, C.J., and Wilson, J., concur in the result.

WILLOCK v. BUI

734 S.W.2d 390 (Tex. App. — Houston
[1st Dist.] 1987, no writ)

Warren, J.

By writ of error, appellant contends that a default judgment entered against him should be set aside because . . . the pleadings were inadequate to support a default judgment. . . .

The pertinent part of appellee's petition reads as follows:

II.

> Defendant, George Michael Willock, is a resident of Houston, Harris County, Texas and may be served with process at his address at 1247 S. Kirkwood, Houston, Texas 77077.

III.

> On January 9, 1985 at approximately 8:00 a.m., Toan Viet Bui sustained serious personal injuries while driving a 1985 Toyota pickup truck which was involved in a rear-end collision, which forced his vehicle into the car in front of him. The automobile which Toan Viet Bui was operating was struck from behind during the collision which involved a Pontiac, Texas license plate number 323-ADH, driven by George Michael Willock. The collision occurred at 1300 Hays Road, Houston, Texas.

IV.

> The collision described in paragraph III above and made the basis of this suit was directly and proximately caused by the negligence of George Michael Willock. On the occasion in question, George Michael Willock was guilty of acts of negligence each of which were a proximate cause of the collision made the basis of this suit.

V.

> Plaintiff alleges that the damages sustained will greatly exceed the minimum jurisdictional limit of this Court.

> WHEREFORE, PREMISES CONSIDERED, Plaintiff prays that Defendants be cited to appear herein and that upon hearing, Plaintiff have judgment against Defendant for his damages, plus interest and costs and

such other and further relief, both general and special, at law or in equity, to which Plaintiff may show himself justly entitled.

Though a part of the petition is inartfully drawn, it nevertheless informs the appellant of the time and the place of the automobile collision, that appellee sustained personal injuries in the collision, and that appellee is contending the collision and the appellee's injuries were proximately caused by the appellant's negligence. Tex. R. Civ. P. 45(b) only requires that the petition "[c]onsist of a statement in plain and concise language of the plaintiff's cause of action." Tex. R. Civ. P. 47 requires that the petition shall contain "(a) a short statement of the cause of action sufficient to give fair notice of the claim involved . . . ," and "(c) a demand for judgment for all the other relief to which the party deems himself entitled."

Pleadings are sufficient if they give the opposing party fair notice of the claim involved. *Castleberry v. Goolsby Bldg. Corp.*, 617 S.W.2d 665 (Tex. 1981).

In order to support a default judgment, it is not necessary that the plaintiff set out in his pleadings, evidence on which he relies to establish his asserted cause of action. *Edwards Feed Mill v. Johnson*, 311 S.W.2d 232 (Tex. 1958). Nor is it a requisite that a petition be technically sufficient to state a cause of action in order to sustain a default judgment. *Id.*

A fair interpretation of the petition is that the appellee claims that he and the appellant were involved in an automobile collision, and that he was injured as a result of the appellant's negligence. The petition adequately informed appellant of the nature of the claim against him in compliance with Tex. R. Civ. P. 45 and 47.

Affirmed.

. . . .

HOYT, J, dissenting.

I respectfully dissent and would sustain the appellant's first point of error, because the appellee's pleadings fail to allege a legal duty owed by the appellant to the appellee.

. . . .

This pleading is insufficient as a matter of law to charge the appellant with a duty of any kind. In fact, the pleading fails to apprise the appellant of what his specific involvement was in the collision. Appellee's assertion that the appellant's vehicle was "involved" in a collision with him, that also involved several other vehicles, does not assert a violation of any duty or responsibility owed by the appellant to the appellee. I would sustain the first point of error, reverse the judgment, and remand this cause to the trial court.

NOTES AND QUESTIONS

(1) *Comparative Analysis.* Compare the pleadings in *White v. Jackson* and *Willock v. Bui* with Federal Form 9, as it was adopted in 1937 to guide federal courts in determining the required level of pleading specificity. ["On June 1, 1936, in a public highway called Boylston Street in Boston, Massachusetts, defendant

negligently drove a motor vehicle against plaintiff who was then crossing said highway. As a result plaintiff was thrown down and had his leg broken and was otherwise injured, was prevented from transacting his business, suffered great pain of body and mind, and incurred expenses for medical attention and hospitalization in the sum of one thousand dollars."] If the federal form is used as a drafting guide, can the *White v. Jackson* petition be revised to comply with Civil Procedure Rules 45 and 47? Is the petition in *Willock v. Bui* in compliance with the specific "act or omission" requirements set forth in *White v. Jackson*? Is it as factually detailed as the federal form?

(2) *The Standard for Sufficiency.* One court of appeals has stated that the test for determining the sufficiency of a pleading is whether an opposing attorney of reasonable competence could, with the pleading before him or her, ascertain the nature and the basic issues of the controversy and the testimony that will probably be relevant. *Daniels v. Conrad*, 331 S.W.2d 411, 415 (Tex. Civ. App. — Dallas 1959, writ ref'd n.r.e.).

(3) *"Magic Words" Are Not Required.* In *Roark v. Allen*, 633 S.W.2d 804 (Tex. 1982), the Roarks sued two physicians for malpractice in the delivery of their son. The child required surgery for skull fractures caused by the use of forceps. The physicians appealed from a judgment for the Roarks. As one point of error they argued that the plaintiffs' petition was insufficient to raise the issue of negligent delivery against one of the doctors inasmuch as the pleading did not state expressly that the doctor was "negligent," that the doctor did not use ordinary care, or that the doctor's negligence during the delivery was the proximate cause of the child's injuries. The Court of Civil Appeals agreed and reversed. The Supreme Court reversed the Court of Civil Appeals on that point and affirmed the trial court's judgment against the doctor:

> The Roarks alleged that Dr. Matthews delivered the child and, as a result of the delivery, the child sustained a fractured skull; the fractures caused the child intense physical pain and mental anguish and caused the parents to incur additional medical expense. We hold this was sufficient to give Dr. Matthews fair notice that he would have to defend against a claim involving the manner in which he delivered the child. We do not consider it fatal that the Roarks did not use the word "negligent" in connection with the delivery or otherwise specifically indicate that Dr. Matthews failed to exercise ordinary care. This can be inferred from the petition as a whole and from the following specific language: "As a result of the delivery, or attempts at delivery, by the Defendants, *jointly and severally*, the infant sustained bilateral depressed skull fractures." (Emphasis added). The phrase "jointly and severally" usually refers to liability; if two defendants are jointly and severally liable, the plaintiff may sue one or the other or both of them for the entire amount of the damages . . . . Such legal terminology, although used vaguely, was sufficient to alert Dr. Matthews that the Roarks intended to hold him liable for some act connected with his delivery of the child. If Dr. Mathews considered the petition obscure, he should have specially excepted to it and he has waived any defect by his failure to do so.

[4] Fair Notice: A Sample Dispute

On the pages that follow, you will encounter a plaintiff's petition, a defendant's answer including special exceptions, a setting for a hearing on special exceptions, the court's order on the exceptions and plaintiff's amended pleading. The elements of the petition and answer are alleged with varying degrees of specificity and care. The answer contains several different kinds of defensive theories. Think about the different functions of the different pleadings and try to discern the strategy of the attorneys.

This material is taken from D. Crump, *The Anatomy of a Civil Suit: Obiedio v. J. Weingarten, Inc.* (1977)*

Original Petition

NO. ___

DELFINA OBIEDIO v. J. WEINGARTEN, INC.	IN THE DISTRICT COURT HARRIS COUNTY, TEXAS 125th JUDICIAL DISTRICT

PLAINTIFF'S ORIGINAL PETITION

To the Honorable Judge of Said Court:

NOW COMES DELFINA OBIEDIO, hereinafter called Plaintiff, complaining of J. WEINGARTEN, INC., hereinafter called Defendant, and for cause of action would respectfully show the Court as follows:

I.

The Defendant, J. WEINGARTEN, INC., is a corporation doing business in the State of Texas, who may be served with Citation by service upon their statutory agent, ABE WEINGARTEN, 600 Lockwood, Houston, Harris County, Texas.

II.

This suit is brought for the recovery of the damages to which your Plaintiff is legally entitled as the result of an accident which occurred on or about May 7, 1969, at the Weingarten Store No. 14, located at 1100 Quitman, Houston, Harris County, Texas. At this time, Plaintiff was getting a shopping cart from a stacked row when she slipped and fell due to the improper manner in which the carts were aligned and the unsafe condition of Defendant's floor. Plaintiff was not guilty of any negligence. On the contrary, Plaintiff's injuries were caused by the failure of J. WEINGARTEN, INC. and its agents to observe the applicable statutory laws and ordinances and their failure to exercise that degree of care in the maintenance of their premises as would have been exercised by a person of ordinary prudence under the same or similar circumstances.

[This petition further alleges that the plaintiff has incurred physical pain, mental anguish and charges for medical services; that she will in all probability incur further such damages in the future; and that her damages are in the sum of $10,000. The petition is signed by Stephen T. Elder as attorney for plaintiff.]

Original Answer

NO. 862,428

DELFINA OBIEDIO v. J. WEINGARTEN, INC.	IN THE DISTRICT COURT OF HARRIS COUNTY, TEXAS 125TH JUDICIAL DISTRICT

DEFENDANT'S ORIGINAL ANSWER

To the Honorable Judge of Said Court:

Comes now J. WEINGARTEN, INC., Defendant in the above styled and numbered cause, and for answer to Plaintiff's Petition would respectfully show the Court:

I.

Defendant specially excepts to the allegations contained in Plaintiff's original petition and more particularly those allegations which provide:

> At this time Plaintiff was getting a shopping cart from a stacked row when she slipped and fell due to the improper manner in which the carts were aligned and the unsafe condition of Defendant's floor;

such allegation being vague and general and does not apprise this Defendant of the manner in which the carts' alignment was improper or the manner in which the condition of Defendant's floor was unsafe or the manner in which J. Weingarten, Inc. was negligent, such allegation wholly failing to apprise your Defendant of the claim being made against it by Plaintiff of which exception Defendant prays judgment of the Court.

II.

Defendant specially excepts to the allegations of Plaintiff's petition and more particularly allegations contained in Paragraph II thereof which provide:

> On the contrary, Plaintiff's injuries were caused by the failure of J. Weingarten, Inc., and its agents to observe the applicable statutory laws and ordinances and their failure to exercise that degree of care in the maintenance of their premises as would have been exercised by a person of ordinary prudence under the same or similar circumstances;

in that such allegation is vague and general and does not apprise this Defendant of:

(a) which statutory laws Plaintiff alleges that J. Weingarten, Inc. has failed to observe;

(b) which ordinances Plaintiff contends J. Weingarten, Inc. failed to observe causing Plaintiff's injuries;

(c) in what manner Defendant, J. Weingarten, Inc., was negligent in failing to maintain their premises,

of which exception Defendant prays judgment of the Court.

III.

As authorized by Rule 92 of the Rules of Civil Procedure, this Defendant denies the allegations of Plaintiff's petition.

IV.

For further and special answer herein, if such be necessary, and in the alternative, this Defendant avers that such injuries and damages as Plaintiff may have sustained were proximately caused by the failure of Plaintiff to exercise that degree of care which would have been exercised by persons of ordinary prudence in the exercise of ordinary care under the same or similar circumstances.

V.

In the further alternative, if such be necessary, this Defendant avers that the sole proximate cause of the occurrence made the basis of Plaintiff's suit was the act or omission of some third person or the condition of some instrumentality over which this Defendant had or exercised no control and for which this Defendant is not in law responsible.

VI.

In the further alternative, if such be necessary, this Defendant avers that the occurrence made the basis of Plaintiff's suit was an unavoidable accident.

WHEREFORE, premises considered, Defendant prays that it go hence without day, with its costs and for general relief.

[A signature block and certificate of service follow.]

Having filed an answer containing several attacks on plaintiff's pleading, Mr. Thompson [defendant's attorney] next took the step of securing a hearing on those attacks (special exceptions), by calling the clerk of the court. On securing a date, he then notified plaintiff's counsel by the following LETTER GIVING NOTICE OF SETTING:

March 5, 1971
Mr. Stephen F. Elder

Attorney at Law
301 Houston First Savings Building
Houston, Texas 77002

Re: No.862,428-*Delfina Obiedio vs. J. Weingarten, Inc.*-125th District Court

Dear Mr. Elder:

Hearing on special exceptions of Defendant, J. Weingarten Inc., will be at 9:00 A.M. on Monday, April 12, 1971 in the 125th Judicial District Court.

Very truly yours,

Order

NO. 862,428

DELFINA OBIEDIO v. J. WEINGARTEN, INC.	IN THE DISTRICT COURT OF HARRIS COUNTY, TEXAS F-125TH JUDICIAL DISTRICT

ORDER

BE IT REMEMBERED on this day came on to be heard Defendant's Special Exceptions to Plaintiff's Original Petition and the Court after considering such exceptions is of the opinion that they should be sustained and it is therefore,

ORDERED, ADJUDGED and DECREED that Defendant's Special Exceptions to Plaintiff's Original Petition be sustained and that Plaintiff be given leave to amend.

SIGNED, RENDERED and ENTERED this _____ day of _____ 1971.

____

JUDGE PRESIDING

APPROVED AS TO FORM:

____

ATTORNEY FOR DEFENDANT

____

ATTORNEY FOR PLAINTIFF

The following instrument was filed by plaintiff's lawyer after plaintiff's deposition was taken and a trial setting was obtained:

Amended Original Petition

NO. 862,428

DELFINA OBIEDIO v. J. WEINGARTEN, INC.	IN THE DISTRICT COURT OF HARRIS COUNTY, TEXAS 125TH JUDICIAL DISTRICT

PLAINTIFF'S FIRST AMENDED ORIGINAL PETITION

TO THE JUDGE AND JURY OF THIS COURT:

This suit is brought by Delfina Obiedio, Plaintiff, against J. Weingarten, Inc., Defendant. The suit is for personal injuries sustained by Mrs. Obiedio.

I.

The Plaintiff has for many years been a resident of Harris County. The Defendant, J. Weingarten, Inc. is a corporation doing business in the State of Texas. Defendant is already before this Court on this matter, so service is not necessary.

II.

This suit is brought for the recovery of the damages to which Mrs. Obiedio is legally entitled as a result of an accident which occurred at the Weingarten's Store No. 14, located at 1100 Quitman, here in Houston, Harris County, Texas on or about the 7th of May, 1969. At that time, Mrs. Obiedio had just come into the store to shop for groceries. To carry her groceries, she sought to get a shopping cart from a row of carts stacked with the baskets inside each other as is customarily done in grocery stores. The carts were in a bad state of repair: the baskets were bent; some of the wheels would not turn and the tubular metal frames of some of the carts were bent. In spite of the state of repair of the carts, Mrs. Obiedio had previously been able to pull one cart away from the stack without difficulty. However, on the occasion in question three or four baskets stuck together and all started rolling toward Mrs. Obiedio. The baskets ran over Mrs. Obiedio, she was knocked off balance and fell to the floor. Mrs. Obiedio was not guilty of any negligence. On the contrary, it is alleged that her injuries were caused by the failure of J. Weingarten, Inc. and its agents to exercise that degree of care in their maintenance of their store as would have been exercised by a person of ordinary prudence under the same or similar circumstances. Specifically, it is alleged that J. Weingarten, Inc. and the company's employees at Store No. 14 ought not to have crammed the bent and broken carts together, or ought to have made sure that they were in sufficiently good repair that an elderly lady could pull a single cart away from a row.

III.

Mrs. Obiedio has required medical care and in reasonable probability will require additional medical care. Her injuries and their effect have caused her to suffer great physical pain and mental anguish. She will probably continue to suffer from such physical pain for a long time in the future, if not for the rest of her life.

Mrs. Obiedio has incurred, and will likely incur, in the future, charges for medical services. These charges represent the usual, reasonable and customary charges for like and similar services in the vicinity where they have been rendered.

By reason of all of the above and foregoing, Mrs. Obiedio has been caused to suffer damages in the reasonable and just sum of TWENTY-FIVE THOUSAND DOLLARS ($25,000) for which sum she now sues.

WHEREFORE, Mrs. Obiedio earnestly asks that upon final trial of this case, she have judgment against J. Weingarten, Inc., for her damages in the reasonable and just sum of TWENTY-FIVE THOUSAND DOLLARS ($25,000.00), that she have interest on the judgment at the legal rates, and that she recover her costs of Court in this behalf expended and that she have such other and further relief, general and special, at law and in equity to which she may show herself justly entitled.

Respectfully submitted,

[signature block and certificate of service follow].

NOTES AND QUESTIONS

(1) *Analyze the Petition.* You have now studied the requirements of "fair notice" of legal and factual theories. Does the plaintiff's initial pleading meet this standard? Does the amended original petition meet this standard? What allegations or claims are problematic in each?

(2) *Analyze the Answer.* What kinds of defenses or defensive theories has defendant's lawyer pleaded in the answer? What is the function of each enumerated paragraph?

Why does the answer not simply end with the third paragraph (the one containing the statement that "Defendant denies the allegations" of plaintiff)? Why are the rest of the paragraphs included (for example, what would happen if defendant tried to rely on contributory negligence at trial without pleading paragraph IV of the answer)? - AFFIRM. DEFENSE gotta be plead

(3) *What Must Defendant Plead?* There is some question whether defendant is required to plead the matters in Paragraphs V and VI of the answer (because "sole proximate cause" and "unavoidable accident" are not affirmative defenses, but instead go to rebut the plaintiff's claim of causal negligence and are called "inferential rebuttal issues"). If there is doubt about the need for pleading a particular claim or defense, what should the lawyer do? What is lost by pleading it?

(4) *Special Exceptions.* The special exception is the vehicle for challenging either form (such as vagueness) or content (such as failure to state a cause of

action) of the petition. What are the special exceptions used for in the *Obiedio* case?

(5) *The Special Exception Hearing.* The hearing on these special exceptions is likely to have been short and informal. The court's docket probably contained 10 or 20 other matters for similar hearings, to be held within an hour or two, before the jury trial or other business of the court for the day. There would be no evidence at the hearing (why not?). The court would probably call both attorneys to come before the bench and inquire what the matter was about, to which defendant's lawyer would probably respond by stating what was contained in the exceptions, in summary form, arguing, perhaps, that "we can't tell whether they mean we're negligent in upkeep of the baskets, or in buying this kind of basket, or in having them stacked wrong, or what." Plaintiff might respond, "Well, Judge, we say in there that the negligence was in the way the carts were aligned and in the way the floor was kept, and I don't see how we could be much more specific." The case is unlikely to be controlled by law specifically on point (there are few cases about shopping cart pleading), and so the court would simply make its own judgment on the matter on the spot, directing the prevailing party to draw an order for the court to sign.

(6) *Strategic Considerations.* What strategy is behind the defendant's desire to make the plaintiff plead more specifically? It is probably not an effort to learn the facts because that can be done through discovery. To identify the strategy, ask yourself this question: What happens if a plaintiff pleads a specific, narrow act of negligence and then at trial, attempts to introduce evidence of a slightly different act of negligence? Incidentally, notice that the defendant's own pleading of contributory negligence is broad and general. Why? What could the plaintiff do to make the defendant be more specific?

Compare the plaintiff's amended original petition with the initial one. Has the plaintiff pleaded very specifically or kept the pleading general? Has she omitted any claims? What, if anything, has been gained by the defendant's exceptions?

[5] Pleading Injuries and Damages

Read Tex. R. Civ. P. 56.

Many kinds of losses are said to be "special damages." What is the consequence of failing to plead for the recovery of an item that falls in that category?

WEINGARTENS, INC. v. PRICE

461 S.W.2d 260 (Tex. Civ. App. — Houston [14th Dist.] 1970, writ ref'd n.r.e.)

JOHNSON, J.

Suit for personal injuries alleged to be in the sum of $17,500 brought by Rosie Price, joined by her husband, James Price, against Weingarten's, Inc. Based on answers to special issues found by the jury judgment was entered for the plaintiffs in the sum of $5,000. Appellant Weingartens duly effects appeal to this Court.

In their petition plaintiffs alleged that Mrs. Price had gone to the Weingartens supermarket to purchase groceries; that while shopping inside the store she tripped and fell over the end of an unattended dolly which was protruding into the aisle way; and that Weingartens had negligently left the dolly in the aisle was proximately causing the injuries made the basis of the suit. The petition then continued as follows:

> "As a result of such negligence, your Plaintiff, Rosie Price, has been damaged in the just and reasonable sum of SEVENTEEN THOUSAND FIVE HUNDRED DOLLARS ($17,500.00) for which sum your Plaintiff, James Price here now sues in her behalf; such damages to your Plaintiffs, consisting of damages for reasonable and necessary medical expenses incurred and to be incurred in the future, past and future physical pain and mental anguish, and loss of services as a wife.
>
> "WHEREFORE, PREMISES CONSIDERED, Plaintiffs pray that the Defendant be cited to appear and answer herein, and that upon final trial hereof, Plaintiff James Price have judgment against the Defendant in the just and reasonable sum of SEVENTEEN THOUSAND FIVE HUNDRED DOLLARS ($17,500.00), as to and for injuries sustained by his wife, Rosie Price; that they have interest on the judgments at the legal rate; that they have all costs of Court herein expended, and that they have such other and further relief, both general and special, at law and in equity, to which they may show themselves to be justly entitled, and in duty bound will ever pray."

In the trial before the jury Mrs. Price testified that prior to her fall she had taken in sewing. She was then asked how much income per month she made from such sewing. Specific objection was then interposed by counsel for the defendant because loss of income had not been pled by the plaintiffs. The court overruled the objection and the witness proceeded to testify that she earned $20 to $25 per month before the accident and that after the accident she had been unable to earn anything.

The court's charge to the jury contained a single damage issue consisting of six elements. The third and fourth of these were as follows:

> "c. Loss of earnings in the past."
>
> "d. Loss of earning capacity which, in reasonable probability, she will sustain in the future."

Specific objection was made by the defendant to the inclusion of these two elements in the court's charge for the reason that loss of income and loss of earning capacity had not been pled. This objection was likewise overruled. The above two elements were included in the damage issue submitted to the jury, and the jury's finding in answer to such issue ($5,000) therefore included consideration of loss of earnings and loss of earning capacity in the future.

Appellant here presents only two points of error. These points are directed to the admission of testimony and the inclusion in the damage issue of the elements of loss of earnings and loss of earning capacity. Weingartens, the appellant, contends here, as it did in the trial court, that there were no pleadings to support the admission of the testimony or the submission of these elements in the damage issue. Appellants contend that the trial court therefore erred and pray that the cause be reversed and remanded. We conclude that appellant's points of error must be sustained . . . .

At the outset in the case at bar it is to be noted that no special exception to the plaintiff's quoted pleading was made by the defendant. It is also to be noted that the plaintiffs made no request at any time for permission to file a trial amendment and none was made. Lastly, we believe it quite clear from the record that the questioned areas of loss of earnings and loss of earning capacity were not tried by consent . . . .

Loss of earnings and loss of earning capacity are items of "special damages" and are not implied from the itemization of other dissimilar "special damages."

Loss of earnings and loss of earning capacity are without support in the petition of the plaintiff. Appellant's points of error are sustained. The judgment of the trial court is reversed and remanded.

NOTES AND QUESTIONS

(1) *General and Special Damages.* General damages are damages that "naturally and necessarily" attend a particular injury. An example of general damages is pretrial pain and suffering, which is presumed to accompany a serious injury. *Pecos & N.T. Ry. Co. v. Huskey*, 166 S.W. 493, 494 (Tex. Civ. App. — Amarillo 1914, writ ref'd). Special damages are damages that tend to vary from person to person. They must be specifically pleaded. Examples of special damages are future pain and suffering and medical expenses. *Young v. Howell*, 236 S.W.2d 247, 248 (Tex. Civ. App. — Texarkana 1951, no writ); *Merchants Bldg. Corp. v. Adler*, 110 S.W.2d 978, 984 (Tex. Civ. App. — Dallas 1937, dis.).

(2) *Loss of Inheritance Damages in Wrongful Death Cases.* In *Yowell v. Piper Aircraft Corp.*, 703 S.W.2d 630 (Tex. 1986), a wrongful death case, defendant Piper argued that the Yowells should not recover loss of inheritance damages because they failed to plead loss of inheritance, a type of special damages that must be specially pleaded. However, the Yowells did allege lost future earnings, indicating that the figures did not include loss of companionship, guidance, and service. Furthermore, the lost earnings figures were supported by allegations of the decedents' life expectancy, work expectancy, salaries, benefits, and other relevant data. Although the court stated that the better pleading practice would have been to use phrases such as "loss of inheritance" or "loss of pecuniary benefit," it concluded such phrases are not required. In effect, the Yowells asked for compensation for their fair share of the decedents' lost earnings. Thus, the pleadings gave fair notice that plaintiffs were seeking lost pecuniary benefits. The court concluded: "Because lost inheritance is a lost pecuniary benefit, we find that the Yowells have pleaded loss of inheritance damages sufficiently to satisfy our liberal rule of pleading." It is, however, the better practice to specifically plead for loss of inheritance damages. [Also be aware that the current court requires considerable evidence to support a finding of lost inheritance, commenting that the relevant factual issues are "virtually imponderable in most cases." *C & H Nationwide, Inc. v. Thompson*, 903 S.W.2d 315 (Tex. 1994)].

(3) *Pleading Damage Measures.* Although a *measure* of damage need not be pleaded specifically, the pleading must be sufficiently detailed to support submission of an appropriate measure. For example, when the action involves damage to personal property, the petition should provide information concerning the value before and after the event if the market-value rule is to be employed. "It is not permissible . . . for the plaintiff to allege his damages under the market value rule and then establish them under the rule which allows a recovery of the reasonable cost of repair." *Tinney v. Williams*, 144 S.W.2d 344, 346 (Tex. Civ. App. — Amarillo 1940, no writ). Also, review *White v. Jackson*, in [3], *above*, with regard to pleading damages.

[6] Alternative or Hypothetical Claims

Read Tex. R. Civ. P. 48.

Sometimes a party may have the right to recover under claims that provide for alternative or inconsistent measures of damages or other remedies. When do they need to choose?

BIRCHFIELD v. TEXARKANA MEMORIAL HOSP.

747 S.W.2d 361 (Tex. 1987)

WALLACE, J.

Kellie Birchfield was born prematurely with a congenitally functionless right eye. Shortly after her release from the hospital, she was diagnosed as having retrolental fibroplasia (RLF) in her left eye and is now totally blind. Her parents, Phillip and Mary Jo Birchfield, individually and as next friends of Kellie, sued Texarkana Memorial Hospital (Wadley) and her three treating physicians, Dr. Jon Hall, Dr. Noel Cowan, and Dr. Betty Lowe. The petition alleged negligence on the part of all four defendants plus a D.T.P.A. action against Wadley under the 1973 version of the Act. Deceptive Trade Practices Act, ch. 143, 1973 Tex. Gen. Laws at 322–43. The jury answered all issues favorably to the Birchfields. The trial court rendered judgment for actual damages against all defendants and exemplary damages against Wadley, but refused to render judgment on the D.T.P.A. action. The Court of Appeals initially affirmed the judgment, but on rehearing, reversed and remanded for trial. We reverse the judgment of the court of appeals and render judgment for the Birchfields.

As a premature infant, Kellie was administered approximately 400 hours of supplemental oxygen without adequate monitoring of arterial blood gases. This occurred even though a 1971 report published by the American Academy of Pediatrics cautioned the medical community about the danger of RLF in premature infants receiving supplemental oxygen, and advised practitioners to closely monitor arterial blood gases of such infants. In the wake of the report Dr. Lowe predicted at a pediatrics section meeting, attended by a Wadley administrator, that the hospital was "going to have blind babies" unless it acquired the facilities to adequately monitor blood gases. However, during the period from 1971 through 1973 Wadley expended approximately $200 per year for nursery improvements. Kellie was born in August of 1974.

The jury found the individual doctors negligent and Wadley both negligent and grossly negligent in failing to properly treat Kellie. It also found that Wadley had violated the D.T.P.A. by holding out to the Birchfields that the hospital was adequately equipped to handle premature babies when it was not. The damage award was $2,111,500 actual damages against all defendants, jointly and severally, plus $1,200,000 exemplary damages against Wadley.

. . . .

DAMAGES

D.T.P.A. Damages

The Birchfields challenge the rulings of both the trial court and the court of appeals concerning questions of damages. At trial, the Birchfields secured jury findings that Wadley violated the Deceptive Trade Practices Act, that the Birchfields were adversely affected by that violation, and that Wadley was negligent and grossly negligent. The Birchfields argue that the courts below erred in failing to award *both* exemplary damages as found by the jury and treble damages under the D.T.P.A. We disagree. This argument overlooks the fact that the jury found that Wadley's deceptive act or practice, as well as each defendants' acts of negligence, were the proximate or producing cause of the *same damages*. *See, Allstate Ins. Co. v. Kelly*, 680 S.W.2d 595, 606 (Tex. App. — Tyler 1984, writ ref'd n.r.e.). The Birchfields' special issues on damages merely requested the jury to fix a sum of money which would compensate Kellie and her parents, "for the damages proximately resulting from the occurrence in question." In the absence of separate and distinct findings of actual damages on both the acts of negligence and the deceptive acts or practices, an award of exemplary damages *and* statutory treble damages would be necessarily predicated upon the same findings of actual damages and would amount to a double recovery of punitive damages. *Id.*

In the alternative, the Birchfields claim that they were entitled to elect whether to recover the exemplary damages as found by the jury or statutory treble damages. In light of our holding that the Birchfields were not entitled to both treble and exemplary damages, they were confronted with a situation where an election would be required. *Kish v. Van Note*, 692 S.W.2d 463, 466–67 (Tex. 1985). The court of appeals held that since the Birchfields, before entry of judgment, failed to unequivocally waive the findings on exemplary damages, they had waived their right to complain on appeal that the trial court erred in failing to award treble damages. We find no support for that proposition. The judgment of the court should be "so framed as to give the party *all the relief* to which he may be entitled." Tex. R. Civ. P. 301, (emphasis added). While a formal waiver by the Birchfields would have been in order, it was not a prerequisite to the recovery of all of the damages to which they were lawfully entitled. *Hargrove v. Trinity Universal Insurance Co.*, 256 S.W.2d 73, 75, 152 Tex. 243 (Tex. 1953). We hold that where the prevailing party fails to elect between alternative measures of damages, the court should utilize the findings affording the greater recovery and render judgment accordingly.

[7] The "Demand for Relief"; Prayer

Read Tex. R. Civ. P. 47.

Dollar Amount Claimed. Civil Procedure Rule 47 was amended in 1977 to provide that an original petition seeking unliquidated damages should contain only the allegation that the damages sought exceed the minimum jurisdictional limits of the court. *See also* C.P.R.C. § 74.053 ("Pleadings in a suit based on a health care liability claim shall not specify an amount of money claimed as damages. The defendant may file a special exception to the pleadings on the ground the suit is not within the court's jurisdiction, in which event the plaintiff shall inform the court and defendant in writing of the total dollar amount claimed. This section does not prevent a party from mentioning the total dollar amount claimed in examining prospective jurors on voir dire or in argument to the court or jury."). The purpose of the amendments was to limit newspaper publicity based on large damage claims in personal injury litigation. In 1990, Rule 47 was amended again to require that pleadings seeking unliquidated damages contain a statement that the damages sought are within the jurisdictional limits of the court, not that they exceed the court's minimum jurisdictional limits (thus accounting for courts that have both a top and a bottom limit on amount in controversy jurisdiction). Although it is proper (indeed, required) for plaintiffs to plead in this way, defendants who want a specific amount pleaded may specially except to the damages pleading and plaintiffs will be ordered to plead an amount for damages. Tex. R. Civ. P. 47 (last sentence).

Before the amendments, a pleading seeking damages "in excess of the minimum jurisdictional limits of the court" would not support a default judgment. *White Motor Co. v. Loden*, 373 S.W.2d 863, 866 (Tex. Civ. App. — Dallas 1964, no writ).

It is not entirely clear what is meant by a claim for "unliquidated damages." In the context of default judgment, a claim is liquidated only if the amount of damages can be calculated accurately by the court from the allegations contained in the petition and an instrument in writing on which the claim is based. *Freeman v. Leasing Assocs., Inc.*, 503 S.W.2d 406, 408 (Tex. Civ. App. — Houston [14th Dist.] 1973, no writ). Would you consider an action on an oral contract to recover a specific agreed dollar sum a liquidated claim? What about a conversion claim involving a finding of the fair value of a chattel as of a specified date? Whether or not "unliquidated" in the technical sense, they are not the kinds of claims that troubled those who lobbied for the prohibition on pleading a damages number.

Use of the General Prayer and Special Prayer. In a general prayer, the pleader requests all relief, legal or equitable, to which the pleader is entitled. The general prayer is ordinarily sufficient to authorize a judgment for any relief, consistent with the cause of action pleaded, that is within the jurisdiction of the court. *Goldberg v. Goldberg*, 392 S.W.2d 168, 171 (Tex. Civ. App. — Fort Worth 1965, no writ). At times, usually when the relief sought is of a non-monetary character, a special (specific) prayer is required. Claims for injunctive relief, rescission, and removal of a cloud on the title to property are examples of when a specific prayer is needed. *See, e.g., Fant v. Massie*, 451 S.W.2d 774, 776 (Tex. Civ. App. — Austin 1970, writ ref'd n.r.e.) (injunction); *Burnett v. James*, 564 S.W.2d 407, 409 (Tex. Civ. App. — Dallas 1978, writ dism'd) (rescission); *West Texas Dist. Baptist Ass'n v.*

Pilgrim Rest Bapt. Ch., 368 S.W.2d 814, 817 (Tex. Civ. App. — Fort Worth 1963, writ ref'd n.r.e.) (title to real property).

A pleader must take great care in making sure that the special prayer is not "inconsistent" with the relief sought under the general prayer. *See Tennessee Life Ins. Co. v. Nelson*, 459 S.W.2d 450, 454–55 (Tex. Civ. App. — Houston [14th Dist.] 1970, no writ). "Inconsistent" in this sense does not mean logically inconsistent but rather is another instance in which the more specific pleading can nullify the effect of the more general one. In *Tennessee Life*, the court held that a prayer for "interest on the amount of the judgment at the legal rate until paid" was inconsistent with a claim for pre-judgment interest, and that the latter could not be recovered even though the petition also contained a general prayer for relief.

Prejudgment Interest and the Prayer. The subject of prejudgment interest has created other difficulties. In *Republic National Bank v. Northwest National Bank of Fort Worth*, 578 S.W.2d 109, 116–17 (Tex. 1978), the Texas Supreme Court ruled that "[w]here prejudgment interest is sought at common law as an element of damages, the plaintiff must plead for it. Such is not the case where prejudgment interest is sought on the basis of a written contract fitting the description of [Texas Finance Code § 302.002]. An award of this statutory interest, or interest *eo nomine* as it is known, may be supported by a prayer for general relief."

[8] Certification and Sanctions for Frivolous Pleadings and Motions

Read Tex. R. Civ. P. 13 and the following provisions of C.P.R.C. chapter 10.

§ 10.001. *Signing of Pleadings and Motions*

The signing of a pleading or motion as required by the Texas Rules of Civil Procedure constitutes a certificate by the signatory that to the signatory's best knowledge, information, and belief, formed after reasonable inquiry:

(1) the pleading or motion is not being presented for any improper purpose, including to harass or to cause unnecessary delay or needless increase in the cost of litigation;

(2) each claim, defense, or other legal contention in the pleading or motion is warranted by existing law or by a nonfrivolous argument for the extension, modification, or reversal of existing law or the establishment of new law;

(3) each allegation or other factual contention in the pleading or motion has evidentiary support or, for a specifically identified allegation or factual contention, is likely to have evidentiary support after a reasonable opportunity for further investigation or discovery;

and

(4) each denial in the pleading or motion of a factual contention is ranted on the evidence or, for a specifically identified denial, is sonably based on a lack of information or belief.

§ 10.002. *Motion for Sanctions*

(a) A party may make a motion for sanctions, describing the specific conduct violating Section 10.001.

(b) The court on its own initiative may enter an order describing the specific conduct that appears to violate Section 10.001 and direct the alleged violator to show cause why the conduct has not violated that section.

(c) The court may award to a party prevailing on a motion under this section the reasonable expenses and attorney's fees incurred in presenting or opposing the motion, and if no due diligence is shown the court may award to the prevailing party all costs for inconvenience, harassment, and out-of-pocket expenses incurred or caused by the subject litigation.

§ 10.003. *Notice and Opportunity to Respond*

The court shall provide a party who is the subject of a motion for sanctions under Section 10.002 notice of the allegations and a reasonable opportunity to respond to the allegations.

§ 10.004. *Violation; Sanction*

(a) A court that determines that a person has signed a pleading or motion in violation of Section 10.001 may impose a sanction on the person, a party represented by the person, or both.

(b) The sanction must be limited to what is sufficient to deter repetition of the conduct or comparable conduct by others similarly situated.

(c) A sanction may include any of the following:

(1) a directive to the violator to perform, or refrain from performing, an act;

(2) an order to pay a penalty into court; and

(3) an order to pay to the other party the amount of the reasonable expenses incurred by the other party because of the filing of the pleading or motion, including reasonable attorney's fees.

(d) The court may not award monetary sanctions against a represented party for a violation of Section 10.001(2).

(e) The court may not award monetary sanctions on its own initiative unless the court issues its order to show cause before a voluntary dismissal or settlement of the claims made by or against the party or the party's attorney who is to be sanctioned.

(f) The filing of a general denial under Rule 92, Texas Rules of Civil Procedure, shall not be deemed a violation of this chapter.

§ 10.005. *Order*

A court shall describe in an order imposing a sanction under this chapter the conduct the court has determined violated Section 10.001 and explain the basis for the sanction imposed.

§ 10.006. *Conflict*

Notwithstanding Section 22.004, Government Code, the supreme court may not amend or adopt rules in conflict with this chapter.

The following excerpt from William V. Dorsaneo III, *Texas Litigation Guide*, Ch. 3, *Professional Responsibility*, discusses a number of additional sources of the attorney's duty to pursue only legitimate, "nonfrivolous" claims and defenses.*

§ 3.07[1]

[a] Disciplinary Rules of Professional Conduct

Lawyers are forbidden to bring or defend proceedings, or to raise or attack particular issues, unless they reasonably believe that there is a nonfrivolous basis for doing so [State Bar Rules, Art. 10 § 9, Rule 3.01]. The comments to the rule give a number of examples of pleadings or contentions that are "frivolous" in this context. For instance, a pleading, motion, or other paper filed with the court is frivolous when the filing is made primarily for the purpose of harassment or to maliciously injure someone [State Bar Rules, Art. 10 § 9, Rule 3.01, Comment 2; see [b], below]. A filing that contains knowingly false statements is also frivolous. On the other hand, a filing is not frivolous simply because the facts have not been substantiated fully or because the lawyer expects to develop vital evidence by discovery. In addition, taking the client's position is not frivolous even though the lawyer believes that the position ultimately may not prevail [State Bar Rules, Art. 10 § 9, Rule 3.01, Comment 3].

[b] Sanctions Under Statute

[i] Relationship of Sanction Provisions

Several Texas rules and statutes, in addition to the Disciplinary Rules of Professional Conduct . . . forbid the filing of frivolous actions and provide for sanctions. Sanctions for filing frivolous pleadings and motions are available under Chapter 10 of the Civil Practice and Remedies Code . . . and have often been imposed under Civil Procedure Rule 13 . . . .

Chapter 10 provides that, notwithstanding the Texas Supreme Court's rulemaking authority under the Government Code [see Gov. C. § 22.004(c)], the Court may not amend or adopt rules in conflict with Chapter 10. However, Chapter 10 does not explicitly repeal or alter current Civil Procedure Rule 13.

Chapter 9 of the Civil Practice and Remedies Code also deals with frivolous pleadings [see C.P.R.C. § 9.001 et seq.]. This chapter was enacted in 1987. In the same year the Texas Supreme Court amended Civil Procedure Rule 13 and added language, pursuant to the Court's rulemaking authority, repealing Chapter 9 to the extent it conflicts with Rule 13 [see Gov. C. § 22.004(c) — adoption of rule by Supreme Court repeals conflicting procedural laws]. When Rule 13 was amended again in 1990, the repealing language was omitted, but it is clear that Chapter 9 was

---

repealed to the extent of any conflict. Moreover, the legislature amended Chapter 9 in 1999 to provide that sanctions may not be imposed under Chapter 9 in any proceeding governed either by the sanctions provision of Chapter 10 or by Rule 13 [see C.P.R.C. § 9.012(h)]. Nevertheless, although Chapter 9 is no longer operative as a basis for sanctions, it is possible that a provision of Chapter 9 that is not in conflict with Chapter 10 or Rule 13 remains in effect. Unlike Chapter 10 or Rule 13, Chapter 9 contains a provision under which the court must report an attorney's conduct to an appropriate State Bar grievance committee if the court imposes sanctions and finds that the attorney has consistently engaged in activity that results in sanctions. The report must contain (1) the name of the attorney, (2) the court's finding that the pleading was signed in violation of the statutory standards, (3) a description of the sanctions imposed against the attorney and the represented party, and (4) the finding that the attorney has consistently engaged in activity that results in sanctions [see C.P.R.C. § 9.013].

The power to sanction may also be implicit in a particular statute or rule or found in the court's inherent power to administer justice [see *Metzger v. Sebek*, 892 S.W.2d 20, 51 (Tex. App. — Houston [1st Dist.] 1994, pet. denied); see [d], below]. When a trial court's order of sanctions refers to a specific rule, either by citing the rule, tracking its language, or both, the reviewing court need not consider whether the sanctions might have been proper under the court's inherent power or some other authority. The reviewing court's role is to determine whether the trial court properly applied the specific rule [see *Metzger v. Sebek*, 892 S.W.2d 20, 51 (Tex. App. — Houston [1st Dist.] 1994, den.); *Aldine Independent School Dist. v. Baty*, 946 S.W.2d 851, 852 (Tex. App. — Houston [14th Dist.] 1997, no writ) — when trial court tracked Rule 13 language, although it did not cite to rule, appellate court limited review to whether sanctions met T.R.C.P. 13 requirements] . . . .

[c] Sanctions Under Civil Procedure Rule 13

[i] Basis for Sanctions

Under Civil Procedure Rule 13, the signature of an attorney or party constitutes a certificate that the attorney has read the pleading, motion, or other paper and that, to the best of the lawyer's knowledge, information, and belief formed after reasonable inquiry, the instrument is neither (1) groundless and brought in bad faith, nor (2) groundless and brought for the purpose of harassment. Additionally, Rule 13 states that an attorney or party may be held in contempt of court for bringing a fictitious suit as an experiment to get an opinion of the court, for filing any fictitious pleading in a cause for the purposes of securing an advisory opinion, or for making statements in a pleading that the attorney knows to be groundless and false if the statements are made for the purposes of securing a delay of the trial of the cause.

The term "bad faith" under Civil Procedure Rule 13 has been held to mean not simply bad judgment or negligence, but the conscious doing of a wrong for a dishonest, discriminatory, or malicious purpose [*Stites v. Gillum*, 872 S.W.2d 786, 794–96 (Tex. App. — Fort Worth 1994, den.); *cf. Campos v. Ysleta General Hosp., Inc.*, 879 S.W.2d 67, 71 (Tex. App. — El Paso 1994, den.)]. There is a presumption under Rule 13 that papers are filed in good faith. Therefore, the burden is on the party moving for sanctions to overcome this presumption [*GTE Communications*

Sys. Corp. v. Tanner, 856 S.W.2d 725, 731 (Tex. 1993)].

Under Rule 13, "groundless" means that there is no basis in law or fact for the pleading and it is not warranted by a good-faith argument for the extension, modification, or reversal of existing law [T.R.C.P. 13; *see also* Donwerth v. Preston II Chrysler-Dodge, Inc., 775 S.W.2d 634, 637 (Tex. 1989) — term "groundless" under T.R.C.P. 13 has same meaning as "groundless" under DTPA; *see also* Bus. & Com. C. § 17.50(c)]. However, the otherwise identical language of Chapter 10 of the Civil Practice and Remedies Code substitutes the phrase "non-frivolous argument" for "good-faith argument."

A general denial under the Civil Procedure Rules does not constitute a groundless pleading in violation of the rule, nor does the amount claimed for damages constitute a groundless claim in violation of the rule [T.R.C.P. 13].

[ii] Right to Seek Court Ruling

A claim or defense set forth in a pleading is not groundless under Civil Procedure Rule 13 merely because relief ultimately is denied. There is a right to seek a court determination of a claim or defense unless the claim or defense is baseless . . . . There is also a right to make a good faith filing of an action before a complete investigation is conducted if such action is necessary to avoid the bar of limitations. Thus, the imposition of sanctions was held to be inappropriate against an attorney who, because of an erroneous interpretation of facts, filed suit on the eve of the running of the statute of limitation, but later dismissed the suit after learning that the claim was unfounded in fact [*Yang Ming Line v. Port of Houston Auth.*, 833 S.W.2d 750, 752–53 (Tex. App. — Houston [1st Dist.] 1992, no writ)].

[iii] Actions Clearly Barred by Law

Rule 13 should be used only "in those egregious situations where the worst of the bar uses our honored system for ill motive without regard to reason and the guiding principles of the law" [*Dyson Descendant Corp. v. Sonat Exploration Co.*, 861 S.W.2d 942, 951 (Tex. App. — Houston [1st Dist.] 1993, no writ)]:

> Innovative changes in the law or applications of the law must by necessity come from creative and innovative sources. For the most part these changes resulted from lawyers advocating positions that may have had little or no basis in law. By their very definition, changes in the law are different from and in disagreement with what has been historically accepted. We cannot allow rule 13 to have a chilling effect on those who seek change in legal precedent. Like other advocates of change, lawyers seeking change in legal precedent may meet with able opposition, even vehement disagreement, and they may even fail at first. They may never succeed, but they must be given an opportunity to try without fear of unjustified persecution.

An action that is clearly barred by existing law may be considered groundless and brought in bad faith or for the purposes of harassment, if the existing law is well settled and no reasonably prudent lawyer could believe that a change in the law would be acceptable. For example, the Fort Worth Court upheld an $18,000 sanctions award against an attorney for filing a counterpetition against a third party in a divorce action for interference with the familial relationship. The sanction was imposed against the attorney after the trial court found that the action filed was an action for alienation of affections, couched in other terms, and was, therefore, abolished by the Family Code. The court of appeals concluded that the pleadings were not seeking a good faith extension of existing law and that the trial court did not abuse its discretion in determining the action to be groundless [*Stites v. Gillum*, 872 S.W.2d 786, 787–96 (Tex. App. — Fort Worth 1994, pet. denied)] . . . .

[d] Sanctions Under Court's Inherent Power

Texas courts have the inherent power to sanction litigants or attorneys whose abusive conduct affects "the core functions of the judiciary," even when the conduct is not specifically proscribed by rule or statute [*Kutch v. Del Mar College*, 831 S.W.2d 506, 509–13 (Tex. App. — Corpus Christi 1992, no writ) — sanction proper for failure to replead, but dismissal of case with prejudice was excessive sanction; *see also Metzger v. Sebek*, 892 S.W.2d 20, 51 (Tex. App. — Houston [1st Dist.] 1994, den.) — adopting rule from *Kutch*]:

> This power [to sanction] includes the power to sanction appropriately for failure to comply with a valid court order incident to one of the core functions of the judiciary . . . . The . . . core functions of the judiciary . . . are: hearing evidence, deciding issues of fact raised by the pleadings, deciding questions of law, entering final judgment and enforcing that judgment . . . . Inherent power to sanction exists to the extent necessary to deter, alleviate, and counteract bad faith abuse of the judicial process, such as any significant interference with the traditional core functions of Texas courts.

The Texas Supreme Court has said that a court has the inherent power to impose sanctions on its own motion in an appropriate case to discipline an attorney's behavior. In this case, the trial court sanctioned two attorneys on its own motion because they tried to circumvent the random assignment of cases to judges. The attorneys had filed what was essentially the same case multiple times, until one of the cases was assigned to a particular judge, and then sought a nonsuit in the other filings. The Court ruled that the imposition of sanctions under these circumstances was not an abuse of discretion, even though the action was taken after the notice of nonsuit was filed and after the defendant had filed a notice of removal to federal court [In re Bennett, 960 S.W.2d 35, 40 (Tex. 1997) — "The practice of filing multiple cases without intent to prosecute most of them, in search of a court perceived to be sympathetic, subverts random assignment procedures that are in place in many multi-court counties and is an abuse of the judicial process. This type of conduct, if tolerated, breeds disrespect for and threatens the integrity of our judicial system."].

In the following case, the court applies chapter 10 to the filing of a lawsuit and request for a temporary restraining order. How does it determine whether the plaintiff's suit was filed in bad faith? How exactly has the lawyer violated chapter 10? Did he also violate Rule 13? Where do oral misstatements to the court fit in?

LOW v. HENRY

221 S.W.3d 609 (Tex. 2007)

WAINWRIGHT, J.

Texas follows a "fair notice" standard for pleading, in which courts assess the sufficiency of pleadings by determining whether an opposing party can ascertain from the pleading the nature, basic issues, and the type of evidence that might be relevant to the controversy. *See Tex. Dep't of Parks & Wildlife v. Miranda*, 133 S.W.3d 217, 230 (Tex. 2004); *Horizon/CMS Healthcare Corp. v. Auld*, 34 S.W.3d 887, 896–97 (Tex. 2000); *Boyles v. Kerr*, 855 S.W.2d 593, 601 (Tex. 1993); *see also* TEX. R. CIV. P. 47(a). However, the actual facts and evidence of a specific case limit this relatively liberal standard. Chapter 10 of the Texas Civil Practice and Remedies Code requires a pleading's signatory to certify that he or she conducted a reasonable inquiry into the allegations and concluded that each allegation or other factual contention in the pleading has or is likely to have evidentiary support. Because the attorney who filed the petition in this case obtained and directed the review of evidence that disproved some of the allegations pled against some of the defendants, the trial court correctly found that the attorney violated Chapter 10. However, we hold that the trial court abused its discretion in not providing a sufficient basis to support the imposition of a $50,000 penalty. We reverse the court of appeals' judgment and remand the case to the trial court for proceedings consistent with this opinion.

I. Factual and Procedural Background

On November 20, 1999, Henry White was admitted to Columbia North Bay Hospital after suffering a stroke. Dr. Stephen Smith treated White in the emergency room for less than one hour. Dr. Robert Low cared for him for four days before White was transferred to another hospital. White was comatose at the time of the transfer. He died in December 1999.

On January 31, 2002, Joyce White (both individually and as representative of her husband Henry White's estate) sued the alleged manufacturers, designers, and distributors of the drug known as Propulsid, Coastal Bend Hospital, Inc. d/b/a Columbia North Bay Hospital, eight physicians, and nurse Donna McMahon for damages flowing from Henry White's death. Although most of the claims involved the drug Propulsid, some alleged that the physicians and hospital were negligent in Henry White's medical treatment.

Attorney Thomas J. Henry represented Joyce White when he filed the petition. His office received copies of Henry White's medical records months before he filed the petition. Henry filed a motion to withdraw as counsel on the same day he filed the petition. Henry continued to represent Joyce White until the trial court granted the motion to withdraw on May 6, 2002.

On May 28, 2002, Dr. Smith filed a motion for sanctions against . . . Henry for alleged violations of Texas Rule of Civil Procedure 13 and chapters 9 and 10 of the Texas Civil Practice and Remedies Code. Dr. Low filed the same motion. Both physicians argued that none of the medical records from the hospital at which the physicians treated White contained any reference to either doctor having prescribed or provided Propulsid to White. On June 10, Joyce White nonsuited the case. The physicians' motions for sanctions remained pending.

The trial court held a hearing on the physicians' motions on July 30, 2002. Henry did not attend or testify but appeared through counsel. On July 31, 2002, the trial court granted the motions and ordered Henry to pay $25,000 in sanctions on each motion, for a total of $50,000. On August 2, 2002, the trial court entered a revised judgment that incorporated findings of fact and conclusions of law. On August 26, 2002, Henry filed a motion for new trial and a motion to vacate, modify, correct, or reform the sanctions order. On September 23, 2002, Henry filed a supplemental motion. On October 15, 2002, the trial court held a hearing on Henry's motions. After hearing more testimony, including Henry's, the trial court ultimately denied admission of all additional evidence and denied Henry's motion to modify the judgment. Henry filed a motion to reconsider, challenging the adequacy of the trial court's findings of fact and conclusions of law for the first time. The trial court denied this motion and rejected as untimely all arguments not contained in the original motion for new trial and motion to vacate, modify, correct or reform the judgment as untimely. Henry appealed.

An en banc court of appeals reversed, holding that because the allegations against the physicians were made in the alternative, sanctions under chapter 10 of the Texas Civil Practice and Remedies Code were inappropriate. The court also held that the physicians' motions did not support sanctions under Chapter 10 for unrelated prior litigation and that the trial court's order failed to meet the specificity requirements of Chapter 10. The dissenting justices argued that the trial court did not abuse its discretion and that Henry waived his other complaints. The physicians petitioned this Court for review.

II. Applicable Law and Standard of Review

We review the imposition of sanctions here under the same standard we review sanctions under Rule 13 — abuse of discretion. *See American Flood Research, Inc. v. Jones*, 192 S.W.3d 581, 583 (Tex. 2006); *Cire v. Cummings*, 134 S.W.3d 835, 838 (Tex. 2004). An appellate court may reverse the trial court's ruling only if the trial court acted without reference to any guiding rules and principles, such that its ruling was arbitrary or unreasonable. *Cire*, 134 S.W.3d at 838–39. To determine if the sanctions were appropriate or just, the appellate court must ensure there is a direct nexus between the improper conduct and the sanction imposed. *Spohn Hosp. v. Mayer*, 104 S.W.3d 878, 882 (Tex. 2003) (citing *TransAmerican Natural Gas Corp. v. Powell*, 811 S.W.2d 913, 917 (Tex. 1991)). Generally, courts presume that pleadings and other papers are filed in good faith. *GTE Commc'ns Sys. Corp. v. Tanner*, 856 S.W.2d 725, 730 (Tex. 1993). The party seeking sanctions bears the burden of overcoming this presumption of good faith. *Id.* at 731.

Chapters 9 and 10 of the Texas Civil Practice and Remedies Code and rule 13 of the Texas Rules of Civil Procedure allow a trial court to sanction an attorney or a party for filing motions or pleadings that lack a reasonable basis in fact or law. Chapter 9 of the Texas Civil Practice and Remedies Code only applies in proceedings in which neither Rule 13 nor Chapter 10 applies. TEX. CIV. PRAC. & REM. CODE § 9.012(h). Rule 13 authorizes the imposition of the sanctions listed in Rule 215.2(b), which only provides for a monetary penalty based on expenses, court costs, or attorney's fees. Because the trial court ordered Henry to pay $50,000 in penalties not based on expenses, court costs, or attorney's fees, and because the trial court's written order specifically orders the penalty pursuant to chapter 10 of the Texas Civil Practice and Remedies Code, we review the trial court's order in light of chapter 10. Chapter 10 provides that:

> The signing of a pleading or motion as required by the Texas Rules of Civil Procedure constitutes a certificate by the signatory that to the signatory's best knowledge, information, and belief, formed after reasonable inquiry:
>
> (1) the pleading or motion is not being presented for any improper purpose, including to harass or to cause unnecessary delay or needless increase in the cost of litigation;
>
> (2) each claim, defense, or other legal contention in the pleading or motion is warranted by existing law or by a nonfrivolous argument for the extension, modification, or reversal of existing law or the establishment of new law;
>
> (3) each allegation or other factual contention in the pleading or motion has evidentiary support or, for a specifically identified allegation or factual contention, is likely to have evidentiary support after a reasonable opportunity for further investigation or discovery; and
>
> (4) each denial in the pleading or motion of a factual contention is warranted on the evidence or, for a specifically identified denial, is reasonably based on a lack of information or belief.

TEX. CIV. PRAC. & REM. CODE § 10.001. Under Section 10.001, the signer of a pleading or motion certifies that *each* claim, *each* allegation, and *each* denial is based on the signatory's best knowledge, information, and belief, formed after reasonable inquiry. The statute dictates that each claim and each allegation be individually evaluated for support. *Id.* The fact that an allegation or claim is alleged against several defendants — so-called "group pleadings" — does not relieve the party from meeting the express requirements of Chapter 10. Each claim against each defendant must satisfy Chapter 10.

Likewise, alternative pleading under Texas Rule of Civil Procedure 48 does not excuse noncompliance with Chapter 10. Pleading in the alternative allows multiple allegations, which may even conflict, to be alleged against a defendant, but there still must be a reasonable basis for each alternative allegation. Pleading in the alternative does not permit alleging a claim with no reasonable basis in fact or law "in the alternative" of a claim that does have support. That is simply not permitted by Texas law. *See* TEX. CIV. PRAC. & REM. CODE § 10.001. Each allegation and factual contention in a pleading or motion must have, or be likely to have, evidentiary support after a reasonable investigation. *Id.*

The language of section 10.001 of the Texas Civil Practice and Remedies Code tracks much of the language in Federal Rule of Civil Procedure 11(b):

> Representations to Court. By presenting to the court (whether by signing, filing, submitting, or later advocating) a pleading, written motion, or other paper, an attorney or unrepresented party is certifying that to the best of the person's knowledge, information, and belief, formed after an inquiry reasonable under the circumstances, —
>
> (1) it is not being presented for any improper purpose, such as to harass or to cause unnecessary delay or needless increase in the cost of litigation;
>
> (2) the claims, defenses, and other legal contentions therein are warranted by existing law or by a nonfrivolous argument for the extension, modification, or reversal of existing law or the establishment of new law;
>
> (3) the allegations and other factual contentions have evidentiary support or, if specifically so identified, are likely to have evidentiary support after a reasonable opportunity for further investigation or discovery; and
>
> (4) the denials of factual contentions are warranted on the evidence or, if specifically so identified, are reasonably based on a lack of information or belief.

Although the text of Rule 11 does not specify that *each* claim, allegation, and denial be based on the signatory's best knowledge, information, and belief, formed after reasonable inquiry, Federal Rule of Civil Procedure 8(e), which allows pleading in the alternative, specifically subjects all such pleadings to the requirements of Rule 11. Neither Rule 8 nor Rule 11 permits a plaintiff "to intentionally ignore relevant evidence in order to assert unfounded claims." *Tibor Mach. Prods., Inc. v. Freudenberg-NOK Gen. P'ship*, 967 F. Supp. 1006, 1014 (N.D. Ill. 1997).

The physicians argue that by filing the pleading in this case, Henry certified that to the best of his knowledge, information, and belief, the factual contentions in the pleading had or were likely to have evidentiary support. A reasonable inquiry into the allegations would have proven otherwise. *See* Tex. Civ. Prac. & Rem. Code § 10.001(3). White's medical records, which were in Henry's possession before he filed the lawsuit, indicated that neither physician ever prescribed or administered the drug to White. The physicians argue that Henry violated Chapter 10 by alleging that they prescribed and administered Propulsid in spite of the information to the contrary in White's medical records. We agree with the physicians.

Undeniably, the petition focuses on Propulsid, a drug used to treat gastric reflux. The first sentence of the fact section of the petition summarizes, "The Plaintiffs are victims of the Defendants' decision to manufacture, market, design, promote, and/or distribute [Propulsid]." The petition claims that Johnson & Johnson, Janssen Pharmaceutica, and Janssen Research Foundation were negligent, negligent per se, and strictly liable for the defective design, marketing, manufacture, and distribution of the drug and for the violation of specified statutes and regulations. The petition also includes fraud and misrepresentation claims against Johnson & Johnson,

Janssen Pharmaceutica, and Janssen Research Foundation regarding the safety and efficacy of the drug. The petition further alleges that collectively the "defendants" breached implied and express warranties. Finally, the petition makes the following sixteen allegations of negligence against the "Defendant Physicians and Hospital" — eight physicians and a hospital:

a. In failing to weigh the substantial risks involved in prescribing the drug against its potential benefits, if any;

b. In failing to try alternate treatments such as antacids and gastric acid reducing agents before prescribing the drug;

c. In failing to advise the Plaintiffs about changes in lifestyle before prescribing the drug;

d. In failing to obtain a careful history of the Plaintiffs and in prescribing the drug in the presence of underlying cardiac conditions and other conditions or family history that would preclude the use of the drug;

e. In failing to determine the Plaintiffs' medications and in prescribing the drug along with contraindicated medications;

f. In failing to perform ECG monitoring at baseline and in failing to refer to prior ECGs performed on the Plaintiffs;

g. In failing to warn or adequately warn the Plaintiffs concerning the contraindications, warnings; precautions, adverse reactions, and drug interactions associated with the use f [sic] the drug;

h. n failing to advise the Plaintiffs concerning any significant changes in the patient package inserts and Physicians' Desk Reference;

i. In failing to advise the Plaintiffs concerning the contents of FDA warnings and "Dear Doctor" letters;

j. In failing to advise the Plaintiffs concerning the reasons for withdrawal of the drug from the market;

k. In failing to warn the Plaintiffs concerning abnormal EGGs [sic] and prolonged QTC intervals;

l. In failing to properly diagnose the cardiac conditions caused by the drug;

m. In failing to properly read and interpret the Plaintiffs' ECGs;

n. In failing to administer the proper treatment for the cardiac conditions caused by the drug;

o. In failing to discontinue the drug; or

p. In failing to continue to monitor the Plaintiffs, including ECG monitoring, electrolyte monitoring, prescription drug monitoring, and cardiac condition monitoring.

In six places — paragraphs a, b, c, d, e, and o — the petition alleges that Drs. Low and Smith provided or prescribed the drug to White. The other paragraphs allege negligent conduct other than prescribing or providing Propulsid to White.

However, Drs. Low and Smith presented undisputed evidence at the trial court that neither doctor ever prescribed or administered Propulsid to White and that a pre-suit review of White's medical records would have confirmed that fact. Dr. Low filed an affidavit with his motion for sanctions swearing that "[a]t no time during [his] involvement with this patient did [he] ever prescribe, provide, administer or order Propulsid for Mr. White." Dr. Smith filed an affidavit making the same statement with his motion. At the July 30, 2002 hearing on the motions, the physicians again testified that they did not administer or prescribe Propulsid. The testimony established that Dr. Smith was White's doctor for less than an hour in the emergency room, and Dr. Low, an internal medicine doctor at Columbia North Bay, provided care to White for four days after he arrived at Columbia North Bay and before his transfer to a facility in Corpus Christi. Dr. Low also confirmed that "anyone familiar with reviewing a medical record could easily have confirmed [Dr. Low's] testimony and the fact that [Dr. Low] had nothing to do with Propulsid had they simply reviewed the record." Dr. Smith testified that White's medical record contains no reference to Dr. Smith's ever prescribing or administering Propulsid to White. In fact, Henry does not dispute Dr. Low's testimony that White had not been taking Propulsid approximately two weeks before his treatment by the physicians. Dr. Smith similarly testified that he was informed that White had not been taking Propulsid "for sometime" before his arrival at the Columbia North Bay emergency room and his subsequent treatment by Drs. Low and Smith.

The evidence at the hearing supports the trial court's conclusion that:

> Based upon the totality of the evidence admitted during the hearing on the Motions for Sanctions, each and all of the allegations brought against Drs. Low and Smith, and therefore the lawsuit brought against these physicians, did not, on January 31, 2002, and do not now, have evidentiary support; nor were they on January 31, 2002, likely to have evidentiary support after a reasonable opportunity for further investigation . . . .

Under chapter 10 of the Texas Civil Practice and Remedies Code, the physicians were not required to specifically show bad faith or malicious intent, just that Henry certified he made a reasonable inquiry into all of the allegations when he did not and that he certified that all the allegations in the petition had evidentiary support, or were likely to have evidentiary support, when some allegations did not. We conclude that the trial court did not abuse its discretion in concluding that Henry failed to meet the standard in Chapter 10.

III. Notice

Henry argues that the trial court violated his rights to due process and due course of law because he was given inadequate notice of the subject matter of the hearing on the physicians' motions for sanctions. First, he argues that he only received notice of the hearing six days before the hearing. Second, he argues that he had no notice that sanctions under chapter 10 of the Texas Civil Practice and Remedies Code were being sought and that his conduct in other cases could be at issue at the hearing. Finally, Henry complains that the trial court's findings were insufficient to support sanctions under chapter 10 of the Civil Practice and Remedies Code. We overrule Henry's complaints.

Section 10.003 of the Texas Civil Practice and Remedies Code requires a court to provide the subject of a sanctions motion with "notice of the allegations and a reasonable opportunity to respond." Both physicians' motions specifically based sanctions on Chapter 10 and contain a certificate of service stating that the motions were sent to Henry in accordance with the Texas Rules of Civil Procedure on May 29, 2002. Henry did not object, made no argument, and provided no evidence that he did not receive the physicians' motions for sanctions at the July 30, 2002 hearing. Only later, at a hearing on Henry's motion for new trial and motion to vacate, modify, correct, or reform the order does Henry suggest that he did not receive adequate notice of the July 30, 2002 hearing. In Henry's brief to the court of appeals, he admits that he received notice of the hearing six days before the hearing. Even assuming that six-day notice was the first notice he received, the proper method to preserve his notice complaint was to bring the lack of adequate notice to the attention of the trial court at the hearing, object to the hearing going forward, and/or move for a continuance. Although Henry was represented by counsel at the July 30, 2002 hearing, he made no such complaint or motion but participated in the hearing. Even if Henry had preserved his notice complaint, *see* Tex. R. App. P. 33.1(a)(1), he had a reasonable opportunity to respond under section 10.003 of the Texas Civil Practice and Remedies Code.

Henry also complains he did not have notice that the physicians sought sanctions under chapter 10 of the Civil Practice and Remedies Code. He argues that the sanctions motions requested relief only under rule 13 of the Texas Rules of Civil Procedure and chapters 9 and 11 of the Texas Civil Practice and Remedies Code. Henry maintains that because the physicians did not move for sanctions under Chapter 10, the trial court abused its discretion in considering evidence of Henry's filings in other lawsuits. Henry's counsel did not object to the lack of notice that the physicians were seeking sanctions under Chapter 10 before or during the July 30, 2002 sanctions hearing. Henry's first complaint that he lacked notice of the subject matter of the hearing was in his motion for new trial. This objection was untimely.

Even if this objection had been timely, Henry had notice that the physicians sought sanctions under Chapter 10. The introductory paragraph of both physicians' motions explicitly state that the motions seek sanctions pursuant to chapter 10 of the Texas Civil Practice and Remedies Code. Further, the allegations made and relief sought are consistent with Chapter 10. Specifically, the motions request the trial court to order Henry to pay a monetary penalty to the Court, a sanction available only under Chapter 10. Tex. Civ. Prac. & Rem. Code § 10.004(c)(2); *see Sterling v. Alexander*, 99 S.W.3d 793, 799–800 (Tex. App. — Houston [14th Dist.] 2003, pet. denied). Because Henry failed to challenge receipt of the motions, he cannot now deny having notice of the content of the motions. *In re B.L.D.*, 113 S.W.3d 340, 350–55 (Tex. 2003). Thus, neither of Henry's notice complaints have merit.

As to Henry's argument that he did not receive notice that his conduct in other cases would be considered at the hearing, again, he failed to timely object. During the testimony of other physicians who had been served with identical pleadings prepared by Henry in other cases, Henry's attorney objected only to the relevance of the testimony. This does not preserve a due process complaint based on lack of notice.

Moreover, Henry waived any objection to the relevance of testimony about Henry's conduct in other proceedings by failing to establish a running exception. During the examination of Dr. Robert Mastin, a defendant doctor in a different suit filed by Henry, Henry's attorney objected to the relevance of the petition in the case. He requested a "running objection as to relevance" without specifying what he intended the objection to cover. The trial court overruled the objection and instructed Henry's attorney to make objections as necessary. Thereafter, Henry's attorney made occasional objections to relevance but failed to object to much of the testimony about his conduct in other cases. The trial court did not abuse its discretion in denying Henry's request for a running objection because his attorney failed to "plainly identif[y] the source of the objectionable testimony, the subject matter of the witness's testimony and the ways the testimony would be brought before the [court]." *Volkswagen of Am., Inc. v. Ramirez*, 159 S.W.3d 897, 907 (Tex. 2004). Thus, even if the testimony about Henry's conduct in other cases is irrelevant, Henry waived his objections to the bulk of that evidence.

Finally, Henry claims that the trial court's order, including the findings of fact and conclusions of law, was not specific enough to support sanctions under chapter 10 of the Texas Civil Practice and Remedies Code. Henry first raised this complaint in his first supplemental motion to vacate, modify, correct, or reform the modified judgment, which he filed on September 23, 2002. As we held in *Moritz, M.D. v. Preiss*, "[r]ead together, Rules 5, 329b(b) and 329b(e) demonstrate that an amended motion for new trial filed more than thirty days after the trial court signs a final judgment is untimely." 121 S.W.3d 715, 720 (Tex. 2003). The trial court signed its revised order granting sanctions, including findings of fact and conclusions of law, on August 2, 2002, fifty-two days before Henry's complaint that the order was not sufficiently specific to support an award of sanctions under Chapter 10. Although we have recognized that "the trial court may, at its discretion, consider the grounds raised in an untimely motion and grant a new trial under its inherent authority before the court loses plenary power," the trial court in this case denied Henry's motion as untimely. *Id.* at 720. On appeal, Henry fails to challenge the trial court's ruling on the timeliness of his post-sanctions motions and thus has waived any complaint about the specificity of the trial court's order. *See* Tex. R. App. P. 33.1(a). Despite Henry's waiver, as discussed below, we conclude that Henry's challenge fails on the merits: the evidence and the trial court's order support an award of sanctions under Chapter 10.

IV. Amount of Sanction

Henry claims that the $50,000 sanction, a $25,000 sanction for the petition filed against each doctor, is excessive. The amount of the sanction is limited by the trial court's duty to exercise sound discretion. *Powell*, 811 S.W.2d at 917. A trial court abuses its discretion when it acts without reference to any guiding rules or principles, not when it simply exercises that discretion in a different manner than reviewing appellate courts might. *Downer v. Aquamarine Operators, Inc.*, 701 S.W.2d 238, 241–42 (Tex. 1985). In *Powell* we held that a sanction under rule 215 of the Texas Rules of Civil Procedure, now rule 215.2, must relate directly to the abuse found and "be no more severe than necessary to satisfy its legitimate purpose." *Powell*, 811 S.W.2d at 917. Texas Rule of Civil Procedure 215.2 allows a trial court to disallow any further discovery; charge certain expenses, costs, or attorney's fees of one party against the offending party; order certain facts to be established as true; limit a party's ability to defend against or bring certain claims; strike pleadings or parts of pleadings; or find a party in contempt of court. In contrast, Chapter 10 authorizes a sanction ordering the offending party to, among other things, pay a penalty into the court, as ordered in this case. TEX. CIV. PRAC. & REM. CODE § 10.004. The only restriction on the amount of the penalty in the language of the statute is that the "sanction must be limited to what is sufficient to deter repetition of the conduct or comparable conduct by others similarly situated." *Id.* § 10.004(b); *see, e.g., Skepnek v. Mynatt*, 8 S.W.3d 377, 380 (Tex. App. — El Paso 1999, pet. denied) (upholding $25,000 sanction to be paid into registry of court under Chapter 10). The legislative history does not shed light on the question.

Generally, a sanction cannot be excessive nor should it be assessed without appropriate guidelines. *See Powell*, 811 S.W.2d at 917.[4] Although this Court has not specifically identified factors for a trial court to consider when assessing penalties under Chapter 10, the absence of an explanation of how a trial court determined that amount of sanctions when those sanctions are especially severe is inadequate. For example, in *Cire v. Cummings*, we held the trial court was required to explain that it considered lesser sanctions before imposing severe, "death penalty" sanctions. In *Powell*, we held that the dismissal of plaintiff's case with prejudice for failing to appear for a deposition was an excessive sanction under Texas Rule of Civil Procedure 215. Because we held that the death penalty sanction at issue was "manifestly unjust," we did not identify specific factors for determining appropriate sanctions. In his concurrence, Justice Gonzalez recognized that the American Bar Association cumulated relevant factors useful to this type of analysis. *Id.* at 920–21 (Gonzalez, J., concurring).[5] Although we do not require a trial court to address all of the factors listed in the report to explain the basis of a monetary sanction under

---

[4] The severity of sanctions is also limited by constitutional standards. TEX. CONST. art. I, § 13; *Pennington v. Singleton*, 606 S.W.2d 682, 690 (Tex. 1980) (noting that the article I, section 13 of the Texas Constitution makes the excessiveness of a fine "a question for the court to decide under the facts of each particular case"); *see also Flores v. Millennium Interests, Ltd.*, 185 S.W.3d 427, 436 (Tex. 2005) (Wainwright, J., concurring). This issue was not raised in this appeal and is not addressed in this opinion.

[5] The ABA's 1988 report was designed, in part, to help bring uniformity to the uneven application of sanctions under Federal Rule of Civil Procedure 11. AMERICAN BAR ASSOCIATION, STANDARDS AND GUIDELINES FOR PRACTICE UNDER RULE 11 OF THE FEDERAL RULES OF CIVIL PROCEDURE, *reprinted in* 121 F.R.D. 101, 104 (1988). The factors are: (a) the good faith or bad faith of the offender; (b) the degree of willfulness, vindictiveness, negligence, or frivolousness involved in the offense; (c) the knowledge, experience, and expertise of the offender; (d) any prior history of sanctionable conduct on the part of the offender; (e) the reasonableness and necessity of the out-of-pocket expenses incurred by the offended person as a result of the misconduct; (f) the nature and extent of prejudice, apart from out-of-pocket expenses, suffered by the offended person as a result of the misconduct; (g) the relative culpability of client and counsel, and the impact on their privileged relationship of an inquiry into that area; (h) the risk of chilling the specific type of litigation involved; (i) the impact of the sanction on the offender, including the offender's ability to pay a monetary sanction; (j) the impact of the sanction on the offended party, including the offended person's need for compensation; (k) the relative magnitude of sanction necessary to achieve the goal or goals of the sanction; (l) burdens on the court system attributable to the misconduct, including consumption of judicial time and incurrence of juror fees and other court costs; . . . (n) the degree to which the offended person's own behavior caused the expenses for which recovery is sought . . . . *Id.* at 125–26 (cited in *Powell*, 811 S.W.2d at 920–21 (Gonzalez, J., concurring)). This nonexclusive list of factors is helpful in guiding the often intangible process of determining a penalty for sanctionable behavior.

Chapter 10, it should consider relevant factors in assessing the amount of the sanction. In addition, the determination of the amount of a penalty to be assessed under Chapter 10, which is not limited to attorney's fees and costs, should nevertheless begin with an acknowledgment of the costs and fees incurred because of the sanctionable conduct. This provides a monetary guidepost of the impact of the conduct on the party seeking sanctions and the burdens on the court system.

The trial court found that the claims brought against the doctors did not meet the evidentiary support requirement in Chapter 10. The trial court also concluded that the lawsuit was groundless, as defined in Texas Rule of Civil Procedure 13. The trial court's order stated that Henry "has consistently engaged in a similar pattern of conduct."

Dr. Low testified that he felt that Henry harassed him by filing the lawsuit. He testified that he lost a day and a half from the office because of the lawsuit but does not quantify this expense and identifies no other out-of-pocket expenses. Dr. Smith testified that he believed Henry felt "bad will toward [him] personally" because Henry filed a suit with no basis in fact against him. Two other physicians, Drs. Mastin and Canterbury, testified that Henry had named them in lawsuits in which they had never treated the plaintiff patients. Both testified about the impact of the lawsuits and intent to sue letters on their malpractice insurance rates: Dr. Mastin testified that his group's rates increased by 68% due in part to three groundless suits filed by Henry's clients; Dr. Canterbury also testified that her practice group faced increased insurance premiums due to groundless pleadings like Henry's.

Although we conclude that the trial court was within its discretion to award sanctions under Chapter 10, we cannot determine the basis of the $50,000 penalty on this record. Given the severity of the sanction, therefore, we remand this case in the interest of justice to allow the parties to present evidence responsive to our guidelines, if necessary, and to allow the trial court to consider the amount of the penalty imposed in light of the guidelines in this opinion. *See Tony Gullo Motors I, L.P. v. Chapa*, 212 S.W.3d 299, 314–15 (Tex. 2006) (remanding because evidence of attorneys fees for entire case is some evidence of what amount of segregated fees would be).

V. Conclusion

We recognize that in some cases, a party may not have evidence that proves each specific factual allegation at the time a lawsuit is filed. Certainly, the law does not require proof of a case without reasonable time for discovery. However, this does not excuse the filing of claims against parties when the attorney filing the lawsuit possesses information that a reasonable inquiry would have determined negated some of the claims made. We affirm the trial court's determination that chapter 10 was violated but hold that the trial court abused its discretion in not more specifically identifying the basis for imposing a $50,000 penalty under chapter 10 of the Texas Civil Practice and Remedies Code. We reverse the judgment of the court of appeals and remand the case to the trial court for proceedings consistent with this opinion.

NOTES AND QUESTIONS

(1) *Pre-Filing Factual Investigation.* The Court notes that Henry had in his possession medical records that demonstrated that Drs. Low and Smith did not prescribe Propulsid to plaintiff's husband, contrary to the allegations of the petition. Suppose that Henry did not have the records, but could have gotten access to them before filing. Would including those accusations still be a violation of Chapter 10? (Hint: What constitutes a "reasonable inquiry"?)

(2) *Pleading in the Alternative.* The petition made allegations of negligence against Drs. Low and Smith in addition to the ones regarding Propulsid, and those allegations were not attacked in the motion for sanctions. Why does the Court conclude that Henry nevertheless violated Chapter 10?

(3) *Sanctions and Alternative Claims.* The Court cites with approval an ABA Report listing factors that a court may consider in assessing sanctions in particular cases. Based on what you can tell from the opinion, how will these factors affect the sanction to be assessed against Henry? Will the alternative, non-sanctionable allegations against the doctors be relevant to this analysis? How much of the doctors' costs were caused by the Propulsid allegations, as opposed to the remainder of the plaintiff's claims?

(4) *Statutory Language Regarding Sanctions.* Chapter 10 contains several discussions of sanctions, some of which seem to reflect a goal of compensating the offended party and some of which seem aimed at deterrence. How do the following sections fit together:

- § 10.002(c) ("The court may award to a party prevailing on a motion under this section the reasonable expenses and attorney's fees incurred in presenting or opposing the motion, and if no due diligence is shown, the court may award to the prevailing party all costs for inconvenience, harassment, and out-of-pocket expenses incurred or caused by the subject litigation.")
- § 10.004(b) ("The sanction must be limited to what is sufficient to deter repetition of the conduct or comparable conduct by others similarly situated.")
- § 10.004(c)(3) ("A sanction may include . . . an order to pay to the other party the amount of the reasonable expenses incurred by the other party because of the filing of the pleading or motion, including reasonable attorney's fees.")

(5) *Payment to the Court.* Notice that the doctors here requested that the sanctions against Henry be paid to the court. This is explicitly authorized by § 10.004(c)(2). Federal Rule 11 has a similar provision and, in fact, payment of sanctions beyond the costs of the Rule 11 motion itself are generally made to the court rather than to the offended party. *See* FED. R. CIV. P. 11(c)(4) ("The sanction may include . . . an order to pay a penalty into court; or, if imposed on motion and warranted for effective deterrence, an order directing payment to the movant of part or all of the reasonable attorney's fees and other expenses directly resulting from the violation.").

§ 6.05 DEFENDANT'S ANSWER

[A] Contents and Primary Function of the Answer

The immediate function of the answer is to avoid judgment by default. Civil Procedure Rule 99 requires the citation to command the defendant to appear by filing a written answer to the plaintiff's petition at or before 10:00 A.M. on the Monday next after the expiration of 20 days after the date of service of the petition and citation. *See* Tex. R. Civ. P. 99. The primary function of the answer is to set forth the defendant's grounds of defense in plain and concise language. *See* Tex. R. Civ. P. 45. A general denial of matters pleaded by the adverse party that are not required to be denied under oath is sufficient to put the adverse party's allegations in controversy. *See* Tex. R. Civ. P. 92. The original answer may include the following:

(1) A special appearance. *See* Tex. R. Civ. P. 120a.

(2) A motion to transfer. *See* Tex. R. Civ. P. 86.

(3) A special exception. *See* Tex. R. Civ. P. 90, 91.

(4) A plea in abatement or to the jurisdiction. *See* Tex. R. Civ. P. 85.

(5) A general denial. *See* Tex. R. Civ. P. 92.

(6) Special denials. *See* Tex. R. Civ. P. 93.

(7) Any matter in avoidance or estoppel (*i.e.*, affirmative defenses). *See* Tex. R. Civ. P. 85, 94.

(8) Inferential rebuttal defenses. *See* Tex. R. Civ. P. 278.

You have already learned the form and function of the special appearance. The motion to transfer is considered in the chapter on venue. This section deals with other matters that may be contained in the defendant's answer.

[B] Use of Defensive Pleas

PRACTICE EXERCISE #15

Which plea or pleas can be used to raise each of the following kinds of defenses or defensive theories?

(1) In a negligence action, the defendant disputes the plaintiff's claim as to how the accident happened.

(2) In a negligence action, the defendant wants to assert the defense of contributory negligence as a total or partial bar.

(3) In a negligence action, the defendant wants to complain that the plaintiff's allegation of the negligence element in the cause of action is vague and confusing as it is alleged.

(4) In a suit on a written instrument purporting to be a contract, the defendant wants to deny execution of the instrument, among other

denials. (Note: a denial of execution of a written instrument is one of the pleadings that Texas requires be made under oath.)

(5) A claim that venue in the case is improper and the action should be transferred to a place of proper venue.

(6) A claim that the defendant, a corporation incorporated and having its principal place of business in Ohio, does not do business in Texas.

(7) A claim that a person needed for just adjudication has not been joined in the suit.

(8) In a suit on a contract for the sale of land, the defendant wants to raise the fact that the petition expressly shows that the alleged contract was oral only and thus seems to violate the statute of frauds.

[C] Special Exceptions

Read Tex. R. Civ. P. 90, 91.

Special exceptions are often used to complain that the opponent's pleading is too vague. What requirements apply to the special exception itself? And what happens if the court sustains a special exception and the plaintiff refuses to re-plead?

McCAMEY v. KINNEAR

484 S.W.2d 150 (Tex. Civ. App. — Beaumont 1972, writ ref'd n.r.e.)

KEITH, J.

Plaintiff appeals from a judgment of dismissal of his suit wherein he sought to recover of the defendant attorney's fees paid to defendant in connection with a patent application. Plaintiff also sought recovery of certain expenses incurred by reason of the alleged inaction of defendant. At the outset we note affirmatively that while plaintiff has prosecuted the appeal with diligence, such comment does not apply to his trial court actions.

On the day the case was specially set for trial upon the "try or dismiss" docket, defendant filed a motion to dismiss plaintiff's cause of action, the allegations being set out in the margin.[1]

The court's order, entered on January 31, 1972, recited that the defendant's motion to dismiss having been heard, and "it appearing to the Court that said motion should be in all things granted; it is therefore ordered, adjudged and decreed that defendant's motion to dismiss be in all things granted."

This order of dismissal was preceded by some unusual maneuvers which require

---

[1] "Defendant would show the Court that it is useless to pick a jury in this cause or to take up the Court's time because said Plaintiff does not state a cause of action in this suit, and it would be a waste of the Court's time and a waste of the Jury's time to pick a jury in this cause, and said suit should be in all things dismissed."

mention at this point. Defendant leveled many exceptions to plaintiff's original petition, some of which were sustained by an order entered May 4, 1970, defendant's exceptions to such action being duly noted. Although plaintiff did not file amended pleadings until the very day of the dismissal (a matter which will be mentioned later), the docket sheet in our record shows that defendant procured three continuances, the last being on October 7, 1971. Upon this latter date, the trial court entered a specific and detailed order setting the case for trial on January 31, 1972, and advised counsel that it would be tried or dismissed upon said date "depending upon any announcements which may or may not be made by counsel at such time."

On January 31, 1972, the date set for trial, plaintiff filed what he denominated a "Trial Amendment" but which was in fact an amended original petition. *See* Rule 71, Texas Rules of Civil Procedure. Our record does not reveal that leave was granted to file the instrument, whatever it might have been, under either Rule 63 or Rule 66, nor does the record show that such instrument ever came to the attention of the trial court before the order of dismissal was entered. On the other hand, the record is equally silent as to any motion to strike the pleading filed in violation of the rules just mentioned.

Plaintiff timely gave notice of appeal from the order of dismissal, duly perfected his appeal, and now assigns many points of error. We do not find it necessary to discuss all of such points of error under our view of the record.

Plaintiff devotes much of his brief to the proposition that the trial court erred in granting the defendant's motion to dismiss, contending that such motion was a general demurrer in legal disguise which is forbidden by Rule 90. Under our view of the record, we do not reach the point. Instead, we turn to the controlling issue in the appeal, the action of the trial court upon the exceptions.

When special exceptions addressed to a pleading are sustained, the party has two options available to him: (a) he may amend to meet the exceptions and this he may do as a matter of right; or, (b) he may stand upon his pleadings, refuse to amend, and test the validity of the ruling upon appeal.

A reasonable time should be allowed a party desiring to amend to conform to the ruling upon the special exceptions; but this is a matter within the sound discretion of the court not to be overthrown except for an abuse of discretion. The plaintiff, being ever under the duty of prosecuting his suit with diligence under the penalty of having it dismissed for want of prosecution, must also use diligence in amending his pleadings after an order sustaining exceptions. 4 McDonald, Texas Civil Practice § 17.18. In our case, the plaintiff waited nearly twenty months — and through three trial settings — before filing his amended pleading upon the very day the case was set upon the "try or dismiss" docket.

Under the circumstances of this case, we hold that the long unexplained delay in filing the amended pleadings amounted in law to a refusal to amend. When a party stands firm on his pleadings, as we have held the plaintiff did in this case, the trial court may dismiss the cause if the remaining allegations fail to state a cause of action.

Having reviewed the remnants of the original petition, after the exceptions had been sustained, we are of the opinion that the remaining allegations of the petition failed to state a cause of action. The trial court was authorized, under these circumstances, to dismiss the case.

The order sustaining the special exceptions was interlocutory in nature and plaintiff had no right of appeal therefrom. However, when the court entered the order of dismissal on January 31, 1972, following plaintiff's failure to amend within a reasonable time, plaintiff's right to appeal was then exercised. We now turn to the validity of the special exceptions and review the action of the trial court in entering the order sustaining such exceptions.[2] Special Exceptions 5, 8, 9 and 10 were worded identically and challenged different parts of plaintiff's pleading. We quote the exception:

> "Plaintiff [sic, *Defendant*] excepts . . . [naming the particular paragraph of the petition] because said allegations are too general; because said allegations are a mere conclusion of the pleader; because no facts are alleged on which said conclusions are based; because said allegations do not inform this defendant of the facts on which the plaintiff intends to rely; because said allegations do not inform this defendant of the proof that he will be required to meet on the trial of this cause and because said allegations are calculated to surprise and prejudice the defendant on the trial of this cause; because said allegations are calculated to cause a mistrial; said allegations should be in all things stricken and of this exception the defendant prays judgment of the Court."

It is obvious that this "special exception" did not comply with the provisions of Rule 91 and even a cursory examination of the allegations attacked shows that in each instance the exception was without merit. The exception quoted was simply a broadside attack and did not "point out intelligibly and with particularity the defect, omission, obscurity, duplicity, generality, or other insufficiency in the allegations in the pleading excepted to" as required by Rule 91. There were other exceptions sustained which are subject to the same criticism and the result of the court's action was to eliminate from plaintiff's pleading the necessary allegations upon which his cause of action was predicated. In effect, such exceptions were "nothing more than the old general demurrer" which was abolished in 1941 when Rule 90 was adopted. *Huff v. Fidelity Union Life Insurance Company*, 312 S.W.2d 493, 499 (Tex. 1958).

These particular exceptions also lacked merit for the reasons pointed out in *Kelly v. Wright*, 188 S.W.2d 983, 985 (Tex. 1945):

> "Rule 91 provides that a special exception shall not only point out the particular pleading excepted to, but shall also point out intelligibly and with particularity the defect, omission, obscurity, duplicity, generality, or other insufficiency in the allegation in the pleading excepted to.
>
> "The exceptions in question merely assert that the petition failed to show any grounds for equitable relief or state a cause of action. They do not point out intelligibly and with particularity the reasons for such conclusions.

[2] In fairness to the trial judge who entered the order of dismissal, we note in our record that the order upon special exceptions was entered by his predecessor upon the bench.

Therefore, the trial court erred in sustaining them."

The object and purpose of pleading is to give fair and adequate notice to the party being sued of the nature of the cause of action asserted against him so that he may adequately prepare his defense thereto. Plaintiff's original petition in this case fairly and adequately advised defendant of the nature of the cause of action being asserted against him. The plaintiff was not required to plead his evidence in detail and if the defendant desired more factual detail as to the basis of the claim, he had but to invoke the discovery processes authorized by the rules.

It follows, therefore, that the trial court having erred in sustaining the special exceptions, likewise erred in dismissing the case. The judgment below must be reversed and the cause remanded. We note, however, that plaintiff, by his inaction below, has delayed a disposition of his case and has contributed to the clogging of the dockets of both the trial and appellate courts. Such action is not to be commended and it is suggested that a repetition of this spectacle could be avoided by utilizing the provisions of Rule 166.

Reversed and remanded.

NOTES AND QUESTIONS

(1) *Refusal to Amend.* It is better practice for the order granting the special exception to set a specific date by which the plaintiff must amend the petition. That eliminates the trickier issue of when a long delay becomes a refusal to amend. When a special exception is properly made and granted, and the plaintiff refuses to amend, the defendant may file a motion to dismiss.

(2) *Opportunity to Amend.* The Texas Supreme Court has often affirmed the need to provide a chance to amend, and the proper action when the trial court denies that opportunity: "Special exceptions are appropriate to challenge a plaintiff's failure to state a cause of action. Tex. R. Civ. P. 91. But once the trial court sustains the special exceptions, if the defect is curable, it must allow the pleader an opportunity to amend. *See Friesenhahn v. Ryan*, 960 S.W.2d 656, 658 (Tex. 1998). If the trial court fails to provide this opportunity, the aggrieved party must prove that the opportunity to replead was requested and denied to preserve the error for review." *Parker v. Barefield*, 206 S.W.3d 119 (Tex. 2006). Note also that "the right to amend does not extend to the privilege of multiple opportunities to amend in the face of repeated grants of special exceptions. If there is no reasonable probability that further amendment would disclose facts legally sufficient to sustain a cause of action, the trial court may properly refuse further leave to amend." *Mowbray v. Avery*, 76 S.W.3d 663, 678 (Tex. App. — Corpus Christi 2002, pet. denied), *citing City of Fort Worth v. Gilliland*, 169 S.W.2d 149, 151 (Tex. 1943).

(3) *Formal Defects.* A general allegation of negligence has long been held to be subject to special exception. "The usual reason for excepting to general pleadings is to obtain further information about and narrow the claims or defenses asserted by the adverse party. One who does not need such information to prepare for trial will probably permit the pleading to go unchallenged . . . ." *Kainer v. Walker*, 377 S.W.2d 613, 615 (Tex. 1964), *overruled and disapproved on other grounds, Burk Royalty Co. v. Walls*, 616 S.W.2d 911, 925 (Tex. 1981). The same logic applies to

other general allegations, e.g., "breach," "default," etc. This philosophy may be changing, as you saw in § 6.04[B][3]. The special exception remains the proper tool to challenge a formal defect in the opponent's pleading.

(4) *Substantive Defects.* Failure to plead a component or constituent element of a "cause of action" is considered a substantive pleading defect. As noted above, however, the defect can be waived. Understand, though, that waiver of the *pleading* defect does not eliminate the requirement of *proof* of all component elements of a ground of recovery or defense at trial. In short, waiver of the pleading defect merely waives the right to have the element *pleaded* — it does not constitute an admission of an unpleaded element. *See* Tex. R. Civ. P. 301. *See* William T. Deffebach & George E. Brown, *Waiver of Pleading Defects and Insufficiencies in Texas*, 36 Tex. L. Rev. 459 (1958).

(5) *Special Exceptions Need to Be Specific, Too.* In interpreting the specificity requirement of Civil Procedure Rule 91, one court has stated that: "An objection should be sufficiently specific so that the opposing party may be informed of the defect and amend his pleadings accordingly, provided the defect be of such a nature that may be cured by an amendment. An objection to pleading made in compliance with the requirements of Rule 91 . . . is similar to a valid objection to the introduction of evidence. It must be informative so that it may be obviated if possible." *Ragsdale v. Ragsdale*, 520 S.W.2d 839, 842 (Tex. Civ. App. — Fort Worth 1975, no writ). Will it always be harmful (reversible) error for the trial court to sustain a general demurrer? *See Kelly v. Wright*, 188 S.W.2d 983, 986 (Tex. 1945), in which the Texas Supreme Court held that even though error was committed in sustaining the demurrer, since it "affirmatively appears from the sworn pleadings of petitioners that they cannot in good faith allege a cause of action . . . it would be a futile and useless procedure to reverse the judgment."

(6) *Confusion with Federal Practice.* In *Castano v. San Felipe Agric., Mfg., & Irrigation Co.*, 147 S.W.3d 444, 453 (Tex. App. — San Antonio 2004, no pet.), the defendant filed a "motion for more definite statement" in place of a special exception. The court held that the motion failed to comply with Civil Procedure Rule 91, since it complained only that Castano's pleadings were "vague and ambiguous" so that they were not able to "frame a responsive pleading" or "properly prepare a defense." Defendants also stated that the pleadings "failed to identify the actions which formed the basis of any liability asserted against them and requested a more definite statement regarding the complaints." The San Antonio court characterized this as nothing more than a general demurrer. Although the defense lawyers seem to have confused state special exception practice with federal motions for more definite statement, the Federal Rules of Civil Procedure also abolished general demurrers, and the motion for more definite statement must "point out the defects complained of and the details desired." Fed. R. Civ. P. 12(e).

(7) *Improper Use of the Special Exception: the "Speaking Demurrer."* Traditionally, a demurrer, whether of the general or special variety, could not be used to set forth factual propositions not appearing in the pleading under attack in order to challenge the validity of the ground of recovery or defense. "Speaking demurrers were not permitted under the former nor is it permitted by present

practice." *Ragsdale v. Ragsdale*, 520 S.W.2d 839, 843 (Tex. Civ. App. — Fort Worth 1975, no writ). On the hearing of the special exception, the allegations of the pleading under attack must be taken as true. An example of a "speaking" demurrer appears in *Travelers Indem. Co. v. Holt Mach. Co.*, 554 S.W.2d 12 (Tex. Civ. App. — El Paso 1977, no writ), a case involving an action on a fidelity bond. The bonding company denied coverage in its answer by a general denial and special pleas concerning exclusions from coverage under the provisions of the bond. On the date of trial, plaintiff's counsel filed an instrument, styled a "Motion to Strike" the special pleas, which stated:

> Defendant has never raised this asserted reason heretofore with its insured, the Plaintiff, as a reason why Defendant's liability to Plaintiff was denied under the policy, and Defendant now attempts to assert a new reason of its alleged non-liability. The law provides that where an insurance company states to an insured its grounds for denial of coverage or liability, that under the circumstances here, the insurance company waives its rights to assert new and additional grounds at trial. Because the new grounds now attempted to be asserted have never heretofore been given by the Defendant insurance com pany as grounds for refusing to defend or assume liability for Plaintiff's claim, the new grounds must be deemed waived and stricken . . . .

What "fact" is the plaintiff trying to assert in the "motion to strike"? Suppose all of the facts, including defendant's failure to previously assert the new ground of defense, were set forth in the special pleas of the defendant; would the motion still "speak"?

Consider the following portion of defendant's Answer to a petition alleging breach of warranty in the sale of real estate. Be prepared to discuss whether or not the special exceptions comply with the requirements of the Rules of Civil Procedure:

DEFENDANT'S ORIGINAL ANSWER

I.

Defendants specially except to said Petition in its entirety because nowhere in said Petition is it alleged that Defendants, or either of them, made any misrepresentations as to presently existing facts, and that in the absence of such allegations said Petition fails to state a ground of recovery upon which relief may be granted. And of this their special exception Defendants pray judgment of the court.

II.

Defendants specially except to Paragraph V of said Petition, wherein it is alleged that certain personal property of the Plaintiffs became damaged in the sum of Fifty Dollars ($50.00) from being mildewed, for the reason that said allegation is too vague, general and indefinite in that it does not specify the particular items of property which allegedly became damaged, and that therefore Defendants are not given fair notice of what Plaintiffs expect to prove under said allegation and are not enabled properly to prepare any defense thereto. And of this their special exception Defendants pray judgment of the court.

III.

Defendants specially except to Paragraph VI of said Petition, wherein it is alleged that Plaintiffs have undergone physical and mental suffering, for the following reasons:

(1) Any promises or representations (if any were made) that Defendants would repair or alter the construction of the floor of Plaintiffs' garage were made after the property had been sold and possession thereof had been delivered to Plaintiffs. Since said promises or representations, if any, were made after the consummation of the sale of the property, Plaintiffs could not have relied upon the representations or promises as an inducement to enter into the contract and, therefore, any damages arising from the failure to perform said representations and promises cannot be recovered in a suit for breach of warranty. And of this their special exception Defendants pray judgment of the court.

(2) The only cause of action alleged by Plaintiffs in their Petition is one of breach of warranty in the sale of real estate, and damages for physical and mental suffering are not recoverable in an action for breach of warranty, the proper measure of damages being the difference between the value of the property as warranted and its value as actually conveyed. Therefore, said allegations as to physical and mental sufferings are immaterial and would be prejudicial to Defendants if read to the jury trying this cause, and said allegation should, therefore, be stricken from the Plaintiffs' Petition. And of this their special exception Defendants pray judgment of the court.

(8) *Presentation of the Special Exception.* The burden is on the party making the special exception to bring it to the attention of the court. *Castilleja v. Camero*, 402 S.W.2d 265, 268 (Tex. Civ. App. — Corpus Christi 1966), *aff'd on other grounds*, 414 S.W.2d 424, 425–28 (Tex. 1967). Despite the literal language of Rule 90, the exception should be presented before trial in order to avoid waiver of the pleading defect.

(9) *Relationship to Summary Judgment Practice.* The summary judgment rule (Tex. R. Civ. P. 166a) provides that the movant may proceed "with or without supporting affidavits." On the one hand, the Supreme Court of Texas has indicated that summary judgment may be rendered on the pleadings when the petition does not state a legal claim or cause of action. *See Castleberry v. Goolsby* in § 6.04[B][2]. On the other hand, the Supreme Court has rejected the idea that a summary judgment is proper merely because the petition fails to adequately state a cause of action. In *Texas Dept. of Corrections v. Herring*, 513 S.W.2d 6, 9–10 (Tex. 1974), the petitioner had been granted summary judgment on the basis that the plaintiff failed to state a cause of action under the Texas Tort Claims Act "since no 'use of tangible property' was alleged as required." The Supreme Court affirmed the reversal of the

summary judgment in the following terms:

> However, the question to be resolved is whether Herring, under the instant circumstances, may be denied the opportunity to amend his pleadings because they were attacked via a summary judgment motion instead of a special exception. It is recognized that a party may plead himself out of court; *E.g.*, the plaintiff may plead facts which affirmatively negate his cause of action . . . . In such instance it is proper to grant the defendant's motion for summary judgment. The instant case is clearly distinguishable however. Here, as we have held, Herring's pleadings were insufficient; that is, they failed to state a cause of action [because they failed to allege an essential element]. The Department of Corrections leveled no special exceptions to Herring's pleadings and thus no opportunity to amend his pleadings to state a cause of action was afforded.
>
> Had the Department of Corrections filed special exceptions which were sustained by the court, Herring would have had an opportunity to amend as a matter of right. *McCamey v. Kinnear*, 484 S.W.2d 150 (Tex. Civ. App. — Beaumont 1972, writ ref'd n.r.e.). But only after a party has been given an opportunity to amend after special exceptions have been sustained may the case be dismissed for failure to state a cause of action.
>
> In the instant case Herring was precluded opportunity to amend his pleadings once the trial court had granted the motion for summary judgment. This court believes that the protective features of special exception procedure should not be circumvented by a motion for summary judgment on the pleadings where plaintiff's pleadings, as here, fail to state a cause of action. To do so would revive the general demurrer discarded by Rule 90, Texas Rules of Civil Procedure . . . .
>
> We agree with the court of civil appeals that the instant motion for summary judgment alleging that the plaintiff's pleadings fail to state a cause of action cannot take the place of a special exception. Accordingly, this case must be returned to the trial court. If the Department of Corrections files a special exception which is sustained and Herring still fails to state a cause of action, then the case may properly be dismissed.

Can you distinguish *Castleberry* from *Herring*? In *Castleberry*, the plaintiff pleaded negligence when intent was required. In *Herring* the plaintiff failed to plead that the state employees used tangible property, a requirement of the Texas Tort Claims Act. The plaintiff did plead that the state employees failed to provide him with adequate medical care when treating his injured eye. Why allow one but not the other an opportunity to amend the pleading after the defect was pointed out?

(10) *What About Stating New Facts in a Motion for Summary Judgment?* If the facts needed to defeat the claim are not in the opponent's pleading, they can form the basis of a motion for summary judgment, which can be based on evidence extrinsic to the pleading. We will consider summary judgments in greater detail in Chapter 11, Disposition Without Trial.

PRACTICE EXERCISE #16
DRAFTING SPECIAL EXCEPTIONS

How would you respond to the following allegations made in an opposing party's pleadings?

1. [In ¶ 5] "Plaintiff and defendant entered into a contract on September 4, 1982. A copy of the contract is attached as Exhibit A, and incorporated herein for all purposes. Defendant breached the contract."

2. [In ¶ 8] "Defendant deliberately misrepresented to plaintiff that the house sold to plaintiff by defendant contained 1500 square feet when in fact it contains only 1300 square feet. This fraudulent act damaged plaintiff in the amount of $10,000." [Hint: this fails to allege that plaintiff relied on the misrepresentation].

3. [In ¶ 6] "During the 2007 Fall semester, Plaintiff was hired by the Defendant university to perform part time clerical work on an as needed basis. Defendant wrongfully discharged Plaintiff from her employment with defendant, because defendant disliked the color of the plaintiff's car." [Hint: *see Tex. Farm Bureau Mut. Ins. Cos. v. Sears*, 84 S.W.3d 604 (Tex. 2002) (at-will doctrine does not require an employer to be reasonable, or even careful, in making its termination decisions).]

[D] The Plea in Abatement

Although the plea is referred to in Civil Procedure Rule 85, the rules do not explain the function of the plea. A plea in abatement is not an attack on the merits of the plaintiff's cause of action. Instead, it argues that some procedural flaw should prevent the case from going forward. One common example is a claim that a different court has dominant jurisdiction over the matter, as is illustrated in the following case. Who should win the race to the courthouse, and under what circumstances will the first filed case lose the right to proceed?

WYATT v. SHAW PLUMBING CO.

760 S.W.2d 245 (Tex. 1988)

RAY, J.

This case arises out of a dispute over the services provided by a plumbing contractor in the construction of a house in Duval County. The issue presented by this appeal involves a plea in abatement filed in a second suit in Nueces County when a prior suit was pending in Duval County. The court of appeals affirmed the Nueces County district court, holding that the decision to grant a plea in abatement was within the discretion of the Nueces County court and there was no abuse of that discretion. We hold that the Nueces County district court was required to grant the plea in abatement because a previously filed suit between the parties was pending. We, therefore, reverse the judgment of the court of appeals and remand the cause to the Nueces County district court with instructions to vacate its judgment and abate all proceedings pending final disposition of the Duval County lawsuit, which was previously filed.

This controversy involves a suit between the parties in the district court of

Duval County and another suit subsequently filed in the district court of Nueces County. Oscar Wyatt was building a house in Duval County. On Wyatt's behalf, Morgan Spear entered into an oral agreement with Shaw Plumbing Company for Shaw to perform work on the house. When Wyatt did not pay Shaw Plumbing for its services, Shaw made a written demand for payment. Following Shaw Plumbing's demand letter, Wyatt filed suit against Shaw in Duval County on February 7, 1983, alleging fraud and violation of the Deceptive Trade Practices Act.

On April 4, 1983, Shaw Plumbing filed a breach of contract suit against Wyatt and Spear in Nueces County to recover for its services. Wyatt filed a plea in abatement in the Nueces County suit based upon the pendency of the previously filed Duval County suit. The Nueces County district court signed an order denying Wyatt's plea in abatement on June 15, 1984. On February 13, 1986, Wyatt filed a second plea in abatement in Nueces County after he agreed to indemnify Spear for any claims against Spear by Shaw Plumbing. The Nueces County district court again denied the plea. Prior to the trial in Nueces County, the trial judge struck Wyatt's pleadings as a sanction for alleged discovery abuse. Judgment was rendered against Wyatt following a jury trial in Nueces County.

It has long been the policy of the courts and the legislature of this state to avoid a multiplicity of lawsuits. The need for judicial economy has recently become more acute because the dockets of our trial courts are overburdened, and litigants must wait far too long for their cases to be heard. In keeping with the policy to avoid multiple lawsuits, Texas Rule of Civil Procedure 97(a) was promulgated. This rule regarding compulsory counterclaims dictates that a pleading shall assert a counterclaim if it meets six elements. A counterclaim is compulsory if: (1) it is within the jurisdiction of the court; (2) it is not at the time of filing the answer the subject of a pending action; (3) the action is mature and owned by the pleader at the time of filing the answer; (4) it arises out of the transaction or occurrence that is the subject matter of the opposing party's claim; (5) it is against an opposing party in the same capacity; and (6) it does not require for its adjudication the presence of third parties over whom the court cannot acquire jurisdiction. *See* Tex. R. Civ. P. 97(a), (d). If a claim meets these elements, it must be asserted in the initial action. A defendant's failure to assert a compulsory counterclaim precludes its assertion in later actions. Shaw Plumbing's suit against Wyatt was a compulsory counterclaim under the requirements of Rule 97(a).

In the case in which Wyatt as plaintiff sued Shaw Plumbing as defendant on tort and DTPA theories, the counties in which venue was proper were: (1) Nueces County, where the defendant had its principal office situated; (2) Duval County, where the construction and plumbing was done, and thus the cause of action arose; or (3) Harris County, where the plaintiff resided at the time the cause of action arose. Wyatt's agent, Morgan Spear, was not a party to the suit brought by Wyatt. Spear was a party, however, to Shaw Plumbing's suit in Nueces County, which was based solely on breach of contract. Because there was a difference in both issues and parties, Shaw argues that the Nueces County district court was not obliged to grant the plea in abatement. We disagree.

When an inherent interrelation of the subject matter exists in two pending lawsuits, a plea in abatement in the second action must be granted. It is not required that the exact issues and all the parties be included in the first action before the second is filed, provided that the claim in the first suit may be amended to bring in all necessary and proper parties and issues. In determining whether an inherent interrelationship exists, courts should be guided by the rule governing persons to be joined if feasible and the compulsory counterclaim rule. *See* Tex. R. Civ. P. 39, 97(a).

Shaw Plumbing should have brought its compulsory counterclaim on the contract in Wyatt's tort and DTPA suit in Duval County. If Shaw Plumbing had joined Morgan Spear, venue would have been proper in the Duval County suit filed by Wyatt, where the cause of action arose. If Wyatt had sued Shaw Plumbing in Nueces County, venue would have also been proper because Shaw's principal office was situated in Nueces County. However, since Wyatt filed suit first, he chose Duval County.

It is well settled that when suit would be proper in more than one county, the court in which suit is first filed acquires dominant jurisdiction to the exclusion of other courts. *Curtis v. Gibbs*, 511 S.W.2d 263, 267 (Tex. 1974); *Cleveland v. Ward*, 285 S.W. 1063, 1070 (Tex. 1926). As long as the forum is a proper one, it is the plaintiff's privilege to choose the forum. *Mutual Sav. & Loan Ass'n v. Earnest*, 582 S.W.2d 534, 535 (Tex. Civ. App. — Texarkana 1979, no writ). Defendants are simply not at liberty to decline to do battle in the forum chosen by the plaintiff.

Abatement of a lawsuit due to the pendency of a prior suit is based on the principles of comity, convenience, and the necessity for an orderly procedure in the trial of contested issues. *See McCurdy v. Gage*, 69 S.W.2d 56, 59, *reh'g overruled per curiam and opinion adopted*, 75 S.W.2d 1107 (Tex. Comm'n App. 1934). The plea in abatement must be raised in a timely manner, however, or it is waived. There has been no waiver in the present case.

There are three exceptions to the rule of *Cleveland v. Ward* that the court where suit is first filed acquires dominant jurisdiction: (1) Conduct by a party that estops him from asserting prior active jurisdiction: (2) lack of persons to be joined if feasible, or the power to bring them before the court; and (3) lack of intent to prosecute the first lawsuit. None of these exceptions applies in this case . . . .

We reaffirm that the rule of *Cleveland v. Ward* is the law regarding conflicts of jurisdiction between Texas courts of coordinate jurisdiction. In the case at bar, both lawsuits involve the same issues. Moreover, the parties in the second suit were either present in the first suit, or parties who should have been joined in the first suit. Since venue was proper in either Duval, Harris, or Nueces County, the court where suit was first filed, Duval County, acquired dominant jurisdiction. The Nueces County district court, therefore, had no discretion to deny Wyatt's plea in abatement.

Accordingly, we reverse the judgment of the court of appeals and remand the cause to the Nueces County district court with instructions to vacate its judgment and abate all proceedings pending final disposition of the Duval County lawsuit.

[Justice Kilgarlin's concurring opinion, which expresses concern about the "race to the courthouse," is omitted.]

GONZALEZ, J. dissenting, joined by Chief Justice Phillips and Justice Mauzy

I agree wholeheartedly with the court's articulation of the rule of dominant jurisdiction. We do not disagree on the law; we disagree on its application to this cause.

Unquestionably, the general rule is that the court in which suit is first filed acquires dominant jurisdiction and that any subsequent suit involving the same parties and the same controversy must be dismissed if, by a plea in abatement, a party calls the court's attention to the pendency on the prior suit. *Curtis v. Gibbs*, 511 S.W.2d 263 (Tex. 1974), *Cleveland v. Ward*, 285 S.W. 1063 (1926). I would not in any way abandon this general rule . . . .

There is still another reason for why the Nueces County trial judge acted properly in refusing to abate the second suit. *Curtis v. Gibbs*, 511 S.W.2d at 267, stated the following exception to the general rule of dominant jurisdiction:

> The plaintiff in the first suit may be guilty of such inequitable conduct as will estop him from relying on that suit to abate a subsequent proceeding brought by his adversary.

In this case, Wyatt filed his DTPA suit against Shaw Plumbing after having already received Shaw Plumbing's thirty day demand letter, and he did so without giving the thirty day notice required of him under the Deceptive Trade Practices — Consumer Protection Act. TEX. BUS. & COM. CODE ANN. § 17.505.

Wyatt's failure to give the required statutory notice enabled him to beat Shaw Plumbing to the courthouse and fix venue in Duval County. The proper remedy for a party's failure to give the required DTPA notice is ordinarily abatement rather than dismissal. Under the circumstances of this case, I would hold that although a party's failure to comply with the statutory notice requirement will not result in dismissal, it is nevertheless a type of "inequitable conduct" that cannot be used as a vehicle for fixing venue. Thus, I would further hold that Wyatt's failure to give the required DTPA notice estops him from relying on his first-filed suit to abate the subsequent suit.

Although the court's opinion acknowledges the exceptions to the general rule of dominant jurisdiction, it summarily states that none apply. Upon analysis, I am unable to reach the same conclusion. Therefore, I dissent from the court's opinion and would affirm the judgment of the court of appeals.

NOTES AND QUESTIONS

(1) *The Plea in Abatement.* A plea in abatement is used to allege reasons, other than venue or jurisdiction, why the case should not proceed or should be dismissed. The following excerpt from the *Texas Litigation Guide*, Ch. 70, *Answer*,* discusses the many uses of the plea in abatement.

§ 70.03[7][a] Nature and Purpose

A plea in abatement may be directed to a wide range of issues; it may be based on any fact that is not in the petition and does not challenge venue or jurisdiction but that presents a reason to suspend or dismiss the case [*see Austin Neighborhoods Council, Inc. v. Board of Adjustment*, 644 S.W.2d 560, 565 n.17 (Tex. App. — Austin 1982, writ ref'd n.r.e.)]. For example, a plea may be used to attack the petition based on matters such as the following:

1. The capacity of the parties . . .
2. A defect in the parties, such as a failure to join parties who should be joined if feasible . . .
3. The pendency of administrative proceedings . . .
4. The pendency of another action involving the same parties and controversy

A common use of the plea in abatement is to allege the action is premature — in other words, to assert that there is a condition precedent to bringing suit that has not yet occurred. For example, in a DTPA action, the complaining party must give written notice to the party complained of as a "prerequisite" to filing suit. *See* Tex. Bus. & Com. C. § 17.505(a). Similarly, written notice of a health care liability claim must be given prior to filing suit. If such notices are not given before suit is filed, the defendant's response should be to file a plea in abatement.

(2) *Mechanics of the Plea.* The following excerpt from *Bryce v. Corpus Christi Area, etc.*, 569 S.W.2d 496 (Tex. Civ. App. — Corpus Christi 1978, writ ref'd n.r.e), discusses the mechanics of the plea:

> A plea in abatement should not only show the grounds upon which the suit is improperly brought, but should also show how it should have been brought, and should always state facts, not conclusions of law. When such a plea is sustained, the suit should not be dismissed until the plaintiff has been given a reasonable opportunity to amend, if it is possible to do so, and thereby remove the obstacle which defeated the suit initially filed. Even if the case is dismissed, it is revived upon the removal of such obstacle which prevented its further prosecution in the first instance.

(3) *Verify It.* Many of the matters that would support abatement are matters which must be verified by affidavit [in other words, they must be sworn to] pursuant to Civil Procedure Rule 93. *See, e.g.*, Tex. R. Civ. P. 93(4). Even if no provision of a rule of procedure or statute requires sworn pleadings, the plea is customarily verified. The sworn pleading or supporting affidavit is not evidence. The party presenting the plea must be prepared to introduce evidence at the hearing.

(4) *Plea to the Jurisdiction Distinguished.* Although both a plea in abatement and a plea to the jurisdiction are dilatory pleas, a plea to the jurisdiction is properly used to urge that the court lacks subject matter jurisdiction over the controversy, whereas a plea in abatement, if sustained, might merely require an abatement (temporary suspension) of the action until the obstacle to its further prosecution is removed or satisfied.

(5) *Comity.* What happens when the suits are filed in different states? "The mere pendency of an action in one state does not require the abatement of a suit in another state between the same parties and involving the same subject matter; however, as a matter of comity, it is customary for the court in which the later action is instituted to stay proceedings for a reasonable time." *Project Eng'g USA Corp. v. Gator Hawk, Inc.*, 833 S.W.2d 716, 724 (Tex. App. — Houston [1st Dist.] 1992, no writ).

(6) *Time for Making a Plea in Abatement.* The rules are silent as to the time for making a plea in abatement. Although the plea is not subject to "due order" rules like special appearance motions and motions to transfer venue, case law supports a requirement that the plea must be urged within a reasonable amount of time after the grounds are apparent. The failure to timely urge a plea in abatement may result in waiver. *Howell v. Mauzy*, 899 S.W.2d 690, 698 (Tex. App. — Austin 1994, writ denied).

[E] Plea to the Jurisdiction

A defendant may want to assert that the trial court lacks the power — jurisdiction — to hear the case. The vehicle for raising this defense is a Plea to the Jurisdiction. One use of such a plea is to raise issues about the amount in controversy or other jurisdictional limits discussed in Chapter 3. Recently, however, the plea to the jurisdiction has become an extremely popular way to urge that the defendant is immune from suit, or that the plaintiff lacks standing. [Using the plea to the jurisdiction often allows an immediate interlocutory appeal if the trial court rules against the defendant's claim.] The proper treatment of this type of plea to the jurisdiction is quite complex, because the facts underlying the issues of immunity and standing often overlap with the merits of the lawsuit. In the following case, the Texas Supreme Court discusses the procedures that should be used in a plea to the jurisdiction arising out of an immunity claim. Be sure to read Justice Brister's dissent carefully, as he highlights the procedural difficulties raised by the majority's approach.

TEXAS DEPARTMENT OF PARKS AND WILDLIFE v. MIRANDA

133 S.W.3d 217 (Tex. 2004)

Justice Wainwright delivered the opinion of the Court with respect to parts I., II., III.A., III.B., III.C.2., III.C.3., III.D., and IV., in which Chief Justice Phillips, Justice Hecht, Justice Owen, and Justice Smith joined, and a plurality opinion with respect to Part III.C.1., in which Chief Justice Phillips, Justice Hecht, and Justice Smith joined.

Justice Jefferson filed a dissenting opinion.

Justice Brister filed a dissenting opinion, in which Justice O' Neill and Justice Schneider joined.

Maria Miranda sustained injuries after a tree limb fell on her at Garner State Park in Uvalde County. Maria and her husband Ray sued the Texas Parks and Wildlife Department, alleging negligence and gross negligence. The Department filed a plea to the jurisdiction, to which it attached supporting evidence, and argued that sovereign immunity barred the Mirandas' claims. The trial court denied the plea to the jurisdiction and a unanimous court of appeals affirmed, holding that the trial court could not consider evidence in support of the plea because the Department did not allege that the Mirandas' pleadings were a sham for the purpose of wrongfully obtaining jurisdiction.

In accord with our decision in *Bland Independent School District v. Blue*, 34 S.W.3d 547 (Tex. 2000), we hold that the trial court in this case was required to examine the evidence on which the parties relied to determine if a fact issue existed regarding the alleged gross negligence of the Department. Due to the unusual confluence of standards erected by the Legislature for waiver of sovereign immunity in the Texas Tort Claims Act and the recreational use statute, plaintiffs must plead gross negligence to establish subject matter jurisdiction. Further, if the plaintiffs' factual allegations are challenged with supporting evidence necessary to consideration of the plea to the jurisdiction, to avoid dismissal plaintiffs must raise at least a genuine issue of material fact to overcome the challenge to the trial court's subject matter jurisdiction. Because the Mirandas failed to raise a genuine issue of material fact regarding the alleged gross negligence of the Department, we conclude that the trial court lacked subject matter jurisdiction over this lawsuit. Therefore, we reverse the judgment of the court of appeals and render judgment dismissing the case.

I. Factual and Procedural Background

The Mirandas' third amended petition contains the following allegations: In April 1998, the Mirandas and their family were camping and picnicking as paying guests at Garner State Park, owned and operated by the Texas Parks and Wildlife Department. The Mirandas asked a park ranger to recommend a campsite that would be safe for children. While standing next to a picnic table at the recommended campsite, a falling tree branch approximately twelve inches in diameter and fifteen feet long struck Maria on the head. As a result of the incident, Maria suffered extensive injuries to her head, neck, and spine. Ray suffered mental anguish and other damages related to his wife's injuries.

On May 7, 1999, the Mirandas filed suit against the Department, alleging negligence and later amended their suit to add gross negligence claims. With respect to the gross negligence claims, the Mirandas alleged that the Department "knew of the dangers of its falling tree branches, failed to inspect, failed to prune, failed to alleviate or remove the danger, and consciously and deliberately failed to warn Plaintiffs of the extremely dangerous condition," "knew that its property contained hidden, dangerous defect [sic] in that its tree branches which have not been inspected or pruned regularly fall," failed "to make safe the dangerous condition of its campsite trees," and "failed to warn or make reasonably safe the dangerous condition of which it was aware." In addition, the Mirandas alleged that the Department's conduct was "willful, wanton, or grossly negligent."

Over a year after the Mirandas filed suit and after the parties conducted discovery, the Department filed a plea to the jurisdiction and motion to dismiss, arguing that the Mirandas' allegations were insufficient to invoke a waiver of the

Department's sovereign immunity under the standard established in the Tort Claims Act and the recreational use statute.[2] The Department attached evidence in support of its plea. The Mirandas filed a response to the Department's plea and their third amended original petition. In their response, the Mirandas stated that they relied on evidence attached to the Department's plea, including written discovery responses from the Department and the deposition the Mirandas took of assistant park manager Craig Van Baarle. At the trial court's hearing on the Department's plea, the parties addressed the allegations in the Mirandas' third amended original petition. The next day, the trial court denied the plea. The Department filed this interlocutory appeal claiming that the trial court erroneously denied its plea to the jurisdiction and motion to dismiss. *Id.* § 51.014(a)(8). The court of appeals affirmed the trial court's denial of the plea, stating that the Mirandas pled a premises defect cause of action based on gross negligence under the recreational use statute. The court of appeals rejected the Department's argument that there was no evidence to support gross negligence, holding that "the trial court was not authorized to inquire into the substance of the claims because the Department did not specifically allege that the Mirandas' allegations were pled merely as a sham for the purpose of wrongfully obtaining jurisdiction." *Id.* (citing *Bland*, 34 S.W.3d at 554 and *Rylander v. Caldwell*, 23 S.W.3d 132, 135 (Tex. App. — Austin 2000, no pet.)).

The Department contends that the court of appeals erred in relying solely upon the conclusory allegations found in the Mirandas' petition to affirm the trial court's denial of the Department's plea to the jurisdiction and in disregarding the Department's evidence submitted with its plea. Specifically, the Department contends that gross negligence is a jurisdictional prerequisite to the Mirandas' claims and that its evidence affirmatively negates gross negligence. The Department further argues that because the Mirandas failed to plead specific facts alleging gross negligence in their petition or introduce evidence to controvert the evidence in the Department's plea, they failed to establish subject matter jurisdiction to proceed with the litigation. . . .

III. The Department's Plea to the Jurisdiction

A. Sovereign Immunity

In Texas, sovereign immunity deprives a trial court of subject matter jurisdiction for lawsuits in which the state or certain governmental units have been sued unless the state consents to suit. *Texas Dep't of Transp. v. Jones*, 8 S.W.3d 636, 638 (Tex. 1999). The Texas Tort Claims Act provides a limited waiver of sovereign immunity. Tex. Civ. Prac. & Rem. Code §§ 101.001-.109. Sovereign immunity includes two distinct principles, immunity from suit and immunity from liability. Immunity from liability is an affirmative defense, while immunity from suit deprives a court of subject matter jurisdiction. The Tort Claims Act creates a unique statutory scheme in which the two immunities are co-extensive: "Sovereign

[2] The Department also moved for summary judgment under Texas Rule of Civil Procedure 166a(b)-(c) and 166a(i). The trial court denied both motions, but the Department does not appeal the trial court's denial of either motion.

immunity to suit is waived and abolished to the extent of liability created by this chapter." TEX. CIV. PRAC. & REM. CODE § 101.025(a). Thus, the Department is immune from suit unless the Tort Claims Act expressly waives immunity.

[The Court then discusses the Tort Claims Act and the Recreational Use Statute and concludes that the Department has waived sovereign immunity only if it is grossly negligent. "Gross negligence involves two components: (1) viewed objectively from the actor's standpoint, the act or omission complained of must involve an extreme degree of risk, considering the probability and magnitude of the potential harm to others; and (2) the actor must have actual, subjective awareness of the risk involved, but nevertheless proceed in conscious indifference to the rights, safety, or welfare of others." *Louisiana- Pacific Corp. v. Andrade*, 19 S.W.3d 245, 246 (Tex. 1999) (citing *Transportation Ins. Co. v. Moriel*, 879 S.W.2d 10, 23 (Tex. 1994)).]

B. Standard of Review

Sovereign immunity from suit defeats a trial court's subject matter jurisdiction and thus is properly asserted in a plea to the jurisdiction. The trial court must determine at its earliest opportunity whether it has the constitutional or statutory authority to decide the case before allowing the litigation to proceed. . . . Whether a court has subject matter jurisdiction is a question of law. *Texas Natural Res. Conservation Comm'n v. IT-Davy*, 74 S.W.3d 849, 855 (Tex. 2002). Whether a pleader has alleged facts that affirmatively demonstrate a trial court's subject matter jurisdiction is a question of law reviewed *de novo*. Likewise, whether undisputed evidence of jurisdictional facts establishes a trial court's jurisdiction is also a question of law. However, in some cases, disputed evidence of jurisdictional facts that also implicate the merits of the case may require resolution by the finder of fact. *See Gates v. Pitts*, 291 S.W. 948, 949 (Tex. Civ. App. — Amarillo 1927, no writ); *Gentry*, 21 S.W. at 570; *see also Valentin v. Hospital Bella Vista*, 254 F.3d 358, 363 n.3 (1st Cir. 2001) (observing that in certain situations, the predicate facts can be so inextricably linked to the merits of the controversy that the district court may "defer resolution of the jurisdictional issue until the time of trial"); *Cameron v. Children's Hosp. Med. Ctr.*, 131 F.3d 1167, 1170 (6th Cir. 1997) ("Whether a district court has subject matter jurisdiction is a question for the court, not a jury, to decide, even if the determination requires making factual findings, unless the jurisdictional issue is inextricably bound to the merits of the case."); *Williamson v. Tucker*, 645 F.2d 404, 413 n.6, 416 n.10 (5th Cir. 1981) (suggesting that a federal district court's role in determining jurisdictional facts may be more limited in cases in which the jurisdictional attack implicates the merits of plaintiff's cause of action). In this case, we address a plea to the jurisdiction in which undisputed evidence implicates both the subject matter jurisdiction of the court and the merits of the case.

When a plea to the jurisdiction challenges the pleadings, we determine if the pleader has alleged facts that affirmatively demonstrate the court's jurisdiction to hear the cause. *Texas Ass'n of Bus. v. Texas Air Control Bd.*, 852 S.W.2d 440, 446 (Tex. 1993). We construe the pleadings liberally in favor of the plaintiffs and look to the pleaders' intent. If the pleadings do not contain sufficient facts to affirmatively demonstrate the trial court's jurisdiction but do not affirmatively demonstrate incurable defects in jurisdiction, the issue is one of pleading sufficiency and the plaintiffs should be afforded the opportunity to amend. If the pleadings affirmatively negate the existence of jurisdiction, then a plea to the jurisdiction may be granted without allowing the plaintiffs an opportunity to amend.

However, if a plea to the jurisdiction challenges the existence of jurisdictional facts, we consider relevant evidence submitted by the parties when necessary to resolve the jurisdictional issues raised, as the trial court is required to do. *See Bland*, 34 S.W.3d at 555 (confining the evidentiary review to evidence that is relevant to the jurisdictional issue). When the consideration of a trial court's subject matter jurisdiction requires the examination of evidence, the trial court exercises its discretion in deciding whether the jurisdictional determination should be made at a preliminary hearing or await a fuller development of the case, mindful that this determination must be made as soon as practicable. *Id.* at 554. Then, in a case in which the jurisdictional challenge implicates the merits of the plaintiffs' cause of action and the plea to the jurisdiction includes evidence, the trial court reviews the relevant evidence to determine if a fact issue exists. The United States Supreme Court and all of the federal circuits have authorized federal district courts to consider evidence in deciding motions to dismiss for lack of subject matter jurisdiction. If the evidence creates a fact question regarding the jurisdictional issue, then the trial court cannot grant the plea to the jurisdiction, and the fact issue will be resolved by the fact finder. However, if the relevant evidence is undisputed or fails to raise a fact question on the jurisdictional issue, the trial court rules on the plea to the jurisdiction as a matter of law.

We acknowledge that this standard generally mirrors that of a summary judgment under Texas Rule of Civil Procedure 166a(c). We adhere to the fundamental precept that a court must not proceed on the merits of a case until legitimate challenges to its jurisdiction have been decided. This standard accomplishes this goal and more. It also protects the interests of the state and the injured claimants in cases like this one, in which the determination of the subject matter jurisdiction of the court implicates the merits of the parties' cause of action. The standard allows the state in a timely manner to extricate itself from litigation if it is truly immune. However, by reserving for the fact finder the resolution of disputed jurisdictional facts that implicate the merits of the claim or defense, we preserve the parties' right to present the merits of their case at trial. Similar to the purpose of a plea to the jurisdiction, which is to defeat a cause of action for which the state has not waived sovereign immunity (usually before the state has incurred the full costs of litigation), the purpose of summary judgments in Texas is " 'to eliminate patently unmeritorious claims and untenable defenses.' " By requiring the state to meet the summary judgment standard of proof in cases like this one, we protect the plaintiffs from having to "put on their case simply to establish jurisdiction." *Bland*, 34 S.W.3d at 554. Instead, after the state asserts and supports with evidence that the trial court lacks subject matter jurisdiction, we simply require the plaintiffs, when the facts underlying the merits and subject matter jurisdiction are intertwined, to show that there is a disputed material fact regarding the jurisdictional issue. *See Huckabee v. Time Warner Entm't Co. L.P.*, 19 S.W.3d 413, 420 (Tex. 2000); *Phan Son Van v. Pena*, 990 S.W.2d 751, 753 (Tex. 1999).

Appellate courts reviewing a challenge to a trial court's subject matter jurisdiction review the trial court's ruling *de novo*. *IT-Davy*, 74 S.W.3d at 855. When reviewing a plea to the jurisdiction in which the pleading requirement has been met and evidence has been submitted to support the plea that implicates the merits of the case, we take as true all evidence favorable to the nonmovant. *See Science Spectrum, Inc. v. Martinez*, 941 S.W.2d 910, 911 (Tex. 1997). We indulge every reasonable inference and resolve any doubts in the nonmovant's favor. *Id.*

In his dissent JUSTICE JEFFERSON criticizes this standard of review as depriving plaintiffs responding to a plea of the procedural protections of a motion for summary judgment, including a twenty-one day notice period or an adequate time to conduct discovery. However, the scheduling of a hearing of a plea to the jurisdiction is left to the discretion of the trial court, which is in the best position to evaluate the appropriate time frame for hearing a plea in any particular case. This procedure does not dramatically differ from that outlined in Texas Rule of Civil Procedure 120a governing special appearances. Although Rule 120a requires any affidavits to be used at a hearing on a special appearance to be served at least seven days before the hearing, it does not specify the length of a notice period and is therefore presumably subject to the three-day notice period of Rule 21. Rule 120a allows the trial court to order a continuance and allow time for discovery if the development of the case requires it. Nothing prevents a trial court from doing the same with a plea to the jurisdiction where evidence is necessary.

Many other procedures in Texas practice — ranging from a trial court's rulings on motions to strike intervention to the timing of a class certification decision to even the alteration of the summary judgment notice periods — also "depend[] . . . upon the wise exercise of discretion by the trial court." *Union Carbide Corp. v. B.D. Moye*, 798 S.W.2d 792, 794 (Tex. 1990) (Hecht, J., concurring). Thus, the Texas civil procedural scheme entrusts many scheduling and procedural issues to the sound discretion of the trial court, subject to appellate review. Of course, Texas practice and rules also allow the parties to request additional time to prepare for certain hearings or to conduct discovery upon a showing of sufficient cause, and the court's ruling on such a motion is reviewed for an abuse of discretion. . . . In any event, the Mirandas do not complain that they had an inadequate opportunity to conduct sufficient discovery, nor did they request a continuance to do so.

C. Waiver of Immunity Based on Premises Defects

1. The Mirandas' Pleadings

The Mirandas contend that their pleadings fall within the Tort Claims Act's waiver of immunity for both premises defects and injuries arising out of conditions or use of property. The Act provides that a state agency is liable for injury and death caused by "a condition or use of tangible personal or real property if the governmental unit would, were it a private person, be liable to the claimant according to Texas law." The Mirandas' pleadings allege injuries caused by a falling tree limb, which falls under the definition of real property. . . . The Mirandas' allegation of an injury caused by a tree limb falling on Maria Miranda constitutes an allegation of a condition or use of real property and is an allegation of a premises defect.

To state a claim under the recreational use statute, the Mirandas must allege sufficient facts to establish that the Department was grossly negligent. [The plurality in this section examines the Mirandas' allegations and concludes that, liberally construed, "the Mirandas stated a claim against the Department for gross negligence." In Section 2, the majority further notes that the Department filed deposition testimony and an affidavit demonstrating its lack of gross negligence and that the Mirandas filed no evidence in response. "We conclude that the evidence in the record establishes that the Department was not grossly negligent and that the Mirandas have failed to raise a fact question regarding the Department's alleged gross negligence. The Mirandas fall short of satisfying the requirements for the Legislature's limited grant of a waiver of sovereign immunity from suit under the applicable statutes. Therefore, the trial court lacked subject matter jurisdiction."]

3. Dissent

In his dissent, Justice Brister takes the view that all pleas to jurisdiction based on immunity must take the form of two "standard" or "established" motions — either special exceptions or motions for summary judgment. This approach might be appropriate, if we were starting from scratch. Given that we are not writing on a blank slate, that pleas have been a useful procedural vehicle in Texas for over 150 years . . . the Court declines to abolish by written opinion such pleas to the jurisdiction.

The plea to the jurisdiction was included in procedural rules promulgated by this Court in 1877 and has been used as a procedural vehicle to challenge subject matter jurisdiction in trial courts for over a century and a half. In fact, as early as 1893, Texas courts indicated that evidentiary challenges to subject matter jurisdiction raised in pleas to the jurisdiction should be considered by trial courts. With such a long lineage, one wonders why a plea to jurisdiction does not qualify as a "standard" or "established" motion. Perhaps a second mention in the Texas Rules of Civil Procedure would suffice.

We decide that refining the rules for considering a plea supported by evidence is a better approach than eliminating the motion. This approach is consistent with precedent, is not disruptive to civil practice going back more than a century, and furthers the legislative purpose of timely adjudicating subject matter jurisdiction when the immunity and liability facts are the same.

There is a suggestion in the dissents that confirming in this opinion the authority of trial courts to consider evidence in a plea to the jurisdiction is unfair to the parties in this case. The facts undercut this assertion. At the trial court, both parties relied on extrinsic evidence in briefing the plea, and both parties had extrinsic evidence on file with the court. Furthermore, plaintiffs expressly stated in their response to the plea that they were relying on "Defendants' responses to discovery requests, and upon the deposition of Craig VanBaarle [the Department's assistant park manager]." In fact, the Mirandas deposed VanBaarle months before the Department filed its plea. There is good reason why Plaintiffs have not argued unfair surprise. Given Texas precedents and the actions of the parties, there was none. . . .

IV. Conclusion

Trial courts should decide dilatory pleas early — at the pleading stage of litigation if possible. Here, the Legislature's mandate is not so simple. By statute, waiver of sovereign immunity for recreational use of the Department's premises can only be effected by a showing that it acted with gross negligence. Due to the standard erected (gross negligence), the determination of whether immunity was waived may require consideration of extrinsic facts after reasonable opportunity for targeted discovery. To preclude consideration of extrinsic facts when necessary to decide a plea to the jurisdiction would require a trial on the merits for many cases that do not need it, waste the resources of the courts and the parties in the case, and involve state courts in rulings on the merits in cases over which they have no jurisdiction.

For the reasons explained, we conclude that the Department established that it was not grossly negligent and that the Mirandas failed to raise a fact issue on that point. Thus, the trial court lacked subject matter jurisdiction over the action. The judgment of the court of appeals is reversed and the Mirandas' action dismissed for lack of subject matter jurisdiction.

[The dissent by Justice Jefferson is omitted. He argues that the Mirandas' petition was insufficient to show any duty by the Department and would remand the case to allow them an opportunity to amend their petition.]

JUSTICE BRISTER, joined by JUSTICE O' NEILL and JUSTICE SCHNEIDER, dissenting.

The Legislature has provided that state park visitors are owed the same duty of care as trespassers; thus, the plaintiffs in this case had to prove the Parks and Wildlife Department caused deliberate, wilful, or malicious injury. All members of the Court agree that either their petition or their summary judgment evidence fails to do so, though we disagree which. . . .

Faced with what appears to be an insupportable allegation like the gross-negligence pleading here, litigants normally have two options: (1) demand more specific facts by special exception, or (2) demand more specific facts by motion for summary judgment. Instead, the Department filed three motions, including a "plea to the jurisdiction" — the white elephant[7] of current Texas motion practice. By use of this plea, the Department was able to force the trial judge (and ultimately this Court) to make an ad hoc decision whether our jurisdiction should be determined by reference to pleadings or evidence. Because it should be litigants rather than judges making that choice, I respectfully dissent.

Pleas to the jurisdiction are nothing new. In his *Commentaries on the Laws of England*, Blackstone lists them as a category of dilatory pleas that (along with pleas of disability and abatement) deny the propriety of the remedy rather than the injury. One hundred years ago, this Court addressed a variety of matters as

---

[7] The OXFORD ENGLISH DICTIONARY (1989) defines "white elephant" as: "a. A rare albino variety of elephant which is highly venerated in some Asian countries. b. fig. A burdensome or costly possession (from the story that the kings of Siam were accustomed to make a present of one of these animals to courtiers who had rendered themselves obnoxious, in order to ruin the recipient by the cost of its maintenance). Also, an object, scheme, etc., considered to be without use or value."

pleas to the jurisdiction, including objections based on personal jurisdiction, subject-matter jurisdiction, dominant jurisdiction, venue, capacity, and conflict of laws.

Since then, there has been a steady shift away from the common-law forms of pleading to the more specific motion practice set out in the rules of civil procedure. For example, a defendant objecting to venue today must file a motion to transfer that complies with the form requirements of Rule 86 and the deadlines of Rule 87. Similarly, a nonresident objecting to personal jurisdiction must file a special appearance that meets the requirements of Rule 120a. In substance, these motions could still be categorized as "pleas to the jurisdiction;" but in form, they must comply with the current rules of civil procedure.

But pleas to the jurisdiction have enjoyed a recent resurgence in the field of governmental immunity. For many years, governmental units were not very particular about the vehicle for asserting immunity, raising it sometimes by general demurrer; special demurrer; special exception; plea to the jurisdiction; plea in abatement; or summary judgment. In 1997, the Legislature amended the Civil Practices and Remedies Code to allow interlocutory appeals "from an interlocutory order . . . [that] grants or denies a plea to the jurisdiction by a governmental unit." We have held this section must be strictly construed, as it is an exception to the general rule that interlocutory orders are not appealable.

As a result, almost overnight a "plea to the jurisdiction" became the motion of choice for asserting immunity; indeed, some appellate courts have refused to consider any other. This development exalts form over substance. For example, before the Legislature's amendment, one governmental entity unsuccessfully asserted immunity by means of a summary judgment and special exceptions; immediately after the effective date, the entity filed the same objection as a "plea to jurisdiction" — and prevailed.

For several reasons, we should put a stop to this resurgence of common-law pleadings in immunity cases. First, it is fraught with uncertainty. Despite hundreds of haphazardly-numbered rules, only once do the Texas Rules of Civil Procedure mention pleas to the jurisdiction, and then only in a rule regarding permissible parts of an *answer* rather than permissible motions. There is *no* rule — no case and no code — that specifies the form, deadlines, or evidentiary requirements for pleas to the jurisdiction generally.

In *Bland Independent School District v. Blue*, [34 S.W.3d 547 (Tex. 2000),] we attempted to bring some order to this resurgence by setting guidelines for handling such pleas. But due to the broad range of issues a plea to the jurisdiction might address, that was not easy to do. As we pointed out in several examples, consideration of some pleas should not go beyond the pleadings, but consideration of others must. When necessary, trial courts must consider evidence relating to the jurisdictional facts, but should not consider evidence relating to the merits, even though the two are sometimes the same. Nor could we be specific about when pleas should be decided, leaving it to the trial court's discretion whether to address the issue at a preliminary hearing or after fuller development of the merits.

The examples given in *Bland* certainly provided more procedural guidance than existed before. But without considering all possible pleas to the jurisdiction, we could not prescribe more definitive rules; until all those disputes come before us, we should probably not try. In the meantime, it will often be unclear *what* the trial court should consider, or *when* it should do so, until the plea is decided (or perhaps even later on appeal). To some observers, this may appear to be drawing up the rules after the game has been played.

From almost any vantage point, the resurgence of pleas to the jurisdiction creates problems in immunity cases. For governmental entities, it results in unnecessary repetition. In this case, the Parks and Wildlife Department could not be sure whether the trial court would consider evidence necessary, so it filed three motions — a no-evidence motion for summary judgment, a traditional motion for summary judgment, and a plea to the jurisdiction. But as counsel for the Department admitted at the hearing, "all three relate to the same set of issues."

Such repetition is unnecessary for interlocutory review. Nothing in the Civil Practice and Remedies Code suggests the Legislature intended to specify a *form* motions had to take for that purpose, rather than their *substance*. Indeed, the opposite is suggested by the Legislature's selection of a common-law term applicable to a broad category of motions, rather than a term pointing to any particular motion in the current rules of civil procedure. It has long been our practice to consider the substance of motions rather than their form; nothing in the legislative history suggests the interlocutory appeal statute was intended to be an exception to that rule.

For plaintiffs, the problems created by the resurgence of pleas to the jurisdiction are even more acute. Defendants uncertain about how to present an immunity defense can simply try a little of everything; plaintiffs, by contrast, may lose their case if they guess wrong. In this case, for example, the Mirandas did not attach any evidence to their responses to the various motions. The lower courts agreed they did not need to, but if we hold otherwise, then the Mirandas will learn three years too late that they should have presented evidence at the jurisdictional hearing.

From a trial judge's vantage point, pleas to the jurisdiction create uncertainty, not just about the rules to be applied but about the role of the judge. This case is one of many in which immunity from suit under the Texas Tort Claims Act is coextensive with immunity from liability. As a result, deciding the jurisdictional question bears a strong resemblance to deciding the merits.

In these circumstances, it is difficult for Texas judges to detect the line between jurisdictional questions they *must* decide before going further and liability questions they *cannot* decide without usurping the function of the jury. Here, the Mirandas convinced the lower courts that whether their pleadings were supported by any evidence was a question solely for the jury. But that is not true if they raised no material facts that could establish a waiver of immunity.

By contrast, returning to standard motions as the vehicles for asserting governmental immunity would clarify what the jurisdictional hearing will be like and simplify many procedural questions. For decades, governmental units have asserted immunity by special exceptions or motions for summary judgment. In many cases (including this one), they still do so today. Relying on standard procedural motions would eliminate many questions about deadlines, forms, and evidence. It would make government entities rather than trial judges decide whether the jurisdictional challenge is directed to the plaintiff's pleadings or the underlying facts. If a governmental unit chooses wrong, it may always try again. But the plaintiff is not required to guess what rules or procedures the trial judge might apply.

Returning to pre-resurgence practice would not change the incidence of governmental immunity. As we recently held, if a plea to the jurisdiction is directed only to the plaintiff's pleadings, we construe them in the plaintiff's favor and allow an opportunity to amend unless they affirmatively negate jurisdiction. This is, of course, identical to the rules governing special exceptions. And when governmental entities wish to rely on evidence, any questions of fact that affect jurisdictional issues must be settled by the jury, the same standard that applies to summary judgments.

Nor can it be argued that courts exceed their jurisdiction by requiring immunity pleas to be brought in standard motions according to settled rules of procedure. As we stated shortly after the rules of civil procedure were enacted:

> Since [the trial court] had the power to sustain the demurrers and grant the motions, it had the power to overrule them. The jurisdiction of a court must be determined, not upon the court's action in deciding the questions presented in a case, but upon the character of the case itself. Jurisdiction is the power to decide, and not merely the power to decide correctly.

Martin v. Sheppard, 201 S.W.2d 810, 812–13 (Tex. 1947).

Of course, returning to established procedural motions will not remove all difficulties with issues of governmental immunity. Judges of goodwill and intellect will still disagree about whether a particular pleading is sufficiently specific, as JUSTICES JEFFERSON and WAINWRIGHT do here. Governmental units may incur unnecessary discovery costs and delays unless judges agree to hear summary judgment motions on jurisdictional matters as early in the case as they might hear a plea to the jurisdiction. And appellate courts must still distinguish between immunity from suit (as to which an interlocutory appeal will lie) and immunity from liability (as to which it will not). But simplification of our procedures should not be rejected because we cannot simplify everything.

If the Texas Legislature mandated interlocutory review of "pleas in bar asserting limitations" (a development devoutly to be wished against), few would suggest such review was available only for motions entitled "Plea in Bar" instead of the summary judgment or special exception forms that have long been used to raise such issues. We should stop making the assumption that the Legislature intended something different for pleas of governmental immunity.

Accordingly, I would reverse and remand for (1) the Parks and Wildlife Department to specify whether its plea to the jurisdiction is a challenge to the pleadings (by special exception) or the evidence (by summary judgment), (2) the Mirandas to respond in compliance with the rules of civil procedure, and (3) the lower courts to address the governmental immunity issue in accordance with the usual rules governing disposition and review of those motions.

NOTES AND QUESTIONS

(1) *No Waiver.* Failure to include the plea to the jurisdiction in the original answer does not waive the jurisdictional challenge. Objections to subject matter jurisdiction may not be waived by the parties and may be raised for the first time after judgment and on appeal. *Texas Ass'n of Business v. Texas Air Control Bd.*, 852 S.W.2d 440, 445 (Tex. 1993) (standing is component of subject matter jurisdiction that can be raised for first time on appeal); *Pan Am. Life Ins. Co. v. Erbauer Constr. Co.*, 805 S.W.2d 395, 395–96 (Tex. 1991).

(2) *Timing of the Trial Court's Decision.* As *Miranda* indicates, the issue of whether a determination of subject matter jurisdiction can be made at a preliminary hearing or should await a fuller development of the merits of the case is left to the trial court's discretion. In exercising this discretion, the trial court must be mindful of the policy that this determination be made as soon as practicable. When the jurisdictional challenge implicates the merits of the plaintiffs' cause of action and the plea to the jurisdiction includes evidence, the trial court reviews the relevant evidence to determine if a fact issue exists. If so, the trial court cannot grant the plea to the jurisdiction, and the fact issue will be resolved by the fact finder. If the relevant evidence is undisputed or fails to raise a fact question on the jurisdictional issue, the trial court rules on the plea to the jurisdiction as a matter of law. This standard is similar to summary judgment practice, which is discussed in Chapter 11.

(3) *Subject Matter of the Case and Jurisdiction.* The more traditional use of the plea to the jurisdiction was to claim that a case had been brought in the wrong court. At times, such pleas to the jurisdiction may be based on a defect in subject matter jurisdiction that appears on the face of the plaintiff's petition. For example, a plea to the jurisdiction may be used to allege that the plaintiff has included a claim that is restricted by a statute or constitutional provision to the jurisdiction of another court. *See Speer v. Stover*, 685 S.W.2d 22, 23 (Tex. 1985) (case concerned matters incident to estate, over which county court had jurisdiction).

(4) *Amount in Controversy and Jurisdiction.* If the jurisdictional plea is based on the assertion that the amount in controversy is not within the trial court's amount in controversy jurisdiction, the plaintiff's pleadings may be determinative because a plea to the jurisdiction cannot be used to require the plaintiff to prove damages. *Bland Indep. Sch. Dist. v. Blue*, 34 S.W.3d 547, 554–55 (Tex. 2000). The plaintiff's allegations in the petition of the amount in controversy control for jurisdictional purposes unless the party challenging jurisdiction pleads and proves that the plaintiff's allegations of the amount in controversy were made fraudulently for the purpose of obtaining jurisdiction.

(5) *Other Types of Pleas to the Jurisdiction.* Pleas to the jurisdiction are also frequently used to assert that the plaintiff lacks standing to bring the claim asserted. *Bland Indep. Sch. Dist. v. Blue*, 34 S.W.3d 547 (Tex. 2000). The plaintiff's failure to exhaust its administrative remedies before filing suit also may be asserted by a plea to the jurisdiction. *See Subaru of Am. v. David McDavid*

Nissan, 84 S.W.3d 212, 221 (Tex. 2002). A plea to the jurisdiction is also the appropriate method for raising the issue of an administrative agency's obligation to hold a hearing on an administrative appeal. *See Cantu v. Perales*, 97 S.W.3d 861, 862–63 (Tex. App. — Corpus Christi 2003, no pet.) (plea to jurisdiction challenging civil service commission's refusal to hold hearing to review firefighter's resignation); *Friends of Canyon Lake v. Guadalupe-Blanco*, 96 S.W.3d 519, 525 (Tex. App. — Austin 2002, pet. denied) (plea to jurisdiction challenging environmental group's filing of suit against conservation and reclamation authority, when group had failed to request contested case hearing under process established by legislature).

[F] The General Denial

Read Tex. R. Civ. P. 92.

Drafting a general denial is extremely simple. The issues surrounding general denials, therefore, usually revolve around whether a defendant's general denial was sufficient to permit him to raise certain issues at trial, or whether those issues required an additional and more specific pleading of some kind. The following case discusses whether an issue is covered by the general denial or whether it should have been raised instead as an affirmative defense.

BAHR v. KOHR

980 S.W.2d 723 (Tex. App. — San Antonio 1998, no pet.)

Angelini, J.

Nature of the Case

Raymond D. Bahr, M.D. and his wife, Patricia Bahr (the "Bahrs") appeal a judgment entered in favor of Bradley D. Kohr and his wife, Vivian E.S. Kohr (the "Kohrs"). The Bahrs filed suit against the Kohrs under the Uniform Fraudulent Transfer Act. *See* Tex. Bus. & Com. Code Ann. § 24.001 *et seq.* After a trial to the bench, the court entered a take-nothing judgment in favor of the Kohrs. In their issues presented, the Bahrs argue that the court erred in admitting parol evidence and evidence regarding separate property when only a general denial was filed . . . .

Factual Background

On or about March 7, 1987, the Bahrs obtained an agreed judgment in Maryland against Dutchman Hereford Co., and Mr. Kohr in the amount of $200,000. Mrs. Kohr was not a party to that suit. The agreed judgment provided for periodic payments and was secured by a ranch in Montana. On or about June 9, 1988, the Kohrs purchased 268 acres of real property in Gillespie County. The 268 acres was conveyed by a general warranty deed which stated that ten dollars and other good and valuable consideration was paid by grantees, Bradley D. Kohr and wife, Vivian E.S. Kohr. On January 31, 1994 the Bahrs recorded the Maryland judgment with the district clerk of Kerr County. Mr. Kohr executed a deed to Mrs. Kohr on February 10, conveying to her as her separate property, 68 acres of the Gillespie County property. The remaining 200 acres were claimed as a homestead by the Kohrs. The Bahrs then instituted this lawsuit, contending that the transfer of the 68 acres was a fraudulent conveyance because Mr. Kohr had no other assets to satisfy the Maryland judgment.

The only witnesses at trial were Mr. and Mrs. Kohr. The Kohrs testified that the money used to purchase the 268 acres came from Mrs. Kohr's separate property money market account. The trial court made the following relevant findings of fact and conclusions of law:

4. The Kohrs sold the New Jersey farm in 1987 for a considerable profit. The Kohrs partitioned the proceeds of the sale of the New Jersey farm between themselves as each other's separate property. Thereafter, the Kohrs kept their separate proceeds segregated from each other's accounts.

5. Brad Kohr used his proceeds from the sale of the New Jersey farm to pay separate business debts he had incurred.

6. Vivian Kohr deposited her share of the proceeds from the sale of the New Jersey farm into account number 0006421 at Flemington National Bank and Trust Company, in Flemington, New Jersey. The account was in Vivian Kohr's name only and was her separate property or her sole management community property.

The court found that the Gillespie County property was purchased from money deposited in Mrs. Kohr's separate account at Flemington National Bank. Thus, the 268 acres were Mrs. Kohr's separate property and a resulting trust was created in favor of Mrs. Kohr. The court found that the conveyance of the 68 acres to Mrs. Kohr from Mr. Kohr clarified the title to the property and was not a fraudulent conveyance.

. . . In their second issue presented, the Bahrs allege that the court erred in admitting the Kohrs' evidence of separate property when only a general denial was filed and an affirmative defense of separate property or separate funds was not pled . . . .

Affirmative Defense

In their second issue presented, the Bahrs allege that the trial court erred by admitting evidence regarding separate funds or separate property because the Kohrs filed only a general denial and failed to plead an affirmative defense of separate property or separate funds. Rule 94 of the Rules of Civil Procedure sets forth a list of specific affirmative defenses, which does not include separate property or separate funds. Tex. R. Civ. P. 94. However, Rule 94 also provides that any other matter constituting an avoidance or an affirmative defense must be specifically pled. An affirmative defense does not tend to rebut the factual propositions asserted in the plaintiff's case, but rather seeks to establish an independent reason why the plaintiff should not recover. *Gorman v. Life Ins. Co. of North America*, 811 S.W.2d 542, 546 (Tex. 1991). "An affirmative defense is one of avoidance, rather than a defense in denial." *Id.* The Kohrs argue that separate property or separate funds are not affirmative defenses and their general denial put in issue the ownership of the Gillespie County property. "A general denial of matters pleaded by the adverse party which are not required to be denied under oath, shall be sufficient to put the same in issue." Tex. R. Civ. P. 92.

The Bahrs point to two cases for the proposition that separate property or separate funds are affirmative defenses. *See Weatherall v. Weatherall*, 403 S.W.2d 524 (Tex. Civ. App. — Houston [1st Dist.] 1966, no writ); *Grogan v. Henderson*, 313 S.W.2d 315 (Tex. Civ. App. — Texarkana 1958, writ ref'd n.r.e.). In *Weatherall*, the trial court awarded damages to a spouse who had contributed community funds to the other spouse's separate property. *Weatherall*, 403 S.W.2d at 525. The court found that the trial court erred in awarding the damages because the pleadings did not assert separate property or more importantly reimbursement. *Id.* at 526. The *Weatherall* case seems to focus more on reimbursement as the affirmative defense that must be plead in order to recover damages. In the *Grogan* case, the court acknowledged that the appellees did not plead separate property as an affirmative defense. *Grogan*, 313 S.W.2d at 320. However, the court found that evidence of separate funds was submitted to the jury without objection and therefore the issue was waived. *Id.* The case does not hold that separate property must be plead as an affirmative defense.

In this case, we do not find that separate property or separate funds are affirmative defenses. In order to prove that Mr. Kohr fraudulently conveyed the Gillespie County property, the Bahrs must necessarily prove the ownership of the property. An affirmative defense must be capable of defeating the plaintiff's cause of action even though the plaintiff proves its case. Without proving that Mr. Kohr owns the property, the Bahrs cannot prevail on their claim. The Kohrs' general denial properly raised the issue of ownership of the Gillespie County property. Thus, the court did not err in admitting evidence regarding separate funds or separate property. We overrule the second issue presented.

NOTES AND QUESTIONS

See Tex. R. Civ. P. 93, 94, 95.

(1) *General Denial.* No particular form of general denial is required. One traditional form is as follows:

> Defendant ____________ [*name*], denies each and every, all and singular, the allegations in Plaintiff's Original Petition, and demands strict proof thereof.

(2) *Argumentative Denials, Alibis, and Converse Theories.* Would evidence that the event was the result of an "Act of God" or an "unavoidable accident" be admissible under a general denial? Traditionally such pleadings, which are called "inferential rebuttal defenses" because they functionally deny some element of the plaintiff's cause of action but do it inferentially rather than directly, had to be specially pleaded before they could be included in the court's charge to the jury. Currently such pleas may not be submitted as jury questions, and so the need to plead them is less clear.

[G] Special Denials

When the procedure rules require that something be denied specifically (and sometimes under oath), the issue cannot be raised at trial if it is not correctly pleaded. Rules 54 and 93 are the most common sources of specific denial requirements. There are also, once again, waiver rules at work: sometimes the plaintiff may waive the right to complain about defects in the defendant's denials. Consider the following cases.

[1] Conditions Precedent

Read Tex. R. Civ. P. 54, 93.

When a defendant wants to deny that a condition precedent has occurred, how specific should its denial be about what didn't happen?

DAIRYLAND COUNTY MUTUAL INS. CO. OF TEXAS v. ROMAN

498 S.W.2d 154 (Tex. 1973)

Walker, J.

This is a suit to recover under the uninsured motorist provisions of an automobile liability insurance policy. On the controlling questions presented for decision, we hold . . . that where the plaintiff avers generally that all conditions precedent have been performed and no attempt is made to raise an issue of notice except by a sham pleading, the defendant is not entitled to a reversal on the ground that the plaintiff failed to establish that a written notice condition was performed . . . .

The suit was brought by George Cruz Roman, Jr., against his insurer, Dairyland County Mutual Insurance Company of Texas, to recover damages for personal injuries sustained by him in an accident that occurred shortly after midnight on July 4, 1970, a few miles north of San Antonio on Interstate Highway 35. Plaintiff, who was accompanied by Mary Lou Valdez, was driving in a northerly direction on the highway when the muffler on his 1956 Chevrolet automobile became dislodged and began dragging on the pavement. He stopped his vehicle on the left side of the roadway and crawled under the car to remove the muffler. After he had completed his work and while he was emerging from under the car, it was struck in the rear by a vehicle driven by Ethan Odoms, an uninsured motorist. Immediately following this collision, an automobile driven by Charlene Hayes in a northerly direction in the right-hand lane of the highway was struck either by Odoms' car or by a piece of debris from the collision. Neither Miss Valdez nor Mrs. Hayes was injured, but plaintiff sustained personal injuries consisting primarily of a large laceration of the face and forehead.

At the time of the accident plaintiff was 19 years of age and was the named insured in an automobile liability insurance policy issued by defendant. He is the only person named as an insured, and his automobile is the only vehicle described in the policy. The policy contained the standard uninsured motorist coverage and the usual general condition requiring written notice of an accident, occurrence or loss to be given by the insured to the company as soon as practicable. Five days after the accident, plaintiff's mother talked with the insurance agent in Uvalde through whom the policy had been acquired and informed him of the details of the accident and that Odoms was uninsured. Neither defendant nor any of its agents received written notice of the accident, however, until August 5, 1970, when defendant was served with the citation and the accompanying petition in this suit . . . .

The provision of the present policy requiring that notice of the accident be given the insurer as soon as practicable is a condition precedent to liability. In the absence of waiver or other special circumstances, failure to perform the condition constitutes an absolute defense to liability on the policy . . . .

This does not mean that defendant is entitled to a reversal of the trial court's judgment because of plaintiff's failure to obtain a finding that proper written notice was given within the time provided in the policy. Plaintiff alleged generally that he had complied with all conditions precedent under the policy. Rule 54, Texas Rules of Civil Procedure, provides that a party who so avers performance of conditions precedent "shall be required to prove only such of them as are specifically denied by the opposite party." Defendant did not specifically deny performance by plaintiff of any condition precedent, but alleged that 

> "Plaintiff has solely [sic] failed to comply with the conditions of said policy, to wit:" followed by a xerographic reproduction of the entire "Conditions" section of the policy. One of the seventeen numbered divisions of the section contains the notice requirement now urged by defendant, but many provisions in the section obviously have no bearing on the present case.

The Court of Civil Appeals recognized that defendant's pleading was not in compliance with Rule 54. It reasoned that while the trial court might have been authorized to disregard the pleading or require a repleader, this had not been done since evidence concerning notice was freely introduced and an issue relating to notice was submitted. There is also a footnote to the opinion suggesting that the deficiency in the pleading may have been waived by plaintiff's failure to except. We do not agree.

In *Sherman v. Provident Am. Ins. Co.*, 421 S.W.2d 652, the insurance company had a somewhat similar pleading that set up all the policy exclusions. Until the case reached this Court, all parties proceeded on the assumption that the exclusions were properly raised by the pleadings. The Shermans, who were plaintiffs there, introduced no evidence to negative the exclusions, because it was their position that the company had the burden of proving that the loss fell within one or more of the exceptions. The trial court instructed a verdict for the company, and the Court of Civil Appeals affirmed. These judgments were affirmed by this Court with two members dissenting. The majority recognized that the company's pleading was in violation of Rule 94, T.R.C.P., but concluded that the trial court's judgment for the company could not be reversed on that ground since no question as to sufficiency of the pleading had been raised in the trial court or preserved on appeal. This holding was based, in some measure at least, on the provisions of Rule 90, T.R.C.P.

Our situation here is the converse of that in *Sherman*. The trial court rendered judgment for plaintiff, and it is the defendant that seeks a reversal. Although evidence concerning notice was admitted and an issue concerning notice was submitted, the trial court overruled defendant's objections and requests that sought submission of an issue inquiring whether written notice containing the information required by the policy was given as soon as practicable. As the case reaches us then, and there being nothing to the contrary in the record, it may fairly be assumed that the trial court chose to disregard defendant's pleading that all policy conditions were breached. Be that as it may, there is no pleading specifically raising the written notice condition as required by Rule 54. In these circumstances defendant will not be heard to complain of the trial court's refusal to submit an issue thereon or of plaintiff's failure to obtain a finding or otherwise establish that the condition was performed. *See* International Sec. Life Ins. Co. v. Maas, 458 S.W.2d 484 (wr. ref. n.r.e.) . . . .

Defendant's other points of error have been considered, and in our opinion they do not warrant a reversal of the judgments below. The judgment of the Court of Civil Appeals is accordingly affirmed.

NOTES AND QUESTIONS

(1) *Application of the Waiver Rule.* As the principal case points out, the literal language of Civil Procedure Rule 90 provides that a waiver of pleading defects resulting from the failure to point them out applies only to the party seeking reversal "on such account." Tex. R. Civ. P. 90. Under this wording, "the anomalous result is that waiver does not depend [entirely] upon the action of the parties, but upon the entry of judgment in the trial court." William T. Deffebach & George E. Brown, *Waiver of Pleading Defects and Insufficiencies in Texas*, 36 Tex. L. Rev. 459, 471 (1958). One court of appeals has held that this means that the plaintiff's failure to except to an improper verification for a denial was not a waiver of the defect when the defendant sought reversal after the trial court disregarded the defendant's defective pleading. *Davis v. Young Californian Shoes, Inc.*, 612 S.W.2d 703, 704 (Tex. Civ. App. — Dallas 1981, no writ); *cf. Federal Parts v. Robert Bosch Corp.*, 604 S.W.2d 367, 369–70 (Tex. Civ. App. — Fort Worth 1980, writ ref'd n.r.e.).

(2) *Special Exception Not Required in Response to a Defective Denial.* Another possible rationale for the conclusion that Roman was not required to specially except to the insurance company's defective pleading is the rule that complaint regarding a defective denial is not waived by a failure to specially except. *See Heusinger Hardware Co. v. Frost National Bank*, 364 S.W.2d 851, 856 (Tex. Civ. App. — Eastland 1963, no writ) ("As stated in Volume 2 McDonald, *Tex. Civil Practice*, pages 657, 658, 'Where the defective plea is in the nature of a denial, and if effective would impose on the pleader's opponent an additional onus of proof, the opponent is not required to except specially. The defective plea is insufficient to require him to make proof and he avoids a waiver of the pleading defect by objecting to any evidence tendered by the pleader or any questions on cross-examination, tending to raise the issue.' ") *See also MG Bldg. Materials, Ltd. v. Moses Lopez Custom Homes, Inc.*, 179 S.W.3d 51 (Tex. App. — San Antonio 2005, pet. denied) (defendant's denial of conditions precedent).

(3) *Relevance of Rule 93.* Do the provisions of Civil Procedure Rule 93(12) or (15) have any relevance or application to the principal case?

(4) *Relationship to Rule 94.* Read the last sentence of Civil Procedure Rule 94. What function does it perform? How does it differ in application from Rule 54?

(5) *Statutory Notice as a Condition Precedent.* It should also be noted that a specific pleading of notice in satisfaction of a particular statutory prerequisite to recovery has been held subject to Civil Procedure Rule 54's imposition of a specific denial requirement. *Investors, Inc. v. Hadley*, 738 S.W.2d 737, 741 (Tex. App. — Austin 1987, no writ) (interpreting second sentence of Rule 54 as requiring specific denial of statutorily required notice of claim under Deceptive Trade Practices Act when plaintiffs specifically pleaded notice even though plaintiffs did not "generally aver" performance of all conditions precedent to recovery).

(6) *Changes in Insurance Law.* While *Dairyland* is a good example of the requirements for raising issues regarding performance of conditions, it is no longer correct with regard to insurance law. First, failure to comply with the notice condition is not a defense to liability unless the insurer shows actual prejudice. *PAJ, Inc. v. Hanover Ins. Co.*, 2008 Tex. LEXIS 8 (Tex. 2008); *see generally* Dorsaneo, Texas Litigation Guide § 341.05. Second, it is now clear that the burden is on the insurer to both plead and prove that the loss sued on was due to a risk or cause coming within a particular exclusion to its coverage. *See* Ins. Code § 554.002 ("In a suit to recover under an insurance . . . contract, the insurer . . . has the burden of proof as to any avoidance or affirmative defense that the Texas Rules of Civil Procedure require to be affirmatively pleaded. Language of exclusion in the contract or an exception to coverage claimed by the insurer or health maintenance organization constitutes an avoidance or an affirmative defense."); Tex. R. Civ. P. 94 (insurer must specifically allege that loss was due to excluded risk).

[2] Verified Denials — Execution

Read Tex. R. Civ. P. 93.

Rule 93 requires a long list of denials to be specially made under oath. What are the consequences of failing to do so?

BAUER v. VALLEY BANK OF EL PASO

560 S.W.2d 520 (Tex. Civ. App. — El Paso 1977, no writ)

Osborn, J.

This is an appeal from a judgment based upon a promissory note and a guaranty agreement. We affirm.

The Valley Bank of El Paso brought suit upon a promissory note of Gateway Investment Company and a written guaranty agreement signed on the same date as the note by Carlton C. Freed and L. F. Bauer, officers of Gateway. Only Mr. Bauer appeals from the judgment in favor of the Bank. In his answer, Mr. Bauer pled a general denial, and also affirmatively alleged that at the time the guaranty was signed, the President of the Bank represented that no reliance would be placed on the guaranty agreement. The note and guaranty agreement were received into evidence with proof that no payment had ever been made on the note. Mr. Bauer testified that he was told he would never be called upon to honor the guaranty. That testimony was contradicted by witnesses for the Bank. In the only issue answered by the jury, they found that the Bank did not make a representation to Mr. Bauer that he would not be guarantying the debt of Gateway.

The Appellant presents six points of error. The first three complain of the entry of judgment for Appellee when there was no special issue requested or answered favorably to the Bank, other than on the defensive issue of misrepresentation. The contention is presented that there should have been issues submitted to the jury as to whether or not there was a meeting of the minds on the guaranty agreement, whether or not there was a binding contract, and whether or not there was any consideration for the agreement.

Appellant did not deny the execution of the guaranty agreement, nor did he assert that the agreement was without consideration. Without a sworn plea under Rules 93(h) and (j), Tex. R. Civ. P., [Rules 93(h) and (j) are now embodied in Rules 93(7) and (9)] those issues were not before the trial Court. Since execution of the guaranty agreement was not an issue, it was only necessary that the agreement be introduced into evidence to prove up its terms. In *Safway Scaffolds Company of Houston v. Sharpstown Realty Company*, 409 S.W.2d 883 (Tex. Civ. App. — Waco 1966, no writ), the court said:

> "In the absence of a verified denial of the execution by defendants or by their authority of the written instruments upon which the pleading is founded, under Rule 93(h), Texas Rules of Civil Procedure, the instruments were received in evidence as fully proved."

The agreement as received into evidence fully proved the indemnity obligation of Mr. Bauer. There being no issue raised on execution, consideration, or ambiguity, there was no issue to present to the jury, other than the defensive issue of misrepresentation and that issue was decided adversely to Appellant. The first three points of error are overruled.

NOTES AND QUESTIONS

(1) *Sworn Denial of Execution of an Instrument.* What is the effect of a properly sworn denial of execution? The denial increases the onus of proof that is placed on the pleader's opponent. *See* Tex. R. Civ. P. 93(7) ("In the absence of such a sworn plea, the instrument shall be received in evidence as fully proved").

(2) *Authentication of Documents.* What is the usual way for authenticating documents? The easiest way is through the request for admissions. Read Tex. R. Civ. P. 198. In *Bauer*, if Bauer had made a sworn denial, Valley Bank would have sent a request for admissions asking him to admit the genuineness of the guaranty agreement. If Bauer had denied the genuineness or had sent a response detailing the reasons why he could neither admit nor deny it, Valley Bank then would have had to produce evidence in accordance with Texas Evidence Rule 901. Under the current discovery rules, a party's production of a document in response to written discovery authenticates the document for use against that party in any pretrial

proceeding or at trial unless — within ten days . . . after the producing party has actual notice that the document will be used — the party objects to the authenticity of the document. *See* Tex. R. Civ. P. 193.7.

(3) *Strict Compliance Required.* Civil Procedure Rule 93(7) requires a sworn denial of an allegation that an instrument was signed by the authority of the party who is being sued on the instrument. If a party fails to file a proper sworn denial, he admits that the contract was signed by him, or with his authority. This may be true even if the name on the contract is not that of the party being sued. Consider the following excerpt from *Baylor University Medical Center v. Van Zandt*, 620 S.W.2d 707 (Tex. Civ. App. — Dallas 1981, no writ) (discussing former Rule 93(h), now Rule 93(7)):

> [A]ppellant pleaded that its suit was on a written contract executed by appellee or an authorized agent of appellee. Appellee did not deny the execution of the contract or the allegation that he or his authorized agent signed it, as required by Tex. R. Civ. P. 93(h). Consequently, appellee has admitted that the contract was signed by him or by his authority. *Public Service Life Ins. Co. v. Copus*, 494 S.W.2d 200 (Tex. Civ. App. — Tyler 1973, no writ). Appellee contends, however, that since it is apparent from the face of the record that neither he nor his authorized agent signed the contract, it was not necessary to deny appellant's allegation under oath as required by rule 93(h). We do not agree. It is not apparent from the face of the record that neither appellee nor *his authorized agent* signed the contract sued upon. Therefore, rule 93(h) applies to this case and, because it was not complied with, appellant established all the requirements . . . [for venue] . . . by its pleadings and its tender into evidence of the contract.

If a sworn denial is properly made, the burden is on the opposing party to show that there was the requisite authority to sign; it is not enough to show the authenticity of the instrument. A brief review of the law of agency will demonstrate that proving authority is generally a more difficult task than proving authenticity.

[3] Verified Denials — Capacity

Texas law requires verification of two categories of allegations concerning capacity. Tex. R. Civ. P. 93(1), (2). The first category of allegations includes any assertion that the plaintiff lacks the legal capacity to sue or that the defendant lacks the legal capacity to be sued. *See Austin Nursing Center, Inc. v. Lovato*, 171 S.W.3d at 849 ("[M]inors and incompetents are considered to be under a legal disability and are therefore unable to sue or be sued in their individual capacities."). Actions may be brought by and against parties only if they actually or legally exist and are legally capable of being sued. Dead persons, decedent's estates, trusts, infants, and incompetents, for example, lack the capacity to sue or be sued. *See Lovato*, 171 S.W.3d at 849; *see also Ray Malooly Trust v. Juhl*, 186 S.W.3d 568, 570 (Tex. 2006). This capacity defense is relatively easy to recognize because it concerns whether the claimant is competent to prosecute any action on the claimant's own behalf and causes no particular difficulty.

The second lack of capacity defense, that the plaintiff is not entitled to recover in the capacity in which the plaintiff sued or that the defendant is not liable in the capacity in which the defendant was sued, is much more problematic. In this context, capacity refers to the authority of the party to assert or defend the particular action that is before the court, such as the legal authority of a personal representative to prosecute a decedent's cause of action, or the legal authority of a bankruptcy trustee to enforce payment obligations owed to a bankrupt.

The distinction between the second capacity defense and the defense that a claimant lacks standing is frequently difficult to identify because both of the defenses contend that the claimant is the wrong person to bring the action. The difficulty is reflected in the interpretation of the second capacity defense that is expressed in a line of Texas cases usually identified with the Texas Supreme Court's opinion in *Pledger v. Schoellkopf*, 762 S.W.2d 145 (Tex. 1988).

In that case, Pledger brought suit against Hunt and Schoellkopf for fraud and tortious interference. The jury returned a verdict for Pledger and judgment was rendered on the verdict. On appeal, the Dallas Court of Appeals reversed the trial court's judgment holding that the causes of action asserted by Pledger belonged to Midway Aircraft Sales, Inc., a corporation in which Pledger, Schoellkopf, and Hunt were shareholders. The Dallas Court reasoned that the Schoellkopfs had not waived this defense by failing to file a verified denial of Pledger's capacity to prosecute the corporate cause of action against them because Pledger was "not suing in any capacity other than his own" and Pledger did not establish that he suffered any damages. The Texas Supreme Court reversed. The Court explained that the Dallas Court's holding that "Rule 93(2) applies only when a party is seeking recovery in a representative capacity" was too narrow an interpretation. Instead, the Court ruled that "Rule 93(2) requires that a verified plea be filed anytime" the record does not affirmatively demonstrate the "plaintiff's or defendant's right to bring suit or be sued in whatever capacity he is suing. TEX. R. CIV. P. 93(2). Its application is not limited to cases of representative capacity only. The rule means just what it says." If Pledger had been seeking damages for Midway, as its representative, it could have been much easier to accept the Supreme Court's per curiam opinion because the issue clearly would be "authority to act for Midway." But there is no question that the Court went further by not limiting the rule's application to cases of representative capacity, presumably to avoid arguments about authority.

Thus, in the absence of a sworn denial of capacity, the claimant's ownership of the claim is presumed or established. The ownership of the claim is a question of capacity, not one of the elements of the plaintiff's claim, and certainly not a question of standing. The Texas Supreme Court's per curiam opinion flatly rejects the court of appeals' reasoning that "[t]he burden is on the plaintiff to prove the elements of his claim, including his ownership of it. The defendant is not burdened with disproving that element of the plaintiff's claim."

The Texas Supreme Court has also held that if a defendant is sued individually along with the defendant's corporation and there is no verified denial of individual liability, then the individual's capacity to be sued is admitted. Accordingly, the individual defendant may be held liable in either an individual or a corporate capacity if there is evidence to support such a judgment. *W.O.S. Constr. Co. v. Hanyard*, 684 S.W.2d 675, 676 (Tex. 1985); *see also Light v. Wilson*, 663 S.W.2d 813,

814 (Tex. 1983) (merits of claim, on other hand, are placed in issue by general denial).

Under the analysis made in these cases, a failure to deny that the plaintiff has sued in the right capacity or that the defendant has been sued in the right capacity obviates the need to prove the plaintiff's ownership of the claim or the basis, like alter ego, for the defendant's liability on the claim, but not the need to prove the validity of the claim itself.

Texas courts have recognized the need to plead the capacity defense in a number of cases. For example, in *The Ray Malooly Trust v. Juhl*, 186 S.W.3d 568 (Tex. 2006), the Texas Supreme Court held that while suits against a trust must be brought against its legal representative — the trustee — and not against the trust itself, the Malooly Trust waived that objection by failing to file a timely verified denial of capacity under Rule 93(1). Similarly, the court in *McBride v. Mail Sys. Coordinator's Panel*, 2008 Tex. App. LEXIS 3906 (Tex. App. — Corpus Christi 2008, no pet.), held that a state agency wanting to claim that it was not a separate legal entity had to raise that defense with a sworn denial of capacity. In *Cox v. Jale Group, Inc.*, 2009 Tex. App. LEXIS 2185 (Tex. App. — Dallas 2009, no pet.), the court noted that shareholders claiming that they were not liable in their individual capacities had to raise that issue with a sworn denial of capacity, without which they could not raise the capacity issue on appeal.

PRACTICE EXERCISE #17
RELATION OF GENERAL DENIALS TO OTHER DEFENSES

Suppose A sues B, who, according to A's allegations, guaranteed C's note to A under the terms of a written guaranty agreement. If B files a general denial, will B be able to introduce evidence that:

(1) The written guaranty is without consideration;

(2) B did not sign the guaranty;

(3) C had paid the note?

[H] Affirmative Defenses

Read Tex. R. Civ. P. 94.

Rule 94 requires that affirmative defenses be pleaded; if they are not, they cannot be raised. The rule also contains a partial list of affirmative defenses, but there are others that are not listed in the rule. Particularly with newer causes of action, it is not always clear whether something is an element of the plaintiff's claim or whether its opposite is part of defendant's affirmative defense. In making the decision, the court will consider things like statutory language, efficiency, probabilities, and public policy. For example, in *Eckman v. Centennial Savings Bank*, 784 S.W.2d 672 (Tex. 1990), the court held that the defendant has the burden to plead and prove the business consumer exception to the Deceptive Trade Practices Act because it is not likely to arise often [and so it would be inefficient to force all plaintiffs to disprove it]; because of the Act's policy to protect consumers; because most plaintiffs will not have $25 million in assets; and because the plaintiff's financial status should not normally be presented to the jury.

Sometimes an affirmative defense will also be subject to the sworn denial requirements of Rule 93. What happens when such an affirmative defense is not made under oath? And can this kind of pleading defect be waived?

ECHOLS v. BLOOM

485 S.W.2d 798 (Tex. Civ. App. — Houston [14th Dist.] 1972, writ ref'd n.r.e.)

BARRON, J.

This suit was brought by appellant Robert Echols for specific performance of an alleged earnest money contract for the sale of a tract of realty. In a trial before the court judgment was rendered in favor of appellees denying the relief sought. The trial court filed requested findings of fact and conclusions of law. In these the court characterized the instrument in question as a contract containing an "option offer" and it found that (1) the option offer was without valuable consideration and was therefore unenforceable, (2) that the offer of sale was withdrawn prior to acceptance, (3) that the entire instrument was procured by fraudulent representations, (4) that the parties contracted while operating under a mutual mistake of fact as to the time for execution of the instrument and (5) that the description of the realty to be conveyed was impermissibly vague.

Appellant's recourse to this Court seeks to reverse the judgment adverse to him by attacking each of the findings recounted above. We think that the issues of consideration for the option and withdrawal of the offer prior to acceptance are dispositive.

The contract of sale included the following paragraph:

> (2) Sellers are to execute this contract as an offer to Buyer and Buyer is to have the right to accept or reject such offer for fourteen (14) days from the date hereof and Seller agrees that such offer shall be irrevocable and shall be binding upon Sellers. If Buyer notifies Sellers within said fourteen (14) day period of Buyer's intention to accept such offer this contract shall be placed with the American Title Company with instructions to proceed forthwith.

This provision embodies a formal offer to sell real estate to appellant, with a concurrent promise by appellees to keep the offer open for two weeks. In other words, two transactions appear — an ordinary offer to sell and a contract not to revoke that offer or to impede performance by conveyance to a third person.

It is axiomatic that to be valid and enforceable a contract establishing an option must be supported by consideration. Often the consideration is, as here, a sum of money to be regarded as a parcel of the total purchase price in the event the option-holder elects to buy. If an option is contained in a contract which itself is supported by a sufficient consideration, no independent consideration for the option itself need appear. However, if no consideration in fact passes, the option giver has power of revocation just as in the case of other revocable offers.

The instrument presently before us was signed and dated July 11, 1969. By its terms appellant was given the power of accepting appellees' offer for fourteen days thereafter, that is, up to and including July 25, 1969. The only possible consideration for such option is the sum of $500 earnest money recited as deposited with a title company as escrow agent "upon the execution hereof." The record conclusively demonstrates that the $500 was not tendered and accepted until July 25, 1969, the last day of the option period. Thus, for the preceding thirteen days of that period no consideration passed in support of the option agreement. As documented above, the absence of consideration rendered the option unenforceable by appellant during that time period. Although consideration for a contract of sale can serve as consideration for an included option agreement as well, we have found no case involving options within sales contracts which enforced the option and held the offer of sale irrevocable from its inception where the contract consideration did not pass until the option period was virtually extinguished.

Appellant contends that, despite the above, appellees failed to file a verified plea of failure of consideration as required by Tex. R. Civ. P. 93(j) [Rule 93(j) is now embodied in Rule 93(9)]. However, appellant failed to except to the nonverification of appellees' pleadings and thus waived his objection. Tex. R. Civ. P. 90; *Smith v. Walters*, 468 S.W.2d 889 (Tex. Civ. App. — Dallas 1971, no writ). It is true that, under Tex. R. Civ. P. 94, failure of consideration must be affirmatively pleaded. We think appellees' first amended answer probably contains a sufficient affirmative plea of failure of consideration. In paragraph I appellees alleged that appellants "in fact, had not deposited such sum ($500)," and in the succeeding paragraph they alleged that, because of false representations that $500 had been paid, appellees "were under the impression that there was consideration for the Contract . . . ." Even so, appellant has waived any complaint under Rule 94 by failing to object. Rather, the issue of failure of consideration appears to have been tried by consent. Tex. R. Civ. P. 67 . . . .

Inasmuch as no enforceable option agreement was consummated, appellees were empowered to revoke their offer of sale prior to appellant's acceptance. Because we are not disposed to disturb the trial court's finding that no acceptance preceded revocation by Dr. Bloom, the trial court's judgment is affirmed.

NOTES AND QUESTIONS

(1) *Affirmative Defenses.* Under Texas law, the party pleading the affirmative defense also has the burden of production and persuasion. While there are exceptions, in almost all cases the defendant has both the burden to plead and the burden to prove an affirmative defense.

(2) *Want of Consideration.* Sometimes it is substantive law that determines whether a defensive theory is an affirmative defense or merely a denial. For example, want of consideration is an affirmative defense in written contract cases. *See Wright v. Robert & St. John Motor Co.*, 58 S.W.2d 67 (Tex. 1933). It therefore must be pleaded as an affirmative defense, and must be verified under Rule 93(9).

(3) *Verified Affirmative Defenses.* What is the logic behind requiring a verification of some affirmative defenses? Is the "onus of proof" shifted by a verified avoidance; in other words, when a defense is properly verified, does it force the plaintiff to prove something that it would otherwise not need to prove? Is the failure to verify waivable at the pleading stage? [Hint: review the court's discussion of waiver and trial by consent in *Echols*.]

(4) *Waiver and the Onus of Proof.* When the defective plea: 1) is a denial; and 2) if the denial were effective, it would impose additional proof requirements on plaintiff; then 3) a special exception is not required to preserve the right to complain about the effective denial. Instead, plaintiff can preserve the right to complain about the defective denial by objecting at trial to evidence raising the denial.

(5) *Waiver and Winning at Trial.* In addition, the existence (or not) of waiver may depend on which party won at trial. Rule 90 provides that waiver is only by "the party seeking reversal on such account."

§ 6.06 AMENDED AND SUPPLEMENTAL PLEADINGS

[A] Amended Pleadings

Read Tex. R. Civ. P. 62-7.

The function of an amended pleading is to add something to or withdraw something from what had been previously pleaded to correct what had been incorrectly stated by the party making the amendment, or to plead new matter that constitutes an additional claim or defense permissible to the action. *See* Tex. R. Civ. P. 62. An amended pleading supersedes its predecessor. Amended pleadings are liberally permitted to be filed "at such times as not to operate as a surprise to the opposite party; provided, that any pleadings, responses or pleas offered for filing within seven days of the date of trial or thereafter . . . shall be filed only after leave of the judge is obtained." *See* Tex. R. Civ. P. 63. *See also Lee v. Key West Towers, Inc.*, 783 S.W.2d 586, 588 (Tex. 1989). The judge may alter the time period in a pretrial order. *See* Tex. R. Civ. P. 63, 66. In several counties, the period has been modified by local rules of procedure.

When a party seeks to amend a pleading within seven days of the date of trial or during the trial (*see* Tex. R. Civ. P. 66) the objecting party must make a complaint to the effect that the new matter constitutes a "surprise" (*see* Tex. R. Civ. P. 63) or otherwise "satisfy the court that the allowance of such amendment would prejudice him in maintaining his action or defense upon the merits." *See* Tex. R. Civ. P. 66. Apparently, in order to test the sincerity of the objecting party, case law requires that party to seek a continuance to complain on appeal that the trial court erred in permitting the amendment. *Myers v. King*, 506 S.W.2d 705 (Tex. Civ. App. — Houston [1st Dist.] 1974, writ ref'd n.r.e.).

In a case tried to a jury, an opposing party need not have objected to the introduction of testimony as a prerequisite to making a complaint concerning the absence of an "issue" from the opposing party's pleadings. In other words, an issue is not tried by implied consent of the parties in a jury case merely because no objection to the admissibility of the testimony concerning the issue was made at the proper time. *See* Tex. R. Civ. P. 67. On the other hand, if no objection is made to the testimony at the proper time, the party who introduced it would ordinarily be entitled to a trial amendment pursuant to Civil Procedure Rule 66 because the "objecting party" would ordinarily be unable to "satisfy the court that the allowance of such amendment would prejudice him . . . ." Tex. R. Civ. P. 66. Rule 67 also provides that written pleadings, before the time of submission, are necessary to the submission of jury questions, as is provided in Civil Procedure Rules 277 and 279. *See* Tex. R. Civ. P. 67. This means that written pleadings are necessary to support a party's right to the submission of jury questions on unpleaded issues even if they are tried by consent. *See Elbaor v. Smith*, 845 S.W.2d 240, 243–44 (Tex. 1992); *Gibbins v. Berlin*, 162 S.W.3d 335, 340–42 (Tex. App. — Fort Worth 2005, no pet.).

In a non-jury case, because there is no submission of jury questions, it appears that "trial by implied consent" may occur merely by virtue of the failure to object at the time the testimony, not otherwise raised by the pleadings of the offering party, introduced without objection. *See Gadd v. Lynch*, 258 S.W.2d 168 (Tex. Civ. App. — San Antonio 1953, writ ref'd). For an excellent discussion of the relationship of the trial amendment rule (Tex. R. Civ. P. 66) to the rule governing amendments to conform issues tried without objection (Tex. R. Civ. P. 67), *see* William T. Deffebach & George E. Brown, *Waiver of Pleading Defects*, 36 Tex. L. Rev. 459 (1958).

The two cases that follow deal with issues of extremely late attempts to secure trial amendments. What should determine whether a request to amend has come too late?

BURNETT v. FILE

552 S.W.2d 955 (Tex. Civ. App. — Waco 1977, writ ref'd n.r.e.)

James, J.

This is an appeal by Plaintiff Burnett from a take nothing judgment rendered against him on a jury verdict, in a suit for personal injuries resulting from an automobile rear-end collision. We affirm the judgment of the trial court.

Plaintiff-Appellant O. J. Burnett sued Defendant-Appellee Virgil E. File for personal injuries allegedly sustained by Plaintiff-Appellant growing out of an automobile accident wherein Defendant-Appellee File allegedly rearended Plaintiff-Appellant Burnett.

Trial was to a jury, which found that Plaintiff-Appellant Burnett was not injured as a result of the collision, in Answer to Special Issue No. 1. Pursuant to said verdict, the trial court entered judgment that Plaintiff-Appellant take nothing.

Plaintiff-Appellant asserts error on the part of the trial court (1) in refusing Plaintiff leave to file a trial amendment, (2) in refusing to submit the definition of "injury" as submitted by Plaintiff, (3) in submitting an erroneous definition of "injury" to the jury, (4) in conditionally submitting Special Issues Nos. 2 through 14 on a positive finding of Special Issue No. 1, and (5) that the jury's answer to Special Issue No. 1 is factually insufficient. We overrule all of Plaintiff's points of error and affirm.

The basis of this suit is an alleged rearend collision that occurred on March 9, 1974, near the intersection of Irving and Hampton Boulevards in Dallas County. Plaintiff was stopped for traffic in front of him at that intersection when he was allegedly hit from the rear by the automobile driven by the Defendant. Plaintiff's Original Petition in this case was filed on July 31, 1974. In October 1974, Defendant filed its answer in the case. Plaintiff filed his Second Amended Original Petition on March 20, 1976, which is the pleading he went to trial upon. In none of said pleadings did Plaintiff allege any aggravation of any pre-existing condition. In other words, in said pleadings Plaintiff alleged personal injuries growing out of the accident of March 9, 1974.

The case proceeded to trial on April 12, 1976, and the jury returned a verdict on April 13, 1976, finding that Plaintiff sustained no injury in the accident. After Plaintiff had rested his case and near the end of the trial, Plaintiff's counsel "served notice" that he intended to file a Trial Amendment of some sort. Plaintiff did tender a Trial Amendment some time after both parties had closed and prior to the submission of the court's charge to the jury. By said Trial Amendment the Plaintiff alleged for the first time that on the occasion of the March 9, 1974, accident in question, he was suffering from a "pre-existing disease or condition" which was "incited, accelerated, and/or aggravated" by the accident in question. Defendant objected to the filing of said Trial Amendment alleging surprise, and because the case was tried on the theory of an original injury, whereupon the trial court denied Plaintiff leave to file such Trial Amendment.

Plaintiff-Appellant contends the trial court abused its discretion in denying him leave to file such Trial Amendment. We do not agree.

The filing of a Trial Amendment is within the sound discretion of the trial court and unless the trial court clearly abuses that discretion no reversible error is shown. Rule 66, Texas Rules of Civil Procedure; *Victory v. State* (Tex. 1942) 158 S.W.2d 760, 763.

The instant case was pleaded by Plaintiff and tried upon the theory that Plaintiff sustained an original injury as the result of the accident of March 9, 1974. It was after both sides had closed and before the court's charge was submitted to the jury that Plaintiff sought leave from the trial court to file the Trial Amendment in question. Had same been granted, it would have changed the entire nature and complexion of the lawsuit. Moreover, there was no explanation by the Plaintiff as to why he was not aware of the "aggravation" basis of his Trial Amendment sooner. In the language of our Supreme Court: "to require the trial court to permit amendments such as the one filed in this case would disrupt orderly procedure and lead to frequent interruptions and interminable delay in concluding expensive jury trials. McDonald's Texas Civil Practice; vol. 2, page 737." *Westinghouse Electric Corp. v. Pierce* (Tex. 1954) 271 S.W.2d 422; *King v. Skelly* (Tex. 1970) 452 S.W.2d 691. Here, the Defendant had the right to assume that the case made by the pleadings and testimony was the case and the only case he was called upon to defend and to prepare his defense accordingly.

Under the record before us, we cannot say the trial court abused its discretion in denying leave to Plaintiff to file the Trial Amendment.

Special Issue No. 1 as submitted to the jury inquired:

> "Do you find from a preponderance of the evidence that O. J. Burnett was injured as a result of the occurrence on March 9, 1974?
>
> "You are instructed that a person is "injured" if he receives damage or harm to the physical structure of the body.
>
> "Answer 'we do' or 'we do not.' To this issue the jury answered 'we do not.' "

Then the court instructed the jury that "if you have answered the above issue 'we do' then you will answer Issues Numbers 2, 4, 6, 8, 10, 12, and 14; otherwise, do not answer them." In this connection, Issues Nos. 2 through 14 were issues inquiring into primary negligence (and proximate cause) of Defendant together with a damage issue.

Plaintiff requested that the trial court define "injury" to the jury as follows:

"You are instructed that a person is 'injured' if he receives damage or harm to the physical structure of the body. Such damage or harm includes such diseases and infections as naturally result therefrom, and the incitement, acceleration, or aggravation of any previously existing disease or condition by reason of such damage or harm to the physical structure of the body."

The trial court refused to submit Plaintiff's proffered definition of "injury," which refusal Plaintiff asserts as error. As stated above, Plaintiff had no pleadings to support such a definition.

However, Plaintiff strongly urges that the issue of "aggravation" was tried by implied consent on the part of the Defendant, under the provisions of Rule 67, Texas Rules of Civil Procedure. We do not agree. The record clearly establishes the Defendant's objection to the Trial Amendment and requested instructions on aggravation as hereinabove set out. In *Harkey v. Texas Employers Ins. Assn.* (Tex. 1948) 208 S.W.2d 919, our Supreme Court held that although the Defendant did not object to the testimony relative to an issue but did object to its submission because it was not pleaded, it could not be held that the issue was tried by consent. In that case the Defendant offered no objection to testimony on an essential issue, but it did object to its submission because it was not pleaded. The Supreme Court held that the issue could not be presumed to have been tried by consent and that submission of such unpleaded essential issue over proper objection constituted reversible error.

In the case at bar, under the record before us, the rule enunciated in *Harkey* applies, and it cannot be said that the issue of aggravation was tried by implied consent . . . .

Finding no reversible error in the record we affirm the trial court's judgment.

GREENHALGH v. SERVICE LLOYDS INS. CO.

787 S.W.2d 938 (Tex. 1990)

Mauzy, J.

The issue in this case is whether a trial court abuses its discretion by allowing a post-verdict amendment increasing the amount of damages in Plaintiff's pleadings to conform to the amount awarded by the jury when Defendant presents no evidence of surprise or prejudice. We hold that under Texas Rules of Civil Procedure 63 and 66, a trial court must allow a trial amendment that increases the amount of damages sought in the pleadings to that found by the jury unless the opposing party presents evidence of prejudice or surprise.

Plaintiff Greenhalgh and Service Lloyds Insurance Company (Service Lloyds), his workers' compensation carrier, agreed to a settlement of Greenhalgh's workers' compensation claim. However, Service Lloyds refused to pay Greenhalgh's medical expenses as required by the settlement. Greenhalgh subsequently filed this bad-faith insurance claim against Service Lloyds. The jury found in favor of Greenhalgh on each of his theories of recovery: breach of the duty of good faith and fair dealing, bad-faith insurance practices, gross negligence, negligence, and intentional infliction of emotional distress. Greenhalgh pleaded for $10,000 in actual damages and $100,000 in punitive damages; the jury awarded $8,000 in actual damages and $128,000 in punitive damages.

Because Greenhalgh had pleaded for only $100,000 in punitive damages, he requested leave to amend his pleadings to conform the amount of damages to that found by the jury and supported by the evidence. In its responsive motion, Service Lloyds alleged that the amendment was prejudicial because Service Lloyds had relied on the $100,000 amount in Plaintiff's pleadings in preparing for trial and in deciding whether to settle the case. The trial court allowed the post-verdict amendment. The court of appeals held that the trial court abused its discretion in allowing the amendment and reduced the punitive damages to $100,000.

The court of appeals reasoned that "because a defendant receives notice of the upper limit of punitive damages only by way of pleadings, it is an abuse of discretion to allow a post-verdict trial amendment increasing punitive damages when proper objections are made." 771 S.W.2d 688, 697. We disagree. The holding of the court of appeals ignores the mandates of the procedural rules regarding amendment of pleadings during trial. *See* Tex. R. Civ. P. 63 and 66.

Not only did the trial court not abuse its discretion in granting the amendment, it would have been an abuse of discretion if the trial court had refused the amendment. Under Rules 63 and 66 a trial court has no discretion to refuse an amendment unless: 1) the opposing party presents evidence of surprise or prejudice, Tex. R. Civ. P. 63 and 66; *Hardin v. Hardin*, 597 S.W.2d 347, 350–51 (Tex. 1980) (Campbell, J., concurring); *see Food Source, Inc. v. Zurich Ins. Co.*, 751 S.W.2d 596, 599 (Tex. App. — Dallas 1988, writ denied); or 2) the amendment asserts a new cause of action or defense, and thus is prejudicial on its face, and the opposing party objects to the amendment. *Hardin v. Hardin*, 597 S.W.2d 347 (Tex. 1980). The burden of showing prejudice or surprise rests on the party resisting the amendment. *Patino v. Texas Employers Insurance Association*, 491 S.W.2d 754, 756 (Tex. Civ. App. — Austin 1973, writ ref'd n.r.e.). Because Greenhalgh's amendment raised no new substantive matters and because there was no showing of surprise or prejudice by Service Lloyds, the trial court properly granted leave to file the amendment.

Service Lloyds relies on appellate court holdings that a trial court abuses its discretion in allowing a post-verdict amendment increasing damages to conform to the verdict. *Burk Royalty Co. v. Walls*, 596 S.W.2d 932, 938 (Tex. Civ. App. — Fort Worth 1980, *aff'd on other grounds*, 616 S.W.2d 911 (Tex. 1981); *Winn-Dixie Texas, Inc. v. Buck*, 719 S.W.2d 251, 255 (Tex. App. — Fort Worth 1986, no writ). We disapprove these holdings because they directly conflict with Rules 63 and 66.

TEXAS RULES OF CIVIL PROCEDURE 63 and 66

It is well established that a party may amend its pleading after verdict but before judgment, *American Produce & Vegetable Co. v. J.D. Campisi's Italian Restaurant*, 533 S.W.2d 380, 386 (Tex. Civ. App. — Tyler 1975, writ ref'd n.r.e.). Rule 63 states:

> Parties may amend their pleadings, . . . as they may desire by filing such pleas with the clerk at such time as not to operate as a surprise to the opposite party; provided, that any amendment offered for filing within seven days of the date of trial *or thereafter*, . . . shall be filed only after leave of the judge is obtained, *which leave shall be granted by the judge unless there is a showing that such amendment will operate as a surprise* of the opposite party.

(Emphasis added).

The language of Rule 63 makes it clear that without a showing of surprise the trial court must grant leave for a party to file the amendment when requested within seven days of trial or thereafter. Thus, a party's right to amend under Rule 63 is subject only to the opposing party's right to show surprise. *Hardin v. Hardin*, 597 S.W.2d 347, 349 (Tex. 1980). However, the trial court may conclude that the amendment is on its face calculated to surprise or that the amendment would reshape the cause of action, prejudicing the opposing party and unnecessarily delaying the trial. *Id.*

An amended pleading that changes only the amount of damages sought does not automatically operate as surprise within the contemplation of Rule 63. *See Drury v. Reeves*, 539 S.W.2d 390, 394 (Tex. Civ. App. — Austin 1976, no writ). A party opposing an amendment increasing damages must present evidence to show that the increase resulted in surprise. Because Service Lloyds presented no evidence of surprise, the trial court properly allowed the amendment as required under Rule 63.

Rule 66 further confirms the propriety of the trial court's granting leave for Greenhalgh to file his amendment. Rule 66 provides in part:

> If during the trial any defect, fault or omission in a pleading, either of form or substance, is called to the attention of the court, the court may

allow the pleadings to be amended and *shall do so freely* when the presentation of the merits of the action will be subserved thereby and the objecting party fails to satisfy the court that the allowance of such amendment would prejudice him in maintaining his action or defense upon the merits.

(Emphasis added). In *Vermillion v. Haynes*, 215 S.W.2d 605, 609 (Tex. 1948), this Court held that the trial court abused its discretion in denying a trial amendment filed after the close of evidence in a nonjury trial. Rule 66 "directs that the court shall 'freely' allow an amendment" when it subserves the merits of the case and the opposing party fails to show prejudice. *Id.*

The "defect" that Greenhalgh sought to cure in his amendment was to conform his pleadings to the evidence and jury findings on punitive damages. Service Lloyds failed to complain in the trial court that the evidence did not support the jury's finding on punitive damages — nor has it made this argument on appeal. We have held that when objections carry neither suggestion nor hint that the opposing party was in any manner surprised or prejudiced, both the spirit and the intent of Rule 66 require that the amendment be permitted. *Id.* Thus the trial court properly allowed the amendment under Rules 63 and 66.

We hold that in the absence of a showing of surprise or prejudice by an opposing party, a trial court must grant leave to a party to amend his or her pleadings to conform the amount of damages requested to that awarded by the jury. We reverse the judgment of the court of appeals and affirm the judgment of the trial court.

[The concurring opinion of Justice Hecht is omitted.]

NOTES AND QUESTIONS

(1) *The Basis for the Amendment.* Consider the following excerpt from *Westinghouse Electric Corp. v. Pierce*, 271 S.W.2d 422, 424–25 (Tex. 1954):

> We do not regard *Vermillion v. Haynes*, 215 S.W.2d 605, as controlling here. In that case, trial was before the court without a jury. It involved a claim for rents. After the close of the testimony and before judgment, the defendant tendered a trial amendment setting up for the first time the defense of limitations. This court held that the trial judge abused his discretion in refusing to allow the amendment. There the amendment sought only to assert a defense in law to facts already established, while here the effort was to change the fact basis of the suit; there the trial was before the court, the new defense offered requiring only a judicial decision of a new law question not theretofore in the suit, while here trial was to a jury, the new matter being entirely factual and requiring an entire reshaping of the defense on the new facts.

> Similarly, the recovery of prejudgment interest does not require any evidentiary proof at trial. It simply requires a mechanical application of the proper formula by the trial court after the verdict has been returned. "This being the case, [the] trial amendment could not have caused any surprise or prejudice . . . . We hold the trial court's refusal of the amendment was

arbitrary and unreasonable and therefore an abuse of discretion."

(2) *Need for Post-Verdict Amendments.* A post-verdict amendment must be made when damages awarded by the jury exceed the amount alleged by the plaintiff. In the absence of such a request, the judgment must conform to the pleadings. *Picon Transp., Inc. v. Pomerantz*, 814 S.W.2d 489, 490 (Tex. App. — Dallas 1991, writ denied). Note, however, that under current law a plaintiff must plead a discovery level, and if the plaintiff chooses Level 1 (suits involving $50,000 or less), he or she may *not* amend after verdict to recover an amount higher than $50,000. *See* Tex. R. Civ. P. 190, Comment 2 (stating that *Greenhalgh* does not apply to such cases).

(3) *Amending Defective Denials.* The cases above involve plaintiffs attempting to amend their petitions. A defendant may also wish to amend its answer. For example, defendant may have failed to verify a special denial. The Texas Supreme Court discussed a request to amend the answer less than seven days before trial in *Chapin & Chapin v. Texas Sand & Gravel*, 844 S.W.2d 664, 665 (Tex. 1992):

> By adding a verified denial in this case, Chapin did not change a single substantive issue for trial. Chapin's position throughout had been that it has already paid for all it got. The only change was procedural: Texas Sand would have been obliged to rebut Chapin's substantive defense and could not simply insist [on] judgment on the pleadings. If Texas Sand had relied upon the absence of a verified denial to the extent that it was unprepared to proceed to trial and would thus have been prejudiced by Chapin's amendment, it would have been entitled to a continuance. However, Texas Sand's counsel stated that he was prepared to prove that all deliveries had been made or accounted for and that the amount claimed was owed. In these circumstances . . . we conclude that the trial court's refusal to allow Chapin to verify its denial was an abuse of discretion.

[B] Supplemental Petitions and Answers

Read Tex. R. Civ. P. 69, 78, 82, 83.

The function of supplemental petitions and answers is limited. They are used to respond to "new matter" contained in the last preceding pleading of the adverse party. *See* Tex. R. Civ. P. 69. Under Texas procedure, unlike in federal court, a party sometimes needs to respond to affirmative defenses if more than a general denial is required. Their supplemental pleading can thus become a kind of affirmative defense to the affirmative defense. What happens if a party fails to file these supplemental pleas?

ROYAL TYPEWRITER CO. v. VESTAL

572 S.W.2d 377 (Tex. Civ. App. — Houston [14th Dist.] 1978, no writ)

Coulson, J.

Appellant, Royal Typewriter Company, plaintiff below, appeals from a take nothing judgment following a nonjury trial in a suit on a contract against appellees

Vestal, Middlebrook, and U. S. Land Development Company, defendants below. Appellant conceded at argument that Middlebrook is not a party to this appeal. We affirm.

On December 5, 1972, a contract was executed by Royal, purportedly with U. S. Land Development Company, for the rental of a copying machine. The agreement was signed by one "Julian Holsten" whose title, as written on the agreement, was "Sales Mgr." The copier was installed on December 8, 1972. On February 21, 1975, Royal filed suit against Vestal, Middlebrook, and U. S. Land Development, alleging that "the Defendants did . . . make and execute" the rental agreement, and that payments totaling $1,254.20 were due and not paid. Royal thus asserted damages resulting from breach of a contract with defendants.

Defendants, in addition to a general denial, pled that they did not execute the contract in question and were not indebted to Royal. Royal filed no additional pleadings. At argument Royal conceded that the actual contract had not been proved and that ratification was the only issue upon which they rely in their appeal to bind defendants. Royal had requested additional findings of fact and conclusions of law on the issue of ratification. The trial judge refused to make any additional findings or conclusions on that issue. We conclude that Royal was not entitled to such additional findings, and cannot prevail upon the theory of ratification in this appeal because ratification was not pled.

The Supreme Court of Texas has held that ratification is a plea in avoidance and thus is an affirmative defense which, in the absence of trial by consent, is waived if not affirmatively pled under Rule 94, Texas Rules of Civil Procedure. *Petroleum Anchor Equipment, Inc. v. Tyra*, 419 S.W.2d 829, 835 (Tex. 1967). The record before this court does not indicate that the issue of ratification was tried by consent. Rule 94 requires that "[i]n pleading to a preceding pleading, a party shall set forth affirmatively . . . any . . . matter constituting an avoidance or affirmative defense." The rule itself is not limited to "defendants" but applies to all parties. When a plaintiff desires to rely on an affirmative matter in avoidance of a defense pled in the defendant's answer, he must allege it in a supplemental petition, unless it is already put in issue by the petition. Rule 94 thus imposes on the plaintiff the requirement that he plead any matter in avoidance on which he intends to rely.

In the case before us, under these principles, once the defendants pled that they did not execute the contract, it then became incumbent upon Royal to file a supplemental pleading asserting ratification if it intended to rely upon that as a defense to defendants' denial of the contract. The purpose of requiring the pleading of affirmative defense is to put the other party on notice of the matters to be relied on and to enable him to ascertain what proof he may need to meet such defenses. In this case defendants asserted, and the evidence supported the conclusion, that they did not make the contract. The contract was signed by a person not a party to the suit. Royal did not establish any actual or apparent authority of Holsten to execute the contract. Thus the contract itself did not bind defendants. After the trial was concluded, and judgment handed down, Royal attempted to obtain a finding on ratification. The trial judge properly refused to make such a finding, and Royal has no basis on which to persuade this court to make a finding on the affirmative defense of ratification which it neglected to plead. The judgment of the trial court is affirmed.

NOTES AND QUESTIONS

(1) *Comparison to Federal Rule.* Federal Rule of Civil Procedure 8(b)(6) expressly provides that "[a]n allegation — other than one relating to the amount of damages — is admitted if a responsive pleading is required and the allegation is not denied. If a responsive pleading is not required, an allegation is considered denied or avoided." Federal Rule 7 allows a reply to an answer only if the court orders one.

(2) *Incorrect Use of Supplemental Pleadings.* If a party wishes to change something in its pleadings, amendment and supplementation are not interchangeable. In *Sixth RMA Partners, L.P. v. Sibley*, 111 S.W.3d 46, 53–54 (Tex. 2003), a partnership sued in its assumed name rather than its legal name. It attempted to correct this problem in its "second supplemental petition." The Supreme Court held that this was an incorrect use of supplementation procedure. Citing long-established principles, the Court compared supplementation and amendments:

> Under the prescribed practice in the district and county courts the original and the supplemental pleadings "constitute separate and distinct parts of the pleading of each party," the former being for the purpose of stating or defending against the cause of action, and the latter for the purpose of replying to the allegations of the opposing party immediately preceding them; whereas an amendment to either, "as contradistinguished from a supplemental petition or answer," is designed to "add something to, or withdraw something from" the amending party's own pleading, so as to cure its deficiencies.

(quoting *Glenn v. Dallas County Bois D'Arc Island Levee District*, 268 S.W. 452 (Tex. 1925)). Therefore, a supplemental pleading would only have been the correct vehicle to correct the plaintiff's name if the name change had been a response to a factual or legal allegation of the defendant's preceding pleading. The factual allegations regarding the plaintiff's true name would properly have been set forth in amended original pleadings. The Supreme Court also held that use of the wrong pleading device was merely a defect of form, and so the defendant's failure to use a timely and specific special exception to point out the problem waived it. *Id.* at 55.

PRACTICE EXERCISE #18

Civil Procedure Rule 94 is entitled "Affirmative Defenses." When is it necessary for a *plaintiff* to assert a "matter constituting an avoidance or affirmative defense"? Read Tex. R. Civ. P. 82.

Suppose A sues B on a promissory note. B files a general denial and alleges that A executed a written release and attaches it to her answer.

(1) If A contends that she did not sign the release, must A file a supplemental petition? Why?

(2) If A contends that the release was without consideration, must A file a supplemental petition? Why?

(3) If A contends the release was procured by fraud, must A file a supplemental petition? Why?

§ 6.07 SPECIALIZED PLEADING FORMS

[A] The Sworn Account Petition

A "sworn account" is a specialized kind of suit on a debt. Traditionally, if the plaintiff pleads it correctly, the defendant would be held to have admitted the account unless it was denied under oath and in exactly the right language. While many of the technicalities have been relaxed in 1984 amendments to Rule 185 (for example, it is no longer necessary to obsess over whether to deny the account is "just or true" or that it is "just and true"), the specialized form remains and failure to file a proper sworn denial can have dire consequences. Should the lack of technically correct pleading allow a party to lose its case? What if the party is not represented by a lawyer?

Read Tex. R. Civ. P. 185.

PANDITI v. APOSTLE

180 S.W.3d 924 (Tex. App. — Dallas 2006, no pet.)

Lang, J.

R.K. Panditi, pro se, appeals the trial court's summary judgment in favor of James N. Apostle, plaintiff below. Apostle has not filed a brief in this appeal. On appeal, Panditi argues the trial court erred when it granted traditional summary judgment in favor of Apostle because Apostle did not properly plead his suit on a sworn account. We conclude the trial court did not err when it granted summary judgment in favor of Apostle. The trial court's summary judgment is affirmed.

I. FACTUAL AND PROCEDURAL BACKGROUND

Apostle, an attorney who formerly represented Panditi, filed a lawsuit against Panditi for breach of contract and a suit on a sworn account to collect his unpaid legal fees as well as attorney's fees incurred in bringing the instant suit for collection. Apostle moved for traditional summary judgment on his sworn account claim arguing Panditi's unsworn general denial did not satisfy Texas Rules of Civil Procedure "185 and 93(1) [sic]," precluding him from denying Apostle's claim. Panditi did not file a response to Apostle's motion for summary judgment. The trial court granted summary judgment in favor of Apostle and "denied all relief not granted in the [summary] judgment." Panditi filed a motion for a new trial which was overruled by operation of law.

II. SUIT ON SWORN ACCOUNT

Panditi argues the trial court erred when it granted traditional summary judgment in favor of Apostle on the ground that Panditi failed to file a sworn denial. He contends he was not required to file a sworn denial because Apostle did not properly plead his suit on a sworn account. Specifically, he claims Apostle's sworn account was defective because Apostle failed to support his petition with evidence that his attorney's fees were reasonable and necessary, and the fees were assessed at the usual and customary rate.

A. Standard of Review

When a defendant fails to file a sworn denial, a court of appeals is limited in what it can consider to set aside a summary judgment on a sworn account because the defendant will not be permitted to dispute the plaintiff's claim. *See Price v. Pratt*, 647 S.W.2d 756, 757 (Tex. App. — Corpus Christi 1983, no writ). However, it is within the province of the court of appeals to determine, as a matter of law, whether the pleadings are sufficient on their face to constitute a sworn account. *See id.*

B. Applicable Law

Rule 185 states an open account includes, "any claim . . . for personal services rendered." *See* Tex. R. Civ. P. 185. Rule 185 is not a rule of substantive law. Rather, it is a rule of procedure regarding the evidence necessary to establish a prima facie right of recovery.

Texas Rule of Civil Procedure 185 provides that when an action is founded on an open account on which a systematic record has been kept and is supported by an affidavit, the account shall be taken as prima facie evidence of the claim, unless the party resisting the claim files a written denial under oath. Also, a plaintiff's suit on a sworn account must "reveal" any offsets made to the account. *See* Tex. R. Civ. P. 185. The account must show with reasonable certainty the name, date, and charge for each item, and provide specifics or details as to how the figures were arrived at. *See Abe I. Brilling Ins. Agency*, 601 S.W.2d 403, 405 (Tex. Civ. App. — Dallas 1980, no writ) (discussing bill for insurance premiums); *see also Powers v. Adams*, 2 S.W.3d 496, 499 (Tex. App. — Houston [14th Dist.] 1999, no pet.) (itemized monthly statements of legal services reflecting offsets, payments, and credits sufficient). Also, a suit on a sworn account must be accompanied by the affidavit of the plaintiff, his agent, or his attorney taken before an officer authorized to administer oaths. The affidavit must state the following: (1) the claim is within the knowledge of the affiant; (2) the claim is just and true; (3) the account is due; and (4) all just and lawful offsets, payments, and credits have been allowed. If there is a deficiency in the plaintiff's sworn account, the account will not constitute prima facie evidence of the debt.

A defendant resisting a suit on a sworn account must comply with the rules of pleading and timely file a verified denial or he will not be permitted to dispute the receipt of the services or the correctness of the charges. *See* Tex. R. Civ. P. 93(10), 185; *Vance v. Holloway*, 689 S.W.2d 403, 404 (Tex. 1985). A defendant's sworn denial must be written and verified by an affidavit. *See* Tex. R. Civ. P. 93(10), 185. However, a defendant is not required to file a sworn denial if the plaintiff's suit on a sworn account was not properly pleaded.

C. Application of the Law to the Facts

Attached to Apostle's petition were four statements addressed to Panditi, dated January 28, 2004, April 2, 2004, May 14, 2004, and July 20, 2004. The statements describe legal services rendered from September 10, 2003 through July 17, 2004. These four statements list the date and type of legal services rendered, the total number of hours spent on those legal services, the total fees for the professional services and expenses, and the total combined amount owed. The last statement dated July 20, 2004, lists the cumulative total fees and expenses owed as $26,684.81. Attached to Apostle's petition was his affidavit which reveals offsets by stating the balance due is $16,334.81:

> The foregoing and annexed account, claim and cause of action in favor of James N. Apostle, in the principle sum of sixteen thousand three hundred thirty four [sic] and 81/100 dollars ($16,334.81), is within the knowledge of affiant, just and true, and that it is due and unpaid and that all just and lawful offsets, payments and credits have been allowed.

Apostle's billing statements and affidavit complied with the requirements of rule 185. *See* Tex. R. Civ. P. 185. As a result, Panditi was required to file a verified denial. *See* Tex. R. Civ. P. 93(10), 185. Panditi did not file a verified denial and he was precluded from denying "the claim, or any item therein." *See* Tex. R. Civ. P. 185. Pursuant to the rules applicable to a sworn account, Apostle presented a prima facie case and was not required to offer additional proof, as argued by Panditi, that the fees and expenses were reasonable and necessary, and assessed at the usual and customary rate.

III. CONCLUSION

The trial court did not err when it granted summary judgment in favor of Apostle. The trial court's summary judgment is affirmed.

[B] Types of Claims and Procedural Requirements

It is important to know which kinds of claims may qualify as "sworn accounts," how to draft a petition to get the sworn account effect, and how to effectively contest sworn account petitions. The following excerpt from chapter 11 of the *Texas Litigation Guide* discusses these issues.*

§ 11.05

. . . [2] Scope of Rule 185

Civil Procedure Rule 185 provides that the following claims are within its scope:

---

1. A claim founded on an open account or other claim for goods, wares, and merchandise "including any claim for a liquidated money demand based upon written contract or founded on business dealings between the parties."

2. A claim for personal services rendered.

3. A claim for labor done.

4. A claim for labor furnished.

5. A claim for material furnished.

Civil Procedure Rule 185 was taken from Article 3736 of the Revised Civil Statutes, which originally encompassed only an action on an open account. In 1931, the statute was amended to include liquidated demands based on written contract or business dealings between the parties and claims for personal services rendered on which a systematic record of accounts has been kept. One purpose of the amendment was to include "accounts stated" as well as "open accounts" in the actions contemplated by the rule [*Hollingsworth v. Northwestern National Ins. Co.*, 522 S.W.2d 242, 245 (Tex. Civ. App. — Texarkana 1975, no writ); *cf. Unit, Inc. v. Ten Eyck-Shaw, Inc.*, 524 S.W.2d 330, 334 (Tex. Civ. App. — Dallas 1975, writ ref'd n.r.e.)]. A second purpose of the amendment was to include claims for personal services rendered [*see Juarez v. Dunn*, 567 S.W.2d 223, 226 (Tex. Civ. App. — El Paso 1978, writ ref'd n.r.e.)]. Subsequently, in 1950, a second amendment added suits for "labor done or labor or material furnished" to the sworn account rule [*see* Tomasic & Kieval, *Sworn Accounts and Summary Judgment Proceedings in Texas: A Proposed Change*, 17 S. Tex. L.J. 147, 150 (1976)].

As a result, the scope of Civil Procedure Rule 185 was expanded by amendment beyond the contours of the common law "sworn account" [*see, e.g., Meaders v. Biskamp*, 316 S.W.2d 75, 78 (1958) — "[i]t has been held that a sworn account is defined according to its popular sense and applies only to transactions between persons, in which there is a sale upon one side and a purchase upon the other, whereby title to personal property passes from one to the other, and the relation of debtor and creditor is created by general course of dealing (which may include only one transaction between the parties). It does not mean transactions between parties resting upon special contract"]. Unfortunately, until 1984, Civil Procedure Rule 185 was entitled "Suit on Sworn Account," even though the body of the rule never has included that term [*see Seisdata v. Compagnie Generale De Geophysique*, 598 S.W.2d 690, 691 (Tex. Civ. App. — Houston [14th Dist.] 1980, ref. n.r.e.) — holding that Rule 185 is not restricted to types of claims described in *Meaders*, which dealt only with the recovery of attorney's fees under former R.C.S. Art. 2226; *Larcon Petroleum, Inc. v. Autotronic Systems*, 576 S.W.2d 873, 875 (Tex. Civ. App. — Houston [14th Dist.] 1979, no writ); *see also Schorer v. Box Service Co.*, 927 S.W.2d 132, 135 (Tex. App. — Houston [1st Dist.] 1996, den.) — concurring opinion, citing Texas Litigation Guide for proposition that scope of Rule 185 has been expanded beyond contours of common-law sworn account rules as discussed in *Meaders v. Biscam* p].

The courts have had difficulty in arriving at a consistent interpretation of the scope of Civil Procedure Rule 185. The most common problem relates to a supposed distinction between "sworn accounts" and "special contracts." A special contract has been defined as "one with peculiar provisions or stipulations not found in the ordinary contract relating to the same subject matter and [which] provisions . . . if omitted from the ordinary contract, the law will never supply" [*Eisenbeck v. Buttgen*, 450 S.W.2d 696, 702 (Tex. Civ. App. — Dallas 1970, no writ) — alleged oral employment contract providing for percentage of gross receipts in addition to set salary as special contract; *Brown v. Starrett*, 684 S.W.2d 145, 146 (Tex. App. — Corpus Christi 1984, no writ)]. There is case law to the effect that a special contract may not be the subject of an action under Rule 185 because "[i]t does not apply to transactions between parties resting upon special contracts other than those giving rise to the transactions mentioned in the rule" [*Hollingsworth v. Northwestern National Ins. Co.*, 522 S.W.2d 242, 244 (Tex. Civ. App. — Texarkana 1975, no writ); *cf. Robinson v. Faulkner*, 422 S.W.2d 209, 212–13 (Tex. Civ. App. — Dallas 1967, writ ref'd n.r.e.) — oral contract for services rendered not qualifying as "sworn account" under T.R.C.P. 185]. Finally, it has also been suggested that the benefits of Rule 185 specifically include an action founded on "any claim for a liquidated money demand based upon a written contract or founded on business dealings between the parties" [*Brown v. Starrett*, 684 S.W.2d 145, 146 (Tex. App. — Corpus Christi 1984, no writ) — "special contract" exception did not apply to oral contract to remodel house; *cf. DeWees v. Alsip*, 546 S.W.2d 692, 694 (Tex. Civ. App. — El Paso 1977, no writ) — suit on promissory note for sale of partnership is not within Rule 185] . . . .

[3] Pleading Requirements — Plaintiff's Petition

To allege a cause of action properly under Civil Procedure Rule 185, a petition should indicate that the claim is within the coverage of the rule and give fair notice of its content . . . . No particularization or description of the nature of component parts of the account or claim is necessary unless the trial court sustains special exceptions to the pleadings [T.R.C.P. 185 — as amended in 1984; McConnico & Bishop II, *Practicing Law with the 1984 Rules: Texas Rules of Civil Procedure Amendments Effective April 1, 1984*, 36 Baylor L. Rev. 73, 99 (1984)].

If a special exception is made and sustained, the petition should be redrafted in conformity with the following principles derived from case law antedating the 1984 amendments to Civil Procedure Rule 185. When the suit is based on the sale of personal property, the petition should show with reasonable certainty the nature of each item sold, the date, and the charges for each item [*Hassler v. Texas Gypsum Co., Inc.*, 525 S.W.2d 53, 55 (Tex. Civ. App. — Dallas 1975, no writ)]. Similarly, when the claim is based on the rendition of personal services, the petition should identify clearly the services rendered [*see Juarez v. Dunn*, 567 S.W.2d 223, 226 (Tex. Civ. App. — El Paso 1978, ref. n.r.e.)]. A computer printout comprising coded numbers was held under the pre-1984 version of Civil Procedure Rule 185 not to be a specific account for purposes of the rule [*Boots, Inc. v. Tony Lama Co., Inc.*, 584 S.W.2d 583, 585 (Tex. Civ. App. — Beaumont 1979, no writ)]. Also, a billing statement from an insurance agent showing a charge for a final audit on a workers' compensation policy, giving the policy number and amount due, was held to be insufficient under the pre-1984 version of Rule 185 because it did not show how the charges were calculated and it could not be determined from the petition why the customer allegedly underpaid the premiums [*Abe I. Brilling Ins. Agency v. Hale*, 601 S.W.2d 403, 404–05 (Tex. Civ. App. — Dallas 1980, no writ)].

The petition should also include allegations that a systematic record has been kept with dates of sales, services, charges, and credits, together with the description of the item or items provided and the charges and payments made [*see Howard v. Weisberg*, 583 S.W.2d 920, 921 (Tex. Civ. App. — Dallas 1979, no writ) — in suit on sworn account based on an express contract for personal services, general statements in affidavit without description of specific items is insufficient to comply with T.R.C.P. 185]. This may be accomplished by copies of invoices and/or a recapitulation sheet using readily understandable terms rather than abbreviations or jargon [*see Goodman v. Art Reproductions Corp.*, 502 S.W.2d 592, 594 (Tex. Civ. App. — Dallas 1973, writ ref'd n.r.e.)].

The claim must be "supported by the affidavit of the party, or his agent or attorney taken before some officer authorized to administer oaths, to the effect that such claim is, within the knowledge of the affiant, just and true, that it is due, and that all just and lawful offsets, payments and credits have been allowed" [T.R.C.P. 185]. The Fourteenth Court of Appeals has held that the supporting affidavit must make clear that the affiant has personal knowledge of the facts. In this case, a defendant claimed that because the affidavit stating the claim was true, just, and correct was executed by an officer of a successor corporation to the one that performed the construction work, it was based on hearsay. The court of appeals rejected this argument, holding that the affidavit was sufficient because the affiant declared that he had personal knowledge of the facts and identified himself as an officer of the successor corporation, formerly the corporation in question [*Requipco, Inc. v. Am-Tex Tank & Equipment*, 738 S.W.2d 299, 301 (Tex. App. — Houston [14th Dist.] 1987, writ ref'd n.r.e.)].

[4] Defenses

The effect of Civil Procedure Rule 185 is to place the burden on the opposing party to deny the account or one or more of its elements by a written denial, under oath [*see* T.R.C.P. 93(10), 185; *Vance v. Holloway*, 689 S.W.2d 403, 404 (Tex. 1985) — per curiam opinion — in absence of verified denial, sworn account is received as prima facie evidence of account and defendant may not contest receipt of items or services or correctness of stated charges; *Nichols v. William A. Taylor, Inc.*, 662 S.W.2d 396, 398 (Tex. App. — Corpus Christi 1983, no writ) — filing of verified denial in form required by T.R.C.P. 185 destroys evidentiary effect of itemized account and forces plaintiff to put on proof of his or her claim]. For example, if the defendant files a properly verified denial of a claim for goods, wares, or merchandise, the plaintiff must show the following elements of a common-law action on account: (1) that there was a sale and delivery of the goods; (2) that the account is just because the prices were charged in accordance with an agreement or are the usual, customary, and reasonable prices for the goods; and (3) that the amount is unpaid [*Nichols v. William A. Taylor, Inc.*, 662 S.W.2d 396, 398 (Tex. App. — Corpus Christi 1983, no writ); *Jones v. Ben Maines Air Conditioning, Inc.*, 621 S.W.2d 437, 439 (Tex. Civ. App. — Texarkana 1981, no writ)].

If the plaintiff has properly pleaded a prima facie case and the defendant fails to file a timely written denial under oath, the defendant may not deny the claim or any item thereof. The lack of a proper denial, however, does not bar the defendant from raising affirmative defenses . . . .

If the plaintiff's own pleadings or exhibits indicate or if other evidence reflects that the defendant was not a party to the original transaction, the defendant may also raise the "stranger to the account" defense; such a defendant is not required to file a sworn denial in accordance with the technical requirements of Rule 185 . . . . It should be noted, however, that a verified denial under Rule 93 of the Texas Rules of Civil Procedure may be necessary to support the defense when, for example, the defendant alleges that he or she is not liable in the capacity sued.

[C] Standard "Sworn Account" Petition

When drafted in compliance with Rule 185, a suit on a sworn account will look something like this.

Original Petition

PLAINTIFF'S ORIGINAL PETITION

TO THE HONORABLE COURT:

_____ [*Name*], plaintiff, complains of _____ [*name*], defendant, and for cause of action shows:

I.

Plaintiff is a corporation, with its principal office and place of business in the City of Houston, Travis County, Texas. Defendant is an individual whose residence is located in Dallas County, Texas. Service of citation may be had on defendant by serving _____ [him *or* her] at defendant's residence at 1234 Elm Street, Dallas, Texas. [Plead discovery level as required by Tex. R. Civ. P. 190].

II.

On the several occasions from March 15, 2005, to August 25, 2005, as more particularly shown on the attached Exhibit A, a verified account representing a liquidated money demand, which is incorporated by reference, plaintiff sold and delivered to defendant goods, wares, and merchandise consisting of paints, solvents, brushes, and tapes, as more specifically itemized on Exhibit A. The sales were made at the special instance and request of defendant, and the goods were sold and delivered in the regular course of business. In consideration of the sales, on which a systematic record has been kept, defendant promised and became bound and liable to pay plaintiff the prices charged for the goods in the total amount of $_____ [*specify*], being a reasonable charge for such items, as further shown on the attached Exhibit A. Despite numerous demands by plaintiff upon defendant for payment, defendant has refused and failed to pay the account, to plaintiff's damage in the sum of $_____ [*specify*], plus interest as alleged below.

[*Add if attorney's fees are sought*]

III.

On January 16, 2006, plaintiff presented defendant with the account. In this connection, plaintiff employed the undersigned attorneys to represent plaintiff and agreed to pay them a reasonable attorney's fee for their service, which plaintiff alleges to be the sum of $_____ [*specify*].

IV.

Plaintiff further shows that under Finance Code § 302.002, interest on open accounts accrues at the rate of 6 percent per annum, commencing on the 30th day after the day on which the sum is due and payable. Plaintiff is, therefore, entitled to prejudgment interest from the 30th day after each unpaid item of the account became due and payable, which was _____ days after the delivery date set forth in the attached Exhibit A, until the date of judgment.

WHEREFORE, plaintiff requests that defendant be cited to appear and answer and that upon final hearing, plaintiff have judgment against defendant for $_____ [*specify*], plus interest before and after judgment as provided by law, attorney's fees in the sum of $_____ [*specify*], and such other and further relief to which plaintiff is justly entitled.

Respectfully submitted,

[signaturc block]

EXHIBIT "A"

[*Set out verified account, e.g.*]

Shipment Date	Item No.	Price/Unit	Total Price
3-15-05	R-25	250 Gls. $5.73	$ 1,432.50
4-12-05	S-1	10 Gls. $3.15	$ 31.50
8-25-05	Misc.	15 units $1.57	$ 23.55
			$1,487.55

[*Affidavit to the Account*]
THE STATE OF TEXAS,
COUNTY OF HARRIS

BEFORE ME, the undersigned Notary Public in and for said County and State, on this day personally appeared John Doe, known to me, and, after being duly sworn, stated on oath that the foregoing and annexed account in favor of John Doe and against Richard Roe for the sum of $1,487.55 is within the knowledge of affiant, just and true, that it is due and unpaid, and that all just and lawful offsets, payments and credits have been allowed.

_______ *signature of affiant*]

SWORN AND SUBSCRIBED TO BEFORE ME, on _______.

[*Seal*]

_______ *signature*]

_______ [*typed or stamped name*]

Notary Public in and for _______ County, Texas

My commission expires ____ [*date*].

NOTES AND QUESTIONS

(1) *Types of Claims.* Review the sample petition and then ask yourself if the pleading would satisfy Rule 185:

(a) Does the petition allege or identify the type of claim involved?

(b) Does it show with reasonable certainty the nature of the items sold?

(c) If the transaction had involved services, how would they be properly identified?

(d) Does the petition show that a systematic record has been kept?

(e) Is the claim "supported by the affidavit of the party, or his agent or attorney taken before some officer authorized to administer oaths, to the effect that such claim is, within the knowledge of the affiant, just and true, that it is due, and that all just and lawful offsets, payments and credits have been allowed"?

(2) *Special Exceptions and Rule 185.* The particularized pleading requirements of Rule 185 were liberalized by the Texas Supreme Court when the rule was amended in 1984. From the standpoint of the particularity required of a claimant, the last sentence of the amended rule appears to require the defendant to specially except to a petition that either contains or incorporates a claim or an account that is not detailed or particularized (*i.e.*, "$5,000 for legal services"). After obtaining more specific information, a party who is resisting a claim can "file a written denial, under oath." How specific or particularized must the denial be? Does a sworn general denial satisfy the literal requirements of the procedural rule? It is still clear that an unverified general denial does not. *Vance v. Holloway*, 689 S.W.2d 403, 404 (Tex. 1985). Is there any penalty for false swearing? For a comprehensive review of the special pleading requirements of Rule 185, see *Requipco, Inc. v. Am-Tex Tank & Equipment*, 738 S.W.2d 299 (Tex. App. — Houston [14th Dist.] 1987, no writ).

(3) *Do We Still Need the Sworn Account?* The sworn account device pre-dates modern rules of pleading, discovery, and summary judgment. It provided a device for an efficient exchange of information and quick disposition of a claim at a time when otherwise there would have been no other procedural mechanism to accomplish those goals. Is sworn account procedure still helpful in modern times, or does it cause confusion and complication that are disproportionate to its function?

[D] Trespass to Try Title

Read Tex. R. Civ. P. *783 through 813.*

[1] General Requirements

A trespass-to-try-title action is the method of determining title to land, improvements on land, or other real property. Prop. C. § 22.001(a). Usually, a trespass-to-try-title suit seeks to clear problems in chains of title or to recover the possession of land unlawfully withheld from an owner who has a right to immediate possession. It embraces all of litigation affecting title to real estate. An action in trespass to try title is purely statutory. Prop. C. §§ 22.001-22.004 and is governed by special pleading and proof requirements established by the Texas Rules of Civil Procedure. T.R.C.P. 783-809. Both of these stem from very early systems for litigating title to property.

In addition to a straightforward title dispute, an action in trespass to try title is the appropriate procedure to remedy situations in which: (1) owners of adjacent parcels dispute the boundary line separating the parcels; (2) a landlord seeks to compel a tenant to vacate premises subsequent to termination of a lease between the landlord and the tenant; (3) a landlord seeks cancellation of a rental contract after notice because of default in rent payments; or (4) parties each claim a conflicting right of possession to realty.

Pleading and proof requirements in trespass to try title cases are specifically set out in the Property Code and the procedure rules. For plaintiffs, the petition must state: (1) the real names of the parties and their residences, if known; (2) a legally sufficient description of the premises; (3) the interest which the plaintiff claims in the premises; (4) that the plaintiff was in possession of the premises or entitled to such possession; (5) that the defendant unlawfully entered upon and dispossessed the plaintiff of the premises and withholds possession; (6) facts showing rents, profits, or damages if claimed; and (7) a prayer for the relief sought. Tex. R. Civ. P. 783. The petition must state the county or counties in which the land is situated and must describe the premises by metes and bounds or with sufficient certainty to identify the property so that possession may be delivered. A faulty description of the disputed property will render the petition defective and may preclude recovery because the court will be unable to identify the land in question. For example, a petition describing the realty only as "House and lot known as 4613 Gaston Avenue in the city of Dallas, being a lot 50 x 150 feet with improvements thereon" was held not to be a sufficient description. *Leach v. Cassity*, 279 S.W.2d 630, 636 (Tex. Civ. App. — Fort Worth 1955, writ ref'd n.r.e.) A plaintiff should *not* include as a part of the subject matter of the action any land or interest in land that is not in dispute. Otherwise, the plaintiff would needlessly risk losing the entire interest in the land, including the undisputed portion, if the plaintiff loses the case. The plaintiff's case must be proven by a preponderance of the evidence, and if the plaintiff fails to satisfy the burden of proof of superior title, the defendant is entitled to judgment without proving any right of title or possession.

The defendant in a trespass to try title action may file the plea of "not guilty," which must state in substance that the defendant is not guilty of the injury complained of in the petition filed by the plaintiff. A plea of not guilty by the defendant constitutes an admission by the defendant for the purposes of the action that the defendant was in possession of the premises sued for, or that the defendant claimed title at the time of commencing the action, unless the defendant states distinctly in the answer the extent of possession or claim, in which case the not guilty plea is an admission to that extent only. In effect, a plea of not guilty relieves the defendant of pleading affirmative defenses except for latent ambiguity and title by limitations; but claims for the value or removal of improvement or for reimbursement of taxes must be specially pleaded.

After the defendant has answered the plaintiff's petition, either party may demand an abstract of title. The abstract enables the requesting party to inspect the opposing party's documents and thereby prepare a more informed defense. After notice and hearing prior to the beginning of trial, a party who fails to file an abstract within the prescribed time period may be precluded by court order from presenting written instruments that are evidence of his or her claim or title at trial. Why do you suppose that a system for land title disputes, created before the advent of modern discovery, would have provided for the exchange of documents of title?

[2] The Declaratory Judgment Alternative

In many situations, such as in boundary disputes, the parties would prefer to use a procedure other than trespass to try title. Unfortunately, the Texas Supreme Court held in 2004 that trespass-to-try-title actions were the sole remedy. The Texas legislature responded with a bill intended to provide greater flexibility.

In the 2004 decision, *Martin v. Amerman*, 133 S.W.3d 262, 265–67 (Tex. 2004), the Texas Supreme Court determined that because the Property Code provides that a trespass-to-try-title action is the sole method of determining title to real property, a plaintiff cannot use the Uniform Declaratory Judgments Act to obtain relief in a boundary dispute between adjoining landowners.

At the time *Martin v. Amerman* was decided, Section 37.004 of the Uniform Declaratory Judgments Act provided generally that "[a] person interested under a deed, will, written contract or other writings constituting a contract or whose rights, status or other legal relations are affected by a statute, municipal ordinance, contract or franchise may have determined any question of construction or validity arising under the instrument, statute, ordinance, contract or franchise and obtain a declaration of rights, status, or other legal relations thereunder." TEX. CIV. PRAC. & REM. CODE § 37.004(a). In addition, section 37.003 provides more generally that declaratory relief is available "in any proceeding in which declaratory relief is sought and a judgment or decree will terminate the controversy or remove an uncertainty." C.P.R.C. § 37.003(c); *see generally* WILLIAM V. DORSANEO, III, TEXAS LITIGATION GUIDE § 45.04. Thus, parties to boundary disputes or other types of cases traditionally brought as trespass-to-try-title actions sometimes sued for declaratory relief instead because proceeding under the DJA offers the following advantages:

- DJA procedures, particularly the pleading and proof requirements, are less technical than trespass-to-try-title action requirements;

- Resort to usual discovery rules is as expedient or more expedient than the process of obtaining an abstract of title and survey of the land;
- An award of additional injunctive relief might aid enforcement of a possessory right in the disputed property; and
- The court has the discretion to award attorney's fees [*see* TEX. CIV. PRAC. & REM. CODE § 37.009] without a prerequisite claim of adverse possession.

Nevertheless, *Martin v. Amerman* made declaratory judgment actions unavailable in boundary disputes.

As a result of 2007 legislation, section 37.004 of the Uniform Declaratory Judgments Act was amended to allow "a person described in Subsection (a)" to use a declaratory judgment action to resolve a land title dispute "under this chapter when the sole issue concerning title to real property is the determination of the proper boundary line between adjoining properties." TEX. CIV. PRAC. & REM. CODE § 37.004(c) (added by Acts 2007, 80th Leg., ch. 305 — effective 6/15/07).

Hence, all of the benefits provided by the DJA should now be available in boundary litigation and, perhaps as significantly, all of the technical difficulties confronting litigants previously required to use trespass-to-try-title actions have been ameliorated by the 2007 legislation. As the Court explained in *Martin v. Amerman*, the "strict pleading and proof requirements applicable to trespass-to-try-title actions have sometimes produced harsh results." 133 S.W.3d at 265. What the Court did not explain, however, is the particularly onerous wrinkle described in *Hejl v. Wirth*, 343 S.W.2d 226, 227 (Tex. 1961), which provides that under then (and now) well-settled (but nonetheless ridiculous) law, if the plaintiff fails to establish title by one of the methods for doing so, the effect of a take nothing judgment is to vest title in the defendant!

But not all boundary disputes involve the "construction or validity" of contracts, wills, deeds, or statutes. *See, e.g., McRae Exploration & Prod., Inc. v. Reserve Petroleum Co.*, 962 S.W.2d 676, 685 (Tex. App. — Waco 1998, pet. denied); *see also* WILLIAM V. DORSANEO, III, TEXAS LITIGATION GUIDE § 280.01. Therefore, the placement of the statutory authorization to use DJA actions to resolve boundary disputes in section 37.004 raises another issue. Can the statutory amendment be construed to include all boundary disputes? In most boundary disputes, the plaintiff will be a "person interested in the land with respect to which the boundary is disputed" under a deed, will, written contract or other writings constituting a contract" even if no issue as to the "construction or validity" of the instrument is involved in the boundary dispute. Hence, it may be argued that the statutory amendment authorizes "a person described by subsection (a)" of section 37.004 to obtain declaratory relief "under this chapter" according to section 37.003(c)'s broader provision. Under this interpretation, relief under the DJA is available to "a person interested under a deed, will, written contract or other "writings constituting a contract" seeking to establish a boundary line under any of the theories that are available to claimants in disputed boundary cases. *See* WILLIAM V. DORSANEO, III, TEXAS LITIGATION GUIDE § 280.01 (discussion of theories used to resolve boundary disputes).

As originally proposed by Representative Will Hartnett, HB 1787 was a broader piece of legislation which permitted declaratory relief to "obtain a determination under [the Declaratory Judgments Act] of title to lands, tenements, or other real property." Unfortunately, the original bill ran into legislative difficulty and was amended before passage.

The original bill would have worked a much more beneficial change in Texas procedural law than the amended one. Normal pleading, discovery, and proof principles applied generally under the Texas Rules of Civil Procedure, coupled with the general availability of declaratory relief provide the same benefits as trespass-to-try-title law practice did in the nineteenth century, without all of the arcane complexity and sometimes harsh results that follow mandatory use of trespass-to-try-title actions to resolve land title disputes. For the same reasons, the legislature should seriously consider the elimination of trespass-to-try-title actions altogether. Only then will the technical traps inherent in trespass-to-try-title litigation be eliminated.

NOTES AND QUESTIONS

(1) *Distinguishing Equitable Actions.* An action in trespass to try title is purely statutory and is governed by special pleading and proof requirements established by the Texas Rules of Civil Procedure. Tex. R. Civ. P. 783-809. The action affords a legal, as distinguished from an equitable, remedy. It is not to be confused with a suit to quiet title or a suit in equity for an injunction to restrain a trespasser. The assertion of a mere equitable right will not support a suit for trespass to try title, but must be brought as a separate suit, such as one to cancel a deed. Once successful in setting the deed aside, a party may proceed later to recover title by trespass to try title. Moreover, an equitable *title*, as distinguished from an equitable *right*, will support an action of trespass to try title.

Trespass to try title actions are concerned with the establishment of title (legal or equitable) and possession. Accordingly, a nonpossessory interest such as an overriding royalty interest, not being a possessory interest, is not suitable for a trespass to try title suit. Similarly, a purchaser under a contract for the sale of realty does not acquire an equitable title until the purchaser has fully performed all obligations under the contract. Until performance, the purchaser has but an "equitable right," which is not sufficient to support an action in trespass to try title.

(2) *Waiver of Objections.* There is authority that predates the supreme court's decision in *Martin* that if a trespass-to-try-title claim is brought as a declaratory action, absent any objection to that procedure any error in permitting a suit under the DJA is waived. *Krabbe v. Anadarko Petroleum Corp.*, 46 S.W.3d 308, 320–21 (Tex. App. — Amarillo 2001, pet. denied). This authority should survive *Martin* because the error in the legal characterization of the claim is neither jurisdictional nor so fundamental as to require reversal in the absence of an objection.

(3) *Proving Title.* The plaintiff in an action in trespass to try title must recover, if at all, on the strength of the plaintiff's own title and may not rely on the weakness of the defendant's title. Recovery by proof of title may be had by proving: (1) a regular chain of conveyances from the sovereignty of the soil; (2) a superior

title out of a common source; (3) title by limitation; or (4) title by prior possession coupled with proof that the possession has not been abandoned. These stringent proof requirements, however, are not applicable to a boundary dispute resolved by a trespass-to-try-title action; instead, a recorded deed is sufficient to show an interest in the disputed property without proof of a formal chain of superior title. *Martin v. Amerman*, 133 S.W.3d 262, 265 (Tex. 2004).

(4) *Defensive Pleadings.* A defendant in a trespass to try title action may simply file a plea of not guilty, which must state in substance that the defendant is not guilty of the injury complained of in the plaintiff's petition. Tex. R. Civ. P. 788. The not guilty plea is a denial of the plaintiff's allegations and puts the burden of proof on the plaintiff to establish all elements necessary to maintain the action and recover title and possession of the disputed premises. Under a plea of not guilty, the defendant may prove any equitable or legal defense except the defense of limitations, which must be specially pleaded. Tex. R. Civ. P. 789.

APPENDIX — PLEADINGS AND THE TEXAS BAR EXAM

Pleadings are a part of every lawsuit, and pleading issues are periodically tested on the Texas Bar Exam. The following are questions from past exams, reprinted with the permission of the Texas Board of Law Examiners, which owns the copyright to these questions. You can see more questions, and the examiners' comments on the answers, by visiting www.ble.state.tx.us/past_exams/main_pastexams.htm, the Board's website.

In considering the questions, keep in mind that on the bar exam your answer is always limited to five lines.

July 2006

Properties, Inc. ("Properties") owns Apartments, located in Nueces County, Texas. Properties' principal office is located in Dallas County, Texas. Sam is employed by Properties as manager of Apartments. Sam is a resident of San Patricio County, Texas. Betsy lives in Apartments. Betsy sustained serious injuries in a fire that consumed her unit in Apartments. The source of the fire was a broken electrical outlet. Betsy had asked Sam to replace the broken outlet weeks before the fire. The outlet had not been replaced prior to the fire.

Betsy filed a lawsuit in Nueces County seeking damages against Properties and Sam, both of whom were served with a copy of the petition and citation three days after the lawsuit was filed.

1. When must Properties and Sam file their answers to the lawsuit to ensure that the answers are timely filed? Explain fully.

2. What remedies does Betsy have if either Properties or Sam does not file an answer on time? Explain fully.

Following the filing of the lawsuit, Properties and its attorneys knew that Sam was at all times acting within the course and scope of his employment prior to and at the time of the fire. However, Properties' attorney later signs and files a pleading in court denying that Sam was acting within the course and scope of his employment.

3. What remedies does Betsy have, and against whom, when she discovers what Properties and its attorneys knew at the time Properties' attorney filed the pleading denying course and scope? Explain fully.

February 2005

Sam, his wife, and their minor daughter, Jane, were on a family vacation in Harris County, Texas, when a truck rear-ended their car. Sam was driving the car. Sam's wife, Martha, and Jane were passengers. All three sustained serious injuries in the collision. The owner of the truck was Pipe Corp, a Texas corporation whose principal place of business has always been Tarrant County, Texas. Bob, Pipe Corp's employee, was driving the truck at the time of the collision. Sam, Martha, Jane, and Bob resided in Nueces County, Texas at the time of the collision. Sam and Martha want to file a lawsuit to recover for the injuries and damages sustained by them and Jane.

1. Sam and Martha decide to sue Pipe Corp and Bob. What must they allege in their Original Petition to state a cause of action? Explain fully.

2. The Original Petition generally alleges that the negligence of the defendants proximately caused damages to the plaintiffs. The Petition, however, does not allege any specific acts of negligence nor a total dollar amount of damages being sought. If the defendants wish to object to the generality of these allegations, what pleading should they file? If the court sustains the objection, what relief, if any, should the court grant? Explain fully.

February 2010

Trey slipped, fell and injured himself while he was shopping at the Home Grocery Store ("Home") at its only location in Collin County. Trey's fall was caused by water on the floor which came from the ice machine. The machine was owned and maintained by Ice Products ("Ice"), whose principal place of business is in Parker County. Trey filed a suit for damages in district court in Dallas County, his county of residence, alleging that Home and Ice were jointly and severally negligent and that their negligence proximately caused his injuries.

1. Trey's original petition is very broad and makes general allegations of negligence against both defendants. What pleading should the defendants file to require the plaintiff to re-plead his case with more definite and specific factual allegations? Explain fully.

2. Home is actually a Texas corporation and not a sole proprietorship as pleaded by Trey. How should Home give notice to the parties and the court that it is a corporation and intends to seek the protection of that status for its shareholders? Explain fully.

3. Ice believes that Trey's suit against Ice is barred by the statute of limitations. Ice does not want to disclose this defense for strategic reasons. Must Ice raise this issue before the case goes to trial and if so, how should Ice assert the defense of limitations? Explain fully.

Chapter 7

PARTIES

SCOPE

This chapter covers issues related to the party structure of a lawsuit. The chapter addresses such topics as joinder of claims and parties by both the plaintiff and the defendant, intervention and voluntary joinder of new parties, interpleader, compulsory joinder, and class actions.

§ 7.01 PERMISSIVE JOINDER OF CLAIMS

Read Tex. R. Civ. P. 51.

The Texas joinder of claims rule (Tex. R. Civ. P. 51) was taken without modification from the 1937 version of its federal counterpart, Fed. R. Civ. P. 18(a). Under the Texas rule, it is clear that in a case involving only one plaintiff and one defendant, there can be no misjoinder of claims, because the claims need not arise from the same transaction or occurrence or series of transaction or occurrences. *Cf.* Tex. R. Civ. P. 40 (requiring commonality for multiple parties).

For example, imagine that Paulette and David are involved in a traffic accident in which Paulette's car is damaged. Coincidentally, David owes Paulette $1,000 because he agreed to pay her to paint his house. Paulette may sue David both for negligence in the traffic accident and for the money owed on the painting contract in the same lawsuit, even though the claims are not related.

The fact that joinder is proper does not necessarily mean that unrelated claims will be tried together. The court may order separate trials in order to prevent any party from being embarrassed, delayed, or put to undue expense by the inclusion of a party against whom he or she asserts no claim and who asserts no claim against him or her. Tex. R. Civ. P. 40(b), 174(b). If the court orders "separate trials" of various claims or defenses under Rule 40(b) or Rule 174(b), the various components remain a single case, so that the judgment is not generally final until all claims and defenses are disposed of. *Van Dyke v. Boswell, O'Toole, Davis & Pickering*, 697 S.W.2d 381, 383 (Tex. 1985); *Hall v. City of Austin*, 450 S.W.2d 836, 837–38 (Tex. 1970). Only one final judgment is entered after all claims and issues involved in the lawsuit have been tried. *In re Koehn*, 86 S.W.3d 363, 366 (Tex. App. — Texarkana 2002, no pet.).

When joinder is not proper, courts will "sever" the improperly joined claims. The court may also order severance "to do justice, avoid prejudice, and further convenience." *Guarantee Fed. Sav. Bank v. Horseshoe Operating Co.*, 793 S.W.2d 652, 658 (Tex. 1990); *Dalisa, Inc. v. Bradford*, 81 S.W.3d 876, 879 (Tex. App. —

Austin 2002, no pet.). Severance is only proper where: 1) the controversy involves more than one cause of action; 2) the severed claim would be the proper subject of a lawsuit if it were asserted independently; and 3) the claim to be severed is not so interwoven with the remaining claims that two trials will involve the same facts and legal issues. It should be understood clearly that "severance" results in two or more independent lawsuits, each with its own docket number and in each of which a final judgment may be rendered. Tex. R. Civ. P. 41.

Although the procedure rules make joinder permissive, there will be times when the rules of claim preclusion will cause a claim that was not brought to be lost forever because it was part of the same "cause of action" as the claims made in the earlier litigation. See Chapter 8 for further discussion of this phenomenon.

§ 7.02 PERMISSIVE JOINDER OF PARTIES BY THE PLAINTIFF

Read Tex. R. Civ. P. 40, 51.

When there are multiple plaintiffs or multiple defendants (or both), Texas civil practice requires some commonality among the claims in the lawsuit. Persons may join as plaintiffs or be joined as defendants when the following conditions are met:

1. The right asserted by or against the parties must be in respect of or arise out of the same transaction, occurrence, or series of transactions or occurrences.
2. The action must present a question of law or fact common to all parties joined.

The inclusion of different counts in the petition, involving some but not all of the parties joined, does not prohibit the joinder. A party need not be interested in obtaining or defending against all the relief demanded, and the judgment may be given in accordance with the respective rights and liabilities of the parties.

The most difficult issue with regard to joinder under Rule 40 deals with the first requirement: when do the claims arise out of the same "transaction, occurrence, or series of transactions or occurrences"? Consider the following case:

RUSSELL v. HARTFORD CASUALTY INS. CO.

548 S.W.2d 737 (Tex. Civ. App. — Austin 1977, writ ref'd n.r.e.)

Shannon, J.

This is an appeal from a summary judgment entered by the district court of Travis County. Appellants, John L. Russell and wife, Linda L. Russell, filed suit against Wendland Farm Products, Inc., Hartford Casualty Insurance Company, Airways Rent-A-Car System, Inc., and Warren Cowley, doing business as Airways Rent-A-Car of Austin, Texas. The district court severed appellants' causes of action asserted against Hartford, Airways Rent-A-Car System, and Cowley from the negligence cause of action asserted by appellants against Wendland. The district court then entered a summary judgment in favor of Hartford, Airways Rent-A-Car System, and Cowley that appellants take nothing. We will affirm that judgment.

On September 11, 1974, a truck owned by Wendland Farm Products, Inc., and operated by its employee, collided with an automobile driven by Mrs. Russell. As a result of the collision Mrs. Russell was injured and her automobile was wrecked.

On the same day an adjuster for Hartford called upon the Russells. The adjuster arranged, at Hartford's cost, to provide a temporary rent car for the Russells' use from Airways Rent-A-Car System, Inc., and Warren Cowley, doing business as Airways Rent-A-Car of Austin, Texas.

Seven days later Hartford canceled the rental car arrangement. On the same day an employee of Airways requested the Russells to return the rent car. They returned the car on the following day. Airways did not charge the Russells for the use of the car.

Because the entry of the summary judgment was grounded upon appellees' theory that appellants failed to state a cause of action, the petition will be examined.

As against Wendland, appellants alleged that their damages were caused proximately by the negligence of Wendland's driver. Appellants sought to recover $264,200 for personal injuries, past and future medical expenses, an unwanted pregnancy, loss of wages, loss of Mrs. Russell's services, and loss of their car. They also sought $900,000 in exemplary damages from Wendland for alleged gross negligence.

The Russells also joined Hartford as a defendant in their negligence suit against Wendland. The Russells pleaded that one basis for Hartford's joinder was that it was the liability carrier for Wendland and, as such, Hartford was bound to pay any judgment obtained against Wendland. As another basis for joinder, the Russells alleged that Hartford was "directly liable" to them by virtue of Tex. Ins. Code Ann. art. 21.21 § 16 (1973).

In the second "count" of the petition, appellants enumerated a litany of wrongs allegedly committed by Wendland, Hartford, Airways and Cowley, and all flowing in some manner from Hartford's cancellation of the rent-car arrangement. For purposes of convenience, these complaints will be termed the "unfair settlement practices" and the "conspiracy" theories.

Under their "unfair settlement practices" theory, the Russells pleaded that Hartford was guilty of engaging in false, misleading, or deceptive acts or practices in violation of Tex. Bus. and Comm. Code Ann. § 17.46(b) by causing confusion or misunderstanding on the part of the Russells as to the "sponsorship and approval" of a rent car by them until Hartford could obtain a comparable replacement vehicle for them; by representing that the Russells had unlimited use of the rent car with respect to time and mileage until Hartford obtained for them a replacement vehicle, and by making false or misleading statements concerning the need for a replacement vehicle or the need for and expense of repair of the Russells' car.

Also, under their "unfair settlement practices" theory, the Russells alleged that

Hartford violated Tex. Ins. Code Ann. art. 21.21 § 4(4) in attempting "to coerce and intimidate" them by canceling the rent-car arrangement.

Finally, the Russells pleaded that Hartford violated Tex. Ins. Code Ann. art. 21.21–2 by knowingly misrepresenting to them pertinent facts or policy provisions relating to Wendland's coverage; by not attempting in good faith to effectuate prompt, fair, and equitable settlement of their claim; and by not attempting in good faith to settle promptly their claim where liability had become reasonably clear under one part of the policy in order to influence settlement under other parts of the policy.

The Russells sought to obtain a recovery from Hartford in the total sum of $45,000 for engaging in such unfair practices.

As another basis for joinder of Hartford, appellants alleged that Wendland "ratified Hartford's wrongful acts." In this connection appellants alleged that their attorney wrote to Hartford offering to settle the property damage aspect of the case for $3200 and advising Hartford of the "damaging effects of their [Hartford's] unfair, and deceptive settlement practices upon the Plaintiffs [the Russells] . . . ." Hartford was requested to send a copy of that letter to its insured, Wendland. The Russells pleaded further that Hartford advised Wendland, and because Wendland unreasonably failed to request Hartford to accept the settlement offer, *Wendland* "ratified" Hartford's unfair settlement practices, and that this somehow furnished a further ground for joinder of *Hartford.*

The Russells' "conspiracy" theory is difficult to summarize. The appellants pleaded that Hartford and Wendland as "First Conspirator" and Airways Rent-A-Car System, Inc., and Cowley as "Second Conspirator" entered into a conspiracy "to injure" the Russells. The conspirators allegedly arranged to furnish a rent car to the Russells without informing them about any limitations on the number of days permitted by the arrangement or by the number of miles allowed to be driven each day and without informing the Russells as to the terms of the cancellation of the rent-car arrangement. Thereafter, the "First Conspirator" directed the "Second Conspirator" to advise the Russells of the cancellation of the arrangement and of the mileage limitations in the arrangement. As a result of such alleged conspiracy Mr. Russell had to arrange for a ride to work and arrangements had to be made with friends, relatives, and neighbors to take Mrs. Russell to the physician and other places. For such damages allegedly flowing from the conspiracy, the Russells sought as their due $540,000.

Under their first point of error, appellants claim that joinder of the liability insurance company was permitted by the exception in Tex. R. Civ. P. 51(b).

In Texas, and in most states, the liability insurance company, in absence of a statute or an express provision of the insurance contract, cannot be sued directly in a tort suit with or without the joinder of the insured. Green, *Blindfolding the Jury*, 33 Texas L. Rev. 157, 158 (1954). That rule is expressed in Tex. R. Civ. P. 51(b) and other rules.[1] Rule 51(b) prohibits the joinder of a liability or indemnity insurance

[1] Similar prohibitions appear in the rules governing third-party practice and counterclaims and cross-claims. Tex. R. Civ. P. 38(b) and 97(f).

company in a tort case unless the insurance company is ". . . by statute or contract directly liable to the person injured or damaged."

Appellants say that any one of the several statutory causes of action asserted by them against the liability insurance company for alleged violations of the Texas Insurance Code and the Texas Business and Commerce Code permits them to join the insurer under the exception in Rule 51(b). Appellants say that the insurer is by those statutes "directly liable to the person injured or damaged."

Appellants' argument ignores the fact that the exception in Rule 51(b) permits the joinder of the liability insurer in tort cases in which a statute has made the insurer directly liable for the injuries or damages resulting from the tortious act of its insured. Appellants' statutory causes of action have nothing to do with the insured's tortious conduct or with injuries or damages flowing from that conduct. The alleged violations of the Texas Insurance Code and the Texas Business and Commerce Code asserted by appellants refer to alleged conduct of the insurer or its adjuster which occurred days or weeks after the tort of its insured, and which, of course, had nothing to do with the tort.

The Rules of Civil Procedure should be construed so as to produce harmony rather than discord. *Ex parte Godeke*, 355 S.W.2d 701 (1962). Rule 51(b) should be read in conjunction with Rule 40. Rule 40 limits the joinder of defendants to situations in which the right to relief asserted against the defendants arises out of the same transaction or occurrence or series of occurrences and if any question of law or fact common to all of them will arise in the action.

In the case at bar, appellants' allegations concerning violations of the Texas Insurance Code and the Texas Business and Commerce Code do not arise out of the truck-automobile collision, nor do the allegations present questions of law or fact common to those presented in the negligence suit. It follows that if there were a legal basis for appellants' suit for violations of the Texas Insurance Code and the Texas Business and Commerce Code against Hartford, still that would not be a basis for the joinder of Hartford in the negligence suit against Hartford's insured.

Contrary to assertions in their brief and in oral argument, appellants did not plead that Hartford was directly liable to them by virtue of some "direct action" provision in the insurance policy issued to Wendland.

We have concluded that Rule 51(b) afforded no basis for the joinder of the liability insurer in appellants' suit for negligence against the insured, Wendland.

. . . .

NOTES AND QUESTIONS

(1) *Rule 40 Language.* Rule 40 also requires that the relief asserted by or against the joined parties be sought "jointly, severally, or in the alternative." As this seems to encompass every method by which relief can be sought, it is not a meaningful limitation on joinder.

(2) *Misinterpretation of Rule 40's Cumulative Requirements.* Despite the clear language of Civil Procedure Rule 40, a number of intermediate appellate courts

have read the procedural rule as if each requirement constituted a separate alternative basis for permissive joinder. For example, in *Lambert v. H. Molsen & Co.*, 551 S.W.2d 151 (Tex. Civ. App. — Waco 1977, writ ref'd n.r.e.), a buyer brought an action against three sellers of cotton who had each separately agreed to sell cotton to the buyer. Because the contracts were executed individually and without joint obligations, the defendants moved to sever. The motions were overruled. The Waco Court said the following:

> Defendants say that Rule 40 requires more than common fact and law questions for joinder of separate causes against several defendants, and that it also requires as a mandatory predicate for the joinder that plaintiff's case against the defendants must arise out of the same transaction or same series of transactions. Thus, they say, they were entitled to the severances as a matter of law. We disagree. Defendants' construction of Rule 40 is too restrictive. It is settled that questions of joinder of parties and causes of action, consolidation, and severance, are addressed to a broad discretion bestowed upon the trial courts in such procedural matters by our rules of civil procedure. Rules 37 to 43, 97, and 174; *Hamilton v. Hamilton*, 280 S.W.2d 588, 591 (1955). Absent a showing of an abuse of the discretion, prejudicial to the complainant, the court's rulings in those matters will not be disturbed on appeal. *Parker v. Potts*, 342 S.W.2d 634, 636 (Tex. Civ. App. — Fort Worth 1961, writ ref'd n.r.e.).
>
> . . . In our case the contracts sued upon are identically worded in every material respect; each was solicited and executed on behalf of Molsen by the same agent; and, as we have said, all raise the same questions of law and fact which are crucial to this dispute. On the trial, the same testimony on trade customs and practices, technical terms and their meaning, expenses saved by Molsen, and micronaire range production statistics dealing with the major factual disputes in the case, was relevant to all defendants. The only fact question not common to all was the landlord's share issue. Jackson conceded during his testimony that the contracts were intended to include the shares of his landlord. Struve and Lambert did not. However, the jury found in favor of Struve and Lambert, so no harm resulted to any defendant on this issue.
>
> Our review of the record has failed to reveal the prejudice to defendants they claim was generated by trying their cases together. We find no abuse of discretion in the court's rulings on the motions for severance. *See Texas Employment Commission v. International Union of Electrical, Radio, And Machine Workers*, 352 S.W.2d 252, 253 (1961); *Hindman v. Texas Lime Co.*, 305 S.W.2d 947, 954 (1957).

This opinion by the Waco court, while it reaches a correct result, misconstrues the meaning of the "same transaction or occurrence or series of transactions or occurrences." The term does not require identity of time and place, but rather a situation in which a significant overlap in evidence will create efficiencies at trial, or one in which there is a logical relationship among the claims. Hence the contract claims described by the court, given the same evidence that was relevant to all of the claims, do meet the "same transaction or occurrence" test as well as that for "common questions of law or fact." The court is also mistaken in suggesting that the requirements listed in the rule are alternative rather than cumulative.

(3) *Relationship of Rules 40 and 51.* Civil Procedure Rules 40 and 51 must be read together. There is some ambiguity in the Texas rules on permissive joinder of claims (Rule 51) and permissive joinder of parties (Rule 40) in certain multiple party/multiple claims hypotheticals. Consider the following excerpt from Louis R. Frumer, *Multiple Parties and Claims in Texas*, 6 Sw. L.J. 135, 144 (1952),* for an analysis of the inter-relationship of Civil Procedure Rules 40, 41, and 51.

> *A* has a cause of action against *B* and *C* on a note executed jointly by them, and another cause of action upon a separate and entirely unrelated note executed jointly by *B*, *C*, and *D*. May *A* join both of these causes of action in one action against *B*, *C*, and *D?* *D* is not concerned with the cause of action solely against *B* and *C*, there are no common questions of law or fact, and the joinder of both causes of action in one petition would be improper. However, if the causes of action are joined, the court should sever the cause of action against *B* and *C* from the cause of action against *B*, *C*, and *D*, ordering that each be docketed as a separate suit. Of course, if the two causes of action were so related as to be within the scope of Rule 40(a), it would be immaterial that *D* is not concerned with the cause of action against *B* and *C*. Note that under that rule a "defendant need not be interested in . . . defending against all the relief demanded. Judgment may be given . . . against one or more defendants according to their respective liabilities."

Under this interpretation, a misjoinder of parties can create a misjoinder of claims. How is the misjoinder problem handled under Rule 40? Does the court have discretion in how it is handled? Why should there be any limitation? Can't the problem be handled by giving the trial judge discretion to grant separate trials when this would be appropriate, economical, and nonprejudicial?

The federal rule was amended in 1966 to deal with interpretive problems involving the last two sentences of Rule 18(a), which is the federal counterpart to Texas rule 51. The federal rule now provides, "A party asserting a claim to relief as an original claim, counterclaim, cross-claim, or third party claim, may join, either as independent or as alternate claims, as many claims, legal, equitable, or maritime, as he has against an opposing party." There is no reference to limitations on claim joinder by the joinder of parties rules (F.R.C.P. 20, the counterpart to Tex. R. Civ. P. 40). The apparent effect of the amendment in federal court is to permit joinder of unrelated claims so long as there is one common claim linking the defendants together. The answer to Professor Frumer's hypothetical would therefore change: joinder would be proper, and severance merely in the discretion of the court. Benjamin Kaplan, *1966 Amendments of the Federal Rules of Civil Procedure (II)*, 81 Harv. L. Rev. 591, 597 (1968).

(4) *Proper Analysis of Rules 40 and 51.* Professor Kaplan indicates that all three of the following hypotheticals would involve proper joinder of claims and parties

---

under the revised *federal* rule.

> *Case I.* Plaintiff sues *A* and *B* in one action for breaches of separate contracts made with each of them respectively: the two contracts arose out of the same transaction and a common question of law or fact will arise. Suppose Plaintiff wants to join in the action claims for libel against *A* and *B* respectively; the libels both arose out of the same transaction but one unconnected with the contract transaction, and a common question of law or fact will arise unconnected with any contract question.
>
> *Case II.* Contract claims against *A* and *B* as in Case I. Plaintiff wants to join in the action a libel claim against *A;* this claim arose out of the same transaction as the contract claims and there is a question of law or fact with respect to the libel that will also arise with respect to the contracts.
>
> *Case III.* Contract claims against *A* and *B* as in Case I. Plaintiff wants to join in the action a libel claim against *A;* this claim did not arise out of the same transaction as the contract claims and there is no question of law or fact regarding the libel that will also arise with respect to the contracts.

The amendment to the federal rule was meant to clarify that joinder is proper in the Case III situation. *But does that mean that the Texas rule must be interpreted to prohibit it?* The Texas rule is worded like the old federal rule. But the drafters of the federal rules clearly considered Frumer's position to be incorrect, and amended the federal rule for purposes of clarity. One could argue that the Texas rule could be interpreted to allow the same kind of joinder as the federal rule, with fairness and efficiency concerns handled by the court's discretion to allow separate trials.

(5) *Consolidation.* As the previous sections demonstrate, Texas has a general policy against a multiplicity of suits for claims that are sufficiently related so that they comprise one convenient unit for trial. This policy is reflected in the rules concerning the joinder of parties and claims, and the Texas Rules of Civil Procedure give trial courts broad discretion to arrange for one suit to replace two or more actions when appropriate to achieve a fair and efficient resolution. Rule 174(a) extends the power to combine things to separate cases pending in the same court. If actions involving a common question of law or of fact are pending before a court, it may order a joint hearing or trial of any or all the matters in issue in the actions, may order all the actions consolidated, and may make any orders concerning proceedings that may tend to avoid unnecessary costs or delay. Tex. R. Civ. P. 174(a). Note that Rule 174 does not include an additional requirement that the actions arise out of the "same transaction or occurrence." Two different types of consolidation are contemplated: (1) merger of actions into one action under one docket number, and (2) joint hearing or trial without actual merger. Suits filed separately may be consolidated by order of the court on the motion of any party or on the court's own initiative at any stage of the action before submission to the jury (or to the court if trial is without a jury) on terms that are just. Tex. R. Civ. P. 41. For a discussion of procedures for joint handling of cases filed in different districts, see § 5.06, Multidistrict Litigation.

(6) *Relationship to Limitations Statutes*. Sections 16.068 and 16.069 of the Civil Practice and Remedies Code allow, under limited circumstances, all parties to amend and add additional grounds of recovery/defense that otherwise might have been time-barred. If a plaintiff's later added claim could have been asserted at the time that the original action was filed (i.e., was not time-barred), it is not time-barred if subsequently added in an amended pleading unless it is wholly based on a new, distinct or different transaction or occurrence. C.P.R.C. § 16.068; *Milestone Prop., Inc. v. Federated Metals Corp.*, 867 S.W.2d 113, 114–18 (Tex. App. — Austin 1993, no writ) (construing C.P.R.C. § 16.068). The same concept applies to a counterclaim or cross-claim if it is filed not later than the 30th day after the defendant's answer day. *See, e.g., Oliver v. Oliver*, 889 S.W.2d 271, 272–74 (Tex. 1994) (holding that wife's counterclaim for fraud arose out of same transaction as husband's divorce action).

(7) *Next Friends and Guardians ad Litem*. Certain kinds of persons either are not capable of appearing as independent litigants, or need some independent guardian to safeguard their interests. Rule 44 provides that "minors, lunatics, idiots, or persons non compos mentis who have no legal guardian" may sue and be represented by "next friends." Next friends have the power to bind the person represented, but any settlement or agreed judgment must be approved by the court. Tex. R. Civ. P. 44. Normally, a child's parent acts as the child's next friend, because parents have the power to represent their children in legal actions. Fam. C. § 151.001(a)(7). The allegations in a petition may identify a party in both his or her individual capacity and as a minor's representative. For example, a parent may, as an individual, seek recovery of medical expenses paid in the treatment of the minor's injuries and, as a minor's representative, may seek recovery for pain and suffering. The rules also include limits on the fees that the guardian ad litem may recover. Tex. R. Civ. P. 173.6.

Rule 173 sets out the procedures governing guardians ad litem, who must be appointed only when the next friend or guardian appears to have a conflict of interest with the party they represent or when the parties agree. The guardian ad litem acts as an officer and advisor to the court, and may take actions such as advising the court as to whether a settlement proposal is in the party's best interest. Tex. R. Civ. P. 173. The guardian's role in the litigation is ordinarily limited, and does not include participation in discovery or trial unless the court specifically orders it because it is necessary due to the conflict of interest between the party and the next-friend. Rule 173 does not apply when the procedures and purposes for appointment of guardians ad litem (as well as attorneys ad litem) are prescribed by statutes, such as the Family Code and the Probate Code, or by other rules, such as the Parental Notification Rules.

§ 7.03 JOINDER OF CLAIMS BY THE DEFENDANT

[A] Counterclaims

Read TEX. R. CIV. P. 97.

Sometimes the defendant also suffered injuries, and wants to bring claims for those injuries against the plaintiff. This is called a counterclaim. Some counterclaims are permissive — if they do not arise out of the same transaction or occurrence as the plaintiff's claims, the defendant may choose a different forum to litigate its claim. Some counterclaims are compulsory — if they arise out of the same transaction or occurrence as the plaintiff's claim, the defendant must bring the counterclaim or lose the right to bring it later. In order for a counterclaim to be compulsory, it must also be "mature." The following case considers when indemnity claims accrue so as to be "mature" and compulsory counterclaims.

INGERSOLL-RAND CO. v. VALERO ENERGY CORP.
997 S.W.2d 203 (Tex. 1999)

ENOCH, J.

Valero sued Kellogg and Ingersoll-Rand for damages caused by malfunctioning equipment. Kellogg and Ingersoll-Rand installed the equipment during an expansion of Valero's oil refinery. Kellogg was the general contractor on the expansion, and Ingersoll-Rand was one of Kellogg's subcontractors. Both Kellogg and Ingersoll-Rand defended by asserting that certain indemnification and hold-harmless provisions in the Valero-Kellogg contract applied. The trial court concluded that the contract's indemnification provisions were enforceable and granted interlocutory summary judgment for Kellogg and Ingersoll-Rand. The court then severed that part of the case, so that Valero could appeal the summary judgment. The court of appeals affirmed, and that judgment is now final.

During that appeal, the trial court abated the remaining claims. After the abatement was lifted, Kellogg and Ingersoll-Rand moved for summary judgment, seeking attorney's fees under the indemnity provisions upheld in *Valero I*. Valero filed its own motion for summary judgment, asserting that Kellogg's and Ingersoll-Rand's claims for attorney's fees were compulsory counterclaims barred by res judicata and by the statute of limitations. The trial court granted Valero summary judgment. The court of appeals affirmed.

The pivotal question in this case is when does an indemnitee's contractual claim for indemnification mature for purposes of the compulsory counterclaim rule. We adhere to the longstanding rule that a claim based on a contract that provides indemnification from liability does not accrue until the indemnitee's liability becomes fixed and certain. Applying this rule, we conclude that Kellogg's and Ingersoll-Rand's indemnity claims did not accrue until the trial court's rendition of summary judgment in *Valero I*. Accordingly, neither res judicata nor limitations bar Kellogg's and Ingersoll-Rand's claims. We reverse the court of appeals' judgment and remand to the trial court for further proceedings.

Valero I

Valero sued Kellogg in 1986 over mechanical malfunctions allegedly resulting from Kellogg's flawed installation of refinery equipment. Valero pleaded fraudulent misrepresentation, breach of contract, violations of the Texas Deceptive Trade Practices Act, breach of implied and express warranties, products liability, negligence, gross negligence, and intentional misconduct. Valero added Ingersoll-Rand as a defendant in 1989, after a piece of equipment supplied by Ingersoll-Rand exploded. The suit eventually came to include a host of cross-claims, counterclaims, and third-party claims not at issue here.

Kellogg and Ingersoll-Rand answered Valero's petition, asserting that the contract's indemnity provision barred Valero's claims . . . . Valero replied that the contract's indemnity provision was unenforceable as against public policy. On this issue, each side filed competing motions for summary judgment.

The trial court granted Kellogg's and Ingersoll-Rand's motions for summary judgment, denied Valero's motion, and rendered judgment that Valero take nothing on its claims against Kellogg and Ingersoll-Rand. That matter was severed, and the remaining issues were abated pending appeal. Valero appealed, and the court of appeals affirmed the trial court's judgment on June 30, 1993. This Court denied Valero's application for writ of error on April 20, 1994, and overruled its motion for rehearing of the application on June 2, 1994. That judgment is final.

Valero II

One of the remaining abated claims was Kellogg's counterclaim for attorney's fees and costs incurred in defending against Valero. Kellogg filed the counterclaim between the time summary judgment was entered and the time the severance order was entered, but more than five years after Valero first sued Kellogg. After the trial court dissolved the abatement, Ingersoll-Rand initiated its own counterclaim against Valero for attorney's fees and costs. This claim was raised more than five years after Valero added Ingersoll-Rand as a defendant.

Kellogg and Ingersoll-Rand filed a joint motion for summary judgment asserting that the contract's indemnity provision, held enforceable in *Valero I*, entitled each to attorney's fees, court costs, and litigation expenses incurred in *Valero I*. Valero responded with a motion for summary judgment, asserting two affirmative defenses: (1) Kellogg and Ingersoll-Rand's counterclaims were compulsory, had not been asserted in *Valero I*, and were therefore precluded by res judicata; and (2) the four-year statute of limitations for breach of contract barred the claims.

Without specifying grounds, the trial court granted Valero's motion for summary judgment, and denied Kellogg and Ingersoll-Rand's motion. The court of appeals affirmed, holding that Ingersoll-Rand's counterclaim was compulsory and barred by res judicata, and Kellogg's claim was barred by limitations. Kellogg and Ingersoll-Rand each petitioned for review.

Because resolution of the issues we consider in Ingersoll-Rand's appeal disposes of issues presented by Kellogg's appeal, we consider Ingersoll-Rand's appeal first.

Ingersoll-Rand's Appeal

The court of appeals held that Ingersoll-Rand's claim for attorney's fees was a compulsory counterclaim that Ingersoll-Rand should have brought in *Valero I*; and, therefore, res judicata barred the claim in *Valero II*. We disagree.

Res judicata prevents parties and their privies from relitigating a cause of action that has been finally adjudicated by a competent tribunal. Also precluded are claims or defenses that, through diligence, should have been litigated in the prior suit but were not. The doctrine is intended to prevent causes of action from being split, thus curbing vexatious litigation and promoting judicial economy. Res judicata, however, does not bar a former defendant who asserted no affirmative claim for relief in an earlier action from stating a claim in a later action that could have been filed as a cross-claim or counterclaim in the earlier action, unless the claim was compulsory in the earlier action. Here, the court of appeals concluded that Ingersoll-Rand's claim was compulsory.

But a counterclaim is compulsory only if: (1) it is within the jurisdiction of the court; (2) it is not at the time of filing the answer the subject of a pending action; (3) the claim is mature and owned by the defendant at the time of filing the answer; (4) it arose out of the same transaction or occurrence that is the subject matter of the opposing party's claim; (5) it is against an opposing party in the same capacity; and (6) it does not require the presence of third parties over whom the court cannot acquire jurisdiction. A claim having all of these elements must be asserted in the initial action and cannot be asserted in later actions.

To meet its summary judgment burden on the affirmative defense that Ingersoll-Rand's claim was compulsory and barred by res judicata, Valero had to prove that Ingersoll-Rand's counterclaim satisfied each element above. Ingersoll-Rand asserts that its indemnity claim for attorney's fees was not compulsory because the claim could not have become mature before the trial court's rendition of summary judgment in *Valero I*.

A claim is mature when it has accrued. To determine the correct accrual date of an indemnity claim we look to the contract's indemnity provision. There are two types of indemnity agreements, those that indemnify against liabilities and those that indemnify against damages. Broad language, like that in this contract, that holds the indemnitee "harmless" against "all claims" and "liabilities" evidences an agreement to indemnify against liability. Such provisions entitle the indemnitee to recover when the liability becomes fixed and certain, as by rendition of a judgment, whether or not the indemnitee has yet suffered actual damages, as by payment of a judgment.

Valero's suit presented the rather anomalous situation of an indemnitor (Valero) acting concurrently as the plaintiff seeking damages from the indemnitee (Ingersoll-Rand). The more common scenario for an indemnification dispute involves three separate and distinct parties: plaintiff (party one), indemnitee (party two), and indemnitor (party three). Despite the unusual factual setting here, we find no persuasive reason not to apply the longstanding rule that a claim under a liability indemnification clause does not accrue, and thus is not mature, until the indemnitee's liability to the party seeking damages becomes fixed and certain.

When Ingersoll-Rand was added as a defendant in *Valero I*, it was entirely conceivable that Ingersoll-Rand might sustain extensive liabilities because of Valero's claims for damages. And Ingersoll-Rand, presumably, would have sought indemnification for all such liabilities under the contract's indemnity provision. Any claim Ingersoll-Rand could have asserted, however, could not have accrued until all of Ingersoll-Rand's potential liabilities to Valero became fixed and certain by rendition of a judgment.

In *Valero I*, the trial court rendered summary judgment for Ingersoll-Rand that Valero take nothing on its claims for damages. That judgment was signed on October 25, 1991. Ingersoll-Rand's liabilities became fixed and certain at zero for Valero's tort, DTPA, and contract damages plus the total amount of attorney's fees and costs incurred in defending against Valero when summary judgment was rendered in *Valero I*. Because Valero demonstrated no time earlier than the date of judgment in *Valero I* by which Ingersoll-Rand's liabilities became fixed and certain, the third element of the compulsory counterclaim rule — maturity of the claim — was not satisfied.

Our reasoning is bolstered by commentary on the analogous federal rule. The Texas compulsory counterclaim rule is based on Rule 13 of the Federal Rules of Civil Procedure. In commenting on Federal Rule 13(a)'s condition that a claim must be mature in order to be compulsory, Professors Wright and Miller state:

> This exception to the compulsory counterclaim requirement necessarily encompasses a claim that depends upon the outcome of some other lawsuit and thus does not come into existence until the action upon which it is based has terminated. For example, . . . *a claim for contribution cannot be compulsory in the action whose judgment is the subject of the contribution suit.* [emphasis added]

Likewise, an indemnity claim cannot be compulsory in the action whose judgment is the subject of the indemnity suit. In a suit for either contribution or indemnity the injury upon which suit might be based does not arise until some liability is established. In this case, as in a contribution claim against a joint tortfeasor, liability could not have been established until judgment was rendered . . . .

The fact that attorney's fees and costs were the only liabilities for which Ingersoll-Rand was eventually entitled to seek indemnity does not change our conclusion. It is true that a counterclaim for attorney's fees will in most cases be compulsory. We do not dispute the legal basis of such a statement because a claim for attorney's fees will generally satisfy the elements of the compulsory counterclaim rule. However, an indemnity claim based on an agreement to indemnify against liabilities has different characteristics than a simple claim for attorney's fees. The attorney's fees are certain to be incurred as soon as an attorney is retained, while liabilities covered by an indemnity agreement in any given case may never be incurred depending on the outcome of the case. This difference is significant.

Consider *Fidelity Mutual Life Insurance Company v. Kaminsky*, [820 S.W.2d 878, 882 (Tex. App. — Texarkana 1991, writ denied)] another case upon which the court of appeals relied. In *Kaminsky* the court concluded that a contractual claim for attorney's fees, even though contingent on the outcome of the suit, was mature and compulsory. The contractual provision on which Dr. Kaminsky relied established his contractual right to attorney's fees contingent on the result of the suit, but it did not indemnify him against other liabilities generally. It was not an indemnification agreement. Thus, the general rule that a cause of action accrues when facts come into existence that authorize the claimant to seek a judicial remedy applied in *Kaminsky*. Dr. Kaminsky's claim for attorney's fees accrued when he first incurred fees.

As we have explained, a specific accrual rule applies to claims for indemnification: an indemnity claim does not accrue until all of the potential liabilities of the indemnitee become fixed and certain. This specific rule is consistent with the general accrual rule. The facts that entitle an indemnitee to seek indemnification through suit come into existence when the indemnitee's liabilities become fixed and certain by judgment.

While attorney's fees will almost always be a component of an indemnitee's total liabilities, we decline to hold that recovery for the attorney's fees component of an indemnitee's potential liability must be pursued before and separate from the remaining components. An indemnification claim does not accrue until all of the indemnitee's liabilities become fixed and certain . . . .

Kellogg's Appeal

Our conclusions above largely dispose of Valero's claims against Kellogg. Like Ingersoll-Rand, Kellogg's claim for attorney's fees did not accrue until summary judgment was rendered in *Valero I*. Consequently, Kellogg's claim was not compulsory . . . .

Conclusion

Kellogg and Ingersoll-Rand's claims for attorney's fees were not compulsory counterclaims and are not barred by res judicata. Further, the claims were filed within the applicable limitations period. Accordingly, we reverse the court of appeals' judgment and remand to the trial court for further proceedings consistent with this opinion.

JUSTICE OWEN did not participate in the decision.

If a counterclaim is compulsory but the defendant does not assert it, the claim may be lost forever. Should that also be true when the first judgment arises through default rather than from litigation of the merits of the case? Consider the contrasting views of the majority and dissent in the following case.

JACK H. BROWN & CO. v. NORTHWEST SIGN CO.

718 S.W.2d 397 (Tex. App. — Dallas 1986, writ ref'd n.r.e.)

GUITTARD, C.J.

The question on this appeal is whether the present suit is barred by a prior default judgment and the compulsory counterclaim rule embodied in rule 97(a) of the Texas Rules of Civil Procedure. The present suit was brought by "Signgraphics," an assumed name of Jack H. Brown & Company, Inc., a Texas corporation, against Northwest Sign Company, an Idaho corporation, for the price of steel pipe furnished for the erection of a Holiday Inn sign in Idaho . . . . Northwest . . . filed a motion for summary judgment asserting that Signgraphics's claim in the present suit is barred by the failure of Signgraphics to present it as a counterclaim in an Idaho suit by Northwest against Signgraphics on a contract for erection of the sign. Although the trial court overruled Northwest's special appearance, it awarded a summary judgment to Northwest based upon the compulsory counterclaim rule and also upon the ground of *res judicata*. Since we agree that the compulsory counterclaim rule applies, we affirm the summary judgment without reaching the *res judicata* question . . . .

The summary judgment proof discloses the following facts. Signgraphics made a written contract with Weston, the operator of a Holiday Inn in Idaho, to fabricate and install a Holiday Inn sign on supporting steel pipe to be provided by Weston. Signgraphics then made a written subcontract with Northwest for installation of the sign. In accordance with the subcontract, Signgraphics made the sign, but Weston had difficulty obtaining the steel pipe. Northwest then asked Signgraphics to supply the pipe. Signgraphics obtained the pipe, shipped it along with the sign to Northwest, and billed Northwest for the pipe. Northwest erected the pipe and installed the sign. Signgraphics refused to pay for the installation, and Northwest refused to pay for the pipe.

In the earlier suit, Northwest sued Signgraphics in Idaho and obtained a default judgment. Northwest brought the Idaho judgment to Texas, obtained an order giving the judgment full faith and credit, and garnished Signgraphics's bank account. *See Northwest Sign Co. v. Jack H. Brown & Co.*, 680 S.W.2d 808 (Tex. 1984). Signgraphics then brought the present suit in Texas for the price of the pipe.

Signgraphics contends that its claim was not a compulsory counterclaim in the Idaho suit because the sale of the pipe was an oral transaction subsequent to and separate from the written subcontract for installation of the sign, on which Northwest brought its suit in Idaho. Since the law of Idaho has not been proved or cited, we assume it is the same as the law of Texas, and apply rule 97(a) of the Texas Rules of Civil Procedure. This rule requires a pleading to assert as a counterclaim any claim against the opposing party "if it arises out of the transaction or occurrence that is the subject matter of the opposing party's claim . . . ."

Decisions under this rule throw little light on the problem of determining what is "the transaction or occurrence that is the subject matter of the opposing party's claim." The only pertinent decision of the Supreme Court of Texas is *Griffin v.*

Holiday Inns of America, 496 S.W.2d 535, 539 (Tex. 1973), which indicates that the compulsory counterclaim rule is broader than the rule of *res judicata.* There the plaintiff had filed a previous suit for the balance claimed on a contract to pave a parking lot and the defendant had counterclaimed for breach of the same contract. Recovery was denied to both parties in the first suit. In the second suit, the plaintiff sued for the same work in *quantum meruit.* The supreme court held that the *quantum meruit* claim was not barred by *res judicata* because it was considered a "different cause of action,"* but it was barred by rule 97(a) because it arose out of the same transaction — the paving of the parking lot — that was the subject matter of the defendant's counterclaim for damages in the first suit.

Other Texas courts have given rule 97(a) a similarly broad interpretation. The rule has been held to apply in the following cases. *Bailey v. Travis*, 622 S.W.2d 143, 144 (Tex. Civ. App. — Eastland 1981, writ ref'd n.r.e.), held that a legal malpractice claim was barred by failure to assert it in a previous suit for attorney's fees. *Corpus Christi Bank & Trust v. Cross*, 586 S.W.2d 664, 666–67 (Tex. Civ. App. — Corpus Christi 1979, writ ref'd n.r.e.), held similarly in a suit against an accountant. *Upjohn Co. v. Petro Chemicals Suppliers, Inc.*, 537 S.W.2d 337, 340 (Tex. Civ. App. — Beaumont 1976, writ ref'd n.r.e.), held that a seller's claim for unpaid invoices was a compulsory counterclaim in a suit against the seller for fraud in bribing the buyer's agent. *Burris v. Kurtz*, 462 S.W.2d 347, 348 (Tex. Civ. App. — Corpus Christi 1970, writ ref'd n.r.e.), held that a suit for alleged impropriety in handling a retail installment contract was barred by failure to assert the claim in a previous suit against the plaintiff on the contract. *Powell v. Short*, 308 S.W.2d 532, 534 (Tex. Civ. App. — Amarillo 1957, no writ), held that a claim of malicious prosecution for giving a worthless check was a compulsory counterclaim in a suit by the payee to collect on the check. *Connell v. Spires*, 264 S.W.2d 458, 459 (Tex. Civ. App. — Eastland 1954, no writ), held that a claim for breach of contract for pasturing cattle was a compulsory counterclaim in a suit to recover the balance due on the contract.

On the other hand, rule 97(a) has been held not to bar a later suit in the following cases. *Reliance Universal, Inc. v. Sparks Industrial Services*, 688 S.W.2d 890, 891 (Tex. App. — Beaumont 1985, writ ref'd n.r.e.), held that a claim by the buyer of material for the sellers' negligence, after delivery, in directing use of materials was not a compulsory counterclaim in a suit by the seller for the price of the materials. *Astro Sign Co. v. Sullivan*, 518 S.W.2d 420, 426 (Tex. Civ. App. — Corpus Christi 1974, writ ref'd n.r.e.), held that a suit by a former employee for his commissions did not arise out of the same transaction as an earlier suit by the employer for conversion of property by the employee after his discharge. *Gulf States Abrasive Manufacturing, Inc. v. Oertel*, 489 S.W.2d 184, 188 (Tex. Civ. App. — Houston [1st Dist.] 1972, writ ref'd n.r.e.), held that claims against a corporation for personal services and conversion of stock were not compulsory counterclaims in a suit by the corporation for breach of fiduciary duties in setting up a competing corporation.

These cases reveal no consistent test of what is the same "transaction or occurrence." We look, therefore, to the decisions and commentaries interpreting

* [Ed note: The Supreme Court overruled this res judicata analysis in *Griffin* in *Barr v. Resolution Trust Corp.*, 837 S.W.2d 627 (Tex. 1992). See § 8.01[A], infra.]

rule 13(a) of the Federal Rules of Civil Procedure, from which Texas Rule 97(a) is taken. The leading case on compulsory counterclaims is *Moore v. New York Cotton Exchange*, 270 U.S. 593 (1926), in which the Supreme Court construed the former equity rule that preceded federal rule 13. The Court adopted a broad interpretation of the rule, holding that a claim that the plaintiff was purloining quotations from the defendant's exchange was a compulsory counterclaim to the plaintiff's suit alleging that the defendant was violating the antitrust laws by refusing to furnish him ticker service. The Court said that "transaction" has a flexible meaning that "may comprehend a series of many occurrences, depending not so much upon the immediateness of their occurrence as upon their logical relationship." *Moore*, 270 U.S. at 610.

Professor Charles Alan Wright has written that this "logical relationship" test is the only satisfactory method of determining whether a counterclaim is compulsory. He analyzes and discards other suggested tests, including whether substantially the same evidence will support or refute both the plaintiff's claim and the counterclaim, whether the issues of fact and law are largely the same, and whether *res judicata* would bar the subsequent suit in the absence of a compulsory counterclaim rule. Wright, *Estoppel by Rule: The Compulsory Counterclaim Under Modern Pleading*, 39 IOWA L. REV. 255, 270–73 (1954); C. WRIGHT, FEDERAL COURTS § 79, at 527–29 (4th ed. 1983). Professor Wright points out that if a counterclaim would be compulsory under any of these three tests it would be so likewise under the "logical relationship" test, but that the converse is not true because some claims that come within the purpose of the compulsory counterclaim rule would not be compulsory under these other tests. 39 IOWA L. REV. at 271, 272. Professor Wright suggests that the purpose of compelling counterclaims is to reduce the volume of litigation and promote the just, speedy, and inexpensive determination of controversies by barring relitigation of the same sets of facts. 39 IOWA L. REV. at 263. Thus, we conclude that application of the rule requires that both claims concern at least some of the same facts. *Plant v. Blazer Financial Services, Inc.*, 598 F.2d 1357, 1360–61 (5th Cir. 1979).

We recognize that the "logical relationship" test does not provide an easy solution in every case, although it does give a broader scope to the rule than any of the other tests. There is no logical relationship when none of the same facts are relevant to both claims. However, whenever the same facts, which may or may not be disputed, are significant and logically relevant to both claims, the "logical relationship" test is satisfied. This test is consistent with the decision of the Supreme Court of Texas in *Griffin*, as well as most, if not all, of the other Texas decisions cited.

In the present case we conclude that the "logical relationship" test is satisfied. Signgraphics's contract with Weston to fabricate and install the sign was the basic transaction out of which arose both the subcontract on which Northwest sued in Idaho and the later oral contract on which Signgraphics sued in the present suit. Performance of both of these contracts was necessary to enable Signgraphics to perform its contract with Weston. Moreover, performance by Signgraphics of its contract to furnish the pipe was necessary to enable Northwest to perform its subcontract with Signgraphics. Evidence of both of the earlier contracts is relevant to the present suit. Thus, although three distinct contracts are involved, there is a logical relationship between them. We hold that Signgraphics's claim arose out of the transaction or occurrence that was the subject of Northwest's claim, and, therefore, that the present suit is barred by rule 97(a).

Signgraphics contends further that its claim should not be barred because the Idaho judgment was based on a default after service on Signgraphics of a nonresident notice that this Court held to be insufficient in *Northwest Sign Co. v. Jack H. Brown & Co.*, 677 S.W.2d 135 (Tex. Civ. App. — Dallas), *rev'd*, 680 S.W.2d 808 (Tex. 1984). However, the sufficiency of the service and the jurisdiction of the Idaho court were upheld by the Supreme Court of Texas in *Northwest Sign Co. v. Jack H. Brown & Co.*, 680 S.W.2d 808 (Tex. 1984). Signgraphics cites no authority supporting the view that the compulsory counterclaim rule does not apply to a default judgment. Nothing in rule 97(a) indicates that it does not apply to default judgment cases. The rule has been applied to cases where the former defendant did not file an answer because his insurer made a settlement with the plaintiff. *Harris v. Jones*, 404 S.W.2d 349, 351–52 (Tex. Civ. App. — Eastland 1966, writ ref'd); *Firemen's Ins. Co. v. L. P. Steuart & Bros.*, 158 A.2d 675, 677 (D.C. 1960). We conclude that a party has no right to let an adverse claim go by default and reserve his counterclaim for a time and place of his own choice. The same policy reasons apply as if he had appeared and defended the opposing claim. Consequently, we hold that Signgraphics's present claim is barred by its failure to present its present claim as a counterclaim in the Idaho suit . . . .

HOWELL, J., dissenting.

I dissent. In stating that a party "has no right" to default his opponent's action and thereafter litigate his counterclaim at "a time and place of his own choice," the majority infers that the Idaho default was a conscious and deliberate strategic maneuver of Signgraphics, the Texas signmaker. The trial court made no such finding, the Idaho signmaker makes no such claim, and the record does not warrant this court to so hold *sua sponte*.

Likewise, the majority holds by inference that the failure of the Texas signmaker to cite authority "supporting the rule that the compulsory counterclaim rule does not apply to a default judgment" is a sufficient ground for an affirmance. The decision harkens back to the medieval rule that if there be no writ, there be no right. Where the law upon a point has not been decided, it is our obligation to declare the law, not to simply affirm because the appellant has no case directly in point.

Sound legal analysis leads to the conclusion that neither the compulsory counterclaim rule, nor any theory of *res judicata* should be applied to default judgment situations. The courts of our nation enter a myriad of defaults against the impecunious. The most frequent reason, by far, that a defaulting defendant fails to meet his underlying obligation is that he has no money; the reason that he defaults is that he has neither a defense, nor funds to retain counsel to present a defense. That class of default is easily distinguishable and is of little present concern because, once a default of that class is entered, it is rarely contested and, more often than not, the plaintiff ultimately realizes little or nothing upon his judgment.

The class of default which is subsequently contested almost always involves mistake, oversight, misunderstanding, and other human failing. In the majority of instances, the failing which leads to the default is not the personal failing of the defaulting defendant but is the failing of the defendant's agent, generally a member of the bar certified as competent to protect the rights of the public by the very court system which has exacted the default.

Defaults are necessarily punitive. In every instance, they represent the forfeiture of the right to present evidence and to be heard as to the merits of the opposing party's claim. Of course, every system for the regulation of human conduct must have its sanctions; experience demonstrates that without *reasonable* sanctions and the *reasonable* application thereof, our judicial system would collapse. This case squarely presents the question of what is a reasonable sanction for the Texas signmaker's Idaho default. Regrettably the majority has avoided rather than answered the core question presented by this record.

The question, having been properly outlined and placed in its proper context is easily answered: The compulsory counterclaim rule is not applicable to default judgments. Neither should a default judgment be granted *res judicata* effect over and beyond the actual res awarded to the plaintiff who prevails upon default.

The law has long recognized the harsh and punitive effect of defaults. Upon default, the plaintiff may not amend; he may not make additional claims, not unless he serves those claims upon the defaulting defendant and obtains subsequent default thereon; he may not recover more than that for which he has sued; the may not state additional grounds for recovery; and if his evidence will not support all relief granted, the default will not as a rule be modified — it will be set aside in its entirety.

These rules have been fashioned by the courts to ameliorate the punitive effect of defaults. The within majority decision violates them. The Idaho signmaker is being given relief that it did not plead; relief to a dollar value in excess of the defaulted Idaho petition is being awarded; relief different in kind is being granted; relief not supported by evidence received at the default hearing is being assessed. The well established law of Texas pertaining to defaults has been traversed *sub silentio*.

The only theoretical justification advanced by the majority is that which it has gleaned from Professor Wright's statement that the law of compulsory counterclaim reduces the volume of litigation and promotes "the *just*, speedy and inexpensive determination of controversies . . . (emphasis added)." Texas has long held that it is not "just" to assess against a defaulting defendant anything over and beyond that which was precisely claimed and precisely put in evidence in the case wherein the default occurred. Professor Wright's analysis, while persuasive as a general proposition, must yield to the Texas concept of proper sanctions against a defaulting defendant. It is to be further noted that the Professor's stated goal of an inexpensive determination is largely inapplicable to defaults. Default hearings are short and summary proceedings; defaults are often granted upon the pleadings or upon affidavit. To exempt defaults from the compulsory counterclaim rule and from the rule of *res judicata* still only requires but one full blown trial upon the merits. The judgment below should be reversed.

NOTES AND QUESTIONS

(1) *Opposing Parties.* Who is an "opposing party" within the meaning of TEX. R. CIV. P. 97(a), (b)? Suppose A, B, and C are involved in a three-car accident. If A sues B and C claiming personal injury damages from them on a theory of negligence, are B and C "opposing parties"? [Not yet.] Would your answer differ if B made a claim for B's own damages against C? [Yes, then they are opposing parties.] Would C be required to make a claim for C's own damages to counter B's claim? [Yes, because it would be a compulsory counterclaim.] As to contribution claims, however, the Texas Supreme Court has held that contribution claims are not "mature" until after liability is fixed, and so a contribution claim cannot be a compulsory counterclaim in the action whose judgment is the subject of the contribution suit. *Ingersoll-Rand, supra.*

(2) *Prohibited Counterclaims.* Are any counterclaims prohibited under Rule 97? *Cf.* John Kennedy, *Counterclaims Under Federal Rule 13*, 11 HOUS. L. REV. 255 (1974). Suppose the counterclaim is above the maximum jurisdictional limits of the court. Is it still proper? [No.] Below the minimum? [Yes, if it is a compulsory counterclaim.] *See* TEX. R. CIV. P. 97(c).

(3) *Procedural Penalty.* Are the consequences of failing to make a counterclaim that is compulsory too harsh? *See* Charles A. Wright, *Estoppel by Rule: The Compulsory Counterclaim Under Modern Pleading*, 38 MINN. L. REV. 423 (1954). Consider the following from John E. Kennedy, *Counterclaims Under Federal Rule 13*, 11 HOUS. L. REV. 255 (1974).*

> It can be persuasively argued that the traditional *res judicata* consequence of totally barring relitigation is too harsh. A more rational consequence than total bar, in this view, would be to make the relitigator pay court costs and attorneys' fees for not raising the claim in the first litigation. This approach minimizes the supposed success of the traditional approach in granting repose to the plaintiff, and in protecting the courts from relitigation.
>
> Another approach, specifically focusing on the compulsion aspect of rule 13(a), takes a different but related tack. It is argued that the consequence of total preclusion ought to be based on a theory of estoppel, when the party has knowingly waived his right to counterclaim, and should not be applied automatically whenever it appears that the defendant had a claim that arose out of the same transaction or occurrence. Although the traditional *res judicata* concept is often recited, the estoppel theory is gaining ground, especially in cases where reasonable grounds can be shown why the attorney did not raise a counterclaim in the previous litigation. For example, when the defense in the first suit was handled by an insurance company attorney, or the case was settled, it is now being recognized that it is more appropriate to apply rule 13(a) on an estoppel or waiver basis.

(4) *Interpretation of the Compulsory Counterclaim Proviso.* Assume that a case is settled by an injured party's insurance agent who obtains a dismissal of a suit filed

against the insured who has filed no counterclaim in the dismissed action. Is the insured a "pleader" as described in TEX. R. CIV. P. 97(a)? What is the proper interpretation of the proviso at the end of subdivision (a)? Isn't this the same type of problem discussed by Professor Kennedy?

(5) *Severance of Compulsory Counterclaim Improper.* Severance of a compulsory counterclaim is improper. To figure out why, think about what makes a counterclaim compulsory to begin with. *See Rucker v. Bank One Texas, N.A.*, 36 S.W.3d 649, 651 (Tex. App. — Waco 2000, pet. denied) (trial court severed claim against guarantors on a line of credit from counterclaim alleging fraudulent inducement to sign the guarantees — court of appeals held that severance of the compulsory counterclaim was an abuse of discretion).

[B] Cross-Claims

Re-read TEX. R. CIV. P. 97(e).

Cross-claims are claims made between co-parties. They could be claims for a party's own damages, or they could be contribution or indemnity claims against a co-defendant.

NOTES AND QUESTIONS

(1) *Compulsory Cross Claims?* Are any cross-claims compulsory? See former C.P.R.C. § 33.017 (Claims Determined in Primary Suit), which provided: "All claims for contribution between named defendants must be determined in the primary suit, but a named defendant may sue a person who is not a party to the primary suit and who has not settled with the claimant." As a result of the repeal of the statute and the permissive language of subdivision (e) of Civil Procedure Rule 97, it appears that cross-claims as cross-claims are permissive. However, claims between co-parties may fall into more than one category. Read the following note.

(2) *Cross-Claims as Counterclaims.* Can a cross-claim also be a counterclaim? When are co-parties also opposing parties? If A sues B and C for damages for personal injuries incurred in a traffic accident, B may sue C for damage to B's car resulting from the same collision. This would be a cross-claim. The cross-claim makes B and C become opposing parties. If C has a claim against B for damages to C's car it becomes a compulsory counterclaim (as well as being a cross-claim), and C may not bring it later in a separate suit.

What about contribution claims? If B brings a cross-claim against C, C could properly assert C's contribution claim (whether or not mature) against B, as it arises out of the same transaction or occurrence as A's claim against B and C. It would be a proper cross-claim. It is also a counterclaim, since B's claim against C makes them opposing parties. What if C would rather not assert the contribution claim now? C would not lose the right to bring the contribution claim in a later suit; it is not compulsory because it is not mature. *See Ingersoll-Rand, supra.*

§ 7.04 PERMISSIVE JOINDER OF PARTIES BY THE DEFENDANT

Read Tex. R. Civ. P. 38, 97(f).

Defendants may want to bring additional parties into the lawsuit. This can be accomplished in two ways under the procedure rules. First, Rule 38 allows a defendant to implead such new parties if the claims are derivative — the original defendant claims that the newly-added party (the third-party defendant) is or may be liable to the defendant or to the plaintiff for all or part of the plaintiff's claim against the defendant. Second, a defendant with a counterclaim against the plaintiff may add a new party to the counterclaim so long as the claims against the plaintiff and the new party arise out of the same transaction or occurrence. Tex. R. Civ. P. 97(f).

Civil Procedure Rule 38 provides that a defendant as a "defending party" may cause a citation and petition to be served on a person who is not, at that time, a party to the action [*see* Tex. R. Civ. P. 38(a)]. The defendant who attempts to bring the new party into the action is called a "third-party plaintiff." The person brought into the action is called a "third-party defendant." Rule 38 further provides that a third-party plaintiff may join or implead a third-party defendant on the ground that the third-party defendant is liable to the third-party plaintiff or to the original plaintiff for all or part of the claim made against the defendant by the original plaintiff. Tex. R. Civ. P. 38(a).

A plaintiff may also take advantage of Rule 38 when the plaintiff is also a "defending party" within the meaning of the rule. Thus, a plaintiff against whom a defendant asserts a counterclaim may implead another person who is or may be liable to the counterclaimant for all or some part of the claims made in the counterclaim. Tex. R. Civ. P. 38(b).

Civil Procedure Rule 97(f) also provides for the joinder of additional parties to a third-party action, counterclaim, or cross-claim in accordance with the provisions of Rules 38, 39, and 40. Accordingly, any defending party against whom claims are made may implead third parties in accordance with the provisions of Rule 38 [*see* Tex. R. Civ. P. 38(a), 97(f)] or join additional parties to counterclaims or cross-claims in accordance with Rules 39 and 40. Tex. R. Civ. P. 39, 40; *see* Tex. R. Civ. P. 97(f).

A defending party's rights to statutory or common-law indemnity may be enforced in a third-party action. Because the rights of indemnity and contribution are derivative of the plaintiff's primary cause of action, neither contribution nor indemnity is recoverable from a third party against whom the plaintiff has no cause of action. Thus, parties protected by common-law or statutory immunity, such as employers protected by the exclusive remedy provision of the Texas Workers' Compensation Act and governmental entities enjoying sovereign immunity, have no liability for contribution to a tortfeasor. *See, e.g., Varela v. American Petrofina Co. of Texas*, 658 S.W.2d 561, 562-563 (Tex. 1983).

The primary and probably only viable ground for joining or impleading a third-party defendant is that the third-party defendant is liable to the defending party for all or part of the plaintiff's claim. The third-party plaintiff may assert claims against the third-party defendant founded on a contractual indemnity theory, a statutory ground of indemnity, or a theory of contribution. Thus, for example, in a case in which a building contractor had agreed to indemnify one landowner, a municipality, against negligence claims brought by neighboring landowners in connection with construction, the municipality was permitted to implead the contractor when such a claim was brought against it by an adjoining landowner. *City of Amarillo v. Stockton*, 310 S.W.2d 737, 739, 158 Tex. 275 (1958). Similarly, a warrantee of title may generally implead the warrantor when suit to quiet title is brought by a third party. *See Jones v. Jimmerson*, 198 S.W.2d 954, 955 (Civ. App. — Texarkana 1947, no writ).

A third-party action for indemnity may be based on an agency relationship between the third-party plaintiff and the third-party defendant. *See Heisey v. Booth*, 476 S.W.2d 782, 783-784 (Civ. App. — Fort Worth 1972, dis.) (third-party plaintiff permitted to implead alleged principal, but recovered nothing because of failure of proof of agency). An indemnity action may also be based on a statutory right to indemnity. For example, the prosecution of a third-party action was properly permitted when an injured construction worker brought an action against a public utility. The utility was permitted to maintain an indemnity action against the plaintiff's employer because a statute gave the utility company a right of indemnity under certain circumstances. *Hernandez v. Houston Lighting & Power*, 795 S.W.2d 775, 776 (Tex. App. — Houston [14th Dist.] 1990, no writ)].

In tort actions in which the third-party plaintiff alleges that some of the damages claimed by the plaintiff were caused by a third person, the third-party plaintiff may join that other person as a third-party defendant in a third-party action for contribution. Tex. Civ. Prac. & Rem. Code § 33.016(a), (b); *see Ryland Group, Inc. v. White*, 723 S.W.2d 160, 162 (Tex. App. — Houston [1st Dist.] 1986, no writ) (interpreting former Tex. Civ. Prac. & Rem. Code § 33.017). The defendant's ability to seek contribution by way of impleader is, however, subject to the trial court's discretionary power to deny joinder when the joinder of a third party would result in an undue delay of trial. *Valley Industries, Inc. v. Martin*, 733 S.W.2d 720, 721 (Tex. App. — Dallas 1987, orig. proceeding).

Not all derivative liability of a potential third-party defendant to a potential third-party plaintiff is a basis for impleader or joinder. Civil Procedure Rule 38 specifically limits the joinder of liability or indemnity insurers in tort cases. The rule provides that the existence of an insurance policy does not permit the impleader of the insurer, unless the insurer is, by statute or contract, liable to the person injured or damaged. Tex. R. Civ. P. 38(c).

Impleader of persons who have settled with the plaintiff to obtain contribution is not permitted, because settling tortfeasors have no liability for contribution [*see* Tex. Civ. Prac. & Rem. Code § 33.015(d) — no defendant has right of contribution against any settling person]. Furthermore, in cases governed by Chapter 33 of the Civil Practice and Remedies Code, it is debatable whether impleader of a third person who has settled with the plaintiff is permissible to obtain common-law indemnity, as distinguished from contractual or statutory indemnity. Under the Civil Practice and Remedies Code, a plaintiff's total recovery is automatically reduced by reason of settlement with some but less than all joint tortfeasors.

Although the statute is silent on the point, it is entirely conceivable that a settling tortfeasor cannot be impleaded for common-law indemnity because of the credit mechanisms provided in the statutory scheme. *See* notes (4) and (5), *infra.*

Persons who were not made parties to the original action may also be added by bringing them in as parties to a counterclaim or cross-claim. This means that persons who are subject to service of process may be joined as additional defendants to a counterclaim or cross-claim if there is asserted against them jointly, severally, or in the alternative, any right to relief relating to, or arising out of, the same transaction, occurrence, or series of transactions or occurrences and if any question of law or fact common to all of them will arise in the action. Tex. R. Civ. P. 40(a), 97(f). However, the court may sever and order a new trial to prevent parties from being embarrassed, delayed, or put to expense by the inclusion of parties against whom they assert no claim and who assert no claim against them. Tex. R. Civ. P. 40(b); *see Jack R. Allen & Company v. Wyler Textiles, Ltd.*, 371 S.W.2d 728, 730 (Civ. App. — Dallas 1963, no writ).

NOTES AND QUESTIONS

(1) *Third-Party Practice under the Tex. R. Civ. P.: Derivative Claims vs. Defendant's Own Damages.* What persons are eligible to be third-party defendants? The rule provides for the bringing of such actions "against a person not a party to the action who is or may be liable to him [i.e., the defendant] or to the plaintiff for all or part of the plaintiff's claim against him [i.e., the defendant]." Assume A, B, and C become involved in a traffic collision. As a result of the collision, all sustain serious bodily injuries. A sues B. May B bring a third-party action against C for B's personal injuries? What about a contribution claim against C for A's claims against B? What was wrong with the chiropractors' claims that excluded them from the operation of Civil Procedure Rule 38?

(2) *Civil Procedure Rule 97(f).* If A, B, and C are involved in a three-car collision and A sues B for damages, can B join C in connection with a counterclaim against A, seeking to recover B's damages in the collision? Could B also include an indemnity claim against A? Yes. This would arise out of the same transaction or occurrence as B's claim against A. *See* Tex. R. Civ. P. 97(f).

If B successfully joins C as a party to B's counterclaim against A, must C assert a claim against A for C's damages even though A has not asserted a claim against C? [No, this would be a cross-claim, and cross-claims are not compulsory.] *See* Tex. R. Civ. P. 97(e). Is A an opposing party as to C? [Not at this point: A has not filed a claim against C.] *See* Tex. R. Civ. P. 97(a). If C chooses to bring a claim against A, must A then bring A's claim against C for his damages in this collision or lose it forever? [Yes. Once C has brought a claim against A for C's damages in the collision, they are opposing parties and A must bring any compulsory counterclaims or lose the right to bring them later. A's claims for A's damages in this accident arise out of the same transaction or occurrence as C's claims for C's damages in this accident, and so A's counterclaim would be a compulsory one.]

(3) *C.P.R.C. § 33.015: Contribution Defendants.* The primary purpose of impleader under modern practice is to provide for the assertion of contribution

claims against tortfeasors who have not been named as defendants by the plaintiff. Subchapter B of Chapter 33 of the Civil Practice and Remedies Code provides contribution rights to defendants who are "jointly and severally liable" to plaintiffs such that they are legally accountable for all damages recoverable by the plaintiff. *See* C.P.R.C. §§ 33.015, 33.016. The joinder of a "contribution defendant" allows the defendant to assert a claim for contribution and to obtain a judgment against the contribution defendant based on an assessment of the contribution shares of each defendant and each contribution defendant. *See* C.P.R.C. § 33.016. It appears that the same tortfeasor can be joined as a "responsible third party" and as a "contribution defendant." *See* C.P.R.C. § 33.004(b).

(4) *C.P.R.C. § 33.004: The Empty Chair Defendant.* As to actions filed after July 1, 2003, Chapter 33 of the Texas Civil Practices & Remedies Code allows a defendant to designate a "responsible third party" in tort and deceptive trade practices claims, for purposes of submitting their percentage of responsibility to the factfinder and determining the appropriate judgment. C.P.R.C. § 33.003(a). A defendant may make this designation, on motion, without joining the responsible third party, although a claimant may seek joinder of that party as a defendant. Third party practice remains an independent basis for joinder.

Section 33.003 provides that the finder of fact is to determine the percentage of responsibility for each claimant, defendant, settling person, and responsible third party who has been designated under Section 33.004. "Responsible third party" is defined as "any person who is alleged to have caused or contributed to causing in any way the harm for which recovery of damages is sought," provided that a seller eligible for indemnity under Civil Practice and Remedies Code Section 82.002 is not a "responsible third party." C.P.R.C. § 33.011(6). Chapter 33 allows the defendant to designate responsible third parties even if the responsible person is a bankrupt, a criminal, a person beyond the court's jurisdiction, or an employer with workers' compensation immunity.

The granting of leave to designate a responsible third party or a finding of fault against that person does not, absent joinder as a defendant, impose liability on the responsible third party and may not be used in other proceedings, on the basis of *res judicata* or collateral estoppel. C.P.R.C. § 33.004(i). That is, the judgment may not be enforced or collected as to a designated responsible third party. The purpose of designation is to place before the fact finder all persons who are potentially responsible for the claimant's injuries for purposes of determining an appropriate judgment based on how the jury allocates percentages of responsibility among the plaintiffs, the defendants, any parties who have settled with the plaintiff and any designated responsible third parties. Because the general rule is that defendants are liable only for the percentage assigned to them, and that a defendant is not jointly and severally liable unless it has been assigned more that fifty percent of the responsibility with respect to a cause of action, designation of responsible third parties is done in an attempt to lower the percentage of responsibility assigned to any one defendant and thereby to avoid joint and several liability. C.P.R.C. § 33.013.

Defendants who wish to assert contribution claims against other responsible parties may also wait and file those claims in a later lawsuit, even one brought after the plaintiff's claims against the responsible parties is barred by limitations. *In re Martin*, 147 S.W.3d 453, 455 (Tex. App. — Beaumont 2004, pet. denied).

Strategically, why would a defendant prefer to designate a responsible third party rather than join them as a contribution defendant? What effect does the jury's liability findings as to a responsible third party have on the originally named defendant's ultimate responsibility on the judgment?

(5) *The Need for Leave of Court.* Civil Procedure Rule 38 provides that leave of court to prosecute a third-party action must be obtained unless the third-party petition is filed "not later than thirty (30) days after he [the defendant] serves his original answer." Tex. R. Civ. P. 38(a). Does this mean the defendant's initial original answer or any original answer? What if leave of court is not obtained? *See Trueheart v. Braselton*, 875 S.W.2d 412, 414 (Tex. App. — Corpus Christi 1994, no writ) (trial court did not abuse discretion in refusing to strike third-party petition filed without obtaining leave of court).

(6) *Venue of Third-Party Actions.* For venue purposes, a third-party action was formerly viewed as a "distinct and severable" controversy or cause of action. *Union Bus Lines v. Byrd*, 177 S.W.2d 774, 776 (1944). This traditional view was altered for negligence cases by the decision in *Arthur Brothers, Inc. v. U.M.C., Inc.*, 647 S.W.2d 244 (Tex. 1982). Section 15.062(a) of the Civil Practice and Remedies Code now provides that venue of the main action governs venue of cross-claims, counterclaims and third-party actions. Furthermore, if an original defendant properly joins a third-party defendant, venue is proper for a claim arising out of the same transaction, occurrence, or series of transactions or occurrences by the plaintiff against the third-party defendant if the claim arises out of the subject matter of the plaintiff's claim against the original defendant. C.P.R.C. § 15.062(b).

PRACTICE EXERCISE #19

Jason McBride, the driver of an 18-wheeler gravel truck proceeding eastbound on Highway 380 in Wise County, Texas was killed when two 200-pound wheels separated from the tractor of another 18-wheeler that was proceeding in the opposite direction and rolled across the center line into the eastbound lane, sideswiping McBride' truck, which toppled over and exploded into a 20-foot-high ball of fire. The westbound rig was operated by Fabian Cardenas, who was employed by Omega Contracting, Inc. Cardenas suffered massive injuries but lived.

A few weeks before the fatal collision, Omega had hired Williams Tire Service to install new tires on its truck. Michael Paige, an employee of Williams Tire Service, actually installed the tires and reattached the wheels to the tractor. Post-accident investigations strongly suggest that the wheels fell off because the lug nuts were not securely tightened when Paige reinstalled the wheels. Before beginning the journey, Cardenas was required by Federal Motor Carrier Safety Regulations to conduct a safety inspection, but he failed to do more than make a visual inspection of the truck on the morning of the collision.

(1) If the personal representative of McBride's estate brings a survival action against Omega Contracting, Inc. and Cardenas claiming that Cardenas' negligence was a proximate cause of the collision and McBride's death, can Omega join Williams Tire Service as a third party defendant? What kind of claim can Omega assert in such an action and what relief is obtainable?

(2) Under the same facts, can Omega or Cardenas, or both, designate Williams Tire Service and Paige as responsible third parties, without making third party claims against them? What benefits would Omega and Cardenas expect to gain by this designation?

§ 7.05 INTERVENTION; VOLUNTARY JOINDER OF NEW PARTIES

In most of the cases in this chapter, the issue is whether a party can be brought into a lawsuit against its wishes. Here we consider a different situation: a person not a party to the lawsuit wants to join the action. When is this proper?

Read TEX. R. CIV. P. *60.*

IN RE UNION CARBIDE CORPORATION

273 S.W.3d 152 (Tex. 2008)

PER CURIAM

In this case, family members who survived John Hall intervened in a pending personal injury suit filed by Kenneth Moffett. Union Carbide, a defendant in both the pending suit and the intervention, filed a motion to strike the intervention. Instead of ruling on that motion, the trial court severed the Halls claims into a new suit that then remained pending in the same court. We conclude that (1) the trial court abused its discretion by failing to rule on Union Carbide's motion to strike before considering whether to sever the intervention; (2) the trial court only had discretion to grant the motion to strike; and (3) Union Carbide does not have an adequate remedy by appeal. We conditionally grant mandamus relief.

On January 27, 2006, Kenneth Moffett filed a personal injury action in the 212th District Court of Galveston County. Moffett alleged that he was exposed to toxic chemicals distributed, marketed, or manufactured by fourteen defendants and that the exposure caused him to develop acute myelogenous leukemia. He claims to have been exposed to the chemicals from 1974 to 2000, including short periods of time in the mid-1970s and in the 1980s when he worked at the Union Carbide facility in Texas City.

On March 5, 2007, family members who survived John Hall intervened in Moffett's lawsuit. They alleged that Hall died from myelodysplastic syndrome caused by his exposure between 1963 and 1998 to toxic chemicals at Union Carbide's Texas City facility. Some, but not all of the defendants sued by the Hall survivors were also defendants in Moffett's suit. Union Carbide was a defendant in both the Moffett and Hall suits. Union Carbide filed a motion to strike the Halls' intervention because the Halls failed to show that they possessed a justiciable interest in the Moffett suit. The trial court conducted a hearing on the motion to strike but did not rule on it. Instead, the trial court severed the Halls' claims into a separate suit and directed the suit to be docketed and maintained on the regular docket of the court. Union Carbide petitioned the court of appeals for a writ of mandamus directing the trial court to rule on and grant its motion to strike. The court of appeals denied the petition.

In this Court, Union Carbide argues that the trial court abused its discretion by both refusing to rule on its motion to strike the intervention and refusing to grant the motion because the Halls did not show a justiciable interest in the Moffett suit. Union Carbide also urges it does not have an adequate appellate remedy and that the benefits of mandamus review outweigh the detriments.

Texas Rule of Civil Procedure 60 provides that "[a]ny party may intervene by filing a pleading subject to being stricken out by the court for sufficient cause on the motion of any party." The rule authorizes a party with a justiciable interest in a pending suit to intervene in the suit as a matter of right. *Guar. Fed. Sav. Bank v. Horseshoe Operating Co.*, 793 S.W.2d 652, 657 (Tex. 1990). Because intervention is allowed as a matter of right, the "justiciable interest" requirement is of paramount importance: it defines the category of non-parties who may, without consultation with or permission from the original parties or the court, interject their interests into a pending suit to which the intervenors have not been invited. Thus, the "justiciable interest" requirement protects pending cases from having interlopers disrupt the proceedings. The parties to the pending case may protect themselves from the intervention by filing a motion to strike. Id. If any party to the pending suit moves to strike the intervention, the intervenors have the burden to show a justiciable interest in the pending suit. *Mendez v. Brewer*, 626 S.W.2d 498, 499 (Tex. 1982).

To constitute a justiciable interest, "[t]he intervenor's interest must be such that if the original action had never been commenced, and he had first brought it as the sole plaintiff, he would have been entitled to recover in his own name to the extent at least of a part of the relief sought" in the original suit. *King v. Olds*, 12 S.W. 65, 65 (Tex. 1888). In other words, a party may intervene if the intervenor could have "brought the [pending] action, or any part thereof, in his own name." *Guar. Fed. Sav. Bank*, 793 S.W.2d at 657.

In this case, the Halls' petition in intervention only briefly addressed their interest in the Moffett suit:

> In the original action, Moffett claims exposure to benzene and benzene-containing products at premises including Union Carbide in Texas City and against some, if not all, of the Defendants that Intervenors are making claims. Intervenors are entitled to a recovery against the defendants and Intervenors' claims [that] arise out of the same transaction and/or series of transactions and have common questions of law and/or fact with the claims in the original action.

Neither party introduced evidence at the hearing on Union Carbide's motion to strike. In their brief the Halls claim to have met their burden of showing that they had a justiciable interest in the Moffett suit. They primarily base their argument on allegations that Hall and Moffett suffered from similar blood disorders resulting from exposure to benzene at Union Carbide's facilities. Yet the Halls do not assert that they could have brought any part of Moffett's claim. While there is a real controversy between the Halls and Union Carbide — whether John Hall's exposure to toxic chemicals while working at Union Carbide caused his disease — the Halls make no claim that their controversy will be affected or resolved by resolution of the Moffett case. Accordingly, the Halls fail to demonstrate a justiciable interest in Moffett's suit and are not entitled to intervene in the Moffett suit.

The Halls assert that even if they did not properly intervene in Moffett's suit, the trial court had discretion to sever their claims rather than striking them. First, the Halls claim that their petition met the standard for permissive joinder found in Texas Rule of Civil Procedure 40, and therefore, the trial court could properly sever their claims under Rule 41. *See* Tex. R. Civ. P. 41 (providing that "actions which have been improperly joined may be severed"). But the joinder standard does not control here because this was an intervention, and the two are distinct. *Compare* Tex. R. Civ. P. 40(a) (providing the requirements to join in an action as a plaintiff), *with Guar. Fed. Sav. Bank*, 793 S.W.2d at 657 (providing the requirements to intervene in an action). Permissive joinder relates to "proper parties to an action who may be joined or omitted at the *pleader's* election." 1 Roy W. McDonald & Elaine A. Grafton Carlson, Texas Civil Practice § 5:29 (2d ed. 2004) (emphasis added). Permissive joinder and intervention are authorized and permitted by separate rules, and the rules provide different processes for addressing the different situations. Tex. R. Civ. P. 41, 60. Because interventions by uninvited participants have potential for disrupting pending suits, trial courts should rule on motions to strike interventions before considering other matters such as severance.

The Halls reference *Boswell, O'Toole, Davis & Pickering v. Stewart*, 531 S.W.2d 380, 382 (Tex. Civ. App. — Houston [14th Dist.] 1975, no writ), in which the court stated that a trial judge may "proceed to trial of the intervention claim; he may sever the intervention; he may order a separate trial; he may strike the intervention for good cause." *See also Saldana v. Saldana*, 791 S.W.2d 316, 320-21 (Tex. App. — Corpus Christi 1990, no writ). However, Rule 60 does not provide for such options as equal alternatives; it provides only that an intervention is "subject to being stricken out by the court for sufficient cause on the motion of any party." Tex. R. Civ. P. 60.

The Halls further argue that mandamus relief is not proper because the Court cannot prescribe the manner in which the trial court exercises its discretion. The Halls' argument assumes that Rule 60 afforded the trial court discretion to refuse to rule on Union Carbide's motion to strike before it considered severing the Hall case from the Moffett case. It did not. The trial court abused its discretion in failing to first rule on the motion to strike. Furthermore, the Halls did not show that they possessed any justiciable interest in the Moffett lawsuit. They did not show that they had standing to have brought and recovered for any part of Moffett's claim. Accordingly, the trial court had no discretion to deny Union Carbide's motion to strike the petition in intervention.

For mandamus to issue, a relator must show that it has no adequate remedy by appeal. *In re Prudential Ins. Co. of Am.*, 148 S.W.3d 124, 135-36 (Tex. 2004). "An appellate remedy is 'adequate' when any benefits to mandamus review are outweighed by the detriments." *Id.* at 136. Union Carbide claims that the benefits of mandamus review outweigh the detriments because (1) the issue presented is one of law that is likely to recur, yet eludes an answer by appeal; (2) the trial court's action effectively establishes a template for circumventing procedures for random assignment of cases in multi-court counties;[2] (3) it will be difficult or impossible to show on appeal that the deprivation of a randomly assigned judge entitles Union Carbide to appellate relief; (4) the effective initiation of suit by intervention and severance deprived Union Carbide of procedural rights afforded to defendants in original actions; and (5) granting mandamus will not result in any, or at most, negligible detriment. We agree with Union Carbide.

Regardless of the other benefits claimed by Union Carbide, there is significant benefit from mandamus relief in regard to the random-assignment-of-cases question. Random assignment of cases is designed to prevent forum-shopping. Practices that subvert random assignment procedures breed "disrespect for and [threaten] the integrity of our judicial system." *See In re Bennett*, 960 S.W.2d 35, 40 (Tex. 1997). We need not consider whether the intervention was intended to circumvent Galveston County's local rule requiring random assignment of cases because regardless of the Halls' intent, the intervention and the trial court's abuse of discretion in failing to rule on and grant the motion to strike resulted in circumvention of the random assignment rule. In regard to any detriment to the parties, the Halls' claims have now been filed as a separate lawsuit that is pending in Galveston County. There will be insignificant detriment to either party or the judicial system if mandamus relief is granted. On balance, mandamus review is warranted because the benefits of establishing the priority that trial courts must give to ruling on motions to strike interventions and re-emphasizing the importance of both appearance and practice in maintaining integrity of random assignment rules outweigh any detriment to mandamus review in this instance. Thus, Union Carbide does not have an adequate remedy by appeal.

Without hearing oral argument, we conditionally grant the writ of mandamus and direct the trial court to vacate its severance order and enter an order granting Union Carbide's motion to strike. *See* Tex. R. App. P. 52.8(c). The writ will issue only if the trial court does not do so.

NOTES AND QUESTIONS

(1) *Proper Parties.* Who is a "proper" party? *See* Tex. R. Civ. P. 40. Don't John Hall's survivors have the same kind of claims against the same defendants as Kenneth Moffett? What kind of "interest" do they have? Did Moffett object to their presence in the suit? What will happen when the case goes back to the trial court?

(2) *Strategy.* Why do you suppose the Halls wanted to intervene in Moffett's case rather than filing their own independent case from the beginning? And why was it worth such enormous effort on Union Carbide's part to prevent the trial court from

[2] Cases such as the Halls' are subject to random assignment in Galveston County. *See* Galveston (Tex.) Dist. Ct. Loc. R. 3.10.

retaining jurisdiction over the severed Hall claims? (Hint: consider the Court's discussion of the inadequacy of the remedy on appeal).

(3) *Intervening as Defendants.* The Court cites *Guaranty Federal,* one of its own older cases involving intervention in a very different context. *Guaranty Federal Sav. Bank v. Horseshoe Operating,* 793 S.W.2d 652 (Tex. 1990), demonstrates another application of the analysis used to scrutinize a challenged intervention. At the request of its borrower, Petrolife, Inc., University Savings had a teller's check issued to Intercontinental as payment for gasoline under a contract. Later, also at Petrolife's request, University Savings stopped payment on the teller's check. When Intercontinental sued University Savings, Petrolife intervened as a defendant. The trial court, *sua sponte,* struck the intervention, but the court of appeals reversed. The Texas Supreme Court agreed that the trial court had abused its discretion and held:

> Rule 60 of the Texas Rules of Civil Procedure provides that "[a]ny party may intervene, subject to being stricken out by the court for sufficient cause on the motion of the opposite party . . . ." TEX. R. CIV. P. 60. An intervenor is not required to secure the court's permission to intervene; the party who opposed the intervention has the burden to challenge it by a motion to strike. *See In re Nation,* 694 S.W.2d 588 (Tex. App. — Texarkana 1985, no writ); *Jones v. Springs Ranch Co.,* 642 S.W.2d 551 (Tex. App. — Amarillo 1982, no writ). Without a motion to strike, the trial court abused its discretion in striking Petrolife's plea in intervention.
>
> Furthermore, under Rule 60, a person or entity has the right to intervene if the intervenor could have brought the same action, or any part thereof, in his own name, or, if the action had been brought against him, he would be able to defeat recovery, or some part thereof. The interest asserted by the intervenor may be legal or equitable. Although the trial court has broad discretion in determining whether an intervention should be stricken, it is an abuse of discretion to strike a plea in intervention if (1) the intervenor meets the above test, (2) the intervention will not complicate the case by an excessive multiplication of the issues, and (3) the intervention is almost essential to effectively protect the intervenor's interest.
>
> Under the facts alleged in Petrolife's plea in intervention and counterclaim and University Savings' response to ICC's motions for partial summary judgment, Petrolife meets the above test. Furthermore, the intervention will not complicate the case by an excessive multiplication of the issues and is almost essential to effectively protect Petrolife's interests. Judicial economy requires that Petrolife intervene and participate in the trial in order to avoid a multiplicity of lengthy lawsuits. It is undisputed that Petrolife's rights and interests will be affected by the judgment in this case. Therefore, we hold that the trial court abused its discretion in striking Petrolife's plea in intervention.

793 S.W.2d at 657–658.

(4) *Prudential Limits on Permissive Intervention.* In *Roberson v. Roberson,* 420 S.W.2d 495 (Tex. Civ. App. — Houston 1967, writ ref'd n.r.e.), a plea in intervention

was filed by a putative wife in a divorce proceeding. The putative wife claimed that Dr. Roberson acquired properties during the time that she lived with him. She asserted a claim to the properties. Her intervention was stricken. Consider the following excerpt from the opinion:

> Appellants first attack the order of the trial court in striking the plea of intervention of Marinelle Pullen. Marinelle makes claim to a portion of the property acquired by Dr. Roberson while she was claiming to be his putative wife . . . . While the striking of a plea in intervention is ordinarily a discretionary matter with the trial court, there are limits to this rule . . . . However, in the case, an alleged putative wife seeks to intervene in a suit between husband and wife for divorce where a division of an abundance of community property is required. The burdens on the court were already heavy before the attempted intervention. The master in chancery had held hearings on several occasions attempting to determine values and the extent of community property before the filing of the intervention. Suit for divorce was filed on April 1, 1964 and the master was appointed on October 13, 1965. After extensive and complicated hearings the master filed his report on September 20, 1966. Depositions were taken and the master held at least five hearings before the plea of intervention was filed on May 25, 1966, more than two years after the suit was filed. Moreover, the issues required to determine the lack of knowledge and innocence of the intervenor and the putative nature of the alleged marriage were entirely distinct transactions involving issues materially different from those already before the court. Marinelle Pullen could have and now can, in a separate suit against one or both parties to this action, protect the interest, if any, she might have in the property involved. Had the trial court allowed such intervention, this suit for divorce between husband and wife and division of community property probably would have been confused and clouded by a new and complicated set of issues. We believe that interminable trouble, confusion and delay would have resulted by the intervention. The trial court was well within his discretion and was correct in striking the intervention under all the circumstances . . . . We hold that intervenor is not a necessary and indispensable party to this action . . . . Broad discretion is accorded the trial judge in the matter of intervention.
>
> Moreover, the apparently tenuous position of intervenor as being an innocent putative wife of Dr. Roberson, and her consequent claim to a part of the property as against the rights of Mrs. Elsie Roberson, adds force to the decision of the trial court in striking the intervention. We overrule appellants' points of error.

Was her intervention stricken because she filed it too late? What does the court mean about complications? What about the nature of her interest?

(5) *Venue Requirements.* An intervening plaintiff needs to establish an independent basis for venue. Review section 15.003 of the Civil Practice and Remedies Code and the cases interpreting that section in Chapter Five.

§ 7.06 INTERPLEADER

Read Tex. R. Civ. P. *43.*

Interpleader is a procedure that enables a person who is merely holding property that is claimed by adverse parties to file suit naming the claimants, deposit the property into the registry of the court and thereby be discharged, and then leave it to the court to determine to which claimant the property belongs. The purpose of the interpleader procedure is to relieve an innocent stakeholder of the vexation and expense of multiple litigation and the risk of multiple liability. The stakeholder must meet several requirements, however, in order to be entitled to use the interpleader device. In addition, attorney's fees are only available to the disinterested stakeholder: one who is not itself claiming a share of the fund. Consider the following case.

CLAYTON v. MONY LIFE INS. CO. OF AMERICA

284 S.W.3d 398 (Tex. 2009)

Gaultney, J.

This is an appeal from the trial court's discharge order granting an interpleader filed by MONY Life Insurance Company of America. We conclude the court did not abuse its discretion by permitting interpleader and granting a discharge related to annuity payments tendered and made in compliance with the court order. However, the trial court erred by dismissing with prejudice certain pre-interpleader claims, and considering MONY's more than two year delay in interpleading the funds, the court erred by awarding MONY attorney's fees from the annuity. We therefore affirm the discharge order in part, reverse the order in part, and remand the case for further proceedings consistent with this opinion.

THE DISPUTE

In exchange for $400,000, MONY issued an annuity contract to appellant in February 2003, shortly before his divorce from Nancy Clayton. MONY made regular monthly payments to appellant under the annuity contract from March 15, 2003, to July 15, 2003. The trial court signed the decree of divorce on June 27, 2003, and the judgment was affirmed on appeal. The judgment provides in part that Nancy is awarded "fifty percent of MONY Annuity i/n/o husband as set out in the qualified domestic relations order to be signed by the court." . . . MONY apparently learned of the divorce decree in July 2003 and stopped making payments to appellant. MONY began depositing the annuity payments into a non-interest bearing account pursuant to its own procedures.

In February 2005, appellant sued MONY, Nancy Clayton, and Jeffery Shelton (Nancy's attorney in the divorce proceeding) on contract and tort claims, all related to the annuity. MONY filed its answer and subsequently filed an amended answer asserting a plea in interpleader. MONY also filed an affidavit of its compliance director. The affidavit explained that the parties had not completed the appropriate paperwork to allow MONY to disburse the annuity after the divorce decree.

Appellant filed a responsive pleading contesting MONY's entitlement to interpleader relief.

The trial court held a hearing to consider the interpleader and heard arguments by counsel. The compliance director's affidavit was not alluded to or admitted into evidence at the hearing. We find nothing in the record indicating any party filed a motion for summary judgment regarding any matter related to MONY's interpleader or appellant's liability claims against MONY. The only evidence offered at the hearing related to MONY's attorney's fees.

Appellant argued MONY was required to pay him the annuity on a monthly basis, and upon receiving the payment, he would pay Nancy Clayton her share. Counsel for Nancy explained that she had to seek and obtain a court order requiring the payment to her by appellant of her share of some of the annuity payments that had been paid directly to him.

MONY argued that the divorce judgment named Nancy as a fifty percent owner of the annuity, and that although appellant had signed some paperwork to effectuate that division, the paperwork had not been completed despite MONY's repeated requests. Counsel for MONY stated, "We've never gotten paperwork that allows us to do anything." MONY maintained that it was "in the middle" of the controversy.

The trial court ordered the annuity payments placed into the registry of the court, awarded MONY attorney's fees from appellant's share of those funds, and dismissed all claims against MONY with prejudice. The trial court severed the interpleader action, making the discharge order final and appealable. Appellant asks this Court to set aside the order.

INTERPLEADER

Texas has long recognized the equitable remedy of interpleader. Presented with conflicting claims to the stake it holds, a stakeholder who does not know which claimant to pay and fears exposure to double or multiple liability for the single stake, may apply to a court for protection. By placing the fund in the control of the court pursuant to court order for the court to decide ownership, the stakeholder is relieved from the potential liability to pay the single fund more than once, and also from the litigation costs attending the rival claims. *See generally State Farm Life Ins. Co. v. Martinez*, 216 S.W.3d 799, 806-07 (Tex. 2007). If a reasonable doubt exists as to the proper party to pay, the interpleader procedure allows the court to make that decision and discharge the stakeholder from that responsibility.

Today, the interpleader procedure is provided in Texas as a remedial joinder-of-parties rule. Rule 43 of the Texas Rules of Civil Procedure authorizes a party to join as defendants persons having conflicting claims against the party. The rival claimants may be "required to interplead when their claims are such that the plaintiff is or may be exposed to double or multiple liability." As set out in Rule 43, "A defendant exposed to similar liability may obtain such interpleader by way of cross-claim or counterclaim." A party presented with multiple claims to property in its possession may join all claimants in a lawsuit, tender the disputed property into the registry of the court, and request a discharge. The trial court decides whether interpleader is appropriate. As is true of all the rules of civil procedure, the objective of Rule 43 is to obtain a just adjudication of the litigants' rights, and toward that end, we construe the rule liberally. *See* TEX. R. CIV. P. 1.

Rule 43 expressly disclaims certain pre-rule restrictions imposed on interpleader practice. The Rule "extended and liberalized the equitable remedy of interpleader." Interpleader under Rule 43 requires only conflicting claims. In *Martinez*, a case involving rival claims to life insurance proceeds, the Supreme Court explained as follows:

> When insurers receive notice of adverse bona fide claims, Texas law does not require them "to act as judge and jury," or to pay one claim and risk liability on the other. Instead, if a reasonable doubt exists in law or fact as to whom the proceeds belong, an insurer should interplead them and let the courts decide.

Martinez, 216 S.W.3d at 806. Interpleader requires the rival claimants to litigate the ownership issue among themselves, rather than with a stakeholder who has no claim to the fund and simply seeks to pay the proper claimant.

In practice, interpleader generally involves two stages. In the first stage, the court determines whether interpleader is appropriate. Generally, the stakeholder is discharged from liability to the rival claimants in the first stage of the process, and so can avoid the cost of additional litigation over the stake it once held, but to which it asserts no claim. In the second stage, after interpleader has been determined to be appropriate, the rival claimants litigate their differences.

RIVAL CLAIMS

To be entitled to interpleader relief, MONY had to establish that it was facing rival claims to the fund, and that a reasonable doubt existed in law or fact as to which claim was valid. Appellant argued that he is the owner of the annuity contract and that MONY refused to transfer the account. He explained he had signed a "Title Change Form," and although MONY had a copy of that document, MONY made no change in the ownership of the annuity. On appeal, he argues there are no rival claims to the annuity, and the risk that payment of the annuity to him alone may leave MONY without a right of reimbursement is "not the kind of exposure to multiple liabilities that would justify [i]nterpleader relief."

It is undisputed that the divorce decree awarded fifty percent of the annuity to Nancy Clayton. Nevertheless, appellant asserted that the contract required MONY to make the annuity payments solely to him, with appellant then disbursing Nancy's share to her. Confronted with a divorce decree awarding Nancy a fifty percent interest in the annuity and two claimants disputing how and to whom the payments should be made, MONY was presented with rival claimants. Pursuant to Rule 43, under the circumstances MONY could "interplead them and let the courts decide."

. . .

TIMELINESS OF INTERPLEADER

Appellant argues MONY filed its interpleader late. He filed suit against MONY, Nancy Clayton, and Shelton on February 14, 2005, along with a request for disclosure and request for production of documents. MONY filed its answer on April 21, 2005, and its discovery responses and objections on May 23, 2005. On August 25, 2005, approximately six months after appellant filed suit and over two years after MONY received notice of the divorce judgment and stopped the payment of the annuity funds to appellant, MONY filed a plea in interpleader.

Delay in filing an interpleader does not bar a party from depositing disputed funds into the registry of the court. The Supreme Court explained in *Martinez* as follows:

> [I]nterpleader is not improper merely because it is delayed; while some courts have listed prompt filing as an interpleader requirement, the rules of procedure require only conflicting claims. When rival claims exist, courts must decide who gets the proceeds no matter how tardy the deposit; we cannot simply "toss the money back out the clerk's window," or return it to a stakeholder who makes no claim to it.

Id. MONY was presented with conflicting claims and its interpleader is not improper merely because it was delayed.

UNCONDITIONAL TENDER

Appellant argues MONY did not make an unconditional tender of the entire annuity, because MONY deposited only $61,492.23, less attorney's fees, into the court's registry, rather than $400,000. In its plea in interpleader, MONY unequivocally disclaimed any interest in the annuity proceeds that had become due. The trial court found that "at the time of the filing of the Plea in Interpleader, MONY unconditionally offered and tendered to the Court the Annuity payments which had become due at that time, $56,937.25." The trial court also found MONY "unconditionally offered and tendered to [the] Court each additional future monthly Annuity payment of $2,277.49 as they became due until further notice from the Court." . . . MONY made an unconditional tender of the annuity payments into the registry of the court for the trial court to determine who should receive the money. That unconditional tender fulfilled the purpose of interpleader.

INDEPENDENT CLAIMS

Appellant argues he has claims against MONY which should not have been discharged. MONY's tender did not include interest on the money it retained in its possession for over two years. Appellant's claim for interest remained in dispute. He asserted causes of action against MONY for breach of contract, fraud, and breach of fiduciary duty. Appellant argues MONY placed his share as well as Nancy's share of the annuity payments in a non-interest bearing account for two years and did not tender the annuity funds by interpleader until months after he sued MONY. According to the pleadings, the conduct giving rise to these causes of action all occurred prior to MONY's August 2005 filing of the interpleader.

NOT A REQ

Courts have sometimes held that independent liability to one of the claimants precludes interpleader; essentially, the stakeholder was required to be "innocent." That restriction did not survive the adoption of Rule 43, however. Rule 43 requires only conflicting claims. Rule 43 provides that it is not grounds for objection that the rival claims "do not have a common origin or are not identical but are adverse to and independent of one another." It is also not grounds for objection that the stakeholder claims it is "not liable in whole or in part to any or all of the claimants." This language indicates that interpleader is not precluded merely because one of the rival claimants alleges the stakeholder is also independently liable to that claimant, and the stakeholder denies that independent liability, but makes no claim to the stake. Rule 43 expressly permits a defendant, exposed to "similar" double or multiple liability, to "obtain such interpleader by way of cross-claim or counter-claim," and the Rule supplements and does not "in any way limit the joinder of parties permitted in any other rules." *Id.*; *see also* Tex. R. Civ. P. 40 (permissive joinder of parties). As the interpleader remedy was applied in *Martinez*, the insurer's pre-interpleader liability for statutory penalties — those penalties that were incurred before the interpleader was filed — did not preclude the filing of the interpleader, or the effect of the tender in halting any subsequent penalties. . . . The possibility of independent liability may affect the final scope of the discharge order, but independent liability does not necessarily preclude the placement of the fund into the registry of the court, or the obtaining of a discharge from further liability for the payment in compliance with the court order.

The trial court erred, however, in dismissing with prejudice appellant's pre-interpleader liability claims against MONY, because there has been no adjudication of the merits of those claims by summary judgment motion or trial. Courts have applied interpleader to discharge parties from liability on related tort and contract claims. However, those cases involved a summary judgment or a judgment after a trial. While independent liability does not necessarily and automatically preclude interpleader under Rule 43, liability for the independent pre-interpleader claims is not necessarily and automatically discharged by the tender. . . .

The discharge order properly discharged MONY from the potential double liability to the rival claimants for the single fund. The interpleader tender did not serve to discharge all liability claims which arose prior to the interpleader, however. Those disputed independent claims must be adjudicated by summary judgment motion or trial.

ATTORNEY'S FEES

"Under the common law, a stakeholder is entitled to recover its attorney's fees from the deposited funds unless there were no rival claimants or the interpleader was unreasonably delayed." *Martinez*, 216 S.W.3d at 803. An award of attorney's fees to the stakeholder from the fund is within the trial court's sound discretion. Appellant argues an award of attorney's fees to MONY under the circumstances was improper, because MONY, having breached the contract with appellant and having violated its fiduciary duty, was not an innocent stakeholder but rather unreasonably delayed payment or tender of the funds. He asserts the deprivation of his funds caused him harm.

MONY says it learned "in or about July 2003" that the divorce decree awarded fifty percent of the annuity to Nancy Clayton. More than two years elapsed, during which time MONY retained all of the annuity payments due appellant and Nancy in a non-interest bearing account. Appellant sued MONY in February 2005. MONY did not file an interpleader action until August 2005. Nothing in the record suggests MONY offered to place the funds into the registry of the court at an earlier time.

Delay in interpleading may be justified or reasonable under some circumstances. *See Martinez*, 216 S.W.3d at 805 ("Some delay before filing an interpleader may benefit all concerned, if settlement can be reached before lawyers must be hired and pleadings filed."). However, the mere existence of an ongoing dispute involving rival claims does not, without more, justify a lengthy delay like that here; rival claims to a single fund are the reason for the existence of the interpleader procedure and not an excuse for its non-use. The record of the hearing in this case does not support an award of attorney's fees to MONY from the annuity funds in light of the delay of more than two years before MONY filed its interpleader.

CONCLUSION

We affirm the trial court's order instructing MONY to deposit the monthly annuity payments into the registry of the court until further order of the court, and discharging MONY of further liability for payments made in compliance with the court order. We reverse the trial court's award of attorney's fees to MONY. We reverse the dismissal of the pre-interpleader independent liability claims and remand the case for further proceedings consistent with this opinion.

NOTES AND QUESTIONS

(1) *Purpose of Interpleader.* The device of interpleader permits a stakeholder to require rival claimants to fight it out. It supplements the other joinder devices. As the rule indicates, it may be asserted by way of cross-claim or counterclaim. Is the device necessary when the stakeholder is not disinterested?

(2) *Innocent Stakeholder.* Texas follows the rule that a disinterested stakeholder who has reasonable doubts as to the party entitled to the funds or property in his or her possession, and who in good faith interpleads the claimants, is entitled to an allowance of attorney's fees. *United States v. Ray Thomas Gravel Co.*, 380 S.W.2d 576, 580 (Tex. 1964). The allowance is usually from the "fund" in controversy. *Vassiliades v. Theophiles*, 115 S.W.2d 1220 (Tex. Civ. App. — Eastland 1938, writ dism'd).

Be sure to distinguish the requirement that a stakeholder be disinterested (aka "innocent") to recover attorney's fees with a requirements for bringing an interpleader action. It is perfectly proper under Rule 43 for a stakeholder who itself claims a share of the fund to use the interpleader device.

(3) *Venue Requirements.* Under the present venue statute, C.P.R.C. § 15.005 would be applicable to interpleader defendants. The issue would be whether the claims arose out of the same transaction, occurrence, or series of transactions or occurrences.

(4) *Subject Matter Jurisdiction.* The value or amount of the fund or property in the possession of the stakeholder appears to control the question of subject matter jurisdiction. *See Vassiliades v. Theophiles*, 115 S.W.2d 1220 (Tex. Civ. App. — Eastland 1938, writ dism'd).

(5) *Possible Due Process Limits: Nonresident Claimants.* A limitation on the availability of interpleader in state court exists when one of the claimants is a nonresident over whom personal jurisdiction cannot be obtained. Presence of the property or fund in question is not sufficient. *New York Life Ins. Co. v. Dunlevy*, 241 U.S. 518 (1916). The Federal Interpleader Act was passed in 1917 in response to *Dunlevy.* The Act obviates the problem by providing for nationwide service of process in the federal courts. 28 U.S.C. §§ 1335, 1397, 2361. *See* Zechariah Chafee, Jr., *Interstate Interpleader*, 33 YALE L.J. 685 (1924); Zechariah Chafee, Jr., *Federal Interpleader Since the Act of 1936*, 49 YALE L.J. 377 (1940).

§ 7.07 COMPULSORY JOINDER OF PARTIES

When are a party's rights so entwined in a controversy that the case should not, in fairness to the current parties or the absent party, go forward without him? Older cases took a very technical approach to these issues, creating categories of parties who were or were not "indispensable." The rule was amended, however, and current cases take a more functional approach. Can a party wait until appeal before raising an issue of the absence of an important party?

Read TEX. R. CIV. P. 39.

BROOKS v. NORTHGLEN ASSOCIATION

141 S.W.3d 158 (Tex. 2004)

JEFFERSON, J.

This is a declaratory judgment action involving eight property owners' challenge to their homeowners association's attempt to increase and accumulate annual assessments and impose late fees. The trial court held that chapter 204 of the Texas Property Code authorized the Board to raise assessments unilaterally. The court of appeals affirmed the trial court's judgment in part and reversed in part. Both parties petitioned this Court for review. We granted the petitions to review the interplay between Texas Property Code chapter 204 and Northglen Association's deed restrictions. We affirm the court of appeals' judgment in part, vacate in part, and reverse and render judgment in part.

I

Background

Northglen Association ("Northglen") is the homeowners association for six Harris County subdivisions or "sections" encompassing more than 1600 single-family residences. Each section is governed by a separate set of deed restrictions through which every property owner is a member of the Association. The restrictions subject each homeowner to an annual assessment that is deposited into a maintenance fund for such services as maintaining common areas, contracting for garbage disposal, and constructing parks.

In 1994, Northglen's Board of Directors amended the deed restrictions to expand the Board and to assess late fees on unpaid assessments. Geneva Brooks and other Northglen property owners ("Brooks") organized a committee, called the Committee to Remove the Board, to remove certain Board members who, they complained, acted outside the bounds of the deed restrictions by adopting the amendments. Northglen responded by suing for injunctive and declaratory relief. Northglen sought an order enjoining the eight homeowners from conveying the false impression that Brooks's committee was formed pursuant to Northglen's bylaws and from other conduct designed to disrupt the Board's activities. Northglen also sought a judgment declaring that its actions in electing the Board and assessing late fees were valid exercises of its authority. Brooks counterclaimed for a declaratory judgment that Northglen had no authority to raise assessments or charge late fees without a vote of the property owners. Northglen eventually nonsuited its claims, and the case proceeded on Brooks's declaratory judgment action.

The trial court granted summary judgment for Northglen, declaring that, without a vote of the homeowners, Northglen had the authority to: (1) raise the assessment for Sections One, Two, and Three; (2) raise the assessment for Sections Four, Five, and Six by ten percent each year or accumulate and assess the increase after a number of years; and (3) charge delinquent homeowners a $35 late fee. Finding that both parties had pursued legitimate interests, the trial court elected not to award attorney's fees.

The court of appeals affirmed the trial court's judgment in part and reversed in part. It reversed as to Sections One, Two, and Three, holding that the deed restrictions did not permit annual assessments exceeding $120. As to Sections Four, Five, and Six, the court of appeals held that because the deed restrictions contained no language expressly forbidding accumulation, Northglen could accumulate previous assessments under Property Code section 204.010(a)(16). The court also held that section 204.010(a)(10) gave Northglen the right to assess a $35 late fee in addition to the interest charge permitted by the deed restrictions. Because the property owners did not have prior notice of the late fee, the court of appeals held that Northglen could not foreclose on any homesteads to collect those fees. The court of appeals affirmed the trial court's denial of attorney's fees.

We hold that Northglen cannot accumulate unassessed fee increases because the language in the deed restrictions prevails over chapter 204, and we reverse that portion of the court of appeals' judgment. We affirm the portion of the court of appeals' judgment restricting increases in assessments to $120 and holding that Northglen has the authority to assess late charges for unpaid fees, in addition to the interest charges described in the deed restrictions. We conclude, however, that Northglen may not foreclose on the property if late charges are not paid. Finally, we affirm the court of appeals' judgment regarding attorney's fees.

II

Jurisdiction

We first consider Northglen's contention that the trial court lacked subject matter jurisdiction because Brooks did not join all Northglen property owners as parties. Northglen argues that Brooks was required to join all property owners in each affected section before the trial court could render a declaratory judgment and, alternatively, that the trial court was without jurisdiction to render a declaratory judgment interpreting the deed restrictions for Sections Three and Six because property owners from those sections were not represented in the lawsuit.

We do not have the benefit of the lower courts' views on jurisdiction because Northglen did not raise the issue either in the trial court or the court of appeals. Northglen contends that the doctrine of fundamental error excuses it from "the usual requirements of preservation of the error or briefing of the . . . argument" because the absence of jurisdiction may be raised for the first time on appeal. We disagree that the absence of parties within the represented sections deprived the court of jurisdiction and therefore reject Northglen's contention as to Sections One, Two, Four and Five; however, because no property owners in Sections Three or Six were joined in the suit, we agree with Northglen that any judgment affecting those sections would be advisory.

A

No one disputes that the trial court had jurisdiction to declare the "rights, status, and other legal relations" for the named homeowners, who are "interested under a deed, . . . written contract, or other writings constituting a contract or whose rights, status, or other legal relations are affected by a statute." Tex. Civ. Prac. & Rem. Code §§ 37.003(a) and 37.004(a). The question, then, is not "whether jurisdiction is lacking," as Northglen asserts, but whether the trial court should have refused to enter a judgment when a subset of the homeowners was not joined in the lawsuit. *See Cooper v. Texas Gulf Indus., Inc.*, 513 S.W.2d 200, 204 (Tex. 1974) ("[the] concern is less that of the jurisdiction of a court to proceed and is more a question of whether the court ought to proceed with those who are present"). To answer that prudential question, we turn to Rule 39, which governs joinder of persons under the Declaratory Judgment Act. Tex. R. Civ. P. 39; *Clear Lake City Water Auth. v. Clear Lake Util.*, 549 S.W.2d 385, 390 (Tex. 1977) (applying Rule 39 to actions under the Declaratory Judgment Act).

Rule 39, like the Declaratory Judgment Act, mandates joinder of persons whose interests would be affected by the judgment. *See* Tex. Civ. Prac. & Rem. Code § 37.006 ("When declaratory relief is sought, *all persons who have or claim any interest that would be affected by the declaration must be made parties.*") (emphasis added); Tex. R. Civ. P. 39 (a) ("A person who is subject to service of process *shall be joined as a party* in the action if . . . he claims an interest relating to the subject of the action.") (emphasis added). Rule 39 determines whether a trial court has authority to proceed without joining a person whose presence in the litigation is made mandatory by the Declaratory Judgment Act.

Clear Lake City Waste Auth., 549 S.W.2d at 390.

Rule 39(a)(1) requires the presence of all persons who have an interest in the litigation so that any relief awarded will effectively and completely adjudicate the dispute. In this case, nothing in the rule precluded the trial court from rendering complete relief among Northglen and the eight homeowners who had sued for a declaration of rights. Although the parties continue to litigate its correctness, the trial court's judgment represents a final and complete adjudication of the dispute for the parties who were before the court. *See Caldwell v. Callender Lake Prop. Owners Improvement Ass'n*, 888 S.W.2d 903, 907 (Tex. App. — Texarkana 1994, writ denied). Rule 39(a)(2) relates to situations in which the absent party:

> Claims an interest relating to the subject of the action and is so situated that the disposition of the action in his absence may (i) as a practical matter impair or impede his ability to protect that interest or (ii) leave any of the persons already parties subject to a substantial risk of incurring double, multiple, or otherwise inconsistent obligations by reason of his claimed interest.

TEX. R. CIV. P. 39.

Section 37.006(a) of the Declaratory Judgment Act, which provides that a trial court's declaration does not prejudice the rights of any person not a party to the proceeding, dispenses with the first of these concerns. *See* TEX. CIV. PRAC. & REM. CODE § 37.006(a). Any non-joined homeowner would be entitled to pursue individual claims contesting Northglen's authority to raise assessments or impose fees, notwithstanding the trial court's judgment in the current case.[2] *See Cooper*, 513 S.W.2d at 204 ("It would be rare indeed if there were a person whose presence was so indispensable in the sense that his absence deprives a court of jurisdiction . . . ").

We appreciate the risk that, unless each homeowner is joined in one suit, Northglen may be subject to inconsistent judgments. TEX. R. CIV. P. 39(a)(2)(ii). Northglen's dilemma, however, is the product of its own inaction. Northglen could have sought relief at trial by urging the court, among other things, to abate the case, join absent homeowners, or grant special exceptions. *See, e.g.*, *Pirtle v. Gregory*, 629 S.W.2d 919, 920 (Tex. 1982); *Dahl v. Hartman*, 14 S.W.3d 434, 436 (Tex. App. — Houston [14th Dist.] 2000, pet. denied). Instead, it waited until the case reached this Court to first raise the specter of multiple or inconsistent judgments.

Northglen counters that the doctrine of fundamental error excuses its failure to preserve error. However, when Rule 39 was amended, a *young law professor* remarked:

> Henceforth, it will be rare indeed when an appellate court properly determines that the trial court lacked jurisdiction to adjudicate a dispute when the nonjoining person's absence is raised for the first time on appeal by one of the parties in the trial court, at least insofar as the judgment affects parties who participated in the trial, directly or indirectly, or who

---

[2] Despite the notoriety this dispute engendered in the neighborhood, the record does not disclose that any other homeowners filed suit or were otherwise disposed to contest Northglen's actions.

> purposely bypassed the proceedings. The doctrine of fundamental error should no longer protect persons from the binding force of judgments when they have had an opportunity to raise the absence of the nonjoined person and waived it.

William V. Dorsaneo, III, *Compulsory Joinder of Parties in Texas*, 14 Hous. L. Rev. 345, 369 (1977) [emphasis added by editors]. We conclude that Northglen "had an opportunity to raise the absence of the nonjoined person and waived it." *Id.*; Tex. R. App. P. 33.1.

[The court then concluded that there was no "case or controversy" as to Sections Three and Six, because there were no "plaintiffs" from those sections before the court. See § 3.05, "Justiciability, Standing, and Related Doctrines," for a discussion of this jurisdictional doctrine.]

NOTES AND QUESTIONS

(1) *Modern Compulsory Joinder Analysis.* In *Provident Tradesmens Bank & Trust Co. v. Patterson*, 390 U.S. 102, 118–19 (1968), the United States Supreme Court rejected in the following terms the contention that there is a predetermined class of persons without whose joinder the action cannot proceed:

> To say that a court "must" dismiss in the absence of an indispensable party and that it "cannot proceed" without him, puts the matter the wrong way around: A court does not know whether a particular person is "indispensable" until it has examined the situation to determine whether it can proceed without him.

The Court also appears to have rejected the following argument:

(1) there is a category of persons called "indispensable parties";

(2) that category is defined by substantive law and the definition cannot be modified by rules;

(3) the right of a person falling within that category to participate in the lawsuit in question is also a substantive matter, and is absolute.

(2) *Persons Who Should Be Regarded as Indispensable.* Various rules and statutes require the joinder of persons who are primarily liable in actions against sureties, guarantors, and other persons who have secondary liability. If their absence is raised by timely plea in abatement in the trial court, will the court require joinder? *See, e.g.*, Tex. R. Civ. P. 30–32; C.P.R.C. § 17.001 (Suit on Contract With Several Obligors or Parties Conditionally Liable) (requiring joinder unless the missing obligor is beyond the reach of process, missing, dead, or "actually or notoriously insolvent").

(3) *Government Entities as Indispensable Parties.* Although the court in *Northglen* indicated it would be "rare indeed" if there were persons whose presence was so indispensable that their non-joinder would deprive the court of jurisdiction to adjudicate between the parties already joined, such instances do exist. For example, in *Motor Vehicle Bd. of the Texas Dep't of Transp. v. El Paso Indep. Auto. Dealers Ass'n, Inc.*, 37 S.W.3d 538, 540–41 (Tex. App. — El Paso 2001, pet. denied),

the intermediate court dismissed the case for want of jurisdiction due to the failure to join the party responsible for enforcing a statute in an action to declare that statute unconstitutional. Why is nonjoinder regarded as a jurisdictional problem in such a case?

(4) *"Rare Indeed." Northglen* affirms that it would be extremely rare to allow a party to raise a compulsory joinder issue for the first time on appeal, even if a statute states that some other person or persons "must be made parties" (as in C.P.R.C. § 37.006). Similarly, in *Cox v. Johnson*, 638 S.W.2d 867 (Tex. 1982), there was failure to join a joint payee of a promissory note. TEX. BUS. & COM. CODE § 3.110(d) provides that when an instrument is payable to two or more persons, it may be enforced *only* by all of them. In spite of the statute and in express disapproval of an earlier holding to the contrary in *Hinojosa v. Love*, 496 S.W.2d 224 (Tex. Civ. App. — Corpus Christi 1973, no writ), the Texas Supreme Court held that the failure to join the other payee was *not* fundamental error. In other words, normal principles of waiver did apply because the statutory requirement could not be raised for the first time on appeal.

What about the interests of the absent party? If A sues B for partition of Greenacre and neither A nor B raises at trial the absence of C (who also claims an interest in Greenacre), is the judgment of the trial court which divided the tract void? Can A or B attack it on appeal on the basis that they were prejudiced by C's absence? What about C's interest? If C knew of the litigation but purposely bypassed it, should we protect C? What if C didn't know? *Cf. Cooper v. Texas Gulf Indep., Inc.*, 513 S.W.2d 200 (Tex. 1974) (judgment against husband not binding on wife when she was not a party to the first suit for cancellation and rescission of a sale of real estate to her and her husband).

§ 7.08 CLASS ACTIONS

Read TEX. R. CIV. P. 42.

A class action is an extraordinary proceeding created to advance judicial economy by trying claims together that lend themselves to collective treatment. In a class action, a party brings or defends a suit on its own behalf and on the behalf of others who are similarly situated. The judgment binds not only the named parties, but also the class members. The class action proceeding is an exception to the general rules that litigation is conducted by and on behalf of the individual named parties and that a judgment binds only the named parties. *Ford Motor Co. v. Sheldon*, 22 S.W.3d 444, 452 (Tex. 2000). The goals of economy and efficiency through class action do not override the paramount objective of a fair and impartial trial for plaintiffs and defendants. *Southwestern Ref. Co. v. Bernal*, 22 S.W.3d 425, 437 (Tex. 2000). The class action proceeding, therefore, cannot enlarge or diminish any substantive rights or obligations of any parties to a civil action. For example, it cannot be used in a way that will alter the parties' burdens of proof, right to a jury trial, or the substantive prerequisites to recovery under a given tort. *Id.*

[A] Texas Supreme Court's Approach to Class Certification

Prior to the 1977 amendments to Civil Procedure Rule 42, the Texas class action rule was modeled on the 1937 version of Federal Civil Procedure Rule 23, which divided class actions into three categories: "true" class actions, which involved claims by or against class members having joint interests; "hybrid" class actions, involving multiple claims against specific property; and so-called "spurious" class actions, involving common questions among multiple claimants. Under the prior version of Rule 42, the Texas Supreme Court expressed considerable hostility to "spurious"/common question class actions, stating that "this provision has no place in state practice." *Commercial Travelers Life Ins. Co. v. Spears*, 484 S.W.2d 577, 579 (Tex. 1972) (stating that Rule 42 "should not be used as a device to enable client solicitation"). Nevertheless, five years later, the Texas Supreme Court largely copied the revised federal rule, which created greatly expanded opportunities for class certification.

The current Texas Rules of Civil Procedure provide that a court may certify a class action if the requirements of Civil Procedure Rule 42 are satisfied, but the court is not required to order class certification. The Texas Supreme Court had the opportunity in recent years to enunciate guiding principles concerning class action practice in Texas courts. *See, e.g., Ford Motor Co. v. Sheldon*, 22 S.W.3d 444 (Tex. 2000); *Intratex Gas Co. v. Beeson*, 22 S.W.3d 398 (Tex. 2000); *Southwestern Refining Co. v. Bernal*, 22 S.W.3d 425 (Tex. 2000); *Henry Schein, Inc. v. Stromboe*, 102 S.W.3d 675 (Tex. 2002). Generally, the Court has endorsed conservative principles for class action treatment. *Schein*, 102 S.W.3d at 688 (stating that "a cautious approach to class certification is essential"); *Bernal*, 22 S.W.3d at 434.

Bernal is the case that sets out the Texas Supreme Court's framework for considering class certification. After *Bernal*, what must plaintiffs' lawyers be prepared to demonstrate when requesting class certification? What are the policies behind these requirements? What difficulties do they create?

SOUTHWESTERN REFINING COMPANY, INC. v. BERNAL

22 S.W.3d 425 (Tex. 2000)

JUSTICE ALBERTO R. GONZALES delivered the opinion of the Court, in which JUSTICE HECHT, JUSTICE OWEN, JUSTICE BAKER, JUSTICE ABBOTT and JUSTICE O'NEILL joined.

The principal issue in this interlocutory appeal is the propriety of certifying a class action of 904 plaintiffs against Southwest Refining Company for alleged personal injuries arising from a refinery tank fire in Corpus Christi, Texas. The trial court certified the class and directed that the class proceed in three phases: the first to determine general liability and gross negligence; the second to determine punitive damages; and the third to determine causation and actual damages. The court of appeals modified the certification order to require determination of the class representatives' actual damages before punitive damages may be assessed for the whole class. Southwest filed this petition for review, contending that this Court has conflicts jurisdiction and that the common issues do not predominate over the individual issues. We agree with both of

Southwest's contentions. Therefore, we reverse the court of appeals' judgment and remand this cause to the trial court for further proceedings consistent with this opinion.

I

On January 26, 1994, at about 7:30 a.m., a slop tank at a Southwest refinery in Corpus Christi exploded. Julia Bernal, Mary De La Garza, Anita Barrerra and Josephine Suarez, four Corpus Christi residents, sued Southwest and four other defendants for extreme fear and mental anguish caused by the sight and sound of the explosion and for personal injuries and property damages caused by toxic exposure. They allege that the explosion and ensuing fire sent a plume of toxic smoke into the air and that soot and ashes from the smoke descended on their homes in the surrounding neighborhoods. Plaintiffs claim that because of the explosion, they suffered respiratory difficulties, skin irritation, eye irritation, headaches, and nausea, and their lawns, foliage, and pets died.

After an additional 900 claimants joined the lawsuit, plaintiffs moved to certify the personal injury claims as a class action consisting of all of the claimants. The trial court granted the motion, certifying the class with nineteen class representatives under Rule 42(b)(4) of the Texas Rules of Civil Procedure. TEX. R. CIV. P. 42(b)(4). And as the plaintiffs requested, the court excluded from the class all claims for property or diminution-in-value damages. The court's order granting the motion provided for a three-phase trial:

> Phase I will address the alleged liability of defendants to the named class representatives on the issues of negligence, strict liability, toxic trespass, nuisance and gross negligence. Phase I will establish whether defendants are liable for the explosion and whether the released materials were capable of causing the harm alleged by the class.
>
> If during Phase I there is a finding of gross negligence, Phase II of the trial will determine the amount to be recovered by the class as punitive damages.
>
> Phase III will determine whether the individual class members can show sufficient specific injuries or damages and whether they were proximately caused by the release due to the tank explosion. The amount of punitive damages, awarded in Phase II, if any, will be proportionately reduced by the number of individuals who can not make the requisite showing of actual damages and proximate cause in Phase III, if any.

The order does not indicate whether the trial court envisioned a single jury deciding all three phases, including the 904 individual damage claims.

Southwest brought an interlocutory appeal seeking to reverse the certification order. It argued that the prerequisites to class certification, most notably the requirement that common issues predominate over individual ones, were not met. It also argued that the trial court erred by splitting the trial into different phases, in which fault and punitive damages would be determined before causation and actual damages.

The court of appeals held that the class certification satisfied the class action prerequisites. While it acknowledged that "individual issues may predominate in determination of causation and damages," it reasoned that the class was maintainable because the modified trial plan called for the individual issues to be litigated separately from the common issues. The court suggested that these issues would not necessarily overwhelm the jury because "it remains to be seen" whether "the issues of causation and damages may be proven [expeditiously] by the use of models, formulas, and damage brochures." In any event, the court suggested, separate juries could be summoned to resolve the individual issues.

However, in response to Southwest's arguments, the court of appeals modified the trial plan to require proof of actual damages by the nineteen class representatives before the jury may resolve punitive damages for the entire class. Under the modified trial plan, phase I remained as the trial court originally ordered, phase II would determine proximate cause and actual damages for the nineteen class representatives, phase III would determine punitive damages for the entire class, and phase IV would determine proximate cause and actual damages for the remaining 885 class members. Southwest petitions for review from this decision, arguing that the trial court's certification order was an abuse of discretion. Southwest contends that the class action is not maintainable because individual issues will predominate over common questions of law and fact. Southwest also objects to the class action as being an inferior and unmanageable method of adjudicating the controversy. Moreover, Southwest argues that liability and damage issues cannot be tried in separate phases and that punitive damages for the entire class cannot be tried until the jury determines actual damages for the entire class. Finally, Southwest maintains that the class is not so numerous that joinder is impracticable, that class counsel have a conflict of interest because they are also counsel for those members who must decide whether to opt out, and that class notice was deficient . . . .

IV

Southwest argues that the trial court abused its discretion by certifying this case as a class action. Rule 42 of the Texas Rules of Civil Procedure governs class certification. Tex. R. Civ. P. 42. The rule is patterned after Federal Rule of Civil Procedure 23; consequently, federal decisions and authorities interpreting current federal class action requirements are persuasive authority. *See RSR Corp. v. Hayes*, 673 S.W.2d 928, 931–32 (Tex. App. — Dallas 1984, writ dism'd). All class actions must satisfy four threshold requirements: (1) numerosity ("the class is so numerous that joinder of all members is impracticable"); (2) commonality ("there are questions of law or fact common to the class"); (3) typicality ("the claims or defenses of the representative parties are typical of the claims or defenses of the class"); and (4) adequacy of representation ("the representative parties will fairly and adequately protect the interests of the class"). *See* Tex. R. Civ. P. 42(a). In addition to these prerequisites, class actions must satisfy at least one of four subdivisions of Rule 42(b). Plaintiffs assert this class action satisfies Rule 42(b)(4), which requires common questions of law or fact to predominate over questions affecting only individual members and class treatment to be "superior to other available methods for the fair and efficient adjudication of the controversy." Tex. R. Civ. P. 42(b)(4); *see also Amchem Prods. Inc. v. Windsor*, 521 U.S. 591, 615 (1997) (discussing the kinds of class actions that can be maintained under federal rule 23(b)); *Green v. Occidental Petroleum Corp.*, 541 F.2d 1335, 1340 (9th Cir. 1976) (observing that certification under federal rule 23(b)(1)(A), the federal counterpart to Texas's Rule 42(b)(1)(A), will ordinarily be inappropriate in an action for damages).

We consider Rule 42(b)(4)'s predominance requirement first because it is one of the most stringent prerequisites to class certification. To aid a court in determining if (b)(4) certification is appropriate, the rule establishes a list of nonexhaustive factors to consider:

> (A) the interest of members of the class in individually controlling the prosecution or defense of separate actions; (B) the extent and nature of any litigation concerning the controversy already commenced by or against members of the class; (C) the desirability or undesirability of concentrating the litigation in the particular forum; (D) the difficulties likely to be encountered in the management of a class action.

TEX. R. CIV. P. 42(b)(4).

Courts determine if common issues predominate by identifying the substantive issues of the case that will control the outcome of the litigation, assessing which issues will predominate, and determining if the predominating issues are, in fact, those common to the class. *See Reserve Life Ins. Co. v. Kirkland*, 917 S.W.2d 836, 839 (Tex. App. — Houston [14th Dist.] 1996, no writ); *Amoco Prod. Co. v. Hardy*, 628 S.W.2d 813, 816 (Tex. App. — Corpus Christi 1981, writ dism'd). The test for predominance is not whether common issues outnumber uncommon issues but, as one court stated, "whether common or individual issues will be the object of most of the efforts of the litigants and the court." *Central Power & Light Co. v. City of San Juan*, 962 S.W.2d 602, 610 (Tex. App. — Corpus Christi 1998, writ dism'd w.o.j.); *see also Glassell v. Ellis*, 956 S.W.2d 676, 686 (Tex. App. — Texarkana 1997, writ dism'd w.o.j.); *Adams v. Reagan*, 791 S.W.2d 284, 289 (Tex. App. — Fort Worth 1990, no writ). If, after common issues are resolved, presenting and resolving individual issues is likely to be an overwhelming or unmanageable task for a single jury, then common issues do not predominate. Ideally, "a judgment in favor of the class members should decisively settle the entire controversy, and all that should remain is for other members of the class to file proof of their claim." *Life Ins. Co. of the Southwest v. Brister*, 722 S.W.2d 764, 772 (Tex. App. — Fort Worth 1986, no writ); *accord Sun Coast Resources Inc. v. Cooper*, 967 S.W.2d 525, 533–34 (Tex. App. — Houston [1st Dist.] 1998, pet. dism'd w.o.j.); *Microsoft Corp. v. Manning*, 914 S.W.2d 602, 611 (Tex. App. — Texarkana 1995, writ dism'd). Before we determine whether individual issues predominate over common ones in this class, we consider how to properly apply the predominance requirement.

V

The predominance requirement is intended to prevent class action litigation when the sheer complexity and diversity of the individual issues would overwhelm or confuse a jury or severely compromise a party's ability to present viable claims or defenses. But the predominance requirement has not always been so rigorously applied. When presented with significant individual issues, some courts have simply remarked that creative means may be designed to deal with them, without identifying those means or considering whether they would vitiate the parties' ability to present viable claims or defenses. *See, e.g., Amerada Hess Corp. v. Garza*, 973 S.W.2d 667, 680 (Tex. App. — Corpus Christi 1996), *writ dism'd w.o.j.*, 979 S.W.2d 318 (Tex. 1998); *Franklin v. Donoho*, 774 S.W.2d 308, 313 (Tex. App. — Austin 1989, no writ) (both expressing faith that, but not suggesting how, the trial court can creatively deal with significant individual issues in a manner that will be both fair and efficient). Other courts have indulged every presumption in favor of the trial court's ruling, viewed the evidence in the light most favorable to that ruling, and frankly acknowledged that if they erred, it would be in favor of certification. *See, e.g., Health & Tennis Corp. of Am. v. Jackson*, 928 S.W.2d 583, 587 (Tex. App. — San Antonio 1996, writ dism'd w.o.j.); *Reserve Life Ins. Co. v. Kirkland*, 917 S.W.2d 836, 839, 843 (Tex. App. — Houston [14th Dist.] 1996, no writ). Still others have postulated that because a settlement or a verdict for the defendant on the common issues could end the litigation before any individual issues would be raised, predominance need not be evaluated until later. *See, e.g., Ford Motor Co. v. Sheldon*, 965 S.W.2d 65, 72 (Tex. App. — Austin 1998), *rev'd*, 22 S.W.3d 444, 43 Tex. Sup. J. 719, 2000 Tex. LEXIS 48 (Tex. 2000); *Union Pac. Resources Co. v. Chilek*, 966 S.W.2d 117, 123 (Tex. App. — Austin 1998, pet. dism'd w.o.j.). Other courts have suggested that the predominance requirement is not really a preliminary requirement at all because a class can always later be decertified if individual issues are not ultimately resolved. *See National Gypsum Co. v. Kirbyville Indep. Sch. Dist.*, 770 S.W.2d 621, 627 (Tex. App. — Beaumont 1989, writ dism'd w.o.j.) ("There can be no danger in this proceeding to Appellant for the trial court recognized in his order that individual issues would have to be addressed, and stated, 'This certification, of course, may be altered, amended or withdrawn at any time before final judgment.' "); *Life Ins. Co. v. Brister*, 722 S.W.2d 764, 775 (Tex. App. — Fort Worth 1986, no writ) (suggesting that when predominance is in doubt, "the most efficient approach for the trial court is to allow class certification at the present time subject to a motion by the defendants after the case has developed to dissolve the class on the grounds that common questions are not predominant at trial.").

We reject this approach of certify now and worry later. In *Amchem Products Inc. v. Windsor*, the United States Supreme Court reemphasized the importance of vigorously applying the predominance requirement in a class-action certification that sought global settlement of current and future asbestos-related claims. There the Supreme Court emphasized the importance of carefully scrutinizing the predominance standard to ensure that the proposed class is "sufficiently cohesive to warrant adjudication by representation." *Amchem Prods. Inc.*, 521 U.S. at 623. Noting that "the predominance criterion is far more demanding" than the commonality requirement, the Court determined that the plaintiffs' shared experience of asbestos exposure might meet the commonality requirement, but failed to predominate over individual issues. *Amchem Prods. Inc.*, 521 U.S. at 623. In effect, the exacting standards of the predominance inquiry act as a check on the flexible commonality test under Rule 42(a)(2).

Courts must perform a "rigorous analysis" before ruling on class certification to determine whether all prerequisites to certification have been met. *See General Tel.*

Co. of the Southwest v. Falcon, 457 U.S. 147, 161 (1982); *see also In re American Medical Sys., Inc.*, 75 F.3d 1069, 1078–79 (6th Cir. 1996). Although it may not be an abuse of discretion to certify a class that could later fail, we conclude that a cautious approach to class certification is essential. The "flexibility" of Rule 42 "enhances the usefulness of the class-action device, [but] actual, not presumed, conformance with [the Rule] remains . . . indispensable." *Falcon*, 457 U.S. at 160. As the Supreme Court stressed in *Amchem*: "Courts must be mindful that the rule as now composed sets the requirements they are bound to enforce . . . . The text of a rule . . . limits judicial inventiveness." *Amchem Prods. Inc.*, 521 U.S. at 620; *see also General Motors Corp. v. Bloyed*, 916 S.W.2d 949, 954 (Tex. 1996) (emphasizing "the importance of the trial court's obligation to determine that the protective requirements of Texas Rule 42 are met").

Thus it is improper to certify a class without knowing how the claims can and will likely be tried. *See Castano v. American Tobacco Co.*, 84 F.3d 734, 744 (5th Cir. 1996). A trial court's certification order must indicate how the claims will likely be tried so that conformance with Rule 42 may be meaningfully evaluated. "Given the plaintiffs' burden, a court cannot rely on [mere] assurances of counsel that any problems with predominance or superiority can be overcome." *Castano*, 84 F.3d at 742. To make a proper analysis, "going beyond the pleadings is necessary, as a court must understand the claims, defenses, relevant facts, and applicable substantive law in order to make a meaningful determination of the certification issues." *Castano*, 84 F.3d at 744. Any proposal to expedite resolving individual issues must not unduly restrict a party from presenting viable claims or defenses without that party's consent. *See* TEX. R. CIV. P. 815; TEX. GOV'T CODE § 22.004(a) (stating that Texas's procedural "rules may not abridge, enlarge, or modify the substantive rights of a litigant"). If it is not determinable from the outset that the individual issues can be considered in a manageable, time-efficient, yet fair manner, then certification is not appropriate. *See General Motors Corp. v. Bloyed*, 916 S.W.2d 949, 959 (Tex. 1996) ("The trial court [found] that 'there is uncertainty as to whether a class action could be properly certified and maintained through trial because there are potentially substantial individual questions of fact and law and obstacles to the manageability of the action on a class basis.' If the trial court believed this to be the case, it should not have certified the class . . . .").

We turn to the application of the class-action device generally in personal injury cases and determine whether individual issues predominate over common ones in this class.

VI

Personal injury claims will often present thorny causation and damage issues with highly individualistic variables that a court or jury must individually resolve. *See generally Amchem Prods. Inc.*, 521 U.S. 591. Thus, the class action will rarely be an appropriate device for resolving them. The drafters of Federal Rule 23(b)(3), the counterpart to our Rule 42(b)(4), recognized this when they observed that personal injury claims are generally inappropriate for class certification:

> A "mass accident" resulting in injuries to numerous persons is ordinarily not appropriate for a class action because of the likelihood that significant

> questions, not only of damages but of liability and defenses of liability, would be present, affecting individuals in different ways. In these circumstances an action conducted nominally as a class action would degenerate in practice into multiple lawsuits separately tried.

39 F.R.D. 69, 103 (1966).

Here, the causation and damages issues are uniquely individual to each class member. The proximity of the explosion to the residents' homes varied from less than one-half of a mile to almost nine miles. There is evidence that prevailing winds blew the smoke away from the residents' homes. When the tank explosion occurred, class members were scattered in locations that varied from less than one mile from the explosion to as far away as Beaumont. Some were inside their homes, others were outside; some were walking, others were driving. One representative, in fact, admitted that he did not think he was exposed to anything from the tank fire and explosion. Another representative did not even know who he was suing or what he was suing over. In his deposition, he expressed his belief that this lawsuit represented claims relating to a 1993 benzene release from a Coastal Corporation plant. Plaintiffs' counsel concede that there are class members who were not or who do not think they were exposed. One of the class members, for example, was in a Beaumont prison when the explosion occurred. Another was in California. Nevertheless, plaintiff's counsel insist that class members who were not or who do not think they were exposed need to be included and represented within the class so that the class can cover the whole spectrum of "less severe cases, medium cases and really good cases."

We conclude that individual issues predominate over common ones in this class. The common-issues phase will establish whether Southwest is legally responsible for the explosion and whether the released materials were capable of causing the harm some members of the class allege. The answers to these questions are necessary in considering Southwest's liability, but they will not establish whether and to what extent each class member was exposed, whether that exposure was the proximate cause of harm to each class member, whether and to what extent other factors contributed to the alleged harm, and the damage amount that should compensate each class member's harm. As for these latter issues, highly individualistic variables including each class member's dosage, location, activity, age, medical history, sensitivity, and credibility will all be essential to establishing causation and damages.

Rule 42(b)(4) requires class treatment to be superior for the fair and efficient adjudication of the controversy. *See* Tex. R. Civ. P. 42(b)(4). Here Southwest is entitled to a fair opportunity to individual determinations of causation and damages for each of the 904 plaintiffs — a difficult undertaking for any jury. Plaintiffs argue that under the trial plan a single jury in a single lawsuit can and will consider the individual issues fairly and efficiently. Plaintiffs assert that they can present their entire case — all four phases of it — in six to eight weeks. First, they plan to offer evidence on most elements of damages using medical records, summaries, and expert testimony. Second, they plan to submit a charge to the jury with damages and proximate cause issues using a matrix format. Plaintiffs urge that this strategy, coupled with the use of models, formulas, and damage brochures, will allow them to litigate phase IV expeditiously and enable the jury to sort through and deliberate each personal injury claim.

With the help of models, formulas, extrapolation, and damage brochures, plaintiffs may indeed be able to present their case in an expeditious manner. Likewise, Southwest may choose to present a timely and efficient defense, making arguments and presenting evidence on only a generalized, class-wide basis. But, while Southwest may not be entitled to separate trials, it is entitled to challenge the credibility of and its responsibility for each personal injury claim individually. *See generally In re Colonial Pipeline*, 968 S.W.2d 938, 942 (Tex. 1998); *Able Supply Co. v. Moye*, 898 S.W.2d 766 (Tex. 1995) (both vindicating defendants' rights, in mass tort cases, to case-by-case discovery on basic medical and causal information).

The class action is a procedural device intended to advance judicial economy by trying claims together that lend themselves to collective treatment. It is not meant to alter the parties' burdens of proof, right to a jury trial, or the substantive prerequisites to recovery under a given tort. Procedural devices may "not be construed to enlarge or diminish any substantive rights or obligations of any parties to any civil action." TEX. R. CIV. P. 815; *see also* TEX. GOV'T CODE § 22.004(a); *In re Ethyl Corp.*, 975 S.W.2d 606, 613 (Tex. 1998) ("The systemic urge to aggregate litigation must not be allowed to trump our dedication to justice, and we must take care that each individual plaintiff's — and defendant's — cause not be lost in the shadow of a towering mass litigation.") (quoting *In re Brooklyn Navy Yard Asbestos Litig.*, 971 F.2d 831, 853 (2d Cir. 1992)). Although a goal of our system is to resolve lawsuits with "great expedition and dispatch and at the least expense," the supreme objective of the courts is "to obtain a just, fair, equitable and impartial adjudication of the rights of litigants under established principles of substantive law." TEX. R. CIV. P. 1. This means that "convenience and economy must yield to a paramount concern for a fair and impartial trial." *In re Ethyl Corp.*, 975 S.W.2d at 613. And basic to the right to a fair trial — indeed, basic to the very essence of the adversarial process — is that each party have the opportunity to adequately and vigorously present any material claims and defenses. If Southwest chooses to challenge the credibility of and its responsibility for each personal injury claim individually, then what may nominally be a class action initially would degenerate in practice into multiple lawsuits separately tried. We therefore conclude that Rule 42(b)(4)'s requirement that class treatment be superior to other available methods for a fair and efficient adjudication has not been satisfied.

Some commentators have urged that courts relax their commitment to individualized treatment of causation and damages in the mass tort context. *See, e.g.*, David Rosenberg, *Class Actions for Mass Torts: Doing Individual Justice by Collective Means*, 62 INDIANA L.J. 561, 567 (1987) (arguing that "bureaucratic justice implemented through class actions provides better opportunities for achieving individual justice than does the tort system's private law, disaggregative processes"); Samuel Issacharoff, *Administering Damage Awards in Mass-Tort Litigation*, 10 REV. LITIG. 463, 493 (1991) ("The legal system is now beginning to confront the conflict between idealized forms of case-by-case adjudication and the reality of injured parties' regularly dying before the litigation of their claims. Against this backdrop of justice routinely denied, proposals for rough-cut justice dispensed on a mass scale must be taken seriously."). Indeed, under intense pressure to manage their mass-tort dockets, some trial courts have dispensed with proof requirements for certain elements and sharply limited defendants' rights to contest plaintiffs' claims, only to be reversed on appeal. *See* Roger H. Transgrud, *Mass Trials in Mass Tort Cases: A Dissent*, 1989 U. Ill. L. Rev. 69, 84–85 (illustrating how mass trials create incentives for improper behavior and decisions by trial judges). For example, in *Cimino v. Raymark Industries, Inc.*, 151 F.3d 297, 304 (5th Cir. 1998), the trial court certified a class of 2,298 asbestos cases and implemented a trial plan in which the trial court planned to award damages for 2,128 cases based on an extrapolation of jury awards for 160 sample cases. Moreover, the trial court refused to allow defendants to contest exposure or causation for the 160 sample cases. *See Cimino*, 151 F.3d at 304–05 & n.16. Instead, the trial court instructed the jury to assume that each plaintiff had sufficient exposure to be a producing cause of an asbestos- related injury. *See Cimino*, 151 F.3d at 304–05 & n.16. In short, defendants were not permitted to contest individual exposure or causation issues for any of the 2,288 nonrepresentative class members and the 160 sample cases. On an appeal from a judgment rendered in 159 of the cases, the Fifth Circuit reversed, holding that the trial plan violated defendants' Seventh Amendment rights and violated Texas's substantive law. *See Cimino*, 151 F.3d at 311–321; *see also Leverence v. PFS Corp.*, 532 N.W.2d 735, 739–40 (Wis. 1995) (reversing judgment in which trial court, over defendants' objections, used aggregative procedures on issues of cause, contributory negligence, and damages in place of individualized jury determination).

Aggregating claims can dramatically alter substantive tort jurisprudence. Under the traditional tort model, recovery is conditioned on defendant responsibility. The plaintiff must prove, and the defendant must be given the opportunity to contest, every element of a claim. By removing individual considerations from the adversarial process, the tort system is shorn of a valuable method for screening out marginal and unfounded claims. In this way, "class certification magnifies and strengthens the number of unmeritorious claims." *Castano*, 84 F.3d at 746; *see also* John A. Siliciano, *Mass Torts and the Rhetoric of Crisis*, 80 Cornell L. Rev. 990, 1010–11 (1995); Francis E. McGovern, *Looking to the Future of Mass Torts: A Comment on Schuck and Siliciano*, 80 Cornell L. Rev. 1022, 1023–24 (1995) (both observing that mass tort cases have a tendency to attract many unmeritorious claims). If claims are not subject to some level of individual attention, defendants are more likely to be held liable to claimants to whom they caused no harm.

Finally, plaintiffs contend that denial of class treatment is, in reality, the complete denial of legal redress for many of the 904 plaintiffs, because many of their claims are simply too small to justify the cost of individual litigation. At oral argument, plaintiffs' counsel stated that "we have injuries that probably do not exceed, for any of the plaintiffs on an individual basis, a thousand dollars." Plaintiffs urge that the most compelling reason to certify a class action is the existence of a "negative value" suit, in which the cost of litigating each individual claim would surpass any potential recovery. *See General Motors Corp. v. Bloyed*, 916 S.W.2d 949, 953 (Tex. 1996); *Castano v. American Tobacco Co.*, 84 F.3d 734, 748 (5th Cir. 1996).

We do not second-guess plaintiffs' contention that, from a financial perspective, some claims may not be worth pursuing if class-action treatment is denied. But proceeding as a class action may very well cost more in the long run, if, as can be expected here, the class must ultimately be dissolved because there is no manageable way, fair to both parties, to resolve the individual issues. And "there is no right to litigate a claim as a class action. Rather, Rule 42 provides only that the court may certify a class action if the plaintiff satisfies the requirements of the rule." *Sun Coast Resources, Inc. v. Cooper*, 967 S.W.2d 525, 529 (Tex. App. — Houston [1st Dist.] 1998, pet. dism'd w.o.j.); *accord Weatherly v. Deloitte & Touche*, 905 S.W.2d 642, 647 (Tex. App. — Houston [14th Dist.] 1995, writ dism'd w.o.j.); *Vinson v. Texas Commerce Bank-Houston N.A.*, 880 S.W.2d 820, 825 (Tex. App. — Dallas 1994, no writ). This class certification does not satisfy those requirements.

VII

When properly applied the class action device is unquestionably a valuable tool in protecting the rights of our citizens. As the United States Supreme Court has stated:

> the very core of the class action mechanism is to overcome the problem that small recoveries do not provide the incentive for any individual to bring a solo action prosecuting his or her rights. A class action solves this problem by aggregating the relatively paltry potential recoveries into something worth someone's (usually an attorney's) labor.

Amchem Prods. Inc. v. Windsor, 521 U.S. 591, 617 (1997) (quoting *Mace v. Van Ru Credit Corp.*, 109 F.3d 338, 344 (7th Cir. 1997)). But fairness and justice to all concerned require adherence to certification standards before a court may allow a case to proceed as a class action. *See General Motors Corp. v. Bloyed*, 916 S.W.2d 949, 954 (Tex. 1996).

We hold that the trial court's certification order was an abuse of discretion because common issues do not predominate. Because of this conclusion we need not consider Southwest's other objections to the class action or trial plan. We reverse the judgment of the court of appeals and remand this cause to the trial court for further proceedings consistent with this opinion.

[Concurring and dissenting opinions are omitted.]

[B] Types of Class Actions

[1] Generally

As the court notes in *Bernal*, in addition to deciding numerosity, commonality, typicality, and adequacy of representation under Civil Procedure Rule 42(a), the court must determine whether the class action can be maintained under one of the following categories listed in rule 42(b):

> Rule 42(b)(1)(A): When the prosecution of separate actions would pose a risk of inconsistent adjudications with incompatible standards of conduct for the opposing party.
>
> Rule 42(b)(1)(B): When the prosecution of separate actions would pose a risk of adjudications that would be dispositive of the interests of the individual members.

Rule 42(b)(2): When an opposing party has acted or refused to act on grounds generally applicable to the class, making final injunctive or declaratory relief for the entire class appropriate.

Rule 42(b)(3): When questions of law or fact common to the members of the class predominate over any questions affecting only individual members, and a class action is superior to other available methods for the fair and efficient adjudication of the controversy.

The first three types listed above are often referred to as "mandatory" classes because the class members cannot withdraw from the class or file individual actions. Tex. R. Civ. P. 42(b)(1), (2). In a mandatory class, the judgment binds all class members who received appropriate notice of the class determination. In contrast, a Rule 42(b)(3) class is referred to as an "opt-out" or "non-mandatory" class because the members may request exclusion from the class and thereby not be bound by the judgment. Tex. R. Civ. P. 42(b)(3), (c)(2)(B).

[2] (b)(1)(A) Classes

A suit may be appropriate for class treatment if it meets the threshold requirements of Rule 42(a) and if the prosecution of separate actions by or against individual members of the class would create a risk of inconsistent adjudications creating incompatible standards of conduct for the party opposing the class. Texas follows federal precedent and requires more than a lack of uniform results to satisfy the requirements of rule 42(b)(1)(a). Proof that separate actions will yield varying results is not sufficient to prove that there is a risk that the adjudications will create incompatible standards of conduct for the party opposing the class. *Henry Schein, Inc. v. Stromboe*, 102 S.W.3d 675, 691 (Tex. 2002). Rather, there must be additional proof, such as proof that the defendant will be unable to comply with one judgment without violating the terms of another judgment. *Id.* An action is not suitable for rule 42(b)(1)(A) certification if each class member's claim would require an individual determination depending on varying circumstances.

[3] (b)(1)(B) Classes

Another type of mandatory class is the rule 42(b)(1)(B) class, in which prosecution of separate actions poses risks to the interests of individual members of the class. If an individual suit creates a risk of an adjudication that, as a practical matter, will dispose of the interests of other members not parties to the suit or substantially impair or impede their ability to protect their interests, class treatment may be available under rule 42(b)(1)(B). This type of class is generally used where there are multiple claimants to a limited fund. For example, one court of appeals held that when a statute imposed a maximum penalty of $100,000 for conduct affecting a class or series of classes, there was a limited fund. A mandatory class was certified to preserve the limited fund for all claimants. *Morgan v. Deere Credit, Inc.*, 889 S.W.2d 360, 369 (Tex. App. — Houston [14th Dist.] 1994, no writ).

The proof of the limited fund must be more than a broad assertion of the existence of a limited fund; there must be evidence for the court to reach a conclusion that a limited fund exists, such as evidence about the financial condition of the defendant. When this type of class is created for settlement purposes only, the value of the limited fund should be proved by more than an agreement by the parties on the settlement value, especially if the class attorneys have the potential to recover enormous fees. *Ortiz v. Fibreboard Corp.*, 527 U.S. 815 (1999).

[4] (b)(2) Classes

If declaratory or injunctive relief is appropriate for the entire class because the party opposing the class has acted or refused to act on grounds applicable to the class, a rule 42(b)(2) class may be certified. For example, a rule 42(b)(2) class was certified when a credit card company improperly sold personal information it obtained from all of its credit card applicants. The conduct affected the entire class of cardmembers in such a way that injunctive relief was appropriate for the class. *American Exp. Travel Related Servs. Co. v. Walton*, 883 S.W.2d 703, 711 (Tex. App. — Dallas 1994, no writ).

The rule 42(b)(2) class has been used in a variety of actions, such as suits to prohibit defendants from charging excessive late fees [*TCI Cablevision of Dallas, Inc. v. Owens*, 8 S.W.3d 837, 843–44 (Tex. App. — Beaumont 2000, pet. dism'd by agr.)] and discriminating against a specific race [*Clements v. League of United Latin Am. Citizens*, 800 S.W.2d 948, 952–953 (Tex. App. — Corpus Christi 1990, no writ).] Courts have also permitted this type of class in suits to determine rights and obligations under contracts, such as consumer financing agreements [*Morgan v. Deere*, 889 S.W.2d 360, 369–70 (Tex. App. — Houston [14th Dist.] 1994, no writ)] and oil and gas pooling agreements [*Wiggins v. Enserch Expl., Inc.*, 743 S.W.2d 332, 334 (Tex. App. — Dallas 1987, dis. w.o.j.)].

[5] (b)(3) Classes

A non-mandatory class may be appropriate if a court finds that (1) questions of law or fact common to the members of the class predominate over questions affecting only individual members and (2) a class action is superior to other available methods for the fair and efficient adjudication of the controversy. Tex. R. Civ. P. 42(b)(3) (renumbered from 42(b)(4) effective January 1, 2004). This class differs from the others in Civil Procedure Rule 42 because the proposed members of the class may opt-out of the class.

In a case involving a class of 20,000 nationwide software consumers, the Texas Supreme Court ruled that common factual and legal issues did not predominate because the trial court's determinations that there was class-wide reliance on the software company's representations and warranties, commonality of damage claims including restitution, consequential damages, and exemplary damages, and that Texas law applied to all of the class members' claims were not supported by the record. *Henry Schein, Inc. v. Stromboe*, 102 S.W.3d 675, 685 (Tex. 2002). The Court approvingly cited a Fifth Circuit case for the proposition that if reliance is necessary to prove actual damages, a class action may not be certified on that issue. *Perrone v. General Motors Acceptance Corp.*, 232 F.3d 433, 440 (5th Cir. 2000). The Court concluded that "[w]e need not and do not decide whether a class asserting a cause of action requiring proof of reliance, like the class alleged here, can ever be certified. We hold only that the plaintiffs in this case have failed to show that individual issues of reliance do not preclude the necessary finding of predominance under Rule 42(b)[3].” *Schein*, 102 S.W.3d at 694. Thus, one court of appeals affirmed the certification of a class action when any reliance would have affected each class member in the same manner and was not individualized, but the Texas Supreme Court has granted the petition to review that decision. *Southwestern Bell v. Marketing on Hold*, 170 S.W.3d 814, 827–28 (Tex. App. — Corpus Christi 2005), *pet. granted*, 2007 Tex. LEXIS 155 (Tex. 2007)

Effective January 1, 2004, the trial court’s order granting or denying a certification under Civil Procedure Rule 42(b)(3) must address eight issues:

1. The elements of each claim or defense asserted in the pleadings.
2. Any issues of law or fact common to the class members.
3. Any issues of law or fact affecting only individual class members.
4. The issues that will be the object of most of the efforts of the litigants and the court.
5. Other available methods of adjudication that exist for the controversy.
6. Why the issues common to the members of the class do or do not predominate over individual issues.
7. Why a class is or is not superior to other available methods for the fair and efficient adjudication of the controversy.
8. If a class is certified, how the class claims and any issues affecting only individual members, raised by the claims or defenses asserted in the pleadings, will be tried in a manageable, time-efficient manner.

This codifies the “rigorous analysis” and “trial plan” requirements of *Bernal*.

NOTES AND QUESTIONS

(1) *Shareholder’s Derivative Action*. When Civil Procedure Rule 42 was originally adopted, it governed both class actions and shareholders’ derivative suits. With the substantial revision of Rule 42 in 1977 so that it generally paralleled Fed. R. Civ. P. 23, reference to derivative suits was dropped. But there was no concomitant adoption of a rule comparable to Fed. R. Civ. P. 23.1. In *Zauber v. Murray Savings Ass’n*, 591 S.W.2d 932 (Tex. Civ. App. — Dallas 1979), *writ ref’d n.r.e. per curiam*, 601 S.W.2d 940 (Tex. 1980), the court held: “In light of the [1977 revision of the rule], the supreme court clearly intended rule 42 to govern only class actions; derivative actions brought in the right of a corporation are governed solely by article 5.14 of the Texas Business Corporation Act.” Civil Procedure Rule 42 was amended in 1984 to correlate the procedural rules with Article 5.14 of the Business Corporation Act. Under current law, derivative suit proceedings are governed by section 21.522 of the Texas Business Organizations Code.

(2) *Bernal’s Trial Plan Requirement Applies Generally*. The Texas Supreme Court has made it clear that a trial plan must be included in every certification order, not only when the Rule 42(b) (3) predominance and superiority requirements are in issue. *State Farm Mut. Auto. Ins. Co. v. Lopez*, 156 S.W.3d

550, 554–56 (Tex. 2004) ("The formulation of a trial plan assures that a trial court has fulfilled its obligation to rigorously analyze all certification prerequisites, and understands the claims, defenses, relevant facts, and applicable substantive law in order to make a meaningful determination of the certification issues.").

(3) *Bernal's "Rigorous Analysis" Requirement Applies to (b)(2) Class Actions.* In order to avoid perceived stricter certification requirements applied to (b)(3) class actions, some practitioners attempted to use (b)(2) actions for declaratory relief coupled with claims for monetary relief. In *Compaq Computer Corp. v. Lapray*, 135 S.W.3d 657 (Tex. 2004), the Texas Supreme Court held that parties cannot evade the "rigorous analysis" requirement by seeking (b)(2) certification. Although Rule 42(b)(2) class actions have no predominance of common issues requirement, the class claims must be "cohesive." As the court explained, in many cases "this analysis will be identical to the 'predominance and superiority' directive undertaken by trial courts certifying (b)(3) classes." Indeed, a (b)(2) class may require "more cohesiveness than [a] (b)(3) class . . . because in [a] (b)(2) action, unnamed members are bound without the opportunity to opt out" unless notice and opt out rights are provided in the certification order.

(4) *"Rigorous Analysis" and Choice of Law.* The "rigorous analysis" in all cases must include considerations of what state or states' law will apply to the issues in the case. This is especially important in cases requesting the certification of a nationwide class. Accordingly, trial courts cannot postpone choice of law questions until after certification, as courts "can hardly evaluate the claims, defenses, or applicable law without knowing what the law is." *Lapray*, 135 S.W.3d at 672. In ruling on motions for class certification, trial courts "must conduct an extensive choice of law analysis before they can determine predominance, superiority, cohesiveness and even manageability." *Id.* The party seeking class certification of a predominance-of-common-questions nationwide class has the burden of establishing the substantive law that will be applicable to the class claims in order to demonstrate that common legal issues predominate over individual issues. Which states' laws will govern an issue in a class action is a question of law for the court to decide. However, determining the state contacts to be considered by the court in making this legal determination involves a factual inquiry.

(5) *Adequacy of Representation.* In *Southwestern Bell Telephone Co. v. Marketing On Hold, Inc.*, 2010 Tex. LEXIS 159 (Tex. 2010), the Court was faced with a class action that satisfied many of the barriers it had erected in earlier cases. Marketing On Hold (MOH) is a company that monitors its customers' telephone bills for inaccuracies, and retains a portion of the money saved. Five customers assigned to MOH their rights to claims against Southwestern Bell — that Bell illegally charged municipal fees to business customers. MOH then filed a class action, as named plaintiff, against Southwestern Bell and sought to be designated the class representative for approximately 6,900 of Southwestern Bell business customers. MOH asserted claims for breach of contract, unjust enrichment, breach of express warranty for services, and negligence per se for illegally charging municipal fees. The trial court certified the case as a state-wide class action, and the court of appeals affirmed the certification. Southwestern Bell appealed to the Texas Supreme Court, and almost three years after oral argument of this

interlocutory appeal, the Court ruled 5-3 (with one Justice not participating) that the certification should be reversed.

The Court held that MOH's assignments were valid and provided standing to sue. "The assignee is not disqualified from serving as a class representative so long as it is not a stranger seeking entrepreneurship in class actions, and it does not distort the litigation process." Further, its claims were typical of the class, numerosity was not a problem, and there were common questions of law and fact. The (b)(3) class also satisfied the predominance requirement, since neither reliance nor damages required burdensome individualized proof.

However, the majority concluded that MOH had not demonstrated that it would adequately represent the class, because its interests might conflict with those of class members. It said that MOH:

> has a materially lesser interest in making itself and the class whole because it was never personally aggrieved by Southwestern Bell's alleged overcharging, and its maximum recovery is less than half the value of any individual claim for damages. . . . For example, because [MOH] never paid the alleged overcharges at issue and can retain at best only thirty-percent of any recovery, [MOH's] incentive in settling quickly in order to minimize litigation expenses differs from class members who have overpaid and may be willing to hold out for a settlement that approximates their actual damages. For the same reason, [MOH's] motivation may encourage pursuit of theories of relief that are more efficient for it, but yield less recovery for absentee class members. . . . The only objective benefit that [MOH] obtained was standing to sue on behalf of the five assigned claimants, and the resultant ability to serve as the class representative and to control the litigation of some 6,900 claims against Southwestern Bell. [MOH] stands in somewhat different shoes from other class members by virtue of its possible recovery pursuant to consulting contracts with other customers who paid the alleged overcharges but have not assigned their claims to [MOH]. [MOH's] motives, different interests, and potentially conflicting interest created by the benefits under the five assignments and consulting contracts distinguish it from the thousands of other class members.

Justices O'Neill, Jefferson, and Medina dissented, characterizing the majority's concerns as "hypothetical conflicts that have no basis in the record." Dismissing the alleged conflicts, the dissent wrote: "the Court theorizes that since [MOH] never paid the overcharges itself, it might have a greater incentive to settle more quickly than other class members who paid the charges and might want more. However, any incentive [MOH] might have to minimize litigation expenses by settling early appears to be no different from that any other class member would have, and [MOH's] incentive to maximize recovery appears to be no different either. Though the Court posits that [MOH] might ultimately pursue theories of relief more efficient for itself at the expense of absentee class members, it does not speculate what those theories might be and none have been asserted. Such speculative conflicts are far too tenuous to render [MOH] inadequate."

Since the majority's adequacy concerns relate specifically to Marketing on Hold, could the plaintiffs amend their claim on remand to instead name individual

Southwestern Bell business customers as the class representatives?

(6) *2004 Changes to Texas Rule of Civil Procedure 42.* As directed by the Texas Legislature in House Bill 4, the Texas Supreme Court amended rule 42 governing class actions. Some of the more noteworthy changes:

a) *The Timing of Certification.* The trial court is directed to determine whether to certify an action as a class action "at an early practicable time" tracking the changes to Federal Rule 23. The comment to rule 42 clarifies: "The amended language is not intended to permit undue delay or permit excessive discovery unrelated to certification, but is designed to encourage good practices in making certification decisions only after receiving the information necessary to decide whether certification should be granted or denied and how to define the class if certification is granted."

b) *Notice to the Class.* The trial court "may" direct appropriate notice to the members of a class certified under rule 42(b)(1) or (2), but "must" direct notice to members of a rule 42(b)(3) class. This notice must be "the best notice practicable under the circumstances, including individual notice to all members who can be identified with reasonable effort." The notice must inform "when and how members may elect to be excluded" and "the binding effect of a class judgment on class members." Further, the trial court may not approve a settlement "unless it affords a new opportunity to request exclusion to individual class members who had an earlier opportunity to request exclusion but did not do so." Class members may object to any proposed settlement.

c) *Class Counsel — Qualifications and Fees.* Rule 42(g) sets forth the requirements and factors the court should consider in appointing class counsel. An attorney appointed to serve as class counsel must fairly and adequately represent the interest of the class. The court in appointing class counsel must consider the work counsel has done in identifying or investigating potential claims in the action; counsel's experience in handling class actions, other complex litigation, and claims of the type asserted in the action; counsel's knowledge of the applicable law; and the resources counsel will commit to representing the class. In addition, the court may consider any other matter pertinent to counsel's ability to fairly and adequately represent the interests of the class.

d) *Attorney's Fees.* The legislature has placed certain restrictions on the recovery of attorney's fees recoverable by class counsel, that are incorporated in rule 42(i). For actions filed after September 1, 2003, the trial court must first determine a "lodestar figure" by multiplying the number of hours reasonably worked times a reasonable hourly rate. The attorney fees award must be in the range of 25% to 400% of the lodestar figure. In making these determinations, the court must consider the factors specified in rule 1.04(b) of the Texas Disciplinary Rules of Professional Conduct. Further, "if any portion of the benefits recovered for the class are in the form of coupons or other noncash common benefits, the attorney fees awarded in the action must be in cash and noncash amounts in the same proportion as the recovery for the class."

(7) *Settling Class Actions.* Effective January 1, 2004, after a suit is certified as a class action under Civil Procedure Rule 42, claims, issues, or defenses of the certified class may be settled, dismissed, or compromised if the following conditions are met:

1. The court must approve any settlement, dismissal, or compromise of the claims, issues, or defenses of a certified class.

2. Notice of the material terms of the proposed settlement, dismissal, or compromise, together with an explanation of when and how the members may elect to be excluded from the class, must be given to all members in such manner as the court directs.

3. The trial court holds a hearing on any settlement, dismissal, or compromise that would bind class members.

4. The trial court finds the settlement, dismissal, or compromise would be fair, reasonable, and adequate.

These safeguards are designed to protect the unnamed class members from an unjust or unfair settlement.

For 42(b)(3) classes, rule 42 also requires that a settlement must afford individual class members, who had an earlier opportunity to request exclusion but did not do so, a new opportunity to request exclusion. Parties seeking settlement approval must also file a statement with the court identifying any agreement made in connection with the proposed settlement, dismissal, or compromise.

The goal of notice is to provide the class members sufficient information to enable them to make informed decisions on whether to object to the class settlement. Thus, the terms of the settlement should be included with specificity. For example, the notice must not only state that attorney's fees will be awarded, but must also include the maximum amount of the attorney's fees class counsel seeks and the method for calculating those fees. This information must be given whether the award is to be subtracted from the funds to be distributed among the class members or is to be paid as a separate amount.

Once objections, if any, have been filed, the court will hold a hearing to determine whether the settlement, dismissal, or compromise is fair, reasonable, and adequate. Case law requires that the hearing must be a plenary hearing where witnesses are sworn and testify in person or by deposition. The hearing may not be based on affidavits alone; there should be an opportunity for the court to question the witnesses and the counsel representing the objecting class members to engage in rigorous cross-examination. *General Motors Corp. v. Bloyed*, 916 S.W.2d 949, 958 (Tex. 1996). The court must examine both the substantive and procedural aspects of the settlement, dismissal, or compromise to determine whether it meets those requirements and was the product of honest negotiations, not collusion. To aid the court in its determination, the court will consider the following factors:

1. Whether the settlement was negotiated at arms' length or was a product of fraud or collusion.

2. The complexity, expense, and probable duration of the case.

3. The current stage of proceedings and amount of discovery completed.
4. The factual and legal obstacles affecting the merits.
5. The possible range of recovery and the certainty of damages.
6. The respective opinions of participants, including the class representative, other class members, and counsel.

After the fairness hearing, the court is empowered to approve the settlement, dismissal, or compromise based on a determination that it is fair, reasonable, and adequate, even though objections may still remain.

(8) *Settlement-Only Classes.* A suit may be certified as a class action even if the only purpose is to settle the class action rather than litigate the case. The settlement-only class is not specifically authorized by Civil Procedure Rule 42, but the use of such a class, with additional safeguards, has been approved in the context of both mandatory and voluntary class actions in federal and state jurisprudence. Actions certified as settlement-only class actions must meet the class certification requirements in Civil Procedure Rule 42(a) and (b) in addition to the fairness requirement in rule 42(e).

An exception that will likely be applied in Texas was developed in *Amchem Prods., Inc. v. Windsor*, in which the United States Supreme Court recognized that in a settlement-only class action, it is unnecessary to prove that the class is manageable for trial, which ordinarily must be proved in a predominance-of-common-questions class. The Supreme Court excuses proof on the manageability of the class at trial because the parties are seeking certification for settlement purposes only, not for litigation purposes. 521 U.S. 591, 620 (1997).

(9) *Effects of Class Judgment.* Judgments in class actions under rule 42(b)(1) and (2) include and describe all persons the court finds to be members of the class, regardless of whether the judgment is favorable to the class. For class actions maintained under Civil Procedure Rule 42(b)(3), judgments, whether or not favorable to the class, must include and specify or describe to whom proper notice was provided, and persons who did not request to be excluded, and persons the court found to be members of the class. TEX. R. CIV. P. 42(c)(3).

In *Citizens Insurance Co. of America v. Daccach*, 217 S.W.3d 430 (Tex. 2007), the Court adopted a broad approach to claim preclusion in the class action setting. In that case, the named plaintiffs originally asserted a number of claims, but sought class certification as to only one. The plaintiffs argued that, because the other issues were not suited to class treatment, the class members could choose to pursue those individual claims separately. The Texas Supreme Court disagreed, and held that the class members would lose any un-asserted claims that were part of the same cause of action as the one as to which the class was certified. For this reason, courts must consider the risk of preclusion when deciding whether to certify a class, and willingness to abandon strong individual claims may demonstrate that the named plaintiff is not adequately representing the class. ("We hold, therefore, that Texas Rule of Civil Procedure 42 requires the trial court, as part of its rigorous analysis, to consider the risk that a judgment in the class action may preclude subsequent litigation of claims not alleged, abandoned, or split from the class action. The trial court abuses its discretion if it fails to consider the preclusive effect of a judgment on abandoned claims, as res judicata could undermine the adequacy of representation requirement." *Id.* at 457.) Preclusion issues may also make notice and opt-out rights particularly important. ("Ultimately, to certify a class in which the representatives have abandoned claims in favor of pursuing certain class claims, raising a risk of preclusion for absent class members, effective notice must be given to these absent members of an identified class regarding the preclusive effect that may attach to their individual claims. The unnamed members may then exercise independent judgment and chose to remain in the class or opt out." *Id.* at 458.)

(10) *Appellate Review of Class Action Certification Orders.* Class certification orders are subject to immediate interlocutory review and may be reviewed by the Texas Supreme Court on petition for review. C.P.R.C. § 51.014(a)(3). An interlocutory appeal of a certification ruling stays not only the trial but "also stays all other proceedings in the trial court."

(11) *Class Action Fairness Act.* In February of 2005, the U.S. Congress passed the Class Action Fairness Act, much of which is codified at 28 U.S.C. § 1332(d). The act grants federal court jurisdiction of class actions in which a class of at least 100 persons has claims that aggregate at least $5 million, and in which there is at least minimal diversity between some class member and some defendant. In addition, defendants may remove such actions even if they are citizens of the state where the action is pending. 28 U.S.C. § 1453. Thus a plaintiff's attorney can no longer prevent removal to federal court by joining a non-diverse defendant or by suing an in-state defendant. This provision may mean that more nationwide consumer class actions are litigated in federal court than in state court, as in some states the federal courts are considered to be more hostile to class certification than are state courts. Whether this will be true in Texas remains to be seen. CAFA also provides that the federal courts should decline jurisdiction of class actions that are primarily local in nature.

PRACTICE EXERCISE #20

George Gunner is a third year law student at Directional University Law School (DULS). During the fall semester, he purchased a book called "Conquering Texas Procedure," a 500-page text that promised that it contained the secret to passing the Civil Procedure and Evidence portion of the Texas Bar Exam. The book's publishers, DTPA Press, went so far as to warrant that those who purchased and studied the book would be guaranteed bar passage because it would so elevate a student's performance in procedure that it would make up for weaknesses in any other portion of the exam. George bought the book, studied it carefully, took the bar exam, and failed (although he did OK on the Texas procedure part).

George sued DTPA Press for fraud and breach of warranty, seeking actual and punitive damages for himself individually and for a class composed of all law students in the United States who purchased DTPA's book but failed to pass the bar exam. His suit is now pending in state district court in Dallas County, Texas.

(1) George filed a motion to certify the class. At the hearing on his motion, George produced evidence that more than 2,000 copies of Conquering Texas Procedure have been sold to U.S. law students (mostly but not exclusively from Texas) since August 1, 2002. He also introduced evidence regarding the qualifications of his lawyers, his own serious devotion to the case, and the adoption by 49 states of the Uniform Commercial Code provisions regarding breach of warranty. George argued that a class action would be manageable because the same written representations were made to each class member (on the back of the book). DTPA Press introduced evidence of different legal standards regarding warranty, consumer legislation, and fraud in the fifty states. They also argued that class members (who cannot all be individually identified) must each prove that they relied on DTPA Press' representations and must individually prove causation and damages. What will George's most significant hurdles be for class certification?

(2) Suppose that George modified his class claim so that only Texas residents who attended Texas law schools are class members. What effect would that have on his quest for class certification?

(3) DTPA Press has made George a settlement offer: they will agree to class certification if the class will accept a free copy of "Conquering Wills & Trusts" as their total compensation. (After all, they need to re-take the bar exam.) They also offer to pay George's lawyers $250,000. Suppose George agrees and submits the proposal to the court for approval. What objections do you expect a class member might make? Should the court approve the settlement?

(4) Assume that George's claims are as originally stated (so that there are class members from Texas, New York, Illinois, New Mexico, Louisiana, Oklahoma, Georgia, and California), and that he claims that each class member has suffered actual damages of at least $100,000 and that defendant should have to pay $5 million in punitive damages. Also assume that DTPA Press is a Texas corporation with its principal place of business in Texas. Could DTPA Press remove this case to federal court under CAFA?

Chapter 8

PRECLUSION DOCTRINES

Scope

This chapter focuses on the effects of prior adjudication on later litigation, traditionally known as "*res judicata*" but in more recent times known as preclusion. The chapter begins by discussing the binding effect of prior litigation on the parties: merger and bar (claim preclusion), collateral estoppel (issue preclusion). It then covers the doctrines of "election of remedies" and "law of the case."

§ 8.01 PRECLUSION

Two different but related doctrines deal generally with the conclusive effects of judgments. "Claim preclusion" (formerly known as "*res judicata*" or "merger and bar") precludes relitigation of a claim when a subsequent suit is brought on the same cause of action, whether or not that claim was actually litigated in the earlier case. "Issue preclusion" (formerly known as "collateral estoppel") precludes relitigation of an issue or issues of fact common to separate causes of action. As will become clear in the sections below, the distinction between claim preclusion and issue preclusion is important in determining the breadth of the estoppel worked by the prior judgment.

[A] Claim Preclusion: The Doctrine of Merger and Bar

Traditionally, it has been considered a great evil to split a cause of action. The policies behind the doctrine reflect the need to bring all litigation to an end, prevent vexatious litigation, maintain stability of court decisions, promote judicial economy, and prevent double recovery. *Barr v. Resolution Trust Corp.*, 837 S.W.2d 627, 629 (1992).

The basic rules and vocabulary are as follows: If a plaintiff recovered in the first action instituted on a particular "cause of action," that cause of action is viewed as having *merged* into the judgment such that it cannot be reasserted. On the other hand, if the plaintiff lost in the first suit on the cause of action, the cause of action and all claims comprising it are said to be *barred* by the judgment. In both cases, the preclusion includes both claims that were actually asserted and those that were not, as long as they are part of the same "cause of action." While these rules are relatively clear cut, courts have had great difficulty in defining the boundaries of particular causes of action, and various methods have been employed to try to do so. In the context of the doctrine of claim preclusion, the following approaches have been considered and used in Texas at one time or another:

1. *Individualized/Same Evidence Approach.* Early Texas authority indicated that if a claim asserted in a second action was technically different from the claim asserted in an earlier lawsuit, the latter action was not barred. *See Moore v. Snowball*, 81 S.W. 5, 7–10 (Tex. 1904). Under this approach to the problem, a single cause of action exists when a particular set of facts is sufficient to individualize a specific rule of law such that it can be distinguished from any other claim against the same party:

> Even a minimal alteration of material facts may constitute a new cause of action, if the alteration makes available a new rule of substantive law . . . . This "small-sized" cause of action generally restricts the operation of *res judicata*; much like the ancient common law forms of action, this concept strictly limits an action according to the rights enforced under it. While acclaimed as a simple and consistent criterion for defining cause of action, this concept has also been criticized as being too narrow for practical application and oblivious to important policy considerations.

ZOLLIE STEAKLEY & WELDON U. HOWELL, *Ruminations on Res Judicata*, 28 Sw. L.J. 355, 361–62 (1974).

2. *Pragmatic Approach.* Alternatively, the doctrine of merger and bar was said to preclude relitigation of matters a party could have interposed, but that the party failed to interpose, in an action between the same parties or their privies in reference to the same subject matter. *Freeman v. McAninch*, 27 S.W. 97 (Tex. 1894), and *Ogletree v. Crates*, 363 S.W.2d 431, 435–36 (Tex. 1963), are examples of this "pragmatic approach." In using the approach, the court considers matters of practicality (e.g., trial convenience, judicial economy, and common usage) and whether the additional facts involved in the second action are so closely related to those litigated in the prior action that it makes sense to consider the two situations as one "cause of action." The main difficulty with the pragmatic approach is that it is inherently unpredictable, owing to heavy reliance on policy factors and judicial discretion, which, in turn, hinder the development of precedent. Steakley & Howell, *supra*, at 362–63.

3. *Procedural Duty Approach.* This approach bears a strong resemblance to and suffers from the same problems as the pragmatic approach. Under the procedural duty approach, however, the focus appears not to be on an abstruse analysis of whether a particular "cause of action" has been split, but rather on whether a procedural duty has been violated in failing to set up in the first suit another claim that bears a relationship to it.

4. *Transactional Approach.* The Restatement (Second) of Judgments adopts a transactional analysis approach to claim preclusion. Under this approach, all claims arising out of the same transaction or series of transactions are barred, even if based on different theories or involving different remedies. RESTATEMENT (SECOND) OF JUDGMENTS § 24.

As shown by the following cases, the Texas Supreme Court has embraced the transactional approach and expressly overruled other tests of what constitutes a cause of action for *res judicata* purposes. Attorneys should therefore approach earlier cases with extreme caution. Think about whether the transactional approach is preferable to its predecessors in terms of predictability, efficiency, and fairness.

BARR v. RESOLUTION TRUST CORP.

837 S.W.2d 627 (Tex. 1992)

GONZALEZ, J.

The issue in this case is whether a claim by Sunbelt Federal Savings against George Barr based on a partnership promissory note and guarantee agreement is barred by the doctrine of res judicata. The trial court granted Barr's motion for summary judgment based on res judicata. The court of appeals, with one Justice dissenting, reversed the trial court's judgment, holding that the doctrine did not apply . . . . We reverse the judgment of the court of appeals and affirm the trial court's judgment.

In 1985, Barr and Ron Knott were partners in the Bar III Venture. On March 14, 1985 Barr III executed a promissory note for $369,750 in favor of Sunbelt's predecessor in interest. The same day, Barr and Knott executed a personal guarantee of the note. In March 1987, Bar III defaulted on the note.

On May 24, 1988, Sunbelt filed two separate lawsuits on the note. In one suit, Sunbelt alleged liability against the partnership as maker of the note and against Knott as guarantor of the note. In the other, Sunbelt alleged that Barr was personally liable because of his unconditional guarantee of the note.

Barr moved for summary judgment in the latter lawsuit on the grounds that the terms of the guaranty agreement were too uncertain to be enforceable. Barr argued that the agreement, a standard form containing a number of options to choose and blanks to complete, was not sufficiently completed to ascertain his liability. The trial court granted the motion, and rendered a final take-nothing judgment. Sunbelt did not appeal the judgment.

Thereafter, Sunbelt amended its pleadings in the suit against the partnership and Knott by adding Barr as a defendant, alleging that his status as a partner created liability for the note. Barr's answer asserted res judicata, among other defenses.

Barr moved for summary judgment on the grounds that the take-nothing judgment in the first lawsuit barred litigation of the claims against him in the second lawsuit. Sunbelt also moved for summary judgment, requesting a judgment on the note. The trial court granted Barr's motion and denied Sunbelt's. This interlocutory judgment became final when the court rendered judgment for Sunbelt on its claims against the partnership and Knott to the full amount of the note.

Sunbelt appealed, arguing that the trial court should have granted its summary judgment instead of Barr's. The court of appeals, with one justice dissenting, determined that the first suit did not bar the second. However, the court concluded that questions of fact prevented rendition in Sunbelt's favor, and thus remanded the case to the trial court. Both Barr and Sunbelt sought review in our court.

Much of the difficulty associated with the doctrine of res judicata is due to the confusion of several related theories. Broadly speaking, res judicata is the generic term for a group of related concepts concerning the conclusive effects given final judgments. *Puga v. Donna Fruit Co.*, 634 S.W.2d 677, 679 (Tex. 1982). Within this general doctrine, there are two principal categories: (1) claim preclusion (also known as res judicata); and (2) issue preclusion (also known as collateral estoppel.) Res judicata, or claims preclusion, prevents the relitigation of a claim or cause of action that has been finally adjudicated, as well as related matters that, with the use of diligence, should have been litigated in the prior suit. *Gracia v. RC Cola-7-Up Bottling Co.*, 667 S.W.2d 517, 519 (Tex. 1984); *Bonniwell v. Beech Aircraft Corp.*, 663 S.W.2d 816 (Tex. 1984). Issue preclusion, or collateral estoppel, prevents relitigation of particular issues already resolved in a prior suit. *Bonniwell*, 663 S.W.2d at 818. Barr's argument, that Sunbelt should have brought all theories of liability in one suit, is the defense of claim preclusion.

Claim preclusion prevents splitting a cause of action. *Jeanes v. Henderson*, 688 S.W.2d 100, 103 (Tex. 1985). The policies behind the doctrine reflect the need to bring all litigation to an end, prevent vexatious litigation, maintain stability of court decisions, promote judicial economy, and prevent double recovery. Zollie Steakley & Weldon U. Howell, Jr., *Ruminations on Res Judicata*, 28 Sw. L.J. 355, 358–59 (1974).

The question that has given courts the most difficulty is determining what claims should have been litigated in the prior suit. Early on, this Court held that res judicata "is not only final as to the matter actually determined, but as to every other matter which the parties might litigate in the cause, and which they might have decided." *Foster v. Wells*, 4 Tex. 101, 104 (1849). We have never repudiated this definition of claim preclusion, and it appears in some form in most definitions of res judicata. *See, e.g., Jeanes v. Henderson*, 688 S.W.2d 100, 103 (Tex. 1985) (res judicata bars not only what was actually litigated but also claims that could have been litigated in the original cause of action). If taken literally, this definition of the rule would require that all disputes existing between parties be joined regardless of whether the disputes have anything in common. This court has resorted to a wide variety of theories and tests to give res judicata a more restrictive application. *See generally* 5 William V. Dorsaneo III, *Texas Litigation Guide* § 131.06[4][b][ii] (1991); Steakley, 28 Sw. L.J. 355.

Even if only cases from more recent times are considered, our holdings with respect to res judicata are difficult to reconcile. In *Griffin v. Holiday Inns of America*, 496 S.W.2d 535 (Tex. 1973), the court determined that a take-nothing judgment in a suit to recover in contract for services and materials did not preclude a subsequent suit to be compensated in quantum meruit. The court rejected the view that a judgment as to one claim is res judicata of all claims or causes of action arising out of the same transaction, and stated that, "[a]s a general rule a judgment on the merits in a suit on one cause of action is not conclusive of a subsequent suit on a different cause of action except as to issues of fact actually litigated and determined in the first suit." *Id.* at 538. The court acknowledged, however, that alternative theories of recovery for the same "claim" may not be brought in different lawsuits.

Thus, in *Griffin*, the court determined that a "cause of action" for res judicata purposes is something more than the set of facts necessary to establish a single theory of recovery but not necessarily the entire transaction between the parties. *Id.* at 537–38. The court gave no guidance on the question of how to make this fine distinction between a mere alternative theory of recovery and a different cause of action. Every theory of recovery has its unique elements of proof. As the *Griffin* case illustrates, only slight variations of the facts to support different theories of the same incident can result in a court finding different causes of action, thus thwarting the purposes of res judicata. *See* Steakley, 28 Sw. L.J. at 361–62.

The court took an entirely different approach in *Westinghouse Credit Corp. v. Kownslar*, 496 S.W.2d 531 (Tex. 1973). In that case Kownslar had guaranteed all promissory notes by the maker. The issue was whether res judicata required that Westinghouse bring in one suit its claims for all notes guaranteed by Kownslar that were then in default. Rather than decide whether there was more than one cause of action involved, the court decided the case solely on whether it appeared that the policies of res judicata required such a result.

This pure policy approach as exemplified by *Westinghouse* makes it virtually impossible to determine in advance what policy will win out in any given case. Without any objective standards, each case is decided ad hoc, and therefore the doctrine is "inherently unpredictable" and "affords little basis for consistency and formulation of precedent." Steakley, 28 Sw. L.J. at 362–63. *Westinghouse* is the only case we have decided solely on policy grounds.

Then, in *Texas Water Rights Comm. v. Crow Iron Works*, 582 S.W.2d 768 (Tex. 1979), the court shifted the focus from the cause of action to the subject matter of the litigation. The question was whether a major lawsuit instigated to sort out water rights to the lower Rio Grande river precluded a subsequent suit based on the claim that during the pendency of that suit the plaintiff had purchased additional rights. The court concluded that the subsequent claim was barred, noting that:

> The scope of res judicata is not limited to matters actually litigated; the judgment in the first suit precludes a second action by the parties of their privies not only on matters actually litigated, but also on causes of action or defenses which arise out of the same subject matter and which might have been litigated in the first suit.

Id. at 771–72. *Accord*, *Gracia*, 667 S.W.2d at 519. Thus this definition is not consistent with earlier formulations of the rule, such as in *Griffin*, that only issues related to a single cause of action are barred in a subsequent suit. While we did not expressly overrule the *Griffin* test in either *Crow Iron Works* or *Gracia* we do so now.

A determination of what constitutes the subject matter of a suit necessarily requires an examination of the factual basis of the claim or claims in the prior litigation. It requires an analysis of the factual matters that make up the gist of the complaint, without regard to the form of action. Any cause of action which arises out of those same facts should, if practicable, be litigated in the same lawsuit. *Gracia*, 667 S.W.2d at 519; *Crow Iron Works*, 582 S.W.2d at 772.

The definition of res judicata in *Gracia* and *Crow Iron Works* is substantially similar to the rule of compulsory counterclaims embodied in the rules of civil procedure. A party defending a claim must bring as a counterclaim any claim that "arises out of the transaction or occurrence that is the subject matter of the opposing party's claim . . . ." TEX. R. CIV. P. 97.

The Restatement of Judgments also takes the transactional approach to claims preclusion. It provides that a final judgment on an action extinguishes the right to bring suit on the transaction, or series of connected transactions, out of which the action arose. Restatement of Judgments § 24(1). A "transaction" under the Restatement is not equivalent to a sequence of events, however, the determination is to be made pragmatically, "giving weight to such considerations as whether the facts are related in time, space, origin, or motivation, whether they form a convenient trial unit, and whether their treatment as a trial unit conforms to the parties' expectations or business understanding or usage." *Id.* § 24(2).

We conclude that the transactional approach to claims preclusion of the Restatement effectuates the policy of res judicata with no more hardship than encountered under rule 97(a) of the rules of civil procedure. Modern rules of procedure obviate the need to give parties two bites at the apple, as was done in *Griffin*, to ensure that a claim receives full adjudication. Discovery should put a claimant on notice of any need for alternative pleading. Moreover, if success on one theory becomes doubtful because of developments during trial, a party is free to seek a trial amendment.

In the case now before us, there is no valid reason to subject Barr to two different lawsuits. In the suit brought previously against Barr, the bank alleged that he executed the guarantee on the same day and as part of the "same transaction" as the promissory note. In both suits Sunbelt seeks to hold Barr primarily liable for payment of the note and seeks the same amount of damages. Both suits require proof establishing the notes of the partnership, that the notes are due, and that the partnership has defaulted. The only factual allegation that Sunbelt pleaded in the second suit that was not in the first is that Barr is a general partner of Bar III Venture.

It is clear that in this case the execution of the partnership note and Barr's guarantee of it were related in time and space and motivation, and the parties considered it as a single transaction. The issues of both claims form a convenient trial unit, whereas separate lawsuits would require significant duplication of effort of the court and the parties involved. With due diligence, the claim that Barr was liable because he is a partner could have been joined in the suit on his guarantee of the partnership note.

We reaffirm the "transactional" approach to res judicata. A subsequent suit will be barred if it arises out of the same subject matter of a previous suit and which through the exercise of diligence, could have been litigated in a prior suit. For these reasons, the judgment of the court of appeals is reversed and that of the trial court is affirmed.

GETTY OIL CO. v. INSURANCE CO. OF N. AMERICA
845 S.W.2d 794 (Tex. 1992)

PHILLIPS, C.J.

The purchaser of certain chemicals brought suit against the seller and its insurers, claiming that they were contractually obligated to provide insurance to cover a judgment against the purchaser in a wrongful death action precipitated by the explosion of the chemicals. The trial court granted summary judgment for the defendants on four grounds . . . . The court of appeals affirmed on the theory of res judicata . . . . We affirm the judgment of the court of appeals in part, reverse in part, and remand the cause to the trial court or further proceedings.

I. Facts and Procedural Background

Getty Oil Company ("Getty") purchased various chemicals from NL Industries, Inc. ("NL") for Getty's oil production and exploration operations in the Midland, Texas, area . . . .

On November 22, 1983, a barrel of chemical emulsifier delivered by NL under Order No. HB-5357 exploded in the vicinity of a Getty well, killing Carl Duncan, an independent contractor working for Getty.

Duncan's estate and survivors brought wrongful death and survival actions in the 130th Judicial Court of Matagorda County against Getty, NL and its subsidiaries, and others. Getty filed a cross-claim against NL, alleging that NL's negligence proximately caused the injury to Duncan, that the chemicals manufactured by NL were defective, and that NL breached warranties in connection with the sale of the chemicals. Getty also asserted a contractual right of indemnity against NL under the terms of HB-5357 . . . , and a contribution claim because of NL's negligence. The jury found Getty 100% negligent and grossly negligent in causing the accident. The trial court rendered judgment on the jury verdict for $3,757,000 actual damages and $25,000,000 punitive damages. The trial court also rendered judgment that "all Cross-Actions for contributions and or indemnity based upon the contracts are denied." Getty appealed the portion of the judgment denying it contribution and indemnity, and the court of appeals affirmed the judgment of the trial court. *Getty Oil Corp. v. Duncan*, 721 S.W.2d 475 (Tex. App. — Corpus Christi 1986, ref. n.r.e.). Getty's insurers, Travellers Insurance Company, Travellers Indemnity Company, and English & American Insurance Company, settled the claim for $14 million.

Getty then filed an insurance claim with NL's insurers. After they refused to honor the claim, Getty sued NL and its primary and excess insurance carriers, Insurance Company of North America ("INA") and Youell and Companies ("Youell"), respectively . . . . NL, INA and Youell jointly moved for summary judgment, . . . [and] on May 3, 1990, the trial court granted the defendants' motions for summary judgment . . . . Getty appealed the summary judgment for defendants, and the court of appeals affirmed on res judicata grounds, holding that Getty's claims were barred because it was seeking the same relief under a different theory that it unsuccessfully sought in the first suit. 819 S.W.2d at 915. Getty now seeks a reversal of the court of appeals' judgment and the trial court's summary judgment.

II. Res Judicata

. . . .

We recently clarified that Texas follows the "transactional" approach to res judicata. *See Barr v. Resolution Trust Corp.*, 837 S.W.2d 627 (Tex. 1992). Under this approach, a judgment in an earlier suit "precludes a second action by the parties and their privies not only on matters actually litigated, but also on causes of action or defenses which arise out of the same subject matter and which might have been litigated in the first suit." *Id.* at 630; *Texas Water Rights Comm. v. Crow Iron Works*, 582 S.W.2d 768, 771–72 (Tex. 1979).

We conclude that Getty's present suit arises out of the same subject matter as its earlier cross-claim against NL asserted in the Duncan suit. The Restatement (Second) of Judgments, which recognizes the transactional test, suggests that factors to consider in determining whether facts constitute a single "transaction" are "their relatedness in time, space, origin, or motivation, and whether, taken together, they form a convenient unit for trial purposes." Restatement (Second) of Judgments 24 cmt. b (1980). Getty's present action against NL arose from the same accident that was adjudicated in the Duncan suit. The present suit also concerns the same contract, HB-5357, and the same section of that contract, the "Insurance and Indemnity" section. Finally, Getty seeks the same relief against NL here as in its earlier cross-claim: reimbursement for Getty's liability to Duncan's estate and beneficiaries. Thus, both Getty's actions against NL derived from the same transaction.

Getty argues that res judicata cannot bar its present claims against NL because these claims did not accrue until judgment was rendered in the Duncan suit. That is, Getty had no liability and hence no need for insurance coverage until liability was assigned. The contingent nature of these claims, however, does not preclude the operation of res judicata. We held in *Barr* that "[a] subsequent suit will be barred if it arises out of the same subject matter of a previous suit and which, through the exercise of diligence, could have been litigated in a prior suit." 837 S.W.2d at 631. Getty could have asserted its present claims in the Duncan suit, with their resolution being contingent on the plaintiffs' claim. Texas Rule of Civil Procedure 51(b) provides:

> Joinder of Remedies. Whenever a claim is one heretofore cognizable only after another claim has been prosecuted to conclusion, the two claims may be joined in a single action; but the court shall grant relief in that action only in accordance with the relative substantive rights of the parties.

See Parkhill Produce Co. v. Pecos Valley Southern Ry. Co., 348 S.W.2d 208 (Tex. Civ. App. — San Antonio 1961, ref. n.r.e.). For example, we have held that an indemnitee may bring a claim against an indemnitor before judgment is assigned against the indemnitee. *See Gulf, Colorado & Santa Fe Ry. Co. v. McBride*, 322 S.W.2d 492, 495 (Tex. 1958); *Mitchell's, Inc. v. Friedman*, 303 S.W.2d 775, 779 (Tex. 1957); *K & S Oil*

Well Service, Inc. v. Cabot Corp., 491 S.W.2d 733, 739 (Tex. Civ. App. — Corpus Christi 1973, ref. n.r.e.). Forcing the indemnity suit to wait for judgment in the liability suit "would contravene the policy of the courts to encourage settlements and to minimize litigation." *Id.*

Getty itself took advantage of this rule in its initial cross-action against NL, in which Getty asserted its claim under the indemnity provision of HB-5357. The fact that Getty had no claim for indemnity against NL until the trial court rendered judgment did not preclude this cross-claim. Likewise, Getty could have brought its other contingent cross-claims against NL in the Duncan action. The fact that Getty's claims against NL were contingent on Getty incurring liability in the Duncan suit does not in and of itself preclude operation of res judicata . . . .

Getty replies that even if INA and Youell were in privity with NL, res judicata would not bar Getty's present claims against them because Getty could not have asserted those claims in the Duncan suit. The insurance policies themselves specifically prohibited any claim from being brought against INA or Youell before the insured's liability was reduced to judgment or compromised. We have held that when such "no action" policy provision exists, "a third party's right of action against the insurer does not arise until he has secured such an agreement or a judgment against the insured." *Great American Ins. Co. v. Murray*, 437 S.W.2d 264, 265–66 (Tex. 1969); *see also State Farm County Mut. Ins. Co. of Texas v. Ollis*, 768 S.W.2d 722, 723 (Tex. 1989).

Moreover, Tex. R. Civ. P. 38(c) prohibited Getty from joining INA and Youell in the Duncan suit. This rule provides, with respect to the joinder of third parties:

> (c) This rule shall not be applied, in tort cases, so as to permit the joinder of a liability or indemnity insurance company, unless such company is by statute or contract liable to the person injured or damaged.

Rule 38(c) has been held to prohibit the joinder of insurers in situations resembling this case. *See Langdeau v. Pittman*, 337 S.W.2d 343, 355 (Tex. Civ. App. — Austin 1960, ref. n.r.e.).

Since Getty could not have asserted its present claims against INA or Youell in the Duncan suit, it is not now precluded by res judicata from bringing these claims. We accordingly reverse the judgment of the court of appeals affirming the trial court's summary judgment against INA and Youell on the grounds of res judicata, and we remand this portion of the cause to the trial court for further proceedings.

MARTIN v. MARTIN, MARTIN & RICHARDS, INC.
989 S.W.2d 357 (Tex. 1998)

Per Curiam

The primary question presented is whether a dismissal with prejudice of a suit to declare a contract valid bars an action for a breach occurring after the dismissal. In the circumstances of this case, we answer no, contrary to the court of appeals, and therefore reverse and remand the case to that court for further proceedings.

Gary Martin sold his stock in Martin, Martin & Richards, Inc. to its other two shareholders, Roneal Martin and Floyd Richards. Under their written contract ("the contract"), Gary was to be paid $200,000 for his interest in MMR and $1.3 million for consulting services. Payments were to be made in equal bimonthly installments over ten years.

Several years later, Roneal and MMR sued Floyd to dissolve their business relationship. Gary was not named as a party. Although MMR had paid Gary all but one installment due up to that point under the contract, he was concerned that Roneal and Floyd might attempt to restructure their relationship so as to evade their contractual obligations to him. Consequently, Gary intervened in the suit to obtain a declaration that the contract was a binding obligation on MMR and that it and any transferees of its assets as a result of the business dissolution would remain liable to Gary for all payments due. Gary also sought to impose a constructive trust on MMR's assets to secure its contractual obligations to him. Roneal and Floyd settled, and Roneal became the sole shareholder of MMR. Although Gary did not take part in the settlement, he approved a proposed order reciting that "all parties . . . desire to dismiss the claims which they had, each against the other, with prejudice." This order, perhaps by mistake, only allocated costs of suit and did not dismiss the case. In a later order not approved by Gary, the district court dismissed with prejudice "all causes of action which were brought, or which could have been brought, by Plaintiffs, Defendants, and Intervenor."

Throughout the litigation MMR had continued to pay Gary installments under the contract as they became due, but a month after the settlement, it ceased payments. Gary immediately sued MMR and later amended his pleadings to name Roneal as a defendant, claiming past installments due and unpaid, as well as future installments based on anticipatory breach. The events of this lawsuit were quite complex, and we describe them only insofar as they are material to the issues now before us. Defendants moved for summary judgment, and four days later, without notice to Gary and before he had filed a response, the district court signed an order granting summary judgment for defendants. Two days after the order was signed, Gary filed a response to defendants' motion. Eleven days later the court issued another order stating that Gary's response had been "received and considered for all purposes, with respect to Defendants' Summary Judgment . . . , and that, after having considered [the response], the Court's prior determination that [defendants' motion] should be granted remains correct in all respects." The court of appeals dismissed Gary's appeal, holding that the order granting summary judgment was interlocutory. Before the judgment was made final in the trial court, Gary died, and his independent executrix, Jan Martin, was substituted as a party in his stead.

Defendants' motion for summary judgment was based on numerous grounds, and the district court did not specify the basis for its ruling. Accordingly, on appeal Martin has attacked all of the grounds in defendants' motion. The court of appeals held that defendants were entitled to summary judgment on one ground — res judicata — and therefore did not consider the other grounds raised by defendants.

"Res judicata, or claims preclusion, prevents the relitigation of a claim or cause of action that has been finally adjudicated, as well as related matters that, with the use of diligence, should have been litigated in the prior suit." The court of appeals reasoned that Gary's intervention in the prior suit raised the same issues regarding the validity of the contract and the obligation owed under it that he attempted to litigate in this action. We have not had occasion to consider whether or to what extent a judgment dismissing a claim for declaratory relief should be given preclusive effect. Forty years ago in *Cowling v. Colligan* we stated that a "judgment is res adjudicata only of present and not of future conditions." More recently, in *Marino v. State Farm Fire & Casualty Insurance Co.*, we reiterated that "a judgment in one suit will not operate as res judicata to a subsequent suit . . . 'where, in the interval, the facts have changed, or new facts have occurred which may alter the legal rights or relations of the parties.' " But these broad pronouncements provide little guidance in resolving the issue in this case.

Section 33 of the *Restatement (Second) of Judgments* states:

> "A valid and final judgment in an action brought to declare rights or other legal relations of the parties is conclusive in a subsequent action between them as to the matters declared, and, in accordance with the rules of issue preclusion, as to any issues actually litigated by them and determined in the action."

The rule as stated does not address what, if any, preclusive effect should be given to a judgment that simply denies declaratory relief without determining the matters presented, although comment c to this section suggests that such a judgment should not preclude subsequent claims or issues. We need not resolve this broad issue here. We decide only that, as a general matter, a judgment dismissing with prejudice a claim for a declaration that a contract is valid does not amount to a declaration that the contract is invalid and does not preclude an action for subsequent breaches. Here, Gary does not appear to have sued for the one installment that had gone unpaid before the judgment in the prior suit, or on grounds that had arisen before that judgment. Thus, we need not decide whether such claims might have been merged in the judgment or otherwise barred . . . .

Accordingly, we grant Martin's application for writ of error, and without hearing oral argument, reverse the judgment of the court of appeals and remand the case to that court for consideration of other issues not previously addressed.

NOTES AND QUESTIONS

(1) *Final Judgment Requirement.* A final judgment has *res judicata* effect despite the pendency of an appeal unless the appeal is by trial de novo. *Scurlock Oil Co. v. Smithwick*, 724 S.W.2d 1, 6 (Tex. 1986); *see also* Restatement (Second) of Judgments § 13, comment f (providing that "[t]he better view is that judgment otherwise final remains so despite the taking of an appeal").

(2) *Relationship to Federal Law — Different, But the Same.* When the first lawsuit is decided in federal court, the *federal* law of *res judicata* (claim preclusion) controls the determination of whether a later state court action is barred, unless the federal court did not possess jurisdiction over the omitted state claims or, even

if the federal court had jurisdiction, it would clearly have declined to exercise it as a matter of discretion. *Eagle Props., Ltd. v. Scharbauer*, 807 S.W.2d 714, 718–21 (Tex. 1990). In *John G. & Marie Stella Kenedy Mem. Found. v. Dewhurst*, 90 S.W.3d 268, 288 (Tex. 2002), the court cited *Eagle Properties* as holding that Texas and federal law is the same. In this connection, the Fifth Circuit Court of Appeals has also adopted the "transactional" analysis discussed in *Barr*. *See Ocean Drilling & Exploration Co. v. Mont Boat Rental Servs. Inc.*, 799 F.2d 213, 217 (5th Cir. 1986). Note also that the U.S. Supreme Court, in *Semtek Int'l Inc. v. Lockheed Martin Corp.*, 531 U.S. 497 (2001), held that in diversity cases, the federal courts will apply federal common law to determine the preclusive effect of federal judgments, but that federal common law will in most cases require applying the preclusion rules of the state in which the rendering federal court sits.

(3) *Withdrawn Claims.* Voluntarily withdrawn claims are subject to the doctrine of claim preclusion. *Jones v. Nightingale*, 900 S.W.2d 87, 88–90 (Tex. App. — San Antonio 1995, writ ref'd). However, the doctrine of *res judicata* does not bar a cause of action created after the entry of judgment in a prior suit when a change in the law or facts subsequent to the first adjudication changes or creates substantive rights not existing until after the first judgment. *See Besing v. Vanden Eykel*, 878 S.W.2d 182, 184 (Tex. App. — Dallas 1994, writ denied).

(4) *Declaratory Judgments.* What is the nature of a declaratory judgment? Why should the preclusive effect of such a judgment differ from that of ordinary judgments? Historically, injunctions have also been treated differently for preclusion purposes, in part because the court's power to amend the judgment for changed circumstances prevents them from being sufficiently final. Would the court's decision in *Martin* have been different if all of the plaintiff's claims had matured prior to the first lawsuit?

(5) *Merger Doctrine. Res judicata* can affect a plaintiff who won as well as one who lost. If the plaintiff fails to bring additional claims arising out of the same cause of action, they are "merged" into the judgment and the plaintiff loses the chance to recover on those claims in a later case. For example, if a plaintiff sues a defendant for negligence and recovers a judgment for personal injuries, the plaintiff cannot later decide to sue for property damages arising out of the same cause of action. The property damages claim is "merged" into the first judgment.

(6) Preclusion and Class Actions. The Texas Supreme Court held in *Citizens Insurance Co. of America v. Daccach*, 217 S.W.3d 430 (Tex. 2007), that claim preclusion also applies in the class action context. If a certified class raises only some of the claims that are part of a single cause of action, the class members are precluded from pursuing the remaining claims. Those other claims are either merged into, or barred by, the result of the class action. The Court rejected the argument that Rule 42(d), which provides that "an action may be brought or maintained as a class action with respect to particular issues," requires a different kind of preclusion analysis for class actions.

[B] Issue Preclusion: Collateral Estoppel

[1] Basic Elements

Issue preclusion (also known as collateral estoppel or estoppel by judgment) involves factual determinations actually litigated in a prior suit rather than matters that should have been but were not litigated. It does not matter whether the matter litigated was part of the same cause of action litigated in the first action. *See generally* McGlinchey, *Collateral Estoppel*, 4 Hous. L. Rev. 73 (1966). The following case discusses the elements of collateral estoppel as well as the policy behind the doctrine. Be sure to focus on the fact that there are three sets of defendants (all blamed for the sulfite that killed Susan Trapnell), so that the distinction between the "potato whitener defendants" and "non potato whitener defendants" is important. Notice also that because of various provisions governing federal court jurisdiction, it was impossible for the Trapnells to litigate all claims against all defendants in a single court.

SYSCO FOOD SERVICES, INC. v. TRAPNELL

890 S.W.2d 796 (Tex. 1994)

Gammage, J.

I.

This case is a products liability death action. The defendants, manufacturers and suppliers of foods containing sulfites, obtained a summary judgment in the trial court. The court of appeals reversed in part and affirmed in part. We affirm.

II.

Susan Trapnell was a chronic asthmatic. She was allergic to sulfites, a food additive used to process and preserve food. Her reactions to sulfites ranged from "asthma attacks" to, in severe cases, "anaphylactic shock." After one particularly serious episode, Susan was referred to Dr. Ronald Simon, an expert in the diagnosis and treatment of sulfite sensitive persons. After testing Susan, Dr. Simon concluded that she was extremely sensitive to sulfites. Dr. Simon advised Susan to avoid certain foods which commonly contain sulfites. He counseled her that when she ate at restaurants, she should ask whether sulfites were in the foods she wished to eat. In case she accidentally ingested sulfites, Susan always carried a hypodermic syringe of epinephrine.

On August 5, 1984, Susan, her husband, Benjamin, and their son, Nicholas, went to the Officer's Club at the Corpus Christi Naval Air Station to dine at the buffet. Before going through the buffet line, Benjamin asked one of the cooks whether any sulfites had been used in the preparation of the fruit salad. The cook, Robert Mangohig, responded that no sulfites had been used, but offered to get Mr. Trapnell some fresh fruit from the kitchen. Mr. Trapnell declined, and the Trapnells went through the buffet line. Susan allegedly served herself fruit from the fresh fruit bowl, hash browns, apple pie filling, and other foods. Within minutes after she began eating, Susan had a violent reaction. The Trapnells immediately tried to leave the Club and go to the hospital. Susan made it only to the Club's lobby before collapsing. Benjamin administered epinephrine from the emergency kit. Before E.M.S. arrived, Susan began having seizures. E.M.S. rushed Susan to the Naval Air Station Hospital, where she arrived with no pulse. At the hospital, emergency room personnel succeeded in bringing Susan's blood pressure back. For the next several days, Susan remained unresponsive to stimuli. Susan's brain activity ceased on August 9, and on August 10, the doctors pronounced her dead. No autopsy was performed.

In summary judgment evidence, experts stated that although sulfites can be ingested from many sources, including air pollution, in their opinion Susan died as a result of eating food containing sulfites. Specifically, they identified three foods that Susan had on her plate as potentially containing sulfites: potato whitener on the fruit salad, apple pie filling, and hash browns.

The sulfite manufacturers and other parties in the chain of distribution are as follows: Potato Whitener:

> Hoechst Celanese Corporation, Specialty Group (formerly known as Virginia Chemicals, Inc.), manufactured sodium metabisulfite and sold it to John Hogan Interests d/b/a First Foods Company, Inc. First Foods manufactured potato whitener from the sodium metabisulfite it acquired from Hoechst Celanese and sold it to Nordhaus. Nordhaus sold potato whitener to Sysco Food Services, Inc. of Sysco Corporation. Sysco sold potato whitener to the Officer's Club.

Hash Browns:

> Allied Corporation manufactured and sold sulfites to Univar Corporation. Univar sold the sulfites to Lamb-Weston, Inc. Lamb-Weston processed hash browns and sold them to Sysco. Sysco sold the hash browns to the Officer's Club.

Apple Pie Filling:

> Allied manufactured sulfites and sold them to McKesson Chemical Company. McKesson then sold sulfites to Zero Pack. Zero Pack added sulfites to apples during processing and sold them to Globe. Globe manufactured apple pie filling and sold it to Labatt Institutional Supply Company. Labatt sold apple pie filling to the Officer's Club.

III.

On May 22, 1986, the Trapnells brought suit against Sysco and other defendants in state district court, alleging negligence, Deceptive Trade Practices, strict liability, and breach of warranty. On December 22, 1986, the Trapnells filed suit against the United States Department of the Navy under the Federal Tort Claims Act ("F.T.C.A."). The Trapnells claimed that the Navy was negligent in using sulfites and in failing to warn Susan of the sulfites in the food they prepared. [Ed. note: The Trapnells were required to sue the Navy in federal court under the F.T.C.A. and therefore could not join all defendants in the state court action.]

On March 30, 1989, the federal district court issued a stay order pending the conclusion of the state suit against the manufacturers and distributors. On June 16, 1989, upon the motion of the defendants, the state district court ordered an abatement in order for the defendants to try to intervene in federal court, have the federal court stay lifted, and have all the parties litigate all claims in federal court. In a September 26, 1989 order, the federal court denied the motion to intervene on the grounds that it did not have jurisdiction over the proposed intervenors . . . . [Ed. note: The federal court did not have diversity jurisdiction for lack of complete diversity. It also lacked supplemental jurisdiction over the claims against the intervenors, because the case pre-dated the supplemental jurisdiction statute, 28 U.S.C. § 1367(a), and supplemental jurisdiction over pendent parties was not allowed. The Trapnells therefore could not join all defendants in the federal court action.]

At this point, the proceedings were at a standstill. The state trial court refused several motions to vacate its order of abatement, for reasons that are not clear from the record. The plaintiffs filed a petition for writ of mandamus in the court of appeals in which they complained of the trial court's January 5, 1990 refusal to lift its abatement order. Holding that the abatement order unconstitutionally deprived plaintiffs of a forum under the "open courts" clause of the Texas Constitution, the court of appeals ordered the trial court to lift the abatement order. *Trapnell v. Hunter*, 785 S.W.2d 426, 429 (Tex. App. — Corpus Christi 1990, original proceeding) (*Trapnell I*) (opinion issued February 1, 1990).

On July 31, 1990, soon after the state court complied with the court of appeals' mandate and the case proceeded to trial, the trial court granted summary judgment as to one of the defendants, First Foods. First Foods' motion for summary judgment alleged that its product did not cause Susan Trapnell's death. During the appeal of the order granting First Foods' summary judgment, the federal court lifted its stay and proceeded to try the plaintiffs' F.T.C.A. claim against the Navy. On September 14, 1990, the federal court, based on its finding that no potato whitener had been added to the fruit salad, held that the Navy was not liable and rendered judgment that the plaintiffs take nothing by their claims. On September 17, 1990, the state trial court granted First Foods' motion to sever all claims against it, including the cross-claims asserted by the other defendants, enabling the plaintiffs to immediately appeal the summary judgment. On April 25, 1991, the state court of appeals reversed First Foods' summary judgment because it concluded that the motion and response raised a fact issue regarding causation. *Trapnell v. First Foods Co.*, 809 S.W.2d 606, 611 (Tex. App. — Corpus Christ 1991, writ denied) (*Trapnell II*). The court of appeals refused to consider First Foods' argument that the plaintiffs were collaterally estopped from relitigating the federal court's finding that potato whitener was not added to the fruit salad, on the grounds that collateral estoppel was not raised as a basis for summary judgment in the trial court. *See Trapnell*, 809 S.W.2d at 608.

Meanwhile, the trial court granted summary judgments in favor of all other defendants, who had asserted in their motions for summary judgment the grounds that (1) collateral estoppel barred relitigation of the federal court's finding that potato whitener was not in the fruit salad, as to the potato whitener defendants and (2) lack of causation as to the other defendants was proven as a matter of law. The court of appeals reversed in part and affirmed in part. 850 S.W.2d 529, 532 (*Trapnell III*). We affirm the court of appeals.

IV.

The central issues are: (1) whether the summary judgment evidence on causation raises a fact issue so as to prevent summary judgment in favor of the hash brown and apple pie filling defendants, and (2) whether the federal court's finding that potato whitener was not in the fruit bowl precludes the Trapnells from litigating the issue in state court.

A. CAUSATION

The first question is whether the summary judgment evidence raises a fact issue sufficient to preclude summary judgment in favor of the potato whitener, hash brown, and apple pie filling defendants. [The court concludes that fact issues preclude summary judgment.]

B. COLLATERAL ESTOPPEL

The court of appeals held that the federal judgment does not preclude the Trapnells from relitigating in state court whether potato whitener was in the fruit bowl. 850 S.W.2d at 535. Although we do not agree with the court's reasoning, we agree that collateral estoppel should not be applied in this case because doing so would not promote the goals served by the doctrine.

The doctrine of collateral estoppel or issue preclusion is designed to promote judicial efficiency, protect parties from multiple lawsuits, and prevent inconsistent judgments by precluding the relitigation of issues . . . . A party seeking to assert the bar of collateral estoppel must establish that (1) the facts sought to be litigated in the second action were fully and fairly litigated in the first action; (2) those facts were essential to the judgment in the first action; and (3) the parties were cast as adversaries in the first action . . . . Strict mutuality of parties is no longer required . . . . To satisfy the requirements of due process, it is only necessary that the party *against whom* the doctrine is asserted was a party or in privity with a party in the first action. *See Eagle Properties*, 807 S.W.2d at 721; *Benson v. Wanda Petroleum Co.*, 468 S.W.2d 361 at 363; Michael Kimmel, *The Impacts of Defensive and Offensive Assertion of Collateral Estoppel by a Nonparty*, 35 GEO. WASH. L. REV. 1010, 1014 (1967).

The court of appeals held that collateral estoppel should not apply because the issue to be estopped was not fully and fairly litigated in the federal trial. However, the court of appeals reached this conclusion only after improperly characterizing the issue to be estopped as "causation," rather than the more narrow issue of whether potato whitener was added to the fruit salad. Since collateral estoppel is an affirmative defense, the potato whitener defendants had the burden of pointing out the issue they wished to be estopped; in their motions for summary judgment and in their briefs before this Court, they have argued only that the limited issue of whether potato whitener was added to the fruit salad has already been litigated. They specifically deny asserting any preclusive effect to any determination of causation by the federal court.

When the issue is properly identified, it becomes clear that this issue was fully and fairly litigated in the federal action. *See* 1 B James Wm. Moore, Moore's Federal Practice § 0.441[3.-3] (June 1983) ("The circumstances in which it can be said that the parties to suits in the federal courts lack a 'full and fair opportunity' to present their claims and defenses are probably very limited."). The issue was necessary to the federal court's judgment that the Navy did not breach its duty to Benjamin Trapnell to adequately respond to his question. The court stated in its September 14, 1990 order that "because this court finds that the Officer's Club staff did not use potato whitener in preparing the fruit bowl, Mangohig's response fulfilled that duty." There was no difference in the burdens of proof on this issue in the federal and state actions. *See* Restatement (Second) of Judgments §§ 28(4), 29 (1982) (stating that even where an issue is actually litigated and determined by a valid and final judgment, and the determination is essential to the judgment, relitigation of the issue in a subsequent action is not precluded when the party against whom preclusion is sought had a significantly heavier burden of persuasion with respect to the issue in the initial action than in the subsequent action); *Scurlock Oil Co. v. Smithwick*, 724 S.W.2d 1, 7 (Tex. 1986) (citing the Restatement); Geoffrey C. Hazard, Jr., *Res Nova in Res Judicata*, 44 S. Cal. L. Rev. 1036, 1044 (1971) (arguing that relitigation of an issue may be warranted where the burden of proof on that issue differs between the first and second actions). Assuming without deciding that Texas law encompasses the theory of alternative liability or the other theories of collective liability urged by the plaintiffs, the plaintiffs still have the preliminary burden of proving by a preponderance of the evidence that Susan was exposed to the allegedly harmful product, i.e., potato whitener. *See* Restatement (Second) of Torts § 433B(2) & (3) (1982) (requiring the plaintiff to first prove that the defendants acted tortiously before shifting the burden to the defendants). The federal court, applying Texas tort liability law, placed the same burden on the plaintiffs with respect to this issue.

We also disagree that the lack of joinder of all defendants in the first action adversely affected litigation of the issue of whether potato whitener was added to the fruit salad. Although the court of appeals correctly notes that joinder of the manufacturers and suppliers of the three food products would be advantageous to the plaintiffs on the general issue of causation, the same is not necessarily true regarding this narrower issue. The Trapnells had every incentive to litigate this issue, and indeed may have been aided by the absence of the other defendants in this regard; they did not have to be concerned with proving their case against the potato whitener defendants so strongly as to cast doubt upon their claims against the hash brown and apple pie defendants.

Nevertheless, we agree with the court of appeals' resolution of this case because we do not believe that the purposes of the doctrine of collateral estoppel would be served by applying it to these facts. *Cf. Lytle v. Household Mfg., Inc.*, 494 U.S. at 553 (holding that "the purposes served by collateral estoppel do not justify applying the doctrine in this case"). Applying collateral estoppel against the Trapnells would not conserve judicial resources, because the parties could still relitigate the issue of whether potato whitener caused Susan Trapnell's death. A fundamental principle of collateral estoppel is that it can only be asserted against one who was a party to or in privity with a party to the prior litigation. *See Blonder-Tongue Lab. v. Univ. of Ill. Found.*, 402 U.S. at 329 ("Some litigants — those who never appeared in a prior action — may not be collaterally estopped without litigating the issue. They have never had a chance to present their evidence and arguments on the claim. Due process prohibits estopping them . . . ."); *Eagle Properties*, 807 S.W.2d at 721 (holding that "it is only necessary that the party against whom the plea of collateral estoppel is being asserted be a party or in privity with a party in the prior litigation"); *Benson*, 468 S.W.2d at 363 ("Due process requires that the rule of collateral estoppel operate only against persons who have had their day in court either as a party to the prior suit or as a privy . . . ."). The non-potato whitener defendants were not parties to the prior federal case, and no one has asserted that they were in privity with the Trapnells or with the Navy. Consequently, if the Trapnells were precluded by collateral estoppel from proceeding against the potato whitener defendants, the non-potato whitener defendants would still be able to argue in their absence that potato whitener was in the fruit salad and that it, not their product, caused Susan's death.[11] The goal of conserving judicial resources by preventing relitigation, then, would not be served. *See Lytle*, 494 U.S. at 553.[12]

In addition, the goal of protecting defendants from being subjected to multiple lawsuits is simply not applicable to the facts of this case. *See Montana v. United States*, 440 U.S. at 153 (stating that the application of collateral estoppel protects parties "from the expense and vexation attending multiple lawsuits"); Steven C. Malin, *Collateral Estoppel: The Fairness Exception*, 53 J. Air L. & Com. 959, 965 (1988) (same). The potato whitener defendants themselves will not have to defend two suits. *Cf. Lytle*, 494 U.S. at 553 (holding that the goal of protecting parties from multiple lawsuits was not implicated).

Application of collateral estoppel also will not necessarily prevent the possibility of inconsistent findings. Since the non-potato whitener defendants are free to raise the potato whitener issue, the jury could exonerate the non-potato whitener defendants on the basis of a finding that the potato whitener was present and caused Susan Trapnell's death. *See Tarter v. Metropolitan Savings & Loan Ass'n*, 744 S.W.2d 926, 928 (Tex. 1988) (holding that the "doctrine of collateral estoppel

---

[11] Indeed, the record indicates that the non-potato whitener defendants have already begun to litigate the potato whitener issue. Hoechst Celanese points out that some of the non-potato whitener defendants such as Allied argued issue preclusion to the trial court, and that all of the defendants joined in a reply brief filed in the court of appeals that argued for preclusion. However, neither Globe nor Lamb-Weston has argued preclusion to this Court. Lamb-Weston specifically asserts that while it is not concerned with the estoppel issue, if this court upholds the court of appeals' reversal of its summary judgment, all defendants should be present in the subsequent trial so that it can fully explore all causation issues. Moreover, the same non-potato whitener defendants that argued issue preclusion below also presented evidence of potato whitener use and causation in their motions for summary judgment and in their appellate briefs to argue that their products did not cause Susan's death.

[12] In addition, issue preclusion is likely to further complicate the trial in state court. *See* Restatement (Second) of Judgments § 29(6) (1982) (listing as a factor weighing against preclusion the fact that "treating the issue as conclusively determined may complicate determination of issues in the subsequent action.").

applies when relitigation could result in an inconsistent determination of the same ultimate *issue*" (emphasis in original)).

Application of collateral estoppel also involves considerations of fairness not encompassed by the "full and fair opportunity" inquiry. *See Blonder-Tongue*, 402 U.S. at 328 (describing the "goal of limiting relitigation of issues where that can be achieved without compromising fairness in particular cases"); *Benson*, 468 S.W.2d at 362–63 ("It has been said that the rule rests upon equitable principles and upon the broad principles of justice."). Given the procedural uniqueness of this case, considerations of fairness are especially important. The Trapnells were prevented from filing all of their claims in one suit by case law that has subsequently been overruled by statute. If collateral estoppel were applied, the Trapnells would face a situation in which they would be foreclosed from litigating the potato whitener issue as to one set of defendants, yet the issue would remain in the case as a defense to the Trapnells' claims against the remaining defendants. Because of a previous suit in a forum dictated by statute, they would be deprived of the opportunity to have all three sets of defendants in one trial.[14]

In sum, applying collateral estoppel in this case would fulfill none of the doctrine's purposes: it would neither conserve judicial resources nor prevent multiple lawsuits. In addition, applying collateral estoppel would be unfair to the Trapnells, whose procedural predicament is not of their own making. Our holding today is a narrow one, given the unusual procedural posture of this case and the fact that statutory changes make it unlikely that this situation will recur in the future. For these reasons, collateral estoppel should not be applied here. Consequently, we need not reach and neither approve nor disapprove of the court of appeals' holding that application of collateral estoppel would violate the Trapnells' right to trial by jury under the Texas Constitution. *See* Tex. Const. art. 1, § 15; art. 5, § 10.

Because we find that there is a question of fact regarding the hash brown and apple pie filling defendants and the federal judgment does not preclude the Trapnells from litigating the issue of whether potato whitener was in the fruit salad, we affirm the judgment of the court of appeals.

[The opinion of Justices Enoch, Hecht, and Gonzalez, concurring in part and dissenting in part, is omitted.]

---

[14] We acknowledge Sysco's concern that refusing to apply collateral estoppel may result in unfairness to it, because if it is found liable to the Trapnells, it cannot seek contribution from the Navy. The court of appeals' argument that the potato whitener defendants' contribution rights are intact because the Navy cannot assert collateral estoppel against them confuses contribution law with the law of collateral estoppel. 850 S.W.2d at 541 n.10. Sysco and the others would be prevented from seeking contribution from the Navy because their contribution claims are derivative of the Trapnells' claims against the Navy. Because of the adverse judgment they suffered in federal court, the Trapnells probably have no further cause of action against the Navy. It would follow that none of the defendants has a derivative cause of action against the Navy . . . . Although we recognize this potential unfairness, it is but one consideration in our analysis. *See* Geoffrey C. Hazard, Jr., *Res Nova in Res Judicata*, 44 S. Cal. L. Rev. 1036, 1043 (1971) (recognizing that collateral estoppel involves a "multiple factor analysis and [is] hence not reducible to categorical rules that have yes-no application"). Moreover, the cases suggest that the focus of our analysis should be unfairness to the party against whom collateral estoppel is being asserted, in this case the plaintiffs . . . .

NOTES AND QUESTIONS

(1) *Offensive Use of Findings.* Most cases involve a party using collateral estoppel as a defense. In *Trapnell,* for example, the potato whitener defendants were arguing that collateral estoppel precluded the plaintiff from trying to establish that the fruit salad contained potato whitener. In some cases, however, a party asserts collateral estoppel as a basis for establishing an element of his or her cause of action. Some jurisdictions have prohibited such offensive use, but in *Bonniwell v. Beech Aircraft Corp.*, 633 S.W.2d 553 (Tex. 1983), the Texas Supreme Court, assessing two law suits stemming from the same plane crash, referred approvingly to the use. The plaintiffs in the first suit sued three defendants on a mixture of negligence and strict liability grounds. The defendants cross-claimed against each other for indemnity and contribution. The jury returned findings regarding the comparative fault of the various defendants that, in turn, determined the cross-claims. The second suit then proceeded to trial, that suit involving different plaintiffs but the same defendants sued on the same grounds as in the first suit. Again, the defendants cross-claimed for indemnity and contribution. Defendant Beech asserted that the issues regarding the cross-claims were identical to those decided in the earlier suit. Thus, Beech argued, relitigation of the issues at the heart of the cross-claims should be barred. Essentially, Beech was asserting the doctrine of collateral estoppel both defensively (as the "defendant" of the cross-claims against it) and offensively (as the "plaintiff" in its cross-claims against the other defendants). The Supreme Court agreed with Beech that relitigation of the issues surrounding the cross-claims was barred and said, regarding offensive use of the doctrine:

> We recognize that the estoppel applied here is essentially offensive collateral estoppel. Application of the doctrine in this fashion is appropriate where the derivative claims of identical parties are based upon issues identical to those litigated in a prior suit. *Southern Pac. Transp. Co. v. Smith Material Corp.*, 616 F.2d 111, 114–15 (5th Cir. 1980). To hold those same issues may again be litigated between these defendants to establish mutual liabilities in a subsequent controversy, would invite inconsistent adjudication contrary to the spirit and purpose of the doctrine of collateral estoppel.

The *Bonniwell* court, in reaching its decision, noted, "Texas courts have adopted the position that mutuality is required only as to the party against whom the plea of collateral estoppel is asserted" [citing *Windmill Dinner Theatre, Inc. v. Hagler*, 582 S.W.2d 585 (Tex. Civ. App. — Dallas 1979, writ dism'd); *Olivarez v. Broadway Hardware, Inc.*, 564 S.W.2d 195 (Tex. Civ. App. — Corpus Christi 1978, writ ref'd n.r.e.); *Hardy v. Fleming*, below; *Benson v. Wanda Petroleum Co.*, below ("When persons against whom collateral estoppel operates have had their day in court, either as parties, privies, or through actual and adequate representation, application of the doctrine meets the requirements of due process")]. The abolition of the mutuality requirement was essential in the landmark federal case allowing offensive use of collateral estoppel by plaintiffs not parties to an earlier action. *See Parklane Hosiery Co. v. Shore*, 439 U.S. 322 (1979) (offensive use was permissible when defendant had full and fair opportunity and strong incentive to litigate issue in earlier action, when plaintiff could not have joined in the earlier suit, and when judicial economy and efficiency would be served).

After handing down its original opinion in *Bonniwell*, on motion for rehearing, the Texas Supreme Court withdrew the opinion and substituted a new opinion in which it concluded that Beech could not use the collateral estoppel doctrine to support its claim because the issue that was litigated in the first suit and that Beech was using as an estoppel in the second suit "was not essential to the judgment" in the first action. *Bonniwell v. Beech Aircraft Corp.*, 663 S.W.2d 816, 818–19 (Tex. 1984). Hencc, the "offensive use" of collateral estoppel issue that is discussed in the original opinion dropped from the case on rehearing.

Several Texas intermediate courts have approved the offensive use of collateral estoppel. *Dover v. Baker, Brown, Sharman & Parker*, 859 S.W.2d 441, 449 (Tex. App. — Houston [1st Dist.] 1993, no writ); *Tankersley v. Durish*, 855 S.W.2d 241, 244 (Tex. App. — Austin 1993, writ denied); *Phillips v. Allums*, 882 S.W.2d 71, 75 (Tex. App. — Houston [14th Dist.] 1994, writ denied) (acknowledging trial court's discretion to apply offensive use doctrine considering fairness factors set forth in *Parklane Hosiery Co. v. Shore*, 439 U.S. 322 (1979)).

(2) *Alternative Grounds and Essential Findings.* As noted in *Trapnell*, one of the requirements for collateral estoppel is that the finding in question was essential to the result in the original suit. Can a result based on multiple findings be "essential"? It appears that the Texas Supreme Court does not generally embrace the concept that is set forth in comment (i) to Section 27 of the Restatement (Second) of Judgments that "[i]f a judgment of a court of first instance is based on determinations of two issues, either of which standing independently would be sufficient to support the result, the judgment is not conclusive with respect to either issue standing alone." *See Eagle Props., Ltd. v. Scharbauer*, 807 S.W.2d 714, 721–22 (Tex. 1990). After quoting the Restatement, the Texas Supreme Court declined to follow it:

> While this alternative reasoning may have had some adverse effect on defendants' desire to appeal the judgment, it is clear that the federal court "rigorously considered" defendants' claims of fraudulent inducement, carefully reviewing each contention. Therefore, applying state law to the circumstances of this case, we hold that the defendants' claims of fraudulent inducement were "actually tried" in the federal court and that the court's findings on fraudulent inducement were "essential" to its judgment for the purposes of preclusion by collateral estoppel . . . . [E]xcept in very unusual cases, the abandonment of estoppel for the reason that a prior judgment rests on multiple grounds is inconsistent with the general rule in federal courts that a party is only entitled to one full and fair opportunity to litigate an issue.

(3) *Lower Court Judgments.* Consider the following sections of the Civil Practice and Remedies Code concerning the preclusive effect of decisions of lower trial courts:

> § 31.004. *Effect of Adjudication in Lower Trial Court.*
>
> (a) A judgment or a determination of fact or law in a proceeding in a lower trial court is not res judicata and is not a basis for estoppel by

judgment in a proceeding in a district court, except that a judgment rendered in a lower trial court is binding on the parties thereto as to recovery or denial of recovery.

(b) This section does not apply to a judgment in probate, guardianship, lunacy, or other matter in which a lower trial court has exclusive subject matter jurisdiction on a basis other than the amount in controversy.

(c) For the purposes of this section, a "lower trial court" is a small claims court, a justice of the peace court, a county court, or a statutory county court.

§ 31.005. *Effect of Adjudication in Small Claims or Justice of the Peace Court.*

A judgment or a determination of fact or law in a proceeding in small claims court or justice of the peace court is not *res judicata* and does not constitute a basis for estoppel by judgment in a proceeding in a county court or statutory county court, except that the judgment rendered is binding on the parties thereto as to recovery or denial of recovery.

These statutory provisions modify the common law so that *res judicata* bars only those claims that were actually litigated in a limited jurisdiction court. *Webb v. Persyn*, 866 S.W.2d 106, 107 (Tex. App. — San Antonio 1993, no writ).

(4) *Collateral Estoppel Based on Finding in Criminal Proceeding.* Should a jury determination of facts in a criminal proceeding serve as the basis for collateral estoppel in a civil action? *See Texas Dep't. of Pub. Safety v. Petta*, 44 S.W.3d 575, 577 (Tex. 2001) (applying collateral estoppel when the facts necessarily found in the criminal action are identical to an issue in the civil proceeding).

[2] The Doctrine of Mutuality

Can strangers to lawsuit #1 use issue preclusion to help their position in lawsuit #2? Think about what would make such a doctrine fair or unfair.

HARDY v. FLEMING

553 S.W.2d 790 (Tex. Civ. App. — El Paso 1977, writ ref'd n.r.e.)

WARD, J.

This is a medical malpractice case where summary judgment was rendered for the Defendant Doctor. Prior to the present suit, the Plaintiff had lost a workmen's compensation suit which was based on the same heart attack which he now claims was caused by the Doctor's negligence. The principal question concerns the correctness of the trial Court's action in sustaining the Defendant's plea of collateral estoppel where the Defendant asserting the plea was not a party or in privity with a party to the earlier litigation. We affirm.

On August 6, 1971, the Plaintiff, Karl Hardy, while at home suffered an apparent heart attack. He immediately placed himself under the care of the Defendant, Dr.

B.K. Fleming, and was thereafter treated by that Doctor for about a month. On September 10th, the Defendant advised the Plaintiff that he could return to full duty work at the Columbian Carbon Black Company at Seminole. The Plaintiff's employment was physically strenuous and required that the Plaintiff sack carbon black, put the sacks on pallets, and move them to a cooler. On September 12th, the Plaintiff returned to his employment on a full duty basis, but, after only a few hours of work, he experienced additional heart problems and, according to him, suffered another heart attack.

Hardy then filed his claim for compensation based on this latter attack, and thereafter instituted suit to recover his benefits under the Texas Workmen's Compensation Act by cause entitled "*Karl Hardy v. Insurance Company of North America*," Cause No. 6463 in the District Court of Gaines County, Texas. Upon trial before a jury, the Court submitted Special Issue No. 1 to the jury inquiring whether Mr. Hardy had sustained a heart attack on September 12, 1971. According to the judgment rendered, the finding to this issue was that the Plaintiff, Karl Hardy, did not sustain a heart attack on September 12, 1971. Based upon that finding, judgment was entered that Hardy take nothing from the Insurance Company of North America. That judgment, which was in July, 1973, has become final.

Hardy next filed this present suit in the District Court of Gaines County to recover his alleged damages sustained from being under the care of Dr. Fleming during August and September, 1971. This malpractice suit was based upon the alleged negligence of the Doctor in: (a) advising Mr. Hardy that he could return to work on a full-time basis when it was not safe to do so; (b) failing to advise Hardy of the nature and extent of the damage done to his heart and of his physical condition; (c) failing to perform such tests and procedures to determine the nature of the damage and injuries done to Hardy's heart as would have been done by a competent and ordinary prudent physician; and (d) failing to refer Hardy to an appropriate medical specialist. The Plaintiff further alleged that he returned to work on the date authorized by Dr. Fleming and, "within four hours, suffered a massive heart attack brought on by the work and exertion associated with his employment."

By way of answer, the Doctor has pled the above matters regarding Cause No. 6463, the submission of the special issue regarding the heart attack on September 12, 1971, the finding by the jury that Hardy did not sustain the heart attack, the final judgment, and that because of the principle of estoppel by judgment, Hardy is now prohibited in the present case from contending that he sustained a heart attack on September 12, 1971. The Doctor filed his first amended motion for summary judgment setting forth two points of law: (1) the doctrine of collateral estoppel bars the present action; and (2) there is no genuine issue of proximate causation in the case. The summary judgment proof consisted of the depositions of the two parties, certified copy of the judgment in Cause No. 6463, the Defendant's answers to the Plaintiff's interrogatories, and the depositions of Dr. William Gordon, Dr. J.B. Jensen, and Dr. Moses Muzquiz, Jr. As stated, the trial Court entered summary judgment for the Defendant on his motion which advanced the two grounds.

The [Plaintiff's] first point attacks the summary judgment on the ground that the doctrine of collateral estoppel is not applicable in this case. The Plaintiff points out that Dr. Fleming had no relationship with the Columbian Carbon Black Company, nor with the Insurance Company of North America. Thus, the issue to be determined is whether Dr. Fleming, who is a stranger to the prior suit, may assert the doctrine of collateral estoppel in this subsequent independent suit brought by the same Plaintiff.

The parties recognize the authorities and agree as to the principles. They agree that the tendency of the Courts has been toward an abandonment of the requirement of mutuality and the retention of the requirement of privity only to the party against whom the plea of collateral estoppel is made in the second case. They disagree as to the present rule in this State . . . .

Originally, mutuality was essential to the invocation of collateral estoppel. *Kirby Lumber Corporation v. Southern Lumber Co.*, 196 S.W.2d 387 (1946). However, the requirement of mutuality is nowhere mentioned in the last definition of collateral estoppel made by the Supreme Court where it was stated:

> "The rule of collateral estoppel, or as sometimes phrased, estoppel by judgment, bars relitigation in a subsequent action upon a different cause of action of fact issues actually litigated and essential to a prior judgment. It has been said that the rule rests upon equitable principles and upon the broad principles of justice . . . . The rule is generally stated as binding a party and those in privity with him . . . ."

Benson v. Wanda Petroleum Company, 468 S.W.2d 361 (Tex. 1971). There, Wanda Petroleum Company had successfully defended a negligence case brought by the Porters. Mrs. Benson then brought her suit for damages for her injuries and those of her deceased husband who owned the automobile and which had been driven by the Porters. The plea of collateral estoppel was held inapplicable to Mrs. Benson's suit as Mrs. Benson was not a party to the former action, had not participated in or exercised any control over the other trial, nor did she have any right to do so, and was not shown to have any beneficial interest in recovery of damages for personal injuries on behalf of the plaintiffs in the other trial. The Supreme Court did not apply the doctrine of mutuality, which would have ended it, but relied instead on the due process test as was originally done in the leading case of *Bernhard v. Bank of America Nat. Trust & Savings Ass'n*, 122 P.2d 892 (Cal. 1942). That case was cited by Justice Steakley in his opinion. *See also Seguros Tepeyac, S.A., Compania Mexicana v. Jernigan*, 410 F.2d 718 (1969). There, the Fifth Circuit, in passing on Texas law and in ignoring any requirement of mutuality, refers to a suggestion that mutuality as an element of collateral estoppel is "a dead letter."

The Plaintiff, Karl Hardy, the one against whom the plea of collateral estoppel is asserted, was the party Plaintiff to the prior adjudication and he lost on his claim that he sustained a heart attack on September 12, 1971. No useful public policy is served by permitting him to relitigate that identical issue in the present suit. Dr. Fleming, the one now asserting the plea, was not a party or in privity with a party to the prior litigation. There is no compelling reason that such be required and, in this fact situation, no satisfactory reason for any requirement of mutuality.

Bernhard v. Bank of America Nat. Trust & Savings Ass'n, supra. The Plaintiff's first point is overruled . . . .

The judgment of the trial Court is affirmed.

NOTES AND QUESTIONS

(1) *Due Process Rights.* Why is there a requirement that the party to be bound by the determination of the issue must have been a party or in privity with a party in the prior case?

(2) *Adverse Consequences of Eliminating Mutuality.* The elimination of the mutuality doctrine can arguably lead to harsh results when the effect of the finding made in the first case on subsequent litigation involving a different party is difficult to foresee. *See* Brainerd Currie, *Mutuality of Collateral Estoppel — Limits of the* Bernhard *Doctrine*, 9 Stan. L. Rev. 281 (1957). Is *Hardy v. Fleming, above*, a case in which the plaintiff would likely have foreseen the consequences of the prior adjudication? At least in the case of offensive, non-mutual collateral estoppel, the court is directed to consider various fairness issues before applying non-mutual estoppel. *Parklane Hosiery Co. v. Shore*, 439 U.S. 322 (1979) (offensive use was permissible when defendant had full and fair opportunity and strong incentive to litigate issue in earlier action, when plaintiff could not have joined in the earlier suit, and when judicial economy and efficiency would be served).

§ 8.02 PARTIES BOUND BY PRIOR ADJUDICATIONS

Sometimes a person who was not actually a party to lawsuit #1 will still be bound because of his or her very close relationship to someone who *was* a party. It is said that those who are in "privity" with the parties may also be bound by the judgment. As you read the next case, think about what kind of relationship to a party will lead to the non-party's being bound by the first judgment.

BENSON v. WANDA PETROLEUM COMPANY

468 S.W.2d 361 (Tex. 1971)

Steakley, J.

The source of the problem here is a collision which occurred on October 29, 1967 in Eastland County, Texas, involving a tractor and trailer owned by Wanda Petroleum Company, respondent, and an automobile owned by Merrel Benson, now deceased, and his wife, Mrs. Lily Benson, which was being driven by Thurman C. Porter. A third party identified as Donald Chalk collided with the Benson vehicle following the initial collision. Separate suits for damages for personal injuries were filed against Wanda in the District Court of Eastland County by Mrs. Benson and by Mr. and Mrs. Porter. The suits were consolidated by the trial court and when called for trial Mrs. Benson took a voluntary non-suit. The trial jury in the Porter suit found Wanda and its driver free of negligence and found Porter guilty of acts of negligence which proximately caused the collision. A take nothing judgment was entered in favor of Wanda.

This suit for damages for personal injuries suffered by her and by her deceased husband was subsequently filed by Mrs. Benson in the District Court of Harris County against Wanda and Chalk. The trial court severed the suit against Chalk and rendered summary judgment in favor of Wanda upon the theory that the fact findings and judgment in the Porter suit were binding on Mrs. Benson. The Court of Civil Appeals affirmed in the stated opinion that the Bensons and Porters were engaged in a joint enterprise as a matter of law, and hence were in privity; and that the Bensons rested under a secondary or derivative liability which must have been considered and determined in the Porter suit. We disagree and so reverse and remand.

The rule of collateral estoppel, or as sometimes phrased, estoppel by judgment, bars relitigation in a subsequent action upon a different cause of action of fact issues actually litigated and essential to a prior judgment. It has been said that the rule rests upon equitable principles and upon the broad principles of justice . . . . The rule is generally stated as binding a party and those in privity with him . . . . Section 83 of the Restatement of Judgments (1942) states that a person who is not a party but who is in privity with the parties in an action terminating in a valid judgment is bound by the rules of res judicata. A comment to this section says in part: "Privity is a word which expresses the idea that as to certain matters and in certain circumstances persons who are not parties to an action but who are connected with it in their interests are affected by the judgment with reference to interests involved in the action, as if they were parties . . . . The statement that a person is bound by . . . a judgment as a privy is a short method of stating that under the circumstances and for the purpose of the case at hand he is bound by . . . all or some of the rules of res judicata by way of merger, bar or collateral estoppel." It has been emphasized that privity is not established by the mere fact that persons may happen to be interested in the same question or in proving the same state of facts . . . . Also, that privity connotes those who are in law so connected with a party to the judgment as to have such an identity of interest that the party to the judgment represented the same legal right . . . . But it is also recognized that there is no generally prevailing definition of privity which can be automatically applied to all cases involving the doctrine of res judicata and the determination of who are privies requires careful examination into the circumstances of each case as it arises . . . . In *Kirby Lumber Corp. v. Southern Lumber Co., supra*, privity was defined as meaning the mutual or successive relationship to the same rights of property; and it was said that persons are privy to a judgment whose succession to the rights of property therein adjudicated are derived through or under one or the other of the parties to the action, and which rights accrued subsequent to the commencement of the action. It has also been said that the Restatement definition corresponds to results generally reached by the courts, the elements of which are summarized in these words: "[t]he word 'privy' includes those who control an action although not parties to it . . . ; those whose interests are represented by a party to the action . . . ; successors in interests . . . ." *Developments in the Law — Res Judicata*, 65 HARV. L. REV. 818, 856 (1952).

The rules of res judicata rest upon the policy of protecting a party from being twice vexed for the same cause, together with that of achieving judicial economy in precluding a party who has had a fair trial from relitigating the same issue . . . . Due process requires that the rule of collateral estoppel operate only against persons who have had their day in court either as a party to the prior suit or as a privy, and, where not so, that, at the least, the presently asserted interest was actually and adequately represented in the prior trial. As to the latter, § 84 of the Restatement of Judgments (1942) states that a person who is not a party but who controls an action is bound by the adjudications of litigated matters as if he were a party where he has a proprietary or financial interest in the judgment or in the determination of a question of fact or of law with reference to the same subject matter or transaction.

The rationale of decisions in other jurisdictions that have considered the problem at hand in the context of the employer-employee relationship is instructive. This is illustrated by *Makariw v. Rinard*, 336 F.2d 333 (3rd Cir. 1964). Rinard took his automobile to YBH Sales and Service, Inc. for servicing, and accompanied YBH's mechanic, Makariw, on a road test. While Makariw was driving, the car hit a "pothole" and skidded into another car and an embankment. Makariw was killed and Rinard was injured. Rinard sued YBH for personal injuries and contended that Makariw's negligence caused the accident. Judgment was in his favor based on findings of negligence against Makariw. Makariw's Administratrix thereafter brought a suit against Rinard under the Pennsylvania Wrongful Death and Survival Acts. The federal district court granted Rinard's motion to dismiss the action on the grounds that any recovery would be barred by the prior finding in the Rinard suit that Makariw had been guilty of negligence, which was conclusive under the doctrine of collateral estoppel; it was reasoned that the derivative liability of the employer for the employee's negligence established the employee's privity with the employer and bound him to the previous fact findings. The court of appeals for the Third Circuit reversed for the stated reason that the legal representative of the employee had not had her day in court on the critical issues which premised her suit and was not bound by a final determination in the prior suit against the employer. Reliance was placed on decisions giving particular emphasis to considerations here present: the plaintiff in the later suit was neither a party to the former action nor in privity with any party in the sense that his rights were derived from one who was a party; and the cause of action always had been that of the present plaintiff who had no voice in the conduct of the prior suit, with no right to examine witnesses or to take other action to protect his interests . . . .

The suit at bar is a separate and distinct action for redress for personal injuries. Mrs. Benson was not a party to the former action instituted by the Porters following her non-suit and they did not represent her in her claims against Wanda, respondent here. It was not shown that Mrs. Benson participated in, or exercised any control over, the trial in the Porter suit, or that she had any right to do so. She was not shown to have any beneficial interest in the recovery of damages for personal injuries on behalf of the Porters. In our view, the requirements of due process compel the conclusion that a privity relationship which will support application of the rules of res judicata does not exist under these circumstances. Accordingly, we hold that the fact findings and judgment in the Porter suit do not bar Mrs. Benson, and that she is entitled to her day in court in prosecuting this action in her own right.

The judgments below are reversed and the cause is remanded for trial.

NOTES AND QUESTIONS

(1) *Other Applications of Privity Concept. Benson* sets forth the general principles by which a person not a party, but in privity with a party, may be bound by a valid judgment. The principal case also presents conditions under which a person would be held *not* to be in privity. What factual situation would adequately demonstrate privity to justify the application of the doctrine of *res judicata*? Consider *Lemon v. Spann*, 633 S.W.2d 568 (Tex. Civ. App. — Texarkana 1982, writ ref'd n.r.e.), demonstrating the application of the concept of privity to individuals on both sides of the versus. In Action 1, Blundell sued George Lemon, Sr., a real estate agent, to impose an equitable lien or enforce specific performance of a contract for the sale of certain land to Blundell and another, Spann. Alternatively, Blundell sought damages for fraudulent conduct on the part of Lemon, Sr. The conveyance to Blundell and Spann had been stopped by the sale of the land to George Lemon, Jr. The sale to Lemon, Jr., had been arranged by Lemon, Sr. In Action 1, Lemon, Sr. obtained a partial summary judgment on the lien and specific performance dimensions of the case and then obtained a severance of those issues from the remaining fraud allegations so that Lemon, Jr. could deal freely with the property. Blundell appealed on the ground that the fiduciary relationship with Lemon, Sr. as real estate agent entitled him to a constructive trust. The Court of Civil Appeals affirmed the lower court's judgment, holding that the matter of fiduciary relationship had not been presented as a fact issue in opposition to Lemon, Sr.'s motion for summary judgment and therefore could not be presented on appeal.

Action 2 was filed before the appellate court decided the appeal of Action 1. In Action 2, Spann and Blundell sued Lemon, Jr., and the estate of Lemon, Sr., who had died in the meantime. They alleged fraud against both Lemons, breach of confidential relationship between Lemon, Sr. and Blundell, and authorization or ratification by Lemon, Jr. of his father's actions. The plaintiffs sought a constructive trust on the land and actual and punitive damages. The case went to trial with Lemon, Jr. as the only defendant. The trial court, based on a jury verdict, imposed a constructive trust on the property. Lemon, Jr. appealed, and the Court of Civil Appeals reversed on the basis of the doctrine of *res judicata*. The plaintiffs contended on appeal that the doctrine did not apply in that there were different parties (Spann as a new plaintiff and Lemon, Jr. as a new defendant) and different issues in the second suit (e.g., pursuit of a constructive trust, which was not sought at the trial court level in the first action). After reviewing the concept of privity in a manner similar to *Benson*, the court responded to the different-parties argument:

> The rights of Harlin Spann and George Lemon, Jr. in the tract of land were mutual to those of Blundell and George Lemon, Sr., respectively. Further, they were derivative. Spann conceded that any interest he had in the property was to be through Blundell. Any judgment against George

> Lemon, Jr. is dependent on first establishing a cause of action against George Lemon, Sr., for fraud or breach of a fiduciary relationship. On these bases we determine that Spann and George Lemon, Jr. were privies to the parties in the first suit.

Regarding the different-issues argument, the court stated:

> [A]ppellees say that, as we recognized in our earlier opinion, they did not litigate the merits of imposing a constructive trust in the prior suit. However, this was an equitable matter which might have been litigated in the first suit seeking to enforce an equitable lien or specific performance. Even appellees recognized this when they asserted it on their earlier appeal as the basis to bar the granting of the partial summary judgment in the first suit. That judgment barred the equitable proceedings seeking a claim against the land and severed the fraud claims seeking damages. The instant judgment imposing a constructive trust is barred because that matter might have been litigated by the parties or their privies in the first suit.

(2) *Types of Claims.* Did *Benson* raise a plea of merger and bar or a plea of collateral estoppel? What about *Lemon*?

§ 8.03 ELECTION OF REMEDIES

As you learned in the chapter on pleadings, parties are allowed to plead in the alternative, including the ability to request inconsistent remedies. At some point, however, a litigant takes an action that constitutes a choice to pursue one remedy and forgo the other. When does that happen?

BOCANEGRA v. AETNA LIFE INS. CO.
605 S.W.2d 848 (Tex. 1980)

Pope, J.

Plaintiff, Janie Bocanegra, sued Aetna Life Insurance Company on a group medical and hospital policy and recovered judgment upon a jury finding that certain medical and hospital services she needed resulted from a non-occupational disease.[1]

Previously Mrs. Bocanegra had filed with the Industrial Accident Board a claim, which she settled, for an occupational injury. The court of civil appeals held the settlement was an election which barred her later suit. That court reversed the judgment of the trial court and rendered judgment for Aetna . . . . We hold that Mrs. Bocanegra did not make an informed election that barred her in this action.

---

[1] The court instructed the jury by using a part of the definition in the group policy:

> You are instructed that the term "NON-OCCUPATIONAL DISEASE" means a disease which does not arise, and which is not caused or contributed to by, or as a consequence of, any disease which arises, out of or in the course of any employment or occupation for compensation or profit.

We reverse the judgment of the court of civil appeals and affirm the judgment of the trial court.

Mrs. Bocanegra began working for Clegg Company in 1965 as a book binder. Her work required her to lift and handle books. As she got out of bed one morning in April of 1975, she experienced a sharp pain in her lower back. She reported for work but did not tell her employer about her pain. On June 3, 1975, again on arising from bed, she had another severe pain, but still did not report any job-related injury. On June 29 the pain became so severe that she went to the emergency room of the Baptist Hospital. Her physician, Dr. Larry Miller, prescribed conservative treatment including two weeks in traction. He told Mrs. Bocanegra that she might have hurt her back at work. Failing to get any relief and after extensive tests, on August 11, she underwent surgery for a slipped disc. Dr. William Dossman performed the surgery. Mrs. Bocanegra never gave notice to her employer that she had sustained an occupational injury, but on August 18, after her operation, she filed with the Texas Industrial Accident Board her Notice of Injury or Occupational Disease and Claim for Compensation. In that notice she wrote, "I was lifting telephone books in the course and scope of my employment and injured my back and body generally." In her accompanying hardship affidavit, she swore, "I was hurt on the job on the above date while working for the above employer." On July 21, she filed a claim under the Aetna group policy on which she checked the box which asked if the claim was based on an accident. She also wrote on that claim form that the accident occurred "At work by lifting and bending." On July 29, she filed a second claim with Aetna on which she checked "No" to the question whether her claim was based on an accident. She also filed a claim with American Security Life Insurance Company on September 13 in which she stated that the accident occurred at work while lifting and bending. On September 17, she filed a similar claim with Presidential Life Insurance Company which gave the same information.

On October 27, Mrs. Bocanegra settled her worker's compensation claim for a general injury for $12,000 which the compensation carrier paid. The settlement agreement was "solely for lost wages and future impaired earning capacity," and it expressly excluded any payment for past or future medical or hospital expenses, the items that are here in question.

Mrs. Bocanegra, after her surgery and the settlement of her claim for an occupational injury, commenced these proceedings against Aetna to recover the amount of her medical and hospital bills. She asserted, and the jury found, that the medical and hospital services resulted from a non-occupational injury. She supported this claim by her own testimony that she was not injured on the job but that she did not know that fact until after her operation. At that time Dr. Dossman, her surgeon, told her that her back problem was the result of a degenerative disc disease that pre-dated but lingered after the onset of the initial back pain. She denied that she at any time ever told her doctors that she had sustained an injury on the job. Dr. Dossman confirmed Mrs. Bocanegra's testimony and testified that, in his opinion, her disc trouble was not related to her occupation. He testified: "About half of the time in this problem there is no known injury or cause of the problem, it just happens. About half of the time there is a history of some specific injury producing the problem." The court of civil appeals concluded that Mrs. Bocanegra's claim for an occupational injury was, as a matter of law, inconsistent with the state of facts upon which she later relied to obtain a judgment in her suit on the health policy that she had a non-occupational injury. The court rendered judgment that she take nothing.

The doctrine of election, although widely criticized,[2] survives in wide-ranging branches of the law that stretch from the widow's election in probate law to the choice in contract law between a suit for damages and one for rescission. *See* 5 Williston on Contracts §§ 683–688 (3d ed. Jaeger 1961). Election, an affirmative defense, has been held to bar remedies, rights, and inconsistent positions arising out of the same state of facts. 25 AM. JUR. 2D *Election of Remedies* § 7 (1966); Annot., 116 A.L.R. 601, 602 (1938). The situations in which an election might arise are so variable that an all-inclusive definition has been elusive, and discussions of the doctrine often borrow terms that may also appropriately relate to other affirmative defenses. For that reason, election is often confused with or likened to judicial estoppel, equitable estoppel, ratification, waiver or satisfaction. Those doctrines sometimes do not reach a situation that equity and good conscience need to reach through the doctrine of election.

A judicial estoppel may arise when a question necessary for the determination of a prior adjudication is decided. It constitutes a bar to a redetermination of that issue in a different cause. *Benson v. Wanda Petroleum Co.*, 468 S.W.2d 361 (Tex. 1971); *Long v. Knox*, 291 S.W.2d 292 (1956); *Houston Terminal Land Co. v. Westergreen*, 27 S.W.2d 526 (1930). Equitable estoppel differs from each of the above defenses, because it requires some deception that is practiced upon a party who relies upon it to his prejudice. *Barfield v. Howard M. Smith Co. of Amarillo*, 426 S.W.2d 834 (Tex. 1968); *Concord Oil Co. v. Alco Oil and Gas Corp.*, 387 S.W.2d 635 (Tex. 1965); *Gulbenkian v. Penn*, 252 S.W.2d 929 (1952). A ratification rests upon a manifestation of assent to confirm one's prior act or that of another. It may occur without any prior litigation and in the absence of any change of position by or prejudice to the other party. *Texas & Pac. Coal & Oil Co. v. Kirtley*, 288 S.W. 619 (Tex. Civ. App. — Eastland 1926, writ ref'd). Waiver, the voluntary relinquishment of a known right, is sometimes spoken of as intentional conduct inconsistent with the assertion of a known right. *Ford v. State Farm Mut. Auto. Ins. Co.*, 550 S.W.2d 663, 667 (Tex. 1977). Full satisfaction will bar a claim because the law will not permit double redress. *James & Co. Inc. v. Statham*, 558 S.W.2d 865 (Tex. 1977); *McMillen v. Klingensmith*, 467 S.W.2d 193 (Tex. 1971); *Bradshaw v. Baylor University*, 84 S.W.2d 703 (1935).

The single underlying principle of the election doctrine has not been found. Estoppel in some form, ratification and unjust enrichment have been suggested as the basic reasons for an election, and in many instances they suffice. *Schenck v. State Line Telephone Co.*, 144 N.E. 592 (N.Y. 1924); *Metroflight, Inc. v. Shaffer*, 581 S.W.2d 704 (Tex. Civ. App. — Dallas 1979, writ ref'd n.r.e.). The court of civil

[2] It has been criticized because of its lack of any fixed legal underpinnings and called the following: a legal weed that judicial gardeners should root out, Hine, *Election of Remedies: A Criticism*, 26 HARV. L. REV. 707, 719 (1913); a legal delusion, Note, *Election of Remedies: A Delusion?* 38 COLUM. L. REV. 292, 293 (1938); an anachronism, Fraser, *Election of Remedies: An Anachronism*, 29 OKLA. L. REV. 1 (1976); a problem child of the law, Merrem, *Election of Remedies*, 8 SW. L.J. 109 (1954); and a remedy that has no independent viability, LaBay, *Election of Remedies: The California Basis*, 19 HASTINGS L. REV. 1233, 1246 (1968).

appeals in this case has, perhaps more soundly, held that inconsistency will bar an action in instances of manifest injustice. Even though the inconsistent position may not fit the mold of a better defined principle, an election will bar recovery when the inconsistency in the assertion of a remedy, right, or state of facts is so unconscionable, dishonest, contrary to fair dealing, or so stultifies the legal process or trifles with justice or the courts as to be manifestly unjust.

A similar loosely defined but useful equitable doctrine is the constructive trust. It is unlike other trusts, but equity raised it up in the name of good conscience, fair dealing, honesty, and good morals. *Omohundro v. Matthews*, 341 S.W.2d 401, 405 (1960). "A constructive trust is the formula through which the conscience of equity finds expression." *Beatty v. Guggenheim Exploration Co.*, 122 N.E. 378, 380 (N.Y. 1919). Equity provides the idea of constructive trusts as a tool to "frustrate skullduggery," 4 R. Powell, *Real Property* § 593 (1949), even though that kind of a trust is also grounded upon elusive principles.[3] Such a trust is purely a creature of equity. Its form is practically without limit, and its existence depends upon the circumstances. *Simmons v. Wilson*, 216 S.W.2d 847, 849 (Tex. Civ. App. — Waco 1949, no writ).

The election doctrine, therefore, may constitute a bar to relief when (1) one successfully exercises an informed choice (2) between two or more remedies, rights, or states of facts (3) which are so inconsistent as to (4) constitute manifest injustice. *See Custom Leasing, Inc. v. Texas Bank & Trust Co. of Dallas*, 491 S.W.2d 869 (Tex. 1973).

A number of seemingly inconsistent positions do not rise to the level of an election which will bar recovery. One may, for example, plead alternative and inconsistent facts without being barred. Rules 48 and 51, Texas Rules of Civil Procedure, authorize such procedures. One who pleads alternative or inconsistent facts or remedies against two or more parties may settle with one of them on the basis of one remedy or state of facts and still recover a judgment against the others based on the pleaded alternative or inconsistent remedies or facts. By analogy, an insurer's voluntary payment to a worker of weekly compensation benefits will not bar the defense that there was no accidental injury. *Lopez v. Associated Employers Ins. Co.*, 330 S.W.2d 522 (Tex. Civ. App. — San Antonio 1959, writ ref'd). *See also Southern Underwriters v. Schoolcraft*, 158 S.W.2d 991 (1942). The basis for the holding was to encourage prompt payments of compensation following injury. A holding that the payments were inconsistent with a denial of an accidental injury or that they constituted an admission of an injury would discourage prompt payment of weekly benefits. *Hartford Accident & Indemnity Co. v. Hale*, 400 S.W.2d 310, 312–13 (Tex. 1966).

There is no election, that is, no inconsistency in choices, when one first unsuccessfully pursues a right or remedy which proves unfounded and then pursues the one that is allowed. *Poe v. Continental Oil & Cotton Co.*, 231 S.W. 717 (Tex. Com. App. 1921, holding approved); *Schwarz v. National Loan & Investment*

---

[3] "Without much conscious purpose or plan we have created this shambling creature. It is time to fence it in." J. Dawson, Unjust Enrichment 26 (1951). "It thus constitutes a fenceless field with hazy boundaries." 4 R. Powell, Real Property § 593, 565 (1949).

Co., 133 S.W.2d 133 (Tex. Civ. App. — Dallas 1939, writ ref'd); *Breland v. Guaranty Building & Loan Co.*, 119 S.W.2d 690 (Tex. Civ. App. — Fort Worth 1938, writ ref'd); 25 Am. Jur. 2d, *Election of Remedies* § 9. One may assert concurrent but inconsistent remedies or distinct causes of action against different persons arising out of independent transactions . . . .

One's choice between inconsistent remedies, rights or states of facts does not amount to an election which will bar further action unless the choice is made with a full and clear understanding of the problem, facts, and remedies essential to the exercise of an intelligent choice . . . . An exception to that rule exists when the choice of a course of action, though made in ignorance of the facts, will cause harm to an innocent party. *Slay v. Burnett Trust, supra* at 394; *Employers' Indemnity Corp. v. Felter*, 277 S.W. 376 (Tex. Com. App. 1925).

This present case aptly illustrates the reason that election should not bar a suit when a previous course of action or a settlement for less than the claim was grounded upon uncertain and undetermined facts. The definition of an occupational disease contained in section 20 of article 8306 is itself complex and difficult:

> Whenever the term "Occupational Disease" is used in the Workmen's Compensation Laws of this State, such term shall be construed to mean any disease arising out of and in the course of employment which causes damage or harm to the physical structure of the body and such other diseases or infections as naturally result therefrom. An "Occupational Disease" shall also include damage or harm to the physical structure of the body occurring as the result of repetitious physical traumatic activities extending over a period of time and arising in the course of employment; provided, that the date of the cumulative injury shall be the date disability was caused thereby. Ordinary diseases of life to which the general public is exposed outside of the employment shall not be compensable, except where such diseases follow as an incident to an "Occupational Disease" or "Injury" as defined in this section.

Under that definition, Mrs. Bocanegra's injury may have been an occupational one which was compensable, it may have been an "ordinary disease of life" which was not, or it may have been both. Tex. Rev. Civ. Stat. Ann. art. 8306, § 22. Many diseases, do not fit neatly within an either/or distribution, and the dispute whether such a condition is compensable or not is an ongoing one. Uncertainty in many complex areas of medicine and law is more the rule than the exception. It would be a harsh rule that charges a layman with knowledge of medical causes when, as in this case, physicians and lawyers do not know them. Mrs. Bocanegra's first physician, Dr. Miller, was of the opinion that the lifting and bending at the work bench was the cause of an occupational injury. Dr. Dossman advised her to the contrary after the surgery. The settlement agreement that Mrs. Bocanegra made with her compensation carrier showed that the carrier disputed liability, the period of time lost for the claimed occupational disease, and past and future medical expenses for which the carrier paid nothing. Mrs. Bocanegra lacked the requisite knowledge to bind her to an informed election.

Some of the Texas decisions cannot be harmonized, and they need discussion. *Seamans Oil Co. v. Guy*, 276 S.W. 424 (1925), while reaching a correct result, intermingles the doctrines of election, estoppel, and satisfaction. J.H. Guy and wife, lessors of an oil and mineral lease instituted suit against Seamans Oil Company and Empire Gas & Fuel Company for the cancellation of the lease. During the pendency of the suit against them, Seamans and Empire Gas could exercise none of the rights accorded by the lease, but they kept the lease alive by tendering timely delay rental payments which the Guys refused to accept. Just before the lease expired by its own terms, the Guys adopted an inconsistent posture, dismissed their suit for cancellation and drew a check on the bank for the delay rentals that they had previously rejected. By that time, the Guys' suit had fully accomplished its purpose to defeat any drilling or other operations. The court held that "[i]t would be shocking to a sense of justice to hold that the Guys could destroy the value of the leasehold by the claim that it did not exist and at the same time collect delay rentals upon the basis that it was a valid lease." The opinion, though primarily grounded upon an election, is an instance of full satisfaction which the Guys had already achieved through their lawsuit. Even though it was dismissed, the suit had fully accomplished the same purpose that a favorable judgment would have achieved. *Seamans* quotes from 10 Ruling Case Law 703, 704:

> If one having a right to pursue one of several inconsistent remedies makes his election, institutes suit, and prosecutes it to final judgment or receives anything of value under the claim thus asserted, or if the other party has been affected adversely, such election constitutes an estoppel thereafter to pursue another and inconsistent remedy. And where the right in the subsequent suit is inconsistent with that set up in the former suit, as distinguished from a merely inconsistent remedy, the party is estopped though the former suit may not have proceeded to judgment. But where the inconsistency is in the remedies it is generally considered that there is no estoppel where the former suit was dismissed without trial or before judgment.

The quotation is an early statement of the election doctrine and contains errors. An election may arise short of one's prosecution of a claim to final judgment. One may also receive something by way of settlement, even of substantial value, under an uncertain claim without making an election which bars recovery against another person. The quotation may be illustrative of some situations which might rise to the level of an election, but it is an unreliable statement of a general rule, and we reject it.

Lomas and Nettleton Co. v. Huckabee, 558 S.W.2d 863 (Tex. 1977), relied upon *Seamans, supra*, in holding there was an election. The Huckabees first asserted in their lawsuit that two insurance companies had insured the Huckabees' real and personal property that was destroyed in a fire. The Huckabees, upon the strength of that state of facts, recovered in a settlement one hundred percent of their claim for the destroyed realty and eighty percent of their claim for the destroyed personalty. Their lawsuit was then dismissed with prejudice. After succeeding with their claim that their property was insured, they adopted the inconsistent position that it was not insured and sued their agent for his neglect. We held that the Huckabees, after successfully asserting their claim on one state of facts and receiving almost the whole of their claim, would not be permitted a second recovery against another party by denying the truth of that state of facts. The case was correctly decided, but the quotation from *Seamans*, as discussed above, includes errors concerning the election doctrine. *Cf. Shriro Corp. v. Ward*, 570 S.W.2d 395 (Tex. 1978).

The court of civil appeals in *Metroflight, Inc. v. Shaffer*, 581 S.W.2d 704 (Tex. Civ. App. — Dallas 1979, writ ref'd n.r.e.), followed but criticized *Huckabee*. As is characteristic of this whole area of law, the opinion mixes equitable estoppel, ratification, satisfaction, judicial estoppel, unjust enrichment and other matters. Perhaps the underlying flaw in the analysis of the court of civil appeals in *Metroflight* is its basic assumption. Metroflight had sued in federal court claiming that it had insurance coverage for losses arising out of a plane crash. The defendant insurer denied coverage but later paid Metroflight eighty percent of the total claim. Metroflight, after dismissing its action in which it asserted insurance coverage, proceeded with a suit against its agent for damages on the basis of the inconsistent fact that the plane was not insured. The trial court held that Metroflight was barred by election. The court of civil appeals affirmed but criticized the *Huckabee* case, which it felt bound to follow. The *Metroflight* court assumed that Metroflight had dismissed its federal court claim asserting insurance coverage because pre-trial discovery had shown that claim to be groundless and certain to fail. This assumption, twice stated, is wrong. The insurer's settlement for eighty percent of the very large coverage-based claim shows the validity and strength of the claim that insurance actually existed.

In *Seamans*, *Huckabee*, and *Metroflight*, the respective plaintiffs realized most or all of what they claimed by asserting facts about which they were certain. By contrast, however, the fact upon which Mrs. Bocanegra relied in settling with her compensation carrier, the nature of her complex disease, was highly uncertain which was evidenced by the small settlement which included none of her hospital and medical bills.

The judgment of the court of civil appeals is reversed and the judgment of the trial court is affirmed.

CAMPBELL, J, concurring.

We should not attempt to draw an artificial distinction between this case and the decisions in *Huckabee* and *Metroflight* merely to avoid an admission that those decisions were erroneous. The claims in those cases were as uncertain as the claims in this case. Except for uncertainty there would obviously have been no compromise and settlement. This decision establishes a rule of law that whether a settlement with a defendant will be deemed an election barring suit against another defendant, upon facts inconsistent with those asserted to obtain the settlement, will be ultimately determined by this Court's opinion as to the degree of uncertainty as to the facts inconsistently asserted.

Seamans Oil Co. v. Guy was not decided upon the law of elections but was decided upon a clear-cut equitable estoppel. This Court in *Huckabee* followed a dictum quotation from Ruling Case Law which is incompatible with recognized principles of Texas procedure and policy. A party may plead and prove totally inconsistent claims and defenses in Texas. *Deal v. Madison*, 576 S.W.2d 409 (Tex. Civ. App. — Dallas 1978, writ ref'd n.r.e.); Rule 48, T.R.C.P.

Settlement agreements are highly favored in the law because they are a means of amicably resolving doubts and preventing lawsuits . . . .

Proper regard for these principles compels a conclusion that a mere compromise and settlement of a claim asserting facts inconsistent to those asserted in a claim against a different defendant should not bar the latter claim. The contrary conclusion, in effect, compels a party to proceed to final judgment against two or more defendants instead of settling with a defendant who is desirous of settlement. This would not diminish assertion of inconsistent claims but would merely diminish settlements.

We should concede our error and expressly overrule *Huckabee* and hold there is no election until final judgment on the merits.

NOTES AND QUESTIONS

(1) *Contours of Election Doctrine.* Do you find it strange that Mrs. Bocanegra could collect under one theory, then turn around and collect under the exact opposite theory? What factors were critical to the court's reasoning? Did it make a difference that the kinds of damages sought by Mrs. Bocanegra across the two actions were different and thus she could not be considered to have obtained a double recovery, prevention of which is one objective of the doctrine of election of remedies? Mrs. Bocanegra could have obtained an award of past and future medical expenses under workers' compensation, but the settlement struck expressly excluded them. What if she had received such medical expenses in the settlement? Did the amount of money involved affect the court's judgment? The medical expenses in question amounted to $4,500. Was it that Mrs. Bocanegra "honestly" asserted inconsistent theories that prompted the court to hold she had not made an election? What if the first action in the *Bocanegra* case had gone to trial rather than settlement? Would the outcome have been different if the issue of whether Mrs. Bocanegra suffered from an occupational or non-occupational disease had been litigated and a judgment rendered based on the way the issue was decided? (The settlement agreement between Mrs. Bocanegra and the workers' compensation insurance carrier stated specifically that, notwithstanding the settlement, liability was disputed.) Would litigation and adjudication have converted the case from an election-of-remedies case into a collateral-estoppel case? *Cf. Hardy v. Fleming*, in § 8.01[B][2].

(2) *Consequences of Successful Prosecution of Claim.* A number of workers' compensation cases have held that the prosecution of a claim in proceedings before the Texas Industrial Accident Board (now the Workers' Compensation Commission (WCC)) on one theory and resulting in an award of benefits accepted by the claimant constitutes an election of remedies and bars relitigation on a different theory or for a different measure of damages. *See Hedgeman v. Berwind Ry. Serv. Co.*, 512 S.W.2d 827 (Tex. Civ. App. — Houston [14th Dist.] 1974, writ ref'd n.r.e.); *Moore v. Means*, 549 S.W.2d 417 (Tex. Civ. App. — Beaumont 1977, writ ref'd n.r.e.); *Le Jeune v. Gulf States Utils. Co.*, 410 S.W.2d 44 (Tex. Civ. App. — Beaumont 1966, writ ref'd n.r.e.). Unlike *Bocanegra*, these cases went to judgment in the first action rather than to settlement. Does the judicial expenditure of time play a role in whether or not the plaintiff is deemed to have made an election in the

earlier action? Reconsider the Supreme Court's statement, "[A]n election will bar recovery when the inconsistency in the assertion of a remedy, right, or state of facts is so unconscionable, dishonest, contrary to fair dealing, or so stultifies the legal process or trifles with justice or the courts as to be manifestly unjust." What does this sentence mean? Does the acceptance or nonacceptance of an award make a difference? In *Grimes v. Jalco, Inc.*, 630 S.W.2d 282 (Tex. App. — Houston [1st Dist.] 1981, writ ref'd n.r.e.), the plaintiff was not deemed to have made an election when he rejected an IAB (now WCC) award obtained on his asserted theory that he was an employee at the time of injury and filed a common law cause of action for negligence asserting he was either an employee or an independent contractor. The *Grimes* court, referring to *Hedgeman*, *Moore*, and *LeJeune*, above, stated:

> These three cases are distinguishable from our case in that in each instance a final board award had been accepted by the claimant or a final judgment had been entered in the compensation claim. In this case the award by the IAB has been appealed and no final judgment has been entered. Under these circumstances we hold that an election of remedies has not been made by the appellant.

See also *Hanks v. GAB Bus. Servs., Inc.*, 644 S.W.2d 707 (Tex. 1982), applying the doctrine in a business dispute in which the plaintiff retained assets under one theory and later tried to pursue a different theory resulting in a different remedy.

(3) *Vitality of Election Doctrine.* After *Bocanegra*, how often do you think the court would find the doctrine of election of remedies applicable? Do you think the court would take the same approach in all kinds of cases? What if the plaintiff had not been Mrs. Bocanegra, an employee lacking knowledge of medicine and seeking workers' compensation benefits, but instead had been a business enterprise pursuing redress? The Supreme Court's position in such a case might be considerably different. *See Hanks v. GAB Bus. Servs., Inc.*, 644 S.W.2d 707 (Tex. 1982), above.

The Supreme Court in *Bocanegra* found that Mrs. Bocanegra did not have the requisite knowledge regarding the nature of her injury to bind her to an informed election between inconsistent theories and remedies. How uncertain and undetermined were the facts in *Hanks*? Is it any more fair to impute knowledge and understanding of contract law to a business enterprise than it is to impute knowledge of medicine to an injured individual like Mrs. Bocanegra?

(4) *Pleading Requirements.* Note that if the affirmative defense of election of remedies is relied on to defeat recovery, it must be specifically alleged. The defense must be presented to the trial court and cannot be urged for the first time on appeal. The *Bocanegra* case demonstrates that the burden of proof on the proponent may be heavy, but, as *Hanks* demonstrates, the doctrine is still viable and should be considered, especially when the doctrine of *res judicata* is unavailable.

§ 8.04 THE LAW OF THE CASE DOCTRINE

The "law of the case" doctrine is defined as that principle under which questions of law decided on appeal to a court of last resort will govern the case throughout its subsequent stages. But when do the courts get to change their minds?

HUDSON v. WAKEFIELD
711 S.W.2d 628 (Tex. 1986)

GONZALEZ, J.

This case involves the refusal of a bank to honor a check given as earnest money under a contract for the sale of land. The issue presented is whether, under the doctrine of the "law of the case," our "limited remand" of this cause precluded the assertion of additional related legal theories or defenses.

Robert Hudson and Andy Wright (Purchasers) sued to enforce specific performance of a contract for the sale of real property owned by Marion and Jean Wakefield (Sellers). In the original proceeding, the trial court granted sellers' motion for summary judgment on the grounds that the instrument on which specific performance was sought never attained the status of a contract because the check for earnest money was returned due to insufficient funds. The court of appeals affirmed, holding that a condition precedent under the contract was that purchasers fulfill the requirements of the earnest-money provision. We reversed the judgments of the lower courts and remanded, holding that, as a matter of law, the earnest-money provision was only a covenant. We then remanded the cause to the trial court to determine whether "the return of the earnest money check because of insufficient funds was such a material breach of the contract as to warrant sellers' repudiation of same." 645 S.W.2d 427, 431 (Tex. 1983).

On remand, the case was fully litigated to a jury. Prior to submission of the charge, the trial court allowed sellers to file a trial amendment which asserted fraud in the inducement. Purchasers objected to the trial amendment and to the court's submission of issues thereon. The record, however, fails to contain a statement of facts so that we cannot determine if purchasers objected to evidence of fraudulent inducement or if it was tried by consent. That court also allowed purchasers to file a trial amendment alleging a new theory dealing with ratification. The trial court then submitted several issues to the jury. Upon motion, the trial court disregarded two of the jury's findings: one, that sellers had ratified the contract; and two, that there had been no breach of contract by the purchasers. The trial court then rendered judgment *non obstante veredicto* for the sellers. In an unpublished opinion, the court of appeals affirmed the judgment of the trial court. We affirm the judgment of the court of appeals.

The question is whether, under the "law of the case" doctrine, our remand of the cause to the trial court to determine whether "the return of the earnest money check because of insufficient funds was such a material breach of the contract as to warrant sellers' repudiation of the same" precludes sellers' trial amendment and submission of issues on a theory of fraudulent inducement which would defeat the existence of a valid contract. Purchasers argue that when we remanded the case, the existence of a valid contract became the "law of the case;" therefore, the only issue which could be decided on remand was whether the contract breach was material.

Law of the Case

The "law of the case" doctrine is defined as that principle under which questions of law decided on appeal to a court of last resort will govern the case throughout its subsequent stages. *Trevino v. Turcotte*, 564 S.W.2d 682, 685 (Tex. 1978); *Governing Bd. v. Pannill*, 659 S.W.2d 670, 680 (Tex. App. — Beaumont 1983, writ ref'd n.r.e.); *Kropp v. Prather*, 526 S.W.2d 283 (Tex. Civ. App. — Tyler 1975, writ ref'd n.r.e.). By narrowing the issues in successive stages of the litigation, the law of the case doctrine is intended to achieve uniformity of decision as well as judicial economy and efficiency. *Dessommes v. Dessommes*, 543 S.W.2d 165, 169 (Tex. Civ. App. — Texarkana 1976, writ ref'd n.r.e.). The doctrine is based on public policy and is aimed at putting an end to litigation. *See Barrows v. Ezer*, 624 S.W.2d 613, 617 (Tex. App. — Houston [14th Dist.] 1981, no writ); *Elliott v. Moffett*, 165 S.W.2d 911 (Tex. Civ. App. — Texarkana 1942, writ ref'd w.o.m.).

The doctrine of the law of the case only applies to questions of law and does not apply to questions of fact. *Barrows*, 624 S.W.2d at 617; *Kropp*, 526 S.W.2d at 285. Further, the doctrine does not necessarily apply when either the issues or the facts presented at successive appeals are not substantially the same as those involved on the first trial. *Barrows*, 624 S.W.2d at 617; *Kropp*, 526 S.W.2d at 285; *Ralph Williams Gulfgate Chrysler Plymouth, Inc. v. State*, 466 S.W.2d 639 (Tex. Civ. App. — Houston [14th Dist.] 1971, writ ref'd n.r.e.). Thus, when in the second trial or proceeding, one or both of the parties amend their pleadings, it may be that the issues or facts have sufficiently changed so that the law of the case no longer applies . . . .

Limited Remand

When this court remands a case and limits a subsequent trial to a particular issue, the trial court is restricted to a determination of that particular issue. *Wall v. East Texas Teachers Credit Union*, 549 S.W.2d 232 (Tex. Civ. App. — Texarkana 1977, writ ref'd); *McConnell v. Wall*, 5 S.W. 681 (Tex. 1887). Thus, in a subsequent appeal, instructions given to a trial court in the former appeal will be adhered to and enforced. *Wall v. Wall*, 186 S.W.2d 57 (1945, opinion adopted); *Dessommes*, 543 S.W.2d at 169. In interpreting the mandate of an appellate court, however, the courts should look not only to the mandate itself, but also to the opinion of the court. *Wells v. Littlefield*, 62 Tex. 28 (1884); *Seale v. Click*, 556 S.W.2d 95, 96 (Tex. Civ. App. — Eastland 1977, writ ref'd n.r.e.). In this regard, we have observed that "the cases are rare and very exceptional in which this court is warranted in limiting the issues of fact, in reversing and remanding a case where the trial has been by jury; and to authorize such interpretation, it must clearly appear from the decision that it was so intended." *Cole v. Estell*, 6 S.W. 175, 177 (Tex. 1887). *See Price v. Gulf Atlantic Life Ins.*, 621 S.W.2d 185, 187 (Tex. Civ. App. — Texarkana 1981, writ ref'd n.r.e.).

A critical factor in our determination of this case is that in the first appeal we reviewed a summary judgment. On review of summary judgments, the appellate courts are limited in their considerations of issues and facts. In such a proceeding, the movant is not required to assert every theory upon which he may recover or defend.[1] Thus, when a case comes up for a trial on the merits, the parties may be different, the pleadings may be different, and other causes of action may have been consolidated. *See Governing Bd. v. Pannill*, 659 S.W.2d 670, 680–81 (Tex. App. — Beaumont 1983, writ ref'd n.r.e.). Other distinctions may be drawn; for instance, in reviewing the evidence to determine whether there are any fact issues in dispute, the appellate court must review the evidence in the light most favorable to the party opposing the motion for summary judgment. *Gaines v. Hamman*, 358 S.W.2d 557, 562 (1962). Thus, the context of a summary judgment proceeding is distinguishable from a full trial on the merits.

The distinction between a summary judgment and a trial on the merits in regard to the law of the case doctrine was made in *Pannill*, where the court noted:

> Also, it is apparent that the record presented on this third appeal, being an appeal after a full and lengthy trial on the merits with the jury acting as a finder of facts, differs in a very material sense from the prior limited appeal. There is no error in the action of the trial court in declining to follow the "law of the case" as pronounced by another Court of Civil Appeals on a vastly different record.

659 S.W.2d at 681. In the case at hand, the trial amendments by purchasers and sellers changed both the scope and nature of the lawsuit.

Purchasers argue that our remand language established the law of the case as to the existence of a valid contract. Therefore, they contend the trial court erred in allowing seller's trial amendment and issues asserting fraud in the inducement. We disagree.

In this case, sellers moved for summary judgment, asserting breach of contract by purchasers as a defense. In summary judgment proceedings, the movant must conclusively establish the essential elements of his asserted theories of recovery or defense. *City of Houston v. Clear Creek Basin Authority*, 589 S.W.2d 671, 678 (Tex. 1979). Breach of contract may have been the only theory which sellers believed they could conclusively establish. In regard to this theory, we held, on a single question of law (condition or covenant), that one of the terms of the contract was a covenant; therefore, a fact question existed and summary judgment was improper. Our holding in the first appeal, however, did not preclude sellers from asserting other defensive theories, including those attacking the validity of the contract, at a subsequent trial on the merits. Therefore, in light of the proceeding in which the question first arose, the trial court properly allowed sellers to assert the defense of fraud in the inducement . . . .

---

[1] It is important to note, that non-movants are required, in a written answer or response to motion, to expressly present to the trial court all issues that would defeat the movant's right to a summary judgment, and failing to do so, they cannot later assign them as error on appeal. *City of Houston v. Clear Creek Basin Authority*, 589 S.W.2d 671, 679 (Tex. 1979).

NOTES

(1) *Law of the Case and the Court of Appeals.* In *Briscoe v. Goodmark Corp.*, 102 S.W.3d 714 (Tex. 2003), the Texas Supreme Court discussed an exception to the law of the case doctrine:

> Under the law of the case doctrine, a court of appeals is ordinarily bound by its initial decision if there is a subsequent appeal in the same case. The law of the case doctrine states as follows:
>
> The "law of the case" doctrine is defined as that principle under which questions of law decided on appeal to a court of last resort will govern the case throughout its subsequent stages. By narrowing the issues in successive stages of the litigation, the law of the case doctrine is intended to achieve uniformity of decision as well as judicial economy and efficiency. The doctrine is based on public policy and is aimed at putting an end to litigation.
>
> A decision rendered on an issue before the appellate court does not absolutely bar re-consideration of the same issue on a second appeal. Application of the doctrine lies within the discretion of the court, depending on the particular circumstances surrounding that case.
>
> The Court has long recognized as an exception to the law of the case doctrine that if the appellate court's original decision is clearly erroneous, the court is not required to adhere to its original rulings. "It would be unthinkable for [the court], after having granted the writ, reconsidered the case, and arrived at the conclusion that the opinion on the former appeal was clearly erroneous, to hold that it is bound by considerations of consistency to perpetuate that error. Our duty to administer justice under the law, as we conceive it, outweighs our duty to be consistent.

(2) *Law of the Case and the Supreme Court.* In *City of Houston v. Jackson*, 192 S.W.3d 764, 769 (Tex. 2006), the Court held that the " 'law of the case' doctrine in no way prevents this Court from considering legal questions that are properly before us for the first time."

Chapter 9

DISCOVERY: PURPOSES, SCOPE, AND USES

Scope

This chapter looks at the purposes, scope, and uses of discovery. More specifically, the chapter begins by considering why discovery matters, the general scope of discovery, and the ethical implications of discovery practice. It then analyzes in detail the meaning of "relevance" for discovery purposes and the extent of privileges protecting relevant information from discovery.

This chapter will, of necessity, refer to various discovery devices, because the cases involve parties using those devices. They are very much like the discovery devices you learned about in your first year Civil Procedure class. In addition, one device — the request for disclosure — specifically makes certain matters discoverable, and so this chapter discusses disclosures. The chapter's focus, however, is on what can and cannot be discovered. The specific devices, their uses, the procedures for litigating discovery disputes, the duty to supplement discovery responses, and sanctions for discovery misconduct are covered in chapter 10.

§ 9.01 AN INTRODUCTION TO THE PURPOSES AND SCOPE OF DISCOVERY

It is difficult to overemphasize the importance of discovery to a trial lawyer. The vast majority of suits involve factual disputes, and even in the minority of suits in which the main question is one of law, the facts must be established. Discovery is the principal means of finding out what the facts are before trial. Therefore, a good trial lawyer must be familiar with the techniques of discovery so that he or she not only understands the rules, but also knows how to use them.

[A] Objectives of Discovery

Attorneys in a lawsuit do not use the discovery devices simply to be using them. Discovery is part of the adversary process. Ultimately, the attorney's goal is to win the case. The aims of discovery contribute to this ultimate goal. However, the smooth functioning of the discovery system depends on attorneys obeying the rules even when judicial oversight is absent, and on attorneys exercising good faith in both making discovery requests and in objecting to discovery.

The primary purpose of discovery is to find out about the event or transaction that is at the heart of the lawsuit. If, during a deposition, an attorney finds out that the opposing party admits to having driven five miles per hour in excess of the speed limit, the attorney has moved, however slightly, toward winning the suit. But note that the strategy is not limited to the discovery of helpful information. If the opposing party contends that the attorney's client ran a red light, the attorney will also try to discover this claimed fact. Having discovered it, the attorney can consider how to explain, qualify, limit, or destroy the contention. It may also help in arriving at a reasonable settlement agreement. Thus, the attorney seeks to discover unfavorable as well as favorable information. The discovery devices are chiefly a method of finding out as much as possible about the lawsuit.

A second function of discovery is to "freeze" the testimony of harmful witnesses. Does the opposing party claim that the plaintiff was traveling at five miles per hour in excess of the speed limit? In that event, the opponent will have difficulty if he or she testifies at trial that the plaintiff was going "at least 80," and will have even more difficulty in maintaining the position that he or she did not see the plaintiff's vehicle until the accident. The deposition does not prevent such a change in testimony, but it can be used to impeach the credibility of the witness if the witness testifies contrary to it. Consequently, skillful litigators are adept at getting witnesses to give definite, specific, and detailed answers during depositions. Their purpose is to "freeze" the testimony, as far as they are able.

A third purpose of discovery is to put useful evidence in a form admissible at trial. Suppose, for example, that the plaintiff's treating doctor has written plaintiff's attorney a letter summarizing the injuries that are the subject of the suit. The doctor's schedule makes it impossible for the doctor to be available for trial, and a subpoena would be unwise because it would be offensive, and make the doctor a hostile witness. Yet the letter itself is not admissible in evidence (it would be excluded as hearsay at a trial), and therefore the doctor's information must be put in a different form. The plaintiff may wish to take the doctor's deposition — not to discover information this time, and not to freeze the doctor's testimony — but simply because the deposition, unlike the letter, will be admissible at trial.

Sometimes discovery is put to a fourth, and ethically improper, use: to harass, annoy, or vex an opposing party. In the right kind of case, most skillful litigators could draft interrogatories within an hour that could cost thousands of dollars to answer. Similarly, skillful attorneys in an adversary system might be tempted to expose trade secrets of an opponent or to make numerous objections to discovery requests in order to increase the opponent's costs and to hide discoverable information. You cannot understand the function of the rules unless you understand that discovery has the potential for harassment and understand how to deal with your opponents' misuse of the process.

[B] The Scope and Limits of Discovery

Discovery extends to matters that are "relevant to the subject matter of the pending action." TEX. R. CIV. P. 192.3(a). The concept of "relevance" for discovery purposes is broad. For example, discovery is not limited to the issues set forth in the pleadings because it extends to the entire subject matter of the controversy that has given rise to the litigation. Moreover, Civil Procedure Rule 192.3 provides, "It is not a ground for objection that the information sought will be inadmissible at the trial if the information sought appears reasonably calculated to lead to the discovery of admissible evidence." TEX. R. CIV. P. 192.3. For instance, hearsay or opinion matters are usually inadmissible at trial — but they can sometimes be discovered. In a deposition, a lawyer might ask: "What's your opinion as to how the accident happened?" or, "What have you heard other people say about the accident?" The examiner can then inquire into the factual observations underlying the opinion or the names of the other people who said something about the accident. In other words, discovery is a kind of investigatory device, and the rules allow a freer hand than the rules of evidence would at trial.

Nevertheless, there are limits. The information may be so slim or remote that its likelihood of turning up admissible evidence is not "reasonable." In such a case, a court might conclude that the information is not "relevant" in the discovery sense. By the same token, when the burden imposed on the party who is the holder of the information sought to be discovered is heavy, the courts may be inclined to view the relevance question with more strictness. Other limits on the extent of discovery are imposed by Civil Procedure Rule 192. The rule exempts from discovery: (1) an attorney's work product; (2) the identity, mental impressions, and opinions of a consulting expert; and (3) any matter protected from disclosure by privilege. *See* Tex. R. Civ. P. 192. These matters are exempt from discovery, not because the information would be irrelevant to the subject matter involved in the pending action, but on policy grounds. In addition to these exemptions, the trial judge has discretion in the interest of justice to make any order necessary to protect "the movant from undue burden, unnecessary expense, harassment, annoyance, or invasion of personal, constitutional, or property rights." Tex. R. Civ. P. 192.6(b).

[C] The Ultimate Policies Underlying the Discovery Rules

Aside from the strategies engaged in by trial lawyers, there are certain overarching societal purposes that the discovery rules are designed to serve. Broad discovery, it is often said, makes the adversary process a better instrument for arriving at the truth. It decreases "Perry Mason" tactics and it discourages trial by ambush. It provides each party with greater knowledge about the case, and thus it arguably leads to fairer trials and, probably, to a higher proportion of disputes settled without trial or to settlements that more closely approximate the merits of the case.

The limits of discovery are, of course, aimed in part at preventing harassment and undue expense. They are also designed to buttress the adversary nature of the system, in that they limit the extent to which a party may get a "free ride" on investigation done by an opponent. Certain privileges are designed to ensure privacy and protection of desirable interpersonal relationships and to serve other purposes.

The "broad-versus-narrow-discovery" controversy has a long history and is still ongoing. The Texas rules may not be the best possible resolution of this controversy; they are simply one possible resolution.

Effective January 1, 1999, the Texas Supreme Court substantially revised the rules governing pretrial discovery. Among other goals, these rules were designed to impose limits on the volume of discovery in an attempt to provide adequate access to information without unnecessarily driving up the costs and delays associated with the discovery practice. As is often true with procedural issues, then, the Texas discovery rules will involve tension between the desire to aid just results and the desire to enhance speed and efficiency.

[D] Limits Created by the "Discovery Levels"

Read Tex. R. Civ. P. 190 and accompanying Comments.

Another way in which the Texas rules try to decrease the expense of discovery is through a set of rules putting limits on the number of times various discovery devices can be used. Every case must be governed by a discovery control plan. In an effort to tailor the amount of discovery to the complexity of the case, there are three levels of discovery plans contained in Civil Procedure Rule 190. Level 1 applies to small cases, Level 2 applies to the majority of cases and is the "default" level, and Level 3 may apply to complex cases (although any case may be governed by a Level 3 plan). Every case must be in some tier at all times. Tex. R. Civ. P. 190.2.

[1] Level 1 Plans

Level 1 applies to two kinds of cases:

1. Any suit in which all plaintiffs affirmatively plead that they seek only monetary relief aggregating $50,000 or less, excluding costs, prejudgment interest and attorneys' fees; and
2. Any suit for divorce not involving children in which a party pleads that the value of the marital estate is more than zero but not more than $50,000.

Because Level 1 is designed for relatively small cases in which only monetary damages are sought, the amount of discovery that can be taken in a Level 1 case is very limited. Each party may have no more than six hours in total to examine and cross-examine all witnesses in oral depositions. The parties may agree to expand this limit to up to 10 total hours, but cannot agree to more than 10 hours without a court order. In addition, any party may serve on any other party no more than 25 interrogatories, excluding interrogatories asking a party only to identify or authenticate specific documents. Other discovery devices are not limited in Level 1, and a party may take full advantage of requests for disclosure, requests for production and inspection, requests for admissions, requests for entry on land, depositions on written questions, and any other discovery device. The Comments provide, however, that depositions on written questions may not be used to circumvent the limits on interrogatories.

All discovery must be conducted during the "discovery period." The discovery period begins when the suit is filed and continues until 30 days before the date set for trial. For purposes of determining the discovery period, "trial" does not include a hearing on a motion for summary judgment. The discovery devices that permit 30 days for a response (such as requests for disclosure, requests for production of documents, and interrogatories) must be served at least 60 days before the date the case is set for trial so that the responses may be served during the discovery period. *See* Tex. R. Civ. P. 194.1, 196.1, 197.1, 198.1.

In addition to providing a scheme for discovery, Level 1 amends the pleading rules to provide that, without leave of court, a party cannot file an amended or supplemental pleading that would remove the case from Level 1 within 45 days before the date the case is set for trial. Leave may be granted only if good cause for filing the pleading outweighs the prejudice to an opposing party. This is significantly different from the general pleading practice under which a party is entitled to amend pleadings without leave of court up until seven days before trial.

A plaintiff's failure to state in the initial pleading that the case should be in Level 1, as provided in Rule 190.1, does not alone make the case subject to Level 2 because the discovery level is determined by Rule 190.2. A plaintiff's failure to plead as required by Rule 190.1 is subject to special exception.

Litigants must be cautious when proceeding in Level 1. This is because "the relief awarded [in Level 1] cannot exceed the limitations of Level 1," i.e.; $50,000 excluding costs, prejudgment interest, and attorney's fees. Tex. R. Civ. P. 190, Comment 2. In other words, if the plaintiff pleads for damages of $49,000 and discovery is conducted under Level 1, the plaintiff cannot recover more than $50,000 in damages even if the jury awards more. And the plaintiff cannot amend his or her pleadings after the verdict to conform the pleadings with the verdict. Comment 2 to Rule 190 specifically provides that "the rule in *Greenhalgh v. Service Lloyds Ins. Co.*, 787 S.W.2d 938 (Tex. 1990) [allowing post-verdict pleading amendments] does not apply." It may be, therefore, that Level 1 will be limited to breach of contract and other similar suits where the damages are subject to an exact calculation, and to small family law cases. Litigants in personal injury and similar suits in which the jury could award damages in excess of $50,000 should probably avoid using Level 1.

[2] Level 2 Plans

Level 2 applies to all cases that do not proceed under Level 1 or Level 3. It will govern discovery in most cases. Because this is the catch-all tier, the amount of discovery permitted and the period during which the parties may conduct discovery is designed to accommodate most litigation. In Level 2, each side is entitled to no more than 50 hours in oral depositions to examine and cross-examine: (1) parties on the opposing side; (2) experts designated by those parties; and (3) persons who are subject to those parties' control. If one side designates more than two experts, the opposing side may take an additional six hours of total deposition time for each additional expert designated. Other witnesses are not subject to the 50-hour limit. As is the case in Level 1, any party may serve on any other party no more than 25 written interrogatories, excluding interrogatories asking a party only to identify and authenticate specific documents. Other discovery devices are not limited in Level 2.

For purposes of the overall deposition time limit, the term "side" means all litigants with generally common interests in the litigation. Comment 6 to Rule 190 explains that the "concept of 'side' . . . borrows from Rule 233, which governs the allocation of peremptory strikes, and from Fed. R. Civ. P. 30(a)(2). In most cases there are only two sides . . . plaintiffs and defendants. In complex cases, however, there may be more than two sides, such as when defendants have sued third parties not named by plaintiffs, or when defendants have sued each other." Thus, a defendant who has brought a third-party action or stated a cross-claim against another defendant is entitled to 50 hours in depositions as to the plaintiff on matters in controversy between the defendant and the plaintiff, and another 50 hours in deposition as to the third-party defendant or cross-defendant on matters in controversy between the defendant and the third-party or cross-defendant. It is not clear that a plaintiff will ever be entitled to more than 50 hours in depositions, except that the court may modify the deposition hours on motion by any party, and must do so when a side or party would be given an "unfair advantage" if the deposition limits were not modified.

Discovery in Level 2 must be conducted during the "discovery period." The discovery period for all cases begins when suit is filed. For cases brought under the Family Code, the discovery period continues until 30 days before the date set for trial. In all other cases, the discovery period ends on the *earlier* of 30 days before the date set for trial, nine months after the date of the first oral deposition, or nine months after the due date of the first response to written discovery. As with Level 1, discovery devices that allow a 30-day response time must be served at least 30 days before the end of the discovery period. The "discovery period" may come to a close considerably before trial in some metropolitan areas.

[3] Level 3 Plans

Level 3 provides for a court-ordered discovery plan. The trial court must, on a party's motion, and may, on its own initiative, order that discovery be conducted in accordance with a discovery control plan tailored to the circumstances of the specific suit. Although Level 3 may be used to provide for additional discovery in complex cases, there is no requirement that the court-ordered plan provide for discovery in excess of Level 1 or Level 2. In fact, Level 3 can be used to limit discovery if a party or the court believes that the discovery allowed by the current level is excessive. Also, a Level 3 plan may simply adopt Level 1 or Level 2 restrictions.

The parties may agree to a Level 3 discovery control plan and may submit an agreed order to the trial court for its consideration. But nothing in the rule requires the court to approve the plan offered by the parties. It is, however, required to render *some* form of Level 3 order if any party moves for one, and to act on the request "as promptly as reasonably possible." Any discovery control plan instituted under Level 3 must include a trial date or date for conference to determine a trial setting, a discovery period during which all discovery must be conducted or all discovery requests must be sent, appropriate limits on the amount of discovery, and deadlines for joining additional parties, amending or supplementing pleadings, and designating expert witnesses. The plan may also address any issue concerning discovery or the matters listed in Civil Procedure Rule 166. In some cases, separate Level 3 plans may be appropriate for different phases of a case.

NOTES AND QUESTIONS

(1) *Choice of Level.* If you represent a plaintiff, what will you consider in initially choosing a level? To what extent can you control the initial level? To what extent is it beyond your control? If you represent a defendant, what will you consider relevant in determining an optimal level? How much control can you exert over the level that applies?

(2) *Moving From Level to Level.* How can cases move among levels? How can a case worth less than $50,000 become a Level 3 case? When would you want it to?

(3) *Modification Orders.* Under what circumstances may a court modify a discovery control plan? When must it do so? May a judge who dislikes the new rules simply "opt out" by form order?

(4) *Modification Agreements.* To what extent can parties agree to modify the limits of the various plan levels? Are there matters to which the parties cannot agree? Note that in order to be enforceable, any agreement of the parties must comply with the documentation requirements of Civil Procedure Rule 11.

§ 9.02 DISCOVERY AND ATTORNEY OBLIGATIONS

[A] Discovery and Ethical Rules

W. Dorsaneo, Texas Litigation Guide § 90.01[4]*

Due to the lack of candor during discovery . . . and judicial dissatisfaction with litigants' unduly adversarial approach to discovery, there was a fairly active use of sanctions for discovery-related misconduct following the 1984 amendments to the Civil Procedure Rules . . . . The Texas Supreme Court, through its rule-making authority and power to regulate the practice of law, has addressed attorneys' obligations during discovery in several ways. Civil Procedure Rule 191.2 mandates a certain degree of cooperation among attorneys engaged in discovery, providing:

> Parties and their attorneys are expected to cooperate in discovery and to make any agreements reasonably necessary for the efficient disposition of the case. All discovery motions or requests for hearings relating to discovery must contain a certificate by the party filing the motion or request that a reasonable effort has been made to resolve the dispute without the necessity of court intervention and the effort failed.

In addition, Civil Procedure Rule 191.3 requires that all discovery requests, notices, responses, and objections be signed. The attorney's signature certifies, among other things, that the discovery request, notice, response, or objection is "not unreasonable or unduly burdensome or expensive, given the needs of the case, the discovery already had in the case, the amount in controversy, and the importance of the issues at stake in the litigation" [T.R.C.P. 191.3(c)(4); *see also* T.R.C.P. 192.4].

Further, the Texas Disciplinary Rules of Professional Conduct, which define proper conduct for attorneys, provide guidelines for proper conduct during discovery. For instance, Rule 3.04 prohibits the habitual violation of established rules of procedure or evidence [State Bar Rules, Art. 10 § 9, Rule 3.04(c)]. A comment to this rule notes that it applies to habitual abuses of procedural rules, including those related to the discovery process [State Bar Rules, Art. 10 § 9, Rule 3.04, Comment ¶ 3]. The Disciplinary Rules also impose duties on lawyers to protect a client's confidential information [*see* State Bar Rules, Art. 10 § 9, Rule 1.05].

[B] Beyond the Ethical Minimum: Lawyer Professionalism and Discovery

Our litigation system is often referred to as "adversarial," meaning that the parties take the main role in compiling and presenting information to a neutral, passive judge. The discovery process, however, is meant to function as an island of cooperation in a sea of adversariness. Not surprisingly, this attitude shift is often difficult for lawyers. Unfortunately, extreme implementation of the adversary mind set sometimes leads lawyers to act like nine-year-olds. In 1989, the Texas Supreme Court adopted the "Texas Lawyer's Creed," which sets out standards of professionalism. The Creed was a direct result of perceived inappropriate conduct by lawyers in pretrial discovery. The Creed is merely aspirational, and can only be enforced through (1) the courts' inherent powers and (2) the rules already in existence. Nevertheless it sets a standard of conduct that should be followed by attorneys in the conduct of discovery.

THE TEXAS LAWYER'S CREED
A Mandate for Professionalism

I am a lawyer; I am entrusted by the People of Texas to preserve and improve our legal system. I am licensed by the Supreme Court of Texas. I must therefore abide by the Texas Disciplinary Rules of Professional Conduct, but I know that Professionalism requires more than merely avoiding the violation of laws and rules. I am committed to this Creed for no other reason than it is right.

I. OUR LEGAL SYSTEM

A lawyer owes to the administration of justice personal dignity, integrity, and independence. A lawyer should always adhere to the highest principles of professionalism.

1. I am passionately proud of my profession. Therefore, "My word is my bond." . . .

5. I will always be conscious of my duty to the judicial system.

II. LAWYER TO CLIENT

A lawyer owes to a client allegiance, learning, skill, and industry. A lawyer shall employ all appropriate means to protect and advance the client's legitimate rights, claims, and objectives. A lawyer shall not be deterred by any real or imagined fear of judicial disfavor or public unpopularity, nor be influenced by mere self-interest.

1. I will advise my client of the contents of this Creed when undertaking representation.
2. I will endeavor to achieve my client's lawful objectives in legal transactions and in litigation as quickly and economically as possible.
3. I will be loyal and committed to my client's lawful objectives, but I will not permit that loyalty and commitment to interfere with my duty to provide objective and independent advice.
4. I will advise my client that civility and courtesy are expected and are not a sign of weakness.
5. I will advise my client of proper and expected behavior.
6. I will treat adverse parties and witnesses with fairness and due consideration. A client has no right to demand that I abuse anyone or indulge in any offensive conduct.
7. I will advise my client that we will not pursue conduct which is intended primarily to harass or drain the financial resources of the opposing party.
8. I will advise my client that we will not pursue tactics which are intended primarily for delay.
9. I will advise my client that we will not pursue any course of action which is without merit.
10. I will advise my client that I reserve the right to determine whether to grant accommodations to opposing counsel in all matters that do not adversely affect my client's lawful objectives. A client has no right to instruct me to refuse reasonable requests made by other counsel.
11. I will advise my client regarding the availability of mediation, arbitration, and other alternative methods of resolving and settling disputes.

III. LAWYER TO LAWYER

A lawyer owes to opposing counsel, in the conduct of legal transactions and the pursuit of litigation, courtesy, candor, cooperation, and scrupulous observance of all agreements and mutual understandings. Ill feelings between clients shall not influence a lawyer's conduct, attitude, or demeanor toward opposing counsel. A lawyer shall not engage in unprofessional conduct in retaliation against other unprofessional conduct.

1. I will be courteous, civil, and prompt in oral and written communications.
2. I will not quarrel over matters of form or style, but I will concentrate on matters of substance.
3. I will identify for other counsel or parties all changes I have made in documents submitted for review.
4. I will attempt to prepare documents which correctly reflect the agreement of the parties. I will not include provisions which have not been agreed

upon or omit provisions which are necessary to reflect the agreement of the parties.

5. I will notify opposing counsel, and, if appropriate, the Court or other persons, as soon as practicable, when hearings, depositions, meetings, conferences or closings are cancelled.

6. I will agree to reasonable requests for extensions of time and for waiver of procedural formalities, provided legitimate objectives of my client will not be adversely affected.

7. I will not serve motions or pleadings in any manner that unfairly limits another party's opportunity to respond.

8. I will attempt to resolve by agreement my objections to matters contained in pleadings and discovery requests and responses.

9. I can disagree without being disagreeable. I recognize that effective representation does not require antagonistic or obnoxious behavior. I will neither encourage nor knowingly permit my client or anyone under my control to do anything which would be unethical or improper if done by me.

10. I will not, without good cause, attribute bad motives or unethical conduct to opposing counsel nor bring the profession into disrepute by unfounded accusations of impropriety. I will avoid disparaging personal remarks or acrimony towards opposing counsel, parties and witnesses. I will not be influenced by any ill feeling between clients. I will abstain from any allusion to personal peculiarities or idiosyncrasies of opposing counsel.

11. I will not take advantage, by causing any default or dismissal to be rendered, when I know the identity of an opposing counsel, without first inquiring about that counsel's intention to proceed.

12. I will promptly submit orders to the Court. I will deliver copies to opposing counsel before or contemporaneously with submission to the court. I will promptly approve the form of orders which accurately reflect the substance of the rulings of the Court.

13. I will not attempt to gain an unfair advantage by sending the Court or its staff correspondence or copies of correspondence.

14. I will not arbitrarily schedule a deposition, Court appearance, or hearing until a good faith effort has been made to schedule it by agreement.

15. I will readily stipulate to undisputed facts in order to avoid needless costs or inconvenience for any party.

16. I will refrain from excessive and abusive discovery.

17. I will comply with all reasonable discovery requests. I will not resist discovery requests which are not objectionable. I will not make objections nor give instructions to a witness for the purpose of delaying or obstructing the discovery process. I will encourage witnesses to respond to all deposition questions which are reasonably understandable. I will

neither encourage nor permit my witness to quibble about words where their meaning is reasonably clear.

18. I will not seek Court intervention to obtain discovery which is clearly improper and not discoverable.

19. I will not seek sanctions or disqualification unless it is necessary for protection of my client's lawful objectives or is fully justified by the circumstances.

IV. LAWYER AND JUDGE

Lawyers and judges owe each other respect, diligence, candor, punctuality, and protection against unjust and improper criticism and attack. Lawyers and judges are equally responsible to protect the dignity and independence of the Court and the profession.

1. I will always recognize that the position of judge is the symbol of both the judicial system and administration of justice. I will refrain from conduct that degrades this symbol.

2. I will conduct myself in court in a professional manner and demonstrate my respect for the Court and the law.

3. I will treat counsel, opposing parties, witnesses, the Court, and members of the Court staff with courtesy and civility and will not manifest by words or conduct bias or prejudice based on race, color, national origin, religion, disability, age, sex, or sexual orientation.

4. I will be punctual.

5. I will not engage in any conduct which offends the dignity and decorum of proceedings.

6. I will not knowingly misrepresent, mischaracterize, misquote or miscite facts or authorities to gain an advantage.

7. I will respect the rulings of the Court.

8. I will give the issues in controversy deliberate, impartial and studied analysis and consideration.

9. I will be considerate of the time constraints and pressures imposed upon the Court, Court staff and counsel in efforts to administer justice and resolve disputes.

NOTES AND QUESTIONS

(1) *Similar Federal Standards in Texas.* Similar concerns about bad behavior in discovery led the federal district judges in the Northern District of Texas to adopt standards for litigators. *Dondi Props. Corp. v. Commerce Sav. & Loan Ass'n*, 121 F.R.D. 284, 287 (N.D. Tex. 1988).

The order notes that attorneys "who persist in viewing themselves solely as combatants, or who perceive that they are retained to win at all costs without regard to fundamental principles of justice, will find that their conduct does not square with the practices we expect of them. Malfeasant counsel can expect instead that their conduct will prompt an appropriate response from the court, including . . . a warm friendly discussion on the record, a hard-nosed reprimand in open court, compulsory legal education, monetary sanctions, or other measures appropriate to the circumstances." *Id.* Courts in the Northern District have ordered sanctions for violations of these standards, including a $25,000 sanction against an attorney whose repeated verbal abuse included characterizing other attorneys, including an Assistant United States Attorney, as "stooges," a "weak pussyfooting 'deadhead' " who "had been 'dead' mentally for ten years," "various incompetents," "inept," "clunks," and the like. *In re First City Bancorporation of Texas*, 270 B.R. 807 (N.D. Tex. 2001). *See also Lelsz v. Kavanagh*, 137 F.R.D. 646 (N.D. Tex. 1991) (ordering attorney removed from case).

(2) *Professional Behavior.* Are you horrified that it was necessary to make rules like, "I will abstain from any allusion to personal peculiarities or idiosyncrasies of opposing counsel," and "I will treat counsel, opposing parties, witnesses, the Court, and members of the Court staff with courtesy and civility and will not manifest by words or conduct bias or prejudice based on race, color, national origin, religion, disability, age, sex, or sexual orientation"? Do you think that aspirational codes will be sufficient to deter this kind of misconduct?

(3) *Drawing the Line.* Professional ethics rules require attorneys to zealously represent the interests of their clients. Yet both the discovery rules and these codes demand that lawyers stop short of abusing the rules for their clients' advantage. As you read the materials in this chapter and Chapter 10, try to discern where the lawyers involved were drawing the line between legitimate discovery behavior and abusive requests or objections.

§ 9.03 THE SCOPE OF DISCOVERY: "RELEVANT" INFORMATION, "NOT PRIVILEGED"

[A] The Discovery "Relevance" Standard; Information "Reasonably Calculated" to Lead to Admissible Evidence

Read Tex. R. Civ. P. 192 and accompanying Comments.

Any analysis of discovery relevance must grow from an understanding of trial relevance. Evidence is relevant for trial purposes if it has "any tendency to make the existence of any fact that is of consequence to the determination of the action more probable or less probable than it would be without the evidence." Tex. R. Evid. 401. This broad standard of relevance must be kept in mind when considering whether information is relevant for purposes of discovery.

Rule 192.3 of the Texas Rules of Civil Procedure defines discovery relevance. Litigants may discover "any matter that . . . is relevant to the subject matter of the pending action, whether it relates to the claim or defense of the party seeking discovery or the claim or defense of any other party." Discovery relevance is broader than trial relevance because trial relevance determinations are based on the issues caused by the parties' pleadings. Moreover, information is not exempt from discovery because it will be inadmissible at trial. Rather, non-privileged information is discoverable if it "appears reasonably calculated to lead to the discovery of admissible evidence."

Section [A] examines how Texas courts determine whether requested material is relevant in the discovery sense. It will also examine certain areas that have generated special consideration in the relevance area. Subsection [B] will focus on the privileges recognized by Texas that limit discovery of relevant information. Subsection [C] will look at ways in which privileges can be waived.

[1] The Relevance Test Generally

K MART CORP. v. SANDERSON
937 S.W.2d 429 (Tex. 1996)

Per Curiam

. . . .

Stacey Thompson sued K Mart, a Michigan corporation, to recover actual and punitive damages not exceeding $30 million for injuries she received when she was abducted from a K Mart store parking lot in Lufkin and raped. Thompson also sued Weingarten Realty Management Company, a Texas corporation. Thompson alleged that these defendants (to whom we refer collectively as K Mart) and others were negligent and grossly negligent in failing to make adequate provisions for her safety . . . .

Thompson . . . served the three following interrogatories on K Mart:

10. Please describe by date and offense type any criminal conduct that occurred in the K Mart store or parking lot in the shopping center in question during the last seven (7) years.

15. Please list all criminal activities at all property owned, leased or managed by both K Mart Corporation or Weingarten Realty Management Company in the State of Texas during the last seven years that relates in any way to the alleged failure to provide adequate security allegedly resulting in any sort of physical injury to any person.

16. Have there been other incidents at K Mart Stores owned by Weingarten Realty Management Company nationwide in which a person was abducted from the premises and raped? If so, please state the date and location of each such incident that occurred within the last ten years.

Thompson also requested production . . . of all documents related to interrogatory 15. K Mart objected to the interrogatories and request as being overly broad and burdensome. The district court overruled K Mart's objections.

In *Texaco, Inc. v. Sanderson*, plaintiffs claimed damages for exposure to toxic chemicals. At plaintiffs' request, the district court ordered production of all documents written by Texaco's safety director concerning "safety, toxicology, and industrial hygiene, epidemiology, fire protection and training." 898 S.W.2d at 814. We granted mandamus relief, holding the request to be so excessively broad as to be "well outside the bounds of proper discovery." *Id.* at 815. The same may be said of Thompson's interrogatory 10. It would require K Mart to give the date of every shoplifting offense for the past seven years, though shoplifting on K Mart's premises has no apparent connection to Thompson's injury or cause of action.

In *Dillard Department Stores, Inc. v. Hall*, plaintiff sued Dillard for false arrest. At plaintiff's request, the trial court ordered Dillard to produce "every claims file and incident report prepared from 1985 through 1990 in every lawsuit or claim that involved allegations of false arrest, civil rights violations, and excessive use of force" for each of its 227 stores located in twenty states. 909 S.W.2d at 491–492. We granted mandamus relief, holding that the requested discovery was "overly broad as a matter of law." *Id.* at 492. Thompson's interrogatories 15 and 16 are likewise overly broad. The likelihood that criminal conduct on the parking lot of a K Mart store or other property owned by Weingarten in El Paso or Amarillo as long ago as 1989, or outside Texas as long ago as 1986, will have even a minuscule bearing on this case is far too small to justify discovery.

A reference in *Loftin* [*v. Martin*, 776 S.W.2d 145 (Tex. 1989)], suggests that interrogatories and depositions may properly be used for a fishing expedition when a request for production of documents cannot . . . . We reject the notion that any discovery device can be used to "fish." The burden of answering interrogatories like those in this case is hardly less to K Mart than producing documents containing the same information. The district court's order . . . exceeded the bounds of discovery permitted by the rules of procedure and was a clear abuse of discretion . . . .

IN RE C.S.X. CORP.
124 S.W.3d 149 (Tex. 2003)

PER CURIAM

Relators filed a petition for writ of mandamus to challenge the trial court's discovery ruling in the underlying negligence litigation. Relators complain that certain interrogatories are overbroad and irrelevant. We agree and conditionally grant mandamus relief.

Real party in interest, Donald Ward, worked periodically as a mechanic, tankerman, and seaman from 1958 to 1998. He worked at National Marine Services for part of 1958 and from 1972 to 1977. In 1998, American Commercial Barge Line acquired National Marine Services. Ward sued American Commercial Barge Line and its subsidiaries — American Commercial Lines, CSX Corporation, National Marine, Inc., and Vectura Group — in 2002. Ward claims that exposure to benzene and other carcinogenic chemicals throughout his career caused him to contract refractory anemia/myelodysplastic syndrome.

During discovery, Ward served interrogatories on all defendants that included the following:

(16) For the time period 1973 to present, please identify and give last known address and telephone number for all persons in the safety and/or industrial hygiene department who had any responsibility for the safety and/or industrial hygiene and/or assessment of the hazards of benzene for this Defendant.

(17) For the time period 1970 to present, please identify and give last known address and telephone number for all safety department workers employed by Defendant.

(18) For the time period 1970 to present, please identify and give last known address and telephone number for all corporate physicians employed by this Defendant.

Relators CSX Corporation, National Marine, Inc., and Vectura Group objected to these interrogatories on the grounds that they are "overbroad, harassing, and seek information that is not relevant and will not lead to the discovery of admissible evidence." Ward then moved the trial court to compel Relators to answer the interrogatories. After a hearing, the trial court modified Interrogatory 17 to exclude purely clerical safety workers. Subject to this modification, the trial court ordered Relators to answer Interrogatories 16, 17, and 18. The court of appeals denied Relators' petition for mandamus relief.

Relators complain that these interrogatories are overbroad for two reasons. First, Relators never employed Ward. They are subsidiaries of American Commercial Barge Line, which also never directly employed Ward, but acquired Ward's former employer, National Marine Services. Therefore, the identity of relators' managerial safety and hygiene personnel and corporate physicians is not relevant to Ward's claims. Second, the requested time period extends twenty-five years beyond the time Ward was employed by American Commercial Barge Line's predecessor in interest, National Marine Services.

Mandamus relief is appropriate only if a trial court abuses its discretion, and there is no adequate appellate remedy. *Walker v. Packer*, 827 S.W.2d 833, 839 (Tex. 1992); *CSR Ltd. v. Link*, 925 S.W.2d 591, 596 (Tex. 1996). The burden of establishing an abuse of discretion and an inadequate appellate remedy is on the party resisting discovery, and this burden is a heavy one. *Canadian Helicopters Ltd. v. Wittig*, 876 S.W.2d 304, 305 (Tex. 1994). A clear abuse of discretion occurs when an action is "so arbitrary and unreasonable as to amount to a clear and prejudicial error of law." *CSR*, 925 S.W.2d at 596.

Generally, the scope of discovery is within the trial court's discretion. *Dillard Dep't Stores, Inc. v. Hall*, 909 S.W.2d 491, 492 (Tex. 1995). However, the trial court must make an effort to impose reasonable discovery limits. *In re American Optical*, 988 S.W.2d 711, 713 (Tex. 1998). The trial court abuses its discretion by ordering discovery that exceeds that permitted by the rules of procedure. *Texaco, Inc. v. Sanderson*, 898 S.W.2d 813, 815 (Tex. 1995).

Our procedural rules define the general scope of discovery as any unprivileged information that is relevant to the subject of the action, even if it would be inadmissible at trial, as long as the information sought is "reasonably calculated to lead to the discovery of admissible evidence." TEX. R. CIV. P. 192.3(a); *see also Eli Lilly & Co. v. Marshall*, 850 S.W.2d 155, 160 (Tex. 1993). Also, a party may obtain discovery of the name, address, and telephone number of persons who have or may have knowledge of any discoverable matter. TEX. R. CIV. P. 192.3(c). Although the scope of discovery is broad, requests must show a reasonable expectation of obtaining information that will aid the dispute's resolution. *American Optical*, 988 S.W.2d at 713. Thus, discovery requests must be "reasonably tailored" to include only relevant matters. *Id.*

Ward argues that Relators have not shown the trial court's order was so arbitrary and unreasonable as to constitute a clear abuse of discretion. *See Johnson v. Fourth Court of Appeals*, 700 S.W.2d 916, 917 (Tex. 1985). According to Ward, the information these interrogatories seek is within the scope of permissible discovery. Ward contends that relevant evidence is not limited to what National Marine Services's employees knew. Ward also argues that employees from Relator's subsidiaries may have information about barge industry custom that is relevant to a negligence claim. *See Boatland of Houston, Inc. v. Bailey*, 609 S.W.2d 743, 748 (Tex. 1980) (in negligence cases, evidence of industry custom at the time of manufacture is admissible to compare the defendant's conduct with industry custom).

We do not find Ward's argument persuasive. Discovery orders requiring document production from an unreasonably long time period or from distant and unrelated locales are impermissibly overbroad. *See American Optical*, 988 S.W.2d at 713; *Dillard*, 909 S.W.2d at 492; *Texaco*, 898 S.W.2d at 815. For example, in *American Optical*, an asbestos-litigation case, the trial court ordered the defendant to turn over every document ever produced relating to asbestos. *American Optical*, 988 S.W.2d at 713. We held the order was overbroad, because "ordering a defendant to produce virtually all documents regarding its products for a fifty-year period is an abuse of . . . discretion." *Id.* In *Dillard*, we held the trial court's order was overly broad, because it required Dillard to produce every incident report filed between 1985 and 1990 in all 227 Dillard stores nationwide. *Dillard*, 909 S.W.2d at 492. The Court explained that "requests for document production may not be used simply to explore." *Dillard*, 909 S.W.2d at 492 (citing *Loftin v. Martin*, 776 S.W.2d 145, 148 (Tex. 1989)). Finally, in *Texaco*, the plaintiffs claimed injurious workplace exposure to benzene and requested all safety and toxicology documents written by the corporate safety director, including those documents regarding other employees' exposure and plants where the plaintiffs never worked. *Texaco*, 898 S.W.2d at 814. The request also extended into a time period during which the plaintiffs did not work with the company. *Id.* This Court held the request was overbroad, because it was "not merely an impermissible fishing expedition; it [was] an effort to dredge the lake in hopes of finding a fish." *Id.* at 815.

A central consideration in determining overbreadth is whether the request could have been more narrowly tailored to avoid including tenuous information and still obtain the necessary, pertinent information. *See American Optical*, 988 S.W.2d at 713. A request to identify all safety employees who worked for Relators over a 30-

year period, even though Ward never worked for Relators or for their parent company for that length of time, qualifies as the kind of "fishing expedition" this Court has repeatedly struck down. *See, e.g.*, *Texaco*, 898 S.W.2d at 815. Accordingly, the discovery request at issue here is overly broad.

Ward additionally argues that the cases involving requests for document production are distinguishable, because such requests are characteristically more burdensome than providing a list of names and addresses. But, as Relators note, this Court has not identified different standards for evaluating various discovery methods. *See K Mart Corp. v. Sanderson*, 937 S.W.2d 429, 431 (Tex. 1996) (relying on cases involving document production requests to reverse a trial court's order compelling K-Mart to answer interrogatories). In *K Mart*, we "reject[ed] the notion that any discovery device can be used to 'fish.' " *Id.*

Finally, Ward claims he needs the identities of thirty years' worth of safety and industrial hygiene employees, as well as the names of corporate physicians, because they might have information on barge industry custom from the applicable time period. *See Bailey*, 609 S.W.2d at 748. Although Ward may discover evidence of industry custom at the time Ward was employed, the interrogatories at issue here impermissibly request information for twenty-five years beyond the applicable time period. *See Texaco*, 898 S.W.2d at 815 (rejecting plaintiff's argument that an overbroad discovery request lacking appropriate limitations as to time, place, or subject matter was relevant to establish defendant's "corporate strategy to ignore safety laws").

If a reviewing court concludes that a trial court's discovery order is overbroad, the trial court has abused its discretion, and the order must be vacated if there is no adequate remedy on appeal. *See American Optical*, 988 S.W.2d at 713; *see also Walker*, 827 S.W.2d at 840. Here, no adequate appellate remedy exists. We have said that where a discovery order compels production of "patently irrelevant or duplicative documents," as this order undoubtedly does, there is no adequate remedy by appeal because the order "imposes a burden on the producing party far out of proportion to any benefit that may obtain to the requesting party." *Walker*, 827 S.W.2d at 843; *see also General Motors Corp. v. Lawrence*, 651 S.W.2d 732, 734 (Tex. 1983). Ward's request could easily be narrowly tailored to obtain information pertinent to the time period during which Ward was employed by National Marine Services.

As written, interrogatories 16, 17, and 18 are overbroad. The interrogatories lack reasonable limitations as to time and subject matter. *See Texaco*, 898 S.W.2d at 815. Accordingly, without hearing oral argument, we conditionally grant mandamus relief and direct the trial court to vacate its order compelling CSX Corporation, National Marine, Inc. and Vectura Group to answer interrogatories 16, 17, and 18. Tex. R. App. P. 59.1. The writ will issue only if the trial court fails to act promptly in accord with this opinion.

IN RE ALLSTATE COUNTY MUTUAL INSURANCE CO.
227 S.W.3d 667 (Tex. 2007)

PER CURIAM

Discovery is a tool to make the trial process more focused, not a weapon to make it more expensive. Thus, trial courts "must make an effort to impose reasonable discovery limits." *In re CSX Corp.*, 124 S.W.3d 149, 152 (Tex. 2003) (per curiam) (quotations omitted). In this suit alleging an insurer reneged on a $13,500 settlement offer, the trial court refused to impose any limit on the plaintiffs' 213 discovery requests. As much of this discovery has no relation or relevance to the scope of the parties' dispute, we grant mandamus relief. *See In re Graco Children's Prods., Inc.*, 210 S.W.3d 598, 600 (Tex. 2006) (per curiam) ("[An] order that compels overly broad discovery well outside the bounds of proper discovery is an abuse of discretion for which mandamus is the proper remedy.") (quotations omitted).

Following a car accident, two plaintiffs (Jorge Karim and Teresita Manllo) brought a single suit against the other driver (Sang Cho), her carrier (Allstate County Mutual Insurance Company), and the latter's adjuster (David Gonzalez). The plaintiffs sent the insurer and its adjuster a total of 89 requests for production, 59 interrogatories, and 65 requests for admission, including requests for:

* transcripts of all testimony ever given by any Allstate agent on the topic of insurance;
* every court order finding Allstate wrongfully adjusted the value of a damaged vehicle;
* personnel files of every Allstate employee a Texas court has determined wrongfully assessed the value of a damaged vehicle; and
* legal instruments documenting Allstate's status as a corporation and its net worth.

Allstate and Gonzalez objected to the discovery. . . . The trial court . . . rejected the objections, and ordered the defendants to respond to all the requests. The Thirteenth Court of Appeals denied mandamus relief without explanation.

The plaintiffs make no effort to justify their hundreds of requests. Nor can they, given what this Court has said repeatedly in similar cases. In *In re CSX Corp.*, we held that "discovery orders requiring document production from an unreasonably long time period or from distant and unrelated locales are impermissibly overbroad." In *K Mart Corp. v. Sanderson*, we held overbroad a request for every criminal act that occurred on the defendant's premises for the last seven years. In *Dillard Department Stores, Inc. v. Hall*, we held overbroad a request for every false imprisonment case in the last five years throughout twenty states. And in *Texaco, Inc. v. Sanderson*, we held overbroad a request for all documents ever written by the defendant's safety director about safety. Like all those requests, the plaintiffs' requests here are overbroad as to time, location, and scope, and could easily have been more narrowly tailored to the dispute at hand. *See CSX*, 124

S.W.3d at 153 ("A central consideration in determining overbreadth is whether the request could have been more narrowly tailored to avoid including tenuous information . . . ").

More important, the plaintiffs' requests and the trial court's order reflect a misunderstanding about relevance. American jurisprudence goes to some length to avoid the spurious inference that defendants are either guilty or liable if they have been found guilty or liable of anything before. *See, e.g.*, Tex. R. Evid. 404 (barring proof of other crimes, wrongs, or acts "in order to show action in conformity therewith"). While such evidence might be discoverable in some cases (e.g., to prove motive or intent), it is hard to see why reneging on some other settlement offer makes it more or less probable that the insurer reneged on this one. Tex. R. Civ. P. 192.3; Tex. R. Evid. 401.

The plaintiffs argue the defendants failed to preserve their objections by failing to provide details regarding why the discovery here was burdensome. But Allstate objected to the plaintiffs' requests as irrelevant (and thus by necessity overbroad). Overbroad requests for irrelevant information are improper whether they are burdensome or not, so the defendants were not required to detail what they might encompass. *See In re CSX Corp.*, 124 S.W.3d at 153; *In re Union Pac. Res. Co.*, 22 S.W.3d 338, 341 (Tex. 1999).

The plaintiffs also argue the defendants waived their objections by obscuring them amidst numerous unfounded objections. *See* Tex. R. Civ. P. 193.2(e). Allstate objected to every one of the plaintiffs' requests on the ground that it owed no discovery to a party with no standing to bring a direct action against it. Even if this objection was unfounded (an issue we do not reach), it did not obscure Allstate's objections regarding relevance and overbreadth.

"Reasonable" discovery necessarily requires some sense of proportion. With today's technology, it is the work of a moment to reissue every discovery request one has ever sent to an insurer before. But by definition such a request is not "reasonably tailored." *See In re Graco Children's Prods.*, 210 S.W.3d 598, 601 (Tex. 2006) (per curiam); *CSX*, 124 S.W.3d at 152. Given the limited scope of the plaintiffs' claims and the amount at issue, the trial court erred by compelling discovery of everything the plaintiffs could imagine asking in any unfair insurance practice case.

Accordingly, without hearing oral argument, we conditionally grant the writ of mandamus and direct the trial court to vacate its discovery order and reconsider the scope of permissible discovery in light of this opinion.

NOTES AND QUESTIONS

(1) *Breadth of Discovery Relevance Test.* How broad is the discovery relevance test in Texas? In determining whether a particular matter is discoverable, would it be proper for a trial judge to deny discovery of marginally relevant information because the burden on the defendant is heavy? Is that what happened in the cases above, or did the Supreme Court of Texas conclude that the information sought had no logical relevance whatever?

(2) *Similar Products.* In products liability cases, the "relevance" of information about different but similar products is often an issue in discovery disputes. The results often turn on factual determinations regarding the degree of similarity. In some cases the courts have ordered discovery of different models and years of products with similar design. *But see In re Merck & Co.*, 150 S.W.3d 747 (Tex. App. — San Antonio 2004, orig. proceeding) (*Vioxx* case, in which the court denied discovery regarding another Merck product called Arcoxia, which had a different chemical structure, a different patent, and which was never sold in the United States).

(3) *Burdensomeness Issues.* The burden of retrieving information depends in part on the manner in which the information is stored. Should the court take into consideration that a party's own decisions about document storage have contributed to the burden of production? *See ISK Biotech Corp. v. Lindsay*, 933 S.W.2d 565 (Tex. App. — Houston [1st Dist.] 1996, no writ).

(4) *The Proportionality Rule.* The 1999 discovery rule revisions added a new proportionality rule, modeled on the federal discovery provisions, that authorizes the court to balance benefit and burden. Tex. R. Civ. P. 192.4. Texas courts may have already been doing such balancing in its relevance decisions; this rule explicitly condones the process.

(5) *Objecting to Relevance.* Can a discovery request be irrelevant on its face? Consider *In re Union Pacific Resources Co.*, 22 S.W.3d 338 (Tex. 1999) (per curiam). In that case, the Texas Supreme Court held that evidence may not always be necessary to support an objection based on relevance. The Court found that the *non*-relevance of the amount of settlement in a separate lawsuit could be determined from the face of the pleadings and existing discovery.

[2] Special Relevance Issues

[a] Witnesses, Witness Statements, People with Knowledge, and Contentions

Read Tex. R. Civ. P. 192.

Within the generic definition of relevance, there are areas in which there are recurring disputes about the scope of discovery. Some of these areas are directly addressed in the rules regarding relevance and disclosure requests. First, Civil Procedure Rule 192.3 provides that a party may obtain discovery of the name, address, and telephone number of any person having knowledge of relevant facts. In addition, a party is entitled to obtain a brief statement of each identified person's connection with the case. This provision is intended to help parties decide how to allocate limited deposition hours by identifying persons whose connection with the case is more substantial than others. The phrase "connection with the case" does not contemplate a narrative statement of the facts a person knows, but should consist of a few words describing the person's identity as it is relevant to the lawsuit. Examples include: "treating physician," "eyewitness," "director," or "plaintiff's mother and eyewitness to the accident." Tex. R. Civ. P. 192, Comment 3. The rules also make clear that an expert is a "person with knowledge of relevant facts" if that expert obtained his or her knowledge of the case first hand, not in preparation for trial or in anticipation of litigation.

Second, the rules allow a party to discover "the statement of any person with knowledge of relevant facts," otherwise called a witness statement. Before the amendments, witness statements were not directly discoverable because they were protected as a species of work product. A "witness statement" is either a "written statement signed or otherwise adopted or approved in writing by the person making it" or a "stenographic, mechanical, electrical, or other type of recording of a witness's oral statement, or any substantially verbatim transcription of such a recording." Tex. R. Civ. P. 192.3(h). Witness statements must be relevant to be discoverable, and privileges such as the attorney-client privilege may be asserted where applicable. However, no work product objections may be asserted to a request for disclosure of witness statements.

Third, a party may obtain discovery of the name, address, and telephone number of any person who is expected to be called to testify at trial. This specific provision of rule 192.3(d) overrules previous cases that protected such information as work product. Even rebuttal witnesses must be disclosed if the party reasonably anticipates their use.

Fourth, a party may obtain discovery of any other party's legal contentions and the factual bases for those contentions. Tex. R. Civ. P. 192.3(j). The information may be discovered through either a request for disclosure under rule 194 or through an interrogatory under rule 197. Note, however, that a party is not required to marshal all of its available proof or all the proof that party intends to offer at trial. Rather, Comment 5 to Civil Procedure Rule 192 notes that the rules do not "require more than a basic statement of those contentions."

[b] Insurance Policies and Settlement Agreements

Read Tex. R. Civ. P. 192.3 (f) and (g).

IN RE DANA CORP.
138 S.W.3d 298 (Tex. 2004)

Per Curiam

The relator, Dana Corporation, filed a petition for writ of mandamus to challenge the trial court's discovery ruling in the underlying asbestos litigation. The real parties in this proceeding, who consist of approximately 1,260 plaintiffs in the underlying case, sought production of Dana's insurance policies since 1930 and also sought to learn the amount of insurance remaining under those policies. The trial court ordered Dana, the defendant in the underlying proceeding, to produce "exact duplicates of any and all commercial general liability insurance policies . . . from 1930 to the present." The trial court also ordered Dana "to produce a knowledgeable witness for deposition to testify regarding such insurance policies." Dana argues that the trial court abused its discretion in two ways: first, by ordering the production of insurance policies that were not shown to be applicable to the underlying litigation; and second, by compelling Dana to produce insurance information beyond the applicable insurance agreements' existence and contents. Because we agree that the trial court's order was overly broad and required the production of insurance policies not shown to be applicable to the underlying litigation, we conditionally grant a writ of mandamus to direct the trial court to modify its order to require production only of those policies "under which [Dana] may be liable to satisfy part or all of a judgment." TEX. R. CIV. P. 192.3(f) . . . .

Dana agrees that the Texas Rules of Civil Procedure mandate disclosure of any insurance agreement that may satisfy part or all of a judgment rendered in the action. TEX. R. CIV. P. 192.3(f) ("[A] party may obtain discovery of the existence and contents of any indemnity or insurance agreement under which any person may be liable to satisfy part or all of a judgment rendered in the action or to indemnify or reimburse for payments made to satisfy the judgment."). Dana argues, however, that in mass toxic-tort litigation, a defendant should not have to mass-produce insurance policies until each of the plaintiffs first establishes (1) which of the company's products is allegedly at fault, and (2) for what periods of time the exposure allegedly occurred. In this case, forty-nine plaintiffs have provided affidavits identifying both the particular products to which they were allegedly exposed and the time periods in which this exposure allegedly occurred.

We do not agree that a special rule should apply in toxic-tort cases. Even in an ordinary case, however, our rules require that a threshold showing of applicability must be made before a party can be ordered to produce multiple decades of insurance policies; only those insurance policies "under which any person may be liable to satisfy part or all of a judgment" are subject to discovery. TEX. R. CIV. P. 192.3(f); *see also In re CSX*, 124 S.W.3d at 152. Thus, while we do not agree that the plaintiffs' request for production should be delayed until each plaintiff has necessarily identified a particular product and a particular period of exposure, we do agree that the insurance policies need not be produced until they are shown to be applicable to a potential judgment.

In this case, the plaintiffs have identified thirteen products at issue in the suit; of these products, each is identified by at least one of the forty-nine affiants as a product to which he or she was exposed. Furthermore, Dana admits that its policies "are general products liability claims policies and provide coverage for all products-based claims asserted against Dana." Consequently, we conclude that these affidavits sufficiently identify the products at issue, and that the trial court did not abuse its discretion by ordering production of Dana's general insurance policies before receiving affidavits of exposure from each plaintiff.

While we conclude that the affidavits sufficiently identified the relevant products, we also conclude that they do not adequately support the time period covered by the trial court's order. The trial court ordered the production of all policies from 1930 to the present. The plaintiffs argue that "with a thousand plaintiffs," the range of potential insurance would "probably" go back to "1930 or '35." The affidavits of exposure, however, reveal that the earliest reported exposure occurred in 1945. Consequently, we hold that plaintiffs have not established the potential applicability of policies covering exposure from 1930 to 1944. Accordingly, the discovery request at issue here is overly broad. *See CSX Corp.*, 124 S.W.3d at

153 (granting mandamus relief when the court's order "impermissibly requested information for twenty-five years beyond the applicable time period").

We must also determine whether the trial court abused its discretion by ordering Dana to produce a witness for deposition to testify regarding its insurance policies. The plaintiffs argue that Texas Rule of Civil Procedure 192.3(f) permits them to conduct discovery regarding insurance coverage, and that such discovery is "needed . . . to find out what policies were there, whether they were exhausted, whether they were close to . . . being exhausted." They note that while the rule itself provides for disclosure of only the "existence and contents" of the policies, the Twelfth Court of Appeals has held that depositions relating to the erosion of insurance coverage fit within the scope of permissible discovery. *In re Senior Living Props., L.L.C.*, 63 S.W.3d 594, 597–98 (Tex. App. — Tyler 2002, orig. proceeding), *mand. abated pursuant to bankruptcy*, 46 Tex. Sup. J. 600 (Tex. 2003). That court noted that Rule 192.3(f) does not preclude "further discovery on insurance issues should the facts of a particular case warrant such discovery," and held that such a deposition could reveal "the extent to which coverage has been eroded or compromised and the number of claims competing for the coverage." *Id.* at 597–98.

We agree that Rule 192.3(f) does not foreclose discovery of insurance information beyond that identified in the rule; however, we also conclude that the plain language of Rule 192.3(f), by itself, does not provide a sufficient basis to order discovery beyond the production of the "existence and contents" of the policies. We therefore disagree wit h the *Senior Living* opinion to the extent it relies on Rule 192.3(f) to suggest that the insurance-erosion information plaintiffs seek in this case is necessarily discoverable. Instead, we hold that a party may discover information beyond an insurance agreement's existence and contents only if the information is otherwise discoverable under our scope-of discovery rule. *See* Tex. R. Civ. P. 192.3(a) ("In general, a party may obtain discovery regarding any matter that is not privileged and is relevant to the subject matter of the pending action, whether it relates to the claim or defense of the party seeking discovery or the claim or defense of any other party.").

Though Rule 192.3(f)'s plain language does not preclude discovery of additional insurance information, the rule's language itself specifically requires only the production of "the existence and contents" of the policies. This specificity prevents our construing the rule, by itself, to require additional discovery about insurance coverage. *See Missouri Pac. R.R. Co. v. Cross*, 501 S.W.2d 868, 872 (Tex. 1973) (holding that the rules of civil procedure "have the same force and effect as statutes" and should be construed in a similar manner). We recognize that to achieve our procedural rules' objective "to obtain a just, fair, equitable and impartial adjudication of the rights of litigants under established principles of substantive law," we typically apply a liberal construction. Tex. R. Civ. P. 1; *see also Cross*, 501 S.W.2d at 872. But relying on Rule 192.3(f) alone to allow discovery of additional insurance information would require us to construe Rule 192.3(f) in a manner contrary to its literal meaning. Consequently, we conclude that, to determine whether information beyond that identified in Rule 192.3(f) is discoverable in a particular case, courts must ascertain if the information is discoverable under Rule 192.3(a)'s general scope-of-discovery test.

[The court then looked at federal cases and concluded that its approach is consistent with treatment of insurance information under the analogous Federal Rules of Civil Procedure.]

We therefore reject the plaintiffs' argument that Rule 192.3(f)'s purpose — to facilitate settlement negotiations — supports broadly reading the rule to allow the discovery requested here.[2] We hold that such discovery is warranted only if the information sought meets the general scope-of-discovery relevance standard under Rule 192.3(a) — *i.e.*, that it "relates to the claim or defense of the party seeking discovery." TEX. R. CIV. P. 192.3(a).

In this case, however, the trial court's order does not specifically address policy erosion; rather, it merely orders Dana "to produce a knowledgeable witness for deposition to testify regarding such insurance policies." Because the witness may be needed to prove up the contents of the policies, and because the plaintiffs are entitled to ask questions relevant to the subject matter of the litigation, we conclude that the trial court did not abuse its discretion in ordering Dana to produce a witness for deposition. At that deposition, Dana is of course free to object to any question regarding policy erosion that does not meet the relevancy standard announced in this opinion.

Accordingly, without hearing oral argument, we conditionally grant mandamus relief. We direct the trial court to modify its order to limit the production of policies to those covering exposure from 1945 to the present. The writ will issue only if the trial court does not modify its order.

NOTES AND QUESTIONS

(1) *Liability Insurance.* Information concerning the existence of liability insurance and indemnity agreements (including the policy limits of the policies) is discoverable, but its discoverability does not make it admissible. TEX. R. CIV. P. 192.3(f).

(2) *Relevance of Policy Limits.* Why should policy limits be "relevant" in the discovery sense? Most liability insurance policies impose a duty of defense on the insurer, so the defendant's lawyer is likely furnished by the insurer. A plaintiff would want to see the policy because Texas law, like the law of other states, imposes excess liability on an insurer if it fails to settle within policy limits under certain circumstances. *G. A. Stowers Furniture Co. v. American Indemnity Co.*, 15 S.W.2d 544 (Tex. Comm'n App. 1929, opinion adopted). Plaintiff's settlement leverage may be increased if plaintiff can create the potential for *Stowers*-based liability. Why else might a plaintiff want the policy?

---

[2] We note that this Court has previously held that determining settlement and litigation strategy is good cause for a party to discover information about the other side's insurance policy limits. *Carroll Cable Co. v. Miller*, 501 S.W.2d 299 (Tex. 1973) (per curiam). But, in *Carroll Cable*, our decision rested on the fact that the actual policies were not available for discovery; this Court held that "it is sufficient showing of good cause that an insurance agreement is not available to the moving party." *Id.* Because the applicable insurance policies are available in this case, we conclude that *Carroll Cable* is distinguishable and does not control the outcome of this case.

(3) *Settlement Agreements.*Civil Procedure Rule 192.3(g) also makes the existence and contents of any settlement agreement discoverable. Tex. R. Civ. P. 192.3(g). As in the case of insurance agreements, its discoverability does not make it admissible. Despite its broad language, this rule has been held to be limited by the general discovery relevance standard. *Palo Duro Pipeline Co., Inc. v. Cochran*, 785 S.W.2d 455, 457 (Tex. App. — Houston [14th Dist.] 1990, orig. proceeding). The court rejected the argument that discovery of settlement agreements is limited to "Mary Carter" agreements (agreements in which a settling defendant retains a financial stake in the plaintiff's recovery against the remaining tortfeasors, and remains a party at trial) or agreements arising out of the same lawsuit. *Id.*

The Corpus Christi Court of Appeals considered whether a settlement agreement in a related case was relevant. It held that when a settlement agreement might disclose whether plaintiff has already been compensated for his injuries under the "one satisfaction" rule, it is relevant for purposes of discovery. The court further noted that this is true even if the discovering party has not yet pleaded its entitlement to a settlement credit. *In re Frank A. Smith Sales, Inc.*, 32 S.W.3d 871 (Tex. App. — Corpus Christi 2000, orig. proceeding).

[c] Net Worth

(1) *Relevance of Defendant's Net Worth.* The Texas Supreme Court held in *Lunsford v. Morris*, 746 S.W.2d 471 (Tex. 1988), that information about defendant's net worth is relevant to the issue of punitive damages and is therefore discoverable. Net worth information is not discoverable under *Lunsford* when no proper claim to punitive damages has been made. For example, in *Al Parker Buick Co. v. Touchy*, 788 S.W.2d 129 (Tex. App. — Houston [1st Dist.] 1990, orig. proceeding), plaintiff's petition did not allege a cause of action entitling him to punitive damages against the individual defendant's employer. Because the petition was legally insufficient to support an award of punitive damages, the net worth discovery sought should have been denied.

The United States Supreme Court has recently downplayed the importance of net worth information in considering punitive damages. In *State Farm Mut. Auto. Ins. Co. v. Campbell*, 538 U.S. 408, 427 (2003), the majority noted, "The wealth of a defendant cannot justify an otherwise unconstitutional punitive damages award." The more important factor is the degree of reprehensibility of defendant's conduct. However, the Court did not hold that net worth was irrelevant to the amount of punitive damages.

(2) *Limits on Net Worth Discovery.* Since *Lunsford*, the Texas Supreme Court has considered what type of financial information can be discovered. In *Sears, Roebuck & Co. v. Ramirez*, 824 S.W.2d 558, 559 (Tex. 1992), the Court held that the trial court had abused its discretion in ordering production of Sears' tax returns. Sears had produced annual reports reflecting its net worth and introduced an affidavit claiming that the annual reports were accurate. Further, Sears proffered evidence that it would take an employee two or three weeks to duplicate the requested five years' worth of tax returns. Under these facts, the Supreme Court held that Sears should not have been ordered to produce the returns.

(3) *Bifurcation of Trials: Punitive Damage Claims.* In a case seeking punitive

damages, the trial court should bifurcate the trial when presented with a timely motion. *See* C.P.R.C. § 41.009; *Transportation Ins. Co. v. Moriel*, 879 S.W.2d 10, 29–30 (Tex. 1994). This does not mean, however, that discovery of net worth should be postponed until after the first part of the trial. The First Court of Appeals has rejected a trial court's attempt to delay the discovery of net worth data until after a finding of liability in a bifurcated trial. *Miller v. O'Neill*, 775 S.W.2d 56 (Tex. App. — Houston [1st Dist.] 1989, orig. proceeding) (also rejecting an overbreadth claim and allowing discovery of income tax returns, financial statements, or net worth statements of defendant and any partnership and professional corporations in which he had an interest for a 10-year period).

[d] Information Sought Solely for Impeachment

Special problems arise when information is sought in order to impeach a person who is expected to testify at trial, especially when the person is not a party. The Texas Supreme Court has held that voluminous financial records of a nonparty medical witness were not "discoverable prior to trial in instances where the potential witness is not a party to the lawsuit and whose credibility has not been put in issue and where the records do not relate directly to the subject matter of the pending suit and are sought to be discovered for the sole purpose of impeachment of such witness by showing his bias and prejudice." *Russell v. Young*, 452 S.W.2d 434, 435 (Tex. 1970).

Four years later, the court distinguished *Russell* and held that appraisal reports prepared by the government's appraisal witnesses relating to land that was not the subject of the condemnation proceedings in which discovery was sought were discoverable. First, "*Russell* presented an attempt at wholesale discovery of the private records of a non-party . . . . In this case the reports sought are not of a private or personal nature." Second, "[t]he condemning authority has designated the appraisers whose reports are sought as witnesses upon whom they will rely at trial." Third, "the reports are not sought solely, or even primarily, to show bias or prejudice. They are sought as evidence of possible inconsistencies in the appraiser's valuation of other [comparable] properties." *Ex parte Shepperd*, 513 S.W.2d 813, 816 (Tex. 1974).

The Texas Supreme Court returned to the issue of impeachment discovery in *Walker v. Packer*, 827 S.W.2d 833 (Tex. 1992). The Court characterized *Russell* as involving "wholesale discovery of financial records of a potential medical witness who was not a party to the lawsuit." In *Walker*, however, the court noted that the plaintiff had presented the trial court with evidence of specific circumstances that indicated bias. Under these circumstances, the Court indicated that some discovery should be allowed:

> [T]he Walkers are not engaged in global discovery of the type disapproved in *Russell*; rather, they narrowly seek information regarding the potential bias suggested by the witness' own deposition testimony and that of his professional colleague. Our rules of civil procedure, and the federal rules upon which they are based, mandate a flexible approach to discovery . . . . Evidence of bias of a witness is relevant and admissible.

Earlier cases suggesting a complete bar to discovery of impeachment materials are therefore incorrect. In addition, the rules about expert discovery make information relevant to the bias of an expert witness clearly discoverable. *See* Tex. R. Civ. P. 192.3(e)(5). There are nevertheless recent cases refusing to allow impeachment discovery, relying on *Russell*. For example, *In re Makris*, 217 S.W.3d 521 (Tex. App. — San Antonio 2006, orig. proceeding), rejected the plaintiffs' request to discover information regarding the income that defendant's medical expert has earned testifying for defendants. Plaintiffs argued that the doctor made a substantial portion of his income from such testimony, and that it would therefore show bias, but the court disagreed:

> We have previously held that Rule 192.3(e)(5) was not intended to overrule the Supreme Court's holding in *Russell v. Young* that personal financial records of a nonparty witness are not discoverable for the sole purpose of showing bias . . . . [*S*]ee *alsoIn re Doctors' Hosp. of Laredo*, 2 S.W.3d 504, 507 (Tex. App. — San Antonio 1999, orig. proceeding) (holding that new rule 192.3(e)(5) did not overrule *Russell*, and does not permit discovery of personal financial records and appointment books of a nonparty witness to show bias).

See also In re Wharton, 226 S.W.3d 452 (Tex. App. — Waco June 15, 2005, orig. proceeding) (holding that Rule 192.3(e)(5) did not overrule *Russell*).

PRACTICE EXERCISE #21

Opal Allen was shopping at her neighborhood Alpha Omega Grocery Store in Dallas. She shopped there regularly and knew the store well. On this particular occasion, while shopping in the produce department, Allen slipped and fell, breaking her wrist. She was taken by ambulance to the local hospital, where she was treated and released. Her injury was severe enough that she was unable to return to her job as a secretary for about a month, and she received no pay check during that period. She has now returned to work, but suffers from chronic pain in the injured wrist, and has permanently lost some mobility as well. She may have to look for other work, as it is very hard for her to type all day.

Consider the following discovery issues that might arise in a slip and fall case brought by Allen against Alpha Omega.

1. You represent Allen. What discovery level will best meet your needs for information and your litigation budget? What steps will you take to try to establish the case at that level?

2. You represent Alpha Omega. What discovery limits would you find appropriate for this lawsuit? If you are unhappy with the initial level, as determined by the pleadings, what steps can you take to change the discovery control plan to one that better suits your client's needs?

3. Allen sent Alpha Omega a request for production of documents seeking all documents concerning injuries to customers or employees in all Alpha Omega stores in Texas for the last five years. If you represented Alpha Omega, what objection would you make to this request? If you represented Allen, how could you redraft the request to get the most essential information while reducing the probable success of objections?

4. Alpha Omega has asked to take the deposition of Allen's adult daughter, Pearl. Pearl was not present when Opal fell, but Alpha Omega believes that one of Opal's friends (who was in the store when Opal fell) may have said something to Pearl that is inconsistent with the friend's current account of the accident. Is Pearl's information relevant in the discovery sense? Is it discoverable?

5. Alpha Omega has brought a third-party action against FruitSafe, the company that manufactured the mats used on the floor in the produce section of this Alpha Omega store. If this case is proceeding under a Level 2 discovery control plan, how many hours of deposition time does each party get, and on what issues?

6. Allen would like to know what witnesses Alpha Omega intends to call to testify at trial. Is this discoverable?

[B] Privileges and Other Limits on Discovery

Even information that is relevant may not be discoverable. There are a number of privileges that, for various policy reasons, protect certain kinds of communications from discovery. These privileges variously come from the procedure rules themselves, from the rules of evidence, from other statutes, and from the U.S. Constitution. This subsection considers the parameters of those privileges, especially those related to trial preparation materials, experts, and the attorney-client privilege.

[1] The Discovery Rule Privileges

Read Tex. R. Civ. P. 192, 194, 195 and accompanying Comments.

Some of the information that is relevant to a lawsuit is actually generated by the parties and their representatives in the course of preparing for that lawsuit. In the federal courts, communications generated in anticipation of litigation are referred to as "work product," and their discoverability is limited. The United States Supreme Court first considered the issue in *Hickman v. Taylor*, 329 U.S. 495 (1947). The case concerned the sinking of a tugboat, in which five people were killed. The tug owners hired an attorney, and the attorney took oral and written statements from witnesses. The controversy before the Supreme Court grew out of a discovery request by a plaintiff's attorney for "copies of all such statements if in writing and, if oral, . . . the exact provisions of such oral statements or reports." The Court rejected an argument that the information requested was covered by the attorney-client privilege, but did create a discovery exemption for the "work product of the lawyer." Note the Texas Supreme Court's discussion of *Hickman* in the *National Tank* opinion below.

Until the 1999 amendments, the Texas Rules of Civil Procedure divided trial preparation materials into four subdivisions, each of which was specifically included in former Civil Procedure Rule 166b(3): (1) work product of an attorney; (2) witness statements; (3) party communications; and (4) information concerning consulting experts who neither testify nor have their work reviewed by testifying experts. The 1999 amendments, however, made a wholesale revision of the trial preparation privileges. Civil Procedure Rule 192 merges the previously undefined "work product" exemption and the party communications exemption into a single two-part "work product" privilege. Significantly, the former separate privileged status for witness statements prepared or taken in anticipation of litigation has been expressly eliminated and witness statements are not work product, even if made in anticipation of litigation. The protection of pure consulting expert information remains, now codified at Civil Procedure Rule 192.3(e).

This section of the chapter examines the work product and expert witness exemptions contained in the discovery rules.

[a] Work Product

Read Tex. R. Civ. P. *192.3(e)(3), (6), 192.5, 194.5.*

Civil Procedure Rule 192.5 provides that work product is not discoverable. "Work product" is defined as material prepared or mental impressions developed in anticipation of litigation or for trial by or for a party or a party's representative. Work product also encompasses a communication made in anticipation of litigation or for trial between a party and a party's representative or among a party's representatives. A party's representatives include the party's attorneys, consultants, sureties, indemnitors, insurers, employees, and agents. Tex. R. Civ. P. 192.5(a).

The primary purpose of the work product rule is to shelter the mental processes, conclusions, and legal theories of the attorney, providing a privileged area in which the lawyer can analyze and prepare the case. *Owens-Corning Fiberglas Corp. v. Caldwell*, 818 S.W.2d 749, 750 (Tex. 1991). The work product exemption protects two related but different concepts. First, the privilege protects the attorney's thought process, which includes strategy decisions and issue formation, and the notes or writing evidencing those mental processes. Second, the privilege protects the mechanical compilation of information in preparation for trial; it protects the documents produced in anticipation of litigation and not the underlying information itself. With respect to an attorney's thought processes, the work product exemption is absolute, subject only to the narrow exceptions listed in Texas Rule of Evidence 503(d). *See* Tex. R. Civ. P. 192.5(c)(5). But with respect to compiled information, the exemption is not absolute. This distinction is carried forward into Civil Procedure Rule 192.5, which draws a distinction between "core work product" and all other work product.

"Core work product" is defined as the work product of an attorney or attorney's representative that contains the attorney's or the attorney's representative's mental impressions, opinions, conclusions, or legal theories. Core work product is not discoverable. Other materials that fall within the definition of work product but do not qualify as core work product (known as "ordinary work product") are discoverable *only* on a showing of substantial need and undue hardship.

Civil Procedure Rule 192.5(c) provides that some types of information are discoverable even if made in anticipation of litigation or for trial:

- Information discoverable under Rule 192.3 concerning expert witnesses, trial witnesses, witness statements, and contentions.
- Trial exhibits if ordered disclosed by the trial court.

- The name, address, and telephone number of any potential party or any person with knowledge of relevant facts.
- Any photograph or electronic image of underlying facts or a photograph or electronic image of any sort that a party intends to offer into evidence.
- Any work product created under circumstances within an exception to the attorney-client privilege under the evidence rules.

In other words, items on the above list are *not* protected as work product.

In order for material to be work product, it must have been produced "in anticipation of litigation." It has always been difficult to apply this phrase to particular communications. When does a party "anticipate" litigation? And when were documents produced for that purpose, as opposed to produced in the ordinary course of business? The following case was decided under the pre-1999 rules. As you read it, consider how it will help you to interpret the meaning of the new rules.

NATIONAL TANK CO. v. BROTHERTON
851 S.W.2d 193 (Tex. 1993)

PHILLIPS, C.J.

. . . .

An explosion occurred on August 23, 1990, at a Wichita Falls manufacturing facility operated by the National Tank Company (NATCO), Relator in this proceeding. The explosion critically injured Rex Willson, a NATCO employee, and two other persons employed by independent contractors. Willson later died from his injuries. Allen Pease, NATCO's General Counsel and Secretary, learned of the explosion the day it occurred and dispatched Henry Townsend, NATCO's safety and risk control coordinator, to investigate. Although not a lawyer, Townsend was employed in NATCO's legal department under Pease's supervision. Pease also immediately notified David Sneed, a brokerage supervisor with American International Adjustment Company (AIAC), a representative of NATCO's liability insurers. Pease explained to Sneed the serious nature of the accident, and recommended that AIAC initiate its own investigation, which it did.

Willson's wife, individually and on behalf of her children and the estate, sued NATCO and several other defendants on January 15, 1991. Shortly thereafter, she requested that NATCO produce any reports prepared in connection with the accident investigation. NATCO objected, asserting the attorney-client, work-product, witness-statement, and party-communication privileges. In an order signed July 25, 1991, the trial court overruled NATCO's objections as to documents prepared prior to October 25, 1990, the date NATCO learned that it had been sued by Frank Kroupa, one of the other persons injured in the explosion. The trial court thus ordered NATCO to produce the documents prepared prior to that date. These documents are 1) the transcripts of four interviews of NATCO employees conducted by Henry Townsend shortly after the accident, 2) the transcripts of nine interviews of NATCO employees conducted by Phil Precht, an AIAC employee, shortly after the accident, and 3) three accident reports prepared by Precht and sent to Pease. The trial court, however, stayed the effect of this order to allow NATCO to seek mandamus relief . . . .

III

We next consider whether the documents are privileged under Texas Rule of Civil Procedure 166b(3)(a) as "the work product of an attorney." "Work product" has generally been defined as "specific documents, reports, communications, memoranda, mental impressions, conclusions, opinions, or legal theories, prepared and assembled in actual anticipation of litigation or for trial." *Wiley v. Williams*, 769 S.W.2d at 717; *Brown & Root U.S.A., Inc. v. Moore*, 731 S.W.2d 137, 140 (Tex. App. — Houston [14th Dist.] 1987, orig. proceeding); *Evans v. State Farm Mut. Auto. Ins. Co.*, 685 S.W.2d 765, 767 (Tex. App. — Houston [1st Dist.] 1985, writ ref'd n.r.e.). NATCO argues, however, that the privilege is not limited to documents prepared in anticipation of litigation. This Court has not previously addressed this issue. To do so, it is necessary to examine some of the history of the work product privilege.

The work product doctrine was created by the United States Supreme Court in *Hickman v. Taylor*, 329 U.S. 495 (1947). In *Hickman*, five crew members drowned when the tugboat J.M. Stark sank in the Delaware River. The boat owner's attorney investigated the accident, obtaining signed statements from some of the witnesses and making memoranda of his conversations with the others. The estate of one of the deceased crew members subsequently sued the boat owner and sought by interrogatories to obtain copies of the witness statements and the attorney's memoranda prepared during the investigation. The defendant objected on the grounds that the requests called "for privileged matter obtained in preparation for litigation" and was "an attempt to obtain indirectly counsel's private files." *Id.* at 499.

The district court ordered production, but the United States Court of Appeals for the Third Circuit reversed and the Supreme Court affirmed the judgment of the appellate court. The Supreme Court could find no existing privilege that applied, but it created a new common law privilege for what it termed the "work product of the lawyer," consisting of interviews, memoranda, briefs and other materials prepared "with an eye toward litigation." *Hickman*, 329 U.S. at 511. The Court justified the privilege as follows:

> Proper preparation of a client's case demands that [the attorney] assemble information, sift what he considers to be the relevant from the irrelevant facts, prepare his legal theories and plan his strategy without undue and needless interference. That is the historical and the necessary way in which lawyers act within the framework of our system of jurisprudence to promote justice and to protect their clients' interests.

Id. The Court indicated that the privilege could be overcome as to factual information otherwise unavailable to the opposing party, but not as to the attorney's "mental impressions." *Id.* at 512.

The *Hickman* work product doctrine was codified in Fed. R. Civ. P. 26(b)(3) in 1970. This rule maintains the distinction between ordinary work product, which is discoverable upon a showing of "substantial need" and "undue hardship," and an attorney's "mental impressions, conclusions, opinions, or legal theories," which are discoverable, if at all, only upon a much higher showing.

This latter category has come to be known as "opinion" or "core" work product. *See In re Murphy*, 560 F.2d 326, 329 n.1 (8th Cir. 1977); Jeff A. Anderson et al., *Special Project, The Work Product Doctrine*, 68 CORNELL L. REV. 760, 817–20 (1983). Federal Rule of Civil Procedure 26(b)(3) has been adopted verbatim by 34 states, and in substantial part by 10 others. *See* Elizabeth Thornburg, *Rethinking Work Product*, 77 VA. L. REV. 1515, 1520–21 (1991).

The structure of the Texas rule is somewhat different from the federal rule, however, as it simply protects the "work product of an attorney." "Work product" is not defined in the rule, and this Court has never specifically defined the term . . . . [T]he term "work product" as used in Rule 166b(3)(a) applies only to materials prepared in anticipation of litigation. It is not necessary to further consider the scope of the work product exemption in Texas, because if the disputed documents were prepared in anticipation of litigation, they are privileged under the witness statement and party communication privileges . . . .

IV

A

[In the context of the old witness statement and party communication privileges, the Court considers how to determine when a communication was made in anticipation of litigation.]

An investigation is conducted in anticipation of litigation if it meets the two-prong test of *Flores v. Fourth Court of Appeals*, 777 S.W.2d 38, 40–41 (Tex. 1989). The first prong of the *Flores* test is objective. The court is required to determine whether a reasonable person, based on the circumstances existing at the time of the investigation, would have anticipated litigation. We stated in *Flores* that "[c]onsideration should be given to outward manifestations which indicate litigation is *imminent*." *Id.* at 41 (emphasis added). Upon further consideration, however, we conclude that the "imminence" requirement impairs the policy goals of the witness statement and party communication privileges. Serving the function filled in many jurisdictions by the work product doctrine, these privileges seek to strike a balance between open discovery and the need to protect the adversary system. As the Supreme Court noted in *Hickman*, a party must be free to assemble information about the case free of undue interference from the other side:

> Were such materials open to opposing counsel on mere demand, much of what is now put down in writing would remain unwritten. An attorney's thoughts, heretofore inviolate, would not be his own. Inefficiency, unfairness and sharp practices would inevitably develop in the giving of legal advice and in the preparation of cases for trial. The effect on the legal profession would be demoralizing. And the interests of the clients and the cause of justice would be poorly served.

Hickman, 329 U.S. at 511. The investigative privileges promote the truthful resolution of disputes through the adversarial process by encouraging complete and thorough investigation of the facts by both sides . . . . At the same time, they do not unduly thwart discovery, as they are limited in scope and can be overcome by a showing of substantial need for the information and undue hardship in obtaining it from other sources.

Considering these policies, we conclude that the objective prong of *Flores* is satisfied whenever the circumstances surrounding the investigation would have indicated to a reasonable person that there was a substantial chance of litigation. The confidentiality necessary for the adversary process is not defeated because a party, reasonably anticipating future litigation, conducts an investigation prior to the time that litigation is "imminent." We accordingly modify *Flores* to the extent that it accords protection only to investigations conducted when litigation is imminent.

We agree with the dissenting justices' characterization of "substantial chance of litigation." This does not refer to any particular statistical probability that litigation will occur; rather, it simply means that litigation is "more than merely an abstract possibility or unwarranted fear." 851 S.W.2d at 216. The underlying inquiry is whether it was reasonable for the investigating party to anticipate litigation and prepare accordingly.

The real parties in interest argue, and some courts of appeals have held, that the objective prong of *Flores* may be satisfied only where the *plaintiff* engages in some action indicating an intent to sue. *See, e.g., Boring & Tunneling Co. v. Salazar*, 782 S.W.2d at 287. *Flores*, however, does not hold this. Rather, it requires the trial court to examine the *totality of the circumstances* to determine whether the investigation is conducted in anticipation of litigation. *Flores*, 777 S.W.2d at 41. Requiring that the plaintiff manifest an intent to sue would also be at odds with the policy goals of the witness statement and party communication privileges. These privileges are designed to promote the adversarial process by granting limited protection to investigations conducted in preparation for litigation. Common sense dictates that a party may reasonably anticipate suit being filed, and conduct an investigation to prepare for the expected litigation, before the plaintiff manifests an intent to sue. *See Wiley*, 769 S.W.2d at 717; *Smith v. Thornton*, 765 S.W.2d 473, 477 (Tex. App. — Houston [14th Dist.] 1988, no writ); *Lone Star Dodge, Inc. v. Marshall*, 736 S.W.2d 184, 189 (Tex. App. — Dallas 1987, orig. proceeding).

We held in *Stringer v. Eleventh Court of Appeals*, 720 S.W.2d 801 (Tex. 1986), that "[t]he mere fact that an accident has occurred is not sufficient to clothe all post-accident investigations . . . with a privilege." *Id.* at 802. We adhere to this holding, but we disapprove *Stringer* to the extent that it holds that the circumstances surrounding an accident can never by themselves be sufficient to trigger the privilege. If a reasonable person would conclude from the severity of the accident and the other circumstances surrounding it that there was a substantial chance that litigation would ensue, then the objective prong of *Flores* is satisfied.

The second prong of the *Flores* test is subjective. There, we held that the party invoking the privilege must have had "a good faith belief that litigation would ensue." 777 S.W.2d at 41. For the reasons previously discussed with respect to the objective prong, however, we conclude that the subjective prong is properly satisfied if the party invoking the privilege believes in good faith that there is a substantial chance that litigation will ensue. It does not further the policy goals of the privilege to require the investigating party to be absolutely convinced that litigation will occur. Also, although not expressly stated in *Flores*, we believe that the subjective prong plainly requires that the investigation actually be conducted for the purpose of preparing for litigation. An investigation is not conducted "in anticipation of litigation" if it is in fact prepared for some other purpose. As with the objective prong, the court must examine the totality of the circumstances to determine whether the subjective prong is satisfied . . . .

The fundamental problem that has plagued other courts is determining whether a "routine" investigation is conducted in anticipation of litigation. The Advisory Committee Notes to the 1970 federal rules amendments provide that "[m]aterials assembled in the ordinary course of business, or pursuant to public requirements unrelated to litigation, or for other nonlitigation purposes" are not protected. *Proposed Amendments to the Federal Rules of Civil Procedure Relating to Discovery*, 48 F.R.D. 485, 501 (1970). Accordingly, many courts have recognized a bright-line "ordinary course of business" exception . . . .

Other courts, however, have rejected a hard and fast ordinary course of business exception, recognizing that a prudent party may routinely prepare for litigation after a serious accident . . . .

We agree that there should be no bright-line ordinary course of business exception. It may very well be that a party routinely investigates serious accidents because such accidents routinely give rise to litigation. As with other investigations, an investigation performed in the ordinary course of business is conducted in anticipation of litigation if it passes both prongs of the *Flores* test. With regard to the subjective prong, the circumstances must indicate that the investigation was in fact conducted to prepare for potential litigation. The court therefore must consider the reasons that gave rise to the company's ordinary business practice. If a party routinely investigates accidents because of litigation and nonlitigation reasons, the court should determine the primary motivating purpose underlying the ordinary business practice.

In summary, an investigation is conducted in anticipation of litigation for purposes of Rule 166b(3) when a) a reasonable person would have concluded from the totality of the circumstances surrounding the investigation that there was a substantial chance that litigation would ensue; and b) the party resisting discovery believed in good faith that there was a substantial chance that litigation would ensue and conducted the investigation for the purpose of preparing for such litigation . . . .

[The concurring opinion of Justice Gonzalez is omitted.]

DOGGETT, J, concurring and dissenting.

While a widow plans a funeral, the corporation in whose facility her husband was killed conducts an investigation. While family and friends mourn, the corporation obtains witness statements and prepares reports concerning the circumstances surrounding the death. If this occurrence is ever considered by a judge and jury, they should be able to hear the plain, unvarnished truth — to learn what really happened when memories were fresh and unpolished by counsel.

But now the majority puts a stop to all of that; it approves concealment of this investigation. As the family buries the victim, the corporation can bury any inconvenient facts it has learned. There is certainly nothing improper about the corporation investigating, but justice may well be defeated if the fruits of that investigation are hidden from the victim as well as other parties who may be forced to defend themselves against charges of wrongdoing. Such unwarranted secrecy defeats the search for truth and violates the previous law of Texas, as the trial judge in Wichita properly recognized. Unfortunately, once again neither an explicit procedural rule nor the prior decisions of this court prevent the continued erection of what is essentially a double standard of justice in Texas. Amply displayed here is the added cost and delay resulting from the majority's eagerness to intrude rather than willingness to accept our existing law.[3] . . .

[b] The Problem of Witness Statements

When *National Tank* was decided, "witness statements" of potential parties and witnesses were protected from discovery "when made subsequent to an occurrence or transaction upon which the suit is based and in connection with the prosecution, investigation or defense of the particular suit or in anticipation of the prosecution or defense of the claims made a part of the pending litigation." Former Tex. R. Civ. P. 166b(3)(c). The former rule also defined the term "witness statement" to include "a written statement signed or otherwise adopted or approved by the person making it, and (ii) a stenographic, mechanical, electrical or other type of recording, or any transcription thereof which is a substantially verbatim recital of the statement made by the person and contemporaneously recorded." Former Tex. R. Civ. P. 166b(3)(c). In federal court, witness statements are protected as a type of ordinary work product. The definition contained in the federal rules and carried forward into the Texas rules was originally developed in discussing a witness's right to receive a copy of his or her own statement.

Now, however, the rules and comments provide that "witness statements" are not privileged, even if taken in anticipation of litigation. The rule drafters intended to make statements signed or adopted by the witness discoverable, but not to make attorneys' notes concerning witness interviews discoverable. Tex. R. Civ. P. 192.3(h). As you read the court's opinion in *Team Transport*, consider the following questions. Did the courts get it right? Should the definition of "witness statement" be changed? What if the statement is given to an attorney (as opposed to a non-attorney investigator)? What if the statement is given to the witness's attorney? *See* Tex. R. Civ. P. 192, comment 9; *see also In re Fontenot*, 13 S.W.3d 111 (Tex. App. — Fort Worth 2000, orig. proceeding). What if the investigator taking the statement is

[3] The lethal explosion occurred on August 23, 1990; Judge Brotherton properly applied Texas law to permit discovery by an order of July 25, 1991; the court of appeals promptly and appropriately rejected mandamus on September 27, 1991. After according National Tank emergency relief in November 1991, this court heard oral argument on March 10, 1992 and now obstructs access to information that could "significantly place the blame for the explosion on . . . National Tank Company . . . ." 851 S.W.2d at 213.

hired by the attorney rather than by the client or an insurance company?

Read Tex. R. Civ. P. 192.3(h).

IN RE TEAM TRANSPORT, INC.

996 S.W.2d 256 (Tex. App. — Houston [14th Dist.] 1999, orig. proceeding)

Wittig, J.

This mandamus proceeding involves a discovery dispute arising out of a personal injury lawsuit. Relator, Team Transport, Inc., complains the trial court clearly abused its discretion by ordering relator to produce a certain letter from relator to its insurance carrier. Finding the trial court was within its discretion to order production of the letter, we deny the petition for writ of mandamus.

BACKGROUND

On December 1, 1998, the real party in interest, Samuel Martinez, filed a personal injury lawsuit against the relator and Michelin North America, Inc. Martinez alleges that on or about October 20, 1998, relator's employee negligently dumped a container full of tires on him at the Michelin tire facility. On April 21, 1999, Martinez filed a motion to compel certain responses to his requests for production of documents. In particular, Martinez sought to compel a response to request number six seeking all investigative reports. Five days later, relator filed a response asserting that several of the documents were protected by the work product privilege. *See* Tex. R. Civ. P. 192.5. Among the documents identified, was a letter dated October 26, 1998, sent by an employee and a company officer to relator's insurance carrier. This letter was subsequently submitted *in camera* to the trial court and to this court. The first paragraph of the letter contains a description of the accident by Johnnie McIlveen, relator's allegedly negligent employee and a witness to the accident. The second paragraph of the letter contains comments by relator's Vice-President, Robert Eagleton, on procedures used at the Michelin warehouse, as those procedures related to the accident. Relator supported its response with several affidavits and correspondence showing the documents were prepared "in anticipation of litigation."

On April 27, 1999, the trial court held a hearing on the motion to compel and orally ruled in favor of Martinez. The following day, relator filed a motion for reconsideration. On May 3, 1999, the trial court signed an order compelling relator to produce the October 26, 1998, letter as a witness statement. In its order, the court specifically found this letter was prepared in anticipation of litigation, however, it ordered production of the letter as a witness statement. *See* Tex. R. Civ. P. 192.3(h). Relator was required to comply with the court's order by 5:00 p.m. on May 6, 1999, unless it filed a petition for writ of mandamus. On the same date it signed the discovery order, the trial court also signed an order denying relator's motion for reconsideration. On May 6, 1999, relator filed this petition for writ of mandamus. *See* Gov. C. § 22.221. The following day, Martinez filed a letter response.

WITNESS STATEMENT v. WORK PRODUCT

Mandamus relief is available if the trial court violates a duty imposed by law or clearly abuses its discretion, either in resolving factual issues or in determining legal issues, when there is no adequate remedy at law. *See Walker v. Packer*, 827 S.W.2d 833, 839 (Tex. 1992). A trial court abuses its discretion by making an arbitrary and unreasonable decision that amounts to a clear and prejudicial error of law. *See Johnson v. Fourth Court of Appeals*, 700 S.W.2d 916, 917 (Tex. 1985). Here, relator complains the trial court clearly abused its discretion in compelling the production of a privileged document. Because the erroneous disclosure of privileged information will materially affect relator's rights and thus, cannot be remedied by appeal, relator's complaint is appropriate for mandamus . . . .

As we described, the trial court found the October 26, 1998 letter was prepared in anticipation of litigation, but ordered production of the letter as a witness statement. Under Rule 192.3(h), "a party may obtain discovery of the statement of any person with knowledge of relevant facts — a 'witness statement' — *regardless of when the statement was made.*" (emphasis added). Thus, the court's ruling was correct provided the letter is a witness statement. Relator all but concedes the first paragraph of the letter prepared by Johnnie McIlveen is a witness statement. However, relator argues the second paragraph of the letter prepared by Robert Eagleton is not a witness statement, but work product. Thus, relator argues the trial court should not have ordered production of the entire letter or should have ordered production of a redacted version of the letter.

"Work product" is defined as follows: (1) "materials prepared or mental impressions developed in anticipation of litigation or for trial by or for a party or a party's representative, including the party's attorneys, consultant, sureties, indemnitors, insurers, employees, or agents;" or (2) "a communication made in anticipation of litigation or for trial between a party and the party's representatives or among a party's representatives including the party's attorney's, consultants, sureties, indemnitors, insurers, employees or agents." *See* Tex. R. Civ. P. 192.5(a). The work product privilege protects "core work product," which includes the attorney's "mental impressions, opinions conclusions or legal theories." *See* Tex. R. Civ. P. 192.5(b)(1). It also protects "other work product" unless the party seeking discovery shows a "substantial need" for the materials and "undue hardship" in obtaining the substantial equivalent of the materials by other means. *See* Tex. R. Civ. P. 192.5(b)(2). "Witness statements" are not work product, however, even if made or prepared in anticipation of litigation or trial. *See* Tex. R. Civ. P. 192.5(c)(1). Relator argues the trial court should not have ordered production of the October 26, 1998, letter because the Eagleton paragraph is a privileged communication between its agent and its insurer and because Martinez has not shown substantial need or undue hardship.

As to the latter contention, relator has not provided the reporter's record of the motion to compel hearing. As the party seeking relief, relator had the burden of providing this court with a sufficient record to establish its right to mandamus relief. *See Walker*, 827 S.W.2d at 837. As to the former contention, based upon our review of the Eagleton paragraph, we find no abuse of discretion by the trial court. Eagleton relates the normal procedures for warehousemen such as Martinez, used at the Michelin warehouse. Because those procedures pertain to the accident, they were included as a follow-up to McIlveen's witness statement. They are part and parcel of that statement. Without citation of authority, relator argues the Eagleton paragraph could not be a witness statement because Eagleton was not a witness to the accident. The rules do not mandate such a requirement. A person with knowledge of relevant facts need not have personal knowledge of the facts. *See* TEX. R. CIV. P. 192.3(c). Further, "the statement of *any person* with knowledge of relevant facts" is discoverable. *See* TEX. R. CIV. P. 192.5(h) (emphasis added). Thus, we cannot say the trial court committed a clear and prejudicial error of law by concluding that the Eagleton paragraph was a witness statement . . . .

[The court also decides that the 1999 rule amendments could be applied to documents created prior to the rule change.]

NOTES AND QUESTIONS

(1) *Duration of Work Product Protection.* Once it has been created, when does work product protection end? The Supreme Court held in *Owens-Corning Fiberglas Corp. v. Caldwell*, 818 S.W.2d 749, 751 (Tex. 1991), that the attorney work product exemption is "perpetual" unless waived. The Court believed that this was necessary in order to further the policies underlying the work product doctrine. "Were the work product protection not continuing, a situation would result in which a client's communications to an attorney, which must be full, frank and open, are protected, Tex. R. Civ. Evid. 503, but the same attorney's work product done in furtherance of such attorney-client relationship is not. This anomaly clearly cannot be allowed."

(2) *Attorney's Notes.* How should a court determine whether an attorney's notes are factual ("other work product") or whether they reveal the attorney's thought processes ("core work product")? Note that Rule 192.5(b)(3) provides that material that "incidentally discloses by inference attorney mental processes" is not protected as work product.

(3) *Discovery of Attorney's Litigation File.* Although it is possible that individual documents located in an attorney's files may be discoverable, the Texas Supreme Court has held that a discovery request for an attorney's "litigation file" is, on its face, an improper invasion of the work product exemption. *National Union Fire Ins. Co. of Pittsburgh v. Valdez*, 863 S.W.2d 458 (Tex. 1993). But an individual document is not privileged simply because it is contained in an attorney's file. A party may not cloak a document with privilege simply by forwarding it to his or her attorney. Thus, although a party may not compel the production of an adverse party's entire file, the party may request individual documents relevant to the case and is entitled to discover nonprivileged documents even if they are kept in the attorney's file.

(4) *The Substantial Need/Undue Hardship Exception.* Work product that is not absolutely protected as "core work product" is subject to discovery if the party seeking discovery "has substantial need of the materials in the preparation of the party's case and . . . is unable without undue hardship to obtain the substantial equivalent of the material by other means." This exception, like the work product

doctrine itself, has its origin in the United States Supreme Court's opinion in *Hickman v. Taylor*, 329 U.S. 495, 511–12 (1947). Following *Hickman*, the Federal Rules of Civil Procedure included a substantial need and undue hardship exception in Rule 26(b)(3). A review of federal law, therefore, may help in understanding this exception. In one Texas case, the Texas Supreme Court concluded that both the substantial need and undue hardship requirements were met when the parties seeking discovery attempted to discover information amassed by the state from responses to civil investigative demands made on third parties. *State v. Lowry*, 802 S.W.2d 669, 673 (Tex. 1991). One court of appeals, noting that the exception is underdeveloped in Texas, looked to federal case law to support its determination that credibility issues and the failing memory of a witness who had been interviewed by opposing counsel satisfied the substantial need and undue hardship exception. *Dillard Dep't Stores, Inc. v. Sanderson*, 928 S.W.2d 319, 321 (Tex. App. — Beaumont 1996, orig. proceeding).

(5) *Policy Issues.* Do you agree that the work product exemption is necessary to encourage lawyers to adequately prepare their cases for trial? *Compare* Elizabeth G. Thornburg, *Rethinking Work Product*, 77 Va. L. Rev. 1515 (1991), *with* Alexandra W. Albright, *The Texas Discovery Privileges: A Fool's Game?*70 Tex. L. Rev. 781 (1992).

PRACTICE EXERCISE #22

For the following questions, assume the same facts as for Practice Exercise #21.

1. Six months before Allen's fall, the store manager discovered that one of the produce clerks had learned of a spill on the floor but had hidden in the employee break room for an hour to avoid cleaning it up. The manager reprimanded the clerk and placed a memo describing the incident in the employee's personnel file. That clerk was also on duty when Allen fell. Assume that Allen has sent a discovery request that covers this document. Is the document protected by the work product privilege?

2. Alpha Omega's insurance company has been investigating Allen's fall. In talking to regular store customers, the investigator learned that the produce department floor was particularly messy on the day of Allen's fall. One of the customers wrote the investigator a letter describing what happened. If Allen properly requests this document, will Alpha Omega have to produce it? Why or why not?

3. Immediately after Allen's fall, Hugh Cumber, a produce department manager, made a list of the names, addresses, and phone numbers of all of the customers in the produce department at the time of the fall. Can Allen discover the list? Can Allen discover the names and contact information?

4. One week after Allen's fall, Alpha Omega's insurer contacted Cumber. The insurance agent questioned Cumber about Allen's accident and tape recorded the conversation. Can Allen discover the recording?

5. Alpha Omega's insurer also interviewed store employees. One of them, Tom Ato, said that he saw squashed grapes on the floor just before Allen's fall. The investigator wrote a memo about this conversation. Since that time, Tom has been called up from the army reserves and sent to Iraq. If Allen properly requests this document, will Alpha Omega have to produce it? Why or why not?

6. Allen's lawyer is preparing for trial. He has put together a trial notebook containing proposed voir dire questions, opening statement, witness questions, and proposed jury questions. If Alpha Omega properly requests production of the trial notebook, will Allen have to produce it? Why or why not?

[c] Expert Witnesses

Read Tex. R. Civ. P. 192.3(e), 192.5(c)(1), 194.2(f), 195.

Generally, experts are used in litigation in two ways. First, an expert may help a litigant prepare the case for discovery and trial. Second, an expert may testify at trial as part of a litigant's effort to persuade the trier of fact. The discovery rules are designed to account for the different uses of experts in the litigation process by differentiating between "consulting experts" (those who help litigants prepare the case) and "testifying experts" (those who act as a witness at trial). The discovery rules permit a party to protect from discovery the identity, mental impressions, and opinions of consulting experts, as long as a testifying expert did not review their impressions or opinions. This is in accord with the general theory that a litigant is entitled to prepare for trial without having to disclose his or her trial strategy. Thus, these experts are permitted to work with the litigant and the attorney behind the scenes. Tex. R. Civ. P. 192.3(e) ("The identity, mental impressions, and opinions of a consulting expert whose mental impressions and opinions have not been reviewed by a testifying expert are not discoverable."); *see also* Tex. R. Civ. P. 192.7(d) ("A consulting expert is an expert who has been consulted, retained, or specially employed by a party in anticipation of litigation or in preparation for trial, but who is not a testifying expert.").

Experts who will play an active role in the trial process receive the opposite treatment. Thus, a person who will testify as an expert at trial is subject to extensive discovery. The same scope of discovery applies to a consulting expert whose mental impressions or opinions have been reviewed by a testifying expert. This is in accord with the general theory of discovery that full disclosure of facts before trial helps achieve justice. Although the 1999 discovery rules are somewhat more complex than prior law concerning the scope of expert discovery, comment 3 to Civil Procedure Rule 192 provides that the rule "is intended to be consistent with *Axelson v. McIlhany*, 798 S.W.2d 550 (Tex. 1990)." *Axelson* is included with the cases in this section.

Litigation regarding the consulting expert exemption has centered on several issues: (1) when was a consulting expert retained in anticipation of litigation or preparation for trial; (2) when can an employee or former employee be designated as a consulting expert; and (3) can an expert be converted from a testifying expert (discoverable) to a consulting expert (exempt) by redesignating the expert's function? The cases that follow show the Texas Supreme Court wrestling with these issues.

LINDSEY v. O'NEILL
689 S.W.2d 400 (Tex. 1985)

Per Curiam

This is an original mandamus action brought by George Lindsey and Betty Lindsey, individually and as next friends of their son, Thomas Daniel Lindsey, to compel Judge O'Neill to rescind his order limiting the scope of their Second Amended Notice of Deposition. This court has jurisdiction over this cause pursuant to Tex. Rev. Civ. Stat. Ann. art. 1733 (Vernon Supp. 1985). Because we believe the trial court's order improperly restricted the scope of discovery as defined by the Texas Rules of Civil Procedure, we conditionally grant the writ.

The Lindseys brought the underlying lawsuit in this cause against several defendants including certain named physicians, several pharmaceutical companies, and Hermann Hospital in Houston, based upon medical malpractice and products liability theories. In the course of conducting pretrial discovery, the Lindseys served their Second Amended Notice of Deposition upon one of the defendants, Travenol Labs, Inc. This deposition notice requested Travenol to produce individuals for deposition on some thirty-nine subject areas. Travenol moved for a protective order and the trial court ordered twenty-one of these subject areas stricken from the notice on the ground that the subjects called for Travenol to produce expert opinion testimony. The trial court struck another eight subjects from the notice on relevancy grounds. As to the remaining subject areas, the trial court limited the scope of permissible inquiry by the Lindseys to only such facts as are, or may lead to, matters relevant to the issues identified by the Lindseys' Seventh Amended Petition. The trial court also quashed the document request which accompanied the deposition notice.

Tex. R. Civ. P. 200 provides that a party may take the deposition of a private or public corporation. Subsection 2b [now Tex. R. Civ. P. 199.2(b)] requires that a deposition notice of a corporation describe with reasonable particularity the matters on which examination is requested. Rule 200 makes no distinction between deposition notices directed toward corporations based upon whether the deposition is to pertain to purely factual matters or matters calling for expert opinion . . . .

No provision exists in the Texas Rules of Civil Procedure exempting the mental impressions and opinions of experts from discovery when these mental impressions and opinions were neither acquired nor developed in anticipation of litigation. Before the trial court may hold an entire category of expert opinion evidence exempt from discovery, there must be proof before it that all such evidence was either acquired or developed in anticipation of litigation. Because the trial court excluded from discovery all of the mental impressions and opinions of experts associated with Travenol without any showing that this information was acquired or developed in anticipation of litigation, we find a conflict between the trial court's order and the Texas Rules of Civil Procedure and, hence, an abuse of discretion on the part of the trial court.

With regard to those subject areas either struck from the Lindseys' deposition notice on relevancy grounds or restricted in scope to the facts relevant to the

Lindseys' claims, we find no abuse of discretion in the trial court's order.

We grant the motion for leave to file petition for writ of mandamus. Pursuant to Tex. R. Civ. P. 483, without hearing oral argument, we grant the writ. We are confident the trial court will comply with our decision. A writ of mandamus will issue only if it fails to do so.

AXELSON, INC. v. McILHANY
798 S.W.2d 550 (Tex. 1990)

GONZALEZ, J.

In this mandamus proceeding, we are asked to direct Judge McIlhany to vacate orders denying pretrial discovery. The court of appeals conditionally granted the petition for writ of mandamus on certain points but denied the petition on other points. Among other things, we are requested to grant relief regarding discovery of a kickback investigation and "dual capacity" witnesses. We conditionally grant the writ.

The underlying suit from which this action arises involves what is believed to be the largest gas well blowout in United States history. Key Well 1-11, located in Wheeler County, blew out in October 1981 and was not brought under control for over a year. Apache Corporation operates the well and, together with El Paso Exploration Company (a/k/a Meridian Oil Production, Inc.), owns the working interest. Numerous lawsuits involving over 100 parties have been filed against Apache and El Paso, alleging that their wrongful acts caused the blowout. All suits against Apache and El Paso have been consolidated.

Plaintiffs include Arkla Exploration, Stephens Production Company and Hobart Key, all of whom own mineral interests in the same field. Tom L. Scott, Inc. and other mineral interest holders ("Scott group") intervened as plaintiffs, alleging a cause of action against Apache and El Paso only. Apache and El Paso responded by adding numerous third-party defendants. Sooner Pipe & Supply Corporation, Hydril Corporation and Babcock & Wilcox Company ("Sooner") were added because they supplied well equipment that allegedly caused the blowout. Axelson, Inc. and its parent corporation, U.S. Industries, Inc. (USI), were added because Axelson manufactured a relief valve that allegedly should have prevented the blowout . . . .

"DUAL CAPACITY" WITNESSES

Several potential witnesses in this case maintain a dual capacity — possessing firsthand knowledge of relevant facts and serving as consulting-only experts for Apache and El Paso. One of these persons, Paul Douglas Storts, is the petroleum engineer who has been in charge of the well from its inception. He also spearheaded the effort to bring the well under control after the blowout. The others include Richard Biel, Joe Fowler and Tom Hill, who were hired by Apache and El Paso to examine the wellhead equipment and have specific knowledge concerning the chain of custody of the wellhead equipment.

Axelson and USI seek to discover all facts known by Storts and his mental impressions and opinions gained while working on the well and consulting. They seek to discover only chain of custody facts from Biel, Fowler and Hill.

The trial court entered several orders from December 1984 through July 1987 limiting discovery. With regard to Storts, the trial court initially quashed his deposition, but later determined that information gained by him while working on the well was discoverable, but that information he gained while doing a combination of working on the well and consulting was not discoverable. With regard to Biel, Fowler, and Hill, the trial court allowed discovery of facts relating only to the Axelson valve. The court of appeals held that the trial court had not abused its discretion and disallowed all other discovery from these experts. We disagree.

The factual knowledge and opinions acquired by an individual who is an expert and an active participant in the events material to the lawsuit are discoverable. This information is not shielded from discovery by merely changing the designation of a person with knowledge of relevant facts to a "consulting-only expert."

The scope of discovery regarding experts who serve in the dual capacity of fact witness and consulting-only expert has not been addressed thoroughly by Texas courts. Barrow and Henderson, *1984 Amendments to the Texas Rules of Civil Procedure Affecting Discovery*, 15 St. Mary's L.J. 713, 729 (1984). The literal text of the exemption, however, resolves the issue presented in this mandamus. The consulting expert exemption protects the identity, mental impressions and opinions of consulting only experts; but not the facts. The rule we announce today, however, "should not extend to consulting [only] experts . . . whose only source of factual information was the consultation." *Id.* In other words, persons who gain factual information by virtue of their involvement relating to the incident or transaction giving rise to the litigation do not qualify as consulting-only experts because the consultation is not their only source of information. We now separately address Axelson's discovery requests regarding Storts, an employee designated as a consulting-only expert, and Biel, Fowler and Hill, experts designated as consulting-only who have factual knowledge of the well equipment.

STORTS

An employee may be specially employed as a consulting-only expert. *See Barker v. Dunham*, 551 S.W.2d 41, 43–44 (Tex. 1977, orig. proceeding). Nevertheless, all employees do not necessarily qualify as "consulting-only" experts. The rules provide requirements that a consulting-only expert must meet. *See* Tex. R. Civ. P. 166b(3)(b). Rule of Civil Procedure 166b(3)(b) provides:

> 3. Exemptions. The following matters are protected from disclosure by privilege:
>
> b. *Experts*. The identity, mental impressions, and opinions of an expert who has been *informally consulted* or of an expert who has been *retained*

> *or specially employed by another party in anticipation of litigation or preparation for trial . . . .*

Id. (emphasis added). Under this rule, a consulting-only expert must be informally consulted or retained or specially employed in anticipation of litigation. An employee who was employed in an area that becomes the subject of litigation can never qualify as a consulting-only expert because the employment was not in anticipation of litigation. On the other hand, an employee who was not employed in an area that becomes the subject of litigation and is reassigned specifically to assist the employer in anticipation of litigation arising out of the incident or in preparation for trial may qualify as a "consulting-only" expert. In any event, a party may discover facts known by an employee acting as a "consulting-only" expert.

In this case, evidence presented to the trial court suggested that Storts was doing a combination of both working on the well and consulting. Storts was hired to work as a petroleum engineer and he worked on Key Well 1-11 before, during and after the blowout. After litigation began Apache asserted that Storts was a consulting-only expert and resisted all discovery of Storts' mental impressions, opinions and facts. On the record before him, the trial judge abused his discretion in denying discovery of Storts' mental impressions, opinions and facts because Storts did not qualify as a consulting-only expert.

Policies previously enunciated by this court support the decision we reach today. This rule aims to effectuate the ultimate purpose of discovery, which is to seek truth, so that disputes may be decided by those facts that are revealed, rather than concealed. *Jampole v. Touchy*, 673 S.W.2d at 573. Additionally, although Apache and El Paso are defendants in this case, they are pursuing a cross claim and "cannot use one hand to seek affirmative relief in court and with the other lower an iron curtain of silence around the facts of the case." *Ginsberg v. Fifth Court of Appeals*, 686 S.W.2d 105, 108 (Tex. 1985, orig. proceeding).

BIEL, FOWLER, & HILL

Axelson sought only factual discovery from Biel, Fowler and Hill regarding the condition of wellhead equipment in addition to the condition of Axelson's relief valve. The trial judge limited the scope of discovery from these consulting-only experts to the Axelson valve. The trial judge abused his discretion in refusing discovery of these facts because the exemption for consulting-only experts does not extend to facts known to them . . . .

TOM L. SCOTT, INC. v. McILHANY
798 S.W.2d 556 (Tex. 1990)

GONZALEZ, J.

This is an original mandamus proceeding involving pretrial discovery of expert witnesses. The relators, Tom L. Scott, Inc. and others, seek relief from orders signed by the respondent, the Honorable Grainger W. McIlhany, denying discovery of six experts retained by various parties to the case. By this mandamus, relators seek to obtain the depositions of these experts. The defendants changed the designation of these experts from "testifying" experts to "consulting-only" experts after they settled with some of the plaintiffs and third-party defendants in the underlying suit. The court of appeals denied the petition for writ of mandamus. We hold that the redesignation under the facts before us violates the purpose of discovery enunciated in *Gutierrez v. Dallas Independent School District*, 729 S.W.2d 691, 693 (Tex. 1987), and in *Jampole v. Touchy*, 673 S.W.2d 569, 573 (Tex. 1984, orig. proceeding), and is, therefore, ineffective. Thus we conditionally grant the writ.

[The Court here sets forth the factual background, which is the same as in the preceding case.]

The initial plaintiffs, Arkla, Stephens and Key (Arkla/Key), and third-party defendants, Sooner, Hydril and Babcock & Wilcox, designated the six experts in question as *testifying* experts. Allegedly, these experts were prepared to deliver damaging testimony against Apache and El Paso. On the morning the Arkla/Key witnesses' depositions were scheduled, Apache and El Paso settled with these parties on the condition that Apache and El Paso gain control of the experts. Following execution of the settlement, Apache and El Paso, along with the settling parties, redesignated all six as consulting-only experts.

The trial court denied requests by the Scott group to depose the experts. Specifically, the Scott group filed a motion to take depositions of the experts, and Judge McIlhany denied it . . . . We next address the critical question presented in this case — whether a party may obtain an adversary's testifying experts and redesignate them as consulting-only experts to avoid discovery.

Designating these experts as testifying experts subjected their work product to discovery. Texas Rule of Civil Procedure 166b(2)(e)(1) [now Tex. R. Civ. P. 192.3] provides in part:

> A party may obtain discovery of the identity and location (name, address and telephone number) of an expert who may be called as an expert witness, the subject matter on which the witness is expected to testify, the mental impressions and opinions held by the expert and the facts known to the expert (regardless of when the factual information was acquired) which relate to or form the basis of the mental impressions and opinions held by the expert.

. . . .

Upon gaining control of the experts, Apache and El Paso redesignated them as consulting-only experts. The settling parties also redesignated the experts as consulting-only experts. Identities and opinions of experts are nevertheless discoverable if they are not engaged in anticipation of litigation and solely for consultation or if their work product has been reviewed or relied upon by testifying experts. *See* Tex. R. Civ. P. 166b(3)(b) [now Tex. R. Civ. P. 192.3(e)]. The trial court allowed the redesignation and refused requests by the Scott group to depose these experts. The Scott group asks us to hold this redesignation invalid.

The primary policy behind discovery is to seek truth so that disputes may be decided by facts that are revealed rather than concealed. *Jampole*, 673 S.W.2d at 573. Privileges from discovery run contrary to this policy but serve other legitimate interests. The policy behind the consulting expert privilege is to encourage parties to seek expert advice in evaluating their case and to prevent a party from receiving undue benefit from an adversary's efforts and diligence. *Werner v. Miller*, 579 S.W.2d 455, 456 (Tex. 1979, orig. proceeding); *see also* D. KELTNER, TEXAS DISCOVERY § 3.110 (1989). But the protection afforded by the consulting expert privilege is intended to be only "a shield to prevent a litigant from taking undue advantage of his adversary's industry and effort, not a sword to be used to thwart justice or to defeat the salutary objects" of discovery. *Williamson v. Superior Court*, 582 P.2d 126, 132 (Cal. 1978); *see also Chuidian v. Philippine Nat'l Bank*, 734 F. Supp. 415, 423 (C.D. Cal. 1990) (interpreting *Williamson* as holding agreements to suppress evidence or conceal discreditable facts are illegal); *Raytheon Co. v. Superior Court*, 256 Cal. Rptr. 425, 427 (Cal. Ct. App. 1989) (interpreting *Williamson* as holding agreements between adversarial codefendants to suppress expert testimony are against public policy).

The redesignation of the experts in this case was an offensive and unacceptable use of discovery mechanisms intended to defeat the salutary objectives of discovery. Attorneys for Apache and El Paso even admitted to the trial judge that the settlements were "expressly contingent" on these experts not being required to give their testimony, and that there might not be a settlement agreement if the depositions were ordered. One of the settling parties expressly told the trial court that he understood the settlement offer would expire upon the depositions being taken. The legitimate purposes and policies behind the consulting expert privilege do not countenance this conduct. We hold that, as a matter of law, the redesignation of experts under the facts of this case violates the policy underlying the rules of discovery and is therefore ineffective. *See Gutierrez*, 729 S.W.2d at 693; *Jampole*, 673 S.W.2d at 573. "If we were to hold otherwise, nothing would preclude a party in a multi-party case from in effect auctioning off a witness' testimony to the highest bidder." *Williamson*, 582 P.2d at 132. Because the redesignation of experts under the facts of this case violates the clear purpose and policy underlying the rules of discovery, the trial court abused its discretion in granting the protective order as to these six experts. We are confident Judge McIlhany will vacate his orders denying discovery and will render orders consistent with this opinion. Should he fail to do so, the clerk of the supreme court is directed to issue the writ of mandamus.

PRACTICE EXERCISE #23

Assume the same facts as for Practice Exercise #21.

1. Every year, all of the locations of Alpha Omega have a customer safety audit. The audit includes an analysis of produce display practices done by engineers. If Allen properly requests the most recent analysis, will Alpha Omega have to produce it? Why or why not?

2. Allen has hired an expert economist to testify about her lost income from her injuries in the fall. What can Alpha Omega discover from and about that expert?

3. Alpha Omega has hired two experts to help defend against Allen's claims. Expert A will testify at trial that Alpha Omega's produce department was designed and maintained in a state of the art fashion. Expert B will not testify, but he has met with Expert A to help develop the testimony and to do some testing on which Expert A will rely. What can Allen discover from or about Expert B?

4. Brock Lee is the senior manager of Alpha Omega's produce department. He knows about stacking and cleaning practices, and was on duty the day Allen fell. Alpha Omega has designated him as a consulting-only expert witness. Allen wants to take his deposition. Should she be allowed to? What will she be allowed to ask about?

5. Alpha Omega hired an expert to be its testifying expert. Later it found a different expert whose opinions are more unequivocally supportive. It wants to redesignate the original expert, who has not yet been deposed, as a pure consulting expert. Any problems?

[2] Other Discovery Privileges

The scope of discovery does not include privileged material. Tex. R. Civ. P. 192.3(a). This allows parties resisting discovery to rely on privileges that exist outside the discovery rules themselves. This section of the chapter discusses some of the other privileges that have been applied to the discovery process. They are based in the federal Constitution, the Texas Rules of Evidence, and other Texas statutes.

[a] Constitutional Privileges

The privilege against self-incrimination can affect civil cases. That privilege extends to testimonial communications that would sustain a conviction, and also to responses that would furnish a link in the chain of evidence needed to prosecute the person claiming the privilege. The privilege should be sustained unless it clearly appears that the person claiming it is mistaken. *Hoffman v. United States*, 341 U.S. 479, 486–87 (1951). On the other hand, the privilege does not bar the compelled production of a tangible thing, such as a document, that contains no self-incriminating testimonial declaration, unless the act of production itself constitutes an incriminating testimonial communication. *Fisher v. United States*, 425 U.S. 391, 409–11 (1976).

Although a person is never compelled to incriminate him or herself, a plaintiff who invokes this privilege during discovery may suffer sanctions. In other words, the plaintiff has several options: (1) bring the action and disclose self-incriminating matter; (2) if possible, limit the action to matters that will not involve disclosure of incriminating material; (3) refrain from suit; or (4) face dismissal or stay on failure to make the required disclosure. In considering the appropriate sanction for a plaintiff asserting privilege, the court must consider a number of factors and must tailor the sanction to the nature of the offensive conduct. *Texas Dep't of Public Safety Officers Ass'n v. Denton*, 897 S.W.2d 757 (Tex. 1995). On the basis that defendants do not have these options, it has been held that a defendant is not subject to sanctions for invoking the privilege. *Duffy v. Currier*, 291 F. Supp. 810,

814 (D. Minn. 1968). The defendant is not, however, the sole judge of the right to invoke the privilege against self-incrimination in a civil case. The judge must decide if the refusal to respond is based on good faith and is justified under the circumstances. *Ex parte Butler*, 522 S.W.2d 196, 197 (Tex. 1975); *Warford v. Beard*, 653 S.W.2d 908, 911 (Tex. App. — Amarillo 1983, no writ). Note also that at trial in civil cases, both the judge and opposing counsel are allowed to comment on a party's claim of the privilege against self-incrimination and suggest that inferences may be drawn from the claim. TEX. R. EVID. 513.

A litigant may also claim a constitutional privilege to challenge discovery requests in violation of First Amendment freedom of association rights. *In re BACALA*, 982 S.W.2d 371 (Tex. 1998); *Tilton v. Moye*, 869 S.W.2d 955 (Tex. 1994); *Ex parte Lowe*, 887 S.W.2d 1 (Tex. 1994). Once the claim of privilege is properly raised, the party seeking associational information has the burden to establish a constitutionally permissible basis justifying its disclosure. *Id.*

[b] Privileges Based on the Texas Rules of Evidence

Read TEX. R. EVID. 501–510.

The Texas Rules of Evidence recognize privileges for required reports privileged by statute (TEX. R. EVID. 502); lawyer-client communications (TEX. R. EVID. 503); husband-wife communications (TEX. R. EVID. 504); communications to clergy (TEX. R. EVID. 505); political vote (TEX. R. EVID. 506); trade secrets (TEX. R. EVID. 507); identity of informers (TEX. R. EVID. 508); physician-patient communications (TEX. R. EVID. 509); and mental health information (TEX. R. EVID. 510). Some of the privileges are absolute, some are conditional, and all are subject to waiver and exceptions. Most have generated little litigation.

Attorney-Client Privilege

The attorney-client privilege, not surprisingly, has proved the most controversial of the privileges. The privilege protects confidential communications between lawyer and client made for the purpose of receiving legal advice. Until quite recently, there was little litigation in Texas regarding the parameters of the attorney-client privilege.

As in other jurisdictions, one of the most difficult privilege questions arises when the "client" is an organization rather than a human being. In such cases, the court must decide who can be a representative of the client, so that communications to and from the representative qualify for the privilege. Different jurisdictions have different approaches to this issue, but they tend to be characterized as falling into two kinds of tests. One approach is the "control group" test. Under a control group analysis, only employees who are quite high in the corporate hierarchy can claim the privilege. While the precise identity of control group employees may be hard to predict, it is generally defined to include persons in a position to control or take a substantial part in a decision about any action which the corporation may take on the advice of the attorney. *City of Philadelphia v. Westinghouse Electric Corp.*, 210 F. Supp. 483 (E.D. Pa.), *petition for mandamus and prohibition denied sub. nom. General Electric Co. v. Kirkpatrick*, 312 F.2d 742 (3d Cir. 1962).

The second approach to the attorney-client privilege in the corporate context is referred to as a "subject matter test." The subject matter test provides a privilege to people with whom an attorney needs to communicate in order to render legal services, regardless of their position in the corporate hierarchy. The United States Supreme Court in *Upjohn Co. v. United States*, 449 U.S. 383 (1981), is often said to have used a subject matter approach. There are broader and narrower ways to define a subject matter test, but generally the test will require that the communication with the attorney be made at the direction of an employee's superiors and that the subject matter on which the attorney's advice is sought is the employee's performance of the duties of his employment. *National Tank Co. v. Brotherton*, 851 S.W.2d 193, 198 (Tex. 1993).

What approach does Texas use? The pre-1997 version of Evidence Rule 503 was interpreted to adopt a control group approach. *National Tank*, 851 S.W.2d 193 (Tex. 1993). Effective March 1, 1998, the Texas Supreme Court amended Evidence Rule 503 to provide coverage to communications made by a lower level employee who "for the purpose of effectuating legal representation for the client, makes or receives a confidential communication while acting in the scope of employment for the client." Tex. R. Evid. 503(a)(2)(B). The Rule 503 version of the privilege is also quite broad in its discussion of the communications encompassed by the attorney-client privilege.

Read the rule, and consider all of the directions in which privileged communications can flow. For example, can communications between employees of a corporate client fall within the definition of attorney-client privilege, as long as the communication is "for the purpose of facilitating the rendition of professional legal services to the client"? Why might corporate litigants prefer attorney-client privilege to work product protection of such communications?

Rule 503. Lawyer-Client Privilege

(a) *Definitions.* — As used in this rule:

(1) A "client" is a person, public officer, or corporation, association, or other organization or entity, either public orprivate, who is rendered professional legal services by a lawyer, or who consults a lawyer with a view to obtaining professional legal services from that lawyer.

(2) A "representative of the client" is:

(A) a person having authority to obtain professional legal services, or to act on advice thereby rendered, on behalf of the client, or

(B) any other person who, for the purpose of effectuating legal representation for the client, makes or receives a confidential communication while acting in the scope of employment for the client.

(3) A "lawyer" is a person authorized, or reasonably believed by the client to be authorized, to engage in the practice of law in any state or nation.

(4) A "representative of the lawyer" is:

(A) one employed by the lawyer to assist the lawyer in the rendition of professional legal services; or

(B) an accountant who is reasonably necessary for the lawyer's rendition of professional legal services.

(5) A communication is "confidential" if not intended to be disclosed to third persons other than those to whom disclosure is made in furtherance of the rendition of professional legal services to the client or those reasonably necessary for the transmission of the communication.

(b) *Rules of Privilege.*

(1) *General Rule of Privilege.* — A client has a privilege to refuse to disclose and to prevent any other person from disclosing confidential communications made for the purpose of facilitating the rendition of professional legal services to the client:

(A) between the client or a representative of the client and the client's lawyer or a representative of the lawyer;

(B) between the lawyer and the lawyer's representative;

(C) by the client or a representative of the client, or the client's lawyer or a representative of the lawyer, to a lawyer or a representative of a lawyer representing another party in a pending action and concerning a matter of common interest therein;

(D) between representatives of the client or between the client and a representative of the client; or

(E) among lawyers and their representatives representing the same client.

(2) *Special Rule of Privilege in Criminal Cases.* — In criminal cases, a client has a privilege to prevent the lawyer or lawyer's representative from disclosing any other fact which came to the knowledge of the lawyer or the lawyer's representative by reason of the attorney-client relationship.

(c) *Who May Claim the Privilege.* — The privilege may be claimed by the client, the client's guardian or conservator, the personal representative of a deceased client, or the successor, trustee, or similar representative of a corporation, association, or other organization, whether or not in existence. The person who was the lawyer or the lawyer's representative at the time of the communication is presumed to have authority to claim the privilege but only on behalf of the client.

(d) *Exceptions.* — There is no privilege under this rule:

(1) *Furtherance of Crime or Fraud.* — If the services of the lawyer were sought or obtained to enable or aid anyone to commit or plan to commit what the client knew or reasonably should have known to be a crime or fraud;

(2) *Claimants Through Same Deceased Client.* — As to a communication relevant to an issue between parties who claim through the same deceased client, regardless of whether the claims are by testate or intestate succession or by *inter vivos* transactions;

(3) *Breach of Duty by a Lawyer or Client.* — As to a communication relevant to an issue of breach of duty by a lawyer to the client or by a client to the lawyer;

(4) *Document Attested by a Lawyer.* — As to a communication relevant to an issue concerning an attested document to which the lawyer is an attesting witness; or

(5) *Joint Clients.* — As to a communication relevant to a matter of common interest between or among two or more clients if the communication was made by any of them to a lawyer retained or consulted in common, when offered in an action between or among any of the clients.

NOTES AND QUESTIONS

(1) *Breadth of Protection Afforded Corporations.* Re-read Evidence Rule 503. How broad a protection does the new attorney-client privilege provide for corporate communications? Notice the directions in which communications are protected, and the number of agents who are included.

(2) *Satisfaction of Confidentiality Requirement.* Consider the requirement that communications must be "confidential." What advice would you give a corporate client about generating, circulating, and storing privileged communications?

(3) *Public Policy Issues.* As a matter of public policy, how broad do you think the corporate attorney-client privilege should be? *Compare* Charles Fried, *The Lawyer as Friend: The Moral Foundations of the Lawyer-Client Relation*, 85 YALE L.J. 1060 (1976), *with* Elizabeth Thornburg, *Sanctifying Secrecy: The Mythology of the Corporate Attorney-Client Privilege*, 69 NOTRE DAME L. REV. 157 (1993).

(4) *Exceptions to Attorney-Client Privilege.* Attorney-client communications are not privileged if they fall within certain exceptions, set out in Texas Rule of Evidence 503(d). The most litigated exception is the crime-fraud exception. TEX. R. EVID. 503(d)(1). There is no privilege if the services of counsel were sought or obtained to enable or aid anyone to commit or plan to commit what the client knew or reasonably should have known to be a crime or fraud. The crime-fraud exception applies only when a prima facie case is made of contemplated fraud. In addition, there must be a relationship between the document for which the privilege is challenged and the prima facie proof offered. *Granada Corp. v. First Court of Appeals*, 844 S.W.2d 223, 227–28 (Tex. 1996).

TRADE SECRETS

Evidence Rule 507 recognizes a privilege not to disclose a trade secret. *See* TEX. R. EVID. 507. In determining whether information qualifies as a trade secret, the Texas Supreme Court applies the following six-factor test:

> (1) the extent to which the information is known outside of his business; (2) the extent to which it is known by employees and others involved in his business; (3) the extent of the measures taken by him to guard the secrecy of the information; (4) the value of the information to him and to his competitors; (5) the amount of effort or money expended by him in

developing the information; (6) the ease or difficulty with which the information could be properly acquired or duplicated by others.

In re Bass, 113 S.W.3d 735, 740 (Tex. 2003) (quoting Restatement of Torts § 757, cmt. b and Restatement of Unfair Competition § 39 reporter's note and cmt. d); *see also In re Union Pacific RR Co.*, 294 S.W.3d 589 (Tex. 2009); *Hyde Corp. v. Huffines*, 314 S.W.2d 763, 776 (1958) ("A trade secret may consist of any formula, pattern, device, or compilation of information which is used in one's business, and which gives him an opportunity to obtain an advantage over competitors who do not know or use it."). The Texas Supreme Court has also recognized that "trade secrets do not fit neatly into each factor every time." *See In re Bass*, 113 S.W.3d 735, 739–40 (Tex. 2003).

In a case involving the Union Pacific Railroad, the Court applied this test and found that the railroad's "confidential rate structures" for handling hazardous materials were trade secrets. This was based on a corporate officer's affidavit stating that "the manner and method that Union Pacific employs to calculate and arrive at shipping rates . . . is confidential, proprietary and a trade secret of Union Pacific. The information is not generally known or readily available to Union Pacific competitors or its customers or other businesses. The information is not even generally known throughout the company. Rather, the information is known only to a limited number of Union Pacific employees and certain management employees." The Court also stated that disclosure of these rates to competitors would give them a pricing advantage, and noted that Congress prohibits the disclosure of these rates in certain instances. *In re Union Pacific RR Co.*, supra, at 592.

The Texas Supreme Court has recently bolstered the significance of the trade secret privilege. Consider the following case and ask yourself: (1) is the protection for trade secrets a true privilege?; (2) what is a trade secret?; and (3) how would the availability of a protective order and the scope of such an order influence the court's decision about the proper treatment of trade secrets?

IN RE CONTINENTAL GENERAL TIRE, INC.
979 S.W.2d 609 (Tex. 1998)

PHILLIPS, C.J.

Under our rules of evidence, a party has a privilege to refuse to disclose its trade secrets "if the allowance of the privilege will not tend to conceal fraud or otherwise work injustice." *See* TEX. R. EVID. 507. The issue is whether Rule 507 protects from discovery a tire manufacturer's chemical formula for its "skim stock," a rubber compound used in tire manufacturing. The trial court ordered the manufacturer to produce the formula under a protective order, and the court of appeals denied the manufacturer's requested mandamus relief without opinion. We hold that, when a party resisting discovery establishes that the requested information is a trade secret under Rule 507, the burden shifts to the requesting party to establish that the information is necessary for a fair adjudication of its claim or defense. Because relator established that the formula was a trade secret, and because the real party in interest did not meet its burden of establishing necessity, we conditionally grant mandamus relief. Nothing in the relief we grant prohibits plaintiffs from seeking to discover the formula under the procedure we set forth.

I.

While Kenneth Fisher was driving his pick-up truck on Highway 190, his left front tire blew out, causing him to lose control of the vehicle. Fisher's truck crossed the median and struck Dora Pratt's car, killing Pratt and her passenger. Pratt's heirs, Luz Enid Rivera, Brenda Beatriz Killens, Gilberto DeJesus Cruz, Dora Maria Cruz, and Toribio Nieves, filed the underlying products liability action against Continental General Tire, the manufacturer of the failed tire.

It is undisputed that the tire failed because its tread and outer belt separated from the inner belt. The belts are made from brass-coated steel cords encased in a skim-stock rubber compound. These belts, along with the other tire components, are assembled into a "green tire," to which heat and pressure are applied in a process called "vulcanization." This process causes the components in the tire, including the skim stock, to chemically bond with each other. Plaintiffs contend that either a design or manufacturing defect in the skim stock prevented the belts of Fisher's tire from properly bonding. To secure evidence to prove this claim, plaintiffs requested Continental to produce the chemical formula for the skim stock used on this tire.

Continental objected, claiming that the formula is a trade secret that Texas Rule of Evidence 507 protects. After a hearing, the trial court ordered Continental to produce the formula, subject to a protective order which the trial court had earlier entered for other confidential material produced by Continental.

The trial court stayed its order pending Continental's efforts to obtain mandamus review. After the court of appeals denied relief, we granted Continental's mandamus petition and heard oral argument.

II.

Continental claims that the skim-stock formula is protected by Texas Rule of Evidence 507, which provides in full:

> A person has a privilege, which may be claimed by the person or the person's agent or employee, to refuse to disclose and to prevent other persons from disclosing a trade secret owned by the person, if the allowance of the privilege will not tend to conceal fraud or otherwise work injustice. When disclosure is directed, the judge shall take such protective measure as the interests of the holder of the privilege and of the parties and the furtherance of justice may require.

Tex. R. Evid. 507. This rule, adopted in 1983, is based on Supreme Court Standard 508, a proposed rule of evidence promulgated by the United States Supreme Court in 1969. *See* 3 McLaughlin, Weinstein's Federal Evidence § 508.01, at 508–5 (2d ed. 1998); *Preliminary Draft of Proposed Rules of Evidence for the United States District Courts and Magistrates*, 46 F.R.D. 161, 270 (1969). Although Congress did not adopt Standard 508 as a federal rule of evidence, *see* McLaughlin, *supra* at

508–5, twenty states, including Texas, have adopted some version of it.

This Court has never addressed the scope of Rule 507. Moreover, of the other jurisdictions adopting Supreme Court Standard 508, only two have directly considered its scope. *See Bridgestone/Firestone v. Superior Court*, 7 Cal. App. 4th 1384, 9 Cal. Rptr. 2d 709 (Cal. Ct. App. 1992); *Rare Coin-It, Inc. v. I.J.E., Inc.*, 625 So. 2d 1277 (Fla. Ct. App. 1993).

In *Bridgestone/Firestone*, the plaintiffs sued the tire manufacturer for wrongful death caused by a tire failure. Claiming that belt separation caused the tire failure, the plaintiffs sought to discover defendant's compound formula. Defendant asserted California's trade secret privilege, which is virtually identical to our Rule 507. *See* CAL. EVID. CODE § 1060. The trial court ordered defendant to produce the formula, and defendant sought interlocutory review.

The court of appeals, in analyzing the rule, first noted that a requesting party must establish more than mere relevance to discover trade secrets, or the statutory privilege would be "meaningless." 9 Cal. Rptr. 2d at 712. "Allowance of the trade secret privilege may not be deemed to 'work injustice' within the meaning of Evidence Code section 1060 simply because it would protect information generally relevant to the subject matter of an action or helpful to preparation of a case." *Id.* Rather, to show "injustice," the party seeking to discover a trade secret

> must make a prima facie, particularized showing that the information sought is relevant and necessary to the proof of, or defense against, a material element of one or more causes of action presented in the case, and that it is reasonable to conclude that the information sought is essential to a fair resolution of the lawsuit.

Id. at 713. The court perceived this as a balancing process, in which the trial court must weigh the interests of both sides and "must necessarily consider the protection afforded the holder of the privilege by a protective order as well as any less intrusive alternatives to disclosure proposed by the parties." *Id.* Applying these principles, the court noted that plaintiffs' expert, although averring generally that the formula could assist him in determining a defect, did not "describe with any precision how or why the formulas were a predicate to his ability to reach conclusions in the case." *Id.* at 716. The court thus determined that the information, although perhaps useful, was not necessary to the plaintiffs' claim. The court consequently denied the discovery.

Similarly, in *Rare Coin-It*, the court was called upon to interpret section 90.506 of the Florida Statutes, a trade secret privilege identical to ours. The court held:

> When trade secret privilege is asserted as the basis for resisting production, the trial court must determine whether the requested production constitutes a trade secret; if so, the court must require the party seeking production to show reasonable necessity for the requested materials.

625 So. 2d at 1278. *See also Inrecon v. Village Homes at Country Walk*, 644 So. 2d 103, 105 (Fla. Ct. App. 1994).

The approach adopted in California and Florida is consistent with the federal courts' treatment of trade secrets. Although Congress did not adopt Supreme Court Standard 508, the federal rules nonetheless allow a court, in the discovery context, to "make any order which justice requires to protect a party or person from . . . undue burden or expense, including . . . that a trade secret or other confidential research, development, or commercial information not be revealed or be revealed only in a designated way . . . ." FED. R. CIV. P. 26(c)(7). Federal courts applying this rule recognize that "there is no absolute privilege for trade secrets and similar confidential information." [citations omitted] Rather, federal courts apply a balancing test with shifting burdens, comparable to that articulated by the California appellate court in *Bridgestone/Firestone.*

In federal court, the party resisting discovery must establish that the information sought is indeed a trade secret and that disclosure would be harmful. The burden then shifts to the requesting party to establish that the information is "relevant and necessary" to his or her case. If the trial court orders disclosure, it should enter an appropriate protective order.

This is ultimately a balancing test, in which the trial court must weigh all pertinent facts and circumstances. *See* WRIGHT & MILLER, § 2043 at 559 ("[T]he burden is on the party seeking discovery to establish that the information is sufficiently relevant and necessary to his case to outweigh the harm disclosure would cause to the person from whom he is seeking the information."). *See also Centurion Indus., Inc. v. Warren Steurer & Associates*, 665 F.2d at 325 ("The district court must balance the need for the trade secrets against the claim of injury resulting from disclosure.").

III.

Our trade secret privilege seeks to accommodate two competing interests. First, it recognizes that trade secrets are an important property interest, worthy of protection. Second, it recognizes the importance we place on fair adjudication of lawsuits. *See* PRELIMINARY DRAFT OF PROPOSED RULES OF EVIDENCE, Advisory Committee's Note to Rule 5-08, 46 F.R.D. at 271 ("The need for accommodation between protecting trade secrets, on the one hand, and eliciting facts required for full and fair presentation of a case, on the other hand, is apparent."). Rule 507 accommodates both interests by requiring a party to disclose a trade secret only if necessary to prevent "fraud" or "injustice." Stated alternatively, disclosure is required only if necessary for a fair adjudication of the requesting party's claims or defenses.

We therefore hold that trial courts should apply Rule 507 as follows: First, the party resisting discovery must establish that the information is a trade secret. The burden then shifts to the requesting party to establish that the information is necessary for a fair adjudication of its claims. If the requesting party meets this burden, the trial court should ordinarily compel disclosure of the information, subject to an appropriate protective order.[3] In each circumstance, the trial court

[3] In this case, for example, the trial court limited access to the information to the parties in this lawsuit, their lawyers, consultants, investigators, experts and other necessary persons employed by counsel to assist in the preparation and trial of this case. Each person who is given access to the

must weigh the degree of the requesting party's need for the information with the potential harm of disclosure to the resisting party . . . .

V.

. . . Plaintiffs concede for purposes of this proceeding that the compound formula is a trade secret. The burden thus shifted to the plaintiffs to establish that the compound formula is necessary for a fair adjudication of this case. The only evidence that plaintiffs presented was deposition testimony from Continental's expert, Joseph Grant, that a compound that "doesn't have the right ingredients in it" could cause a belt separation. But Grant stated in his affidavit that the physical properties of a tire cannot be determined from an examination of a compound formula; rather, the finished tire itself must be tested. Further, plaintiffs do not contest Continental's assertions that the plaintiffs have no other manufacturers' compound formulas with which to compare Continental's formula. The plaintiffs contended at oral argument before this Court that their expert has found sulfur on the belt surfaces of this tire, and that plaintiffs need Continental's formula to determine whether sulfur is a regular component of the skim stock or whether it was a foreign material improperly introduced during manufacture. Regardless of whether this theory might otherwise justify discovery of the compound formula, an issue on which we express no opinion, plaintiffs presented no evidence supporting this theory to the trial court. Under these circumstances, given the highly proprietary nature of the information, the plaintiffs have not carried their burden under Rule 507 of demonstrating that the information is necessary for a fair trial.

We accordingly conclude that the trial court abused its discretion. Because the trial court has ordered Continental to produce privileged, trade secret information, Continental has no adequate remedy by appeal. *See Walker v. Packer*, 827 S.W.2d 833, 843 (Tex. 1992) . . . .

For the foregoing reasons, we conditionally grant mandamus relief directing the trial court to vacate its order compelling Continental to produce the belt skim-stock formula. We reiterate that nothing in our decision prohibits plaintiffs from seeking to discover the formula under the procedure we have set forth.

HANKINSON, J., did not participate in the decision.

PHYSICIAN-PATIENT AND MENTAL HEALTH INFORMATION

Texas created a physician-patient privilege and a comparable privilege protecting mental health information from disclosure when the Texas Rules of Evidence were adopted. Nevertheless, a party may be required to disclose medical and mental health records despite assertions of the physician/patient privilege pursuant to Evidence Rule 509 and the confidentiality of mental health information as provided in Evidence Rule 510. Exceptions to the medical and mental health privileges apply

documents must agree in writing to keep the information confidential, and all documents must be returned to Continental at the conclusion of the case.

when records sought to be discovered are relevant to a condition at issue relied on as part of any party's claim or defense. In this instance, the trial court, on request, is to perform an *in camera* inspection to assure the proper balancing of interest occurs before production is required. If a condition is part of a party's claim or defense, the patient records should be revealed only to the extent necessary to provide relevant evidence pertaining to the alleged condition. The Texas Supreme Court rejected the argument that the 1988 amendments to Evidence Rules 509(e)(4) and 510(d)(5) were meant solely to codify the *Ginsberg* offensive use doctrine, but rather represent "a significant departure from the historical scope of the patient-litigant privilege."

The exception terminates the privilege whenever any party relies upon the condition of the patient as part of its claim or defense even though the patient has not personally placed the condition at issue, and even though the patient is not a party to litigation. This interpretation will abrogate much of the control patients once exercised over the release of their medical records. *R.K. v. Ramirez*, 887 S.W.2d 836, 842 (Tex. 1994). However, in *Ramirez*, the Supreme Court explained the test for determining whether a party relies upon a medical or mental condition as part of the party's claim or defense for purpose of the litigation exception:

> Communications and records should not be subject to discovery if the patient's condition is merely an evidentiary or intermediate issue of fact, rather than an "ultimate" issue for a claim or defense, or if the condition is merely tangential to a claim rather than "central" to it . . . . As a general rule, a . . . condition will be a "part" of a claim or defense if the pleadings indicate that the jury must make a factual determination concerning the condition itself.

The medical records of non-parties were held to be discoverable within the Rule 509(d)(4) exception in *In re Whiteley*, 79 S.W.3d 729 (Tex. App. — Corpus Christi 2002, orig. proceeding). Defendant doctor based his defense on his extensive success with the procedure performed on plaintiff, thus making the records of those other patients relevant. This is a good example of a situation in which the records become discoverable even though the patient has not personally placed the condition at issue and in which the patient is not a party to the litigation. In contrast, the court in *In re Christus Health Southeast Texas*, 167 S.W.3d 596 (Tex. App. — Beaumont, 2005, orig. proceeding), found that non-party patients' records were not sufficiently central to the plaintiff's claims to be discoverable. Note that Tex. R. Civ. P. 196.1(c) requires a party seeking the medical records of a non-party to serve a copy of the request on the non-party if patient identity will be disclosed unless the court, on a showing of good cause, concludes that service is not required. The provisions of HIPAA, discussed below, will also affect the discoverability of medical records in litigation, particularly with respect to non-party medical records.

[c] Other Statutory Privileges

(1) *Hospital Committee Privilege.* In *Barnes v. Whittington*, 751 S.W.2d 493 (Tex. 1988), the Texas Supreme Court interpreted a statutory privilege granted to hospital committee records and proceedings. The Court held that this privilege protects only documents created by or at the direction of the committee for

committee purposes. Documents gratuitously submitted to the committee are not protected. Since *Barnes* was decided, the statutory hospital committee privilege has been recodified as Section 161.032 of the Health and Safety Code. The privileges from disclosure under the former Medical Practice Act (now recodified as Title 3 of the Occupations Code) extend to documents and files generated for and by a hospital credentialing committee in its investigation and review of a physician's initial application for staff privileges. *See Memorial Hospital-The Woodlands v. McCown*, 927 S.W.2d 1, 3 (Tex. 1996). The Court has limited the employment review facet of the medical peer review privilege to decisions regarding physicians, but extended the privilege to the work of both physician and non-physician health care workers when the committee is considering the quality of medical and health care services. *See In re Living Centers of Texas, Inc.*, 175 S.W.3d 253 (Tex. 2005) (also discussing privileges for medical committees, nursing peer review committees, and the quality assessment and assurance privilege).

(2) *Waiver of Statutory Committee Privileges*. In *In re The University of Texas Health Care Center*, 33 S.W.3d 822 (Tex. 2000), the Texas Supreme Court considered a claim that the Health Care Center had waived its privilege by answering an interrogatory in a way that included the recommendations of the peer review committee. The Texas Supreme Court rejected this argument, noting that section 5.06 of the former Medical Practice Act provided that only a committee may execute a waiver, and the waiver must be in writing. Therefore, "the voluntary production of information about the [Committee's] recommendations in response to a discovery request does not waive the privilege that protects the documents received, maintained, or developed by the committee from discovery." *Id.* at 827.

(3) *Public Health Statutes*. Various other public health statutes contain reporting and confidentiality requirements that might become relevant during discovery disputes. For example, the Communicable Disease Prevention and Control Act contains extensive reporting and confidentiality requirements concerning communicable disease test results. HEALTH & SAFETY C. § 81.103; *but see Gulf Coast Regional Blood Ctr. v. Houston*, 745 S.W.2d 557 (Tex. App. — Fort Worth 1988, orig. proceeding) (holding statute inapplicable to court proceedings).

In addition, another statute makes the medical and donor records of a blood bank confidential. *See* HEALTH & SAFETY C. § 162.003. However, the statute also provides that the blood bank may be required by a court of competent jurisdiction, after notice and hearing, to provide a recipient of blood from the blood bank with results of tests, with donor identification deleted, of the blood of every donor of blood transfused into the recipient. HEALTH & SAFETY C. § 162.010. Under certain circumstances, a court may order discovery relating to the donor. HEALTH & SAFETY C. § 162.011; *see also Gulf Coast Regional Blood Ctr. v. Houston*, 745 S.W.2d 557 (Tex. App. — Fort Worth 1988, orig. proceeding) (pre-statute case; order requiring blood center to identify blood donors in wrongful death action based on blood transfusion resulting in death from AIDS not violation of right to privacy); *Tarrant County Hosp. Dist. v. Hughes*, 734 S.W.2d 675 (Tex. App. — Fort Worth 1987, orig. proceeding) (same).

(4) *Health Insurance Portability and Accountability Act (HIPAA)*. In 1996, Congress passed a statute designed to provide a uniform minimum standard of

confidentiality for medical records. HIPAA requires the Department of Health and Human Services to issue regulations implementing the Act. HIPAA preempts state laws less protective of patient privacy than the federal act. One section of the regulations governs disclosures pursuant to court order or other discovery provision. 45 C.F.R. § 164.512(e) (2001).

HIPAA affects pretrial discovery and other mandated forms of disclosure in judicial and administrative proceedings. Under the regulations, a covered entity may disclose individually identifiable personal health information (PHI) in the course of any judicial or administrative proceeding only if certain requirements are met. 45 C.F.R. §§ 164.512(e)(i), (ii). In response to an order from the court or tribunal, it may disclose the PHI expressly authorized by the order (and only that information). In the absence of an order — for example, in response to a subpoena or other discovery request — the covered entity can disclose PHI if the party seeking the information provides "satisfactory assurance" 1) that the individual whose protected health information is in issue has been notified of the request; or 2) the party has made reasonable efforts to secure a proper qualified protective order (QPO). A QPO may come from a court, or may be agreed by the parties. It must prohibit use of the information for any purpose other than the litigation and must require the PHI (and all copies) to be returned to the covered entity at the end of the litigation.

HIPAA's requirements may arguably provide a party to litigation with a general duty to resist discovery until the requirements are met. For instance, in one case, a hospital included a claim of "HIPAA privilege" in its response to a discovery request. The plaintiff contended that de-identified information concerning nonparty patients was needed to dispute the hospital's defense that no beds had been available for the treatment of the plaintiff. Under the plaintiff's view, such information should have been discoverable under HIPAA exemptions. The court conditionally granted mandamus. *In re Christus Health Southeast Texas*, 167 S.W.3d 596, 598 (Tex. App. — Beaumont 2005, orig. proceeding). While the court's ultimate decision did not turn on the application of HIPAA, but rather on other discovery issues, it did note that the hospital "filed a response to the motion to compel entirely ignoring [plaintiff's] claim that HIPAA provided an exception to the general rule prohibiting disclosure of protected information." *Id.* It is likely that as time goes by there will be more litigation regarding the meaning and impact of HIPAA.

Although HIPAA does not create a private right of action, covered entities that were not parties to litigation have refused to disclose individually identifiable patient information, fearing penalties under state law or HIPAA. Courts so far have been willing to craft protective orders requiring disclosure of relevant health records to the parties involved in litigation while also protecting the privacy rights of non-parties. Some parties to litigation have also objected to the disclosure of health information, citing HIPAA. In these cases, the courts have been unwilling to permit a litigant to deny its opponent access to information relevant to the lawsuit. *See generally* Rebecca H. Bishop, Note, *The Final Patient Privacy Regulations Under the Health Insurance Portability and Accountability Act: Promoting Patient Privacy or Public Confusion?*, 37 GA. L. REV. 723 (2003). The federal Office of Civil Rights also has helpful information about the meaning and coverage of

HIPAA on its website, www.hhs.gov/ocr/hipaa.

The Texas Supreme Court has recently considered whether HIPAA affects litigation-related ex parte communications. In *In re Collins*, 286 S.W.3d 911 (Tex. 2009), Kelly Regian, the plaintiff in a medical malpractice case, argued that HIPAA prohibited defendant's counsel from conferring ex parte with her other treating physicians. (The plaintiff is required to disclose their identities and provide a release allowing the disclosure of medical records by § 74.052 of the Civil Practice and Remedies Code). The Court rejected this argument, saying:

> The Regians argue that, to the extent section 74.052(c) authorizes ex parte communications with non-party treating physicians, it is preempted by HIPAA. As we have said, we do not decide whether section 74.052(c) authorizes ex parte communications in every situation; instead, we hold that in this case, the Regians failed to make the showing necessary to obtain a protective order. In any event, however, HIPAA itself allows the disclosure of protected health information if the patient has executed a valid, written authorization conforming to the requirements of 45 C.F.R. § 164.508(c). 45 C.F.R. 164.508(a) (2008). The Regians do not dispute that the authorization Kelly signed conforms to those requirements. Rather, they contend the authorization is not a valid HIPAA release because it was not voluntary, as Kelly was required to sign it as a condition of bringing this suit.
>
> First, while it is true that the Regians could not have proceeded with their suit if Kelly had not executed the authorization, it was their choice to file the suit in the first instance. . . . HIPAA preempts state law only if it would be impossible for a covered entity to comply with both the state and federal requirement, or if it would undermine HIPAA's purposes. While several courts have held that HIPAA preempts state law procedures that would allow ex parte contacts between health care providers and defendants and their representatives, none of them involve situations in which the patient has executed a written release compliant with 45 C.F.R. § 164.508. Because section 74.052(c) authorizes disclosure under the exact same terms as 45 C.F.R. § 164.508, it would not be impossible for a health care provider to comply with both laws. Moreover, while the privacy of medical information is the primary goal of the privacy rules, the rules balance that interest against other important needs. Reducing the costs of medical care is a concern underlying both HIPAA and section 74.052(c). In this case, the legislatively prescribed form authorizes disclosure only to the extent the information would "facilitate the investigation and evaluation" or defense of the health care claim described in the Regians' notice. TEX. CIV. PRAC. & REM. CODE § 74.052(c). Accordingly, under the circumstances presented, we conclude that HIPAA does not preempt section 74.052(c).

Id. at 920.

(5) *Lobbying Activities.* The Government Code prohibits the public disclosure of a written or otherwise recorded communication from a citizen of Texas to a member of the legislature unless either party authorizes disclosure. Gov. C. § 306.004. This provision was held to prevent discovery in a civil case of documents submitted to

lobbyists for use in advocating legislation and copies of documents distributed to state representatives in support of proposed legislation. *Inwood West Civic Ass'n v. Touchy*, 754 S.W.2d 276, 278 (Tex. App. — Houston [14th Dist.] 1988, orig. proceeding) (homeowners' associations denied discovery of Houston Cable's lobbying efforts in support of law giving cable companies free access to utility easements across private property).

(6) *Reporter's Privilege.* In 2009, the legislature adopted a statutory provision recognizing a qualified testimonial privilege for journalists. *See* C.P.R.C. chapter 22 (civil cases). Section 22.023 provides that compulsory process may not be used to "compel a journalist to testify regarding or to produce or disclose in an official proceeding: (1) any confidential or nonconfidential information, document, or item obtained or prepared while acting as a journalist; or (2) the source of any information, document, or item described by Subdivision (1)." Communication service providers and news media receive the same protection. However, the person seeking the protected information may overcome the privilege by making a "clear and specific showing" that all reasonable efforts have been exhausted to try to get the information from alternate sources, and that "the interest of the party subpoenaing the information outweighs the public interest in gathering and dissemination of news, including the concerns of the journalist." C.P.R.C. § 22.024. The subpoena must not be overbroad, and may not be used to obtain peripheral, nonessential, or speculative information. Rather, the information, document or item must be "relevant and material to the proper administration" of the proceeding in which it is sought." In case that is not emphatic enough, the statute goes on to require that, in order to overcome the privilege, the information sought must be "essential to the maintenance of a claim or defense of the person seeking the testimony, production, or disclosure." *Id.* The statute also provides a procedure to be used to litigate these privilege claims, and requires that the privilege holder be given adequate notice and an opportunity to respond.

(7) *Public Information Act.* The Public Information Act provides for public access to a wide variety of public information maintained by government bodies. *See* Gov. C. § 552.001 et seq. Certain types of information are exempt from the public disclosure requirement. These exceptions from disclosure do not create new privileges from discovery, nor is the Act intended to affect the scope of discovery under the Texas Rules of Civil Procedure. Gov. C. § 552.005. Nevertheless, the Texas Supreme Court has created some privileges based on exceptions to the Act. For example, information held by law enforcement agencies and prosecutors relating to their criminal investigations is privileged from discovery in civil actions against the officers or prosecutors. *Hobson v. Moore*, 734 S.W.2d 340, 341 (Tex. 1987).

(8) *Electronic Communications Privacy Act.* In a recent case, the plaintiffs sought production of a copy of computer backup tapes belonging to defendant CI Host, Inc. The trial court had ordered CI Host to produce the tapes over CI Host's objection that the ECPA protected the information. At the first discovery hearing, CI Host presented no evidence to support its objection. At a second hearing, it presented only summary affidavits and conceded that some information on the tapes were not protected by the ECPA. The trial court therefore did not abuse its discretion in overruling the objection and ordering the tapes produced. Because the discovery dispute involved potentially private information, the Texas Supreme

Court remanded the case to the trial court to consider how to best address the privacy of CI Host's customers. *In re CI Host, Inc.*, 92 S.W.3d 514 (Tex. 2002).

§ 9.04 WAIVER OF PRIVILEGES

[A] Offensive Use

Even when a party has a privilege to withhold certain material, that privilege can be waived. Sometimes the waiver results from the party's failure to properly assert or prove the privilege. That situation is discussed in [B], below. A party can also lose a privilege by making offensive use of privileged material.

Privileges are created to shield particular kinds of private communications from disclosure in a lawsuit. However, the courts have sometimes found it unacceptable for a party to create a situation in which the privileged information is relevant, but then refuse to disclose that information, claiming privilege. In other words, an evidentiary privilege is intended to be a "shield" but not a "sword," and a person who makes his own privileged communication relevant in the lawsuit may find that he or she has waived that privilege.

Texas first addressed this issue in the context of a psychotherapist-patient privilege. In *Ginsberg v. Fifth Court of Appeals*, 686 S.W.2d 105 (Tex. 1985), the Texas Supreme Court held that when medical records concerning communications between the plaintiff and her psychiatrist regarding a business transaction that was the subject matter of her claim against the discovering party were relevant, the court was within its discretion to hold the medical records discoverable. In *Republic Insurance Co. v. Davis*, 856 S.W.2d 158 (Tex. 1993), the Court applied the doctrine to the attorney-client privilege and articulated a three-pronged test for its application. First, the party asserting the privilege will waive it only if the party is seeking affirmative relief (filing a declaratory judgment action is not seeking affirmative relief). Second, the privileged information must be such that the information, if believed by the fact finder, in all probability would be outcome determinative. It is not enough that the privileged information is relevant, or even that it contradicts a position the party is taking in the current lawsuit. Third, disclosure of the privileged communication must be the only means by which the aggrieved party may obtain the evidence. Texas thus has adopted a more limited "offensive use" waiver than many states, and shaped it so that plaintiffs are more likely than defendants to find that they have waived a privilege by putting the privileged information in issue. *Compare* Richard L. Marcus, *The Perils of Privilege: Waiver and the Litigator*, 84 MICH. L. REV. 1605 (1986), *with* Elizabeth G. Thornburg, *Attorney-Client Privilege: Issue-Related Waivers*, 50 J. AIR L. & COM. 1039 (1985).

The Texas Supreme Court has also discussed the proper procedure to follow when deciding the appropriate sanction for offensive use. *See Texas Dep't of Public Safety Officers Ass'n v. Denton*, 897 S.W.2d 757 (Tex. 1995) (suggesting several factors to consider and requiring that, as with any sanction, a direct relationship must exist between the offensive conduct and the sanction imposed). *See also* James L. Cornell, *Piercing the Iron Curtain of Silence: The Doctrine of Offensive*

Use Waiver, 60 Tex. B.J. 304 (April 1997).

[B] Not a Waiver of Privileges: Inadvertent Production

Read Tex. R. Civ. P. 193.3(d); Tex. R. Evid. 512.

A claim of privilege is not defeated by a disclosure that was compelled erroneously. Tex. R. Evid. 512. The privilege is also not defeated if the disclosure was made without an opportunity to claim the privilege. Tex. R. Evid. 512.

A claim that the disclosure was inadvertent does not fall within either of these exceptions. The discovery rules have a specific provision concerning the inadvertent production of privileged documents. A party who produces material or information "without intending to waive a claim of privilege" does not waive the privilege claim if the producing party amends the response, identifies the material or information produced, and states the privilege asserted. Note that the emphasis is on the intent to *waive*, not the intent to *produce* the material. The amended response must be served within 10 days, or a shorter time if ordered by the court, after the producing party actually discovers the inadvertent production. If the producing party amends the response to assert a privilege, the requesting party must promptly return the specified information or material and any copies, subject to any ruling by the court denying the privilege claim. Tex. R. Civ. P. 193.3(d).

Although a party does not have an obligation to notify an opponent that apparently privileged information was inadvertently disclosed, the party should be aware of the implication of the timing rules. For example, if the party holding the material discloses the inadvertent production for the first time at trial, his or her opposing party may demand its return at that time and will preserve the privilege by doing so. *Warrantech Corp. v. Computer Adapters Services, Inc.*, 134 S.W.3d 516 (Tex. App. — Fort Worth 2004, no pet.) (party successfully asserted privilege at trial for document inadvertently produced three years earlier).

These anti-waiver provisions become more complex when the inadvertent production is made to a party's own testifying expert witness rather than directly to an opponent. In the following case, the Texas Supreme Court discusses the fate of documents that had been protected as work product but which were provided to a testifying expert. See if you can state the basis for the court's holding: is it based on the language of the rules or on broader principles of discovery?

IN RE CHRISTUS SPOHN HOSPITAL

222 S.W.3d 434 (Tex. 2007)

SNAP BACK PROVISION

O'Neill, J.

In this medical malpractice mandamus proceeding, the defendant hospital seeks to recover privileged documents that were mistakenly provided to its designated testifying expert witness. We must decide whether Texas Rule of Civil Procedure 193.3(d), known as the "snap-back" provision, preserves the privilege over Rule 192.3(e)(6)'s mandate that all documents provided to a testifying expert are discoverable. We hold that the inadvertent nature of the production in this case preserved the privilege under Rule 193.3(d) and entitled the hospital to recover the documents upon realizing its mistake, provided the hospital's designated expert does not testify at trial. The hospital has not attempted to name another testifying expert, instead indicating an intent to rely upon the expert to whom the documents were disclosed. So long as the hospital stands upon its testifying expert designation, Rule 192's plain language and purpose and the policy considerations that surrounded its amendment compel the conclusion that the documents may not be snapped back. Accordingly, we deny the hospital's petition for writ of mandamus without prejudice to any right the hospital might have to designate another testifying expert and recover the privileged documents.

I. Background

When Mona Palmer notified Christus Spohn Hospital Kleberg of her intent to file a health care liability claim arising out of her daughter Brandi Lee Palmer's death, the Hospital's internal investigator, Sandra Northcutt, conducted an investigation. That investigation generated a number of documents, labeled "CONFIDENTIAL COMMUNICATION PREPARED IN ANTICIPATION OF LITIGATION," which form the basis of this mandamus action. The Northcutt documents include Northcutt's memoranda summarizing her interviews with Hospital employees and her correspondence to and from Hospital counsel. A paralegal newly employed by the Hospital's counsel sent the Northcutt documents to the Hospital's only expert witness on standard-of-care issues, Nurse Kendra Menzies. According to the Hospital's counsel, the paralegal had recently moved to Texas from California, where she understood that all materials forwarded to an expert witness remained confidential. She assumed the same rule applied in Texas.

Menzies' expert report on Brandi Lee Palmer listed the documents she reviewed in forming her opinion; the Northcutt documents do not appear on that list. Plaintiff's counsel sought to depose Menzies, and issued a subpoena duces tecum requesting all documents furnished to and reviewed by Menzies in connection with her consultation in the lawsuit. Among the materials Menzies brought to the deposition were the Northcutt documents. This was the first time that the Hospital's and Palmer's counsel learned the privileged documents had been forwarded to Menzies. When questioned about the documents that had been transmitted to her, Menzies testified, "I didn't read every bit. But, yes, I glanced through everything in the box."

The Hospital filed an "Objection, Assertion of Privilege, and Motion to Return Privileged Documents" pursuant to Rule 193.3(d) of the Texas Rules of Civil Procedure, known as the "snap-back" provision, seeking to recover the documents mistakenly produced to Menzies. At the hearing on this issue, Menzies testified by affidavit that she did not read the documents but rather "glanced" at them "merely to identify what they were," and upon determining that they were not relevant to her needs, "tossed them back in the box." The trial court overruled the Hospital's claim of privilege, stating it was "unclear that [Menzies] did not see certain specified documents." The court of appeals denied the Hospital's request for mandamus relief. We granted the Hospital's request for mandamus review to consider the application of Rule 193.3(d)'s snap-back provision to the Northcutt documents. Mandamus is appropriate if we conclude that the documents are in fact privileged and have been improperly ordered disclosed by the trial court. *See In re Bass*, 113 S.W.3d 735, 738 (Tex. 2003).

II. Discussion

A. The Parties' Arguments

The Hospital claims the Northcutt documents were created or generated in connection with the Hospital's internal investigation conducted in anticipation of litigation; therefore, the work-product privilege shields them from discovery. *See* Tex. R. Civ. P. 192.5(a), (b). According to the Hospital, the privilege was not lost when the documents were transmitted to Menzies because waiver can only occur when privileged documents are voluntarily and knowingly disclosed, not when disclosure is inadvertent. The Hospital claims this principle is embodied in Rule 193.3(d)'s snap-back provision, which mandates the return of privileged documents that have been inadvertently produced. Because it properly invoked Rule 193.3(d)'s snap-back provision, the Hospital argues, the trial court erred in determining that the privilege was waived. The Hospital further contends that Rule 192.3(e)(6), which mandates disclosure of all documents provided to a testifying expert, is not implicated because the Northcutt documents were not "prepared by or for the expert," and even if they were, Menzies did not read them. Tex. R. Civ. P. 192.3(c). Under these circumstances, the Hospital claims, the snap-back rule that protects the work-product privilege against inadvertent disclosure prevails.

For purposes of this appeal, Palmer does not dispute the privileged nature of the documents, nor does she challenge the Hospital's assertion that it complied with the snap-back procedures that Rule 193.3(d) requires for the return of inadvertently produced documents. Rather, Palmer contends Rule 193.3(d)'s snap-back provision does not apply to information that Rule 192.3 makes discoverable once it is provided to a testifying expert. Palmer further challenges the Hospital's statement that Menzies did not "read" the inadvertently transmitted documents, arguing a fact issue exists regarding the extent of her review. In any event, Palmer contends, whether or not Menzies actually relied upon the documents in forming her opinion is not dispositive, because implicit in Rule 192.3's disclosure requirement is the notion that documents an expert chooses to regard and those she chooses to disregard in forming an opinion are both relevant and necessary for effective cross-examination.

We begin by examining the discovery rules in dispute, applying the same rules of construction that govern the interpretation of statutes. *See BASF Fina Petrochemicals Ltd. v. H.B. Zachry*, 168 S.W.3d 867, 871 (Tex. App. — Houston [1st Dist.] 2004, pet. denied); *see also In re Emeritus Corp.*, 179 S.W.3d 112, 114 (Tex. App. — San Antonio 2005, orig. proceeding) (holding that a rule of procedure is subject to the same rules of construction as statutes). When a rule of procedure is clear and unambiguous, we construe the rule's language according to its plain or literal meaning. *See Texas Dep't of Transp. v. Needham*, 82 S.W.3d 314, 318 (Tex. 2002).

B. Discovery from Testifying Experts

Texas Rule of Civil Procedure 192.3(e), which defines the scope of permissible discovery from experts, provides in pertinent part as follows:

> A party may discover the following information regarding a testifying expert . . .
>
> (3) the facts known by the expert that relate to or form the basis of the expert's mental impressions and opinions formed or made in connection with the case in which the discovery is sought, regardless of when and how the factual information was acquired; (4) the expert's mental impressions and opinions formed or made in connection with the case in which discovery is sought, and any methods used to derive them; (5) any bias of the witness; (6) *all documents*, tangible things, reports, models, or data compilations *that have been provided to, reviewed by, or prepared by or for the expert in anticipation of a testifying expert's testimony* . . . .

TEX. R. CIV. P. 192.3(e) (emphasis added). We must first decide whether this rule applies to the Northcutt documents; if it does not, the documents retain their privileged nature and may be recovered pursuant to Rule 193.3(d)'s snap-back feature.

Rule 192.3(e)(6) was promulgated in 1999 to replace former Rule 166b, which permitted discovery of only those "documents . . . prepared by an expert or for an expert in anticipation of the expert's trial and deposition testimony." TEX. R. CIV. P. 166b(2)(e)(2) (repealed). Under this former rule, privileged work product lost its protected status if the material provided to the expert was, in fact, relied upon by the expert as the basis for his or her testimony. *See D.N.S. v. Schattman*, 937 S.W.2d 151, 156 (Tex. App. — Fort Worth 1997, orig. proceeding) (noting that privilege is waived when an expert relies on a privileged document as the basis for the expert's opinion); *Aetna Cas. & Sur. Co. v. Blackmon*, 810 S.W.2d 438, 440 (Tex. App. — Corpus Christi 1991, orig. proceeding) (holding that an expert witness's possession of documents did not automatically waive attorney-client and work-product privileges). Thus, under the pre-amendment rule, if an expert did not rely on a privileged document, it was not discoverable.

To avoid the discovery disputes that frequently arose over what material an expert may or may not have relied upon, the rule was amended in 1999 to include more expansive language. In addition to documents "prepared by or for the expert," the rule now mandates discovery of documents "that have been provided to, [or] reviewed by" a testifying expert. TEX. R. CIV. P. 192.3(e)(6). The Hospital's argument that the Northcutt documents were prepared by or for the Hospital rather than by or for the expert, and that Menzies did not read them in any event, erroneously ignores the rule's disjunctive language. Whether or not the documents were actually "read" by or prepared for Menzies, they were clearly "provided to" the Hospital's testifying expert and thus fall within Rule 192.3(e)(6)'s plain language.

It is true, as the Hospital claims and Palmer does not dispute, that the Northcutt documents constitute work product under Rule 192.5, and that work product is carefully protected from discovery under our rules. TEX. R. CIV. P. 192.5(a)(1), (2). However, Rule 192.5(c)(1) specifically states that work product loses its protected status when it is provided to a testifying expert:

> (c) Even if made or prepared in anticipation of litigation or for trial, the following is not work product protected from discovery:
>
> (1) information discoverable under Rule 192.3 concerning experts . . . .

TEX. R. CIV. P. 192.5(c)(1). Because the Northcutt documents were provided to the Hospital's testifying expert, the work-product privilege does not protect them unless the snap-back provision requires their return.

C. The Snap-Back Provision

The snap-back provision was designed to protect the inadvertent disclosure of privileged material in order to reduce the cost and risk involved in document production. TEX. R. CIV. P. 193 cmt. 4. The snap-back provision states that:

> A party who produces material or information without intending to waive a claim of privilege does not waive that claim under these rules or the Rules of Evidence if — within ten days or a shorter time ordered by the court, after the producing party actually discovers that such production was made — the producing party amends the response, identifying the material or information produced and stating the privilege asserted.

TEX. R. CIV. P. 193.3(d). The rule is focused on the intent to waive the privilege, not the intent to produce the material or information. *Id.* at cmt. 4.

The snap-back provision has typically been applied when a party inadvertently produces privileged documents to an opposing party. *See Warrantech Corp. v. Computer Adapters Servs.*, 134 S.W.3d 516, 525 (Tex. App. — Forth Worth 2004, no pet.) (holding that inadvertent production of privileged letter to opposing counsel did not waive the privilege under Rule 193.3(d)); *see also In re Parnham*, 2006 Tex. App. LEXIS 8252 (Tex. App. — Houston [1st Dist.] 2006, orig. proceeding) (applying snap-back rule when privileged documents were inadvertently provided to opposing counsel during discovery); *In re AEP Tex. Cent. Co.*, 128 S.W.3d 687, 693–94 (Tex. App. — San Antonio 2003, orig. proceeding) (holding that privileged legal memorandum inadvertently produced to the opposing side must be returned under the snap-back provision). In this case, however, the privileged material was produced by a party to its own testifying expert, invoking Rule 192.3(e)(6)'s overlapping directive that all materials provided to a testifying expert must be produced.

The tension between the snap-back provision that protects privileged documents and the expert-disclosure requirement presents an issue of first impression for our Court. In resolving this tension, we consider the respective interests the rules were designed to protect.

D. Competing Interests

As we have said, the snap-back provision was designed to ensure that important privileges are not waived by mere inadvertence or mistake. Under the rule, a party who is less than diligent in screening documents before their production does not waive any privilege that might attach to them, presuming the party complies with Rule 193.3(d)'s procedures. TEX. R. CIV. P. 193.3(d) cmt. 4. By permitting the recovery of documents inadvertently produced to the opposing side, the rule preserves the important interests that the work-product doctrine was designed to protect, while at the same time visiting no harm upon the recipient for having to return documents it was not entitled to in the first place. Under Rule 193.3(d), the production of documents without the intent to waive a claim of privilege does not waive the claim.

The concepts of waiver and the intent required to effect it, however, do not appear in our testifying-expert disclosure rule. *See* TEX. R. CIV. P. 192.5(c)(1). Rule 192.5, which governs work product, speaks not in terms of waiver but rather states that documents and tangible things provided to a testifying expert under Rule 192.3, "even if made or prepared in anticipation of litigation or for trial . . . *is not work product* protected from discovery." *Id.* (emphasis added). Thus, it appears from the rule's plain language that documents and tangible things provided to a testifying expert lose their work-product designation irrespective of the intent that accompanied their production.[2] This makes sense in light of the important interests the expert-production requirement was designed to serve.

The expert witness occupies a unique place in our adversarial system of justice. *See E.I. du Pont de Nemours & Co. v. Robinson*, 923 S.W.2d 549, 553 (Tex. 1995). Considered to have "knowledge, skill, experience, training, or education," that will "assist the trier of fact to understand the evidence or to determine a fact in issue," the expert is generally held out to be, and is seen by the jury as, an objective authority figure more knowledgeable and credible than the typical lay witness. *See Robinson*, 923 S.W.2d at 553. For this reason, juries are prone to rely on experts to tell them how to decide complex issues without independently analyzing underlying factors. *See id.* As the Supreme Court has noted, " '[e]xpert evidence can be both powerful and quite misleading because of the difficulty in evaluating it.' " *Daubert v. Merrell Dow Pharms., Inc.*, 509 U.S. 579, 595 (1993) (quoting Jack B. Weinstein, *Rule 702 of the Federal Rules of Evidence Is Sound; It Should Not Be Amended*, 138 F.R.D. 631, 631 (1991)).

Coupled with the expert's vast potential for influence is the fact that experts are generally unfettered by firsthand-knowledge requirements that constrain the ordinary witness. While lay witnesses may only testify regarding matters of which they have personal knowledge, expert witnesses may testify about facts or data not personally perceived but "reviewed by, or made known" to them. If the facts or data are of a type upon which experts in the field reasonably rely in forming opinions on the subject, the facts or data need not even be admissible in evidence. Thus, in many instances, experts may rely on inadmissible hearsay, privileged communications, and other information that the ordinary witness may not. Moreover, an expert may state an opinion on mixed questions of law and fact, such as whether certain conduct was negligent or proximately caused injury, that would be off limits to the ordinary witness.

Armed with these advantages, the expert witness paints a powerful image on the litigation canvas. And it is typically the hiring attorney who selects the materials

[2] We note that only documents are at issue in this case. No discovery request regarding whether the Hospital's counsel provided information to Menzies orally is before us, and we voice no opinion on whether such discovery would be permitted.

that will provide color and hue. Just as a purveyor of fine art must examine the medium used in order to distinguish masterpiece from fake, a jury must understand the pallet from which the expert paints to accurately assess the testimony's worth. Given the importance that expert testimony can assume, the jury should be aware of documents and tangible things provided to the expert that might have influenced the expert's opinion. In terms of determining what effect documents provided to an expert had in shaping the expert's mental impressions and opinions, the attorney's intent in producing the documents is irrelevant.

In light of these important policy concerns that underlie the expert-disclosure rule, we conclude that Rules 192.3(e)(6) and 192.5(c)(1) prevail over Rule 193.3(d)'s snap-back provision so long as the expert intends to testify at trial despite the inadvertent document production. That is, once privileged documents are disclosed to a testifying expert, and the party who designated the expert continues to rely upon that designation for trial, the documents may not be retrieved even if they were inadvertently produced. Of course, inadvertently produced material that could not by its nature have influenced the expert's opinion does not evoke the concerns the expert-disclosure rule was designed to prevent and the policy concerns underlying the rule's disclosure requirement would presumably never arise. In that event, there would be nothing to prevent the snap-back rule's application, although we note that a party seeking snap-back under such circumstances would bear a heavy burden in light of the disclosure rule's underlying purpose.

Our holding comports with federal case law interpreting the federal expert-disclosure rule, which is similar to our own.

E. The Federal Rule

Before the federal expert-disclosure rule was amended in 1993, interpretation of the rule's disclosure requirement was generally mixed. Some courts favored a protective approach, precluding discovery unless the party seeking production could demonstrate a substantial need for the material in preparing the case and show that obtaining equivalent material elsewhere would be unduly hard. . . .

Changes to the federal rules in 1993, like the amendment to our own rule thereafter, significantly increased the scope of permissible discovery from expert witnesses. Federal Rule of Civil Procedure 26(a)(2)(B) now provides for the disclosure of information "considered by" an expert in forming an opinion. Fed. R. Civ. P. 26(a)(2)(B). The Advisory Committee notes state that "[g]iven this obligation of disclosure, litigants should no longer be able to argue that materials furnished to their experts to be used in forming their opinions — whether or not ultimately relied upon by the expert — are privileged or otherwise protected from disclosure when such persons are testifying or being deposed." At least with respect to testifying experts, "[i]t appears that counsel should now expect that any written or tangible data provided to testifying experts will have to be disclosed." 8 Charles A. Wright, Arthur R. Miller & Richard L. Marcus, Federal Practice & Procedure: Civil §§ 2016.2, 2031.1 (1994).

Since the rule change, the overwhelming weight of federal authority interprets the rule to favor full disclosure, requiring the protections afforded attorney work product to yield to the interests that arise once privileged material is disclosed to the testifying expert. In *TV-3, Inc. v. Royal Insurance Co. of America*, 193 F.R.D. 490 (S.D. Miss. 2000), for example, the court drew a "bright line" in favor of discovery:

> [O]nly the most naive of experienced lawyers or judges could fail to realize that in our present legal culture money plus the proper "marching orders" will get an "expert" witness who will undertake to prove most anything. The courts and the Fifth Circuit Court of Appeals in particular have begun to wrestle with ways to put some bridle on this legal phenomenon. *See, e.g., Daubert v. Merrell Dow Pharmaceuticals, Inc.*, 509 U.S. 579 (1993). It is most consistent with this trend to say that when an attorney hires an expert both the expert's compensation and his "marching orders" can be discovered and the expert cross-examined thereon. If the lawyer's "marching orders" are reasonable and fair, the lawyer and his client have little to fear. If the orders are in the nature of telling the expert what he is being paid to conclude, appropriate discovery and cross-examination thereon should be the consequence. Such a ruling is most consistent with an effort to keep expert opinion testimony fair, reliable and within the bounds of reason.

Id. at 492 (citation omitted). While these cases did not involve inadvertent disclosure, the courts' policy analysis would apply irrespective of counsel's intent in producing the documents. . . .

G. The Northcutt Documents

Having determined that our expert-disclosure rules preclude the snap-back of documents inadvertently produced so long as the expert remains designated to testify at trial, we must decide whether the Hospital's claim that Menzies did not read the documents affects our analysis. According to the Hospital, Menzies did not sufficiently review the Northcutt documents such that Rule 192.3(e)(6) requires their disclosure. In order to waive the privilege, the Hospital claims, the documents must have been used in arriving at the expert's mental impressions and opinions.

As we have said, Rule 192.3(e)(6) requires the production of "all documents . . . that have been *provided to*, reviewed by, *or* prepared by or for the expert . . . ." TEX. R. CIV. P. 192.3(e)(6) (emphasis added). By disjunctively requiring the production of documents "provided to" the expert, our rule appears to be broader than the federal rule, which mandates disclosure of information that is "considered by the witness in forming the opinions." FED. R. CIV. P. 26(a)(2)(B). Thus, the Hospital's claim that Menzies did not sufficiently consider the documents to warrant their production is immaterial.

We note that an expert's choice not to utilize certain information does not necessarily mean that the information plays no part in forming the expert's opinion. Materials both accepted and rejected by an expert are indicative of the process by which the expert went about forming his or her opinion and may provide an effective basis for cross-examination. *See* Plunkett, 69 TEMP. L. REV. at 480 ("[A] litigant can most effectively cross-examine an opposing expert by confronting that expert with a relevant piece of evidence upon which he or she did not rely. Materials rejected by an expert, therefore, also form part of the basis of the expert's opinion."); *In re Air*

Crash Disaster at Stapleton Int'l Airport, 720 F. Supp. 1442, 1444 (D. Colo. 1988) (stating that "[i]n forming an opinion, an expert 'relies' upon material he finds unpersuasive as well as material supporting his ultimate position"); *Eliasen v. Hamilton*, 111 F.R.D. 396, 400 n.5 (N.D. Ill. 1986) (noting that documents an expert both relies upon and rejects are important for cross-examination). In *Tracy*, for example, the Supreme Court of Missouri rejected the notion that an expert must rely on a document for it to be subject to the disclosure rule, stating:

> [t]o hold otherwise would allow the expert witness or the party retaining the expert witness to select which documents to produce after the expert has reviewed the documents in preparation for the expert's testimony. It is appropriate, at deposition or trial, to cross-examine an expert witness as to information provided to the expert that may contradict or weaken the bases for his or her opinion regardless of whether the expert relied upon or considered the information.

State ex rel. Tracy v. Dandurand, 30 S.W.3d at 835 (citations omitted); *see also Karn v. Ingersoll Rand*, 168 F.R.D. at 635 (stating that " '[c]onsidered,' which simply means 'to take into account,' clearly invokes a broader spectrum of thought than the phrase 'relied upon,' which requires dependence on the information"). Moreover, the fact that an expert chooses to ignore certain materials that have been provided may indicate a bias on the expert's part, or a proclivity toward a predetermined result. *See* Easton, 32 Ariz. St. L.J. at 563–64; *see also United States v. City of Torrance*, 163 F.R.D. 590, 594 (C.D. Cal. 1995) (stating that "the documents considered but rejected by the expert trial witness could be even more important for cross-examination than those actually relied upon by him").

In this case, when questioned about her review of the Northcutt documents, Menzies testified: "I didn't read every bit. But, yes, I glanced through everything in the box." In her Affidavit attached to the Hospital's First Amended Objection, Menzies attested:

> Any other documents or materials contained in that box I glanced at merely to identify what they were and when I recognized that they were not something that I would need or want to read, I tossed them back into the box. I did not, under any circumstances, read or rely upon any of the following in the formulation of my opinions, nor in the preparation of my report . . . .
>
> Frankly, I did not even know that they were in the box until Mr. Todd Taylor, at my deposition, taken on August 16, 2004, took them from my box, showed them to me and asked me if I had read or relied upon any information contained therein. It is my recollection that I testified as testifying here, that I did not.

After considering Menzies' testimony, the trial court stated that its decision to deny the Hospital's objection was based not only on delivery of the documents to Menzies, but also on her testimony "that she reviewed and glanced at some of the documents — at the documents in the box." Based on her testimony, the trial court concluded it was "unclear that she did not see certain specified documents."

We agree that it is unclear from the record to what extent Menzies reviewed the

Northcutt documents, although at the very least she "glanced" at them "to identify what they were." The plain language of Rule 192.3(e)(6) makes it immaterial whether she reviewed the documents; they were discoverable because they were provided to her. Under these circumstances, the trial court did not abuse its discretion in denying the request of the Hospital, which continued to rely upon Menzies as its testifying expert, for return of the documents.

We are sympathetic to the Hospital's concerns over losing valuable work-product protections when documents are produced to a testifying expert by mistake. But the producing party in such a situation is not without a remedy. An attorney who discovers that privileged documents have been inadvertently provided to a testifying expert may presumably withdraw the expert's designation and name another. *See Tracy*, 30 S.W.3d at 835–36. Although such a course may entail additional expense and perhaps delay, these concerns do not outweigh countervailing concerns that require full disclosure from an expert who will testify. If leave of court is necessary for an alternative designation — when, for example, the expert designation deadline has passed — courts should carefully weigh the alternatives available to prevent what may be akin to a death-penalty sanction for the party forced to trial without a necessary expert. The Hospital did not pursue such a course in this case, however, and we voice no opinion on the trial court's discretion in that regard.

Finally, the Hospital contends that, even if discoverable for purposes of deposing Menzies, the Northcutt documents should otherwise retain their privilege and not be used for other purposes or at trial. Since Menzies has already been questioned about the documents, the Hospital argues, their discovery should be confined to that context. Specifically, the Hospital seeks to quash Sandra Northcutt's deposition, which has been postponed pursuant to the parties' agreement pending the outcome of this mandamus proceeding. We decline to opine on the potential admissibility of the Northcutt documents at trial, as that issue is premature. And in light of Rule 192.5(c)'s provision that information discoverable under Rule 192.3 "is not work product protected from discovery," we cannot say that the trial court abused its discretion in denying the Hospital's motion to quash Sandra Northcutt's deposition.

NOTES AND QUESTIONS

(1) *Snap Back and Production by Non-Parties.* The Beaumont Court of Appeals considered another variant on the "snap back" rule: what if the person who produced the documents is not a party to the lawsuit? *In re Certain Underwriters at Lloyds of London*, 294 S.W.3d 891, 902-03 (Tex. App. — Beaumont 2009, orig. proceeding), involved a discovery dispute in which notes reflecting conversations between a consultant and an attorney were produced by the consultant in response to a subpoena duces tecum for a deposition. After holding that the notes were protected by the work product doctrine, the court considered whether their production had waived the privilege. The discovering party argued that it had not, quoting the language of Rule 193.3(d): "A *party* who produces material or information without intending to waive a claim of privilege does not waive that claim under these rules or the Rules of Evidence if — within ten days or a shorter time ordered by the court, after the producing party actually discovers that such production was made — the producing party amends the response, identifying the

material or information produced and stating the privilege asserted." (emphasis added). Reading the rule literally, it applies only if a "party" produces the material, and if "party" means "litigant," the person who produced the privileged documents was not a party.

In order to protect privilege holders, the court read the word "party" broadly, and found that the snap back provisions applied in this case. Thus, so long as the privilege holders followed the procedures outlined in rule 193.3, they could reclaim their privileged documents.

A Houston court reached a different conclusion in *In re Oturno*, 2008 Tex. App. LEXIS 3396, at *5 (Tex. App. — Houston [14th Dist.] 2008, orig. proceeding). In *Ortuno*, the Fourteenth Court of Appeals reasoned that Rule 193.3 could not be used to remedy the production of a patient's privileged medical record because the record had been produced by a nonparty to the suit, a hospital.

(2) *When Does It Stop Being Work Product?* The Court in *Christus* states that material provided to a testifying expert witness is not work product. Therefore, the snap-back provisions of Rule 193.3(d) do not apply — the materials supplied to the expert are simply not privileged. Presumably the transformation occurs the instant the materials get to the testifying expert, because the Court rejects an argument that privilege is only lost if the expert "reviews" the material, and this interpretation is consistent with the language of the discovery rules.

(3) *Intangible Work Product.* Attorneys also communicate orally with their experts. These communications are treated differently from written materials. They are not covered by the automatic disclosure provisions of Rule 194.2(f)(4)(A). However, if a testifying expert's deposition is taken, Rule 192.3(e)(3) makes "facts [made] known to the expert that relate to or form the basis of the expert's mental impressions and opinions" discoverable. Suppose an attorney orally provides information to a testifying expert "without intending to waive a claim of privilege." Does the *Christus* holding cover this situation?

(4) *Attorney-Client Privilege.* In *Christus*, the hospital did not claim that the mistakenly-produced memos were protected by the attorney-client privilege. What if they had been? The Court relies both on the technical language of Rule 194 and on the policy of truth-testing underlying expert discovery. Only the latter would apply when the documents or other information provided to the expert are protected by attorney-client privilege. Suppose an attorney inadvertently provides to the testifying expert a memo from the client to the lawyer. How do you predict the Texas Supreme Court would react? Would the snap-back provision apply?

(5) *Changing Witnesses.* What would happen if the hospital re-designates Nurse Menzies as a non-testifying expert? The Court suggests that if the hospital decides not to use the expert who was provided the work product, then those documents would not be discoverable after all. Is this consistent with the Court's conclusion that — once provided to the testifying experts — the documents were *not* work product? What if Nurse Menzies then assisted the new testifying expert in preparing testimony for the case?

(6) *New Federal Rule of Evidence 502.* In September of 2008, the U.S. Congress adopted a new Rule 502 of the Federal Rules of Evidence, and this rule can affect

issues of waiver even in state courts, particularly when state litigation follows related federal litigation. It also makes court no-waiver orders binding on other courts, even state courts, and the legislative history indicates that this will be true even if the order was entered as part of an agreement between the parties. Rule 502 provides as follows:

Rule 502. Attorney-Client Privilege and Work Product; Limitations on Waiver. The following provisions apply, in the circumstances set out, to disclosure of a communication or information covered by the attorney-client privilege or work-product protection.

(a) Disclosure made in a Federal proceeding or to a Federal office or agency; scope of a waiver. When the disclosure is made in a Federal proceeding or to a Federal office or agency and waives the attorney-client privilege or work-product protection, the waiver extends to an undisclosed communication or information in a Federal or State proceeding only if:

(1) the waiver is intentional;

(2) the disclosed and undisclosed communications or information concern the same subject matter; and

(3) they ought in fairness to be considered together.

(b) Inadvertent disclosure. When made in a Federal proceeding or to a Federal office or agency, the disclosure does not operate as a waiver in a Federal or State proceeding if:

(1) the disclosure is inadvertent;

(2) the holder of the privilege or protection took reasonable steps to prevent disclosure; and

(3) the holder promptly took reasonable steps to rectify the error, including (if applicable) following Federal Rule of Civil Procedure 26(b)(5)(B).

(c) Disclosure made in a State proceeding. When the disclosure is made in a State proceeding and is not the subject of a State-court order concerning waiver, the disclosure does not operate as a waiver in a Federal proceeding if the disclosure:

(1) would not be a waiver under this rule if it had been made in a Federal proceeding; or

(2) is not a waiver under the law of the State where the disclosure occurred.

(d) Controlling effect of a court order. A Federal court may order that the privilege or protection is not waived by disclosure connected with the litigation pending before the court--in which event the disclosure is also not a waiver in any other Federal or State proceeding.

(e) Controlling effect of a party agreement. An agreement on the effect of disclosure in a Federal proceeding is binding only on the parties to the agreement, unless it is incorporated into a court order.

(f) Controlling effect of this rule. Notwithstanding Rules 101 and 1101, this rule applies to State proceedings and to Federal court-annexed and Federal court-mandated arbitration proceedings, in the circumstances set out in the rule. And notwithstanding Rule 501, this rule applies even if State law provides the rule of decision.

(g) Definitions. In this rule:

(1) "attorney-client privilege" means the protection that applicable law provides for confidential attorney-client communications; and

(2) "work-product protection" means the protection that applicable law provides for tangible material (or its intangible equivalent) prepared in anticipation of litigation or for trial.

APPENDIX — SCOPE OF DISCOVERY AND THE TEXAS BAR EXAM

Most lawsuits involve at least some discovery, and discovery issues are frequently tested on the Texas Bar Exam. The following are questions from past exams, reprinted with the permission of the Texas Board of Law Examiners, which owns the copyright to these questions. You can see more questions, and the examiners' comments on the answers, by visiting www.ble.state.tx.us/past_exams/main_pastexams.htm, the Board's website.

In considering the questions, keep in mind that on the bar exam your answer is always limited to five lines.

February 2005

Sam, his wife, and their minor daughter, Jane, were on a family vacation in Harris County, Texas, when a truck rear-ended their car. Sam was driving the car. Sam's wife, Martha, and Jane were passengers. All three sustained serious injuries in the collision. The owner of the truck was Pipe Corp, a Texas corporation whose principal place of business has always been Tarrant County, Texas. Bob, Pipe Corp's employee, was driving the truck at the time of the collision. Sam, Martha, Jane, and Bob resided in Nueces County, Texas at the time of the collision. Sam and Martha want to file a lawsuit to recover for the injuries and damages sustained by them and Jane.

1. Plaintiffs allege in the Original Petition that discovery should be conducted under Level 2 of the Texas Rules of Civil Procedure. Under a Level 2 discovery plan, what are the limitations on the discovery period, the total time for oral depositions, and the total number of interrogatories. Explain fully.

2. Plaintiffs propound Requests for Disclosure on Defendants. List five categories of information that can be obtained under such Requests. Explain fully.

July 2004

On March 30, 2004, Paul was injured in a collision with an 18-wheeler truck in Bell County, Texas. We-Haul, Inc. ("We-Haul"), a Delaware corporation, owned the truck and employed the driver, Daniel. We-Haul has its headquarters in Oklahoma. At the time of the accident, Paul was a resident of Grayson County, Texas, and

Daniel was a citizen of France and admitted as a permanent resident of Dallas County, Texas.

1. The case is assigned Discovery Level 2. When does the discovery period begin and end? Explain fully.

2. Paul sends interrogatories to We-Haul asking for the names of all impeachment and rebuttal witnesses it expected to call at trial. We-Haul objects, claiming violations of work product privilege and trial strategy. Paul files a motion to compel. How should the court rule? Explain fully.

3. We-Haul retained Dr. Critic as a consulting expert to review [Paul's doctor's] records and opinions. Dr. Critic provided We-Haul's counsel with his report. Paul moves to compel production of the report. How should the court rule? Explain fully.

February 2010

Trey slipped, fell and injured himself while he was shopping at the Home Grocery Store ("Home") at its only location in Collin County. Trey's fall was caused by water on the floor which came from the ice machine. The machine was owned and maintained by Ice Products ("Ice"), whose principal place of business is in Parker County. Trey filed a suit for damages in district court in Dallas County, his county of residence, alleging that Home and Ice were jointly and severally negligent and that their negligence proximately caused his injuries.

1. Trey and his attorney want to know if Home and Ice have liability insurance to cover any of the claims brought in this suit. Ice's attorney informally tells Trey's attorney that Ice has no insurance. Home's attorney makes no reply about insurance coverage. What document can Trey serve to determine whether either defendant is covered by insurance? Explain fully.

2. By way of interrogatories, Home inquires of Trey whether he has sustained other accidental personal injuries, before or after the incident made the basis of the lawsuit. Trey objects to the interrogatory as being irrelevant. Home sets the objection for hearing. How should the court rule? Explain fully.

Chapter 10

DISCOVERY: METHODOLOGY OF THE INDIVIDUAL DEVICES

SCOPE

In Chapter 9, we examined the scope of discovery. This chapter examines the individual discovery devices used to secure discoverable information. The discovery rules allow discovery from both parties and non-parties. This chapter will examine both written and oral discovery devices. The chapter also covers the procedures for litigating discovery disputes, the duty to amend or supplement discovery responses, and the sanctions that can be imposed for violations of the discovery rules.

§ 10.01 THE INDIVIDUAL DISCOVERY DEVICES: AN INTRODUCTION

[A] The Discovery Devices Provided by the Rules

In the first year of law school you are likely to have had a course covering the federal approach to discovery. Although there are important differences, the Texas discovery rules are similar. The discovery rules contemplate discovery among parties to the suit as well as discovery from persons and entities that are not parties. There are six devices that may be used to accomplish formal discovery: (1) requests for disclosure; (2) requests for production and inspection (including pretrial subpoenas) and for entry on land; (3) interrogatories; (4) requests for admissions; (5) depositions (both depositions on oral examination and depositions on written questions); and (6) requests for physical and mental examination. The use of these devices is subject to numerical limits, depending on the case's Discovery Level. These limits were discussed in Chapter 9.

1. *Requests for Disclosure.* The discovery rules create a mechanism requiring, on request, disclosure of basic information described in Civil Procedure Rule 194.2, including identity of parties and potential parties, legal theories, damage calculations, persons with knowledge of relevant facts, information about testifying experts, witness statements, and insurance and settlement agreements. It is likely that they will be used in most cases, especially cases with significant limits on the use of other discovery devices.

2. *Oral Depositions.* Depositions are questions asked of a witness before trial in the presence of a court reporter, with opposing parties having the right to be present and ask questions also. The term "deposition" is also used to describe the session at which questions are asked and answered. This type of discovery may be used both as to party and nonparty witnesses. It is set up by a written notice to all

other parties and, for a nonparty witness, issuance of a subpoena. Depositions are usually the most effective means for obtaining useful information from adverse witnesses because the examiner may ask follow-up questions in the event of evasive, incomplete, or unexpected answers.

3. *Depositions on Written Questions.* As an alternative to the oral deposition, a party may send written questions to a person authorized to administer a written deposition to the deponent. The other side may, in response, issue cross-questions. This is a weak form of discovery for several reasons, including the fact that the deposition officer cannot revise the questions or ask follow-up questions. The device was historically used most frequently for authentication of documents. Now, however, production of a document authenticates the document for use against the party that produced it unless specific objection procedures are followed. TEX. R. CIV. P. 176.5, 193.7. The deposition on written questions may thus be used less frequently as documents may be acquired from nonparties through subpoena without need for an oral or written deposition. *See* TEX. R. CIV. P. 176, 205. However, deposition of the records custodian may still be required in order to prove that the documents are admissible business records.

4. *Interrogatories.* Interrogatories are written questions directed by one party to another, to be answered under oath. Because this discovery device allows time for the opponent to consider the response, and because opposing counsel generally determines the form of the answers, responses are frequently evasive. Thus, interrogatories are not an effective method for getting incriminating information from an adverse party. However, interrogatories may be an inexpensive way to get basic background information. Some of the information formally secured through interrogatories will now be sought through requests for disclosure. Parties may serve on any other party no more than 25 written interrogatories (excluding interrogatories asking a party only to identify or authenticate specific documents) unless they get court permission. Interrogatories may be directed only to parties. Written discovery from nonparty witnesses must be obtained by the similar but separate mechanism of the deposition on written questions.

5. *Requests for Admissions.* A party opponent may be requested to admit or deny factual propositions submitted to the party, including the genuineness of documents. This kind of discovery is useful for eliminating issues about which there is no real dispute.

6. *Production and Inspection of Documents, Tangible Things, and Realty.* The request to produce constitutes the basic method for obtaining discovery of documents and other tangible things from other parties to the action. Under the request procedure, a party sends to another party a written request listing the documents, tangible things or realty the party wishes to photograph, copy, or inspect. The request procedure applies only to parties but is similar to the procedure for nonparties. Production of tangible items from nonparties involves the use of a notice and subpoena.

7. *Motions for Physical or Mental Examination.* On motion showing good cause, the court may order that a physical or mental examination be had of a person whose condition is in controversy.

[B] Discovery Timing

In a complicated suit justifying the use of several different kinds of discovery, the "first wave" of discovery, as it is called, usually consists of identifying documents, witnesses, or business entities that need to be investigated. Thus the first devices used may be a request for disclosure and a set of interrogatories, because they are an efficient means for getting background information. In addition to the discovery allowed under the request for disclosure, a party might want further background information such as the identity and location of documents and other tangible things relevant to the case. The opponent may be asked to identify the persons having knowledge of the transaction or occurrence involved in the action, the corporations or other business entities for which they have acted, the officers or employees of those businesses, and the identity and location of any tangible evidence relating to the issues. In a complex suit the proper conduct of this first wave is essential to a successful effort.

Once the basics are thus established, the "second wave," often consisting of requests for document production, will be conducted. While human testimony may vary, documents contain what they contain, and they are useful to have available when taking depositions. Nowadays, attorneys must gather information about the client's and opponent's computer systems in order to efficiently discover electronically-stored information (ESI). Failure to deal with format issues from the beginning of the discovery process can result in a significant waste of time and money. Failure to discover ESI can result in a significant loss of relevant information.

The "third wave" may be depositions of witnesses or parties who know about the transaction at issue. These depositions may even lead to a fourth or fifth wave of discovery, as the attorneys attempt to discover through depositions not only what the deponents know, but also the existence of other sources of information. In this sense discovery may double back on itself, as depositions reveal documents that were not produced, additional questions that should be asked, or additional persons who should be deposed. Depositions of expert witnesses come late in the process, making it more likely that the experts have had access to all of the relevant facts and time to develop and document their opinions.

Finally, requests for admissions may be used as a last step in the discovery process to obtain admissions of matters that the discovery process has shown to be undisputed and to secure admissions concerning the authenticity of documents to be introduced at trial.

Cost considerations affect and limit discovery strategy in any given law suit. An automobile accident in which injuries are minor may justify only a brief deposition or two, if even that. A complex products liability or intellectual property case, on the other hand, may easily call for the expenditure of hundreds of thousands of dollars in attorney's fees for discovery. It is not unusual for thousands of documents to be produced in such a case. There will be more documents and more persons with information relevant to such suits, and the stakes will justify larger expenditures on discovery.

Discovery is also available, to at least a limited extent, both before the lawsuit and after judgment. A person may petition the court for an order authorizing the taking of a deposition on oral examination or on written questions either (1) to perpetuate or obtain the person's own testimony or that of any other person for use in an anticipated suit; or (2) to investigate a potential claim or suit. Tex. R. Civ. P. 202. The court must order a deposition if, and only if, it finds that either (1) allowing the petitioner to take the requested deposition may prevent a failure or delay of justice in an anticipated suit; or (2) the likely benefit of allowing the petitioner to take the requested deposition to investigate a potential claim outweighs the burden or expense of the procedure. Tex. R. Civ. P. 202.4(a). If one of these standards is met, Civil Procedure Rule 202 provides authority for pre-trial depositions to discover information about prospective claims or defenses. The scope of discovery in depositions before suit is the same as if the anticipated suit or potential claim had been filed. Tex. R. Civ. P. 202.5.

A deposition taken before suit may be used in a subsequent suit as permitted by the rules of evidence. Tex. R. Civ. P. 202, Comment 2. For example, if the deposed person is no longer available to testify at the later trial, the deposition testimony may be admitted as an exception to the hearsay rule, provided the party against whom the testimony is offered, or a person with a similar interest, had an opportunity and similar motive to develop the testimony by direct, cross, or redirect examination. If the deposed person testifies at the trial, the deposition testimony may be available for impeachment.

A court may restrict or prohibit the use of a pre-suit deposition in order to protect a person who was not served with notice of the deposition from any unfair prejudice. The Supreme Court of Texas intended Civil Procedure Rule 202 to accommodate competing concerns of plaintiffs and defense lawyers regarding the extent to which plaintiffs should be permitted to obtain pre-suit depositions without notice to potential parties. It was alleged that some plaintiffs had used former Civil Procedure Rule 737, which was incorporated into Civil Procedure Rule 202, to "set up" defendants by obtaining one-sided depositions of key witnesses without notice to the prospective defendant. Because these depositions could be used for impeachment, they "pinned down" the witnesses' testimony. Under Civil Procedure Rule 202.5, if a person attempts to use Civil Procedure Rule 202 abusively or to circumvent deposition notice requirements, such as to "set up" a defendant rather than for good faith investigation of a potential claim, the trial court is authorized to forbid the use of the deposition for any purpose, including impeachment. For a helpful discussion of pre-suit discovery, see Lonny S. Hoffman, *Access to Information, Access to Justice*, 40 U. Mich. J.L. Reform 217 (2006).

The Rules of Civil Procedure also provide for discovery in the context of enforcing a judgment. Generally, the rules governing and related to pre-trial discovery proceedings apply in like manner to proceedings after judgment. Tex. R. Civ. P. 621a. Frequently, a party who loses a lawsuit resists efforts to satisfy or otherwise abide by the court's judgment. The party may refuse to point out any property for levy and execution, assert spurious claims of exemption, attempt to transfer assets to third parties, or otherwise alter financial relationships and holdings to frustrate collection efforts. When judgment debtors are less than forthright about their ability to satisfy the judgment, there is little that the sheriff or constable holding a writ of execution can do. Usually, the judgment creditor is equally uninformed, having no information about the adversary's holdings or dealings, and is thus not in a position to help the levying officer or to ask the court for assistance under the turnover statute. However, when faced with such an obstacle, a judgment creditor does have some tools to help solve the problem.

To gain information to assist a successful litigant's efforts to collect or enforce the judgment, a judgment creditor may use any devices authorized by the Texas Rules of Civil Procedure for pre-trial discovery, including written interrogatories, depositions, and requests for the production of documents. In doing so, the judgment creditor may inquire about any matter relevant to collection of the judgment or any matter reasonably calculated to lead to the discovery of information relevant to enforcement. The broad scope of permissible post-judgment discovery does have limits, however. For example, it is beyond the scope of such discovery to attempt to relitigate issues determined in the lawsuit itself or bring in others not parties to the original action.

Judicial supervision of post-judgment discovery proceedings will be conducted in the same court that rendered the judgment and under the same rules as supervision of pre-trial discovery. Of particular importance when dealing with a recalcitrant judgment debtor are the sanctions available for discovery abuse. In the context of post-judgment discovery, monetary sanctions against the party or attorney advising the party to abuse the discovery process are the usual sanctions for failure to respond properly, although court orders holding a person in contempt and assessing a fine or jail sentence are also authorized.

PRACTICE EXERCISE #24

Use of Discovery Devices. What device or devices might you use to obtain each of the following items of information? Explain.

(1) Information related to medical expenses of a plaintiff in a suit for personal injuries, including such matters as the doctors consulted, the amount of money paid, and the treatment the patient underwent. You represent the defendant.

(2) The bank statements or cancelled checks of the plaintiff for these expenditures.

(3) In an action on a contract, the genuineness of the copy of the contract in your client's possession, which you wish to establish for trial.

(4) In a suit over an automobile accident, the opposing party's version of facts surrounding the accident.

(5) Records maintained by an automobile repair shop, which is not a party to the suit, concerning the condition of the brakes of the automobile driven by the opposing party.

§ 10.02 DISCOVERY DEVICES

[A] Written Discovery

Read Tex. R. Civ. P. 176, 193, 194, 196, 197, 198, 205 and accompanying Comments.

The discovery rules define written discovery as "requests for disclosure, requests for production and inspection of documents and tangible things, requests for entry onto property, interrogatories, and requests for admission." TEX. R. CIV. P. 192.7(a). This section will examine those devices, as well as the use of a subpoena to command the production of documents without the need for a deposition.

[1] Requests for Disclosure

The adversarial approach to pretrial discovery is superseded in the rules by a type of disclosure practice for commonly discoverable matters. The procedural mechanism for implementing this disclosure is a new discovery device: the request for disclosure. TEX. R. CIV. P. 194. Civil Procedure Rule 194.1 specifies the exact language of the request. A standard request for disclosure, which is not subject to objection, allows a party to obtain disclosure of a broad range of information and documents, including the following (TEX. R. CIV. P. 194.2):

(1) The correct names of the parties to the lawsuit.

(2) The name, address, and telephone number of any potential parties.

(3) The legal theories and, in general, the factual bases of the responding party's claims or defenses (although the responding party need not marshal all evidence that may be offered at trial).

(4) The amount and any method of calculating economic damages.

(5) The name, address, and telephone number of persons having knowledge of relevant facts, and a brief statement of each identified person's connection with the case

(6) Specific information concerning testifying experts.

(7) Any indemnity and insuring agreements described in Rule 192.3(f).

(8) Any settlement agreements described in Rule 192.3(g).

(9) Any witness statements described in Rule 192.3(h).

(10) In a suit alleging physical or mental injury and damages from the occurrence that is the subject of the case, all medical records and bills that are reasonably related to the injuries or damages asserted or, in lieu thereof, an authorization permitting the disclosure of such medical records and bills.

(11) In a suit alleging physical or mental injury and damages from the occurrence that is the subject of the case, all medical records and bills obtained by the responding party by virtue of an authorization furnished

by the requesting party.

Disclosure is intended to provide basic discovery of these specific categories of information, not automatically in every case, "but upon request, without preparation of a lengthy inquiry, and without objection or assertion of work product." A responding party may, however, assert applicable privileges other than work product. Tex. R. Civ. P. 194, Comment 1. Generally, a response must be filed within 30 days after service of the request (or 50 days after service for a defendant served before the defendant's answer is due). Tex. R. Civ. P. 194.3. However, a longer period is authorized for a party to designate experts and to furnish expert information. Tex. R. Civ. P. 195.2.

The request for disclosure will tend to replace the use of interrogatories for certain commonly relevant factual matters and, together with a specific rule on discovery regarding testifying expert witnesses, eliminates the use of interrogatories in the discovery process concerning testifying experts. Tex. R. Civ. P. 195.1. This is especially important given the reduced limits on the number of interrogatories that can be used in most cases.

Unlike answers to interrogatories, disclosure responses need not be verified, but they are subject to a general certification requirement contained in Rule 191.3 concerning the propriety, completeness, and accuracy of the response.

NOTES AND QUESTIONS

(1) *Use of Requests.* When might you choose not to use all of the available requests for disclosure? [Except for requests that would be irrelevant to your case, you should routinely use them.]

(2) *Privilege Assertions.* Under what circumstances might you assert a privilege in response to a disclosure request? [You cannot assert a work product privilege in response to a disclosure request, nor can you assert medical privilege with regard to the last two items. You may still assert attorney-client, trade secret, or other applicable privileges.]

(3) *Timing Considerations.* What strategic considerations might affect the timing of your use of requests for disclosure? [Generally the disclosures provide information that you need at the beginning of the discovery period — things that you will use in framing your requests for production of documents, in deciding who to depose, and the like. Because there is a time limit for all of discovery, the disclosure request should generally be sent as soon as it is available under the rules.]

(4) *Designation of Experts.* Does a party have to designate experts if that party has never received a request for disclosure under Civil Procedure Rule 194.2(f)? [No. *See also* Tex. R. Civ. P. 195 (listing discovery available regarding expert witnesses).]

[2] Interrogatories to Parties

Interrogatories are governed by Civil Procedure Rule 197. Interrogatories are written questions that may be served on parties to the lawsuit to inquire about matters within the scope of discovery, except for certain matters with regard to expert witnesses. An interrogatory may request a party to provide the identity and location of relevant documents, inquire whether a party makes a specific legal or factual contention, and may ask the responding party to state the legal theories and to describe in general the factual bases for the party's claims or defenses. They may not, however, be used to require the responding party to marshal all of its available proof or the proof the party intends to offer at trial. Tex. R. Civ. P. 197.1.

The responding party must serve a written response within 30 days after service of the interrogatories (except that a defendant served with interrogatories before the defendant's answer is due need not respond until 50 days after the service of the interrogatories). The response must include the party's answers to the interrogatories and may include objections and assertions of privilege. A party's attorney must sign all discovery responses, including interrogatory responses and objections. In addition, the responding party must sign the answers under oath, except: (1) when answers are based on information obtained from other persons, the party may so state; and (2) interrogatories about persons with knowledge of relevant facts, trial witnesses, and legal contentions can be signed by the party's agent or attorney. Tex. R. Civ. P. 197.2. Interrogatory answers can be used only against the responding party. Tex. R. Civ. P. 197.3.

The number of interrogatories that can be directed to a party is limited by the various discovery control plans. *See* Tex. R. Civ. P. 190 (default limit is 25 for all discovery levels).

NOTES AND QUESTIONS

(1) *Objections and Privilege Assertions.* A party might object to interrogatories on relevance grounds, or might assert a privilege in response to a particular interrogatory. Neither, however, excuses the responding party from answering the interrogatories to the extent no objection is made. Objections must be in writing and must be made within the time for response. The responding party must state the legal or factual basis for the objection and the extent to which the party is refusing to comply. An objection not made within the time required, or that is obscured by numerous unfounded objections, is waived unless the court excuses the waiver for good cause shown. Tex. R. Civ. P. 193.2. The rules also provide a procedure for asserting privilege claims as to written discovery. *See* Tex. R. Civ. P. 193.3. Any party may at any reasonable time request a hearing on an objection or claim or privilege. Tex. R. Civ. P. 193.4.

(2) *Reference to Business Records.* When the answer to an interrogatory may be derived or ascertained from public records, from the responding party's business records, or from a compilation, abstract, or summary of the responding party's business records, *and* the burden of deriving or ascertaining the answer is substantially the same for the requesting party as for the responding party, the responding party may answer the interrogatory by specifying and, if applicable,

producing the records. Tex. R. Civ. P. 197.2(c). When might you tender business records instead of answering an interrogatory? When would you choose not to do so, even if the Civil Procedure Rules would allow it?

PRACTICE EXERCISE #25

Opal Allen was shopping at her neighborhood Alpha Omega Grocery Store. She shopped there regularly and knew the store well. On this particular occasion, while shopping in the produce department, Allen slipped and fell, breaking her wrist. She was taken by ambulance to the local hospital, where she was treated and released. Her injury was severe enough that she was unable to return to her job as a secretary for about a month, and she received no pay check during that period. She has now returned to work, but suffers from chronic pain in the injured wrist, and has permanently lost some mobility as well.

Consider the following discovery issues that might arise in a slip and fall case brought by Allen against Alpha Omega.

1. You represent Alpha Omega. You were served with interrogatories one day before the day your Answer was due. How long do you have to answer those interrogatories?
2. You represent Allen. In your interrogatories to Alpha Omega you would like to define "identify" with regard to a person to include the person's home address, work address, phone number, and email address, so that whenever an interrogatory asks Alpha Omega to identify someone, it must include that information as well as the person's name. Would that make each "identify" interrogatory count as five questions?

[3] Production and Inspection of Documents and Tangible Things From Parties

[a] In General

Civil Procedure Rule 196 governs requests for production and inspection sent to parties, as well as requests for entry on land owned by a party or nonparty. To request the production or inspection of a document or tangible thing in another party's possession, custody, or control, the discovering party must serve a request no later than 30 days before the end of the discovery period. The request must specify the items to be produced or inspected, "either by individual item or by category, and describe with reasonable particularity each item and category." If the request is for the medical or mental health records of a nonparty, the requesting party must also serve the nonparty with the request for production. Tex. R. Civ. P. 196.1.

The responding party must serve a written response within 30 days after service of the request (except that a defendant served with a request before the defendant's answer is due need not respond until 50 days after service of the request). The response must state with respect to each item or category of items whatever objections and assertions of privilege the responding party wishes to make. Tex. R. Civ. P. 196.2. In addition, the responding party must produce the requested documents and tangible things not subject to objection or assertion of privilege, and must provide the discovering party with a reasonable opportunity to inspect them. The items produced must be organized either as they are kept in the usual course of business or labeled to correspond with the categories in the request. Tex. R. Civ. P. 196.3. Another provision addresses the problem of data in electronic or magnetic form. *See* Tex. R. Civ. P. 196.4.

Questions often arise as to how specific the requests must be before the responding party has a duty to comply with the request or assert specific objections or privileges. Could a party successfully request "all documents relevant to this lawsuit"? Comment 2 to Rule 193 states "An objection to written discovery does not excuse the responding party from complying with the request to the extent no objection is made. But a party may object to a request for 'all documents relevant to the lawsuit' as overly broad and not in compliance with the rule requiring specific requests for documents and refuse to comply with it entirely. *See Loftin v. Martin*, 776 S.W.2d 145 (Tex. 1989)."

In addition to issues regarding drafting specificity, courts must also decide whether a party has sufficient "possession, custody, or control" to require it to produce particular documents. Read Tex. R. Civ. P. 192.3(b) and 192.7(b). In reading the following case, consider what kind of relationship between party and information meets this test.

IN RE KUNTZ

124 S.W.3d 179 (Tex. 2003)

Justice Smith delivered the opinion of the Court, in which Chief Justice Phillips, Justice Hecht, Justice Owen, Justice Jefferson, Justice Schneider, Justice Wainwright, and Justice Brister joined.

In this mandamus proceeding, we decide a question of first impression regarding the proper interpretation and application under the Texas Rules of Civil Procedure of the phrase "possession, custody, or control." *See* Tex. R. Civ. P. 192.3(b), 192.7(b). The respondent trial court, in an action filed against relator Hal Kuntz in his individual capacity, ordered Kuntz to produce documents that he had access to at his place of employment. It was undisputed that Kuntz's employer had actual physical possession of the relevant documents, that the documents were owned by a client of Kuntz's employer, and that the client claimed the documents contained its privileged trade secrets. In this Court, Kuntz asserts that his mere ability to access the documents does not constitute possession, custody, or control. We agree and, accordingly, conditionally grant the requested writ.

. . . .

II

Texas Rule of Civil Procedure 192.3 is entitled "Scope of Discovery." Rule 192.3(a) provides: "In general, a party may obtain discovery regarding any matter that is not privileged and is relevant to the subject matter of the pending action . . . ." Tex. R. Civ. P. 192.3(a). Rule 192.3(b) provides:

> A party may obtain discovery of the existence, description, nature, custody, condition, location, and contents of documents and tangible things . . . that constitute or contain matters relevant to the subject matter of the action. A person is required to produce a document or tangible thing that is within the person's possession, custody, or control.

Tex. R. Civ. P. 192.3(b).

Texas Rule of Civil Procedure 192.7(b) sets forth the following definition: "*Possession, custody, or control* of an item means that the person either has physical possession of the item or has a right to possession of the item that is equal or superior to the person who has physical possession of the item." Tex. R. Civ. P. 192.7(b) (emphasis in original); *see also GTE Communications Sys. Corp. v. Tanner*, 856 S.W.2d at 729 ("The right to obtain possession is a legal right based upon the relationship between the party from whom a document is sought and the person who has actual possession of it.").

Under Texas Rule of Civil Procedure 196.1, a party may request that another party to the pending action produce a document or tangible thing. Texas Rule of Civil Procedure 205 governs discovery from nonparties, including a request for production of a document or tangible thing.

III

The live pleading in the underlying suit, Vesta Kuntz's Sixth Amended Petition to Enforce Division of Agreement Incident to Divorce, For Declaratory Judgment or, Alternatively to Clarify, or Reform Agreement, states:

2. Vesta L. Kuntz, Movant, is an individual residing in Harris County, Texas.

3. Hal G. Kuntz, Respondent, is an individual residing in Harris County, Texas. His counsel is being furnished a copy of this pleading . . . .

5. On October 7, 1983 the parties were married. On June 30, 1999 the parties were divorced. The Court approved an Agreement Incident to Divorce ("AID") as a just and right division of the parties' property. A true copy of the AID is attached as Exhibit "A." Paragraph *5.4* of the AID under the subheading "Future MOXY Royalty" provides as follows:

> Husband by virtue of employment or as a partner of CLK may earn additional interests in oil and gas leases and properties which Husband may acquire by assignment from McMoRan Offshore Exploration Co. ("MOXY") or its successors or predecessors in the future. All such interests which have not been assigned by MOXY shall be the property of Husband, except Wife will have the right to *25%* of all overriding royalty interests, if any, from MOXY assigned to Husband after the date of divorce that results [sic] from projects on which CLK forwarded letters of recommendation to MOXY to drill during the marriage.

McMoRan Oil & Gas, L.L.C. ("MOXY"), successor to McMoRan Offshore Exploration Company, is an independent oil and gas company engaged in the exploration, development, and production of oil and gas. The company's operations are primarily conducted offshore in the Gulf of Mexico and onshore in the Gulf Coast area, and its offices are located in New Orleans. CLK Company, L.L.C. ("CLK") is MOXY's primary geological and geophysical consultant. CLK has offices in both New Orleans and Houston. MOXY is CLK's only client.

Hal Kuntz is a minority owner and the general manager of CLK. He works at CLK's Houston office. As general manager, Hal is in charge of CLK's day-to-day operations and answers only to the company's board, of which he is one of four members.

CLK is in the business of evaluating oil and gas prospects for MOXY. After evaluating a property, CLK creates and forwards to MOXY a letter of recommendation ("LOR") detailing its findings and recommendations. A copy of each LOR is traditionally maintained in both of CLK's offices. Hal and other CLK principals have unrestricted access to those copies.[1]

The consulting agreement between MOXY and CLK provides that data and information obtained or compiled by CLK for MOXY belongs exclusively to MOXY and prohibits disclosure of that data and information to a third party without MOXY's written consent. CLK's operating agreement obligates Hal to maintain the confidentiality of data and information acquired during his employment and prohibits him from disclosing it to a third party without the written consent of CLK's board.

In May 2001, Vesta filed a motion to compel discovery, requesting that Hal be ordered "to produce all LORs that are 'positive' from October 7, 1983 (date of marriage) to June 30, 1999 (date of divorce) in an unredacted form." She had previously, pursuant to Texas Rule of Civil Procedure 196.1, requested that Hal produce "all the LORs written during the marriage." In response to the motion, Hal asserted that he did not have possession, custody, or control of the documents and, that the requested documents were MOXY's privileged trade secrets.

While the aforementioned motion was pending, Hal requested permission from both MOXY and CLK to release the relevant documents. MOXY and CLK, in separate letters, denied Hal's written request. In August 2001, the letters were filed as exhibits in the trial court.

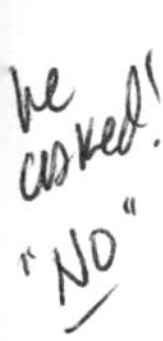

On September 18, 2001, a hearing was held on the motion to compel discovery. On December 11, 2001, the trial court signed an order resolving the motion. Hal was ordered to "produce all Letters of Recommendation for the period beginning on October 7, 1983 through June 30, 1999 generated by CLK Company or any of such company's partners or employees that contain a positive recommendation." Approximately 2,000 LORs satisfy the order's criteria for production.

In his petition for writ of mandamus, Hal requests that we: "(1) order

---

[1] Hal testified:

> QUESTION: Does CLK have copies of [the relevant LOR's].
>
> ANSWER: Yes, they do.
>
> QUESTION: You've certainly got access to them, don't you.
>
> ANSWER: I can access them, but I don't control them.

Respondent to vacate the Order dated December 11, 2001, requiring Hal Kuntz to disclose MOXY's trade secrets; (2) vacate any finding that Hal Kuntz has possession, custody, or control of MOXY's trade secrets; and (3) grant Hal Kuntz such other and further relief to which he may be justly entitled."

IV

Hal asserts that he does not have possession, custody, or control of the relevant letters of recommendation. Specifically, Hal asserts that, in his individual capacity, he does not have physical possession of the requested documents and has no legal right to obtain physical possession of the documents from either CLK or MOXY. In sum, Hal argues that he "should not be ordered to produce documents in the physical possession of his corporate employer in this suit brought against him individually."

Noting that the "testimony in this case is unequivocal that the LORs were in Hal's offices and he could get them anytime he wants," Vesta asserts that "Hal has the actual possession, custody and control of the documents, so he cannot refuse to produce the same." She does not argue that Hal has a legal right to obtain physical possession of the documents from either CLK or MOXY.

MOXY appeared as amicus in the courts below in support of Hal. In this Court, MOXY, also as amicus, asserts that "the trial court improperly circumvented the Texas Rules of Civil Procedure related to obtaining nonparty discovery and improperly infringed on MOXY's constitutional rights by depriving MOXY of its property without due process of law." In addition, MOXY argues:

> Hal Kuntz, as an employee of CLK, lacks both physical possession of MOXY's trade secret LORs or any "right to possess" MOXY's trade secret LORs. At best, all that Hal Kuntz has is access to MOXY's trade secret LORs and that access is strictly limited to use of the LORs in furtherance of his employer's services performed for MOXY. Like a bank teller with access to cash in the vault, Hal Kuntz has neither possession nor any right to possess MOXY's trade secret LORs.

V

Hal's mere access to the relevant letters of recommendation does not constitute "physical possession" of the documents under the definition of "possession, custody, or control" set forth in Texas Rule of Civil Procedure 192.7(b). *Cf. In re Grand Jury Subpoena (Kent)*, 646 F.2d 963, 969 (5th Cir. 1981) ("The [employee's] subpoena, if upheld, would be illegal because it would direct her to produce documents not in her possession, custody, or control. Because [employee] had mere access, her compliance with the subpoena would have required that she illegally *take* exclusive possession of [her employer's] documents and deliver them to the grand jury.") (emphasis in original); *American Maplan Corp. v. Heilmayr*, 203 F.R.D. 499, 501–02 (D. Kan. 2001) (denying motion to compel defendant, president and minority shareholder of nonparty corporation, to produce nonparty corporation's documents in suit brought against defendant in his individual capacity). Thus, we conclude that the trial court abused its discretion in ordering Hal to produce the documents.

If required to produce the relevant LORs, Hal would be forced to violate the confidentiality provisions contained in both CLK's operating agreement and the consulting agreement between MOXY and CLK, potentially subjecting himself to a suit for significant damages. *See, e.g., IBP, Inc. v. Klumpe*, 101 S.W.3d 461 (Tex. App. — Amarillo 2001, pet. denied) (suit brought by employer against employee arising out of disclosure of trade secrets by employee in response to request for production). Because an appellate court would not be able to cure the trial court's discovery error, we further conclude that Hal does not have an adequate remedy by appeal.

Based on the foregoing, we conditionally grant the writ of mandamus and direct the trial court to vacate its December 11, 2001 order. We are confident that the trial court will promptly comply, and the writ will issue only if it does not.

[Justice Hecht, joined by Justice Owen, Justice Schneider and Justice Wainwright, agreed with the majority opinion and also concurred on the ground that the LORs are trade secrets and Vesta has not established that they are "essential to the fair adjudication of her claims." Justice O'Neill concurred in the judgment only.]

NOTES AND QUESTIONS

(1) *Requests for "All Documents" Can be Proper.* A request for "any and all documents" does not itself violate the specificity requirements of Rule 196 that items be described with "reasonable particularity," as long as the request is further restricted to a particular type or class of documents. *Davis v. Pate*, 915 S.W.2d 76, 79 (Tex. App. — Corpus Christi 1996, orig. proceeding) (approving request to "Please produce any and all documents which evidence, reflect or pertain in any way to any lost profits you contend you suffered as a result of the conduct of the Bank of Robstown").

(2) *Avoidance of Overbroad Requests.* In *K Mart Corp. v. Sanderson*, 937 S.W.2d 429 (Tex. 1996), the court considered a challenge based on *Loftin* to plaintiff's request for production of documents. Plaintiff Stacey Thompson was abducted from a K Mart parking lot and raped. She alleged that defendants were negligent and grossly negligent in failing to make adequate provisions for her safety. In three separate requests for production, Thompson requested K Mart to produce all documents "which relate to, touch or concern the allegations of this lawsuit," all documents "reflecting the incident made the basis of this lawsuit," and any document "which is not work product which relates in any way to this incident." The Texas Supreme Court held: "Thompson requested all documents relating to the incident in which she was injured, not all documents which support K Mart's position or which relate to the claims and defenses in the cause of action. Because the incident was an isolated occurrence, we think a reasonable person would understand from the request what documents fit the description. It would be better, of course, to be more specific. We do not hold that a request as broad as Thompson's is proper in every circumstance. Here, however, the district court did not abuse its discretion in enforcing Thompson's requests, except for requiring production of work product." 937 S.W.2d at 430–31.

(3) *No "Fishing Expeditions" Are Permitted.* The Texas Supreme Court also noted in *K-Mart* that no discovery device may be used to "fish." How would you distinguish between "fishing" and "thorough discovery"? Perhaps it's merely a question of whose discovery is involved: *your* fishing expedition, *my* thorough discovery. For a discussion of the uses of the "fishing" metaphor and its impact, see Elizabeth Thornburg, *Just Say 'No Fishing': The Lure of Metaphor*, 40 U. Mich. J.L. Reform 1 (2006).

(4) *Drafting Considerations.* How can you draft requests for production that comply with Rule 196's specificity requirement? Where will you get the necessary information? In order to draft with sufficient specificity, you must carefully analyze your case. Think about the kinds of records that are likely to exist. Also consider the extent to which information beyond your own individual client's situation may or may not produce probative evidence from which inferences may be drawn. This will involve considerations of both geography and time frame. If your clients have information about the workings of the opponent's business, they may be helpful. You can also get information about documents through deposing people with knowledge of relevant facts. In some cases, your expert witness may be able to suggest the types and scope of information that should exist and that would be relevant.

(5) *Possession, Custody, or Control.* One court of appeals has required an alter-ego or single business enterprise relationship between parent and subsidiary companies before either can be required to produce a document belonging to the other. *In re U-Haul Internat'l, Inc.*, 87 S.W.3d 653 (Tex. App. — San Antonio 2002, orig. proceeding). This approach is consistent with the Texas Supreme Court's interpretation of "possession, custody or control" in the *Kuntz* case.

[b] Electronic Discovery

Read Tex. R. Civ. P. 196.4.

As technology continues to create new media in which information is stored, the courts are faced with issues about the discoverability of electronic information such as e-mails, text messages, voice mail, internet searches, instant messages, digital spreadsheets, and digital versions of documents. The issues become particularly difficult if the information has been "deleted" but is still retrievable either on an individual computer or through company backup tapes. Electronic discovery also raises issues about the discoverability of embedded data and metadata. (Think, for example, of the information available when one clicks on "Properties" or "Track Changes" in a Word document or from the formulas underlying Excel spreadsheets.)

In the following case, the Supreme Court considers the procedures that should be used in searching for deleted data: what showing must be made before a search for deleted material may be undertaken; who can do the search; and what protections should be in place to protect the discovered party from the disclosure of confidential information, privileged matters, and irrelevant information. Notice the extent to which the Texas court is influenced by e-discovery doctrine developed in the federal courts.

IN RE WEEKLEY HOMES, L.P.

295 S.W.3d 309 (Tex. 2009)

O'NEILL, J.

ON PETITION FOR WRIT OF MANDAMUS

In this mandamus proceeding, we must decide whether the trial court abused its discretion by ordering four of the defendant's employees to turn over their computer hard drives to forensic experts for imaging, copying, and searching for deleted emails. Because the plaintiff failed to demonstrate the particular characteristics of the electronic storage devices involved, the familiarity of its experts with those characteristics, or a reasonable likelihood that the proposed search methodology would yield the information sought, and considering the highly intrusive nature of computer storage search and the sensitivity of the subject matter, we hold that the trial court abused its discretion.

I. Background

In October 2002, relator Weekley Homes, L.P., a homebuilder, entered into an agreement with Enclave at Fortney Branch, Ltd. (Enclave), a residential real estate developer, to purchase 136 developed lots in a subdivision pursuant to a take-down schedule (the Builder Contract). In November 2004, after Weekley had purchased some of the lots from Enclave pursuant to the Builder Contract, Enclave and HFG Enclave Land Interests, Ltd. (HFG) entered into an agreement whereby Enclave would sell and convey seventy-four of the remaining developed lots to HFG (the Warehouse Contract). Under the Warehouse Contract, Enclave also assigned to HFG its rights to those seventy-four lots under the Builder Contract such that Weekley would be obligated to purchase those lots from HFG.

One day before the Warehouse Contract's execution, Weekley executed a Consent to Assignment and Estoppel Certificate (the Estoppel Certificate), in which Weekley made various express representations, warranties, and covenants to HFG about the state of Enclave's performance under the Builder Contract up to that point. According to HFG, it relied upon the Estoppel Certificate when it agreed to the terms of the Warehouse Contract.

Enclave allegedly failed to perform various obligations owed to HFG under the Warehouse Contract, and HFG sued Enclave in August 2006. Two months later, HFG subpoenaed documents from a number of third parties, including Weekley. After reviewing several of the documents Weekley produced, HFG's counsel began asking Weekley about the possible existence of other potentially responsive documents relating to the subdivision. In response, Weekley eventually produced approximately 400 additional pages of documents in March 2007. According to HFG, information contained in the documents led it to believe Weekley had made a number of material misrepresentations in the Estoppel Certificate relating to Enclave's performance under the Builder Contract.

In June 2007, HFG added Weekley as a defendant to its pending suit against

Enclave, seeking damages for common law fraud and fraudulent inducement, statutory fraud, fraud by nondisclosure, negligence per se, and negligent misrepresentation. In July and December 2007, HFG served Weekley with requests for production including requests that Weekley produce a broad variety of emails to and from Weekley and its employees relating to Enclave, the subdivision, and the Builder Contract. HFG specifically requested emails between Enclave and Russell Rice (Weekley's Division President), Joe Vastano (Weekley's Area President), Scott Thompson (Weekley's Project Manager for the subdivision), and Biff Bailey (Weekley's Land Acquisitions Manager) (collectively "the Employees"), relating to Enclave and the Builder Contract. HFG received thirty-one responsive emails, one of which discussed a third-party engineering analysis (the Slope Stability Analysis) predating the Estoppel Certificate and Warehouse Contract and addressing the existence of multiple unsafe subdivision lots that required remedial measures. Weekley produced a copy of the Slope Stability Analysis, but did not produce any additional communications to or from the Employees discussing it. Considering the safety issues HFG contends the Slope Stability Analysis highlighted, and that Weekley allegedly spent $92,000 to remedy those issues, HFG was unconvinced that there was only one email discussing the report.

HFG moved to compel Weekley to "search for any emails stored on servers or back up tapes or other media, [and] any email folders in the email accounts of [the Employees]." At the hearing on HFG's motion, John Burchfield, Weekley's General Counsel, testified that "each [Weekley] employee has an [email] inbox that's limited in size. And once you bump that size limit, you have to start deleting things off the inbox in order to be able to receive any more emails." Burchfield further testified that "[Weekley] forces [employees] to clear out [their] inbox[es] on a regular basis," so that deleted emails will only be saved if an employee "back[s] them up on [the employee's] own personal hard drive somehow." And while deleted emails are saved on backup tapes, they are only retained "[f]or a thirty-day cycle." The trial court denied HFG's motion.

Email Storage Policy

Based upon information learned at the hearing, HFG filed a "Motion for Limited Access to [Weekley's] Computers" directing its discovery efforts at the Employees' hard drives. In essence the motion would, at HFG's expense, allow any two of four named PricewaterhouseCoopers forensic experts to access the Employees' computers "for the limited purpose of creating forensic images of the hard drives." According to the motion, the experts would "make an evidentiary image of the [hard drives] using a procedure that is generally accepted as forensically sound." Once the images are created, the experts would search the images for deleted emails from 2004, the relevant year, containing twenty-one specified terms: slope stability, retaining wall, Holigan, HFG, fence, mow!, landscap!, screening wall, LSI, limited site, Alpha, entry, earnest money, Legacy, defective, lot 1, lot 8, grading, substantial completion, letter of credit, and Site Concrete. Once the responsive documents had been identified, extracted, and copied to some form of electronic media by the experts, Weekley would have the right to review the extracted data

> and designate which documents or information [Weekley] claims are not relevant, not discoverable, or are subject to any claim of privilege or immunity from which they are withheld under such claims, identifying such withheld documents by page identification number, directory and subdirec-

tory identification, statement of claimed privilege or immunity from discovery, and brief description of the information in question as is required by Tex. R. Civ. Pro. 193.3.

After reviewing the extracted data, Weekley would be required to furnish HFG with any responsive documents that were not being withheld. According to the Motion, should HFG, its counsel, or the experts incidentally observe privileged or confidential information, the information would be maintained in strict confidence and otherwise valid privileges or confidentiality rights would not be waived. Failure to comply with the order's confidentiality provisions would subject the violator to penalties and contempt of court.

At the hearing on HFG's motion, Weekley complained about the intrusiveness of the suggested protocol, pointing out that the forensic experts would have access to private conversations, trade secrets, and privileged communications stored on the Employees' hard drives. Weekly also complained that requiring the Employees' hard drives to be "taken out of commission" for imaging would be burdensome and disruptive. And Weekley complained that HFG failed to show the feasibility of "obtain[ing] data that may have been deleted in 2004" using the protocol set forth in the Motion. [Weekley does not contend that the relevant computers or hard drives are unavailable, so access to the actual hard drives in use by the Employees during the relevant time period is not an issue.]

The trial court granted HFG's motion, and Weekley sought mandamus relief from the court of appeals. In a brief memorandum opinion, the court of appeals denied Weekley's petition. We granted oral argument in this case to determine whether the trial court abused its discretion by allowing forensic experts direct access to Weekley's Employees' electronic storage devices for imaging and searching.

II. Analysis

A. Rule 196.4's Application

1. Emails are electronic information

Texas Rule of Civil Procedure 192.3(b) provides for discovery of documents, defined to include electronic information that is relevant to the subject matter of the action. *See* Tex. R. Civ. P. 192.3(b) cmt. — 1999. Rule 196 governs requests for production of documents, and Rule 196.4 applies specifically to requests for production of "data or information that exists in electronic or magnetic form." As a threshhold matter, Weekley contends the trial court abused its discretion because HFG did not comply with Texas Rule of Civil Procedure 196.4 governing requests for production of electronic or magnetic data. HFG responds that Rule 196.4 does not apply because deleted emails are simply documents governed by the general discovery rules. According to HFG, Rule 196.4 only applies to spreadsheets and statistics, not emails and deleted emails.

We see nothing in the rule that would support HFG's interpretation. Emails and deleted emails stored in electronic or magnetic form (as opposed to being printed out) are clearly "electronic information." *See* Conference of Chief Justices, Guidelines for State Courts Regarding Discovery of Electronically-Stored Information v (2006), *available at*

http://www.ncsconline.org/images/EDisCCJGuidelinesFinal.pdf

Accordingly, we look to Rule 196.4 in analyzing HFG's requests.

B. Rule 196.4's Requirements

1. Specificity

Weekley argues that HFG failed to comply with Rule 196.4 because it never specifically requested production of "deleted emails." Rule 196.4 provides that, "[t]o obtain discovery of data or information that exists in electronic or magnetic form, the requesting party must specifically request production of electronic or magnetic data and specify the form in which the requesting party wants it produced." Tex. R. Civ. P. 196.4. As we have said, email communications constitute "electronic data," and their characterization as such does not change when they are deleted from a party's inbox. Thus, deleted emails are within Rule 196.4's purview and their production was implied by HFG's request. However, for parties unsophisticated in electronic discovery, such an implication might be easily missed. Rule 196.4 requires specificity, and HFG did not specifically request deleted emails. HFG counters that it did not know how Weekley's computer system and electronic information storage worked, and thus did not know what to ask for. But it is a simple matter to request emails that have been deleted; knowledge as to the particular method or means of retrieving them is not necessary at the requesting stage of discovery. Once a specific request is made the parties can, and should, communicate as to the particularities of a party's computer storage system and potential methods of retrieval to assess the feasibility of their recovery.[6] But even though it was not stated in HFG's written request that deleted emails were included within its scope, that HFG thought they were and was seeking this form of electronic information became abundantly clear in the course of discovery and before the hearing on the motion to compel. The purpose of Rule 196.4's specificity requirement is to ensure that requests for electronic information are clearly understood and disputes avoided. Because the scope of HFG's requests was understood before trial court intervention, Weekley was not prejudiced by HFG's failure to follow the rule and the trial court did not abuse its discretion by ordering production of the deleted emails. To ensure compliance with the rules and avoid confusion, however, parties seeking production of deleted emails should expressly request them.

Weekley additionally complains that HFG's "Motion for Limited Access to [Weekley's] Computers" is not a permissible discovery device. We agree with HFG, however, that the motion was, in effect, a motion to compel and the trial court properly treated it as such.

---

[6] The federal rules recognize the importance of early communication between parties on how electronic information is stored. *See* Fed. R. Civ. P. 16(b), 26(f). While the Texas rules have no counterpart, early discussions between the parties or early discovery directed toward learning about an opposing party's electronic storage systems and procedures is encouraged.

C. The Trial Court Abused Its Discretion in Allowing Access to Weekley's Hard Drives on this Record

1. The appropriate procedures under the rules

Weekley next contends that, even if a motion to compel may be used to access another party's hard drives, the trial court abused its discretion by permitting the experts to rummage through the Employees' computers in search of deleted emails that may no longer exist. Such an invasive procedure is only permissible, Weekley argues, when the requesting party has produced some evidence of good cause or bad faith, together with some evidence that the information sought exists and is retrievable. According to Weekley, HFG failed to make such a demonstration. HFG responds that inconsistencies and discrepancies in a party's production justify granting access to a party's hard drives. Additionally, HFG claims it was not required to show the feasibility of retrieval because it is well-settled that deleted emails can, at least in some cases, be retrieved from computer hard drives. Once again, we turn to Rule 196.4 for guidance.

When a specific request for electronic information has been lodged, Rule 196.4 requires the responding party to either produce responsive electronic information that is "reasonably available to the responding party in its ordinary course of business," or object on grounds that the information cannot through reasonable efforts be retrieved or produced in the form requested. Once the responding party raises a Rule 196.4 objection, either party may request a hearing at which the responding party must present evidence to support the objection. TEX. R. CIV. P. 193.4(a). To determine whether requested information is reasonably available in the ordinary course of business, the trial court may order discovery, such as requiring the responding party to sample or inspect the sources potentially containing information identified as not reasonably available. *See* TEX. R. CIV. P. 193.4(a); *cf.* TEX. R. CIV. P. 196.7 & cmts. — 1999; *accord* FED. R. CIV. P. 26(b)(2)(B) notes of the advisory committee to the 2006 amendments. The trial court may also allow deposition of witnesses knowledgeable about the responding party's information systems. *See* TEX. R. CIV. P. 195.1. Because parties' electronic systems, electronic storage, and retrieval capabilities will vary in each case, trial courts should assess the reasonable availability of information on a case-by-case basis.

Should the responding party fail to meet its burden, the trial court may order production subject to the discovery limitations imposed by Rule 192.4. If the responding party meets its burden by demonstrating that retrieval and production of the requested information would be overly burdensome, the trial court may nevertheless order targeted production upon a showing by the requesting party that the benefits of ordering production outweigh the costs. TEX. R. CIV. P. 192.4. Like assessing the reasonable availability of information, determining the scope of production may require some focused discovery, "which may include sampling of the sources, to learn more about what burdens and costs are involved in accessing the information, what the information consists of, and how valuable it is for the litigation in light of information that can be obtained by exhausting other opportunities for discovery." FED. R. CIV. P. 26(b)(2)(B) notes of the advisory committee to the 2006 amendments; *see also* TEX. R. CIV. P. 196.7. To the extent possible, courts should be mindful of protecting sensitive information and should choose the least intrusive means of retrieval. And when the court orders production of not-reasonably-available information, the court "must also order that the requesting party pay the reasonable expenses of any extraordinary steps required to retrieve and produce the information." Tex. R. Civ. P. 196.4.

Because HFG did not initially specifically request deleted emails as Rule 196.4 requires, Weekley had no obligation to object in its response that deleted emails were not "reasonably available . . . in its ordinary course of business." *Id.* However, because HFG's motion to compel clarified the scope of its original request, Weekley was required in its response to HFG's motion and at the subsequent hearing to make the Rule 196.4 showing. Our limited record does not reflect whether Weekley met its burden. However, the trial court's ultimate decision to order imaging of the Employees' hard drives and forensic examination implies a finding that the deleted emails were not reasonably available and required extraordinary steps for their retrieval and production. We must decide, then, whether the measures the trial court crafted for retrieving the Employees' deleted emails were proper under the circumstances presented. Although Rule 196.4 does not provide express guidelines for the manner or means by which electronic information that is not reasonably available in the ordinary course of business may be ordered produced, the federal rules and courts applying them offer some guidance.

2. The federal rules

Beginning in 2000, the federal Committee on Rules of Practice and Procedure began intensive work on the subject of computer-based discovery because of growing confusion in the area. *See* Comm. on Rules of Practice and Procedure, Summary of the Report of the Judicial Conference 22 (2005), *available at* http://www.uscourts.gov/rules/Reports/ST09-2005.pdf. The Committee's purpose was to "determine whether changes could be effected to reduce the costs of discovery, to increase its efficiency, to increase uniformity of practice, and to encourage the judiciary to participate more actively in case management when appropriate." In 2005, the Committee proposed amendments to the Federal Rules to better accommodate electronic discovery. The amendments were supported by The American Bar Association Section on Litigation, the Federal Bar Council, the New York State Bar Association Commercial and Federal Litigation Section, and the Department of Justice, and most of the amendments were unanimously approved by the Committee. The amendments were ultimately approved by the Judicial Conference and the United States Supreme Court, and have been in effect since December 1, 2006. Although we have not amended our rules to mirror the federal language, our rules as written are not inconsistent with the federal rules or the case law interpreting them.

Under Federal Rule of Civil Procedure 26(b)(2)(B), a trial court may order production of information that is not reasonably available only "if the requesting party shows good cause." In determining whether the requesting party has demonstrated "good cause," the court must consider, among other factors, whether

> the burden or expense of the proposed discovery outweighs its likely benefit, considering the needs of the case, the amount in controversy, the parties' resources, the importance of the issues at stake in the action, and the importance of the discovery in resolving the issues.

FED. R. CIV. P. 26(b)(2)(C)(iii). The Texas rules do not expressly require a "good cause" showing before production of not-reasonably-available electronic information may be ordered, but they do require a trial court to limit discovery when

> the burden or expense of the proposed discovery outweighs its likely benefit, taking into account the needs of the case, the amount in controversy, the parties' resources, the importance of the issues at stake in the litigation, and the importance of the proposed discovery in resolving the issues.

TEX. R. CIV. P. 192.4(b). Thus, both the federal rule and ours require trial courts to weigh the benefits of production against the burdens imposed when the requested information is not reasonably available in the ordinary course of business. We see no difference in the considerations that would apply when weighing the benefits against the burdens of electronic-information production; therefore we look to the federal rules for guidance.

Providing access to information by ordering examination of a party's electronic storage device is particularly intrusive and should be generally discouraged, just as permitting open access to a party's file cabinets for general perusal would be. The comments to the federal rules make clear that, while direct "access [to a party's electronic storage device] might be justified in some circumstances," the rules are "not meant to create a routine right of direct access." FED. R. CIV. P. 34 notes of the advisory committee to the 2006 amendments. When allowing such access, the comments to Rule 34 warn courts to "guard against undue intrusiveness." *Id.*

3. Federal case law

Since the 2006 amendments to the federal rules were promulgated, federal case law has established some basic principles regarding direct access to a party's electronic storage device. As a threshold matter, the requesting party must show that the responding party has somehow defaulted in its obligation to search its records and produce the requested data. *See The Scotts Co. v. Liberty Mut. Ins. Co.*, 2007 U.S. Dist. LEXIS 43005, at *5 (S.D. Ohio 2007); *Diepenhorst v. City of Battle Creek*, 2006 U.S. Dist. LEXIS 48551, at *10 (W.D. Mich. 2006); *Powers v. Thomas M. Cooley Law Sch.*, 2006 U.S. Dist. LEXIS 67706, at *14 (W.D. Mich. 2006). The requesting party should also show that the responding party's production "has been inadequate and that a search of the opponent's [electronic storage device] could recover deleted relevant materials." *Diepenhorst*, 2006 U.S. Dist. LEXIS 48551, at *9. Courts have been reluctant to rely on mere skepticism or bare allegations that the responding party has failed to comply with its discovery duties. *The Scotts Co.*, 2007 U.S. Dist. LEXIS 43005, at *6; *Powers*, 2006 U.S. Dist. LEXIS 67706, at *15;[7] *cf. Balfour Beatty Rail, Inc. v. Vaccarello*, 2007 U.S. Dist. LEXIS 3581, at *7 (M.D.

---

[7] *See also White v. Graceland Coll. Ctr. for Prof'l Dev. & Lifelong Learning, Inc.*, 2009 U.S. Dist. LEXIS 22068, at *13 (D. Kan. 2009) (allowing direct access where requesting party's expert noted discrepancies in the metadata of certain produced emails); *Matthews v. Baumhaft*, 2008 U.S. Dist. LEXIS 42396, at *5 (E.D. Mich. 2008) (allowing direct access upon a showing of responding party's discovery misconduct); *Ferron v. Search Cactus, L.L.C.*, 2008 U.S. Dist. LEXIS 34599, at *8 (S.D. Ohio 2008) (allowing direct access where responding party "failed to fulfill his 'duty to preserve information because of pending or reasonably anticipated litigation'") (quoting FED. R. CIV. P. 37 notes of the advisory committee to the 2006 amendments).

Fl. 2007) (denying access to responding party's hard drives where requesting party failed to demonstrate responding party's non-compliance with its discovery duties); *see also McCurdy Group v. Am. Biomedical Group, Inc.*, 9 Fed. Appx. 822, 831 (10th Cir. 2001) (noting that skepticism alone is not sufficient to permit direct access to an opponent's electronic storage device).

Even if the requesting party makes this threshold showing, courts should not permit the requesting party itself to access the opponent's storage device; rather, only a qualified expert should be afforded such access, *Diepenhorst*, 2006 U.S. Dist. LEXIS 48551, at *7; *accord In re Honza*, 242 S.W.3d 578, 583 n.8 (Tex. App. — Waco 2008, pet. denied) (noting that "the expert's qualifications are of critical importance when access to another party's computer hard drives or similar data storage is sought"), and only when there is some indication that retrieval of the data sought is feasible. *See Calyon v. Mizuho Sec. USA Inc.*, 2007 U.S. Dist. LEXIS 36961, at *17-18 (S.D.N.Y. 2007); *Antioch Co. v. Scrapbook Borders, Inc.*, 210 F.R.D. 645, 652 (D. Minn. 2002). Due to the broad array of electronic information storage methodologies, the requesting party must become knowledgeable about the characteristics of the storage devices sought to be searched in order to demonstrate the feasibility of electronic retrieval in a particular case. And consistent with standard prohibitions against "fishing expeditions," a court may not give the expert carte blanche authorization to sort through the responding party's electronic storage device. *See Thielen v. Buongiorno USA, Inc.*, 2007 U.S. Dist. LEXIS 8998, at *7-8 (W.D. Mich. 2007). Instead, courts are advised to impose reasonable limits on production. Courts must also address privilege, privacy, and confidentiality concerns.

Finally, federal courts have been more likely to order direct access to a responding party's electronic storage devices when there is some direct relationship between the electronic storage device and the claim itself. For example, in *Ameriwood Industries v. Liberman*, 2006 U.S. Dist. LEXIS 93380, Ameriwood sued several former employees claiming they improperly used Ameriwood's computers, confidential files, and confidential information to sabotage Ameriwood's business by forwarding its customer information and other trade secrets from Ameriwood's computers to the employees' personal email accounts. 2006 U.S. Dist. LEXIS 93380, at *2, *9. Based in part on the close relationship between Ameriwood's claims and the employees' computer equipment, the trial court justified "allowing an expert to obtain and search a mirror image of [the employee] defendants" hard drives. *Id.*, at *6. Similarly, in *Cenveo Corp. v. Slater*, 2007 U.S. Dist. LEXIS 8281, Cenveo sued several former employees for improperly using its computers, confidential trade information, and trade secrets to divert business from Cenveo to themselves. *Id.*, at *1. Borrowing from *Ameriwood*, the district court authorized a similar order "[b]ecause of the close relationship between plaintiff's claims and defendants' computer equipment." *Id.* at *4. Finally, in *Frees, Inc. v. McMillian*, 2007 U.S. Dist. LEXIS 4343, a former employee was sued for using company computers to remove certain proprietary information. 2007 U.S. Dist. LEXIS 4343, at *2. Noting that the employee's computers would be "among the most likely places [the employee] would have downloaded or stored the data allegedly missing," *id.*, at *5, the court allowed direct access to the employee's work and home computers.

4. HFG did not make the necessary showing

In this case, HFG's motion relied primarily upon discrepancies and inconsistencies in Weekley's production. According to HFG, Weekley only produced "a handful of emails from Russell Rice, and one email from Biff Bailey," Weekley's Division President and Land Acquisitions Manager respectively, while producing "no emails from the email accounts of Scott Thompson or Joe Vastano, both of whom . . . were very involved with the [s]ubdivision." Additionally, HFG expressed concern about the limited number of emails relating to the Slope Stability Analysis it received despite the importance of that report. Beyond Weekley's meager document production, HFG relied upon Burchfield's testimony that Weekley employees do not save deleted emails to their hard drives, and that Burchfield had "no earthly idea . . . whether [the deleted emails are] something a forensic specialist could go in and retrieve."

From this testimony, the trial court could have concluded that HFG made a showing that Weekley did not search for relevant deleted emails that HFG requested. But it does not follow that a search of the Employees' hard drives would likely reveal deleted emails or, if it would, that they would be reasonably capable of recovery. HFG's conclusory statements that the deleted emails it seeks "must exist" and that deleted emails are in some cases recoverable is not enough to justify the highly intrusive method of discovery the trial court ordered, which afforded the forensic experts "complete access to all data stored on [the Employees'] computers." The missing step is a demonstration that the particularities of Weekley's electronic information storage methodology will allow retrieval of emails that have been deleted or overwritten, and what that retrieval will entail. A complicating factor is the some two-and-a-half years that passed between the time any responsive emails would have been created and the time HFG requested them. Under these circumstances, it is impossible to determine whether the benefit of the forensic examination the trial court ordered outweighs the burden that such an invasive method of discovery imposed. *Compare Honza*, 242 S.W.3d at 583 n.8.

5. This case differs from *Honza*

We understand the trial court's predicament, as state law in this area is not clearly defined and the parties' discovery postures shed more heat than light upon the situation. That being the case, the trial court apparently followed the protocol set forth in the only Texas case to address a similar situation. *See Honza*, 242 S.W.3d 578. In *Honza*, A & W Development, L.L.C. assigned to Wesley F. Honza and Robert A. Honza the right to purchase a tract of land under a real estate contract. Under the terms of the assignment, A & W retained the right to purchase a portion of the assigned tract for construction of a street. According to A & W, an earlier version of the assignment made no mention of a purchase price upon exercise of the right because the consideration negotiated for the partial assignment included what the Honzas should receive for the street. When A & W decided to exercise its right, the Honzas demanded that A & W pay additional consideration. A & W sued the Honzas seeking declaratory relief and alleging various theories of recovery. In the course of discovery, the Honzas produced two drafts of the partial assignment in electronic form. However, they did not produce or otherwise make available metadata associated with those documents. The first trial resulted in a mistrial, after which A & W moved to gain access to the Honzas hard drives to obtain the metadata necessary to identify the points in time when the partial assignment draft was modified. *Id.* The trial court granted A & W's motion, crafting a protocol similar to the one ordered in this case. The court of appeals affirmed the trial court's order, *id.* at 579, and we denied mandamus relief.

Despite the undeniable similarities between the *Honza* order and the one presented here, there are several important distinctions concerning the contexts in which the two orders were granted. First, in *Honza*, A & W sought metadata associated with two documents that had already been shown to exist; indeed, the Honzas produced those documents in electronic form in response to discovery requests propounded before the first trial. Because the Honzas were required to preserve that evidence once it had been requested, there was a reasonable likelihood that a search of the Honzas' computers would reveal the information A & W sought. In this case, on the other hand, the potential for successful recovery of the Employees' deleted emails over a two-and-a-half-year period is much less clear.

Moreover, in *Honza* there was a direct relationship between the hard drives sought and A & W's claims. As the court of appeals noted, identification of the points in time when the partial assignment draft was modified directly concerned "the issue of whether [the Honzas] altered the partial assignment after the parties concluded their agreement but before the document was presented for execution." In contrast, although the deleted emails HFG seeks in this case might reveal circumstantial evidence that the representations Weekley made in the Estoppel Certificate were misleading, there is no claim that the Estoppel Certificate itself was tampered with. While we recognize that a more tenuous link between the electronic storage device and the claim itself is not dispositive, it is a factor trial courts should consider.

Finally, in *Honza* there was extensive testimony from A & W's expert about his experience and qualifications before access to the Honzas' computers was ordered. Although Weekley does not directly challenge the qualifications of HFG's forensic experts, nothing was presented to show that the experts were qualified to perform the search given the particularities of the specific storage devices at issue, or that the search methodology would likely allow retrieval of relevant deleted emails. Absent some indication that the experts are familiar with the particularities of the Employees' hard drives, that they are qualified to search those hard drives, and that the proposed methodology for searching those hard drives is reasonably likely to yield the information sought, *Honza* does not support the trial court's order. We conclude that by ordering forensic examination of Weekley's hard drives without such information, the trial court abused its discretion.

Because the trial court abused its discretion by granting HFG's motion without the requisite showing, we need not reach Weekley's alternative arguments that the search terms the trial court ordered are overly broad, or that the trial court's order improperly requires Weekley to create the equivalent of a "privilege log" as to irrelevant documents that the search might produce. However, because trial courts should be mindful of protecting sensitive information and utilize the least intrusive means necessary to facilitate discovery of electronic information, the trial court should consider these arguments on remand.

D. Summary of Rule 196.4 Procedure

A fundamental tenet of our discovery rules is cooperation between parties and their counsel, and the expectation that agreements will be made as reasonably necessary for efficient disposition of the case. TEX. R. CIV. P. 191.2. Accordingly, prior to promulgating requests for electronic information, parties and their attorneys should share relevant information concerning electronic systems and storage methodologies so that agreements regarding protocols maybe reached or, if not, trial courts have the information necessary to craft discovery orders that are not unduly intrusive or overly burdensome. The critical importance of learning about relevant systems early in the litigation process is heavily emphasized in the federal rules. Due to the "volume and dynamic nature of electronically stored information," failure to become familiar with relevant systems early on can greatly complicate preservation issues, increase uncertainty in the discovery process, and raise the risk of disputes. FED. R. CIV. P. 26(f) notes of the advisory committee to the 2006 amendments.

With these overriding principles in mind, we summarize the proper procedure under Rule 196.4:

- the party seeking to discover electronic information must make a specific request for that information and specify the form of production. TEX. R. CIV. P. 196.4.

- The responding party must then produce any electronic information that is "responsive to the request and . . . reasonably available to the responding-party in its ordinary course of business."

- If "the responding party cannot — through reasonable efforts — retrieve the data or information requested or produce it in the form requested," the responding party must object on those grounds.

- The parties should make reasonable efforts to resolve the dispute without court intervention. TEX. R. CIV. P. 191.2.

- If the parties are unable to resolve the dispute, either party may request a hearing on the objection, TEX. R. CIV. P. 193.4(a), at which the responding party must demonstrate that the requested information is not reasonably available because of undue burden or cost, TEX. R. CIV. P. 192.4(b).

- If the trial court determines the requested information is not reasonably available, the court may nevertheless order production upon a showing by the requesting party that the benefits of production outweigh the burdens imposed, again subject to Rule 192.4's discovery limitations.

- If the benefits are shown to outweigh the burdens of production and the trial court orders production of information that is not reasonably available, sensitive information should be protected and the least intrusive means should be employed. TEX. R. CIV. P. 192.6(b). The requesting party must also pay the reasonable expenses of any extraordinary steps required to retrieve and produce the information. TEX. R. CIV. P. 196.4.

- Finally, when determining the means by which the sources should be searched and information produced, direct access to another party's electronic storage devices is discouraged, and courts should be extremely cautious to guard against undue intrusion. . . .

III. Conclusion

We conditionally grant the writ of mandamus and order the trial court to vacate its Order. We are confident the trial court will comply, and our writ will issue only if it does not. We note that HFG is not precluded from seeking to rectify the deficiencies we have identified.

NOTES AND QUESTIONS

(1) *Requesting Electronically-Stored Information.* A party who wants e-discovery must specifically ask for it. Civil Procedure Rule 196.4 provides, "To obtain discovery of data or information that exists in electronic or magnetic form, the requesting party must specifically request production of electronic or magnetic data and specify the form in which the requesting party wants it produced." Before embarking on discovery (or representing the discovered party), the lawyer should become well-informed about the nature of the client's data as well as its capacity to "read" various types of data. In negotiating the format in which data will be produced, consider carefully whether documents will be produced in a format the contains embedded data and metadata or in a format in which those components have been removed. Embedded "Comments," for example, might contain privileged communications between attorney and client.

(2) *Cost of Producing Electronic Data.* The court in *Weekley Homes* discusses in detail the proper procedure for allowing discovery of data on a computer hard drive, but does not discuss who bears the cost of such searches. Civil Procedure Rule 196.4 provides that electronic data that is "reasonably available to the responding party in its ordinary course of business" must be produced, but that the responding party may object if it cannot "through reasonable efforts" retrieve the data or information requested or produce it in the form requested. The rule further provides that if the court nevertheless orders production that requires "extraordinary steps" to retrieve and produce information, it is the requesting party who must pay the reasonable expenses of those steps. This is different from the federal rules, which give the court discretion to allocate the costs of retrieving data that is not readily available. Which do you think is the better approach?

(3) *Spoliation.* Electronic data is also more easily changed or deleted than hard copy documents. Litigants must be particularly careful to avoid deletion of electronically-stored information after a discovery request or document retention order is in place. In the federal courts, parties have been severely sanctioned for destroying electronic files. *See, e.g., Zubulake v. UBS Warburg*, 229 F.R.D. 422 (S.D.N.Y. 2004) (sanctions for deletion of emails). The new federal electronic discovery rules create a partial safe harbor, providing that, "Absent exceptional circumstances, a court may not impose sanctions under these rules on a party for failing to provide electronically stored information lost as a result of the routine,

good-faith operation of an electronic information system." FED. R. CIV. P. 37(e). Thus, a client can be advised that having a document retention policy and following it may protect them from adverse consequences when documents have been discarded. *See, e.g.*, *Stevenson v. Union Pacific R.R.*, 354 F.3d 739, 747 (8th Cir. 2004). Note that this will not protect litigants from sanctions when they have engaged in brazen destruction of electronic data.

A recent Texas case considers a claim of spoliation and, citing *Weekley Homes*, distinguishes *Zubulake* and finds that the destruction of backup tapes was not improper. *MRT, Inc. v. Vounckx*, 299 S.W.3d 500, 508-511 (Tex. App. — Dallas 2009, no pet.).

(4) *Early Planning.* The new federal discovery rules also urge the parties to discuss "any issues about disclosure or discovery of electronically stored information, including the form or forms in which it should be produced" in an early discovery planning conference. FED. R. CIV. P. 26(f)(3). While the Texas rules do not explicitly require such a conference, identifying the nature of electronic information that will be subject to discovery and making decisions about format and procedures for its discovery at an early stage can be extremely helpful and may avoid later disputes and unnecessary expense. The Texas Supreme Court in *Weekley Homes* specifically recommends early planning and consultation regarding electronic discovery.

[4] Getting Documents and Things From Nonparties by Subpoena Without Deposition

Rule 176 governs the issuance, service, and use of subpoenas. TEX. R. CIV. P. 176. A subpoena may be used to command the person to whom it is directed to do either or both of the following: (1) attend and give testimony at a deposition, hearing, or trial; or (2) produce and permit inspection and copying of designated documents or tangible things in the possession, custody, or control of that person. TEX. R. CIV. P. 176.2. Thus, a pretrial subpoena may be used as a separate discovery device for obtaining production of documents from nonparties without taking an oral or written deposition.

The rule provides a subpoena range under which a person "may not be required by subpoena to appear or produce documents or other things in a county that is more than 150 miles from where the person resides or is served" for discovery subpoenas served on persons whose appearance or production may not be compelled by notice alone. TEX. R. CIV. P. 176.3. Similarly, the Civil Practice and Remedies Code defines the subpoena range this way: "A witness who is represented to reside 150 miles or less from a county in which a suit is pending or who may be found within that distance at the time of trial on the suit may be subpoenaed in the suit." C.P.R.C. § 22.002. The subpoenas may be issued by a court clerk, a licensed attorney, or an officer authorized to take depositions in Texas. *See* TEX. R. CIV. P. 176.4; C.P.R.C. § 22.001; GOV. C. § 52.021.

A person responding to a subpoena need not appear in person at the time and place of production unless the person is also commanded to attend and give testimony, either in the same subpoena or a separate one. Specific procedures for making objections to a subpoena and for moving for a protective order are set forth in Civil Procedure Rule 176. A person who properly objects or moves for protection "before the time specified for compliance" need not comply with the contested part of the subpoena "unless ordered to do so by the court." Tex. R. Civ. P. 176.6(d). (Note, however, that for oral depositions under Civil Procedure Rule 199.4, a motion for protective order only stays the oral deposition if the motion is filed by the third business day after service of the notice of deposition.) The party requesting the subpoena may seek a court order enforcing it "at any time" after the motion for protection is filed. Tex. R. Civ. P. 176.6(e).

Another procedural rule also applies to document discovery from nonparties. Tex. R. Civ. P. 205. This rule requires that a party seeking discovery by subpoena without deposition from a nonparty must serve on the nonparty *and* all parties a copy of the form of notice "required under the rules governing the applicable form of discovery . . . at least ten days before the subpoena compelling production is served." Tex. R. Civ. P. 205.2; 205.3. The rule also contains other specific provisions concerning the production of documents without depositions and requests for production of medical or mental health records of nonparties.

NOTES AND QUESTIONS

(1) *Need for Testimony.* When using a subpoena to discover documents from a nonparty, when would you need the person subpoenaed to testify in addition to producing the documents? Consider issues of both authentication and admissibility. [Although production of the documents authenticates them as to that party, they may need to be authenticated to be used against others. In addition, if you want to introduce the documents in evidence, you would need to have the testimony required to overcome a hearsay objection — for example, testimony proving them to be admissible as business records. *See, e.g.*, Tex. R. Evid. 803(6) (records of regularly conducted activity); 902(10) (self-authentication of business records).]

(2) *Procedural Requirements.* Suppose you want to subpoena nonparty X to produce documents without deposition. When do you need to send a notice? When in relation to that should the witness be served with a subpoena? How long a period must you allow between the subpoena and the production? [The notice to produce documents must be served at least 10 days before the subpoena compelling production is served. Tex. R. Civ. P. 205.2. The subpoena, in turn, must be served "a reasonable time before the response is due but no later than 30 days before the end of any applicable discovery period." Tex. R. Civ. P. 205.3.]

(3) *Enforcement of Subpoenas.* What happens when a person ignores a subpoena? [It may be enforced by the court through a writ of attachment, but only if the subpoena process is strictly followed. *See* Tex. R. Civ. P. 176.8. *See also Kieffer v. Miller*, 560 S.W.2d 431 (Tex. Civ. App. — Beaumont 1977, no writ) (refusing to use attachment to enforce the subpoena because the affidavit failed to swear that the witness fee had been tendered).]

PRACTICE EXERCISE #26

Assume the same facts as for Practice Exercise #25.

1. You represent Alpha Omega. You have received a document production request from Allen that, read fairly, requires production of a very damaging internal memo. You wish it were privileged, but it is not. You would like to place it in the middle of a very large file full of grape invoices. Do the discovery rules allow that?

2. You represent Brock O. Lee, a produce company delivery man. He delivered a large quantity of pre-bagged grapes to Alpha Omega on the day of Allen's fall. Lee has been served with a subpoena to produce all documents reflecting his delivery of grapes to Alpha Omega from 1990 to the present. One of these documents is a letter from his employer's lawyer to all delivery people describing possible company liability if the grapes are not properly handled. Lee never throws much of anything away, and has boxes of this stuff in his garage. However, he doesn't keep his business records separate from his personal records and it is all mixed up with old birthday cards, newspapers, and tax returns. Advise Lee on his possible responses to the subpoena, including both the substance of the response and the procedure for responding.

3. You represent Allen. She has received the following Request for Production of Documents from Alpha Omega: "Please produce any and all books, records, reports, or other documents in your possession, custody, or control that relate to this case." Any problems? What should you do?

4. You represent Allen. You have learned from your neighbor, a former Alpha Omega employee, that the Alpha Omega where Allen fell maintains an extensive database: (1) describing every incident in which a customer has fallen in the store; (2) identifying each Alpha Omega employee who has ever been reprimanded or discharged for failure to follow store safety policies; and (3) listing all products recommended by Alpha Omega's national office to maximize produce department safety. You would love to get at this information, and would be even more ecstatic if you could search it on your own computer. What will you do to maximize your chance of getting this information, and getting it in usable form?

[5] Requests for Admissions

Requests for admissions try to identify facts that are not disputed. They are governed by Civil Procedure Rule 198. A party may serve on another party written requests that the other party admit the truth of any matter within the scope of discovery, including statements of opinion or of fact or of the application of law to fact. Each matter for which an admission is requested must be stated separately. Tex. R. Civ. P. 198.1. The responding party must serve a written response on the requesting party within 30 days after service of the request (except that a defendant served with a request before the defendant's answer is due need not respond until 50 days after service of the request). Tex. R. Civ. P. 198.2(a).

Unless the responding party states an objection or asserts a privilege, the responding party must specifically admit or deny the request or explain in detail the reasons that the responding party cannot admit or deny the request. Lack of information or knowledge is not a proper response unless the responding party states that a reasonable inquiry was made but that the information known or easily obtainable is insufficient to enable the responding party to admit or deny. Tex. R. Civ. P. 198.2(a).

If a response is not timely served, the request is considered admitted without the necessity of a court order. Tex. R. Civ. P. 198.2(c). This is a significant consequence, in that a matter admitted under Civil Procedure Rule 198 is conclusively established as to the party making the admission unless the court permits the party to withdraw or amend the admission. The court may permit the party to withdraw or amend the admission if: (1) the party shows good cause for the withdrawal or amendment; and (2) the court finds that the parties relying on the responses and deemed admissions will not be unduly prejudiced and that presentation of the merits of the action will be subserved by permitting the party to amend or withdraw the admission. Tex. R. Civ. P. 198.3. The following case discusses these requirements.

STELLY v. PAPANIA

927 S.W.2d 620 (Tex. 1996)

Per Curiam

We consider whether a trial court abuses its discretion by allowing a party to withdraw and amend its original answers to a request for admissions. We hold that a trial court does not abuse its discretion when the moving party shows: (1) good cause; (2) that the party relying on the responses will not be unduly prejudiced; and (3) that the withdrawal will serve the purpose of legitimate discovery and the merits of the case. Accordingly, we reverse the judgment of the court of appeals and remand the case to that court to determine the merits of the appeal.

After delivering a pizza to Ermon Stelly's house, Michael Papania slipped on a patch of mud in what he believed to be Stelly's front yard. As a result, he suffered a broken leg. Papania sued Stelly and the City of Port Neches. He alleged that the City created the mud patch when it worked on the sewer line in front of Stelly's home.

Papania sent Requests for Admissions to both Stelly and the City. Stelly mistakingly admitted that he owned the premises on which Papania fell. Papania non-suited the City and the trial court later dismissed all of Papania's claims against the City with prejudice. Later, Stelly discovered that the City owned the land where Papania fell. A surveyor's report revealed that Stelly's boundary line ended seven feet before the street curb.

Stelly moved to withdraw and amend his previous admissions. He also moved for summary judgment on grounds that he did not: (1) own the property by the street; (2) actively cause the alleged defective condition on the City's property; and (3) have a duty to keep the City's land safe.

The trial court granted both motions. The court of appeals reversed and remanded. That court held that the trial court abused its discretion because Stelly did not show that his new responses would not prejudice Papania. Because the new responses formed the basis for Stelly's motion for summary judgment, the court of appeals reversed the judgment and remanded the case for trial.

Stelly argues that the trial court did not abuse its discretion because the surveyor's report about who actually owned the land provided good cause for Stelly to amend his responses to Papania's request for admissions. Stelly also contends that his amended admissions did not prejudice Papania because: (1) Papania's claim against the City was barred because he did not give timely notice under the Texas Tort Claims Act; and (2) even if Papania had relied on Stelly's original admission, Stelly's ownership could not absolve the City of responsibility for creating a hazard. We agree.

This case presents a unique situation. We have never considered whether a party can withdraw its original response to a request for admission and substitute it with a new response. Moreover, decisions from the courts of appeals are limited to cases where parties seek to withdraw deemed admissions. *See, e.g.*, *Burden v. John Watson Landscape Illumination, Inc.*, 896 S.W.2d 253, 256 (Tex. App. — Eastland 1995, writ denied); *North River Ins. Co. of New Jersey v. Greene*, 824 S.W.2d 697, 700 (Tex. App. — El Paso 1992, writ denied); *Employers Ins. of Wausau v. Halton*, 792 S.W.2d 462, 465 (Tex. App. — Dallas 1990, writ denied). Although this case does not involve deemed admissions, we find these cases instructive.

A party may withdraw a deemed admission "upon a showing of good cause for such withdrawal . . . if the court finds that the parties relying upon the responses . . . will not be unduly prejudiced and that the presentation of the merits of the action will be subserved thereby." Tex. R. Civ. P. 169(2). After the rule was amended in 1988, "good cause" became the threshold standard for withdrawal of deemed admissions. *Halton*, 792 S.W.2d at 465. A party can establish good cause by showing that its failure to answer was accidental or the result of a mistake, rather than intentional or the result of conscious indifference. *Greene*, 824 S.W.2d at 700; *see Halton*, 792 S.W.2d at 465.

A trial court has broad discretion to permit or deny the withdrawal of deemed admissions. *Halton*, 792 S.W.2d at 464. An appellate court should set aside the trial court's ruling only if, after reviewing the entire record, it is clear that the trial court abused its discretion . . . .

The purpose of the rules of civil procedure is to obtain a just, fair, equitable and impartial adjudication of the litigants' rights under established principles of substantive law. *See* Tex. R. Civ. P. 1. The "ultimate purpose of discovery is to seek the truth . . . ." *Jampole v. Touchy*, 673 S.W.2d 569, 573 (Tex. 1984). The discovery rules were not designed as traps for the unwary, nor should we construe them to prevent a litigant from presenting the truth. *See Burden*, 896 S.W.2d at 256. As we stated:

> The primary purpose of [Rule 169] is to simplify trials by eliminating matters about which there is no real controversy, but which may be difficult

> or expensive to prove. It was never intended to be used as a demand upon a plaintiff or defendant to admit that he had no cause of action or ground of defense . . . .

There is evidence in the record to support the trial court's order allowing Stelly to withdraw his admissions. Stelly presented affidavit testimony that, upon discovering the faulty admissions, he immediately filed his motion to withdraw them and amend his responses. He offered the surveyor's affidavit and report to show "good cause." The report and affidavit showed that he did not own the property where Papania fell. Papania offered no controverting evidence.

Papania was not prejudiced by the withdrawal for two reasons. First, his failure to comply with the notice provision under the Texas Tort Claims Act precluded his suit against the City regardless of who owned the land. Secondly, even if Stelly's original admission were true and he did own the land, it would not affect Papania's ability to sue the City for creating the alleged hazard.

Because the trial court properly conducted a hearing on both motions and based its decision on evidence in the record, we cannot say that it abused its discretion. The court of appeals incorrectly concluded that the trial court abused its discretion on a procedural point. It, therefore, declined to consider the merits of Stelly's duty, if any, to Papania. We disagree. Without hearing oral argument the Court remands this case to the court of appeals to determine whether the trial court properly granted Stelly summary judgment. *See* Tex. R. App. P. 170 and 184(c).

WHEELER v. GREEN
157 S.W.3d 439 (Tex 2005)

Per Curiam

Based on sixty-four deemed requests for admissions, the trial court granted summary judgment terminating Sandra Wheeler as joint managing conservator of her daughter, appointing Darrin Green as sole managing conservator (with exclusive rights to determine the child's residence, education, and medical care), and finding Sandra liable for maliciously prosecuting Darrin. Darrin's attorney neglected to point out in his summary judgment motion that Sandra — appearing pro se — actually *had* filed responses six months before the motion was heard, but two days after they were due. Sandra asserts the summary judgment was error, and under the facts presented here we agree.

Sandra gave birth to a daughter in December 1998. She sued to establish Darrin's paternity in February 1999. By final order in January 2000, Darrin agreed to pay child support and both parents were appointed joint managing conservators.

A succession of disputes regarding visitation and allegations of neglect followed, with Darrin eventually seeking modification to appoint him as sole managing conservator. On January 11, 2002, Darrin's attorney mailed sixty-four requests for admissions, which in his own words "requested admissions on every element of each claim set forth in Movant's live petition."

A certified receipt shows Sandra received them on January 19. The instructions informed her to respond "within 30 days after service of this request." *See* TEX. R. CIV. P. 198.2(a).

Sandra sent her responses to Darrin's attorney by mail on February 15, twenty-seven days after she received the requests. But this was actually thirty-five days after the "mailbox rule" deems they were served on her, thus making them two days late. *See* TEX. R. CIV. P. 21a (providing service occurs upon mailing and extending response time by three days).

Darrin's attorney moved for summary judgment, attaching the requests for admission but saying nothing about the responses he had in his file. Sandra — still pro se — filed no response but attended the summary judgment hearing. In fact, she did so twice, as the visiting judge announced at the first setting that the docket was too full and ordered them to return the next morning. When they did, he granted Darrin's motion.

Sandra thereafter obtained an attorney, who filed a motion for new trial, attached her responses, and argued they were timely. The motion asserted the requests should not have been deemed admitted, the summary judgment should be set aside, and that Sandra would pay Darrin's costs if it was. This motion, too, was denied.

Sandra appealed, asserting that summary judgment based on nothing but the deemed admissions was erroneous. The court of appeals affirmed, pointing out that Sandra never responded to the summary judgment and never moved to withdraw her deemed admissions, and that "even in custody cases, a complete failure to follow the rules of pleading and practice cannot be ignored." While we agree that no one can ignore the rules, we disagree that the rules here require judgment against Sandra by default. . . .

We . . . held in *Carpenter* [*v. Cimarron Hydrocarbons Corp.*] that the standards for withdrawing deemed admissions and for allowing a late summary-judgment response are the same. 98 S.W.3d 682, 687–88. Either is proper upon a showing of (1) good cause, and (2) no undue prejudice. *Id.*; *see* TEX. R. CIV. P. 166a(c), 198.3.

Good cause is established by showing the failure involved was an accident or mistake, not intentional or the result of conscious indifference. *Carpenter*, 98 S.W.3d at 687–88; *Stelly v. Papania*, 927 S.W.2d 620, 622 (Tex. 1996) (per curiam). While Sandra argued only that her responses were timely, the trial court could not have concluded otherwise without noting that she was mistaken as to when "service" occurs. And while Sandra did not move to file a late response to the summary judgment motion, she came to argue her case at both hearings only because she was again mistaken as to what a summary judgment "hearing" was. On this record, the lower courts could have concluded that Sandra was wrong on her dates and wrong on how to correct them, but not that either was the result of intent or conscious indifference.[1]

Undue prejudice depends on whether withdrawing an admission or filing a late

---

[1] By contrast, if the same elementary mistakes had been made by a lawyer, such a conclusion might well be warranted.

response will delay trial or significantly hamper the opposing party's ability to prepare for it. *Carpenter*, 98 S.W.3d at 687; *Stelly*, 927 S.W.2d at 622; *see also Wal-Mart Stores, Inc. v. Deggs*, 968 S.W.2d 354, 357 (Tex. 1998) (per curiam) (finding no undue prejudice from withdrawing store manager's deemed admissions as plaintiff had already deposed him). As Sandra's proof attached to her motion for new trial showed, Darrin's attorney received her responses two days late but six months *before* the summary judgment motion was heard. The lower courts could not have concluded on this record that Darrin would suffer any undue prejudice if the admissions were withdrawn.[2]

We recognize that trial courts have broad discretion to permit or deny withdrawal of deemed admissions, but they cannot do so arbitrarily, unreasonably, or without reference to guiding rules or principles. *Stelly*, 927 S.W.2d at 622. While requests for admissions were at one time unique in including an automatic sanction for untimely responses, failure to comply with any discovery requests now bears similar consequences. *See* Tex. R. Civ. P. 193.6(a). Nevertheless, we have held for all other forms of discovery that absent flagrant bad faith or callous disregard for the rules, due process bars merits-preclusive sanctions, and have applied this rule to:

- depositions, *see TransAmerican Natural Gas Corp. v. Powell*, 811 S.W.2d 913, 918–19 (Tex. 1991);
- interrogatories, *see Chrysler Corp. v. Blackmon*, 841 S.W.2d 844, 846, 850 (Tex. 1992);
- requests for production, *see id.* at 849–50; *GTE Communications Sys. Corp. v. Tanner*, 856 S.W.2d 725, 729–30 (Tex. 1993); and
- requests for disclosure, *see Spohn Hosp. v. Mayer*, 104 S.W.3d 878, 883 (Tex. 2003) (per curiam).

When requests for admissions are used as intended — addressing uncontroverted matters or evidentiary ones like the authenticity or admissibility of documents — deeming admissions by default is unlikely to compromise presentation of the merits. *See Stelly*, 927 S.W.2d at 622 (stating requests for admissions were intended to "eliminate matters about which there is no real controversy" and were "never intended to be used as a demand upon a plaintiff or defendant to admit that he had no cause of action or ground of defense"). But when a party uses deemed admissions to try to preclude presentation of the merits of a case, the same due-process concerns arise. *See TransAmerican Natural Gas Corp.*, 811 S.W.2d at 917–18.

Of the sixty-four admissions deemed here, none sought to discover information: nine deemed circumstances changed so modification was proper, twenty-five deemed modification in the child's best interest, twenty-seven deemed Sandra

[2] The rule governing admissions includes as part of the undue-prejudice inquiry that the "presentation of the merits [must] be subserved" by permitting withdrawal. Tex. R. Civ. P. 198.3(b). The two are different sides of the same coin, as presentation of the merits will suffer: (1) if the requesting party *cannot* prepare for trial; and also (2) if the requestor *can* prepare but the case is decided on deemed (but perhaps untrue) facts anyway.

liable for malicious prosecution, and three deemed her liable for child support, attorney's fees, and exemplary damages.

This record contains no evidence of flagrant bad faith or callous disregard for the rules, nothing to justify a presumption that Sandra's case lacks merit, and nothing to suggest Darrin was unable to prepare for trial without the admissions. *See id.* at 918; *cf. Cire v. Cummings*, 134 S.W.3d 835, 843 (Tex. 2004) (affirming dismissal based on destruction of tapes at heart of case). Further, Sandra offered to pay for any expenses Darrin incurred because her responses were late. *See* TEX. R. CIV. P. 215.4. We hold under the facts presented here that the trial court should have granted a new trial and allowed the deemed admissions to be withdrawn upon learning that the summary judgment was solely because Sandra's responses were two days late. *See Spohn Hosp.*, 104 S.W.3d at 883 (holding late production of witness statements insufficient to justify deeming facts on merits).

We certainly agree that pro se litigants are not exempt from the rules of procedure. *Mansfield State Bank v. Cohn*, 573 S.W.2d 181, 184–85 (Tex. 1978). Having two sets of rules — a strict set for attorneys and a lenient set for pro se parties — might encourage litigants to discard their valuable right to the advice and assistance of counsel. But when a rule itself turns on an actor's state of mind (as these do here), application may require a different result when the actor is not a lawyer. Recognizing that Sandra did not know what any lawyer would does not create a separate rule, but recognizes the differences the rule itself contains.

Accordingly, without hearing oral argument, we reverse the court of appeals' judgment, and remand to the trial court for further proceedings consistent with this opinion.

NOTES AND QUESTIONS

(1) *Unifying Standards for Sanctions that Affect the Merits.* In *Wheeler*, the Court explicitly invokes the due process limits on sanctions that it has adopted for other discovery devices. For a discussion of these limits generally, see section 10.05.

(2) *Actual vs. Deemed Admissions.* A party who responds by actually admitting the requests, as was the case in *Stelly*, is bound by those admissions unless the court allows an amendment. Similarly, if the party who receives Requests for Admissions does not respond in a timely way, as in *Wheeler*, the requests are "deemed admitted" and the admitting party must ask the court for permission to amend the responses. As Rule 198 provides, no court order is needed to create "deemed admissions."

(3) *Interaction with Summary Judgment Practice.* In both of the cases above, parties were allowed to amend or withdraw their admissions. Note, though, that admissions may form the basis for all or part of a summary judgment order. For a discussion of the summary judgment process, see Chapter 11.

(4) *Use of Admissions.* Admissions can never be used *by* the party answering them — only *against* that party.

(5) *Improper Refusals to Admit; Sanctions.* Suppose a party denies a request and the matter constituting the subject matter of the request is established in a subsequent trial. Does the requesting party have any recourse? *See* Tex. R. Civ. P. 215.4(b) (providing for cost shifting sanctions).

(6) *Waiver of Right to Rely on Admission.* Admissions are conclusively binding in a way that interrogatories and other forms of discovery are not. An admission once admitted, deemed or otherwise, is a judicial admission. As such, a party may not introduce evidence contrary to the admission. Nevertheless, a party relying on a judicial admission must protect the record by objecting to the introduction of controverting evidence. Otherwise, the right to rely on the admission is waived. *See Marshall v. Vise*, 767 S.W.2d 699 (Tex. 1989) (in a non-jury trial, party who elicited testimony contrary to admissions in his favor and failed to object to such testimony has waived the right to rely on the admissions).

PRACTICE EXERCISE #27

Assume the same facts as for Practice Exercise #25.

1. You represent Allen. In addition to suing Alpha Omega you have sued Produce R Us, the company that you believed manufactured the produce bins that allowed slippery fruit to fall to the floor. Before the statute of limitations ran, you sent Produce R Us a request to admit that it manufactured the bins in the Alpha Omega store in which Allen fell. They failed to respond. Now, after it is too late to sue anyone else, they have requested permission to withdraw the deemed admission. It turns out that the bins were actually manufactured by Grapes to Go, an unrelated entity. What will you argue to the judge in opposition to the Produce R Us motion for leave to withdraw the deemed admission?

2. Assume that the judge has refused to give Produce R Us permission to withdraw the deemed admissions. Now you are trying the case, and the Area Manager of Produce R Us is on the witness stand. The Produce R Us lawyer has just asked her, "Did your company manufacture the produce bins for Alpha Omega?" What should you do?

[B] Oral and Other Non-Written Discovery

Depositions (oral and on written questions) and motions for physical and mental examinations are governed by different procedures from those specially addressed to written discovery. This section examines these discovery devices.

Read Tex. R. Civ. P. 176, 191, 193.3, 195.4, 196.2(a), 199, 200, 201, 203 and accompanying Comments.

[1] Depositions — General Considerations

Before taking a deposition, an attorney should consider the reasons for choosing the deposition device and for choosing the particular witness. A deposition may serve a variety of purposes. It may be a vehicle for the discovery of facts. It may serve to preserve the testimony of witnesses who may not be available at the time of the trial. It may force witnesses to adopt under oath one particular version of the facts, which may be used for impeachment if the witnesses change their testimony at a later time. Depositions also serve as a forum for the evaluation of an opposing party's witnesses and counsel and for observing one's own client and witnesses under cross-examination.

Before a notice of deposition is prepared, a number of preliminary decisions must be made. The objectives of the particular deposition should be clearly identified. A deposition may, for instance, be exploratory in nature, or it may be intended to cement and preserve a particular witness' testimony. Therefore, consideration should be given to the timing and sequence of depositions. In some cases, early depositions will be necessary; in others, depositions will be more productive after other discovery methods are used.

Among the decisions that need to be made are whether the deposition should be taken orally or on written questions. Practical difficulties or the nature of the subject matter may make a deposition on written questions, rather than the more flexible but more expensive oral deposition, the better choice. In light of the variety of recording techniques available, thought must be given to whether a method such as videotaping should be used as a supplement or alternative to the customary stenographic transcription. A videotaped deposition will generally have considerably more impact at trial than a written transcript read into the record.

Finally, the time limits on oral depositions must be considered. Unless otherwise agreed or ordered by the court, oral depositions are limited to six hours per side for each individual witness (TEX. R. CIV. P. 199.5(c)) and are further limited to a total number of hours allowed for all witnesses, depending on the discovery control plan used. *See* TEX. R. CIV. P. 190. Thus, counsel must reserve oral depositions for those witnesses whose testimony is most essential, and obtain information from other individuals through depositions on written questions, which are not so limited, or through other discovery devices.

[2] Notice and Formalities for Depositions

How do you compel a person to appear for a deposition? The answer to this question depends on whether the deponent is a party to the lawsuit. A deponent who is a party, or who is retained by, employed by, or otherwise subject to the control of a party, can be compelled to attend merely by serving a notice of oral or written deposition on the party's attorney. TEX. R. CIV. P. 199.3; 200.2. The content of the notice for oral depositions is specified in Rule 199.2. For a deposition on written questions, the direct questions to be propounded to the witness must be attached to the notice. Tex. R. Civ. P. 200.3(a). Below is an example of an oral deposition notice.

Notice of Deposition

____________ [*Plaintiff*] v. ____________ [*Defendant*]	IN THE ____________ COURT ____________ COUNTY, TEXAS ____________ JUDICIAL DISTRICT

NOTICE OF INTENT TO TAKE ORAL DEPOSITION OF ____ [*name of witness*]

TO: ____ [*Names of witness and of parties to action*] and to their attorneys of record.

PLEASE TAKE NOTICE that _____ [*name of party noticing deposition*] will take the oral deposition of _____ [*name of individual witness or organization*]. The deposition will take place at _____ [*place*] at [*time*] on _____ [*date*]. All parties are invited to attend and examine the witness as prescribed by the Texas Rules of Civil Procedure.

[*Optional. Include if named witness is organization rather than individual*].

We intend to question _____ [*name of organization/witness, e.g., ABC Corporation*] about _____ [*describe with reasonable particularity matters on which examination is requested*] We therefore request that _____ [*e.g., ABC Corporation*], pursuant to Civil Procedure Rule 199, a reasonable time before the deposition, designate one or more individuals to testify on its behalf and notify us and all other parties of the names of the designated individuals, their position or relationship with _____ [*e.g., ABC Corporation*] and the matters on which each individual will testify.

[*Optional. Include in order to request production of documents or things*].

REQUEST FOR PRODUCTION

Further, _____ [*name of party noticing deposition*] requests that _____ [*name of individual witness or organization*], produce at the deposition the following _____ [*documents or things*] _____ within the witness's possession, custody, or control, as required by the Texas Rules of Civil Procedure: _____ [*list or cross-reference annexed exhibit containing list of documents or items*].

[signature and certificate of service]

NOTES AND QUESTIONS

(1) *Sufficiency of Deposition Notice.* This notice complies with the requirements of the discovery rules in most situations. Under certain circumstances, additional provisions would need to be added. For example, requests to use means other than

stenographic recording require notice (either as part of the notice or separately) at least five days prior to the deposition. Tex. R. Civ. P. 199.1(c). Also, if someone other than "the witness, parties, spouses of parties, counsel, employees of counsel, and the officer taking the oral deposition" will attend the deposition, the notice must include that information. Tex. R. Civ. P. 199.2(b)(4); 199.5(a)(3).

(2) *Production of Documents.* What is the shortest amount of time in which a party could be compelled to respond to a request for documents? For parties, subpoenas may not be used to circumvent the normal time allowance for document production. They must therefore be given at least 30 days to respond (or 50 days if the request is served before the defendant's answer is due). Those documents need to be described with "reasonable particularity." Tex. R. Civ. P. 196.1(b); 196.2(a).

(3) *Subpoenas.* As noted above, non-parties cannot be required by mere notice to produce documents. The test is whether the proposed deponent is subject to the party's control. One Texas court has held that a corporation's outside directors are not subject to the corporation's control and therefore must be subpoenaed. *In re Reaud*, 286 S.W.3d 574 (Tex. App. — Beaumont 2009). When a notice will not suffice, a subpoena is used to secure attendance and, if requested, production of documents. Below is an example of a subpoena form..

SUBPOENA REQUIRING APPEARANCE AT DEPOSITION AND PRODUCTION OF DOCUMENTS OR TANGIBLE EVIDENCE

TO: _____ [*Name and address of person or organization to whom subpoena is directed*]

Greetings: YOU ARE COMMANDED to attend and give testimony at a deposition on oral examination at the following time and place: _____ [*specify*].

YOU ARE ALSO COMMANDED to appear and produce and permit inspection [and copying] of the _____ [*e.g., documents or tangible evidence*] identified in the attached deposition notice at the same time and place.

DUTIES OF PERSON SERVED WITH SUBPOENA

You are advised that under Texas Rule of Civil Procedure 176, a person served with a discovery subpoena has certain rights and obligations. Rule 176.6 provides:

(a) *Compliance required.* Except as provided in this subdivision, a person served with a subpoena must comply with the command stated therein unless discharged by the court or by the party summoning such witness. A person commanded to appear and give testimony must remain at the place of deposition, hearing, or trial from day to day until discharged by the court or by the party summoning the witness.

(b) *Organizations.* If a subpoena commanding testimony is directed to a corporation, partnership, association, governmental agency, or other organization, and the matters on which examination is requested are described with reasonable particularity, the organization must designate one or more persons to testify on its behalf as to matters known or reasonably available to the organization.

(c) *Production of Documents or Tangible Things.* A person commanded to produce documents or tangible things need not appear in person at the time and place of production unless the person is also commanded to attend and give testimony, either in the same subpoena or a separate one. A person must produce documents as they are kept in the usual course of business or must organize and label them to correspond with the categories in the demand. A person may withhold material or information claimed to be privileged but must comply with Rule 193.3. A nonparty's production of a document authenticates the document for use against the nonparty to the same extent as a party's production of a document is authenticated for use against the party under Rule 193.7.

(d) *Objections.* A person commanded to produce and permit inspection and copying of designated documents and things may serve on the party requesting issuance of the subpoena before the time specified for compliance written objections to producing any or all of the designated materials. A person need not comply with the part of a subpoena to which objection is made as provided in this paragraph unless ordered to do so by the court. The party requesting the subpoena may move for such an order at any time after an objection is made.

(e) *Protective Orders.* A person commanded to appear at a deposition, hearing, or trial, or to produce and permit inspection and copying of designated documents and things may move for a protective order under Rule 192.6(b) before the time specified for compliance either in the court in which the action is pending or in a district court in the county where the subpoena was served. The person must serve the motion on all parties in accordance with Rule 21a. A person need not comply with the part of a subpoena from which protection is sought under this paragraph unless ordered to do so by the court. The party requesting the subpoena may seek such an order at any time after the motion for protection is filed.

Warning

Failure by any person without adequate excuse to obey a subpoena served upon that person may be deemed a contempt of the court from which the subpoena is issued or a district court in the county in which the subpoena is served, and may be punished by fine or confinement, or both.

This subpoena is issued at the request of _____ [*name of party*], a party to the above-described action, whose attorney of record is _____ [*name of attorney*] . . . .

---

(4) *Use for Discovery.* A subpoena may not be used for discovery to an extent, in a manner, or at a time other than as provided by the discovery rules. Tex. R. Civ. P. 176.3(b). Thus, a deposition subpoena to a party is subject to Rules 196, 199, and

200 and a deposition subpoena to a nonparty is subject to Rule 205. TEX. R. CIV. P. 176, cmt. 2.

(5) *Who May Issue or Serve Subpoenas?* An oral deposition must be taken before an officer authorized by law to take depositions. TEX. R. CIV. P. 199.1(a). Generally, this means that the officer must be certified as a shorthand reporter by the Texas Supreme Court. *See* GOV. C. §§ 52.001, 52.021. The officer must administer the oath to the witness and record the testimony, objections, and other statements during the deposition at the time they are given or made. After the deposition, the officer must prepare and certify a transcript or other recording of the deposition, serve it on all parties, and file it with the court. *See* Tex. R. Civ. P. 203. Any officer authorized to take depositions in Texas may also issue subpoenas, and must do so immediately on a request accompanied by a notice to take the deposition. Tex. R. Civ. P. 176.4. Subpoenas may also be issued by an attorney authorized to practice in Texas. TEX. R. CIV. P. 176.4. A subpoena may be served at any place within the state of Texas by any sheriff or constable of the State of Texas, or any person who is not a party and is 18 years of age or older. TEX. R. CIV. P. 176.5.

(6) *Written Depositions.* A deposition on written questions of a witness who is alleged to reside or to be located in Texas may be taken by a Texas notary public as well as a clerk of a district or county court and a judge of a county court. *See* C.P.R.C. § 20.001 (reprinted below). A subpoena may be issued by "an officer authorized to take depositions in this state." TEX. R. CIV. P. 176.4. Thus, a Texas notary public may both issue a subpoena and take a deposition on written questions. Although no modern cases address the issue, the Texas Supreme Court has held that an attorney for a party cannot take a written deposition even though the attorney is a notary public because "he must be impartial between the parties, and whatever gives to his relation the character of employment by one party will disqualify the officer and subject the deposition, on proper objection, to be suppressed." *Clegg v. Gulf, C. & S.F. Ry. Co.*, 137 S.W. 109, 111 (Tex. 1911).

(7) *Where Can a Deposition Be Taken?* This answer also depends on whether the witness is a party or a non-party. Imagine the following situations:

(a) You represent a party in a suit filed in Houston over an automobile accident that happened in Houston. Both you and your client live and work in Houston. You receive a notice from the opposition to take your client's oral deposition in the opposing party's lawyer's office, which is in El Paso, where the opponent resides. What would you do in response?

You would file a motion for protective order or motion to quash the notice of deposition. If the motion is served by the third business day after service of the notice, the deposition is stayed until the motion can be ruled on. TEX. R. CIV. P. 199.4. You would argue that El Paso is not one of the locations allowed by Rule 199: your client neither resides nor is employed there, it is not the location of the suit, and it is not a "convenient" location for the deposition. (It is also unclear whether the language "subject to the foregoing" in Rule 199.2(b)(2) restricts the court's ability to designate a convenient place that is *not* one of the pre-approved locations.)

(b) You notice your opponent for deposition in your Houston office. He doesn't want to appear there. Is that a proper place for the opponent's deposition?

Yes. Under Rule 199.2(b)(2), the county of suit is one of the locations permitted for deposition. Nonetheless, your opponent may object to having the deposition taken in your office and request another "convenient" place for the deposition.

(c) The only nonparty eyewitness to the accident lives and works in Dallas. Where can you take that deposition?

Since non-parties must be subpoenaed, the places for those depositions (absent agreement) are limited by the subpoena power. *See* official comments to Rule 199. Rule 199 limits proper deposition locations for non-parties to counties where the witness lives, is employed, or regularly transacts business in person or, perhaps, at some other "convenient" location. Rule 176, in turn, provides that a witness may not be deposed in a county more than 150 miles from where the witness resides or is served. The exact calculation of this range is therefore a bit unclear as to, for example, whether you could take the deposition in Collin County so long as it is within 150 miles of the witness's residence, or whether Rule 199 limits you to Dallas County or some other "convenient" location. In any case, since you will be wanting the cooperation of the non-party witness, it would be best not to inconvenience the witness more than necessary, and you can safely take the deposition anywhere in Dallas County that is within 150 miles of the witness' home.

(d) A lawsuit is pending in Tarrant County against defendant Omnimart, and the underlying cause of action arose in Tarrant County. Omnimart's CEO, Sam Omni, lives in Bentonville, Arkansas. Ignore for a moment the limits on "apex" depositions discussed in note 8 below and assume that Mr. Omni can be deposed. Can his deposition be taken in Fort Worth?

Cases decided under the old discovery rules allowed the deposition in Fort Worth, finding that it was not an inconvenient location. *See Wal-Mart Stores, Inc. v. Street*, 761 S.W.2d 587 (Tex. App. — Fort Worth 1988, orig. proceeding).

(e) Plaintiff sues a Japanese corporation in Dallas County. Its CEO, Mr. Yamamoto, is also a resident of Japan. Assume that Texas has personal jurisdiction over the defendant, that Mr. Yamamoto may be deposed under the requirements for "apex" depositions, and that a number of events giving rise to the lawsuit happened in Dallas County. Can Mr. Yamamoto be compelled, over his objection, to come to Dallas County to be deposed because it is the location of the lawsuit, or does this degree of inconvenience (a distance of more than 6000 miles) require that the deposition be taken somewhere closer to Japan?

The answer to this question is unclear. However, in a situation involving a more tangentially-involved foreign defendant, the Eastland Court of Appeals found a Texas deposition to be excessively inconvenient. *In re*

Turner, 243 S.W.3d 843, 846-848 (Tex. App. — Eastland 2008, orig. proceeding) (suggesting that trial court require the parties to find an alternative method — such as a telephone deposition — in order to get the required information from a defendant residing in Hong Kong).

(8) *"Apex" Depositions.* You have seen that a deposing party may notice the deposition of an opposing entity by designating specific subject areas. TEX. R. CIV. P. 199.2(b). But what if you specifically want to depose the CEO? In *Crown Central Petroleum Corp. v. Garcia*, 904 S.W.2d 125 (Tex. 1995), the Court described the procedure for considering such a request:

> When a party seeks to depose a corporate president or other high level corporate official and that official (or the corporation) files a motion for protective order to prohibit the deposition accompanied by the official's affidavit denying any knowledge of relevant facts, the trial court should first determine whether the party seeking the deposition has arguably shown that the official has any unique or superior personal knowledge of discoverable information. If the party seeking the deposition cannot show that the official has any unique or superior personal knowledge of discoverable information, the trial court should grant the motion for protective order and first require the party seeking the deposition to attempt to obtain the discovery through less intrusive methods. Depending upon the circumstances of the particular case, these methods could include the depositions of lower level employees, the deposition of the corporation itself, and interrogatories and requests for production of documents directed to the corporation. After making a good faith effort to obtain the discovery through less intrusive methods, the party seeking the deposition may attempt to show (1) that there is a reasonable indication that the official's deposition is calculated to lead to the discovery of admissible evidence, and (2) that the less intrusive methods of discovery are unsatisfactory, insufficient or inadequate. If the party seeking the deposition makes this showing, the trial court should modify or vacate the protective order as appropriate. As with any deponent, the trial court retains discretion to restrict the duration, scope and location of the deposition. If the party seeking the deposition fails to make this showing, the trial court should leave the protective order in place.

In *Crown Central*, the Court faced the issue in the context of a board chairman with no personal knowledge of the facts involved in the litigation. In *In re Alcatel USA, Inc.*, 11 S.W.3d 173 (Tex. 2000), the "apex" deposition rules were extended to apply even to a CEO who was personally involved in some of the actions giving rise to the litigation, requiring a showing that the executive "arguably has unique or superior personal knowledge" before his or her deposition can be taken over objection. *See also In re BP*, 244 S.W.3d 840 (Tex. 2008) (refusing to set aside agreement regarding "apex" depositions despite corporate officer's public statements about facts underlying the litigation).

(9) *Depositions Taken Outside Texas.* The rules also contain special provisions regarding taking depositions outside of Texas. Civil Procedure Rule 201 applies both to oral and written depositions and applies both in sister states and in foreign

countries. Comment 1 to this rule notes that the rule itself "does not . . . address whether any of the procedures listed are, in fact, permitted or recognized by the law of the state or foreign jurisdiction where the witness is located. A party must first determine what procedures are permitted by the jurisdiction where the witness is located before using this rule." For example, some civil law countries do not allow the taking of testimony by private attorneys without the involvement of the local judiciary. *See* R. Doak Bishop, *International Litigation in Texas: Obtaining Evidence in Foreign Countries*, 19 Hous. L. Rev. 361 (1982).

(10) *Issuance of Subpoenas for Witnesses Outside Texas.* Who can issue an enforceable subpoena for an out-of-state deponent? To answer this question, the law of the place of deposition must be consulted. Many, if not most, other states have statutory or rule provisions similar to Civil Procedure Rule 201.2. This rule provides that a Texas court will enforce a mandate, writ, or commission issued by a court of record of another state or foreign jurisdiction that requires a witness' oral or written deposition testimony in Texas. As long as the foreign mandate, writ, or commission was issued by a court of record of any other state or foreign jurisdiction, the Texas court will enforce it in the same manner and by the same process used for taking testimony in a Texas proceeding. Tex. R. Civ. P. 201.2. Rule 201.2 is based on section 20.002 of the Civil Practice and Remedies Code. *See* Tex. R. Civ. P. 201, cmt. 3. Another option is a common law procedure called letters rogatory (codified in Rule 201.1(c)), wich provides a mechanism to obtain assistance from courts or other appropriate authorities in sister states.

(11) *Who May Be the Deposition Officer Outside Texas?* May a Texas lawyer bring a Texas court reporter along to take a deposition out of state? Civil Procedure Rule 201.1(b) allows a party to "take the deposition by notice in accordance with these rules as if the deposition were taken in the State." It also allows the deposition officer to be a person authorized to administer oaths in the place where the deposition is taken. Rule 201, however, must be read in connection with Section 20.001 of the Civil Practice and Remedies Code. This statute provides:

§ 20.001. Persons Who May Take a Deposition.

(a) A deposition on written questions of a witness who is alleged to reside or to be in this state may be taken by: (1) a clerk of the district court; (2) a judge or clerk of a county court; or (3) a notary public of this state.

(b) A deposition of a witness who is alleged to reside or to be outside this state, but inside the United States, may be taken in another state by: (1) a clerk of a court of record having a seal; (2) a commissioner of deeds appointed under the laws of this state; or (3) any notary public.

(c) A deposition of a witness who is alleged to reside or to be outside the United States may be taken by: (1) a minister, commissioner, or charge d'affaires of the United States who is a resident of and is accredited to the country where the deposition is taken; (2) a consul general, consul, vice-consul, commercial agent, vice-commercial agent, deputy consul, or consular agent of the United States who is a resident of the country where the deposition is taken; or (3) any notary public.

Comment 2 to Civil Procedure Rule 201 characterizes C.P.R.C. § 20.001 as providing a "nonexclusive list of persons who are qualified to take a written deposition in Texas and who may take depositions (oral or written) in another state or outside the United States." Taken together, these rules and statutes mean that a Texas notary public may serve as the deposition officer. The Texas certified shorthand reporter statute neither requires nor prohibits Texas certified shorthand reporters from acting as deposition officers for depositions taken outside Texas. If the reporter is a notary public, he or she may take the out-of-state deposition. For depositions in foreign countries, counsel must also check to see whether a U.S. court reporter would need to have a work visa before being allowed to work as court reporter in that country.

To what extent can these limits be circumvented by taking the deposition by "telephone or other remote electronic means" under Civil Procedure Rule 199.1(b)? The officer taking the deposition may be located with the party noticing the deposition instead of with the witness if the witness is placed under oath by a person who is present with the witness and authorized to administer oaths in that jurisdiction. TEX. R. CIV. P. 199.1(b).

(12) *Modification of Procedural Requirements by Agreement.* What if the parties would like to extricate themselves from some of the deposition requirements? Civil Procedure Rule 191.1 provides that "[e]xcept where specifically prohibited, the procedures and limitations set forth in the rules pertaining to discovery may be modified in any suit by the agreement of the parties or by court order for good cause." Comment 1 to this rule notes that the parties' ability to vary the rules by agreement is "broad but not unbounded . . . . Thus, for example, parties can agree to enlarge or shorten the time permitted for a deposition and to change the manner in which a deposition is conducted, notwithstanding Rule 199.5, although parties could not agree to be abusive toward a witness."

[3] Conduct During Oral Depositions

Given the time limits on an oral deposition, the rules contain procedures intended to encourage focused examination and to discourage spats between counsel. *See Paramount Communications v. QVC Network*, 637 A.2d 34, 58 (Del. 1994) (Addendum). Under the rules, regardless of the type of case:

1. No "side" may examine or cross-examine an individual witness for more than six hours. TEX. R. CIV. P. 199.5(c). If the time limits for deposition have expired or if the deposition is being conducted or defended in violation of these rules, a party or witness may suspend the deposition to obtain a ruling. TEX. R. CIV. P. 199.5(g).

2. Private conferences between the witness and the witness' attorney during the actual taking of the deposition are improper except to determine whether a privilege should be asserted. TEX. R. CIV. P. 199.5(d).

3. The language and content of objections is limited. The only approved objections are: "Objection, leading," "Objection, form," and "Objection, nonresponsive." Argumentative or suggestive objections or explanations

waive objection and may be grounds for terminating the deposition. Tex. R. Civ. P. 199.5(e).

4. Instructions not to answer are allowed "to preserve a privilege, comply with a court order or these rules, protect a witness from an abusive question or one for which any answer would be misleading, or secure a ruling." Tex. R. Civ. P. 199.5(f).

5. An attorney must not object to a question at oral deposition, instruct the witness not to answer a question, or suspend the deposition unless there is a good faith factual and legal basis for doing so at the time. Nor may the attorney ask a question without a good faith legal basis. Tex. R. Civ. P. 199.5(h).

6. Because the deposition rules incorporate the procedures and limitations applicable to requests for production or inspection (including the 30-day period for responses by parties to requests for production of documents), party depositions duces tecum can no longer be used to circumvent the 30-day minimum of the document production rule when the witness is a party. Tex. R. Civ. P. 199.2(b)(5).

NOTES AND QUESTIONS

(1) *Corporate Representatives — Time Limits.* Civil Procedure Rule 199.5(c) provides, "No side may examine or cross-examine an individual witness for more than six hours. Breaks during depositions do not count against this limitation." When an entity rather than a person is the deponent, Comment 2 notes that "[f]or purposes of Rule 199.5(c), each person designated by an organization under Rule 199.2(b)(1) is a separate witness."

(2) *Agreements of Counsel.* The discovery rules have long allowed parties to vary the rules regarding making and waiving objections at depositions. Counsel often begin a deposition by entering into a series of stipulations whose explicit purpose is to modify the rules' effect. The form of the stipulations, which are often added to the deposition by the court reporter simply on the direction of the parties that it be prefaced by "the usual agreements," might appear like this:

> It is agreed, stipulated, and understood by and between the parties hereto, acting by and through their respective counsel, that all formalities incident to the taking of the deposition, except for that of the signature of the witness to this deposition, which may be obtained before any notary public or other person authorized to administer oaths, are hereby expressly waived; and that the deposition when so taken may be introduced in evidence by any of the parties on the trial of said cause. It is further agreed, stipulated and understood by and between the parties hereto that all objections may be reserved until the time of trial. The signature of counsel for the respective parties to this agreement and stipulation are hereby expressly waived.

If such a stipulation is entered into at a deposition, what impact will the agreement have on the requirements of Civil Procedure Rules 199.5, 200.3, and 176.6(c)? *See*

TEX. R. CIV. P. 191.1 ("Except where specifically prohibited . . . [a]n agreement of the parties is enforceable if it complies with Rule 11 or, as it affects an oral deposition, if it is made part of the record of the deposition."). Remember this problem when considering [4], *below*, regarding use of depositions at hearings and trials. Also keep in mind that the wording of such stipulations is not fixed. The parties may agree, for example, to reserve the right to object until time of trial *except* as to the form of individual questions. Why might this proviso be advisable? Local practice on stipulations differs. A lawyer who is asked by an opponent, "Do you want to make the usual agreements?" and who is uncertain what they are should never hesitate to ask, "What usual agreements do you mean?"

PRACTICE EXERCISE #28

Assume the same facts as for Practice Exercise #25.

1. Kay Rett, one of the produce managers for Alpha Omega, was deposed by Allen. During the deposition, she waited for about 30 seconds after each question was asked (apparently considering it carefully), asked for many words to be defined for her, talked *really* slowly, fumbled through the documents needed to answer various questions, and generally ran out the clock. After six hours of this, Allen's attorney still had a number of questions he wanted to ask, but Alpha Omega's lawyer called time and terminated the deposition. Does Allen have any recourse?

2. Also during Rett's deposition, Allen's attorney had carefully led her through a series of questions about maintenance policies. Just after he asked the most crucial question, Alpha Omega's attorney made the following objection: "She can't answer that question — you're trying to make her admit that she was more worried about her staff budget than about customer safety and that's just ridiculous!" Was this a proper objection? Explain fully.

3. You represent Allen. You have noticed the deposition of Alpha Omega as a corporation, specifying the subject matter about which you will inquire. Alpha Omega has identified and produced three people to answer various parts of your questions. How much time, absent agreement or court order, do you have to question these corporate deponents?

[4] Use of Depositions at Hearings or Trials

Same Proceeding

The use of a deposition as evidence at trial is governed by Civil Procedure Rule 203 and by the Texas Rules of Evidence. All or part of a deposition may be used for any purpose in the *same* proceeding in which it was taken. The term "same proceeding" includes a proceeding in a different court but involving the same subject matter and the same parties or their representatives or successors in interest.

A deposition is admissible against a party joined *after* the deposition was taken only if either (1) the deposition is admissible under the former testimony exception to the hearsay rule, or (2) the party has had a reasonable opportunity to re-depose the witness and has failed to do so. The former testimony exception to the hearsay rule allows a deposition to be used if (1) the declarant is unavailable as a witness, and (2) the party against whom the deposition testimony is offered, or a person with a similar interest, had an opportunity and similar motive to develop the testimony by direct, cross, or redirect examination. *See* Tex. R. Evid. 804(b).

Another Proceeding

A deposition from *another* proceeding may be used in the current proceeding to the extent permitted by the Texas Rules of Evidence. Generally, depositions taken in a different proceeding are hearsay, but are admissible if they meet the requirements of the "former testimony" exception to the hearsay rule described above. This will only be proper if the declarant is unavailable. A declarant is considered "unavailable as a witness" in any of the following situations (Tex. R. Evid. 804(a)):

1. The court rules, on the basis of privilege, to exempt the declarant from testifying concerning the subject matter of the former testimony.
2. The declarant persists in refusing to testify concerning the subject matter of the prior testimony, despite an order of the court to do so.
3. The declarant testifies to a lack of memory of the subject matter of the prior testimony.
4. The declarant is unable to be present or to testify at the hearing because of death or then-existing physical or mental illness or infirmity.
5. The declarant is absent from the hearing, and the proponent of the declarant's statement has been unable to procure the declarant's attendance or testimony by process or other reasonable means.

Before the adoption of the Texas Rules of Evidence, the Texas Supreme Court had held that a witness whose deposition could be taken outside of Texas was not "unavailable." *Hall v. White*, 525 S.W.2d 860, 862 (Tex. 1975). It is probable that this same interpretation will be given to the "or testimony" language of Evidence Rule 804(a)(5).

A declarant is not considered unavailable as a witness if the declarant's exemption, refusal, claim of lack of memory, inability, or absence is due to the procurement or wrongdoing of the proponent of the statement for the purpose of preventing the declarant from attending or testifying. Tex. R. Evid. 804(a).

NOTES AND QUESTIONS

(1) *Tactical Use of Depositions.* In terms of tactics, what sort of witness might you prefer to present by deposition even though available? What sort of witness would you prefer to present live? Suppose that you have an important expert witness who will be unavailable on the day of trial, but you do not wish to lose the impact of his or her personal presentation. What possibility do the rules offer?

(2) *Method of Presenting Deposition Testimony.* How does one actually introduce a deposition into evidence? Unless it is read into evidence or somehow conveyed to the jury, it is not part of the evidence considered by the jury, and unless it is offered, it is not part of the trial record. The usual method is for two people to read the deposition, one reading the questions and the other than answers. Be aware of the possible issues raised by overly dramatic readings or emphasis of parts of the deposition record. One major difficulty with the reading of a deposition before a jury is that it loses much of the impact of live testimony. Indeed, some trial lawyers are concerned that jurors, seeing persons in front of them reading material from a little booklet, may not consider it in the same category as the rest of the evidence. One solution is to have the judge explain the procedure to the jury. The increasing use of videotape depositions also solves some of the problem. The videotape of the deposition can be shown to the jury; it is best to deal with issues of which portions will be shown and evidence objections to various questions or answers before the trial begins.

(3) *Available Trial Objections.* Although the deposition as an entirety is admissible, there may still be questions or answers within the deposition that are objectionable. One must therefore also consider whether such objections have been preserved so that they may be raised. Review Rules 199.5(e) and 203. What objections are required at the deposition? Which ones may be made at trial? Which ones can be made after the deposition but require notice before the trial commences?

Objections to questions during the oral deposition are limited to "Objection, leading" and "Objection, form." Objections to testimony during the oral deposition are limited to "Objection, nonresponsive." These objections are waived if not stated during the oral deposition and in the prescribed words. All other objections need not be made or recorded during the oral deposition to be later raised with the court. An objection to the form of a question includes objections that the question calls for speculation, calls for a narrative answer, is vague, is confusing, or is ambiguous. Tex. R. Civ. P. 199, Comment 4. If necessary to preserve a privilege, the attorney should instruct the witness not to answer the question.

Time limitations also apply to the right to challenge the accuracy of the deposition transcript and other irregularities. The witness waives the right to make changes to the transcript if she does not do so within 20 days of the date the transcript was provided to her attorney. Tex. R. Civ. P. 203.1(b). A party may object to any errors and irregularities in the manner in which the testimony is transcribed, signed, delivered, or otherwise dealt with by the deposition officer by filing a motion to suppress all or part of the deposition. If the deposition officer properly delivers the deposition transcript or non-stenographic recording to the proper person at least one day before the case is called to trial with regard to a deposition transcript, or 30 days before the case is called to trial with regard to a non-stenographic recording, the party must file and serve a motion to suppress before trial commences to preserve the objections. Tex. R. Civ. P. 203.5.

PRACTICE EXERCISE #29

Assume the same facts as for Practice Exercise #25.

1. Ruby Humphreys, another Alpha Omega customer, also slipped and fell in the same Alpha Omega store when trying to pull a grocery cart out of the stack. Humphreys has her own lawsuit pending against Alpha Omega. In that lawsuit, she took the deposition of Alpha Omega's national store design consultant. His testimony turned out to be very damaging to Alpha Omega. Can Allen use the deposition in her case? What if the consultant has been transferred to the Alaska office? What if the consultant has died?

2. The deposition of Allen's husband was taken by videotape. Since his health is poor, it will be very difficult for him to testify at trial. The following exchange is contained within the transcript of his deposition. You may assume that there were no agreements modifying the usual deposition rules. Will you be able to prevent Alpha Omega from using the following deposition excerpt in evidence?

> Q (by Alpha Omega's lawyer): So, Mr. Allen, do you claim that your wife is in constant terrible pain?
>
> A Yes, I would agree with that.
>
> Q (by Alpha Omega's lawyer): Mr. Allen, what did you tell your wife's lawyer about her symptoms?
>
> Q (by Allen's lawyer): Objection. Attorney-client privilege.
>
> Q (by Alpha Omega's lawyer): The court reporter isn't a judge, Mr. Allen, so please answer my question.
>
> A (by witness): I told him that she can still mow the lawn, run the vacuum cleaner, and do the laundry.

[5] Motions for Physical or Mental Examinations

Unlike the other discovery devices that are designed to work without the intervention of the judge, a requirement that a party undergo a mental or physical examination requires a court order. When is there a sufficient need for such an exam to be ordered over the objection of the person to be examined? Consider the following case.

COATES v. WHITTINGTON

758 S.W.2d 749 (Tex. 1988)

SPEARS, J.

At issue in this mandamus proceeding is whether a plaintiff who claims mental anguish damages in a personal injury action may be required to submit to a mental examination . . . . Judge Mark Whittington granted the motion [to compel] and ordered Mrs. Coates to undergo the examination. The court of appeals denied Mrs. Coates' motion for leave to file petition for writ of mandamus. We hold that the trial court abused its discretion by ordering Mrs. Coates to submit to a mental examination. We therefore conditionally grant relator's petition for writ of mandamus.

Mrs. Coates was injured when she inadvertently sprayed her arm with Drackett's "Mr. Muscle Oven Cleaner" while cleaning her stove top. She suffered severe second degree burns and permanent scarring on her left forearm as a result of the incident. Mrs. Coates brought a products liability action against Drackett, seeking damages for pain and suffering, physical impairment, lost earnings, medical expenses, and mental anguish. In response, Drackett pleaded contributory negligence, misuse, and pre-existing condition. Drackett moved for an order compelling Mrs. Coates to submit to a mental examination pursuant to Rule 167a [now Rule 204] of the Texas Rules of Civil Procedure, claiming that her mental anguish was pre-existing and may have contributed to the incident with the oven cleaner. The trial judge denied the motion. Drackett then sought a rehearing of its motion, asserting that Mrs. Coates had placed her mental condition "in controversy" by pleading mental anguish damages. Drackett also claimed that there was "good cause" for the mental examination because Mrs. Coates alleged that she experienced "depression and general mental problems at the time she used the oven cleaner." Judge Whittington granted Drackett's motion and ordered that Mrs. Coates submit to a mental examination by a court appointed psychologist. Judge Whittington ordered that the examination address: (1) the relationship of Mrs. Coates' prior problems to the occurrence made the basis of the suit, if any; and (2) the relationship of Mrs. Coates' prior problems to the prayer for mental anguish damages, if any. The court of appeals denied Mrs. Coates' motion for leave to file petition for writ of mandamus . . . .

The more significant issue in this case, however, is whether the trial court abused its discretion by ordering Mrs. Coates to undergo a mental examination. Rule 167a was derived from Rule 35 of the Federal Rules of Civil Procedure and largely duplicates the language of the original federal rule. Federal courts' construction of Rule 35 is thus helpful to an analysis of Rule 167a. The United States Supreme Court has held that federal Rule 35 requires an affirmative showing that the party's mental condition is genuinely in controversy and that good cause exists for the particular examination. *Schlagenhauf v. Holder*, 379 U.S. 104, 118 (1964). In *Schlagenhauf*, the Court expressly stated that these two requirements are not met "by mere conclusory allegations of the pleadings — nor by mere relevance to the case." *Id.* Similarly, Rule 167a, by its express language, places an affirmative burden on the movant to meet a two pronged test: (1) the movant must show that the party's mental condition is "in controversy"; and (2) the movant must demonstrate that there is "good cause" for a compulsory mental examination. In the absence of an affirmative showing of both prongs of the test, a trial court may not order an examination pursuant to Rule 167a.

Drackett maintains that Coates' mental condition is in controversy because she has pleaded for mental anguish damages. In support of its position, Drackett relies on *Schlagenhauf*, 379 U.S. at 119, where the United States Supreme Court stated:

> A plaintiff in a negligence action who asserts mental or physical injury . . . places that mental or physical injury in controversy and provides the

defendant with good cause for an examination to determine the existence and extent of such asserted injury.

In *Schlagenhauf*, however, the court also warned that sweeping examinations of a party who has not affirmatively put his mental condition in issue may not be routinely ordered simply because the party brings a personal injury action and general negligence is alleged. *Id.* at 121. Further, federal courts that have applied Rule 35 in light of *Schlagenhauf* have consistently distinguished "mental injury" that warrants a psychiatric evaluation from emotional distress that accompanies personal injury. *Compare Anson v. Fickel*, 110 F.R.D. 184, 186 (N.D. Ind. 1986) (mental condition is in controversy when plaintiff claims mental problems that required confinement in a psychiatric hospital) *and Lowe v. Philadelphia Newspapers, Inc.*, 101 F.R.D. 296, 298–99 (E.D. Pa. 1983) (mental condition is in controversy when plaintiff claims severe emotional distress and seeks to prove damages through testimony of psychiatrist) *with Cody v. Marriott Corp.*, 103 F.R.D. 421, 423 (D. Mass. 1984) (mental condition is not in controversy when plaintiff claims emotional distress and does not claim a psychiatric disorder requiring psychiatric or psychological counseling).

In her suit against Drackett, Mrs. Coates asserts that she has suffered the type of emotional distress that typically accompanies a severe second degree burn and permanent scarring. In her deposition, she described her mental anguish as feelings of embarrassment and self-consciousness because the scar is ugly and noticeable in public. She is not alleging a permanent mental injury nor any deep seated emotional disturbance or psychiatric problem. Mrs. Coates' mental anguish claim is, therefore, for the emotional pain, torment, and suffering that a plaintiff who has been burned and scarred would experience in all reasonable probability. *Compare Moore v. Lillebo*, 722 S.W.2d 683, 688 (Tex. 1986). Further, the record reflects that Mrs. Coates has not sought any type of psychiatric treatment as a result of the incident and, equally important, does not propose to offer psychiatric or psychological testimony to prove her mental anguish at trial.

To permit Drackett to compel a mental examination because Mrs. Coates has claimed mental anguish damages would open the door to involuntary mental examinations in virtually every personal injury suit. Rule 167a was not intended to authorize sweeping probes into a plaintiff' psychological past simply because the plaintiff has been injured and seeks damages for mental anguish as a result of the injury. Plaintiffs should not be subjected to public revelations of the most personal aspects of their private lives just because they seek compensation for mental anguish associated with an injury.

Drackett also contends that Mrs. Coates' mental condition has been placed in controversy by virtue of its contributory negligence claim. With regard to that claim, it is Mrs. Coates' *conduct* that is in controversy. The jury will be asked to decide whether Mrs. Coates was negligent in her use of the oven cleaner. Whatever mental processes underlay her conduct, it is the nature of that conduct, not the reasons for it, that is in issue. Rule 167a clearly does not contemplate that a plaintiff would be subjected to a probing psychiatric incursion into his or her entire psychological past on the strength of a defendant's contributory negligence claim.

The second requirement of Rule 167a is that the movant show "good cause" for compelling an examination. Drackett maintains that it showed good cause by its reference to Mrs. Coates' pre-existing personal problems which, Drackett asserts, may have caused Coates to injure herself with the oven cleaner. Drackett specifically refers to Mrs. Coates' marital problems, her concerns regarding her son's medical problems, and the fact that she had to take a lower paying job when her original employer re-located. Drackett places significance on the fact that Mrs. Coates had seen a doctor two or three times before the incident with the oven cleaner and had complained of depression and problems eating and sleeping. Drackett further emphasizes that on the day of Mrs. Coates' injury, the examining physician in the hospital emergency room noted in the medical record, "Husband states patient depressed — denies suicidal tendencies." Drackett insists that this notation suggests that Mrs. Coates was suicidal and may have misused the oven cleaner intentionally or with indifference to her welfare.

The "good cause" and "in controversy" requirements of Rule 167a are necessarily related. *See Schlagenhauf*, 379 U.S. at 118–19. Mrs. Coates' prior problems are clearly peripheral to the issues in this case, and, consequently, they are not "in controversy." Drackett, however, attempts to meet the "in controversy" requirement by contending that Mrs. Coates' prior problems affected her mental state at the time she used the oven cleaner and they thus provide "good cause" for compelling a mental examination. Mrs. Coates' prior problems and attendant complaints of depression are distinct from the mental anguish she claims as a result of her injury. Drackett has failed to show any connection or "nexus" between Mrs. Coates' pre-injury depression and her post-injury embarrassment.

It is well settled that a tortfeasor takes a plaintiff as he finds him. *Driess v. Frederich*, 11 S.W. 493, 494 (Tex. 1889); *Thompson v. Quarles*, 297 S.W.2d 321, 330 (Tex. App. — Galveston 1956, writ ref'd n.r.e.). Regardless of Coates' personal problems at the time of the incident with the oven cleaner, she is entitled to recover the damages resulting from the incident "conditioned as [she] was at the time of the injury." The fact that Mrs. Coates had personal problems at the time of her injury does not, in itself, relieve Drackett of liability, and does not, absent a showing of some connection to her allegation of mental anguish, provide good cause for compelling a mental examination.

A routine allegation of mental anguish or emotional distress does not place the party's mental condition in controversy. The plaintiff must assert mental injury that exceeds the common emotional reaction to an injury or loss. Assuming it is shown that a party has put his mental condition in controversy, good cause for the compelled examination must also be shown. The "good cause" requirement of Rule 167a recognizes that competing interests come into play when a party's mental or physical condition is implicated in a lawsuit — the party's right of privacy and the movant's right to a fair trial. A balancing of the two interests is thus necessary to determine whether a compulsory examination may properly be ordered.

The requirement of good cause for a compulsory mental examination may be satisfied only when the movant satisfies three elements. First, that an examination is relevant to issues that are genuinely in controversy in the case. It must be shown that the requested examination will produce, or is likely to lead to, evidence of relevance to the case. *See Schlagenhauf*, 379 U.S. at 117–18. Second, a party must show a reasonable nexus between the condition in controversy and the examination sought. Neither of these requirements has been satisfied in this case. The mere pleading of mental anguish is inadequate to establish the necessity of plaintiff's submission to a mental examination. Finally, a movant must demonstrate that it is not possible to obtain the desired information through means that are less intrusive than a compelled examination. *See Schlagenhauf*, 379 U.S. at 118; *Marroni v. Matey*, 82 F.R.D. 371, 372 (E.D. Pa. 1979). The movant must demonstrate that the information sought is required to obtain a fair trial and therefore necessitates intrusion upon the privacy of the person he seeks to have examined. *See Lowe v. Philadelphia Newspapers, Inc.*, 101 F.R.D. 296, 298 (E.D. Pa. 1983). Drackett has made no showing that the information it seeks cannot be obtained by other discovery techniques. Mrs. Coates' privacy interests require, at minimum, that Drackett exhaust less intrusive means of discovery before seeking a compulsory mental examination. If, however, a plaintiff intends to use expert medical testimony to prove his or her alleged mental condition, that condition is placed in controversy and the defendant would have good cause for an examination under Rule 167a.

We hold that the trial judge abused his discretion in ordering Mrs. Coates to undergo a mental examination. We conditionally grant Mrs. Coates' petition for writ of mandamus. The writ will issue only if the trial judge refuses to rescind his order.

NOTES AND QUESTIONS

(1) *"Good Cause" and "In Controversy" Requirements.* What does it take to supply these two requirements for a mental or physical examination in Texas? Consider the Court's holdings (1) that Mrs. Coates' pre-existing depression did not put her condition "in controversy" or create "good cause" and (2) that the defendant's inferences that she may have had suicidal tendencies (or other reason for misusing the product) also did not meet the requirements. Try to give an example of evidence that *might* be developed by the defendant, that *would* support an order requiring an examination in this case.

Schlagenhauf v. Holder, cited in the principal case, is the leading federal decision on point. The United States Supreme Court there reversed a decision that required a bus driver to submit to examinations in four different specialties, ranging from psychiatry to ophthalmology. The bus driver's deposition showed that on two occasions the driver had driven into other vehicles from the rear in moving traffic while the other vehicles were plainly visible and there was plenty of room to stop. The Court indicated that the only kind of examination that could be ordered under the governing rule was an examination of the driver's eyes.

(2) *Strategic Use of the Request for Examination.* Consider the facts of *Coates*. Can you think of any reason, in addition to relevance, that may have motivated the requests to compel the mental and physical examinations of the plaintiff?

(3) *Limits on Trial Conduct. C.E. Duke's Wrecker Service, Inc. v. Oakley*, 526 S.W.2d 228 (Tex. Civ. App. — Houston [1st Dist.] 1975, writ ref'd n.r.e.), illustrates another aspect of Civil Procedure Rule 204. What should plaintiff do if plaintiff *offers* to submit to examination, but defendant refuses to undertake any examination and simply argues instead, at trial, that plaintiff's medical witnesses

are not credible? Rule 204.3 provides that, in this situation, "the party whose mental or physical condition is in controversy must not comment to the court or jury on the party's willingness to submit to an examination, or on the right or failure of any other party to seek an examination."

In the *Oakley* case, despite this rule, the plaintiff's counsel asked his client in the presence of the jury whether she had "been willing to be examined by anyone that [defendant's] counsel might choose in the form of a doctor [to] determine the nature of your injury?" Over objection, plaintiff answered, "Yes." Plaintiff also introduced an interrogatory and answer in which defendant declined to have its physician examine the plaintiff, and plaintiff argued to the jury that if the plaintiff were not injured, defendant "would have got their own doctor." When the defendant appealed a judgment for the plaintiff, the plaintiff argued that this information was appropriately put before the jury to counteract the "unfair and unjust" impression that defendant had created by attacking the credibility of plaintiff's treating doctor (who was plaintiff's brother). Nevertheless, following the rule, the court of appeals reversed.

Consider whether this rule is fair to such a plaintiff, who must produce evidence but cannot point out a defendant's refusal to do likewise. Is this result in accord with the policies underlying discovery? Consider, also, what a plaintiff might lawfully do to counteract the impression thus created. Could the plaintiff argue, for example, that although the plaintiff has brought expert evidence, the defendant "has brought you absolutely no evidence to contradict the extent of injuries of the plaintiff"? This argument does not appear to violate the letter of Civil Procedure Rule 204, and it is different from that in *Oakley*. Is the difference great enough to make a difference in result?

[6] Discovery From Experts

(1) *Method of Discovery Relating to Experts Generally.* The type of expert will, in some respects, dictate the discovery devices that may be used. Generally, discovery regarding testifying experts is accomplished through requests for disclosure and depositions. Tex. R. Civ. P. 194.2(f), 195. For consulting experts whose impressions and opinions have been reviewed by a testifying expert, discovery is accomplished through interrogatories, requests for production, and depositions. *See* Tex. R. Civ. P. 195, Comment 1 (Rule 195 does not limit permissible methods of discovery concerning consulting experts whose mental impressions or opinions have been reviewed by testifying expert). In addition, some distinctions are made between experts who are retained by, employed by, or otherwise subject to the control of the responding party and experts who are not retained, employed, or controlled by the responding party.

(2) *Retained Testifying Experts.* A party may request that another party designate and disclose information concerning a testifying expert who is retained by, employed by, or under the control of the responding party (collectively called a "retained expert") only through a request for disclosure under Rule 194 and through depositions and reports as permitted by Rule 195. Tex. R. Civ. P. 195.1. Using a request for disclosure, the requesting party may discover the following information regarding a retained testifying expert:

1. The expert's name, address, and telephone number.
2. The subject matter on which the expert will testify.
3. The general substance of the expert's mental impressions and opinions and a brief summary of the basis for them.
4. All documents, tangible things, reports, models, or data compilations that have been provided to, reviewed by, or prepared by or for the expert in anticipation of the expert's testimony.
5. The expert's current resume and bibliography.

Before the 1999 amendments to the discovery rules, discovery regarding experts was through interrogatories, requests for production, depositions, and written reports. Regarding testifying experts, the request for disclosure is a substitute for interrogatories and requests for production. The standardized form of the request for disclosure is designed to avoid needless, time-consuming objections to discovery. The request for disclosure may, however, obtain less information than could be obtained through an interrogatory under the former practice. This is because a party is entitled to discover only the "general substance" of the expert's mental impressions and opinions and a "brief summary" of the basis for them. Tex. R. Civ. P. 194.2(f). Under the former practice, it was common practice to serve interrogatories requesting full disclosure of the expert's mental impressions and opinions and the basis for them.

In addition to disclosure under Civil Procedure Rule 194, a party may obtain discovery concerning the subject matter on which the expert is expected to testify, the expert's mental impressions and opinions, the facts known to the expert (regardless of when the factual information was acquired) that relate to or form the basis of the testifying expert's mental impressions and opinions, and other discoverable matters, including documents not produced in disclosure, only by oral deposition of the expert and by a report prepared by the expert as provided in Civil Procedure Rule 195.5. Tex. R. Civ. P. 195.4. An expert's deposition, like any other deposition, is limited to six hours unless the parties agree to, or the court orders, additional time. Tex. R. Civ. P. 191.1, 199.5(c).

(3) *Timing for Testifying Expert Discovery.* The time for making a designated expert available for deposition is complicated and depends on two factors: (1) whether the party designating the expert is seeking affirmative relief, and (2) whether a report for the designated expert has been produced. The intent of the rule is to give a party who is not seeking affirmative relief a chance to learn the opinions and impressions of an opponent's experts before being required to designate his or her own experts. Thus, in almost all circumstances, a party seeking affirmative relief must either make his or her retained experts available for deposition, or provide a report from those experts, before the opponent is required to designate experts or make them available for depositions. *See* Tex. R. Civ. P. 195.3; Tex. R. Civ. P. 195, Comment 3 ("In scheduling the designations and depositions of expert witnesses, the rule attempts to minimize unfair surprise and undue expense. A party seeking affirmative relief must either produce an expert's report or tender the expert for deposition before an opposing party is required to designate experts. A party who does not wish to incur the expense of a report may

simply tender the expert for deposition, but a party who wishes an expert to have the benefit of an opposing party's expert's opinions before being deposed may trigger designation by providing a report."). This rule applies only to retained experts, because it is presumed that a party has the ability to make a retained expert available for deposition, but may not have the ability to make an expert who is not retained available for deposition.

If a party is seeking affirmative relief and a report of the expert's factual observations, tests, supporting data, calculations, photographs, and opinions is not produced when the expert is designated, the party must make the expert available for deposition reasonably promptly after the expert is designated. TEX. R. CIV. P. 195.3(a)(1); TEX. R. CIV. P. 195.2 (schedule for designating experts). If the deposition cannot be concluded, due to the actions of the designating party, more than 15 days before the deadline for designating experts by parties not seeking affirmative relief, the deadline for designating those other experts must be extended, but only for experts who will be testifying on the same subject as the expert who could not be promptly deposed. TEX. R. CIV. P. 195.3(a)(1).

The rules do not state whether the deadline for designating other experts is extended by operation of the rules under these circumstances or if it must be extended by court order. If extended by operation of rule, there is no provision stating how long the deadline is extended. One reading of Rule 195.3(a)(1) suggests that the deadline is automatically extended to 15 days after the conclusion of the designated expert's deposition. However, because the rule is not clear on this point, it is a safer practice to either extend the deadline by agreement or seek a court order setting a new deadline. *See* TEX. R. CIV. P. 11 (requisites of agreements by parties); TEX. R. CIV. P. 191.1 (parties may agree to modify discovery rules).

If a report of the expert's factual observations, tests, supporting data, calculations, photographs, and opinions is produced when the expert is designated, the party need not make the expert available for deposition until reasonably promptly after all other experts have been designated. TEX. R. CIV. P. 195.3(a)(2); TEX. R. CIV. P. 195.2 (schedule for designating experts). In this situation, the rules presume that the party not seeking affirmative relief has sufficient information from the expert's report to designate his or her own experts without first taking the designated expert's deposition.

A party who is not seeking affirmative relief must make retained testifying experts available for deposition reasonably promptly after the expert is designated and the experts testifying on the same subject for the party seeking affirmative relief have been deposed. TEX. R. CIV. P. 195.3(b). Thus, absent an agreement of the parties to the contrary or some other unusual circumstance, the experts of a party who is seeking affirmative relief will be deposed before the experts of a party who is not seeking affirmative relief.

The rule differentiates between parties who seek affirmative relief and parties who do not. But in many cases, all parties seek affirmative relief, either through the plaintiff's claims or the defendant's counterclaims or cross-claims. Under Civil Procedure Rule 195.3(a), if a party seeks affirmative relief, the party must designate and produce for deposition all of the party's experts without regard to whether a particular expert will testify only in defense to another party's claim.

The deposition timing provisions may also be difficult to apply in multi-party cases. Of course, many cases will be governed by a court-ordered discovery control plan under Level 3 of Civil Procedure Rule 190, which may alleviate some difficulties. Otherwise, litigants should attempt to work out timing problems by agreement or, as a last resort, through court intervention.

(4) *Reducing Expert Opinions to Writing.* If the discoverable factual observations, tests, supporting data, calculations, photographs, or opinions of a retained testifying expert have not been recorded and reduced to tangible form, the court may order these matters reduced to tangible form and produced in addition to the deposition. Tex. R. Civ. P. 195.5. Failure to prepare and produce a court-ordered expert report may result in a sanction against the party for whom the expert will testify. *Ramirez v. Volkswagen of America, Inc.*, 788 S.W.2d 700, 703 (Tex. App. — Corpus Christi 1990, writ denied). A party cannot, by request for production or request for disclosure, compel another party to create an expert report if one is not already in existence. Instead, the party must move for an order requiring the creation of such a report. *Loftin v. Martin*, 776 S.W.2d 145, 147 (Tex. 1989).

(5) *Testifying Experts Not Retained by the Responding Party.* In some circumstances, a party may designate as a testifying expert a person who the party has not retained, does not employ, and does not otherwise control. Using a request for disclosure, the requesting party may discover the following information regarding such an expert:

1. The expert's name, address, and telephone number.
2. The subject matter on which the expert will testify.
3. Documents reflecting the general substance of the expert's mental impressions and opinions.

Tex. R. Civ. P. 194.2(f). This is a much narrower disclosure requirement than is applicable for a retained expert. All other information regarding the expert must be obtained through a deposition or a subpoena in accordance with Civil Procedure Rules 176 and 205.

(6) *Consulting Experts Whose Mental Impressions or Opinions Were Reviewed by Testifying Expert.* Neither Civil Procedure Rule 194 (providing for a request for disclosure to obtain information about experts) nor Civil Procedure Rule 195 (providing for discovery regarding experts) applies to consulting experts whose impressions or opinions were reviewed by a testifying expert. Thus, discovery related to consulting experts is available through interrogatories, requests for production, and depositions, just as it was before the 1999 amendments to the discovery rules. *See* Tex. R. Civ. P. 195, Comment 1 ("This rule does not limit the permissible methods of discovery concerning consulting experts whose mental impressions or opinions have been reviewed by a testifying expert."). Further, as was the case before the 1999 amendments, a party is not entitled to obtain a court-ordered report from a consulting expert.

§ 10.03 RESISTING DISCOVERY

Read Tex. R. Civ. P. 191, 193.

A lawyer litigating discovery disputes must be aware of the procedures for handling disputes about the scope of discovery. Failure to act properly may waive a party's right to discovery or to assert an objection to discovery. The burdens of making appropriate discovery requests and asserting and proving objections to discovery are the subject of a considerable body of case law. In addition, the discovery rules contain important procedures and information about the waiver of objections.

(1) *Duty to Make Complete Response.* When responding to written discovery, a party must make a complete response, based on all information reasonably available to the responding party or the responding party's attorney at the time the response is made. Tex. R. Civ. P. 193.1. In addition, Civil Procedure Rule 191 contains specific provisions regarding the signing of various discovery documents. Signing a disclosure constitutes a certification that "to the best of the signer's knowledge, information, and belief, formed after a reasonable inquiry, the disclosure is complete and correct as of the time it is made." Tex. R. Civ. P. 191.3(b). Signing a discovery notice, response, or objection constitutes a certification that "to the best of the signer's knowledge, information, and belief, formed after a reasonable inquiry, the notice, response, or objection: (1) is consistent with the rules of civil procedure and [the] discovery rules and warranted by existing law or a good faith argument for the extension, modification, or reversal of existing law; (2) has a good faith factual basis; (3) is not interposed for any improper purpose, such as to harass or to cause unnecessary delay or needless increase in the cost of litigation; and (4) is not unreasonable or unduly burdensome or expensive, given the needs of the case, the discovery already had in the case, the amount in controversy, and the importance of the issues at stake in the litigation." Tex. R. Civ. P. 191.3(c).

(2) *Objecting to Written Discovery.* An individual discovery request may be objectionable for a number of reasons. For example, a request for "all documents relevant to the lawsuit" is overly broad and not in compliance with the rule requiring specific requests for documents. *Loftin v. Martin*, 776 S.W.2d 145, 148 (Tex. 1989). A request may be objectionable because it asks for information or material that is simply not relevant to the subject matter of the pending action, or is not within the scope of discovery, such as a request for the identities of purely consulting experts. Sometimes the request, although overly broad, seeks some discoverable information. For example, a request for income tax returns for a 15-year period may be overly broad, but a request for income tax returns for a five-year period may be appropriate. In addition, the time, manner, and place for complying with the request may be objectionable. A party wanting to assert this kind of objection to a discovery request should do so in writing and should state specifically the legal or factual basis for the objection and the extent to which the party is refusing to comply with the request. A party must make objections to written discovery within the time for making the response. Tex. R. Civ. P. 193.2(a). An objection that is not made within the time required is waived unless the court excuses the waiver for good cause shown.

(3) *Withholding Privileged Information.* It is no longer proper to *object* to assert a privilege. Tex. R. Civ. P. 193.2(f). Instead, a claim of privilege is asserted by *withholding* the privileged information or materials and *informing* the requesting party that responsive information or materials have been withheld due to privilege. Tex. R. Civ. P. 193.3(a). In addition to withholding the information or material, the party must state: (1) that information or material responsive to the request has been withheld; (2) the request to which the information or material relates; and (3) the privilege or privileges asserted. Tex. R. Civ. P. 193.3(a). Although the rules provide that failure to timely state an objection results in a waiver of the objection, the rules do not set out the consequences for failing to assert a privilege in a timely manner. Under precedent interpreting the rules before the 1999 amendments, failure to timely assert a privilege resulted in waiver of the privilege. In language similar to the current rule, the former rule required a specific pleading of the "particular exemption or immunity from discovery" relied on by the party. Former Tex. R. Civ. P. 166b(4). Failure to specifically state the privilege may result in waiver of the privilege. At least one new case decided under the current rules reaches the same conclusion. *In re Anderson*, 163 S.W.3d 136 (Tex. App. — San Antonio 2005, orig. proceeding). Note, however, that under the new rules, assertions of privilege should *not* be made prophylactically against the threat of waiver, but only when the information is actually withheld. Tex. R. Civ. P. 193, Comment 3. Note also that under Civil Procedure Rule 193.3(d), a party that has produced a document without claiming the privilege may seek to amend its response to claim the privilege and recover the document.

(4) *Request for and Description of Withheld Information and Materials (Privilege Log).* After receiving a response indicating that information or material has been withheld, the party seeking discovery may serve on the withholding party a written request that the withholding party identify the information and material withheld. Tex. R. Civ. P. 193.3(b). Within 15 days of service of that request, the withholding party must serve a response. The response, often called a "privilege log," must: (1) describe the information or materials withheld, without revealing the privileged information itself or otherwise waiving the privilege, in such a manner as will enable the other parties to assess the applicability of the privilege; and (2) assert a specific privilege for each item or group of items withheld. Tex. R. Civ. P. 193.3(b). *See Weisel Enterprises, Inc. v. Curry*, 718 S.W.2d 56 (Tex. 1986). Under prior law, failure to adequately provide this information could amount to a waiver of the privilege.

(5) *New Exception: Post-Consultation Attorney-Client Communications.* There is one significant exception to the procedure stated in the rule for asserting a privilege. Rule 193.3(c) provides that:

> a party may withhold a privileged communication to or from a lawyer or lawyer's representative or a privileged document of a lawyer or lawyer's representative
>
> (1) created or made from the point at which a party consults a lawyer with a view to obtaining professional legal services from the lawyer in the prosecution or defense of a specific claim in the litigation in which discovery is requested, and

(2) concerning the litigation in which the discovery is requested.

In other words, a party need not state in the response that such information or document has been withheld, and need not list the information or document in a privilege log. In essence, parties withholding such information assert and rule on their own privilege claims, and the discovering party will not even be informed that the documents exist.

(6) *Inadvertent Production and Compelled Disclosure: "Snap-Back."* The discovery rules contain a specific provision concerning the inadvertent production of privileged documents. A party who produces material or information "without intending to waive a claim of privilege" does not waive the privilege claim if the producing party amends the response, identifies the material or information produced, and states the privilege asserted. *See In re Christus Spohn Hospital*, 222 S.W.3d 434 (Tex. 2007). Note that the emphasis is on the intent to *waive*, not the intent to *produce* the material. The amended response must be served within 10 days, or a shorter time if ordered by the court, after the producing party actually discovers the inadvertent production. If the producing party amends the response to assert a privilege, the requesting party must promptly return the specified information or material and any copies, subject to any ruling by the court denying the privilege claim. TEX. R. CIV. P. 193.3(d).

Although a party does not have an obligation to notify an opponent that apparently privileged information was inadvertently disclosed, the party should be aware of the implication of the timing rules. For example, if the party holding the material discloses the inadvertent production for the first time at trial, his or her opposing party may demand its return at that time and will preserve the privilege by doing so. *Warrantech Corp. v. Computer Adapters Services, Inc.*, 134 S.W.3d 516 (Tex. App. — Fort Worth 2004, no pet.) (party successfully asserted privilege at trial for document inadvertently produced three years earlier).

(7) *Hearing and Ruling on Objections and Assertions of Privilege.* Any party may at any reasonable time request a hearing on an objection or claim of privilege. However, a party need not request a ruling on that party's own objection or assertion of privilege to preserve the objection or privilege. TEX. R. CIV. P. 193.4(b). If there is a hearing, the party making the objection or asserting the privilege must present any evidence necessary to support the objection or privilege, and the burden will be on the objecting party to do so. Failure to meet this burden may also result in waiver of the privilege. The evidence may be in the form of live testimony presented at the hearing or of affidavits. If the evidence is in affidavit form, the affidavits must be served at least seven days before the hearing or at such other reasonable time as the court permits. They may not be tendered for ex parte consideration. Often, the documents themselves are the only evidence of the privilege. They should be submitted to the court for *in camera* inspection. TEX. R. CIV. P. 193.4(a).

(8) *Privileged Material as Evidence.* A decision to use the privileged material as evidence at a trial or hearing also waives the privilege and requires prior disclosure of the material. A party may not use material or information withheld from discovery under a claim of privilege, including a claim sustained by the court, at any hearing or trial without timely revealing the information in an amended or

supplemental response to the discovery. Tex. R. Civ. P. 193.4(c).

(9) *Protective Orders.* The discovery rules conceive of a motion for protective order as a device for objecting to discovery that is distinct from the objection or the assertion of a privilege. Tex. R. Civ. P. 192.6. Civil Procedure Rule 192.6 provides that a person should not move for a protective order "when an objection to written discovery or an assertion of privilege is appropriate." This seems to imply that protective orders are the appropriate procedural device only for material that is discoverable but the person from whom discovery is sought wants to object to something such as the time or place of discovery. Tex. R. Civ. P. 192.6(a). On the other hand, Rule 192.6(b) refers to using a protective order to protect the movant from the invasion of personal, constitutional, or property rights. Is it ultimately helpful to think of "objections," "assertions of privilege," and "motions for protective order" as three separate categories, each with its own rules and procedures?

(10) *Raising and Litigating Trade Secret Claims.* How was a protective order used in the litigation underlying *Continental General Tire*? (*See* § 9.03[B][2][b].) Review that case in order to examine the procedures that were used in litigating the trade secret dispute: what procedure was used to assert trade secret protection? how did the party seeking discovery respond? what additional information did the objecting party provide under Rule 193.3(b)? what kind of evidence did the discovering party present to try to show that the information was "necessary for a fair adjudication of its claims"? In *Continental General Tire*, both sides agreed that the information sought was a trade secret. If this were disputed, however, the objecting party would have to present evidence that the information is a trade secret.

The following case discusses the proper procedures for litigating discovery disputes under the new rules. As you read it, focus on what exactly each party did in order to assert or challenge a claim of privilege, and whether their efforts were sufficient. Be sure to notice both pleading requirements and proof requirements, and note impact of the burden of proof.

IN RE E.I. DUPONT DE NEMOURS & CO.

136 S.W.3d 218 (Tex. 2004)

Per Curiam

In the suit underlying this petition for mandamus, nearly 400 plaintiffs sued E.I. DuPont de Nemours ("DuPont") and over 100 other defendants for alleged asbestos-related injuries from 1935 to the present. In response to the plaintiffs' discovery request, DuPont asserted claims of attorney-client and/or work product privilege with respect to 607 documents.

On May 12, 2003, the trial court issued an order requiring DuPont to turn over most of the documents, ruling that DuPont had not made a prima facie showing of privilege. A divided court of appeals declined to grant mandamus relief. DuPont now seeks relief from this Court. DuPont contends that the trial court abused its discretion by holding a hearing on the plaintiffs' global challenge to all of the documents identified in its privilege log. DuPont further argues that the trial court abused its discretion by finding that DuPont had not made a prime facie showing of privilege for the documents at issue and refusing to conduct an in camera inspection of the documents before rejecting its privilege claims.

The court of appeals declined to grant DuPont mandamus relief. We agree with the court of appeals that the trial court did not abuse its discretion in holding a hearing on the plaintiffs' global challenge to DuPont's privilege claims. However, we conditionally grant the writ insofar as we conclude that DuPont made a prima facie showing of privilege for many of the approximately 530 documents that the trial court ordered produced without conducting an in camera review.

In response to plaintiffs' requests for production, DuPont produced over 55,000 pages of documents that go back more than 60 years. However, DuPont stated that it was withholding 607 documents, citing the attorney-client privilege found in Texas Rule of Evidence 503 and the work-product privilege set forth in Texas Rule of Civil Procedure 192.5. After the plaintiffs requested a privilege log,[1] DuPont timely served the log describing the documents withheld. The plaintiffs then requested a hearing challenging DuPont's privilege claims for all of the documents. In response, DuPont filed an affidavit from its paralegal Walter Connor in support of its privilege claims and tendered the documents listed on the privilege log to the court for in camera inspection. In his affidavit, Connor stated, in relevant part:

> I have reviewed all names listed on the DuPont-Brignac privilege log that are identified as "DuPont Legal." I compared each "DuPont Legal" name for each document on the privilege log with a DuPont human resources database for the legal department. Each name that is identified as "DuPont Legal" on the privilege log is a name of a person who was, at the time indicated on the document, a DuPont attorney or DuPont paralegal as confirmed by the comparison with the human resources database.

Connor further averred:

> I have reviewed and am familiar with the definitions of client, representative of client, lawyer, representative of a lawyer, and confidential as

[1] A "privilege log" is the commonly used term for a response pursuant to Texas Rule of Procedure 193.3(b) that: "1) describes the information or materials withheld that, without revealing the privileged information or otherwise waiving the privilege, enables other parties to assess the applicability of the privilege, and 2) asserts a specific privilege for each item or group of items withheld." The dissenting court of appeals opinion noted:

> The log is sufficiently detailed for the real parties in interest to assess the applicability of the specific privilege being asserted. *See* Tex. R. Civ. P. 193.3(b). For example, "DUP Bates Range 0903484-3484, Date 741029," a document from "Austin RE (DuPont Legal)" to "Mfg Environmental Committee," copied to "Bonczek RR (DuPont Legal); Galloway WR; Helmers EN; Hildrew JC; Meany DM; Reichert RJ; Schmutz JF (DuPont Legal), and Sebree DB (DuPont Legal)," is a "Memo between DuPont counsel requesting legal advice and comments re: proposed amendments to regulations concerning national emissions standards for hazardous air pollutants."

Neither the trial court nor the court of appeals majority opinion concluded that the log inadequately described the documents and the plaintiffs do not so argue in this court.

> defined in Rule 503 of the Texas Rules of Evidence. Based on my review of the DuPont human resources database for the legal department, the documents listed on the DuPont-Brignac privilege log, and the definitions in Rule 503, all the documents on the DuPont-Brignac privilege log with "DuPont Legal" names associated with a claim of attorney-client privilege indicate a lawyer or a representative of a lawyer engaging in confidential communications with a client or a representative of a client regarding professional legal services, or a lawyer or representative of a lawyer rendering professional legal services or performing a requested task for a client or a representative of a client involving the rendering of professional legal services.

Finally, Connor also stated:

> I have reviewed and am familiar with the definition of "work product" as defined in Rule 192.5 of the Texas Rules of Civil Procedure. Based on my review of the DuPont human resources database for the legal department, the documents listed on the DuPont-Brignac privilege log, and the definitions in Rule 192.5, all the documents on the DuPont-Brignac privilege log with "DuPont Legal" names associated with a claim of work product indicate material prepared or mental impressions developed in anticipation of litigation or for trial by or for DuPont or its representatives, or a communication in anticipation of litigation or for trial between DuPont and its representatives or among its representatives.

On April 29, 2003, the court conducted a hearing on DuPont's assertions of privilege. The court overruled DuPont's claims of privilege except as to 76 documents, which were ordered to be delivered for in camera review. The trial court excepted those 76 documents listed on the privilege log that were associated exclusively with members of "DuPont Legal," meaning that the author, recipient, and all parties that received copies of the document were members of "DuPont Legal." The trial court ordered DuPont to produce the remainder of the documents, consisting of: 1) documents with no "DuPont Legal" names associated, and 2) documents with both "DuPont Legal" and non-"DuPont Legal" names associated.

The parties do not dispute that mandamus relief is generally available in this type of case. Mandamus relief is appropriate "to correct a clear abuse of discretion or the violation of a duty imposed by law when there is no other adequate remedy by law." *Johnson v. Fourth Court of Appeals*, 700 S.W.2d 916, 917 (Tex. 1985). "[A] clear failure by the trial court to analyze or apply the law correctly will constitute an abuse of discretion and may result in appellate reversal by extraordinary writ." *Walker v. Packer*, 827 S.W.2d 833, 839 (Tex. 1992). Mandamus is proper when the trial court erroneously orders the disclosure of privileged information because the trial court's error cannot be corrected on appeal. *Id.* at 843. As DuPont would lose the benefit of the privilege if the documents at issue are disclosed, even if its assertions of privilege were later upheld on appeal, we conclude that this Court may provide mandamus relief in this case.

The party who seeks to limit discovery by asserting a privilege has the burden of proof. *Jordan v. Fourth Court of Appeals*, 701 S.W.2d 644, 648–49 (Tex. 1985). However, if a party asserting privilege claims makes a prima facie showing of privilege and tenders documents to the trial court, the trial court must conduct an in camera inspection of those documents before deciding to compel production. *Arkla, Inc. v. Harris*, 846 S.W.2d 623, 631 (Tex. App. — Houston [14th Dist.] 1993, orig. proceeding); *Shell Western E & P, Inc. v. Oliver*, 751 S.W.2d 195, 196 (Tex. App. — Dallas 1988, orig. proceeding). We have recognized:

> Generally, a trial court conducts an in camera inspection to determine if a document is in fact privileged. If it is not privileged, then it may become evidence that the factfinder may consider. If the document is privileged, it is not subject to discovery and may not be considered by the factfinder, even when the factfinder is the trial court.

Goode v. Shoukfeh, 943 S.W.2d 441, 448 (Tex. 1997). The trial court abuses its discretion in refusing to conduct an in camera inspection when such review is critical to the evaluation of a privilege claim. *State v. Lowry*, 802 S.W.2d 669, 673–74 (Tex. 1991); *Loftin v. Martin*, 776 S.W.2d 145, 148 (Tex. 1989); *Thibodeaux v. Spring Woods Bank*, 757 S.W.2d 856, 860 (Tex. App. — Houston [14th Dist.] 1988, no writ); *Shell Western E & P*, 751 S.W.2d at 196.

The prima facie standard requires only the "minimum quantum of evidence necessary to support a rational inference that the allegation of fact is true." *Texas Tech Univ. Health Sci. Ctr. v. Apodaca*, 876 S.W.2d 402, 407 (Tex. App. — El Paso 1994, writ denied). The documents themselves may constitute sufficient evidence to make a prima facie showing of attorney-client or work product privilege. *Weisel Enters., Inc. v. Curry*, 718 S.W.2d 56, 58 (Tex. 1986).

The plaintiffs argue that Connor's affidavit is lacking in specificity. However, an affidavit, even if it addresses groups of documents rather than each document individually, has been held to be sufficient to make a prima facie showing of attorney-client and/or work product privilege.

In *Monsanto*, the affidavit of the corporate representative asserted that a log of 117 documents involved "in-house and/or outside attorneys for Monsanto, or other Monsanto employees, representatives or agents." *In re Monsanto Co.*, 998 S.W.2d at 927. The court of appeals held that this representation constituted a prima facie showing of the attorney-client and work product privilege. *Id.* In *Toyota*, the affidavit submitted by the defendant stated that one group of documents consisted of "[c]ommunications to Toyota counsel for the purpose of requesting legal advice or facilitating the rendition of professional legal service." *In re Toyota Motor Corp.*, 94 S.W.3d at 821. This representation was also found to be sufficient to establish a prima facie case of privilege. *Id.* at 823–24. In *Shell Western E & P*, Shell established a prima facie case of attorney-client privilege where a Shell affiant swore that the "documents . . . were written by a lawyer to a client" and "consist of communications from a client to a Shell . . . lawyer . . . ." *Shell Western E & P*, 751 S.W.2d at 196. However, an affidavit is of no probative value if it merely presents global allegations that documents come within the asserted privilege. *Ryals v. Canales*, 767 S.W.2d 226, 229 (Tex. App. — Dallas 1989, orig. proceeding). The plaintiffs contend that the affidavit at issue here is not probative because it is conclusory. The plaintiffs maintain that Connor's affidavit is indistinguishable from the affidavit found insufficient to support attorney-client privilege in *In re Temple-Inland, Inc.*, 8 S.W.3d 459 (Tex. App. — Beaumont 2000, orig. proceeding).

However, the affidavit in *Temple-Inland* that was found to be conclusory merely stated that production "would violate the attorney-client privilege." *Id.* at 462. Connor's affidavit more closely resembles the affidavits in *Monsanto* and *Toyota*, as it sets forth the factual basis for the applicability of the attorney-client and/or work product privileges to the documents at issue. Additionally, while Connor did not attest to the specific contents of each of the 607 documents at issue, the plaintiffs are unable to identify any such legal requirement and do not dispute that the log submitted by DuPont contains a summary of each document. Thus, we find that the specificity of Connor's affidavit and the log taken together are reasonably adequate to establish a prima facie case of privilege given that the documents at issue go back more than 60 years.

The plaintiffs also contend that Connor's affidavit is not probative because it is not based on personal knowledge. For an affidavit to have probative value, an affiant must swear that the facts presented in the affidavit reflect his personal knowledge. *Humphreys v. Caldwell*, 888 S.W.2d 469, 470 (Tex. 1994). Connor swore that his statements were based on his "personal knowledge of the facts stated in the affidavit." Even though Connor later explained that his determinations were "[b]ased on [his] review of the DuPont human resources database for the legal department," an affiant's acknowledgment of the sources from which he gathered his knowledge does not violate the personal knowledge requirement. *See Grotjohn Precise Connexiones Int'l v. JEM Fin., Inc.*, 12 S.W.3d 859, 866 (Tex. App. — Texarkana 2000, no pet.). Therefore, we hold that Connor's affidavit satisfies the personal knowledge requirement.

Three discrete categories of documents are in dispute. First, there are the documents which have only "DuPont Legal" names associated with them. The trial court ordered an in camera review of these 76 documents. Second, there are those documents that have both "DuPont Legal" and other names associated with them. The trial court denied DuPont's claim of privilege with respect to these documents without ordering an in camera review. Finally, there are those documents which do not have any "DuPont Legal" name associated with them. The trial court also rejected DuPont's claim of privilege concerning these documents.

We conclude that the trial court did not abuse its discretion in sustaining DuPont's privilege claims with respect to the first category of documents. The log submitted by DuPont combined with Connor's affidavit clearly make a prima facie case that those documents with only "DuPont Legal" names associated with them are covered by the attorney-client and/or work product privileges. Consequently, the trial court correctly determined that DuPont was entitled to at least an in camera review of those documents.

We also conclude that DuPont established a prima facie case of privilege with respect to the second category of documents, which contained both "DuPont Legal" and other names. Thus, we find that the trial court erroneously rejected DuPont's privilege claim as applied to these documents without at least subjecting them to an in camera review.

There is no presumption that documents are privileged, and there is no presumption that a party listed on the privilege log is an authorized person under the rule governing the privilege. *Cigna Corp. v. Spears*, 838 S.W.2d 561, 565–66 (Tex.

App. — San Antonio 1992, orig. proceeding). Nevertheless, Connor provided sufficient indication of the relationship between the "DuPont Legal" and the non-"DuPont Legal" persons on the privilege log to establish a prima facie case of privilege. In his description of the allegedly privileged documents, Connor identified the non-"DuPont Legal" persons on the privilege log as authorized parties for purposes of attorney-client and/or work product privilege. Connor swore that the documents allegedly privileged as attorney-client materials "indicate a lawyer or representative of a lawyer engaging in communication . . . or performing a requested task . . . for a client or representative of a client." The implication of this statement is that, whatever the relationship between the "DuPont Legal" and the non-"Dupont Legal" parties listed on the privilege log, it was a relationship within the scope of the attorney-client and/or work product privilege and the fact that the hundreds of documents at issue span more than 60 years, this statement combined with the log summarizing each document is sufficient to establish at least a prima facie case of privilege that is then subject to in camera review.[4] Because DuPont has established a prima facie case of privilege as to the second category of documents, which bear both "DuPont Legal" and non-"DuPont Legal" designations, we conclude that it was entitled to an in camera review before being required to produce these documents.

Finally, we agree with the trial court that DuPont has not established a prima facie case of privilege with respect to the third category of documents containing no "DuPont Legal" names. Connor's affidavit offers no evidence to justify privilege assertions concerning these documents. Connor's affidavit attested to the privileged nature of "[a]ll the documents on the DuPont-Brignac privilege log with 'DuPont Legal' names associated with a claim of attorney-client privilege" and "[a]ll the documents on the DuPont-Brignac privilege log with 'DuPont Legal' names associated with a claim of work product privilege." The affidavit was silent as to any claim of privilege regarding the documents that do not bear a "Dupont Legal" name. Accordingly, we agree with the appeals court that the trial court did not abuse its discretion in ruling that DuPont failed to make a prima facie case of privilege with respect to those documents containing no "Dupont Legal" names.

DuPont also argues on appeal that the plaintiffs' global challenge to their privilege claims was not sufficient to place those claims at issue. DuPont contends that the trial court abused its discretion by allowing a hearing based on the plaintiffs' global challenge to DuPont's entire privilege log. DuPont maintains that, prior to the hearing, the plaintiffs should have been required to particularize their objections to specific documents in the privilege log.

DuPont cites two cases in support of its argument. First, DuPont references *In re Carbo Ceramics, Inc.*, 81 S.W.3d 369 (Tex. App. — Houston [14th Dist.] 2002, orig. proceeding), but this case is inapposite. In *Carbo*, the court found that the

---

[4] Evidence corroborating or rebutting a prima facie case of privilege could be found upon in camera review. The documents themselves may contain evidence indicating the positions held by the non-"DuPont legal" recipients and the extent to which their duties relate to the matters upon which legal advice is being given. Plaintiffs are also entitled to put on their own evidence on privilege issues. *See* Tex. R. Civ. P. 193.4. For example, plaintiffs could submit interrogatories seeking additional information about the individuals listed as authors or recipients of disputed documents.

plaintiff "did not challenge the privileged nature of all privileged documents," but instead placed only one letter at issue. *Id.* at 375. *Carbo* is distinguishable because it is not disputed here that the plaintiffs challenged the privileged nature of all documents in the log. DuPont also relies on *Monsanto*, which held in part:

> When the party asserting a privilege has made a prima facie case for its claim, the requesting party has the burden to point out to the court which specific documents or groups of documents it believes require inspection. Otherwise, trial judges will be required to inspect untold numbers of documents. The requesting party should be in a position to do so based upon (1) the contents of the privilege log, (2) other discovery and documents, (3) discovery specifically designated to test the claim of privilege, and (4) the evidence at the hearing.

In re Monsanto Co., 998 S.W.2d at 925.

It is clear that *Monsanto* stands only for the proposition that the party seeking discovery must specify its challenges to the privilege log after the party asserting privilege claims has made a prima facie case. The discovery rules provide that any party may request a hearing on a claim of privilege and the party asserting the privilege must present any evidence necessary to support the privilege. Tex. R. Civ. P. 193.4(a). This provision does not contain a requirement that the party seeking discovery specify their rationale for objecting to each document before requesting a hearing.[5] Accordingly, the trial court did not abuse its discretion by holding a hearing on the plaintiffs' objection to DuPont's privilege log, which challenged whether DuPont had established a prima facie case of privilege for all of the documents it withheld.

For the foregoing reasons, we conditionally grant DuPont's petition for mandamus relief from the trial court ruling insofar as the ruling denied DuPont's privilege claim without conducting an in camera review with respect to the documents containing both "DuPont Legal" and non-"DuPont Legal" names. Accordingly, pursuant to Texas Rule of Appellate Procedure 52.8 and without hearing oral argument, we direct the trial court to vacate in part its May 12, 2003 order and to conduct further proceedings consistent with this opinion. We are confident that the trial court will promptly comply, and our writ will issue only if it does not.

---

[5] We hold simply that the trial court did not abuse its discretion by holding a hearing. We do not suggest that a trial court would abuse its discretion by requiring, at such a hearing or otherwise, that the proponent of the discovery request state their objection to the claimed privilege specifically as to each document on the privilege log. Where large numbers of documents are at issue, such an approach may promote judicial economy by focusing in camera review on those documents where there is a genuine dispute as to the application of the privilege and by clarifying the nature of the dispute so the court can hone in on the probative content of each document.

PRACTICE EXERCISE #30

Assume the same facts as for Practice Exercise #25.

1. In her Petition, Allen seeks damages for lost earning capacity, as she will no longer be able to maintain the secretarial job she has held for the last ten years. (She is now 53 years old.) Alpha Omega has sent Allen a discovery request asking for all of her tax returns or other income statements from age sixteen through the present. Allen thinks that's asking a bit much. How should Allen's lawyer complain to the court about the request?

2. Allen has sent Alpha Omega a discovery request asking for copies of all correspondence regarding Allen's claim. Some of the responsive documents are memos between Alpha Omega employees; others were sent to or from Alpha Omega's lawyers. How should Alpha Omega respond?

3. Assume that Alpha Omega has taken the correct action to complain about the request in question 2. If Allen believes that the request was proper, what should she do next? How should Alpha Omega respond? In what ways can Allen or Alpha Omega bring this dispute to the attention of the trial court? Who will have the burden of producing any evidence relevant to the dispute?

4. During document production in the case, Alpha Omega produced about ten large boxes of documents. In going through the documents, Allen's lawyer was elated to find a memo from one of Alpha Omega's lawyers to the company president. The letter includes this sentence: "We have repeatedly warned you that your choice not to put 'unsightly' floor mats in the produce department puts you at risk for liability when customers fall in your store. In fact, at some point after repeated falls you might be said to be grossly negligent and risk the imposition of punitive damages." Allen's lawyer plans to dramatically use this letter at trial. Will that plan be successful?

§ 10.04 AMENDMENT AND SUPPLEMENTATION OF DISCOVERY RESPONSES

Read Tex. R. Civ. P. 193.5, 193.6, 195.6 and accompanying Comments.

ALVARADO v. FARAH MFG. CO., INC.
830 S.W.2d 911 (Tex. 1992)

HECHT, J.

. . . .

I

While employed by Farah Manufacturing Company, Jose Luis Lerma Alvarado experienced chest pains and was diagnosed as having a pulmonary embolism.

Alvarado consulted with an attorney and filed a worker's compensation claim. After receiving medical treatment, Alvarado was released by his physicians to return to work but was restricted from sitting or standing still for long periods of time. This restriction prevented Alvarado from resuming the work he had done before his illness, which required long periods of standing. Farah had other jobs which Alvarado could perform, and he requested reassignment to one of them; but Farah advised him that there were no openings in any of those jobs. In accordance with the collective bargaining agreement which governed Alvarado's employment, Farah placed him on "sustained layoff" status, listing him with other employees in the same status. Whenever a job opening occurred in a particular department, the collective bargaining agreement required that Farah fill the position from the employees on the list, first from those who had worked in that department, by seniority, then from the others on the list, also by seniority. After one year on the list, an employee's seniority and recall rights automatically terminated.

Farah never recalled Alvarado to work, and all his rights under the collective bargaining agreement were eventually terminated. The union did not complain of Alvarado's termination. Nevertheless, Alvarado filed this action for damages against Farah, claiming that Farah had job openings which it should have offered him but did not do so in retaliation for his filing a worker's compensation claim. Thus, Alvarado claims that Farah violated Tex. Rev. Civ. Stat. Ann. article 8307c. Farah denies that it violated article 8307c and asserts that it never recalled Alvarado to work because it never had an opening for a job that Alvarado was both physically able to do and eligible to take under the seniority system which Farah had to follow.

Shortly after filing suit, Alvarado directed interrogatories to Farah, the first two of which asked:

1. Please state the name, address, telephone number, and employer of all persons having knowledge of the occurrences made the basis of this suit.

2. Please state the name, address, telephone number, and employer of each potential witness that you may use in the trial of this case.

Farah responded with interrogatories to Alvarado, the first two of which were identical to those quoted above. Neither Alvarado nor Farah objected to these interrogatories; both answered them by identifying several persons.

Six days before trial was set to begin, Alvarado subpoenaed two witnesses to testify who had never been identified in answer to Farah's interrogatories. One of these witnesses, Jacqueline Arrambide, had formerly been employed by Farah in a non-union position. Like Alvarado, Arrambide had sued Farah claiming that she had been terminated in retaliation for asserting a claim for worker's compensation benefits. On the first day of trial, before voir dire commenced, Farah moved to exclude the testimony of Arrambide for the reason that she had not been identified in answer to its interrogatories. The trial court denied Farah's motion. After Farah rested its case, Alvarado called Arrambide as a witness on rebuttal. Again Farah objected, and again the trial court overruled, the objection. Arrambide testified that Farah had fired her one week after Farah found out that she had hired an attorney to make a worker's compensation claim for injury to her back. She testified that the reason she was given for her termination was poor attendance at work, even though she had missed only a few days work for medical treatment.

The jury found that Farah violated article 8307c with respect to Alvarado, and that he should be awarded $139,080 actual damages and $1,000,000 exemplary damages. The trial court rendered judgment on the verdict.

II

A

Rule 215(5) of the Texas Rules of Civil Procedure states:

> A party who fails to respond to or supplement his response to a request for discovery shall not be entitled to present evidence which the party was under a duty to provide in a response or supplemental response or to offer the testimony of an expert witness or of any other person having knowledge of discoverable matter, unless the trial court finds that good cause sufficient to require admission exists. The burden of establishing good cause is upon the party offering the evidence and good cause must be shown in the record.

To say that this rule has proven to be problematic is perhaps an understatement. On ten occasions in the eight years since the rule was first promulgated in 1984, this Court has written on whether a witness not identified in response to a discovery request should have been allowed to testify. *Sharp v. Broadway Nat'l Bank*, 784 S.W.2d 669 (Tex. 1990) (per curiam); *Rainbo Baking Co. v. Stafford*, 787 S.W.2d 41 (Tex. 1990) (per curiam); *McKinney v. National Union Fire Ins. Co.*, 772 S.W.2d 72 (Tex. 1989); *Clark v. Trailways, Inc.*, 774 S.W.2d 644 (Tex. 1989); *Boothe v. Hausler*, 766 S.W.2d 788 (Tex. 1989) (per curiam); *Gee v. Liberty Mut. Fire Ins. Co.*, 765 S.W.2d 394 (Tex. 1989); *E.F. Hutton & Co. v. Youngblood*, 741 S.W.2d 363 (Tex. 1987) (per curiam); *Gutierrez v. Dallas Indep. Sch. Dist.*, 729 S.W.2d 691 (Tex. 1987); *Morrow v. H.E.B., Inc.*, 714 S.W.2d 297 (Tex. 1986) (per curiam); *Yeldell v. Holiday Hills Retirement and Nursing Center, Inc.*, 701 S.W.2d 243 (Tex. 1985). In eight of these cases the trial courts admitted testimony which had not been timely identified in response to discovery requests; in none of them did the Court hold that "good cause sufficient to require admission" was shown.

The trial courts in these cases have given various reasons for allowing testimony despite the failure to comply with discovery rules. These reasons seem to share a basic rationale, sometimes expressed and other times implicit, that admitting the testimony allowed a full presentation of the merits of the case. In the present case, for example, the trial court permitted a previously undisclosed witness to testify "in the interest of justice in getting everything on the table, which this court tries to do when possible . . . ." While it is certainly important for the parties in a case to be afforded a full and fair opportunity to present the merits of their contentions, it is not in the interest of justice to apply the rules of procedure unevenly or inconsistently. It is both reasonable and just that a party expect that the rules he has attempted to comply with will be enforced equally against his adversary. To excuse noncompliance without a showing of good cause frustrates that expectation.

The salutary purpose of Rule 215(5) is to require complete responses to discovery so as to promote responsible assessment of settlement and prevent trial by ambush. *See Clark*, 774 S.W.2d at 646; *Gee*, 765 S.W.2d at 396; *Gutierrez*, 729 S.W.2d at 693. The rule is mandatory, and its sole sanction — exclusion of evidence — is automatic, unless there is good cause to excuse its imposition. The good cause exception permits a trial court to excuse a failure to comply with discovery in difficult or impossible circumstances. *See Clark*, 774 S.W.2d at 647 (inability to locate witness despite good faith efforts or inability to anticipate use of witness' testimony at trial might support a finding of good cause). The trial court has discretion to determine whether the offering party has met his burden of showing good cause to admit the testimony; but the trial court has no discretion to admit testimony excluded by the rule without a showing of good cause.

We have repeatedly addressed what factors, standing alone, are not in themselves good cause. Included among these are inadvertence of counsel, *Sharp*, 784 S.W.2d at 672; *E.F. Hutton*, 741 S.W.2d at 364; lack of surprise, *Sharp*, 784 S.W.2d at 671; *Gee*, 765 S.W.2d at 395 n.2 (lack of surprise is not the standard, but may be a factor); *Morrow*, 714 S.W.2d at 298; and uniqueness of the excluded evidence, *Clark*, 774 S.W.2d at 646. The reasons in each instance are intuitive. If inadvertence of counsel, by itself, were good cause, the exception would swallow up the rule, for there would be few cases in which counsel would admit to making a deliberate decision not to comply with the discovery rules. Determining whether a party is really surprised by an offer of testimony not formally identified in discovery is difficult. The better prepared counsel is for trial, the more likely he is to have anticipated what evidence may be offered against his client, and the less likely he is to be surprised. It would hardly be right to reward competent counsel's diligent preparation by excusing his opponent from complying with the requirements of the rules. As we explained in *Sharp*:

> A party is entitled to prepare for trial assured that a witness will not be called because opposing counsel has not identified him or her in response to a proper interrogatory. Thus, even the fact that a witness has been fully deposed, and only his or her deposition testimony will be offered at trial, is not enough to show good cause for admitting the evidence when the witness was not identified in response to discovery.

784 S.W.2d at 671. Finally, if good cause could be shown simply by establishing the unique importance of the evidence to the presentation of the case, only unimportant evidence would ever be excluded, and the rule would be pointless.

To relax the good cause standard in Rule 215(5) would impair its purpose. Counsel should not be excused from the requirements of the rule without a strict showing of good cause. The difficulty with the rule lies not so much in the requirement of strict adherence, but in the severity of the sanction it imposes for every breach. The consequences of the rule should not be harsher in any case than the vice the rule seeks to correct. The sole sanction should not be the exclusion of all evidence not properly identified in discovery; rather, as with other failures to comply with discovery, the trial court should have a range of sanctions available to it to enforce the rules without injustice. "The punishment should fit the crime." *TransAmerican Natural Gas Corp. v. Powell*, 811 S.W.2d 913, 917 (Tex. 1991).

As written, however, Rule 215(5) prescribes a single sanction for failing to supplement discovery, and we are not free to disregard its plain language. Nor should we revise the rule by opinion. The Legislature has provided that notice be given before rules amendments become effective. TEX. GOV. C. § 22.004. In addition, this Court has structured the rules revision process to encourage advice and comment from the bench and bar, and from the public generally. Any revision in Rule 215(5) should be left to those processes, which are underway.

Last year the Court appointed task forces to study the conduct of discovery and the imposition of sanctions, and to make recommendations for revisions in the rules. The Court's Rules Advisory Committee, the State Bar's Committee on the Administration of Justice, and other groups have undertaken similar studies. While those processes are at work, we adhere to the language of the rule and our consistent precedent.

We note, however, that the trial courts are not without power to prevent the enforcement of Rule 215(5) from operating as an injustice in a particular case. When a party has failed to timely identify evidence in response to discovery requests, the trial court has the discretion to postpone the trial and, under Rule 215(3), to impose an appropriate sanction upon the offending party for abuse of the discovery process. Such sanction may be used to compensate the non-offending party for any wasted expense in preparing for trial. Although the trial court should not allow delay to prejudice the non-offending party, the trial court should ordinarily be able to cure any prejudice by a just imposition of sanctions.

B

In the instant case each party inquired of the other the identity of all potential witnesses. Although they might both have successfully objected to the interrogatory, having undertaken to answer it, they were required to do so fully, and to supplement their answers in accordance with the rules. *See Gutierrez*, 729 S.W.2d at 693. Alvarado never supplemented his answers to identify Arrambide as a witness, even though he knew at least six days before trial when he subpoenaed her that she would be a witness. Alvarado does not contend that he did not know of Arrambide until he subpoenaed her. Rather, as good cause to admit Arrambide's testimony over Farah's objection, Alvarado argued at a pretrial hearing that Farah had long known of Arrambide because she had sued Farah herself on a similar claim, that Farah had deposed Arrambide in her own case although not in Alvarado's, and that Arrambide would be called as a rebuttal witness. The trial court did not make a specific finding of good cause but simply overruled Farah's objection. The fact that Farah was aware of Arrambide and had deposed her in another case, is not, either in itself or in the circumstances of this case, good cause for allowing Arrambide to testify. Neither is Alvarado's use of Arrambide as a rebuttal witness. Alvarado was asked to identify "each potential witness that you may use in the trial of this case." Arrambide was clearly a potential witness, at least when Alvarado subpoenaed her, and Alvarado clearly indicated to the trial court prior to trial that he intended to call her to testify. She could just as well have testified during Alvarado's case in chief as in rebuttal. We hold that Alvarado's tactical decision prior to trial to call Arrambide on rebuttal was not good cause for failing to comply with discovery. *See Walsh v. Mullane*, 725 S.W.2d 264, 264–65 (Tex. App. — Houston [1st Dist.] 1986, writ ref'd n.r.e.). To hold otherwise would be to encourage the very kind of gamesmanship that Rule 215(5) is intended to prevent.

Later during the trial, when Alvarado called Arrambide to the witness stand and Farah renewed its objection, Alvarado asserted a further reason as good cause for allowing Arrambide to testify. Alvarado argued that Arrambide's testimony was necessary to rebut unexpected testimony by Farah's personnel director during its case in chief that Farah would rehire employees with physical limitations. Even if Alvarado's argument had merit, it could hardly support his pretrial decision to call Arrambide as a rebuttal witness. Moreover, the testimony Alvarado claims was unexpected was essentially immaterial. Regardless of whether Farah would or would not rehire employees with physical limitations, Alvarado asserted, and Farah's personnel director admitted, that Alvarado did not have any such limitations precluding his return to work. Alvarado argues, somewhat inconsistently, that he did not call Arrambide to rebut specific testimony by Farah's personnel director, but to impeach him generally. Farah's personnel director was deposed prior to trial, and his credibility was known to be in issue before trial commenced. To the extent Arrambide's testimony was used generally to impeach him, Alvarado certainly knew before trial that she was a potential witness.

We therefore hold that the trial court erred in admitting Arrambide's testimony. The question remains whether that error was harmful. *See Gee*, 765 S.W.2d at 396 (erroneous admission of surprise witness' testimony is not harmful if that testimony is "merely cumulative of properly admitted testimony"), citing *McInnes v. Yamaha Motor Corp.*, 673 S.W.2d 185, 188 (Tex. 1984); *accord McKinney*, 772 S.W.2d at 76. Arrambide testified that she had been fired by Farah one week after the company became aware that she had hired an attorney to file a compensation claim. She was the only witness to testify to these facts; her testimony was not cumulative. It was intended to show that Farah had a pattern of firing employees for filing compensation claims. Alvarado's insistence on using her testimony indicates how important he thought it was to his case. Under the circumstances, we hold that the error in admitting Arrambide's testimony was reversible . . . .

Whether Rule 215(5) should be revised is an issue which we leave to the processes which exist to study such matters. In this case, consistent with the plain language of the rule and our prior precedent, we affirm the judgment of the court of appeals.

Justice Doggett, J., not sitting.

[The dissent of Justice Mauzy is omitted.]

NOTES AND QUESTIONS

(1) *Impact of 1999 Amendments.* Since the *Farah* case was decided, the 1999 amendments have codified certain rules and changed others. Specifically:

(a) Amendments or supplementation of responses to *written* discovery is required "reasonably promptly" on learning that a prior response was "incorrect or incomplete" or is no longer "correct or complete." The "in substance misleading" limit, which itself replaced the former "knowing concealment" standard, is eliminated. TEX. R. CIV. P. 193.5(a).

(b) Formal supplementation of responses to written discovery is required for identification of fact witnesses, trial witnesses, or experts.

(c) Informal supplementation of responses to written discovery under a "has been made known" standard applies to other information.

(d) "An amended or supplemental response must be in the same form as the initial response and must be verified by the party if the original response was required to be verified by the party, but the failure to comply with this requirement does not make the amended or supplemental response untimely unless the party making the response refuses to correct the defect within a reasonable time after it is pointed out." TEX. R. CIV. P. 193.5(b). *See also State Farm Fire & Cas. Co. v. Morua*, 979 S.W.2d 616 (Tex. 1998) (discussing need to verify supplemental discovery responses).

(e) Amendment or supplementation less than 30 days prior to trial is presumptively not made "reasonably promptly."

(f) A duty exists to supplement the deposition or report of a retained expert, but only with regard to mental impressions and opinions and their basis. There is no general duty to supplement deposition testimony. TEX. R. CIV. P. 195.6.

(g) A failure to make, amend, or supplement a discovery response in a timely manner precludes introduction of the evidence or testimony of the witness (other than a named party) who was not identified unless the party seeking to introduce the evidence or call the witness establishes good cause *or* the lack of unfair surprise or unfair prejudice. Regardless of whether such a showing is made, the court may grant a continuance or temporarily postpone the trial to allow a response and to allow opposing parties to conduct discovery. TEX. R. CIV. P. 193.6

(2) *Exclusion of Depositions.* The deposition of an undisclosed witness should be excluded as well as his or her live testimony. *New Braunfels Factory Outlet Ctr., Inc. v. Ihop Realty Corp.*, 872 S.W.2d 303, 311 (Tex. App. — Austin 1994, no writ).

(3) *Exclusion of Documents.* The duty to supplement also extends to documents requested during discovery, and exclusion is a proper sanction. What if the information that was not produced by the party actually harms that party and *helps* the opponent? Exclusion of the information is not, in that situation, a meaningful sanction. In that situation the court may order other sanctions.

(4) *Effect of Nonsuit.* Sanctions excluding witness testimony or other evidence do not survive a nonsuit and have no effect on a subsequently filed action. *Aetna Cas. & Sur. Co. v. Specia*, 849 S.W.2d 805 (Tex. 1993).

(5) *The "Named Party" Exception.* Suppose a named party is an entity rather than a human. If one of its employees is not disclosed in response to a proper discovery request, will that employee's testimony be allowed as that of a "named party" or is that exception limited to people? Under pre-1999 case law, an

undesignated party witness could be allowed to testify "when identity is certain and when his or her personal knowledge of relevant facts has been communicated to all other parties through pleadings by name and response to other discovery at least thirty days in advance of trial." *Smith v. Southwest Feed Yards*, 835 S.W.2d 89, 91–92 (Tex. 1992).

(6) *Non-Party Identification.* Is the trial court empowered to prohibit testimony of a fact witness who is identified in response to a request for disclosure but whose connection to the case is not revealed? *See Beam v. A.H. Chaney, Inc.*, 56 S.W.3d 920, 922–23 (Tex. App. — Fort Worth 2001, pet. denied) (responding party's failure to disclose witness' connection to case, absent a showing of good cause or lack of surprise or prejudice triggers automatic exclusion under Rule 193.6). How automatic is the sanction? Is it necessary to object to the defective response? *See F & H Inv., Inc. v. State*, 55 S.W.3d 663, 671 (Tex. App. — Waco 2001, no pet.) ("A party has no duty to remind another party to abide by the Rules of Civil Procedure.").

(7) *Time to Designate Experts.* How soon after retaining a testifying expert must the expert be identified in response to a request for disclosure? *See* Tex. R. Civ. P. 195.2. May counsel wait until he or she knows what the expert's opinion will be before a duty to supplement and disclose arises? *See* Tex. R. Civ. P. 193.5(b), 195.6; *see also Snider v. Stanley*, 44 S.W.3d 713, 716–17 (Tex. App. — Beaumont 2001, pet. denied) (upholding exclusion of expert trial testimony because expert was not designated "reasonably promptly."). The *Snider* court noted the current rules define a testifying expert as one who may be called to testify at trial and not necessarily a witness who a party expects to call as a witness at trial, and held that the obligation under Rule 195 to supplement and identify arises when an expert is retained, employed, or otherwise is in control of party.

(8) *"Reasonably Promptly."* What does Rule 193.5 mean when it says that an amended or supplemental response must be made *reasonably promptly* after the party discovers the necessity for such a response? We know there is a presumption that supplementation made *less than* 30 days before trial was not made reasonably promptly. Tex. R. Civ. P. 193.5(b). The Corpus Christi Court of Appeals rejected an argument that a reverse presumption also exists: that supplementation made *more than* 30 days before trial is timely. Thus a delay of nine months after certain witness statements became discoverable demonstrated that the supplemental production was *not* reasonably timely. *See Matagorda County Hosp. Dist. v. Burwell*, 94 S.W.3d 75 (Tex. App. — Corpus Christi 2002), *rev'd on other grounds*, 189 S.W.3d 738 (Tex. 2006).

What if an expert witness has been disclosed and deposed, but his or her testimony is modified within 30 days of trial? Rule 195.6 requires a party to supplement an expert witness' deposition testimony with regard to the expert's mental impressions or opinions and the basis for them. In *State Farm Fire & Cas. Co. v. Rodriguez*, 88 S.W.3d 313 (Tex. App. — San Antonio 2002, pet. denied), the court of appeals affirmed the trial court's decision to strike the testimony of an expert witness when defendant failed to produce the PowerPoint presentation used with the expert's testimony despite numerous requests from plaintiff. The presentation also contained information not previously disclosed as a basis for the expert's testimony. In some instances, the change in an expert's opinion does not require supplementation. For example, an expert may refine calculations or perfect a report up until trial. *See Exxon Corp. v. West Tex. Gathering Co.*, 868 S.W.2d 299, 305 (Tex. 1993) (no exclusion if changes are not material). *See also Foust v. Estate of Walters*, 21 S.W.3d 495, 504 (Tex. App. — San Antonio 2000, pet. denied) (expert may refine calculations and perfect reports through the time of trial); *Mares v. Ford Motor Co.*, 53 S.W.3d 416, 419 (Tex. App. — San Antonio 2001, no pet.) (minor refinements in expert testimony do not require exclusion of expert testimony).

An expert may also change an opinion without supplementation if the change is an "expansion of an already disclosed subject." *Navistar Int'l Transp. Corp. v. Crim Truck & Tractor Co.*, 883 S.W.2d 687, 691 (Tex. App. — Texarkana 1994, writ denied). A party may not present a material alteration of an expert's opinion without supplementation. The line between refinements and material changes is not always clear. *See Norfolk So. Ry. Co. v. Bailey*, 92 S.W.3d 577 (Tex. App. — Austin 2002, no pet.).

§ 10.05 SANCTIONS FOR FAILURE TO PROVIDE DISCOVERY

Read Tex. R. Civ. P. 215 and accompanying Comment.

The placement of the theoretically cooperative discovery process within a system that is otherwise adversarial often means that parties fail to comply with the discovery rules, even though the law provides a duty to make discovery. Proper discovery therefore depends on adequate power in the court to enforce the discovery rules. Consider how the following cases deal with the tension between allowing courts to enforce the discovery rules and preventing trial courts from imposing unduly harsh sanctions.

TRANSAMERICAN NATURAL GAS v. POWELL
811 S.W.2d 913 (Tex. 1991)

HECHT, J.

In this original mandamus proceeding, TransAmerican Natural Gas Corporation seeks to compel the Hon. William R. Powell, Judge of the 80th District Court, to set aside his orders imposing sanctions for discovery abuse. The district court struck TransAmerican's pleadings, dismissed its action against Toma Steel Supply, Inc., and granted Toma an interlocutory default judgment on its counterclaim against TransAmerican, reserving for trial only the amount of damages due Toma. We conditionally grant the writ of mandamus.

I

The underlying case is a complex, multi-party action arising out of Toma's sale of allegedly defective pipe casing to TransAmerican. TransAmerican withheld payment for the casing, apparently some $2.3 million, and sued Toma in April 1987 for damages allegedly caused by its use. Toma counterclaimed for $52 million damages resulting from TransAmerican's refusal to pay for the casing. Numerous other parties also joined in the litigation.

On July 3, 1988, the district court issued a docket control order pursuant to Rule 166 of the Texas Rules of Civil Procedure, which set a discovery cutoff date of April 3, 1989. The order allowed discovery to be conducted beyond that date only upon agreement of the parties.

On March 7, 1989, Toma noticed the deposition of TransAmerican's president, K. Craig Shephard, to take place March 16. Two days later TransAmerican's counsel, who at that time was one of the attorneys in its legal department, telephoned Toma's counsel to inform him that Shephard could not be available on March 16 because of a previously scheduled deposition in another case. When counsel could not agree on another date for Shephard's deposition, TransAmerica filed a motion for protection to quash the deposition notice and postpone the deposition. The motion stated that it would be submitted to the trial court for ruling on March 17.[1] However, the trial court did not rule on the motion on that date.

Beginning April 3, the deadline set by the district court for completion of discovery, the parties' smoldering discovery problem started to flare. On that date, counsel for TransAmerican and Toma agreed that Shephard would be deposed after April 10 on a date to be agreed upon. Despite this understanding, counsel again failed to agree upon a date, and on April 19 Toma noticed Shephard's deposition for May 2 without TransAmerican's consent. On April 20, upon receipt of this second deposition notice, TransAmerican's counsel wrote a letter to Toma's counsel informing him that Shephard would not be available May 2 because, as before, he already had a deposition in another matter scheduled for that day. Toma's counsel replied by letter that he would not agree to reschedule the deposition. On April 27, TransAmerican reset the date for submission of its motion for protection to the trial court for ruling to May 12. By this time, of course, the motion was moot, and it is not apparent why TransAmerican continued to seek a ruling. TransAmerican did not move the trial court to postpone the May 2 deposition.

Also on April 27, Shephard's other deposition scheduled for May 2 was cancelled, leaving him available to be deposed by Toma. However, Trans-American's counsel did not advise Toma's counsel that Shephard's schedule had changed so that he could be deposed on May 2 after all, nor did Shephard appear on May 2 as noticed. TransAmerican ascribes its failure to produce Shephard for deposition to miscommunication concerning his schedule changes between attorneys in its legal department. Toma alleges that Shephard's failure to appear was purposeful and part of TransAmerican's intentional obstruction of the discovery process.

---

[1] The local rules governing civil cases in Harris County provide: "Motions shall state a date of submission which shall be at least 10 days from filing, except on leave of court. The motion will be submitted to the court for ruling on that date or later." Rule 3.3.2, Local Rules of the Civil Trial Division of the Harris County District Courts (1987). The March 17 submission date stated in TransAmerican's motion was only three days from the date of filing and the day after the deposition was scheduled.

On May 8, Toma filed a response to TransAmerican's March 14 motion for protective order, even though it acknowledged that that motion was moot. Toma included in its response, however, a motion for sanctions against TransAmerican based on Shephard's failure to appear at the May 2 deposition. In return, TransAmerican filed its own sanctions motion on May 11, urging that Toma's motion for sanctions was itself an abuse of the discovery process. Toma's and TransAmerican's motions for sanctions both stated that they would be submitted to the court for ruling on May 12, the date set for submission of TransAmerican's original motion for protection.

On May 12, without hearing oral argument, the district court signed an order granting Toma's motion for sanctions and striking TransAmerican's pleadings in their entirety. TransAmerican moved for reconsideration, which the district court denied after hearing argument of counsel but refusing to hear any evidence. Based upon his May 12 order striking TransAmerican's pleadings, the district court issued an order on October 6 dismissing TransAmerican's action with prejudice, rendering an interlocutory default judgment against TransAmerican and in favor of Toma on its counterclaim, and setting the case for trial solely on the issue of the damages to be awarded Toma.

TransAmerican sought mandamus relief from the court of appeals to compel the district court to set aside his May 12 and October 6 orders. A divided court of appeals denied TransAmerican leave to file its petition for writ of mandamus in an unpublished per curiam opinion. TransAmerican then moved for leave to file its petition in this Court. We granted the motion in order to review the propriety of the discovery sanctions imposed by the district court.

II

The sanctions imposed by the district court are among those authorized for various discovery abuses under Rule 215 of the Texas Rules of Civil Procedure. The district court did not specify what provision of Rule 215 it relied upon. The portions of the rule applicable to the circumstances here are paragraphs 2(b)(5) and 3. Paragraph 2(b)(5) provides in part:

> If a party or an officer . . . of a party . . . fails to comply with proper discovery requests or to obey an order to provide or permit discovery-, . . . the court in which the action is pending may, after notice and hearing, make such orders in regard to the failure as are just, and among others the following:
>
> . . . .
>
> (5) An order striking out pleadings or parts thereof, . . . or dismissing with or without prejudice the action or proceedings or any part thereof, or rendering a judgment by default against the disobedient party . . . .

At the time of the district court's rulings, paragraph 3 of Rule 215 stated in part:

> If the court finds a party is abusing the discovery process in seeking, making or resisting discovery . . . , then the court in which the action is pending may impose any sanction authorized by paragraphs (1), (2), (3), (4),

(5), and (8) of paragraph 2b of this rule. Such order of sanction shall be subject to review on appeal from the final judgment . . . .

In our view, whether an imposition of sanctions is just is measured by two standards. First, a direct relationship must exist between the offensive conduct and the sanction imposed. This means that a just sanction must be directed against the abuse and toward remedying the prejudice caused by innocent party. It also means that the sanction should be visited upon the offender. The trial court must at least attempt to determine whether the offensive conduct is attributable to counsel only, or to the party only, or to both. This we recognize will not be an easy matter in many instances. On the one hand, a lawyer cannot shield his client from sanctions; a party must bear some responsibility for its counsel's discovery abuses when it is or should be aware of counsel's conduct and the violation of discovery rules. On the other hand, a party should not be punished for counsel's conduct in which it is not implicated apart from having entrusted to counsel its legal representation. The point is, the sanctions the trial court imposes must relate directly to the abuse found.

Second, just sanctions must not be excessive. The punishment should fit the crime. A sanction imposed for discovery abuse should be no more severe than necessary to satisfy its legitimate purposes. It follows that courts must consider the availability of less stringent sanctions and whether such lesser sanctions would fully promote compliance.

These standards set the bounds of permissible sanctions under Rule 215 within which the trial court is to exercise sound discretion. The imposition of very severe sanctions is limited, not only by these standards, but by constitutional due process. The sanctions the district court imposed against TransAmerican are the most devastating a trial court can assess against a party. When a trial court strikes a party's pleadings and dismisses its action or renders a default judgment against it for abuse of the discovery process, the court adjudicates the party's claims without regard to their merits but based instead upon the parties' conduct of discovery. "[T]here are constitutional limitations upon the power of courts, even in aid of their own valid processes, to dismiss an action without affording a party the opportunity for a hearing on the merits of his cause." *Societe Internationale v. Rogers*, 357 U.S. 197, 209–10 (1958), *citing Hammond Packing Co. v. Arkansas*, 212 U.S. 322, 350–51 (1909), and *Hovey v. Elliott*, 167 U.S. 409 (1897); *accord Insurance Corp. of Ireland, Ltd. v. Compagnie des Bauxites de Guinee*, 456 U.S. 694, 705–06 (1982). Discovery sanctions cannot be used to adjudicate the merits of a party's claims or defenses unless a party's hindrance of the discovery process justifies a presumption that its claims or defenses lack merit. *Insurance Corp. of Ireland, Ltd. v. Compagnie des Bauxites de Guinee*, 456 U.S. 694, 705–06 (1982); *Rogers*, 357 U.S. at 209–10; *Hammond Packing*, 212 U.S. at 350–51. However, if a party refuses to produce material evidence, despite the imposition of lesser sanctions, the court may presume that an asserted claim or defense lacks merit and dispose of it. *Insurance Corp. of Ireland*, 456 U.S. at 705–06. Although punishment and deterrence are legitimate purposes for sanctions, *National Hockey League v. Metropolitan Hockey Club, Inc.*, 427 U.S. 639 (1976) (per curiam); *Bodnow Corp. v. City of Hondo*, 721 S.W.2d 839, 840 (Tex. 1986), they do not justify trial by sanctions, *Hammond Packing*, 212 U.S. at 350–51; *Hovey*, 167 U.S. at 413–14. Sanctions which are so severe as to preclude presentation of the merits of the case should not be assessed absent a party's flagrant bad faith or counsel's callous disregard for the responsibilities of discovery under the rules. *See National Hockey League*, 427 U.S. at 642–43.

In the present case, it is not clear whether TransAmerican or its counsel or both should be faulted for Shephard's failure to attend his deposition. Moreover, there is nothing in the record to indicate that the district court considered imposition of lesser sanctions or that such sanctions would not have been effective. If anything, the record strongly suggests that lesser sanctions should have been utilized and perhaps would have been effective. The district court could have ordered Shephard's deposition for a specific date and punished any failure to comply with that order by contempt or another sanction. He also could have taxed the costs of the deposition against TransAmerican and awarded Toma attorney fees. The range of sanctions available to the district court under Rule 215 is quite broad. The district court dismissed TransAmerican's claims against Toma and rendered default judgment for Toma on its counterclaim solely because, as the record before us establishes, TransAmerican's president failed to present himself for his deposition.[6]

Nothing in the record before us even approaches justification for so severe a sanction.[7] We recognize that we affirmed a similar sanction in *Downer v. Aquamarine Operators, Inc.*, 701 S.W.2d 238, 241–42 (Tex. 1985). In that case the trial court struck defendant's answer and rendered a default judgment against it based upon the failure of defendant and his employees to appear for their deposition on three separate occasions without explanation. Even assuming that *Downer* was correctly decided, the instant case does not show the same pattern of abuse present in *Downer*. Furthermore, *Downer*'s approval of the sanction of default judgment was specifically based upon the facts of that case, and the holding in that case is limited to those facts. Rendition of default judgment as a discovery sanction ought to be the exception rather than the rule.

There are cases, of course, when striking pleadings, dismissal, rendition of

---

[6] Toma's motion for sanctions was based solely upon Shephard's failure to attend his deposition. As Toma itself stated in its response to TransAmerican's motion to refile its pleadings after they were struck: "On May 12, 1989, the Court granted [Toma's] Motion for Sanctions against [TransAmerican] for TransAmerican's refusal to agree to a date certain for Mr. Craig Shephard's deposition and for the failure of its President, Mr. Craig Shephard, to appear for a properly noticed deposition on May 2, 1989, and struck TransAmerican's pleadings in their entirety." Notwithstanding this rather clear statement in the trial court, during this mandamus proceeding Toma has suggested that the district court properly sanctioned TransAmerican because it had abused the discovery process on other occasions. TransAmerican disputes Toma's assertions. While the district court would have been entitled to consider a pattern of discovery abuse in imposing sanctions, the record does not reveal the existence of any such pattern, Toma did not complain of one, and the district court does not appear to have found one.

[7] The district court made no findings to support the sanctions imposed. Rule 215 does not require a trial court to make findings before imposing discovery sanctions, and we do not add such a requirement here. We note only that we do not have the benefit of any explanation by the district court for the severity of its ruling. It would obviously be helpful for appellate review of sanctions, especially when severe, to have the benefit of the trial court's findings concerning the conduct which it considered to merit sanctions, and we commend this practice to our trial courts. *See Thomas v. Capital Security Services, Inc.*, 836 F.2d 866, 882–83 (5th Cir. 1988). Precisely to what extent findings should be required before sanctions can be imposed, however, we leave for further deliberation in the process of amending the rules of procedure.

default and other such extreme sanctions are not only just but necessary. *See National Hockey League*, 427 U.S. at 642. In this case, however, the record before us establishes that the severe sanctions the district court imposed against TransAmerican were manifestly unjust in violation of Rule 215.

III

We next consider whether TransAmerican has an adequate remedy by appeal. If it does, then the writ of mandamus must be denied. *State v. Walker*, 679 S.W.2d 484, 485 (Tex. 1984). Rule 215 paragraph 3 states that orders imposing discovery sanctions "shall be subject to review on appeal from the final judgment." Today we have held in *Braden v. Downey*, 811 S.W.2d 922 (Tex. 1991), that sanctions should not be imposed in such a way that effective appellate review is thwarted. Whenever a trial court imposes sanctions which have the effect of adjudicating a dispute, whether by striking pleadings, dismissing an action or rendering a default judgment, but which do not result in rendition of an appealable judgment, then the eventual remedy by appeal is inadequate. Specifically, in this case TransAmerican does not have an adequate remedy by appeal because it must suffer a trial limited to the damages claimed by Toma. The entire conduct of the litigation is skewed by the removal of the merits of TransAmerican's position from consideration and the risk that the trial court's sanctions will not be set aside on appeal. Resolution of matters in dispute between the parties will be influenced, if not dictated, by the trial court's determination of the conduct of the parties during discovery. Some award of damages on Toma's counterclaim is likely, leaving TransAmerican with an appeal, not on whether it should have been liable for those damages, but on whether it should have been sanctioned for discovery abuse. This is not an effective appeal.

We therefore hold that when a trial court imposes discovery sanctions which have the effect of precluding a decision on the merits of a party's claims — such as by striking pleadings, dismissing an action, or rendering default judgment — a party's remedy by eventual appeal is inadequate, unless the sanctions are imposed simultaneously with the rendition of a final, appealable judgment. If such an order of sanctions is not immediately appealable, the party may seek review of the order by petition for writ of mandamus. Although not every such case will warrant issuance of the extraordinary writ, this case does. TransAmerican's remedy by appeal from a final judgment eventually to be rendered in Toma's favor is inadequate . . . .

Accordingly, we hold that TransAmerican is entitled to the mandamus relief it seeks. We are confident that Judge Powell will vacate his orders of May 12 and October 6, after which he may conduct further proceedings consistent with this opinion. Our writ of mandamus will issue only in the event he fails promptly to comply.

[The concurring opinions of Justices Gonzalez and Mauzy are omitted.]

NOTES AND QUESTIONS

(1) *Just Sanctions Must Not be Excessive.* The Texas Supreme Court further limited the trial court's ability to impose death penalty sanctions in *Chrysler Corp. v. Blackmon*, 841 S.W.2d 844 (Tex. 1992). In that case, plaintiff accused Chrysler of needless delay, failing to produce crash tests and other requested information, and falsely stating that Chrysler had fully complied with discovery requests. The trial court made findings supporting plaintiff's accusations, and struck Chrysler's pleadings and rendered a default judgment against Chrysler on all issues. The Supreme Court found this to be an abuse of discretion for four reasons:

> First, there is no direct relationship between the offensive conduct and the sanction imposed. As we stated in *Transamerican*, the sanction must be directed against the abuse and toward remedying the prejudice caused an innocent party. We do not doubt that a failure to produce documents can prejudice a party's efforts to assert or defend a claim. But here, there has simply been no showing that the Garcias are unable to prepare for trial without the additional crash-test reports they seek. Furthermore, the record fails to demonstrate Chrysler's ability to produce the missing crash-test reports. There is no evidence in the record that the missing tests exist or are within Chrysler's possession, custody, or control, either actual or constructive. A party cannot be penalized for failure to produce documents under such circumstances. *See* TEX. R. CIV. P. 166b(2)(b).
>
> The Garcias also contend that Chrysler failed to disclose all similar lawsuits, pointing to the omission of a single lawsuit. Chrysler explains that this omission occurred because the case was classified on its computer as an "air bag" case, rather than a "seatbelt" case. Once Chrysler was advised that the Garcias considered their request to include this type of suit, it made an additional search and disclosed ten air bag suits in advance of the April lst deadline. The Garcias have made no showing as to how they have been hindered in their preparation for trial by this omission.
>
> It seems obvious that the Garcias would be prejudiced by the expenditure of attorneys' fees and expenses in pursuing motions to compel discovery and sanctions. However, reimbursement of those expenses would appear to be better calculated to remedy such prejudice than would death penalty sanctions.
>
> Second, striking Chrysler's pleadings and rendering a default judgment on liability is more severe than necessary to satisfy the legitimate purposes of sanctions for discovery abuse. Judge Blackmon himself conceded as much in his letter to counsel . . . requesting alternative sanction proposals.
>
> Third, no lesser sanction was first imposed. Although potentially exposed to a substantial daily fine, such fine was never imposed because there was no judicial determination that Chrysler failed to meet Judge Dunham's deadline for production of the items specified in his Order. Thus, we do not consider the conditional fine to be, as the Garcias argue, an imposition of a required lesser sanction.

> Fourth and perhaps most significantly, death penalty sanctions should not be used to deny a trial on the merits unless the court finds that the sanctioned party's conduct "justifies a presumption that its claims or defenses lack merit" and that "it would be unjust to permit the party to present the substance of that position [which is the subject of the withheld discovery] before the court." This record contains no evidence to justify such a presumption. In fact, the record conclusively refutes any such suggestion. Nor do we find any evidence in the record of flagrant bad faith or counsel's callous disregard for the obligations of discovery.

841 S.W.2d at 849–50.

(2) *Must "Lesser" Sanctions be "Tested"?* Also in *Chrysler*, the Texas Supreme Court declared that a trial court may not impose death penalty sanctions without first imposing lesser sanctions:

> Sanctions that by their severity, prevent a decision on the merits of a case cannot be justified "absent a party's flagrant bad faith or counsel's callous disregard for the responsibilities of discovery under the rules." Even then, lesser sanctions must first be tested to determine whether they are adequate to secure compliance, deterrence, and punishment of the offender.

841 S.W.2d 849 (quoting *TransAmerican*, 811 S.W.2d at 918). However, in *Cire v. Cummings*, 134 S.W.3d 835 (Tex. 2004), the Court upheld a trial court's order analyzing the available sanctions and offering a reasoned explanation as to the appropriateness of death penalty sanctions, without the actual "testing" of the lesser sanctions (party destroyed tapes that were the only objective evidence of her claim in order to avoid producing them).

(3) *Role of Trial Judge's Factual Findings.* In *TransAmerican*, the Court had suggested that trial court findings would be helpful in determining whether the sanctions imposed were within the trial court's discretion. However, in *Chrysler v. Blackmon*, 841 S.W.2d 844 (Tex. 1992), the Court addressed the issue of the appellate treatment of such findings:

> Although the trial court made extensive findings, only two appear pertinent to the *Transamerican* standards: whether Chrysler's discovery abuse justifies the presumption that its defenses to the suit lack merit; and, whether the conditional monetary sanctions order . . . can be fairly characterized as a lesser sanction. We have reviewed the entire record and conclude that it contains no evidence that would justify the presumption of lack of merit of Chrysler's defense; further, we conclude that the conditional monetary sanctions order is not the type of lesser sanction required before the imposition of death penalty sanctions, which we contemplated in *Transamerican* . . . . While trial court findings in a death penalty sanctions case can be helpful in demonstrating how the court's discretion was guided by a reasoned analysis of the purposes sanctions serve and the means of accomplishing those purposes, especially in complex cases where the record is voluminous, such findings must be pertinent to the *Transamerican* standards and supported by the record. Findings specifically

tied to an appropriate legal standard are the only type of findings that can be truly beneficial to appellate review.

841 S.W.2d at 852–53.

(4) *The 1999 Amendments.* The 1999 amendments to the discovery rules do not make any substantive changes in Rule 215 except for the elimination of subdivision 5 of former Rule 215 (failure to respond to or supplement discovery) and the inclusion of former Rule 203 (failure of party or witness to attend or seek subpoena; expenses) as a part of Rule 215. Discovery sanctions were treated as a separate problem by the Supreme Court Advisory Committee and a separate Task Force on Discovery Sanctions. The court has taken no action to amend the rules based on the Task Force recommendations.

(5) *Understanding Civil Procedure Rule 215.* Read Tex. R. Civ. P. 215. As you can see, a broad range of sanctions is available to the trial court. In determining what kind of sanction to apply, the court should consider the severity of the violation, its impact on the litigation, the degree of fault underlying the violation, and the need to deter litigants from violating the discovery rules. Courts continually stress that discovery sanctions must be supported by evidence showing why the dollar amount chosen is appropriate. *See Stromberger v. Turley Law Firm*, 251 S.W.3d 225 (Tex. App. — Dallas 2008, no pet.).

(6) *Community Service.* In *Braden v. Downey*, 811 S.W.2d 922 (Tex. 1991), the Court characterized the sanction of ordering the attorney to perform community service as "creative." It noted, however, that should the attorney wish to challenge the imposition of this type of sanction, the trial court should defer the time for performance until after an opportunity to appeal. The court of appeals in *Hill & Griffith Co. v. Bryant*, 139 S.W.3d 688 (Tex. App. — Tyler 2004, pet. denied), affirmed the trial court's order that an attorney perform fifty hours of community service with a legal aid program for her bad faith failure to produce a document during discovery.

(7) *Sanctions as Damages.* In *Firestone Photographs, Inc. v. Lamaster*, 567 S.W.2d 273 (Tex. Civ. App. — Texarkana 1978, no writ), the court ordered a defendant who refused to produce a witness for deposition to pay a daily fine (with the amount of the fine doubling periodically) for each day of noncompliance. When the case was called to trial, plaintiff waived all of the relief asked for in the petition and sought judgment for the accumulated sanctions, up to the amount originally sought by plaintiff. The court entered judgment for plaintiff for $65,245 in sanctions, plus attorney's fees. The court of appeals found this sanction to be within the discretion of the trial court.

(8) *Other Death Penalty Sanctions.* Death penalty sanctions commonly consist of striking pleadings or rendering default judgment, but may include any sanction that is case determinative. *See Adkins Serv., Inc. v. Tisdale Co.*, 56 S.W.3d 842, 845 (Tex. App. — Texarkana 2001, no pet.) (trial court's exclusion of testimony that supported the assignment of the right to pursue lawsuit constituted a death penalty sanction because it precluded assignee's ability to recover).

PRACTICE EXERCISE #31

Assume the same facts as for Practice Exercise #25.

1. Allen v. Alpha Omega is now approaching trial — the case is set #1 on the docket in two weeks. During discovery, Allen sent a request for disclosure including all of the topics allowed under Civil Procedure Rule 194. Alpha Omega provided a list of persons having knowledge of relevant facts, but did not include the name of Bree Sample, a customer who witnessed the accident. Alpha Omega's lawyer did orally mention Sample to Allen's lawyer during a telephone conversation a couple of months ago. Alpha Omega has now listed Sample as a person who it will call to testify as a witness at trial pursuant to the court's Pretrial Order under Rule 166. Under what circumstances should the trial judge allow Sample to testify?

2. Alpha Omega's testifying expert was deposed about a month before trial. At that time he testified that he had not yet completed his analysis, but believed that Alpha Omega took adequate precautions to prevent falls. During the deposition, Allen's lawyer punched significant holes in the basis for that testimony. Now, at trial (and without prior warning), the expert wants to testify about additional tests that he did between deposition and trial. Should he be allowed to testify about these tests and their effect on his opinion?

3. Assume that the trial court allowed Sample to testify. Her testimony mirrored that of Hugh Cumber, an Alpha Omega employee. The jury found that Allen's negligence was 55 percent responsible for her injuries, and thus she collects nothing. You represent Allen on appeal. What will you have to show to obtain reversal on the ground that Sample should not have been allowed to testify?

4. Before trial, Allen's lawyer intended to take the deposition of Mack N. Tosh, another Alpha Omega customer. He sent the proper notice of deposition to all parties. Unfortunately, he did not subpoena Tosh who, being unenthusiastic about this deposition thing, failed to show up to be deposed. The Alpha Omega lawyer, however, traveled from his office in the big city to Tosh's hometown, where the deposition was to be taken, and while he was traveling his hourly fee meter was running. What sanctions are available to Alpha Omega?

APPENDIX — DISCOVERY DEVICES AND THE TEXAS BAR EXAM

Most lawsuits involve at least some discovery, and discovery issues are frequently tested on the Texas Bar Exam. The following are questions from past exams, reprinted with the permission of the Texas Board of Law Examiners, which owns the copyright to these questions. You can see more questions, and the examiners' comments on the answers, by visiting the Board's website at www.ble.state.tx.us/past_exams/main_pastexams.htm.

In considering the questions, keep in mind that on the bar exam your answer is always limited to five lines.

July 2006

Properties, Inc. ("Properties") owns Apartments located in Nueces County, Texas . . . . Sam is employed by Properties as manager of Apartments . . . . Betsy lives in Apartments. Betsy sustained serious injuries in a fire that consumed her unit in Apartments. The source of the fire was a broken electrical outlet. Betsy had asked Sam to replace the broken outlet weeks before the fire. The outlet had not been replaced prior to the fire. Betsy filed a lawsuit . . . seeking damages from Properties and Sam.

1. Betsy's attorney wants to notice Properties' oral deposition to inquire about a variety of topics relevant to the issues in the lawsuit. Other than time and place for the deposition, what must the notice state? Explain fully.

2. Assuming Properties does not object to the notice of deposition, what must it do to comply with the notice? Explain fully.

3. If Properties wants to object to the time and place of the deposition, what pleading must it file and when? Explain fully.

4. Betsy had vacated Apartments after the fire. Betsy subsequently retains an expert who now wants access to Apartments prior to completing his report. What pleadings must Betsy's attorney file for her expert to have access to Apartments? What must the pleading state? Explain fully.

5. If Properties wants to respond to Betsy's pleading seeking access to Apartments, when must Properties file its response? What must the response state? Explain fully.

6. In the course of discovery, Betsy serves Requests for Admission on Sam, through his attorney, who forwards the Requests to Sam. The Requests state that responses are due within 31 days of service. Sam never respond to the Requests. What is the effect of Sam's failure to respond to the Requests for Admissions? Explain fully.

7. What must Sam's attorney do and show if he wants to avoid the effect of Sam's failure to respond to the Requests for Admissions? Explain fully.

July 2005

Laura has been a lifelong resident of Harris County, Texas. She was injured on January 15, 2002, when she slipped and fell in a grocery store in Dallas County, Texas. The owner and operator of the store was Food, Inc . . . . [Laura consulted a lawyer, who recommended that she file a lawsuit.]

1. Defendant served interrogatories on Plaintiff, seeking the names of the persons Plaintiff expects to call as witnesses at trial, including all rebuttal and impeachment witnesses. Plaintiff objected. How should the Court rule? Explain fully.

2. Plaintiff serves a notice to take the oral deposition of Defendant, a corporation, with a subpoena duces tecum to produce certain documents at the deposition. How much notice must be given for the deposition, as noticed? If Defendant wants to object to the notice, what must it do and when must it do it? Explain fully.

3. During the deposition of Defendant's corporate representative, Defendant's lawyer repeatedly interrupts the questioning with objections that suggest answers

to the witness. What are the only objections permitted during an oral deposition? What remedies are available to Plaintiff's lawyer if Defendant's lawyer goes beyond what is permitted under the rules? Explain fully.

4. Plaintiff was treated by a number of doctors for her injuries. Defendant wants to obtain the medical records from those doctors without taking their oral depositions. How can Defendant obtain the records in admissible form? Explain fully.

5. After obtaining Plaintiff's medical records, Defendant decides that it wants Plaintiff to be examined by another qualified doctor. What must Defendant do to obtain such an independent examination? Explain fully.

February 2009

Paul, a resident of Nueces County, Texas, went to the local hardware store, Supplies, Inc., ("Supplies"), to purchase an electric saw. Supplies is a Texas corporation with its principal place of business in Nueces County, Texas. After purchasing the saw, Paul asked David, a salesman for Supplies, to demonstrate how the saw operated. When David turned on the saw, its blade came loose, resulting in serious injuries to Paul's arm. David is a resident of San Patricio County, Texas. In addition to working for Supplies, David is also a representative for the manufacturer of the saw, Tools, Inc., ("Tools"), a Delaware corporation. Tools regularly advertises and sells its products in Texas through hardware stores like Supplies.

Paul sues David, Supplies, and Tools in a state district court in Nueces County, Texas. Paul's lawsuit seeks damages resulting from the injuries he sustained in the incident in question. All of the defendants are properly served with citation and a copy of the original petition.

1. When Paul filed his original petition, he also filed a Request for Production, which was served on each of the Defendants along with the citation and a copy of the original petition. When must each Defendant file responses to the Requests for Production? Explain fully.

2. The parties want to proceed with written discovery before scheduling oral depositions. Identify five permissible forms of discovery under the Texas Rules of Civil Procedure.

3. Paul's attorney sends Tools attorney a request for admission asking Tools to admit within 31 days of service of the request, that Tools was the manufacturer of the electric saw in question. Forty (40) days after Tools attorney received the request for admission, he served Paul's attorney with a response denying the request for admission. What is the effect of that response and what must Tool's attorney do and show to change that result? Explain fully.

4. All of the Defendants want to independently verify the nature and extent of Paul's injuries. How can that be accomplished? Explain fully.

5. Assume that Paul receives a discovery request from a Defendant calling for the production of material that Paul's attorney considers to be privileged. How can Paul's attorney preserve the privilege? Explain fully.

6. In response to a request for production from Paul, Supplies' attorney inadvertently produces communications between Supplies and its attorneys. What must

Supplies' attorney do to avoid a waiver of the attorney-client privilege with respect to the communications that were produced? Explain fully.

7. During Paul's deposition, his attorney wants to object to questions being asked by Supplies' attorney. What objections to questions can Paul's attorney make during the deposition? What objections to testimony can be made during the deposition?

Chapter 11

DISPOSITION WITHOUT TRIAL

SCOPE

While some cases proceed all the way to trial, others end before they get to that point. If the defendant fails to appear and answer, the plaintiff may be entitled to a default judgment. And if the litigation presents no "genuine issue of material fact," the court may dispose of the case through summary judgment.

§ 11.01 JUDGMENT BY DEFAULT

Read Tex. R. Civ. P. 239 through 243.

There are three types of judgments that are similar to each other and to which the term "default judgment" has been applied from time to time by Texas courts.

(1) The true default judgment exists when the defendant has failed to appear on "answer day," the result being the entry of an interlocutory or final judgment. *Frymire Eng'g Co., Inc. v. Grantham*, 524 S.W.2d 680 (Tex. 1975).

(2) A "nihil dicit" judgment exists when the defendant has appeared (usually by filing a dilatory plea or motion) but has had a plea or motion not dealing with the merits of the case overruled, leaving the defendant with no answer. *See Butler v. Butler*, 577 S.W.2d 501 (Tex. Civ. App. — Texarkana 1978, writ dism'd).

(3) A failure to appear at trial case is different from both of the foregoing in that the only "default" is a failure to appear at trial in response to a proper trial setting notice. *See* TEX. R. CIV. P. 245; *Smith v. Smith*, 544 S.W.2d 121 (Tex. 1977).

Generally speaking, the true default and the nihil dicit cases are similar. There is an admission of liability but not damages, unless the damages are liquidated and proved by an instrument in writing. If damages are unliquidated or not proved by an instrument in writing or both, then "the court shall hear evidence as to damages." *See* TEX. R. CIV. P. 243.

In the failure-to-appear-at-trial case, there is no admission of liability because there is an answer on the merits, *i.e.*, plaintiff must prove both liability and damages. Of course, the answer might itself be an insufficient response. *See, e.g.*, TEX. R. CIV. P. 185. A decision of the Texas Supreme Court appears to hold that a failure to appear at trial case (characterized by the Court as a post-answer-default-judgment case) is to be treated the same as a *no-answer*-default-judgment case with respect to the requirement that the petition (or other pleading for affirmative relief) must give "fair notice" of the claims for relief. *See Stoner v. Thompson*, 578 S.W.2d 679, 685 (Tex. 1979).

The need to prove unliquidated damages can include more than merely putting a number on the plaintiff's injuries. Consider the following case.

MORGAN v. COMPUGRAPHIC CORP.

675 S.W.2d 729 (Tex. 1984)

RAY, J.

Margie F. Morgan brought this suit against Compugraphic Corporation and Solutek Corporation under theories of negligence and strict liability, alleging that the two corporations were jointly and severally liable for injuries she had incurred as a result of inhaling chemical fumes emitted from a typesetting machine installed in her office. Solutek timely answered, but Compugraphic filed no answer. After hearing evidence as to damages pursuant to Texas Rule of Civil Procedure 243, the trial court rendered default judgment against Compugraphic in the amount of $200,000 and then severed Morgan's cause of action against Compugraphic from her suit against Solutek. Compugraphic appealed by writ of error to the Dallas Court of Appeals. The court of appeals reversed and remanded the cause for a trial on the merits holding that: (1) Morgan had the burden of proving that her injuries were proximately caused by the acts of Compugraphic; (2) Morgan had presented no competent evidence of proximate cause; and (3) the trial court's severance of Morgan's suit against Compugraphic from her suit against Solutek was improper.

Morgan contests the correctness of each of these holdings before this court. Upon consideration of the court of appeals holding that it was incumbent upon Morgan to prove proximate cause, we reach the somewhat different conclusion that Morgan was required to prove a causal nexus between her injuries and her exposure to chemical fumes. We find some competent evidence in the record which establishes such a causal nexus. We further find that the court of appeals erred in holding that the trial court's severance of Morgan's causes of action was improper. We reverse the judgment of the court of appeals and remand the cause to that court for a determination of whether there was factually sufficient evidence to support an award of $200,000.

The only evidence as to the facts of this case consists of Morgan's testimony before the trial court at the assessment of damages hearing, at which Compugraphic did not appear. Morgan is a secretary employed by Frito-Lay, Inc. Morgan testified that she had always been in good health prior to returning to work from a vacation in November of 1979. Upon her return to work, Morgan found that a typesetting machine had been installed near her desk. The machine was manufactured and installed by Compugraphic and used chemicals manufactured by Solutek. Morgan testified that the machine was positioned in such a way that the back of it was only two inches from her face as she worked. Soon after Morgan came back to work, she began to develop problems with her breathing. After working four or five days near the machine, she began to experience blurred vision, headaches, stomach problems, and swelling of the eyes, lips, and nasal passages. About a month after she began to suffer these symptoms, Morgan learned that two chemical leaks in the typesetter had been discovered and repaired. Morgan's health continued to decline after the repair. She testified that she began to develop frequent skin rashes as well as a number of problems with her circulatory, digestive and nervous systems. She further testified that she has to administer histamine shots to herself twice each day.

We first reach the question of whether a party who secures a default judgment against a non-answering defendant must, at a Rule 243 hearing, present evidence proving the cause of the damages. Rule 243 reads as follows:

> If the cause of action is unliquidated or be not proved by an instrument in writing, the court shall hear evidence as to damages and shall render judgment therefor, unless the defendant shall demand and be entitled to a trial by jury in which case the judgment by default shall be noted, a writ of inquiry awarded, and the cause entered on the jury docket.

At issue in this case is the meaning of the phrase "the court shall hear evidence as to damages." Morgan contends that "evidence as to damages" refers only to evidence establishing the fact of damages and does not include evidence pertaining to the cause of those damages. Morgan cites as support two long-standing rules of Texas jurisprudence. One rule is that a judgment taken by default on an unliquidated claim admits all allegations of fact set out in the petition, except the amount of damages. *See Stoner v. Thompson*, 578 S.W.2d 679, 684 (Tex. 1979); *Long v. Wortham*, 4 Tex. 381 (1849). The other rule, a corollary of the first, holds that if the facts set out in the petition allege a cause of action, a default judgment conclusively establishes the defendant's liability. *Tarrant County v. Lively*, 25 Tex. Supp. 399 (1860); *Clark v. Compton*, 15 Tex. 32 (1855); *Wall v. Wall*, 630 S.W.2d 493, 496 (Tex. Civ. App. — Fort Worth 1982, writ ref'd n.r.e.).

Morgan's argument is flawed because it combines two distinct aspects of causation which exist in a personal injury case such as this. In a personal injury case, the plaintiff typically alleges that the defendant's conduct caused an event — an automobile accident, a fall, or in this case, the release of chemical fumes — and that this event caused the plaintiff to suffer injuries for which compensation in damages should be paid. Thus, at trial the plaintiff must establish two causal nexuses in order to be entitled to recovery: (a) a causal nexus between the defendant's conduct and the event sued upon; and (b) a causal nexus between the event sued upon and the plaintiff's injuries.[1]

The causal nexus between the defendant's conduct and the event sued upon relates to the liability portion of plaintiff's cause of action. Here, we use the term

---

[1] The distinction between these two causal nexuses is illustrated by contrasting the standard jury issues regarding proximate and producing cause with the issue regarding damages for personal injuries. The issues on proximate and producing cause inquire as to the defendant's liability for the event upon which suit is based: Proximate Cause Issue: "Do you find from a preponderance of the evidence *that such action was a proximate cause of the occurrence in question*?" 1 State Bar of Texas, *Texas Pattern Jury Charges* PJC 3.01 (1969) (emphasis supplied). Producing Cause Issue: "Was that defect *a producing cause of the occurrence in question*?" 3 State Bar of Texas, *Texas Pattern Jury Charges* PJC 71.01A (1982) (emphasis supplied).

The damages issue inquires as to whether there is a causal link between the event sued upon and the plaintiff's injuries: "Find from a preponderance of the evidence what sum of money, if any, if paid now in cash, would fairly and reasonably compensate [plaintiff] for his *injuries*, if any, *resulting from the occurrence in question*." *Id.*, PJC 80.03 (emphasis supplied).

"liability" to mean legal responsibility for the event upon which suit is based. In a negligence action, liability is usually established by proving that the defendant's negligence was a proximate cause of the event sued upon; in a products liability action in which a manufacturing defect is alleged, liability is established by proving that a product was placed in the stream of commerce containing a defect which was a producing cause of the event made the basis of suit. It is this causal nexus between the conduct of the defendant and the event sued upon that is admitted by default. From the rule that a default judgment conclusively establishes the defendant's liability, it follows that a default judgment admits that the defendant's conduct caused the event upon which the plaintiff's suit is based.

Whether the event sued upon caused any injuries to the plaintiff is another matter entirely. The causal nexus between the event sued upon and the plaintiff's injuries is strictly referable to the damages portion of the plaintiff's cause of action. Even if the defendant's liability has been established, proof of this causal nexus is necessary to ascertain the amount of damages to which the plaintiff is entitled. This is true because the plaintiff is entitled to recover damages only for those injuries caused by the event made the basis of suit; that the defendant has defaulted does not give the plaintiff the right to recover for damages which did not arise from his cause of action. *See Mitchell v. Town of Ahoskie*, 129 S.E. 626 (N.C. 1925). To hold, as we do, that a defaulting defendant does not admit that the event sued upon caused any of plaintiff's alleged injuries is entirely consistent with the rule that a judgment taken by default admits all allegations of fact set out in the petition, except for the amount of damages. Proving that the event sued upon caused the plaintiff's alleged injuries is part and parcel of proving the amount of damages to which the plaintiff is entitled. The causal nexus between the event sued upon and the plaintiff's injuries must be shown by competent evidence. *See Gerland's Food Fair, Inc. v. Hare*, 611 S.W.2d 113 (Tex. Civ. App. — Houston [1st Dist.] 1980, writ ref'd n.r.e.). *Accord Smith v. Sayles*, 637 S.W.2d 714 (Mo. App. 1982). We conclude that the mandate of Rule 243 that the court hear "evidence as to damages" makes it incumbent upon a party who obtains a default judgment in a personal injury action to present competent evidence of a causal nexus between the event sued upon and the party's alleged injuries.

It remains to apply the rules set forth in the foregoing discussion to the case before us. Morgan alleged in her petition that Compugraphic negligently installed a typesetting machine, or, alternatively, installed a defective typesetting machine, and that as a result of this conduct chemical fumes were released into Morgan's office, causing her a variety of injuries. The event sued upon is thus the release of chemical fumes into Morgan's office. By its default, Compugraphic admitted that its negligence was a proximate cause of the release of chemical fumes into Morgan's office. Compugraphic further admitted by its default that a defect in the typesetting machine was a producing cause of that event. However, Compugraphic's default did not establish that the release of chemical fumes caused Morgan any injuries. At the Rule 243 hearing, Morgan had the burden of presenting competent evidence of a causal nexus between the release of chemical fumes and her alleged injuries.

This brings us to the issue of whether Morgan presented some competent evidence that her alleged injuries were caused by the release of chemical fumes into her office. We do not attempt here to detail all such evidence; rather, our task is to determine if there is some evidence to support the trial court's judgment. As stated previously, Morgan's testimony was the only evidence presented at the Rule 243 hearing. Morgan concedes that she is a layperson not qualified to give expert medical testimony. Lay testimony is adequate to prove causation in those cases in which general experience and common sense will enable a layman to determine, with reasonable probability, the causal relationship between the event and the condition. *Lenger v. Physician's General Hospital, Inc.*, 455 S.W.2d 703, 706 (Tex. 1970). Generally, lay testimony establishing a sequence of events which provides a strong, logically traceable connection between the event and the condition is sufficient proof of causation. *Griffin v. Texas Employers' Insurance Association*, 450 S.W.2d 59, 61 (Tex. 1969).

In the instant case, the evidence shows that Morgan had always been in good health prior to returning to work from her vacation. Upon returning to her job, she worked with her face two inches from a typesetting machine which, it is admitted by default, was leaking chemical fumes. Soon after resuming her employment, that is, soon after being exposed to the fumes emanating from the typesetting machine, Morgan experienced problems with "breathing and swelling and the like." After four or five days of being constantly exposed to these fumes during her working hours, Morgan developed symptoms such as watering of the eyes, blurred vision, headaches and swelling of the breathing passages. We believe this evidence establishes a sequence of events from which the trier of fact may properly infer, without the aid of expert medical testimony, that the release of chemical fumes from the typesetting machine caused Morgan to suffer injury. We thus conclude that there is some evidence in the record to support the trial court's award of damages. *See Hurst v. Sears, Roebuck & Co.*, 647 S.W.2d 249, 253 (Tex. 1983). . . .

We reverse the judgment of the court of appeals and remand the cause to that court for a consideration of Compugraphic's point of error asserting that the evidence is factually insufficient to support an award of $200,000.

NOTES AND QUESTIONS

(1) *Proving Damages in a Default Judgment Case.* Why does Justice Ray conclude that evidence of causation is part of proof of damages? How difficult a burden does this conclusion impose on plaintiffs in personal injury cases? You should note that the Court's attitude about the sufficiency of the plaintiff's testimony to prove a causal nexus between the event and her injuries may be inconsistent with the Court's more recent decisions, which may require the use of expert testimony. *See, e.g., Broders v. Heise*, 924 S.W.2d 148, 151–54 (Tex. 1996); *cf. Uniroyal Goodrich Tire Co. v. Martinez*, 977 S.W.2d 328, 338–39 (Tex. 1998).

(2) *Post-Answer Defaults and Jury Trial.* Notwithstanding a prior demand for a jury trial, under Civil Procedure Rule 220, a party who commits a post-answer default by failing to appear at trial waives the right to a jury trial. *Bradley Motors, Inc. v. Mackey*, 878 S.W.2d 140, 141 (Tex. 1994).

(3) *Reversal of a Default Judgment Due to Lack of a Proper Record.* A party who obtains a default judgment by presenting evidence of unliquidated damages must ensure that a reporter's record is available to the defaulted party. This means

that a court reporter must be present to take down the necessary testimony presented by the plaintiff at the default hearing. *See, e.g.*, *Morgan Express, Inc. v. Elizabeth-Perkins, Inc.*, 525 S.W.2d 312 (Tex. Civ. App. — Dallas 1975, writ ref'd).

(4) *The Court Reporter's Duty.* Appellate Rule 13.1(a) provides that the official court reporter must attend court sessions and make a full record of the proceedings, unless excused by agreement of the parties. In *Rogers v. Rogers*, 561 S.W.2d 172 (Tex. 1978), the Texas Supreme Court explained that a "defaulted" party is not required to rely on the unaided memory of the trial judge, quoting the following language from *Robinson v. Robinson*, 487 S.W.2d 713, 714 (Tex. 1972): "if an appellant exercises due diligence and through no fault of his own is unable to obtain a proper record of the evidence introduced, this may require a new trial where his right to have the case reviewed on appeal can be preserved in no other way."

(5) *Evidence of Damages.* Can the plaintiff use affidavits rather than live testimony to prove up unliquidated damages at a default judgment hearing? The Texas Supreme Court says yes. In *Texas Commerce Bank v. New*, 3 S.W.3d 515, 516–17 (Tex. 1999) (per curiam), the Court held that bank officers' affidavits identifying the total amount owed (as a consequence of the defendants' check-kiting scheme) supported a default judgment as to damages, and an affidavit from the bank's general counsel supported the award of attorneys' fees. To the extent that the affidavits were hearsay, they still supported the judgment because they were admitted without objection. *See* TEX. R. EVID. 802 ("Inadmissible hearsay admitted without objection shall not be denied probative value merely because it is hearsay."). In Dallas County, some courts dispense with the formality of conducting prove-up hearings by relying completely on affidavits filed by plaintiffs concerning damages.

(6) *Notice of Default Judgment Hearing.* Is the Plaintiff required to give the Defendant notice of the default judgment hearing? Should notice be required? *Continental Carbon Co. v. Sea-Land Serv., Inc.*, 27 S.W.3d 184, 189 (Tex. App. — Dallas 2000, pet. denied) (Plaintiff is not required to provide notice of the default judgment hearing to a non-answering defendant before the trial court renders the default judgment).

(7) *Default Judgment After Amended Petition.* For many years, if a plaintiff amended his petition to seek more onerous relief, he was required to re-serve citation on the defendant in order to support a default judgment based on the amended pleading. *Weaver v. Hartford Accident and Indemnity Co.*, 570 S.W.2d 367, 370 (Tex. 1978). However, the Texas Supreme Court has now held that the adoption of Civil Procedure Rule 21a changed that. Now, defendants who have been properly served with citation and plaintiff's original petition may be served with an amended petition under Rule 21a: "by delivering a copy to the party to be served, or the party's duly authorized agent or attorney of record, as the case may be, either in person or by agent or by courier receipted delivery or by certified or registered mail, to the party's last known address, or by telephonic document transfer to the recipient's current telecopier number, or by such other manner as the court in its discretion may direct." No new service of citation is required. *In re E.A.*, 287 S.W.3d 1, 4 (Tex. 2009). Note, however, that due process requires at least

constructive notice of the amended petition. *Id.* at 5-6.

§ 11.02 SUMMARY JUDGMENT

[A] Standards and Procedure for Granting

[1] Traditional Motions

Read Tex. R. Civ. P. 166a(a), (b), (c), (e).

What Is Summary Judgment?

The procedure known as "summary judgment" allows for the early determination of some or all of the claims and defenses raised by the pleadings in the case, without a full-scale trial. It provides a speedy means for the disposition of controversies that do not present fact issues. As characterized by one court of appeals, the remedy of summary judgment permits the court to weed out non-meritorious causes of action or defenses without the expense of time or money caused by protracted trials. *See, e.g., Thomas v. Medical Arts Hosp. of Texarkana*, 920 S.W.2d 815, 818 (Tex. App. — Texarkana 1996, pet. denied).

To accomplish these purposes, a trial court is empowered to grant a motion for summary judgment and render judgment for the movant when it is conclusively shown that the moving party is entitled to judgment as a matter of law. The court must be satisfied that either (1) there are no genuine issues of material fact and the movant's summary judgment evidence establishes an entitlement to judgment as a matter of law [traditional motion] or (2) there is no evidence of one or more essential elements of a claim or defense on which the adverse party has the burden of proof ["no evidence"' motion]. Tex. R. Civ. P. 166a(c), (i). The resulting judgment may be rendered on the whole case for all the relief requested or it may resolve some issues, claims, or defenses and leave the disputed facts for determination by trial. Tex. R. Civ. P. 166a(e). For example, the court may find that no question of fact exists as to a defendant's liability, and render judgment accordingly, but reserve the assessment of damages for a full evidentiary trial in the usual manner. Tex. R. Civ. P. 166a(a).

Motion Must Specify Grounds

As with any pre-trial motion, a motion for summary judgment must be in writing and state the grounds relied on and the relief or order sought. Tex. R. Civ. P. 21, 166a(c); *see City of Houston v. Clear Creek Basin Authority*, 589 S.W.2d 671, 677 (Tex. 1979). The movant is free to assert several grounds, a common tactic especially in defense of personal injury cases when the defendant claims there is no duty owed to the plaintiff, no evidence to support some key element of the plaintiff's case, and the establishment of an affirmative defense as a matter of law.

The Texas Supreme Court has called for strict enforcement of the requirement that the motion specifically state the grounds for the summary judgment sought. The Court has held that grounds set out in a brief attached to and filed with the motion could not be considered. *McConnell v. Southside Indep. School Dist.*, 858 S.W.2d 337, 339–42 (Tex. 1993); *Stiles v. Resolution Trust Corp.*, 867 S.W.2d 24, 26 (Tex. 1993) (trial court is restricted to ruling on issues raised in motion, response, and any subsequent replies); *Jeter v. McGraw*, 79 S.W.3d 211, 216 (Tex. App. — Beaumont 2002, pet. denied) (summary judgment may not be granted on grounds not raised by motion). Of course, the motion may be accompanied by supporting affidavits, discovery products, or both, as necessary to support the grounds stated in the motion. Tex. R. Civ. P. 166a(a), (c). The movant may attach a brief or memorandum of authorities to guide the trial court in following the movant's legal reasoning. But the accompanying documents cannot be referenced or relied on to set out any grounds for the relief sought in the motion; their only purpose is to support the grounds specified directly in the motion itself. *See Wilson v. Parker*, 904 S.W.2d 628, 629 (Tex. 1995) (summary judgment evidence does not have to be in motion or response, only specification of grounds relied on).

Prevailing on the Traditional Motion for Summary Judgment

1. Plaintiff Moves for Summary Judgment on Its Cause of Action

To prevail on summary judgment, a movant must conclusively establish all elements of its cause of action as a matter of law. Tex. R. Civ. P. 166a(c); *Nixon v. Mr. Property Management*, 690 S.W.2d 546, 548 (Tex. 1985). To prevail and put the burden on the non-movant to raise a genuine issue of material fact, the movant must conclusively establish, by proper summary judgment evidence, all essential elements of the claim. *MMP, Ltd. v. Jones*, 710 S.W.2d 59, 60 (Tex. 1986).

Examples of claims that are particularly good candidates for summary judgment by establishing all the elements include the following:

- Suits on promissory notes
- Claims based on open or stated accounts
- Claims based on unambiguous written instruments
- Actions for declaratory judgment by liability insurer as to duty to defend

2. Defendant Moves for Summary Judgment Based on Its Affirmative Defense

A party defending a claim may obtain a summary judgment by conclusively establishing all the elements of a pleaded affirmative defense. In doing so, the party must sustain the burden of proving that there are no disputed issues of fact that would prevent judgment in its favor as a matter of law; any factual disputes as to the elements of the claimant's cause of action are immaterial if an affirmative defense is established. Tex. R. Civ. P. 166a(c).

Examples of affirmative defenses capable of proof by summary judgment evidence include the following:

- Unambiguous release of liability
- Res judicata
- Governmental immunity of employee acting in good faith

- Expiration of time prescribed by controlling statute of limitation

3. Defendant Moves for Traditional Summary Judgment, Negating an Element of Each of Plaintiff's Claims

A party resisting a claim may establish that no genuine issue of fact exists, justifying a "take-nothing" judgment as a matter of law, by negating at least one of the key elements of each of the claimant's theories of recovery. The movant need not negate all conceivable theories on which the claimant might recover; rather, the movant is only required to negate the theories raised by the pleadings.

In tort cases, an essential element of the cause of action often challenged by summary judgment proceedings is the existence of a particular duty alleged to have been breached by the defendant. In the absence of a duty, the defendant is entitled to judgment in its favor as a matter of law. Although the question of duty is a question of law, there may also be a question concerning the existence of the facts that would trigger the duty claimed to have been breached. By establishing that those facts do not exist as a matter of law, the defendant is entitled to summary judgment. For example, in a premises liability case, the summary judgment evidence may prove that the owner of the premises had no right to control the conduct of an independent contractor and thus had no duty to maintain a safe job site to avoid injury to the plaintiff.

Other examples of an essential element of a claim successfully negated by the adverse party are the following:

- The existence of outrageous conduct, as an element of the tort of intentional infliction of emotional distress
- In an action for libel, the fact that the newspaper article in question was reasonably capable of a defamatory meaning
- Causation and damages, as key elements of a claim for legal or medical malpractice
- Notice of the claim, as required for an action under the Texas Tort Claims Act

---

The following case is an example of the court considering a traditional summary judgment motion.

SCIENCE SPECTRUM, INC. v. MARTINEZ

941 S.W.2d 910 (Tex. 1997)

CORNYN, J.

In this premises liability case we decide whether Science Spectrum, Inc., which occupied premises adjacent to that in which Arthur Martinez was injured, owed a legal duty to Martinez by virtue of its control of the premises where his injury occurred, or its creation of a dangerous condition. Based on Science Spectrum's motion for summary judgment and proof that it did not exercise control over the premises, the trial court granted the motion. The court then severed Martinez' claims against Science Spectrum from those alleged against the remaining defendants, thus rendering a final summary judgment. The court of appeals reversed and remanded, holding that "by creating a condition in the area adjacent to the leased space it controlled, Science Spectrum became responsible." 946 S.W.2d 86, 89 (citing *Wal-Mart Stores, Inc. v. Alexander*, 868 S.W.2d 322, 324 (Tex. 1993)). We disagree with the court of appeals' interpretation of *Alexander* as applied to the facts of this case, but for the reasons that follow, we affirm its judgment.

On June 7, 1990, Martinez was electrocuted when he cut through a live electrical wire while in the course and scope of his employment. Martinez and members of his immediate family (the Martinezes) sued numerous defendants, including Furr's, Inc.; Robert B. Bain, the Executor of the Estate of H.R. Gibson, Sr.; Smith & Fitzpatrick, d/b/a The 50th Street Caboose; and Science Spectrum, Inc., the sublessee of the premises adjacent to those where Martinez was working at the time of his injury.

The 50th Street Caboose, a restaurant in Lubbock, occupies part of a large building owned by the Estate of H.R. Gibson, Sr., but leased to and formerly occupied by Furr's, Inc. Furr's at one point partitioned the building and subleased portions to smaller businesses. Science Spectrum subleased a portion of the building and, as part of its sublease, agreed to construct a partition wall to enclose its leased space. It erected the partition in January 1989.

About one year later, Smith & Fitzpatrick, Inc. (S&F) subleased the premises adjacent to Science Spectrum and began to construct the 50th Street Caboose. Martinez was employed by S&F when he was injured. Although S&F had hired an electrical contractor to rewire its premises, S&F's foreman instructed Martinez to remove conduit and electrical wires to facilitate the rewiring. Following the foreman's assurances that there was no power to the 50th Street Caboose's space, Martinez began to remove the wiring. In so doing, he cut into a hot wire and was electrocuted.

Later, it was learned that although the electrical power to the 50th Street Caboose's premises had been turned off, the hot wire that Martinez cut was connected to an air conditioning compressor service in building over the 50th Street Caboose. The hot wire, as it was originally routed in 1969, traveled from Science Spectrum's premises through its ceiling, over the partition wall it had erected, through the 50th Street Caboose's ceiling, and out to the compressor.

The Martinezes alleged that the defendants, including Science Spectrum, "were negligent in creating and/or allowing a dangerous condition to exist on the premises which they controlled or with regard to the Science Spectrum, on adjoining premises." More specifically, the Martinezes alleged that Science Spectrum created the dangerous condition on the 50th Street Caboose's premises "by constructing a partition wall over said wiring in such a way as to create an unknown and disguised danger to individuals such as the Plaintiff, Arthur Martinez."

In its motion for summary judgment, Science Spectrum claimed in part that it owed no legal duty to Martinez because it had no control over, nor any right or duty to control, the premises where the accident occurred. The Martinezes responded that Science Spectrum caused the partition wall to be constructed in such a way that it created a condition that "in connection with the negligent acts of other co-defendants herein was a proximate cause" of Arthur's injuries. Science Spectrum replied and produced summary judgment evidence that it did not install, reroute, or alter the air compressor's wiring in any way.

Of course, summary judgment for a defendant is proper only when the defendant negates at least one element of each of the plaintiff's theories of recovery, *Gibbs v. General Motors Corp.*, 450 S.W.2d 827, 828 (Tex. 1970), or pleads and conclusively establishes each element of an affirmative defense. *City of Houston v. Clear Creek Basin Auth.*, 589 S.W.2d 671, 678 (Tex. 1979). When reviewing a summary judgment, we take as true all evidence favorable to the nonmovant and indulge every reasonable inference in the nonmovant's favor. *Nixon v. Mr. Property Management Co.*, 690 S.W.2d 546, 549 (Tex. 1985).

In reversing Science Spectrum's summary judgment the court of appeals primarily relied on our decision in *Wal-Mart Stores, Inc. v. Alexander*, 868 S.W.2d 322 (Tex. 1993). In that case, we held that an occupier of premises is legally responsible for adjacent premises that it actually controls. *Id.* at 324. . . .

Science Spectrum argues that the court of appeals erred in relying on *Alexander* to find that a fact issue existed regarding Science Spectrum's liability for creating a dangerous condition on the adjacent premises, because Science Spectrum had no control over the premises on which Martinez was injured. We agree.

The summary judgment evidence shows that (1) Science Spectrum's sublease required it to erect a dividing wall to enclose its space within the building; (2) in erecting the wall, Science Spectrum did not install, reroute, modify, or change the wire feeding electricity to the air compressor servicing its space; (3) the 50th Street Caboose later occupied and controlled the premises adjacent to Science Spectrum; and (4) Martinez was injured when performing work for and on the 50th Street Caboose's premises. Viewing this evidence in the light most favorable to the Martinezes, we hold that the court of appeals erred in relying on *Alexander*. By simply erecting a wall around its own leased premises to separate that space from the rest of the building, Science Spectrum did not exercise control over the area adjacent to its premises in a way analogous to the facts in *Alexander*. This conclusion, however, does not end our inquiry.

A motion for summary judgment must itself expressly present the grounds upon which it is made, and must stand or fall on these grounds alone. *McConnell v. Southside Indep. Sch. Dist.*, 858 S.W.2d 337, 341 (Tex. 1993); *see* Tex. R. Civ. P. 166a(c) ("The motion for summary judgment shall state the specific grounds therefor."). In other words, in determining whether grounds are expressly presented, we may not rely on briefs or summary judgment evidence. *See McConnell*, 858 S.W.2d at 341.

The Martinezes alleged that Science Spectrum was liable for creating a dangerous condition on the adjacent premises. We have recognized that under some circumstances, one who creates a dangerous condition, even though he or she is not in control of the premises when the injury occurs, owes a duty of due care. *See City of Denton v. Van Page*, 701 S.W.2d 831, 835 (Tex. 1986) (citing *Strakos v. Gehring*, 360 S.W.2d 787, 790 (Tex. 1962)). Science Spectrum's motion for summary judgment addressed only the issue of its control [not of whether it had] created a dangerous condition. Because it did not raise this ground in its motion, we hold that Science Spectrum is not entitled to a summary judgment on this claim.

Accordingly, we affirm the court of appeals' judgment and remand this cause to the trial court for further proceedings consistent with this opinion.

[The dissenting opinion of Justices Enoch, Gonzalez and Hecht is omitted.]

[2] No Evidence Motions

Read Tex. R. Civ. P. 166a(i) and Comment to 1997 change.

The Texas Supreme Court amended the summary judgment rule effective September 1, 1997, to embrace the federal approach to motions that are based on challenges to a ground of recovery or defense on which the nonmovant would have the burden of proof at trial. Formerly, in order for a defendant to be entitled to summary judgment, he or she was required, by competent proof, to disprove as a matter of law at least one of the essential elements of the plaintiff's cause of action, *Lear Siegler, Inc. v. Perez*, 819 S.W.2d 470, 471 (Tex. 1991), or establish one or more affirmative defenses as a matter of law, *Jennings v. Burgess*, 917 S.W.2d 790, 793 (Tex. 1996). By this amendment, the Texas rules adopted the approach taken by the United States Supreme Court in *Celotex Corp. v. Catrett*, 477 U.S. 317 (1986). In *Celotex*, Chief Justice Rehnquist wrote that "the plain language of [federal] Rule 56(c) mandates the entry of summary judgment, after adequate time for discovery and upon motion, against a party who fails to make a showing sufficient to establish the existence of an element essential to that party's case, and on which that party will bear the burden of proof at trial." 477 U.S. at 322.

As a result of the amendment, a defendant may obtain a summary judgment without conclusively negating an element of the plaintiff's cause of action. Rather than attempting to negate the claimant's case, the movant can assert that there is no evidence to support one or more specific elements of the claim and put the burden on the claimant to present summary judgment evidence to raise an issue of fact.

As a practical matter, the party opposing a no-evidence motion ordinarily will produce evidence the same as when the movant attempts to negate a key element of the opponent's claim or defense. The key difference, however, is that the opposing party will be required to produce evidence in response to the no-evidence motion even though the movant's evidence does not conclusively establish the nonexistence of the element. *See Pena v. Van*, 960 S.W.2d 101, 105 (Tex. App. — Houston [1st Dist.] 1997), *rev'd on other grounds*, 990 S.W.2d 751 (Tex. 1999) (defendant's motion unsuccessful as attempt to negate proximate cause but might have been successful as a no-evidence motion).

The following case is an example of a no-evidence motion for summary judgment. Can you see how it differs from the traditional motion?

MOORE v. K MART CORP.

981 S.W.2d 266 (Tex. App. — San Antonio 1998, pet. denied)

HARDBERGER, C.J.

Appellant, Janet K. Moore ("Moore"), appeals the trial court's summary judgment granted in favor of K Mart Corporation d/b/a K Mart Super Center ("Kmart"). Moore brought suit against Kmart for the personal injuries she allegedly sustained when she tripped and fell on Kmart's premises. Kmart filed a no-evidence motion for summary judgment, asserting that there was no evidence that a dangerous condition existed on its premises or, alternatively, there was no evidence that Kmart had actual or constructive knowledge of any such condition.

PROCEDURAL HISTORY

Moore filed suit against Kmart on September 11, 1996. In her petition, Moore alleged that on April 8, 1996, she was walking to the photograph counter when she tripped and fell where the carpet and floor tile inside Kmart's store was separated by a black rubber border. Moore contended that the carpet area next to the border depressed lower than the border when she stepped onto the carpet, causing her to trip on the border. Moore asserted that the depression of the carpet in this manner was a condition on Kmart's premises that posed an unreasonable risk of harm to her, and Kmart had actual or constructive knowledge of the condition. Moore further contended that one of Kmart's employees created the condition by pushing shopping carts across the border. Moore concluded that the condition proximately caused her fall, resulting in her injury.

On September 18, 1997, Kmart moved for summary judgment under rule 166a(i) of the Texas Rules of Civil Procedure. Kmart asserted that no evidence of any dangerous condition existed. If the court found that such a condition did exist, Kmart argued in the alternative that it did not have actual or constructive knowledge of such a condition. Although not required by the rule, Kmart attached deposition excerpts in support of its position.

The first excerpt attached to Kmart's motion was from Moore's deposition. Moore testified that on the date that she fell, she did not go back and see what had caused her to trip and she did not tell anyone that the border had caused her to fall. Moore stated that she knew the black border caused her to trip because there was "nothing else there."

The second excerpt attached to Kmart's motion was from the deposition of Estella Duque, the Kmart employee to whom Moore reported the incident several days later. Duque stated that she personally inspected the carpet and did not see anything wrong with the border. Duque stated that she could not move the border with her hand, and the border did not move even after she kicked it with her foot.

In response to Kmart's motion, Moore filed the following summary judgment evidence: (1) her opposing affidavit; (2) excerpts from her deposition; and (3) excerpts from two other Kmart employees' depositions, together with an exhibit from one of those depositions. In her affidavit, Moore stated that she returned to the store three days after her fall and stepped on the carpet by the black border where she fell. Moore further stated that the depression of the carpet at least one half inch below the black border caused her to stumble because there was nothing else in the area that could have caused her fall. Two weeks after her fall, Moore again returned to the store and noticed the black border was pulled away from the carpet in the shopping cart area, which was 18–20 feet from where she fell. Because dust and debris were on the tile floor where the border had pulled away from the carpet, Moore believed the black border had been pulled away for at least two weeks. Moore contended that the border being pulled away from the carpet created the same condition that had caused her to fall. In her deposition, Moore stated that she could tell that the border had been pulled away from the carpet in the shopping cart area for some time because there were footprints on the exposed tile area.

Moore also relied upon excerpts from the depositions of Derrick Hayes and Robert Bender, who were both Kmart employees. Hayes stated that the carpet and floor tile were inspected by taking a couple of shopping baskets and running them over the edging every other day. Bender testified that the carpet had pulled away from the border in the shopping cart area. Bender stated that the condition was caused by the carts pushing against the border as they were turned into the shopping cart area. Bender estimated that the condition had existed for two days, and when he noticed it, he pushed the border back under the carpet because it was still tacky. Bender stated that other than this one occurrence, he had never seen this condition on the border. Bender also admitted that another person had reported tripping or stumbling at the border area in August of 1996, and when Bender inspected the area, he saw that the border had slightly separated from the carpet.

STANDARD OF REVIEW

"A no-evidence summary judgment is essentially a pretrial directed verdict," and we apply the same legal sufficiency standard in reviewing a no-evidence summary judgment as we apply in reviewing a directed verdict. Judge David Hittner and Lynne Liberto, *No-Evidence Summary Judgments Under the New Rule*, in State Bar of Texas Prof. Dev. Program, 20 Advanced Civil Trial Course D, D-5 (1997). We review the evidence in the light most favorable to the respondent against whom the no-evidence summary judgment was rendered, disregarding all contrary evidence and inferences. *Merrell Dow Pharmaceuticals, Inc. v. Havner*, 953 S.W.2d 706, 711 (Tex. 1997); *Connell v. Connell*, 889 S.W.2d 534, 538 (Tex. App. — San Antonio 1994, writ denied). A no-evidence summary judgment is improperly granted if the respondent brings forth more than a scintilla of probative evidence to raise a genuine issue of material fact. TEX. R. CIV. P. 166a(i); Judge David Hittner and Lynne Liberato, *No-Evidence Summary Judgments Under the New Rule, in* State Bar of Texas Prof. Dev. Program, 20 Advanced Civil Trial Course D, D-5 (1997); *see also Merrell Dow Pharmaceuticals, Inc. v. Havner*, 953 S.W.2d at 711. Less than a scintilla of evidence exists when the evidence is "so weak as to do no more than create a mere surmise or suspicion" of a fact. *Kindred v. Con/Chem, Inc.*, 650 S.W.2d 61, 63 (Tex. 1983). More than a scintilla of evidence exists when the evidence "rises to a level that would enable reasonable and fair-minded people to differ in their conclusions." *Merrell Dow Pharmaceuticals, Inc. v. Havner*, 953 S.W.2d at 711.

Having set forth the standard we must apply in reviewing a no-evidence summary judgment, we must further understand the meaning of the terms "genuine" and "material fact," as they are used in rule 166a(i). For clarification of these terms, we t urn to federal law. *See* Judge David Hittner and Lynne Liberato, *No-Evidence Summary Judgments Under the New Rule, in* State Bar of Texas Prof. Dev. Program, 20 Advanced Civil Trial Course D, D-5 (1997).

Materiality is a criterion for categorizing factual disputes in relation to the legal elements of the claim. *Anderson v. Liberty Lobby, Inc.*, 477 U.S. 242, 249 (1986). The materiality determination rests on the substantive law, and only those facts identified by the substantive law to be critical are considered material. *See id.* Stated differently, "[o]nly disputes over facts that might affect the outcome of the suit under the governing law will properly preclude the entry of summary judgment." *Id.*

A material fact issue is genuine if the evidence is such that a reasonable jury could find the fact in favor of the non-moving party. *Anderson*, 477 U.S. at 249; *Matsushita Electric Industrial Co., Ltd. v. Zenith Radio Corp.*, 475 U.S. 574, 588 (1986). If the evidence simply shows that some metaphysical doubt as to the fact exists, or if the evidence is not significantly probative, the material fact issue is not "genuine." *Anderson*, 477 U.S. at 250–51; *Matsushita Electric Industrial Co., Ltd.*, 475 U.S. at 587–88.

DISCUSSION

The elements in a premises liability negligence case are as follows:

(1) Actual or constructive knowledge of some condition on the premises;

(2) That the condition posed an unreasonable risk of harm;

(3) That the owner/operator did not exercise reasonable care to reduce or eliminate the risk; and

(4) That the owner/operator's failure to use such care proximately caused the plaintiff's injuries.

Motel 6 G.P., Inc. v. Lopez, 929 S.W.2d 1, 3 (Tex. 1996). With regard to Moore's claim, Kmart's motion for summary judgment asserted that there was no evidence of the following elements: (1) the existence of a condition that posed an unreasonable risk of harm; and (2) actual or constructive knowledge of the condition.

1. Condition Posing Unreasonable Risk of Harm

Viewing the evidence in the light most favorable to Moore, Moore stated that she tripped over the border separating the floor tile and carpet. Three days after she fell, she went back to the store, stepped on the carpet by the border where she fell, and the carpet depressed at least one half inch below the border. Moore stated that if the border had been under the edge of the carpet, the carpet would not have depressed, and she would not have stumbled and fallen. Although a Kmart employee testified that she did not discover such a condition when she inspected the area, we must disregard her testimony as contrary. *Merrell Dow Pharmaceuticals, Inc. v. Havner*, 953 S.W.2d 706. The Kmart employee designated as safety coordinator was responsible for checking the border by running shopping carts over the edging or border throughout the store every other day. One Kmart employee testified that when the carpet is pulled away from the border it is a potential trip hazard.

Moore testified that the carpet depressed because the border was not under the edge of the carpet. Moore's testimony that this condition existed at the location where she fell three days after her fall is evidence that "rises to a level that would enable reasonable and fair-minded people to differ in their conclusions" with respect to whether the condition existed at the time Moore fell. *Merrell Dow Pharmaceuticals, Inc. v. Havner*, 953 S.W.2d at 711. Moore's testimony, coupled with the Kmart employees' actions and testimony that recognize this condition to be a potential trip hazard, is some evidence that a condition existed that posed an unreasonable risk of harm.

2. Actual or Constructive Knowledge of the Condition

Moore relies on the Texarkana court's decision in *K Mart Corp. v. Rhyne*, 932 S.W.2d 140 (Tex. App. — Texarkana 1996, no writ), in support of her contention that Kmart had actual or constructive knowledge of the condition. In *Rhyne*, the plaintiff slipped and fell on a three-inch metal plate protruding from the concrete floor. *Id.* at 142. The metal plate was embedded in the middle of a concrete walkway and was used to hold a pipe that ran between the concrete and the fence to stabilize the fence. *Id.* The assistant manager, who completed an accident report, admitted that the metal plate was a dangerous and hazardous condition and that it was Kmart's responsibility to repair the condition. *Id.*

The case was tried to a jury, which awarded damages to the plaintiff. *See id* at 141. On appeal, Kmart argued that there was legally insufficient evidence for the jury to infer Kmart's actual or constructive knowledge of the condition that injured the plaintiff. *Id.* at 142. The appellate court noted that the assistant manager testified that the most probable explanation for the condition was that a Kmart employee in a fork lift truck broke the pipe while setting tables in the garden area. *Id.* at 142–43. The assistant manager further testified that the employee must have hit the pipe with great force to dislodge it and, therefore, should have assessed the situation after the impact. The Texarkana court held that the jury could have inferred actual or constructive knowledge from the assistant manager's testimony that the Kmart employee working in the area should have known of the condition based on the likely cause of the condition or from the physical condition of the metal plate itself, which extended three inches up from the floor in the middle of the aisle. *See id.* at 143.

In this case, there is no evidence Kmart had actual knowledge of the condition. However, in order for Kmart to prevail in a no-evidence summary judgment, there also must be no evidence that Kmart had constructive knowledge of the border condition. *Motel 6 G.P., Inc.*, 929 S.W.2d at 3–4.

Unlike the evidence in *Rhyne*, the evidence in this case does not support an inference that Kmart should have known of the condition based on the physical nature of the condition itself. However, constructive knowledge can be found if a reasonably careful inspection would have revealed an unreasonable risk. *Corbin v. Safeway Stores, Inc.*, 648 S.W.2d 292, 295 (Tex. 1983); *Johnson v. Tom Thumb Stores, Inc.*, 771 S.W.2d 582, 587 (Tex. App. — Dallas 1989, writ denied).

A Kmart employee inspected the edging every other day. The nature of this inspection was described as follows:

Question: Okay. Do you know — do you have any personal knowledge of how they would do inspections of he [sic] carpet and floor tile?

Answer: Robert Bender — I have knowledge of Robert Bender. He would come and our [sic] the store — whole store daily. He'd take a couple of baskets and run it over the tile and see how it would handle up — how it would hold up to the baskets running over it.

Question: And he would do this every day?

Answer: He would do it approximately every other day.

Question: Every other day?

Answer: Yes.

Question: And what I'm understanding is he would take a cart and kind of roll it across the floor tile and the carpet both?

Answer: The edging.

Question: The edging?

Answer: Uh-huh. And the carpet.

Question: Would he do this everywhere the edging was in the store?

Answer: Yes, sir.

Question: And he would do this like every other day?

Answer: Yes, sir.

While this is evidence that an inspection was undertaken based on the possibility that the border might pull away from the carpet, there is no evidence that such an inspection revealed or should have revealed the border condition that allegedly caused Moore to fall. Although an inference could be made that the inspections undertaken by Kmart in this manner were not reasonable, *see Johnson*, 771 S.W.2d at 589, there is no evidence that a different, reasonably careful inspection would have revealed the condition. Therefore, we agree with the trial court that Moore presented no evidence of actual or constructive knowledge and affirm the trial court's judgment.

NOTES AND QUESTIONS

(1) *Sufficiency of No Evidence Motions.* A comment to the 1997 amendments to Civil Procedure Rule 166a states that "[p]aragraph (i) authorizes a motion for summary judgment based on the assertion that, after adequate time for discovery, there is no evidence to support one or more specified elements of an adverse party's claim or defense. . . . The motion must be specific in challenging the evidentiary support for an element of a claim or defense; paragraph (i) does not authorize conclusory motions or general no-evidence challenges to an opponent's case." Does this comment mean that the movant must only identify one or more elements of the plaintiff's claim and assert that, after adequate time for discovery, no evidence has been discovered that would be sufficient to authorize submission of the claim to the jury? Does it mean more than that? *See In re Mohawk Rubber Co.*, 982 S.W.2d 494, 497–98 (Tex. App. — Texarkana 1998, no pet.) ("The rule requires a motion to be specific in alleging a lack of evidence on an essential element of the plaintiffs' alleged cause of action, but it does not require that the motion specifically attack the evidentiary components that may prove an element of the cause of action. The specificity requirement is designed to avoid conclusory no-evidence challenges to an opponent's cause of action. The rule requires a specific challenge to the evidentiary support for an element of a claim or defense. Causation is a specific element of tort liability.").

(2) *Defending the No Evidence Motion.* The comment to Rule 166a also states that "[t]o defeat a motion made under paragraph (i), the respondent is not required to marshal its proof; its response need only point out evidence that raises a fact issue on the challenged elements. The existing rules continue to govern the general requirements of summary judgment practice. A motion under paragraph (i) is subject to sanctions provided by existing law (Tex. Civ. Prac. & Rem. Code §§ 9.001–10.006) and rules (Tex. R. Civ. P. 13)." Regardless of whether the motion is a traditional motion or a non-evidence motion, summary judgment evidence must be in admissible form. *See* Tex. R. Civ. P. 166a(f) ("Supporting and opposing affidavits shall be made on personal knowledge, shall set forth such facts as would be admissible in evidence, and shall show affirmatively that the affiant is competent to testify to the matters stated therein.").

(3) *Adequate Time for Discovery.* A no evidence summary judgment motion is not proper until adequate time for discovery has been afforded. Whether a non-movant has had adequate time for discovery is a case specific inquiry. An adequate time for discovery is determined by the nature of the cause of action, the nature of the evidence necessary to controvert the motion, and the length of time the case has been active in the trial court. *Tempay, Inc. v. TNT Concrete & Construction, Inc.*, 37 S.W.3d 517, 522 (Tex. App. — Austin 2001, pet. denied). Lawsuits presenting only questions of law will ordinarily require no or minimal discovery, while a case dependent upon factual determinations may require extensive discovery. A non-movant asserting it has not had sufficient time for discovery, must, before a summary judgment hearing, "file either an affidavit explaining the need for further discovery or a verified motion for continuance." *McClure v. Attebury*, 20 S.W.3d 722, 728 (Tex. App. — Amarillo 1999, no pet.).

[3] Hybrid Motions

A request for a no-evidence summary judgment may be combined in a single motion with a request for a traditional summary judgment. The fact that evidence may be attached with respect to the traditional summary judgment motion does not foreclose a party from also asserting that there is no evidence with regard to a particular element. *Binur v. Jacobo*, 135 S.W.3d 646, 650–51 (Tex. 2004). When the two types of motions are combined, care should be taken to include headings that clearly delineate and segregate the portions seeking a traditional summary judgment from those seeking a no-evidence summary judgment. This will make it easier for the court to apply the appropriate standards to each motion. Nevertheless, if a motion clearly sets forth its grounds and otherwise meets Rule 166a's requirements, it is sufficient.

[B] Procedure and Evidence

[1] Summary Judgment Proof

In order for a party to successfully support or oppose a motion for summary judgment, the evidence offered to the court must meet the requirements of the summary judgment and evidence rules. In the following case, the Texas Supreme Court discusses the requirement that, like a witness at trial, a person signing a summary judgment affidavit must have personal knowledge of the information provided.

KERLIN v. ARIAS

274 S.W.3d 666 (Tex. 2008)

PER CURIAM.

This is another suit claiming title to a substantial part of Padre Island. Unlike our recent case concerning heirs of Juan Jose Balli, *see Kerlin v. Sauceda*, 263 S.W.3d 920 (Tex. 2008), this one was brought by heirs of his nephew, Jesus Balli. The heirs seek to set aside an 1847 deed (and thus all sales in the ensuing 161 years) on the basis of fraud. The trial court granted summary judgment against the heirs, but the court of appeals reversed. As the only evidence of fraud in 1847 is an affidavit by one of the current heirs — who could not possibly have personal knowledge of those events — we reverse.

The 72 alleged heirs asserted in their petition that the 1847 deed was fraudulent because it was signed by Jesus Balli's father, even though Jesus was not a minor under either Texas or Mexican law at the time. They sued Gilbert Kerlin, who apparently had no contact with them or their ancestors, but owned substantial acreage in South Padre Island from 1942 until 1961.

Kerlin moved for summary judgment on several grounds, including that the deed was valid. In support, Kerlin tendered the deed — not the original in Spanish signed in Matamoros in 1847, but a certified English translation filed in the Nueces County deed records later that same year. The translated deed affirmatively states that:

- Jesus Balli was a minor at the time the deed was signed;
- his lawful guardian was his father, who had the power to administer and convey his son's property;
- it was in his son's best interest to sell the land because the war between the United States and Mexico made it uncertain whether his title would be recognized; and
- his father accordingly sold the Padre Island property to Nicolas Grisanti on his son's behalf.

The heirs did not contest this document's authenticity. Nor did they challenge the accuracy of the translation. The statements in the translated deed are competent to prove the facts stated therein under the rules of evidence. *See* TEX. R. EVID. 803(14), (16).

The heirs' only responsive summary judgment evidence was a 2003 affidavit by Eva Castillo, in which she avers that Jesus Balli was not a minor in 1847 because he was 22 years old and had married. Kerlin objected to the affidavit on several grounds, including lack of personal knowledge and hearsay.

We agree with Kerlin that this affidavit creates no fact issue on fraud. Summary judgment affidavits "shall be made on personal knowledge, shall set forth such facts as would be admissible in evidence, and shall show affirmatively that the affiant is competent to testify to the matters stated therein." TEX. R. CIV. P. 166a(f). This affidavit fails on each count.

First, the only representation Castillo makes about the truth of her affidavit is that "[a]ll statements contained herein are true and correct to the best of my personal knowledge and belief." To have probative value, an affiant "must swear that the facts presented in the affidavit reflect his personal knowledge." *In re E.I. DuPont de Nemours and Co.*, 136 S.W.3d 218, 224 (Tex. 2004). An affiant's *belief* about the facts is legally insufficient. *Ryland Group, Inc. v. Hood*, 924 S.W.2d 120, 122 (Tex. 1996); *Brownlee v. Brownlee*, 665 S.W.2d 111, 112 (Tex. 1984).

Second, Castillo says she is competent to make the affidavit because she "heard testimony" in the Juan Jose Balli case, "reviewed documents" related to the heirs' claims, and "read historical accounts about Padre Island." Her testimony about these out-of-court sources was hearsay and carries no probative weight over Kerlin's objection. *See* TEX. R. EVID. 802; *Gracey v. West*, 422 S.W.2d 913, 916 (Tex. 1968).

Third, nothing in the affidavit affirmatively shows how Castillo could possibly have personal knowledge about events occurring in the 1840s. An affidavit showing no basis for personal knowledge is legally insufficient. *Humphreys v. Caldwell*, 888 S.W.2d 469, 470 (Tex. 1994); *Radio Station KSCS v. Jennings*, 750 S. W.2d 760, 762 (Tex. 1988). Accordingly, Castillo's affidavit does not raise a fact issue about whether Jesus Balli was a minor at the time his father sold his interest in Padre Island. . . .

The court of appeals . . . faulted Kerlin for not responding to the heirs' assertions by providing "evidence of Jesus' age or marital status at the time of the deed signing." But Kerlin presented prima facie evidence that the 1847 deed was valid; he did not have any duty to prove these additional details unless the heirs could raise a fact question regarding them. This they did not do.

The summary judgment record here raises no fact question that the 1847 deed was fraudulent. Accordingly, we grant Kerlin's petition for review, and without hearing oral argument, we reverse the court of appeals' judgment and render judgment that the heirs take nothing. Tex. R. App. P. 59.1.

[2] Preserving Complaints About Summary Judgment Evidence

Read Tex. R. Civ. P. 166a(c), (d), (f), (g), (h).

The procedures involved in moving for or opposing summary judgment are riddled with technical requirements with which the attorney must comply or risk losing the client's right to assert its arguments on appeal. Subdivision (c) of Rule 166a makes it plain that "[i]ssues not expressly presented to the trial court by written motion, answer or other response shall not be considered on appeal as grounds for reversal." In addition, one of the trickiest is the rule that objections to the form of summary judgment evidence must be made in a timely way in the trial court, while defects in the substance may be made for the first time on appeal. Tex. R. Civ. P. 166a(f). Unfortunately, the line between "form" and "substance" is unclear and appellate cases are inconsistent.

Case law continues to develop concerning the point at which the defective nature of summary judgment proof is so integral to its probative value that the defect is deemed to be one of substance rather than form. For example, an affidavit's failure to state that the affiant had personal knowledge of the facts stated in it, or that the affiant was competent to testify on the matters in the affidavit, has been held to be a formal defect that can be waived absent objection. In contrast, other courts found that an objection that an affidavit includes conclusions and opinions constitutes an objection involving substance, not form, and may be raised on appeal despite never having been raised in the trial court. Some arguably technical defects have occasionally been treated as substantive defects. For example, a party's reliance on verified pleadings as summary judgment proof has been ruled a substantive proof problem, which required no trial court objection. Similarly, the absence of a jurat on a summary judgment affidavit has been held to be a substantive defect, although the decisions are not uniform on this point.

To complain about formal defects on appeal, a complaining party must not only object to the form, but must also obtain a ruling at or prior to the summary judgment hearing. But if a litigant's summary judgment proof is substantively defective, the trial court is not required to provide an opportunity to correct the defect.

The following case articulates a method for distinguishing between formal and substantive defects. How clear is the distinction to you? In the absence of clarity, what strategy will you adopt when opposing summary judgment?

MATHIS v. BOCELL

982 S.W.2d 52 (Tex. App. — Houston [1st Dist.] 1998, no pet.)

HEDGES, J.

In this medical malpractice case, Nancy Mathis, M.D. and Gary Mathis ("plaintiffs") appeal from a summary judgment granted in favor of appellees, James R. Bocell, M.D. and Thomas Cain, M.D. In their sole point of error, Nancy and Gary Mathis complai n that (1) the summary judgment evidence did not establish the absence of material fact issues and (2) the affidavits of Drs. Bocell and Cain were legally insufficient to support a summary judgment. We reverse and remand.

BACKGROUND

[In September, 1992, Nancy Mathis had arthroscopic knee surgery, during which the surgeon placed ethibond sutures over Mathis' meniscal tear. After the surgery and in the following months, Mathis continued to have swelling and an apparent infection in the knee. Mathis went to Dr. Bocell for treatment on many occasions, complaining of swelling. Bocell prescribed antibiotics and provided follow-up care, including an aspiration of the knee and an arthroscopic examination to determine whether infection was present. Bocell found no sutures and believed the tissue was in good condition. Mathis later sought treatment from Dr. Cain, still complaining of swelling. Dr. Cain also performed an arthroscopy and claimed to have removed two ethibond sutures. Mathis continued to have problems until November, 1993, when a third doctor performed an arthroscopy and removed two sutures.]

PROCEDURAL HISTORY

In their original petition, Nancy and Gary Mathis sued Bocell alleging that Bocell failed to (1) properly diagnose, manage, and treat Nancy's post-operative infection and knee, (2) timely perform a subsequent irrigation and debridement of her knee in face of her recurring infection, and (3) use reasonable skill, care, and diligence to correctly perform a thorough irrigation and debridement of her knee in March 1993. Bocell moved for summary judgment arguing that nothing he did fell below the standard of care so as to cause or contribute to the damages of which plaintiffs complained. In support of his motion for summary judgment, Bocell attached his own affidavit.

Plaintiffs filed a response arguing that genuine issues of fact exist as to whether Bocell was negligent and whether that negligence caused Nancy Mathis' injury. Plaintiffs attached the affidavit of their expert, Dr. Julio V. Westerband, to controvert the facts stated in Bocell's affidavit. In his reply to plaintiffs' response, Bocell argued that Westerband's affidavit was fatally defective because plaintiffs did not attach the medical records upon which Westerband relied in forming his opinion. In response, plaintiffs filed a motion for leave to supplement Westerband's affidavit with those medical records. The record does not indicate whether the trial court ruled on this motion. The trial court granted Bocell's motion for summary judgment but did not rule on Bocell's objection to Westerband's affidavit.

While Bocell's motion for summary judgment was pending, plaintiffs amended their petition, adding Cain as a defendant. . . .

Cain moved for summary judgment arguing that he did not breach the relevant standard of care. In support of his motion for summary judgment, Cain attached his own affidavit. In their response to that motion for summary judgment, plaintiffs argued that (1) Cain's affidavit did not detail the standards of reasonably prudent orthopedic care and treatment for patients like Nancy Mathis; (2) Cain's affidavit did not detail how he met the standards of reasonably prudent orthopedic care; (3) Cain's affidavit was based on medical records not attached as summary judgment proof; (4) Cain's affidavit was conclusory; (5) genuine issues of material fact existed on negligence and causation because of inconsistencies between Cain's affidavit and the medical records; and (6) Westerband's affidavit, which was attached to the response along with the medical records he relied upon in forming his opinion, created genuine fact issues regarding whether Cain breached the standard of care and whether that breach caused her injuries. In his reply, Cain argued that Westerband's affidavit lacked credibility and did not raise a fact issue because Westerband never reviewed Cain's records.

The trial court granted Cain's motion for summary judgment, overruled plaintiffs' procedural and evidentiary objections to Cain's motion for summary judgment, and granted Cain's objections to the conclusory nature of Westerband's affidavit.

STANDARD OF REVIEW

In reviewing a summary judgment, we must take all evidence favorable to the nonmovant as true and grant every reasonable inference in favor of the nonmoving party. *Nixon v. Mr. Property Management Co.*, 690 S.W.2d 546, 548–49 (Tex. 1985). If differing inferences may reasonably be drawn from the summary judgment evidence, a summary judgment should not be granted. *Id.* at 549. The movant's own evidence may establish the existence of a genuine issue of material fact on the plaintiff's claim. *Armbruster v. Memorial Southwest Hosp.*, 857 S.W.2d 938, 941 (Tex. App. — Houston [1st Dist.] 1993, no writ).

The elements of a medical negligence claim are: (1) a duty to conform to a certain standard of care; (2) a failure to conform to the required standard; (3) actual injury; and (4) a reasonably close causal connection between the conduct and the injury. *Armbruster*, 857 S.W.2d at 940. A defendant seeking a summary judgment must prove conclusively that the plaintiff cannot prevail. *Griffin v. Rowden*, 654 S.W.2d 435, 435–36 (Tex. 1983); *Armbruster*, 857 S.W.2d at 940. This may be accomplished by proving at least one element of the claim conclusively against the plaintiff. *Gray v. Bertrand*, 723 S.W.2d 957, 958 (Tex. 1987); *Armbruster*, 857 S.W.2d at 940–41. If the movant negates an element of the plaintiff's claim, the plaintiff must produce controverting evidence raising a fact issue on the element or elements negated. *Armbruster*, 857 S.W.2d at 941. The plaintiff must prove by competent medical evidence either that the defendant did something other health care providers using ordinary care would not have done or that it failed to do something they would have done under the same circumstances. *Birchfield v. Texarkana Memorial Hosp.*, 747 S.W.2d 361, 366 (Tex. 1987); *Armbruster*, 857 S.W.2d at 941.

SUMMARY JUDGMENT FOR THE APPELLEES

The threshold question in a medical malpractice case is the standard of care, which must be established so the fact finder can determine if the defendant deviated from it. *Armbruster*, 857 S.W.2d at 941. In such cases, the court must be guided solely by an expert's opinion. *Id.* A summary judgment may be based on an expert's uncontroverted testimony if the testimony is clear, positive, direct, otherwise credible, free from inconsistencies, and capable of being readily controverted. TEX. R. CIV. P. 166a(c). The affidavit of an interested expert who is also a party to the case can support summary judgment if it meets these requirements. *Anderson v. Snider*, 808 S.W.2d 54, 55 (Tex. 1991). However, an expert cannot merely state that he knows the standard of care and conclude that it was met. *Armbruster*, 857 S.W.2d at 941.

Dr. Bocell

In addition to setting out his credentials and qualifications in orthopedic surgery, Bocell's affidavit [described Nancy Mathis's condition on each visit, described the medical care provided on each visit, stated his familiarity with the standard of care involved in orthopedic and arthroscopic surgery, and stated his reasons for believing he had met the standard of care].

Plaintiffs contend that Bocell's affidavit did not specifically establish the orthopedic standard of care and, therefore, is insufficient to sustain the summary judgment. We disagree. An interested expert's affidavit is sufficient to establish compliance with the standard of care if the affiant (1) states that he is familiar with the applicable standard of care, (2) states with specificity each examination and treatment performed, (3) states that the acts of the physician were consistent with the appropriate standard of care, and (4) states that there was no causal connection between the physician's acts and the plaintiff's injury. *Griffin v. Methodist Hosp.*, 948 S.W.2d 72, 74 (Tex. App. — Houston [14th Dist.] 1997, no writ); *see also Wheeler v. Aldama-Luebbert*, 707 S.W.2d 213, 215–17 (Tex. App. — Houston [1st Dist.] 1986, no writ) (expert affidavit stated with specificity each examination, each operative procedure, and each treatment administered to plaintiff; affidavit stated that expert knew what standard of care was for plaintiff and that treatment and diagnosis of plaintiff was standard of care and was same standard of care used by other reasonably prudent physicians acting under same or similar circumstances).

In this case, Bocell's affidavit met the requirements set out in *Griffin*. First, Bocell's affidavit described with specificity each examination and treatment he performed on Nancy Mathis from September 1992, through September 1993. Second, Bocell's affidavit stated he was familiar with the standard of care involved in orthopedic surgery, pre-operative assessment of patients, the technical aspect of orthopedic surgery, post-operative care, and the recognition and treatment of complications. Third, Bocell's affidavit stated that the standard of medical doctors in his field of practice requires patients such as Nancy Mathis to be "evaluated, diagnosed, and for treatment recommendations to be made to the patient and treatment rendered as required in accordance with the patient and the manor [sic] in which the patient is presented." Fourth, Bocell's affidavit stated that the evaluation, diagnosis, and treatment of Nancy Mathis, which he described in the affidavit, met or exceeded the standard of care in Houston. Finally, Bocell's affidavit states there was no causal connection between the infectious process in Nancy Mathis' knee and the presence of sutures during his treatment of her. We conclude that Bocell's affidavit was sufficient to establish compliance with the standard of care.

Plaintiffs also contend that fact issues exist as to whether Bocell was negligent in failing to remove the ethibond sutures and whether such failure to remove these sutures proximately caused Nancy Mathis' injuries. They assert that although Bocell denied that he was negligent and that he proximately caused Nancy Mathis' injuries, Westerband's controversion of Bocell's testimony raised genuine issues of material fact. Before we examine whether the Westerband affidavit raised a fact issue, we must decide whether the Westerband affidavit is proper summary judgment evidence.

Rule 166a requires that certified or sworn copies of all records or papers referred to in a supporting or opposing affidavit be attached to the affidavit. Tex. R. Civ. P. 166a(f). The last sentence of rule 166a(f) provides: "Defects in the form of affidavits or attachments will not be grounds for reversal unless specifically pointed out by objection by an opposing party with opportunity, but refusal, to amend." Plaintiffs argue that Bocell waived his objections to the defective nature of Westerband's affidavit because Bocell did not get a written ruling on his objection to plaintiffs' failure to attach medical records to Westerband's affidavit. A party must also obtain a ruling on an objection as to defects of form of an affidavit, or the objection is waived. *McConnell v. Southside Indep. Sch. Dist.*, 858 S.W.2d 337, 343 n. 7 (Tex. 1993); *Roberts v. Friendswood Dev. Co.*, 886 S.W.2d 363, 365 (Tex. App. — Houston [1st Dist.] 1994, writ denied). Thus, Bocell waived his objection to the lack of medical records attached to Westerband's affidavit if the defect is of the type that a party must object to and receive a ruling.

There is conflicting authority concerning the difference between a defect of substance and a defect of form in summary judgment evidence. Among the courts of appeals, there is contradiction, if not confusion, distinguishing the two. Rule 166a(f) refers only to "defect of form": there is no mention of its counterpart, defect of substance. The application of one or the other is crucial because formal defects must be objected to and ruled upon by the trial court, while substantive defects may be raised for the first time on appeal.

The concept of defect in form in summary judgment proof first appeared in *Youngstown Sheet & Tube Co. v. Penn*, 363 S.W.2d 230, 234 (Tex. 1962). The movant's summary judgment affidavits were allegedly defective because (1) they did not state that they were made on the personal knowledge of the affiants; (2)

they did not affirmatively show that the affiants were competent to testify to the matters stated therein; (3) sworn or certified copies of the documents referred to in the affidavit were not attached; and (4) they contained conclusions and hearsay. The nonmovant failed to object on any grounds in the trial court. The supreme court found that although there was no merit to the fourth ground, the affidavits were defective based on the other three grounds. The court concluded that "The deficiencies which [nonmovant] now urges appear to be purely formal, and it may be assumed that they would have been corrected upon proper exception in the trial court." *Id.* at 234. It went on to state that "objections of this kind may not be raised for the first time on appeal when it fairly appears from the record that there is no genuine issue as to any material fact and that the moving party is entitled to judgment as a matter of law." *Id.*

The first mention of "substantive defect" appeared in *Landscape Design and Construction, Inc. v. Warren*, 566 S.W.2d 66, 67 (Tex. Civ. App. — Dallas 1978, no writ). In that case, the nonmovant argued that the movant's affidavit was defective because it did not reflect whether the affiant had personal knowledge of the facts recited in the affidavit supporting the motion for summary judgment. The movant urged that the defect was a mere formal defect which was waived by the defendant's failure to object in the trial court. The appellate court rejected that argument, explaining that "[a] defect is rendered 'formal' only when it fairly appears *from the record* that, despite the deficiency, there is no genuine issue as to any material fact and that the moving party is entitled to judgment as a matter of law." *Id.* at 67 (emphasis in the original). The court concluded that the defect was "substantive," rather than "formal" and that no objection to the affidavit was necessary to preserve error on appeal. *Id.*

In interpreting rule 166a(f), several courts have held that the failure to attach copies of the documents relied upon in forming an expert opinion is a defect in substance, and therefore, can be raised for the first time on appeal. *See, e.g.*, *Gorrell v. Texas Utils. Elec. Co.*, 915 S.W.2d 55, 60 (Tex. App. — Fort Worth 1995) (failure to attach sworn or certified affidavits of the extraneous documents referred to in the affidavit was defect in substance and trial court was not required to give offering party the chance to amend), *writ denied*, 954 S.W.2d 767 (Tex. 1997) ("We neither approve nor disapprove of the conclusion of the court of appeals that the failure to attach copies of documents referenced in the affidavit of an expert witness 'constituted a defect in the substance of the affidavit.' "); *Rodriquez v. Texas Farmers Ins. Co.*, 903 S.W.2d 499, 506 (Tex. App. — Amarillo 1995, writ denied) ("Failure to attach copies of the documents relied upon in forming. . . . [expert's] opinion was a fatal defect in the substance of the affidavit, and the trial court properly excluded it from consideration"); *Ceballos v. El Paso Health Care Sys.*, 881 S.W.2d 439, 444–45 (Tex. App. — El Paso 1994, writ denied) ("The failure to attach to, or serve with, Dr. Krumlovsky's and Nurse Williams' affidavits sworn or certified copies of the medical chart or other record referred to therein is not simply a *defect in the form of his affidavit*, but rather is a *defect in the substance* thereof. This is true because there is no way to tell from these affidavits on what specific entries, notations or statements entered on the medical chart they are basing their respective opinions.") (emphasis in original).

Other courts have held that the failure to attach copies of the documents relied upon in forming an expert opinion is a waivable defect in form. *See, e.g.*, *Martin v. Durden*, 965 S.W.2d 562, 565 (Tex. App. — Houston [14th Dist.] 1997, pet. denied) ("[W]e find the failure to attach sworn or certified copies of documents relied upon in expert opinion is merely a defect in form which is waived on appeal if not raised in the trial court."); *Noriega v. Mireles*, 925 S.W.2d 261, 265–66 (Tex. App. — Corpus Christi 1996, writ denied) ("If there is a dispute as to what is contained in the medical records, we agree that the failure to attach the medical records to the summary judgment affidavit would be a substantive defect. . . . [W]here there is no dispute regarding the contents of the medical records and the treatment the patient received, and in which the disputed issue relates to additional treatment that the patient clearly did not receive but arguably should have, the failure to attach the relevant medical records to the expert witness's affidavit is a formal, rather than a substantive defect."); *Knetsch v. Gaintonde*, 898 S.W.2d 386, 389–90 (Tex. App. — San Antonio 1995, no writ) (characterizing the failure to attach documents to summary judgment affidavit as a defect in form but ultimately disposing of case on substantive ground that affidavit itself raised issue of material fact).

How can this conflict be resolved? We believe that the best way to analyze these defects is on the basis of admissibility versus competency of evidence. A defect is substantive if the evidence is incompetent, and it is formal if the evidence is competent but inadmissible. *See* Address by Justice Sarah B. Duncan, *No-Evidence Motions for Summary Judgment: Harmonizing Rule 166a(i) and its Comment*, 21st Annual Page Keeton Products Liability and Personal Injury Law Conference (November 20–21, 1997) 25–26. Formal defects may be waived by failure to object, and if waived, the evidence is considered. Substantive defects are never waived because the evidence is incompetent and cannot be considered under any circumstances. *See* Address by Justice Sarah B. Duncan at 26 ("If evidence is incompetent, it necessarily has no probative value because it either does not relate to a controlling fact, or, if material, does not tend to make the existence of that fact more or less probable; therefore, there is no need to object to the erroneous introduction of incompetent evidence either to preserve the error in its admission or to ensure it is not treated as 'some evidence.' ") (citing *Aetna Ins. v. Klein*, 325 S.W.2d 376 (1959)).

Following this reasoning, we conclude that the failure of Westerband to attach the medical records on which he relied is a defect of form. Clearly, the affidavit is competent: it recites Mathis' medical history; it establishes the affiant as an expert in the field in which he is testifying; and it presents his expert opinion. The lack of underlying documents on which he relied makes the evidence inadmissible, not incompetent. Therefore, Bocell waived his objection when he failed to obtain a ruling by the trial court.

Having determined that Bocell waived his objection to the failure to attach the medical records to Westerband's affidavit, we will now examine whether Westerband's affidavit raises fact issues regarding whether Bocell was negligent and whether such negligence proximately caused Mathis' injury. . . .

According to Westerband, had Bocell been aware that he should have been looking for ethibond sutures, which are nonabsorbable, he might have meticulously scrutinized the knee to find the presence of such sutures. Nevertheless, Bocell opined that it "would have been an inappropriate course of action to have removed the good tissue visualized. . . . in order to get down to the underlying sutures with no signs of infection, redness or irritation in the tissue."

Contrary to Bocell's assertion that there was no evidence of any infectious process relating to the presence of sutures during his treatment of Nancy Mathis, Westerband opined that Nancy Mathis suffered a chronic infection as a result of the retained ethibond sutures. Given these two contradicting statements as well as the inconsistencies regarding whether Bocell should have scrutinized the tissue more closely for the presence of ethibond sutures, we conclude that material fact issues exist. Thus, the trial court erred in granting summary judgment in favor of Bocell.

Dr. Cain

In response to Cain's motion for summary judgment, plaintiffs again relied on the affidavit of Westerband. Attached to Westerband's affidavit were the medical records upon which Westerband relied in forming his opinion. Plaintiffs argue that material fact issues exist as to whether Cain was negligent. . . .

Contrary to Cain's assertion that the infection, if any, in Nancy Mathis' knee did not relate to the presence of sutures in her knee, Westerband opined that the failure to remove the retained ethibond sutures caused and prolonged Nancy Mathis' infection. Given these two contradicting statements as well as the inconsistencies in the number or type of sutures removed, we conclude that material fact issues exist. Thus, the trial court erred in granting summary judgment in favor of Cain.

CONCLUSION

We sustain point of error one. We reverse the summary judgments granted in favor of Bocell and Cain and remand the cause for further proceedings.

NOTES AND QUESTIONS

(1) *Drafting the Motion for Summary Judgment.* The grounds for a summary judgment must be expressly set forth in the motion itself. *See* Tex. R. Civ. P. 166a(c). Although exceptions should be urged in the trial court if the grounds for summary judgment are only expressed in an accompanying brief, failure to except does not result in waiver. *See McConnell v. Southside School Dist.*, 858 S.W.2d 337, 341–42 (Tex. 1993). Summary judgment evidence need not be referenced in the motion itself. *Wilson v. Burford*, 904 S.W.2d 628, 629 (Tex. 1995). If the grounds for a summary judgment are unclear or ambiguous, a party should specially except to the motion to preserve that complaint for appellate review. *See Clement v. City of Plano*, 26 S.W.3d 544, 550 (Tex. App. — Dallas 2000, no pet.).

(2) *Role of Pleadings.* In general, summary judgment is not usually granted "on the pleadings," as the preceding materials show. They may, however, form the basis for a summary judgment by defining the issues to which the summary judgment

evidence is relevant, as when summary judgment is granted for a defendant when the plaintiff states no cause of action other than those that are defeated by the defendant's summary judgment materials. In *Hidalgo v. Surety Savings & Loan Ass'n*, 462 S.W.2d 540, 543 n.1 (Tex. 1971), the Supreme Court explained as follows:

> We are not to be understood as holding that summary judgment may not be rendered, when authorized, *on the pleadings*, as, for example, when suit is on a sworn account under Rule 185, Texas Rules of Civil Procedure, and the account is not denied under oath as therein provided, or when the plaintiff's petition fails to state a legal claim or cause of action. In such cases summary judgment does not rest on proof supplied by pleading, sworn or unsworn, but on deficiencies in the opposing pleading.

(3) *Summary Judgment Proof.* Neither a motion for summary judgment nor the response constitutes summary judgment proof. Civil Procedure Rule 166a provides that summary judgment proof may be made by: (1) affidavits; (2) discovery on file; (3) stipulations; and (4) certified or sworn records. Tex. R. Civ. P. 166a(c). The motion for summary judgment and supporting proof is to be filed and served no later than 21 days before the hearing. If service of the motion is by mail, the motion must be served no later than 24 days before the hearing under Tex. R. Civ. P. 4. *Lewis v. Blake*, 876 S.W.2d 314, 316 (Tex. 1994). A response in opposition and any supporting proof is to be filed and served no later than seven days before the hearing. Late filed proof will not be considered on appeal, unless leave of the trial court appears of record or in a written agreement of counsel.

(4) *Formal and Substantive Defects.* What is the difference between a formal defect in summary judgment proof and a substantive defect? Given the inconsistency of the case law, the safest course is generally to object at the trial level. The risk of tipping the opponent to a possibly fatal defect in time for its correction must be balanced against the likelihood of waiving the argument if there is an appeal. Counsel should also consider that the chance of success before the trial judge may be improved by pointed objections to hearsay, improper conclusions, or other inadmissible evidence in an affidavit, whether or not an objection is necessary to preserve the issue for appeal. The following areas should be examined carefully for objectionable defects:

- Defects in Motion Itself. If a motion for summary judgment clearly presents certain grounds but not others, no objection is required. Similarly, if the grounds for summary judgment are not expressly presented in the summary judgment motion itself, the motion is legally insufficient, even if the non-movant fails to object to the motion. But if the statement of grounds in the motion is unclear, vague, or ambiguous, an objection to the motion is required "to ensure that the parties, as well as the trial court, are focused on the same grounds." *McConnell v. Southside School Dist.*, 858 S.W.2d 337, 342–43 (Tex. 1993).
- Affidavit Not Based on Personal Knowledge of Affiant. In an area that remains unsettled, most court opinions have held that the failure to state that the affiant had personal knowledge of the facts stated in the affidavit is a defect of form such that an objection is required to preserve the complaint.

- Failure to Attach Sworn or Certified Copies of Papers Referred to in Affidavit. Civil Procedure Rule 166a(f) requires that sworn or certified copies of all papers or parts of papers referred to in an affidavit must be attached and served with the affidavit. The safest practice is to object to the opponent's failure to attach material referenced in an affidavit, because there appears to be a conflict of authorities on whether the defect is one of substance or form.

- Absence of Jurat in Affidavit. The decisions are not consistent on the issue of whether the absence of a technically correct jurat is a defect in form or substance. Some decisions reason that the fact that a statement intended as a supporting affidavit has no jurat means that the statement is not sworn and, thus, is not an affidavit. Under this approach, the defect is considered to be a substantive one that is not waived by failure to object in the trial court, and therefore can be raised for the first time on appeal. Other decisions have concluded that the current Texas statutory requirements for affidavits do not necessarily require a jurat. *See* Gov. C. § 312.011(1); *Residential Dynamics, LLC v. Loveless*, 186 S.W.3d 192, 197 (Tex. App. — Forth. Worth 2006, no pet.).

- Affiant's Competence to Testify. To qualify as valid summary judgment evidence, an affidavit must state facts showing that the affiant is competent to testify to the matters stated in the affidavit. If no objection is made to the affidavit's failure to show the affiant's competence to testify, the defect is waived.

- Conclusory Statements. A "conclusory statement" is a statement that does not provide the underlying facts to support the conclusion. For example, the affidavit of a construction company's president was held to be conclusory and not competent evidence to support the company's summary judgment motion when the matters set forth in the affidavit were not based on the president's personal knowledge but rather were based on what he had been told by other people. In many cases, the dividing line between conclusory statements and opinions can be thin and hard to determine. An objection that an affidavit is conclusory is chiefly viewed as an objection to the substance of the affidavit that can be raised for the first time on appeal. The case law is particularly clear that conclusory statements by an expert are insufficient to support or defeat summary judgment.

- Statements of Opinion. Despite the obvious difficulty of distinguishing a conclusion from an opinion, there is some suggestion in the case law that even though an affidavit containing a conclusion is substantively defective, an objection that an affidavit contains a statement of opinion must be made in the trial court because the defect is formal rather than substantive. Other court decisions treat both statements of opinion and conclusions as incompetent summary judgment proof.

- Hearsay. The prohibition against hearsay affidavits is not absolute. Prior to the adoption of the Texas Rules of Evidence, inadmissible hearsay could never form the basis of a summary judgment, even in the absence of an objection by the non-movant. Under Evidence Rule 802, however, inadmissible evidence admitted without objection is not denied probative value merely because it is hearsay. In the absence of an objection, hearsay in an affidavit is competent summary judgment proof. Accordingly, modern cases hold that an objection that an affidavit contains hearsay is an objection to the form of the affidavit and must be made in the trial court.

- Authentication. Defects in the authentication of attachments in support of a motion for summary judgment or response are usually considered to be defects of form that are waived absent an objection. However, it has also been held that a complete absence of authentication is a defect in substance that is not waived by the failure to object. Thus, when a party made no attempt to authenticate loan documents, correspondence, and court records submitted in response to a summary judgment motion, and the evidence was neither identified nor referenced in the party's affidavit, none of this evidence was properly before the trial court, and this objection could be urged for the first time on appeal. Statements deemed "conclusory" can also eliminate the proper authentication of summary judgment evidence. For example, in *Trejo v. Laredo Nat'l Bank*, 185 S.W.3d 43 (Tex. App. — San Antonio 2005, no pet.), the court held that a conclusory affidavit meant that photographs were unauthenticated, and therefore the opponent could object to them for the first time on appeal.

(5) *Affidavits of Experts.* Ordinarily, the testimony of an expert witness does no more than raise an issue to be determined by the trier of fact; it usually does not establish any fact as a matter of law. Moreover, a conclusory statement in an affidavit of an expert witness is insufficient to create a question of fact to defeat summary judgment. *See IHS Cedars Treatment Ctr. of DeSoto v. Mason*, 143 S.W.3d 794, 803 (Tex. 2003) (statement that alleged negligent conduct constituted negligence that was proximate cause of injuries was conclusory because it failed to explain causal nexus).

Expert testimony, however, may establish a fact conclusively for summary judgment purposes if: 1) the subject matter is such that the trier of fact must be guided solely by the opinion testimony of experts; 2) the testimony is clear, positive, and direct, free from contradictions and inconsistencies; and 3) the evidence is uncontroverted but could have been readily controverted.

Expert testimony can establish a fact only when it is an issue on which a jury "must be guided solely" by expert opinion. This means that an expert opinion may establish a fact as a matter of law only when the fact is one that lay people cannot determine without expert assistance. Issues of causation and the standard of care in professional malpractice cases are typical examples of issues necessitating the guidance of experts.

Summary judgment evidence (whether by affidavit or deposition) must meet all the requirements for admissibility under the rules of evidence the same as if it was being offered in an ordinary trial. The Texas Supreme Court has said that "no difference obtains between the standards for evidence that would be admissible in a summary judgment proceeding and those applicable at a regular trial." *United Blood Serv. v. Longoria*, 938 S.W.2d 29, 30 (Tex. 1997). There are some admissibility requirements that frequently present problems in the summary judgment context. For example:

- The summary judgment evidence must establish an expert witness' qualifications as an expert on the particular issue made the subject of the testimony.
- An expert's opinion must be based on a reliable foundation, amounting to more than an unsupported speculation or subjective belief, and satisfy the requirements discussed in *E.I. DuPont de Nemours & Co. v. Robinson*, 923 S.W.2d 549, 556–60 (Tex. 1995).
- An expert's conclusory statements will be ignored unless the facts supporting the conclusions are set out in the testimony. The expert's affidavit must set out the reasoned basis for the expert's conclusions.
- An expert opinion as to a mixed question of law and fact is admissible so long as the opinion is based on proper legal concepts and a statement of the underlying facts used to support it. In this connection, it is not necessary for the expert to state the definitions of the legal terms used and sought to be proved, although that may be the better practice. The testimony must describe conduct or circumstances that equate to the elements in the legal definition.

(6) *Reliance on Deposition Excerpts.* Authentication is not required as a condition to the use of deposition excerpts as summary judgment proof. *McConathy v. McConathy*, 869 S.W.2d 341, 342 (Tex. 1994). The excerpts need not include a copy of the court reporter's certificate or an original affidavit of counsel certifying the accuracy of the copied deposition testimony. Civil Procedure Rule 166a dispenses with the necessity of authenticating deposition excerpts for use as summary judgment evidence. *See* Tex. R. Civ. P. 166a(d). However, two courts of appeals have concluded that a litigant must present to the court deposition testimony on which the motion for summary judgment relies. In *E.B. Smith Co. v. USF & Guar.*, 850 S.W.2d 621 (Tex. App. — Corpus Christi 1993, writ denied), the court interpreted the term "specific references" in Civil Procedure Rule 166a(d) to require that the party "show the court language from an unfiled deposition or other unfiled discovery document before the court rules on the summary judgment motion." *Accord Salmon v. Miller*, 958 S.W.2d 424, 428 (Tex. App. — Texarkana 1997, writ denied). Thus, the prudent practitioner filing a summary judgment motion will attach copies of unfiled discovery products on which the motion relies.

(7) *Is an Oral Hearing Required?* There is no live testimony at the summary judgment hearing, only the argument of counsel. (All proof is written and is required to be timely filed well in advance of the hearing.) May the trial court dispense with the hearing? The Texas Supreme Court denied application for writ of error to review a summary judgment rendered without affording a hearing, despite the nonmovant's request for a hearing. *See Adamo v. State Farm Lloyds Co.*, 864 S.W.2d 491, 492 (Tex. 1993) (Doggett, J., dissenting).

(8) *Motion for New Trial following Summary Judgment.* The Texas Supreme Court reviewed the denial of a motion for new trial following a summary judgment in *Carpenter v. Cimarron Hydrocarbons Corp.*, 98 S.W.3d 682 (Tex. 2002). The

nonmovant had notice of the hearing and discovered its failure to respond before the hearing. The Court held that under those circumstances, a motion to allow a late-filed summary judgment response should be granted when a litigant establishes good cause for failure to timely respond by showing: 1) the failure to respond was not intentional or the result of conscious indifference, but the result of accident or mistake; and 2) allowing the late response will not cause undue delay or otherwise injure the party seeking summary judgment. The trial court's ruling denying leave to file a late response was held not to be an abuse of discretion under this standard, as the nonmoving party offered no explanation for the failure to timely respond to the summary judgment motion. The Court did not address what standard should apply when a nonmovant does not discover its failure to respond until after the summary judgment hearing or rendition of judgment.

(9) *More Time to Respond.* Rule 166a provides that a party faced with a motion for summary judgment may file an affidavit explaining the reasons she needs additional time to gather affidavits or do discovery in order to oppose the motion. This additional time is not a matter of right, however. The non-movant must justify the request, as this excerpt demonstrates:

COOPER v. CIRCLE TEN COUNCIL BOY SCOUTS OF AMERICA

254 S.W.3d 689 (Tex. App. — Dallas 2008, no pet.)

Lang-Miers, J.

This is an appeal from the trial court's order granting summary judgment in favor of Circle Ten Council Boy Scouts of America and awarding it attorney's fees as the prevailing party in a declaratory judgment action. The sole issue below was whether Circle Ten Council is a governmental body for purposes of the Texas Public Information Act. The trial court concluded it was not. We affirm the trial court's summary judgment and the award of attorney's fees.

FACTUAL AND PROCEDURAL BACKGROUND

Jay Sandon Cooper sent Gene Stone, Scout Executive and Chief Executive Officer of Circle Ten Council, a letter pursuant to the TPIA requesting disclosure of information relating to the operation of the Dallas Police Department's Explorer program. Stone replied that Circle Ten Council is a private organization and not subject to the TPIA's disclosure requirements. Cooper then filed this lawsuit pro se seeking a declaration that Circle Ten Council is a governmental body subject to the TPIA and required to disclose the information. Circle Ten Council moved for summary judgment on the ground that it is not a governmental body as a matter of law and for attorney's fees as sanctions under chapter 10 of the civil practice and remedies code for filing a frivolous lawsuit. Circle Ten Council attached Stone's affidavit as summary judgment evidence.

. . . In this pro se appeal, Cooper argues that the trial court . . . erred by granting summary judgment in favor of Circle Ten Council without affording him adequate time for discovery [and] abused its discretion by granting summary judgment before discovery was completed as required by the pretrial scheduling order.

. . . .

B. Was summary judgment premature?

1. Continuance of summary judgment hearing based on motion

. . . Cooper contends that it was error to grant summary judgment without allowing him additional time for discovery. We review a trial court's decision whether to grant a party additional time for discovery before a summary judgment hearing for an abuse of discretion. *Tenneco, Inc. v. Enter. Prods. Co.*, 925 S.W.2d 640, 647 (Tex. 1996).

A party contending that he has not had an adequate opportunity for discovery before a summary judgment hearing must file either an affidavit explaining his need for additional discovery or a verified motion for continuance. *Id.; see* Tex. Rs. Civ. P. 166a(g), 251, 252. The affidavit must describe the evidence sought, explain its materiality, and set forth facts showing the due diligence used to obtain the evidence prior to the hearing. In considering whether the trial court abused its discretion, we consider such factors as the length of time the case had been on file before the hearing, the materiality of the discovery sought, whether the party seeking the continuance exercised due diligence in obtaining the discovery, and what the party expects to prove.

Cooper did not comply with the rules. Although he filed a response to the summary judgment motion, he did not file a verified motion for continuance, and that fifteen-page document only states, in two short paragraphs on pages eight and thirteen, that he has not had adequate time for discovery. He does not specifically ask for a continuance in the response, nor does he ask for a continuance in his prayer for relief. He also did not file an affidavit setting forth specific details concerning his need for additional time for discovery. *See* Tex. Rs. Civ. P. 166a(g), 251, 252. Instead, in the last sentence of the three-page affidavit he filed in opposition to the summary judgment, Cooper "requests that the Court refuse the Defendant's application for judgment as premature, and order that discovery continue in accordance with the Texas Rules of Civil Procedure." He did not provide any specific details in his response or affidavit regarding the type of discovery he anticipated, stating only "that given full opportunity for discovery of the facts in this case, Plaintiff will establish Defendant is a 'governmental body.' " As a result, the trial court did not have a basis on which to weigh the materiality of the requested discovery.

Additionally, Cooper did not provide any information regarding the diligence on his part in obtaining the discovery prior to the hearing. *See Lee v. Haynes & Boone, L.L.P.*, 129 S.W.3d 192, 198 (Tex. App. — Dallas 2004, pet. denied). In fact, the record in this case reflects that Cooper requested the information from Circle Ten Council over two years before he filed this action. A trial court may presume that a plaintiff investigated his own case prior to filing the lawsuit. It also shows that the case was on file over four months before the summary judgment motion was filed and the hearing on the motion was held thirty-eight days after the motion was filed. And generally it is not an abuse of discretion to deny a motion for continuance when the party has received the twenty-one days' notice required by rule 166a(c). *Lee*, 129 S.W.3d at 198.

We conclude that the trial court did not abuse its discretion by denying his request for relief. . . .

2. Continuance of summary judgment hearing based on pretrial scheduling order

. . . Cooper contends that summary judgment was premature because it was granted before the date established in the pretrial scheduling order for completion of discovery had passed. He does not cite any authority to support his position that a motion for summary judgment filed under rule 166a(c) cannot be granted prior to the date established by the court for completion of discovery. In fact, rule 166a(b) allows a party to file a motion at any time. *Cf.* Tex. Rs. Civ. P. 166a(b) ("A party against whom a . . . declaratory judgment is sought may, at any time, move with or without supporting affidavits for a summary judgment in his favor") *with* Tex. Rs. Civ. P. 166a(i) ("After adequate time for discovery, a party without presenting summary judgment evidence may move for summary judgment on the ground that there is no evidence of one or more essential elements of a claim . . . on which a adverse party would have the burden of proof at trial."). Additionally, we previously concluded that Cooper did not present sufficient facts to support his claimed need for additional time for discovery. We conclude that the trial court did not abuse its discretion by granting summary judgment prior to the date established by the court for completion of discovery.

APPENDIX — DISPOSITION WITHOUT TRIAL AND THE TEXAS BAR EXAM

Issues related to summary judgment procedure are common in practice and have appeared on the bar exam. The following are questions from past exams, reprinted with the permission of the Texas Board of Law Examiners, which owns the copyright to these questions. You can see more questions, and the examiners' comments on the answers, by visiting the Board's website at www.ble.state.tx.us/past_exams/main_pastexams.htm.

In considering the questions, keep in mind that on the bar exam your answer is always limited to five lines.

February 2004

X Corp is a Texas corporation with headquarters in Travis County, Texas. X Corp has developed a thriving online consulting business with a customer base in Texas and the four surrounding states. Paul and Don, both Texas citizens, were the original co-founders of X Corp; Paul is President and Don is Vice-President. Paul and Don disagree over issues of management and compensation.

A competitor in the same market, Y Corp (an Oklahoma corporation with headquarters in Tulsa), recruits Don to come work for it as President. He accepts, but continues to live in Texas. Don hires his old college roommate Larry, an Oklahoma citizen, to manage the Oklahoma territory. X Corp wishes to bring suit against Y Corp, Don, and Larry for interference with contractual relations, improper use of trade secrets and customer lists, and breach of Don's covenant not to compete after he left X Corp.

Assume that X Corp has not produced any evidence in discovery, whether fact or expert opinion, on damages. X Corp employees who have been deposed have not expressed opinions on quantifying the amount of damages allegedly sustained by X Corp and caused by Y Corp, Don and Larry. Y Corp files a "no evidence" motion for summary judgment against X Corp. What must X Corp do to prevent the Court from granting the summary judgment in favor of Y Corp? Explain fully.

February 2005

Sam, his wife, and their minor daughter, Jane, were on a family vacation in Harris County, Texas when a truck rear-ended their car. Sam was driving the car. Sam's wife, Martha, and Jane were passengers. All three sustained serious injuries in the collision. The owner of the truck was PipeCorp, a Texas corporation whose principal place of business has always been in Tarrant County, Texas. Bob, PipeCorp's employee, was driving the truck at the time of the collision. Sam, Martha, Jane and Bob resided in Nueces County, Texas at the time of the collision. Sam and Martha want to file a lawsuit to recover for the injuries and damages sustained by them and by Jane.

In its responsive pleadings, PipeCorp claims that Bob was not within the course and scope of his employment at the time of the collision. Plaintiffs' counsel believes that the evidence conclusively establishes otherwise. Plaintiffs want the court to rule on this issue before trial. What pleading can Plaintiffs file to seek a ruling on this issue and when can they file it? Explain fully.

February 2001

Paul Palmer, a resident of Bell County, has filed a negligence, breach of warranty, and product liability suit in state district court in Hill County, Texas. Palmer alleges that a curling iron, which he had bought for his daughter from Dad's Department Store ("Dad's"), was defective, overheated, and caused a fire in his home. Palmer, who is uninsured, seeks to recover the cost of repairing the damage to his home and for injuries to his minor daughter, and he alleges damages in excess of $50,000. Palmer sued two defendants: the retailer, Dad's, a sole proprietorship in Waco, Texas (McLennan County); and Kurlee, Inc., the manufacturer, a Vermont corporation with its headquarters in Vermont.

One year after filing the suit, Palmer has no expert witness on causation. Dad's has an expert witness who opines that the fire was caused solely by faulty wiring in the house and that it had nothing to do with the curling iron that was in the general area where the fire originated. Dad's would like for you to explore ways to conclude the case without a trial. Given this factual background, name two variations of a motion Dad's can file to seek a pretrial adjudication of the case. Explain the difference between the two variations.

July 2009

Extra Good Plumbing ("Extra") was a Texas sole proprietorship with a principal place of business in Nueces County, Texas. Bill resided in Kleberg County, Texas.

Bill requested that Extra send an employee to his residence to check a possible gas leak. Extra dispatched an employee, Ray, to Bill's residence. Ray resides in Brooks County, Texas. Ray had been a plumber for one month. Ray discovered a gas valve leak inside Bill's residence. Ray told Bill he could try to replace the valve, but that he was not certified to replace any type of leaking gas valve. Bill told Ray he did not care about any certification and that he wanted Ray to replace the valve. Ray turned the gas off at Bill's gas meter. Ray installed a replacement valve manufactured by Plumber Parts, Inc. ("Parts"). Parts is not a Texas corporation, but it had over $2,000,000 in sales in Texas in the year of the valve replacement.

In spite of a city ordinance to the contrary, Bill turned his gas back on at the gas meter without contacting the local gas utility. The next day, Bill's house exploded and he sustained serious personal injuries. Bill hired a lawyer to sue Ray and Extra for his personal injuries sustained in the explosion and fire. Extra brought Parts into the case as a third-party defendant.

Parts' expert and the Fire Marshall believe that the valve in question was not defective, but rather that the valve was improperly installed by Ray and that the valve's design was not a cause in fact of the explosion and fire. Discovery is complete. What motion or motions should Parts file in order to be dismissed from the case? What documents should be attached to the motion or motions? Explain fully.

Chapter 12

SETTLEMENT AND ALTERNATIVE DISPUTE RESOLUTION

SCOPE

In Texas as elsewhere, very few disputes actually proceed all the way to a trial on the merits. This chapter discusses ways in which a case may be resolved before trial not by a ruling on the merits but by agreement of the parties. Instead, the litigation ends with voluntary dispositions such as settlement and alternative dispute resolution techniques.

§ 12.01 SETTLEMENT AND ITS EFFECTS

[A] General Attributes of Settlement Agreements

Most legal disputes are resolved before litigation. Most lawsuits are settled before trial. Indeed, a large portion of the pretrial process could be characterized as preparation for settlement rather than preparation for trial. Consider the following excerpts from William V. Dorsaneo III, *Texas Litigation Guide.**

§ 102.01 Preparation for Settlement

[1] Considerations and Tactics

From the moment that a trial lawyer undertakes a case, the possibility of settlement is an important consideration. Factors of time and expense and the possibility of fee- and cost-shifting encourage both lawyer and client to work toward termination of a dispute short of an actual trial. A plaintiff seeking money damages prefers cash in hand today rather than after the levy of execution on a judgment, possibly much later. Many defendants prefer to compromise and substitute a certain result for the uncertainty involved in placing the dispute in a jury's hands. Obviously, neither party intends to "sell out," and a satisfactory settlement, like the trial of a lawsuit, depends on a proper functioning of the adversary system.

In negotiating the compromise and settlement of a legal dispute, attorneys are, in effect, selling, buying, and bargaining. As salesmen or negotiators, they must know their "product" well. Preparation for settlement negotiations will vary depending on the amount or extent of the matter in controversy and the probabilities of successfully advocating the client's cause in court.

Timing the commencement of settlement negotiations may well depend on the scope of counsel's preparation and investigation. Many successful plaintiff's attorneys work toward settlement before suit is filed by accumulating statements, reports, photographs, and medical bills into a settlement brochure by which the defense can "see the product" underlying the plaintiff's demands. Others may deliver to their adversary a copy of a petition and memorandum of law when the theory of the cause of action is important to the dispute. Once suit is filed and appearances have been made by all parties, skillful use of pretrial procedures may prepare counsel for settlement negotiations. Other procedures, such as special exceptions, partial summary judgment, or severance of claims or parties, may narrow the issues in aid of compromise.

The defendant may invoke the statutory offer of settlement procedure, which may enhance the prospects for settlement, but also interjects substantial risk into the settlement process.

Alternative dispute resolution procedures designed to aid the settlement process may also provide an opportunity to settle or to enhance the likelihood of settlement ofthe claims made in litigation. The Texas Alternative Dispute Resolution Procedures Act allows a court, on its own motion or the motion of a party, to refer a pending dispute to an appropriate alternative dispute resolution procedure, to be determined by the court after conferring with the parties.

During the preparation process, the trial lawyer should ascertain the positive and negative factors affecting the client's position and evaluate the client's chances of recovery or defense. The lawyer must be prepared not only to zealously try the case but also to advance the client's cause in negotiations knowledgeably and realistically, seeking a result that is advantageous to the client but consistent with requirements of honest dealing with others [*see* State Bar Rules, Art. 10 § 9, Preamble: A Lawyer's Responsibilities, Comment 2]. The lawyer must be prepared to advise the client of the reasonableness and effects of any proposed settlement, for it is the client's decision whether to accept a settlement offer [*see* State Bar Rules, Art. 10 § 9, Rule 1.02(a)(2); *but see* State Bar Rules, Art. 10 § 9, Rule 1.02, Comment 3 — rights of client may be limited in class actions, insurance defense cases, and cases in which client has waived right of consent; *see also* Liberty Steel Co. v. Guardian Title Co., 713 S.W.2d 358, 361 (Tex. App. — Dallas 1986, no writ) — when settling party is indemnitee, third-party indemnitor has right, if granted in indemnity contract, to approve any settlement before it becomes final].

[2] Admissibility of Settlement Offers and Agreements

Counsel must consider whether and under what circumstances an offer or agreement of settlement will be admissible in evidence. As a general rule, neither furnishing nor accepting a valuable consideration in compromising a disputed claim is admissible to prove liability for or invalidity of a claim or its amount [T.R. Evid. 408; Bounds v. Scurlock Oil Co., 730 S.W.2d 68, 70 (Tex. App. — Corpus Christi 1987, ref. n.r.e.) — jury might take settlement agreement as admission of liability; *see also* T.R.C.P. 167.6 — evidence relating to offer made under offer of settlement statute is not admissible except for purposes of enforcing settlement agreement or obtaining litigation costs]. Offers or promises to furnish or accept consideration to compromise a claim are also inadmissible for the same purposes. Finally, evidence of conduct or statements made in compromise negotiations is inadmissible under the same circumstances [T.R. Evid. 408]. Similarly, communications relating to the subject matter of a dispute made by a participant in any alternative dispute resolution procedure are confidential, and may not be used as evidence against the participant in any judicial or administrative hearing [C.P.R.C. § 154.073(a)].

[B] Offers of Settlement Under Rule 167

Read Tex. R. Civ. P. 167.

Overview

The Texas Legislature adopted an Offer of Settlement statute as a part of House Bill 4 (and as new Chapter 42 of the Civil Practices and Remedies Code), that can significantly affect settlement strategies and potentially the ultimate judgment rendered in Texas civil suits. It provides for shifting of certain "litigation costs" when an offer to settle is rejected and the ultimate judgment is less favorable to the offeree, by a 20 percent margin. The litigation expenses to be shifted and imposed on the party who "unreasonably" rejected an offer (even though they may win the case), include post-rejection costs, reasonable attorney's fees, and fees for two expert witnesses. Recently, the Texas Supreme Court promulgated Rule 167 of the Texas Rules of Civil Procedure implementing this new fee shifting mechanism. The rule applies to suits filed after January 1, 2004, involving monetary claims. It does not, however, apply to: 1) class actions; 2) shareholder's derivative actions; 3) actions by or against a governmental unit (defined as "the state, a unit of state government or a political subdivision of the state"); 4) actions brought under the Family Code; 5) actions to collect workers' compensation benefits; or 6) actions filed in a justice of the peace court. It should also be noted that Rule 167 does not apply to any offer made in a mediation or arbitration proceeding.

Putting Fee Shifting in Play — The Defendant's Declaration

While the offer of settlement statute is a "two way" provision that allows both plaintiffs and defendants to shift litigation costs when an offer is "unreasonably" rejected, before the offer of settlement rule is operative, a "defendant" must file a declaration that the "settlement procedure allowed by this chapter is available in the action." In a multi-defendant case, the declaration by one defendant does not inure to the benefit of the other: "If there is more than one defendant, the settlement procedure allowed by this chapter is available only in relation to the defendant that filed the declaration and to the parties that make or receive offers of settlement in relation to that defendant."

A "defendant" that may file the declaration and put fee shifting in play includes "a person from whom a claimant seeks recovery on a claim, including a counterdefendant, cross-defendant, or third party defendant." C.P.R.C. § 42.002(c). Thus, a plaintiff, as a counterdefendant, for example, may file the declaration and invoke potential fee shifting.

Rule 167.2 (a) allows the declaration to be filed not later than 45 days before the case is set for a conventional trial on the merits. Rule 167 affords the trial court discretion to amend this time limit on motion, and for good cause.

The Offer of Settlement

Rule 167 provides that an offer of settlement may not be made:

(1) before a defendant's declaration is filed;

(2) within 60 days after the appearance in the case of the offeror or offeree, whichever is later;

(3) within 14 days before the date the case is set for a conventional trial on the merits, except that an offer may be made within that period if it is in response to, and within seven days of, a prior offer.

Rule 167.2 (b) directs that the offer:

(1) be in writing;

(2) state that it is made under Rule 167 and Chapter 42 of the Texas Civil Practice and Remedies Code;

(3) identify the party or parties making the offer and the party or parties to whom the offer is made;

(4) state the terms by which all monetary claims — including any attorney fees, interest, and costs that would be recoverable up to the time of the offer — between the offeror or offerors on the one hand and the offeree or offerees on the other may be settled;

(5) state a deadline — no sooner than 14 days after the offer is served — by which the offer must be accepted;

(6) be served on all parties to whom the offer is made.

Extreme caution must be taken in adding any additional conditions to the offer to settle as some conditions will invalidate the opportunity for fee shifting. The rule admonishes: "An offer may be made subject to reasonable conditions, including the execution of appropriate releases, indemnities, and other documents. An offeree may object to a condition by written notice served on the offeror before the deadline stated in the offer. A condition to which no such objection is made is presumed to have been reasonable. Rejection of an offer made subject to a condition determined by the trial court to have been unreasonable cannot be the basis for an award of litigation costs under this rule."

An offer of settlement is served by the offeror upon the offeree. It is not filed with the court. While the statute is silent as to its admissibility, Rule 167 expressly provides that the offer of settlement is inadmissible except for purposes of enforcing a settlement agreement or obtaining litigation costs.

Be sure to understand that an offer to settle may be made under Rule 167, with potential "fee shifting" consequences or outside the rule with no fee shifting potential.

Withdrawal of Offer

An offer may be withdrawn before it is accepted. Withdrawal is effective when written notice of the withdrawal is served on the offeree. Once an unaccepted offer has been withdrawn, it cannot be accepted or be the basis for imposing litigation expenses under this rule.

Successive Offers

Rule 167 allows for successive offers. An offeror faced with an unaccepted offer, may want to improve its chances of recovery of its costs and attorneys' fees by improving the offer which further enhances the chances of settlement, thereby fulfilling the objective of the rule. Specifically, Rule 167 provides, "A party may make an offer after having made or rejected a prior offer. A rejection of an offer is subject to imposition of litigation expenses under this rule only if the offer is more favorable to the offeree than any prior offer.

Offer "Void" Upon Subsequent Joinder of Parties

Chapter 42 mandates that "[i]f the offering party joins another party or designates a responsible third party after making the settlement offer, the party to whom the settlement offer was made may declare the offer void." Rule 167 requires a timely objection within 15 days after service of the offeror's pleading (that joins another party) or designation.

Acceptance of Offer of Settlement

Rule 167 provides, "An offer that has not been withdrawn can be accepted only by written notice served on the offeror by the deadline stated in the offer. When an offer is accepted, the offeror or offeree may file the offer and acceptance and may move the court to enforce the settlement." Presumptively, the acceptance must mirror the offer.

Rejection of Offer of Settlement

An offer that is not withdrawn or timely accepted is rejected. The date of rejection is important because if fee shifting is warranted, the date of rejection is the "starting" date for computing the fees to be shifted.

Consequences of Rejection of Offer — Triggering the Fee Shifting Event

Shifting of certain litigation expenses is mandated when an offeree rejects a settlement offer made under Rule 167 and the judgment rendered is significantly less favorable than the rejected offer. A judgment is significantly less favorable to the rejecting party than is the settlement offer when: 1) the offeree is a claimant and the judgment would be less than 80 percent of the offer; or 2) the offeree is a defendant and the judgment would be more than 120 percent of the offer.

Litigation Expenses Shifted

The litigation costs that may be recovered by the offering party are limited to those litigation costs "actually made and the obligations actually incurred directly in relation to the claims covered by a settlement under this rule" by the offering party after the date the rejecting party rejected the settlement offer and run "from the time the offer was rejected to the time of judgment." The litigation expenses recoverable include: 1) court costs; 2) reasonable fees for not more than two testifying expert witnesses; and 3) reasonable attorney fees. The reasonableness of the fees to be shifted is determined by the trial court.

Rule 167.5(b) provides that when litigation costs are to be awarded against a party, the party, on motion and for good cause shown, may be allowed to conduct discovery in relation to the reasonableness of those costs. However, if the court determines that the litigation costs are reasonable, "it must order the party requesting discovery to pay all attorneys fees and expenses incurred by other parties in responding to such discovery." It would seem that discovery would be timely once the amount of the monetary award is determined, as that award will determine whether fees are to be shifted.

There is a cap on the litigation expenses that may be shifted that is tied to the Plaintiff's recovery. Specifically, Chapter 42 provides:

> (d) The litigation costs that may be awarded under this chapter may not be greater than an amount computed by:
>
> (1) determining the sum of:
>
> (A) 50 percent of the economic damages to be awarded to the claimant in the judgment;
>
> (B) 100 percent of the noneconomic damages to be awarded to the claimant in the judgment; and
>
> (C) 100 percent of the exemplary or additional damages to be awarded to the claimant in the judgment; and
>
> (2) subtracting from the amount determined under Subdivision (1) the amount of any statutory or contractual liens in connection with the occurrences or incidents giving rise to the claim.

Chapter 41 of the Civil Practices and Remedies Code defines "economic damages" as "compensatory damages intended to compensate a claimant for actual economic or pecuniary loss." "Noneconomic damages" are defined as "damages awarded for the purposes of compensating a claimant for physical pain and suffering, mental or emotional pain or anguish, loss of consortium, disfigurement, physical impairment, loss of companionship and society, inconvenience, loss of enjoyment of life, injury to reputation and all other nonpecuniary losses of any kind other than exemplary damages." "Exemplary damages" means "any damages awarded as a penalty or by way of punishment but not for compensatory purposes."

If the claimant is responsible for litigation costs in an amount less than the claimant's recovery, "those litigation costs shall be awarded to the defendant in the judgment as an offset against the claimant's recovery from that defendant."

Presumably, if the defendant is responsible for litigation costs, the recovery of those costs becomes a part of the judgment.

May a prevailing plaintiff under the Offer of Settlement rule double recover fees incurred after the defense rejects the offer when the plaintiff obtains a more favorable judgment and an independent statutory basis exists to recover fees? No. Rule 167.4(e) prohibits double recovery of litigation costs:

> A party who is entitled to recover attorney fees and costs under another law may not recover those same attorney fees and costs as litigation costs under this rule.

May a defending party utilize the offer of settlement scheme to attempt to cut off the plaintiff's right to recover statutory or contractual attorney's fees from the date of refusal to the date of judgment? Yes. Rule 167.4 (f) expressly provides that:

> A party against whom litigation costs are awarded may not recover attorney fees and costs under another law incurred after the date the party rejected the settlement offer made the basis of the award.

Trial Court Discretion to Deny Fee Shifting Is Very Limited

It appears that Chapter 42 of the Civil Practice & Remedies Code makes the award of litigation costs mandatory once a "significantly less favorable judgment is entered" as defined by the statute. The effect is a non-rebuttable presumption of unreasonableness where the party rejecting the settlement offer suffers a less favorable judgment by a 20 percent margin from the offer.

[C] The Effects of Settlement on Remaining Claims

McMILLEN v. KLINGENSMITH

467 S.W.2d 193 (Tex. 1971)

Pope, J.

Joyce Lynn McMillen and husband sued Dr. William Klingensmith and Dr. Henry E. Martinez for negligence in the treatment of Joyce McMillen's injuries which she suffered in an automobile collision with a car driven by William Robert Perkins. Mrs. McMillen and her husband released Perkins from all claims upon his payment of $7,900. The McMillens then instituted suit against the two physicians who moved for summary judgment grounded upon the release. The trial court and the court of civil appeals rendered judgment for the defendant doctors, holding that the release of the original tort-feasor operated to release the subsequent tort-feasors also. We reverse those judgments and remand the cause to the trial court.

The collision occurred on June 2, 1967. Mrs. McMillen was hospitalized in Clarendon, Texas, for emergency treatment, including an emergency tracheostomy. She was then transferred to an Amarillo hospital where the two defendant physicians treated her. On June 9, 1967, Mrs. McMillen was released from the hospital, and accompanied by a nurse, returned to her home in California.

On May 2, 1968, Mrs. McMillen and her husband, upon receipt of $7,900, signed a release which named Perkins only and discharged him

> "from any and all actions, causes of action, claims, demands, damages, costs, loss of services, expenses and compensation, on account of, or in any way growing out of, any and all known AND UNKNOWN personal injuries and property damage resulting or to result from the accident that occurred on or about the 2nd day of June, 1967, at or near Clarendon, Texas.
>
> I/we hereby declare and represent that the injuries sustained are permanent and progressive and that recovery therefrom is uncertain and indefinite, and in making this release and agreement it is understood and agreed that I/we rely wholly upon my/our own judgment, belief and knowledge of the nature, extent and duration of said injuries. . . .
>
> This release contains the ENTIRE AGREEMENT between the parties hereto, and the terms of this release are contractual and not a mere recital."

On May 22, 1969, the McMillens filed suit against Doctors Klingensmith and Martinez, asserting that their negligent diagnoses and treatment resulted in permanent damage to her larynx. The two doctors answered and moved for summary judgment, contending that the release of Perkins was also a release of them. The legal question presented is whether the McMillens may maintain an action for damages against the doctors for malpractice after releasing from liability the named tort-feasor whose conduct made the services of the doctors necessary. . . .

The rule that a release of an original tortfeasor also releases a malpracticing physician finds its basis in the broader common-law rule known as the unity of release rule. The unity of release rule is based upon the idea that there is such a unity of the obligation or injury that a release of one is release of all. After a re-examination of this common-law rule, we have now determined to place our decision in this case upon a broader base. . . .

The legal basis for the unity of release rule has been challenged by every legal scholar who has examined it. Underlying much of the criticism is the idea that there has beena confusion of satisfaction of a claim with release of a cause of action. As expressed by Prosser: "A satisfaction is an acceptance of full compensation for the injury; a release is a surrender of the cause of action, which might be gratuitous, or given for inadequate consideration." Prosser, *Joint Torts and Several Liability*, 25 CAL. L. REV. 413, 423 (1937). Unless the settlement with one of the tortfeasors fully satisfies the injured party, the release of one party should, according to Prosser, release only the tortfeasor who makes the partial settlement.

Those jurisdictions which purport to follow the unity of release rule have, nevertheless, looked with favor upon devices, such as the "covenant not to sue" or a reservation of a cause against others, which are used to skirt the rule. Texas is among those jurisdictions which hold that such devices will save the cause against another tortfeasor when a release would be fatal to it. . . . These judicial efforts to avoid the harsh common-law rule have also been challenged for their artificial reasoning. They have been declared. . . . to be less than forthright, judicial fudging, and a trap for the unwary who do not notice in a document such nice distinctions.

Mr. Justice Rutledge, while serving on the court of appeals for the District of

Columbia wrote *McKenna v. Austin*, 134 F.2d 659 (D.C. Cir. 1943). He thoroughly examined the foundation and rationale of the unity of release rule. He said that it arose historically by an inappropriate transference of the metaphysics of the property concepts of joint estates and survivorship to the law of obligations independent of property. He summarized the practical reasons for abandoning the rule by saying:

> The rule's results are incongruous. More often than otherwise they are unjust and unintended. Wrongdoers who do not make or share in making reparation are discharged, while one willing to right the wrong and no more guilty bears the whole loss. Compromise is stifled, first, by inviting all to wait for the others to settle and, second, because claimants cannot accept less than full indemnity from one when doing that discharges all. Many, not knowing this, accept less only to find later they have walked into a trap. The rule shortchanges the claimant or overcharges the person who settles, as the recurring volume and pattern of litigation show. Finally, it is anomalous in legal theory, giving tortfeasors an advantage wholly inconsistent with the nature of their liability.

The Supreme Court of Alaska, writing in *Young v. State*, 455 P.2d 889 (Alaska 1969), reviewed the several alternatives which that jurisdiction could adopt, and it chose the path of simplicity. It wrote:

> In our opinion the rule which will bring most clarity to this area of ambiguous and conflicting release rules is one under which a release of one tortfeasor does not release other joint tortfeasors unless such tortfeasors are specifically named in the release. We are of the further view that adoption of this rule will insure that the intent of the parties to the release is given effect and will greatly minimize the possibility of any party being misled as to the effect of the release.

The rule is a simple one. Unless a party is named in a release, he is not released. A rule of this type is fairer and easier to apply. It avoids many of the problems arising from the present rule which often requires proof by parol evidence of the releasor's subjective intent at the time the release was executed. With a slight modification we adopt the rule suggested by the Alaska court. We hold that a release of a party or parties named or otherwise specifically identified fully releases only the parties so named or identified, but no others. Our holding in this case shall not affect releases presently in existence where it appears from the language of the release and other circumstances that it was the intention of the releasor to release the named parties and other persons generally identified. The release presently before us names only William Robert Perkins and makes no reference to any other parties.

In holding as we do, we preserve the rule that a claimant in no event will be entitled to recover more than the amount required for full satisfaction of his damages. *Bradshaw v. Baylor University*, 84 S.W.2d 703 (Tex. 1935). One of the problems considered by thecourt in *McKenna v. Austin, supra*, was that of disturbing the law concerning the adjustment of rights between tortfeasors after a release of one tortfeasor. In deciding *McKenna* both Justice Rutledge for the majority and Judge Stephens in dissent, discussed this problem in connection with their choice of the better rule. We regard this as less a problem in Texas than in *McKenna* by reason of our decision in *Palestine Contractors, Inc. v. Perkins*, 386 S.W.2d 764 (Tex. 1965), which concerned true joint tortfeasors. *See also* Hodges, *Contribution and Indemnity Among Tortfeasors*, 26 Tex. L. Rev. 150, 170–172 (1947). We feel that these authorities are also instructive on the effects of a release on the relative rights and liabilities of successive tortfeasors. The impact of a release effective only as to the named original tortfeasor on the extent of the liability of the successive tortfeasor is not yet before us. We reserve judgment on that problem.

This case is before us as a result of the trial court's judgment sustaining the defendant physicians' motion for summary judgment. This judgment was based solely on the conclusion that the release, which named only Perkins, released all other tortfeasors including the doctors. Under our present decision disapproving the unity of release rule, this conclusion was erroneous and the summary judgment for the doctors must fall. The judgments of the courts below are reversed and the cause is remanded for trial.

NOTES AND QUESTIONS

(1) *The New Rule: Parties Not Identified in a Release Are Not Released.* Before the decision of the Texas Supreme Court in *Knutson v. Morton Foods, Inc.*, 603 S.W.2d 805 (Tex. 1980), it was held that if the liability of a person not named in the release was strictly vicarious, the release of the active tortfeasor would serve as a release of the party whose liability was derivative or vicarious. *See Spradley v. McCrackin*, 505 S.W.2d 955–959 (Tex. Civ. App. — Tyler 1974, writ ref'd n.r.e.). In *Knutson*, the Court held that the release of an employee (Chastain) did not operate as a release of an employer (Morton Foods) despite the fact that the employer was entitled to indemnity from the employee. In April, 1974, Dorothy Chastain and Wilma Knutson were in an automobile accident. At the time of the accident, Mrs. Chastain was allegedly delivering snack items for Morton Foods. The Knutsons sued the Chastains and Morton Foods, seeking recovery from Morton Foods under the theory of respondeat superior. The Knutsons alleged that Dorothy Chastain was acting on behalf of her husband, who was an employee of Morton Foods. The Knutsons then entered into a covenant not to sue with the Chastains upon their paying the Knutsons ten thousand dollars. The agreement specifically reserved the Knutsons' cause of action against Morton Foods, provided that the sum paid was in complete satisfaction of claims against the Chastains, and stated that the Knutsons agreed to indemnify the Chastains to the extent of $10,000 in the event Morton Foods obtained indemnity against the Chastains.* In holding thatthis settlement

* The relevant provisions of the covenant were:

II. Plaintiffs expressly reserve their cause of action against Morton Foods, Inc., arising out of the incident described in plaintiffs' pleadings;

III. This covenant does not release and is not intended to release plaintiffs' cause of action, or any part thereof, against Morton Foods, Inc., arising out of the incident described in plaintiffs' pleadings;

IV. It is further understood and agreed that in the event judgment should be rendered in any suit arising out of the occurrence made the basis of this suit in favor of plaintiffs and against Morton Foods, Inc., and Morton Foods, Inc. subsequently seeks to obtain indemnity and contribution against the Chastains by way of suit against the Chastains, the plaintiffs will agreement with Chastain did not release Morton Foods, the Court justified its conclusion in the following terms:

> The Chastains may, as argued, be subjected to an indemnity suit by Morton Foods. It is true that the Chastains are not completely protected from all liability arising out of the accident. Moreover the Knutsons, under their agreement to indemnify the Chastains up to $10,000, may have to return that sum to the Chastains. Morton Foods says, therefore, that this suit by the Knutsons, a subsequent claim for indemnity by Morton Foods against Chastain, and the Chastains' claim for indemnity up to $10,000 against the Knutsons, presents an undesirable circuity of action and undermines the original settlement if Knutson has to give back the $10,000.
>
> There are reasons, however, which favor a recognition of partial settlements and the application of *Klingensmith* to this case and situation. We have long recognized that encouraging settlement and compromise is in the public interest. *Gilliam v. Alford*, 6 S.W. 757 (Tex. 1887); *Fidelity-Southern Fire Ins. Co. v. Whitman*, 422 S.W.2d 552 (Tex. Civ. App. — Houston [14th Dist.] 1967, writ ref'd n.r.e.). The instant decision will aid in the achievement of that goal. A plaintiff will be able to settle with a tortfeasor who acts for another without being fearful of losing his cause of action against the party who may be liable under *respondeat superior.* At the same time, the party who is liable under *respondeat superior* will retain complete access to the courts for a full adjudication of his liabilities and his rights to indemnification.
>
> The Knutsons and Chastains knew about these possibilities, and they were exposed to these obligations to indemnify when they executed the release. They contracted with those possibilities in mind. Paragraph IV of the release, quoted above, fully states the rights of the parties. Only the Knutsons and the Chastains will be affected by the fact that this agreement may fail to protect the Chastains from all future liability, or may subject the Knutsons to a circuitous course of litigation resulting in the return of the $10,000 to the Chastains. Ironically, the only party that is troubled by the incompleteness, or wisdom, of this release is Morton Foods. Morton Foods, however, neither participated in the negotiation of this instrument, nor paid any consideration for its release from liability.
>
> Morton Foods, who was not a party to the settlement agreement, is the only one who does not want to give it the force expressed in the document, but it is no more prejudiced by the settlement than if none had been made. Morton Foods has actually been benefitted since the partial settlement made by the Chastains to the plaintiffs reduces Morton Foods' liability. We see no reason why we should be more concerned with the potential

---

hold harmless and indemnify defendants Chastain and their insurer for any such judgment to the extent of the payment herein recited;

V. It is specifically agreed that the sum paid to plaintiffs and their attorney is in complete and final satisfaction of any and all claims for damages, of whatsoever kind and character, which plaintiffs, or anyone claiming through them or on their behalf, may have against defendants Chastain or their insurer.

problems that the Knutsons and Chastains may encounter as a result of this settlement than they were at the time they executed the release. Accordingly, we conclude that the policies expressed in *Klingensmith* outweigh the perceived dangers in permitting parties to enter into an incomplete release, or one that may lead to a circuity of action, when the parties themselves are not disturbed by those possibilities.

In *Klingensmith* we adopted, with slight modifications, the rule that was proposed by the Alaska Supreme Court in *Young v. State*, 455 P.2d 889 (Alaska 1969). In *Alaska Airlines, Inc. v. Sweat*, 568 P.2d 916 (Alaska 1977), the Alaska Supreme Court addressed the exact question that is posed in this case; whether the rule established in *Young* and *Klingensmith*, requiring the identification of a party in a release before his liability would be extinguished, should beextended to include cases in which the non-released defendant was liable solely under the theory of *respondeat superior.* In answering the question affirmatively, as we do, that court declared:

"[B]ased on our reasoning in *Young*, we would reach the same result at common law by giving effect to the obvious intent of the parties to the covenant. The policy favoring termination of litigation and encouraging settlement agreements should here prevail." 568 P.2d at 930.

We disapprove the holding in *Spradley v. McCrackin*, 505 S.W.2d 955 (Tex. Civ. App. — Tyler 1974, writ ref'd n.r.e.).

(2) *A Party Not Named Must Be Otherwise Specifically Identified to Be Released.* The *McMillen* case abolished the unity of release rule in favor of a rule that only a "party or parties named or otherwise specifically identified" in a release are released. This formulation of the release rule differs from the Alaska approach and has produced its own difficulties. When are unnamed parties "otherwise specifically identified"? The Texas Supreme Court answered the question in *Duncan v. Cessna Aircraft Co.*, 665 S.W.2d 414 (Tex. 1984). Agreeing with the court of appeals' interpretation that "otherwise specifically identified" means "sufficiently particular so that a stranger to the release could readily identify the released party even though the party's name is lacking," the Supreme Court held that merely naming a general class of tortfeasors, e.g., "all corporations," in a release would not absolve all persons literally encompassed in the general language. Rather, the tortfeasor must be identified by name or "with such descriptive particularity that his identity or his connection with the tortious event is not in doubt."

In another case cited with approval in *Duncan*, a release executed by a patient that named and released a doctor "as well as all other persons, firms and corporations of [and] from all claims and causes of action arising from as in any way connected with medical treatment by the said [doctor] and the claims and causes of action. . . . which were or could have been asserted in said cause No. 77-653 in the District Court of Guadalupe County, Texas" was held not to specifically identify a second doctor who failed to diagnose the problem caused by the first doctor's medical treatment. Although the release was signed after the second doctor's treatment had occurred, it was made before a lawsuit was filed against the second doctor and in connection with a settlement of a lawsuit which had been brought against the doctor who was named in the release. *Lloyd v. Ray*, 606 S.W.2d 545, 546–47 (Tex. Civ. App. — San Antonio 1980, writ ref'd n.r.e.).

(3) *Statutory Rules for Tort and DTPA Cases.* In certain kinds of cases, the effect of a settlement with one tortfeasor on the remaining defendants is quite complex. Depending on when the case was filed [which affects which version of the law applies], the plaintiff may have to credit the remaining defendants with some or all of the settlement proceeds. The result turns on both the defendants' percentage of responsibility under the proportionate responsibility statute and on whether the credits are based on a percentage or on the dollar amount paid in settlement. In addition, medical malpractice cases are calculated differently from other torts.

The adjudicative effect of settlement in tort cases is currently governed by Chapter 33 of the Civil Practice and Remedies Code, which includes the 1995 proportionate responsibility statute, as further amended in 2003 and again in 2005. Chapter 33 applies to any tort cause of action and to any action brought under the Deceptive Trade Practices Act in which a defendant, settling person, or responsible third party is found responsible for a percentage of the harm for which relief is sought, with certain exceptions. C.P.R.C. § 33.002. Another important adjudicative effect of a settlement is that no defendant has a right of contribution against any settling person. C.P.R.C. § 33.015(d). But nothing in Chapter 33 affects any common law or statutory right of indemnity owed by any settling person. C.P.R.C. § 33.017.

The basic rule of proportionate responsibility is that a claimant's award of actual damages is reduced by a percentage equal to the claimant's percentage of responsibility. C.P.R.C. § 33.012(a). The claimant's award may be further reduced by a credit based on a settlement. C.P.R.C. § 33.012(b).

- In cases that are either filed on or after June 9, 2005, or in which the trial or a retrial begins on or after that date, Chapter 33 of the Civil Practice and Remedies Code reduces a claimant's damages with respect to a cause of action by the sum of the dollar amounts of all settlements, except in medical malpractice cases. C.P.R.C. § 33.012(b).

- In older cases — those filed on or after July 1, 2003, but before June 9, 2005, and in which no trial or retrial begins on or after June 9, 2005 — Chapter 33 reduces a claimant's damages by a percentage equal to each settling person's percentage of responsibility, as determined by the finder of fact, except in medical malpractice cases. *See* former C.P.R.C. § 33.012(b).

- In medical malpractice cases, the claimant's damages are reduced, at the defendant's election, by the sum of the dollar amounts of all settlements *or* by a percentage equal to each settling person's percentage of responsibility as found by the trier of fact. C.P.R.C. § 33.012(c). A medical malpractice defendant must make the election in writing before the issues of the action are submitted to the trier of fact. If no defendant makes an election, or if defendants make conflicting elections, an election for a dollar-for-dollar credit is deemed to have been made by all defendants. C.P.R.C. § 33.012(d).

Because the settlement credit is applied to the damages found by the trier of fact, unless a claimant has recovered in settlement enough money to reduce the recoverable damages to an amount less than a severally liable defendant's percentage of responsi bility multiplied by the damages found by the trier of fact, only defendants that are jointly and severally liable can benefit from reductions in the amount of recovery grounded on a settlement credit. In a case decided by the Texas Supreme Court in 1994, the Court interpreted the predecessor statute to mean that a defendant having no joint and several liability would not be entitled to any share of a settlement made by another person with the claimant, even though the other defendants would have their liability reduced by the amount of the settlement. *See C&H Nationwide v. Thompson*, 903 S.W.2d 315, 321 (Tex. 1994); *see also Roberts v. Williamson*, 111 S.W.3d 113, 122–24 (Tex. 2003) (applying same approach to case governed by 1995 amendments). Using this method of calculation, the settlement credit will benefit a severally liable defendant *only* if the credit is large enough to reduce the amount of the settling claimant's recovery below the upper limit of the dollar liability of the severally liable defendant. *See* Dorsaneo, *Commentary*, 2001 Texas Torts Update 276 (Sept.).

This result has even more potential significance under the current statute because only one defendant can be jointly and severally liable in most cases. Except in a few situations involving intentional harm, a defendant must be found more than 50% responsible before joint and several liability kicks in — and math makes it impossible for that to include more than one defendant. *See* C.P.R.C. § 33.013. The inclusion in the jury charge of non-defendants who are designated as "responsible third parties" will also tend to reduce the percentage of fault that the jury assigns to any one party. C.P.R.C. § 33.004(a). There will therefore be more and more cases resulting only in several liability.

The unavailability of any share of the pertinent credit to reduce the amount of liability of severally liable defendants means that the plaintiff's recovery is not reduced by any settlement credit unless a defendant is jointly and severally liable or unless the judicially created "one satisfaction" or "one recovery rule" would otherwise be violated. *See* CTTI Priesmeyer, Inc. v. K&O Ltd. P'ship, 164 S.W.3d 675, 683–85 (Tex. App. — Austin 2005, no pet.) (trial court properly denied settlement credit under "one satisfaction rule" because settlement credits are available only as to jointly and severally liable def endants, and defendant on contract claim cannot be jointly and severally liable in absence of joint contract or promise of same performance). For example, assume the amount awarded by the jury is $100,000. If the percentage allocation is 10 percent to P, 45 percent to D-1, 35 percent to D-2, and 10 percent to the Settling Party (SP), P can recover 45 percent ($45,000) of the amount awarded by the jury from D-1 and 35 percent ($35,000) from D-2, for a total of $80,000 and may keep the amount of the settlement, unless the settlement reduces the amount the plaintiff can recover under Section 33.012(a) (below $80,000). Thus, if the amount of the settlement is more than $10,000, the "one recovery" rule and the cap created by Section 33.012(b) would limit the liability of D-1, D-2, or both by establishing the maximum recovery obtainable by the plaintiff. In other words:

JURY FINDINGS:

P	10%	.10	x	$100,000	=	$ 10,000
D-1	45%	.45	x	$100,000	=	$ 45,000

D-2	35%	.35	x	$100,000	=	$ 35,000
SP	10%	.10	x	$100,000	=	$ 10,000
Total	100%				=	$100,000

PROPORTIONATE LIABILITY AND SETTLEMENT CREDITS

Cap on amount P can recover absent settlement = $90K ($100K − $10K)

Absent settlement, P can recover from D-1 & D-2 = $80K ($45K + $35K)

D-1 and D-2 are only severally liable (<50%)

If settlement = $5K, cap on amount P can recover = $85K ($100K − $10K − $5K)

D-1 and D-2 combined will pay $80K. Doesn't exceed cap. No settlement credit to these Ds.

If settlement = $15K, cap on amount P can recover = $75K ($100K − $10K − $15K)

D-1 and D-2 combined will not have to pay more than $75K. One or both will benefit from the settlement credit.

[D] The Consent Judgment/Enforcement of the Settlement

Read Tex. R. Civ. P. 11.

LEAL v. CORTEZ

569 S.W.2d 536 (Tex. Civ. App. — Corpus Christi 1978, no writ)

Bissett, J.

The question presented by this appeal is whether the trial judge rendered judgment in accordance with an agreement between the parties which was dictated into the record. Fidel Leal and wife, Magdalena Leal, brought this suit against Narciso Cortez and other named defendants, where, among other things, they sought a recovery of certain lands. During the course of a jury trial all parties announced in open court that they had reached a settlement of the lawsuit. The terms of the settlement were then dictated into the record and the jury was discharged. Several months later a dispute arose between the parties as to whether a certain promissory note was to be made payable to Gloria Leal Cortez, as insisted by plaintiffs, or to the Cortez Trust, as contended by defendants. Following a hearing relating to the sole issue in disagreement, judgment was rendered that the note be made payable to the Cortez Trust. Plaintiffs have appealed.

Two points of error are brought forward. Plaintiffs contend that the trial court erred:1) in rendering judgment when neither they nor the defendants mutually agreed upon all the terms of the judgment; 2) in not rendering a judgment which conformed to all of the terms of the agreement. They ask that the judgment of the trial court be reversed and the cause remanded, or, in the alternative, that the judgment be reversed and judgment rendered in accordance with the settlement agreement as the same appears in the record.

Rule 11, T.R.C.P., provides:

> "No agreement between attorneys or parties touching any suit pending will be enforced unless it be in writing, signed and filed with the papers as part of the record, or unless it be made in open court and entered of record."

In a judgment by consent, the terms must have been definitely agreed upon by all parties, and either reduced to writing, signed by all parties and filed among the papers of the case, or made in open court and dictated into the record. *McIntyre v. McFarland*, 529 S.W.2d 857 (Tex. Civ. App. — Tyler 1975, no writ); *Behrens v. Behrens*, 186 S.W.2d 697 (Tex. Civ. App. — Austin 1945, no writ).

It is absolutely essential that the parties themselves agree upon all the terms, provisions and conditions of the agreed settlement; the trial court has no power to supply terms, provisions or conditions not previously agreed to by the parties; and the trial court is without authority to render an agreed judgment that does not fall strictly within the terms of the agreement dictated into the record by the parties themselves. *Matthews v. Looney*, 123 S.W.2d 871 (Tex. Com. App. 1939, opinion adopted); *Pope v. Powers*, 120 S.W.2d 432 (Tex. Com. App. 1938, opinion adopted). Further, it is not sufficient that a party's consent to the agreed judgment may at one time have been given; consent must exist at the very moment the trial court undertakes to make the agreement the judgment of the court. *Burnaman v. Heaton*, 240 S.W.2d 288 (1951); *Wilmer-Hutchins I.S.D. v. Blackwell*, 529 S.W.2d 575 (Tex. Civ. App. — Dallas 1975, writ dism'd).

In the case at bar, on the morning of April 13, 1977, during the trial before the jury, Mr. Hollis Rankin, Jr., counsel for plaintiffs, and Mr. Tony Martinez, counsel for defendants, announced that they had reached a settlement of all matters in dispute. The trial judge then instructed counsel for the parties to dictate into the record the terms of settlement. This was done. It was agreed by both Mr. Rankin and Mr. Martinez, who represented to the court that each had full authority from his respective clients to settle the suit, that Gloria Leal Cortez was to be conveyed as her sole and separate estate free and clear of all indebtedness approximately 100 acres of land, and the remainder of the lands in dispute was to be conveyed by the Cortez Trust to the plaintiff Fidel Leal for the total consideration of $130,000.00, to be paid $13,000.00 in cash and the execution and delivery of a note for the remaining balance of $117,000.00, to be paid in 15 equal annual installments, with interest at 7 1/2% per annum; it was further agreed that a second lien on the land to be conveyed by the Cortez Trust to Leal "will be given on this land to Gloria Leal Cortez as her sole and separate property to secure this."

A short time after the agreement was dictated into the record, and before the jury was discharged, counsel advised the trial court that they had decided to change some of the terms of the original agreement of settlement. The following statements were then dictated into the record:

"MR. RANKIN: The agreement that we have heretofore dictated is the same with the exception that the property will be conveyed to the Cortez Trust.

MR. MARTINEZ: All right. The property previously described as the property going to Gloria Leal Cortez.

MR. RANKIN: The hundred-acre tract.

MR. MARTINEZ: Right. Shall remain in the Cortez Trust; either way, as we see fit to do.

MR. RANKIN: I would prefer to deed it.

MR. MARTINEZ: As you wish. It shall be deeded to the trust.

THE COURT: All right, Gentlemen, have you recited the amendment in the agreement now?

MR. RANKIN: Yes, sir.

THE COURT: Now, do I understand now that as amended the agreement now comprises the settlement entered into by all parties?

MR. RANKIN: That is correct, Your Honor.

MR. MARTINEZ: Yes, sir.

THE COURT: And that you have settled all your differences?

MR. RANKIN: We have settled the differences. The only change was that the hundred acres is to be deeded directly to the Cortez Trust.

THE COURT: And the necessary instruments will be executed by all parties by agreement to effect the agreement, the settlement; is that correct?

MR. RANKIN: Yes, Your Honor.

MR. MARTINEZ: Yes, Your Honor.

THE COURT: Any reason why the jury should not be discharged?

MR. RANKIN: No, Your Honor.

MR. MARTINEZ: No, Your Honor."

Whereupon, the jury was discharged. Later, and before judgment was rendered, a dispute arose with respect to the identity of the payee of the note. Plaintiffs contended that the payee, under the terms of the agreement, was Gloria Leal Cortez. Defendants contended that all parties to the original agreement, as amended, agreed that the Cortez Trust was to be the named payee. On September 26, 1977, a hearing was had, wherein the following statements were made:

"THE COURT: All right, Gentlemen, the Court set a hearing for today with respect to an agreement that had been entered into while a jury was waiting in this cause, and I will hear from you.

What seems to be your differences, Gentlemen?

MR. MARTINEZ: Your Honor, on behalf of Dr. Cortez, I guess we tried this way back in April, but since that time Mr. Rankin had submitted to me a proposed judgment in this cause in accordance with our agreement and, obviously, there was a discrepancy in understanding exactly what was meant or said back on April the 13th of 1977 with regard to a note for a hundred and thirty thousand dollars.

It was my understanding and the way that I read the notes of the court reporter from that time that the note was to be payable to the Cortez Trust, and the Cortez Trust would, in turn, deed the properties over to Mr. and Mrs. Leal.

Mr. Rankin feels that the note was meant to have been to Gloria Leal Cortez, and that is our sole and only dispute that we have as of right now. And my client's understanding at that time was that it was going to go strictly to the Cortez Trust and he is staunch about the fact that it should so reflect in the judgment.

MR. RANKIN: Your Honor, my recollection of the record — and Your Honor has it before you — was that we dictated an agreement providing that certain land, roughly a hundred and one and a fraction acres and a note for a hundred and thirty thousand or a hundred and thirty thousand dollars payable $13,000.00 down and the balance over a period of years at a certain percent should be given to Gloria Cortez as her sole and separate estate, and certain other terms and conditions, and this was dictated into the record.

THE COURT: Yes. As I look at the recitations with which I have beenfavored now, and as I recall this situation, you gentlemen agreed that everything was going to go to Gloria Leal Cortez in her separate right.

MR. RANKIN: Yes, sir.

THE COURT: And that then a phone call was made in between and then the agreement was off.

MR. RANKIN: He said it was off.

THE COURT: And it came back because of the fact that the Defendant Narciso Cortez would not agree.

MR. RANKIN: That is right. Unless she agreed to convey to —

THE COURT: You then came back and returned and at that time Mr. Leal had taken ill the day before.

MR. RANKIN: Yes, sir.

THE COURT: And then everybody returned and said it would go to the trust.

MR. RANKIN: The land, Your Honor.

THE COURT: Well, as I noticed, the record only made reference to the land specifically.

MR. RANKIN: That is right, sir.

THE COURT: But I remember the holdup between the parties was the fact that there was a projection by which she was to receive everything in her separate right. This was disagreeable. And then they talked to Mr. Leal and you came back and said that — so the problem as between both parties appears to be as to whether a hundred thirty thousand dollars was a part of the land.

MR. RANKIN: That is right.

THE COURT: I will give you one of two choices: I will declare a mistrial and we'll start trying this case again, or I will rule on the motion for a verdict from the evidence I heard in the case.

There was perjury in this case, my recollection is. I will give you one of two choices.

MR. RANKIN: Your Honor, let me talk to my clients and I will give you a —

THE COURT: Go ahead and discuss it, but I was very displeased by the fact that there was perjury."

After a short recess, the hearing continued, and the following statements were madc:

"THE COURT: All right, Gentlemen, I will hear you.

MR. RANKIN: All right, Your Honor. For the plaintiffs, as I understand, the Court said that he would declare a mistrial or the Court would enter a judgment in accordance with his understanding of the agreement, and we are prepared for the Court to enter a judgment in accordance with the agreement as it was made and appears in the record.

THE COURT: Very well. Both sides ready, Gentlemen?

MR. MARTINEZ: Yes, sir.

THE COURT: Both sides ready?

MR. MARTINEZ: Yes, sir.

MR. RANKIN: Yes, sir.

THE COURT: All right. It is my opinion from all of the circumstances that took place at that time that it was the intention of the parties that all of the matters go into the Cortez Trust.

That is my opinion, Gentlemen, and I am going to so rule."

A judgment was then rendered which stated that the parties "had reached an agreement and settlement of this lawsuit," wherein the said 100 acres "is to be conveyed" to the Cortez Trust, and the Cortez Trust will convey certain described lands to plaintiffs, and that "plaintiffs shall give defendant Cortez Trust a note for $117,000.00," payable in 15 equal annual installments, "and further the sum of $13,000.00 should be paid to defendant Cortez Trust by plaintiffs."

It is plaintiffs' position that in the original agreement of settlement, it was agreed by all parties that the 100 acres would be conveyed to Gloria Leal Cortez free and clear of liens and as her separate property and estate and that the remaining lands (544 acres) would be conveyed by the Cortez Trust to Fidel Leal; and, also, that $13,000.00 in cash was to be paid to Gloria Leal Cortez and a note in the amount of $117,000.00 was to be executed to her as payee, which was to be secured by a second lien on the 544 acres. They admit that the original agreement was amended so as to provide that the 100 acres would be conveyed to the Cortez Trust instead of to Gloria Leal Cortez, but say that this was the only change made by the amendment. They further contend that at the hearing on September 26, 1977, that they agreed to the rendition of a judgment in accordance with the agreement as it was made and appears in the record, and did not agree to a rendition of judgment based on the trial judge's interpretation of the agreement.

The original agreement does not specifically provide that the note in question shall be made payable to Gloria Leal Cortez. With respect to the original agreement, all that was said concerning any deferred consideration for the transaction was:

> "[t]he total consideration will be $130,000.00, $13,000.00 cash, the balance in 15 equal installments, with interest at 7 1/2 per cent per annum, and a second lien will be given on this land to Gloria Leal Cortez as her sole and separate property to secure the payment of this."

The implication from the above-quoted statement is that the parties agreed that a note payable to Gloria Leal Cortez would be executed. Further, after the statement was dictated into the record, counsel for both plaintiffs and defendants, in the initial settlement agreement, used the word "note" in their discussions clarifying some of the terms of settlement, and agreed that the "note" would be an "on or before note" which would contain a "prepayment clause." No mention of the note was made when the agreement was amended.

We tend to agree with plaintiffs' contention that the trial court, in rendering judgment, failed to follow the final agreement made by the parties. Statements by counsel for each side have already been delineated. The amendment to the initial settlement did not refer to the note in question. The amendment affected only the disposition of the 100 acres. This is made clear by the last part of Mr. Rankin's statement, which was not contradicted by Mr. Martinez, when he represented unto the trial court:

> "We have settled the differences. The only change was that the hundred acres is to be deeded directly to the Cortez Trust."

After the trial court told the parties that they had a choice of either a mistrial or the rendition of judgment "from the evidence I heard in the case," Mr. Rankin said:

> "[w]e are prepared for the court to enter a judgment in accordance with the agreement as it was made and appears in the record."

There was no agreement by counsel for plaintiffs to be bound by the judgment of the trial court according to the trial court's understanding of the settlement terms. The court below had no power to alter the agreement or supply additional terms; it only had the power to put the agreement as made by the parties themselves into judgment form. The trial court may not enter a valid consent judgment when consent of one of the parties is lacking. *Burnaman v. Heaton, supra*. A judgment by agreement must fall strictly within the stipulations and agreements of the parties. *Edwards v. Gifford*, 155S.W.2d 786, 788 (1941). Where the trial court undertakes to make an agreement of the parties the judgment of the court, and consent is lacking in the case, the judgment of the trial court must be reversed and the cause remanded for a new trial. *Carter v. Carter*, 535 S.W.2d 215, 217 (Tex. Civ. App. — Tyler 1976, writ ref'd n.r.e.). Accordingly, we sustain plaintiff's first point of error.

The circumstances suggest that the parties were not in agreement as to the identity of the payee of the note in question. It is apparent that both defendants' counsel and the trial judge were under the impression that the settlement agreement, as finally reached, provided that the note would be payable to the Cortez Trust. It is likewise apparent that plaintiffs' counsel was under the impression that the final settlement provided that the note would be made payable to Gloria Leal Cortez.

We hold that the judgment was not in accordance with the agreement of the parties which was dictated into the record. Plaintiffs' second point is sustained.

An argument can be made that we should reverse the judgment of the trial court with respect to the note in question. However, we do not believe that we should do so under the record here presented. Since it is evident that there was an honest misunderstanding between the parties, we believe, and so hold, that the ends of justice would be better served by a reversal and remand of the case for a new trial.

NOTES AND QUESTIONS

(1) *The* Burnaman *Rule: A Consent Judgment Cannot Be Rendered if Consent of One of the Parties Is Lacking.* Notice that there is a difference between a settlement agreement and an agreed judgment. Just what is the difference? *See Burnaman v. Heaton*, 240 S.W.2d 288 (1951), cited in *Leal, above*.

An agreed judgment, as the preceding case shows, cannot be rendered unless both parties are in agreement at the time the judgment is made. What if the settlement agreement does not satisfy the technical requirements of Civil Procedure Rule 11? Rule 11 imposes other distinct requirements. The Texas Supreme Court has held that such an agreement may not be enforced in derogation of Rule 11's requirements. *See Kennedy v. Hyde*, 682 S.W.2d 525, 528–29, 530 (Tex. 1984) (holding that compliance with Rule 11 and the *Burnaman* rule are both necessary because "Rule 11 is a minimum requirement for enforcement of all agreements concerning pending suits, including but not limited to, agreed judgments."). A settlement agreement, on the other hand, can be enforced contractually if it has been properly made under contract law.

With this distinction in mind, consider the following hypothetical situation. The plaintiff and the defendant enter into a complete settlement agreement, unambiguous in its terms, and they shake hands and sign it. The agreement provides for an agreed take-nothing judgment to be rendered on joint motion of the parties in exchange for a payment by defendant. The parties begin to walk down to the courthouse carrying a proposed form of agreed order, but the plaintiff begins thinking that the settlement does not provide him with enough money. As the parties stand before the judge, the plaintiff states, outright, "I've changed my mind and I no longer agree to the settlement." What courses of action are available to the defendant now?

(2) *Rationale of* Leal v. Cortez. What is the basis of the decision in *Leal v. Cortez*? Is it that the judgment was not what the parties agreed? Is it that the agreement to the judgment was not in effect at the time of the entry of judgment? Is it that there never *was* an enforceable agreement in the first place? Is it a combination of these rationales? What should be done next by the parties relying on the "settlement"?

(3) *A Settlement Agreement May Be Enforced Over One Party's Objection.* Although a party may revoke consent to settlement any time before the trial court's rendition of judgment, liability may still result for breach of contract. *S & A Restaurant Corp. v. Leal*, 892 S.W.2d 855, 857 (Tex. 1995). Thus, a Rule 11 agreement to settle is enforceable even though a party withdraws consent before the agreement is filed withthe court. *Padilla v. LaFrance*, 907 S.W.2d 454, 461 (Tex. 1995). For a case in which a settlement agreement was enforced, see *National Maritime Union v. Altman*, 568 S.W.2d 441 (Tex. Civ. App. — Beaumont 1978, no writ). The plaintiff sued for certain pension benefits. After some discovery and while a trial setting was pending, the parties agreed orally on a settlement. The plaintiff then sent a letter to the defendant offering to settle for $12,000. The defendant responded with a letter enclosing a proposed judgment, a proposed set of releases and a letter stating that if the papers met with the plaintiff's approval, the plaintiff should return them signed, and the defendant would enter them and send a check. The plaintiff signed and returned the papers. The defendant then discovered that its records showed that the plaintiff was owed a lesser sum, and it repudiated the settlement agreement. The plaintiff then filed a motion to enforce the settlement agreement contractually, and the trial court did so, entering a judgment substantially similar to that proposed initially by the defendant. The court of civil appeals affirmed. It pointed out that there was no question of lack of authority by the attorney, no question of overreaching and no contractual defense. The court emphasized the distinction between "the *Burnaman* Rule and the enforcement of an agreement to settle a case." The agreement here was contractually enforceable, and the judgment was not made as an agreed judgment. Hence, *Burnaman* did not apply.

§ 12.02 ALTERNATE DISPUTE RESOLUTION

[A] ADR Overview

In 1987, the 70th Legislature enacted a number of statutes providing for Alternative Dispute Resolution. *See* C.P.R.C. §§ 154.001–154.073. The following excerpt analyzes and summarizes the legislation.

1987 ALTERNATIVE DISPUTE RESOLUTION PROCEDURES ACT: AN OVERVIEW*

The Act is found beginning at Section 154.001 of the Texas Civil Practice and Remedies Code. Significantly, the act begins by clearly stating, "It is the policy of the State to encourage the peaceable resolution of disputes. . . . and the early settlement of pending litigation through voluntary settlement procedures." It is the responsibility of the courts — appellate, district, county, family, probate, municipal, and justice of the peace — to carry out this policy.

To implement the policy, the Act allows a court, on its own motion, or the motion of a party, to refer a pending dispute to an ADR procedure and to appoint neutral third parties to preside over such procedures. The court must confer with the parties to determine the most appropriate ADR procedure and notify the parties of its determination. The parties have 10 days after receipt of the notice to file a written objection to the referral. If the court finds a reasonable basis exists for an objection, an ADR referral may not be used.

Sections 154.023–027 contain broad descriptions of a number of ADR procedures such as mediation, mini-trial, moderated settlement conferences, summary jury trials, and arbitration. This list, however, is not inclusive. Flexibility exists to adapt procedures to individual disputes. The descriptions also will serve as a useful source for both judges and attorneys as ADR procedures are integrated into the Texas judicial system. It is important to note that each section stresses that the results of an ADR procedure are not binding on the parties. Therefore, while participation can be required, acceptance of the outcome is not.

Section 154.052 addresses the qualifications of impartial third parties in ADR procedures, an area which received careful review. The Act requires a minimum of 40hours of training in dispute resolution techniques and 24 additional hours for those involved in parent-child disputes. Waivers, however, may be based on other training and experience. While these qualifications give the parties and the judge broad latitude in selecting a neutral third party, it is important that those selected have the qualifications to perform competently.

The list of duties of neutral third parties contained in Section 154.053 is equally important because it helps to maintain the uniformity of the procedures and it gives notice to everyone involved of what should be expected. Only when these conditions are met will ADR be successfully integrated into Texas' court system. The duties emphasize "encouraging" and "assisting" a settlement and strictly forbid coercion. Finally, the Act specifies that a written ADR agreement is enforceable as any other written contract and may be incorporated in the court's final decree and that communications during the procedure are strictly confidential.

Assessing the impact of this legislation, especially at this early stage, presents a challenge. It is important that we, as members of the Texas Bar, look at this not as a change to be feared but rather as an opportunity. As former Texas Chief Justice John Hill has pointed out, ADR does not deny rights; it adds options. Under this

* Krier & Nadig, 51 Tex. B.J. 22–24 (1988).

Act, due process rights are protected. While the parties can be directed to participate, they are free to reject the results and are not thereafter prejudiced.

We are convinced of ADR's potential. Its impact in Texas will be significant if the Bar will help it to reach its full potential. . . .

We doubt there is a person reading this journal who is unaware of or unconcerned by the too-often negative public perception of the legal profession. The judicial system is viewed as being too fraught with complexities, delays, expenses, and various other obstacles. It is too often perceived not as a place to solve problems, but as a place which causes or adds to problems. We must change that perception and that will require substantive change in the way we settle disputes.

ADR can be part of that change — that progress — by providing every person access to justice through the most expeditious, inexpensive, and appropriate process. The continued development of alternatives is vital to our judicial system. If we do this, not only ADR, but our entire judicial system, can be brought to its full potential and help us to meet the growing demands of society.

[B] Mediation

[1] The Third-Party Facilitator — Qualifications

Alternative dispute resolution procedures generally require the services of one or more impartial third-party facilitators, who conduct the procedure, issue an advisory opinion, or mediate between the parties. There is no certification or licensure of third-party facilitators in Texas, although there are certain minimal requirements for impartial third parties appointed in court-referred procedures. Generally, however, consulting attorneys and their clients must be responsible for assuring that a particular third party is competent and appropriate to handle any particular dispute. Even in a court-referred procedure, the court must confer with the parties to determine the most appropriate procedure. C.P.R.C. § 154.021(b). At the conference, the parties may recommend an appropriate third party to the court, or the parties may agree on an appropriate third party and request the court to appoint that person. C.P.R.C. § 154.051. If the court appoints a third party who is not well qualified to aid in resolving the particular dispute, the party should consider filing an objection to referral. C.P.R.C. § 154.022.

A capable third-party facilitator must be able to:

1. Listen actively.
2. Analyze problems, identify and separate the issues involved, and frame the issues for resolution.
3. Serve all parties and remain free from favoritism or bias toward either party.
4. Use clear, neutral language in speaking and writing.
5. Demonstrate sensitivity to strongly felt values of the parties, including gender, ethnic, and cultural differences.

6. Deal with complex factual materials.
7. Project an appropriate presence that reflects an overt commitment to honesty, dignified behavior, and control of diverse parties.
8. Identify and separate personal values from the issues under consideration.
9. Help parties assess their alternatives and invent creative options.
10. Help parties identify principles and criteria that will guide their decision making.
11. Help parties make informed choices.

A third party should also adhere to ethical standards and continue to improve his or her competence through training, study, and practice.

If a court refers a pending dispute to an alternative procedure, the court may appoint one or more impartial third parties to facilitate the procedure. Generally, to qualify for appointment, the third party must have completed 40 hours of classroom training in dispute resolution techniques conducted by an organization approved by the court. If the case involves a parent-child relationship, the third party must have completed an additional 24 hours of training in family dynamics, child development, and family law. In appropriate circumstances, however, the court in its discretion may appoint a third party who does not meet the statutory qualifications if the court bases its appointment on legal or other professional training or experience in particular dispute resolution processes.

[2] Duties of Impartial Third Parties

The function of a third-party facilitator is to encourage and assist the parties in reaching a settlement of their dispute, but without compelling or coercing the parties to enter into a settlement agreement. C.P.R.C. § 154.053(a). Ethical guidelines provide that the third party should act diligently and in good faith to carry out the procedure, and should accept responsibility only in cases in which he or she has sufficient knowledge regarding the appropriate process and subject matter to be effective. The third party should ensure that the parties are informed about the nature of the procedure, the role of the third party, and the bases of compensation and other charges. The third party should remain impartial, avoid conflicts of interest or the appearance of conflicts of interest, and maintain strict confidentiality of the procedure. The third party also has an ethical obligation to ensure that the parties have considered the interests of unrepresented parties, such as children in family litigation. Ethical standards may also impose duties that apply outside of the particular procedure, such as a duty to maintain and improve professional skills, refrain from certain advertising practices, educate the public about dispute resolution procedures, or provide pro bono services.

[3] Impartiality of Third Parties

Third parties appointed in court-referred procedures must be impartial. C.P.R.C. § 154.051(a). However, Texas law does not further define the standards for determining impartiality. Generally, the third party should remain free from favoritism or bias and committed to serving all parties as opposed to a single party. The third party should have no personal interest in the dispute, show no predisposition on the types of issues involved, and should not disclose any circumstances that may create or give theappearance of a conflict of interest or that may reasonably raise a question as to impartiality.

Issues of impartiality may arise in the following situations:

1. When a third party has previously provided services to one or more of the parties. Under some professional standards of practice, a third party is prohibited from participating if he or she has previously provided services to any of the parties or even to the parties together.

2. When a third party has biases or strong views relating to the issues to be mediated. In this situation the third party has a duty to disclose the biases or views.

3. When the third party meets separately with a party, a party's consulting attorney, or a party's child or other relative. However, separate meetings may be appropriate in some contexts. For example, some mediators hold separate caucuses with each party as part of the mediation process. Any separate meetings should take place with the knowledge and consent of all parties.

4. When the third party has some financial, business, or personal relationship to a party or interest in the subject of the dispute. In these circumstances, the third party must disclose the actual or potentially conflicting interest to the parties.

The third party's obligation to be impartial does not relieve him or her of the obligation to raise questions about the fairness and feasibility of proposed settlement options.

[4] Orders to Mediate

Voluntary mediation has become popular as a method of assisting the parties to resolve their dispute. In addition, it has become extremely common for trial courts in Texas to order the parties to mediation, even over the objection of one or both parties. Further, the orders sometimes purport to require the parties to "negotiate in good faith" or to appear with a person having settlement authority, including an insurer. Are such orders enforceable? The following article discusses these issues.

Robert K. Wise
MEDIATION IN TEXAS: CAN THE JUDGE REALLY MAKE ME DO THAT?
47 S. Tex. L. Rev. 849 (2006)*

Under the Texas ADR Act, a Texas court may, on its own initiative or on a party's motion, refer any civil case for resolution by an ADR procedure, including mediation. A Texas court is required to confer with the parties to determine if ADR is appropriate and, if so, which ADR procedure should be used. However, a Texas court can order mediation without the parties' consent, even if one or all of the parties believe mediation will be futile. If the court determines that a case is appropriate for mediation, it must notify the parties of its determination. A party then has ten days from receipt of the mediation referral order to object to it. An order referring a case to mediation before the ten-day objection period expires is void.

If a party objects and if the objection has a reasonable basis, the court cannot refer the case to mediation. Of course, if the court determines that the objection has no reasonable basis, it can make the referral. . . .

Three issues arise in the context of what a mediation referral order can properly require. They are:

- Can the order require the litigants to settle, make bona fide settlement offers, or negotiate in good faith at the mediation?
- Can the order require the litigants and their insurers to attend the mediation?
- Can the order require "good faith" or "meaningful" mediation participation by the litigants?

A. A Texas Court Cannot Order Litigants to Settle at Mediation or Even to Make Bona Fide Settlement Offers or to Negotiate in Good Faith at Mediation

Although it is clear that a Texas court can order even the most recalcitrant litigant and his or her attorney to mediation, it is equally clear that a court cannot force a settlement on an unwilling litigant. As noted in *Decker v. Lindsay*,

> the policy of section 154.002 [of the Texas ADR Act] is consistent with a scheme where a court refers a dispute to an ADR procedure, requiring the parties to come together . . . , but no one can compel the parties to negotiate or settle a dispute unless they voluntarily and mutually agree to do so.

In other words, there simply is no judicial power to coerce a settlement, and it is a litigant's prerogative not to settle. Accordingly, it is impermissible to sanction or otherwise penalize a party for failure to make or accept a reasonable settlement offer during mediation. . . .

Of course, if a court cannot coerce a settlement, it necessarily follows that it also cannot order a party to make a "bona fide" settlement offer at mediation. . . .

B. The Scope of Mediation Attendance

A typical mediation order provides that "all parties, any insurance company having an interest, and their counsel, are ordered to attend all mediation sessions scheduled by the mediation center or the mediator. At least one such person for each party and insurance company shall have full settlement authority." Thus, three issues arise in connection with mediation attendance. First, can a court require the parties to attend? Second, if a court can require them to attend, can it also order attendance by a representative of a governmental body or other type of organization, such as a corporation, with full settlement authority? Third, can the court require attendance of a representative of a party's insurer with full settlement authority? Each issue is discussed below.

1. Attendance by Parties with Full Settlement Authority

It is widely believed that party attendance at mediation is essential for its success. Aside from the fact that party participation brings settlement authority to the mediation that might be lacking when only the parties' attorneys attend, a party benefits from attending mediation because his or her attendance:

- provides the party with the opportunity to tell his or her "story," thus often providing the "day in court" the party may be seeking;
- directly informs the party about the strengths and weaknesses of both his or her and the opposing party's positions and arguments;
- directly informs the party about the strengths and weaknesses of his or her and the opposing party's attorney;
- provides information that may help the party identify opportunities for creative problem solving and resolution; and
- improves the likelihood of settlement because the ultimate decisionmaker is present.

Not only do the parties benefit from attending mediation, but courts and commentators also have concluded that the mediation process suffers when governmental or other organizational parties do not send representatives with full settlement authority to the mediation. As noted by one federal district court:

> During the ADR conference, all parties have the opportunity to argue their respective positions. In the Court's experience, this is often the first time that parties, especially corporate representatives, hear about the difficulties theywill face at trial. As a practical matter this may also be the first time that firmly held positions may be open to change. For ADR to work, the corporate representative must have the authority and discretion to change her opinion in light of the statements and arguments made by the neutral and opposing party.
>
> Meaningful negotiations cannot occur if the only person with authority to actually change their mind and negotiate is not present. Availability by telephone is insufficient because the absent decision-maker does not have the full benefit of the ADR proceedings, the opposing party's arguments, and the neutral's input. The absent decision-maker needs to be present and hear first hand the good facts and the bad facts about their case. Instead, the absent decision-maker learns only what his or her attorney chooses to relate over the phone. This can be expected to be largely a recitation of what has been conveyed in previous discussions. Even when the attorney attempts to summarize the strengths of the other side's position, there are problems. First, the attorney has a credibility problem: the absent decision-maker wants to know why the attorney's confident opinion expressed earlier has now eroded. Second, the new information most likely is too much to absorb and analyze in a matter of minutes. Under this dynamic it

> becomes all too easy for the absent decision-maker to reject the attorney's new advice, reject the new information, and reject any effort to engage in meaningful negotiations. It is quite likely that the telephone call is viewed as a distraction from other business being conducted by the absent decision-maker. In that case the absent decision-maker will be preoccupied with some other matter. . . . [Thus, the] easiest decision is to summarily reject any offer and get back to the business on her desk.
>
> . . . Occasionally parties may use the absence of the decision-maker as a weapon . . . to "gain information about [its] opponent's case, strategy, and settlement posture without sharing any of its own information- .". . . . Mediation becomes a stealth discovery session, to the unfair benefit of the party whose decision-maker is not in attendance . . . . "Meanwhile, the opposing side has spent money and time preparing for a good-faith, candid discussion toward settlement."

Oddly, nothing in the Texas ADR Act expressly authorizes a court to order the parties to attend mediation, and no case discusses a Texas court's authority to do so. Nonetheless, Texas courts almost uniformly order individual parties to attend mediation and governmental and other organizational parties to send a representative with full settlement authority to mediation. And, a party or an attorney who fails to comply with such an order can be sanctioned severely.

A Texas court's authority to require parties to attend mediation and to require governmental and other organizational parties to send a representative with full settlement authority to mediation is implicit in the Texas ADR Act and also is within a Texas court's inherent power. The fact that a Texas court has the power to order a governmental or other organizational party to send a representative with full settlement authority to mediation, does not, however, mean that it should always do so or that an order requiring a governmental or other organizational party to do so never constitutes an abuse of discretion. To the contrary, ordering a governmental or other organizational party to send a representative with full settlement authority to mediation may constitute an abuse of discretion when the case involves complex or novel issues or large sums of money. This is because the ultimate settlement authority for government bodies, corporations, and other organizations often is vested in a board or commission. Thus, "there may be no one with on-the-spot settlement authority, and the most that should be expected is access to a person who would have a major role in submitting a recommendation to the body or board with ultimate decision-making responsibility." Furthermore, Texas governmental bodies are subject to the Texas Open Meetings Act ("TOMA"), which requires a meditation to be open to the public if it is likely to lead to a settlement or decision . . . .

2. Attendance by Insurers with Full Settlement Authority

Nonparty insurers often play important roles in the settlement of civil cases. Their subrogation rights to the monetary recovery of their insureds named as plaintiffs, as well as their duties involving defense costs and judgment payments on behalf of their insureds named as defendants, significantly affect settlements . . . .

Settlement efforts also can be delayed significantly if the defendant is uncertain about its ability to fund a settlement or is unsure about its insurance coverage.

Further, the defendant and his or her insurer may disagree regarding the existence or scope of insurance coverage or the insurer's duty to defend. Thus, when the insurer's agreement is needed to achieve a settlement, a common practice in mediation referral orders is to require an insurer's representative with full settlement authority to attend the mediation.

Surprisingly, no case has directly considered the question of a Texas court's authority to order a party's insurer to attend mediation. Courts in other jurisdictions, however, have taken three approaches regarding their authority to order a nonparty insurer's mediation attendance in the absence of an explicit statute or court rule authorizing it to do so.

The first approach holds that a trial court has authority to order an insurer to send a representative with full settlement authority to the mediation under its "inherent power."

The second approach reads the mediation statute or rule literally, resulting in no court power to order an insurer to attend a mediation unless such authority is expressly provided in the controlling statute or rule.

The third approach . . . reasons that because the legal and financial interests of the insurer and insured are "aligned," an order directing the insured *party* to produce a person with full settlement authority can effectively "coerce cooperation" from the nonparty *insurer* (emphasis added).

The language in the Texas ADR Act and general principles of Texas law make it clear that Texas courts lack authority to order a party's insurer to attend mediation. Significantly, nothing in the Texas ADR Act authorizes a Texas court to order an insurer or other nonparty to attend, or otherwise participate in mediation. To the contrary, every section of Subchapter 154B of the Act, which outlines the specific ADR procedures, refers only to "parties," and not to their insurers or other nonparties . . . . If the Texas Legislature had intended to make insurers or other nonparties subject to ADR referral orders, it clearly would have specified this requirement in the Texas ADR Act and would have further required the ADR notice to be sent to both the parties and their insurers . . . .

The conclusion that a Texas court cannot order a party's insurer to attend mediation is supported by three additional factors. First, the only Texas case to directly consider the question has held that a Texas court lacks authority to order a nonparty to attend mediation. In *Nueces County v. De Pena*, the Corpus Christi Court of Appeals held that a trial court had no authority to order the County Judge of the defendant county to attend mediation because he was not a party to the lawsuit . . . .

Second, the conclusion that a trial court has no authority to order a party's insurer to mediation is supported by the fact that Texas trial courts are courts of limited jurisdiction that have only the power specifically granted to them by the Texas Constitution and the legislature. Of course, nothing in the Texas Constitution, the Government Code, the Texas ADR Act, or the Texas Rules of Civil Procedure gives a Texas trial court jurisdiction over a nonparty, such as an insurer, in ADR. To the contrary, a Texas trial court only has jurisdiction over parties to the lawsuit — plaintiffs by virtue of their filing of the lawsuit, defendants (or third-party defendants) by virtueof service of process, voluntary appearance, or waiver of service, and nonparties by virtue of service of a subpoena. Tellingly, Texas Rule of Civil Procedure 176 does not authorize subpoenas to be issued for mediation; rather, it allows subpoenas to be issued only for "a deposition, hearing, or trial" or the production of "documents or tangible things." . . .

Third, the conclusion that a trial court has no authority to order a party's insurer to mediation is supported by the insurer's relationship to a lawsuit. In Texas, as in most states, an insurer is not, and cannot be named as a defendant in a lawsuit against its insured. To the contrary, in such lawsuits the insurer is simply a nonparty that has either a contractual obligation to indemnify the insured for his or her loss and to pay any of the insured's defense costs or a subrogation right to all or a portion of the insured's recovery. Although this relationship may make the insurer interested in the lawsuit's outcome, it does not make it a party to the lawsuit and subject to the trial court's jurisdiction and orders. As the insurer is not a party, it is axiomatic that the trial court has no jurisdiction to impose any obligation on it because, as previously discussed, the court's authority extends only to parties and to subpoenaed nonparties in limited non-ADR contexts.

An analogous example illustrating this important distinction is the imposition of sanctions for discovery abuse. Texas Rule of Civil Procedure 215 allows a trial court to impose sanctions against a party or its attorney for discovery abuse. It, however, does not allow a court to sanction the party's insurer even though it is paying for the party's defense or engaged the wrongdoing attorney.

C. Good-Faith Mediation Participation

Mediation referral orders use a variety of terms to describe the form of participation expected of the litigants. Many such orders require "good faith" or "meaningful" mediation participation. Nothing in the Texas ADR Act, however, expressly requires parties to participate in mediation meaningfully or in good faith, and the Texas ADR Act and Texas decisions, as well as the policy underlying mediation, clearly indicate that a mediation referral order cannot require such participation . . . .

Notwithstanding its inability to order good faith or meaningful mediation participation, a Texas court can do a great deal to ensure that mediation is productive and the parties' participation is meaningful. Rather than imposing a broad "good faith" or "meaningful" participation requirement, a mediation referral order should delineate specifically what the parties are required to do in connection with mediation. For example, the mediation referral order may specify: (1) the date mediation must be completed; (2) how many mediation sessions are required; (3) who is required to attend each mediation session; (4) whether the parties are to exchange the names of their potential mediation attendees; (5) whether the parties are to submit to the mediator or to each other premediation position papers that set forth basic information about the dispute, such as its background, its legal and factual issues, the parties' positions on the issues, the relief sought, and the most recent offers and counteroffers; (6) whether the parties are to exchange key documents before mediation; and (7) how long the participants must remain at the mediation. Of course, a mediation participant can be sanctioned if he or she fails to comply with any such requirement. Moreover, such requirements do not violate the Texas ADR Act's confidentiality provisions because they relate to actions and conduct occurring before or after the mediation and do not involve the disclosure of communications or conduct occurring during mediation.

V. Conclusion

As evidenced by the foregoing discussion, many Texas courts, without conferring with the parties, routinely issue mediation referral orders that impose improper requirements on the litigants. In addition, many Texas practitioners blindly follow such orders because of their unfamiliarity with the Texas ADR Act's mediation requirements and the principle of mediation confidentiality. Under the Texas ADR Act, it simply isimproper for a Texas court to (1) require the parties to settle, make bona fide settlement offers, or negotiate in good faith at mediation, (2) order a party's insurer to send a representative to mediation, or (3) require good faith or meaningful mediation participation. Although a court clearly can require the parties to attend mediation, it may abuse its discretion by ordering a single mediation session in cases involving complex or novel issues for large sums of money, or by requiring governmental or other organizational parties to send a representative to mediation with full settlement authority.

Both Texas courts and practitioners should pay more attention to mediation referral orders. Before issuing such an order, the court should confer with the parties and their attorneys to determine whether an ADR procedure is appropriate and, if so, whether mediation is the best procedure for the case. If mediation is appropriate, the parties and the court should further confer about the appropriate number of mediation sessions, who should attend each session, and, if an insurer's attendance is needed, whether the insured party can obtain the insurer's attendance. In addition, the mediation referral order, rather than imposing a general good faith or meaningful participation requirement on the parties, should specifically delineate what the parties are required to do in connection with mediation and how long they are required to attend. Finally, if a Texas court's mediation referral order imposes improper requirements on a party, he or she should promptly object to the order and, if the court fails to modify it, seek immediate mandamus relief.

[C] Arbitration

Increasingly, claimants find that they are barred from going to court by an obscure clause in a contract they signed before any dispute had arisen. As Justice Hecht recently noted:

> During the five years I served as a judge of the 95th District Court in Dallas County, from 1981 to 1986, I never once received a motion to compel arbitration, nor do I recall during my first years on the Supreme Court of Texas seeing a petition challenging the denial of such a motion. The first came late in 1991, resulting in our decision the following year regarding *Jack B. Anglin Co. v. Tipps*. We noted that eight years earlier the United States Supreme Court had referred to a "national policy favoring arbitration." Since *Tipps*, cases involving arbitration issues have become a large part of our docket (citing 25 cases decided since 1992).

> Institutional litigants — like employers, insurers, securities dealers, health care providers, contractors, and home builders — have in the past decade increasingly insisted on arbitration agreements with employees, customers, and clients. Institutional litigants, usually defendants, perceive binding arbitration as less expensive, less risky, or more favorable for other reasons. Even trial lawyers, who generally deplore this migration to arbitration, often insist on arbitration agreements with clients. Unquestionably, a large number of disputes that would have resulted in litigation, and often probably in trials, are now resolved by binding arbitration. This trend would appear to have contributed to the decline in civil jury trials in both the state and federal systems.*

So when are arbitration agreements binding? To answer this question, one must consult both state and federal law.

Texas General Arbitration Statute

The Texas general arbitration statute authorizes certain agreements concerning arbitration and provides procedures for implementing them. The statute validates provisions in written contracts to submit to arbitration any future controversy arisingbetween the parties. C.P.R.C. § 171.001. The precise language of the agreement is not important and need not contain the terms "binding" or even "arbitration," provided there is operative language by which the parties agree to submit their future disputes for resolution by a third party. The Texas Arbitration Act necessarily contemplates that an arbitration award will be binding. Thus, even if an agreement does not explicitly specify that the arbitration will be binding, a court may infer that this was the intention of the parties.

The statute does not apply to collective bargaining agreements, and claims for workers' compensation are not subject to arbitration under the statute. C.P.R.C. § 171.002(a)(1), (4); *see* Lab. C. § 102.001 (provisions for voluntary arbitration of existing disputes between employer and employee). In addition, certain arbitration agreements are excluded from coverage unless the agreement to arbitrate is in writing and is signed by both parties and their attorneys. These requirements apply to all contracts by which an individual person (as distinguished from a corporation, partnership, or other legal entity) agrees to pay or furnish a consideration of $50,000 or less to acquire any real or personal property, services, money, or credit. C.P.R.C. § 171.002(a)(2), (b). Similarly, an arbitration agreement concerning a claim for personal injury is not enforceable under the statute unless each party to the claim agrees to arbitrate in writing on the advice of counsel, and the agreement is signed by each party and each party's attorney. C.P.R.C. § 171.002(a)(3), (c). These limitations make it unlikely that statutory arbitration would be available for small claims, medical malpractice actions, or uninsured motorist claims involving personal injury as long as they do not involve interstate commerce.

A signed, written agreement to arbitrate may be revoked by a party on any ground that exists at law or in equity for the revocation of a contract, such as fraud.

---

* Justice Nathan L. Hecht, *The Vanishing Civil Jury Trial: Trends in Texas Courts and an Uncertain Future*, 47 S. Tex. L. Rev. 163, 175–76 (2005).

C.P.R.C. § 171.001(b). However, the fraudulent inducement must relate to the agreement to arbitrate itself and not to the underlying contract. It is not sufficient to avoid arbitration that fraud induced some part of the contract that is submitted to arbitration.

A court may not enforce an agreement to arbitrate if the court finds the agreement was unconscionable at the time the agreement was made. C.P.R.C. § 171.022. However, an arbitration clause in a contract is not unconscionable per se. For example, one court of appeals held that an arbitration clause in a home loan agreement was not unconscionable even though (1) the borrower was not told of the clause or its effects, (2) the contract was presented as a "standard" earnest money contract, (3) the borrower did not receive any separate consideration for foregoing the right to trial, (4) the contract was prepared by the lender, and (5) the borrower was not represented by counsel. Barring fraud or misrepresentation, the parties to a contract are presumed to know and agree to the contents of a contract signed by them.

Federal Arbitration Act

The Federal Arbitration Act applies to written arbitration provisions in maritime transactions and in contracts "evidencing a transaction involving commerce." 9 U.S.C. § 2. The scope of "involving commerce" is very broad and is the functional equivalent of "affecting commerce," signaling the intent of Congress to fully exercise its Commerce Clause power. *Allied-Bruce Terminix Co. v. Dobson*, 513 U.S. 265, 272–74 (1995). *See In re Nexion Health at Humble, Inc.*, 173 S.W.3d 67, 69 (Tex. 2005) (Medicare funds crossing state lines constitutes interstate commerce); *Cappadonna Elec. Mgmt. v. Cameron County*, 180 S.W.3d 364, 369–70 (Tex. App. — Corpus Christi 2005, no pet.) (FAA governed agreement involving construction of county jail complex); *Associated Glass, Ltd. v. Eye Ten Oaks Invests., Ltd.*, 147 S.W.3d 507, 511 (Tex. App. — San Antonio 2004, no pet.) (FAA applied when windows that were subject of contract were subject of interstate commerce by shipment from Georgia to Texas).

The term "commerce" must also be broadly construed. A contract involves commerce under the FAA if the transaction that is the subject of the contract itself involves interstate commerce. In addition, a contract involves commerce if the underlying transaction requires the interstate flow of materials, supplies, services, and personnel. Substantial interstate activity is not required if the contract involves persons from different states and the contract involves interstate travel, mail, and transfer of materials. *See In re FirstMerit Bank, N.A.*, 52 S.W.3d 749, 754 (Tex. 2001) (retail installment financing agreement for purchase of mobile home was governed by FAA when bank was Ohio corporation and purchasers were Texas residents); *see also* Jack B. Anglin Co., Inc. v. Tipps, 842 S.W.2d 266, 270 n.6 (Tex. 1992) ("some courts have focused on whether the contract itself indicates that the parties contemplated substantial interstate activity, so that the fortuity of diverse citizenship or ancillary travel across state lines would not alone trigger application of the Federal Act.").

To be enforceable as a written contract, the agreement must only be evidenced by a writing. It does not have to be signed by either party. *In re AdvancePCS*

Health L.P., 172 S.W.3d 603, 606 (Tex. 2005). Further, the requirements noted above under the Texas general arbitration statute that certain contracts are not enforceable unless signed by the party's attorney do not limit the enforceability of an agreement under the federal statute. *Palm Harbor Homes, Inc. v. McCoy*, 944 S.W.2d 716, 721 (Tex. App. — Fort Worth 1997, no writ). Otherwise, under the FAA, an agreement to arbitrate that is valid under general principles of contract law and involves interstate commerce is "valid, irrevocable, and enforceable." 9 U.S.C. § 2.

The Texas Supreme Court has held that non-signatories to a contract containing an arbitration clause may be bound by the arbitration requirement under the "direct benefits estoppel" theory. *In re Weekley Homes, L.P.*, 180 S.W.3d 127, 132–35 (Tex. 2005). In *Weekley Homes*, the Court ruled that a party to a contract containing an arbitration clause could compel arbitration of a personal injury claim brought by a nonparty because the nonparty had obtained benefits from the contract. While the boundaries of direct-benefits estoppel are not always clear, non-parties generally must arbitrate claims if liability arises from a contract with an arbitration clause rather than from general law, and the nonparty deliberately seeks substantial benefits from the contract. A party may use six theories to bind non-signatories to arbitration agreements: (1) incorporation by reference; (2) assumption; (3) agency; (4) alter ego; (5) equitable estoppel; and (6) third-party beneficiary. *In re Kellogg Brown & Root, Inc.*, 166 S.W.3d 732, 739 (Tex. 2005).

The Scope of the Arbitration Clause

When a dispute arises between contracting parties whose contract includes an arbitration agreement, a trial court that is asked to compel or to prevent arbitration or to confirm or to vacate an arbitration award must determine whether the dispute concerns issues that are subject to arbitration under that agreement. *In re D. Wilson Constr. Co.*, 2006 Tex. LEXIS 644 at *13 (Tex. 2006). Determination of whether a given dispute falls within the scope of an arbitration clause is a matter of contract interpretation that must be performed by a court. *In re Vesta Ins. Group, Inc.*, 192 S.W.3d 759, 762 (Tex. 2006) (tortious interference claim subject to arbitration); *In re Dillard Dep't Stores, Inc.*, 186 S.W.3d 514, 515–16 (Tex. 2006). However, the court should focus on the factual allegations of the claim, rather than the legal causes of action asserted. The burden is on the party opposing arbitration to show that the claims fall outside the scope of the arbitration agreement as interpreted by the court.

The Texas Supreme Court has addressed the question of whether an arbitrator or a court should rule on class certification issues when the contracts at issue committed all disputes arising out of the agreement to the arbitrator, holding that such authority rests with the arbitrator. *In re Wood*, 140 S.W.3d 367, 368 (Tex. 2004). In so deciding, the Court relied on a U.S. Supreme Court decision holding, as a matter of contract interpretation, that when the parties agreed to submit all disputes to an arbitrator under the FAA, issues of class arbitration are for the arbitrator to decide. *Green Tree Fin. Co. v. Bazzle*, 539 U.S. 444, 452 (2003).

Because of the FAA policy that favors arbitration over litigation, whenever the scope of an arbitration clause is reasonably in doubt, the court should decide the interpretationquestion in favor of arbitration. *Mitsubishi Motors v. Soler Chrysler-*

Plymouth, 473 U.S. 614, 626 (1985). A court should not deny arbitration unless it can be said with positive assurance that an arbitration clause is not susceptible of an interpretation that would cover the dispute.

Claims within the scope of an arbitration clause are arbitrable under the Federal Arbitration Act even though they are based on statutory rights. *Shearson/American Express, Inc. v. McMahon*, 482 U.S. 220, 226–28 (1987) (claims under Securities Exchange Act are arbitrable, unless party resisting arbitration shows that Congress intended to preclude waiver of judicial remedies for statutory rights). For example, claims based on the Deceptive Trade Practices Act are arbitrable under the Federal Arbitration Act. *Ommani v. Doctor's Associates, Inc.*, 789 F.2d 298, 299–300 (5th Cir. [Tex.] 1986) (arbitration of claims for breach of contract, negligence, fraud, and violations of DTPA).

Under federal law, after it is determined that the subject of a dispute falls within an arbitration clause, any procedural questions that grow out of the dispute and bear on its final resolution are questions for the arbitrator. Thus, an issue about whether a party has complied with the procedural prerequisites to arbitration under their contract is for the arbitrator to decide.

A party is ordinarily entitled to seek a stay of litigation in a case involving a dispute referable to arbitration. Regardless of which party seeks the stay, unless the parties contract otherwise, the burden to initiate arbitration rests on the party seeking relief, who may waive the right to arbitrate by delay. However, a party against whom a claim is asserted does not waive its right to arbitrate by failing to initiate arbitration of that claim, even though that party may be the one who sought the stay of litigation. The burden to initiate arbitration rests on the plaintiff as the party seeking relief. *In re Bruce Terminix Co.*, 988 S.W.2d 702, 705–06 (Tex. 1998).

Compelling Arbitration

Under the Texas Arbitration Act, if a party to an arbitration agreement that falls within the scope of the Texas general arbitration statute refuses to arbitrate a dispute, the other party is entitled to obtain a court order compelling the parties to proceed with arbitration. The statute provides that the party desiring arbitration must make an "application" for an order compelling arbitration. C.P.R.C. § 171.021. At least in the context of pending civil litigation, it seems that the application should be made in the form of a motion to compel arbitration.

If the party opposing arbitration denies the existence of the agreement to arbitrate, the court must proceed summarily to determine whether an agreement within the statute exists. C.P.R.C. § 171.021(b). The party seeking to compel arbitration must establish the existence of an enforceable arbitration agreement, and show that the claims raised fall within the scope of that agreement. Once the party establishes a claim within the arbitration agreement, the trial court must compel arbitration and stay its own proceedings. C.P.R.C. § 171.021(b); *In re Oakwood Mobile Homes, Inc.*, 987 S.W.2d 571, 573 (Tex. 1999). Disputes regarding interpretation of the arbitration agreement are determined according to ordinary contract principles. Because the statute requires a summary proceeding, the court must act speedily and without delay. Thus, a court abuses its discretion if it delays its decision until after discovery on the merits has been completed. Similarly, a court may not defer a ruling on arbitration until after the parties mediate their dispute.

The Federal Arbitration Act provides two parallel devices for enforcing an arbitration agreement: a stay of litigation in any case raising a dispute referable to arbitration, and an affirmative order to engage in arbitration. A stay merely arrests further action by the court until any arbitration is complete, but an order compelling arbitration affirmatively orders the parties to engage in the process of arbitration.

In many cases, a stay is adequate to protect the right to arbitration. If, however, the party opposing arbitration is the one from whom payment or performance is sought, an order compelling arbitration would be necessary to ensure that the dispute is resolved.

The two remedies are independent. A court may order a stay even when it may not compel arbitration. Similarly, a motion to compel arbitration is not a prerequisite to a motion for a stay. Moreover, an order compelling arbitration may be sought even after a court has already refused to stay proceedings. A court also has power to both stay proceedings and compel arbitration.

Although the substantive provisions of the Federal Arbitration Act, Sections 1 and 2, are applicable in state courts as well as federal courts, the United States Supreme Court has not held that the specific remedies provisions of the Act apply in state court. There is no federal policy favoring arbitration under a certain set of federal rules; the policy is to ensure that arbitration agreements can be enforced according to their terms. Therefore, a choice-of-law clause in a contract with an arbitration agreement may be interpreted to adopt state procedural rules governing the conduct of arbitration without offending federal policy. *Volt Info. Sciences v. Stanford Univ.*, 489 U.S. 468, 476 (1989) (Act does not preempt California statute permitting court to stay arbitration pending resolution of related litigation between party to arbitration agreement and third party not bound by agreement).

Proceedings instituted in state court with respect to arbitration agreements covered by the Federal Arbitration Act are governed by Texas procedural law when the federal policy favoring arbitration will not be frustrated. *Jack B. Anglin Co., Inc. v. Tipps*, 842 S.W.2d 266, 268–69, 272 (Tex. 1992).

Waiver of Arbitration

The issue of waiver usually arises when one party to pending litigation is seeking to stay the litigation and compel the other party to arbitrate. Waiver may be found when it is shown that a party acted inconsistently with its right to arbitrate and this action prejudiced the other party. *In re Oakwood Mobile Homes, Inc.*, 987 S.W.2d 571, 574 (Tex. 1999). The right to arbitrate future disputes may be waived by either party to the agreement. However, the burden to prove waiver is a heavy one. *Perry Homes v. Cull*, 258 S.W.3d 580 (Tex. 2008). Arbitration is strongly favored, and accordingly there is a strong presumption against waiver. *Id.* (nevertheless finding waiver).

Waiver must be intentional. This intent may be implied from a party's actions only if the facts demonstrate that the party seeking to enforce arbitration intended to waive its arbitration rights. *In re Fleetwood Homes of Texas, L.P.*, 257 S.W.3d. 692 (Tex. 2008) (discussing potential trial setting and sending discovery day before moving to compel arbitration did not waive arbitration); *EZ Pawn Corp. v. Mancias*, 934 S.W.2d 87, 90 (Tex. 1996). Whether a waiver has been accomplished by implication is determined in each case from the totality of the circumstances. *Perry Homes, supra.*

There is no waiver in the absence of prejudice to the opposing party. *Fleetwood Homes; Perry Homes; Prudential Sec., Inc. v. Marshall*, 909 S.W.2d 896, 898–899 (Tex. 1995) (no waiver when party invoked judicial process to strike intervention and by resisting discovery). Mere delay in making a demand for arbitration does not constitute waiver in the absence of actual prejudice. *EZ Pawn Corp. v. Mancias*, 934 S.W.2d 87, 91 (Tex. 1996); *Home Club, Inc. v. Barlow*, 818 S.W.2d 192, 193 (Tex. App. — San Antonio 1991, orig. proceeding) (no waiver of right to arbitrate dispute despite delay of almost 13 months from time suit was filed until motion for stay was filed); *cf. Spain v. Houston Oilers, Inc.*, 593 S.W.2d 746, 747–48 (Civ. App. — Houston [14th Dist.] 1979, no writ) (three-year delay between filing of suit and motion to compel arbitration was unreasonable and prejudicial per se).

A party does not waive its right to enforce an arbitration clause by merely taking part in litigation unless it has substantially invoked the judicial process to its opponent's detriment. *In re Fleetwood Homes of Texas, L.P.*, 257 S.W.3d. 692 (Tex. 2008) (discussing potential trial setting and sending discovery day before moving to compel arbitration did not waive arbitration); *In re Citigroup Global Markets, Inc.*, 258 S.W.3d. 623 (Tex. 2008) (party's statements about what discovery might be saved by transfer to MDL court was not enough to substantially invoke judicial process); *Perry Homes v. Cull*, 258 S.W.3d 580 (Tex. 2008); *In re Vesta Ins. Group, Inc.*, 192 S.W.3d 759, 763 (Tex. 2006) (no waiver when party sent standard requests for disclosure, noticed four depositions, and sent request for production); *In re Bruce Terminix Co.*, 988 S.W.2d 702, 704 (Tex. 1998) (no waiver when defendant filed answer and propounded set of 18 interrogatories and set of 19 requests for production, but moved to abate judicial proceedings and compel arbitration less than six months after plaintiff filed suit).

Even substantially invoking the judicial process does not waive a party's arbitration rights unless the opposing party proves that it suffered prejudice as a result. Similarly, if the discovery is relevant to non-arbitrable issues that must be decided by the court, waiver does not occur merely because the discovery may also be relevant to arbitrable issues. Thus, when a party repeatedly requested arbitration but also carried out extensive discovery on the question of whether the contract containing the arbitration clause had been rescinded (which was non-arbitrable in this case), the court found that no waiver had taken place. *In re Certain Underwriters at Lloyd's*, 18 S.W.3d 867, 875–76 (Tex. App. — Beaumont 2000, no pet.) (party should not be required to choose between seeking rescission or seeking arbitration on other, arbitrable issues). In contrast, a party that conducts discovery about every aspect of the merits and then waits to the eve of trial to request arbitration to gain an unfair advantage by manipulating the litigation process by switching to arbitration when trial is imminent waives arbitration rights. *Perry Homes v. Cull*, 258 S.W.3d 580 (Tex. 2008).

[D] Other Types of ADR

[1] Mini-Trial

A mini-trial is a structured but nonbinding procedure designed to aid settlement negotiations. At a mini-trial, the parties and their counsel present their positions before selected representatives for each party or before an impartial third party. The purpose of the procedure is to define the issues and develop a basis for realistic settlement negotiations. The impartial third party may issue an advisory opinion, but the opinion is not binding unless the parties agree that it is binding and afterwards enter into a written settlement agreement. C.P.R.C. § 154.024. If the parties do execute a written settlement agreement, the agreement is enforceable in the same manner as any written contract, subject to contract defenses such as mistake or fraud. The terms of the agreement may be incorporated in the final decree of a court that has referred the case to mini-trial. C.P.R.C. § 154.071.

The mini-trial has been used most often in complex business litigation, but it need not be limited to this area. The mini-trial enables each party to hear the arguments of the other party as well as the opinion of an impartial neutral party, who may be selected because of his or her expertise in the subject matter of the dispute. Because the procedure is nonbinding, the disputant does not give up control over the dispute or forfeit the right to proceed with litigation. The process is confidential, and communications at the proceedings and any opinion issued may not be used in court or communicated to the judge in later litigation. If the procedure is successful, the disputants will save the considerable time and expense of litigation.

A mini-trial generally follows these steps:

1. Agreement by the parties to take part in a mini-trial, or referral by a court.

2. Selection by the parties of the neutral party or selected representatives who will hear the case.

3. Limited discovery and exchange of information to the extent agreed on by the parties.

4. The mini-trial, at which attorneys for each party make informal, summary presentations of their side of the case, aided by expert or other witnesses if necessary. The trial may include question and answer sessions between the parties, and the neutral party or selected representatives may ask questions or comment on the strengths and weaknesses of each party's case. The trial may be as brief as one or two days.

5. An advisory opinion by the neutral party.

6. Negotiations between the parties or their attorneys resulting in settlement, or a return to litigation or some other dispute resolution process such as binding arbitration.

The mini-trial may be especially effective when normal negotiations have broken down. The mini-trial allows the parties to dispute the matter in an adversarial context, but without the binding consequences of litigation or arbitration. A mini-trial may be inappropriate in factually complex cases because of the lessened opportunity for fact determination.

[2] Moderated Settlement Conference

The moderated settlement conference, like the similar mini-trial procedure, is designed to aid settlement negotiations by providing a forum for case evaluation. At the conference, the parties and their counsel present their positions before a panel of impartial third parties, who may issue a nonbinding advisory opinion. This objective evaluation of the case may provide a basis for further negotiations. C.P.R.C. § 154.025. The moderated settlement conference should be distinguished from mediation, in which a neutral third party holds discussions with the parties to aid them in reaching an agreement, but does not make any judgment on the issues. C.P.R.C. § 154.023. The moderated settlement conference should also be distinguished from a mandatory settlement conference, which may be required by a court, but which does not include presentation of the case to a neutral panel.

The conference is usually a brief procedure of less than one day. The panel commonly consists of three attorneys agreed to by the parties who may have special experience or expertise in the area of the dispute. The panel is provided summaries of the case by each party, but does not review the case file. At the conference, each party or the party's attorney will make a 15- to 30-minute presentation, with time allowed for questions by the other party and the panel and for rebuttal. After brief summation by each side, the panel will deliberate and then give an opinion on the issues. The parties and their attorneys may then proceed with ordinary settlement negotiations. If the parties reach a settlement and execute a written settlement agreement, the agreement is enforceable in the same manner as any written contract, subject to contract defenses such as fraud or mistake. The conference is conducted in confidence and the results may not be disclosed to the court in subsequent litigation proceedings. Because the procedure is designed to aid the parties in reaching a settlement, it is most effective when the parties are open to settlement but have not been able to resolve their dispute through ordinary negotiations.

[3] Summary Jury Trial

In a summary jury trial, the parties and their counsel present their positions before a panel of jurors, usually six, who may issue a non-binding advisory opinion. The procedure is designed to aid in settlement negotiations by providing a reasonable prediction of the outcome of a full jury trial. C.P.R.C. § 154.026. Summary jury trial is most appropriate when the case turns on factual disagreements, and is comparable to summary judgment procedures for questions of law. For instance, summary jury trialmay be useful to determine how a jury will apply a reasonableness standard of liability in a given case. *See* Thomas D. Lambros, *The Judge's Role in Fostering Voluntary Settlements*, 29 VILL. L. REV. 1363 (1983-84). *But see* Charles F. Webber, Comment, *Mandatory Jury Trial: Playing by the Rules?*, 56 U. CHI. L. REV. 1495 (1989) (arguing against compelled summary jury trial).

The summary trial is conducted by the court in generally the same manner as an ordinary trial, but is much briefer and less formal, generally taking less than one day. The jury selection process is usually conducted by the attorneys, so that they may gain a knowledge of the jurors in order to better evaluate the eventual verdict. The jurors are not told that the verdict is merely advisory. Attorneys for the parties present the evidence in summary form and do not generally call witnesses. Although the rules of evidence are relaxed at the summary trial, the attorneys are limited to representations based on evidence that will be admissible at trial. The judge then instructs the jury panel, who deliver a verdict. After the verdict is read, the jury is usually informed of the advisory nature of the proceedings, and the parties and their counsel discuss the verdict with the jury in order to determine the members' views on the facts of the case. After the summary trial, the parties and their attorneys continue with settlement negotiations. If the parties reach a settlement and execute a written agreement, the agreement is enforceable in the same manner as any written contract, subject to contract defenses such as fraud or mistake. The court may incorporate the terms of the agreement in the final decree disposing of the case. C.P.R.C. § 154.071.

APPENDIX — SETTLEMENT, ADR, AND THE TEXAS BAR EXAM

Some lawsuits are settled informally or through alternative dispute resolution devices. ADR is very common in practice, and related issues have appeared on the bar exam. The following are questions from past exams, reprinted with the permission of the Texas Board of Law Examiners, which owns the copyright to these questions. You can see more questions, and the examiners' comments on the answers, by visiting the Board's website at www.ble.state.tx.us/past_exams/main_pastexams.htm.

In considering the questions, keep in mind that on the bar exam your answer is always limited to five lines.

February 2005

Sam, his wife, and their minor daughter, Jane, were on a family vacation in Harris County, Texas when a truck rear-ended their car. Sam was driving the car. Sam's wife, Martha, and Jane were passengers. All three sustained serious injuries in the collision. The owner of the truck was PipeCorp, a Texas corporation whose principal place of business has always been in Tarrant County, Texas. Bob, PipeCorp's employee, was driving the truck at the time of the collision. Sam, Martha, Jane and Bob resided in Nueces County, Texas at the time of the collision. Sam and Martha want to file a lawsuit to recover for the injuries and damages sustained by them and by Jane.

During a mediation before trial, Plaintiffs told the mediator that they would accept significantly less in settlement than the amount they would seek at trial. The case did not settle. At trial, defense counsel calls the mediator to testify about what Plaintiffs said at mediation. What objection should Plaintiffs' counsel make and how should the court rule? Explain fully.

February 2001

Paul Palmer, a resident of Bell County, has filed a negligence, breach of warranty, and product liability suit in state district court in Hill County, Texas. Palmer alleges that a curling iron, which he had bought for his daughter from Dad's Department Store ("Dad's"), was defective, overheated, and caused a fire in his home. Palmer, who is uninsured, seeks to recover the cost of repairing the damage to his home and for injuries to his minor daughter, and he alleges damages in excess of $50,000. Palmer sued two defendants: the retailer, Dad's, a sole proprietorship in Waco, Texas (McLennan County); and Kurlee, Inc., the manufacturer, a Vermont corporation with its headquarters in Vermont.

Palmer has waited patiently for one year while discovery is conducted. He wants to settle and move on with repairing his house and would like to resolve the case by mediation.

1. As Palmer's counsel what strategy do you have available to force the defendants to attend a mediation?

Assume that a mediation is held but that neither Kurlee, Inc. nor Dad's offer anything to settle with Palmer. Instead, they swagger and sneer that they would never pay anything to Palmer because they do not like him, regardless of whether he has a meritorious case.

2. What remedy, if any, does Palmer have with the Court to either seek sanctions against Defendants for their conduct or to require that they return to a second mediation and to negotiate in good faith by making realistic offers to Palmer?

At the original mediation, Palmer hears the Kurlee, Inc. party representative say to the mediator that Kurlee, Inc. had 10 reports in the last year of house fires related to the identical model of curling iron. This is very inconsistent with Kurlee, Inc.'s discovery responses.

3. Palmer wants you as his attorney to subpoena the mediator to testify in court about what he heard Kurlee, Inc.'s representative say. What advice do you give Palmer on this and for what reasons?

TABLE OF CASES

[References are to pages]

A

B

[References are to pages]

C

[References are to pages]

D

[References are to pages]

E

F

[References are to pages]

G

[References are to pages]

H

[References are to pages]

I

J

K

L

[References are to pages]

M

[References are to pages]

N

[References are to pages]

O

P

[References are to pages]

Q

R

S

[References are to pages]

T

[References are to pages]

U

V

[References are to pages]

W

Y

Z

INDEX

[References are to sections.]

A

C

[References are to sections.]

[References are to sections.]

[References are to sections.]

L

M

P

[References are to sections.]

[References are to sections.]

[References are to sections.]

W